LAROUSSE

Dictionary of

BELIEFS
and
RELIGIONS

LAROUSSE
Dictionary of BELIEFS and RELIGIONS

Editor
Rosemary Goring

Consultant Editor
Dr Frank Whaling

LARROUSSE
Larousse plc
43–45 Annandale Street, Edinburgh EH7 4AZ
Larousse Kingfisher Chambers Inc.
95 Madison Avenue, New York, New York 10016

First published in the UK in hardcover by W & R Chambers Ltd 1992

First published in the US in hardcover under the Larousse imprint 1994

First published in paperback under the Larousse imprint 1994 (UK), 1995 (US)

10 9 8 7 6 5 4 3 2 1

British Library Cataloging in Publication Data for this book
is available from the British Library

Library of Congress Cataloging in Publication Data for this book
is available from The Library of Congress

ISBN 0-7523-0000-8

Editorial Manager: Min Lee

Illustrations by David Brogan and John Marshall

Typeset by the Charlesworth Group, Huddersfield

Printed in Great Britain by Clays Ltd, St Ives plc

Contents

Acknowledgements

For a variety of contributions, help and advice we would like to thank the following: Kim Baxter, Lancaster College of Higher Education; Nigel Billen, *Scotland on Sunday*; Wendy Dossett, St David's University College, University of Wales, Lampeter; Nila Joshi, Ethnic Services Department, McDonald Road Library, Edinburgh; Simon Smith, University of Leeds; Bruce Wallace, Dean Education Centre, Edinburgh; Professor P M Warren, University of Bristol; Dr James D White, Institute of Soviet and East European Studies, University of Glasgow.

Contributors

Dr Jonathan G Campbell
Lecturer in Jewish Studies
Department of Theology and Religious Studies
St David's University College
University of Wales
Lampeter

Dr Gavin D Flood
Lecturer in Indian Religions
Department of Theology and Religious Studies
St David's University College
University of Wales
Lampeter

Dr G B Hall
Senior Lecturer
Department of Divinity
University of St Andrews

Dr Phillip Hillyer
Theological Author and Editor

Valérie Huet
Moses and Mary Finley Fellow
Darwin College
Cambridge

Dr Philip G Kreyenbroek
Specialist in Iranian Studies
School of Oriental and African Studies
University of London

Dr David Law
Gifford Research Fellow
University of St Andrews

Andrew Mein
Research Student
University of Edinburgh

Dr Peter McEnhill
Minister
Anderston Kelvingrove Church
Glasgow

Robert Parker
Fellow and Tutor in Greek and Latin Languages and Literature
Oriel College
Oxford

Dr Ronald A Piper
Lecturer in New Testament Languages and Literature
University of St Andrews

Professor D W D Shaw
Professor in Divinity and Principal of St Mary's College
University of St Andrews

Elizabeth Templeton
Freelance Theologian,
Editor of *Trust* newsletter and
Co-ordinator of Threshold Theological Resource Centre, Edinburgh

Professor Andrew Finlay Walls
Director of the Centre for Christianity in the Non-Western World
University of Edinburgh

Dr Frank Whaling
Director of the Religious Studies Centre and
Senior Lecturer in the Department of Theology and Religious Studies
University of Edinburgh

Preface

Belief in anything, whether it be an earth goddess or a monthly horoscope, is guaranteed to be alien or almost incomprehensible to those who do not hold the same ideas. Yet, while it is easy to dismiss another's beliefs as irrational or misguided, it is rare to hold absolutely no personal opinion about what lies behind our existence. The variety of theories and divinities to which the question of life is attributed is endless, and has provided the source of some of the most heated conflicts in history. But on one level there is a similarity between, for example, a Carmelite nun praying before a crucifix, an Algonquin kneeling in the forest and communing with Kitshi Manitou, the Great Spirit, and a Muslim facing Mecca at the rallying chant of a muezzin. Each of these believers, obviously, would see great and possibly insurmountable differences in their worship; for a start, none of them is contacting the same spirit. But, while the varying natures of their deities cannot be lightly dismissed, not least because the essence of their gods dictates the character of their religion, all three are nevertheless witness to what some anthropologists see as humankind's natural religiosity: a need to be in touch with a superior force whose presence can be invoked, placated or challenged, and who, as a result of appropriate human responses, can influence the lives of believers.

For some, particularly in more modern times, faith in the supernatural is considered primitive and, at best, a little pathetic. Paul Radin, for example, considers that religious belief stems from neurosis and insecurity, while philosophers such as Feuerbach have tried to prove that belief in the divine is simply a projection of the human need to believe that there is some design and deliberate — if obscure — order behind an otherwise inexplicably painful universe. Equally persuasive arguments, however, can be put forward by those whose experience of their god, or contact with the spirit world, convinces them beyond doubt and scepticism of the reality of their faith.

Whatever an individual's personal conviction, there can be no gainsaying the influence wielded by the multitude of systems of belief, both current and past. The aim of this dictionary is to provide a sweeping and comprehensive outline of the most prevalent modern religions and ideologies. As well as these, we also look at major historical faiths, such as Ancient Near Eastern, Greek or Roman religions, whose influence is still evident in artistic, architectural or literary remains, or whose concepts have underlain subsequent religious structures.

The intention behind our selection of material has been three-fold. First, to give a detailed insight into the various strands of thought and convictions that have joined together in shaping a particular creed. So, for example, within Buddhism we cover (among other subjects) the concept of the original, primordial Buddha (Adi-Buddha), describe the content of the main Buddhist scriptures (eg Abhidharma, Agama, Heart Sutra, Lotus Sutra, Diamond Cutter Sutra), and look at various meditational techniques (eg jhana, samatha). Our second purpose has been to highlight not just the differences but also the points of similarity between faiths. So, for instance, a common concern for the socially deprived is seen running through many major religions, as does an emphasis on initiation, devotion and adherence to clearly-defined moral codes.

Thirdly, we hope that by explaining the reasons behind certain rituals, customs or beliefs we will remove some of the suspicion or uncertainty that commonly veil attitudes to other cultures or opinions. Out of this we hope may come a greater understanding of the views of others, however incompatible they may be with one's own private theology.

On a more practical level: to keep the text as uncluttered as possible we have omitted all diacritical marks except where a word has its own entry, in which case the full and correct spelling is given in parenthesis following the headword. Most entries are supplemented by a short string of other relevant articles, although these suggestions for further browsing cannot, of course, be exhaustive. For a better idea of all the material available on a certain faith we recommend the Entries by Subject listings (pp 588–605), where you see at a glance all the articles given under a specific category. For dating we use the convention BCE (Before the Common Era) and CE (Common Era), rather than the more Christian-centred BC and AD; they do, however, indicate exactly the same periods.

Finally, although we have tried to give as wide and fair a spread of information as possible, we appreciate that there may well be unintentional gaps, and we would welcome suggestions for further articles.

Rosemary Goring

A

Aaron (15th–13th century BCE) Biblical patriarch and elder brother of Moses, first high priest of the Israelites and said to be the founder of the priesthood. He was spokesman for Moses to the Egyptian pharaoh in his attempts to lead their people out of Egypt, and performed various miracles with his rod. Later he gave in to the demands of the rebellious Israelites in the desert and organized the making of a golden calf for idolatrous worship. He and his sons were ordained as priests after the construction of the Ark of the Covenant and the Tabernacle, and Aaron was confirmed as hereditary high priest by the miracle of his rod blossoming into an almond tree (hence various plants nicknamed 'Aaron's Rod'). He is said to have died at the age of 123. ▷ Ark of the Covenant; golden calf; pharaoh; Moses; Tabernacle

Abailard ▷ Abelard

Abbas (al-'Abbās ibn 'Abd al-Muṭṭalib) (566–652) Uncle of Muhammad, at first hostile to him, but ultimately the chief promoter of his religion. He was the founder of the Abbasid dynasty of rulers. ▷ Abbasids; Muhammad

Abbasids ('Abbāsids) An Arab dynasty which traced its descent from al-Abbas, an uncle of the prophet Muhammad, and which held the caliphate from 749 to 1258. The Abbasids were swept to power by the Hashimiya (from Hashim, grandfather of al-Abbas and great-grandfather of Muhammad), a revolutionary movement which opposed the rule of the Umayyads and demanded that government should reside in the hands of the prophet's own family. In 747 an uprising in the province of Khurasan led by the Hashimite representative Abu Muslim found strong support throughout Persia and Iraq, and after the proclamation of Abul Abbas al-Saffah (d.754), great-great-grandson of al-Abbas, as caliph (749), his forces defeated the Umayyad Marwan II and his Syrian troops at the Great Zab (750). Al-Saffah's brother al-Mansur firmly established Abbasid rule, and was succeeded in turn by his own son al-Mahdi (c.744–785), and grandson al-Hadi (764–86). The age of Harun al-Rashid and his son al-Mamun (786–833) was the apogee of the Abbasid caliphate, which ruled an empire stretching from North Africa to Central Asia, with Baghdad as its capital. Yet from this time the Abbasids became increasingly unable to prevent the fragmentation of the Muslim polity. In the 10th century a rival caliphate, the Fatimids, took over North Africa and Egypt, while the caliphs themselves fell under the domination of the Persian Buyids (945–1055) and then of the Turkish Seljuks. Eventually al-Nasir (c.1155–1225), who reigned from 1180, recovered some independence and re-established the Abbasids as a regional power in Iraq, but his successors were unable to withstand the onslaught of the Mongols. The capture of Baghdad by the khan Hülegü (1258), and the subsequent execution of al-Mustasim, effectively ended the Abbasid caliphate, although his uncle, al-Mustansir, was carried off to Cairo by Baybars, sultan of Egypt (1261), where the family continued to hold a titular caliphate under Mamluk tutelage until the Ottoman conquest (1517). ▷ caliphate; Muhammad

abbey A building or group of buildings used by a religious order for worship and living. It houses a community under the direction of an abbot or abbess as head, who is elected for a term of years or for life. Abbeys were centres of learning in the Middle Ages. ▷ monasticism

Abdias, Book of ▷ Obadiah, Book of

Abduh, Muhammad ('Abduh) (1849–1905) Muslim reformer, born in Egypt. He was associated with other Muslim reformers such as al-Afghani, and Sir Muhammad Iqbal, in the attempt to reinterpret Islam in the light of the modern world. While studying in Paris he met al-Afghani, and together they established a reforming religious society called the Unbreakable Bond (*Urwah al-Wuthqa*) and a journal called *The Minaret* (*al-Manar*). In 1885 Abduh went to Beirut to teach Muslim theology, and in 1888 he returned to Egypt, becoming Grand Mufti of Egypt in 1889. From this position he was able to advance Islamic modernization ideas through the Salafiyyah Movement, which embodied his and Afghani's notions. He influenced the modern development of al-Azhar University in Cairo, becoming a member of its Supreme Council (1894), and publishing *The Message of Unity* (*Risalat at-Tawhid*) in 1897. His emphasis upon the need for an Islamic renaissance, on reason, the need to reinterpret the Quran, on a unified Islamic law, and on adaptation to the modern scientific world-view influenced a number of educated Muslims, not only in Egypt but also in countries such as India, through Aligarh Muslim University, and Indonesia, through the Muhammadiyah Movement. ▷ Afghani, al-; Azhar, al-; Iqbal, Sir Muhammad; Islamic modernism

Abdul-Baha ('Abdu'l-Bahā 'Abbās) (1844–1921) The eldest son of Bahaullah, he succeeded his father as leader of the Bahai tradition in 1892. He had been born on that day in 1844 when the Bab had proclaimed himself to be the 'Gate of God', thus inaugurating the Bahai religion. By the time of his death, Abdul-Baha had played a crucial part in the formation of the religion. During the time of Bahaullah's exile (from 1868) he helped to organize the consolidation and advance of Bahai affairs, and saw the expansion of the Bahai community beyond Iran and into 23 other countries. His role was pivotal as leader, teacher, and writer. Some of his writings are included with the writings of Bahaullah and Shoghi Effendi, forming Bahai texts. His visits to the West were important in projecting the Bahais as a world religion, and his enunciation of the Bahai universal principles bolstered the inclusivism, religious liberalism, social vision and global awareness that became hallmarks of Bahai teaching. He was succeeded as leader by his grandson Shoghi Effendi. ▷ Bahaullah; Bab, the; Shoghi Effendi

à Becket, Thomas ▷ Becket, St Thomas à

Abel ▷ Cain

Abelard, or **Abailard, Peter** (1079–1142) Boldest theologian of the 12th century, born near Nantes, France. While a lecturer at Notre-Dame, he fell in love with Héloïse, the 17-year-old niece of the canon Fulbert. When their affair was discovered, Fulbert threw Abelard out of the house. The lovers fled together to Brittany, where Héloïse gave birth to a son, Astrolabe, and returned to Paris, where they were secretly married. Héloïse's furious relatives took their revenge on Abelard by breaking into his bedroom one night and castrating him. Abelard fled in shame to the abbey of St Denis to become a monk, and Héloïse took the veil at Argenteuil as a nun. After Abelard's teaching on the Trinity was condemned as heretical, he retired to a hermitage, which later became a monastic school known as Paraclete. He then became abbot of St Gildas-de-Rhuys, Paraclete being given to Héloïse and a sisterhood. Later, at Cluny, he lived a strictly ascetic life, studying theology tirelessly, and recanted some of the doctrines that had given most offence. Again, however, his adversaries, headed by Bernard of Clairvaux, accused him of heresies, and he was found guilty by a council at Sens. On his way to Rome to defend himself, he died at the priory of St Marcel, near Chalon. His remains were buried by Héloïse at Paraclete, and hers were laid beside them in 1164. ▷ asceticism; Bernard of Clairvaux, St; heresy; monasticism; theology; Trinity

Abhidharma (Pali: Abhidhamma) The third part of the Buddhist scriptures, the first being the *Vinaya* or the monastic discipline of the Buddhist tradition, and the second being the *Suttas* or discourses of the Buddha. The three parts together are called the *tipitaka*, or three baskets, and are also known as the Pali Canon. The Abhidharma brings out the thematic structure and the logical development of the Buddha's teachings. It is abstract, technical and impersonal by contrast with the discourses of the Buddha in the second part, which is personal and engaging. It analyses a comprehensive set of Buddhist terms and doctrines and places a special emphasis on consciousness. Various states of consciousness are described, and their constituent elements, or *dharmas*, are analysed. These constituent elements are interdependent and inter-related. Although inviting study, application and memory, the underlying purpose of the Abhidharma was ultimately not theoretical but meditational, and aimed at liberating human beings from craving and suffering by giving them insight into the impermanence (*anicca*) of things and the unreality of the self (*anatman*). Although originating in India, in Ceylon the Abhidharma was elaborated into a deeper system by Buddhaghosa around 430CE, and a recognized introduction was written by Anuruddha in the 11th century. ▷ anatman; Buddhaghosa; sutta-pitaka; tipitaka; vinaya-pitaka

ablutions, Islamic The religious purpose of Islamic ablutions is to prepare the Muslim for meaningful ritual activity by removing impurities of body and soul. Ablutions are of three kinds. The greater ablution (*ghusl*) involves washing the whole body with water. It is necessary for a ceremony of conversion to Islam, for a ceremony of preparation for pilgrimage, for entering a mosque, and before touching an Arabic Quran. The lesser ablution (*wudu*) involves a brief washing with water of the feet, hands and face, and usually takes place before the five sets of daily prayers. Where water is not available, or where there is a legitimate problem connected with the use of water, a third ablution (*tayammum*) can be performed, involving the use of a water substitute such as earth or sand or unworked stone. As well as being preparations for effective ritual, Islamic ablutions involve an elaborate set of washing actions that constitute a ritual in their own right. As well as symbolizing purification, they also symbolize the interconnection between body, mind and intention. ▷ mosque; pilgrimage; prayer; Quran

Abraham (c.2000–1650BCE) Revered in the Old Testament as the father of the Hebrew people. According to Genesis he came from the Sumerian town of Ur ('Ur of the Chaldees') in modern Iraq, and migrated with his family and flocks via Haran (the ancient city of Mari on the Euphrates) to the 'Promised Land' of Canaan, where he settled at Shechem (modern Nablus). After a sojourn in Egypt, he lived to be 175 years old, and was buried with his first wife Sarah in the cave of Machpelah in Hebron. By Sarah he was the father of Isaac (whom he was prepared to sacrifice at the behest of the Lord) and grandfather of Jacob ('Israel'); by his second wife Hagar (Sarah's Egyptian handmaiden) he was the father of Ishmael, the ancestor of 12 clans; by his third wife Keturah he had six sons who became the ancestors of the Arab tribes. He was also the uncle of Lot. Abraham is traditionally regarded as the father of the three great monotheistic religions: Judaism, Christianity and Islam. ▷ Christianity; Genesis, Book of; Hagar; Ishmael; Islam; Jacob; Judaism; Lot; Old Testament

Abraham in Islam Known as Ibrahim in Arabic, Abraham is seen by Muslims as a patriarch of Islam, an ancestor of Muhammad (through his son Ishmael), and the one who, together with Ishmael, rebuilt the Kabah in Mecca. He is revered not as an ordinary prophet (*nabi*) but as a messenger (*rasul*) of outstanding importance who established primordial monotheism, and it is Abraham's primordial monotheism that Islam sees itself as restoring and fulfilling after its distortion by the Jews and Christians. Abraham is thus eminent in a line of special messengers which includes Noah, Moses, Jesus and Muhammad, and which culminates in the latter, who is seen as the seal of the prophets. ▷ Adam and Eve; Jesus Christ in Islam; Mecca; Moses; Muhammad; nabi; Noah; prophets in Islam

Abram ▷ Abraham

absolution A declaration of forgiveness of sins. In Christian worship it is understood as God's gracious work in Jesus Christ, pronounced by a priest or minister either in private after confession or as part of the liturgy in public worship. ▷ Christianity; confession; liturgy; priest; sin

Abu-Bakr (Abū-Bakr) (c.570–634) The first Muslim caliph, one of the earliest converts to Islam. He became chief adviser to Muhammad, who married his daughter Aïshah, and on the death of the prophet was elected leader of the Muslim community, with the title *khalifat Rasubul Allah*, 'successor of the messenger of God' (632). In his short reign of two years he put down the 'Apostasy', a religious and political revolt directed against the government in Medina, and set in motion the great wave of Arab conquests over Persia, Iraq and the Middle East. ▷ caliphate; Islam; Medina; Muhammad

Abu Hanifah (Abū Hanīfah al-Nu'mān ibn Thābit ibn Zūtā) (700–67) Muslim theologian and jurist, born in Kufah, Iraq, the originator of one of the four schools of Islamic Law which became known as the Hanafi School. The grandson of a slave who had been given freedom, he studied at Medina and elsewhere, and later traded in silks in Kufah, where he also taught Islamic theology and law. The Hanafi School became important through the work of Abu Yusuf and Shaibani, 'the two doctors', and was adopted by the Abbasid caliphs as a major school of law. It is now the dominant Islamic law school in Central Asia, Egypt, India and Turkey. Abu Hanifah and his school are known for their breadth of legal interpretation and their willingness to use analogy and personal judgement in their legal practice, even though Abu Hanifah had in fact been traditional and rational. The Hanafi School's method is fairly literal and formal when compared with the approach of other Islamic schools, concentrating upon the external act rather than individual intent. Nevertheless it gives greater play than do other Islamic schools to legal stratagems in order to circumvent the positive aspects of the law. ▷ Abbasids; Baghdad; Islamic law schools

Acts of the Apostles A New Testament book, the second part of a narrative begun in

Luke's Gospel, which traces the early progress of Jesus's followers in spreading the Christian faith. It begins with the resurrection and ascension of Jesus, but concentrates largely upon the growth of the Jerusalem Church, its spread to Samaria and Antioch, and the missionary journeys of Paul to Asia Minor, the Aegean lands, and Rome. ▷ apostle; Jesus Christ; Luke, Gospel according to; New Testament; Paul, St

Adalbert, St (939–97) Apostle of the Prussians, born in Prague, and chosen Bishop of Prague in 982. The hostility of the corrupt clergy whom he tried to reform obliged him to withdraw to Rome. He carried the Gospel to the Hungarians, the Poles, and then the Prussians, by whom he was murdered, near Gdansk. He was canonized in 999. His feast day is 23 April. ▷ apostle; missions, Christian

Adam and Eve Biblical characters described in the Book of Genesis as the first man and woman created by God. Adam was formed from the dust of the ground and God's breath or spirit (Genesis 2.7); Eve was made from Adam's rib. Traditions describe their life in the garden of Eden, their disobedience and banishment, and the birth of their sons Cain, Abel, and Seth. Their fall into sin is portrayed as a temptation by the serpent (Satan) to disobey God's command not to eat the fruit of the tree of the knowledge of good and evil (Genesis 3). ▷ Bible; Cain; Genesis, Book of; Satan

Adi-Buddha (Ādi-Buddha) The notion of the primordial or original Buddha found especially in Tantric Buddhism in Nepal and Tibet. The earlier Buddhist tradition had thought more in terms of a historical succession of Buddhas, whereas Tantric Buddhism thought in terms of five Buddhas, who could be seen as different but co-existing forms of a primordial, self-existing Buddha. This did not constitute the Adi-Buddha as a creator God, or indeed as a God in any form. He is conceived not as the creator of the five Buddhas but as their constituent principle and as the central principle of Buddhahood. The earliest evidence for the concept of the Adi-Buddha dates back to the 7th century CE, but it has a prehistory in early Buddhist teachings about the Buddha who, when he died, is said to have passed into a state that was undefinable but was not nothingness. Later Mahayana Buddhists talked about the three bodies of the Buddha: his earthly body, his blissful body, and his truth body. The truth body (*dharmakaya*) was the unity behind all aspects of the Buddha. The Adi-Buddha is a slightly more personal elaboration of this concept of the truth body in Tibetan circumstances; in Japan the notion of the Adi-Buddha was adapted under the name of Maha Vairocana. ▷ dharmakaya; Mahayana Buddhism; nirvana; Tantric Buddhism; trikaya; Vairocana

Adi Granth (Ādi Granth) One of the names given to the main Sikh scripture. After the succession of 10 human gurus ended in 1708, the *Adi Granth* succeeded them as Guru of the Sikh tradition and it became more commonly known as the *Guru Granth Sahib*. It was compiled by the fifth guru, Guru Arjan, in 1603 and 1604, and includes works of the first five Sikh gurus, along with devotional works of Kabir and other members of the Sant tradition at that time. The word 'Adi' means primal or original. The *Adi Granth* is primal in two senses: first because it is the original and most important of the Sikh scriptures—the *Dasam Granth* completed in 1734 is secondary; more importantly it is primal in the sense that it uncovers the truth about God, the Primal Being, which had been true from all eternity. It is symbolic of the fact that true Sikhism predated its historical appearance. The present *Adi Granth* includes works by the tenth guru that have been added later to Guru Arjan's original version; it is written in Gurumukhi, a modern Punjabi script, and it is treated with deep physical respect as being the embodied Guru of the Sikh tradition. ▷ Arjan, Guru; Dasam Granth; Guru Granth Sahib; guru, Sikh; Kabir; Sant tradition

adoptionism The understanding of Jesus as a human being of sinless life adopted by God as son, usually thought to be at the time of his baptism by John in the River Jordan. Such teaching was declared heretical, in that it implied that Jesus could not have had a fully divine nature. Associated with Arianism, it figured in 4th-century controversies over the person of Christ, in Spain in the 8th century, and in some scholastic theology (eg Abelard, Lombard). ▷ Abelard, Peter; Arius; Jesus Christ; John, St (the Baptist); Lombard, Peter

Adrian IV, also **Hadrian**, originally **Nicholas Breakspear** (c.1100–1159) Pope, the first and only Englishman to hold this title. Born in Langley, Hertfordshire and educated at Merton Priory and Avignon, became a monk in the monastery of St Rufus, near Avignon, and in 1137 was elected its abbot. Complaints about his strictness led to a summons to Rome, where the pope, Eugenius III, recognized his qualities and appointed him cardinal-bishop of Albano in 1146. In 1152 he was sent as papal legate to Scandinavia to reorganize the church, where he earned fame as the 'Apostle of the North'. He was elected pope in 1154. One of his early acts is said to have been the issue of a controversial bill granting Ireland to Henry II. Faced with rebellion in Rome he excommunicated the whole city. He also excommunicated the powerful William I the Bad of Sicily, but was later glad to accept him as an ally. In 1155 he crowned Frederick I, Barbarossa as Holy Roman Emperor in front of his massed army in a show of strength in support of the papacy; but their relationship quickly deteriorated when Adrian tried to impose feudal overlordship over him, and for the rest of his papacy Adrian was engaged in a bitter struggle with him for supremacy in Europe. ▷ papacy

Advaita Vedanta (Advaita Vedānta) One of the most influential of the orthodox schools of Hindu philosophy presents the monistic philosophy that distinctions are illusory and reality is non-dual (*advaita*) in its essence. This means that the individual self, though perceived as being distinct, is ultimately identical with the absolute (*Brahman*). This absolute is beyond all predicates and without qualities, though it is nevertheless referred to as being (*sat*), consciousness (*cit*) and bliss (*ananda*). The Advaitins maintained that only knowledge of this non-dual absolute could release beings from the cycle of transmigration (*samsara*), in contrast to the Mimamsa school which claimed that only ritual action was efficacious in purifying the soul. For the Advaitins the ever-present reality of Brahman has to be known directly though experience, in the same way that, for example, silver seen on the beach turns out to be a shell upon inspection. This direct knowledge of the absolute bestows liberation in life (*jivanmukti*) by eradicating ignorance (*avidya*) or illusion (*maya*), which is also the eradication of karma built up over innumerable previous lifetimes. The most famous philosopher of this school was Shankara (788–820), who accepted that devotion to a personal Lord (Ishvara) was useful but was a lower level of truth than knowledge of the absolute, impersonal Brahman. Perhaps the greatest exponent of Advaita after Shankara was Shri Harsha (1125–80), who used logic, particularly *reductio ad absurdum* arguments, to defeat opposing schools such as the Nyaya-Vaisheshika. Other forms of Advaita Vedanta include Vallabha's Shuddhadvaita and the Vishishtadvaita of Ramanuja. ▷ Ishvara; jivanmukti; Mimamsa; Nyaya; Vaisheshika

Advent In the Christian Church, the four weeks before Christmas, beginning on the Sunday nearest 30 November (Advent Sunday); a period of penitence and preparation for the celebration of the first coming of Christ at Christmas, and for his promised second coming to judge the world. ▷ Christian year; Christmas; Jesus Christ

Adventists Those Christians whose most important belief is in the imminent and literal Second Coming of Christ. Found in most periods of history and in most denominations, a separate movement began in the USA with William Miller (1781–1849), who predicted Christ's return (and the end of the world) in 1843–4, and whose followers eventually formed a denomination called Seventh Day Adventists. They believe that the Second Coming of Christ is delayed only by a failure to keep the Sabbath (Friday evening to Saturday evening), which, along with Old Testament dietary laws, is held to rigorously. ▷ Jesus Christ; millenarianism; Seventh Day Adventists

Aesir and Vanir Aesir (plural of *as*, a god) is the collective term used in Norse literature for the Germanic pantheon (12 in number, according to Snorri Sturluson, apart from the *Asyniur*, goddesses). More strictly, it stands for that majority group among the gods which includes Odin, Thor, Balder, Tyr, Heimdall and Loki, who share a common origin. Living with them in their city, Asgard, are some deities of the Vanir, of different origin: Njord, with his son Freyr and fair daughter Freya. There are echoes in the literature of an ancient war between Aesir and Vanir which ended in alliance and an exchange of hostages. In general the Aesir display military prowess, much needed against the frost giants, the persistent enemies of Asgard. The Vanir, on the other hand, are the source of fertility and plenty (though it is clear that Thor's help was often invoked in relation to weather). Such are the deities of the present age; they will perish in battle at Ragnarok, which will seal the doom of the gods, and that era will give way to a new one.

The double origin of the deities has been variously interpreted. Sturluson believed that the Vanir were originally from the Black Sea area, near the Don mouth, and the Aesir their neighbours; Odin and the others represent migrating heroes and leaders who founded the various Germanic kingdoms. Later writers have pointed to the difference of function; Odin and Thor are the natural patrons for a warrior, Freyr or his sister for a farmer. Some see the stories as reflecting religious change, whereby the original gods, the Vanir, were largely displaced by later cults of the Aesir. A passage in *Voluspa* suggests the opposite—the corruption of the Aesir by the wealth represented by the Vanir. We know little for certain about the interrelations of the Germanic deities in still earlier times; pre-Norse sources are too fragmentary. ▷ Balder; Freya; Odin; Ragnarok; Sturluson, Snorri; Thor; Tyr, Tiwaz, Tu; Voluspa

aesthetics in religion This refers to the aesthetic dimensions of religion such as painting, sculpture, architecture, music, dance and drama, which for many people have been more important than scriptures or doctrines, since they do not depend upon a knowledge of reading and writing. Thus the stained-glass windows of a medieval Christian cathedral give a visual interpretation of Jesus; the five *mudras* (hand-gestures) of the Buddha or Buddha images convey an immediate picture of the Buddha as teacher, giver of spiritual gifts, source of meditation, dispeller of fear and spiritual example; a Shiite Muslim passion play poignantly relives the suffering of Husayn, and the annual open-air acting of the story of Rama brings it to life for an Indian community. Some religious traditions have favoured aesthetic expressions of religion more than others. Thus the Muslim restraint on portraying God or human beings has diminished the importance of painting and sculpture in Islam, and increased the importance of calligraphy, mosque architecture and Persian carpets; and whereas Orthodox Christians have made beautiful icons, Protestant Christians have frowned upon them. Religious structures tell their own aesthetic story; the pointed spire of a church, the dome of a mosque, and the many-crannied roof of a Hindu temple are symbolic. There is a sacred geometry of cubic dimensions built into the Greek altar at Delphi, the holy of holies in Solomon's temple, the Sumerian ark, the Vedic fire altar, and the sacred Muslim Black Stone, in the Kabah ('cube'), at Mecca. The aesthetics of religion engage not only the mind but also the emotions and whole personality of the believer. ▷ Buddha image; calligraphy, Islamic; cathedral; Delphi; Husayn; icon; mosque; mudras; passion play; Rama; sacred geometry

Afghani, al- (Jamāl ad-Dīn al-Afghānī) (1838–97) Muslim activist reformer and modernist, born in Iran but brought up in Afghanistan. Throughout his career he travelled widely in the Muslim world and the West. From 1871 to 1879 he wrote and taught in Cairo, and in the early 1880s he met Muhammad Abduh in Paris. Together they established a reforming religious society called the Unbreakable Bond (Urwah al-Wuthqa) and a journal called *The Minaret* (*al-Manar*). In 1886 and 1889 al-Afghani was invited by the Shah to Iran, and in the 1890s he supported the pan-Islamic ideals of the Ottoman Sultan in Turkey. His aim was to reinvigorate Islam and to free it from undue Western influence. To achieve this he was willing to reinterpret Islam in the light of the modern world, thus bringing him under suspicion from the Muslim religious leaders, the *ulama*. His political interventions were opportunistic rather than systematically conceived, yet by his dynamism, his pamphlets, his oratory, and his charisma he inspired many young and educated Muslims around the world to become interested in Islamic reforming modernism. Collaborators such as Muhammad Abduh gave a more philosophical foundation to the Salafiyyah Movement (inspired by al-Afghani), which became the institutional mouthpiece of the Islamic Reform Movement. ▷ Abduh, Muhammad; Iqbal, Sir Muhammad; Islamic modernism; ulama

African Independent churches A name given to modern religious movements in Africa which see themselves as churches within the Christian tradition but which did not derive in their present form from Western mission sources. ('Independent' refers to origin, not to government; almost all African churches are independent in the sense of 'self-governing'.) Until recently two main types occurred. 'Ethiopian' churches (so-called because some of them used this title, symbolizing an African Christianity older than the Western missions) arose from dissatisfaction with missionary leadership, a desire for African self-expression, or rejection of some aspect of missionary policy. In all other respects Ethiopian churches maintained the patterns established by the missions. Ethiopian churches frequently appeared in the early days of colonialism and became a special feature in South Africa; but with independence in Church and State their importance has declined. By contrast, 'Prophet-healing' churches, often called 'aladura' or 'spiritual' in West Africa and 'Zionist' in southern Africa, have burgeoned since independence.

Remodelling the church on the basis of African readings of Scripture, they point to the powerful effect of the divine Spirit, demonstrated in prophecy, revelation and healing, in the Bible; they apply these to African situations, offering intelligible ways of coping with guilt, sickness, stress, and the fear of witchcraft and sorcery. Frequent, though not universal features are uniforms, assigned roles of ranks, and codes of spiritual discipline. Worship typically involves dancing, the use of African instruments and much congregational participation. Credal matters are not usually emphasized, but explicit rejection of the historic Christian formularies is rare. Churches vary greatly in size (many are small and local, while the Kimbanguist church in Zaire has a membership in millions); in organization and leadership; in acceptance of elements of traditional religion (though complete rejection of traditional fetish magic and diviners is usual); and in openness to other churches (some belong to national councils of churches, a few to the All Africa Conference of Churches and the World Council of Churches, and many to various associations of Independent churches). In recent years some countries have seen a new form of independent church, stressing empowerment by the Spirit, Bible reading, and radical Christian obedience, but using modern media and rejecting those features of the prophet healing churches closest to traditional life. Older churches of mission origin have increasingly recognized the extent to which the Independent churches have identified modern African needs and aspirations. ▷ aladura; Christianity in Africa; Harris, William Wadé; Lenshina, Alice Mulenga; Maria Legio; Zionist churches

African Methodist Episcopal Church A Church formed at a national meeting of Black Methodists in 1816 in the USA, the culmination of a movement begun in 1787. It expanded rapidly after the Civil War, and today has over 1000000 members. In 1841 it established the first black publishing house in the USA. ▷ Methodism

African religions In this context the term refers to the traditional religious systems of African peoples south of the Sahara, and stands for those aspects of ancestral belief and custom which relate to the transcendent world. Many of these African peoples are now wholly or partly Christian or Muslim, but the traditional religions and these universal faiths continue to interact, and the way in which traditional believers articulate their faith is often affected by this interaction.

African spirit dance

There is a wide variety of traditional religious systems across Africa. In most of them, the understanding of the spirit world includes four significant components: God, the supreme being, usually with a personal name; divinities who are the spiritual rulers of localities or of specific activities or departments of life; ancestral spirits; and power, either, like the Melanesian *mana*, conceived impersonally, or manifested in places or objects. (There may be other inhabitants of the spirit world who receive no attention, unless a propitiatory offering to keep them away. These are spirits with whom no relationship is expected or desired.) One way of classifying the religious systems is according to the relative prominence in normal life of the four components: thus there are God-dominated, divinity-dominated and ancestor-dominated systems. Sometimes one or other component is missing. Thus for the Gikuyu (Kikuyu) of Kenya, God (*Ngai*) is the sole recipient of worship, and there is no place for divinities, whereas the Acholi show no clear recognition of any supreme being or divinities. The relative importance of a component is not determined by ethnic or linguistic affinity. For example, though the religions of Bantu-speaking peoples are often ancestor-dominated, there are important exceptions, and Nilotic peoples range from the God-dominated Nuer to the Acholi, who appear to have no place for God at all. Frequently the supreme being is recognized as creator and moral governor of the world, while active religion is directed more to divinity or ancestors. Sometimes, indeed, divinities are seen as extensions, refractions or accessible representatives of the supreme being, who is

recognized without temples, priesthood or regular worship (though he may be approached in an emergency).
Like other religions, African religions develop and change, both under external influences (war, conquest, intermarriage, epidemic) and internal influences (prophets, reformers, synthesizers). Borrowings (eg cults or shrines) from neighbours are also common. Their highly practical orientation usually makes divination important; evil and misfortune have their causes in the personal, social and spiritual realms, so diagnosis must be by spiritual means; and witchcraft, though perhaps itself not a religious phenomenon, can only be effectively combated by spiritual means. The ritual dimension of traditional religions is manifest both in community ritual activities (most noticeable among agricultural peoples, for example at planting and harvest time) and in the crises of personal and family life (such as the ceremonies at birth, puberty or death). ▷ ancestors, African; Dinka religion; divination, African; Modimo; Mulungu; Mwari; Nuer religion; Shilluk religion; supreme beings; witchcraft and sorcery, African

Afro-Brazilian religions Brazil is unique in Latin America in the variety and depth of the interaction of its racial, cultural and religious influences. No other country has received so many people from Africa, nor has such a variety of indigenous Amerindian elements. From the days of slavery certain features of African religions became fused with folk Catholicism. In the 20th century, with urbanization and industrialization, a synthesis has emerged, producing in effect new complete religious systems. African divinities have merged with Christ and the saints in devotion, ritual and the quest for healing and divination. Seance and possession trance are so marked that these Afro-Brazilian religions are often collectively called Spiritism. Despite the opposition of the Church authorities of the country with the largest Catholic population in the world, most participants would also call themselves Catholics. The largest movement, Umbanda, is urban and multi-racial, with a large middle-class element. Its membership is estimated at between 30 and 40 million, and its decentralized structure leads to great local variations. In the Candomblé movement, prominent in Bolivia, strong elements of Yoruba religion from Nigeria have been preserved; Xangu and Batuque represent similar formulations elsewhere. Macumba, more characteristic of Rio de Janeiro, displays Bantu influences, especially Kongo from Zaire, as well as Amerindian elements. ▷ African religions; Christianity in Latin America

afterlife The notion of survival of the human person in some form after physical death. This assumes a wide variety of forms in different religions, but some such notion is common to nearly all. Afterlife may be conceived as eternal, or beyond time; everlasting, without end, or temporary; subject to cessation through release or absorption into a greater reality or into deity. It need not imply survival of the whole embodied person, survival of a disembodied soul being frequently postulated. ▷ Akhira; Sheol

afterlife, Ancient Egyptian concept of The Ancient Egyptians had a keen interest in the afterlife, which they saw as very similar to this life, but better. Fundamental to entry was the preservation of the body in a recognizable form and great care was taken in the mummification of corpses. In the Old Kingdom hopes of the afterlife were focused on the king, but these became gradually democratized. Sometimes the dead were thought to enter heaven as one of the stars or as a member of the crew of Re's solar boat. Alternatively they might live on in the tomb, where regular offerings were brought for their sustenance. Perhaps the dominant conception was that of the realm of Osiris in the underworld. On death the deceased came before Osiris and 42 judges to plead their innocence and have their hearts balanced against Maat. If successful they entered the underworld where they lived an idealized earthly life based on agriculture and in a land that was an improved replica of Egypt. As in so much of their religion the Egyptians appear to have tolerated several different conceptions at once without difficulty. ▷ Anubis; funerary practices; Ka; Maat; mummification; Osiris; Re; Thoth; underworld

afterlife, Ancient Near Eastern concept of In contrast to Egypt, the conception of afterlife in the rest of the Ancient Near East seems almost uniformly gloomy. In Mesopotamia it was believed that immortality was only for the gods, and mortals were doomed to go down to the realm of Nergal and Ereshkigal after they died. This was called the 'land of no return' and was conceived of as a dark and dusty city on the underside of the world, not unlike the Israelite Sheol. There is some evidence of a judgement of the dead, this being the responsibility of the sun god Shamash, a favourable judgement making death a little more tolerable. The Hittites and Canaanites appear equally pessimistic about the prospects of the dead, although the Hittites considered their kings divine after death and there was also a royal funerary cult at Ugarit. ▷ Ancient Near Eastern religions; Hittite religion; Nergal; Shamash; Sheol; Ugarit

afterlife, Christian concept of This is enshrined in the credal statement 'I believe in the resurrection of the body and the life everlasting', which opposes all ideas of the survival of the soul alone, reincarnation, or extinction. Belief in the resurrection of Christian believers, founded on reflection on the resurrection of Jesus (as in 1 Corinthians 15), is accompanied by belief in a second coming of Christ (*parousia*), last judgement and general resurrection for all humankind, in which good is rewarded and evil punished (as in Matthew 25 and Revelation 20), and the powers of evil, already defeated by the death of Christ, are finally routed. Biblical eschatology and teaching about the afterlife leave a number of questions unanswered. Some, such as the nature of heaven or of hell (which many theologians would define simply as separation from the presence of God, an outcome denied by universalism), have been the subject of Christian art and mythology. Others, such as those relating to the question of how sinful human beings could ever be in heaven, in the presence of a holy God, have been approached through the traditional Roman Catholic doctrines of limbo and purgatory. A more recent question, which has become acute since the 19th century, about the eternal destiny of people who have not heard the Christian message or have faithfully followed another religion, is a matter of continuing debate. Rahner's idea, for example, of 'anonymous Christians' has been found lacking. Universalism satisfies some theologians. Many suggest that this issue, along with other unanswered questions about the afterlife, should be left to the justice and mercy of God. ▷ angelology, biblical; demonology, biblical; eschatology; limbo; parousia; purgatory; Rahner, Karl; resurrection; saint, Christian view of; universalism

afterlife, Greek concept of Traditional Greek religion was a religion of this world, and this emphasis was scarcely altered by the widespread expectation that there would, or might, be an afterlife of some kind. The soul that goes to Hades after death, in Homer's description (8th/7th century BCE), is a kind of futile wraith, 'without strength': 'I had rather work as a labourer for a poor master on earth...than be king of all the souls of the dead', says the great Achilles. Only a very few exceptionally favoured heroes are translated to the islands of the blessed; a few great sinners are punished. By the 5th century BCE the idea had gained strength that *all* souls might fare better or worse in accord with their conduct in life, and there existed rites, most notably the Eleusinian Mysteries, that gave their initiates 'hopes' of a better lot in the afterlife. From the same date we also find occasional traces of a belief in a quite new kind of afterlife, amid the stars. But (certain sects and speculative philosophical movements aside) the fundamental this-worldly orientation of Greek religion remained unaltered, and it is rare to find a claim about the afterlife that is not qualified by a phrase such as '*if* any consciousness remains after death'. ▷ Greek religion; Mysteria; Orphic/Pythagorean movement; soul

Agama (Āgama) A Sanskrit term used in Mahayana Buddhism for a collection of the discourses of the Buddha. There are four of these Agamas, and they are similar to the four sections of the discourses of the Buddha found in the Theravada *tipitaka* or Pali Canon. As in the *tipitaka*, these four Agamas form a third of the 'three baskets' of scripture. This particular 'basket' concentrates upon discourses said to have been given by the Buddha at particular times and places, and on particular themes. The style is popular and is adapted to the purpose of apologetics and teaching. It includes allegories, illustrations, parables, popular stories, and similes. Each major school of Buddhism has its own Agamas. The term is also used in other Indian religious traditions. In the Jain tradition it designates the Jain scriptural texts. In the Hindu tradition it refers to later post-Vedic Sanskrit scriptures which have a mainly ritualistic emphasis and are taken to have been revealed by each of the three main personal deities, Shiva, Vishnu, and the goddess Devi. ▷ Jainism; Mahayana Buddhism; scriptures; Shiva; Theravada Buddhism; tipitaka; Vishnu

ages of the world This is the notion that the world undergoes various stages of development that can be divided into separate ages. The simplest division is into the periods before and after a certain event or date. Thus the Christian calendar divided events into those that took place before and after Christ, and the Muslim calendar into events before and after the migration (hegira) of Muhammad from Mecca to Medina. At a wider level there is the notion of world-periods, for example the three periods of 3000 years in

Zoroastrian thought, and the notion of distinct periods put forward in St Augustine's *City of God* (Adam to the Flood, the Flood to Abraham, Abraham to David, David to the Exile, the Exile to Christ, the present period, and an 'eternal day' of rest). In some cultures and movements there is the idea of the repetition of world-periods in a succession of cycles. An extreme example of this is the notion of a repeated 5000-year cycle of four declining periods of 1250 years each (the golden, silver, iron and copper ages) in the thought of the new religious movement, the Brahma Kumaris, and this concept is found, with expanded ages, in ancient Greek thought. At a much wider level of cosmic recurrence the same notion of four declining ages is found in Hindu, followed by Buddhist and Jain, thought. The four ages, or *yugas*, are essentially the same—the golden age, the silver age, the iron age, and the copper age—but they are of monumental length. During these ages there is a continual decline until the fourth and final age, which is a time of unrighteousness and disruption which will eventually end. After that there will be a period of rest, following which a new cycle will begin. ▷ Augustine, St (of Hippo); Brahma Kumaris/Raja Yoga movement; hegira; Muhammad; yugas

Aggadah, or **Haggadah** Jewish interpretative development of the narrative and theological sections of the Bible. The word means 'narration', derived from a Hebrew verb 'to tell'. Like Halakhah, which is concerned with human behaviour, Aggadah denotes the content of parts of Rabbinic and later Jewish literature. Aggadah compensates for omissions, clarifies obscurities, and harmonizes contradictions in the Bible; it covers subjects such as God's nature, divine mercy, and the character of the Messiah. Aggadah normally takes the form of *midrash*, ie overt scriptural interpretation, in contrast to Halakhah, which is usually expressed independently of Scripture. However, there is also Aggadah which is not midrashic. An important aggadic collection is the Midrash Rabbah (the 'Great Midrash') from the second half of the first millennium CE, commenting on the Pentateuch. The section on Genesis, called Genesis Rabbah, is the oldest and includes development of the Aqedah or 'binding of Isaac' from Genesis 22.1–19. Despite the importance of such traditions, the Aggadah is essentially creative and speculative, leaving room for dissent; this contrasts with the Halakhah, which remains definitive and obligatory. The designation Aggadah is preferable to Haggadah, enabling a distinction between it and the (Passover) Haggadah, which is the liturgical retelling in Jewish homes of the Exodus story at Passover. ▷ Aqedah; Haggadah; Halakhah; midrash; Pentateuch

Aggeus ▷ **Haggai, Book of**

aggiornamento The process of making the life, doctrine, and worship of the Roman Catholic Church effective in the modern world. This was initiated by Pope John XXIII at the Second Vatican Council. ▷ John XXIII; Roman Catholicism; Vatican Councils

Agni Fire and the god of fire in Hinduism. In the Veda Agni is a god who inhabits the realm of the earth (along with the hallucinogenic Soma plant with which he is sometimes identified) and is the link between heaven and earth, between the gods and humans. Agni conveys offerings in the fire to the other world and brings the heat of the other world to human households. Indeed Agni also devours the bodies of the dead on the funeral pyre and conveys them to the realm of the ghosts (*preta-loka*) from whence they will join the world of the ancestors (*pitri-loka*). In the Brahman household Agni is the focus of the daily *agnihotra* ritual, in which offerings of clarified butter are made to him. Agni is identified with the sun and with other forces involving 'heat', such as the fire of digestion and the fire of passion. ▷ Veda

agnosticism The view that the existence of God cannot be known since it cannot be proved. It falls between theism and atheism; while the theist claims that God exists, and the atheist denies his existence, the agnostic claims ignorance. T H Huxley was the first to use the term in the context of religious scepticism (1869), and today it can have several meanings in addition to the first. It can be used to indicate either a non-religious lifestyle, or an emotive anti-Christian stance; or can simply be used as a synonym for atheism. ▷ atheism; theism

Agricola, Johann, real name **Schneider** or **Schnitter**, also called **Magister Islebius** (1492–1566) German reformer, born in Eisleben, one of the most zealous founders of Protestantism. Having studied at Wittenberg and Leipzig, he was sent by Luther to Frankfurt (1525) to institute Protestant worship there. In 1536 he was appointed to a chair at Wittenberg, but resigned it in 1540 because of his doctrinal opposition to Luther. He died while court preacher in Berlin. He wrote many theological books, and made a collection of German proverbs. ▷ Luther, Martin; Protestantism; Reformation

Ahab (9th century BCE) King of Israel c.869–850BCE and son of Omri (d.c.875BCE). He was a warrior king and builder on a heroic scale, extending his capital city of Samaria and refortifying Megiddo and Hazor. He fought in the alliance that withstood the Assyrians at the battle of Karkar (853). To extend his alliances in the north he married Jezebel, daughter of the King of Tyre and Sidon, who introduced Phoenician style and elegance to Ahab's court and the worship of the Phoenician god, Baal, in a temple in Samaria. This aroused the furious hostility of the prophet Elijah. Ahab was killed in battle against the Syrians at Ramoth Gilead. ▷ Baal; Elijah

ahimsa (ahiṃsâ) The principle of respect for all life and the practice of non-injury to living things, found in certain Hindu sects, Buddhism, and especially Jainism. It is based on the belief that violence has harmful effects on those who commit it, including an unfavourable future rebirth. The rule of non-violence was applied by Mahatma Gandhi in the political sphere during India's struggle for independence. ▷ Buddhism; Gandhi, Mohandas Karamchand; Hinduism; Jainism; karma

Ahmadiyya (Aḥmadiyyah), or **Ahmadis** An Islamic religious movement founded in 1889 in India by Mirza Ghulam Ahmad (c.1839–1908), who was believed to be the Messiah Mahdi prophesied in the Quran. In 1914 the sect split into two, a Qadiyani and a Lahori branch, neither having any dealings with the other, but both spreading the movement across the world. The sect is rejected by orthodox Islam, which cannot accept Ghulam Ahmad's claim to be a prophet following Muhammad, since the traditional belief is that Muhammad was the last manifestation of God. Marked by its missionary zeal, the movement is active in Asia, Africa, and Europe. In 1974, after several years of vicious demonstrations against the sect, its followers were declared to be heretical and were officially banned from the orthodox Islam community. ▷ heresy; Islam; Mahdi; Muhammad

Ahmad Khan, Sir Sayyid (1817–98) Muslim reformer, born in India, who advocated the modernization of Islam and India in the light of Western education and scientific ideals. A similar modernizing movement had already been promoted from the end of the 18th century by Raja Rammohun Roy and his successors in Hindu India. Sayyid Ahman Khan spurred similar aspirations in Muslim India by founding a Muslim College at Aligarh in 1875, which in 1920 became Aligarh Muslim University, offering a modernist rather than a traditional curriculum. He had served in the East India Company, and as a magistrate had been helpful to beleaguered foreigners at the time of the 1857 independence movement. However, his main aim was to see the establishment of an environment in India where different religions could coexist and co-operate in the life of a progressive modern state. ▷ Islamic modernism; Rammohun Roy

Ahriman ▷ **Angra Mainyu**

Ahura Mazda (Ahurā Mazda) ('Wise Lord') The name for God used by Zoroaster and his followers. The world is the arena for the battle between Ahura Mazda and Angra Mainyu, the spirit of evil; a battle in which Ahura Mazda will finally prevail and become fully omnipotent. ▷ Angra Mainyu; light and darkness; Zoroastrianism

ahura The Old Iranian word *ahura* meant 'lord', the Old Indian equivalent being *asura*. In pre-Zoroastrian times the word could probably be used for great gods, and also for temporal rulers. In Zoroastrianism the word ahura and adjectives derived from it are used for beneficent divine beings, in contradistinction to *daeva*, 'demon', or 'evil supernatural being'. Apart from Ahura Mazda ('Lord Wisdom') himself, the title ahura is used of Mithra, and of the water divinity Apam Napat; the plural, ahuras, can denote beneficent divine beings generally. ▷ Ahura Mazda; daevas; Zoroastrianism

Aidan, St, known as the 'Apostle of Northumbria' (d.651). Monk from the Celtic monastery on the island of Iona in Scotland, he was summoned in 635 by King Oswald of Northumbria to evangelize the north. He established a church and monastery on the island of Lindisfarne, of which he was appointed the first bishop, and from there he travelled throughout Northumbria founding churches. He died in the church he had built at Bamburgh; his feast day is 31 August. ▷ missions, Christian; monasticism

Ainu Historically a physically distinct people in Japan, but now intermarried with other

Japanese and culturally assimilated; their own language and religion has largely disappeared. Traditionally hunters and fishermen, today many are factory workers and labourers. ▷ Japanese religion

Airyanam Vaejah Literally the 'homeland of the Aryans', a term used in Zoroastrian tradition to denote the original, ideal homeland of the Iranians. According to the Vendidad, a text which forms part of the Avesta, Ahura Mazda created Airyanam Vaejah as the best place on earth. There has been some academic speculation as to where this mythical country was thought to be, but the belief that such an ideal country existed at all was probably more important to Zoroastrians than its exact location. ▷ Ahura Mazda; Zoroastrianism

Ajanta An ancient Buddhist site about 50 miles from Aurangabad in Maharashtra in India, which contains 30 monastic dwelling caves and worship places cut out of the rocks. Rediscovered in 1819 after a thousand years of neglect, it is important for art history and research into Buddhism. It contains two phases of Buddhist development: a Hinayana phase from about the 2nd century BCE to the 2nd century CE, and a Mahayana phase from about the 5th to 7th centuries. The early phase shows less readiness to portray the Buddha in his own right, and has a greater emphasis upon stupas, which are present in some of the shrine rooms. In the later phase there is a proliferation in paintings and sculptures of Buddhas and bodhisattvas of various kinds, as well as portrayals of animals, birds, flowers and humans. The main episodes of the life of the Buddha are amply represented at Ajanta: his sudden confrontation with suffering in the form of illness, old age, and death, and his temptations by Mara. Also near to Aurangabad are the Ellora caves which contain important shrines cut out of the hillside for devotees of the Buddhist, Hindu and Jain traditions, although they date slightly later than most of the Ajanta finds, being from the 5th to 9th centuries. ▷ bodhisattva; Buddha; Hinayana Buddhism; Mahayana Buddhism; Mara (Buddhist); stupa

Ajivika (ājīvika) A school of world-renouncers (*shramanas*) at the time of the Buddha (5th century BCE). The Ajivikas, whose leader was Gosala, believed that life was governed by fate (*niyati*) and that each soul went through a process of reincarnation, experiencing every possible life form until it reached perfection and final release. This process took billions of years, the highest point being the Ajivika ascetic who, upon death, would attain final peace.

Akali Dal (Akālī Dāl) An Akali is a Sikh devoted to God, who is known as *Akal Purukh*, the Timeless One. The name was first used of irregular Sikh warriors who resisted oppression by the Mughal emperors at the end of the 17th century, and who defended Sikh rights against later authorities. The Akali Dal, which means the army of the Akalis, was formed in 1920 in connection with the attempt by Sikhs to wrest control of their temples, the gurdwaras, from private ownership. The Akali Dal is now a political party centred in the Punjab, supporting Sikh interests at state and national levels. It is also a major influence on the committee that manages gurdwaras in the Indian states of Haryana, Himachal Pradesh, and the Punjab, thus retaining some religious as well as political significance. ▷ Akal Purukh; gurdwara; Nihangs; Punjab

Akal Purukh (Akāl Purukh) A Sikh term for God meaning the 'Timeless One'. It is probably the main name for God in Sikh theological usage, but at the more popular level the term *Vahiguru*, God as the Eternal Guru, is more favoured. Although implicitly denying the Hindu notion of avatara—the idea that God comes down to earth—as well as the Hindu notion that God can be revered in image form, its resonance and meaning are positive rather than negative. God is changeless, is never born and never dies, is beyond time and space, is transcendent and immanent, and is present everywhere. As the creator he is both personal and compassionate, and 'he' is father and mother, in other words he is not bound by sexual metaphors. The Akal Purukh is trustworthy, inwardly knowable, and offers release from the round of rebirths as well as sustenance in this life. Other names for God, such as Vahiguru, *Satnam* (the True Name), *Sat Guru* (the True Guru), and *Nirankar* (the Formless One) have tended to coalesce with Akal Purukh in the Sikh view of the Godhead. ▷ Akali Dal; God; Mul Mantra; Nam; Nirankar; Sat Guru

Akbar the Great, properly **Jalal ud-Din Muhammad Akbar** (1542–1605) Mughal emperor of India, born at Umarkot, Sind. He succeeded his father, Humayun, in 1556, and took over the administration from his regent in 1560. Within a few years he had gained control of the whole of India north of the Vindhya Mountains. He constructed roads, established a uniform system of weights and measures, and adjusted taxation. He was unusually tolerant towards non-Muslims, and greatly encouraged literature and the arts. ▷ Islam; Mughal Empire

à Kempis, Thomas ▷ Kempis, Thomas à

akhand path (akhaṇḍ path) A reading of the Sikh scripture, the *Guru Granth Sahib*, continuously from beginning to end. A relay of readers takes part in this event, which lasts for about 48 hours. The reading is to be clear, well-enunciated and unrushed. It differs from an ordinary *path*, a reading of part of the scripture, and from a *saptahik path*, where the reading of the whole scripture may last for seven days. The practice probably dates back to the 18th century, but it grew more popular in the 19th century when printed scriptures became more widely available. An akhand path may be used on special family occasions such as weddings, deaths, or removals, and in some major Sikh temples it may be a more permanent feature of worship. It often concludes with a bhog ceremony which includes the distribution of specially-blessed food. ▷ Guru Granth Sahib; Karah Prasad

Akhenaton, also Akh(e)naten or Amenhotep (Amenophis) IV (14th century BCE) A king of Egypt, of the 18th dynasty, who renounced the old gods and introduced a purified and universalized solar cult. One of his wives was Nefertiti. ▷ Ancient Egyptian religion; pharaoh

Akhira The Islamic notion of the afterlife. This was contingent upon the Final Judgement, according to which the righteous would attain paradise and the unrighteous would be consigned to hell. Paradise could be seen either in physical terms as a beautiful garden filled with material and aesthetic attractions, or in spiritual terms, namely the joy and bliss of personally knowing Allah. Hell was seen as a physical place of fire and torment, with a variety of places to fit the nature of the transgressions committed by its occupants. Like the Christian notion of purgatory, it could be seen as a temporary rather than a permanent abiding-place. ▷ afterlife; heaven; hell; Paradise; purgatory; sin

akhlaq (akhlāq) One of the Islamic terms for ethics, another being *ihsan*. The Islamic tradition inherited various earlier ethical strands, especially from Persia and Greece, and integrated them into the Quranic world-view that lay at the heart of Islam. Miskawayh (d.1030) wrote a significant work on philosophical ethics, the *Tahdhib al-Akhlaq*, and a still deeper synthesis emerged in the work of al-Ghazali, who assimilated Miskawayh's treatise into the ethical tradition of the Quran and sunnah. Al-Ghazali's summary of Islamic morality was also influenced by mystical Sufism. This Sufi influence later increased and in the modern period Islamic modernism, as seen in the work of leaders such as al-Afghani, Muhammad Abduh and Sir Muhammad Iqbal, reacted against Sufi quietism in a more activist direction. Partly influenced by Western ethical philosophy, they advocated deeper social and political activism as well as concern for individual and family ethics. In some neo-fundamentalist circles in contemporary Islam there has been a return to the original morality of the Quran, as found behind the medieval synthesis that had incorporated elements from Persia and Greece. ▷ Abduh, Muhammad; Afghani, al-; Ghazali, Abu Hamid Mohammed al-; Iqbal, Sir Muhammad; Islamic modernism; Quran; Sufism; sunnah

Akitu The New Year festival in Ancient Babylon during the first millennium BCE, which took place over the first 11 days of the spring month of Nisan. The most important festival in the Babylonian calendar, it celebrated the national god Marduk's activity in creation and his rise to kingship over the gods by a reading of the creation epic *Enuma Elish*. Part of the festival involved the ritual humiliation and reinvestiture of the Babylonian king as an act of atonement for both king and city and as a token renewal of his kingship. As in Sumerian New Year festivals, the determination of destinies and probably a celebration of sacred marriage followed. The name Akitu also applies to the *bit akitu* (Akitu house), a building just outside the city in which part of the celebration took place. ▷ Asshur; cosmogony, Ancient Near Eastern; kingship, Ancient Near Eastern; Marduk; New Year festivals, Ancient Near Eastern

Akiva ben Joseph, Rabbi, also Akibah (c.50–135) Leading scholar and famous teacher in the formative period of rabbinical Judaism. A pupil of Rabbi Eliezer, he is credited with extensive exegetical attempts to relate Jewish legal traditions to scriptural texts, and with providing the basis for the Mishnah by his systematic grouping and codification of the *halakhoth* (legal traditions). He apparently supported the revolt against Rome under Bar Kokhbah in 132, and was martyred by the Romans soon afterwards. ▷ Bar Kokhbah; Halakhah; Judaism; Mishnah

al- ▷ main name

aladura A Yoruba (Nigeria) word meaning 'one who prays', applied 1 to a movement of religious revival in Western Nigeria following World War I; 2 to a group of churches which emerged from the movement; 3 to African Independent churches of the prophet-healing type as a whole, especially in West Africa.
The revival movement began with a prayer group among Yoruba Anglicans in Ijebu-Ode during the 1918 influenza epidemic. The group stressed prayer and fasting and experienced visions and healing. It grew in the Depression years, especially through the charismatic preaching of Joseph Babalola, a steamroller driver, producing a movement towards Christianity in areas previously little touched, as well as exciting religious and political fervour. In the early 1930s a link was established with British Pentecostalism, though for most of the movements this was a temporary liaison. Churches originating from the movement include Faith Tabernacle, the Christ Apostolic Church, the Church of the Lord (Aladura) and the many divisions of the Cherubim and Seraphim. The spread of these churches beyond Yorubaland, and the parallel features in many African churches elsewhere, has facilitated wider use of the term. ▷ African Independent churches; Zionist churches

alaya-vijnana (ālaya-vijñāna) One of the eight or nine kinds of consciousness in Buddhist thought and psychology elaborated mainly by the *Yogacara* school of Mahayana Buddhism. Alaya-vijnana is the 'store-consciousness', the storehouse of tendencies built up over successive births and deaths. It is from this storehouse that everyday experiences are formed. Although in dynamic flux, being constantly added to and subtracted from, it is this seed-store that becomes modified to appear as the mental and physical worlds of daily living. The theory is an attempt to explain how a person can be reborn many times and yet not be a permanent 'self'. The alaya-vijnana is the persisting element or basic consciousness in each person within the ongoing cycle of births and deaths, yet it is not equivalent to a 'self'. Meditation and mental insight are required to understand it and to transform it. The notion of alaya-vijnana was propounded in India in the 4th century CE by Asanga and his younger brother Vasubandhu, and expounded more fully 200 years later by Dharmapala. When Dharmapala was translated into Chinese the theory became important there. ▷ anatman; Asanga; bhavana; Dharmapala, Anagarika; Vasubandhu; Yogacara

Albertus Magnus, St, Count of Bollstädt (c.1200–1280) German philosopher, bishop, and Doctor of the Church, often called the 'Doctor Universalis' (Universal Doctor), born in Lauingen. He studied at Padua, and joined the Dominican order, becoming a teacher of theology. His most famous pupil was Thomas Aquinas. In 1254 he became provincial of the Dominicans in Germany, and in 1260 was named bishop of Ratisbon. In 1262 he retired to his convent in Cologne to devote himself to literary pursuits, and died there. He excelled all his contemporaries in the breadth of his learning, and helped to bring together theology and Aristotelianism. He was canonized in 1932. His feast day is 15 November. ▷ Aquinas, St Thomas; Aristotle; Dominicans; scholasticism; theology

Albigenses, or **Albigensians** Followers of a form of Christianity which in the 11th and 12th centuries especially had its main strength in the town of Albi, in south-west France. It was derived from 3rd-century followers of the Persian religious teacher, Mani, whose ideas gradually spread along trade routes to Europe, especially Italy and France. Also known as Cathari or Bogomiles, they believed life on earth to be a struggle between good (spirit) and evil (matter). In extreme cases they were rigidly ascetic, with marriage, food, and procreation all condemned. They believed in the transmigration of souls. Condemned by Rome and the Inquisition, they were devastated in the early 13th-century crusade against them, which also broke down the distinctive civilization of Provence in France. ▷ Cathars; Christianity; Inquisition; Mani

Albinus ▷ **Alcuin**

alchemy The search for a substance sometimes called the 'philosopher's stone' that will change base metals into gold, and endow human beings with longevity, immortality or spiritual perfection. Alchemy is a subtle alliance of chemistry and spirituality which, although questioned by scientific chemistry, has been an important factor in material and spiritual exploration. It was a significant element in religious Taoism in China between the 5th and 9th centuries, and various works on it were included in the Taoist Canon. They focused on the search for longevity and immortality by exploring through alchemy the theories of yin and yang, the five elements (earth, fire, metal, water, wood), and the mystical trigrams of the *I Ching*. European alchemy had its origins in Alexandria and Gnostic thought whereby base metals 'stood for' human beings, the philosopher's stone became the vehicle to eternal life, and change became the evolution from ignorance to spiritual perfection. Chinese and Greek alchemy came to the Arab world and thence to Europe where it was an important spiritual and scientific factor from the 14th to 17th centuries, even involving scholars such as Isaac Newton (1643–1727). After the scientific revolution of the 17th century it became reduced to insignificance in the West but interest in it has revived recently through the work of Carl Jung and new age thought, and in South-East Asia it has never really died out. ▷ Gnosticism; I Ching; Jung, Carl Gustav; new age religion; Taoism; yin and yang

alchemy, Chinese This has usually been associated with three aims: primarily with the search for immortality, but also with the search for perfection of spirit and for elevation into the hierarchy of the gods. The two key forms of alchemy were concerned firstly with achieving immortality, perfection of spirit, and appointment to the celestial hierarchy through working on metals and chemicals, and secondly with achieving these aims inwardly through meditation and breath control. Essentially alchemy was associated with a kind of mysticism. It was also often connected with and existed alongside religious Taoism. The oldest surviving book on alchemy, written by Wei Po Yeng in the 2nd century CE, quotes concepts from the *Tao Te Ching*, the *I Ching*, and yin/yang theory, and is an interesting combination of alchemy, breath control and meditation. In this the impression is given that internal self-cultivation is a more dominant concern than the literal cultivation of gold out of base metals, although that was attempted as well. ▷ Chinese pantheon; I Ching; immortality; Tao Te Ching; yin and yang

Alcuin, originally **Ealhwine** or **Albinus** (c.735–804) Writer, theologian, and adviser of the emperor Charlemagne, and thus a major influence on the Carolingian revival of learning. He was born in York and educated at the cloister school, of which in 778 he became master. Invited to Charlemagne's court (781), he devoted himself to the education of the royal family. As a result, the court became a school of culture for the hitherto almost barbarous Frankish Empire. In 796 he settled in Tours as abbot; the school there soon became one of the most important in the empire. His works comprise poems; works on grammar, rhetoric, and dialectics; theological and ethical treatises; lives of several saints; and over 200 letters.

Alexandria, Catechetical School of A school of theology which flourished in Alexandria from the 2nd century to the end of the 4th century CE, and was also influential in Caesarea and Rome. Probably founded by Panctaenus, its greatest teachers were Clement of Alexandria and Origen, who tried to blend classical philosophy with Christian teaching, emphasizing the unity of the divine, and an allegorical interpretation of scripture. It displayed spiritualizing and mystical tendencies, and is generally contrasted with the contemporary School of Antioch. ▷ Athanasius, St; Christology; Clement of Alexandria, St; Origen

Alexandria, Christianity in Alexandria was founded by Alexander the Great in 332BCE and was long renowned as the intellectual centre of Hellenistic Judaism that produced Philo and *The Wisdom of Solomon*. It continued as the capital city of the Roman administration of Egypt, as important as Rome and Antioch (which also became centres of early Christianity). Nothing definite is known about the origins of Christianity in Alexandria, but later unsubstantiated tradition connects the city with the preaching of St Mark.

The Alexandrian theological school, the Didaskaleion, produced scholars like Clement of Alexandria and his famous pupil Origen, followed later by Arius and Athanasius. Under the influence of neo-platonism, it championed the use of philosophy in theology, logos Christology (with a stress on the divinity of Christ tending towards the extremes of Apollinarianism and Monophysitism, and away from the opposite heresies of adoptionism and Nestorianism that followed from the stress on Christ's humanity by the rival school of Antioch), and mystical and allegorical interpretation of scripture. Christian Alexandria (like the Jewish Alexandria that produced the Septuagint, the 2nd-century BCE Greek version of the Old Testament) became the source of Greek versions of the Bible, probably including the famous 4th-century Codex Vaticanus and Codex Sinaiticus, which are often considered the most useful of all the surviving manuscripts. ▷ adoptionism; Arianism; Athanasius, St; Clement of Alexandria, St; Mark, St; Nestorians; Origen; Septuagint

Algonquin, or **Algonkin religion** The Algonquin language family of Native American peoples (which includes, among others, the Arapaho, Blackfoot, Cheyenne, Cree, Lenape or Delaware and Ojibwa) cover an area of Central and Eastern North America from the sub-Arctic to far south of the Great Lakes. Despite this variety of habitat and way of life, and so many neighbouring cultural influences, there are many common elements. The key religious concept is manitou, 'the mysterious', 'the supernatural'. Belief in the supreme God (*Kitshi Manitou*), the pillar of the universe (to whom the pillar at the centre of the cult house points), is older than Algonquin contact with Christianity. Under him are sun and moon, the thunder gods, the earth mother, the masters of the animals (a master for each species on which life depends). The Great Hare (or white deity) is a culture hero, creative and benign; his twin, Wolf, represents darker forces. There is a trickster figure Wisaka (popularly 'Whiskey Jack') and a baleful monster, the *windigo*. In the vision quest seekers may meet their personal guardian spirits, and receive their own medicine bundle. The society of Midewiwin guards occult knowledge, with the medicine lodge as its ritual focus; shamanistic healing is practised, and the northern Algonquin know the shaking tent. ▷ Manitou; medicine bundle; medicine lodge; shaking tent; vision quest; windigo

Ali ('Ali ibn Abī Ṭālib (d.661) Cousin and son-in-law of Muhammad and fourth caliph. He converted to Islam while still a boy, and later married the prophet's daughter Fatimah. He withdrew, or was excluded from, government during the caliphates of Abu-Bakr and Omar, and disagreed with Uthman in the interpretation of the Quran and application of the law. Although not involved in the death of Uthman he was elected caliph soon after, but encountered considerable opposition, led by Muawiya, governor of Syria, which was the beginning of a major division within Islam which has persisted to the present day. The issue was still undecided when he was murdered in the mosque in Kufa, his capital, by a member of a third Muslim party, the Kharijites. ▷ Abu-Bakr; caliphate; Kharijites; Muhammad; Omar; Quran; Shiism; sunnah; Uthman

Allah (Allāh) The Muslim name for God. In pre-Islamic Arabia Allah had been a supreme deity but not the only one. In the Quran Allah is portrayed as the sole, unique God as in the basic Muslim statement of faith 'Allah is Allah and Muhammad is his prophet'. His unity (*tauhid*) is stressed over the ultimate deviation of polytheism (*shirk*). Allah is omnipotent and dominant but also compassionate. He is the transcendent Lord who is the creator and sustainer of the world and the bestower of its gifts. He is also the judge who will reward believers and the righteous, and punish unbelievers and the unrighteous. Later theologians distinguished the attributes of Allah belonging to his essence, namely Life, Knowledge, Power, Will, Hearing, Sight and Speech, from other attributes such as creating and sustaining, belonging to his action. There is also a classical list of the 99 names of Allah known as the 'Most Beautiful Names' that can be used in prayer and worship. Muslim thinkers later debated the relation of Allah's omnipotence to the possibility of human free will, and the relation of Allah's justice to his mercy. They also discussed the ethics of philosophizing about Allah rather than accepting his revelation unquestioningly, and they questioned the relationship between his mysterious presence and his transcendent otherness. The debate continues. ▷ God; Muhammad; Quran; shirk; Sufism

almsgiving The making of gifts of money, food or clothing to the poor and the needy. This is widely recognized as a fundamental religious duty and figures strongly in Buddhism, Judaism, Christianity and Islam, though not so strongly in the ancient religions of Mesopotamia, Greece and Rome. Sometimes the giving of alms earns divine merit for the donor.

almsgiving, Buddhist Almsgiving is an important aspect of Buddhist life. At the ordinary level it is manifested in generosity and a willingness to give in a general sense, including hospitality to one's neighbours. At a higher level it may take the form of giving the wherewithal to build a Buddhist monastery, pagoda or shrine. Above all, within the Buddhist context, it has taken the form of layfolk giving alms to Buddhist monks. This mainly consists of food, although occasionally it can be clothes and other items, and in Theravada countries such as Sri Lanka it may involve giving food to monks daily and providing occasional special meals for them. Although almsgiving is recognized as a way of gaining merit, emphasis is placed in Buddhist thought on the intention and unselfishness latent in the act. An everyday mark of being a lay Buddhist, it is part of the general ethical practice built into Buddhist life. ▷ pancasila; sila

Altamira Palaeolithic limestone cave of c.13 500BCE on the north Spanish coast near Santander, celebrated for its vivid ceiling paintings of game animals (principally bison, bulls, horses, hinds, and boars), some being over 2 m/6½ ft long. Though discovered in 1879 by local landowner Marcellino de Sautuola, its authenticity was not established before 1902. It is now a world heritage site. ▷ prehistoric religion

altjiranga, or **alcheringa** A fundamental concept held in aboriginal religion. It refers to the time known as 'the Dreaming' or 'the Dreamtime'—the period before living memory (but possibly relatively recent) when their heroic ancestors roamed the world and created it as they now know it. These forebears shaped the landscape by giving parts of themselves to it, eg their eyes for waterholes, their tails for trees. They also created the different types of animal and plant species, and laid down laws for living by. ▷ Australian Aboriginal religion; creation myths

Alvar (Ālvār) The name given to particularly fervent devotional Hindu saints of the Vaishava tradition, prominent between the 2nd and 10th centuries CE, who travelled through southern India, composing and singing poetry, much of which has subsequently become sacred text. The word Alvar means 'diver', and is attributed to one who enters into the depth of mystical experience. Alvars are closely associated with the Tamils of Southern India. ▷ Hinduism; Vishnu

Amar Das, Guru (Amar Dās) (1479–1574) Third of the 10 Sikh gurus, born in the Punjab, India. He became guru in 1552, succeeding Guru Angad, and was in turn succeeded by his son-in-law Guru Ram Das. Amar Das strengthened the growing Sikh community, and deepened its system of pastoral oversight by organizing it into 22 geographical units and by giving women more preaching responsibility. He also developed the structure and self-awareness of the Sikh community by increasing the importance for Sikhs of the Baisakhi and Divali festivals, and by building a bathing centre in Goindwal as a pilgrimage place for Sikhs in addition to Hardwar. He deepened the importance of the *Langar*, the practice of sharing food together in a gurdwara, which had already been established by Guru Nanak. During his time as guru he met the Mughal emperor Akbar, and through his efforts the political significance of the growing Sikh movement developed further. ▷ Akbar the Great; Angad, Guru; Baisakhi; Divali/Deepavali; guru, Sikh; Langar; Nanak; Ram Das, Guru

Amaterasu The sun goddess of Japan who is the supreme *kami* (sacred power) of the Shinto pantheon. She is mentioned in the original chronicles of Shinto, the *Kojiki* and *Nihongi*, as the goddess through whose grandson the imperial line of Japan became established. The divine origin of the emperor was thus justified, and this theory held until the end of World War II. She became enshrined at Ise at an early date as a sacred figure and, as Shinto and Buddhism drew closer together, she became associated with the sun Buddha Vairocana and they were worshipped jointly at the Ise shrines. Her symbol is a mirror, which is the symbol of the sun, but despite her importance she is not portrayed in art form. ▷ Ise shrines; kami; Vairocana

Ambedkar, Bhimrao Ranji (1893–1956) Indian politician and champion of the depressed castes, born in a Ratnagiri village on the Konkan coast of Bombay, the son of an Indian soldier. Educated at Elphinstone College, Bombay, Columbia University, New York, and the London School of Economics, he became a London barrister and later a member of the Bombay legislative assembly and leader of 60000000 untouchables. In 1941 he became a member of the governor-general's council. Appointed Law Minister in 1947, he was the principal author of the Indian constitution. He resigned in 1951 and with some thousands of his followers he publicly embraced the Buddhist faith not long before his death. His dedicated work for the outcasts strengthened Indian public opinion which secured a better life for them. His publications include *Annihilation of Caste* (1937). ▷ Buddhism; caste

Ambrose, St (c.339–397) Roman churchman, and one of the four Latin Doctors of the Church (with St Augustine, St Jerome, and Gregory the Great). Born in Trier, the son of the prefect of Gaul, he practised law in Rome and in 369 was appointed consular prefect of Upper Italy, whose capital was Milan, and which was then the centre of controversy between Catholics and Arian 'heretics'. When the bishopric fell vacant in 374, Ambrose was chosen to be bishop by universal acclamation, even though he was still only a catechumen undergoing instruction. He was quickly baptized, and consecrated bishop eight days later. He fought for the integrity of the church at the imperial court, resisted the empress-regent Justina over the introduction of Arian churches, and even forced the emperor himself, Theodosius I, 'the Great', to do public penance over the massacre of Thessalonica in 390. He introduced the use of hymns, and made many improvements in the service, such as the Ambrosian ritual and Ambrosian chant. His feast day is 7 December. ▷ Arius; Augustine, St (of Hippo); Gregory I, the Great; heresy; Jerome, St

Amerindian religions ▷ Native American religions

Amesha Spentas An Avestan term meaning 'Beneficent Immortals'. In the Zoroastrian tradition the term is most often used to denote the six divine helpers of Ahura Mazda who form a Heptad together with him, and each of whom is in charge of part of his Creation, viz, Vohu Manah, 'Good Thought' (in charge of beneficent animals), Asha Vahishta, 'Best Righteousness' (fire), Khshathra Vairya, 'the Sovereignty that must be chosen' (metals), Spenta Armaiti, 'Beneficent Devotion' (earth), Haurvatat, 'Wholeness' (water), Ameretat, 'Immortality' (plants). In early Zoroastrianism the divinity Spenta Mainyu, 'Beneficent Spirit', was probably held to be part of this group, forming a heptad with the other six Amesha Spentas, but his concept lost much of its individuality in the course of time. In a few late texts the term Amesha Spentas appears to be used loosely to denote divinities generally. ▷ Ahura Mazda; Avesta; Zoroastrianism

Ameer Ali (Sayyid Amīr 'Alī) (1849–1928) Muslim modernizing reformer, born in India. He was associated with other Indian Muslim reformers such as Sir Sayyid Ahmad Khan and Sir Muhammad Iqbal in the attempt to reinterpret Indian Islam in the light of the modern world. Influenced by Western humanist writers including Gibbon and Shakespeare, his greatest work, *The Spirit of Islam*, was first published in 1873. His aim was to revive Islam from what he saw as stagnation. He hoped to defend it against attack from the West, as well as from internal enemies, and from Westernization. At the same time he wanted to enable it to adjust to Western education, science and democracy through a rational and apologetic presentation of Islamic history and principles. He therefore felt that the problem of evil, and the Quran itself, could be approached figuratively and metaphorically rather than literally. He represents one of the most effective illustrations of modern Islamic liberalism. ▷ Iqbal, Sir Muhammad; Islamic modernism; Ahmad Khan, Sir Sayyid; Quran

Amidah (Hebrew 'standing') The principal component of the daily prayers of Talmudic Judaism, recited while standing, and said silently except when in a congregational service. It consists of 19 (originally 18) benedictions, firstly in praise of God, secondly asking for his help (petitions), and closing with thanksgiving. An altered form of the prayer is also recited on sabbaths and festivals. ▷ Judaism; Shema; Talmud

Amida worship The worship of Amida Buddha in Japanese Pure Land Buddhism. In India Amida has been known as the bodhisattva Amitabha, and the original Pure Land Sutra had been Indian, but in China a separate Pure Land school emerged that became and remains strong, and Pure Land Buddhism was introduced from China into Japan by Ennin in 847CE within the Tendai school. The first major Japanese Pure Land (*Jodo*) school was founded in 1175 by Honen (1130–1212), based upon faith in the grace of Amida Buddha through repetition of Amida's name, which produces rebirth in Amida's Pure Land or paradise. Shinran (1173–1262) innovated by ending priestly celibacy, and by stressing that Amida's grace was available despite continuing sin on the basis that if a good person can receive Amida's grace, how much more so can a bad person. The True Pure Land (*Jodo Shinshu*) school, which became the largest Pure Land group, emerged as a result of his work. Behind Amida worship lay the theory that a third phase in Buddhist history had arisen due to the 'decline of history' in which the harder way to salvation based on self-effort was no longer appropriate, and what was needed was faith and reliance on 'other-power', the mercy and grace of Amida Buddha. Amida sits on a lotus seat, has a huge halo, and is said to have 84000 marks or virtues; his Pure Land is a paradise where beings can remain until they attain nirvana. Repeating the *nembutsu*, 'I put my faith in Amida Buddha', is an important element in Amida worship; if said with sincerity, it can bring salvation. ▷ bodhisattva; Ennin; Honen; Jodo; Jodo Shinshu; nembutsu; Tendai

Amish A conservative offshoot of the Mennonites which emerged in Switzerland around 1693 under the leadership of the Anabaptist Jakob Amman (c.1645–c.1730). Migration to the USA, particularly in the 1870s, led to the formation of more liberal groups. Only the

Old Order Amish (founded 1720–40) still maintain their founder's strict regulations on dress, customs, and non-co-operation with the state. ▷ Mennonites

Amos (835–765BCE) Old Testament prophet, the earliest prophet in the Bible to have a book named after him. A herdsman from the village of Tekoa, near Bethlehem of Judaea, he denounced the iniquities of the northern kingdom of Israel. ▷ Old Testament; prophet

Amos, Book of One of the 12 so-called 'minor' prophetic writings in the Hebrew Bible/Old Testament; attributed to the prophet Amos, who was active in the Northern kingdom of Israel in the mid 8th century BCE. It proclaims judgement on Israel's neighbours for idolatry, and on Israel itself for social injustices and ethical immorality. ▷ Amos; Israel, tribes of; Old Testament; prophet

amrit A form of drink used by Sikhs in their ritual and on special occasions. The word means 'nectar'. It is a solution of sugar-crystals dissolved in water by being stirred by a double-edged sword while the Sikh scriptures are being recited. Amrit is especially important in connection with naming and initiation rituals. During the *amrit sanskar*, the ceremony of initiation, it is drunk in cupped hands by the candidates for initiation, and sprinkled on parts of their head. Amrit also has allegorical and spiritual significance. An amrit bani is an immortal saying, with the inference that such a saying from the Sikh scripture is nectar. The notion of amrit is also applied to God's Name (*Nam*), and God's Word (*Shabad*). Thus physical amrit can point to spiritual nectar, and vice versa. ▷ five Ks; Nam; Shabad

Amritsar City in the Punjab, north-west India, the centre of the Sikh religion. It was founded in 1577 by Guru Ram Das around a sacred tank, known as the pool of immortality. The Golden Temple, found at the centre of the tank, is particularly sacred to Sikhs; under the gold and copper dome is kept the sacred book of the Sikhs, the *Adi Granth*. The city was the centre of the Sikh empire in the 19th century, and of modern Sikh nationalism. In recent times, the storming of the Golden Temple by Indian soldiers during its occupation by Sikh radicals was a cause of the assassination in 1984 of Indira Gandhi by Sikh bodyguards. ▷ Adi Granth; Punjab; Ram Das, Guru; Sikhism

Amun (also **Amen, Amon**) From the Middle Kingdom onwards the supreme deity in Ancient Egyptian religion. Although mentioned as a primeval god in the tradition of Hermopolis, it was as a local god of Thebes that Amun achieved prominence. When the princes of Thebes became rulers of Egypt, Amun became the supreme state god, worshipped throughout Egypt. He was particularly venerated in the New Kingdom (c.1567–1085BCE), and as royal patron was given the qualities of the sun god Re, as the god Amun-Re. Amun was worshipped as one of the Theban Triad with his consort Mut and their son Khons. Amun's priests acquired considerable political power, and the god's persecution by the heretic pharaoh Akhenaton may have been partly a reaction to this, but Amun was firmly reinstated by Akhenaton's successors. Not just a royal god, he was worshipped by ordinary people as a protector of the needy. Amun was associated as a creative deity with the ram and the goose, and was often depicted as a man wearing a tall plumed head-dress. ▷ Akhenaton; Atenism; Re; Thebes

Anabaptists The collective name given to groups of believers stemming from the more radical elements of the 16th-century Reformation; also known as Rebaptizers. They believed in the baptism of believing adults only, refusing to recognize infant baptism. They emphasized adherence to the word of scripture, strict Church discipline, and the separation of Church and State. Being prepared to criticize the state, they frequently suffered savage persecution. They were associated with Thomas Münzer and the Zwinglian prophets in Wittenberg (1521); the Swiss brethren in Zürich (1525); and Jan Mattys (died 1534) in Münster (1533–4), where the Anabaptists achieved supremacy; and spread to Moravia, north and west Germany, the Low Countries (especially the Mennonites in Holland), and later the USA. They were the forerunners of the Baptists, who are in many respects their spiritual heirs. ▷ baptism; Baptists; Mennonites; Münzer, Thomas; Reformation; Zwingli, Huldreich

anaconda The anaconda, the great rain forest snake, has special significance for some of the Arawak, Carib and Warrau hunting groups of Guyana and the Caribbean fringe of South America. There are several versions of a myth of the anaconda as lord of the animals, in which his many-hued skin gives birds, and sometimes all animals, their colours. This makes the anaconda valued by hunters, who wear snakeskin headbands. Plants which give supernatural powers to the hunter are thought to have grown from the ashes of the primordial anaconda.

anagamin (anāgāmin) A term used in Theravada Buddhism for the 'non-returner', one who will not be reborn into this world at the end of this life. It is a third stage of life for a person of advanced spirituality. The first stage is that of 'entering the stream', an entry which will culminate eventually in the end of all rebirths. The second stage is that of the 'once-returner', one who has only one more life to live on earth after this one. In the third stage the Buddhist overcomes the five remaining fetters that bind humans to the sensual world of birth and death, namely belief in a soul, doubt, belief in rituals, sensuality and ill-will. When he dies he will not return to the world but will live in the heavenly sphere. There he will become an *arahat*, or saint. ▷ arahat; bodhisattva; Theravada Buddhism

anagarika (anagārika) An Indian, mainly Buddhist, term meaning a 'non-householder'—one who has left home and renounced its comforts in order to go out and seek the meaning of life. This notion of leaving the household to become a wandering seeker, or a holy person, was common in ancient India and is still honoured today. It was after he left his palace and family in order to seek the answer to the problem of suffering and to attain enlightenment that Sakyamuni became 'the Buddha', the enlightened one. The early followers of the Buddha also became non-householders, and they looked to householders for the necessities of life that would sustain them. Buddhist scriptures describe various motives for becoming an anagarika: 'I am subject to birth, decay, death, sorrow, lamentation, suffering and depression of heart; being thus afflicted how now if I were to seek for an end of all this mass of suffering?' (*Majjhima Nikaya* I.192). By leaving the householder status, obstacles of family and lack of opportunity to engage in good acts and conquer suffering could be overcome, in spite of the possible decline in material benefits that would ensue. ▷ bodhi; Buddha; tipitaka

Anahita (Anāhitā) Prominent female divinity known in the Zoroastrian tradition as Ardvi Sura Anahita, 'the moist, mighty pure one'. This composite name was probably the result of the identification of an originally Eastern Iranian river goddess, Ardvi Sura Harahvaiti, with the goddess Anahiti/Anahita. The cult of the latter divinity, perhaps inspired by that of the goddess Ishtar in neighbouring Babylonia, appears to have been very popular in Western Iran at the time when Zoroastrianism first became prominent there. The evidence of the Pahlavi books suggests that the Zoroastrian priesthood remained aware of the originally separate identities of Ardvi Sura and Anahita. The divinity is particularly associated with water, with prosperity and with women's affairs. ▷ Pahlavi; Zoroastrianism

analogy, argument from One of the theories postulating the existence of God. Popular in the 18th and 19th centuries, it maintained that the universe is like a mechanism; therefore if a mechanism requires a maker, so does the universe. ▷ God, arguments for the existence of

Ananda (Ānanda) (5th–6th century BCE) Cousin and favourite pupil of the Buddha. Noted for his devotion to the Buddha, and a skilled interpreter of his teachings, he was instrumental in establishing an order for women disciples. ▷ Buddha; Buddhism

Ananda Marg (Ānanda Mārg) A new religious movement founded in India in 1955 by Anandamurti. It means literally the 'way of joy'. Compared with some other new religious movements of Indian origin, such as the Raja Yoga movement and Divine Light mission, it has strong social and political motivation as well as a spiritual input. Ananda Marg spread to the West after 1970. It is based upon a lifestyle that combines bodily purity, correct diet, appropriate posture and social service with a systematic programme of meditation. Celibacy, although not absolute, is recommended for seriously involved members, and procreation in marriage is the only motive for which sexual union is allowed. There has been a strong sense of commitment to the leader of the movement, as evidenced by the fact that when he was imprisoned by the Indian authorities some followers burnt themselves to death in support of him. Although present in the West it tends to be traditionally Hindu in its basic orientation. ▷ Divine Light Mission; new religious movements in the West; Raja Yoga

Anat, or **Anath** Canaanite goddess of love and war, sister and probably consort of Baal. In the Ras Shamra texts Anat is often described by the epithet 'virgin', and presented as the violent helper of Baal in his struggles. When Baal has been killed by Mot, god of death and sterility, she mourns him and searches for him in the underworld, where she releases him by killing his adversary Mot, an action described in terms reminiscent of the harvest. After the Hyskos invasion (17th century BCE) Anat became known in Egypt as the consort of Baal-Sutekh, and was chosen as personal patron by the pharaoh Rameses II (1304–1237BCE). In the Hellenistic period she was fused with the goddess Astarte and worshipped as Atargatis, the 'Syrian Goddess'. ▷ Aramaean religion; Astarte; Baal; Canaanite religion; Ras Shamra texts; Seth; Ugarit

anatman (anātman; Pali: anatta) The Buddhist idea of the 'no-self'. According to Theravada Buddhist teaching it is one of the three basic qualities of worldly existence. It is closely allied to the notion of *anicca* or impermanence, because if everything in the universe is impermanent and in flux there can be no such thing as a permanent and enduring self. There is only a temporary coming together of constituent elements (*skandhas*) with no central motor activating them or holding them together. There are bodily acts, feelings, and thoughts—but no actor, feeler, or thinker. And those acts, feelings and thoughts are themselves in constant flux: they appear and then they vanish. Therefore the notion of an ongoing personal identity is an illusion which produces attachment to one's own selfhood, and the selfishness that results from this makes it impossible to attain nirvana. It is essential to overcome the delusion of 'self' so that release from the round of rebirths can occur. Various Buddhist meditational disciplines are aimed at building up the truth of the 'no-self' in a person. Philosophically there was absolute opposition to the Hindu notion of the self (atman) as a permanent entity. Within Buddhism there have arisen approximations to the concept of the self in the notion of *pudgala* (person by another name), in the Mahayana theory of the *alaya-vijnana* (storehouse-consciousness), and in the idea of the Buddha nature. However, even they have avoided any sense of the reality of the empirical self. The self appears to be real, but a good part of salvation lies in realizing that this is not the case. ▷ alaya-vijnana; atman; nirvana; rebirth; skandhas; Theravada Buddhism

ancestor reverence, Chinese Ancestor veneration is a long-standing element within Chinese life. It dates back to the early Shang dynasty, founded about 1500BCE, and has persisted down to the present day, outlasting the attempts of the Cultural Revolution of 1966 to 1976 to annihilate it. One of the Chinese Classics, the *Classic of Rites*, summarizes the various ritual features that are part of ancestor reverence. A number of factors have helped to preserve the veneration of ancestors in China. Confucian funeral rites feed into it, it maintains family unity and continuity, it bolsters filial piety and, in religious terms, the ancestor benefits the living from the transcendent world while the ancestor's soul is helped by the offerings of the living in this world. This applies especially to the *po* soul which normally lives in the burial ground and can become malevolent if not assuaged. Ancestors normally wield power for three to five generations and are then replaced by others nearer to the memory of the living. In the Confucian tradition ancestor reverence before the special altars in ancestral halls is very important, whereas more informal ancestor reverence is practised using altars set up in the home. ▷ Chinese religion in Taiwan and Hong Kong (20th century); Chinese religion on the China mainland (20th century)

ancestors, African For most African peoples, the ancestors form one of the most important (for some *the* most important) elements in the spirit world. Only in a minority of African primal religions is prayer or worship directly and regularly offered to God; in many more the ancestors mediate between God and the family or community, and prayer may be directed to or through them. The religious significance of the ancestors is a reflection of the importance and the solidarity of the family in Africa. Death does not destroy that solidarity; 'the living dead', as John Mbiti calls them, as elders of the family, maintain their interest in the family and have a right to be respected and consulted about family matters, just as they would have when living. Indeed, they may have sanctions to require respect, neglect of the ancestors, or their wishes or standards, possibly bringing illness or misfortune.

The veneration of ancestors means that ancestral status is not accorded to unworthy people—to the sort of people who are best forgotten. Nor does it usually belong to 'unlucky' people—those who died violently (unless, perhaps, as honourable warriors) or of unclean diseases. Nor, naturally, does it belong to those who die without children, one reason why childlessness in Africa is deemed such a tragedy.

In addition to genealogical ancestors within a particular family, communal heroes of the past—those who are 'fathers of their people'—may be venerated. And on some occasions the help of particular ancestors may be sought; those who in life had a special expertise may be called on when that skill is needed. In practice genealogical ancestors are not regularly venerated beyond a few generations back. Just as proper funerary rites are necessary for a recently-departed member of the family, commemorative offerings will be made at anniversaries. Offerings may also be required to propitiate neglect or wrong-doing (and thus remove the misfortune that has followed), as thanks for benefits secured, or to pass on to God, or to some ruling divinity.

Ancient Egyptian religion The isolation of Ancient Egypt (c.3100–30BCE) and unique geography of the Nile Valley were influential in the development of distinctive and persistent religious ideas. The early worship of tribal deities developed into the often animal-headed local and state gods, many of which represented forces in the natural world which needed to be entreated through worship and sacrifice. The pharaoh played an important role as an incarnation of the god Horus and was himself responsible for the cult of all the gods. In the 14th century BCE Akhenaton made an unsuccessful attempt to establish Aten, the sun's disc, as sole national deity. The Egyptians were optimistic about the afterlife, for which they made elaborate preparations, including the mummification of corpses and building of large funerary monuments such as the pyramids. Over the 3000 years of Ancient Egyptian civilization developments in belief were balanced by a deep conservatism, and the religion was very tolerant of contradictory ideas. ▷ afterlife, Ancient Egyptian concept of; Akhenaton; animal cults; Atenism; funerary practices, Ancient Egyptian; Horus; mummification; Nile; pharaoh; pyramids

Egyptian god Anubis weighing the souls of the dead

Ancient Near Eastern religions The civilizations of the Ancient Near East covered an area stretching from Asia Minor and Mesopotamia through Syria and Palestine to Egypt. There was always considerable contact between the various peoples of this region and they shared many religious ideas. Mesopotamia was the home of the earliest urban society, that of Sumer (4th and 3rd millenia BCE), and Sumerian religion was adopted to a large extent by the Semitic Babylonians and Assyrians, despite their different ethnic background and language. Although they promoted their own national gods above those of the Sumerian pantheon, these and other invaders of the region merged into a common Mesopotamian religious tradition which remained stable over many centuries. Assyro-Babylonian influence was always felt strongly on the borders of Mesopotamia. To the north the Hurrians and Hittites in Asia Minor adopted many Mesopotamian ideas while retaining strong traditions of their own. In western Persia the Elamite kingdom was a distinctive religious centre, viewed by Mesopotamians as a land of witches and magic. In Syria and Palestine the West Semitic peoples (Aramaeans, Canaanites and Phoenicians) formed another relatively unified cultural area, although one about which there is much less information. The most important discovery for the study of West Semitic religion has been the site of ancient Ugarit at Ras Shamra on the Syrian coast. The nature of the available evidence makes it hard to write a comprehensive study of Ancient Near Eastern religions. Late literary sources are often unreliable and archaeological evidence limited. Such evidence as exists is almost all concerned with state religion, temples and kings, and it is extremely difficult to construct a picture of the religious life of ordinary people. ▷ Canaanite religion; Elamites; Hittite religion; Hurrian religion; Phoenician religion

Andrewes, Lancelot (1555–1626) English prelate and scholar, born in Barking. Educated at Ratcliffe, Mechant Taylors' School, and Pembroke Hall, Cambridge, he took orders in 1580, and in 1589, through Walsingham's influence, was appointed a prebendary of St Paul's and Master of Pembroke Hall. In 1597 Queen Elizabeth made him a prebendary, and in 1601 dean, of Westminster. He rose still higher in favour with King James VI and I, who appreciated his learning and oratory. He attended the Hampton Court Conference, and took part in the translation of the Authorized Version of the Bible (1607). In 1605 he was consecrated bishop of Chichester; in 1609 he was translated to Ely, and in 1618 to Winchester. A powerful preacher and defender of Anglican doctrines, he is considered one of the most learned theologians of his time. His *Private Prayers*, written in Greek, were published posthumously. ▷ Authorized Version of the Bible

Andrew, St One of the 12 apostles, brother of Simon Peter, a fisherman converted by John the Baptist. Tradition says he preached the gospel in Asia Minor and Scythia, and was crucified in Achaia (Greece) by order of the Roman governor. The belief that his cross was X-shaped dates only from the 14th century. The patron saint of Scotland and Russia, his feast day is 30 November. ▷ apostles; disciples (early Christian); John, St (the Baptist)

Angad, Guru (Aṅgad, Gurū) (1504–52) Second of the Sikh gurus, born in the Punjab, India. He became a disciple of the first guru, Guru Nanak, and was installed by him as second guru in 1539. His original name was Lehna, but it was changed by Guru Nanak to Angad, meaning 'limb', because Guru Nanak's own sons were less worthy than Lehna to lead the Sikh community after his death. Guru Angad wrote a number of hymns, 62 of which are included in the Sikh scripture, the *Guru Granth Sahib*. He was especially important for finalizing the Gurumukhi alphabet, which is the form of the Punjabi language used in the Sikh scriptures and in the Indian Punjabi language in general. His time as guru was crucial in consolidating the Sikh community and ensuring that after Guru Nanak's death it would continue to develop into the religious tradition that it later became. ▷ Amar Das, Guru; Guru Granth Sahib; guru, Sikh; Nanak

Angakok The term used by the peoples of the Central Arctic for a shaman or sorcerer. It applies to a person who has a 'helping spirit', and involves a variety of techniques or initiation practices for making contact with the basic power of the universe (*sila*) from which one obtains divinatory and curative powers. ▷ shamanism

angelology, biblical In biblical thought angels are human or divine messengers of God, distinguished by function (the Greek *angelos* simply means 'messenger') rather than outward appearance. Their role is to communicate or carry out the will of God for individuals or nations. In the Old Testament God is also represented in a special way by the 'angel of Yahweh', who is sometimes indistinguishable from him. Individual angels entrusted with God's will for humankind are part of the countless 'heavenly host' of angels who continually worship and praise him.
In the New Testament angels are involved in announcements of Christ's birth and resurrection, and they come to strengthen him at times of crisis such as his temptations in the desert and agony in Gethsemane before the crucifixion. They are also said to be guardians of individuals (for example, giving messages to Peter and Paul in dreams) and churches. They take part in God's final judgement of the world (Revelation 15–16), but as created beings are held to be inferior to Christ. New Testament hints of a hierarchy among angels, with Michael being the chief archangel, are considerably developed in the speculations of Jewish and Christian post-biblical literature, which also develops the idea of demonic or fallen angels mentioned in Genesis 6. ▷ demonology, biblical

angels Spiritual or heavenly beings acknowledged in most religions. Usually angels, as opposed to demons, are benevolent towards the human and earthly, and are frequently believed to act as agents or messengers of the gods or God. They are often organized in hierarchies.

angels, Islamic The Quran often mentions angels, who are seen as celestial beings living in a supernal world. Although many in number, four of them who are archangels are of particular importance: Gabriel, who helped to bring the Quran to the world; Michael; Israfil, who will sound the last trumpet at the end of time; and Israil, the angel of death. Another archangel, Iblis, or Satan, fell from that position by disobeying God's injunction to bow down before Adam, and it was he who tempted Adam and Eve in the Garden of Eden and bears the responsibility for this event. Ordinary angels are superior to human beings in general, but inferior to the prophets, and although closer to God they cannot truly know God, whereas faithful human beings can. ▷ Adam and Eve; Eden, Garden of; Gabriel; Iblis; malaikah; Quran; Satan

angels, Jewish From Second Temple times (c.515BCE–70CE) traditional Judaism has included belief in angels, who praise God, protect the faithful and fulfil divine commands and errands; others are wicked, banished from heaven due to pride or lust. However, the prevalence and detailed role of angels vary, even in the Bible, where it is sometimes unclear that Hebrew *malakh* ('messenger', whether human or superhuman) means 'angel'. Angels are hardly mentioned in the Pentateuch's priestly material or in much of the prophetic corpus, but are prominent in Ezekiel, Zechariah and Daniel. Similarly, although absent from the Mishnah, other parts of the talmudic literature of post-biblical times discuss the nature and function of angels. Thus, formed on the second or fifth day of creation, angels can fly, speak Hebrew and tell the future; although innumerable, four archangels are supreme: Gabriel, Michael, Raphael, and Uriel. Mystical texts go even further, viewing angels as emanations of divine light, while the medieval Jewish philosopher Maimonides equated them with Aristotle's incorporeal intelligences. In the modern period, Conservative and Reform Judaism tend to view traditional angelology as the product of a by-gone age; it must either be discarded or interpreted symbolically. However, Orthodoxy still holds to belief in angels with varying literalness. ▷ angelology, biblical; angels; Kabbalah; Maimonides

Angkor Thom The ancient capital of the Khmer Empire (South-East Asia). The moated and walled city was built on a square plan, extending over 100 square kilometres, and was completed in the 12th century. Abandoned in the 15th century, it was rediscovered in 1861. Angkor Wat is the largest of the temples surrounding the site—linked, richly-sculptured sanctuaries on a massive platform, the work of Suryavarman III (1112–52).

Anglican Communion A fellowship of some 26 independent provincial or national Churches, several extra-provincial dioceses, and Churches resulting from unions of Anglicans with other Churches, spread throughout the world, but sharing a close ecclesiastical and doctrinal relationship with the Church of England. Most of these Churches are found in the British Commonwealth, and owe their origins to missionary activities of the Church of England in the 19th century; a major exception is the Episcopal Church in the USA, which was fostered by the Scottish Episcopal Church. Churches from non-Commonwealth countries, such as Brazil, China, and Japan, are also part of the Anglican Communion.

The Communion is based on co-operation, since there is no worldwide uniform authority, but every 10 years the Archbishop of Canterbury invites bishops throughout the Anglican Communion to take part in the Lambeth Conference, a consultative body that considers issues of common concern even though it has no final policy-making authority. The 1968 Lambeth Conference also set up an Anglican Consultative Council to act during the 10-year intervals. ▷ Church of England; Episcopal Church, Protestant

Anglicanism ▷ Church of England

Anglican-Roman Catholic International Commission ▷ ARCIC

Anglo-Catholicism A movement within the Church of England, the term first appearing in 1838. It stresses the sacramental and credal aspects of Christian faith, and continuity and community with the wider Catholic Church, especially with Roman Catholicism. ▷ Church of England; Roman Catholicism

Angra Mainyu An Avestan term meaning 'evil spirit'; the later (Middle and New Persian) equivalent is Ahriman. According to Zoroastrian teaching Angra Mainyu is the leader and creator of the forces of evil, the evil opponent of Ahura Mazda. The opposition between Ahura Mazda and Angra Mainyu has a central place in the teachings of the prophet Zoroaster, who emphasized the need for people to choose between them, and the moral obligation to collaborate with the

Angra Mainyu or Ahriman, spirit of evil

forces of Ahura Mazda in order to overcome the evil wrought by Ahriman. According to later Zoroastrian texts the world was created as a theatre of war, in order to enable Ahura Mazda to vanquish Angra Mainyu in a limited place, during a limited time. The history of the world as we know it will end with the defeat of Angra Mainyu at the End of Time. ▷ Ahura Mazda; Avesta; Bundahishn; evil; Frashokereti; Zoroaster

animal cults In predynastic Egypt animals were revered as tribal deities and they continued to play an important part in the religion of the historical period. Among the most characteristic features of the Egyptian gods are their animal or bird heads; it was believed that a god could manifest himself in his sacred species of animal, just as he could dwell in a cult statue. In some cases only one individual was singled out as the object of a cult, such as the Apis bull, which was sacred to Ptah. In other cases all members of a species were venerated; for example ibises and baboons were sacred to Thoth, cats were sacred to the goddess Bast. In the late period (c.800BCE onwards) animal cults became extremely popular and many thousands of sacred animals were mummified and buried in animal cemeteries at holy places throughout Egypt. ▷ Apis; mummification; Ptah; Thoth

animal slaughter, Jewish In Judaism there is a clearly-defined body of regulations known as *shehitah* ('slaughter'), concerning the slaughter of animals and birds for food. Its aim is to ensure that death for animals should be as quick and as painless as possible and that the maximum amount of blood be removed. This means that a very sharp knife is applied to the throat, severing the trachaea, oesophagus and jugular. Beforehand a blessing is pronounced, and it must be checked that the blade is both clean and smooth. Only meat from animals killed in this way is pure (kosher), and since medieval times only a licensed *shohet* ('slaughterer'), trained in the theory and practice of shehitah, is permitted to slaughter animals for food. Further, because of the religious importance attached to correct shehitah, only those regarded as suitably pious were permitted to train as slaughterers. Traditionally, the Jewish community or *kehillah* has regulated its own shehitah and sale of kosher meat, resulting in the shehitah tax used to pay for various communal needs such as education and charity. ▷ Halakhah; kashrut; kehillah

animism A belief in spiritual beings thought capable of influencing human events, based on the idea that animals, plants and even inanimate objects have souls like humans. The 19th-century anthropologist Edward Tylor regarded it as the earliest form of religion, a view not accepted by modern anthropologists. ▷ Tylor, Sir Edward Burnet

ankh A cross with a loop for its upper vertical arm; in Ancient Egypt, an emblem of life. ▷ Ancient Egyptian religion

Annas (1st century) Israel's high priest, appointed in 6CE and deposed by the Romans in 15CE, but still described later by this title in the New Testament. He apparently questioned Jesus after his arrest (John 18) and Peter after his detention (Acts 4). His other activities are described in the works of Josephus Flavius. ▷ Jesus Christ; Josephus Flavius; New Testament; Peter, St

Annunciation The angel Gabriel's foretelling to Mary of the birth of Jesus and of the promise of his greatness (Luke 1.26–38). Many of the features of this account are parallel to the annunciation of the birth of John the Baptist (Luke 1.5–25). The feast day is also known as Lady Day. ▷ Gabriel; Jesus Christ; John, St (the Baptist); Mary; New Testament

anointing the sick The ritual application of oil performed in cases of (usually) serious illness or preparation for death. In the Roman Catholic and Orthodox Churches, which claim scriptural authority for the practice, it is recognized as a sacrament to be performed by a priest. It was formerly sometimes called extreme unction. ▷ Roman Catholicism; Orthodox Church; sacrament

Anselm, St (1033–1109) Scholastic philosopher and prelate, and Archbishop of Canterbury, born in Aosta, Piedmont. He left Italy in 1056 and settled at the Benedictine abbey of Bec in Normandy to study with Lanfranc, the prior and master of the famous school. In 1063 he himself became prior on Lanfranc's departure to Caen, and then abbot after the death of Herluin in 1078. Finally he moved to England to succeed Lanfranc as Archbishop of Canterbury in 1093 and held that position until his death. He was distinguished as a churchman and a philosopher, but his strong principles brought him into conflict with both William II and Henry I and he was temporarily exiled by both kings. He was eventually reconciled with Henry and on his death was buried next to Lanfranc at Canterbury. He was canonized in 1494. Much influenced by Augustine, he sought 'necessary reasons' for religious beliefs: his main arguments are presented in the *Monologion* (1076) and the *Proslogion* (1077–78), the latter containing the famous 'ontological argument' for the proof of the existence of God. He also wrote philosophical dialogues and important works on the Incarnation (*Cur Deus Homo*) and on logic. His feast day is 21 April. ▷ Augustine, St (of Hippo); God, arguments for the existence of; Incarnation; Lanfranc; ontological argument; scholasticism

Anthony, St ▷ Antony, St

anthropology of religion One of the three social sciences of religion, along with the psychology and sociology of religion. It has tended to focus upon the religion of small-scale primal societies and has been centred within the discipline of anthropology. Anthropologists living in a primal society study the religion of that society as one aspect of the whole rather than in isolation. In its early days the anthropology of religion was dominated by the theory of the evolution of religion and by the search for the origins of religion, with different anthropologists believing in different origins. For Frazer the origin was magic, for Tylor it was animism, for Schmidt it was original monotheism, and for others it was pre-animism, totemism, fetishism, or polytheism. Later anthropologists moved in two main directions. They abandoned great theories and explanations of religion and concentrated on its role in society, going out to live in the societies they were studying. They asked, with Lévy-Bruhl, whether there were primitive modes of thought that were different from the modern mentality; they analysed the symbols and myths and looked at the ritual practice of primal religion; and they examined auxiliary ritual practices such as magic, ecstasy, possession, and spirit-mediumship. While the social anthropology of religion concentrated upon these topics and saw religion as part of society, the cultural anthropologists saw religion as the set of beliefs, practices and institutions that explains the origin and nature of cultural order and preserves its existence. Another main division has been between functional anthropologists, who analysed the function of religion in society, and structural anthropologists, such as Lévi-Strauss, who work from structures of the mind and language back to religious phenomena rather than vice versa. ▷ Frazer, Sir James George; Lévi-Strauss, Claude; Lévy-Bruhl, Lucien; origin of religion; psychology of religion; Schmidt, Wilhelm; social sciences of religion; sociology of religion; Tylor, Sir Edward Burnet

anthropomorphism The application to God or gods of human characteristics, such as a body (as in Greek mythology), or the mental, psychological, or spiritual qualities of human beings. It is often used to indicate insufficient appreciation of transcendence and mystery of the divine. ▷ God; mythology; transcendence and immanence

anthroposophy A modern spiritual and cult movement founded by Rudolph Steiner. He reacted to materialism by seeking a direct apprehension of the spiritual world, and in working out his theories he has had a small but growing impact on agricultural, educational, sociological and religious concepts. Influenced by Goethe and by Hindu notions taken from the theosophical movement, he believed that the universe and human beings (who are immortal selves subject to rebirth) have descended from higher 'astral' and 'etheric' stages of consciousness in which they are enmeshed. Through the life and work of Jesus Christ, the decline was arrested and a new spiritual advance inaugurated. This development involves a reintegration of will, thought and feeling in human beings and of the material, intellectual and spiritual life in general so that a better world will emerge. In anthroposophy, through concentration and meditation, a person is able to have an intuitive awareness whereby the lower self is able to form a vision of the higher self, and to work towards it in an integral way. The word *anthropos* (meaning 'man') suggests rightly that anthroposophy is more human-centred than God-centred. ▷ Jesus Christ; materialism; rebirth; Steiner, Rudolph; Theosophical Society

Antichrist A notion found in the Bible in the Johannine Letters (1 John 2.18, 22, 4.3; 2 John 7) and in the Apocrypha and Revelation, referring sometimes to a single figure and at other times to many who are adversaries and deceivers of God's people. In later centuries, it was conceived as a supreme evil figure, often identified with one's opponents. In Islam the concept of Antichrist (*Alchira*; *Qiyama*) has specific significance as the figure whose arrival will indicate that the end of the world is close. ▷ Akhira; Apocrypha, New Testament; Apocrypha, Old Testament; John, Letters of; Qiyama; Satan

Anti-Cult movement A movement that is concerned to curb the advance of cults that have arisen in the Western world since the 1960s. It consists often of evangelical Christians, parents of youngsters converted to cults, people who have left a cult and reacted against it and, occasionally, concerned citizens and politicians. Their objections are that the beliefs of the cults are wrong and that the conduct of their members is anti-social. Charges are made of brainwashing, fortune building, undermining families, unusual behaviour, and activities unwelcome to the host society. Complaints have been made about many cults, including the Unification Church, Scientology, Children of God, and Hare Krishna. The Anti-Cult movement has engaged in in-depth psychiatric counselling, deprogramming and even kidnapping in order to counteract the work of cults among young people. Recently some liberal Christians and human rights activists have begun to question the propriety of the methods used by the Anti-Cult movement, and its tendency to use the emotive word 'cult' indiscriminately. As they point out, many major religious traditions, including Christianity, began as 'cults' or new religious movements. ▷ Children of God; Hare Krishna movement; new religious movements in the West; scientology; Unification Church

Antioch, early Christianity in The city of Antioch in Syria (now Turkish Antakya) was founded c.300BCE by Seleucus I Nicator. It became the third largest city of the Roman empire (after Rome and Alexandria) and headquarters of the first Gentile Christian church, second in importance only to the church in Jerusalem. It was at Antioch that the followers of Jesus were first called 'Christians' (according to Acts 11.26). Antioch was the starting point of Paul's missionary journeys (during the first of which he visited another Antioch, in Pisidia, now west-central Turkey), and representatives of the church there successfully argued at the Council of Jerusalem (see Acts 15; Galatians 2) that evangelism among the Gentiles (non-Jews) should not be hampered by insisting that would-be converts to Christianity should first adopt circumcision and other Jewish practices. This decision prevented the Christian church as a whole splitting into ex-Jewish and ex-Gentile factions at the beginning of its existence.
The Antiochine theological school, under the influence of the philosophy of Aristotle rather than Plato, took a more rational, historical and literal approach to scripture than the rival school of Alexandria, and tended to stress the humanity rather than the divinity of Christ (a position whose extremes led to the heresies of adoptionism and Nestorianism). Notable figures connected with Antioch apart from Nestorius include the bishop-martyr and epistle-writer St Ignatius (c.35–107) and the biblical expositor St John Chrysostom. Antioch was the seat of several church councils in the 3rd to 6th centuries, but declined in influence as the power of the see of Constantinople increased. ▷ adoptionism; Chrysostom, St John; Ignatius (of Antioch), St; Nestorians; Syrian Christianity

antipope In the Roman Catholic Church, a claimant to the office of pope in opposition to one regularly and canonically appointed. Antipopes featured prominently in the period of Great Schism in the Western Church (1378–1417). They included Clement VII and Benedict XIII (in Avignon, France) and Alexander V and John XXIII (in Pisa, Italy). ▷ Great Schism; papacy

anti-Semitism A late 19th-century term describing hostility towards Jews and/or Judaism. Strictly speaking all descendants of Shem are Semites (see Genesis 10.1), but anti-Semitism is normally associated only with Jewry. While scholars disagree over the precise connection between prejudice against Jews as a race, a largely modern phenomenon, and anti-Judaism on religious grounds, the former undoubtedly has roots in the latter. The Graeco-Roman period produced some anti-Jewish literature and activity, but only with Christianity did a consistent anti-Judaism appear.
This originates in the New Testament, which subtly transfers the blame for Jesus's death from politically-motivated Roman and Jewish rulers to the Jews en masse as a specifically religious grouping (eg 1 Thessalonians 2.14–16). As the Church became Gentile and ignorant of Judaism, this trait intensified in Patristic and Medieval times. Because they had murdered Jesus, Jews were thought to have forfeited the covenant; they were likened to Esau, who lost his birthright, and to Cain, who killed his brother. In art Jews were portrayed as ruthless, godless, and the embodiment of evil; in folklore they engaged in ritual murder of Christians, desecration of the Eucharistic Host, and plots to overthrow Christendom. Further, their commercial and money-lending activities encouraged comparison with Judas who betrayed Jesus for silver. At the Reformation, Luther hoped the Jews would accept his reading of the Hebrew Scriptures. When they did not, he was enraged and in 1542

published a tract called *Von den Juden und ihren Lügen* ('On the Jews and their Lies'), calling for synagogues to be burned and Jewish worship prohibited. Even after the Enlightenment prejudice remained embedded in Western culture and fuelled modern anti-Semitism. In this the focus shifted from the religious to the racial, so that Jews were considered a social menace responsible for society's ills. This culminated in the Nazis' Final Solution to the so-called *Judenfrage* ('Jewish problem').
Since then there have been important changes. Jews themselves have gained political power in order to prevent a repetition of the Nazi Holocaust, while many Christians have acknowledged their tradition's role in that tragedy. In contrast anti-Semitism has increased within the Islamic world in recent times, with the Arab-Israeli conflict encouraging anti-Semitic propaganda in various Arab and Muslim countries. ▷ covenant; Holocaust; Israel, State of; Luther, Martin; Nazi Party; Reform Judaism

Antony, or **Anthony, St**, called **the Great**, or **Antony of Egypt** (c.251–356) Religious hermit, one of the founders of Christian monasticism, born in Koman, Upper Egypt. Having sold his possessions for the poor, he spent 20 years in the desert, where he withstood a famous series of temptations, often represented in later art. In 305 he left his retreat and founded a monastery near Memphis and Arsinoë. In about 355, although over 100, he made a journey to Alexandria to dispute with the Arians; but retired soon after to his desert home, where he died. His feast day is 17 January. ▷ Arius; monasticism

Anubis Ancient Egyptian god associated with death. Anubis is represented as a jackal-headed man or a crouching jackal, and is the god responsible for embalming and the protection of tombs. His worship was widespread throughout Egypt, and as son of Nephthys by Osiris he became associated with the supreme god of the dead. In the Osirian legends he, with Isis and Nephthys, embalmed the body of Osiris and performed the burial rites for him. In later times the process of embalming was supervised by a priest wearing a jackal mask to represent Anubis. Important in the judgement of the dead, Anubis oversaw the balancing of the deceased's heart against Maat, and passed on the result to Thoth and to Osiris. ▷ afterlife; Isis; Maat; mummification; Nephthys; Osiris; Thoth

anukampa (anukampā) A Buddhist term meaning to 'quake' or 'tremble with' (*anukampa*), a reference to the empathy that is aroused in a person by seeing the distress of others. It was the motivating force behind the teaching of the Buddha and his disciples, and is allied to notions of friendship and mercy. It can be used of a monk who shows his empathy for his lay supporters by various means including graciously receiving their food and gifts. It is similar to the notion of compassion (*karuna*), but karuna developed the technical meaning of meditationally offering compassion to all beings, and in later Mahayana Buddhism became allied with wisdom as one of the two supreme Buddhist virtues. Anukampa remained more prosaic and less technical as human empathy and kindness. ▷ bhikkhu; Buddha; karuna; Mahayana Buddhism; wisdom

Apis The Egyptian bull-god, representing or incarnating the Ptah of Memphis. An actual bull was selected from the herd, black with a triangular white patch on the forehead, and kept at Memphis; after death it was mummified and placed in a special necropolis, the Serapeum. ▷ Ancient Egyptian religion; mummification; Ptah

apocalypse (Greek 'revelation of the future') A literary genre which can be traced to post-Biblical Jewish and early Christian eras; it especially comprises works in highly symbolic language which claim to express divine disclosures about the heavenly spheres, the course of history, or the end of the world. The most famous example is the Book of Revelation in the New Testament. ▷ Bible; Pseudepigrapha; Revelation, Book of

Apocalypse of John ▷ Revelation, Book of

Apocrypha, New Testament Christian documents, largely from the early Christian centuries, which are similar in title, form, or content to many New Testament works, being called Gospels, Acts, Epistles, or Apocalypses, and often attributed to New Testament characters, but not widely accepted as canonical. Some derive from Gnosticism or heretical circles, but others are just of a popular nature. ▷ Apocrypha, Old Testament; Gnosticism; Gospels, apocryphal; Nag Hammadi texts; New Testament

Apocrypha, Old Testament (Greek 'hidden things') Usually, a collection of Jewish writings found in the Greek version of the Hebrew

Bible (the Septuagint), but not found in the Hebrew Bible itself; in a more general sense, any literature of an esoteric or spurious kind. Most of these writings were also in the Latin version of the Christian Bible approved at the Council of Trent (the Vulgate), so Roman Catholics tend to consider them as inspired and authoritative, and designate them as deuterocanonical, while Protestants and most others attribute less authority to them, referring to them as Apocrypha. Corresponding to this distinction, non-Catholic Bibles tend to locate the Apocrypha as a separate collection between the two Testaments or after the New Testament, while Catholic Bibles tend to place the writings among the Old Testament works themselves.

There is not complete agreement over which writings are to be included in this collection. Modern studies tend to limit the Apocrypha to 13 writings found in most Septuagint manuscripts, and to exclude additional works found only in the Vulgate, which are then assigned to a much larger body of writings called the Old Testament Pseudepigrapha. The Apocrypha would thus include: 1 Esdras, Tobit, Judith, Additions to the Book of Esther, Wisdom of Solomon, Ecclesiasticus (or Sirach), 1 Baruch, Letter of Jeremiah, Prayer of Azariah and Song of the Three Young Men, Susanna, Bel and the Dragon (the last three being Additions to the Book of Daniel), 1 and 2 Maccabees. Roman Catholics consider all of this list to be deuterocanonical except for 1 Esdras. Most of the Apocrypha were composed in the last two centuries BCE. ▷ Azariah, Prayer of; Baruch; Bel and the Dragon; Bible; Ecclesiasticus/Esdras/Esther/Judith/Maccabees/Tobit, Book(s) of; Jeremiah, Letter of; Manasseh, Prayer of; Old Testament; Pseudepigrapha; Septuagint; Susanna, Story of; Wisdom of Solomon

Apollonian religion This concept is used, by modern writers, in one of two interrelated ways: **1** since Apollo's famous oracle at Delphi was the most prestigious religious institution of classical Greece, and had particular authority in matters of cult, it is sometimes supposed that a distinctive 'Apollonian' interpretation of Greek religion and morality was voiced through it (touching on questions of bloodguilt and purification, for instance); **2** Friedrich Nietzsche in *The Birth of Tragedy* (1872) drew a famous contrast between Apollo and Dionysus, in which Apollo was taken as a symbol of the rational, controlled, lucid aspects of Greek culture, Dionysus of the opposite. The ancients would have recognized the characteristics of Apollo on which these modern images are based (though they might have wished to stress others too); but they never spoke of 'Apollonian' any more than they spoke of 'Artemisian' or 'Aphrodisian' religion. Apollo was merely one god—a particularly important god it is true—from the array of gods who collectively were the objects of worship. ▷ Dionysiac religion; Greek religion; Nietzsche, Friedrich Wilhelm

apologetics (Latin *apologia*, 'defence') A branch of theology which justifies Christian faith in the light of specific criticisms or charges. It mainly emerged in the 2nd century in answer to those who saw Christianity as immoral or godless. Early apologists included Aristides, Tatian and Justin Martyr. Converted from Platonism to Christianity by the witness of Christian martyrs, Martyr wrote an influential *Apology* (c.155) to Emperor Antoninus Pius. Later apologists include Origen, Eusebius of Caesarea, and Augustine of Hippo, whose *City of God* is one of the most memorable apologies ever written. ▷ Augustine, St (of Hippo); Eusebius of Caesarea; Justin, St; Origen; Tatian

apostle In its broadest sense, a missionary, envoy, or agent; more narrowly used at times in the New Testament to refer to the 12 chosen followers of Jesus (less Judas Iscariot, replaced by Matthias according to Acts 1) who witnessed the resurrected Jesus and were commissioned to proclaim his gospel. At times the term also included Paul and other missionaries or itinerant preachers (Acts 14.14; Romans 16.7). ▷ Acts of the Apostles; Jesus Christ; Paul, St

Apostles' Creed A statement of Christian faith widely used in Roman Catholic and Protestant Churches, and recognized by the Orthodox Churches. It stresses the trinitarian nature of God (as Father, Son, and Holy Spirit) and the work of Christ. In its present form, it dates from the 8th century, but its origins go back to the 3rd century. ▷ Christianity; Trinity

Apostolic Constitution One of the most solemn documents issued in the name of a pope, concerned with major matters of doctrine or discipline for the Roman Catholic Church at large. ▷ Roman Catholicism

apostolic succession The theory that a direct line of descent can be traced from the original apostles of Christ through episcopal succession to the bishops of the present-day Church which supports it, guaranteeing preservation of the original teaching of the apostles. This is now disputed by most New Testament scholars, and rejected by many Churches. ▷ episcopacy

apsaras A term used in Hindu and Buddhist thought to refer to celestial nymphs. In ancient Indian mythology they were said to reside in Indra's heaven. One school of thought views them as personifications of water-saturated clouds and mists. They are beautiful, often appear as willing consorts to men and gods, and are sometimes seen as those sent to test the motivation and fortitude of spiritual aspirants. As the Buddhist pantheon developed they were incorporated into it as those who glorified the Buddha and rejoiced at his conception and enlightenment. For example, they bathed, massaged and anointed his pregnant mother's body. The apsaras have been represented in art and sculpture as well as in literature, and there are well-known images of them in many places, including the celebrated Lung Men Caves near Loyang in China. ▷ Buddha; Indra; Lung Men Caves

apu A Quechua word, usually translated as 'Lord', with a wide range of meaning. Before the Spanish conquest it could be used with the name of a divinity (eg Apu Inti, the Inca sun god) but more usually had a wider sense. The famous oracle Apurimac can be translated 'the Lord who speaks', or 'the powerful one who speaks'. Equally apu might denote an ancestor, or one of the high peaks, remote, mysterious and sacred. The word thus related the ideas of authority, power, ancestry and height. Early missionaries, anxious to avoid the associations of Quechua words for divinity, used apu as 'Lord' in the Christian sense, also linking it with the Spanish loan word '*Dios*', 'God'. For Quechua, however, this use of *Apu Dios* did not itself exclude the other apus; it might, in fact, imply them. The word, while extended in its connotations, has thus retained much of its ambivalence of reference. ▷ Christianity in Latin America; huaca; Inca religion

Aqedah or **Akedah** In Jewish tradition the name given to the story in Genesis 22.1–19 about Abraham's attempted sacrifice of Isaac. This was a favourite passage for aggadic development in post-biblical times, eg in the targums to Genesis 22 and in Genesis Rabbah 55–6. Such texts develop the story considerably, especially the roles of Abraham and Isaac. Abraham is commended for his willingness to give up his only son, despite his miraculous birth and central place in God's plan. Isaac is praised for his readiness to be sacrificed; one text even has him ask to be bound tightly to stop him from shaking and rendering the sacrifice unacceptably blemished should the knife slip. Aqedah means 'binding', but in the developed tradition God's intervention at the last minute does not prevent him from accounting the sacrifice to have taken place. The merit produced by this will help later generations of the Jewish people when in trouble. It has been argued that this element deliberately paralleled Christian thought on the death of Jesus, but this is by no means certain. ▷ Abraham; Aggadah; Isaac; targum; sacrifice

Aqida (Aqīdah) The Islamic term for creed. The most basic Islamic statement of faith is to be found in the simple affirmation that 'Allah is Allah and Muhammad is his prophet', which is said daily by most Muslims. However, more elaborate and more systematic statements of belief became necessary to oppose heresy and to present the positions of particular Muslim schools. An earlier short creed was the Fiqh Akbar ascribed to Abu Hanifah. Later and more comprehensive creeds arose out of the Asharite and Shafiite schools, and others. Although creeds came into being in both the Sunni and Shiite traditions within Islam, there is no single definitive Muslim creed approved by an authoritative body. Correct belief is not as important within Islam as it is, for example, in Christianity. ▷ Abu Hanifah; Ashari, al-; Shafii, al-; fiqh; Shiism; sunnah

Aquinas, St Thomas (1225–74) Italian scholastic philosopher and theologian, of the family of the Counts of Aquino, born in the castle of Roccasecca, near Aquino. He was educated by the Benedictines of Monte Cassino, and at the University of Naples; and, against the bitter opposition of his family, in 1244 entered the Dominican order of mendicant friars. His brothers kidnapped him and kept him a prisoner in the paternal castle for over a year; in the end he made his way to Cologne to become a pupil of the great Dominican luminary, Albertus Magnus. In 1248 the heretofore 'Dumb Ox' was appointed to teach under Albert, and began to publish commentaries on Aristotle. In 1252 he went to Paris, and taught there, with growing reputation, until in 1258, by then a doctor, he was summoned by the pope to teach successively in Anagni, Orvieto, Rome and Viterbo. He died at Fossanuova on his way to defend the

papal cause at the Council of Lyon, and was canonized in 1323.
Like most of the other scholastic theologians, Aquinas had no knowledge of Greek or Hebrew, and was almost equally ignorant of history; but his prolific writings display intellectual power of the first order and he came to exercise enormous intellectual authority throughout the church. He was the first among 13th-century metaphysicians to stress the importance of sense perception and the experimental foundation of human knowledge. Through his commentaries he made Aristotle's thought available and acceptable in the Christian West, and in his philosophical writings he tried to combine and reconcile Aristotle's scientific rationalism with Christian doctrines of faith and revelation. His best-known works are two huge encyclopedic syntheses. The *Summa contra Gentiles* (1259–64) was supposedly written as a handbook for Dominican missionaries; it deals chiefly with the principles of natural religion. His *Summa Theologiae* (1266–73) was still uncompleted at his death but contains his mature thought in systematic form and includes the famous 'five ways' or proofs of the existence of God. His influence on the theological thought of succeeding ages was immense. Aquinas was known as the *Doctor Angelicus* and the only other scholastic theologian who rivalled him was the *Doctor Subtilis*, Duns Scotus. The Franciscans followed Scotus, and the Dominicans Thomas, and thenceforward medieval theologians were divided into two schools, Scotists and Thomists, whose divergencies penetrate more or less every branch of doctrine. Thomism now represents, with few exceptions, the general teaching of the Catholic Church. His feast day is 7 March. ▷ Albertus Magnus, St; Aristotle; Dominicans; Duns Scotus, John; Franciscans; Roman Catholicism; scholasticism

Arabi, Ibn (Ibn 'Arabī, Abū Bakr Muḥammad Muhyi-d-Dīn) (1165–1240) Arab mystic poet, born in Murcia, Spain, known as the 'sultan of the Gnostics'. Moving with his family to Seville when he was young, he studied there under Andulasian spiritual masters and by the age of 16 had accumulated a huge store of knowledge. Serious illness, however, in which he was visited by visions, made him abandon ordinary life, and his wife, and on his recovery he spent several years in asceticism and pilgrimage, which took him to Jerusalem and Mecca. It was in Mecca that he wrote *The Interpreter of Longings*, poetry dedicated to a Persian sheik's daughter. Further travels introduced him to Sufism, and he became increasingly sought after for his wisdom. He settled eventually in Damascus. A great influence on Sufi philosophy, his writings present in obscure language a form of pantheism, and he was viewed with suspicion by some since his ideas went beyond the bounds of orthodox Islam. His many writings include his valued commentary on the Quran, *Kitab al-Futuhat al-Makkiyya* (Meccan Revelations), and *Kitab fusus al-hikam* (1229, The Wisdom of the Prophets). ▷ mysticism; pantheism

Arabic A language of the southern Semitic group within the Hamito-Semitic family, spoken by over 150 million as a mother-tongue. Its spread outside the Arabian peninsula was concomitant with the spread of Islam in the 7th–8th centuries. The language has two forms. *Colloquial Arabic* exists as the vernacular varieties of the major Arabic-speaking nation-states, such as Egypt, Morocco, and Syria, which are not always mutually intelligible. *Classical Arabic*, the language of the Quran, provides a common, standard written form for all the vernacular variants, and a common medium for affairs of state, religion, and education throughout the Arabic-speaking world. The language is written from right to left. ▷ Islam; Quran

arahat (Sanskrit: arhat) A Theravada Buddhist term from the verbal root *arh* meaning 'to be worthy'. It designates a saint who is worthy because he has reached the goal of life by gaining insight into the real nature of things and by overcoming the need to be born again into the world. He has arrived at the end of the eightfold path, and has achieved the highest stage of realization known to Theravada Buddhism. As the *Dharmapada* 96 puts it: 'calm is his mind, calm is his speech, calm is his behaviour who, rightly knowing, is wholly freed, perfectly peaceful and equipoised'. Freed from negative defects, the arahat has positive qualities of mindfulness, loving kindness and compassion. He knows his own past rebirths, the rebirths of others, and his own freedom from rebirths. Becoming an arahat is the last of four stages in Theravada Buddhist spirituality, the first three being to 'enter the stream', to be a 'once-returner', and to be a 'no-returner'. The Buddha himself was an outstanding pathfinder among the arahats. Mahayana Buddhists contrasted the arahat of the Theravada Buddhists unfavourably with their own bodhisattva ideal of ultimate concern for others. Instead of forsaking rebirth, like the arahat, when the opportunity came, the bodhisattva would be willing to be reborn repeatedly out of compassion for suffering beings so that they too could be freed from rebirth. ▷ bodhisattva; Buddha; Dharmapada; eightfold path; Mahayana Buddhism; Theravada Buddhism; saint

Aramaean religion The Aramaeans were a West Semitic people who spoke a language distinct from that of Canaan and Phoenicia. By the 11th and 10th centuries BCE they had settled in a number of city states in Syria, particularly around Damascus and the upper course of the Euphrates. Their religion was complex and polytheistic, with many local variations, and as the Aramaeans controlled trade routes between Mesopotamia, Asia Minor, and Canaan they were open to influences from all directions. The chief god was Hadad the storm god, who is identifiable with the Mesopotamian Adad and Canaanite Baal. He was the national god from whom the Aramaean kings received their authority. Other deities worshipped testify to foreign influence, such as the Phoenician Melqart and Mesopotamian Shamash, Nergal and Marduk. The Babylonian moon god Sin was very popular, especially in northern Syria. In the Hellenistic period the 'Syrian goddess' Atargatis was worshipped widely; she was a fertility goddess, the consort of Hadad, and probably an amalgamation of Anat and Astarte. The evidence available for the study of Aramaean religion is not substantial, and little is known of personal beliefs and practices. ▷ Anat; Ancient Near Eastern religions; Astarte; Baal; Babylonian religion; Canaanite religion; Marduk; Nergal; Shamash

archbishop A bishop appointed to have jurisdiction over other bishops; often, the head of a province. The title sometimes refers to a bishop exercising special functions. In Eastern Churches, a hierarchy of archbishops is recognized. ▷ bishop

archdeacon A clergyman in the Anglican Church responsible for the administration of the whole or such part of a diocese as the bishop may authorize. The office formerly existed also in Roman Catholic and Eastern Orthodox Churches. ▷ Anglican Communion

architecture, Christian Although Christian worship does not require any particular architectural setting, it became convenient after Constantine made it the state religion of the Roman empire and the numbers of converts grew, to move from private houses to larger, specially designed public buildings. These basilicas or halls embody the basic single-room pattern of building which has been adopted at all periods except the medieval (1200–1600) and Gothic Revival (c.1850–1950), where the separation of clergy and congregation was reflected in a variety of two-room (sanctuary and nave) designs. The use of the worship space varies with ecclesiastical tradition. Protestant churches and chapels can often be identified by the prominence given to the pulpit, since in this tradition preaching is stressed; liturgical renewal has prompted many churches to bring the altar or communion table used for the Eucharist more into the centre of the building. Some 20th-century religious buildings, such as the pilgrimage chapel of Notre Dame du Haut, at Ronchamp, Vosges (1955) by Le Corbusier (1887–1965), the rebuilt Coventry Cathedral (1962) by Sir Basil Spence (1907–76), and Liverpool Roman Catholic Cathedral (1960–7) make a religious statement as powerful as that made by the great medieval churches. Other modern churches are multipurpose, combining worship and community facilities or sheltered housing. Political independence and a trend of indigenization in worship has led to some churches in former European colonies being built on local models, as in adaptations of the Hindu ashram style in India for Christian worship. A similar freeing from European models can be discerned in some recent religious art. ▷ iconography and symbolism, Christian

architecture, Islamic Islam has not been a great exponent of the visual arts because of its theological ban on the representation of divine, human and animal forms. It developed calligraphy, pottery, carpets, figurative art and ceremonial art, but above all it developed its own architecture. An important aspect of this development was the emergence of the mosque as an architectural genre. This took two major forms: the Arab mosque with its many columns, and the Iranian mosque with its central court and semi-circular vaults. Important early courtyard city mosques were built in Cairo, Cordoba, Damascus, Kufa, Qayrawan and Samarra. They adapted to their environment, and in the cases of the Dome of the Rock in Jerusalem, the Great Mosque in Damascus and later the Great Mosque in Istanbul, they adapted or rebuilt existing buildings. Forms of mosque architecture were applied to other buildings such as madrasa colleges, convents, charitable institutions, mausoleums (including the Taj Mahal), and various secular buildings. As Islamic civil engineering became more sophisticated, so did Muslim architecture. Within the mosques and palaces that arose there was the opportunity for such arts as calligraphy, arabesques, ceramics, the use of semi-precious stones and miniature painting to develop. ▷ art, Islamic; calligraphy, Islamic; Jerusalem in Islam; mosque; Taj Mahal

architecture, Sumerian and Assyrian One of the earliest instances of architecture, dating from the 4th millennium BCE, located on the Euphrates delta on the Persian Gulf. It is characterized by the use of brick arches, domes, and vaults, typically decorated with a surface geometrical pattern of red, black, and brown mosaics, as at the ziggurat temple of Warka (c.2900–2340BCE). It was later adapted by the Assyrians in northern Mesopotamia for buildings such as the vast 23-acre Palace of Saragon at Khorsabad (c.722–705BCE). ▷ ziggurat

ARCIC An acronym for the Anglican–Roman Catholic International Commission, instituted in 1966 by Pope Paul VI and Archbishop of Canterbury Michael Ramsey. The Commission meets regularly, and produces statements on areas of substantial agreement between the two Churches on important points of doctrine. ▷ Anglican Communion; Roman Catholicism

Ardas (Ardās) A Sikh formal prayer which ends, and sometimes begins, most Sikh rituals. It means 'petition', the petition of a servant to a master, and by implication the petition of a devotee to God. It contains three stages. The first recalls the work of the 10 Sikh gurus and other important events in Sikh history; then there is the invocation to God to bless the Sikh community and the whole world; finally there are prayers of petition for the special needs of the local congregation and community. Particular circumstances and personal intercessions can be introduced. The Ardas is written down in the *Rahit Maryada*, the Sikh Code of Conduct of 1945, but the written version can be varied to suit local practice. ▷ guru, Sikh; Rahit Maryada

Arianism ▷ Arius

Aristotle (384–322BCE) Greek philosopher and scientist, one of the most important and influential figures in the history of Western thought. He was born in Stagira, a Greek colony on the peninsula of Chalcidice, the son of the court physician to the king of Macedon (who was father of Philip II and grandfather of Alexander the Great). In 367 he went to Athens and was first a pupil then a teacher at Plato's Academy, where he stayed 20 years until Plato's death in 347. Speusippus succeeded Plato as head of the Academy and Aristotle left Athens for 12 years. He spent time in Atarneus in Asia Minor (where he married), in Mytilene, and in about 342 was appointed by Philip of Macedon to act as tutor to his son Alexander (then 13). He finally returned to Athens in 335 to found his own school (called the Lyceum from its proximity to the temple of Apollo Lyceius), where he taught for the next 12 years. His followers became known as 'peripatetics', supposedly from his restless habit of walking up and down while lecturing. Alexander the Great died in 323 and there was a strong anti-Macedonian reaction in Athens; Aristotle was accused of impiety and with the fate of Socrates perhaps in mind he took refuge at Chalcis in Euboea, where he died the next year.

Aristotle's writings represented an enormous, encyclopedic output over virtually every field of knowledge: logic, metaphysics, ethics, politics, rhetoric, poetry, biology, zoology, physics and psychology. The bulk of the work that survives actually consists of unpublished material in the form of lecture notes or students' textbooks, which were edited and published by Andronicus of Rhodes in the middle of the 1st century BCE. Even this incomplete corpus is extraordinary for its range, originality, systematization and sophistication, and his work exerted an enormous influence on medieval philosophy (especially through St Thomas Aquinas), Islamic philosophy (especially through Averroës), and indeed on the whole Western intellectual and scientific tradition. The works most read today include the *Metaphysics* (the book written 'after the *Physics*'), *Nicomachean Ethics*, *Politics*, *Poetics*, the *De Anima* and the *Organon* (treatises on logic). ▷ Aquinas, St Thomas; Averroës, Ibn Rushd; Plato; Socrates

Arius, Greek **Areios** (c.250–336) Libyan theologian, the founder of the heresy known as 'Arianism'. Trained in Antioch, he became a presbyter in Alexandria. There about 319 he maintained, against his bishop, that the Son was not co-equal or co-eternal with the Father, but only the first and highest of all finite beings, created out of nothing by an act of God's free will. He secured the adherence of clergy and laity in Egypt, Syria, and Asia Minor, but was deposed and excommunicated in 321 by a synod of bishops at Alexandria. Eusebius of Nicomedia absolved him, and in 323 convened another synod in Bithynia, which pronounced in his favour. In Nicomedia, Arius wrote a theological work in verse and prose, called *Thaleida*, some fragments of which remain. The controversy became fierce, and to settle it the emperor Constantine I convoked the memorable Council of Nicaea, or Nice, in Bithynia (325). Three hundred and eighteen bishops, mainly from the East, were present, as well as priests, deacons, and acolytes. Arius boldly expounded and defended his opinions. It was principally by the reasoning of Athanasius that the Council was persuaded to define the absolute unity of the divine essence, and the absolute equality of the three persons. All the bishops subscribed to it except two, who were banished, along with Arius, to Illyricum. Arius was recalled in 334, but Athanasius refused to readmit him to church communion, and the controversy went on all over the East. In 336 Arius went to Constantinople, where the emperor commanded the bishop to admit him to the sacrament. But a day or two before the Sunday appointed for the purpose, he died suddenly—poisoned by the orthodox, said his friends; by the direct judgement of God, according to his enemies. After his death the strife spread more widely abroad: the Homoousian doctrine (identity of essence in Father and Son) and the Homoiousian (similarity of essence) seemed alternately to prevail; and synods and counter-synods were held. The West was mainly orthodox, the East largely Arian or semi-Arian. There was a good deal of persecution on both sides; but Julian 'the Apostate' (361–3) and his successors extended full toleration to both parties. Arianism was at last virtually suppressed in the Roman Empire under Theodosius in the East (379–95) and Valentinian II in the West. Among the Germanic nations, however, it continued to spread through missionary efforts, the Lombards being the last to come round (in 662). John Milton held Arian or semi-Arian views. The Arian controversy was revived in England by the philosopher Samuel Clarke and William Whiston, but Arianism was superseded by Unitarianism. ▷ Athanasius, St; bishop; Constantine I; Nicaea, Council of; Unitarians

Ariyaratna, A T (b.20th century) Lay Buddhist leader in Sri Lanka, best known for his foundation of the Sarvodaya Sharmadana movement which has been working for about 30 years to better the condition of poor village folk throughout Sri Lanka. Ariyaratna was prompted by the examples of Mahatma Gandhi and Vinoba Bhave in India to engage in social service and development work inspired by religious motives. He took his students from a well-known high school in Colombo to work in surrounding villages and to help the villagers, to enable them to help themselves, and to give them a sense of self-worth. The motivation behind his work was Buddhist, but it had a more universal religious perspective as well. Ariyaratna's Sarvodaya Sharmadana movement has worked in thousands of villages and involved nearly half a million people in its operations. It has received international support and acclaim in its own right and as an example of a Buddhist movement deeply involved in social and economic matters as well as spiritual endeavours. ▷ Bhave, Vinoba; Gandhi, Mohandas Karamchand; Sinhalese Buddhism

ariya sacca The four 'noble truths' taught by the Buddha which form the core of Theravada Buddhist teaching and of Buddhist teaching in general. They are noble because they are true, because they were taught by a noble person (the Buddha), and because they produce a state of nobility. The four noble truths are: that all forms of existence, and especially human existence, are characterized by suffering (*duhkha*); that suffering is caused by desire and craving (*tanha*); that suffering can end by means of the elimination of craving; and that the cessation of craving is achieved by means of the eightfold path. Duhkha is usually translated as 'suffering', but it has a wider meaning than pain or problems, and includes unsatisfactoriness and dis-ease. It thus includes times of happiness in that even pleasant experiences and satisfactions, although real, are fleeting and therefore subject to 'suffering' and rebirth. The quest of the Buddha was to understand and overcome suffering, and having achieved this he set out to help others to do the same. In the four noble truths the Buddha played the role of a spiritual doctor who diagnosed the basic dilemma of life (suffering), identified its cause (craving), worked out its cure (the cessation of craving), and advised a course of treatment to bring about the cure (the eightfold path). ▷ Buddha; dependent origination; duhkha; eightfold path; tanha; Theravada Buddhism

Arjan, Guru (Gurū) (1536–1606) Fifth of the 10 Sikh gurus, born in the Punjab, India. He was chosen by his father, Guru Ram Das, to succeed him, and he became guru in 1581. He was important for three reasons. Firstly, he completed the building of the Golden Temple (Harimandir) in Amritsar which had been begun by his father. Secondly, he authorized the first authoritative compilation of the chief Sikh scripture, the *Adi Granth*, and installed it in the Golden Temple (1604). Thus the Sikh 'canon' of scripture began to emerge. Thirdly, it was during his time as guru that relations with the Mughal emperors began to deteriorate. Guru Arjan was arrested by Jehangir in 1605, and died in Mughal captivity, thus being honoured as a kind of martyr. Confrontations with the Mughals followed in the time of the sixth guru, Guru Hargobind, and the tendency towards greater Sikh militancy in the face of aggression became established. ▷ Adi Granth; Amritsar; guru, Sikh; Hargobind, Guru; Harimandir; Ram Das, Guru; Mughal empire

ark ▷ Ark of the Covenant; Noah

Ark of the Covenant A portable wooden chest overlaid with gold, with a cherub with extended wings mounted at each end of the golden lid (the 'mercy seat'). In the Hebrew Bible/Old Testament it is described as having many successive functions—containing the two tablets of the Decalogue, serving as a symbol of the divine presence guiding Israel, and acting as a safeguard in war. It was constructed under Moses, taken into battle in David's time, housed in the Temple under Solomon, but is now lost. Torah scrolls are still kept in containers called 'arks' in Jewish synagogues. ▷ David; Moses; Old Testament; Solomon; Ten Commandments; Torah

Armageddon A place mentioned in the New Testament (Rev 16.16) as the site of the final cosmic battle between the forces of good and evil in the last days of the world. The name is possibly a corruption of 'the mountains of Megiddo' or some other unknown location in Israel. ▷ eschatology; New Testament; Revelation, Book of

Arminianism The doctrine propounded by Arminius. It presented five fundamental arguments: **1** predestination is open only to believers **2** Christ died to save everyone, but only believers will be saved **3** people can only be brought to believe through grace—without God's grace belief is impossible **4** grace can be resisted **5** believers might still lose their faith and forfeit salvation. The followers of Arminianism outlined these concepts in their *Remonstrance to the States-General*, asking for changes to the catechism then accepted in the Low Countries. Their beliefs caused fierce controversy, leading to the exile of those who preached them. Arminianism was well received by English theologians, becoming firmly incorporated in later English theology. ▷ Arminius, Jacobus; heresy

Arminius, Jacobus, properly **Jakob Hermandszoon** (1560–1609) Dutch theologian, born in Oudewater. He studied at Utrecht, Leiden, Geneva and Basle, and was ordained in 1588. Despite early opposition to the doctrine of predestination he was made professor of theology at Leiden in 1603. In 1604 his colleague Gomarus attacked his doctrines and from this time on he was engaged in a series of bitter controversies. Arminius asserted that God bestows forgiveness and eternal life on all who repent of their sins and believe in Jesus Christ; he wills that all men should attain salvation, and only because he has from eternity foreseen the belief or unbelief of individuals has he from eternity determined the fate of each—thus rejecting the high calvinistic doctrine of absolute predestination or election. In 1608 Arminius besought the States of Holland to convoke a synod to settle the controversy; but, worn out with worry and disease, he died before it was held. Arminius was less Arminian than his followers, who continued the strife for many years and influenced the development of religious thought all over Europe. In England Laudians and Latitudinarians were Arminian in tendency; Wesleyans and many Baptists and Congregationalists are distinctly anti-calvinist. ▷ Baptists; Calvinism; Congregationalism; election; Jesus Christ; predestination; salvation; theology

Arnauld, Antoine (1612–94) French philosopher, lawyer, mathematician and priest, born into a famous family associated with the Jansenist movement and community at Port Royal. Known as 'the Great Arnauld', he was a controversialist, and his attacks on the Jesuits and his activities as head of the Jansenist sect in France led to his expulsion from the Sorbonne, persecution, and ultimately refuge in Belgium. While at Port Royal he collaborated with Pascal and Nicole on the work known as the *Port Royal Logic* (1662). ▷ Pascal, Blaise

art, Ancient Egyptian The art which flourished under the pharaohs from c.3000BCE until the conquest of Egypt by Alexander the Great (332BCE). Largely funerary in character, it reflected a rigidly conservative society and religion, and its style remained static. Tombs were decorated with wall paintings and reliefs, and contained portrait statues of the dead, together with household utensils, including fine work in metal, ivory, and terracotta for use in the next world. Human figures were invariably painted with profile head, single large front-view eye, frontal shoulders, and side-view legs. Statues such as the sphinxes similarly combined profile and front view in a way reflecting the shape of the original block. Mummy-cases were often richly decorated. ▷ Ancient Egyptian religion

art, Assyrian The art associated with Assyria, dating from c.1500BCE, to the destruction of Nineveh (612BCE). Stylistically akin to Babylonian art, the best-known examples are the gigantic stone winged and human-headed lions which guarded entrances, and the wall decorations in the form of stone bas-reliefs, originally painted, representing battles and hunting scenes. Human figures tend to be stylized somewhat in the Egyptian manner, but animals are beautifully drawn in lively movement. ▷ Assyria; art, Ancient Egyptian; art, Babylonian; architecture, Sumerian and Assyrian

art, Babylonian The art associated with ancient Babylonia (the southern part of modern Iraq), dating from c.2500BCE, until the conquest of the country by Alexander III (331BCE). What survives is religious and courtly, such as the stylized stone statues of Gudea (eg in the Louvre) made c.2100BCE, the wall-paintings and coloured bas-reliefs representing religious sacrifices, royal ceremonies, and (as in neighbouring Assyria) comparatively realistic hunting scenes. Figures follow the typical Ancient Near-Eastern conventions, with frontal bodies, profile heads and legs, and large staring eyes. Precious metals occur in the objects from the royal cemetery at Ur, made c.2500BCE. ▷ art, Assyrian; art, Ancient Egyptian; Babylon

art, Christian Christianity, unlike Judaism and Islam, has had only temporary periods of opposition to representation of the divine: those of the iconoclastic controversy (c.725–842) in the Eastern Church, and those of post-Reformation Protestant churches in the West. These aside, there have been two main traditions of Christian art: the highly stylized and formal art of the early Christian catacombs, illuminated manuscripts, icons of the Byzantine period and medieval wall paintings stressing the majesty of God; and more varied representational art depicting themes from the Old and New Testament. Notable examples of the latter include the Florentine frescoes of Fra Angelico (c.1400–55), the *Last Supper* (1498) by Leonardo da Vinci (1452–1519), the Sistine Chapel paintings (1508–12) by Michaelangelo (1475–1564), the Isenheim altarpiece (1516) by Matthias Grunewald (?1480–1528), and etchings and sketches by Rembrandt (1606–69). Christian values have been less widely shared in society since the 18th century, and consequently artistic expression of religious themes has been more occasional and individualistic. Notable examples include the engravings of William Blake (1757–1827) and Georges Rouault (1871–1958), *The Resurrection* (1922–7) and other paintings of Stanley Spencer (1891–1959), the stained glass and painted tiles (1951) of the Chapel of the Rosary, Vence (near Nice) by Henri Matisse (1869–1954), the painting of *Christ of St John of the Cross* (1951) by Salvador Dali (1904–89), and the *Christ in Majesty* (1962) tapestry for the new Coventry Cathedral by Graham Sutherland (1903–80). Generally speaking, modern art, like existentialism, reflects a culture full of doubts and questions rather than faith and certainties.

art, Islamic Art in Islam has taken a different form from aesthetic endeavour in other religions because of Islam's lack of stress upon the representation of living beings. This arose partly from the Quran's attack upon images, which were seen to be a form of idolatry and therefore unacceptable in art. In addition, Allah was seen to be the divine creator and it was therefore inappropriate for human beings to copy or usurp God's creative power. This taboo was later written into Islamic law. In spite of this, Muslim art outside the Arab world, in countries such as India, Persia and Turkey, has made some use of living creatures, both human and animal. However, mainstream Islamic art has concentrated upon aesthetic forms such as calligraphy, architecture and carpets. Artistic representation has been primarily of vegetable and arabesque forms, and of the sacred Arabic script. This tendency is in contrast to the luxuriant nature of artistic representations in religions such as

detail of an Arabic arabesque from the Alhambra in Granada

Hinduism, where the emphasis upon the importance of myth and symbol enables living beings to be richly depicted. ▷ Allah; architecture, Islamic; creation myths; Hinduism; law and religion; mythology; Quran; symbolism

art, Jewish For most of its history Jewish art has been intimately connected with Jewish religion, and its production controlled by the understanding of the prohibition against images. Thus, while Exodus 20.4 proscribes all images and Deuteronomy 27.15 any idolatrous depictions of God, a liberalization in favour of the latter took effect from the beginning of the rabbinic period. Thus the 3rd-century CE synagogue at Dura Europas included wall-paintings depicting the scene in Ezekiel 37.1–14; the 6th-century Palestinian Beit Alfa synagogue utilized mosaic representations of the Aqedah and traditional Jewish symbols such as the ark of the covenant and menorah. The Zodiac was also employed, but it is unclear whether this was purely decorative or carried some deeper meaning. During the 13th to 15th centuries European Jews produced illuminated manuscripts, especially texts of the Haggadah; these included depictions of ritual utensils and traditional motifs such as the future restoration of the Temple. Only with Jewish emancipation from the late 18th century have there arisen individual Jewish artists in the modern sense. However, the difficulty then lies in deciding whether it takes a Jewish artist, a Jewish subject-matter or both to constitute Jewish art. ▷ Aqedah; Aggadah; menorah; music, Jewish

art, Palaeolithic The art of the Old Stone Age, created c.30000 years ago, the oldest known art in the world. Preserved in limestone caves in France and Spain are impressive murals representing hunting scenes, with realistic drawings of horses, bulls, and many animals now extinct or no longer found in Europe. Small sculptures were also made, the best-known being the 'Venus of Willendorf', a stylized 11.5 cm/4½-inch stone carving of a pregnant woman. Such works were not made as 'art' in the modern sense; the paintings are often found only in virtually inaccessible chambers deep within the ground, and were presumably done for magical purposes. ▷ Lascaux; Palaeolithic religion; Venus of Willendorf

Arthur (6th century) Semi-legendary King of the Britons and national hero. He may originally have been a Romano-British war leader in the west of England called Arturus; but he is represented as having united the British tribes against the invading Saxons, and as having been the champion not only of his people but of Christendom as well. He is said to have fought stubbornly against the invaders in a series of momentous battles, starting with a victory at 'Mount Baden' and ending with defeat and death at 'Camlan' 20 years later; after which he was buried at Glastonbury. The *Anglo-Saxon Chronicle* makes no mention of him, however; he first appears in Welsh chronicles long after the event. The story of Arthur blossomed into a huge literature, interwoven with legends of the Holy Grail and courtly ideas of a round table of knights at 'Camelot', in such writers as Geoffrey of Monmouth, Chrétien de Troyes, Layamon, and Sir Thomas Malory. ▷ Grail, Holy

arupa-loka (arūpa-loka) A term used in Buddhist cosmology to designate the 'formless world'. This is superior to the two lower worlds which are the sensual world and the world of form, but it is still within the sphere of rebirth. The lowest world, the world of the senses, incorporates five realms of rebirth: the lower animal, ghostly and hellish realms, and the higher human and godly (*deva*) realms. However, all these realms take sensory objects seriously. The second world, the world of form (*rupa-loka*), is the realm of more refined gods beyond the senses of smell, taste and touch. The third world, the formless world (arupa-loka), is even higher than this, beyond all shape and form. It is in this realm that the four most advanced forms of purely mental rebirth take place. Beings are reborn into the formless world by virtue of concentration, and the deeper the concentration the higher the state of formlessness obtained. The Buddha is said to have turned down the possibility of rebirth even into this exalted world because his final goal was the nirvana lying beyond the sphere of rebirth. ▷ Buddha; nirvana; rebirth

Aryans (Āryans) Tribes of Indo-European pastoral nomads who entered India from the north west between 1500 and 1000BCE. They subjugated what remained of the Indus Valley civilization and moved slowly east across northern India, finally settling in the Ganges Plain which became known as the 'Aryan homeland' (*aryavarta*). The Aryans introduced into India a tripartite social structure which became the basis of the Hindu caste system, of priests (*brahmanas*), warriors or nobles (*kshatriyas*), and commoners (*vaishyas*). The indigenous populations of India were placed at the bottom of this scale as the serfs (*shudras*). We know of Aryan religion from the earliest Hindu scriptures, the *Rig Veda*, which comprises hymns to the deities (*devas*) of their pantheon. These gods, theoretically numbering 33 though actually more, were associated with a hierarchical cosmology of sky, atmosphere and earth. Among the sky gods were Varuna, the god of moral order, the benevolent deity Visnu, and the sky-father Dyaus, related to the Greek god Zeus; among the atmospheric gods were the warrior Indra, the wind Vayu and the storm gods (Maruts); and among the terrestrial gods were Agni the fire god and the hallucinogenic plant-god Soma. These gods were the object of praise and sacrifice. Hinduism developed from this Aryan religion, absorbing into it non-Aryan religious ideas and practices as it developed. ▷ Veda

Arya Samaj (Ārya Samāj) A Hindu reform movement founded in Bombay in 1875 by Dayananda Sarasvati. The aims of the Arya Samaj were to restore Hinduism to what it perceived as its original purity, found in the Vedas and stripped of later accretions such as image-worship, child-marriage and polygamy. Among the 10 principles of the Arya Samaj formulated by Dayananda are that God is an unchanging, blissful, formless intelligence, who cannot be represented in an idol; that the Vedas contain all true knowledge; and that each person should be highly moral and promote the well-being of all. The ultimate well-being is liberation (*moksha*), in which the soul is emancipated while yet retaining its distinct identity apart from God. The Arya Samaj promoted a moral vision of kindness and goodwill to all, though its attitude to the caste system remained ambiguous: Dayananda advocated the four classes (varnas) as being a systematization of qualities gained by merit rather than by birth. Indeed the Arya Samaj instigated a rite of purification (*shuddhi*) which allowed low castes and untouchables, who had given up Hinduism in favour of Islam or Christianity, to be reintegrated into the tradition as 'high caste' Hindus. In 1893 there was a split in the movement between the conservatives who advocated traditional Hindu education and vegetarianism, and the liberals who advocated 'modern' education and freedom of diet, the former group having more influence than the latter. The Arya Samaj became nationalistic and was in conflict with the Muslims and Sikhs, especially in the Punjab during the partition (1947). ▷ caste; Dayananda Sarasvati; Veda

Asanga (Asaṇga) (4th century) Indian Buddhist philosopher, born in Peshawar, founder of the *Yogacara* school, an important philosophical branch within Mahayana Buddhism. He was taught by Maitreya, who may have been either a human teacher of that name or the heavenly Maitreya. He converted his half-brother Vasubandhu to Mahayana Buddhism, and Vasubandhu in turn is traditionally considered to be a great Mahayana thinker and writer. In addition to his works on Yogacara philosophy Asanga also wrote the *Compendium of the Mahayana* and the *Collection of Abhidharma*. He thus synthesized the Mahayana and Abhidharma insights into the Yogacara tradition; he also emphasized the importance of meditation and the withdrawal of the mind from sensory objects as prerequisites for true wisdom. His school stressed the notion of the 'eight consciousnesses', the concept of the 'storehouse-consciousness' (*alaya-vijnana*), and the view of consciousness itself as somehow existing whereas the self and separate entities do not exist. For this reason it was sometimes referred to as the Idealist school of Buddhism. Asanga also deepened the notion of what a Buddha is in the Mahayana tradition. ▷ Abhidharma; alaya-vijnana; bhavana; Mahayana Buddhism; Maitreya; meditation; Vasubandhu; Yogacara

Asbury, Francis (1745–1816) English-born American churchman, the first Methodist bishop in America, born in Handsworth, Staffordshire. In 1771 he was sent as a Methodist missionary to America. He founded the Methodist Episcopal Church in 1770, and in 1784 was consecrated as superintendent. In 1785 he assumed the title of bishop. He died in Richmond, Virginia. ▷ Methodism

ascension The raising up from the earthly to the heavenly sphere. In certain ancient myths, the hero attains heaven and release from earthly existence by his own effort. In the Old Testament certain holy men, eg Enoch the patriarch and Elijah the prophet, are reported as being translated by God to heaven. In the New Testament, explicit reference to the ascension of Jesus (Luke 24.51 and Acts 1.2–9) and belief in his exaltation gave rise in the Christian tradition to the inclusion of confession (in eg the Apostles' Creed) of belief in Christ who 'ascended into heaven and sits on the right hand of God the Father Almighty'. This confession does not relate so much to a physical elevation of the body of Christ 'upwards' to a physical heaven as to a recognition by the Church of the status of the resurrected Christ as one with God the Father.

Theologically, it indicates his transcendence over all limitations of time and space, but also the universal availability of Christ, as well as his lordship over all humanity and all creation. For this reason, the ascended Christ figures prominently in the history of Christian art and iconography.
In the Christian calendar, Ascension Day is recognized as a feast, and is the sixth Thursday, ie 40 days, after Easter, to correspond to the chronology of Acts 1.3, though not in line with other New Testament accounts in which the resurrection and ascension of Jesus coincide. ▷ Christian year; Easter; Jesus Christ; heaven; resurrection

Ascension, Feast of In the Christian calendar, the sixth Thursday (being 40 days—see Acts 1) after Easter. It commemorates Jesus's last appearance to his disciples, his being 'lifted up' or 'taken away' from them, prior to the attestation of his later presence to them through the Holy Spirit. ▷ Easter; Holy Spirit; Jesus Christ

asceticism A variety of austere practices involving the renunciation or denial of ordinary bodily and sensual gratifications as a means to achieving greater spiritual awareness. These may include fasting, meditation, a life of solitude, the renunciation of possessions, denial of sexual gratification, and, in the extreme, the mortification of the flesh by such means as wearing heavy chains, self-flagellation, sleeping on a spiked bed or self-mutilation. Asceticism is most prevalent in religions in which the conflict between good and evil, soul and body, or God and the world, are emphasized.

Ashari, al- (al-Ash'arī, Abū-l-Ḥasan 'Ali ibn Ismā'īl) (873/874–935/936) Islamic theologian and philosopher, born in Basra. He studied with the sect of Mutazilites, with whom he broke in a crisis of confidence at the age of 40. In 915 he moved to Baghdad and associated for a while with disciples of Ibn Hanbal, but gradually evolved his own theology and gathered around him his own school of followers. His major work is *Maqalat*, and he was particularly concerned to defend the idea of God's omnipotence and to reaffirm traditional interpretations of religious authority within Islam. ▷ Ibn Hanbal; Islam

Asher, tribe of One of the 12 tribes of ancient Israel, said to be descended from Jacob's eighth son Asher (Genesis 30.12f). Its territory included the narrow coastal plain from Carmel to the outskirts of Sidon and bordered on the east by the Galilean hills. ▷ Israel, tribes of

Asherah, or **Athirat** Ancient Canaanite goddess, known widely in the Ancient Near East. In the Ras Shamra texts she is portrayed as consort of the supreme god El, and mother of the gods. Called Lady Athirat of the Sea (although the significance of that title is not made clear), she also appears in texts from Mesopotamia, Egypt, and South Arabia. Before the discovery of the Ras Shamra texts most information about Asherah came from the Hebrew Bible where, as a Canaanite fertility goddess associated with Baal, her worship is condemned. The word asherah is also used to mean a cultic object or place, probably representing the goddess. ▷ Baal; Canaanite religion; El; Ras Shamra texts; Ugarit

Ashkenazim Jews of central and eastern European descent, as distinguished from Sephardic Jews, who are of Spanish or Portuguese descent. The terms arose in the Middle Ages when Europe and western Asia were divided between Christian and Islamic countries. Cut off, the Ashkenazim developed their own customs, traditions of interpretation of the Talmud, music, and language (Yiddish). ▷ Judaism; Sephardim

Ashoka (Aśoka) (3rd century BCE) Ruler of the Mauryan empire in North India (c.268–239BCE), who in the later part of his reign became a Buddhist and helped to extend the Buddhist tradition beyond India so that it became a world religion. He had become a nominal Buddhist in about 260BCE, but in the aftermath of his bloodthirsty conquest of the Kalinga region, which helped to extend his empire across India from sea to sea, he was filled with remorse and vowed that his kingdom would no longer be filled with the drums of battle but with the sound of the dharma. We know about him from the Pali chronicles of Buddhist monks, and from the rock and pillar edicts that he himself inscribed. Ashoka worked for the moral improvement of his people by legislation, by stressing virtues such as contentment, gentleness, mercy and truth, by advocating non-violence (ahimsa), and by allowing religious tolerance. His work was of help to the mission of Buddhism in that he sent embassies to Egypt, Macedonia and Syria, to East Asia, to southern Indian kingdoms and above all to Ceylon where, in about 250BCE, his son succeeded in introducing Theravada Buddhism. Although not a Hindu, Ashoka is ranked among the three or four greatest rulers of India. ▷ ahimsa; dharma; Theravada Buddhism

ashram An Indian religious community whose members lead lives of austere self-discipline and dedicated service in accordance with the teachings and practices of their particular school. A well-known ashram was that of Mahatma Gandhi. ▷ Gandhi, Mohandas Karamchand

ashrama (āśrama) In Hindu tradition, any of the four stages of life: the pupil, the householder, the forest-dweller and, when all human bonds have been broken, the total renunciation of the world. Seldom followed in practice, these four stages represent the ideal way of life. Each stage has its own rules of behaviour. ▷ ashram; Hinduism

Ashura ('Āshūrā') An important day for the two main branches of Muslims, the Sunnis and the Shiites, though for different reasons. It is the tenth day of *Muharram*, the first month of the Muslim year. When Muhammad went to Medina he adopted this date from the Jews as a day for fasting, and it is still observed as such by a number of Sunni Muslims. Historically it was superseded in importance by the longer and more significant fast of Ramadan. Among the Shiites it is the day when the death of Husayn at Karbala in 680 at the hands of the soldiers of Caliph Yazid is commemorated. It is preceded by nine days of mourning; on the ninth day there is a fast, and on the tenth day a passion play is performed. Some Shiites parade through the streets wounding themselves as a symbol of sadness that their ancestors abandoned Husayn. Representations of Husayn's tomb are also carried through the streets, and it is a day of solemnity, weeping and awe for Shiite Muslims around the world and especially in Iran. ▷ Husayn; Medina; Muhammad; Ramadan; Shiism; Sunnis

Ashvaghosha (Aśvaghoṣa) (1st–2nd century) The name of an important Buddhist writer or writers whose biographical details are uncertain. An Ashvaghosha was a contemporary of King Kanishka, the Mahayana Buddhist ruler of the Kushan empire in north-west India in the 1st and early 2nd century. He wrote three important Sanskrit works (*Buddha Carita*, *Saundarananda* and *Sariputra-Prakarana*) as well as a number of lyrical poems, and according to Tibetan tradition is said to have played an influential part in formalizing the doctrines agreed by the fourth Buddhist Council convened by Kanishka in Kashmir or Jalandar. An important summary of Mahayana Buddhist doctrines in Chinese, translated with the title *Treatise on the Awakening of Faith in the Mahayana*, is also attributed to Ashvaghosha, but the nature of its teaching suggests that it is later than the volumes mentioned above and was therefore written by a different Ashvaghosha. Whether there was one or more Ashvaghosha, the name is a significant one in Buddhist thought. The earlier *Buddha Carita* is the first example of a formal life of the Buddha, and the later *Treatise on the Awakening of Faith in the Mahayana* is a formal summary of the various elements of Mahayana Buddhism. ▷ Buddha; Buddhist Councils; Kanishka; Mahayana Buddhism

Ash Wednesday The first day of Lent. The name derives from the ritual, observed in the ancient Church and continued in Roman Catholic and some Anglican Churches, of making a cross on the forehead of Christians with ashes which have previously been blessed. The ashes are obtained by burning the branches used in the previous year's Palm Sunday service. ▷ Lent

Asmoneans ▷ Maccabees

Assassins The name given to the Nizari branch of the Ismaili tradition within Shiite Islam by the medieval Crusaders. It is taken from the Arabic word *hashashin*, meaning smokers of cannabis, which was probably used by the Assassins to produce ecstasy. The term has become widely used in connection with the practice of assassination in which the Assassins sometimes engaged. Their founder was al-Hasan al-Sabbah, who went to Egypt from Persia in 1078 and supported Nizar unsuccessfully as successor to the Ismaili leadership (hence the name Nizari). Al-Hasan seized the fort of Alamut (1090), which became the centre of Assassin strength in parts of Iraq, Persia and Syria until it was finally captured by the Mongols in 1256. In 1164 a successor, also named Hasan, claimed that he was the Ismaili Imam and that a new age had begun for the Ismaili tradition, but this claim was repudiated by a later successor, Jalal ad-Din. After the fall of Alamut in 1256 remnants of the Nizari or Assassin tradition survived and splits occurred; their main strength currently is among the Khojas in India. ▷ imam; Ismailis; Shiism

Assemblies of God A Christian Pentecostalist denomination formed in the USA and Canada in the early 20th century. It promotes mission work all over the world, and believes baptism by the Holy Spirit to be evidenced by speaking in tongues. ▷ Holy Spirit; glossolalia; Pentecostalism

Asshur (also **Ashur**, **Assur**) National god of Assyria. Asshur is the name of the god, of the nation, and of the first Assyrian capital city, and it is difficult to know which of these is the original use. An outsider in the traditional Mesopotamian pantheon, Asshur's development reflects the growth of Assyria as an imperial power; as Asshur achieved greater importance he came to take elements of Enlil, Marduk, and other Sumero-Babylonian deities into his nature. He replaced Marduk in the Assyrian version of *Enuma Elish*, the Babylonian creation epic which was recited at the akitu-festival. The Assyrian king was high priest of Asshur, and even more involved in cultic duties than many Ancient Near Eastern monarchs. Despite the attempts of Assyrian theologians to enhance his prestige Asshur remained very much a national god, never having much significance outside Assyria. ▷ Assyrian religion; Akitu; Babylonian religion; Enlil; kingship, Ancient Near Eastern; Marduk; Sumerian religion

Assumption The claim that, on the death of the Virgin Mary, mother of Jesus Christ, she was 'assumed' (taken up, body and soul) to heaven. This was believed by some Christians in the ancient Church, widely accepted thereafter in Roman Catholic and Orthodox Churches, and defined by Pope Pius XII as an article of faith in 1950. ▷ Mary

Assyria The name given first to the small area around the town of Assur on the Tigris in Upper Mesopotamia, and then much later to the vast empire that the rulers of Assur acquired through conquering their neighbours on all sides. At its height in the 9th and 8th centuries BCE, the Assyrian Empire stretched from the eastern Mediterranean to Iran, and from the Persian Gulf as far north as the mountains of eastern Turkey. The empire was destroyed in an uprising of Medes and Babylonians in 612BCE. ▷ Nimrod; Nineveh

Assyrian religion As part of the Mesopotamian religious tradition Assyrian religion shared many features with the religion of the Sumerians and especially the Babylonians, with whom they shared a common language. The Assyrian pantheon was the same but headed by the national god Asshur; the goddess Ishtar was especially popular and her warlike aspect stressed. The Assyrian king was high priest of Asshur and had an even more pronounced cultic role than many Ancient Near Eastern monarchs. Divination was as popular as in Babylonia and the best source of Mesopotamian omen texts is the library assembled by the Assyrian king Asshurbanipal (7th century BCE). Astrology was a form of divination favoured by the late Assyrian kings, and in Assyria generally there was more emphasis on atmospheric and astral phenomena than in Babylonian religion. ▷ Ancient Near Eastern religions; Asshur; astrology, Ancient Near Eastern; Babylonian religion; divination, Ancient Near Eastern; Ishtar; Sumerian religion

winged bull, an Assyrian entrance guard

Astarte, or **Ashtart**, **Athtart**, **Ashtoreth** West Semitic goddess, worshipped throughout the ancient Levant. Astarte is mentioned in the Ras Shamra texts and also in inscriptions from Phoenicia, where she was very important. Her name is equivalent to the Babylonian Ishtar, whose characteristics she probably shared. The worship of Ashtoreth and Baal is condemned in the Hebrew Bible as an intrusion of the Canaanite fertility cult. ▷ Baal; Ishtar; Phoenician religion; Ras Shamra texts

astrology A system of knowledge whereby human nature can be understood in terms of the heavens. It relies upon precise measurement and a body of symbolism which has come to be associated with each of the signs of the zodiac and the planets (including the sun and moon). It rests on a foundation of ancient philosophy, particularly on the idea that the force which patterns the heavens likewise orders humanity. As with religion, it is a source of both trivial superstition and profound insight. The most significant stages in the development of astrology took place in the first millennium BCE in Mesopotamia and Greece. From there it spread worldwide, developing distinct branches and great variation in method. It blossomed most in those periods representing peaks of cultural achievement—Classical Greece, Renaissance Europe, and Elizabethan England. Today it thrives in several Eastern countries, and in the West is undergoing something of a revival, though the modern emphasis is on self-knowledge rather than on predicting events. ▷ horoscope

astrology, Ancient Near Eastern The earliest astrology developed in Mesopotamia in the 3rd and 2nd millenia BCE, although it is probably better described as the study of astral omens. It was believed that events in the heavens had their counterparts on earth, and the observation of the heavenly bodies was one of the recognized forms of divination in Babylonia and Assyria. Omens were systematically collected and grouped in four categories, covering the moon, the sun, the planets and meteorological phenomena. Under the late Assyrian kings (c.700 BCE) astral omens became the most important form of state divination and teams of observers sent in regular reports from all over the kingdom. The omens were understood to be significant principally for affairs of state, and often had military interpretations. The more individualistic approach of modern astrology and the invention of the zodiac were very late developments, the first known horoscope being cast for a child born on 29 April 410BCE. Babylonian astrology was exported to Hellenistic Egypt and was influential in the development of later Graeco-Roman astrological techniques. ▷ Assyrian religion; divination; horoscope

astrology, Tibetan Astrology is very important in the folk religion of Tibet. Most Tibetans will consult an astrologer at various times in their life or even annually. Indeed, a person's health and prosperity are contingent upon astrological forces known as the 'wind horse' (*rlung-rita*). The astrologers are lamas called *tsi-pa* (*rtsis-pa*) who draw up horoscopes for birth, marriage, death, the year or for one's whole life. Tibetan astrology is based on the Chinese system rather than the Indian one (which is derived from Greek astrology). In the Tibetan system astrological time is based on the 12- and 60-year cycles of Jupiter. Each of the 12 years in a cycle is associated, as in the Chinese system, with an animal (namely the mouse, ox, tiger, hare, dragon, snake, horse, sheep, monkey, bird, dog and pig). For the 60-year cycle these animals are combined with the five elements: wood, fire, earth, iron and water. The drawing-up of horoscopes is quite complex, involving the use of an astrologer's board and coloured counters, though the basic principle behind it is the attraction and repulsion of astrological forces. In drawing up an annual horoscope, for example, the year in which a person was born will be contrasted with the year at the time of prediction, so if one was born in the water-horse year and if the year of prediction is the earth-mouse year, then there will be conflict because the horse and the mouse are antagonistic. There are degrees of affinity and repulsion between astrological forces which are modelled on human relationships exemplified by the terms mother, son, friend and enemy. For example, wood is mother to water, so there is an attraction between them, whereas water is the enemy of fire, so they repulse each other. ▷ lama; Tibetan religion

asura In ancient and later Indian thought this term is given to a class of non-human beings, or anti-gods, who are at war with the heavenly beings, or gods (*devas*). The main asura in the Hindu Veda was Vritra, a cosmic serpent who lived in the waters of chaos, and fought and lost against Indra, who represented order and cosmos. The notion of asura is related to the Iranian notion of *ahura*. However, in Iranian Zoroastrian thought ahura has a positive sense, and Ahura Mazda is the Zoroastrian term for God. In Hindu thought the meaning is reversed so that asura has a negative and evil connotation. In the *tipitaka* or Pali Canon of Theravada Buddhism asura is also seen negatively, as a spirit-host at war with the heavenly beings. The asuras themselves are subject to rebirth, and for a human being to be reborn as an asura is seen to be a very low and unhappy attainment resulting from various misdeeds. ▷ Ahura Mazda; Indra; Theravada Buddhism; tipitaka; Veda; Zoroastrianism

Atenism In Ancient Egypt, the system of solar monotheism adopted by the pharaoh Akhenaton (14th century BCE). Aten (or Aton) is the Egyptian word for the sun disc, depicted as the round solar disc with rays which end in hands, and originally seen as an aspect of the sun god Re. Under his two predecessors the disc had become personalized and worshipped in its own right, but Akhenaton's innovative system considered the Aten the only deity worthy of worship, and he persecuted other deities, especially the dominant Amun. Atenism worshipped the physical sun, concentrating on the light and warmth it provided for all people and its perceived blessings of life, beauty and love. An interest in art led to new, more naturalistic styles of painting and sculpture. Akhenaton himself lost none of the traditional status of the pharaoh and was sole intermediary between the Aten and the world. The new religion had little effect on the beliefs of the common people, and among the ruling classes was very disruptive and unpopular. Atenism collapsed soon after Akhenaton's death, and the old gods were reinstated by the successors of this 'heretic pharaoh'. ▷ Akhenaton; Amun; Ancient Egyptian religion; art, Ancient Egyptian; pharaoh; Re

Ateshgah A Persian word meaning 'place (or throne) of fire'. In the later Zoroastrian tradition the word is mainly used for a fire-temple of the first or second degree (ie an Atesh Bahram or an Atesh Adaran), and also for the fire-chamber in the temple where the sacred fire is 'enthroned'. ▷ fire; Zoroastrianism

Athanasian Creed A statement of Christian faith, written in Latin probably in the 5th century. Called *quicunque vult* after the opening words, it remains a historic statement of Trinitarian doctrine, still sometimes used liturgically. The Greek text is known in Eastern Churches, but with the omission of the *filioque* clause. ▷ Athanasius, St; Filioque; Trinity

Athanasius, St (c.296–373) Greek Christian theologian and prelate, born in Alexandria. In his youth he often visited the celebrated hermit St Antony, and himself for a time embraced an anchorite's life. He was only a deacon when he distinguished himself at the great Council of Nicaea or Nice in 325. In 326 he was chosen patriarch of Alexandria and primate of Egypt, and was newly installed when Arius, banished on the condemnation of his doctrine at Nicaea, was recalled, and recanted. Athanasius refused to comply with the will of Emperor Constantine that the heretic should be restored to communion. Hence, and on other charges brought by the Arians, he was summoned by the emperor to appear before the synod of Tyre, in 335, which deposed him. The sentence was confirmed by the synod of Jerusalem in 336, when he was banished to Trèves. In 338 he was restored; but in 341 he was again condemned by a council of 97 (mainly Arian) bishops in Antioch. Orthodox synods in Alexandria and Sardica protested in his favour, and he was again restored to office (349). Under the Arian emperor Constantius he was again condemned and forcibly expelled, whereupon he retired to a remote desert in Upper Egypt. Under Julian 'the Apostate', toleration was proclaimed to all religions, and Athanasius once more became Patriarch of Alexandria (361). His next controversy was with the heathen subjects of Julian, by whom he was compelled again to flee from Alexandria, and he hid in the Theban desert until 363, when Jovian ascended the throne. After holding office for a short time he was expelled again by the Arians under the emperor Valens who, after petitions from the orthodox Alexandrians, soon restored the patriarch to his see, in which he continued till his death. Athanasius was the great leader during the most trying period in the history of the early Christian church. His conscientiousness, his wisdom, his fearlessness, his commanding intellect, his activity and patience, all mark him out as an ornament of his age. His writings, polemical, historical, and moral, are simple, cogent, and clear. The polemical works treat chiefly of the Trinity, the Incarnation and the divinity of the Holy Spirit. The so-called *Athanasian Creed* (representing Athanasian beliefs) was little heard of until the 7th century. His feast day is 2 May.

Atharva Veda The fourth section of the Vedas, the revealed scriptures (*shruti*) of Hinduism. Although containing material which may be as old as the *Rig Veda*, most of the *Atharva Veda* is later than the other Samhita portions of the Veda (namely the *Rig*, *Sama*, and *Yajur*). The *Atharva Veda* contains hymns to the gods of the Vedic pantheon, along with magical spells and incantations for curing disease, for rain, for material prosperity and for subduing enemies. Unlike other Vedic texts, the *Atharva Veda* is not closely associated with the cult of sacrifice and may have originated in non-Aryan contexts. Indeed its authenticity has sometimes been questioned within the tradition. ▷ Aryans; Veda

atheism The denial of the existence of God or gods. It includes both the rejection of any specific belief in God or gods, and the view that the only rational approach to claims about divine existence is one of scepticism. Justification of atheism is often made on the grounds that some branch of science or psychology has rendered belief in God or gods superfluous, or that experiential verification of religious belief is lacking. Theists argue that such justification has not proved to be logically grounded. ▷ God; humanism; Marx, Karl; scepticism; secular alternatives to religion; theism

Atisha (Atīśa) (982–1054) The most important figure in the restoration of Buddhism in Tibet, born near Vajrasana in India. He went on a missionary tour to Tibet in 1042, and remained there until his death. He had an impressive boyhood in India, and by the age of 30 had mastered the chief scriptures of the four main Buddhist schools. It was as a 60-year-old monk-professor that he went to Tibet at the invitation of a regional king to spearhead a Buddhist renaissance. He helped to reform the Buddhist community in Tibet, stressed the importance of celibacy, and deepened the Tibetan insight into Buddhist doctrine. Due to his influence, his chief disciple set up the Kadampa school which stressed monastic discipline. He also influenced two other new schools: the Kagyupa school, founded by Marpa (1012–96), which set out a system of yoga based on whispered transmission from master to pupil; and the Sakyapa school, which became famous for its scholarship. Atisha arranged Tibetan Buddhist teaching in a series of levels with a purified Tantrism at the top. His synthesis has remained important in the ensuing history of Tibetan Buddhism. He also discovered in Tibet some Sanskrit Mahayana Buddhist manuscripts, such as the Avatamsaka Sutra, that had been lost; he had them copied and sent back to India. ▷ celibacy; Mahayana Buddhism; Mahayana Sutras; Tantric Buddhism; Tibetan religion; yoga

atman (ātman) (Sanskrit, 'soul' or 'self') In Hinduism, the human soul or essential self. In the teaching of the Upanishads, it is seen as being one with the absolute, and is identified with *Brahman*. ▷ Advaita Vedanta; Brahman; Hinduism; Upanishads

atonement In Christian theology, the process whereby sinners are made 'at one' with God, through the life, death, and resurrection of Jesus Christ. No one theory is recognized as authoritative, but the theories of Irenaeus (stressing 'victory' over evil), Anselm (stressing 'satisfaction' made to God), and Abelard (stressing the force of example of Christ) have been commonly held. ▷ Abelard, Peter; Anselm, St; Irenaeus, St

attributes of God, Islamic In Islam the attributes of God are to some extent bound up with the names of God. Quran 112 proclaims 'He is God, One, God, the Everlasting Refuge, who has not begotten, and has not been begotten, and not equal to Him is any one'. The *shahadah* underlines the belief that 'Allah is Allah, and Muhammad is his prophet'. In the Quran, God is creator, sustainer, redeemer, and judge; he is the mighty one, the wise, the one who sees and hears and knows; he is the merciful (*rahman*), the first, the last, the holy one, the giver of peace. Later the '99 beautiful names of God' summarized the attributes of Allah. They were separated into names of the essence and names of the qualities of God, and into names of the majesty and names of the beauty of God. Later Islamic movements stressed certain attributes of God as being the key to his nature, for example the Kharijites emphasized his attributes of judgement, and the Murji'ites his attributes of freedom. The Mutazilites acknowledged only the names of the essence of God, thus downgrading other names and attributes that seemed to give God human attributes. Synthesizers such as al-Ashari attempted to harmonize these different viewpoints. Within Shiite Islam there was a greater emphasis than among the Sunnis on the transcendence, mystery, unity and ineffability of God. Some modern philosophers have attempted to understand God in terms of scientific theory; for example Iqbal saw God in terms of the theory of creative evolution. Some recent neo-fundamentalist thinkers have returned to the literalism of the Quran in order to understand the nature of the attributes of God. ▷ Allah; Ashari, al-; divine names in Islam; Iqbal, Sir Muhammad; Mutazilites; Quran; shahadah

atua The general term for spirit beings in Polynesia, including the Maori of New Zealand. It can be applied to the supreme being (Tangeroa in Samoa, Tonga and Tahiti, and perhaps, though this is disputed, the archaic Io in New Zealand), and to the personified forces of nature, and the rulers of departments of life—war, agriculture, the underworld. However, it is used equally of inferior local deities, little regarded outside their own area, and a host of other beings—ancestral spirits, a medium's 'familiars', ghosts, or even phenomena that are exceptional or inexplicable, such as a strange disease. The higher myths of the high gods and departmental atua constituted a specialist matter in which most people did not meddle.

Atum (also **Tem**, **Tum**) Ancient Egyptian sun god, and original god of creation according to the Heliopolis theology. Atum arose out of the waters of Nun and willed himself into being on the primeval hill. By copulating with himself, he created the first pair of gods, Shu and Tefnut, and through them the whole Heliopolitan ennead. As creator of the divine order, Atum was called 'Lord of the Two Lands' and was most commonly represented as a bearded man, wearing the double crown of Upper and Lower Egypt and carrying the ankh sceptre. By the 5th Dynasty (c.2494–2345BCE) Atum was identified with the supreme sun god Re as Re-Atum. Later he became specifically identified with Re in his evening aspect, the setting sun. ▷ ankh; creation myths; ennead; Heliopolis theology; primeval hill; Re

Augsburg Confession A statement of faith composed by Luther, Melanchthon, and others for the imperial Diet of Augsburg (1530), the official text being written by Melanchthon in 1531. The earliest of Protestant Confessions, it was presented to Charles V by seven Lutheran princes and two cities, and was intended to set down their beliefs in defence against various criticisms levelled at Lutheran theology. It consisted of 28 articles covering all aspects of doctrine, and showing the reforms of so-called abuses which they considered had begun to corrupt the Catholic Church. The Confession became authoritative for the Lutheran Church, and its influence can be seen on the Thirty-nine Articles. ▷ Luther, Martin; Lutheranism; Melanchthon, Philip; Thirty-nine Articles

Augustine, St, Aurelius Augustinus, also known as **Augustine of Hippo** (354–430) The greatest of the Latin Church fathers, born in Tagaste in Numidia (modern Tunisia). His father was a pagan, but he was brought up a Christian by his devout mother, Monica. He went to Carthage to study and had a son, Adeonatus, by a mistress there. Carthage was a metropolitan centre and he was exposed there to many new intellectual fashions and influences. He became deeply involved in Manichaeism, which seemed to offer a solution to the problem of evil, a theme which was to preoccupy him throughout his life. In 383 he moved to teach in Rome, then in Milan, and became influenced by scepticism and then by neo-platonism. After the dramatic spiritual crises described in his autobiography he finally became converted to Christianity and was baptized (together with his son) by St Ambrose in 386. He returned to North Africa and in 396 became bishop of Hippo, where he was a relentless antagonist of the heretical schools of Donatists, Pelagians and Manichaeans, and a champion of orthodoxy. He remained in Hippo until his death in 430, as the Vandals were besieging the gates of the city. He was an unusually productive writer and much of his work is marked by personal spiritual struggle. The *Confessions* (400) is a classic of world literature and a spiritual autobiography as well as an original work of philosophy (with a famous discussion on the nature of time). *The City of God* (412–27) is a monumental work of 22 books which presents human history in terms of the conflict between the spiritual and the temporal, which will end in the triumph of the City of God, whose manifestation on earth is the Church. His feast day is 28 August. ▷ Ambrose, St; Donatists; Manichaeism; neo-platonism; Pelagianism

Augustine, St (of Canterbury) (d.604) Italian churchman, the first Archbishop of Canterbury. He was prior of the Benedictine monastery of St Andrew in Rome, when, in 596, he was sent, with 40 other monks, by Pope Gregory I to convert the Anglo-Saxons to Christianity, and establish the authority of the Roman see in Britain. Landing in Thanet, the missionaries were kindly received by Æthelbert, King of Kent, whose wife Bertha, daughter of the Frankish king, was a Christian. A residence was assigned to them in Canterbury, where they devoted themselves to monastic exercises and preaching. The conversion and baptism of the king contributed greatly to the success of their efforts among his subjects, and it is recorded that in one day Augustine baptized 1000 persons in the River Swale. In 597 he went to Arles, and there was consecrated Bishop of the English. His efforts to extend his authority over the native British (Welsh) Church, with whose bishops he held a conference in 603 in Aust on the Severn, were less successful. He died in 604, and in 612 his body was transferred to his abbey of Saints Peter and Paul. His feast day is 26 May. ▷ Benedictines; Gregory I, the Great, St; missions, Christian

Augustinians A religious order united in 1255 following the monastic teaching and 'rule' of St Augustine (of Hippo); also known as the Augustinian or Austin Friars; in full, the Order of the Hermit Friars of St Augustine (OSA). It established missions and monasteries throughout the world, and was responsible for founding many famous hospitals. There are also Augustinian nuns of second or third orders ('tertiaries'). ▷ Augustine, St (of Hippo); Orders, Holy; monasticism

Aurobindo Ghose (1872–1950) Indian philosopher, poet and mystic, born in Calcutta into a high-caste Bengali family. Educated at Cambridge and a proficient linguist, he returned to India in 1892 and became a professor at Baroda and Calcutta. In 1908 he was imprisoned by the British authorities in India for sedition, and studied yoga in jail. Renouncing nationalism and politics for yoga and Hindu philosophy, he founded an ashram in 1910 at Pondicherry, then French territory. As an experiment in community living, the ashram, known as Auroville, continued to attract Western visitors long after Aurobindo's death, even if few could grasp the underlying philosophy: salvation of society by the influence of the individual attainment of supermind or higher consciousness through integral yoga, as expressed in *The Life Divine* (1940), *The Synthesis of Yoga* (1948), *Aurobindo on Himself* (1953) and many other books. ▷ ashram; Hinduism; mysticism; yoga

auspicia In Roman religion the signs of the gods inscribed in nature, which were then to be deciphered. Etymologically the term means observation (*spicere*) of birds (*aves*), but in fact the signs of birds constitute only one part of the signs of auspicia. Five types of auspicia are listed: **1** those coming form the sky, such as thunder and lightning. These were considered the most important; **2** those coming from certain birds which were divided into two classes—the singing-birds giving auguries by singing or speaking, and the flying-birds giving auguries by their flight, both types being messengers of Jupiter; **3** those deduced from the way sacred chickens atem-these auspicia were used mainly on military expeditions; **4** those from quadrupeds and reptiles, these auspicia never being taken on behalf of the state; **5** any kind of auspicia which do not belong to the categories above. The auspicia were essentially practical and were not intended to inform on future events but rather to obtain an affirmative or negative response for a proposed course of action. Public auspicia were taken by augurs or magistrates qualified to do so at events such as elections, or in the course of wars, and took place in a delimited area (the *templum*)—the sacred space to which the taking of the auspicia was restricted. ▷ divination; Roman religion; templa

Austin Friars ▷ Augustinians

Australian Aboriginal religion The Aboriginal population of Australia at the time of the first European contact has been estimated at 300000. This small population, scattered over a vast area, was (and is) marked by great ethnic and linguistic variety. The transformation of Australia by its European population has meant that the traditional styles of Aboriginal life are feasible only in the areas of the north, west and centre of the sub-continent, and that the connections with ancestral land and sacred sites have frequently been disturbed.

Fundamental to Australian religion is the concept of the Dreaming. In this period all the world's creative achievements took place. Various beings emerged from the formless land or from the sea. Some took human form, others the shape of animals; some partook of more than one essence, and were both human and animal, or even human and plant. As they went about they formed the earth and all the features of the environment; their steps may be traced today in the marks which they left. They determined the divisions of land and of art, rituals, songs and myths. They established social organization and relationships and the proper division of labour. They established economic activities, hunting and planting and gathering. They made the spirit beings, set up the sacred objects and set the heavenly bodies on high. The Dreaming was not, however, simply a past event; people and things today are organically connected to the events of the Dreaming. The Dreaming is thus a charter for things today, the establishment of norms to be followed, a principle of order. There has been controversy about whether Aboriginal people recognized a high God in the sky over all; it seems clear that several Australian peoples did, though the sky father was not the focus of religious activity. Nearer to hand were the totemic spirits who bound each group together, giving them a special relationship with some other species of the creation. The principal rituals related to the crises of life (initiation of boys at puberty requiring a physical ordeal) and to increase and harvest ceremonies for the community. ▷ altjiranga; wondjina

authority, Christian Questions of authority arose early among Christians in relation to controversy about belief or practice. Paul's appeal (Galatians 2) to direct revelation from the risen Christ concerning circumcision bypassed both apostolic precedent and existing Scriptural warrants. Many subsequent

arguments about doctrine or conduct have involved subsidiary disagreements about how and whether God's self-disclosure can be definitively recognized. For most Christian churches, Scripture and the early councils of the undivided church (eg Nicaea and Chalcedon) have, in principle, set the standard, though the interpretation of both is often problematic. Roman Catholicism has tied authority primarily to *ex cathedra* papal pronouncements, though since Vatican II these have been set in the context of the collegiate responsibility of the bishops and of the reception of the whole Church. For those involved in the Reformation, authority was affirmed to reside in Scripture alone, though subsequent divisions within Protestantism showed this not to be self-evident in practice. The will of the courts of the Church, the conscience of the individual, distinctive charismatic gifts, etc are variously emphasized by different denominations as the way of determining the correct interpretation.
In the 20th century attention has been brought to the issue by the Ecumenical Movement, where long-divided churches seek to find a common voice: by feminism, which challenges most past accounts of authority as patriarchal constructs; and by liberation theology, which disputes any authority not grounded in the committed struggle for justice and peace. ▷ Council of the Church; ecumenism; feminist theology; liberation theology; Paul, St; Vatican Councils

Authorized Version of the Bible The English translation of the Bible commissioned by King James VI and I, and accomplished by a panel of leading scholars of the day; widely called the King James Bible. They used Greek and Hebrew texts, but were also indebted to earlier English translations. Noted for its literary excellence, the 'Authorized Version' gained wide popular appeal after its first publication in 1611, but was never formally 'authorized' by king or Parliament. ▷ Bible

auto-da-fé (Portuguese 'act of faith') The public burning at the stake of heretics and sinners condemned by the Spanish Inquisition. It was last carried out in Spain in 1781, and in Mexico in 1815. ▷ Inquisition

Avalokiteshvara (Avalokiteśvara) The name given to the most popular bodhisattva within the Mahayana Buddhist tradition, who is seen as the embodiment of compassion. He made the classical vow of the bodhisattva that he would not immediately become a Buddha and enter into nirvana, but would remain a bodhisattva and continue to be reborn until all beings were saved, in other words until the end of time. He is able to help human beings when they call upon him in great need, and devotion is offered to him in a kind of Buddhism of faith. When the Indian Avalokiteshvara was taken from India into China, Korea and Japan he gradually became transformed into a female bodhisattva named Kuan Yin in China and Kannon in Japan. Avalokiteshvara, in male or female form, has been widely represented in art and sculpture since the 5th century in the Ajanta caves in India. In particular Kuan Yin has been enshrined not only in Buddhist temples in China, Korea and Japan, but also in Taoist temples and those belonging to Chinese popular religion. This bodhisattva's compassion is seen to operate at two levels: by actual intervention in the problems of human beings, and by awakening persons to their own Buddha nature within. ▷ Ajanta; bodhisattva; Buddha; Buddha nature; Kuan Yin; Mahayana Buddhism; nirvana; Taoism

Avalokiteshvara

Avatamsaka Sutra (Avataṃsaka Sūtra) One of the Mahayana Sutras, the sacred texts of Mahayana Buddhism. It was especially important in the Hua Yen school of Chinese Buddhism founded by Tushun (557–640), which gave the Avatamsaka Sutra the leading role in its synthesis of Buddhist teaching. The sutra gave a full description of the 10 stages of the path that is to be followed by the great Mahayana saints known as bodhisattvas. Literally meaning the 'Flower Ornament' *sutra*, it reveals a beautiful array of spiritual flowers for the Buddhist believer. At one point it describes the spiritual journey of a young man named Sudhana who is seeking to find out how to become a bodhisattva. Near the end of the journey he sees a great tower where all the bodhisattvas live, and in it he finds a world of unsurpassed beauty, the description of which attempts to give insight through images into the inconceivable world of reality. It is like a net of precious jewels where each jewel reflects every other jewel in a welter of interdependent beauty; and it is like the notion of a hologram where everything is significant, in that every individual thing contains the meaning of the whole. The Hua Yen school interpreted the Avatamsaka Sutra in terms of the three bodies of the Buddha, the notion of emptiness, and the importance of mind and consciousness, but essentially it pointed out that every being that exists is important and is to be respected because all beings belong together in the resplendent tower of the Buddha who is himself the 'resplendent one'. ▷ bodhisattva; Buddha; emptiness; Hua Yen; Mahayana Buddhism; trikaya; Vairocana

avatara (avatāra) In Hinduism, the descent to earth of a deity in a visible form. The idea derives from the tradition associated with the deity Vishnu, who from time to time appears on earth in animal or human form in order to save it from destruction or extraordinary peril. Past forms which Vishnu has assumed include a boar, a crocodile and a fish. His most famous appearances have been as Rama and Krishna. The deity is expected to return in the last of his shapes at a time when the world is depraved beyond hope, with the purpose of destroying the world and subsequently recreating it. ▷ Hinduism; Krishna; Rama; Vishnu

Ave Maria ▷ **Hail Mary**

Averroës, Arabic name: **Ibn Rushd** (1126–98) The most famous of the medieval Islamic philosophers, born in Cordoba, son of a distinguished family of jurists. He was himself kadi (judge) successively in Cordoba, Seville and Morocco, and wrote on jurisprudence and medicine in this period as well as beginning his huge philosophical output. In 1182 he became court physician to Caliph Abu Yusuf, but in 1185 was banished in disgrace (for reasons now unknown) by the caliph's son and successor. Many of his works were burnt, but after a brief period of exile he was restored to grace and lived in retirement in Marrakesh until his death. The most numerous and important of his works were the *Commentaries on Aristotle*, many of them known only through their Latin (or Hebrew) translations, which greatly influenced later Jewish and Christian writers and offered a partial synthesis of Greek and Arabic philosophical traditions.

Avesta The scriptures of Zoroastrianism, written in Avestan, a language of the Eastern branch of the Indo-European family. Traditionally believed to have been revealed to Zoroaster, only the *Gathas*, a set of 17 hymns, may be attributed to him. Few portions of the original survive. ▷ Zoroastrianism

Avicenna, Arabic name: **Ibn Sina** (980–1037) Arab philosopher and physician, born near Bokhara. Renowned for his precocious and prodigious learning, he became physician to several sultans, and for some time vizier in Hamadan, in Persia, where he died. He was one of the main interpreters of Aristotle to the Islamic world, and was the author of some 200 works on science, religion and philosophy. His medical textbook, *Canon of Medicine*, remained a standard work for many years. ▷ Aristotle

avidya (avidyā; Pali: avijjā) A term used by Hindus and Buddhists which has the basic meaning of ignorance. In early Hinduism it denoted ignorance of correct religious procedures, but from the time of the Upanishads in the 6th century BCE, and especially in Vedanta thought, it developed the meaning of basic spiritual ignorance about the true nature of things, above all ignorance about the true nature of one's own self (atman) and its identity with *Brahman*, the absolute reality behind the universe. This ignorance involves one in a continual round of rebirths until, through realization of the truth, one obtains liberation (*moksha*) and is not reborn again. In the Buddhist context avidya meant in concrete terms ignorance of the four noble truths of the Buddha, although it coincided with Hindu thought as indicating also an inability to grasp the true nature of things. Ignorance was a key link among the 12 links in the Buddhist chain of dependent origination—by overcoming ignorance one could interrupt the operation of the chain, overcome delusion, and move along the path to enlightenment and nirvana. ▷ ariya sacca; atman; Brahman; Buddha; dependent origination;

enlightenment; moksha; nirvana; Upanishads; Vedanta

Axial Age The name given by Karl Jaspers to a significant epoch in human history which centred on the 6th century BCE when religious factors were vital in new developments in world history. Great religious leaders arose simultaneously in four different areas of the world: the Middle East, India, China and Europe. In the Middle East the Hebrew prophets were active, and there was the elaboration of Zoroaster's earlier work in Persia. In India the great Hindu Upanishads, one of the keys to Hindu scripture, emerged, the Buddhist tradition arose out of the life of the Buddha, and the Jain tradition arose out of the life of the Mahavira. In China Confucius was active, and the early currents of the Taoist tradition were beginning to flow. In Greece the rise of the Ionian philosophers prefigured the glory of Greek philosophy and the rise of Europe. We can attempt to give sociological, cultural, economic and spiritual reasons to account for the Axial Age—the main thing is that it happened. On the basis of the work of the religious leaders and movements mentioned above, over the next 2000 years four great civilizations were to rise that would be roughly equal, parallel, and separate. They were the Middle East, which would be revived by the rise of Islam; Europe, stemming from Greece and leading into Christian civilization; India, building up a multi-religious civilization based upon Hindu roots; and China, establishing its glory on the basis of its three traditions—the Confucian, the Taoist and the Mahayana Buddhist. The balance of civilizations established by the Axial Age would only be disturbed by the rise of the West in the 16th century. ▷ Buddha; Confucius; Mahavira; Taoism; Upanishads; Zoroaster

ayatollah An honorific title given to prestigious Shiite Muslim leaders in Iran, literally 'a sign of Allah'. The title only emerged in the 20th century, but its origins are to be found in the emergence in 18th-century Iran of the powerful Usuli School of Twelve-Imam Shiites. This school stressed the authority of jurists (*Mujtahids*) who, because of their eminence and piety, were able to make independent judgements on Islamic law. By the end of the 19th century there were hundreds of these jurists, and early in the 20th century the title of Ayatollah was introduced to distinguish jurists of high quality and large following. A leading ayatollah is said to partake of some of the authority of the Shiite Hidden Imam, and his rulings are made available to followers around the world. Leading ayatollahs are sometimes given the title of Ayatollah al-Uzma—'the greatest sign of Allah'—to distinguish them from the rank of lesser ayatollahs. Since the Iranian revolution in 1979 ayatollahs such as Khomeini and his successors have achieved political as well as religious significance. ▷ Allah; imam; Khomeini, Ayatollah; Shiism; Twelvers

Aylward, Gladys (1902–70) English missionary in China, born in Edmonton, London. She left school at 14 to become a parlourmaid, but her ambition was to go as a missionary to China. In 1930, she spent her entire savings on a railway ticket to Tientsin in northern China. With a Scottish missionary, Mrs Jeannie Lawson, she founded an inn, the famous Inn of the Sixth Happiness, in an outpost at Yangcheng. From there, in 1938, she trekked across the mountains leading over a hundred children to safety when the war with Japan brought fighting to the area. After nine years spent with the Nationalists, fulfilling her mission by caring for the wounded, she returned to England in 1948, preached for five years, then in 1953 settled in Taiwan as head of an orphanage. ▷ missions, Christian

Ayur Veda Medicine or the science of long life (*ayur*) in Hinduism and the texts (*shastras*), especially by Caraka, about this. Medicine to promote a long and healthy life is an important part of Hinduism, as caring for mind and body promotes spiritual growth. Amongst the topics dealt with by Ayur Vedic texts are the aetiology of disease, cures for disease, preventative medicine, and embryology discussed in the context of reincarnation. Causes of disease are not only physical—the bodily humours of phlegm, bile and wind—but also mental—the qualities (*gunas*) of passion (*rajas*) and darkness (*tamas*). Cures are based on the theory that medicine should contain the opposite qualities to those of the humours which cause disease. Thus a 'hot' disease, such as a fever, should be cured by 'cool' medicine. ▷ guna; shastras; Veda

Azad, Mawlana (Āzād, Mawlānā Abū-l-Kalām) (1888–1958) Indian Muslim. He advocated that Muslims should take a full and active part in the new secular state of India after the partition of the subcontinent at the end of the British Raj, rather than look for inspiration towards the new Islamic state of Pakistan. For a time he was himself an Indian cabinet minister, and he wrote a commentary on the Quran in Urdu, the *Tarjuman* *al-Quran*, in which he argued that all spiritual religion is essentially one. In order to recapture the essence of Islam, which he felt had been obscured, it was important to allow the Quran to interpret itself. He tried to do this in his commentary, and in it he also interpreted various basic Quranic ideas in terms of Western thought. His views were welcomed by more Westernized and secular Muslims who saw their religious tradition as a private, spiritual and communal matter rather than as a legal and political entity. ▷ Islamic modernism; Quran

Azariah, Prayer of One of three Additions to the Book of Daniel in the Old Testament Apocrypha or Catholic Bible, usually linked with the Song of the Three Young Men; known also as the *Benedictus es* in Catholic forms of worship. It depicts a lamentation for the sins of Israel by Azariah (Abednego in Daniel 1.6ff), one of those cast into the furnace for their adherence to Israel's religion. ▷ Apocrypha, Old Testament; Daniel, Book of

Azariah, Vedanayakam Samuel (1874–1945) Indian prelate, and first Indian bishop of the Anglican Church of India, Burma and Ceylon, born in Vellalanvillai, Madras State. A firm believer in co-operation between foreign and Indian church workers (on which topic he addressed the Edinburgh World Missionary Conference in 1910), and in the development of indigenous leadership in a united Indian Church, he was appointed bishop of Dornakal, Andhra Pradesh, in 1912. Bringing to his post experience gained with the Tinnevelly and National missionary societies, and the YMCA, he took a leading role in the Tranquebar (1919) and Nagpur (1931) conferences for church union, and was Chairman of the National Christian Council of India, Burma and Ceylon from 1929.

Azhar, al- The best-known university in the Muslim world, situated in Cairo in Egypt. Meaning 'the resplendent', it has been at the forefront of Muslim higher education since its foundation in 969 by General al-Jawhar. Initially it was instituted by the Egyptian Fatimid dynasty to instruct preachers and teachers in the Ismaili doctrines. It gave an impetus to the foundation of other institutions of higher education around the Muslim world, and predated the establishment of universities in Europe. The challenge it posed to the Sunni Abbasid caliphs led to Sunni colleges being founded in Iraq and Persia, and by Saladin and others in Palestine and Syria. Later it became less sectarian, influencing Islamic education generally, and in recent times through the work of reforming Muslims such as Muhammad Abduh it has influenced the rise and development of Islamic modernism. Some of its traditions, such as public disputations, the use of black academic robes, and the division between undergraduate and graduate bodies, were inherited by European universities. ▷ Abbasids; Abduh, Muhammad; Islamic modernism; Sunnis

Aztec religion The Aztec, a Nahuatl-speaking people, arrived in the Valley of Mexico early in the 14th century CE, establishing their centre at Tenochtitlan, in modern Mexico City. Over the next century and a half their power expanded, and by the time the Spaniards arrived they dominated much of Central America. In religion they retained much of the heritage of the Maya classical period and its successor civilizations, including the calendar and learned, ritual, artistic and magical traditions of the priests. The religious orientation of the state remained; the supreme ruler, the *tlatoani*, represented Huitzilopochtli, the national god, as both governor and priest. Toltec influence was particularly strong and the worship of Quetzalcoatl was actively promoted. What developed massively,

Coatlicue, Aztec mother goddess

which was not only associated with but also required military expansion, was human sacrifice.

A clear picture of Aztec religion is not easy to obtain, despite, or perhaps because of, the unusually rich monumental and literary sources. On the one hand the pantheon of gods is enormous, as might be expected in so wide an empire. Even among the major divinities there are many names, including Huitzilopochtli, perhaps the original patron of the ethnic group; the town god of Tenochtitlan, sun god and war god; the rival Toltec deities Quetzalcoatl and Tezcatlipoca; and Tlaloc the rain-god on whom the soil depends. On the other hand, a distinct tendency towards monotheism can be observed not only in a priestly abstraction such as Ometeotl, the source of creation, but in the use of language suggestive of the supreme being in relation to Huitzilopochtli, Quetzalcoatl, his brother Xolotl and Tezcatlipoca, so that several named divinities partake of the supreme being. The Texcoco king Nezhuacoyotl (d.1472) actually established the worship of an imageless, invisible supreme being, Tloque Nahuaque. Similarly, there are many forms of the mother goddess related to earth or to the moon, some as dramatic as Coatlicue, the 'serpent-skirted'; but all may be regarded as forms of Teteoinnan, mother of goddesses. There is also an oscillation in such figures as Huitzilopochtli and Quetzalcoatl between sky god and national culture hero, and a dualistic habit of mind by which opposites are combined. (Quetzalcoatl and Tezcatlipoca are in opposition, but both are sky gods, and ultimately both are necessary.)

Little is known of popular religion outside the priestly class. A practice which surprised the Spaniards was the stress on confession and on moral, as well as ritual, purification before worship. ▷ calendar, Meso-American; calmecac; goddess worship; human sacrifice, Meso-American; Maya religion; priesthood, Meso-American; Quetzalcoatl; Templo Mayor; Tezcatlipoca; Toltec religion

B

Baal Canaanite storm and fertility god whose name means 'lord', 'owner'. His worship was widespread in the ancient Levant, where he was also known by the name Hadad. Baal features prominently in the Ugaritic Ras Shamra texts. Son of the god Dagan, he has his home on Mount Zaphon to the north of Ugarit; his sister and consort is the goddess Anat. As storm god he is represented wielding a thunderbolt, and as god of the rains he is also a god of vegetation and fertility, responsible for the agricultural process. In the Ugaritic epics Baal fights various enemies to achieve supremacy over the gods, the two most important of these being Yam, the sea, and Mot, the god of death and sterility. In his conflict with Mot, Baal's death and resurrection reflect the annual agricultural process where the summer drought was ended by the autumn rains. Before the discovery of the Ras Shamra texts most information about Baal came from the Hebrew Bible, where his fertility cult is consistently condemned as an alien Canaanite intrusion into the religious and political life of Israel. The prophets and the Deuteronomic literature present one of the most persistent sins of both rulers and people as being a turning away to worship Baal or 'the Baals' instead of Yahweh. ▷

Baal

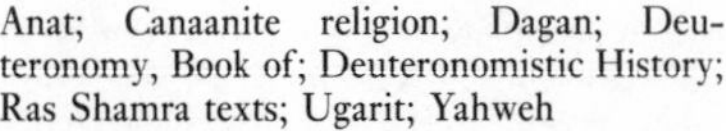

Anat; Canaanite religion; Dagan; Deuteronomy, Book of; Deuteronomistic History; Ras Shamra texts; Ugarit; Yahweh

Baal Schem Tov (literally Master of the Good Name), properly **Israel ben Eliezer** (1700–60) Polish Jewish teacher and healer, the founder of modern Hasidism. Born in the Ukraine, he was orphaned young and received scant formal education. While holding a variety of jobs, including labourer and ritual slaughterer, he became interested in the Kabbalah, studying this and receiving spiritual instruction from various teachers. Settling in Medzhibozh, Podolia, he established a reputation as a healer and mystic. Offering religious knowledge and direction in a manner accessible to those who were poorly educated, he attracted a large following for his ideas. These included the importance of cultivating a joyous spiritual approach to life without resort to severe asceticism, and stressed the place of prayer rather than the study of texts. ▷ Hasidism; Kabbalah

Bab, the (the Bāb, Sayyid 'Alī Muḥammad Shirazi) (1819–50) The title meaning the 'Gate', claimed by Sayyid Ali Muhammad Shirazi in Iran in 1844 when he proclaimed that he was the 'Gate of God'. A group known as the Babis followed him. From 1844 to 1848 they became an unorthodox movement within Islam, united by the Bab's own writings, but when they seceded from Islam (1848) persecution and division followed, and the Bab was finally executed by the Iranian rulers. His followers split into two groups. One, known as the Azali Babis, followed his designated successor Subhi Azal; the other, a larger and more successful movement, followed Subhi Azal's half-brother, Bahaullah, who at Ridvan Garden in Baghdad in 1863 declared that he was the manifestation of God foreseen by the Bab, and they became known as the Bahais. The Bab wrote a number of works, the two main ones being the *Qayyumul-Asma* and the *Bayan* (1847). He set up a code of laws for the Babis, but although his tendency towards legalism, militancy and religious exclusivism became transformed in the Bahai tradition along more tolerant, non-violent lines, he is still venerated within the Bahai movement. ▷ Babis; Bahaism; Bahaullah; Ridvan Garden

Babalola, Joseph ▷ aladura

Babel, Tower of Probably the site of an important temple shrine in the ancient city of Babylon. In the Bible (Genesis 11.1–9) the legend is related of how its construction led to the confusion of languages, and the consequent dispersion of peoples, as a punishment by God for human pride. ▷ Babylon; Genesis, Book of

Babis (Bābīs) The followers of the Bab, a leading figure in the early history of the Bahai tradition. From 1844 to 1848 the early Babis, although unorthodox, were basically Islamic, and were united by the writings of the Bab, notably the Arabic and Persian versions of his *Bayan*. In 1848 they seceded from Islam, a move which resulted in persecution and fragmentation. The Bab saw himself as a forerunner of a future manifestation of God whom Bahais take to be Bahaullah. However, Bahaullah's half-brother Subhi Azal claimed that the Bab had appointed him as his successor, and his followers split off and became known as the Azali Babis. At the Ridvan Garden Bahaullah declared that he was the manifestation of God, and the mainstream Bahai tradition followed him. The Azali Babis remained small and the future of the religion lay with those who became known as the Bahais. ▷ Bab, the; Bahaism; Bahaullah; Ridvan Garden

Babylon From the 18th century BCE, the capital of the Babylonian Empire, situated on the River Euphrates south of Baghdad (modern Iraq). Its massive city walls and 'hanging gardens', attributed by classical tradition to Semiramis, wife of Shamshi-Adad V (823–811BCE), regent (811–806), were one of the wonders of the ancient world. Semi-subterranean vaulted rooms provided with hydraulic lifting gear in the later Palace of Nebuchadnezzar (604–562BCE) have been claimed as remains of the gardens, but their site is not definitely known. ▷ Babylonian religion

Babylonian Captivity The name generally given to the deportation of the Jews to Babylon by Nebuchadnezzar. It is also used metaphorically to describe the exile of the popes to Avignon (1309–77). ▷ Babylon

Babylonian religion The religion of the Babylonians formed part of the common Mesopotamian tradition and was largely continuous with that of their Sumerian predecessors. They preserved Sumerian as a language for religious affairs long after it ceased to be spoken, although it was gradually replaced by their own Akkadian language. They took over the Sumerian pantheon, often translating the names of the gods into Akkadian forms. Important deities included Anu (An), Enlil, Ea (Enki), Sin (Nanna), Shamash (Utu), Ishtar (Inanna), and Tammuz (Dumuzi). The local god of the city of Babylon was Marduk who, in time, became head of the whole pantheon; his rise to power was commemorated at the annual Akitu festival and in the creation epic *Enuma Elish*. The Babylonians had a great interest in omens, and seers used various methods of divination to determine the outcome of almost any important activity. Magic was commonly used by incantation-priests to drive away the demons, who were greatly feared for the suffering they could cause. Because of the success of the Babylonian empires the influences of Babylonian religion can be found among the Assyrians and other peoples in Mesopotamia and beyond. ▷ Akitu; Ancient Near Eastern religions; Assyrian religion; cosmogony; divination; Ea; Enlil; Ishtar; kingship, Ancient Near Eastern; literature, Ancient Near Eastern; magic, Ancient Near Eastern; Marduk; Nergal; Shamash; Sumerian religion

Badarayana (Bādarāyaṇa) (between 1st and 7th centuries) The author of the *Brahma* or *Vedanta Sutra* which summarized Upanishadic teachings in a series of short aphorisms. The Brahma Sutra constitutes one of the three scriptural bases of the Vedanta tradition, along with the *Bhagavad Gita* and the Upanishads. Vedanta theologians wrote commentaries on the Brahma Sutra, interpreting it from their own philosophical perspective. Shankara's commentary interprets Badarayana from a monistic (*advaita*) perspective, saying that there is no difference between the self (atman) and the absolute (*Brahman*), while Ramanuja interprets him from the perspective of 'qualified non-dualism' (*vishishtadvaita*), saying that there is some distinction. In order to found a philosophical school formally, a teacher would write a commentary on the Brahma Sutra. ▷ Advaita Vedanta; Bhagavad Gita; Shankara; Upanishads; Vedanta

Badr, Battle of A decisive battle fought and won in 623 at Badr, 90 miles south of Medina, by Muhammad's Muslims of Medina against the forces of Mecca. Muhammad had migrated from Mecca to Medina in the Hegira of 622, and this was the first major clash between his Medina Muslims and his former townsfolk of Mecca. The Muslim force, numbering 305, defeated an army of about 1000 men. Although a small battle, it had great implications, giving the Muslims credibility elsewhere in Arabia, and reinforcing their belief that Allah was with them, thus giving them the opportunity to fight as a disciplined body. To have fought at Badr became a Muslim mark of honour. Mecca was later incorporated within Islam, and by the time Muhammad died (632) Islam was dominant in Arabia and poised to expand under the early caliphs into the Middle East and North Africa. ▷ caliphate; hegira; Mecca; Medina; Muhammad

Baeck, Leo (1873–1956) German-Jewish religious leader, born in Lissa, Prussia. He was rabbi (1912–42) in Berlin, and when the Nazis came to power became the political leader of German Jewry and spent 1942–5 in the Theresienstadt concentration camp. After the war he lectured in Britain. His chief publications were *The Essence of Judaism* (1936) and *The Pharisees and Other Essays* (1947). ▷ Nazi Party

Bahaism (Bahā'īsm) A religious movement arising out of the Persian Islamic sect Babi in the 1860s, when Mirza Husayn Ali, known as Bahaullah, declared himself the prophet foretold by the founder of the Babi movement, Ali Mohammed Shirazi. Bahaism teaches the oneness of God, the unity of all faiths, the inevitable unification of humankind, the harmony of all people, universal education, and obedience to government. According to Bahaullah, God is unknowable in himself, yet he revealed himself in various manifestations, including Abraham, Moses, Zoroaster, the Buddha, Jesus Christ, Muhammad, and the Bab, culminating in Bahaullah. God was the creator, and the purpose of human life was to know and worship God. God was also One, and fundamentally all religions and humankind are one. Prejudice of all sorts—including the unequal treatment of women and men—is unacceptable. Individuals are encouraged to seek religious truth for themselves as part of total truth, eg scientific discoveries are not seen as incompatible with faith. Cultural diversity is welcomed within an overall search for world government which would eliminate extremes of poverty and wealth, and which would be helped by a universal auxiliary language such as esperanto. Putting emphasis on social goals as well as spiritual truths, the Bahai tradition plays an important part in attempting to unify the human race, as well as in the spiritual development of individuals. There are no initiation rituals, ministers, or sacraments in Bahaism. However, certain practices are incumbent upon followers. These include the obligation to pray every day; to fast from sunrise to sunset during the 19 days of the Bahai Fast; to consider work as part of overall worship; to be ready to teach others 'the cause of God'; to avoid drugs and alcohol; to follow Bahai marriage in monogamy and other respects; to follow the current government and not engage in politics; to avoid gossiping and back-stabbing; to attend the Bahai Feast which occurs every 19 days; and to observe Bahai holy days, such as the birth of Bahaullah and the martyrdom of the Bab. Bahai worship, which forms part of the 19-Day Feast, consists of prayers and reading from the scriptures. Houses of worship have been set up, or are being set up, in each continent, centred on a school, hospital, orphanage, etc.

The supreme governing body of the Bahai tradition consists of nine members, democratically elected by national delegates. Known as the Universal House of Justice, it was first elected in 1963, and has since met every five years. It is based at Haifa in Israel. ▷ Abraham; Bab, the; Bahaism, sacred texts of; Bahaullah; Buddha; calendar; esperanto; Jesus Christ; Moses; Muhammad; Zoroaster

Bahaism, sacred texts of There is no single Bahai scripture, but the Bahais accept as their sacred texts all the writings of Bahaullah as interpreted and extended by Abdul-Baha and Shoghi Effendi, his successors. A number have been translated from the original Persian and Arabic into English, including *The Most Holy Book* (*al-Kitab al-Aqdas*, 1873), summarizing his main legal recommendations for the Bahai community; *The Book of Certitude* (*Kitab-i Iqan*, 1862), giving a clear account of his main teachings on the nature of God and the overlap between doctrine and ethics; *The Hidden Words* (*Kalimat-i Maknunih*, nd), a collection of poetic statements containing religious and ethical injunctions; and *The Seven Valleys* (*Haft Vadi*), a mystical work describing the stages of spiritual growth. His other letters, prayers, exhortations and meditations contained his last major work, *Epistle to the Son of the Wolf*. Bahais consider that Bahaullah's works are inspired, containing God's revelation for the present age. ▷ Abdul-Baha; Bahaism; Bahaullah; Shoghi Effendi

Bahaism in Iran The Bahai tradition began in Iran when the Bab (1819–50) proclaimed himself the 'Gate' in 1844, and more especially when Bahaullah (1817–92) proclaimed himself the one-to-come forecast by the Bab, and took the exclusive and somewhat aggressive Babi religion that he inherited in a more tolerant and pacific direction. Bahaullah went into exile in 1863, but the Bahai movement continued to grow in Iran. Mainly better-educated converts were made from Iranian Jews, Zoroastrians and Shiite Muslims, who were attracted to its modernity and lay appeal. It reached its zenith around the turn of the century, and after that the Iranian Bahais relied on natural increase rather than converts, and the main Bahai expansion took place elsewhere. Problems for the Bahais in Iran included the rise of Shiite fundamentalism, their own lack of numbers, the 'political' image they acquired, their support of modern and Western ideas including female emancipation, and their view that Bahaullah was a further prophet after Muhammad, who for Muslims had been the 'seal' of the prophets. Persecution has taken place during most of the Bahai sojourn in Iran, and at times it has occurred on a grand scale, not least during the period of the Islamic Republic after 1979. The Iranian Bahais have a strong internal cohesion, and a conviction that they are a religious movement that is no longer just an offshoot of Shiite Islam but an authentic world religion in its own right. ▷ Bab, the; Bahaism in the Third World; Bahaism in the West; Bahaullah; Muhammad; Shiism

Bahaism in the Third World The Bahai religious tradition began in Iran in the mid 19th century, and had its main strength in that country until the beginning of the 20th century. During the first half of the 20th century it expanded into the West, and this was important for its breakaway from Iranian Shiite Islam. Since World War II, and especially in recent years, it has expanded significantly into the Third World, where it now has its main strength, and for this reason it is fair to call Bahaism a world religion in its own right. From the 1870s there were small groups of Bahais in India, the Far East and Latin America, but they consisted either of a small Iranian minority or of a small number of Western-educated middle-class groups. Since World War II an attempt has been made to convey the Bahai message to the Third World masses. A number of Amerindians have become Bahais in countries such as Bolivia, Ecuador and Panama. In India the results have been even more impressive. In the Malva area of Madhya Pradesh in central India from 1961 Bahai teachers used visual aids, music, local training centres and social networks to convey their teaching, portraying Bahaullah as the tenth and final avatar of Vishnu. It is estimated that from there being less than a thousand Bahais in India in 1961 there are now over two million, and by 1983 45 per cent of the 25014 Local Assemblies of Bahais in the world were in India. This spectacular growth in the Third World and among different social groups has deep implications for the future development of the Bahai tradition, and it is adapting to the new millieux and the indigenous strengths of the Third World. ▷ avatara; Bahaism in Iran; Bahaism in the West

Bahaism in the West The growth of the Bahai religious tradition in the West has been important for its emergence as a world religion. The expansion in the West has happened in four stages. First there was the attraction for the West of Bahai universalism with its stress on world peace and unity, women's rights, progressive revelation, religious tolerance, and the value of science. Secondly, as Westerners increased in the movement, there was a greater stress on organization, and the increased sense that the Bahais represented a revealed religion in their own right as well as a universal outlook. Thirdly, there was a developing sense of the significance of good administration and planned expansion in local Western communities which stressed internal Bahai strengths as well as world issues. And finally, in recent times there has been a more rapid expansion and a greater social diversity among Bahai converts in the West, for example among American rural blacks as well as well-educated urban whites. During the middle years of this century the Bahai social principles and stress on world unity and peace were attractive, especially to some Western liberal Protestants. The same principle held true during the youth movements of the 1960s, although in recent times the fellowship of the Bahai community has been an important factor in attracting and keeping people in the Bahai tradition. The Bahai expansion in the West was significant for its break with the world of Iranian Shiism, but the focus of expansion has now moved from the West to the Third World—and as Bahais have adapted to the West and used its strengths, so too is it likely that they will adapt to and utilize the strengths of the Third World. ▷ Bahaism in Iran; Bahaism in the Third World; Shiism

Bahaullah (Bahā'u'llāh) (1817–92) Meaning literally the 'glory of God', this is the religious name of the effective founder of the Bahai

Bahaullah

tradition, Mirza Husayn Ali Nuri, who was born in Teheran in Persia. Bahaullah was an early follower of the Bab, who was executed in 1850, and he himself underwent persecution during that period. While in prison in 1852 he had a mystical experience that gave him a premonition of his future role, and in 1863 at Ridvan Garden in Baghdad he declared that he was 'He whom God shall manifest', the one-to-come forecast by the Bab. Although his leadership was disputed by a minority who supported the claims of his brother, Bahaullah became the leader of the mainstream Bahai community. He spent short periods of exile in Istanbul and Adrianople, and then lived out the rest of his life in extended exile at Bahji near Acre in Palestine. It was there that he wrote most of the works which have become important for the Bahai tradition, including *Kitab-i-Agdas* (the most holy book), which is a seminal Bahai text. In practice Bahaullah reoriented the Bahai movement he had inherited. It had been a breakaway Shiite Muslim movement, known as Babism, which had a somewhat authoritarian stance. Bahaullah transformed it into a universal religion, a new dispensation, with a stress upon one God, one humanity, world peace, women's rights, the unity of all religions, universal education, and the value of science. During his lifetime the organization of the movement was strengthened and it began to spread within the Middle East, although its later worldwide spread was to begin under the leadership of his son Abdul-Baha and his successors. Bahaullah is seen as the latest in a succession of divine manifestations including Abraham, Krishna, the Buddha, Jesus, Muhammad and the Bab, and in practice Bahai piety looks upon Bahaullah as an object of devotion. ▷ Abdul-Baha; Abraham; Bab, the; Babis; Bahaism, sacred texts of; Buddha; Jesus Christ; Krishna; Muhammad; Ridvan Garden

Bahya ibn Paquda (fl.later 11th century) Jewish moral philosopher from Saragossa in Spain. He is known for his contribution in the field of ethics. In particular, he wrote a work entitled *Book of Directions to the Duties of the Heart*, in which he set out to systematize Jewish ethics. He stressed that inner spiritual devotion, the 'duties of the heart', should always accompany outward obedience to God's *mitzvot*, the 'duties of the limbs'. Such devotion ought to be the driving force behind all religious and moral activity, so that a person desires in his innermost being to perform God's commandments. Clearly influenced by Sufism or Islamic Mysticism, Ibn Paquda went on to classify the various duties of the heart in hierarchical order, with the pure love of God as the highest. But as well as love of God, faith, and humility, the duties include the study of philosophy and science, both of which increase man's knowledge of God and of the wonders of creation. Ibn Paquda was thus the first among his contemporaries to treat these subjects as worthy spiritual pursuits in their own right. ▷ Maimonides; mitzvah; philosophy, Jewish; Sufism

Baillie, John (1886–1960) Scottish theologian, born in Gairloch, Ross-shire, son of the Free Church minister there. Educated at Inverness Academy, he studied philosophy at Edinburgh, and trained for the ministry at New College, Edinburgh, then at Marburg and Jena. During World War I he served with the YMCA in France. After the war he went to the USA, where he was Professor of Christian Theology at Auburn Theological Seminary, New York (1920–7), and Roosevelt Professor of Systematic Theology at Union Seminary, New York (1930–5). Back in Scotland he was Professor of Divinity at New College from 1935 to 1936. He published a number of theological works, including the modern devotional classic, *Diary of Private Prayer* (1937), and *Our Knowledge of God* (1939). A key contributor to mid-century religious, social and intellectual life in Scotland, he was chairman of the influential church committee that produced the report *God's*

Will for Church and Nation (1946) in favour of the Welfare State and state intervention in the economy. ▷ Presbyterianism

Baisakhi (Baisākhī) A Sikh festival (generally celebrated on 13 April) commemorating the founding in 1699 of the *Khalsa* order of baptized Sikhs by the tenth guru of Sikhism, Guru Gobind Singh. ▷ Gobind Singh, Guru; Khalsa; Sikhism

Balder, Baldur or **Baldr** Norse god, the most handsome and gentle of the children of Odin and Frigga; the name means 'bright'. He taught human beings the use of herbs for healing. Frigga made a spell so that nothing which grew out of or upon the earth could harm him, but Loki made Hodur (Balder's blind brother) throw a dart of mistletoe at him. Balder died, but will return after Ragnarok to the new earth. ▷ Germanic religion; Loki; Odin; Ragnarok

ball game A feature of Meso-American civilizations was a ritual team ball game. The ball court was usually situated in the sacred area of the city, near a temple. It was shaped like an 'I' with a carved 'goal' at each side, and raised seats for spectators. A rubber ball was used, the teams employing hips and shoulders. The clue to its significance is given in the late Maya-Quiche epic, *Popoh Vuh*, which speaks of the sacred twins, Hunahpu and Zbalanque (the sun and the moon?), engaging in a ball game against the powers of the underworld. Thus, the court represents the universe and the players take part in a ritualized version of the cosmic struggle of darkness and light by which the universe and its fruitfulness are maintained. In later times the game seems to have lost some of its religious significance. There are parallels among North American peoples, eg in the lacrosse played between the two moieties (natural 'teams') into which some Native American communities were divided. ▷ Maya religion; Toltec religion

Balthasar, Hans Urs von (1905–88) Swiss Catholic theologian, born in Lucerne. The author of some 60 books on theology, philosophy and spirituality, he was remarkable for drawing considerable inspiration for his theology from the religious experiences of the mystic Adrienne von Speyr (1902–67), with whom he formed a secular institute after leaving the Jesuits. His chief work, *Herrlichkeit* (1961–9, translated as *The Glory of the Lord: A Theological Aesthetics*, 1983–), is a 20th-century statement of a theology of the beautiful, the good, and the true, holding that in the Incarnation of Christ God transformed the meaning of culture. ▷ Incarnation; Jesuits; Jesus Christ; mysticism; theology

Banaras, or **Varanasi** The most important sacred city of Hinduism, situated on the banks of the holy river Ganges. Banaras—also called Kashi, the city of light—is sacred to Shiva. It is an ancient city, at least as old as the Buddha who preached there, filled with temples and shrines amongst its winding, narrow streets. Pilgrims from all over India visit Banaras to worship at its shrines and temples, to consult astrologers, and to bathe in the purifying waters of the Ganges and so expiate bad karma. Alongside the bathing *ghats*—long lines of steps going into the river down which the pilgrims walk to bathe—are the burning ghats where the dead are cremated. To die in Banaras is to ensure liberation (*moksha*) at death and many elderly Hindus undertake the journey or are taken to the city to die. Indeed whereas in other Indian cities the cremation grounds are outside the city to the south, because they are considered to be polluting, in Banaras they are in the midst of the city, for to die there is an auspicious occasion. Banaras has been a great centre of Sanskrit learning, many great teachers such as Shankara have taught in the city, and it still retains a Sanskrit university as well as Banaras Hindu University. Banaras is mentioned in many Sanskrit texts, such as the Puranas, and is extolled in two treatises devoted to the city. ▷ Buddha; Ganga; Puranas; Shiva

Bantu religion ▷ **African religions; Modimo; Mulungu**

baptism The ceremonial ritual symbolizing initiation into a church. The practice of cleansing by water was known in some pre-Christian religions, where it represented transformation, promising immortality or regeneration. In the Jewish tradition people were immersed in water seven days after initiation. John the Baptist is thought to have shared this tradition. Jesus Christ's baptism by John signified the start of his ministry, but baptism (explicitly commanded, according to Matthew 28.19) did not become an essential feature of initiation to the Christian Church until some time after Christ's death. At first, baptism involved total immersion in water and was for adults only (being converts to Christianity). The ritual included confession of faith, renunciation of the devil, anointment with oils and the laying on of hands and consecration of the water. The rite symbolized dying to sin and rising to life in Christ, and as such was necessary to salvation. Because of this, and to remove 'original sin', baptism of infants increasingly became the standard practice in the Church. In churches stemming from the Reformation, baptism was retained as the standard Christian initiation, symbolizing the initiative and unmerited grace of God. Anabaptists, however, believing that baptism must be preceded by confession of faith, restricted the rite to confessing adults. ▷ Anabaptists; John, St (the Baptist); original sin

Baptists A world-wide communion of Christians, who believe in the baptism only of believers prepared to make a personal confession of faith in Jesus Christ. They have certain links with the 16th-century Anabaptists, but mainly derive from early 17th-century England and Wales, where Baptist churches spread swiftly, and in the USA, where a very rapid increase took place in the late 19th century. Strongly biblical, the emphasis in worship is on scripture and preaching. Individual congregations are autonomous, but usually linked together in associations or unions. The Baptist World Alliance was formed in 1905. ▷ Anabaptists; baptism

Barabbas (1st century) Political rebel and murderer (as described in Mark 15, Luke 23) who was arrested but apparently released by popular acclaim in preference to Pilate's offer to release Jesus Christ. He was possibly also called 'Jesus Barabbas' (in some manuscripts of Matthew 27.16–17). ▷ Jesus Christ

Barclay, William (1907–78) Scottish theologian and religious writer and broadcaster, born in Wick, Caithness. Educated in Motherwell, and at the universities of Glasgow and Marburg, he was ordained in the Church of Scotland in 1933. After 13 years as a parish minister in Renfrew, he returned to academic work in 1946 as a lecturer at Trinity College in Glasgow, specializing in Hellenistic Greek, and in 1963 was appointed Professor of Divinity and Biblical Criticism, from which post he retired in 1974. During his career he wrote many serious academic studies, particularly on Graeco-Roman thought, but it is for his popular writings and broadcasts, in which he spoke plainly to the ordinary person about Christian teaching and beliefs, that he is best remembered and greatly loved. His first popular book, *A New Testament Wordbook*, was published in 1955, and like many of his books grew from his contributions to the *British Weekly* journal. He was a prolific writer, producing well over 60 books, and broadcasting on radio and television; his series of televised talks for Lent 1965 formed the basis of his *New People's Life of Jesus*. He was involved in the preparation of the New English Bible. His *Daily Study Bible* (New Testament) won international acclaim and was published in many languages. In 1968 he published his own translation of the New Testament. ▷ biblical criticism; Church of Scotland; New English Bible; New Testament

bardo (bar do) The intermediate state between death and rebirth in Tibetan Buddhism. At death an individual's consciousness (*vijnana, rjam-shes*) enters the bardo which lasts for up to 49 days, before being reborn (according to karma) in one of the human or non-human states of rebirth. Experiences in the bardo in a subtle or bardo body depend upon a person's spiritual maturity. Thus at the moment of death a spiritually mature consciousness will experience a beam of light, the clear light of emptiness, entering which results in liberation (nirvana). If the consciousness cannot remain fixed in the pure light, it will fall away into lower realms, experiencing peaceful and wrathful deities, until attracted by a copulating couple. The consciousness will then enter the woman's womb and the process of birth will begin again. The *Tibetan Book of the Dead* or *Liberation through Hearing in the Intermediate State* (*Bar-do-thos-grul*), which is read to the dying and recently deceased, says that these bardo visions should be recognized as manifestations of a person's own mind. The visions of the clear light and the bardo are important in Naropa's six yogas or spiritual exercises which cultivate them in order to facilitate liberation at death. The bardo is also said to occur between thought-moments; thus a person dies and is reborn with each thought. ▷ emptiness; karma; Naropa; nirvana; rebirth; Tibetan religion

Bar Kokhbah, or **Cocheba** (Aramaic 'son of the star') The popular name of Simeon ben Koseba, who led the second major and unsuccessful revolt of Palestinian Jews against their Roman rulers in 132CE. He was killed in 135 after holding out in the Judaean hills. The virtual dispersion of the Jewish population of Judaea followed this failed revolt. ▷ Diaspora Judaism; Akiva ben Joseph

Barmen Declaration A German Protestant manifesto, drawn up at the Synod of Barmen in May 1934 in response to what was perceived as the Nazification of the German-Christian Church. Largely compiled by Karl Barth, it formed a stern declaration in the belief that Jesus Christ, as the one Word of God, was the *only* source of revelation, and that no images were to be revered in his place. ▷ Barth, Karl; crisis theology; Jesus Christ; Nazi Party

Bar Mitzvah (Jewish phrase: 'son [*bar*]/ daughter [*bat*] of the commandment') Jewish celebrations associated with reaching the age of maturity and of legal and religious responsibility, being 13 years plus one day for boys. The child reads a passage from the Torah or the Prophets in the synagogue on the Sabbath, and is then regarded as a full member of the congregation. Non-Orthodox synagogues have a Bat Mitzvah ceremony for girls at 12 years plus one day. ▷ Judaism; rites of passage

Barth, Karl (1886–1968) Swiss theologian, born in Basle. He studied at Berne, Berlin, Tübingen and Marburg. Whilst pastor in Safenwil, Aargau, he wrote a commentary of St Paul's epistle to the Romans (1919) which established his theological reputation. He became professor at Göttingen (1921), Münster (1925), and Bonn (1930), refused to take an unconditional oath to Hitler, was dismissed and so became professor at Basle (1935–62). His theology begins with the realization of human wickedness, the principal sin being humans' endeavour to make themselves rather than God the centre of the world. Barth therefore re-emphasized the finiteness of humanity and made God's grace once again the pivot and goal of our life. God's unquestionable authority and 'otherness' was the key to his theology. But Barth was criticized in that his own reasoned exposition of antiphilosophical theology itself constituted philosophy and that he prescribed belief in a divinity who failed to explain the nature of humanity. His many works include the monumental *Church Dogmatics* (1932) and *Knowledge of God and the Service of God* (1938). ▷ grace; Paul, St; theology

Baruch (7th–6th century BCE) Biblical character, described as the companion and secretary of the prophet Jeremiah (see Jeremiah 36), possibly of a wealthy family. His name became attached to several Jewish works of much later date, known as 1 Baruch (the Book of Baruch); 2 (the Syriac Apocalypse of) Baruch; and 3 (the Greek Apocalypse of) Baruch. There is also a Christian Apocalypse of Baruch in Ethiopic. ▷ Apocrypha, Old Testament; Jeremiah, Book of; Pseudepigrapha

Basil, St, known as **The Great** (c.329–379) One of the greatest of the Greek fathers, born in Caesarea, in Cappadocia, the brother of Gregory of Nyssa. He studied at Byzantium and Athens, lived for a time with hermits in the desert, and in 370 succeeded Eusebius of Caesarea as bishop of his native city. A fierce opponent of Arianism, he improved monastic standards and wrote many seminal works. His feast day is 2 January. ▷ Arius; Eusebius of Caesarea; Fathers of the Church; Gregory of Nyssa

Basle, Council of (1431–49) A controversial Council of the Church. It was intended to continue the work of the Council of Constance, against heresy, and initiating reform, but fell into dispute with Pope Eugenius IV for asserting the authority of the Council over that of the pope. When the pope attempted to dissolve it, the Council appointed Felix V, the last of the antipopes. ▷ antipope; Council of the Church

Basmalah, Bismillah An important Muslim formula meaning 'In the Name of God, the Merciful, the Compassionate'. It is often uttered by Muslims, sometimes many times a day, and every significant piece of business is begun with it. The Basmalah is said before meals in a way similar to the Christian grace before food. Meals and other activities begun with the Basmalah are often ended with the *Hamdalah*: 'Praise to God'; these expressions tend to go together. The Basmalah is also important aesthetically as a motif in calligraphy, manuscripts and architectural ornamentation. It is held to be efficacious and is used in talismans and charms. Its stress upon the mercy and compassion of Allah forms an important element in Muslim belief which balances the judgement of Allah with his mercy. ▷ Allah; calligraphy, Islamic

Islamic formula Basmalah, Bismillah

Bat Mitzvah ▷ Bar Mitzvah

Baur, Ferdinand Christian (1792–1860) German Protestant theologian and New Testament critic, born in Schmiden, near Stuttgart. He was Professor of Theology at Tübingen from 1826, and founded the 'Tübingen School' of theology, the first to use strict historical research methods in the study of early Christianity. ▷ New Testament; Protestantism; theology

Baxter, Richard (1615–91) English Nonconformist clergyman, born in Rowton, Shropshire. His education was irregular, but he acquired immense knowledge by private study. In 1638 he was made deacon by the Bishop of Worcester. Originally a Conformist, like his family and friends, he found himself led to adopt some of the Nonconformist views as minister in Kidderminster (1640–60). In 1642, on the outbreak of the Civil War, he retired to Coventry, and ministered for two years to its garrison and inhabitants. His sympathies were almost wholly with the Puritans, and after the Battle of Naseby he acted as army chaplain, and was present at the sieges of Bridgwater, Bristol, Exeter, and Worcester. He went back to Kidderminster (1647), but his uncertain health caused him to retire to Rouse-Lench, Worcestershire, where he wrote the first part of *The Saint's Everlasting Rest* (1650). At the Restoration he was appointed a royal chaplain, but in 1662 the Act of Uniformity drove him out of the Church of England. The Act of Indulgence in 1672 permitted him to return to London, where he divided his time between preaching and writing. But in 1685 he was brought, for alleged sedition in his *Paraphrase on the New Testament*, before Judge Jeffreys, who treated him in the most brutal manner, calling him a dog, and swearing it would be no more than justice to whip such a villain through the city. Condemned to pay 500 marks, and to be imprisoned till the fine was paid, he lay in King's Bench prison for nearly 18 months. ▷ Church of England; Nonconformists; Puritanism

beatification The formal process by which the title 'Blessed' is granted by the pope to Roman Catholics of exemplary faith and life who are considered worthy of public veneration after their deaths. It allows such persons to be honoured in a particular part or region of the Catholic Church, and is a necessary preliminary to canonization as a universally recognized saint. ▷ canonization; saint, Christian view of

Beatitudes The common name for the opening pronouncements of blessing upon the poor, the hungry, and others in Jesus's Sermon on the Mount, reported in Matthew's gospel (nine listed in Matthew 5.3–10) and the Sermon on the Plain in Luke's gospel (four listed in Luke 6.20–3). These take the form 'Blessed are the poor in spirit, for theirs is the kingdom of heaven. Blessed are those who mourn, for they shall be comforted' etc. ▷ Jesus Christ; Sermon on the Mount

Becket, St Thomas à (1118–70) English saint and martyr, Archbishop of Canterbury, born in London, the son of a wealthy Norman merchant. Educated at Merton Priory and London, he was trained in knightly exercises at Pevensey Castle, studied theology at Paris, and became a notary. About 1142 he entered the household of Theobald, Archbishop of Canterbury, who sent him to study canon law at Bologna and Auxerre. At the papal court in 1152 he prevented the recognition of King Stephen's son Eustace as heir to the throne; in 1155, the year after Henry II's accession, he became chancellor and the first Englishman since the Norman Conquest who had filled any high office. A brilliant figure at court, he showed his knightly prowess in the Toulouse campaign (1159) and was also a skilled diplomat and a perfect host. The change, then, was all the more drastic when in 1162 he was created Archbishop of Canterbury. He resigned the chancellorship, turned a rigid ascetic, showed his liberality only in charities, and became as zealous a servant of the church as had ever been seen before by king or archbishop. He soon figured as a champion of its rights against the king and had courtiers, several nobles and other laymen excommunicated for their alienation of church property. Henry II, who, like all the Norman kings, endeavoured to keep the clergy in subordination to the state, in 1164 convoked the Council of Clarendon, which adopted the so-called 'Constitutions', or laws relating to the respective powers of Church and State. To these Becket at first declared he would never consent; but afterwards he was induced to give his unwilling approval. Henry began to perceive that Becket's notions and his own were utterly antagonistic, and exhibited his hostility to Becket, who tried to leave the country. For this offence Henry confiscated his goods, and sequestered the revenues of his see. A claim was also made on him for 44000 marks, as the balance due by him to the crown when he ceased to be chancellor. Becket appealed to Pope Alexander III and escaped to France. He spent two years at the

Cistercian abbey of Pontigny in Burgundy; and then went to Rome, and pleaded personally before the pope, who reinstated him in the See of Canterbury.
Becket then returned to France, and wrote angry letters to the English bishops, threatening them with excommunication. Several futile efforts were made to reconcile him with Henry, but in 1170 an agreement was reached. The result was that Becket returned to England, entering Canterbury amid the rejoicings of the people, who regarded him as a shield from the oppressions of the nobility. Fresh quarrels soon broke out and excommunications were renewed. Henry's impetuously voiced wish to be rid of 'this turbulent priest' led to Becket's murder in Canterbury Cathedral in 1170 by four knights, Hugh de Merville, William de Tracy, Reginald Fitzurse, and Richard le Breton. Becket's martyrdom forced confessions from the king. He was canonized in 1173 and Henry II did public penance at his tomb in 1174. In 1220 his bones were transferred to a shrine in the Trinity chapel, until it was destroyed during the Reformation in 1538. This was the popular place of pilgrimage which Chaucer described in the prologue to the *Canterbury Tales*. ▷ martyr; pilgrimage

Bede, the Venerable, St (c.673–735) Anglo-Saxon scholar, theologian and historian, born near Monkwearmonth, Durham. At the age of seven he was placed in the care of Benedict Biscop at the monastery of Wearmouth, and in 682 moved to the new monastery of Jarrow in Northumberland, where he was ordained priest in 703 and remained a monk for the rest of his life, studying and teaching. His devotion to church discipline was exemplary and his industry enormous. Besides Latin and Greek, classical as well as patristic literature, he studied Hebrew, medicine, astronomy and prosody. He wrote homilies, lives of saints, lives of abbots (*Historia abbatum*), hymns, epigrams, works on chronology (*De Temporum Ratione*, and *De sex Aetatibus Mundi*), grammar and physical science (*De natura rerum*), and commentaries on the Old and New Testaments; and he translated the Gospel of St John into Anglo-Saxon just before his death. His greatest work was his Latin *Historia Ecclesiastica Gentis Anglorum* (Ecclesiastical History of the English People), which he finished in 731, and is the single most valuable source for early English history. It was later translated into Anglo-Saxon by, or under, King Alfred. He was canonized in 1899; his feast day is 27 May. ▷ monasticism

Beecher, Henry Ward (1813–87) American Congregationalist clergyman and writer, born in Litchfield, Connecticut, son of Lyman Beecher, and brother of Harriet Beecher Stowe. Educated at Amherst College, Massachusetts, he preached in Indianapolis, and in 1847 became the first pastor of Plymouth Congregational Church, in Brooklyn, New York, where he preached what he held to be the gospel of Christ, contended for temperance, and denounced slavery to an immense congregation. He favoured the Free-soil Party in 1852, and the Republican candidates in 1856 and 1860; and on the outbreak of the Civil War in 1861 his church raised and equipped a volunteer regiment. On the close of the war in 1865 he became an earnest advocate of reconciliation. For many years he wrote for *The Independent*; and after 1870 edited *The Christian Union* (later *Outlook*). A charge of adultery (1874) was not proved. He repeatedly visited Europe and lectured in Britain. His many writings included *Seven Lectures to Young Men* (1844), *Summer in the Soul* (1858), *Yale Lectures on Preaching* (1874), and *Evolution and Religion* (1885). ▷ Congregationalism

Beelzebub (Greek Beelzebul) In the New Testament Gospels, the 'prince of demons', the equivalent of Satan. He is possibly linked with the Old Testament figure Baal-zebub ('lord of flies'), the god of Ekron, or with the Canaanite Baal-zebul ('lord of the high place'). ▷ Satan

Bektashi (Bektashī) An Islamic dervish order found in Turkey. Their name is derived from an Anatolian dervish named Hadjdji Bektash who lived in the 12th century. They became a Sufi Order and eventually became connected with the Janissaries. Absorbing some Christian teachings, they engaged in popular mysticism, and believed in the transmigration of souls. They wrote fervent lyrical poetry, and allowed women to take part in their services unveiled. Their beliefs were syncretistic and radical. Like the other dervish orders in Turkey, they were dissolved in 1925, but they still exist in parts of the former Ottoman Empire. They wear a white cap with four or 12 folds, the four representing the four gates of Islam, and the 12 representing the 12 imams. In their respect for the 12 imams and in their great veneration of Ali they are Shiite in sympathy and belief. ▷ Ali; dervish; imam; Shiism; Sufism; syncretism

Bel and the Dragon An addition to the Book of Daniel, part of the Old Testament

Apocrypha, or Chapter 14 of Daniel in Catholic versions of the Bible. It contains two popular tales, probably from the 2nd century BCE: one of how Daniel discredited Bel (patron god of Babylon) and its priests, and the other of Daniel in the lion's den. ▷ Apocrypha, Old Testament; Daniel, Book of

Bell, George Kennedy Allen (1885–1958) English prelate and ecumenist, born on Hayling Island, Hampshire. Educated at Oxford, he was ordained in 1907, and became chaplain to Archbishop Randall Davidson (1914–24), Dean of Canterbury (1924–9), and Bishop of Chichester (1929–58). A strong supporter of the ecumenical movement, and friend of Niemöller and Bonhoeffer, he risked misunderstanding during World War II by his efforts towards peace with Germany and his condemnation of the policy of saturation bombing. His published works included *Randall Davidson* (1935), *Christianity and World Order* (1940), *Christian Unity: The Anglican Position* (1948) and *The Kingship of Christ* (1954). ▷ Bonhoeffer, Dietrich; ecumenism; Niemöller, Martin

Bellarmine, Robert Francis Romulus, St (1542–1621) Italian Jesuit theologian, born in Montepulciano, near Siena. He entered the order of Jesuits in Rome in 1560, and studied theology at Padua and Louvain. In 1570 he was appointed Professor of Theology at Louvain, but returned to Rome in 1576 to lecture at the Roman College on controversial theology. In 1592 he became rector of the Roman College, was made a cardinal in 1599 against his own inclination, and in 1602 Archbishop of Capua. After the death of Clement VIII, he evaded the papal chair, but was induced by Paul V to hold an important place in the Vatican from 1605 till his death. Bellarmine, who was canonized in 1930, was the chief defender of the Church in the 16th century. A friend and admirer of Galileo, he nonetheless was required to inform him of the pope's prohibition of his teaching of the heliocentric system (1616), yet his learning and moderation gained him the praise even of the Protestant philosopher Pierre Bayle. In the 17th century, stone beer jugs with a caricature of his likeness, called bellarmines, were produced by Flemish Protestants to ridicule him. His feast day is 17 May. ▷ Jesuits

Benedict XV, originally **Giacomo della Chiesa** (1854–1922) Pope (1914–22), born in Pegli, Sardinia, Italy. He was ordained at 24, and after some years in the papal diplomatic service became Archbishop of Bologna (1907) and cardinal (1914). He was elected to succeed Pius X (1914), made repeated efforts to end World War I, and organized war relief on a munificent scale.

Benedictines A religious order following the 'rule' of St Benedict of Nursia. Properly known as the Order of St Benedict (OSB), it follows four basic principles, namely study and learning; stability—ie members of the order often remaining in the same monastery/nunnery all their lives; group prayer; and obedience to the abbot. The order consists of autonomous congregations, and has a long tradition of scholarship and promotion of learning. ▷ Benedict of Nursia, St

Benedict of Nursia, St (c.480–c.547) Italian religious, the founder of Western monasticism, born in Nursia near Spoleto. Educated at Rome, he became convinced that the only way of escaping the evil in the world was in seclusion and religious exercise; so as a boy of 14 he withdrew to a cavern or grotto near Subiaco, where he lived for three years. The fame of his piety led to his being appointed the abbot of a neighbouring monastery at Vicovaro, nominally observing the oriental rule; but he soon left it, as the morals of the half-wild monks were not strict enough. Multitudes still sought his guidance; and from the most devoted he founded 12 small monastic communities. He ultimately established a monastery on Monte Cassino, near Naples, afterwards one of the richest and most famous in Italy. In 515 he is said to have composed his *Regula Monachorum*, which became the common rule of all Western monasticism. In addition to the usual religious exercises, the rule directs that the monks shall employ themselves in manual labours, imparting instruction to the young, copying manuscripts for the library, etc. He was declared the patron saint of all Europe by Pope Paul VI in 1964. His feast day is 21 March. ▷ monasticism

Benjamin, tribe of One of the 12 tribes of ancient Israel, said to be descended from Jacob's youngest son by Rachel (Genesis 35.16–18, 24). Its ancient territories included the land between the hill country of Ephraim and the hills of Judah. Saul, first king of Israel, and the prophet Jeremiah were of this tribe. ▷ Israel, tribes of; Jacob; Jeremiah, Book of; Saul

Berdyaev, Nikolai (1874–1948) Russian religious philosopher, born an aristocrat in Kiev. He developed strong revolutionary sympathies as a student and supported the 1917 Revolution. He secured a professorship at Moscow but his unorthodox spiritual and libertarian ideals led to his dismissal in 1922. He moved to found in Berlin an Academy of the Philosophy of Religion which he later transferred to Clamart, near Paris, where he died. He described himself as a 'believing freethinker' and his fierce commitment to freedom and individualism brought him into conflict with both ecclesiastical and political powers. His main ideas are developed in his journal *The Path* and his books *Freedom and the Spirit* (1927), *The Destiny of Man* (1931) and *Dreams and Reality* (1949).

Bergson, Henri (1859–1941) French philosopher, born in Paris, son of a Polish Jewish musician and an English mother. He became professor at the Collège de France (1900–24), and won the 1927 Nobel Prize for Literature. He was a highly original thinker who became something of a cult figure. He contrasted the fundamental reality of the dynamic flux of consciousness with the inert physical world of discrete objects, which was a convenient fiction for the mechanistic descriptions of science. The *élan vital*, or 'creative impulse', not a deterministic natural selection, is at the heart of evolution, and intuition, not analysis, reveals the real world of process and change. His own writings are literary, suggestive and analogical rather than philosophical in the modern sense, and he greatly influenced such writers as Marcel Proust (to whom he was connected by marriage), Georges Sorel and Samuel Butler. His most important works were *Time and Freewill* (1889), *Matter and Memory* (1896), and *Creative Evolution* (1907).

Berkeley, George (1685–1753) Irish Anglican bishop and philosopher, born at Dysert Castle, Kilkenny, and educated at Kilkenny College and Trinity College, Dublin (where he remained, as fellow and tutor, until 1713). His most important books were published in these early years: *Essay towards a New Theory of Vision* (1709), *A Treatise concerning the Principles of Human Knowledge* (1710) and *Three Dialogues between Hylas and Philonous* (1713). In these works he developed his celebrated claim that 'to be is to be perceived'—that the contents of the material world are 'ideas' that only exist when they are perceived by a mind. In 1713 he visited London, then travelled in Italy and France for some years. He returned to Ireland in 1721 with a newfound concern about social corruption and national decadence (expressed in his anonymous *Essay towards preventing the Ruin of Great Britain*). In 1724 he became Dean of Derry, but became obsessed with a romantic scheme to found a college in the Bermudas to promote 'the propagation of the gospel among the American savages'; after years of intensive lobbying in London for support and subsidies he sailed for America in 1728 with his new wife and made a temporary home in Rhode Island. He waited there nearly three years: the grants did not materialize, he never reached Bermuda and the college was never founded. He returned first to London and then in 1734 became Bishop of Cloyne, and his remaining literary work was divided between questions of social reform and of religious reflection, both interests being represented in the curious work *Siris* (1744), which moves from the medicinal virtues of tar-water to reflections on idealism and the Trinity. In 1752 he resigned his episcopate and moved to Oxford, where he died. ▷ Anglican Communion

Bernardines ▷ **Bernard of Clairvaux, St**

Bernard of Clairvaux, St (1090–1153) French theologian and reformer, born of a noble family in Fontaines, near Dijon, Burgundy. In 1113 he entered the Cistercian monastery of Cîteaux; and in 1115 became the first abbot of the newly-founded monastery of Clairvaux, in Champagne. He was canonized in 1174. His studious, ascetic life and stirring eloquence made him the oracle of Christendom; he founded more than 70 monasteries; and, known as the 'Mellifluous Doctor', is regarded by the Catholic Church as the last of the fathers. He drew up the statutes of the Knights Templars in 1128; he secured the recognition of Pope Innocent II; and it was his glowing eloquence at the Council of Vézelay in 1146 that kindled the enthusiasm of France for the Second Crusade. The influence of St Bernard as a spiritual teacher through his fervid piety and living grasp of Christian doctrine was a wholesome antidote to the dry and cold scholasticism of the age. Yet he showed a harsh severity towards Abelard and others whose views he rejected. His writings comprise more than 400 epistles, 340 sermons, a Life of St Malachy, and distinct theological treatises. The monks of his reformed branch of the Cistercians are often called Bernardines. His feast day is 20 August. ▷ Abelard, Peter; Cistercians; Fathers of the Church; monasticism; scholasticism

Besant, Annie, née **Wood** (1847–1933) English theosophist, born in London of Irish parentage, the sister-in-law of Sir Walter

Besant. After her separation in 1873 from her husband, the Rev Frank Besant, she became in 1874 Vice-President of the National Secular Society. A close associate of Charles Bradlaugh, she was an ardent proponent of birth control and socialism. In 1889, after meeting Madame Blavatsky, she developed an interest in theosophy, and went out to India, where she became involved in politics, being elected President of the Indian National Congress from 1917 to 1923. Her publications include *The Gospel of Atheism* (1877) and *Theosophy and the New Psychology* (1904). ▷ Blavatsky, Helena Petrovna; theosophy

Beza, or **Bèze, Theodore** (1519–1605) French religious reformer, born of the noble family of De Besze at Vézelay, Burgundy. He studied Greek and law at Orléans. He became known as a writer of witty (but indecent) verses in *Juvenilia* (1548), and settled with brilliant prospects in Paris. He lived for a time in fashionable dissipation, but after an illness he took a more serious view of life and, marrying his mistress, in 1548 went with her to Geneva, where he joined Calvin. From 1549 to 1554 Beza was Professor of Greek at Lausanne, publishing a drama on *The Sacrifice of Abraham*. In 1559, with Calvin, he founded the academy at Geneva and became Professor of Theology and first rector there. In a work on the punishment of heretics (1554) he had approved of the burning of Servetus. During the civil war in France he was chaplain to Condé, and later to Coligny. In 1563 he once more returned to Geneva, and on Calvin's death (1564) the care of the Genevese Church fell upon Beza's shoulders. He presided over the synods of French reformers held at Rochelle in 1571 and at Nîmes in 1572. His best-known work is the Latin New Testament. ▷ Calvin, John; Servetus, Michael

Bhagavad Gita (Bhagavad Gītā) (Sanskrit 'The Song of the Lord') A poem forming part of the Hindu epic, the *Mahabharata*, consisting of an eve of battle dialogue between the warrior prince Arjuna and Lord Krishna (in the person of his charioteer). Most Hindus regard the poem, with its teaching that there are many valid ways to salvation, but that not all are universally appropriate, as the supreme expression of their religion. ▷ Hinduism; Krishna; Mahabharata

Bhagavata Purana (Bhāgavata Purāṇa) A 10th-century Sanskrit text probably from South India, containing stories of the god Krishna's childhood and youth in Vrindaban. The text portrays Krishna as a mischievous child who keeps stealing the butter and as a handsome youth who plays games with the *gopis*, the young cowherd women of Vrindaban. The gopis constantly long for Krishna and the sound of his flute, which makes them leave their husbands to go to him. In one story Krishna steals their clothes whilst the gopis are bathing and climbs a tree. To retrieve them, they are forced to leave the water naked, which is said to be an image of the nakedness of the soul before God. In contrast to the majestic (*aishvarya*) Krishna of the *Bhagavad Gita*, the Krishna of the *Bhagavata Purana* is a sweet (*mathura*) and erotic youth who loves and is loved by the gopis. The *Bhagavata Purana* became the central text of *Vaishnava bhakti* traditions, particularly the Bengali Vaishnavism of Chaitanya and the sect of Vallabha. The Bhagavata Purana also inspired Sanskrit court poetry such as Jayadeva's *Gitagovinda* and the poetry of Candidas and Vidyapati. ▷ Bhagavad Gita; Chaitanya; Krishna; Vallabha

bhakti Loving devotion to God, recommended as the most effective path to God in most of the religious texts of popular Hinduism. Devotees are drawn into a close personal relationship to God and, in surrender to him, receive grace, however lowly their station. ▷ Hinduism

Bhakti Yoga Devotion (bhakti) to a personal God as a means of attaining liberation (*moksha*) in Hinduism. In the *Bhagavad Gita*, Bhakti Yoga is a path higher than the yogas of action (karma) or knowledge (*jnana*). Bhakti to a personal deity who is a saviour, rather than knowledge of an impersonal absolute, has been more appealing at a popular level of Hinduism and is reflected in the myths, rituals and devotion of the Sanskrit texts called Puranas, particularly the *Bhagavata Purana*. While bhakti in the *Bhagavad Gita* is reverence to a majestic Lord, indeed the devotee Arjuna trembles before his awe-inspiring vision, from about the 7th century a bhakti movement spread from South India which was even more strongly emotional, emphasizing complete self-surrender to God and ecstasy. These bhakti traditions tended to use vernacular languages rather than Sanskrit and to worship local forms of deities: the Vaishnava Alvars and Shaiva Nayanmars wrote devotional poetry in Tamil, while the Virashaivas wrote in Kannada. Vaishnavism has produced some great bhakti theologians such as Ramanuja, who developed a theology in which life's spiritual aim was not union with an impersonal absolute, as Shankara had said, but loving communion with God. Two schools developed from him, the 'cat' bhakti school which said that souls were saved entirely by God's grace, as a mother cat picks up her kittens, and the 'monkey' school which claimed that some effort was needed for salvation, as a baby monkey clings to its mother's back. The Vaishnava devotee Chaitanya, from whom a branch of Bengal Vaishnavism developed, advocated dancing and chanting God's names as a means of salvation. Shaiva bhakti developed with the Shaiva Siddhanta and in the north the Sants, such as Kabir (15th century) and Nanak, from whom Sikhism developed, advocated devotion to a transcendent God without qualities (*nirguna*). ▷ Bhagavad Gita; Bhagavata Purana; Chaitanya; karma; moksha; Shaiva Siddhanta; Shankara; Sikhism

bhavana (bhāvanā) The Buddhist term for meditation which includes various forms of mind-culture. The aim of meditation is to produce the conditions that are conducive to the maturing of the mind so that a person can see things as they are. The ultimate fruit is insight into the nature of things which arises by itself when the time is ripe. There are two main types of Buddhist meditation: calm meditation based upon stilling the mind, and insight meditation based upon increasing insight. The relationship between these has varied. Sometimes calm meditation has been seen as a preliminary to insight meditation; sometimes greater weight and time has been given to insight meditation. For some the two types of meditation are separate yet complementary, and for others they need to be harmonized and integrated together. Manuals of meditational discipline have been produced for Buddhists, notably that of Buddhaghosa for Theravada Buddhism and that attributed to Asanga for Mahayana Buddhism. Traditionally monasticism has been felt to be essential for sustaining deep meditation, and laymen have been left with the more practical matters of engaging in good works and building up merit. However Mahayana Buddhism has laid more stress upon the meditational potential of laymen and upon realising the Buddha nature in practical life-situations. More flexible and simplified patterns of meditation aimed partly at lay folk are increasingly common, for example in varieties of Zen and in new forms of Theravada insight meditation. ▷ Asanga; Buddhaghosa; Mahayana Buddhism; monasticism; Theravada Buddhism; Zen Buddhism

Bhave, Vinoba (1895–1983) Indian reformer, a member of Gandhi's movement. Whilst studying Sanskrit at Banaras he heard Gandhi speak and in 1916 decided to join Gandhi's ashram near Ahmedabad. Some years later Gandhi sent Bhave to set up an ashram at Wardha. Bhave was imprisoned as a result of Gandhi's non-violent campaigns of civil disobedience and ideals of 'grasping the truth' (*satygraha*). In 1948 Gandhi was assassinated and Bhave found himself partly leading the movement. He started the 'land-giving' or *bhudan* movement in 1951, which tried to persuade wealthy landowners, with some success, to donate land to the poor. He also advocated government by the people (*lokniti*), not by politicians, and wanted to see complete decentralization with self-sufficient villages running their own affairs. This would in fact constitute freedom from all outside government. ▷ Banaras; Gandhi, Mohandas Karamchand

bhikku (Sanskrit: bhikṣu) The term for an ordained Buddhist monk. Before the time of the Buddha there were already various kinds of Hindu ascetics who had left home and renounced the worldly life of the householder. The early Buddhists innovated by setting up permanent monasteries and by giving a more corporate slant to the life of the monk. The sangha, the Buddhist community, is the only religious community centred on monks, and although some other religions do have monks their role has been stressed less than in Buddhism. Even so there remains a close relationship between Buddhist monks and laymen. Regulations for monks and monastic life were written into the scriptures as one of the three parts of the *tipitaka* or Pali Canon. The two rituals of 'going forth' for admission into a monastic order and of ordination into the order, remain important. The monk has time and opportunity to search for enlightenment. His role—and her role in the case of nuns—has also been to act as an exemplary model for lay folk, to exercise a teaching function, to engage in scholarship, and to exert a moral influence upon the leadership of the wider community. ▷ bodhi; enlightenment; rituals; sangha; tipitaka

bhog A ceremony used in Indian religions, especially the Sikh tradition. Within the Sikh community it is used at the end of worship and after important occasions in the life of a Sikh assembly. It means literally 'pleasure', and symbolizes the pleasure felt at the faithful discharge of worship, and this often takes material shape in the form of special food. Bhog is used by Sikhs at the end of uninterrupted, or partially interrupted, readings of the *Guru Granth Sahib*, which takes 48 hours or longer to complete. After the last passage has been read, a special Ardas form of prayer is offered, a random reading is made which is taken to be God's will, or *Hukam*, for the departing congregation, and special food known as *Karah Prasad* is distributed to everyone present. This food has been blessed and consists of equal portions of clarified butter, sugar and wholemeal flour. ▷ akhand path; Ardas; Guru Granth Sahib; Hukam; Karah Prasad

Bible Either the Christian Scripture or the Jewish Scripture, those works recognized as sacred and authoritative writings by the respective faiths. The Christian Scriptures are divided into two testaments: the Old Testament (which corresponds roughly to the canon of Jewish Scriptures), and the New Testament. The Old Testament, or Hebrew Bible, is a collection of writings originally composed in Hebrew, except for parts of Daniel and Ezra that are in Aramaic. These writings depict Israelite religion from its beginnings to about the 2nd century BCE. The New Testament is so called in Christian circles because it is believed to constitute a new 'testament' or 'covenant' in the history of God's dealings with his people, centring on the ministry of Jesus and the early development of the apostolic churches. The New Testament writings were in Greek.

The process of determining precisely which writings were to be accepted in the Jewish or Christian Scriptures is known as the formation of the canon of Scripture. The earliest step towards establishing the canon of Jewish Scriptures was probably the fixing of the Law, viz the Pentateuch (the Books of Genesis, Exodus, Leviticus, Numbers, and Deuteronomy), in about the 4th–3rd century BCE. In addition, a group of writings known as the Prophets appears to have been recognized by the grandson of Ben Sira (c.117BCE). The remaining books of the Hebrew Bible are called the *Writings* (eg the Books of Psalms, Proverbs, Job) and were seemingly the last to be settled. It was only c.100CE that the final selection of authorized Jewish Scriptures was complete, following a decision taken by the council at Jabneh. The Greek translations of the Hebrew Bible (the Septuagint) contained some other writings which were not accepted at Jabneh.

The early Christians largely accepted the Jewish Scriptures, but frequently had access to the larger collection of writings in the Septuagint and some other translations of the Hebrew Bible. Debates about the precise limits of the 'Old Testament' continued into the Reformation period, with a difference eventually resulting between the Protestant and Roman Catholic Churches. At the Council of Trent (1546), the Catholics accepted as deuterocanonical several works which Protestants labelled as Apocrypha and considered of secondary value. Protestant Churches in general have accepted only the writings of the Hebrew canon in their versions of the Old Testament.

Early Christians, however, also began to collect specifically 'Christian' writings. In the 2nd century, Irenaeus testifies to a growing recognition of exactly four Gospels, the Acts, and 13 Pauline letters as authoritative for the Church. Soon this was the basis for a 'New Testament', although a number of other disputed works were also being considered. The first evidence for a canonical list which completely matches that widely accepted for the New Testament today was the 39th Easter letter of Athanasius (367), which designates 27 books of the New Testament alongside the canon of the Old Testament, although debate continued for some years in the East about the Book of Revelation, and in the West over the Letter to the Hebrews.

While the limits of the canon were effectively set in these early centuries, the status of Scripture has been a topic of scholarly discussion in the later church. Increasingly, the biblical works have been subjected to literary and historical criticism in efforts to interpret the texts independent of church and dogmatic influences. Different views of the authority and inspiration of the Bible also continue to be expressed in liberal and fundamentalist churches today. What cannot be denied, however, is the enormous influence which the stories, poetry, and reflections found in the biblical writings have had, not only on the doctrines and practices of two major faiths, but also on Western culture, its literature, art, and music. ▷ Authorized Version of the Bible; Apocrypha, New Testament; Apocrypha, Old Testament; Bible Society; canon; Christianity; Judaism; New Testament; Old Testament; Pseudepigrapha

Bible Society An agency for the translation and dissemination of the Bible. The first was the Van Canstein Bible Society, formed in Germany in 1710, but the modern movement really began with the British and Foreign Bible Society, formed in London in 1904. The United Bible Society now provides a world-wide network of autonomous societies, Protestant and evangelical in the main, responsible for the translation of the Bible in well over 1500 languages, and distributing copies at subsidized prices. ▷ Bible

biblical criticism The application of general literary critical methods to the biblical documents. There are three main aims: **1** To establish the original text from the thousands of variant manuscripts that exist. This is the function of *textual criticism*, which was once called 'lower criticism' to distinguish it from the 'higher criticism' of literary and historical investigation. **2** To establish the sources of the present text. *Source criticism* is concerned with the literary sources behind surviving manuscripts; *tradition* and *form criticism* examine the stages and forms in which the tradition was handed down orally before being written down; *historical criticism* seeks to illuminate the historical context of documents and their sources; *redaction criticism* considers the editorial contribution of the authors in selecting from their sources. **3** To assess the biblical text in its present form. *Structuralism* analyses the literary structure of individual sections of scripture to establish how the writer seeks to communicate with the reader. *Canon criticism* takes a larger view, evaluating biblical books as a whole, separately and together as part of the Old Testament and New Testament canon. ▷ Bible; form criticism

biblical history The Bible spans the whole of existence, opening with an account of the creation of the universe (Genesis), and closing with a vision of a new heaven and earth (Revelation). The historical period opens with the wanderings of the patriarchs (21st–19th century BCE), followed by the exodus from Egypt under Moses (15–13th century BCE). Later historically verifiable and significant dates include those of the United Kingdom under David (c.1010BCE) and Solomon (970), the Divided Kingdom (930), the fall of Jerusalem (586), and the restorations under Zerubbabel (538), Ezra (458) and Nehemiah (432). The period between the Old and New Testaments, known to us through intertestamental literature, saw the Jews living peaceably under the Persian and Greek empires until provoked into successful revolt by the religious insensitivity of Antiochus Epiphanes (175–164BCE). The ensuing Hasmonean priest-king dynasty lasted until the Romans took over (63BCE). Jesus Christ was born (c.6–5BCE) before the death of Herod in 4BCE, and was crucified in 30CE. The exact chronology of the life of the apostle Paul is a matter of scholarly debate: traditional schemes date his conversion to Christianity to about 35, the missionary journeys to 46–57, his chief epistles to 49–57, his first imprisonment in Rome to 59–61 (or 61–3), and the pastoral epistles (if genuine), his second imprisonment and his martyrdom to 64 (or 68). The first written Gospel (Mark) probably dates from 65, shortly before the destruction of Jerusalem in 70CE. Matthew and Luke are usually dated 70–80, and John, the epistles of John and Revelation to dates between 90 and 110. The apostle John is traditionally held to have died in 95. Some would argue that the persecution in Revelation relates to the time of Nero (around 68) rather than Domitian (90–95), and a few would date the whole New Testament before the destruction of Jerusalem. ▷ Corinth, early Christianity in; Ephesus, early Christianity in; intertestamental literature; Jerusalem, early Christian Church at; Rome, early Christian Church at

biblical theology Christian theology which seeks to expound a unity of and integrity in biblical interpretation. Throughout the centuries there have been many attempts to construct theologies of the Old and New Testaments. Gerhard Kittel's *Theological Wordbook of the New Testament* (Germany, 1935) is an outstanding example. ▷ Bible; theology

bidah (bid'ah) The notion of innovation in Islam. It can be interpreted in a creative way, in which case it refers to 'good innovation' (*bidah hasanah*), or in an uncreative way, in which case it refers to 'deviation' from the norm. In the latter case it is the counterpart to what Christians mean by heresy, with the difference that in Islam it is more likely to refer to practice than to belief. For some Muslims it may refer to any religious practice that was not present in early Islam, that is to say in the Quran or in the traditions arising out of Muhammad's sayings. Insofar as this would nullify later developments such as the building of minarets, many Muslims would apply it only to innovations that contradict the basic spirit of Islam. Otherwise the possibility of innovation and creative development would become impossible as the Islamic tradition advances within the flux and process of historical change. ▷ minaret; Muhammad; Quran; sunnah

Biruni, al- (al-Bīrūnī, Abū Rayḥān) (973–1048) Islamic scholar, born in Uzbekistan. Interested in many fields of knowledge, he contributed to various different forms of learning. He travelled to India, and while he was there learnt Sanskrit, translated into

Arabic Patanjali's *Yoga Sutras*, wrote the *Book of India* (*Kitab al-Hind*), and formed an early bridge between Islam and the Hindu and Indian worlds. His knowledge of Hinduism helped him to create his theory of universal history, and he ranks as an early exponent of comparative religion and world history. He wrote to and met the great Muslim philosopher Avicenna, and discussed Aristotle's *Physics* with him. His own scientific work centred upon studies of abstract physics and maths, of the physical world, of animals and plants, and of human beings. In 1018 at Nandana near modern Islamabad in Pakistan he calculated the radius and circumference of the earth with relatively small deviations from present knowledge. In his book on astronomy he also calculated latitude and longitude. In the midst of his epoch-making discoveries and studies he preserved his own Islamic faith and was able to view his vast scholarship within the wider context of Allah, thus combining scientific integrity with spirituality. ▷ Allah; Aristotle; Avicenna; Patanjali; yoga

bishop An ecclesiastical office, probably equivalent to pastor or presbyter in the New Testament, and thereafter generally an ordained priest consecrated as the spiritual ruler of a diocese in Orthodox, Roman Catholic, and Episcopal Churches. In some other Churches (eg certain Methodist Churches), the term is equivalent to 'overseer', or supervising minister. The office was abolished by many Protestant Churches at the Reformation, but in many churches which retain it, it is considered to be essential for the identity of the Church and the transmission of the faith. The issue of whether women as well as men may be consecrated bishop aroused great controversy at the end of the 1980s, especially following the first such appointment (Rev Barbara Harris, as Bishop of Massachusetts) by the Episcopal Church of the United States in 1989. ▷ apostolic succession; archbishop; Christianity; episcopacy; Reformation

Bistami, al- (Bisṭāmī, Abū Yazīd Ṭayfūr) (fl.9th century) Ecstatic Islamic mystic, born in Bistam in North Iran and buried there in 874. His father was a Zoroastrian and his spiritual master was Abu Ali Sindi, probably from Sind. Thus Zoroastrian influences from Iran and elements of Hinduism from Sind may have influenced his ecstatic Sufi mysticism and his paradoxical sayings. One of his statements—'Lover and Beloved and Love are One. Glory be to Me'—seemed to imply divinity in himself, and caused misunderstanding amongst some Sufis, but his yearning for Allah and his desire for God alone became legendary. Another strain of Sufi mysticism, seen in al-Junayd of Baghdad, was less emotional, more dry, and less inclined to imply that union with Allah was linked to deification. Al-Bistami left no writings, and his sayings were gathered in later compilations such as *The Book of Illumination* by al-Sarraj. While disquiet remained about the wording of some of his statements, his tomb at Bistam became a place of pilgrimage for more orthodox Sufis. ▷ ecstacy; Hallaj, al-; Junayd, al-; mysticism; Sufism

Black Elk (?1858–1950) Amerindian holy man from Lakota, who grew up when his people, the Teton Oglala, still hunted bison. He was a cousin of the famous visionary Crazy Horse, and fought at Wounded Knee (1890). He travelled widely in the USA and Europe, in the latter with Buffalo Bill's entourage. Becoming a Catholic, he served as a catechist, while retaining his reverence for and acceptance of Native American tradition. He became famous when J G Neihardt published *Black Elk speaks* in 1932, an account of Black Elk's life and his interpretation of his people's tragic history, described by him as 'a broken hoop'. Interest in Black Elk was further revived by Joseph Epes Brown who established relations with him in 1947 and recorded his account of the sacred pipe of his people and the seven rites. Black Elk had many visions; one of the most powerful, seen while performing the Ghost Dance, was of the wanekia, the saviour of his nation; he later interpreted this in Christian terms, seeing him as the son of the Great Spirit. His version of Sioux history and religion, mediated through his son Benjamin Black Elk, has been highly influential, though not unchallenged. ▷ calumet; Ghost Dance; Sioux religion

Black Friars ▷ **Dominicans**

black Mass A blasphemous caricature of the Roman Catholic Mass, in which terms and symbols are distorted, and Satan is worshipped instead of God. ▷ blasphemy; Mass; Satan

Black Muslims A Muslim group among the Afro-Americans of America, especially the USA, which was also known as 'the Nation of Islam'. The Black Muslims are dedicated to improving their economic, ethical, religious and social position in the face of dominant white and Christian society. Although elements of their work can be traced to the start of the century, they date back as a group to the work of W D Fard Muhammad who came from Arabia to the USA in 1930 and worked among the blacks of Detroit until he disappeared in 1934. His successor Elijah Muhammad (1897–1975) and Elijah's lieutenant Malcolm X built up the movement which looked back to W D Fard Muhammad as a prophet and as the Mahdi. In its stress upon the black race, its exaltation of W D Fard Muhammad, and its denial of life after death the movement diverges from mainstream Islam. It has offered service and dignity especially to deprived blacks in the USA through social welfare programmes, a strict ethical code, educational and business projects, dietary laws, its interpretations of Islam, and its exhortations to prayer and worship. In 1975 Wallace D Muhammad succeeded his father Elijah Muhammad as leader, and whites were allowed to become members of the movement, which changed its name to 'The World Community of al-Islam in the West'. ▷ Islam; Mahdi; Malcolm X

Black Stone The most sacred object in the Kabah, the most important shrine for Muslims, which is in Mecca in Arabia, and is regarded as the centre of the Muslim world. The Black Stone is considered to be the foundation of the Kabah and is set in its south-eastern corner, a few feet above the ground. It dates back to pre-Islamic times and is probably a meteorite. Mainly black in colour, it is ovoid in shape, and is set in a silver casing. Muslims often kiss it when they visit the Kabah, but it is not an object of worship, prayers and worship being offered to Allah, not to the stone. During its history it has been damaged, and in 930 the Qarmatians raided Mecca and stole it for 21 years. Muslim tradition says that it came down from heaven, that Adam put it in the original Kabah, and that Gabriel gave it to Abraham to put in the rebuilt Kabah. It was originally thought to have been white, but turned black as humankind's sins multiplied. ▷ Abraham in Islam; Adam and Eve; Allah; Gabriel; pilgrimage

Black Stone

Blake, William (1757–1827) English poet, painter, engraver, and mystic, born in London, the son of an Irish hosier. In 1771 he was apprenticed to James Basire, the engraver, and after studying at the Royal Academy School he began to produce watercolour figure subjects and to engrave illustrations for magazines. His first book of poems, *Poetical Sketches* (1783), was followed by *Songs of Innocence* (1789) and *Songs of Experience* (1794), which include some of the purest lyrics in the English language and express his ardent belief in the freedom of the imagination and his hatred of rationalism and materialism. His mystical and prophetical works include the *Book of Thel* (1789), *The Marriage of Heaven and Hell* (1791), *The French Revolution* (1791), *The Song of Los* (1795), *Vala* and many others, which mostly have text interwoven with imaginative designs, printed from copper treated by a peculiar process, and coloured by his own hand or that of his wife, Catherine Boucher. Among his designs of poetic and imaginative figure subjects are a superb series of 537 coloured illustrations to Edward Young's *Night Thoughts* (1797) and twelve to Robert Blair's *The Grave* (1808). Among the most important of his paintings are *The Canterbury Pilgrims* which the artist himself engraved; *The Spiritual Form of Pitt guiding Behemoth* (now in the National Gallery); *Jacob's Dream*; and *The Last Judgment*. Blake's finest artistic work is to be found in the 21 *Illustrations to the Book of Job* (1826), completed when he was almost 70, but unequalled in modern religious art for imaginative force and visionary power. At his death he was employed on the illustrations to Dante. He is also known as a wood engraver. During his life he met with little encouragement from the public; but William Hayley, John Flaxman, and Samuel Palmer were faithful friends, and by John Linnell's generosity he was in his last days saved from financial worry. All through his life he was upheld by the most real and vivid faith in the unseen, guided and encouraged—as he believed—by perpetual visitations from the spiritual world. ▷ art, Christian; mysticism

blasphemy Any word, sign, or action which intentionally insults the goodness of or is offensive to God. Until the Enlightenment, it was punishable by death. Blasphemy was classed as heretical if it openly asserted something contrary to faith, and as non-heretical if it involved careless or insulting speech about God. In many Christian countries it is technically a crime, and is extended to include the denial or ridicule of God, Christ or the Bible; but the law is seldom invoked. It is also a crime in certain non-Christian (eg Islamic) countries. The contemporary relevance and range of application of the law of blasphemy became a particular issue in the UK in 1979 with the prosecution for blasphemous libel against *Gay News* and its editor for publishing in 1976 an illustrated poem dealing with a homosexual fantasy about the crucified Christ. Since then there have been several attempted prosecutions against various works, perhaps the most notable furore being that sparked in 1989, following the publication of Salman Rushdie's book, *The Satanic Verses* (1988). The Muslim community considered this work offensive to their religion, and an official death threat was issued by Iran's Ayatollah Khomeini, against Rushdie as a blasphemer. ▷ heresy; Khomeini, Ayatollah Ruhollah; satanic verses

blasphemy, Islamic view of The Muslim view of blasphemy is wider than merely mockery of God. In Islamic law it includes mockery of Muhammad, of the Quran, and of angels, and blasphemy may also include certain suspect theological positions and mystical claims. Blasphemy cannot be committed by a minor, an insane person, or someone who acts under duress. Punishment for blasphemy varies, but death is usually a last resort, and repentance is often held to be meaningful. At certain times in Islamic history certain theological positions (for example Avicenna's views that the world is eternal, that there is no bodily resurrection, and that God has no knowledge of particular details) were regarded as blasphemous, and suspicion was also cast upon mystical statements such as al-Bistami's 'Glory be to Me!' and al-Hallaj's 'I am the Truth'. Although al-Hallaj was crucified in Baghdad in 922, this was mainly for political reasons, and there is no absolute consensus in concise legal terms as to what blasphemy is in practice. ▷ Avicenna; Hallaj, al-; Muhammad; Quran

Blavatsky, née **Hahn, Helena Petrovna** (1831–91) Russian-born American theosophist, born in Ekaterinoslav. She had a brief marriage in her teens to a Russian general, but left him and travelled widely in the East, including Tibet. She went to the USA in 1873, and in 1875, with Henry Steel Olcott, founded the Theosophical Society in New York. She later carried on her work in India. Her psychic powers were widely acclaimed but did not survive investigation by the Society for Psychical Research, although this did not deter her large following, which included Annie Besant. Her writings include *Isis Unveiled* (1877). ▷ Besant, Annie; theosophy

Blessed Virgin (Mary) ▷ Mary

blessing The utterance of a wish, request or direction that good should follow, pronounced over a person or an object; or the benefit which follows from such utterances. In primitive religions, such pronouncements were believed to be effected by magic and to last until counteracted by a superior power. In mature religions, the subject is God or the divine, and the agent or utterer is often, though not necessarily always, a person of spiritual authority. In the Jewish and Christian scriptures there are frequent examples of blessings by God, of a people, or individuals or sacred objects; by patriarchs and holy men; and by Jesus, of children brought to him, of loaves and fishes, bread and wine, and notably in 'the Beatitudes' (Matthew 5.3–12). Blessings in liturgical form such as the Aaronic (Numbers 6.24–6) play an important part in Jewish and Christian worship, which regularly ends with a 'benediction'. These are often accompanied by ritual gestures such as the raising or laying on of hands, the sign of the cross and anointing with oil. Prayer uttered before meals is frequently called a 'blessing' but is really an expression of praise and thanksgiving. In the Roman Catholic Church, a service in which the congregation is 'blessed' by the consecrated host is also called a Benediction. ▷ Beatitudes

Bodhgaya, (Budh Gayā) A sacred Buddhist site in Bihar, India. Since the 3rd century BCE, shrines have marked the spot where Gautama Buddha attained enlightenment. ▷ Buddha

bodhi An Indian term used especially in Buddhism, meaning 'enlightenment' or 'awakening', from the Sanskrit root *budh*, to awake. There are three kinds of enlightenment: that of the disciple who hears the Buddha and is enlightened; that of someone who is enlightened independently and in isolation; and that of a universal Buddha who is enlightened independently but then passes enlightenment on to others. For Theravada Buddhism especially the enlightenment of Gautama Buddha was normative. On the night of that event he sat in deep meditation and remembered first of all his past lives; he then grasped the basic meaning of the suffering built into the life of the world, and finally he found the answer to the problem of suffering in the four noble truths that became central to Buddhism. His enlightenment was an experience with a content, but the main stress was upon the experience rather than the doctrinal belief lying behind it, and this emphasis upon seeking and experiencing rather than on orthodox belief has been typical of Buddhism. The tree under which the Buddha had his experience was called the bodhi tree, the tree of enlightenment, and the place where the experience happened was called Bodhgaya, the place of enlightenment. ▷ ariya sacca; enlightenment; Gautama; suffering; Theravada Buddhism

Bodhidharma (6th century) Indian monk and founder of the Chan (or Zen) sect of Buddhism. Born near Madras, he travelled to China in 520, where he had a famous audience with the emperor. He argued that merit applying to salvation could not be accumulated through good deeds, and taught meditation as the means of return to Buddha's spiritual precepts. ▷ Buddha; Buddhism; Zen Buddhism

bodhisattva (literally 'enlightened existence') In Mahayana Buddhism, one who has attained the enlightenment of a Buddha but chooses not to pass into nirvana, voluntarily remaining in the world to help lesser beings attain enlightenment. This example of compassion led to the emphasis in Mahayana on charity towards others. ▷ Buddhism; Dalai Lama; enlightenment; Mahayana Buddhism; nirvana

bodily marks In many cultures bodily marks such as birthmarks, deformities and unusual features have been regarded as outward signs of religious or magical significance, linked with reincarnation, election to special tasks, witchcraft, and so on. Religion has also been used to shape bodily marks as signs of identity. In some cultures this includes the practice of circumcision and clitoridectomy on young boys and girls. Tattooing is also common in some primal tribes, and scarification is a quicker and more painful form of scarring the body which sometimes takes place at rites of initiation. Body-painting with chalk, paint, charcoal and other substances that can be washed off is also common in some religious traditions. For example, in the Hindu holy city of Banaras, Hindu sects have their own particular combinations of forehead marks in different coloured paints (three yellow lines is a common sign of Shiva, and a combination of white and red is a common sign of Vishnu) and up to 100 sets of Hindu forehead marks are to be found. Bodily marks of deeply religious significance include the 32 'auspicious marks' associated with the Buddha, the marks associated with the Muslim Mahdi-to-come (which were present on the 19th-century Sudanese Mahdi), and the stigmata that have appeared on the bodies of Christians such as St Francis of Assisi, regarded as signs of deep identification with the passion of Christ. ▷ Banaras; Buddha; Francis of Assisi, St; Mahdi; reincarnation; Shiva; Vishnu; witchcraft

Boethius, Anicius Manlius Severinus (c.480–524) Roman philosopher and statesman, sometimes described as 'the last of the Roman philosophers, the first of the scholastic theologians'. Born of a patrician Roman family, he studied at Athens and there gained the knowledge which later enabled him to produce the translations of and commentaries on Aristotle and Porphyry that became the standard textbooks on logic in medieval Europe. He became consul in 510 during the Gothic occupation of Rome and later chief minister to the ruler Theodoric; but in 523 he was accused of treason and after a year in prison at Pavia was executed. It was during his imprisonment that he wrote the famous *De Consolatione Philosophiae*, in which Philosophy personified solaces the distraught author by explaining the mutability of all earthly fortune and demonstrating that happiness can only be attained by virtue, that is, by being like God. The *Consolatione* was for the next millennium probably the most widely read book after the Bible. ▷ scholasticism

Boff, Leonardo (1938–) Brazilian Franciscan liberation theologian, born of Italian stock in Concordia, Santa Catarina. He was ordained in Brazil in 1964, and studied at Würzburg, Louvain, Oxford and Munich, and became professor of systematic theology in Petrópolis, Rio. His best-known work, *Jesus-Christ Liberator* (1972, English trans, 1978), offers hope and justice for the oppressed rather than religious support of the status quo in Church and society. He has written several books on reforming church structures from grass-roots 'basic communities', including *Church: Charism and Power* (1984), which provoked official ecclesiastical censure. Besides collaborating with his brother Clodovis on introductions to liberation theology, he has written widely on other themes, including *St Francis: A Model for Human Liberation* (1985) and *The Maternal Face of God* (1988). ▷ liberation theology

Bogomiles ▷ Albigenses; Cathars

Böhme, or **Boehme, Jakob** (1575–1624) German theosophist and mystic, born of poor parents in Altseidenberg near Görolitz in Upper Lusatia. As a boy he tended cattle, later becoming a shoemaker, but in 1600 he had a mystical experience and from then on devoted much of his time to meditation on divine things. About 1612 he published *Aurora*. It contains revelations and meditations upon God, Man, and Nature, and shows a remarkable knowledge of the Scriptures and of the writings of alchemists. It was condemned by the ecclesiastical authorities of Görlitz, and he was cruelly persecuted, but in 1623 he published *Der Weg zu Christo* and *Mysterium*. His chief aim was to explain the origin of things, especially the existence of evil. God is the *Ungrund* or *Urgrund*, the original and undistinguished unity, at once everything and nothing. However, this has in itself the principle of separation whereby all things come into existence. It is through the principle of negation, which can be identified with evil, that creation is explained. Böhme's philosophy is in fact an application of the principle of contradiction to explain the great problems of philosophy and religion; but the difficulties are only concealed or shifted about under a cloud of mystical language, in which a system of triads, suggested by the Christian doctrine of the trinity, has an important place. His influence spread beyond Germany to Holland and England. Newton studied him; Henry More was influenced by him; William Law might be called a disciple; John Pordage (1608–98) and Jane Leade (1623–1704) were leaders of the Philadelphians, a Böhmenist sect. Points of contact with Spinoza, Fichte, Schelling, and Hegel revived interest in his speculations in Germany in the 19th century. ▷ alchemy; Hegel, Georg Wilhelm Friedrich; Law, William; More, Henry; mysticism; Spinoza, Baruch; theosophy; Trinity

Bon, Bon po Along with Buddhism, one of the two main religions of Tibet. Bon has been regarded by some scholars, as well as the tradition itself, as the pre-Buddhist, indigenous religion of Tibet. More recent scholarship, however, indicates that, while founded on an earlier tradition, it probably emerged during the 11th century. The tradition traces its origin to Shenrab, of whom the historical Buddha Shakyamuni is said to be a manifestation, Bon claims that its country of origin was Tazig, to the west of Tibet, from where it entered Zhang Zhung, from whose language or dialect its texts were translated into Tibetan. Bon scriptures are divided into two groups: the *Kanjur*, containing myths, doctrines and biographies of Shenrab, and *Katen*, containing commentarial material, ritual and iconographic texts. The name bon refers to 'teaching' or 'religion' and is akin to the Tibetan word *chos* which translates dharma. Bon contains doctrines that are virtually identical to those held by Tibetan Buddhism about buddhahood, the bodhisattva ideal, and so on. Particularly important are the *dzogchen* doctrines held in common with the Nyingmapas, which maintain that there is an ineffable state beyond all manifestation and beyond all Buddhas. Bon is also concerned with exorcism and magic. These interests are codified in the doctrine of the nine stages of development, ranging from concerns with divination to the highest Tantric practice. The name 'Tibet' is derived from Bon (Bod). ▷ bodhisattva; Buddha; Buddhism; dharma; Kanjur; Nyingmapa; Tibetan religion

Bonaventure, or **Bonaventura, St,** originally **Giovanni di Fidanza** (1221–74) Italian theologian, born near Orvieto, Tuscany, and known as 'Doctor Seraphicus'. In 1243 he became a Franciscan, in 1253 a professor of theology at Paris, in 1257 general of his order, and in 1273 Cardinal Bishop of Albano. He died, from sheer ascetic exhaustion, during the Council of Lyon. In 1482 he was canonized by Sixtus IV, and in 1587 Pope Sixtus V declared him the sixth of the great Doctors of the Church. His mysticism attracted Luther, though he promoted Mariolatry, celibacy, and a high view of transubstantiation. His most important works are the *Breviloquium* (a dogmatic); the *Itinerarium Mentis in Deum*; *De Reductione Artium ad Theologiam* (a commentary on Peter Lombard); and his *Biblia Pauperum*, or 'Poor Man's Bible'. His feast day is 14 July. ▷ Franciscans; Lombard, Peter; Luther, Martin; mysticism

Bonhoeffer, Dietrich (1906–45) German Lutheran pastor and theologian, and opponent of Nazism, born in Breslau, the son of an

Dietrich Bonhoeffer

eminent psychiatrist. He was educated at Tübingen and at Berlin, where he was influenced by Karl Barth. He left Germany in 1933 in protest against the Nazi enforcement of anti-Jewish legislation, and worked in German parishes in London until 1935, when he returned to Germany, to become head of a pastoral seminary of the German Confessing Church until its closure by the Nazis in 1937. He became deeply involved in the German resistance movement and in 1943 was arrested and imprisoned until 1945, when he was hanged at Flossenbürg. His controversial writings, of increasing importance in modern theology, include *Sanctorum Communio* (1927) and *Act and Being* (1931), on the nature of the Church, and the best-known and most-interpreted, *Ethics* (1949) and *Widerstand und Ergeburg* (1951, translated as *Letters and Papers from Prison*, 1953), on the place of Christian belief and the concept of Christ in the modern world. ▷ Barth, Karl; Confessing Church; Lutheranism; Nazi Party

Boniface, originally **Wynfrith, St** (c.680–c.754) Anglo-Saxon missionary, born in Wessex (probably in Crediton in Devon), and known as 'the Apostle of Germany'. From childhood a Benedictine monk in Exeter, he taught in the monastery of Nursling near Romsey, where he was elected abbot in 717. He declined this dignity in order to spread Christianity among the Frisians, but a war put an end to his immediate plans. He returned to Nursling, but set out again in 718 with a commission from Pope Gregory II to preach the gospel to all the tribes of Germany. He met with great success in Thuringia, Bavaria, Friesland, Hesse and Saxony, everywhere baptizing multitudes, and was consecrated Bishop (723), Archbishop and Primate of Germany (732). He founded many bishoprics. His chief life work was bringing all aspects of life in the Frankish kingdom into accordance with Roman Catholic order and suppressing the irregularities of Irish or Columban Christianity. In 747 Mainz became his primatial seat; but in 754 he resigned the archbishopric, and had resumed his missionary work among the Frisians when he was killed at Dokkum, near Leeuwarden, by 'pagans'. His feast day is 5 June. ▷ Benedictines; Roman Catholicism

Book of Common Prayer The official directory of worship or service-book of the Church of England, widely honoured and followed in churches of the Anglican Communion. Largely composed by Archbishop Cranmer, it was first introduced in 1549, and revised in 1552, 1604 and finally 1662. Until 1975, revisions in England required the approval of Parliament. It is generally considered a landmark of English prose. ▷ Church of England; Cranmer, Thomas; liturgy

book of hours A prayer book, popular in the Middle Ages, and known in England as a 'Primer'. It typically contained the 'Little Office of Our Lady', psalms of penitence, and the 'Office of the Dead' (usually in Latin).

Booth, William (1829–1912) English religious leader, founder and 'general' of the Salvation Army, born amid poverty in Nottingham. In 1844 he was converted and became a Methodist New Connexion minister on Tyneside. There he grew restless, seeing the Lord's requirements as loosing the chains of injustice, freeing the captive and oppressed, sharing food and home, clothing the naked, and carrying out family responsibilities. Thus in 1865 he began in London's East End 'The Christian Mission' which in 1878 developed into the Salvation Army. Though often imprisoned for preaching in the open air, his men and women fought on, waging war on such evils as sweated labour and child prostitution. Booth's Army spread throughout the world, with a whole new network of social and regenerative agencies. Gradually opinion changed: he was made freeman of London, honorary doctor of Oxford, was a guest at Edward VII's coronation, and opened the US Senate with prayer. His book, *In Darkest England and the Way Out* (1890), tells of his philosophy and motivation. His eldest son, William Branwell Booth (1856–1929), was chief of staff from 1880 and succeeded his father as general (1912). His second son, Ballington Booth (1857–1940), was commander of the army in Australia (1883–5) and the USA (1887–96) but resigned after a disagreement with his father and founded a similar organization, Volunteers of America. One of William Booth's daughters, Evangeline Cora Booth (1865–1950), became a US citizen and was elected general in 1934. A granddaughter, Catherine Branwell Booth (1884–1987), was a commissioner in the Army. ▷ Methodism; Salvation Army

Borobudur A Buddhist sanctuary built between 750 and 850 in Java, Indonesia. The monument comprises eight stepped terraces cut into the sides of a natural mound and culminating in a central shrine (stupa). It is renowned for the abundance and intricacy of its relief sculptures. ▷ stupa

bo-tree ▷ peepul

Brahma (Brahmā) The personified creator god of Hinduism. The deities Vishnu, Shiva, and Brahma form the '*Trimurti*' of classical Indian thought. As Vishnu and Shiva represent opposite forces, Brahma represents the balance between them. Brahma is the all-inclusive deity behind all the gods of popular Hinduism. ▷ Brahman; Brahmanism; Hinduism; Shiva; Trimurti; Vishnu

Brahma Kumaris/Raja Yoga Movement A new religious movement arising out of the Hindu tradition that began in the 1930s through the vivid religious experience in Hyderabad Sindh of a diamond merchant, Dada Lekhraj. Known by a new name, Prajapita Brahma, he became the inspirational instrument and channel of the movement and he encouraged leadership to pass into the hands of female leaders, where it still remains. The Brahma Kumaris moved, after persecution, from Hyderabad to Karachi and finally, after World War II, to Mount Abu in Rajasthan, India, where their headquarters are now. They recommend a total lifestyle including vegetarian diet, abstinence from alcohol and smoking, celibacy, and an enhanced quality of life, but their central emphasis is on meditation and spiritual knowledge gained from God through the spiritual university, to which they gain membership when they join a local branch. In recent years they have become active in the United Nations, for instance in the Global Co-operation Movement that they inspired. Although separate from Hinduism and present in 60 countries with 250000 members, the ideas of the movement are influenced by the Hindu background. They believe that we are nearing the end of the present age of decline (*kali-yuga*); a new golden age is at hand; humans are essentially souls rather than bodies; the soul is a point of light that can radiate out to God and others; soul-consciousness is gained by mental union with God; and God is vitally active at this time. This body of ideas is circulated in messages or *murlis* that are given daily at Brahma Kumari centres around the world, thus uniting them. The movement is unique in being led by women and in working eagerly for the world, even though its end is shortly anticipated. ▷ Golden Age; new religious movements in the West

Brahman In Hinduism, the eternal, impersonal Absolute Principle. It is the neuter form of Brahma, and is equated with cosmic unity. ▷ atman; Brahma; Brahmanism; Hinduism

Brahmanas and **Aranyakas** (Brāhmanas and Araṇyakas) Parts of the Veda, the revealed scriptures (*sruti*) of Hinduism. The Brahmanas and Aranyakas are classified after the four Samhitas (*Rig*, *Sama*, *Yajur*, *Atharva*) and before the Upanishads. The Brahmanas are texts concerned with sacrifice and speculation about its magical nature. For the sacrifice to be effective, correct ritual procedures were deemed to be necessary, though in some hymns knowledge of these procedures is thought to be equally effective. Such speculations paved the way for the Aranyakas which maintained that the purely mental performance of the sacrifice is as effective as its actual performance. The Aranyakas also identify the sacrificer with the sacrifice and speculate that there is an inner essence or self (atman) to a human being. Such ideas are the precursors of those in the Upanishads which develop from the Aranyakas. Indeed the term 'Aranyaka' means 'forest treatise' which implies that these texts were composed in reclusive forest settings as were the Upanishads. ▷ Atharva Veda; Upanishads; Veda

Brahmanism An early religion of India (though not the earliest), to which, historically, Indians have looked as the source of their religious traditions. It came to dominance during the Vedic Period (c.1200–500BCE) and was a religion of ritual and sacrifice. It gave supremacy to the Brahman class, who exercised priestly authority over all aspects of life through their responsibility for the transmission of the sacred traditions and the performance of sacrificial rituals. ▷ Brahmanas; Brahmans; Hinduism; Veda

Brahmans The highest of the four Hindu social classes. A priestly class, the Brahmans dominated Indian society for many centuries. Owing to modern economic and social changes, many of their descendants took up secular occupations. Recently they have come under critical attack from some lower-caste movements, particularly in southern India where their influence has been strongest. Believed to be the only ones capable of performing certain religious rituals, such as sacrifices, they were also responsible for teaching the Veda scriptures, and gained the reputation of intellectual superiority. As well as wielding great religious power they were often consulted or employed by rulers. Membership of the Brahman caste involved various observances, such as avoiding work with lowly materials like leather and, usually, following a vegetarian diet. ▷ Brahmanism; Hinduism; Veda

Brahma Sutra ▷ Badarayana

Brahmo Samaj (Brahmo Samāj) (literally 'Divine Society') A theistic movement founded by Rammohun Roy in 1828 which argued that reason should form the true basis of Hinduism. Influenced by Islam, Christianity, and modern science, it sought a return to the purity of Hindu worship through an emphasis on monotheism, the rejection of idol-worship, and the reform of Hindu social practices. ▷ Hinduism; monotheism; Rammohun Roy; theism

Brandon, Samuel George Frederick (1907–71) English scholar of religion, born in Devonshire and educated at the College of the Resurrection, Mirfield, and Leeds University. Ordained in 1932, he served in curacies and as an army chaplain until 1951. Although retaining an interest in Christian studies, and becoming widely known for his provocative views on the bearing of political views on the life of Christ (*The Fall of Jerusalem and the Christian Church*, 1951, *Jesus and the Zealots*, 1967, *The Trial of Jesus of Nazareth*, 1968) his appointment as Professor of Comparative Religion at Manchester University in 1951 focused his attention upon comparative religion, and from 1970 to 1972 he was Secretary-General of the International Association for the History of Religions. The question of the approach of different religions to time and history fascinated him. Developing this theme in *Time and Mankind* (1951), *Man and His Destiny in the Great Religions* (1962), and *History, Time and Deity* (1965), he paved the way methodologically for later comparative religionists, such as Geoffrey Parrinder. ▷ comparative religion; history of religion; Parrinder, Geoffrey; study of religion

Breakspear, Nicholas ▷ Adrian IV

Brethren (in Christ) A Church founded in the late 18th century in Pennsylvania, USA, deriving from Mennonite tradition. Pietistic, evangelical, and missionary, it soon spread to Canada, and now, although numerically small, supports missionary churches in Asia, Africa, and Central America. ▷ Mennonites; missions, Christian; Pietism

breviary A book of liturgical material, eg psalms, hymns, lessons, prayers, used in the Daily Office, and required to be recited by all priests and clerics in major orders of the Roman Catholic Church. It was revised by Pope Paul VI in 1971, to incorporate the recommendations of the Second Vatican Council. ▷ liturgy; Orders, Holy; Roman Catholicism; Vatican Councils

British Humanist Association The name of a well-known institution founded in 1963 to bring together humanist groups within Great Britain. Its long-term background lies in a humanist tradition dating back to the Greek enlightenment, the Renaissance, the European Enlightenment, and 19th-century agnosticism. The more immediate background lies in movements such as the National Secular Society, founded in 1866 by Charles Bradlaugh, the Rationalist Press Association, founded in 1899, and the Ethical Union, founded in 1928. A dinner, chaired by Sir Julian Huxley, was held in the House of Commons to inaugurate the British Humanist Association in 1963, and the Association's second president, Professor A J Ayer, edited *The Humanist Outlook* in 1968. The British Humanist Association organizes humanist publicity and literature, brings together local groups, sets up courses and conferences, helps with counselling, promotes projects, and engages in political action, with the general aim of spreading, cultivating and defending humanist ideals. Its assumption is that humanism is an alternative to religion and a different approach to thinking about and wrestling with human life in this world. Its worldview is centred upon a cluster of ideas, including freedom of thought, liberal values and moral education, which it claims can be seen in separation from religion. ▷ agnosticism; atheism; humanism; religious education; secular alternatives to religion

Browne, Robert (c.1550–c.1633) English clergyman, founder of the Brownists, born in Tolethorpe, Rutland. After graduating from Cambridge in 1572 he became a schoolmaster in London, and an open-air preacher. In 1580 he began to attack the established church, and soon after formed an independant church on congregational principles, at Norwich. Committed to the custody of the sheriff, he was released through the influence of his kinsman, William Cecil, Lord Burghley; but in 1581 he was obliged to take refuge with his followers, at Middelburg, in Holland. In 1584 he returned, via Scotland, to England, and reconciling himself to the Church, in 1586 became Master of Stamford Grammar School, and in 1591 Rector of Achurch, Northamptonshire. Of a very violent temper, he was sent to Northampton jail at the age of 80 for an assault on a constable, and he died in jail. The Brownists may be said to have given birth to the Independents or Congregationalists. ▷ Congregationalism

Brunner, (Heinrich) Emil (1889–1966) Swiss Reformed theologian, born in Winterthur, near Zürich. Following service as a pastor (1916–24), he became Professor of Systematic and Practical Theology at Zürich (1924–55), and was visiting professor at the International Christian University, Tokyo (1953–5). The author of nearly 400 books and articles, his reputation outside the continent was established by translations of two of his books, *The Mediator* (1927) and *The Divine Imperative* (1937). *The Divine–Human Encounter* (1944) reveals his debt to Martin Buber's 'I–Thou' understanding of the relationship between God and humankind, but in 1934 he parted company with the dialectical theology of the early Karl Barth by holding that there *was* a limited universal revelation of God in creation. ▷ Barth, Karl; Buber, Martin; God; Reformed Churches

Bruno, Giordano (1548–1600) Italian philosopher and scientist, born in Nola near Naples. He became a Dominican friar but was too unorthodox to stay in the order, and travelled widely, lecturing and teaching, in France, Germany, England and Italy. He propounded an extreme pantheistic philosophy whereby God animated the whole of creation as 'world-soul', and his enthusiastic championship of Copernicus and his astronomy brought him into conflict with the Inquisition. He was arrested in 1592 in Venice and after a seven-year trial was burned at the stake in Rome. ▷ Dominicans; Inquisition; pantheism

Buber, Martin (1878–1965) Austrian Jewish theologian and philosopher, born in Vienna. He studied philosophy at Vienna, Berlin and Zürich. He then became attracted to Hasidism, founded and edited a monthly journal *Der Jude* (1916–24), taught comparative religion at Frankfurt (1923–33), and directed a Jewish adult education programme until 1938 when he fled to Palestine to escape the Nazis and became Professor of Social Philosophy at Jerusalem. He published profusely on social and ethical problems, but is best known for his religious philosophy expounded most famously in *Ich und Du* (1923), contrasting personal relationships of mutuality and reciprocity with utilitarian or objective relationships. ▷ comparative religion; Hasidism; Nazi Party

Bucer, or **Butzer, Martin** (1491–1551) German Protestant reformer, born in Schlettstadt, Alsace. He joined the Dominicans, and studied theology at Heidelberg, but in 1521 left the order, married a former nun, and settled in Strasbourg. He adopted a middle course in the disputes about the Eucharist between Luther and Zwingli. In 1549 he became professor of divinity at Cambridge, where he influenced the writing of the Book of Common Prayer of 1552, and made many attempts to mediate between the conflicting religious groups of the time. His chief work was a translation and exposition of the Psalms (1529). ▷ Book of Common Prayer; Luther, Martin; Protestantism; Reformation; Zwingli, Huldreich

Buchman, Frank (Nathan Daniel) (1878–1961) American evangelist, founder of the 'Group' and 'Moral Rearmament' movements, born in Pennsburg, Pennsylvania. He was a Lutheran minister in charge of a hostel for under-privileged boys in Philadelphia (1902–7), travelled extensively in the East, and, in Oxford, in 1921, believing that there was an imminent danger of the collapse of civilization, founded the 'Group Movement'. It was labelled the 'Oxford Group' until 1938, when it rallied under the slogan 'Moral Rearmament'. After World War II the movement emerged in a more political guise as an alternative to capitalism and communism. Sir Keith Holyoake, Prime Minister of New Zealand, said of Buchman that 'He has done as much as any man of our time to unite the peoples of the world by cutting through the prejudices of colour, class, and creed'. ▷ evangelicalism; Lutheranism; Moral Rearmament

Buddha (c.563–c.483BCE) The founder of Buddhism, 'the enlightened one', born the son of the rajah of the Sakya tribe in Kapilavastu, north of Benares. His personal name was Siddhartha; but he was also known by his family name of Gautama. When about 30, he left the luxuries of the court, his beautiful wife, and all earthly ambitions for the life of an ascetic; after several years of severe austerities he saw in meditation and contemplation the way to enlightenment. For some 40 years he taught, gaining many disciples and followers, and died at Kusinagara in Oudh. ▷ Buddhism; enlightenment

Buddhaghosa (5th century) Indian Buddhist thinker who became the leading writer and authority for Theravada Buddhism. Around 430 he went to study at Anuradhapura in Ceylon, and it was in that land that he built up a formidable reputation as a Theravada commentator on the *tipitaka* or Pali Canon. He translated local commentaries in the Sinhala language into Pali, thus making them more accessible. His own commentaries became authoritative. In his main work, the *Visuddhimagga*, 'The Path of Purification', he summarized the *Abhidharma* theory, interpreted the Pali Canon, and summed up the theory and method of Buddhist meditation. He set out 40 potential objects of 'calm meditation', including devotional objects such as the qualities of the Buddha himself, and more negative objects such as the gory details of the body to counteract lust. He also recommended devotional chanting as a prelude to meditation. He thus not only revitalized Pali Buddhist scholarship at a time when Sanskrit had increased in importance, but also developed a coherent Theravada system of philosophy, and influenced the nature of Buddhist meditational practice. At the end of his life he returned to India and died at Gaya in Magadha. ▷ Abhidharma; bhavana; meditation; Theravada Buddhism; tipitaka

laughing Buddha

Buddha image In the early history of the Buddhist tradition the Buddha was not represented in image form. Early symbols used by Buddhists for devotional reasons included stupas where the ashes of the Buddha and other relics might be buried, and the bodhi tree under which the Buddha had experienced enlightenment. Other early Buddhist symbols that were used iconographically included the wheel that symbolized the Buddha's teaching, and his royal parasol. The first Buddha images arose in the Indian Kushana empire of Kanishka around the 2nd century CE. This was a Mahayana Buddhist kingdom, and the rise of a sense of devotion to the Buddha fostered by the new Mahayana teaching may well have been a contributory factor in the rise of Buddha images.

Two kinds of Buddha image were made: the more Indian type of Buddha figures originated from Mathura, and the more Hellenistic type from Gandhara in north-west India. Craftsmen making the images drew upon the tradition of the Buddha as having 32 characteristics of a 'Great Man', typical features including a top-knot of hair or turbaned head, elongated ears, and a mark on the forehead. Also important are the different kinds of hand-gestures (*mudras*) made by the Buddha which symbolize events in his life and immediately 'tell a story' to the Buddhist believer. Buddha images are common throughout the Buddhist world and appear in different sizes, shapes and styles according to region. For example at the Lung Men Caves near Loyang in China there are almost 100000 Buddha images varying from over 18 metres to a few centimetres in size. ▷ bodhi; Gandhara; Kanishka; Lung Men Caves; Mahayana Buddhism; mudras; wheel of law

Buddha nature The notion of an inner potential that is possessed by all living beings. Generally people are ignorant of this inner treasure and this kingdom within, but when they wake up to and uncover it they advance spiritually. Buddha nature is a kind of spiritual embryo that is present within all beings and holds out the promise to all people that they can eventually become Buddhas because they all have the potential for buddhahood. This notion was developed in Mahayana Buddhism and was linked to the idea of the *tathagatagarbha*, the Buddha-potential. It became very important in Zen Buddhism. The purpose of Zen meditation was to unfold the Buddha nature within, and the aim of life was to act in the world in such a way as to manifest the Buddha nature to others. This could be done by performing humble tasks such as cooking, gardening and sweeping, all with an inner calmness, and by doing everything in life spontaneously and naturally. Although conceptually very different from the Christian notion that all humans are made in the image of God and from the Hindu notion that all humans are endowed with an atman or self, the notion of the Buddha nature is nevertheless somewhat similar in that it posits a universal possibility and hope for all human beings. ▷ atman; Buddha; tathagata; Zen Buddhism

Buddha Sasana (Buddha Sāsana) A term meaning 'Buddha-discipline', which is often used in Asian countries as a synonym for 'the Buddhist religion'. It is equivalent to the notion of 'the Buddhist religious tradition' involving the community, rituals, ethics, social involvement and spirituality originating from the Buddha. For example, Buddha Sasana councils have been set up in lands such as Burma, Sri Lanka and Thailand by government agencies as councils connected with the Buddhist religion. In Theravada Buddhism it has the more particular meaning of the nine specific forms in which the teaching of the Buddha is found, namely analysis, discourse, exegesis, marvels, previous birth-stories, proclamation, prose, sayings, and verse. ▷ Buddha; Theravada Buddhism; religion

Budh Gaya ▷ Bodhgaya

Buddhism A tradition of thought and practice originating in India c.2500 years ago, and now a world religion, deriving from the teaching of Buddha (Siddhartha Gautama), who is regarded as one of a continuing series of enlightened beings. The teaching of Buddha is summarized in the four noble Truths, the last of which affirms the existence of a path leading to deliverance from the universal human experience of suffering. A central tenet is the law of karma, by which good and evil deeds result in appropriate reward or punishment in this life or in a succession of rebirths. Through a proper understanding of this condition, and by obedience to the right path, human beings can break the chain of karma. The Buddha's path to deliverance is through morality (*sila*), meditation (*samadhi*), and wisdom (*panna*), as set out in the eightfold path. The goal is nirvana, which means 'the blowing out' of the fires of all desires, and the absorption of the self into the infinite. All Buddhas are greatly revered, and a place of special importance is accorded to Gautama.

There are two main traditions within Buddhism, dating from its earliest history. Theravada Buddhism adheres to the strict and narrow teachings of the early Buddhist writings: salvation is possible for only the few who accept the severe discipline and effort necessary to achieve it. Mahayana Buddhism is more liberal, and makes concessions to popular piety: it teaches that salvation is possible for everyone, and introduced the doctrine of the bodhisattva (or personal saviour). As Buddhism spread, other schools grew up, among which are Chan or Zen, Lamaism, Tendai, Nichiren, Pure Land and Soka Gakkai. Recently Buddhism has attracted growing interest in the West. The only complete canon of Buddhist scripture is called the *tipitaka* or Pali Canon. It forms the basic teaching for traditional Theravada Buddhism, but other schools have essentially the same canon written in Sanskrit. Mahayana Buddhists acknowledge many more texts as authoritative.

Underlying the diversity of Buddhist belief and practice is a controlling purpose. The aim is to create the conditions favourable to spiritual development, leading to liberation or deliverance from bondage to suffering. This is generally seen as involving meditation, personal discipline, and spiritual exercises of various sorts. This common purpose has made it possible for Buddhism to be very flexible in adapting its organization, ceremony, and pattern of belief to different social and cultural situations. Reliable figures are unobtainable, but over 1000 million people live in lands where Buddhism is a significant religious influence. ▷ Ananda; ariya sacca; bodhisattva; Buddha; Chan; Dalai Lama; eightfold path; Gautama; karma; Mahayana Buddhism; mandala; mantra; Nichiren Buddhism; nirvana; pagoda; Pure Land Buddhism; sangha; Sanskrit; sila; samadhi; Soka Gakkai; Tantra; Tendai; Theravada Buddhism; tipitaka; Zen Buddhism

Buddhism in South-East Asia Theravada Buddhism is a very significant religious force in South-East Asia in the states of Burma, Cambodia, Laos and Thailand. According to tradition, Buddhism was introduced into the area by missions from the Indian emperor

Ashoka in the 3rd century BCE. Evidence is sparse but it appears that up to the 10th century CE various branches of the Hindu and Buddhist traditions were present in South-East Asia in scattered proportions. From the 11th to 15th centuries Theravada Buddhism grew in influence and there were significant contacts with Ceylon where the movement was strong. Buddhist states arose in Burma, Cambodia, Laos, Java and Thailand, including the Angkor state in Cambodia and the Pagan state in Burma; and, in spite of Indonesia and Malaysia going in a Muslim direction, the Theravada nature of the rest of South-East Asia was becoming clear. In the modern period, with the exception of Thailand which was never colonized, Theravada Buddhism in South-East Asia was challenged by imperial occupation, Christian missionaries, and the Western world view. It has responded in three somewhat contrasting ways to political crisis in Burma, Cambodia and Laos, to psychological crisis in Thailand, and to change everywhere. Firstly, many active lay associations have arisen, such as the World Fellowship of Buddhists centred in Bangkok, and yet there has also been an increasing veneration of monks, to some of whom miracles have been ascribed. Secondly, there has been a significant upturn in meditative seriousness among laymen as well as monks, and yet there has also been an increase in social involvement as in the activist ethical projects of people such as the Thai monk Buddhadasa. Thirdly, there has been an increase in syncretism and quasi-magical practices at the local level, while at the more official and purist level there has been a reassertion of classical teachings stressing liberation (nirvana) and the truth of the no-self (*anatman*). ▷ Ashoka; Islam in South Asia; nirvana; Sinhalese Buddhism; Theravada Buddhism

Buddhism in the West A Western interest in Buddhism began during the 19th century as a result of colonial contacts with Buddhist countries and the start of academic studies of the Buddhist tradition. The Theosophical Society founded by Madame Blavatsky and Colonel Olcott, and continued by Annie Besant, included Buddhist elements in its thought. The visits to the West by Buddhists such as Anagarika Dharmapala, who spoke at the World Parliament of Religions at Chicago in 1893, quickened interest, and a small Buddhist movement began in the USA and Europe at the beginning of the 20th century, tending to stress the nontheistic, practical and logical nature of Buddhism in its Theravada rather than Mahayana aspects. After World War II Zen Buddhism came into vogue due to the work of Daisetz Teitaro Suzuki and Zen practitioners who set up Zen groups in the USA. Tibetan Buddhism arrived in the West after the flight of the Dalai Lama from Tibet, and Tibetan Buddhist centres which attracted Western followers were set up around the West, including Eskdalemuir in Scotland where the largest Buddhist temple in Europe was built. Theravada groups encouraged by institutions such as the Naha Bodhi Society also came into being in different parts of the English-speaking West. Although still often led by Buddhists originating from Buddhist lands, Western Buddhist communities are increasingly being guided by Western Buddhist leaders who have been trained by knowledgeable Buddhists in Asia or in the West, and these Western leaders are becoming increasingly prominent. In the last 20 years many more groups have been formed which tend to attract thinking Westerners and to have some sort of allegiance to Theravada, Zen or Tibetan Buddhism. More Westerners tend to be attracted to the Buddhist than to the Hindu or Muslim traditions, and although their numbers are still small their significance is growing. ▷ Besant, Annie; Dalai Lama; Dharmapala, Anagarika; Mahabodhi Society; Mahayana Buddhism; Suzuki, Daisetz Teitaro; Theosophical Society; Theravada Buddhism; Tibetan religion

Buddhist Councils According to the Buddhist tradition there have been a number of significant councils in Buddhist history. Tradition agrees on the three earliest ones, held at Rajagaha in the monsoon season following the death of the Buddha (c.483BCE), at Vesali about 100 years later, and at Pataliputra (Patna) in the reign of Ashoka (c.250BCE). There is also agreement about the last one, held in 1956CE at Rangoon in Burma to celebrate the 2500th anniversary of the Buddha's enlightenment. Some countries, for example Burma and Sri Lanka (formerly Ceylon), acknowledge six valid councils, the other two being in Ceylon c.90CE and 1865CE; whereas Thailand acknowledges 10 valid councils, the other six being in Ceylon c.220BCE, c.27BCE, c.90CE, and 1044CE, and in Thailand in 1477CE and 1788CE. The first council at Rajagaha was important because it established the text of two of the three parts of the *tipitaka* or Pali Canon, namely the discourses of the Buddha (*sutta-pitaka*) and the monastic discipline (*vinaya-pitaka*). The second council at Vesali was important because it settled serious disputes about the monastic discipline. At the third council in

Patna, associated with Ashoka, harmony was restored in the Buddhist community in the face of dissensions caused by the growth of the Sarvastivadin viewpoint. The final council held at Rangoon in 1956 was an important event in the modern acceptance of Buddhism as an ecumenical world religion, and at its end the whole Pali tipitaka was recited by the assembled monks, and the revised edition of the text was later published. ▷ Ashoka; bodhi; Buddha; enlightenment; Sarvastivada; sutta-pitaka; tipitaka; vinaya-pitaka

Bulgakov, Sergei Nikolayevich (1871–1944) Russian philosopher, economist, and Orthodox theologian, born in Livny, Central Russia. Professor of Political Economy at Kiev (1901–6) and then Moscow (1906–18), he became disillusioned with socialism after 1906 and became a priest in 1918. Expelled from Russia in 1923 like many other clergy, he was appointed Dean and Professor of the Orthodox Theological Academy in Paris (1925–44), where he expounded Sophiology, following Vladimir Soloviev and Florensky's interpretation of the Eastern fathers. Bulgakov's belief that Sophia (the Divine Wisdom) mediates between God and the world implied a fourth person of the Trinity and attracted accusations of heresy. There are English editions of *The Orthodox Church* (1935) and *The Wisdom of God* (1937). Autobiographical notes and extracts from other French and Russian works appear in *A Bulgakov Anthology* (1976). ▷ heresy; Trinity

Bultmann, Rudolf Karl (1884–1976) German Protestant theologian, born in Wiefelstede, Oldenberg. Professor of New Testament at Marburg (1921–51), he maintained that while form criticism of the Gospels showed it was next to impossible to know anything about the historical Jesus Christ, faith *in* Christ, rather than belief *about* him, was what mattered. The Gospels' existential challenge was, however, blunted for modern man by difficulties with miracles and other aspects of the New Testament world-view, which therefore needed to be 'demythologized'. Such controversial views provoked sharp reaction: ultimately towards more confidence in the historicity of the Gospels or to a humanistic existentialism unconcerned with their subject. His books include *The History of the Synoptic Tradition* (1921), *Jesus and the Word* (1934), *Kerygma and Myth* (1953), Gifford Lectures on *History and Eschatology* (1957), *Jesus Christ and Mythology* (1960), *Theology of the New Testament* (2 vols, 1952–5), *Existence and Faith* (1964), and *The Gospel of John* (1941). ▷ demythologizing; existentialism, Christian; form criticism; Jesus Christ; Protestantism

Bundahishn A Middle Persian (Pahlavi) work, whose title means 'Primal Creation'. The last important reworking of the written text probably dates from the late 9th or 10th century, but the work is based on a much older oral tradition, and preserves elements of an extremely archaic picture of the world. The main themes of the Bundahishn are the cosmogony, the nature of the creations, and the history of the early mythical Iranian dynasty of the Kayanians. The work was based on the *Zand*, the Middle Persian translation and exegesis of the Avesta. Its account of the cosmogony is of fundamental importance for our understanding of Zoroastrianism: it describes how, in the Beginning, Ahura Mazda dwelt on high, in the light, while Angra Mainyu lurked in the depths, in darkness. Ahura Mazda, being omniscient, was aware of the antagonism of Angra Mainyu, and of the need to eliminate evil from the universe through a struggle in a limited battleground, the world. To this end he first created an ideal, intangible, light prototype of the world; Angra Mainyu sought to attack this, but was repulsed. The two antagonists then made a pact to fight each other for a limited time. After this Ahura Mazda created the world in physical form, but still ideal, light and motionless. Finally, Angra Mainyu attacked again, and penetrated the world, bringing darkness, death, evil and corruption, and causing the transition from a motionless state to a dynamic one. This is the world of Mixture (*gumezishn*), in which we now live, and which will come to an end when the powers of evil have ultimately been defeated. ▷ Ahura Mazda; Angra Mainyu; Avesta; cosmogony; Frashokereti; Pahlavi; Zoroastrianism

Bunyan, John (1628–88) English writer and preacher, born in Elstow near Bedford, son of a 'brasever' or tinker. In 1644 he was drafted into the army, in June 1645 he returned to Elstow, and there, about 1649, married a poor girl who brought with her two books which had belonged to her father: the *Plain Man's Pathway to Heaven* and the *Practice of Piety*. About this time Bunyan began to experience those deep religious experiences which he described so vividly in *Grace Abounding* (1666). In 1653 he joined a Christian fellowship which had been organized by a converted Royalist major, and about 1655 he was asked by the brethren to address them.

This led to his preaching in the villages round Bedford; and in 1656 he was brought into discussions with the followers of George Fox, which led to his first book, *Some Gospel Truths Opened* (1656), a vigorous attack on Quakerism. Edward Burrough, the Quaker, replied to this; Bunyan answered him in *A Vindication of Gospel Truths Opened* (1657). In November 1660 he was arrested while preaching in a farmhouse near Ampthill. During the 12 years' imprisonment in Bedford county gaol which followed, Bunyan wrote *Profitable Meditations* (1661), *I Will Pray with the Spirit* (1663), *Christian Behaviour* (1663), *The Holy City* (1665), *The Resurrection of the Dead* (1665), *Grace Abounding* (1666) and some other works. He was released after the Declaration of Indulgence of 1672, under which he became a licensed preacher, and pastor of the church to which he belonged.

In February 1673, however, the Declaration of Indulgence was cancelled, and on 4 March, a warrant, signed by 13 magistrates, was issued for his arrest. Brought to trial under the Conventicle Act, Bunyan was imprisoned for six months in the town gaol. It was during this later and briefer period in prison that he wrote the first part of *The Pilgrim's Progress*. When first issued in 1678 it contained no Mr Worldly Wiseman, and many passages were added in the second and third editions (1679). It is essentially a vision of life recounted allegorically as the narrative of a journey. There followed the *Life and Death of Mr Badman* (1680), the *Holy War* (1682), and *The Pilgrim's Progress, Second Part* (1684), containing the story of Christiana and her children. Bunyan became pastor at Bedford for 16 years until his death after a ride through the rain from Reading to London. He was buried in Bunhill Fields, the *Campo Santo* of the Nonconformists. ▷ Friends, Society of; Fox, George; Nonconformists

bushido The Japanese notion of 'way of the warrior', which stemmed from Zen Buddhism and was partly indebted to Confucianism and Shinto. The samurai code until 1868, which taught personal loyalty to a master, death rather than capture/surrender, and stoic indifference to material goods. Like European knights, samurai rode into battle in armour. The bushido tradition is still seen in modern times; eg Japanese officers carried swords in World War II. ▷ samurai

Bushnell, Horace (1802–76) American Congregational minister and theologian, pioneer of liberal theology and the Social Gospel movement. He was born in Bantam, near Lichfield, Connecticut, and graduated from Yale in law and theology, becoming pastor of North Congregational Church, Hartford, Connecticut (1833–59). In his most controversial book, *God in Christ* (1849), he restated the doctrines of the Trinity and the Atonement subjectively, in terms of their effects on humanity rather than as giving information about God. *Christian Nurture* (1847, 2nd ed 1861) had a significant effect on the development of religious education. ▷ Social Gospel

Buston (1290–1364) Tibetan scholar who systematized Buddhist scriptures into the Tibetan Buddhist canon. He was largely responsible for classifying the texts into the *Kanjur*, the word of the Buddha, and the *Tanjur*, commentaries and independent treatises. By the time of Buston, Tibetan translations of Buddhist Sanskrit texts were voluminous and his criteria for their inclusion in the Kanjur were whether they could be traced to a Sanskrit original and whether they were disclosed by one of the three turnings of the wheel of dharma (the 'lower' teachings of the 'Hinayana', the Mahayana emptiness teachings, and the teachings of the consciousness-only tradition). Tantras of the Nyingmapas could not be so related and were rejected, even though these texts, the 'Old Tantras', predate much of the material in the Kanjur, Buston also wrote a history of Buddhism in India and its introduction to Tibet. ▷ Buddha; dharma; emptiness; Hinayana Buddhism; Kanjur; Mahayana Buddhism; Nyingmapa; Tanjur

Butler, Joseph (1692–1752) English moral philosopher and theologian, born in Wantage, Berkshire. From early on he seemed destined for the Presbyterian ministry, but in 1718 he graduated from Oriel College, Oxford, took Anglican orders, and was appointed preacher at the Rolls Chapel where he preached the *Fifteen Sermons* (published in 1726). That work sets out his ethical system, which he tries to base firmly on the empirical complexity of human nature and the distinctive human faculty of conscience, and which argues the ultimate compatibility of self-love and benevolence. He became, successively, Bishop of Bristol (1738), Dean of St Paul's (1740) and Bishop of Durham (1750). His other great work was *The Analogy of Religion* (1736), a defence of revealed religion against the deists. ▷ deism; Anglican Communion

C

Cabbala ▷ Kabbalah

Cabrini, St Francesca Xavier (1850–1917) Italian-born American nun, born Maria Francesca in Sant' Angelo, Lodigliano. She founded the Missionary Sisters of the Sacred Heart (1880), emigrated to the USA in 1889 and became renowned as 'Mother Cabrini' for her social and charitable work. She founded 67 houses for the order in the USA, Buenos Aires, Paris and Madrid. Canonized in 1946, she was the first American saint. Her feast day is 13 November. ▷ monasticism

Cadbury, Henry Joel (1883–1974) American Quaker scholar, born in Philadelphia. Educated at Haverford College and at Harvard, he taught Bible at Haverford, Bryn Mawr, and Harvard, where he subsequently became Professor of Divinity (1934–54). Active in the work of the American Friends Service Committee (he had two stints as chairman) and member of many learned societies, he wrote prolifically. Among his works were *Style and Literary Method of Luke* (1920), *The Peril of Modernizing Jesus* (1937), *George Fox's Book of Miracles* (1948), *The Book of Acts in History* (1955), and *Friendly Heritage* (1972). ▷ Friends, Society of

Cain Biblical character, the eldest son of Adam and Eve, the brother of Abel and Seth. He is portrayed (Genesis 4) as a farmer whose offering to God was rejected, in contrast to that of his herdsman brother Abel. This led to his murder of Abel, and his punishment of being banished to a nomadic life. ▷ Adam and Eve; Bible; Enoch

cakras 'Wheels' or centres of power located within the body in Hinduism. According to the esoteric anatomy of Tantra, the body is traversed by a channel (*nadi*) from the region of the anus/base of the spine to the crown of the head (the *sushumna*). On either side of this are two channels running from the nostrils to the base of the sushumna. The cakras are located along the sushumna's axis. The number and location of the cakras can vary in different tantras, but the version of the *Kubjikamata Tantra* became the standard. In this system cakras are located in the region of the anus, at the generative organs, at the navel, heart, throat, between the eyes and at the 'thousand-petalled lotus' at the crown of the head. The power (*shakti*) of Kundalini dwells in the base cakra and once awakened rises to the thousand-petalled lotus, piercing the cakras as she rises, where she unites with Shiva and the yogin experiences the bliss of union with the absolute. In Buddhist Tantra there are only four cakras, at the navel, the heart, the throat and between the eyes/crown of the head. In Kundalini Yoga each cakra is visualized and they are depicted as lotuses, each with a specific number of petals, with a specific colour, deity and mantra. For example the heart cakra, called the 'unstruck' (*anahata*), has twelve petals, each with a letter of the Sanskrit alphabet, with the 'seed syllable' *yam* at its centre. ▷ Kundalini; Shakti

calendar A system of marking the passage of time by division into regular periods (eg days, months, years). The lunar calendar month is based on the cycles of phases of the moon, while the solar calendar is based on the rotation of the earth around the sun. Commemorations of particular days or seasons are of especial significance in many religions (eg the liturgical year in Christianity), and indeed may account for the origin of calendars in the first place.

calendar, Christian ▷ Christian year

calendar, Islamic The Islamic calendar dates from the migration of Muhammad from Mecca to Medina in 622, rather than from the time when he began to receive the revelations of the Quran in 610. Emphasis was thus placed upon the beginning of Islam as an integrated and successful community in 622 as the key to the start of the calendar. It includes only lunar months, and therefore a year in the Muslim calendar contains 354 days rather than the 365 days of the Gregorian solar calendar that we use. Consequently the year 0 in the Muslim calendar is equal to the year 622CE in the Western calendar, and 100 years in the Western calendar is equal to 103 years in the Muslim lunar calendar. In international practice Muslims tend to use the Western Gregorian calendar for general matters, and the Muslim calendar for religious matters. ▷ Hajj; Mecca; Medina; Quran

calendar, Jewish The Jewish calendar is lunar-solar, arranged primarily according to the moon's cycles, but with reference to the sun to maintain seasonal harmony. Late biblical and Second Temple literature (eg the Dead Sea Scrolls) shows disagreement on whether the sun or moon should have priority, but the moon became paramount and has remained so. Since medieval times years have been dated from the creation of the world, so that, for example, 1992 is 5752. The yearly cycle has 12 months, each beginning with the new moon, and either 29 or 30 days long; the year has 354 or 355 days. Beginning with Nisan, which falls in March/April, the months are: Nisan (or Aviv), Iyyar, Sivan, Tammuz, Av, Elul, Tishri, Cheshvan (or Marcheshvan), Kislev, Tevet, Shevet, and Adar. However, in order to match the solar year and to ensure festivals take place in season, an extra 13th month is added in the 3rd, 6th, 8th, 11th, 17th and 19th year of every 19-year cycle. This comes after Adar, renamed Adar Rishon ('First Adar'), and is called Adar Sheni ('Second Adar'). While Nisan begins the religious year, the Bible points to a competing new year in the Autumn, starting on 1 Tishri; later tradition calls this Rosh Hashanah ('head of the year'). Thus Judaism, like other cultures, begins the year at different points for varying purposes. ▷ Dead Sea Scrolls; hagim; Mishnah; Rosh Hashanah

calendar, Meso-American The priesthoods of the Meso-American civilizations developed an intricate, and remarkably accurate, calendrical system. Alongside a solar year of 365 days ran a sacred year of 260 days (20 weeks of 13 days, each day with its due sacred colour and associated symbols relating it to the world of the gods). The sacred calendar (Tonalpohualli) was important both for public purposes (auspicious and inauspicious days for state activities) and private purposes (horoscopes etc) and occupied much specialist activity. Every 52 years the new year of the solar and ritual calendars coincided, indicating a time of cosmic renewal and, at least in late Aztec times, one requiring a symbolic break with the past (breaking of pots, dowsing of fires, sweeping) and special (human) sacrifice. The so-called Aztec calendar stone of Tenochtitlan is not strictly a calendar, though it bears 20 day signs. Dating from 1500CE, and massive in size, it is a map of time. The four past ages or 'suns' are represented in their relation to the present Aztec age, the 'sun of movement'. At the centre is the sun god; a sacrificial knife hangs, tongue-like, from his mouth. ▷ Aztec religion; Maya religion; priesthood, Meso-American

calendar, Sikh The Sikh calendar is centred upon the Sikh New Year's Day, when the important festival of Baisakhi is celebrated. This happens on the day in April—usually the 13th—when the sun passes from one sign of the zodiac into another. This time is known as *samgrand*, and some Sikhs gather for worship on the samgrand day every month. The position is complicated by the fact that other Sikh festivals, for example Divali and those festivals connected with the lives of the Sikh gurus, are celebrated according to the lunar calendar. They therefore vary in date every year, whereas the New Year's Day/Baisakhi is fixed by the sun's movements. Sikhs have no weekly sacred day, and visits to Sikh temples happen daily, although important events are often fixed on convenient days, for example Friday in Muslim lands, and Sunday elsewhere when it happens to be a holiday. Sikhs generally follow the Gregorian and Common Era calendar, although traditionally they have also used the Samvat calendar attributed to King Vikramaditya which starts at 58BCE. According to this Guru Nanak, the effective founder of the Sikh tradition, was born in 1469CE or in Samvat 1526. ▷ Baisakhi; Divali/Deepavali; gurdwara; guru, Sikh; Nanak

calendar stone ▷ calendar, Meso-American

caliphate A Muslim institution that dates from the death of Muhammad in 632. Caliphs, 'successors', were chosen to succeed Muhammad as leaders of the Muslim community. They did not inherit Muhammad's prophetic role but in principle they inherited his temporal and spiritual authority. The first four caliphs, Abu-Bakr, Omar, Uthman and Ali (632–61), were of special importance and are regarded by Sunni Muslims as the 'rightly guided caliphs' who, together with Muhammad, constituted a kind of golden age for early Islam. The early centre of the caliphate was at Medina. After the first four caliphs the office became hereditary, and under the Umayyad caliphs (661–750) the centre moved to Damascus; under the Abbasid caliphs (750–1258) it moved to Baghdad. After the sack of Baghdad by the Mongols in 1258, the office remained nominally with the Abbasids based in Cairo, but in 1517 it was claimed by the Ottoman Turks and it remained with them until the Turkish National Assembly prompted by Kemal Ataturk abolished it in

1924. Although latterly powerless, the caliphate was a symbolic focus of unity for Muslims, and since its demise there have been occasional attempts to revive it. The Shiite branch of Islam gave it less credence and preferred to stress the role of its imams and, latterly, ayatollahs. ▷ Abu-Bakr; Ali; ayatollah; Medina; Muhammad; Omar; Ottoman Turks; Shiism; Sunnis; Uthman

calligraphy, Islamic The art of calligraphy is a highly significant part of Muslim aesthetics, second only in importance to architecture. Because figurative arts are seen as a kind of idolatry and are virtually prohibited in Islam, calligraphy has been given a greater emphasis among Muslims than in other traditions. The Islamic stress upon the Quran in Arabic as the Word of God means that its expression in writing and its representation in architecture highlight the value of calligraphy. In turn the frequent use of calligraphy in books and on buildings reinforces the importance of the Arabic language and the Quran. As Islam spread out of Arabia around the Middle East, the Arabic Quran and Muslim calligraphy spread with it. Different styles of calligraphy emerged, ranging from the formal and decorative Kufic to the more flowing naskhi and the more commonly written rukah styles. Hand-scripted Qurans became a major artistic glory in the Muslim world, and ministers and rulers as well as scholars and others became interested in calligraphy as a means of aesthetically representing their faith. ▷ Arabic; art, Islamic; idolatry; Quran

Call to Prayer (adhān) A distinctive practice within the Muslim world whereby believers are called to prayer a few minutes before the five sets of daily prayer begin. It is made by the muezzin from the minaret of a mosque or from the door of a prayer-place. It takes the form of a loud chant made by a professional chanter or by a ritually pure adult male, and it contrasts with the Christian call to prayer by means of bells and the Jewish call to prayer by horns. The caller faces in the direction of Mecca and chants while raising his hands to his ears. The words of the call to prayer are familiar to all Muslims and to those who live near mosques: 'God is most great [four times]. I testify that there is no god but God. I testify that Muhammad is the messenger of God. Come to prayer. Come to salvation. God is most great [twice]. There is no god but God [once]'. The phrase 'Prayer is better than sleep' is included at the dawn prayer, and there are slight variations in the Shiite version. The words of the call to prayer include the shahadah, the Muslim short statement of faith, and they contain a convenient short summary of basic Muslim belief. ▷ Mecca; mosque; muezzin; prayer; shahadah; Shiism

calmecac Literally 'row of houses', this was the Aztec priestly school, situated in the sacred area, where sons of the nobility attended in preparation for the priesthood (*teopixque*), law, government or military service, all of them sacral functions. The calmecac was under the patronage of Quetzalcoatl himself. Training there was physically and mentally rigorous, for priests needed to distinguish themselves in war and administrators had to be soundly instructed in the sacred mysteries. The instructors were known as *tlamatinime* ('knowers of things') and their lectures, when formally viewed as passing on orally the sacred tradition, as *huehuetlatolli* ('old, old word'). ▷ Aztec religion; priesthood, Meso-American; Quetzalcoatl

calumet Originally a French local attribution, this term is now often applied to all pipes and smoking materials used in Native American worship. Smoking as a means of prayer and of communion is widespread across North America. Some have derived it from the shaman's sucking pipe, which is the source both of the inhalations that assisted ecstatic

Islamic calligraphy (17th century CE)

vision and the means of withdrawal of dangerous alien substances from the sufferer's body. Indigenous patterns of understanding are reflected in the stories of the archetypal pipe. The best known, that of the Oglala Sioux, speaks of the gift of the pipe by White Buffalo Woman. The pipe, by its bowl, stem, carvings and attached feathers, represents earth, vegetation, animals and birds. Praying with the pipe accordingly means praying with and for everything. This 'calf pipe' is kept, venerated but rarely shown, at Green Grass, South Dakota. The great flat pipe of the Arapaho is similarly guarded. It is held to represent the supreme being himself; hence, under ordinary circumstances, it cannot be looked upon. Pipes, or parts of them, seem to be a frequent element in medicine bundles. Recent years have seen reinterpretations of the sacred pipe in Christian terms. ▷ medicine bundle; shamanism; Sioux religion

Calvary (Latin *calvaria*, 'skull', trans Semitic *Golgotha*) The site where Jesus was crucified, presumed to be a place of execution just outside Jerusalem. The term appears in the Authorized Version of the Bible (Luke 23.33). ▷ crucifixion; Jesus Christ

Calvin, John (1509–64) French theologian and reformer, born in Noyon, in Picardy, where his father, Gérard Caulvin or Cauvin, was *procureur-fiscal* and secretary of the diocese. He studied Latin in Paris from 1523, and later as a law student in Orléans was inspired by the Scriptures. From Orléans he went to Bourges, where he learned Greek, published an edition of Seneca's *De clementia* and began to preach the reformed doctrines. After a short stay in Paris (1533), now a centre of the 'new learning' and of religious excitement, he visited Noyon. He went to Nerac, Saintonge, the residence of the Queen of Navarre, Angoulême, and then to Paris again. Persecution raged so hotly that Calvin was no longer safe in France; at Basel in 1536 he issued his *Christianae Religionis Institutio*, with the famous preface addressed to Francis I. After a short visit to Italy, to Renée, Duchess of Ferrara, he revisited his native town, sold his paternal estate, and set out for Strasbourg, via Geneva, where Guillaume Farel persuaded him to remain and help in the work of reformation. The citizens had asserted their independence against the Duke of Savoy, and magistrates and people eagerly joined with the reformers. A Protestant Confession of Faith was proclaimed, and moral severity took the place of licence. The strain, however, was too sudden and extreme. A spirit of rebellion broke out under the 'Libertines', and Calvin and Farel were expelled from the city (1538). Calvin, withdrawing to Strasbourg, devoted himself to critical labours on the New Testament, and here in 1539 he married the widow of a converted Anabaptist.

In 1541 the Genevans, wearying of the Libertine licence, invited Calvin to return and after some delay he agreed. Through his College of Pastors and Doctors, and his Consistorial Court of Discipline, he founded a theocracy, which was virtually to direct all the affairs of the city, and to control the social and individual life of the citizens. His struggle with the Libertines lasted 14 years, when his authority was confirmed into an absolute supremacy (1555). During that long struggle controversies also occurred between Calvin and Castellio, Bolsec, and Servetus. Servetus, whose speculations on the Trinity were abhorrent to Calvin, was apprehended at Vienna by the Catholic authorities (to whom Calvin forwarded incriminating documents), and was sentenced to be burned. He escaped and, in Geneva, on his way to Italy, was subjected to a new trial, condemned, and burnt to death (1553). Calvin's intolerance was approved by the most conspicuous Reformers, including the gentle Melanchthon. Through Beza he made his influence felt in the great struggle in France between the Guises and the Protestants. None can dispute Calvin's intellectual greatness, or the powerful services which he rendered to the cause of Protestantism. Stern in spirit and unyielding in will, he was never selfish or petty in his motives. He rendered a double service to Protestantism: he systematized its doctrine, and organized its ecclesiastical discipline. His commentaries embrace the greater part of the Old Testament and the whole of the New Testament except Revelation. In 1559 he founded a theological academy at Geneva that became the university. ▷ Beza, Theodore; Calvinism; Melanchthon, Philip; Protestantism; Reformation; Servetus, Michael

Calvinism A term with at least three applications. 1 The theology of the 16th-century Protestant reformer, John Calvin. 2 The principal doctrines of 17th-century Calvinist scholars, including the 'five points of Calvinism' affirmed by the Synod of Dort (1618–19). 3 More broadly, the beliefs of those Churches in the Reformed tradition which arose under the influence of Calvin, and the impact they had on the societies and cultures in which they took root. Historically, Calvinism has emphasized the sovereignty of God, the Bible as the sole rule of faith, the doctrine of predestination, and justification by faith alone. There has been a Neo-Calvinist renewal in the 20th century under the influence of the theologian Karl Barth. ▷ Barth, Karl; Calvin, John; Church of Scotland ; Knox, John; predestination; Presbyterianism; Protestantism; Reformed Churches

Camara, Helder Pessoa (1909–) Brazilian Roman Catholic theologian and prelate, born in Fortaleza, Ceará State. Archbishop of Olinda and Reçife, north-east Brazil, from 1964 to 1984, he has been a champion of the poor and of non-violent social change in his native Brazil and in the Catholic Church at large through his influence at Vatican Council II, and received international recognition with the award of the Martin Luther King Jr Peace Prize (1970) and the People's Prize (1973). His theological and devotional writings have been translated into many languages, especially *Race Against Time* (1971), *Revolution Through Peace* (1971) and *Hoping Against All Hope* (1984). ▷ Roman Catholicism; Vatican Councils

Campbell, Joseph (1904–87) American scholar of comparative mythology, born in New York, and educated at Columbia University and the universities of Paris and Munich. For most of his career he taught at Sarah Lawrence College in the USA. He was influenced by Carl Jung, and was a member of Jung's Eranos Circle which met yearly in Zurich after 1933. He completed and edited four of the key works of the great Indologist Heinrich Zimmer, and he also edited a number of the Eranos Yearbooks. His *magnum opus*, a direct attempt to apply Jung's ideas to comparative mythology, was *Masks of God: Primitive Mythology* (1959), *Oriental Mythology* (1962), *Occidental Mythology* (1964), and *Creative Mythology* (1968). His method was to bring together examples of myth in their thousands and to assemble them in a pattern which was meaningful not only academically but also in the human struggle for identity, as, for example, in the myth of the hero. Through television, Campbell latterly sought to show the direct relevance of religious symbols, myths and archetypes to modern life, 'as statements of certain spiritual principles, which have remained as constant throughout the course of human history as the form and nervous structure of the human physique itself'. ▷ Jung, Carl Gustav; mythology; psychology of religion

Campion, Edmund (1540–81) English Jesuit martyr, the son of a London tradesman. He was educated at Christ's Hospital and St John's College, Oxford, and was ordained an Anglican deacon in 1569; but he hankered after the old religion, and went to Dublin to help re-establish the university there. Suspected of leanings towards Rome, and fearing arrest, he escaped to Douai, and in 1573 joined the Society of Jesus in Bohemia. In 1580 he was recalled from Prague, where he was Professor of Rhetoric, to accompany Robert Parsons on the Jesuit mission into England. The audacity of his controversial manifesto known as Campion's 'Brag and challenge', which was followed by his *Decem Rationes*, or 'Ten Reasons', greatly irritated his opponents. In July 1581 he was caught near Wantage, and sent up to London, tied on horseback, with a paper stuck on his hat inscribed 'Campion, the seditious Jesuit'. Thrice racked, he was tried on a charge of conspiracy of which he was innocent, and hanged. With other sufferers in the same cause he was beatified by Leo XIII in 1886, and canonized in 1970. His feast day is 1 December. ▷ Counter-Reformation; Jesuits

Canaan The land of the ancient Semitic-speaking peoples (the coastal areas of modern Israel and Syria), but perhaps also extending inland to the Jordan River and the Dead Sea. It was divided into various city-states during the early 2nd millennium BCE, but mostly fell under the control of Israelites and other powers from the late 13th century BCE. The name can be traced to one of the sons of Ham (Genesis 9–10). ▷ Ham

Canaanite religion For a long time the only evidence for Canaanite religion was the religious polemic of the Hebrew Bible and some late Phoenician sources, but recent archaeological discoveries have shed more light on the subject. The most significant of these was at Ras Shamra on the Syrian coast, the site of ancient Ugarit. The religion of the Canaanites was polytheistic, and they worshipped a large pantheon, the most important of whom were probably the gods El and Baal and the goddesses Asherah, Anat, and Astarte. The predominance of the fertility cult reflects the importance of the rains for agriculture in the dry climate of Syria-Palestine, and can be seen in the myth of Baal and Mot. The gods were worshipped in open-air shrines, the 'high places' of the Hebrew Bible, as well as in temples. The cult was principally sacrificial, and the terms for sacrifices at Ugarit are very similar to those found in Ancient Israel. The king played an important role in the ritual, following the Ancient Near Eastern pattern.

The conception of life after death was probably the same gloomy one found in Israel and Mesopotamia, although there is evidence that Ugaritic kings were deified when they died. Canaanite religion provided the basic pattern for the religion of the Phoenicians and was very influential upon the Philistines. The Israelites adopted some aspects of Canaanite belief and practice, but others were denounced as alien intrusions into pure Yahweism. ▷ afterlife, Ancient Near Eastern; Anat; Asherah; Astarte; Baal; Dagan; El; Philistine religion; Phoenician religion; Ras Shamra texts; Reshef; sacrifice, Ancient Israelite; Ugarit

Candomblé ▷ **Afro-Brazilian religions**

canon 1 In Christianity, a list of the inspired writings regarded as comprising Holy Scripture. The precise limits of the Old and New Testament canons were debated in the early Christian centuries, and Protestants and Roman Catholics still differ regarding the inclusion of some works. The term is also sometimes used to comprise the rules regarding liturgy, the life and discipline of the Church, and other decisions of the Councils. ▷ Apocrypha, New Testament/Old Testament; Bible; canon law; Council of the Church; Pseudepigrapha 2 The prayer of consecration in the Roman Catholic Mass. ▷ Mass 3 The ecclesiastical title of clergy attached to cathedrals or certain endowed churches; either secular or, if living under semi-monastic rule, regular (eg Augustinian). In the Church of England, residentiary canons are the salaried staff of a cathedral, responsible for the upkeep of the building; non-residentiary canons are unsalaried, but have certain privileges, including rights with regard to the election of bishops. ▷ cathedral

canonization The culmination of a lengthy process in the Roman Catholic Church whereby, after a long process of enquiry, a deceased individual is declared a saint, or entitled to public veneration. Following examination by a group called the Congregation of Rites (a body set up by the pope), a person whose case is considered valid is first beatified and later, if agreed, made into a saint. The process of bestowing sainthood involves among other things amassing sufficient evidence of miracles achieved by supplication to the proposed saint, or at least evidence of the answering of prayers made in his or her name. It confers various honours, such as a feast day, and the dedication of churches to his/her memory. In the Orthodox Church there is a similar but less formal procedure. ▷ beatification; Roman Catholicism; Orthodox Church; saint

canon law In the Roman Catholic Church, a body of rules or laws to be observed in matters of faith, morals, and discipline. It developed out of the decisions of the Councils of the Church, and the decrees of popes and influential bishops. A notable compilation was made by Gratian in his *Decretum* (1140), which, with later additions, formed the *Corpus Juris Canonici* (completely revised in 1917). Pre-Reformation canon law is observed in the Church of England, subject to revisions such as the Book of Canons (1604–6) and Code (1964–9). ▷ canon; Codex Juris Canonici; Council of the Church

Canticles ▷ **Song of Solomon**

cantor, or **hazzan** From the middle ages synagogues employed an official cantor to chant the liturgy; before then any competent member of the congregation could perform this task; as the liturgy grew in complexity and as general knowledge of Hebrew declined a specialized role was required. With time the office of hazzan acquired great prestige, and in return for his efforts the cantor would often receive good wages and tax-exemptions. The corollary of this was that a prospective hazzan had to be in possession of certain qualities: a good voice, smart appearance, familiarity with the liturgy, and an upright character. Nonetheless, it was not uncommon for the dual role of the cantor as both artist and spiritual role-model to create problems. For example, a hazzan of excellent voice might be preferred by those for whom this was paramount; others would favour someone of notable piety at the expense of musical talent. The 19th century brought considerable changes. Cantors composed new melodies under the influence of the Western musical tradition. In contrast, early Reform Judaism opted for a plain reading of the liturgy instead of chanting, with choir and organ for set pieces. ▷ Orthodox Judaism; Reform Judaism; worship, Jewish

capitalism A set of economic arrangements which developed in the 19th century in Western societies following the Industrial Revolution. The concept derives from the writings of Marx and rests upon the private ownership of the means of production by the capitalist class, or bourgeoisie. The workers, or proletariat, own nothing but their labour, and although free to sell their labour in the market, they are dependent upon the capitalist class which exploits them by appropriating the surplus value created by their labour. Non-Marxist economists define capitalism as one in which most property is privately owned and goods are sold freely in a competitive market, but without reference to exploitation, except where monopoly situations occur. Capitalism may be an ideological stance: Marx saw it as one stage in a historical process, finally being replaced by socialism. It has been the most productive economic system to date, though it has brought with it massive environmental and social problems, such as pollution and unemployment. ▷ Marx, Karl; Marxism; secular alternatives to religion

Capuchins (Italian *capuche*, a kind of cowl) A monastic order stemming from the Franciscans; in full, the Order of Friars Minor of St Francis Capuccinorum; abbreviated as OM Cap or OSFC. It was formed in 1529 by Matteo di Bassi (c.1495–1552), and observes a very strict rule, stressing poverty and austerity. ▷ Franciscans; monasticism

cardinal A name originally given to one of the parish priests, bishops, or district deacons of Rome, then applied to a senior dignitary of the Roman Catholic Church, being a priest or bishop nominated by a pope to act as counsellor. His duties are largely administrative, as head of a diocese, a curial office, an ecclesiastical commission, or a Roman congregation. The office carries special insignia, such as the distinctive red cap (biretta). ▷ Cardinals, College of; Roman Curia

Cardinals, College of An institution consisting of all the cardinals of the Roman Catholic Church, technically of threefold structure: bishops, priests, and deacons. It originates from the reforms of Pope Urban II (reigned 1088–99). In 1586 its number was restricted to 70, but this limit was removed by Pope John XXIII in 1958. It is responsible for the government of the Church during a vacancy in the papacy, and since 1179 has been responsible for the election of a pope. ▷ cardinal; Roman Catholicism

cargo A theme in 20th-century Melanesian religious movements. In 1920 a movement emerged at Vailala in what is now Papua New Guinea. Marked by glossolalia and prophecy, this movement proclaimed that a new age was dawning; the ancestors were about to return in ships leaving rich cargoes of Western consumer goods, and the whites would be expelled. People should prepare by moral reformation, by rituals which included marching and drilling, and by getting massive feasts ready for the ancestors. This was an early example of a pattern that became so common that the term 'cargo cult' was applied to Melanesian new religious movements generally. This is misleading since 'cargo', standing for the miraculous supply of goods, is only one and not necessarily the central feature of the movements.

The movements, which received an impetus from the dramatic and unprecedented events of World War II in the Pacific, take different forms, and various sources contribute. The traditional Melanesian myth of the two brothers (open to a new interpretation in the light of experience of black-white relations) and the return of the ancestors is focused in the light of Christian teaching about the kingdom of God and the coming of Christ, and Christian morality is interpreted as a new law. Contemporary experience revealed new goods arriving by ship or plane (Melanesians saw nothing of the manufacturing processes), always controlled by whites. Cargo stands for indigenous well-being, about to be realized. Disappointed expectations do not always destroy the movements; the prophecy is reinterpreted, or the cargo postponed. While new movements continue to arise in Melanesia, the cargo element is not always present. ▷ Christianity in Australasia; glossolalia; Melanesian religion

Carmelites A Roman Catholic monastic order originating in the 12th century from the Hermits of Mount Carmel (Israel), seeking the way of life of the prophet Elijah; properly known as the Order of the Brothers of the Blessed Virgin Mary of Mount Carmel, or White Friars; abbreviated OCarm. They flourished as mendicant friars in Europe. Carmelite nuns were officially recognized in 1452, and reformed by Teresa of Ávila in Spain (1562) as strictly cloistered Discalced Carmelites (ODC). (The term 'discalced' derives from the practice of wearing sandals instead of shoes and stockings.) The male order was similarly reformed by St John of the Cross, and in 1593 was recognized as a separate order. The older order specialized in teaching and preaching; the Discalced mainly in parochial and foreign mission work. ▷ Elijah; John of the Cross, St; monasticism; Teresa of Ávila, St

Carthusians A Roman Catholic monastic order founded in 1084 by Bruno of Cologne in Chartreuse, near Grenoble, France; properly known as the Order of Carthusians; abbreviated OCart. The monks practise strict abstinence and live as solitaries; lay brothers live in a community. Membership is small, but the order maintains houses in many parts of Europe. At the mother-house, 'La Grande Chartreuse', a famous liqueur is distilled, the profits being distributed to local charities. ▷ monasticism

Cassian, John, St (?360–c.435) Romanian-born monk and theologian. He spent some years as an ascetic in the Egyptian deserts, before being ordained by St John Chrysostom at Constantinople in 403. He instituted several monasteries in the south of France, including the Abbey of St Victor at Massilia (Marseilles), which served as a model for many in Gaul and Spain. Cassian was one of the first of the 'semi-Pelagians'. He was the author of *Collationes* (on the Desert Fathers), and a book on monasticism. His feast day is 23 July. ▷ asceticism; Chrysostom, St John; monasticism; Pelagianism

caste An endogamous group which is the basis of the system of social stratification in Hinduism. Caste is central to Hinduism and one could define a Hindu as being a person born into a particular caste. When the Aryans came to India they brought with them a three-tiered social structure of priests (*brahmanas*), warriors (*kshatriyas*), and commoners (*vaishyas*), to which they added the serfs (*shudras*), the indigenous population of India which itself was probably hierarchically structured. This class (varna) system is given sanction by the *Rig Veda* (10.90) which describes each of the classes coming from the body of the sacrificed primal person (*purusha*). The Brahmans or Brahmins came from his head, the thinkers of society; the warriors came from his arms, society's strength; the commoners came from his thighs, society's support; and the serfs came from the feet. This class system and the caste system which derives from it, is therefore regarded as a sacred structure by orthodox Hindus, in harmony with natural or cosmic law dharma). The class system developed into the caste (*jati*) system which we know today. There are thousands of castes within India based on inherited profession and ideas of purity and pollution. The higher castes are regarded as ritually more pure than the lower, whose professions deal with polluting substances, such as leather workers in contact with the skins of dead animals, sweepers in contact with dirt and bodily effluents and barbers in contact with hair, a polluting substance once separated from the body. Although the practice is legally outlawed, some castes are so polluting that they are called the 'untouchables'; Gandhi called them the 'children of God' (Harijans). Marriage between castes is strictly forbidden and transgressors are severely punished. More precisely marriage is endogamous within a caste, but exogamous within a sub-caste: that is, a person must marry within their general caste, but outside of the caste in their village. Within a Hindu village castes are strictly segregated with the untouchables living beyond the village boundary. Castes regarded as being within the upper three classes are known as the 'twice born' because, at about 12, boys undergo an initiation ceremony (*upanaya*), during which they are invested with a sacred thread, the symbol of upper caste males. ▷ Aryans; Gandhi, Mohandas Karamchand; Veda

catechism A manual of Christian doctrine, in question-and-answer form. It derived from the early Church period of instruction for new converts, and was later applied to the instruction of adults baptized in infancy. Such manuals became popular after the Reformation, eg Luther's Little Catechism (1529) and the Heidelberg Catechism (1563). These were intended for instruction, preparation for confirmation, and confessional purposes. Some have avoided the question-and-answer format, such as the Roman Catholic 'New Catechism' of 1966. ▷ Christianity; Luther, Martin; Reformation

Cathars (Greek *kathari*, 'pure ones') Originally, 3rd-century separatists from the Church, puritan and ascetic, following the teaching of the 3rd-century Roman bishop, Novatian. In the Middle Ages, as a sect, they were known in Bulgaria as Bogomiles and in France as Albigenses. Celibate, they rejected sacraments and held 'good' and 'evil' to be separate spheres ('dualism'). They survived until the 14th century, when they were finally exterminated by the Inquisition. ▷ Albigenses; celibacy; dualism; Inquisition; sacrament

cathedral (Latin *cathedra*, 'chair') The chief church of a bishop of a diocese; originally, the church which contained the throne of the bishop, then the mother church of the diocese. The most famous are the Western European Gothic cathedrals built in the Middle Ages, such as those at Rheims, France (1211–90), and Westminster Abbey, London (mostly 1245–1506). In many towns, they were the centre around which social and cultural as well as religious life developed. Colloquially, the term is often now used to refer to any church of great size. ▷ bishop; church; architecture, Christian

Catherine of Siena, St, properly **Caterina Benincasa** (1347–80) Italian mystic, the daughter of a dyer in Siena. She became a Dominican at the age of 16, and so is their patron saint. Her enthusiasm converted hardened sinners, and she prevailed on Pope Gregory XI to return from Avignon to Rome. Christ's stigmata were said to have been imprinted on her body in 1375. She wrote devotional pieces, letters, and poems; her *Dialogue*, a work on mysticism, was translated in 1896. She was canonized in 1461. Her feast day is 30 April. ▷ Dominicans; mysticism; stigmata

Catholic Church (Greek *katholikos*, 'general', 'universal') 1 As in the Apostles' Creed, the universal Church which confesses Jesus Christ as Lord. ▷ Apostles' Creed; Jesus Christ 2 Christian Churches with episcopal order and confessing ancient creeds. ▷ episcopacy 3 Specifically, the Roman Catholic Church and other Churches recognizing the primacy of the pope, as distinct from Protestant and Orthodox Churches. ▷ papacy; Roman Catholicism

cave art ▷ art, Palaeolithic

celibacy The religiously motivated commitment to life-long abstention from sexual relations. Evidence of such commitments abounds in all major religions, eg Priests of Cybele, Buddhist monks and Vestal Virgins as well as monks, nuns and Roman Catholic priests in the Christian tradition, and occasionally among Jewish sects. The motivation for the requirement of, and desire for, celibacy is complex: purification; the Graeco-Roman separation of body and soul, the former being corruptible and impure, so that celibacy was a measure to protect the soul from contamination by the sensual desires of the body; the aim to be free of distraction from religious service; the belief that in the last times there would be no marrying or giving in marriage.

In the Christian tradition, it was related to the rise of hermits and the monastic movements dating from the 4th century CE, celibacy being required of monks and nuns in religious orders as a sign of total commitment to Christ or, in the case of nuns, marriage to the Church. It gradually (after 385CE) became obligatory for secular clergy as well, and remains the law for priests of the Roman Catholic Church, though not, in certain circumstances, for deacons. It is to be considered as a gift from God by those who practise it. In Orthodox Churches, celibacy is required of bishops but not of priests. Since the time of the Reformation, when it was condemned by eg Martin Luther as a manifestation of 'justification by works' as opposed to 'faith', celibacy has not been required of Protestant ministers. Certain Anglican religious communities, however, require it, as do some Reformed communities such as Taizé (France). ▷ monasticism; nun; priesthood; renunciation

Celtic Church The original Church in the British Isles, retaining its administrative and practical independence from the Anglo-Roman Church until the Synod of Whitby (663–4). Contacts with European Christianity were developed as early as the 4th century. The organization was largely monastic, with an abbot rather than a bishop acting as leader. The emphasis was on the ascetic life, and on scholarship and art as well as mission. The Church was active in Ireland, Scotland, Wales, and England (eg Saints Patrick, Ninian, Columba), and in the 6th century in continental Europe. ▷ Christianity; Columba, St; Patrick, St

Central Asian Buddhism Buddhism was present in Central Asia by the 2nd century BCE and it remained a strong influence there until the 11th century CE, when most of the region moved in the direction of Islam. Indian merchants who were Buddhists traded along the Silk Route that led from north-west India to China. Sometimes wandering monks went with them and Buddhist centres were set up, stretching from north-west India and Afghanistan into the oases of what is now Soviet Central Asia and Sinkiang in China. Buddhism reached China by the 1st century CE and, up to the middle of the 3rd century, Central Asian Buddhism, through its missions along the trade routes, had an important influence on Chinese Buddhism. Other religions were also present in Central Asia up to the 11th century, including Nestorian Christianity, Manichaeism, Zoroastrianism and Judaism, and there was a fascinating interchange of religious ideas in this area. The nature of the local terrain has enabled documents, paintings and iconography to be recovered from this region, giving important information about early Buddhism and other religions. It was the Mahayana form of Buddhism that had a strong presence in Central Asia, although other schools such as the Mahasanghika and Sarvastivada were present as well. ▷ Judaism; Mahasanghika; Mahayana Buddhism; Manichaeism; Sarvastivada; Zoroastrianism

centre of the world ceremonies Ceremonies found in many cultures associated with sacred places or objects symbolizing the 'centre of the world'. The centre of the world is not, in this context, conceived geographically or geometrically but rather as the place or a place forming the sacred heart of reality, differing in kind from ordinary everyday reality but giving form and substance to everything that is real. Because of its sacred nature, there is no inconsistency in the recognition of more than one such centre. In different cultures in China and India, for example, a large number of 'centres of the world' may be recognized. These symbolic centres take many forms: whole sacred cities (eg among the Incas and Aztecs of South America), the sacred mountain (eg Mount Meru in Hinduism and Buddhism; Mount Gerizim, the 'navel of the earth' for the Hebrews; the Black Stone in Islam); the cosmic tree; the bridge or ladder; also sanctuaries, temples, and cathedrals, even houses. In certain traditions (eg Tantric schools), the centre may be located within the human body.

The centre of the earth is the place where the mundane and the supernatural unite and communication between the human and the divine takes place. During, and as a result of, ceremonies associated with the centre, sacred power may be generated and spread abroad. Its importance is underlined by the imaging of the *axis mundi* in many traditions and in various forms—intricately woven fibres, drums, the 'cat's cradle' of children's games. Also often associated with it are certain sounds or music, to symbolize the crossing from one level of reality to another.

Cephas ▷ **Peter, St**

Cernunnos Representations abound in the Celtic lands of a man-like figure bearing horns or antlers. One such, from Gaul, is labelled 'Cernunnos' and this name is used for convenience to designate all images of the Celtic horned god. Cernunnos is often shown squatting, with a torque at the neck, and a ram-headed serpent in attendance. Sometimes he is surrounded by animals, recalling a story in the Mabinogion of a mysterious master of the animals who receives worship. Some representations are phallic, or bear other fertility symbols; others suggest instead an association with warfare. In general, known Celtic deities have simply local significance; Cernunnos alone is found throughout the Celtic realms. Theories that the horned god is also the Father God represented by the Irish Dagda remain, however, speculative. ▷ Dagda; Mabinogion

Cernunnos

Cerularius, Michael (d.1058/9) Patriarch of Constantinople (from 1043) at the time of the formal split between the Eastern (Greek or Orthodox) and Western (Latin or Roman Catholic) Church in 1054. When the Greek churches in Italy had been forced to adopt Latin practices, Cerularius responded by ordering that the Latin churches in Constantinople should adopt Greek customs. They refused, so he closed them in 1052. Stormy clashes with Cardinal-Bishop Humbert of Silva Candida (d.1061, the chief representative of a delegation sent to Constantinople in 1054 by Pope Leo IX (1048–54) to resolve the matter), led to Cerularius being excommunicated and to the legates being anathematized in return. The break of 1054 brought to a head tensions between East and West that had begun in 858 in struggles over authority between Photius, Patriarch of Constantinople and Pope Nicholas I (858–67), and continued with doctrinal disputes about the *filioque* clause in the Nicene-Constantinopolitan creed (whether or not the Holy Spirit should be said to proceed 'from the Father *and the Son*'). The incidents of 1054 may have been the theological and institutional point of no return, but it was the Crusaders' sack of Constantinople in 1204 that sealed the division between the two churches in popular consciousness. ▷ Creeds,

Christian; Nicene Creed; Orthodox Church; papacy; Photius

Chaitanya (c.1486–1533) Indian Hindu mystic, born in Nadia, Bengal. A Sanskrit teacher before becoming an itinerant holy man; following conversion in 1510 to a life of devotion to Krishna, he spent the latter part of his life in Puri, inspiring disciples in both Bengal and Orissa with his emphasis on joy and love of Krishna, and the place of singing and dancing in worship. Though he wrote little, he is also remembered for influencing the development of Bengali literature, previously held as much inferior to Sanskrit. ▷ Krishna; mysticism; Sanskrit

Chaitanya movement A 15th-century sect of the *Krishna* bhakti movement, the forerunner of the Hare Krishna movement. Established in Bengal, it emphasizes music, dance, and ecstatic trance in its worship. ▷ bhakti; Chaitanya; Hare Krishna movement

chakras ▷ cakras

Chalcedon, Council of (451) A Council of the Church which agreed that Jesus Christ is truly God and truly man, two natures in one person (the 'Chalcedonian definition'). The definition is generally accepted by the Churches, though from the beginning there was uneasiness about its interpretation, and recently it has come under sustained criticism. ▷ Christology; Council of the Church

Chalmers, Thomas (1780–1847) Scottish theologian and preacher, born in Anstruther, Fife. Educated at St Andrews University, he was ordained minister of Kilmany in 1803. He carried on mathematical and chemistry classes at St Andrews in 1803–4, and in 1808 published an *Inquiry into National Resources*. In 1815 he became minister to the Tron parish in Glasgow, where his magnificent oratory, partly published as *Astronomical Discourses* (1817) and *Commercial Discourses* (1820), took the city by storm. In 1823 he became Professor of Moral Philosophy at St Andrews, where he wrote his *Use and Abuse of Literary and Ecclesiastical Endowments* (1827). In 1827 he was transferred to the professorship of theology in Edinburgh, and in 1832 published a work on political economy. In 1833 appeared his Bridgewater treatise, *On the Adaptation of External Nature to the Moral and Intellectual Constitution of Man*. Meanwhile, the struggles in regard to patronage became keener, until in 1843 Chalmers led the Disruption, in which he, followed by 470 ministers, seceded from the Church of Scotland, and founded the Free Church of Scotland, whose swift and successful organization was mainly due to his indefatigable exertions. He was the first moderator of its Assembly, and Principal of the Free Church College from 1843 to 1847, when he completed his *Institutes of Theology*. His works, in 34 volumes, deal especially with natural theology, apologetics and social economy. As a religious orator Chalmers was unrivalled. ▷ apologetics; Church of Scotland; natural theology

Chan (Ch'an) A general term for meditation in Chinese Buddhism, referring to a school which dates from perhaps the 6th century. It combines Mahayana Buddhist teachings with those of Taoism to form an outlook emphasizing meditative experience as opposed to an intellectual approach. It is better known in the West by its Japanese name Zen. ▷ Buddhism; Mahayana Buddhism; Taoism; Zen Buddhism

Chan, Wing-Tsit (1901–) Chinese scholar of religion, born in Canton. Educated at Lingnan University and Harvard, he became professor at Dartmouth College, New Hampshire (1942) in Chinese culture and philosophy, and later Professor of Philosophy at Chatham College, Pittsburgh. He enriched the study of Chinese religion by the quality of his translations of Chinese classics into English, eg *A Source Book in Chinese Philosophy* (1963), *Neo-Confucian Writings of Wang Yang-Ming* (1963), *The Way of Lao Tzu* (1963), *The Platform Sutra* (1963), while other works cover Chinese religion and philosophy from pre-Confucian times to contemporary Marxist China. His own neo-Confucian sympathies are brought to bear upon his studies of the neo-Confucian giants, Chu Hsi and Wang Yang-Ming, and his interest in modern China is seen in *Religious Trends in Modern China* (1953) and *Chinese Philosophy in Mainland China 1949–1963* (1966). At a crucial time he has interpreted Chinese religion and thought both for the West and for China itself. ▷ China mainland, Chinese religion in (20th century); Chinese Buddhism; Chinese religion (20th century) in Taiwan and Hong Kong; Chu Hsi; neo-Confucianism; Wang Yang-Ming

Chandrakirti (Candrakīrti) (late 6th century) Indian philosopher and teacher of Mahayana Buddhism. Together with Shantideva he gave to the Madhyamika school of Buddhist philosophy a new vigour and clarity of exposition. The Madhyamika viewpoint had been introduced by the great Nagarjuna in the 2nd century CE in somewhat difficult and complicated language, and Chandrakirti gave it a definitive and structured scholastic system. He also founded a school called the Prasangika-Madhyamika school, and his main teaching is set out in his commentary on Nagarjuna entitled the 'Clear-Worded' or *Prasannapada*. He made important contributions in his commentaries and writings to the Mahayana Buddhist understanding of such significant concepts as dependent origination, emptiness (*shunyata*), the two levels of truth, and nirvana. ▷ dependent origination; emptiness; Madhyamika; Mahayana Buddhism; Nagarjuna; nirvana

Channing, William Ellery (1780–1842) American clergyman, born in Newport, Rhode Island. He graduated at Harvard in 1798, and in 1803 was ordained to the Congregational Federal Street Church in Boston, where his sermons were famous for their 'fervour, solemnity, and beauty'. He was ultimately the leader of the Unitarians. In 1822 he visited Europe and made the acquaintance of Wordsworth and Coleridge. Among his Works (6 vols, 1841–6) were his *Essay on National Literature*, *Remarks on Milton*, *Character and Writings of Fénelon*, *Negro Slavery*, and *Self-culture*. ▷ Unitarians

Chan patriarchs (Ch'an) The Chan school was a tradition in Chinese Buddhism which derived its name from the Indian Sanskrit word for meditation (*dhyana*) and later became known in Japan as Zen. It sought an immediate awareness of reality by means of awakening to the Buddha nature within. According to Buddhist traditional records Bodhidharma brought Chan from India to China in 520CE and became its first patriarch. There was a special transmission of the patriarchate from Bodhidharma down to the fifth patriarch Hung Jen (601–74). After that there was a split between two of Hung Jen's disciples who were both recognized as the sixth patriarch by the schools that formed around them. Shen Hsiu (c.600–702) became the leader of the northern school of Chan, which taught the necessity of overcoming false thinking with pure thinking, and the need to evolve gradually towards an awareness of reality. Hui Neng (638–713) became the leader of the southern school of Chan, which stressed the possibility of achieving a sudden awareness of reality rather than receiving it as the culmination of a gradual process of purification and growth. After the great persecution of the Buddhists in 845 Chan survived in two main schools which also became transplanted to Japan; eventually it formed an alliance with Pure Land Buddhism and became harmonized with this tradition in China. ▷ Bodhidharma; Buddha nature; dhyana; Hui Neng; Pure Land Buddhism; Zen Buddhism

chanting, Hindu Part of Hindu daily and occasional ritual. Brahman priests will chant verses or mantras in Sanskrit from the sacred scriptures of Hinduism, the Veda, during daily ritual (*pujas*) to the gods and during occasional rituals such as weddings, sacred-thread investitures and funerals. Chanting the Veda has been an important practice in transmitting the tradition from teacher to student through the generations, before the text was committed to writing. There is great accuracy in the text transmitted in this way. ▷ Veda

chapel Originally, a place to house sacred relics; now generally a church. In England and Wales, the term is used of Nonconformist places of worship; in Northern Ireland and Scotland, of Roman Catholic churches. It may also be a place of worship belonging to a college or institution, and may further denote the chancel of a church or cathedral, or part of a cathedral containing a separate altar. ▷ church; Nonconformists; Roman Catholicism

charismatic movement A movement of spiritual renewal, which has its roots in the Pentecostal Church. Taking a variety of forms in Roman Catholic, Protestant, and Eastern Orthodox Churches, it emphasizes the present reality and work of the Holy Spirit in the life of the Church and the individual. It is sometimes accompanied by speaking in tongues (glossolalia). ▷ glossolalia; Holy Spirit; Pentecostalism

Charlemagne, (Carolus Magnus, Charles the Great) (747–814) King of the Franks and Christian emperor of the West, grandson of Charles Martel and the eldest son of Pepin III the Short. On Pepin's death in 768 the Frankish kingdom was divided between Charlemagne and his younger brother Carloman; three years later, on Carloman's death, he became sole ruler. The first years of his reign were spent in strenuous campaigns to subdue and Christianize neighbouring kingdoms, particularly the Saxons to the north-east (772–7) and the Lombards of northern Italy (773), where he was crowned King of Lombardy. In 778 he led an expedition against the Moors in Spain, but withdrew the same year when his presence was required elsewhere; the celebrated rearguard action at Roncesvalles in which Roland, his chief paladin, is said to have been overwhelmed, gave rise to the heroic literature of the *Chanson de Roland*. In 782 the Saxons rose again in rebellion and destroyed a Frankish army at Süntelberg, which Charlemagne avenged by beheading 4500 Saxons. Other risings followed, but in 785 the Saxon leader, Widukind, submitted and accepted baptism, and became a loyal vassal. In 788, Charlemagne deposed the ruler of Bohemia and absorbed it into his empire. Farther to the east he subdued the Avars (Turko-Finnish nomads) in the middle Danube basin (795–6) to create an eastern 'March' to buttress his frontiers; to the west he created the so-called 'Spanish March' on the southern side of the Pyrenees (795). In 800 he swept into Italy to support Pope Leo III against the rebellious Romans, and on Christmas Day, 800, in St Peter's Church, was crowned by the pope Emperor of the Romans as 'Carolus Augustus'. The remaining years of his reign were spent in consolidating his vast empire which reached from the Ebro in northern Spain to the Elbe. Bishoprics were founded in the Saxon country; many of the Slavs east of the Elbe were subjugated. The emperor established his capital and principal court at Aachen (Aix-la-Chapelle), where he built a magnificent palace and founded an academy to which many of the greatest scholars of the age, such as Alcuin of York, were invited. He himself could speak Latin and read Greek, and letters and Latin poems ascribed to him are still extant. He zealously promoted education, architecture, bookmaking and the arts, created stable administrations and good laws, and encouraged agriculture, industry and commerce. He fostered good relations with the east, and in 798 Harun al-Raschid, the Caliph of Baghdad, sent ambassadors and a gift of a white elephant. His reign was a noble attempt to consolidate order and Christian culture among the nations of the West, a Carolingian renaissance, but his empire did not long survive his death, for his sons lacked both his vision and authority. He was buried in Aachen.

Chen Yen The name given to the school of Tantric Buddhism in China. The term is derived from the Indian Sanskrit word mantra meaning 'mystical word'. Chen Yen came into China through the work of Shubhakarasimha in 716CE, and was expanded by other figures such as Amoghavajra (705–74), but although for a time it gained imperial favour it never became deeply rooted. It grew much more popular in Japan through the work of Kukai, who went to China in 804 and returned to Japan with some of the rituals, texts and teachings of Chen Yen to found the Shingon school in his native land. Especially important for the Shingon school was the *Mahavairocana Sutra*, which had been translated from Sanskrit into Chinese by Shubhakarasimha. There was an infusion of life into Chinese Tantric Buddhism from Tibet during the Yuan dynasty (1279–1368), but the school that survived was as much Tibetan as Chinese, and the intrinsic vitality of Chen Yen had declined. ▷ Kukai; mantra; Shingon; Tantric Buddhism; Tibetan religion

cherubim, singular **cherub** In the Hebrew Bible/Old Testament, winged celestial creatures or beasts of various descriptions. Their roles include guarding the tree of life in the Garden of Eden (Genesis 3.24), being stationed on the cover of the Ark of the Covenant (Exodus 25.18–22), adorning Solomon's temple (1 Kings 6.23ff), and accompanying the throne chariot of God (Ezekiel 1, 10). ▷ angel; Ark of the Covenant; Eden, Garden of; seraphim; Solomon

Cheyenne religion The Cheyenne are a Plains branch of the Algonquin family, now living almost at the geographical centre of the USA but formerly settled in North Dakota. Archaeological remains indicate a change from a largely agricultural to a hunting culture in the late 18th century. The Cheyenne partake of many of the regular features of Algonquin religion, while sharing institutions common among Plains people, such as the Sun Dance, with its lodge built as a model of the universe. The Cheyenne creation story involves a sacred hat and four sacred arrows, a highly regarded communal possession. Local divinities are recognized; the Black Hills are a spirit homeland. The Cheyenne were affected by the Ghost Dance movement in the 19th century and more recently by the peyote movement. ▷ Algonquin religion; creation myths; Ghost Dance; peyote; Sun Dance

Children of God A new religious movement, also known as the Family of Love, that emerged out of the Jesus Movement within evangelical Christianity. It was critical of the institutional church which it felt had compromised too much with the world. It began in California in 1968 under the leadership of David Berg who, as Moses David, circulated 'Mo' letters to his followers on minute details of belief and practice. It opposed the materialism of both the capitalist and communist systems and believed that, in the millennium that would soon appear, those two systems would disappear and the future would be left to the Children of God and like-minded godly people. It evoked a strong commitment mainly from young people, some of whom were motivated to leave college or work to live in fellowship communes and to help to spread the movement. Their high-profile proselytism brought strong reactions from the public, and they were accused of making sexual inducement a means of obtaining new members. Although they have gained much publicity, it is unlikely that their committed membership has been over 10000 at any one time, because the turnover has never been high and the actions of the Anti-Cult movement brought unwelcome attention to certain facets of their fundamentalist-type Christianity. ▷ Anti-Cult movement; Jesus movement; millennium; new religious movements in the West

Children's Crusade A movement in 1212 of thousands of children (some as young as six) from Germany and France, aiming to reach the Holy Land and recapture Jerusalem from the Turks. Some reached Genoa, Italy, but did not embark; some reached Marseilles, France, whence they were shipped to North Africa and sold into slavery. ▷ Crusades

Chilembwe, John ▷ **Providence Industrial Mission**

Chinese Buddhism Buddhism first entered China from India in the 1st century CE via the Central Asian oases along the Silk Route, and by the end of the Han dynasty (220CE) it had established a reasonable presence in China. The difficulties in spreading the Buddhist tradition in China were formidable: it was a foreign religion, its Sanskrit language was foreign, it believed in rebirth, it placed little stress on the family, and it centred on monks. By taking advantage of the disruption that accompanied the fall of the Han empire, by matching their concepts with those of the neo-Taoists, by skilful translations of texts into Chinese, by using gradual missionary methods in the south which was more settled, and by using more vigorous missionary methods in the north when it was overrun by barbarians, the Buddhists helped their religion take root in China. Great translators such as Kumarajiva (344–413) did excellent work in translating the *Mahayana Sutras* into Chinese, and indigenous Chinese schools began to emerge that were unknown in India, including Chan (Zen), said to have been introduced by Bodhidharma in 520CE, and Pure Land, developed by Tan Luan (476–542). Chinese Buddhism became so successful that the Tang dynasty saw it as 'an empire within the empire' and persecuted it in 845, after which only the Chan and Pure Land schools remained strong. They drew closer together and became more harmonized. An attempt was made by the Marxist government of Mao (1949 onwards) to subdue Buddhism and other religions in China, and its lands were nationalized and its monks forced to engage in secular employment. Since 1978, Buddhism and other religions have been reviving in China. ▷ Chan; Kumarajiva; Mahayana Sutras; Mao Zedong; Pure Land Buddhism

Chinese pantheon The Chinese pantheon is very extensive. It includes many deities and spirits from local areas who are present in local homes and temples as well as gods from Buddhist and Taoist pantheons. Because of the diffused nature of popular Chinese religion there has been assimilation and amalgamation between some of these deities. There tends however to be a distinction between the Chinese pantheon on the one hand, and nature gods, Taoist immortals, and Buddhas and bodhisattvas on the other. At the family level there is the worship of household gods and the veneration of ancestors; at the neighbourhood level, in cities and country areas, there is the worship of local gods responsible for those areas; at the state level there has been the worship of state gods which in early China centred on the worship by the ruling classes of *Tien* (heaven), *Ti* (earth) and the royal ancestors. Later some of the gods of popular religion became more important than others. They include the Jade Emperor (Yu-Huang), who was seen to be the ruler of the heavenly court, and under him a series of gods responsible for particular ministries in his court, such as epidemics, fire, healing, sacred mountains, thunder and wind. They were often, though not always, human beings who had become deified over a period of time. Some of the more popular gods include Tsao Chun, the god of the stove who oversees domestic matters, Chang Huang, the god responsible for cities, Fu Shen, the god of happiness, and Tsai Shen, the god of wealth. ▷ bodhisattva; Buddha; Tien; Yu-Huang

Chinese religion in Taiwan and Hong Kong (20th century) With the partial decline of traditional religious forms in mainland China, there has been a flourishing of these forms in Taiwan and Hong Kong alongside the growth of science and technology. The three ways of Confucianism, Taoism and Buddhism have mingled with Chinese folk religion. The Confucian tradition has underscored family and communal ethical values in business and family relations, especially in regard to filial piety; Taoist priests have combined their search for immortality with their ritual role in exorcism, healing and balancing the forces of yin and yang; and Buddhist monks have officiated at funeral services, advocated rebirth into the Pure Land of Amitabha Buddha, and set an example of controlled living in a hectic society. At the popular level New Year and other festivals, the burning of paper gods, ancestor reverence, local temples, and family rituals have continued. With the heavy building programme in these offshore islands the art of geomancy has been in increasing demand in order to ensure an auspicious site. Particular deities such as the goddess of mercy Kuan Yin, the Jade Emperor (Yu-Huang), Amitabha Buddha, the Buddha himself, and the Heavenly Empress have commanded worship, and on their special days crowds are attracted to the festivities. Other religious traditions such as Islam, Protestant Christianity and Catholic Christianity have also established their presence, together with various new religious movements, in the market of religious forms available in these market-oriented areas. ▷ ancestor reverence, Chinese; Buddha; Chinese pantheon; Chinese religion in Taiwan and Hong Kong (20th century); Chinese religion on the China mainland (20th century); festivals, Chinese; Kuan Yin; Pure Land Buddhism; Yu-Huang

Chinese religion on the China mainland (20th century) With the end of the Manchu dynasty at the beginning of this century, the civil service exam system based on the Confucian Classics, which had lasted for nearly 2000 years, ended in 1905, and the Confucian imperial rites ended in 1912. The Taoist, Buddhist and Chinese folk religious traditions continued, as did a less formal Confucian presence, and the more foreign traditions of Islam and Protestant and Catholic Christianity were also present. After the rise of a communist government in 1949 the major religions were designated as 'religion' and were grudgingly tolerated, whereas Chinese folk religion was designated as 'superstition' and was persecuted. In the 1950s government-aided associations assisted in the continuation of the Buddhist, Catholic, Christian (equals Protestant), Muslim, and Taoist traditions, but all of them, especially the Buddhists, were affected by the secularization of their lands and religious leaders. During the Cultural Revolution (1966–76) most places of worship were closed, many religious leaders were exiled to the countryside, and an attempt was made to prohibit all religious activities, with the exception of some Muslim ones. This resulted in religious traditions being driven underground. Since 1978 all religious traditions have been tolerated more freely and have begun to revive in China. They administer their own affairs, have opened or re-opened many buildings and some seminaries, have commissioned new leaders, have crowds coming to their services and rituals, and new adherents flocking into their communities. It is more difficult to assess whether folk religion has revived after the attempts to stifle it, but it appears that ancestor reverence, local temples, popular festivals, and a concern for household and local gods have remained and are now on the increase. New Confucian institutes have also been opened and the Christian churches have become Chinese in their ethos and outlook. ▷ Chinese religion in Taiwan and Hong Kong (20th century)

Ching Ming (Ch'ing Ming) The Chinese Festival of Pure Brightness which happens around the 5th of April on the 106th day after the winter solstice. It is a festival which centres upon visits made by families to the graves of their ancestors. The graves are tidied and swept, and sacrifices of food and wine are made to the ancestors. After this ritual there is often a picnic on the site when the living, so to speak, share a feast with the dead. Grave sites are carefully selected, according to the art of geomancy, and when it is not possible immediately to determine the most auspicious place for the grave, the dead person's remnants are placed in a sealed jar which is laid on a hillside. Where this is the case the jar is visited by family members during Ching Ming. When a person cannot get home for Ching Ming he or she may offer a sacrifice from a distance on the principle that it will reach the ancestors anyway. However, wherever possible it is a time for returning home and Chinese living in the West go home every few years for a long stay to cover the period of the New Year and Ching Ming festivals. ▷ ancestor reverence, Chinese; festivals Chinese; funerary practices, Chinese; Yuan Tan

Ching Tu Tsung (Ching T'u Tsung) (Pure Land) The Pure Land school in Chinese Buddhism. The original *Pure Land Sutras* were written in India in Sanskrit, and described how the Buddha Amitabha came to superintend a paradise or 'Pure Land' as the fruit of his deep service and devotion. He vowed to give the opportunity to those who would put their faith in him and in his Pure Land to be reborn there and to go on to enlightenment from it. He also lit up his Pure Land by means of rays of light from his body. A cult of Amitabha was initiated in China by Hui Yuan in 402CE, and an active Pure Land school was set up by Tan Huan (476–542) and strengthened by Tao Cho (562–645) and Shan Tao (613–81). Emphasis was placed upon repeating the phrase 'I put my faith in Amitabha Buddha' with sincerity. This was held to be an easy way of gaining rebirth in the Pure Land followed by enlightenment at a time of degeneration that was held to coincide with the last of three declining periods of Buddhist history. In addition to repeating the name of Amitabha Buddha with sincerity, meditation, worshipping before a Buddha image, hymn-singing and the chanting of *sutras* were all part of Pure Land practice. After the great persecution of the Buddhists in 845, Pure Land remained popular and began to amalgamate with Chan, the other strong element in Chinese Buddhism. It was introduced from China to Japan by Saicho, who founded the Tendai sect which became the touchstone of Pure Land in Japan. ▷ Buddha image; Chan; enlightenment; rebirth; Tendai

Chinvat Bridge (from the Avestan *Cinvat peretu*, 'Bridge of the Separator') The bridge which, according to Zoroastrian teaching, the souls of the dead must cross on the fourth morning after death in order to reach Paradise or Hell. The concept may have a pre-Zoroastrian origin, referring to the 'separation' between this world and the hereafter. In Zoroaster's *Gathas* (songs), however, the term 'separator' also seems to have connotations of judgement, separating the good from the wicked. The Chinvat Bridge was thought to rest upon the highest mountain in the world, Mount Hara. There are various accounts of what happens at the bridge when the soul crosses it. Some describe a formal judgement there; others state that the soul will be met by its *daena*, its spiritual essence, which has the shape of a beautiful girl if the deceased has been righteous, and that of a repulsive hag if the person has been a sinner. ▷ Avesta; Zoroastrianism

chod (gCod) A practice in Tibetan Buddhism aimed at realizing the empty and illusory nature of all appearances. Practitioners go to a lonely, unfrequented place, such as a cemetery or mountain, and there ritually evoke wrathful and malevolent powers or beings. In one form of the rite, practitioners visualize their bodies as corpses which are dismembered by a wrathful goddess, an aspect of the Buddha's wisdom, who then offers the dismembered parts to a host of malevolent beings or demons who devour them. In another form practitioners visualize themselves as the goddess, who flays her own body, offering her skin and bones to demons and wild animals. At the end of the ritual, the goddess and the malevolent beings are absorbed within the practitioners who should realize that these ferocious forms were produced by their own minds and are essentially empty. In this way they realize the identical nature of *samsara* and nirvana. The ritual's philosophical justification is found in the *Prajnaparamita Sutras*. The chod rites probably originated in the Tantric cremation ground traditions of India, though tradition attributes their origin to the female yogini Macig (Ma-gcig, d.c.1150). ▷ nirvana; prajnaparamita; samsara; Tibetan religion

Chololian ▷ Tollan

Chondogyo (Ch'ŏndogyo) (Literally, the Religion of the Heavenly Way) An indigenous Korean religion founded in 1860 by Ch'oe Suun (1824–64). Although influenced by the Confucian and Taoist traditions it was a reaction against the traditional religions of Korea and against Christianity, and was an attempt to appeal directly to the religious consciousness of the Korean masses. After Suun's martyrdom at the hands of the government, his successors Ch'oe Haewol (1827–98) and Sohn Uiam (1861–1922) built up the movement until it became a major Korean religion. The Chondogyo scriptures comprise the writings of the first three founders, and Suun's writings are especially important. Chondogyo played a significant part in modernizing Korea after 1894, in opposing Japanese imperialism after 1919, and in not acquiescing in communism in North Korea after 1945. It stresses the immanence of God in the whole of life, and sees human beings as 'bearing divinity' and as being called to treat other humans 'as God'. It emphasizes the need for a co-operative kingdom of God on earth based on faith, sincerity, steadfastness, and simplicity. Five practices are recommended: a formula chanted every evening at nine o'clock; the use of water as a symbol of spiritual purity; a Sunday worship service; regular offerings of rice to the church, and prayers of various sorts, including the silent *simgo*, or heart address.

Christ ▷ Jesus Christ

Christadelphians (Greek 'brothers of Christ') A Christian sect, founded by John

Thomas (1805–71) in the USA in 1848. They were originally called Thomasites until, forced to organize themselves officially in order to defend their pacifism during the Civil War, they adopted the name of Christadelphians. Teaching a return to primitive Christianity, they claim that Christ will soon come again to establish a theocracy lasting for a millennium and based in Jerusalem. Christadelphians are congregational in organization, and there are no ordained ministers. They believe in the complete accuracy of the Bible, and claim that only true believers will go on to life after death, all others being consigned to oblivion. Adult followers must be baptized in order to attain full salvation; they do not practise infant baptism. ▷ baptism; millenarianism

Christian ethics Sometimes known as moral theology, this deals with the application of Christian principles to moral issues. It may seek to guide particular individual decisions (by detailed drawing on previous cases of a similar kind, as in Catholic or Anglican casuistry, or by simply applying the 'law of love' to current circumstances, as in modern Protestant 'situation ethics'), give general advice on the matter concerned, or frame rules or laws that society can adopt. The theological basis of Christian ethics is found in the doctrines of God, creation, man, sin, grace and redemption. As created beings men and women are to be valued for themselves as individuals and are meant to be thankful stewards rather than exploitative owners of the rest of God's creation. Although good behaviour does not obtain salvation or favour with God, conversion should result in practical holiness in all areas of life, so that the rule or kingdom of God may spread through church and society.

The fact that the achievement of these ideals is limited by personal or corporate greed, fear, ignorance, weakness or other manifestation of sin, means that Christian ethics has to allow for failure and forgiveness. This is especially true when dealing with individuals in a pastoral situation such as a family or marriage problem, although attempts to distinguish between personal and social ethics fail to recognize that nothing is purely one or the other. Attitudes to divorce, for example, affect society as a whole as well as the individuals most closely concerned. Changes to legislation on working hours or minimum wages can achieve more good for people than championing one particular case of poverty. Yet the poor person trying to feed a family has immediate needs (which may be met by personal charity) as well as long-term requirements.

The relationship between Christian ethics and the ethics of society in general has been as varied as relationships between Church and State. Some churches (or movements within them such as Liberal Protestantism, the social gospel movement, political theology, and liberation theology) have sought to influence and Christianize society. Others (which would be classed as 'sects' rather than 'churches' by sociologists) hold that the values of the kingdom of God can only be realized within the Christian community. The ethical views of the churches have sometimes coincided with the views of the state, sometimes (as with the abolition of slavery) promoted a position that was eventually accepted out of enlightened self-interest, and sometimes (as with the adoption of pacifism or the abandonment of the 'just war' theory in the nuclear age) seemed unrealistic or unpatriotic. It can also be argued that on some issues, such as women's rights, many churches have lagged behind changes in secular society. ▷ Church and State; grace; kingdom of God; Liberal Protestantism; liberation theology; humankind, Christian view of; marriage/divorce, Christian; political theology; redemption; sin; Social Gospel; Christianity, women in

Christian Fellowship Church A movement in New Georgia, Solomon Islands, one of the numerous Melanesian new religious movements which approximates to an Independent church of the African pattern. It began in the 1950s, with the work of a charismatic preacher, Silas Eto, in the Methodist Church. The missionary leadership distrusted its ecstatic and visionary elements (*taturu*) and the movement was established as a separate church in 1961. It has since become a major social and economic force in the Western Solomons. It retains the preaching of Christ as redeemer (and makes much use of the crucifix image), but in its liturgy has added 'Holy Mama' to the persons of the Trinity. Eto is addressed as Holy Mama, but the concept is not identical with his person, and members of the church appear to hold various views of the founder's status. ▷ cargo; Jesus Christ

Christianity (Greek *christos*, 'anointed') A world religion centred on the life and work of Jesus of Nazareth in Israel, and developing out of Judaism. The earliest followers were Jews who, after the death and resurrection of Jesus, believed him to be the Messiah or Christ, promised by the prophets in the Old

Testament, and in unique relation to God, whose Son or 'Word' (Logos) he was declared to be. During his life he chose 12 men as disciples, who formed the nucleus of the Church as a society or communion of believers, called together to worship God through Jesus Christ, who would come again to inaugurate the 'kingdom of God'. Christians believe that God is one, and is the creator. Humankind, as his creation, is essentially good, but in practice is sinful. The only way for humankind to attain true goodness is through God's grace; Jesus Christ, as the Son of God, is the means of grace. God is believed to be one in essence but threefold in person, comprising the Father, Son and Holy Spirit or Holy Ghost (known as the Trinity). Jesus Christ, while the Son of God, is also wholly human because of his birth to Mary. The Holy Spirit is the touch or 'breath' of God which inspires people to follow the Christian faith. The Bible is thought to have been written under its influence.

At the heart of the Christian faith is the conviction that, through Jesus's life, death and resurrection, God has allowed humans to find salvation. Belief in Jesus as the Son of God brings forgiveness of all sin. Christians believe that Jesus will return at the end of the world to judge between the good and the bad, the good joining him in heaven, or 'the kingdom of God', the bad being consigned to hell. The Gospel ('Good News') of Jesus was proclaimed first by word of mouth, but by the end of the 1st century it was committed to writing and became accepted as the authoritative scripture of the New Testament, understood as the fulfilment of the Jewish scriptures, or Old Testament. Through the witness of the 12 earliest leaders (Apostles) and their successors, the Christian faith, despite sporadic persecution, quickly spread through the Greek and Roman world, and in 315 was declared by Emperor Constantine to be the official religion of the Roman Empire. It survived the break-up of the Empire and the 'Dark Ages' through the life and witness of groups of monks in monasteries, and formed the basis of civilization in the Middle Ages in Europe.

Major divisions, separated as a result of differences in doctrine and practice, are the Eastern or Orthodox Churches, the Roman Catholic Church, acknowledging the Bishop of Rome (the pope) as head, and the Protestant Churches stemming from the split with the Roman Church in the Reformation. All Christians recognize the authority of the Bible, read at public worship, which takes place at least every Sunday, the first day of the week, to celebrate the resurrection of Jesus Christ. Most Churches recognize at least two sacraments (baptism, and the Eucharist/ Mass/ Communion/ Lord's Supper) as essential. The impetus to spread Christianity to the non-Christian world in missionary movements, especially in the 19th and 20th centuries, resulted in the creation of numerically very strong Churches in the developing countries of Asia, Africa, and South America. A powerful ecumenical movement in the 20th century, promoted by, among others, the World Council of Churches, has sought to recover unity among divided Christians. ▷ Adventists; African Methodist Episcopal Church; Anabaptists; Anglo-Catholicism; architecture, Christian; art, Christian; Assemblies of God; Baptists; Bible; Brethren (in Christ); Calvinism; Christadelphians; Christian Science; Christians of St Thomas; Christology; Church of Scotland; Confessing Church; Congregationalism; Constantine I; Copts; Dutch Reformed Church; ecumenism; Episcopal Church, Protestant; evangelicalism; Friends, Society of; Greek Orthodox Church; heaven; hell; Jesus Christ; Judaism; Lutheranism; Mary; Methodism; millenarianism; Mormons; Nonconformists; North India, Church of; Orthodox Church; Pentecostalism; Presbyterianism; Protestantism; Reformation; Reformed Churches; Roman Catholicism; Russian Orthodox Church; sacrament; salvation; Salvation Army; secular Christianity; South India, Church of; United Church of Christ; Waldenses; World Council of Churches

Christianity, persecution of Christians have been persecuted by the State at various times, from Nero and the Roman emperors before Constantine to 20th-century Marxist and Islamic states. Such testing has often produced a more active and committed Christian community, bearing out Tertullian's famous observation that 'the blood of the martyrs is the seed of the church'. It is also true that during periods when Church and State have worked together, dominant Christian communities have often persecuted or oppressed minority Christian (or other, particularly Jewish) groups. The Crusades, for example, were experienced both as an attack by Christianity on Islam, and as a battle between the Western (Latin) and Eastern (Greek) churches. Such persecutions were undertaken for both political and religious reasons: to maintain social stability and to punish so-called heretics and schismatics for the good of their souls and as a warning to others. The Reformation and Counter-Reformation periods can supply many examples. The wish to escape such persecution or interference was a prime motive for 17th-century emigration from Europe to North America, and underlies the USA's constitutional separation of Church and State. The 20th century has seen severe persecutions of both Christians (the Armenian massacres in Turkey and Russia) and Jews (the Holocaust in Nazi Germany), but belief in religious freedom has gained a measure of international acceptance through the United Nations. ▷ anti-Semitism; Armenia, Christianity in; Church and State; Constantine I; Crusades; Holocaust; Tertullian; toleration

Christianity, sex and In Christian teaching marriage is the place for sex, as a unique expression of love between a man and a woman committed to each other for life. But marriage is not the greatest human good; it may have to be foregone (as in the vow of celibacy in monasticism) in order to do the will of God. There is also a more negative strain of thought in Christianity, going back to Augustine's view that original sin was transmitted through the sexual act, that distrusts sex (although its outright rejection by Montanism and Manichaeism were counted as heresies). Associated with this is an ambivalent attitude to women, connected with the image of Eve the temptress. A few women, like the Virgin Mary and a handful of outstanding female saints, are highly honoured, but women are allowed no place in the priesthood or official ministry of most churches.
Many Christians practise artificial contraception, including Roman Catholics, for whom its banning was reinforced in 1968 by the encyclical *Humanae vitae*. Some accept abortion under certain circumstances, and some question the biblical and traditional rejection of homosexuality. Others, who wish to maintain traditional teaching within the churches, would nevertheless support civil rights movements that opposed social or legal discrimination against women, homosexuals, or other minority groups. ▷ Augustine, St (of Hippo); Manichaeism; marriage/divorce, Christian; monasticism; Montanism; original sin; Christianity, women in

Christianity, women in Feminist theology, especially since mid 20th-century movements for women's liberation, argues that men have used the Bible to subjugate women and that there is an unacceptable male bias in theology and church organization. God is usually described in terms associated with maleness, hymns often assume by their language that all believers are men, and women (if not now cast in the role of Eve-like temptresses or as distractions from the spiritual life) are given passive or secondary roles. A few, like the Virgin Mary and a handful of outstanding female saints, are highly honoured; but women are allowed no place in the priesthood in Roman Catholicism or the Orthodox Church. The Church of England, under pressure from sister churches of the Anglican Communion who have gone much further, has ordained women deacons since 1987. Further developments are hampered by fear of causing a split in the Church or endangering reunion talks with Catholicism or Orthodoxy. Even those Protestant churches worldwide that now give women official parity with men (approximately one third) often make them subservient in ministry and function, despite the fact that they have, like Catholicism's reliance on nuns, depended on women for much foreign mission work.
Arguments for and against the ordination of women to a large extent revolve around the interpretation of scripture. Were the practice of Jesus (appointing only male apostles, although he had a number of important female supporters and friends) and the teaching of Paul (on the headship of man over woman) necessary adaptations to the cultural situation of the time or a permanent guide to the Church, however social norms might change? Or, as supporters of women's rights argue, has the time now come for Paul's other teaching (Galatians 3.28) that 'in Christ' there are no separate categories of 'male' and 'female', to be realized to the same degree as it was eventually accepted in both Church and society that there is no permanent division of humanity into the 'slave' and the 'free'? ▷ feminist theology; Christianity, sex and; ministry, Christian

Christianity in Africa The origins of African Christianity are unknown. The New Testament ascribes the carrying of Christ's cross to a man from North Africa (Luke 23.26) and describes the conversion of an official from the Sudanese kingdom of Meröe (Acts 8.26–40), stories that are firmly retained in modern African Christian consciousness.
Egypt and Roman North Africa had flourishing Christian communities by the 2nd century CE, and these developed as two of the principal centres of early Christian life and thought. A 4th-century shipwreck led to the foundation of a church in the Horn of Africa, the seed of Ethiopian Christianity. By 600CE Christianity had spread across Africa almost to the physical limits of the ancient world: the Sahara, the Atlas mountains, the Upper Nile

rapids. Thereafter, however, with the rise of Islam and the Arab conquest, the churches of Egypt and Sudan were eroded; a series of developments virtually extinguished the Christianity of Roman Africa; the Ethiopian Church was cut off from the larger Christian communities.

A new chapter of Christian implantation began in the late 15th century as Catholic missionaries accompanied Portuguese exploration, trade and settlement along the West African coast, along and around the lower Zaire river and southwards, and in Mozambique. The most striking development was the wholly African Christian kingdom of Kongo. However, by the 18th century the Catholic presence, outside Angola and Mozambique, had faded. A new impetus came, however, from the Protestant churches, especially of Europe. African former slaves from the New World founded the first modern church of tropical Africa in Sierra Leone in 1792; Sierra Leone was to play a major part in the spread of Christianity elsewhere in West Africa. Around the same time missionary work was beginning in South Africa. Not until the 1840s, and then on a very restricted scale, did missions reach East Africa; not until the 1880s, in Uganda, was a significant response seen there. By this time Roman Catholic activity had resumed on a large scale, with France now in the forefront, and new missionary orders developed specifically for African service. Missions were well established before the division of Africa among the European powers took place in the 1880s. A notable movement towards Christianity occurred during and after World War I in West Africa, partly due to charismatic African figures (the prophet William Wadé Harris being the best known).

The first generations of nationalist and post-independence leaders were much influenced by mission education and church experience. In 1900, there were perhaps 10 million professing Christians in the African continent; in the early 1990s there are probably between 200 and 300 million, making sub-Saharan Africa one of the world's most concentrated areas of Christianity. In the 20th century numerical growth has been accompanied by developing forms of the Church, differing from the Western model and collectively known as African Independent churches. In most areas a vernacular name is used for the God of the Bible, thus rooting Christianity locally.

Contemporary African Christianity is often engaged with such questions as the relation of the Christian faith to the traditional religious past; healing (against a background of minimal medical services and deep-set belief in the spiritual causation of illness); the development of indigenous modes of worship; attitudes to the ancestors (amid an understanding of the family in which ancestors play a vital part). In Southern Africa, issues include the struggle for Black liberation (political, economic, psychological and theological); and in some countries there is the problem of relations between Christianity and Islam in a politically volatile situation. ▷ African Independent churches; Ethiopian churches; Harris, William Wadé

Christianity in Armenia Armenia was the first nation to make Christianity the state religion, after St Gregory the Illuminator (c.240–332) baptized King Tiradates III in 301. St Mesrob (c.345–440) translated the Bible into Armenian in the 5th century. The Armenian Apostolic Church rejected the findings of the Council of Chalcedon (451) and so became classed as monophysite (deemed to hold that the incarnate Christ had a single, divine nature, and so was too unlike human beings to be able to save them), resisting reunion with the Roman or Greek churches. Some Armenians belong to a Uniate church that is in communion with Rome. Armenia was divided between the Byzantine and Roman empires in 390, the start of centuries of foreign domination by Persians, Arabs, Mongols, Turks and Russians. Armenian Christians have endured much persecution. Over one million were massacred or deported from the Turkish Ottoman Empire (now Turkey) between 1915 and 1917, as part of a process that was to reduce the Christian population of Turkey from 20 per cent to less than 1 per cent by 1970. In Soviet Armenia (founded 1920) the church experienced state suppression, but evangelical revival since the 1970s has resulted in claims that half the population now attend church ▷ Chalcedon, Council of; Uniate churches

Christianity in Australasia The first major encounter of Christianity with any part of Australasia came with a Catholic mission to Guam in 1668. Further missionary effort was delayed until the end of the 18th century, with the London Missionary Society in the lead, following the new Western interest in the Pacific which had been stimulated by the voyages of Cook and Baugainville. By 1816 Christianity was the 'natural profession' in Tahiti; the Wesleyans later saw similar success in Tonga. In each case conversion took place in turbulent times and with the assistance of strong rulers. Early success also came to the American mission in Hawaii. Other places proved resistant, and response varied from island to island. A critical development came with the emergence of churches in Samoa and the Cook Islands (Raratonga) which sent large numbers of Polynesian evangelists to other islands. Roman Catholic missions appeared from 1827. Early response to Christianity in Polynesia was often in terms of indigenous ideas of *mana* and *tabu*, the new religion being seen as possessing greater power, and requiring proper practice of a ritual code; however, religious revivals often followed a generation or two after the first major impact.

In New Zealand, after a long period of rejection, the Maori moved towards Christianity in large numbers in the 1830s and 1840s. Massive white settlement, however, created resistance and probably inhibited growth of an indigenous Maori church; Maori Christianity was for some time an appendage of the white (*pakeha*) church. The existence of the Maori translation of the Bible, however, assisted Maori religious revivals and Maori versions of Christianity, such as Ringatu. The Ratana movement began as revival and led to a new Maori expression of Christianity, associated with political consciousness and stress on land rights.

During the 19th century, prior to the large-scale aquisitions by the colonial powers, Polynesia and Fiji presented a series of Christian Pacific states. (In Fiji the importation under colonial rule of a large population of Hindu plantation workers complicated the situation.) Christian penetration of most Melanesian societies was slower, but by the 20th century islands of the Solomons, New Hebrides (Vanuatu) and others had large Christian populations. Melanesia has also seen many new religions, often (though not invariably) linked to the idea of 'cargo' or supernatural wealth. By contrast with Africa, 'Independent churches' displaying indigenous versions of Christianity are not common (an exception is the Christian Fellowship Church in the Solomons). On Tanna (in Vanuatu) the John Frum cargo movement seems to have replaced Christianity as the main religious profession. Papua New Guinea and Irian Jaya, which together make up the mountainous island of New Guinea, are still seeing Christian expansion; the latter, now incorporated into Indonesia, also has Islamic settlements.

Australian religious history reflects the conflict in lifestyle between the white invaders and the Aboriginal population. Though a majority of Aboriginals became Christian, their conversion generally followed the breakdown of traditional life; more recently some reconciliation of Christianity and traditional lifestyles is being seen. White Australia adopted a secular state; its expressions of Christianity reflect not dissimilar patterns to those of Western Europe. ▷ Australian Aboriginal religion; Christian Fellowship Church; Maori religion; tabu

Christianity in Eastern Europe Christianity has a long history in this region. The apostle Paul or his associates may have preached in Illyricum, the Roman province corresponding to modern Yugoslavia. Bulgaria, Hungary and Poland were Christianized in the 9th and 10th centuries. East Germany was deeply affected by the 16th-century Protestant Reformation. Twentieth-century Eastern Europe has been principally shaped by the two World Wars, with many geographical boundaries being fixed following World War I and communism imposed after World War II. Czechoslovakia and Yugoslavia were created in 1918, bringing together culturally and religiously separate areas: Catholicism and Protestantism in Czechoslovakia; Orthodoxy and Catholicism in Yugoslavia. East Germany, split off from West Germany from 1949 to 1990, was chiefly Protestant (though a quarter of the population expressed no religious beliefs), so the reunified nation has become slightly more Protestant than Catholic.

Church-state relations under communism have varied. Roman Catholicism's unique position in Poland, where 95 per cent claim to be Christian believers, was strengthened in 1978 by the election of Cardinal Karol Wojtyla (1920–) as Pope John Paul II, but Catholicism in Hungary lost the privileges it had enjoyed before 1949. The Bulgarian and Romanian Orthodox Churches enjoyed some protection against religious persecution in return for supporting their governments; other Christian denominations in these countries remained more independent, though subject to sporadic persecution and harassment. Church-state relations were more relaxed in Yugoslavia than elsewhere in Eastern Europe, but its neighbour Albania, a Communist republic independent of Moscow, in 1967 declared itself the 'first atheist state in the world', and set about destroying all forms of organized religion, both Christian and Muslim.

Christianity in Latin America The first large-scale encounters of Christian Europe with Central and South America took place with the Aztec in Mexico and the Inca in Peru. Both empires were only a century or so

old, and each had an empire-wide state religion with an official priesthood. The Spanish conquest and the depopulation because of war and disease which followed brought the collapse of the empires and the state religions, leaving the religion of rural peoples tied to local sacred places and ancestral kin. This religion had always been largely independent of the state religions. As European peoples entered other parts of the continent they met peoples with similar rural religious practices and no other old or 'high' civilizations. Early missionary effort (Franciscan and Jesuit) sought to introduce Christianity on the model known in Spain. This involved the destruction of pre-Christian shrines and the mass introduction of the indigenous people to Christian teaching. Missionaries also sought to restrain the rapacity and brutality of Spanish adventurers and settlers, leading to political conflict and compromise and sometimes to separate church-directed and church-protected communities (eg Jesuit reservations in Paraguay). Gradually, and in varying degrees, a new Catholic society arose, especially on the basis of people of mixed race and notably with the emergence of locally-born priests who had spoken Amerindian languages from childhood (peoples of mountain and deep forest areas were often left outside). The resultant Christianity was not, however, wholly on the Spanish model; translation into Quechua, Aymara and other vernaculars introduced new dimensions. Sometimes popular religion was little changed in externals; the same festivals and dances took place at the same time as Christian rites and with the old gods and goddesses transformed into saints. A further factor was the arrival in Brazil and Cuba and the Caribbean fringes of numbers of Africans for the plantations. These were rapidly brought formally into the Church, but the African beliefs and practices which they brought still have a strong effect on religion. There was no doubt, however, of the strength of Catholic devotion; and the Church's acknowledgement of a Mexican Indian's vision of the Virgin in 1531, a virgin moreover with dark, Indian features (Our Lady of Guadelupe) was a recognition that the new Christian lands were not going to be governed entirely by the traditions of the old.
The break with Spain and the emergence of new republics in the early 19th century had little immediate effect on the church, but new countries often wanted to encourage immigration and some, especially Argentina, acquired substantial Protestant communities. The developments of the 20th century have been striking. Central America and some South American countries have seen a rapid growth of Protestantism, and Latin American Protestantism has frequently taken a Pentecostal form. Within the Roman Catholic Church there have been developments such as the theology of liberation—radical criticism of traditional Christianity for its toleration of oppression and injustice—and the emergence of the 'basic ecclesial communities', small socially-concerned Christian groups expressing liberation theology in church life. ▷ Afro-Brazilian religions; Inca religion; liberation theology

Christianity in Russia The first Christian sovereign of Russia was St Vladimir I (c.956–1015), who was baptized and adopted Christianity as the state religion in 988. Monasticism was established soon afterwards and spread rapidly. The Russian Orthodox Church achieved independence in 1589, with the creation of the patriarchate of Moscow, but became completely state-controlled under Peter the Great (1676–1725) in 1720. The association of the Church with the czars led to severe persecution following the Communist Revolution of 1917. About half of the 126 million people killed or sent to prisons and labour camps for political offences between 1917 and the death of Joseph Stalin (1879–1953) were Christians. There was renewed persecution from 1959 to 1964 under Nikita Khrushchev (1894–1971).
Since then, Church-state relations have varied. Limited privileges were accorded to registered congregations that were under the jurisdiction of the state-controlled hierarchy of the Orthodox Church. Clergy who rejected this hierarchy, and unregistered or illegal congregations of all Christian denominations—including Uniates in the western Ukraine, Baptists and Pentecostalists—faced sporadic or sustained opposition. The so-called 'underground church' also included many thousands of secret listeners to religious radio broadcasts from the West.
The attempts of Mikhail Gorbachev (1931–) to liberalize Soviet society from 1985 onwards through *glasnost* ('openness') and *perestroika* ('restructuring'), were favourable to religious believers, but by 1991 the accelerating breakdown of the Soviet Union into a looser association of independent republics made predictions of future developments difficult. Whatever happens is likely to reinforce the regional differences that have existed since the Soviet Union's inception. Outside the Russian republic itself, Armenia and Georgia have strong independent Orthodox Churches, Roman Catholicism is widespread in Lithu-

ania, while the six central Asian republics are overwhelmingly Muslim. ▷ Armenia, Christianity in; Uniate churches

Christianity in the Middle East Christianity is of Middle Eastern origin. Beginning among Palestinian Jews it became in the course of four centuries the dominant faith of all the lands of the East Mediterranean, and a substantial factor in the rest of the Middle East. The emergence of a new world power based in Arabia first brought Islam to these lands in the 7th century CE, and a gradual but steady erosion of the Christian population followed. Christianity has survived in some degree, however, in all parts of the Middle East outside Arabia. The majority of Middle Eastern Christians belong to churches which were there before the rise of Islam, their differences arising from developments in the early Christian centuries. Description of these churches is complicated since terminology and interpretation common in the West is sometimes strange or unacceptable to the churches themselves.

In general, the ancient churches of the Middle East belong to three main families: 1 Churches of the Eastern Orthodox tradition, the same family as the Greek and Russian Orthodox churches. Jerusalem, Antioch, Alexandria and Constantinople, each a major centre of the early church, are still each the focus of a patriarchate. That of Constantinople has 'first among equals' status; that of Antioch (Arabic in language and outlook, with substantial populations in Syria and Lebanon), is the largest. That of Jerusalem, the leading church on the West Bank and in Jordan, has an Arab membership and clergy but, for historical reasons, Greek bishops. All the patriarchates except Jerusalem have important immigrant congregations outside the Middle East, and Alexandria has a lively daughter church among Africans in Kenya and Uganda. 2 Churches of the Oriental tradition which reflect the unacceptability to many Syrian and Egyptian Christians of the formulations of the Council of Chalcedon (451CE) and its association with imperial domination. The missionary enthusiasm of one of these churches, called 'Nestorian' in the West, took Christianity across Central Asia and into China between the 6th and 13th centuries. Today, the 'Church of the East', or Assyrian Church, is a mere fragment, centred in Iraq but with half its membership in the USA. Among those churches called Monophysite in the West, the Church of Armenia (the first Christian nation) has also seen frequent persecution and political difficulties. The Syrian Orthodox Church is significant in Syria, Iraq, Lebanon and Turkey, as well as in South India. Strongest of all the ancient churches today is the Coptic Orthodox Church of Egypt, encompassing more than 12 per cent of the national population. 3 Uniate, or 'Eastern Rite' churches are former parts of ancient churches of the Eastern or Oriental traditions now in communion with the Roman Catholic Church, but retaining their own liturgies, language and customs. They are known as the Chaldean (of some influence in Iraq), Melkite, Syrian Catholic, Armenian Catholic and Coptic Catholic churches. The largest of them, the Maronite Church of Lebanon, disclaims the title uniate, claiming always to have been in union with Rome.

In addition to the ancient Eastern churches, Roman Catholic, Anglican and Protestant churches are found in many parts of the Middle East, deriving from immigration or missionary work (usually directed to the Muslim community) from Europe or North America. The Christian population in the Gulf states consists principally of immigrant workers from India (mostly Catholic, but some Protestant) and other countries eastward. ▷ Christianity; Islam

Christian Kabbalah A period in Christian history from about 1400 to 1700, when the Jewish Kabbalah was interpreted in terms of Christian thought, and Christianity was seen as fulfilling the Kabbalah. Pico della Mirandola (1463–94) showed how the Kabbalah demonstrated Christ's divinity, how the Jewish threefold sephirah confirmed the doctrine of the Trinity, and how the Kabbalah's insights coincided with the Christian mysticism found in the neo-platonism of Pseudo-Dionysius. Johannes Rechlin (1455–1522) argued for the importance of the Kabbalah and its mystical interpretation of numbers, words and sacred geometry, both as a confirmation of the truth of Christian theology, and as a means to convert Jews to Christianity, and the following century witnesed many conversions of Jews to Christianity, albeit for other reasons in addition to the persuasiveness of Christian Kabbalah. Since the 18th century its influence has waned, and its theory that the Jewish Kabbalah is proved or fulfilled by Christianity is no longer seen to be relevant or viable. ▷ Kabbalah; neo-platonism

Christian Science A movement, founded by Mary Baker Eddy in the 19th century, which seeks to reinstate the original Christian message of salvation from all evil, including sickness and disease as well as sin. The first

Church of Christ, Scientist, was established in 1879 in Boston, USA, followed in 1892 by the present worldwide organization, with its headquarters in Boston. The Bible and Eddy's *Science and Health with Key to the Scriptures* (1875) are the principal texts of the movement. God, who is seen as both maternal and paternal, is believed to be spirit and the good creator; accordingly, sin, sickness, death, and matter itself only seem real to mistaken human belief. Health is restored, not by recourse to medical treatment, but by applying to all aspects of life practices in keeping with the principle of divine harmony. Members must not turn to orthodox medical practitioners, but are to seek help from special Christian Science healers, whose training is based on the Bible and *Science and Health*. In recent years, mainly because of recourse to outside medical help, the number of followers has declined. The internationally known newspaper, *The Christian Science Monitor*, is published by the society. ▷ Christianity; Eddy, Mary

Christians of St Thomas A group of Indian Christians living on the Malabar coast. They take their name from the apostle Thomas, who is said to have brought Christianity to India, though they were founded by Nestorians in the 5th century. They are now part of the Syrian Church, and have their own patriarch. ▷ Nestorians; Orthodox Church; Thomas, St

Christian year This takes its shape from weekly (Sunday) and annual (Easter) celebrations of the resurrection of Christ on the first day of the week (Matthew 28.1; Mark 16.2; Luke 24.1; John 20.1). The first Christians met for worship on the first day of the week, rather than the seventh (the Jewish Sabbath). The date of Easter is related to that of the Jewish Passover and new moon, so (on the Roman method of calculation) it can fall on any Sunday between 21 March and 25 April.

The Western Church's year begins with the season of Advent (celebrating Christ's first and second (future) coming), a four-week period of preparation for the nativity at Christmas (25 December). This is celebrated in the Eastern Church at Epiphany (6 January), which the West links with the baptism of Jesus. The Eastern liturgical calendar celebrates the ten Sundays before Easter. In the West the 50-day period before Easter, called Lent, begins on Ash Wednesday. It marks the period of Christ's temptations in the desert (Matthew 4.1–11; Mark 1.13; Luke 4.1–13) and is used as a time of spiritual self-examination. Good Friday (marking the crucifixion of Jesus) and Easter are followed 40 days later by Ascension Day (a Thursday) and 10 days afterwards by Pentecost (or Whitsunday). Trinity Sunday, celebrating the mystery of Trinity, is the following Sunday.

During the medieval period many other festivals connected with the Virgin Mary and the saints were added to the liturgical calendar. Protestant churches abandoned these commemorations at the Reformation, and many still keep only Sundays and Easter as days of special celebration. The liturgical calendars of churches of the Anglican Communion allow, but do not necessarily require, commemoration of the anniversaries of locally or universally acclaimed Christians. ▷ Ascension, Feast of; Christmas; crucifixion; Easter; Epiphany; Jesus Christ; Pentecost; saint, Christian view of; Trinity

Christmas The Christian festival commemorating the birth of Jesus, observed annually by most branches of the church on 25 December but by some denominations in January. The practice of celebrating Christmas on 25 December began in the Western Church early in the 4th century; it was a Christian substitute for the pagan festival held on that date to celebrate the birth of the unconquered sun. Many Christmas customs are of non-Christian origin; for example, Christmas trees (introduced into Britain from Germany) and holly and mistletoe decorations are of north European pagan origin. The first Christmas cards were produced in the 1840s. ▷ Ancient European religion; Christian year; Jesus Christ

Christology The orderly study of the significance of Jesus Christ for Christian faith. Traditionally the term was restricted to the study of the person of Christ, and in particular to the way in which he is both human and divine. Latterly, an emphasis on the inseparability of Christ's person and work has meant that Christology often encompasses enquiry into his saving significance (*soteriology*) as well. ▷ Christianity; soteriology

Chronicles, or Paralipomenon, Books of Two books of the Hebrew Bible/Old Testament, originally a single work, perhaps also linked with the books of Ezra and Nehemiah, thereby presenting a history of Judah from its beginnings to its restoration under Ezra and Nehemiah. It has many parallels with the Books of Samuel and Kings, but the Chronicler's interests lie predominantly in the

Temple and its cult. ▷ Ezra/Kings/Nehemiah/Samuel, Book(s) of; Old Testament; Temple, Jerusalem

Chrysostom, St John (c.347–407) Syrian churchman, and one of the Doctors of the Church, born in Antioch, and named *Chrysostomos* from the Greek meaning 'Golden-Mouthed'. Trained by his pious mother Anthusa, he studied oratory for the career of advocate; but, in his 23rd year, was baptized and ordained an *anagnóstés* or 'Reader'. After six years spent as a monk in the mountains, illness forced him to return in 380 to Antioch, where he was ordained deacon in 381 and priest in 386. The eloquence and earnestness of his preaching secured for him the reputation of the greatest orator of the Church; and in 398 the emperor Arcadius made him Archbishop of Constantinople. Chrysostom bestowed much of his revenues on hospitals, sought to reform the lives of the clergy, and sent monks as missionaries into Scythia, Persia and other lands. His zealous reproof of vices moved the empress Eudocia to have him deposed and banished in 403—first to Nicaea, and then to the Taurus mountains, and finally to Pityus on the Black Sea. Compelled to travel there on foot, with his bare head exposed to a burning sun, the old man died on the way to Comana, in Pontus. His body was brought to Constantinople and reburied with honour in 438. His works are numerous, and consist of *Homilies*, *Commentaries* on the whole Bible, part of which have perished, *Epistles*, *Treatises* on Providence, the Priesthood, etc, and *Liturgies*. His feast day is 27 January.

Chthonian gods The Greeks sometimes distinguished between the gods of heaven and 'chthonian' or earth gods (from *chthon*, meaning earth). The most prominent chthonians were Hades, god of the underworld, and his wife Persephone (who, however, according to myth, commuted between the upper and lower worlds); there were lesser chthonians too, such as the Eumenides or Furies, and even 'heavenly' gods such as Zeus or Hermes could also have a chthonian aspect. Since the earth was seen as the source of life and growth, the chthonians had a positive as well as a frightening side: Persephone was the daughter of Demeter, goddess of corn, and was closely linked with agricultural fertility herself. Scholars have often supposed the worship of the chthonian gods predated that of the Olympians in Greece (as some myths in part suggest); but in fact the two groups only gain their full meaning by contrast with one another, like the black and white pieces in chess. ▷ Greek religion; Olympian pantheon; underworld

Chthonian religion A Greek concept indicating reverence for the gods of the earth. It derives from the Greek word *chthon*, meaning earth. Chthonian religion, with its emphasis on veneration for gods of the earth, contrasted with Greek Olympian religion, which emphasized veneration for gods of the sky. In addition to being associated with the sky, Zeus and the other gods identified with Mount Olympus were of Indo-European origin whereas the Chthonian gods were of Aegean origin. The Chthonian gods were associated with the fertility of the earth and with the under-world of the dead. Amphiaros and Trophonius were examples of Chthonian gods; there was also an apparent attempt to assimilate them into Zeus under the title of Zeus Chthonius. ▷ Greek religion

Chuang Tzu (c.369–c.286BCE) Taoist philosopher, born in Meng in the Sung state of China. A minor government official, he became famous as the main author of the key Taoist work that bears his name, the *Chuang Tzu*. Together with the *Tao Te Ching* it is the most important work in philosophical Taoism, and has influenced not only the Taoist tradition but also the Buddhist tradition and Chinese life in general. It is more personal, more anecdotal and less political than the *Tao Te Ching*. It stresses the notion of the Tao as an all-embracing Way by means of which everything is produced, sustained and transformed. It cannot be summed up in words which obscure it, it must be intuited as a whole. The *Chuang Tzu* advocates naturalness and spontaneity rather than formality and moral order, an inner mysticism rather than an intellectual education, yielding rather than aggression, and creative inaction rather than activism and ethical striving. It complements the opposite concepts of the Confucian tradition within the wider whole of Chinese religion. In its emphasis on natural beauty, harmony and seeking for inner emptiness of the mind, it anticipates some of the insights of the Chan and Zen traditions. ▷ Chan; Taoism; Tao Te Ching; Zen Buddhism

Chu Hsi (1130–1200) Chinese philosopher, born in Fulkien, China, the leading architect of the neo-Confucianism that dominated China until this century. Having passed the government exams at the age of 19 he obtained a succession of civil service posts, but his real contribution was intellectual. He established or revived various Confucian academies, including the White Deer Grotto in the present Kiangsi province. He reorganized the Confucian Canon to include a group of Four Books: the *Analects of Confucius*, the *Book of Mencius*, the *Great Learning*, and the *Doctrine of the Mean*, on which he wrote commentaries. They became the basis of the Chinese civil service examinations from 1313 to 1905, and his work thus moulded Chinese culture and philosophy for 600 years. He reinterpreted and systematized the Confucian tradition by gathering together, into a brilliant synthesis, insights from Confucius, Mencius, the Great Learning, the Doctrine of the Mean, the earlier neo-Confucians, and even the Taoists and Buddhists whom he outwardly opposed. It is a striking coincidence that at a parallel time in history great syntheses were being created elsewhere in the world by Aquinas and Bonaventure in the Christian tradition, Maimonides in the Jewish tradtion, Ramanuja in the Hindu tradition, and (somewhat earlier) al-Ghazali in the Muslim tradition. Towards the end of his life Chu Hsi fell into trouble because of his radical philosophical opinions but nearly 1000 people attended his funeral and before long his position was vindicated. His school became known as the school of principle (*li*) and, although another school known as the school of mind developed in neo-Confucianism due to the work of Wang Yang Ming (1472–1529), it was Chu Hsi's thought that triumphed. ▷ Ghazali, Abu Mohammed al-; Aquinas, St Thomas; Bonaventure, St; Confucian Canon; li; Maimonides; Mencius; neo-Confucianism; Ramanuja; Wang Yang-Ming

Chung Yuan (Chung Yüan) The Chinese Festival of All Souls, or Hungry Ghosts, which is predominantly Buddhist and occurs on the fifteenth day of the seventh lunar month. From this day until the end of the month those who have died unprepared—the homeless, those without descendants, and those without a grave—have offerings made to help them in their time of need with the aim of preventing them from causing mischief. The offerings include such things as paper houses, paper money, clothes and food that it is thought will be of assistance in the spirit world. The paper objects are burnt in local fires and sometimes thrown into rivers to help deceased souls who have drowned and have no graves. In Buddhist temples worship is held on behalf of hungry souls, and paper boats are sometimes made which are burnt on the festival day, so that the unprepared deceased souls can escape from their predicament into another rebirth which will help them to the eventual goal of nirvana. ▷ ancestor reverence, Chinese; festivals, Chinese; funerary practices, Chinese; nirvana

Chung Yung The Chinese name of a small Confucian book entitled *The Doctrine of the Mean*. It was originally a chapter in the *Li Chi* (The Records of Ritual and Protocol) compiled during the 2nd century BCE, but it was given special prominence by the great neo-Confucian philosopher Chu Hsi (1130—1200). It was one of the Four Books that he added to the Confucian Canon, the other three being the *Analects of Confucius*, the *Book of Mencius*, and the *Great Learning*. They became the basis of the Chinese civil service examinations from 1313 to 1905. The *Chung Yung* is traditionally ascribed to the grandson of Confucius, and it advocated the Golden Mean or the Middle Way. As *Analects* 6.27 puts it: 'How transcendent is the moral power of the Middle Way'; the *Chung Yung* advocates moderation and compromise as helpful philosophies in politics and in human relations. ▷ Chu Hsi; Confucian Canon

church In architecture, a building used for public religious worship, especially Christian. First adapted by the early Christians from the Roman basilicas and martyrias, it was later developed in the Romanesque architecture of the 11th and 12th centuries into the now more usual Latin cross plan, typically consisting of nave with side aisles, transepts, chancel, and apse, such as Pisa Cathedral (mainly 1063–1118) and the Panthéon (Sainte Geneviève), Paris (1757–90), architect J G Soufflot. The centrally-planned circular or Greek cross plan was briefly favoured in Renaissance Italy, such as Santa Maria della Consolazione, Todi (1508–1604). In the 20th century, church design has become increasingly eclectic, most famously the Chapel of Notre Dame, Ronchamp, France (1950–5), architect Le Corbusier; the Roman Catholic Cathedral, Liverpool (1960–7), architect Frederick Gibberd; and also in numerous smaller, usually urban churches. ▷ cathedral; architecture, Christian

Church, Christian The term 'church' is applied in several ways. It may refer to the totality of believers in Jesus Christ since the resurrection (also known as the 'church universal', the 'invisible church', or the 'communion of saints'), to particular historical divisions (Roman Catholic Church, Baptist Church), and to local congregations and the buildings in which they worship. The New Testament describes the church by several images, including 'people of God' and 'body of Christ'. The Nicene Creed confesses belief in a church that is 'one' (undivided), 'holy' (in call and life), 'catholic' (universal in extent and membership—no type or class of person may be excluded), and 'apostolic' (based on the apostles' teaching). The Reformers (who, like the Orthodox Church in 1054, rejected the pope's claim to sole apostolic authority and guardianship of the one true church) identified the church as the place where the Gospel was truly preached, the sacraments rightly administered and church discipline upheld. Recent Roman Catholic thinking about the church has an outward or missionary dimension, describing it as the sacrament (sign and example) of the kingdom of God and the unity of humankind.

The scandal of disunity in the church, which was emphasized in the 19th and early 20th centuries by missionaries exporting the historical divisions of European Christianity to colonial countries, has been a strong motive behind ecumenical co-operation in the World Council of Churches. There have been a few reunions among Protestant churches on a national level (as with the Church of South India and the Church of North India), and other discussions or negotiations continue. Some Anglo-Catholics argue that Roman Catholicism's traditional claims to absolute authority might eventually be modified to the extent that the pope could become the world focus of Christian unity. Others (particularly from the expanding churches of the Third World) would say that discussions about church unity are of negligible importance compared to the need to tackle issues of social disunity, poverty, justice, and the survival of the planet. ▷ ecumenism; kingdom of God; Nicene Creed; North India, Church of; papacy; South India, Church of; World Council of Churches

Church and State The relation between Church and State in Christianity is governed by the belief that ultimate allegiance is due to God alone. Christians can support the State when it fulfils its role of ensuring a stable society in which Christian values can be pursued (as the apostle Paul viewed the Roman Empire of his day), but when the State opposes Christian belief and principles it must be resisted (as the Book of Revelation portrays the Roman empire of a later period), even to the point of accepting martyrdom. With Constantine's acceptance of Christianity, long periods ensued in which the interests of Church (Roman Catholicism) and State (the Holy Roman Empire) were often identical. This was still true, though in a more fragmented way, at the Reformation, with the emergence of European nation-states accompanied by the formation of State churches. Such close relations between Church and State could lead to a confusion of roles in both directions: indiscriminate Church support for State policies or State persecution of (Christian or other) religious minorities. Historically, reactions to this situation have included **1** the formation of churches with no state connections; **2** the disestablishment of State churches; **3** constitutional separation between Church and State (as in the USA); and **4** calls for states to be religiously neutral and guarantee freedom of religion for all (a principle actively denied by totalitarian states). ▷ Constantine; persecution; Revelation, Book of; Roman Catholocism; sects, Christian view of; toleration

Church discipline All Church law and custom that is not prescribed by Scripture and, more particularly, the discipline or way of life required of Church members. Both may be codified in canon law or in compilations such as *The Book of Common Order* (1556) and *The First Book of Discipline* (1560) developed by John Knox from Calvin's ideals, as put into practice in Geneva. Individuals who fail to keep the Church's discipline may be admonished, as in the early Church (Matthew 18, 1 Corinthians 5). The ultimate sanction against offenders is excommunication or refusal of fellowship and the sacrament of Holy Communion (Eucharist), and (in situations where Church and State work hand in hand) handing over to the state for punishment. The term 'discipline' is also used (in the sense of spiritual or monastic discipline) to refer to practices of self-denial such as fasting, and (as 'the discipline') to a type of scourge of knotted cords used in penance. ▷ Church and State

Churches of Christ A religious movement whose origins lie in the work of Thomas and Alexander Campbell and Barton Stone in the 19th century in the USA. It preaches a restoration of New Testament Christianity, and rejects all creeds and confessions. Later there was a split which led to the Disciples of Christ being distinguished from the Churches of Christ. ▷ Christianity

Church of England The official state Church of England, a national Church having both Protestant and Catholic features, based on episcopal authority, and with the monarch of England formally as its head. It originated when Henry VIII broke with the Roman

Catholic Church (c.1532–4) and was declared by Parliament to be 'the supreme head on earth of the English Church'. The Church remained largely Catholic in character, however, until reforms of doctrine and liturgy under Edward VI, when the new Book of Common Prayer appeared (1549, 1552), the later edition being significantly more Protestant in its features. Under Elizabeth I the moderately Protestant set of doctrinal statements, known as the Thirty-nine Articles, emerged. She and James I resisted efforts towards a Catholic revival and Puritan attempts to take a more Calvinist stance, but under Charles I a presbyterian form of government was temporarily established until the episcopacy and Prayer Book were restored under Charles II.

While a general attitude of toleration now exists, the tension of Catholic and Protestant inclinations tends to persist in the Church of England, as well as the tensions introduced by the newer influences of evangelicalism and liberalism. The Church of England today consists of some 44 dioceses in the two provinces of Canterbury and York, with over 16000 churches and other places of worship. Local parishes are arranged into rural deaneries and dioceses, with each diocese led by a bishop and sometimes assisted by a suffragan or assistant bishop. The parish structure is fundamental to the organization of the church, but increasingly team ministries, priests-in-charge, and non-stipendiary priests have found a place in addition to parish priests and curates. The Church also supports its own missionary organizations and societies. The largest societies are the Mothers' Union and the Church Army, the latter being engaged in social welfare work. In 1970 the General Synod was established for the purpose of reaching decisions and expressing views on issues of interest to the Church. It also appoints several committees, boards, and councils to advise it. There are over 500 members, divided between the three houses: the Houses of Clergy, of Bishops, and of Laity. It meets three times a year and is presided over by the Archbishops of Canterbury and York. In addition, there are synods of clergy and laity at diocesan level.

The Church of England has especially close relations in Britain with the Church in Wales and the Scottish Episcopal Church. The spread of Anglicanism more widely through the world, particularly in Commonwealth countries, has given the Church of England a prominent role in the Anglican Communion at large. ▷ Anglican Communion; Book of Common Prayer; episcopacy; Protestantism; Reformation; Thirty-nine Articles

Church of Scotland The national Church in Scotland, founded at the Reformation of 1560 under the leadership of John Knox. It comprises a larger proportion of the population than most Protestant Churches in the English-speaking world, with a strong missionary tradition, especially in Africa and India. It maintains links with and supports many Churches in developing countries. It is presbyterian in its governing organization and discipline; laymen or elders (ordained) play a leading part with ministers in church courts at local, congregational level (in Kirk Session), district level (presbyteries, overseeing congregations in a given area), provincial synods, and the General Assembly. Ministers (women and men), who are ordained by presbytery, are alone authorized to administer the sacraments of baptism (of infants as well as adults) and the Lord's Supper (communion). Historically renowned for scholarship in Reformed theology, it has occupied a position in the world Reformed community out of proportion to its size. ▷ Knox, John; Presbyterianism; Protestantism; Reformed Churches; sacrament

Church of the New Jerusalem ▷ New Church

Church organization Following the fairly fluid organization of the early Church recorded in Acts and the Epistles, three main types of Church organization and government developed: episcopacy, presbyterianism, and independency.

Episcopacy holds to a threefold ministry of bishops, priests and deacons. The basic unit of the church is the parish under the charge of a priest, who may be assisted by the ministry of deacons. Parishes are grouped geographically into dioceses under a bishop, and dioceses into provinces under an archbishop or Metropolitan. In the Roman Catholic Church this hierarchy is governed by the pope. In the Anglican Communion (the worldwide fellowship of independent national Anglican Churches), the Archbishop of Canterbury is the senior Metropolitan, considered first among equals. In the Orthodox Church, bishops (whose areas are called parishes) come under patriarchs of self-governing (autocephalous) dioceses.

Presbyterianism follows Calvin in maintaining that presbyter and bishop in the New Testament denote the same office and that all presbyters have the same authority. Each local

congregation is governed by its teaching and ruling elders and ministered to by deacons. Presbyters from local congregations also govern in regional and national assemblies.
Independency argues that the New Testament never refers to regional or national churches. There is only the local congregation governed by all its members meeting together (as in Congregationalism) or by elected elders. Local churches may associate with others for mission or charitable work, for example, but such associations have no authority over them. ▷ Church, Christian; episcopacy; Presbyterianism

circuit riders Early itinerant Methodist preachers on horseback who regularly covered a circuit of churches and also carried their messages to new settlements. They were instrumental in the rapid expansion of early Methodism. ▷ Methodism

circumcision In males, the removal of all or part of the foreskin of the penis, in females the removal of some or all of the external genitalia. In males, it may be performed for health reasons, but the practice is of ancient origin as an important religious rite of initiation among Semites, African and Polynesian tribes, South American peoples and American Indians. Its motivation is complex: health, a covenant with the gods, entry to maturity or a particular group or class, insurance of immortality or against infertility. In Islam, it is obligatory, usually performed on boys between the ages of seven and thirteen. In Judaism, male babies are circumcized on the eighth day after birth, as an external sign of their entry into the people of God's covenant associated with Abraham (Genesis 17.9–14). So important is it that the word is sometimes used as a synonym for the covenant. In Christianity, the requirement of circumcision was early removed, baptism being considered the true circumcision (Colossians 2.11–15). Female circumcision, though not so widespread, may antedate male circumcision, and is still practised among certain tribes of Asia, Africa and South America, and by certain Muslims in India and Western Asia. ▷ covenant

Cistercians A religious order formed by Benedictine monks and led by St Robert of Molesme in Citeaux, France, in 1098, under a strict rule, with an emphasis on solitude, poverty, and simplicity. The order was prominent in the Middle Ages, with leaders including Bernard of Clairvaux. By the 13th century it had over 500 houses in Europe, but thereafter declined. In the 17th century it was divided into communities of Common Observance (now abbreviated SOCist) and of Strict Observance (in full, the Order of the Reformed Cistercians of the Strict Observance, abbreviated OCSO). The latter were revived in France after the Revolution by Trappists (former members of the monastery of La Trappe). Common Observance is now prominent in the USA and parts of Western Europe, with an abbot-general in Rome; Strict Observance, with a mother-house in Citeaux and an abbot in Rome, is active in France, Switzerland, England, and Poland. ▷ Benedictines; Bernard of Clairvaux, St; monasticism; Trappists

civil religion Within a society, the investing of certain social, civic or political traditions with religious or quasi-religious value. It is characterized by the observing of special festivals and rituals, honouring special political creeds, commemorating great events, rulers and heroes. Thus in certain societies, kings or rulers are worshipped, in Ancient Greece and Rome city states were honoured by public festivals and rites, and in the Middle Ages towns and cities developed their own quasi-religious feasts and rituals.
Civil religion tends to grow with and boost aspirations of nationalism, especially where traditional religion declines. Typical was the religion instituted in France during the period 1793–4, by Robespierre. This had its own rites and liturgies, celebrating the French Revolution, the revolutionary state and significant events and people in it. The growth of nationalism in the 19th century saw patriotism in various European countries and in the USA develop with quasi-religious fervour. Phrases like 'la belle France', 'Mother Russia', 'God's own country' (USA), 'the American Way of Life' and dates like 14 July in France or 4 July in the USA evoked a religious response and appropriate celebration.
According to the sociologist Émile Durkheim, in *The Elementary Forms of Religious Life* (1912), some form of religion must survive as long as there are human societies, since in his opinion the object of religious worship is not a transcendent God but the force of society. ▷ Durkheim, Émile; rituals

Clement of Alexandria, St (Titus Flavius Clemens) (c.150–c.215) Church Father, probably born in Athens, but lived chiefly in Alexandria. He became head of the catechetical school (c.180–201) and together with his pupil Origen made it a celebrated centre of learning, until he was forced to flee to Palestine during the persecutions of Emperor Severus. His chief surviving works are *Quis dives salvetur?* ('Who is the Rich Man that is Saved?') and the trilogy comprising *Protrepticus* ('Exhaltation to the Greeks'), *Paedagogus* ('The Tutor') and *Stromateis* ('Miscellanies'). His feast day is 5 December. ▷ Alexandria, Catechetical School of; Fathers of the Church; Origen

clergy Ordained ministers of the Christian or other religion, as holders of an allotted office, in contradistinction to the laity (the word comes from the Latin *clericus*, clerk, clergyman, priest, thus Anglican 'clerk in holy orders'). In Orthodox, Roman Catholic and Anglican churches, the term includes bishops, priests and deacons, also members of religious orders. In Protestant and non-episcopal churches, it includes ministers and pastors. Their appointment is by ordination or consecration, which is not only a human act but the sealing of a divine calling or vocation. The powers of the clergy include administration of the sacraments, preaching and the exercise of spiritual leadership in a congregation, hence their divine appointment. In hierarchical churches (ie Orthodox, Roman Catholic and Anglican), the powers of the priests and deacons are exercised with the authority of the bishop. In conciliar or non-episcopal churches (eg Presbyterian, Congregational, Baptist) there is no higher office in the Church than that of minister of the Word and Sacrament.

In some countries, clergy enjoy certain civil rights (following those introduced in the Roman Empire in the 4th and 5th centuries CE) such as the right to conduct weddings, immunity from jury service, and even the benefit of certain charges on land (eg 'tithes'). ▷ abbey; archbishop; archdeacon; bishop; canon; cardinal; curate; deacon; Holy Orders; ordination; priest; rector; sacrament; vicar

Codex Juris Canonici (Latin 'code of canon law') A code of canon or church law regulating the Roman Catholic Church. The codification, authorized by Pope Pius X in 1904, was completed in 1917, with revisions recommended by a commission set up in 1963. ▷ canon law; Roman Catholicism

Coke, Thomas (1747–1814) Welsh Methodist churchman, born in Brecon. He graduated in 1768 from Oxford, and became an Anglican curate in Somerset, but in 1777 joined the Methodists, and was attached to the London circuit. In 1784 he was appointed by John Wesley as the superintendent of the Methodist Church in America. He visited the USA nine times, and assumed the title of bishop in 1787. He died while crossing the Indian Ocean on a missionary voyage to Ceylon. He published, besides religious works, extracts from his American *Journals* (1790), a *History of the West Indies* (3 vols, 1808–11), and, with Henry Moore, a *Life of Wesley* (1792). ▷ Methodism; Wesley, John

Colossians, Letter to the New Testament writing attributed to Paul while he was in prison. It bears many similarities to the Letter to the Ephesians, but there is much current debate about whether the work is genuinely from Paul. It was apparently written to counter false teachers at Colossae who claimed a higher spiritual knowledge associated with an ascetic and ritualistic way of life and with the worship of angels (Colossians 2.8–23). ▷ asceticism; Ephesians, Letter to the; New Testament; Paul, St; Pauline Letters

Columba, St, also known as **Colmcille** ('Colm of the Churches') (521–97) Irish apostle of Christianity in Scotland, born into the royal warrior aristocracy of Ireland at Gartan in County Donegal. According to his 7th-century biographer, Adomnán, he studied under St Finnian at Clonard with St Ciaran. In 546 he founded the monastery of Derry. In 561, however, he was accused of having been involved in the bloody battle of Cuildreimhne, for which he was excommunicated and sentenced to exile; it was perhaps in this battle that he received the wound that left a livid scar on his side. In 563, at the advanced age of 42 and accompanied by 12 disciples, he set sail to do penance as a missionary, and found haven on the Hebridean island of Iona, where he founded a monastery that became the mother church of Celtic Christianity in Scotland. From Iona he travelled to other parts of Scotland, especially to the north to evangelize amongst the Picts, and won the respect of the pagan King Brude (Bridei) at his stronghold near Inverness (possibly the hillfort at Craig Phadrig). He and his missionaries founded numerous churches in the islands of the Hebrides (hence his Gaelic name of Colmcille). A formidably energetic administrator, he organized his monastery on Iona as a school for missionaries, and played a vigorous role in the politics of the country. Although he spent the last 34 years of his life in Scotland, he visited Ireland on occasions, and towards the end of his life he founded the monastery of Durrow in Ireland. He was renowned as a man of letters; he wrote hymns, and is credited with having transcribed 300 books by hand. However, he was also revered as a warrior saint, and his supernatural aid was frequently invoked for victory in battle. He died on Iona and was buried in the abbey. His feast day is 9 June. ▷ Celtic Church; missions, Christian; monasticism

Columban, or **Columbanus, St** (543–615) Irish missionary, 'the younger Columba', born in Leinster. He studied under St Comgall at Bangor in Down, and c.585 went to Gaul with 12 companions, and founded the monasteries of Anegray, Luxeuil and Fontaine in the Vosges country. His adherence to the Celtic Easter involved him in controversy, and the vigour with which he rebuked the vices of the Burgundian court led to his expulsion in 610. After a year or two at Bregenz, on Lake Constance, he went to Lombardy, and in 612 founded the monastery of Bobbio, in the Appenines, where he died. His writings, all in Latin, comprise a monastic rule, 6 poems on the vanity of life, 17 sermons and a commentary on the Psalms (1878). His feast day is 23 November. ▷ missions, Christian; monasticism

Commentaries on the Quran These Muslim commentaries were based upon the oral traditions of Muhammad and his companions, and especially upon the work known as the *Ocean of Knowledge*, by the nephew of Muhammad, Ibn al-Abbas. Commentaries giving background information about the Quran and some straightforward interpretations of the text were known as *tafsir*; commentaries that gave deeper allegorical and mystical insights were known as *tawil*. Orthodox Muslims stressed that allegorical and mythical interpretations of the Quran found in tawil should not contravene the outward interpretations found in tafsir. Many Islamic commentaries on the Quran were influenced by Jewish *midrash* precedents which used the method of parable as well as exegesis to bring out the meaning and intention of the text. Influential early commentaries include *The Comprehensive Explanation of Koranic Exegesis* by al-Tabari (d.923) and *The Light of Revelation and the Secrets of Interpretation* by al-Baydawi (d.1282). Some later commentaries were Shiite in interpretation and others, such as that of Ibn Arabi, were Sufi in inspiration. ▷ Arabi, Ibn al-; midrash; Muhammad; Quran; Shiism; Sufism; Tabari, Abu Jafar Mohammed Ben Jariral-; tafsir

Communion, Holy ▷ **Eucharist**

communism A political ideology which has as its central principle the communal ownership of all property, and thereby the abolition of private property. Although examples of early social and religious groupings based on communal sharing of property have been cited, modern communism is specifically associated with the theories of Karl Marx. Marx saw the emergence of a communist society as being the final stage in a historical process that was rooted in human needs, preceded by feudalism, capitalism, and (a transitional stage) socialism. Communism, according to Marx, would abolish class distinctions and end the exploitation of the masses inherent in the capitalist system. The working class, or proletariat, would be the instrument of a revolution that would overthrow the capitalist system and liberate human potential. A fully developed communist system would operate according to the principle of 'from each according to his ability, to each according to his needs'; and as there would be no need for a state to regulate society, it would 'wither away'. Marx's writings have provided a powerful ideological basis for communist and many socialist parties and governments, which have legitimized their policies by reference to Marxism or some variant of it.

As Marx had only set out the general principles of communism, and had not described in detail how a communist system would operate, a great deal of scope was left for different interpretations of Marxism and different opinions on what the features of a communist system should be. The most important interpretation of Marxism was that by Lenin (1870–1924), who argued that the workers ought to be led by a disciplined and centralized party organization. This variant of Marxism was known as Maxism-Leninism, and was the ideology of the Russian Communist Party (later renamed the Communist Party of the Soviet Union) which came to power in Russia in 1917. Under the leadership of Lenin and then of Stalin, the economic system that was established in the Soviet Union was a highly centralized one, in which goods were produced and distributed according to an all-embracing economic plan. The political régime became increasingly monolithic, Lenin outlawing all political parties except the Communist Party. Under Stalin's rule the communist régime became particularly opressive, all individual initiative being stifled in the interests of the state.

The Russian Communist Party provided the ideological leadership for communist parties throughout the world. With the creation of the Communist International in 1919 it was laid down that only those parties which accepted the discipline, leadership and organizational structure of the kind of party Lenin had created would be allowed to join. The great expansion of the Soviet type of communism occurred in the years following World War II, when East European countries such as Poland, Hungary, Czechoslovakia, Yugoslavia, Romania, East Germany and Bulgaria joined the communist bloc. Communist governments were also established in China and North Korea in this period. Almost simultaneous with the expansion of the communist bloc dissension began to appear within it. First Yugoslavia and then China challenged the supremacy of the Soviet Party in the international communist movement. During the 1950s and 1960s Soviet military power was deployed to prevent East European countries such as Hungary, Poland and Czechoslovakia breaking away from the Soviet model of communism. Nevertheless, economic reform movements emerged in the countries of Eastern Europe during the 1960s and 1970s, spreading to China in the 1980s. When Mikhail Gorbachev became leader of the Soviet Communist Party in 1985 a far-reaching programme of reform was launched in the Soviet Union to counter the inefficiencies of the centralized economic system.

Under Gorbachev the leading role of the Communist Party in the country was removed, and other political parties were able to put up candidates for election to the democratized state institutions. Attempts were made to decentralize the economy. The hold of the Soviet Union over the countries of Eastern Europe was relaxed, and these in rapid succession overthrew their communist régimes. Democratization and decentralization, however, had the effect of stimulating nationalism and separatism in the Soviet Union, and by the end of 1991 the Union had disintegrated into a number of independent countries, all of which renounced their communist past. The disintegration of Soviet communism demonstrated the fallacy of some of the assumptions on which it had been based: that nationalism would disappear; that planning was superior to a market economy; and that world historical development was on the side of communism. It does not, however, signify the end of communism as a political ideology, because it can be argued that the Soviet model was only one of the possible variants. ▷ Lenin, Vladimir Ilyich; Marx, Karl; Marxism-Leninism; secular alternatives to religion

comparative religion The objective investigation of the religions of the world by scientific and historical methods. Its approach is descriptive and comparative, and is not concerned with questions of the truth or falsity of the beliefs it examines. Max Müller, often called 'the father of comparative religion', did much to bring a knowledge of the world's religions to the notice of the English-speaking world. The discipline has contributed greatly to our knowledge of religions by identifying recurring patterns of belief and practice among religions widely separated by culture and geography, as well as by indicating what is distinctive in each religion. ▷ Müller, (Friedrich) Max; religion

Comte, Auguste (1798–1857) French philosopher and social theorist, born in Montpelier. Usually regarded as the founding father of sociology, he was an unconventional and rebellious student at the École Polytechnique in Paris (1814–16), made a meagre living for a while teaching mathematics, and from 1818 came strongly under the influence of the social reformer Claude Saint-Simon. His professional and personal life then became more precarious: in 1824 he broke violently with Saint-Simon; in 1825 he married, briefly and unhappily; in 1826 he began teaching philosophy, but suffered a breakdown, and although he continued teaching privately, he was largely supported in his later years by J S Mill, George Grote and other friends. He nonetheless completed at least two major works: the *Cours de Philosophie positive* (6 vols, 1830–42) and the *Système de Politique positive* (1851–4). His 'Positivism' sought to expound the laws of social evolution, to describe the organization and hierarchy of all branches of human knowledge, and to establish a true science of society as a basis for social planning and regeneration; in this vision 'Humanity' itself becomes the object of religious reverence and love—'Catholicism minus Christianity', as it was dubbed by T H Huxley. ▷ Mill, John Stuart; positivism

concepts in religion Concepts, in the form of doctrines or beliefs, are an important element in many religious traditions. They engage the use of the intellect and reason, and are often formed into orthodox systems through the medium of theology. In some religious traditions they are of prime importance, for example in Christianity, where theology combined the precision of Greek philosophical thought with the need to express concepts accurately in order to avoid heresy, which was seen as doctrinal deviation. Thus the conceptual formulations of the person of Christ and the nature of the Trinity were seen to be of crucial importance. By contrast the Muslim and Jewish traditions have seen heresy in terms of practical rather than doctrinal deviation, and the four noble truths of the Buddha have been of second-order rather than primary importance to Buddhists. In India Buddhists were able to repudiate the Hindu concepts of God (*Brahman*) and the self (atman) and yet live side by side with Hindus, and in China Confucians and Taoists were able to complement one another while differing conceptually. In some cases differences in concepts have been significant, for instance the theory of reincarnation as opposed to the theory of one life, and the different notions of Jesus held by Christians, Jews and Muslims. There is continuing discussion in various religious traditions as to whether conceptual truth has to do with doctrinal propositions or with persons, and as to whether it is merely a matter of intellect or a matter of faith engaging the whole personality. ▷ ariya sacca; atman; Brahman; Buddha; heresy; Jesus Christ; reincarnation; Trinity

conciliarism The theory that the General Council (consisting of all bishops) has supreme authority in the Church. It gained prominence in disputes concerning the authority of the papacy in the Western Church in the Middle Ages, but declined after 1460 when Pope Pius II forbade appeals from a pope to a General Council. Interest revived with the recognition of corporate or collegial authority of bishops at the Second Vatican Council (1962–6). ▷ bishop; Council of the Church; papacy; Vatican Councils

Cone, James Hal (1938–) American theologian, chief advocate of Black theology in the USA, born in Arkansas. A professor of systematic theology at Union theological seminary, New York, he has written extensively. His angry criticisms of the presuppositions of white theology in *A Black Theology of Liberation* (1970) were followed by the more measured *God of the Oppressed* (1975), *For My People* (1984), *Speaking the Truth* (1986), and the autobiographical *My Soul Looks Back* (1987); he also edited *Black Theology: A Documentary History* (1979) with Gayraud S Wilmore. ▷ theology

Confessing Church A Church formed in Germany by Evangelical Christians opposed to Nazism and the Nazi-supported 'German Christian Church Movement'. Its Synod of Barmen published the *Barmen Declaration* (1934), which became influential in Germany and beyond as a basis for resistance to oppressive civil authorities, It was succeeded in 1948 by the 'Evangelical Church in Germany'. ▷ Barth, Karl; evangelicalism; Nazi Party

confession 1 A declaration or profession of faith, originally by an individual martyr, later by a group or church. Such a document became common after the Reformation. ▷ Augsburg Confession; Westminster Confession of Faith; martyr; Reformation 2 An acknowledgement of sin, made either corporately in the course of public worship or privately and individually as auricular confession, 'into the ear' of a priest. ▷ priest; sin

confirmation The Christian sacrament of initiation, the nature and theology of which have been understood in varying ways in Christian history. In early usage, it was difficult to distinguish baptism from confirmation as acts of initiation into Christian belief, but by the Middle Ages there was a tendency in the West to separate the two, so that confirmation was performed only by the laying on of hands (or by anointing with oil, or both) by a bishop. Children are not usually confirmed before reaching seven years of age, and many Churches prefer them to reach adolescence. In Anglicanism it is often viewed as the young person assuming personal responsibility for earlier baptismal vows. The Second Vatican Council ordered that the rite should be revised so as to emphasize more clearly its character of initiation. ▷ baptism; sacrament; Vatican Councils

Confucian Canon A collection of works that have been regarded as seminal by the Confucian tradition. The original Five Classics were, according to tradition although not in fact, edited by Confucius himself. They are: the *Classic of Odes* (*Shih Ching*) which is a book of 305 early Chinese poems; the *Classic of Rites* (*Li Ching*) which contains three important books of ritual; the *Classic of History* (*Shu Ching*) which contains documents of early Chinese history; the *Spring and Autumn Annals* (*Chun Chiu*) which narrates the history of Confucius's home state of Lu; and the *Classic of Changes* (*I Ching*) which is a book of divination and philosophy. They became the basis of the Chinese civil service examinations from the time of the later Han dynasty (206BCE–220CE). The present Confucian Canon was reorganized by Chu Hsi (1130–1200) to centre upon the Four Books: the

Analects of Confucius, the *Book of Mencius*, the *Great Learning*, and the *Doctrine of the Mean* (the latter two being chapters in the Classic of Rites). From 1313 to 1905 they were the basis for the Chinese civil service exams. Later Confucians such as Tai Chen (1723–77) attempted to go back beyond the Four Books and give priority to the original Five Classics, but without success. ▷ Chu Hsi; I Ching; Mencius

Confucian Exam System A Confucian Academy was opened in 124BCE to train aspiring civil servants in the Confucian Classics, and from then until the fall of the Manchu dynasty in 1905 these provided the basis of the civil service exams. There were five classics which, according to tradition, had been edited by Confucius. They were the *Book of Poetry*, the *Book of Rites*, the *Book of History*, the *Spring and Autumn Annals*, and the *Book of Changes*. During the neo-Confucian movement in the Sung dynasty, Chu Hsi (1130–1200CE) established the authority of four more books as part of the Confucian Canon, namely the *Analects of Confucius*, the *Doctrine of the Mean*, the *Great Learning*, and the *Book of Mencius*, which were then incorporated as sources for the civil service exams. From Chu Hsi's time until it was abolished in 1905, the imperial exam system, based on the Confucian Canon, held influence in China as the way of access into government service. With its departure the outward authority of the Confucian tradition also disappeared. ▷ Chu Hsi; Confucian Canon; Confucius; I Ching; Mencius

Confucianism The oldest school of Chinese thought, Confucianism has two ethical strands. One, associated with Confucius and Hsün Tzu (c.298–238BCE), is conventionalistic; we ought to follow traditional codes of behaviour for their own sake. The other, associated with Mencius and the medieval Neo-Confucians, is intuitionistic; we ought to do as our moral natures dictate. ▷ Confucius

Confucius, Latin for **K'ung Fu-tzu, the Master K'ung** (551–479BCE) Chinese philosopher, born of an aristocratic but impoverished family in the state of Lu, part of the present province of Shantung. When he was three his father died, and he married at 19, becoming a government official in Lu with a retinue of disciples, mostly young gentlemen whom he was preparing for government service. He was promoted to ministerial rank and enjoyed a successful and highly popular career, which eventually attracted jealousy and

Confucius

hostility and led to a breach with the ruler. In 497 he left Lu and for over ten years became an itinerant sage, wandering from court to court seeking a sympathetic patron and attended by a company of his disciples. In about 485 he returned to Lu and spent his final years teaching and possibly writing. After his death his pupils compiled a volume of memorabilia, the *Analects*, which record the master's sayings and doings, but most of the other works attributed to him are later compilations which, like the philosophy of 'Confucianism' itself, are probably only loosely related to his own teachings. He emerges as a great moral teacher who tried to replace the old religious observances with moral values as the basis of social and political order. In his Way (tao) he emphasized the practical virtues of benevolence (jen), reciprocity (shu), respect and personal effort which were to be interpreted pragmatically with regard to individual circumstances and cases rather than any abstract system of imperatives. Succeeding generations revered him and Confucianism became, and remained until recently, the state religion of China, although its influence declined following the end of the monarchy (1911–12) and particularly after the Communist Revolution of 1949. ▷ Confucianism

Congregationalism A movement which sees the Christian Church as essentially a gathered community of believers, covenanting with

God, keeping God's law, and living under the Lordship of Christ. It derived from the Separatists of the 16th-century Reformation in England, of whom Robert Browne was an early leader. Persecution drove the Congregationalists to Holland and the USA (the Pilgrim Fathers, 1620). Church affairs, including calling a minister and appointing deacons to assist, are regulated by members at a 'Church Meeting'. As a world denomination, it has a strong missionary tradition. One denomination formed the International Congregational Council in 1949, which merged with Presbyterians as the World Alliance of Reformed Churches in 1970. With a strong tradition of tolerance and freedom of belief, its major contribution to ecumenism has been its insistence on the importance of the local church in the event of union with other denominations. ▷ Browne, Robert; Christianity; ecumenism; missions, Christian; Pilgrim Fathers; Presbyterianism; Reformation

conscience A phenomenon common to all cultures, however it may be termed, pointing to consciousness of the innermost nature of the human being. It was originally applied generally to inward knowledge, but gradually acquired the sense of a faculty or principle for making moral judgements. It is by virtue of the judgements of conscience that feelings of moral justification or guilt arise. Where moral law is recognized, it is through conscience that the demands of the moral law are mediated. The existence of conscience serves to stress the inner life and individual responsibility as against external rules and authority. Religiously, it has been equated with the voice of God, relating the moral life of the individual to God, and passing this under judgement.

There has been much debate about whether conscience is a faculty natural to the human being and responding positively or negatively to a moral law or to God, or whether it is a disposition conditioned in some way by society. Thus, for Rousseau it was an instinct leading to morality, carrying no implication of obligation, for Kant it was a human, interior court of justice of incomparable dignity. Darwin and Spencer explained it in evolutionary terms, Durkheim accounted for it sociologically, and Freud psychologically as the 'super-ego'.

More recently, it has been seen not as something which the human being has (ie a capacity or faculty), but rather as something which the human being is, driving humans towards reponsible decisions and the realization of value. ▷ moral theology; soul

consciousness, states of The attempt, evident in most major religions and many philosophical traditions, to identify and describe various conditions of the human being in which experiences going beyond ordinary everyday occurrences are received. A 'higher' state of consciousness is said to give access to a higher, otherwise inaccessible level of reality. In such higher levels, sensitivity to the ultimately real or the divine, as well as deepened self-awareness, is claimed. In mystical religion, such a higher state is often induced by special techniques. Recognition of such states of consciousness, which may vary in intensity and in the level of reality to which they give access, is found eg in Hinduism and the Sufi tradition, both of which name four states, the Christian mystical tradition (such as Meister Eckhart), and also in some philosophical traditions, eg Platonism).

The idea of different states of consciousness, long familiar to mystics, has been the subject of investigation by psychologists since the time of F A Mesmer (18th century). In the early 20th century William James maintained that normal, waking or 'rational' consciousness was by no means the only form of consciousness. Many psychologists have followed Freud and Janet in insisting that all alleged states of consciousness other than that of the normally developed ego are really the work of subconscious or unconscious forces. Others, like Jung, with his postulation of a collective unconscious and his concept of archetypes, or more recently Sir Alister Hardy, seem more open to the reality of different states of consciousness, giving access to authentic experience and knowledge, and yielding both a refined and enlarged perspective on life. ▷ Hardy, Sir Alister; Jung, Carl Gustav; mysticism

consecration The investing of particular persons, places or objects with special religious significance, so that they achieve sacred status. Some such practice is common to most religions. Consecration depends on divine assistance, can only be performed by one or more persons already consecrated themselves, and may be either permanent or temporary, requiring renewal. 1 Of persons, in the Christian tradition, consecration is performed once only and is for the benefit of others or the community (eg celebrating Mass or administering the sacraments generally). The Roman Catholic bishop or priest is seen as an agent, through the mediation and as representative of Jesus Christ, of divine grace for the world. The effectiveness of the action does not depend on the sanctity or purity of life of the minister or priest. In other traditions, consecration tends to be more for the benefit of the recipient, and may be repeated regularly so that the purity of eg the Buddhist monk's life may be maintained. Sometimes, as in Hinduism and Judaism and Christian monastic orders, all actions and all life may be seen as consecrated to God. 2 Of places such as churches, temples, pagodas, and shrines, consecration is accomplished by appropriate ritual performed by duly authorized agents in order to provide fitting places for the dwelling of the divine being, or for the traces of relics of holy persons. 3 Of objects, such as vessels or food used in ritual acts, consecration may be performed, and in Hinduism images are set apart as the manifestation of the god, mediating the presence of the divine. ▷ priest; sacrament

Conservative Judaism A denomination within Judaism which arose in response to radical developments in American Reform Judaism towards the end of the 19th century. Against such trends, Sabato Morais (1823–97) and others led a conservative reaction which attempted to steer a course between Orthodoxy and Reform. Morais became President of the Jewish Theological Seminary of America in New York, where the movement's rabbis are still trained. Conservative Judaism's aim was to allow adjustment to the modern world whilst simultaneously holding on to biblical and talmudic legislation. It accepted the need to view Jewish belief and practice over the centuries critically, but maintained that an authentic Judaism must be marked by adherence to Torah. Also influential was Solomon Schechter (1847–1914). He contributed to the development of Conservative Judaism in its desire to synthesize traditional Jewish teaching and worship with modern requirements. This has meant, for example, that Hebrew remains in the liturgy but women are not required to be segregated in a special gallery; recently, despite some opposition, the movement has accepted women for ordination. Although strongest in America, with its Seminary and policy-making body called the Rabbinical Assembly, the influence of Conservative Judaism has now spread to Europe and Israel as well. ▷ Orthodox Judaism; Reform Judaism; Torah

Constantine I, called **the Great,** properly **Flavius Valerius Aurelius Constantinus** (c.274–337) Roman Emperor, born in Naissus, in Upper Moesia. He was the eldest son of Constantius Chlorus and Helena, and first distinguished himself as a soldier in Diocletian's Egyptian expedition (296), next under Galerius in the Persian war. In 305 the two emperors Diocletian and Maximian abdicated, and were succeeded by Constantius Chlorus and Galerius. Constantine joined his father, who ruled in the West, at Boulogne on the expedition against the Picts, and before Constantius died (306) he proclaimed his son his successor. Galerius did not dare to quarrel with Constantine, yet he granted him the title of Caesar only, refusing that of Augustus. Political complications now increased until in 308 there were six emperors at once—Galerius, Licinius and Maximian in the East; and Maximian, Maxentius his son, and Constantine in the West. Maxentius drove his father from Rome, and after some intrigues Maximian died by suicide (309). Maxentius threatened Gaul with a large army. Constantine, crossing the Alps by Mont Cénis, thrice defeated Maxentius, who was drowned after the last great victory at the Milvian Bridge near Rome (312). Before the battle a flaming cross inscribed 'In this conquer' was said to have caused Constantine's conversion to Christianity; and the edict of Milan (313), issued conjointly with Licinius, gave civil rights and toleration to Christians throughout the empire. Constantine was now sole emperor of the West, and by the death of Galerius in 311 and of Maximian in 313, Licinius became sole emperor of the East. After a war (314) between the two rulers, Licinius had to cede Illyricum, Pannonia and Greece. Constantine for the next nine years devoted himself vigorously to the correction of abuses, the strengthening of his frontiers and the chastizing of the barbarians. Having in 323 again defeated Licinius, and put him to death, Constantine was now sole governor of the Roman world. He chose Byzantium for his capital, and in 330 inaugurated it under the name of Constantinople ('City of Constantine').

Christianity became a state religion in 324, though nonconformity was not persecuted. In 325 the great Church Council of Nicaea was held, in which the court sided against the Arians and the Nicene Creed was adopted. Yet it was only shortly before his death that Constantine received baptism. The story of his baptism at Rome by Pope Sylvester I in 326, and of the so-called *Donation of Constantine*, long treated as an argument for the temporal power of the papacy, is utterly unhistorical. His later years were vicious, seeing the execution of his eldest son Crispus (326) for treason and of his own second wife Fausta (327) on some similar charge. He proposed to divide the empire between his three sons by Fausta: Constantius, Constantine II and Constans I; but in 340 Constantine II lost his life in war with Constans. ▷ Arius; Christianity; Nicaea, Council of; Nicene Creed

consubstantiation A theory attributed to Luther, describing the presence of Christ in the Eucharist 'under or with the elements of bread and wine'. It is to be contrasted with the Roman Catholic doctrine of transubstantiation. ▷ Eucharist; Luther, Martin; transubstantiation

contemplation This is a non-discursive mental prayer in which attempts to reason or decide are laid aside for a simple turning in love towards God, as taught within Christianity in the anonymous 14th-century English classic, *The Cloud of Unknowing*. A distinction is often made between active or 'natural' contemplation, which can be learned, and the higher levels of passive or 'infused' contemplation, which are a gift of God. The different degrees or types of Christian contemplation are exhaustively analysed in the works of the 15th-century Spanish mystics St Teresa of Ávila and St John of the Cross. ▷ discursive meditation; John of the Cross, St; prayer; Teresa of Ávila, St

conversion A change in affiliation from one religion to another, or the transition from non-involvement to belief in a religion. It also designates a change involving a transformation and reorientation affecting every aspect of a person's life, which can occur suddenly or gradually. ▷ religion

conversion, Jewish In Jewish tradition it is through the mother that Jewishness is passed on. Nevertheless Judaism has always been open to non-Jews wishing to convert. Accordingly, throughout history there have been individuals and occasionally whole communities who have gone over to Judaism. In addition to sincerity, three things are required for conversion: the offering of an appropriate sacrifice, circumcision for males, and purificatory immersion in a miqveh. Since the destruction of the Temple in 70CE the first is no longer possible. General attitudes towards proselytes in post-biblical times were positive; apart from minor restrictions, they were considered fully Jewish. Nonetheless, and despite some notable and well-documented cases, converts to Judaism under Christian and Muslim rule were relatively few, since in the eyes of those communities such apostates were thought worthy of death. Thus proselytism was rendered impracticable even if prospective converts approaching the Jewish community were in theory to be welcomed. However, the belief that Gentiles who are monotheists and adhere to a basic morality will have a share along with Israel in the Olam haBa enabled many to countenance this situation. Such a tendency has received confirmation in modern times, both Christianity and Islam now being viewed more positively than previously. ▷ Gentiles; miqveh; Olam haBa; Reform Judaism

Convocation A gathering of Church of England clergy, originally in the provinces of Canterbury and York, to regulate affairs of the Church. The Upper House consists of the archbishop and bishops; the Lower House of representatives of the lower clergy. Since the early 20th century the two convocations meet together, all now forming the Church Assembly, which meets two or three times a year, with powers regulated by Parliament. ▷ Church of England

Copts A Christian tradition mainly present in the Muslim lands of Egypt and the Sudan. The Coptic Church separated from the Orthodox Church after the Council of Chalcedon in 451. The Copts were Monophysites who believed that Jesus Christ had a divine nature only, rather than a human and a divine nature which was the orthodox belief. They had links with the other Monophysite churches in Armenia, Ethiopia and Syria, and have retained their liturgy in the Coptic Egyptian language. Since the Muslims over-ran Egypt in 642, the Copts have existed within the Islamic world, and have suffered occasional persecutions and gradual but relentless conversion to Islam. In general affairs they have adopted the Arabic language, but they have kept alive Egyptian Christian monasticism, maintained the Coptic liturgy, evolved an impressive Coptic religious art, and liturgically maintained the rich order of worship of St Basil. They are well represented in Egyptian professional life given their numbers, which are in excess of three million, but small in proportion to their environment. ▷ Basil, St; Chalcedon, Council of; Monophysites

Corinth, early Christianity in Corinth was a great commercial seaport on the shortest route from the Adriatic to the Aegean, linking Europe and Asia. Following destruction of most of the ancient Greek city in 146BCE, Corinth was rebuilt as a Roman colony in 46BCE. It was well known for its temple of Aphrodite, and as a cosmopolitan centre of pleasure and vice. Paul stayed in Corinth for 18 months on his second missionary journey. Some Jews there became Christians, others took him to court for teaching an unlawful religion, but the case was dismissed (Acts 18). Paul established (c.50CE) a mainly Gentile church which, although active and generous, caused him much heartache, as his two epistles to the Corinthians, written a few years later, show. Some converts were tempted to revert to the pagan practices they had just left, others found their new Christian freedoms too heady to bear or supported divisive factions within the church. Paul's first epistle, besides showing how he tackled church problems, gives insights into early Christian worship (including the earliest account of the administration of the Lord's Supper or Eucharist, 1 Corinthians 11), and contains the celebrated 'Hymn to Love' (1 Corinthians 13). ▷ Eucharist

Corinthians, Letters to the Two New Testament writings, widely accepted as genuinely from the apostle Paul to the Church that he founded in Corinth. The first describes his efforts to deal with a variety of ethical and doctrinal problems dividing the Church at Corinth; the second is his response to later developments in this Church, to the efforts to collect funds for the Jerusalem Church, and to charges against him by opponents. ▷ Corinth, early Christianity in; New Testament; Paul, St; Pauline Letters

Corpus Juris Canonici (Latin, 'body of canon law') The chief collection of church or canon law of the Roman Catholic Church and, to an extent, of the Anglican Churches. It includes the decrees of popes and canons, and rules formulated by the Councils, eg the Decretals of Gregory IX. Canon law exercised considerable influence on the development of civil and international law. The 'Corpus' was succeeded in the Roman Catholic Church by the Codex Juris Canonici (1918). ▷ canon law; Codex Juris Canonici

corroboree A term used by 19th-century settlers in New South Wales, Australia, for any Aboriginal ceremonial or festive gathering which included singing and dancing. Later it came into common use among non-Aborigines, but it fails to mark the distinction between religious ceremonies and non-religious performance practised by Aboriginal peoples. When used in a religious sense the term refers to those ceremonies in which Aborigines try to re-enact the activities of the altjiringa or Dreamtime. These occasions can be a communal festivity, where everyone can watch, or can consist of specifically male or female rituals, from which members of the opposite sex are excluded. Body-painting and the marking of the ceremonial site are an important part of the performance. ▷ Australian Aboriginal religion

cosmic law The principles underlying the general order of things in the cosmos; of human beings, the basis of human right and justice. Most religious traditions hold to belief in an ordered universe, such that individual events are not meaningless. Thus there is a parallelism in meaning between, for example, dharma in the Indian tradition and in Buddhism, where it represents the teaching of the Buddha; *tao* in Taoism and Confucianism; and natural law and moral law in the Western philosophical tradition. It can be reflected in a law affecting and regulating ethical behaviour, and also in injunctions for the religious life.

In Ancient Greece, belief in blind fate or chance was counterbalanced by an acceptance of a law of harmony and proportion in human affairs. The *Logos* (literally 'Word') was the eternal rational order of the cosmos, and in the Christian tradition, this principle is held to be 'incarnated' or 'made flesh' in Jesus Christ (John 1.14). Judaism, Christianity and Islam all hold to belief in a personal God, whose will and purpose is the basis of order in the universe. Christianity develops a doctrine of Providence, which in extreme form maintains that 'God wills in eternity whatever comes to pass in time'. This is now frequently modified by the assertion that God's will is realized through the exercise of human freedom. The existence of natural law or a moral law native to all human beings has been questioned by positivist philosophies. Nevertheless, reliance on some kind of order in the universe is the presupposition of scientific enquiry and is basic to religions of both East and West. ▷ natural theology; predestination

cosmogony An account of the origin of the cosmos, frequently with implications as to its composition and evolutionary behaviour. Most religions and cultures recognize as authoritative particular accounts of its origin, creation or emanation. These usually take the form of myths or stories of the gods, as a result of whose activities (often conflicts) the cosmos comes into being. They are significant for determining the relation to God or the gods of the cosmos and creatures in the cosmos. ▷ Bundahishn

cosmogony, Ancient Near Eastern No complete Sumerian account of creation has survived, but from other texts it is possible to see that the world arose out of the primal sea and that the four cosmic deities An, Enlil, Enki and Ninhursag were largely responsible for its ordering. Sumerian myths of origins are more concerned with the institution of the world order and the beginnings of society. The best-known and preserved Ancient Near Eastern cosmogony is that of *Enuma Elish*, the Babylonian creation epic, which recounts the raising of Marduk to supreme god and was recited annually at the Akitu festival. The primeval fresh and salt waters, Apsu and Tiamat, gave birth to the generations of gods, including the four cosmic deities. They came into conflict and Apsu was killed by Ea (Enki), provoking Tiamat to avenge her consort. Marduk alone had the courage to stand up to her. After defeating and killing her, he used her body to make the basic parts of the universe. Later, to relieve the gods of the need to work, he created humankind from the blood of her servant Kingu. The service of the gods is seen persistently in the Ancient Near East as the only reason for human existence. The motif of conflict with the sea occurs elsewhere in the Ancient Near East, and in some parts of the Hebrew Bible the battle between Yahweh and the sea or sea monsters is related to creation. ▷ Akitu; creation myths; Ea; Enlil; Marduk; Tiamat; Yahweh

cosmogony, Jewish In traditional Judaism theories about the origin of the universe are based on Genesis 1; a branch of esoteric mysticism called maaseh bereshit grew up around its interpretation, as also the maaseh merkavah on Ezekiel 1. However, too much speculation on such matters was frowned upon by most rabbis of talmudic times, whose chief interest was the Halakhah. Nonetheless, mainstream opinion insisted on creation out of nothing, as opposed to ideas of the eternity of matter found in Greek philosophy. Thus on the first day 10 things were formed: heaven and earth, *tohu* and *vohu* (Hebrew for 'without form and void', in Genesis 1.2, and understood as two primeval elements), light and darkness, wind and water, day and night. Equating personified Wisdom (Proverbs 8.22) with the Torah, it was also held that God himself consulted the latter as a blueprint for the universe and formed it accordingly. Further, everything created by the Deity must be perfect, including death, the *yetzer ra* ('evil inclination'), suffering and hell; ultimately each of these contributes to human well-being. In modern times, the traditional understanding of Genesis 1 has come into conflict with scientific knowledge. However, many Jews would now interpret the creation story and its later elaborations symbolically. ▷ creationism; Halakhah; humankind, Jewish view of; Merkavah Mysticism; symbolism

cosmological argument An argument for the existence of God as the first cause of all things, championed especially by Aquinas. The argument appeals to the intuitions that the existence of the universe cannot be explained by things *in* the universe, and that there should be only one first cause. ▷ Aquinas, St Thomas; God, arguments for the existence of

cosmology The study of the cosmos and its nature. In religion, it assumes authoritative forms establishing the relation of the natural world and the human beings in it to the divine. These forms are usually couched in myths or stories of God or the gods as a result of whose activities the cosmos not only comes into being, but is maintained. Cosmology forms the framework within which reality is interpreted.

cosmology, Ancient Near Eastern Sumerian cosmology follows a pattern which was also applicable in other parts of the Ancient Near East. The universe comprised heaven and earth, which were fixed immovably in the primeval sea from which they had originally emerged. Heaven and earth were divided by the atmosphere, out of which was made the planets and constellations. The sky itself was a fixed firmament or vault which kept out the waters. Underneath the earth was another hollow space, the realm of the dead, ruled by Nergal and Ereshkigal.

cosmology, Greek The world envisaged by traditional Greek mythology contained, working from the top, 'heaven', in which was the home of the gods, Mount Olympus; the air (often divided into two parts, one above the other, *aither* and *aer*); earth, round which flowed Ocean, the source of all rivers; the underworld, Hades; and still further down Tartarus, a region to which rebellious or defeated gods were expelled. The growth of pre-Socratic philosophy and of geography caused various elements of this world-view to be modified or jettisoned: the historian Herodotus (c.430BCE), for instance, was strongly influenced by geographical thought and denied that the traditional 'Ocean' existed. More importantly, there emerged in pre-

Socratic thought the idea that the universe is an ordered *kosmos* (*kosmos* means order), governed by inflexible natural laws. ▷ pre-Socratic philosophy; Greek religion and philosophy

cosmology, Hindu This is hierarchical in concept with higher, more subtle worlds located above the lower, material universe. The earliest cosmological speculations occur in the *Rig Veda* where three levels of earth, atmosphere, and sky or heaven are measured out by one of the gods (either Indra, Varuna or Vishnu). Each of these realms is also the home for a different class of gods: thus Soma and Agni dwell in the realm of the earth, Indra and Vayu the wind in the atmosphere, and Varuna and Dyaus in the sky. The *Rig Veda* also contains a famous creation hymn (10.129) which asks the unanswerable question of what was before existence and non-existence. One of the general features of later Hindu cosmologies is that the level of the universe corresponds to a person's state of mind or level of awareness: the macrocosm corresponds to the microcosm. Thus a yogi with a purified and concentrated consciousness can access higher cosmological levels or worlds. This is illustrated by the *Mandukya Upanishad* in which the three levels of awareness: waking, dreaming and deep sleep, are identified with the three parts of the mantra AUM. Beyond these levels is the transcendent 'fourth' state (*turya*), identified with the silence beyond sound and with the absolute (*Brahman*). The idea of the cosmos as a manifestation of sound is a very important Hindu idea, being articulated in schools of Sanskrit grammar (*vyakarana*) which regarded language as a gross manifestation of the subtle power of speech (*vac*). This idea was elaborated in Tantra where Shiva, who is a 'mass of sound', manifests the sound-worlds of the universe as coagulations of his essence. In Hindu cosmology generally, the universe is manifested from the absolute during vast cosmic cycles and contracted; a process mythologically represented as Vishnu lying asleep on the cosmic ocean, waking and manifesting the universe from a lotus which grows from his navel. When Vishnu goes back to sleep the universe contracts back into him. During these vast cycles of time, civilizations rise and fall, passing through a series of morally degenerative stages (*yugas*) until, during the last, dark age (*kali yuga*)—which we are in at present—Vishnu will appear, incarnate upon a white horse, and will reinstitute a golden age. ▷ Brahman; Indra; mantra; Shiva; Tantric Hinduism; Upanishads; Veda; Vishnu; yugas

cosmology, Jain The Jain tradition is atheistic; there is no concept of the creation of the universe by God. The cosmos is seen to be eternal and indestructible, and within it there are 'living' and 'material' components in perpetual flux. In the universe there are various heavens and hells. At the summit of the universe live the *tirthankaras* and other liberated souls, and they are superior to the gods who live in the heavens below them. In the middle part of the universe below the heavens live humans, animals and other living beings, subject to the law of rebirth and karma. When souls are liberated they rise from the middle to the summit of the universe where they abide for eternity in bliss. The part of the middle world that relates to human beings goes through cycles of progress and decline similar to those believed to occur in other Indian religions. Below the middle part of the universe are various hells. ▷ jiva; karma, Jain; Mahavira

Council of the Church In the Orthodox and Roman Catholic Churches, a meeting of bishops of the whole Church to regulate doctrine and discipline. The last Ecumenical Council (of the undivided Church) is generally held to be the Second Council of Nicaea (787). The Roman Catholic Church recognizes a Council if called by a pope, and its decisions, if approved by the pope, as infallible, with guaranteed assistance of the Holy Spirit, and binding on the whole Church. Non-Roman Catholic Churches recognize the World Council of Churches (formed in 1948), but infallibility is not claimed. ▷ Basle/Chalcedon/Lateran/Nicaea/Vatican, Councils (of); bishop; conciliarism; infallibility; Orthodox Church; papacy; Roman Catholicism

Counter-Reformation A general movement of reform and missionary activity in the Roman Catholic Church from the mid 16th century, stimulated in part by the Protestant Reformation. It included the revival of the monastic movement (eg Capuchins, 1528; Oratorians, 1575), especially the creation of the Jesuit Order. It provided for the enforcement of disciplinary measures by the Roman Inquisition; its doctrinal formulations were made by the Council of Trent; and liturgical and moral reforms were introduced throughout the Church. There was a strong influence from mystics (eg John of the Cross, Teresa of Ávila) and devotional teachers (eg Francis of Sales). In a secular sense, the term also refers to the success of Roman Catholic powers in Europe in the late 16th century and early 17th century. ▷ Capuchins; Francis Xavier, St; Inquisition; Jesuits; John of the Cross, St; liturgy; monasticism; Oratorians; Reformation; Roman Catholicism; Teresa of Ávila, St

covenant In the Hebrew Scriptures, the agreement between God and his chosen people which was the basis of Jewish religion. It is especially identified with the giving of the law to Moses on Mount Sinai, when God promised to lead the Jewish people from captivity as slaves in Egypt to the promised land. This agreement was preceded by covenants with Abraham and Noah. Some New Testament writers portray the death of Jesus as a 'new covenant', and many Christians believe that this agreement replaces the 'old' Jewish covenant. ▷ Abraham; Judaism; Moses; Noah; Sinai, Mount; Ten Commandments; Torah

Covenanters Originally, signatories (and their successors) of the National Covenant (1638) and the Solemn League and Covenant (1643) in Scotland, who resisted the theory of 'Divine Right of Kings' and the imposition of an episcopal system on the Presbyterian Church of Scotland. When declared rebels, they resorted to open-air preaching. Until Presbyterianism was restored in 1690, they were savagely persecuted, with imprisonment, execution without trial, and banishment (eg to Holland or the USA). ▷ Church of Scotland; episcopacy; Presbyterianism

Coverdale, Miles (1488–1568) English Protestant reformer and biblical scholar, born in Yorkshire. He studied at Cambridge, was ordained priest at Norwich in 1514, and joined the Augustinian Friars at Cambridge, where he was converted to Protestantism. He lived abroad from 1528 to 1534 to escape persecution, and in 1535 published in Zürich the first translation of the whole Bible into English, with a dedication to Henry VIII. The Prayer Book retains the Psalms of this translation, and many of the finest phrases in the Authorized Version of 1611 are directly due to Coverdale. In 1538 he was sent by Thomas Cromwell to Paris to superintend another English edition of the Scriptures. Francis I had granted a licence, but during the printing an edict was issued prohibiting the work. Many of the sheets were burned, but the presses and types were hastily carried over to London. Grafton and Whitchurch, noted printers, were thus enabled to bring out in 1539, under Coverdale's superintendence, the 'Great Bible', which was presented to Henry VIII by Cromwell. The second 'Great Bible', known also as 'Cranmer's Bible' (1540), was also edited by Coverdale, who on Cromwell's fall found it expedient to leave England. While abroad he married, and acted as Lutheran pastor in Rhenish Bavaria. In March 1548 he returned to England, was well received through Cranmer's influence, and in 1551 was made Bishop of Exeter. On Mary I's accession he was deprived of his see, but was allowed to leave the country, at the earnest intercession of the King of Denmark, whose chaplain, Dr Macchabaeus (MacAlpine), was Coverdale's brother-in-law. Returning to England in 1559 he did not resume his bishopric, but in 1564 he was collated by Grindal to the living of St Magnus, near London Bridge. This he resigned in 1566 due to his growing Puritan scruples about the liturgy. ▷ Augustinians; Authorized Version of the Bible; Cranmer, Thomas; Protestantism; Puritanism

cow in Hinduism A sacred animal in Hinduism, the cow is treated with reverence and is not killed. Respect for the cow can be seen as an expression of the ideal of non-violence (ahimsa) and reverence for the 'mother', representing both the ideal and the Mother Goddess. The five products of the cow—milk, clarified butter, curds, urine and dung—are regarded as purifying, and small quantities of these products might be ingested in a ritual context. These products have a practical aspect as well: milk, clarified butter and curds form an important part of a Hindu's diet, while cow urine is used as a cleansing agent and dried cow dung is used as fuel.

Cragg, Albert Kenneth (1913–) English scholar in the Christian dialogue with Islam. Educated at Jesus College, Oxford, and Tyndale House, Bristol, he was ordained priest in the Church of England in 1937. He has served in parishes and pastoral appointments in Beirut, Birkenhead, Canterbury, Longworth Berkshire, and Jerusalem; he has held academic appointments in Beirut, Hartford Connecticut and Sussex University; he has been an Assistant Bishop in Jerusalem, Chichester, Wakefield and Oxford; and has been a visiting lecturer or professor at Union Seminary in New York, Virginia Theological Seminary, and the Universities of London, Cambridge and Ibadan. He has brought to his varied tasks a sympathetic insight into the Muslim tradition gained through actual dialogue with Muslims and an intimate academic knowledge of Islam. This has been brought out in a succession of 24 books, including *The Call of the Minaret* (1956), *Sandals at the Mosque* (1959), *The Dome and the Rock* (1964), *Counsels in Contemporary Islam* (1965), *Christianity in World Perspective* (1968), *The House of Islam* (1969), *The Event of the Qur'an* (1971), *The Wisdom of the Sufis* (1976), *Muhammad and the Christian* (1983) and *Jesus and the Muslim* (1985). Cragg has combined a firm Christian faith with the ability in some sense to see the world as Muslims see it, and he has attempted to interpret Christians and Muslims to one another within the context of today's world. ▷ Muhammad; Quran; Sufism

Cranmer, Thomas (1489–1556) English prelate and Archbishop of Canterbury, born in Aslacton or Aslockton, Nottinghamshire. He was sent in 1503 by his widowed mother to Jesus College, Cambridge, where in 1510 he obtained a fellowship. He forfeited it by his marriage with 'Black Joan' of the Dolphin tavern, but regained it on her death before the year's grace was up, and took holy orders in 1523. During an epidemic of the plague he left Cambridge for Waltham in 1529 with two pupils. Here he met John Foxe and Stephen Gardiner and with them discussed Henry VIII's proposed divorce from Catherine of Aragon. Cranmer suggested an appeal to the universities of Christendom, which pleased Henry, and he subsequently became a counsel in the suit. He was appointed a royal chaplain and Archdeacon of Taunton; was attached to the household of Anne Boleyn's father (Anne at the time being Henry's paramour); and was sent on two embassies, to Italy in 1530 and to Charles V in Germany in 1532.

At Rome, Pope Clement VII made him grand penitentiary of England. At Nuremberg he met and married a niece of the reformer Osiander; soon afterwards a royal summons requested him to return as Warham's successor, as Archbishop of Canterbury. He sent his wife secretly over, and himself following, was consecrated in March. He took the oath of allegiance to the pope, with a protest that he took it 'for form's sake'. In May Cranmer pronounced Catherine's marriage null and void *ab initio* and the private marriage to Anne Boleyn, four months earlier, valid; in September he stood godfather to Anne's daughter Elizabeth. In 1536 he annulled Henry's marriage with Anne Boleyn, divorced him from Anne of Cleves (1540), informed him of Catherine Howard's premarital affairs, then strove to coax her into confessing them (1541). He did what he dared to oppose the Six Articles of 1539, which sought to impose uniformity of dogma; one of these made the marriage of priests punishable with death, whereupon he sent his wife away to Germany and did not recall her until 1548.

He was a kindly and humane man by nature, but nevertheless his episcopacy saw the burning of Frith and Lambert for denying transubstantiation (1533–8), of Friar Forest for upholding the papal supremacy (1538), of two Anabaptists (1538), of Joan Bocher for denying Christ's humanity (1550), and of a Dutch Arian (1551). He promoted the translation of the Bible and a service-book, and curtailed the number of holy days. In 1547 Henry died, and Cranmer sang mass of requiem for his soul. He had been slowly drifting into Protestantism, but now was quickly swept into great religious changes. In 1548 he compiled Edward VI's First Prayer Book (which converted the mass into communion), composed the 42 articles of religion (1553), later called the Thirty-nine Articles, and in 1552 rephrased the Prayer Book.

During this reign, as during the preceding one, he meddled little with affairs of state though he was one of the council of regency. What he did do was not too creditable. In gross violation of the canon law he signed Thomas Seymour's death warrant (1549); he had a chief hand in the depostion and imprisonment of bishops Bonner, Gardiner and Day; and, won over by the dying boy-king's pleading, he reluctantly subscribed the instrument diverting the succession from Mary to Lady Jane Grey (1553). By this he was guilty of conscious perjury, yet when the 12-days' reign was over he made no attempt to escape. On 14 September he was sent to the Tower, on 13 November was arraigned for treason, and, pleading guilty, was condemned to die. In March 1554 he went to Oxford where he bravely faced his trial before the papal commissioner, whose jurisdiction he refused to recognize. In October, from jail, he witnessed Latimer's and Ridley's martyrdom; and on 14 February 1556 he was formally degraded. In rapid succession he signed seven increasingly submissive recantations. The last he transcribed on 21 March, and he was immediately taken to St Mary's Church, where he heard that he was to be burnt. When the time came for him to read his recantation, he retracted all that he had written. Taken to the stake, he thrust his right hand into the flame and kept it there, crying: 'This hath offended! Oh this unworthy hand!' Among Cranmer's 42 writings are his Prefaces to the Bible (1540) and the First Prayer Book (1549); the *Reformatio Legum Ecclesiasticarum* (1571), and *A Defence of the Doctrine of the Sacrament*

(1550). ▷ Latimer, Hugh; Protestantism; Ridley, Nicholas; Thirty-nine Articles

creationism Originally, and in Catholic theology, the belief that God creates a soul for each human individual at conception or birth. In medieval times this was thought to occur on the 40th day after conception for males, and for females after 80 days' conception. Augustine considered creationism and original sin to be contradictory beliefs, but Aquinas held that disbelief in this tenet constituted heresy. The term is now commonly applied to the belief that the Genesis account of creation in the Bible accurately describes the origins of the world and humanity. It is opposed to the theory of evolution, and some evangelical conservative Christians claim there is scientific evidence to support creationism, though this has not been supported by other scientists. ▷ Aquinas, St Thomas; Augustine, St (of Hippo); Darwinism; evangelicalism; Genesis, Book of; heresy

creation myths Accounts in story form of the bringing into existence of the universe and its inhabitants. Such myths are of decisive importance in particular cultures for the understanding of the relation of the universe to the divine, and of the human being's responsibilities in it. ▷ altjiranga; primeval hill; Nun; Theogonies, Greek; wondjina

wondjina, a figure from aboriginal creation myth

creation myths, Greek The Book of Genesis opens with an account of the creation of the universe, culminating in the creation of man. Early Greek mythical accounts of the origins of the universe, by contrast, take the form of Theogonies, narratives of the birth of the gods, and have no place for the origins of humankind—although a misogynistic myth about the first woman, Pandora, appears in the poet Hesiod (7th century BCE). Instead, we find myths about the origins of particular Greek peoples, which often explained how they emerged from the soil of what was, therefore, very literally their native land. Not until the end of the 5th century BCE is the myth that the human race was fashioned from clay by Prometheus attested. ▷ Chthonian religion; creation myths; Genesis, Book of; Greek religion; Theogonies, Greek

creeds Creeds are concise statements that summarize the essential beliefs of a religious tradition. They are regarded as authoritative, they are often used in rituals, and they establish the doctrinal position of a religious community in the wider world. They are especially important in Christianity, which has valued theology and doctrinal orthodoxy more than other religions, but they are present in other traditions as well. The three Christian creeds are the Apostles' Creed, the Nicene Creed and the Athanasian Creed; Judaism values the medieval creed of Maimonides and the one-line formula of the Shema, 'Hear, O Israel: the Lord our God is one God'; in Islam the *shahadah* is a brief statement of faith, 'Allah is Allah and Muhammad is his prophet'; the three refuges of Buddhism are equivalent to a Buddhist creed, 'I take refuge in the Buddha, the Dharma and the Sangha'; and similar formulae are to be found in the Sikh *Japji* and the Zoroastrian *Avesta*, although not so obviously in Hinduism. Sometimes what amounts to longer creeds are found in the form of articles or confessions of faith. The Reformation confessions of faith such as the Augsburg Confession of the Lutheran tradition of 1530 and the Westminster Confession of the Reformed tradition of 1646 set out particular Protestant positions. In Islam, the *aqidahs* of the Sunni law schools, and in Judaism the summaries of faith of Philo and Moses Maimonides, perform similar functions, although they are not used in worship and are not authoritative for the whole tradition. ▷ Apostles' Creed; Aqida; Athanasian Creed; Augsburg Confession; Avesta; Japji; Maimonides; Nicene Creed; Philo Judaeus; shahadah; Shema; Westminster Confession of Faith

Creeds, Christian The New Testament contains brief confessions of faith such as 'Jesus is Lord' (Romans 10.9) and other doctrinal summaries that may have been used at early baptismal services. These developed into longer but still concise statements of Christian belief that were widely, if not almost universally, accepted through the approval of Councils of the Church, especially the (so-called) Apostles' Creed from the West and the Nicene Creed from the East, which are used in worship as well as for teaching. Creeds, including the less well known (and misnamed) Athanasian Creed which stresses the doctrines of the Incarnation and the Trinity, are not complete statements of Christian faith. Issues that arose after the 4th and 5th centuries, such as the Reformation questioning of the Roman Catholic understanding of church order, government, sacraments and ministry, are dealt with in longer but subsidiary documents. These include the Augsburg Confession (Lutheran, 1530), the Thirty-Nine Articles (Anglican, 1563, 1571), the Westminster Confession (Presbyterian, 1647) and the Savoy Declaration (Congregationalist, 1658). Twentieth-century attempts at Church union and ecumenical co-operation have also produced statements of faith to link acceptance of the historic Creeds with other areas of agreement. ▷ Apostles' Creed; Athanasian Creed; Augsburg Confession; Congregationalism; Council of the Church; Nicene Creed; Thirty-nine Articles; Trinity; Westminster Confession of Faith

Creeds, Islamic There is no universal creed in Islam, and doctrinal beliefs as such are not as important as in the Christian tradition. Although not a creed as such, the Muslim statement of faith, the *shahadah*, 'Allah is Allah, and Muhammad is his prophet', is the touchstone of Islam. Later more formal creeds were introduced, but none was as formative for Islam as the great Christian creeds were for Christianity or even Maimonides' creed for Judaism. An influential creed in early Islam was that of al-Ashari (873–935), which rejected the allegorical interpretation of the Quran, and affirmed the Quranic views that the Quran is uncreated, that all happens according to God's will, that God is the sole creator, that human deeds are subject to the creation and predestination of God, that Muslim believers will know the beatific vision on the day of resurrection, that hell is not in prospect for believers in God's unity, that the Islamic tradition's doctrines are trustworthy, and that the four early caliphs represent the foundational age of Islam. Other notable, but again not authoritative, creeds have been those of Abu Hanifah (700–67), al-Shafii (767–820), and al-Ghazali (1058–1111). ▷ Ashari, al-; creeds; Ghazali, Abu Hamid Mohammed al-; Maimonides; Muhammad; Shafii, al-; shahadah

cremation, Buddhist Cremation was introduced into China and Japan under Buddhist auspices. In China the practice of ancestor veneration had made burial of complete bodies the normal procedure, but when Buddhism entered China Buddhist monks and nuns practised cremation and it became more common. In Japan it was given imperial blessing when the empress Jito was cremated in 704, and thereafter the Buddhists became responsible for its implementation. At present, funeral and cremation rites are a primary function of the majority of Buddhist priests and temples in Japan. ▷ funerary practices

crisis theology A type of Protestant theology initiated after World War I under the inspiration of Karl Barth, and very influential during the 1920s and 1930s. The term 'crisis' essentially applied to the judgement (Greek *krisis*) of God upon all merely human social, moral, and religious endeavours. The approach exercised a decisive influence on the Declaration of Barmen (1934) which, in opposition to the readiness of the so-called 'German Christians' to integrate the racialist ideology of the German National Socialists into Christian doctrine, affirmed Jesus Christ as God's sole and sufficient revelation and denied any revelations in nature, history, or race apart from him. ▷ Barmen Declaration; Barth, Karl; Christianity; Christology; Nazi Party; revelation

cross The main symbol of Christianity, but a widespread religious symbol even in pre-Christian times. For Christians it represents the crucifixion and resurrection of Jesus Christ, who was nailed to a cross and left to die, then considered the most demeaning form of execution. The sign of the cross may be invoked as an affirmation of faith, or as a prayer, benediction or dedication. Until the 4th century Christians were wary of using this symbol. With the conversion of Constantine, however, persecution ended, and the cross, along with the labarum symbol, became immensely popular. ▷ crucifixion; labarum; symbolism

Crowley, (Edward) Aleister, originally **Alexander** (1875–1947) English writer and 'magician'. He became interested in the occult while an undergraduate at Cambridge at the time of the 'magic revival' of the late 19th century, and was for a time a member of the Order of the Golden Dawn which W B Yeats also joined. Expelled for extreme practices, he founded his own order, the Silver Star, and travelled widely, settling for several years in Sicily with a group of disciples at the Abbey of Thelema near Cefalù. Rumours of drugs, orgies and magical ceremonies involving the sacrifice of babies culminated in his expulsion from Italy. In 1921 a series of newspaper articles brought him the notoriety he craved—he liked to be known as 'the great beast' and 'the wickedest man alive'—and certainly many who associated with him died tragically, including his wife and child. ▷ occult

crucifix A model of a cross, showing the crucified Christ. Early crucifixes (6th century) portray Christ as victorious and alive, but by the 9th century he was being depicted in a state of suffering. In the West, before the Reformation, the crucifix was given a central—some later said idolatrous—significance, forming a focus of worship, either private or public. In the 20th century there has been fresh emphasis on the use of crucifixes in the Roman Catholic Church. ▷ cross; Jesus Christ; Reformation

crucifixion A common form of capital punishment in the Roman world, in which a person was nailed or bound to a wooden cross by the wrists and feet, and left to die. The method, probably borrowed from the Carthaginians, was inflicted only upon slaves and people of low social status (*humiliores*). It was regularly preceded by flagellation, as happened in the case of Christ himself, whose crucifixion became one of the key events of his life, leading to his death and later resurrection. ▷ cross; crucifix; Jesus Christ

Crusades Holy Wars authorized by the pope in defence of Christendom and the Church. They were fought against the infidels in the East, Germany, and Spain, against heretics and schismatics who threatened Catholic unity, and against Christian lay powers who opposed the papacy. Crusaders committed themselves with solemn vows, and by the 13th century were granted the full Indulgence; ie remission of all punishment due for sin and an assurance of direct entry into heaven. Papal authorizations of war against Islam continued to be made until the 18th century. ▷ Islam

Crusades, Islamic view of In contrast to the effects of the Crusades on Europe—where trade was stimulated, the power of the Italian city-states was increased, military orders such as the Templars and Hospitalers were established, Constantinople was sacked, the church was strengthened, and chivalry renewed—the effect upon Islam was relatively small. During the Crusades Saladin (1138–93) ended the Fatimid dynasty of Egypt, founded his own Ayyubid dynasty, and consolidated his hold upon Syria, Palestine and Egypt. However, in 1260 his dynasty ended, and from the Muslim viewpoint the Crusades were a local matter concerning a minute area of the Islamic world, and thus were of passing interest. One result was that ill-feeling increased between Muslims and Christians, and some Christians who had lived in relative peace within the Muslim world came under increased pressure because of the conduct of their Western brethren. ▷ Crusades

Culavamsa (Culavaṃsa) The 'short chronicle' which continues the story of the Buddhist history of Ceylon begun in the *Mahavamsa*. This had dealt with the period up to the 4th century CE; the *Culavamsa* takes the narrative from 302CE to the 19th century. It is written in the Pali language and appears to be the work of two main authors who wrote in the 13th and 18th centuries. The last chapter, which deals with the arrival of the British in Ceylon, must have been added later still. The existence of these narrative histories of Buddhism in Ceylon (the *Mahavamsa*, *Dipavamsa* and *Culavamsa*) shows the importance attached to the Buddhist tradition as the 'state religion' of Sri Lanka. ▷ Dipavamsa; Mahavamsa; Sinhalese Buddhism

Culdees Originally, monks in the Irish church in the 8th century and the Scottish Church in the 9th century, who later became secular clergy. In Scotland they were respected for their high ideals and spirituality, and survived in St Andrews until the 14th century. ▷ Celtic Church; monasticism

Cullmann, Oscar (1902–) German biblical scholar and theologian, born in Strasbourg. As professor at Basle (from 1938) and Paris (from 1948), he was the chief representative in New Testament studies of the 1950s and 1960s 'biblical theology' movement and an exponent of the concept of Salvation-history (*Heilsgeschichte*). In *Christ and Time* (1951), *Salvation in History* (1967), and *Immortality of the Soul or Resurrection of the Dead?* (1958), he maintains that biblical thinking is essentially historical. God reveals Himself in historical events, not the isolated personal challenges of Bultmann's existential demythologizing approach. He has also written *The Christology of the New Testament* (1959), *Peter: Disciple, Apostle, Martyr* (1953), and several studies of early Church worship and practice. ▷ biblical theology; Bultmann, Rudolf Karl; demythologizing

cult Any set of beliefs and practices associated with a particular god or group of gods, forming a distinctive part of a larger religious body. The focus of the worship or devotion of a cult is usually a god or gods, spirit or spirits, associated with particular objects and places. The focus of devotion may be an animal (eg the whale cult in Inuit (Eskimo) religions), a particular deity (eg the Hindu cult devoted to Shiva), or even a deified human being (eg the emperor cult in ancient Rome). ▷ animal cults; cargo; religion; sect

curate Strictly, a Christian clergyman admitted to the 'cure of souls' and having the 'cure' or charge of a parish. Popularly, the term is used of an assistant or unbeneficed clergyman, helping or temporarily replacing the priest, rector, vicar, or other incumbent of the parish. ▷ priest; rector; vicar

Curia Romana ▷ Roman Curia

Cuthbert, St (c.635–687) Anglo-Saxon churchman and missionary, born probably in Lauderdale, in the Scottish Borders (then part of Northumbria). In 651 he was a shepherd boy there, and while watching his flock by night had a vision which made him resolve to become a monk. The same year he entered the monastery of Old Melrose, and in 660 accompanied its abbot, St Eata, to a new foundation at Ripon. In consequence of the dispute about Easter, Eata returned to Melrose (661), and Cuthbert, having accompanied him, was elected prior. He travelled widely in the north of England as a missionary, and many miracles were reported. In 664 he left Melrose for the island monastery of Lindisfarne, of which he became prior, his old master, Eata, being abbot. But in 676 he left Lindisfarne for a hermit's cell built with his own hands on Farne Island (Inner Farne). Here, in 684, he was visited by Ecgfrith, King of Northumbria, who came entreating him to accept the bishopric of Hexham. He reluctantly complied, but shortly after exchanged the see of Hexham for that of Lindisfarne. Still thirsting after solitude, at the end of two years he returned to his cell, where he died. His body was elevated with a coffin-reliquary in 689, and the magnificent Lindisfarne Gospels book was made for the occasion. The fame of St Cuthbert had been great during his life; it became far greater after his death. Churches were dedicated to him from the Trent and Mersey to the Forth and Clyde. His body remained (incorrupt, as was believed) at Lindisfarne till 875, when the monks moved it inland at the time of the Viking incursions. After many wanderings it found a resting-place at Chester-le-Street in 883; in 995 it was moved first to Ripon and then, in 999, to Durham. Here, enclosed in a costly shrine, and believed to work miracles daily, it remained till the Reformation. The grave was opened in 1826, when inside a triple coffin his skeleton was found, still apparently entire, wrapped in five robes of embroidered silk. His feast day is 20 March. ▷ monasticism

Cyprian, St, Thascius Caecilius Cyprianus (c.200–258) Christian martyr, born probably in Carthage, and one of the great Fathers of the Church. After teaching rhetoric in Carthage, he became a Christian about 245. He was made a bishop in 248, when his zealous efforts to restore strict discipline soon brought him a host of enemies. In the persecution under Decius he had to seek safety in flight; and after his return to Carthage in 251 the rest of his life was a constant struggle to hold the balance between severity and leniency towards the 'lapsed' (ie, those who had conformed for a time to heathenism). Excommunicated by Pope Stephen I for denying the validity of heretic baptism, at a synod in Carthage in 256 Cyprian maintained that the Roman bishop, in spite of St Peter's primacy, could not claim judicial authority over other bishops. He wrote a treatise on church unity, *De unitate ecclesiae*. During the persecution of the reign of Valerianus he was beheaded in Carthage. His feast day is 6 September. ▷ Fathers of the Church; Peter, St

Cyril, St (827–69) Christian missionary, born in Thessalonica. He and his brother, St Methodius (826–85) were known as the Apostles of the Slavs. Cyril, who is traditionally regarded as the inventor of the Cyrillic alphabet, had been a disciple of Photius, and was surnamed 'the philosopher'. He preached the gospel to the Tartar Khazars to the north east of the Black Sea (c.860), while Methodius evangelized the Bulgarians of Thrace and Moesia (c.863). At the request of the Duke of Moravia the brothers prepared a Slav translation of the Scriptures and chief liturgical books. Their use of the vernacular in the liturgy aroused the opposition of the German Roman missionaries, and the brothers were summoned to Rome to explain their conduct. Cyril died there in 869. Methodius, who in the same year was consecrated at Rome Bishop of the Moravians, completed the evangelization of the Slavs. Called to Rome a second time in 879 to justify his celebration of the mass in the native tongue, he gained the approval of Pope John VIII, returned to his diocese in 880, and probably died at Hradištë on the Morava. Both brothers were recognized as saints by the Roman Catholic Church, after having been condemned as Arians by several popes. Their feast day is 7 July. ▷ evangelist; Photius

Cyril of Alexandria, St (376–444) Theologian, one of the Fathers of the Church, born in Alexandria. He became Patriarch of Alexandria in 412, and vigorously implemented orthodox Christian teaching. He expelled the Jews from the city (415), and relentlessly persecuted Nestorius, whose doctrine was condemned at the Council of Ephesus (431). His feast day is 9 June (East) or 27 June (West). ▷ Fathers of the Church; Nestorians; theology

D

daevas (daēvas) The original meaning of the Avestan word was 'the shining ones', referring to heavenly gods. The Old Indian equivalent, *deva*, is still used for 'god'. In Zoroastrianism, however, the word has acquired a pejorative meaning, 'evil supernatural being, demon'. In the Zoroastrian tradition, the daevas are the evil opponents of the *ahuras*. The older theory that devas/daevas and asuras/ahuras represented rival factions in the Indo-Iranian pantheon from a very early age has now been widely abandoned. It seems more likely that, during the migration of the proto-Indian and proto-Iranian tribes from the South Russian steppes, the cult of the warlike god Indra became prominent among the proto-Indians, partly eclipsing the traditional veneration for the high gods Mitra and Varuna. At some stage this cult, which emphatically addressed Indra and his entourage as devas, seems to have spread among the proto-Iranians, provoking Zoroaster's furious reaction, Indra is still one of the most prominent daevas in Zoroastrianism. ▷ ahuras; Avesta; Indra; Zoroastrianism

Dagan, or **Dagon** Ancient West Semitic fertility god. His name may be related to the common Semitic word for corn, but there is little evidence about his characteristics. One of the two temples found at Ugarit was dedicated to him. He features in offering lists, but appears in the Ugaritic mythological texts only in the phrase 'Baal, son of Dagan'. In earlier times he was worshipped in Syria and Western Mesopotamia, and from the Hebrew Bible it appears that he was the chief god of the Philistines, with cult centres at Gaza and Ashdod. ▷ Ancient Near Eastern religions; Baal; Canaanite religion; Philistine religion; Ras Shamra texts; Ugarit

Dagda, the One of the Tuatha Dé Dannan, or old Irish spirit beings. These are clearly pre-Christian divinities, though in the surviving literature (written down in Christian times) they are presented rather as heroes, and any signs of regular worship have been removed. The Dagda is found throughout Ireland. He is described as 'the good god' (ie 'good at everything, omnicompetent') and father of all (Eochaid Ollathair). His signs are a huge club, a beautiful cauldron, and a marvellously effective harp. He is generally benign. Brigit, the triple goddess, is his daughter; the Morrigan, 'the great queen' and one of the triad of war goddesses, is one of his partners; his sons married the three goddesses of Ireland. Some have argued that he is the pre-Christian supreme god, but this is uncertain. In the stories as we have them, Lug is sometimes pre-eminent, and in some the Dagda is made to look ridiculous. Still more doubtful are identifications with Celtic gods known elsewhere in Europe; Cernunnos, for instance, or the club-carrying figure on the hill at Cerne Abbas. ▷ Cernunnos; Lug; matres, matrones

Daimon, Daimones Although 'demon' derives from the Greek word *daimon*, there is nothing demonic about early Greek daimones. There was, in fact, no place for demons in the early Greek world view, which lacked a devil. Daimon is simply, in many contexts, another word for god (*theos*); by way of differentiation, one can note, at most, a tendency to apply theos to divine power conceived personally, daimon to a more impersonal, unidentified force. Another common early application of daimon is to the fate or fortune of an individual: the common Greek word for 'happy, blessed', is *eudaimon*, 'of good daimon', and its opposite is 'of evil daimon' (*kakodaimon*). A famous saying of the philosopher Heraclitus (c.500BCE) plays on and reverses this concept: 'character is daimon to man', in other words, a person's fortune is not externally given but comes from his or her own character. It was Plato in the 4th century BCE who began the process of change that transformed daimon into demon, when he declared the daimones to be a distinct class of beings intermediate between gods and men. ▷ Greek religion; Plato

dakhma An Iranian word deriving from the Indo-European root for 'to bury', and denoting a place for the disposal of the dead. In the older Zoroastrian tradition, there appear to be some discrepancies in the use of the word, perhaps because slightly different traditions existed within the Zoroastrian community. In later Zoroastrianism the word always refers to a 'Tower of Silence'—a round stone structure, usually set well apart from

dakhma

places of human habitation, in which Zoroastrians place their dead. This way of disposing of the dead ensures that the earth as such is not defiled by the corpse, which is held to be extremely polluting, and that the bones will be picked clean by vultures, a process involving a minimum of corruption. Later, the bones are thrown into a pit filled with quicklime, where they disintegrate. The dakhma itself is felt to pose a great threat to purity, and can only be entered by professional corpse-bearers who have to take ritual precautions against polluting influences, and undergo rites of purification when they leave the profession. Some sections of the Zoroastrian commmunity are now strongly in favour of abandoning this ancient way of disposing of the dead, which has become impracticable in many places, but others staunchly adhere to it. ▷ Zoroastrianism

Dalai Lama The title of the hierarch of the Gelugpa tradition of Tibetan Buddhism and political ruler of Tibet from the 17th century to 1959. The title dalai (meaning 'ocean') was given by the Mongol ruler Altan Khan to Sonam Gyamtsho (1543–88), the third head of the Gelugpa order, because he was so impressed by the lama and the Buddhist teachings. The title was retrospectively attributed to the first and second Gelugpa hierarchs who followed from the tradition's founder Tsongkhapa (1357–1419). With Mongol support the fifth Dalai Lama, Ngawang Lopsang Gyatso (1617–82), became the political leader of Tibet. The Dalai Lamas ruled Tibet until the present Dalai Lama fled from Chinese persecution after their invasion in 1951, when Tibet became a province of the People's Republic of China. Each successive Dalai Lama is believed to be a reincarnation of the previous one. They are also thought to be manifestations of the bodhisattva Avalokiteshvara. The present Dalai Lama, Tenzin Gyatso, now lives in exile along with thousands of Tibetans who hope that one day he will be re-established as the political head of Tibet. ▷ Avalokiteshvara; bodhisattva; Dalai Lama; Gelugpa; lama; Tibetan religion; Tsongkapa

Dalai Lama (Tenzin Gyatso) (1935–) Spiritual and temporal head of Tibet. Born in Taktser, in Amdo province, into a peasant family, he was designated the fourteenth Dalai Lama in 1937 by the monks of Lhasa who were convinced, from his actions, that he was the reincarnation of the Compassionate Buddha. He was enthroned at Lhasa in 1940, but his rights were exercised by a regency until 1950. He fled to Chumbi in southern Tibet after an abortive anti-Chinese uprising in 1950, but negotiated an autonomy agreement with the People's Republic the following year and for the next eight years served as nominal ruler of Tibet. After China's brutal suppression of the Tibetan national uprising of 1959 he was forced into permanent exile, settling, with other Tibetan refugees, at Dharamsala in Punjab, India, where he established a democratically-based alternative government. A revered figure in his homeland, the Dalai Lama has for long rejected Chinese overtures to return home as a figurehead, seeking instead full independence. In 1988, however, he modified this position, proposing the creation of a self-governing Tibet in association with China. Active in promulgating Buddhist teachings, he regards compassion as Buddhism's highest ideal. He was awarded the 1989 Nobel Prize for Peace in recognition of his commitment to the non-violent liberation of his homeland. ▷ Buddha; Tibetan religion

Dal Khalsa (Dāl Khālsā) Originally a Sikh standing army set up after the Baisakhi festival of 1748. Replacing a temporary army that had gathered occasionally when the need was great, it was formed into 11 units, each with its own commander, and was led by Baba Jassa Singh Aluwalia (1718–83), a Sikh military leader. New entrants could join whichever unit they wished, and although in principle the units were equal in numbers, in practice they varied in size. In 1978 the name Dal Khalsa was given to a new political party in the Indian state of the Punjab. Promoted by a Sikh leader, Giana Zail Singh, its aim was to give another voice to Sikh political aspirations in the Punjab and in wider India, in addition to that of the Akali Dal. ▷ Akali Dal; Baisakhi; Khalsa; Punjab

Daly, Mary (1928–) American feminist and theological writer, born in Schenectady, New York. She studied theology at St Mary's College, Indiana, and Fribourg University, Switzerland, and has taught at Fribourg (1959–66) and Boston College (from 1969). Having analysed the effects of male bias in *The Church and the Second Sex* (1968), she abandoned her attempts to reform official Roman Catholic attitudes and became a post-Christian radical feminist in *Beyond God the Father* (1973). Her emphasis on pre-Jewish/Christian religion and women's personal experience is developed in *Gyn/Ecology: The Metaethics of Radical Feminism* (1978) and *Pure Lust: Elemental Feminist Philosophy* (1984). ▷ feminist theology; Christianity, women in

Damiani, Pietro, or **St Peter Damian** (1007–72) Italian ecclesiastic, born in Ravenna, and one of the Doctors of the Church. As a boy he herded swine, but in 1035 he joined the hermitage at Fonte Avellana and rose to be Cardinal and Bishop of Ostia (1057). He supported the policy of Hildebrand (Gregory VII) without sharing his arrogance, and laboured strenuously to reform the clergy, then at a low ebb of immorality and indolence. His feast day is 23 February. ▷ Gregory VII, St

Damien, Father Joseph, originally **Joseph de Veuster** (1840–89) Belgian Roman Catholic missionary, born in Tremelo. He is renowned for his great work among the lepers of the Hawaiian island of Molokai, where he lived from 1873 until his death from the disease. ▷ missions, Christian

Dan, tribe of One of the 12 tribes of ancient Israel, said to be descended from the fifth son of Jacob, Dan's mother having been Bilhah, Rachel's maid. Its territory was vaguely defined, but was initially a coastal plain surrounded by the territories of Ephraim, Benjamin, and Judah; later the tribe was forced to migrate north near the sources of the Jordan River. ▷ Israel, tribes of; Jacob; Rachel

Daniel, Book of A book of the Hebrew Bible/Old Testament named after Daniel, its main character. It falls into two parts: chapters 1–6 contain narrative accounts of Daniel and his three companions, ostensibly set during the Babylonian Exile in the 6th century BCE; chapters 7–12 describe apocalyptic revelations of Daniel recorded as first-person visions. Although some date the work in the 6th century BCE, many prefer a later date of the 3rd–2nd century BCE, with several stages of compilation. The **Additions** are three works found joined to the Book of Daniel in some ancient Greek versions and in the modern Catholic Bible, but part of the Protestant Apocrypha. ▷ Apocrypha, Old Testament; Azariah, Prayer of; Bel and the Dragon; Old Testament; Song of the Three Young Men; Susanna, Story of

darshan (darśan) The 'seeing' of a sacred image or person in Hinduism. Darshan is an important part of Hindu worship, during which the devotee will look at the image of a deity and so 'receive its darshan' or be blessed by it. Sometimes an image will only be revealed on occasion and the darshan of some images in temples is restricted to the upper castes. Because the image (*murti*, *arca*) of the deity is regarded as the deity, to behold the image is to receive a blessing and spiritual power. The darshan of a holy man or guru is especially efficacious. ▷ guru; Hinduism; iconography, Hindu

Darwin, Charles Robert (1809–82) English naturalist, born in Shrewsbury, the originator (with Alfred Russel Wallace) of the theory of evolution by natural selection. The grandson of Erasmus Darwin and of Josiah Wedgwood, he was educated at Shrewsbury grammar school and studied medicine at Edinburgh (1825–7). Then, with a view to entering the Church, he entered Christ's College, Cambridge, in 1828. Whilst still a student at Edinburgh he was a member of the local Plinian Society; he took part in its natural history excursions, and read before it his first scientific paper—on Flustra or sea-mats. His biological studies seriously began at Cambridge, where the botanist John Stevens Henslow encouraged his interest in zoology and geology. He was recommended by Henslow as naturalist to HMS *Beagle*, then about to start for a scientific survey of South American waters (1831–6) under its captain, Robert Fitzroy. He visited Tenerife, the Cape Verde Islands, Brazil, Montevideo, Tierra del Fuego, Buenos Aires, Valparaiso, Chile, the Galapagos, Tahiti, New Zealand, Tasmania, and finally the Keeling Islands, where he started his famous theory of coral reefs. During this long expedition he obtained the intimate knowledge of the fauna, flora and geology of many lands which equipped him for his later investigations. By 1846 he had published several works on the geological and zoological discoveries of his voyage, on coral reefs, volcanic islands, etc—works that placed him at once in the front rank of scientists.

He formed a friendship with Sir Charles Lyell, was Secretary of the Geological Society from 1838 to 1841, and in 1839 married his cousin, Emma Wedgwood (1808–96). From 1842 he lived at Downe, Kent, as a country gentleman, keeping a garden, conservatories, pigeons and fowls.

The practical knowledge thus gained (especially as regards variation and interbreeding) proved invaluable; private means enabled him to devote himself unremittingly, in spite of continuous ill-health, to science. At Downe he addressed himself to the great work of his life—the problem of the origin of species. After five years collecting the evidence, he 'allowed himself to speculate' on the subject, and in 1842 drew up some short notes, enlarged in 1844 into a sketch of conclusions for his own use. These embodied in embryo the principle of natural selection, the germ of the Darwinian Theory; but with constitutional caution Darwin delayed publication of his hypothesis. However, in 1858 Alfred Russel Wallace sent him a memoir on the Malay Archipelago, which, to Darwin's surprise, contained in essence the main idea of his own theory of natural selection. Lyell and Joseph Hooker persuaded him to submit a paper of his own, based on his 1844 sketch, which was read simultaneously with Wallace's before the Linnean Society on 1 July 1858, neither Darwin nor Wallace being present at that historic occasion. Darwin now set to work to condense his vast mass of notes, and put into shape his great work on *The Origin of Species by Means of Natural Selection*, published in November 1859. That epoch-making work, received throughout Europe with the deepest interest, was violently attacked, particularly by those who believed that Darwin's theories directly contradicted the biblical view of humankind's divine creation. In the end, however, Darwin succeeded in obtaining recognition (with or without certain reservations) from almost all competent biologists.

From the day of its publication Darwin continued to work on a great series of supplemental treatises: *The Fertilisation of Orchids* (1862), *The Variation of Plants and Animals under Domestication* (1867), and *The Descent of Man and Selection in Relation to Sex* (1871), according to which the human race was derived from a hairy quadrumanous animal belonging to the great anthropoid group, and related to the progenitors of the orang-utan, chimpanzee and gorilla. In it Darwin also developed his important supplementary theory of sexual selection. Later works were *The Expression of the Emotions in Man and Animals* (1873), *Insectivorous Plants* (1875), *Climbing Plants* (1875), *The Effects of Cross and Self Fertilisation in the Vegetable Kingdom* (1876), *Different Forms of Flowers in Plants of the same Species* (1877), *The Power of Movement in Plants* (1880) and *The Formation of Vegetable Mould through the action of Worms* (1881). Though not the sole originator of the evolution hypothesis, nor even the first to apply the concept of descent to plants and animals, Darwin was the first thinker to gain for that concept a wide acceptance among biological experts. By adding to the crude evolutionism of Erasmus Darwin, Lamarck and others his own specific notion of natural selection, he supplied to the idea a sufficient cause, which raised it at once from a hypothesis to a verifiable theory. He also wrote a biography of Erasmus Darwin (1879). ▷ Darwinism

Darwinism The view, first proposed by Charles Darwin, that the world and its living species have evolved over millions of years: in other words, that neither is a static creation of God, but are both instead constantly changing. Darwin outlined a theory of 'natural selection', in which those species best suited to a particular environment will survive over those less well adapted, and will continue to adapt as circumstances change. With *The Origin of the Species* (1859) he outlined his evidence for his theories of evolution. These were seen by many as a direct and therefore heretical contradiction of the biblical creation story as revealed in the sacred texts of Judaism, Islam and Christianity. ▷ creation myths; Darwin, Charles Robert

Dasam Granth A Sikh sacred text, meaning 'the Book of the tenth [guru]'. Associated with the tenth Sikh guru, Guru Gobind Singh, it was not completed until 1734, a few years after his death. It is secondary to the main Sikh scripture, the *Guru Granth Sahib*. Containing over 2000 poems, it is 1428 pages in length, and has no single unifying theme. Written in the Gurmukhi Punjabi script, the language of the original poems could be Hindi, Persian, or Sanskrit. The *Jap Sahib* and other verses from it attributed to Guru Gobind Singh, are used in Sikh initiation rituals and elsewhere, but it is likely that some of the poems in the *Dasam Granth* were written by Guru Gobind Singh's court poets rather than by himself, and in fact it contains a series of reinterpretations of the stories of Krishna (a Hindu deity) as well as a number of non-religious legends. ▷ Adi Granth; Gobind Singh, Guru; Guru Granth Sahib; rites of passage; Krishna

David (Hebrew, 'beloved') First king of the Judean dynasty of Israel. He was the youngest son of Jesse of Bethlehem, and distinguished himself by slaying the Philistine champion, Goliath. Saul appointed him to a military command, and gave him his daughter Michal as a wife, but David had soon to flee from the king's jealousy. In the cave of Adullam, near Gath, he gathered a troop of 400 free-booters, with whom he ranged through the country between Philistia and the Dead Sea. Saul's expeditions against him put him to great straits, and for over a year David became a vassal of the Philistine King of Gath. After the death of Saul and Jonathan at Gilboa, he reigned for seven-and-a-half years in Hebron over the tribe of Judah, while Ishbosheth, Saul's son, ruled the rest of Israel. On the death of Ishbosheth, all Israel chose David as king. He conquered the independent city of Jebus (Jerusalem) and made it the political and religious centre of his kingdom, building a palace for himself on its highest hill, Zion (the 'city of David'), and placing the Ark of the Covenant there under a tent. In the course of a few years the conquest of the Philistines, Moabites, Aramaeans, Edomites and Ammonites reduced the whole territory from Egypt to the Euphrates. The last years of his 32-year reign in Jerusalem were troubled by attempted revolutions by his sons Absalom and Adonijah. The death of the greatest of the kings of Israel took place at earliest in 1018, at latest in 993BCE. He was succeeded by Solomon, his son by Bathsheba. ▷ Ark of the Covenant; Israel, tribes of; Judah, tribe of; Solomon; Zion

Dayananda Sarasvati (1824–83) Founder of the Hindu reform movement, the Arya Samaj. Born and raised in a Shaiva Brahman family, at the age of ten Dayananda Sarasvati was initiated into the worship of the linga, the sacred symbol of Shiva. However, he became disillusioned with image-worship when he saw mice running over the image at an all-night vigil in the temple during the Shivaratri festival. If the image were truly the 'body' of God, then, Dayananda thought, he would not allow it to be defiled in this way. Dayananda became a renouncer (*sannyasin*), found a guru who taught him Sanskrit and after three years left the guru to propagate what he saw as a return to pure or original Hinduism. This was the Hinduism of the Vedas which, Dayananda said, contained no image-worship, nor immoral practices such as child-marriage. The various gods in the Veda were really different names for the one, supreme being. He also accepted reincarnation and karma and the ideal of liberation (*moksha*) in which the soul was liberated but retained its separation from God. These ideas were articulated in his *Light on Truth* (*Satyartha Prakas*) and codified in the principles of the Arya Samaj, the organization which he founded in 1875 to propagate his vision. ▷ Arya Samaj; guru; karma; linga; moksha

day of judgement ▷ **judgement of the dead**

deacon (Greek *diakonos*, 'servant') An official of the Christian Church appointed to assist the minister or priest in administrative, pastoral, and financial affairs. The office developed into a third order of ministry after bishops and priests. In the late 20th century, ecumenical factors revived interest in an order of deacons (the diaconate). In many churches, deaconesses are a separate order of parish assistants. ▷ clergy; ecumenism

Dead Sea Scrolls Parchment scrolls in Hebrew and Aramaic, many representing books of the Old Testament. A thousand years older than previously known copies, they were found accidentally in 1947 and 1952–5, concealed in pottery jars in 11 caves near Qumran on the Dead Sea. They are thought to represent the library of an ascetic Jewish sect, the Essenes, hidden when their settlement was overrun by the Roman army in 68CE. ▷ Essenes; Old Testament; Qumran, community of

dean (Italian *decem*, 'ten') Originally, in a monastery, a monk in charge of 10 novices. Later, the term denoted a senior clergyman (after the bishop) in a cathedral chapter or diocese. In lay terms, it is used of a head of a university college or faculty. ▷ cathedral; clergy; monasticism

death ceremonies, Sikh When a Sikh is dying a famous prayer of Guru Arjan, called the *Sukhmani Sahib*, is read containing the couplet of peace 'The name of God is sweet ambrosia, source of inner peace and joy. The name of God brings blissful peace to the hearts of the truly devout'. In line with Indian custom the body is usually cremated on the day of death, or on the day after when death occurs late in the day. The body is prepared by members of the family, it is dressed, and it bears the five Ks (shorts, comb, bangle, uncut hair and sword), and a turban in the case of a man. During the funeral the important *Sohila* hymn is read from the Sikh scripture, the *Guru Granth Sahib*, and when the body is burnt the ashes are scattered in a nearby river, preferably the River Sutlej in the Punjab. After that there is a reading of the whole *Guru Granth Sahib* at intervals, and at the end of this reading, nine days after the funeral service, a *bhog* ceremony is held with all the family present ending with the sharing of special food. Outside India death ceremonies may be adapted to local conditions, for example in Britain the body may be taken for a funeral service in the local Sikh temple, the gurdwara. ▷ Arjan, Guru; bhog; five Ks; gurdwara; Guru Granth Sahib; turban

'death of God' theology A form of theology whose roots were in the 19th century, but which became popular, especially in the USA, in the mid 1960s. It sought to assert the rationality of the Christian faith and belief in the uniqueness of Christ, without belief in a transcendent God, some of its exponents claiming that since modern people found it impossible to believe in God, the Church ought to manage without him as well. One of its beliefs is that God has removed himself to allow contemporary humankind complete freedom. It is associated with such theologians as William Hamilton (1924–), Paul van Buren (1924–), Gabriel Vahanian (1927–), and Thomas JJ Altizer (1927–), who claimed Hegel, Nietzsche ('God is dead'), and Bonhoeffer as their intellectual forerunners. ▷ Bonhoeffer, Dietrich; Hegel, Georg Wilhelm Friedrich; Nietzsche, Friedrich Wilhelm; theology

Decalogue ▷ Ten Commandments

Dedication, Feast of ▷ Hanukkah

Deepavali ▷ Divali/Deepavali

deification The transformation, development or growth of a being or thing into a god. This was a widespread and ancient practice, generally implying the immortalization of the subject by various means: liberation of the soul from the body, magic, particular rituals, spiritual knowledge, and in the case of animals, mummification. It was especially prominent in the religions of Ancient Greece and Rome, as in the case of Alexander the Great and the Roman Emperors. It was, however, by no means confined to that civilization: Egyptian pharaohs and the Buddha were deified, while in Christianity, Jesus Christ, insofar as he is recognized as the incarnation of the Second Person of the Trinity, is a prime instance, though certain early Greek fathers referred deification to the raising up of the redeemed to share in the life of God himself.
In the mystery religions, it is equivalent to absorption into, or communion with, the deity. It is the aim of asceticism, that the soul, being purified from the contamination of the body, might be released (from the cycle of reincarnation) to its immortal god-like status. Other forms of deification were achieved through rituals or initiations identifying the subject with a particular god (eg Dionysos, Cybele); or, in Gnosticism, through 'heavenly knowledge' whereby the subject was regenerated into immortality; or through magical formulas (eg the cult of Mithra, 3rd century CE); or funeral rites and funerary practices, such as portraying a god with the same features as the dead person. ▷ funerary practices; mystery religions

deism Originally, belief in the existence of a god or gods; today, belief in the existence of a supreme being who is the ground and source of reality but who does not intervene or take an active interest in the natural and historical order. It also designates a largely British 17th-century and 18th-century movement of religious thought emphasizing natural religion as opposed to revealed religion, and seeking to establish reasonable grounds for belief in the existence of God; represented by, among others, Lord Herbert of Cherbury (1583–1648), Matthew Tindal (1657–1733), and Anthony Collins (1676–1729). ▷ theism

deity The divine, or that which transcends the human being or the material world. In many ways, it seems synonymous with God or the gods, but it is not identical. It is not a proper name, like Yahweh or Allah, yet deity can be applied to either, as it can to Brahman, and is not worshipped as such. It is rather more abstract than the one God or particular gods. It has been used defensively, as by the 18th- and 19th-century European Deists, who wanted to affirm belief in a first cause or supreme being without subscribing to the existence of the personal God of Christian theism. Deity may refer not just to God or the gods but to all the powers, forces, and energies which various religious traditions recognize as coming from beyond the human or mundane realm. In most traditions there is a relation between deity and the origin of the cosmos, the latter being derived from or dependent on the former. It can also be seen as symbolizing the perfection or perfect realization of the human, symbolizing both freedom and infinity, justice and peace, or being understood as the divinized human being (eg the

Christ, or *atman-brahman*). This has led some philosophers (eg Feuerbach), sociologists (eg Marx) or psychologists (eg Freud) to present deity as an illusory projection from human experience and need. ▷ Brahman; God; transcendence and immanence

Delilah Biblical character, who at the instigation of the Philistines enticed Samson to reveal the secret of his great strength—his uncut hair, according to his Nazirite vow. She contrived to cut his hair to weaken him (Judges 16). ▷ Judges, Book of; Samson

Delphi, Greek **Dhelfoí**, formerly **Pytho** Village and ancient site in Fokis department, Greece, on the slopes of Mount Parnassós. It was renowned throughout the ancient Greek world as the sanctuary of Apollo and the seat of his oracle; remains of the temple and precincts were excavated in the 19th century. ▷ Delphi, Oracle of; Greek religion

Delphi, Oracle of The oracular shrine of Apollo at Delphi in central Greece. It was the most prestigious oracle in the Graeco-Roman world, for centuries being consulted by states about public policy and by individuals about private matters. On the payment of a fee, enquirers put their questions to Apollo's medium, a priestess called the Pythia. Her ecstatic responses (oracles) were notorious for their ambiguity. ▷ Delphi; oracle

Deluge ▷ **Flood, the**

demonology, biblical In Old Testament thought, God the creator and sustainer of all is seen as the source of both good and evil. Evil spirits are understood to work within his authority, and the Satan who tested Job is seen more as a heavenly prosecutor assessing the extent of human virtue than an evil being intent on destroying it. Speculation on the distant origins of evil, through a rebellion of supernatural beings against God, is more a characteristic of the intertestamental literature that built on the story of fallen angels having offspring by human women (Genesis 6).

The New Testament Gospels portray Jesus tempted by the devil at the outset of his public ministry to misuse his divine powers for personal gain (Matthew 4.1–11); Luke 4.1–13), and see his exorcism of evil spirits as a sign of the coming of the kingdom of God. The Epistles argue that although a very real struggle between good and evil continues, both within the individual and in the world at large, the final outcome is guaranteed by the death of Christ. According to the Book of Revelation, persecution of Christians and other activities of the devil are restricted by God, and his final defeat at the end of the age is assured. ▷ angelology, biblical; intertestamental literature; kingdom of God; Revelation, book of; Satan

demythologizing A method of interpreting the Bible, systematized by Rudolf Bultmann. He attempted to understand the so-called 'mythical' language of biblical times, which presupposed a pre-scientific world-view, by interpreting it 'existentially', thus making it meaningful to the modern scientifically-minded world. In so doing he argued that many major beliefs of Christianity, such as Christ's resurrection, are only myth, and, since they have no historical reality, must be re-explained in terms acceptable to people today. In response to this, critics of demythologizing claim that this approach adopts a materialistic and essentially godless framework as the standpoint from which to judge biblical truth, thus missing the point that if 'myth' is any story dealing with God, any form of discussion of him must inevitably involve myth, without necessarily being untruthful. ▷ Bible; Bultmann, Rudolf Karl; existentialism; Heidegger, Martin; hermeneutics; mythology

deontological ethics Any normative ethical theory which emphasizes principles of rightness and wrongness independent of good and bad consequences, in contrast to teleological or consequentialist theories. Thus a deontological theory might imply that slavery is unjust even if it might maximize a particular society's welfare on balance, or that one ought to keep a promise made to a dying person even though no one would benefit thereby. Deontologists typically try to ground moral judgements in such notions as natural rights, personal dignity, or (in theological versions) God's commands. ▷ teleological ethics

dependent origination (paṭicca-samuppāda; Sanskrit; pratītya-samutpāda) A central concept of the Buddhist tradition, which is related to the four noble truths (*ariya sacca*). It was very important in the Buddha's own teaching, and one of his disciples stated that 'whoever sees dependent origination sees dharma, and whoever sees dharma sees dependent origination' (*Majjhima Nikaya* I.191). The theory argues that everything arises and exists in dependence on other things. Nothing (except nirvana) is independent. Everything is related to everything else and is conditioned by everything else in a chain of 12 interdependent links. The 12 links are: spiritual ignorance, constructing activities, consciousness, mind and body, six sense-bases, sensory stimulation, feeling, craving, grasping, existence, birth, and ageing and death. Thus ageing and death and the suffering connected with them arise ultimately from spiritual ignorance, and they will cease and nirvana will be gained with the cessation of spiritual ignorance. The real problem is not sin but spiritual ignorance, which is not just an intellectual defect but a lack of understanding of reality which can be overcome by meditational insight. The theory of dependent origination underlies the four noble truths, explains the working of rebirth, shows how there can be no permanent self lying behind the links of the chain, and illuminates the concept of impermanence (*anicca*). It was reckoned by the Buddha to be one of the key elements in his thinking. ▷ anatman; ariya sacca; Buddha; dharma; duhkha; nirvana

dervish A member of the Sufi, mystical sects which emerged throughout the Islamic world in the 12th century. Dervishes were known for their ecstatic prayer rituals, in which they often engaged in whirling dances. There are various orders, each with its own rule and ritual. ▷ Bektashi; ecstacy; Sufism

dancing dervish

Descartes, René (1596–1650) French philosopher and mathematician, undoubtedly one of the great figures in the history of Western thought and usually regarded as the father of modern philosophy. He was born near Tours in a small town now called la-Haye-Descartes, and was educated from 1604 to 1614 at the Jesuit College at La Flèche. He did in fact remain a Catholic all his life, and he was careful to modify or even suppress some of his later scientific views, for example his sympathy with Copernicus, mindful no doubt of Galilei's condemnation by the Inquisition in 1634. He studied law at Poitiers, graduating in 1616; then from 1618 he enlisted at his own expense for private military service, mainly in order to travel and to have the leisure to think.

He was in Germany with the army of the Duke of Bavaria one winter's day in 1619 when he had his famous intellectual vision in the 'stove-heated room': he conceived a reconstruction of the whole of philosophy, and indeed of knowledge, into a unified system of certain truth modelled on mathematics and supported by a rigorous rationalism. From 1618 to 1628 he travelled widely in Holland, Germany, France and Italy; then in 1628 returned to Holland where he remained, living quietly and writing until 1649. Few details are known of his personal life, but he did have an illegitimate daughter called Francine, whose death in 1640 at the age of five was apparently a terrible blow to him. He published most of his major works in this period, the more popular ones in French, the more scholarly ones first in Latin. The *Discourse de la Méthode* (1637), the *Meditationes de prima Philosophia* (1641) and the *Principia Philosophiae* (1644) set out the fundamental Cartesian doctrines: the method of systematic doubt; the first indubitably true proposition, *cogito ergo sum*; the idea of god as the absolutely perfect Being; and the dualism of mind and matter. Other philosophical works include *Regulae ad directionem ingenii* ('Rules for the Direction of the Mind', composed in the later 1620s, but unfinished and published posthumously in 1701) and *Traité des Passions de l'âme* (1649, 'Passions of the Soul'). He also made important contributions in astronomy, for example with his theory of vortices, and more especially in mathematics, where he reformed algebraic notation and helped found coordinate geometry.

In 1649 he left Holland for Stockholm on the invitation of Queen Kristina who wanted him to give her tuition in philosophy. These lessons took place three times a week at 5 am and were especially taxing for Descartes whose habit of a lifetime was to stay in bed meditating and reading until about 11 am. He contracted pneumonia and died. His last words were supposedly 'ça mon âme, il faut partir' ('So my soul, a time for parting'). He was buried in Stockholm but his body was later removed to Paris and eventually transferred to Saint-Germain-des-Prés. ▷ dualism; God; Inquisition; philosophy; rationalism

Desert Fathers Third- and fourth-century Christians who left the relative comfort of town and village life to seek God in the desert, following the biblical tradition of Israel's wilderness wanderings, John the Baptist's life and Jesus's period of testing in the desert. With Constantine's legalization of Christianity, physical detachment from the world took the place previously taken by the prospect of martyrdom. The removal of external distractions revealed that the real battle between good and evil went on within the individual's soul. One should therefore submit one's own religious experiences to the discernment of an older and wiser Father, and avoid judging other people. Our knowledge of the Desert Fathers is based on lives of notable pioneers like St Anthony of Egypt (?251–355) and St Pachomius (d.346); general collections of *Apothegmata* or pithy sayings, whose teaching was systematized by Evagrius Ponticus (c.345–399) and transmitted to Western monasticism in the writings of John Cassian; and the histories of Rufinus (c.345–410) and Palladius (c.365–425). ▷ Cassian, John; Constantine I; monasticism

Deuteronomistic History The theory that the biblical narratives from Deuteronomy to 2 Kings were essentially the work of a historian or historians in the mid 6th century BCE, though scholars differ about the date and the nature of the activity, with some accepting only a Deuteronomistic 'revision' of earlier narratives during the exilic period. It portrayed Israel's fate in terms of her leaders' compliance or disregard for Israel's Law and the true prophets. ▷ Deuteronomy/Joshua/Judges/Kings/Samuel, Book(s) of; Old Testament

Deuteronomy, Book of The fifth and last book of the Pentateuch, in the Hebrew Bible/Old Testament. Its title means 'a repetition of the law' (from the Septuagint's mistaken rendering into Greek of Deuteronomy 17.18, where the Hebrew means 'a copy of the law'). It was traditionally attributed to Moses, but many date it much later, c.7th century BCE. It surveys Israel's wilderness experiences, and presents an extensive code of religious laws and duties. ▷ Deuteronomistic History; Old Testament; Pentateuch; Septuagint

Devil ▷ Satan

devils From Greek *diabolos* (translated in the Latin Septuagint *diabulus*), in the plural or as a common noun, spirits or supernatural creatures, generally (but not invariably) evil or malign, agents capable of affecting human and other behaviour for ill. Such characters are found in most religions (eg jinn or *shaytans* in Islam, *asuras* and associated beings in Hinduism, fallen angels or evil spirits in Judaeo-Christian tradition). They are usually depicted as male, but female devils are not unknown. In the singular, the Devil (cf *Mara* in Buddhism, *Angra Mainyu* in Zoroastrianism) is the embodiment of evil, the chief of evil spirits or fallen angels. In the Old Testament the name Satan is more common, but in the New Testament the Devil is frequently referred to, sometimes represented as a serpent (Revelation 12.9) or as a tempter (Matthew 4.1). In religious literature the Devil or a devil or demon can assume many different guises, human or animal. Irrational or

Tibetan devil

destructive human behaviour can be explained by devil- or demon-possession, as if a person's will was taken over by some evil force. Belief in this does not presuppose belief in a single personification of evil ('the Devil') but only belief in the existence of evil spirits or devils. Sometimes, they are accounted for by postulating the survival in the form of evil spirits of the hostile dead. ▷ angels; Beelzebub; Bible; demonology, biblical; hell; jinn; Satan

devotion In religion, attitudes and consequent actions of awe, respect, love, and submission towards the divine. Possible objects of devotion vary widely. In monotheistic religions, the object is primarily God, or the Deity or Supreme Being, and in others, a deity or other divine object. Devotion can, however, be exercised and expressed towards almost anything with which the primary object is associated. Thus typical objects of devotion would include saints (Christianity), ancestors (Hinduism, Confucianism, African religions), Hindu *gurus*, *immams* in Islam, Buddhas and bodhisattvas in Buddhism. Apart from people, relics of holy individuals (eg bones of saints), geographical locations such as cities (eg Mecca, Jerusalem), mountains (in Shinto), and rivers (eg Ganges), cultic objects (eg Torah in Judaism, the host of the Roman Catholic Mass) have all been accepted as worthy of devotion.

Devotion may be exercized individually, or corporately by a worshipping community (monastic or otherwise), in structured or unstructured form. In many communities, churches and religious orders it takes the form of corporate worship, including prayer and meditation, usually contemplative. In some cases, such as Sufism, it includes music and dancing, and in others (eg certain Hindu forms) it becomes passionate and frenzied. Individually, devotion may be expressed by asceticism and pilgrimage. It is sometimes expressed through social action, it being understood that true devotion to God can only be expressed by service to humanity. This form would be exemplified in Christianity by Mother Teresa of Calcutta and in Hinduism by Mahatma Gandhi. ▷ asceticism; Mary; prayer; worship

dhanb One of the Islamic terms for sin. There is no notion of original sin within the Muslim tradition because although Adam fell and was expelled from the Garden of Eden the responsibility for sin was Satan's rather than Adam's. The fault, dhanb, lay with Adam, hence the exile from Eden, but this did not imply inherent guilt or a state of original sin. Islam distinguishes between two categories of sin: dhanb, which is a fault or limitation; and *ithm*, which is more serious in that it includes the will and intention to sin, whereas dhanb does not. The Muslim concept of the sinlessness of the prophets, and the Shiite concept of the sinlessness of their imams, implies that dhanb or fault was possible in them, but not ithm or wilful transgression. The answer to dhanb is to get rid of it; the answer to ithm is to repent and receive God's forgiveness. This is possible in regard to all sins except the ultimate sin which is shirk—polytheism or denying the unity of God. Early sects such as the Kharijites and the Mutazilites took a more serious view of sin than the mainstream Islam of their time, and it was in response to their views that the later and more lenient theology of sin arose with the Muslim tradition. ▷ Adam and Eve; Eden, Garden of; Fall, the; Kharijites; Mutazilites; original sin; polytheism; Shiism; shirk; sin, Islamic view of

dharma (Pali: dhamma) This refers to the teaching of the Buddha, but has a deeper meaning than mere outward doctrine. The dharma has always been true, and it pre-existed the Buddha, but it was uncovered by him when he lived in India in the 6th century BCE, just as it has been uncovered in other ages by other Buddhas. The first main facet of dharma in the sense of the Buddha's teaching centres on the four noble truths: that life is characterized by suffering (*duhkha*), suffering is caused by craving (*tanha*), suffering is ended by the elimination of craving, and the elimination of craving comes by means of the eightfold path. The second main facet of dharma as the Buddha's teaching centres on his summary of the three characteristics of existence: duhkha, which is dealt with in the four noble truths (*ariya sacca*); *anicca*, which is the principle of impermanence behind everything; and *anatman*, which is the notion that there is no such thing as an enduring and abiding self. When the Buddha taught he was said to be 'turning the wheel of the dharma', which includes righteous living as well as doctrine. The dharma is valued as one of the three jewels (*tri-ratna*) of the Buddhist world, the other two being the Buddha himself, and the Buddhist community, the *sangha*. A second meaning of dharma within the Theravada Buddhist tradition relates to the notion of dharmas as ultimate constituents of human existence. Theravada Buddhism claimed that there were a fixed number of such dharmas, of which some were material and others were psychological. This theory of particular dharmas was opposed by the Mahayana Buddhists. ▷ anatman; ariya sacca; Buddha; duhkha; eightfold path; Mahayana Buddhism; sangha; tanha; Theravada Buddhism

Dharmapada (Pali: Dhammapada) A popular and influential book which is part of the Theravada Buddhist *tipitaka* or Pali Canon. It has 423 verses arranged in 16 chapters, and is included in the *sutta-pitaka*, the discourses of the Buddha. In its shortness and popularity it has similarities to the Hindu scripture the *Bhagavad Gita*, which is a well-loved part of the larger epic, the *Mahabharata*. The Dharmapada includes many pithy sayings and proverbs that summarize important aspects of Buddhist moral teaching and wisdom. Its anthology of sayings is regarded by Theravada Buddhists as a kind of synopsis of the central facets of Buddhism, and as such it is owned by many Buddhists and learnt by heart by some. The Dharmapada has been translated into English on a number of occasions. Literally meaning 'verses on dharma', it has become a quick introduction for a number of non-Buddhists as well as Buddhists to the doctrines and ethics of the religion. Examples of verses are: 'The giving up of evil, the cultivation of all that is good, cleansing of one's mind, this is the teaching of the Buddhas'(183); and 'Conquer the angry man by love; conquer the ill-natured man by goodness; conquer the miser with generosity; conquer the liar with truth'(223). ▷ Bhagavad Gita; Buddha; dharma; Mahabharata; sutta-pitaka; Theravada Buddhism; tipitaka

dharmakaya One of the bodies of the Buddha within the Mahayana Buddhist concept of the *trikaya*, the three bodies of the Buddha. The Theravada Buddhists had concentrated upon the historical Buddha who had lived in India in the 6th century BCE. The Mahayana Buddhists had a wider view of Buddahood. They were less interested in the earthly body of the Buddha (*nirmanakaya*) and placed greater emphasis on the celestial body of the Buddha (*sambhogakaya*), and even more stress on the dharmakaya: the absolute, formless, ineffable, and truth body of the Buddha. At the absolute level of truth within Mahayana Buddhism only the dharmakaya was ultimately real; the other two bodies were 'form bodies', provisional ways of referring to and realizing the dharmakaya. At the conventional level the other two bodies were real, but at the ultimate level it was the dharmakaya that was the all-encompassing, self-existent reality. Within Mahayana Buddhism there are many earthly and celestial Buddhas, and lying behind them is the dharmakaya, which represents the essence of Buddhahood. It is the inner nature shared by all Buddhas, and it is the ultimate nature of self-existent reality itself. ▷ Buddha; dharma; Mahayana Buddhism; sambhogakaya; Theravada Buddhism; trikaya

Dharmapala, Anagarika, originally **Don David Hewavitarne** (1864–1933) Buddhist reformer, born in Ceylon. In 1881 he took the name of Anagarika Dharmapala ('defender of dharma'), and worked for the renewal of Buddhism in his own country and throughout the world, as well as for independence for the land that would become Sri Lanka. He reacted against his experience in a somewhat dogmatic Christian school and became a dedicated Buddhist reformer. In 1891 he visited Bodhgaya in North India, the site where the Buddha had experienced his enlightenment, and was upset to find it undeveloped and in Hindu hands. He founded the Mahabodhi Society as an international Buddhist organization to promote the Buddhist way of life and to win back the Bodhgaya site for Buddhism, which eventually happened in 1949. Dharmapala also visited the World Parliament of Religions at Chicago in 1893, and by his presence and speeches created a new interest in Buddhism in the West. In Ceylon he became looked upon as a kind of bodhisattva. His work was significant in promoting a new energy, dynamism and activism, especially among Buddhist laymen, and he worked for the re-establishment of Ceylon as a Theravada Buddhist nation. He also opposed the caste system and worked for social reform, and wanted to revitalize the Buddhist tradition in Ceylon and elsewhere at a time when it had reached a low ebb. ▷ Bodhgaya; bodhi; bodhisattva; Buddhism in the West; caste; Mahabodhi Society; Sinhalese Buddhism; Theravada Buddhism

dhikr An Arabic word meaning 'remembrance', it refers especially to the practice among Sufi Muslims of prolonged repetition of the name of God or of a sacred formula. This may be done silently or aloud, alone or with others. The practice is validated by Quran 33.41: 'O believers, remember God often and give him glory at dawn and in the evening'. For Sufis it is a method of spiritual concentration taught by a spiritual master and aided by a supporting set of doctrines and rituals. Sometimes the word dhikr is used for a Sufi ceremony in general, but it refers especially to the invocation of the Divine

Name at the heart of the ceremony. Particular forms of dhikr include dancing on a fixed spot by Whirling Dervishes, when the invocation of the name of God is reduced to silence and the dance becomes a rhythmic expression of dhikr, which may produce ecstasy. For Sufis dhikr is God's own act as well as a human act; it is God invoking himself as well as being invoked by a believer. ▷ dervish; divine names in Islam; Mevlevis; Quran; Sufism

dhimmis (dhimmīs) The term given by Muslims to 'protected peoples'. At first this referred to what the Quran called 'the people of the book', that is to say to the monotheistic traditions that had a revealed scripture such as the Christian, but it was later implicitly extended to include others, such as Zoroastrian and Hindu, who came within the orbit of the expanding Muslim empire. The dhimmis were given legal protection but had social restrictions placed on them ranging from the trivial to the very severe. They had to pay a form of tax and in return for this were able to avoid military conscription. They were not allowed to proselytize and, although protected, they were essentially second-class citizens. In practice a number of them gradually converted to Islam. In the 19th and 20th centuries the above-mentioned restrictions have been relaxed in most Islamic countries due to the exigencies of modern life. ▷ Quran

dhyana (dhyāna; Pali: jhāna) A Sanskrit term, meaning meditation, which is important in the Jain, Hindu and Buddhist traditions. The word *chan* in Chinese Buddhism and the word *zen* in Japanese Buddhism are derived from the word dhyana, a general designation for meditation which is of central significance in Buddhism. Within the Hindu tradition, dhyana is the seventh of the eight stages of yoga. At the sixth stage specific attention is paid to an object of meditation, such as an image. At the seventh stage of dhyana there is penetration into the inward essence of the object so that the meditator has a prolonged and deep sense of self-awareness, the essence of the object of meditation, and the act of meditating. At the eighth stage of union, or *samadhi*, the differences between the meditator, the object of meditation and the awareness of meditating dissolve and a higher stage of non-dual consciousness is achieved. In Hinduism dhyana is sometimes used in a more general way to indicate the way of meditation and inwardness in contrast to the way of devotion or to the way of works and active service in the world. ▷ Chan; jhana; meditation; Patanjali; samadhi; Zen Buddhism

dialectical materialism A central doctrine of Marxism. Its claims are that quantitative changes in matter yield qualitative changes (for example, the emergence of mind); that nature is a unity of contradictory opposites; and that the result of one opposite (thesis) clashing with another (antithesis) is a synthesis that preserves and transcends the opposites. ▷ Marxism

Diamond Cutter Sutra One of the sacred texts of the Mahayana tradition of Buddhism. It is probably the best known and most significant of the section of *Mahayana Sutras* known as the *prajnaparamita* (perfection of wisdom). It points out how the perfection of wisdom 'cuts like a diamond', and probably originates from the 4th century CE in India. It takes the form of a sermon, preached by the Buddha to his disciple Subhuti, which describes the career of a bodhisattva. It became very influential and popular in China. The great Chan patriarch Hui Neng found sudden enlightenment while hearing it being recited by a monk. It was printed soon after the invention of printing in China, and a copy printed in 868 is said to be the oldest existing printed book in the world. ▷ bodhisattva; Chan; Hui Neng; Mahayana Sutras; prajnaparamita

Diana Roman goddess, associated with the moon, virginity, and hunting. She was considered to be equivalent to the Greek Artemis, whose cult was primarily at Ephesus; hence

Diana

the cult of 'Diana of the Ephesians', who was a fertility goddess. ▷ Roman religion

Diaspora (Greek 'scattering', Hebrew *golah* or *galut*, 'exile') The Jews scattered in the world outside the land of Israel, from either voluntary or compulsory resettlements, such as the Assyrian and Babylonian deportations in the 8th century and 6th century BCE, or later dispersions in the Graeco-Roman period; also known as the Dispersion. The Babylonian Talmud and the Septuagint were important literary products of those Jews that had settled 'abroad'. ▷ Assyrian religion; Babylonian religion; Judaism; Talmud

Diaspora Judaism Judaism and Jews outside Palestine ('diaspora' is Greek for 'dispersion'). Several reasons explain a sizeable Jewish Diaspora throughout history: exile imposed upon its inhabitants by conquerors of Palestine, emigration in times of strife, and the attraction of foreign trade and travel. From the exile of Jews to Babylon in the 6th century BCE a Jewish Diaspora has existed in different parts of the world. Only the restoration of a Jewish state under the Maccabees and the 19th-century revival of Jewish nationalism (culminating in the founding of the State of Israel in 1948) encouraged significant return to the land. Otherwise the greater part of Jewry through most of history has lived in North Africa and Europe or in Babylon. This situation was reinforced with the formation of Rabbinic Judaism, and Christian and Muslim rule in the Holy Land. From the 17th to 19th centuries many Diaspora Jews emigrated to the USA in the face of continued anti-Semitism. Even today, despite the Nazi concentration camps and the founding of the State of Israel, the majority of Jews still live in the Diaspora. ▷ Ashkenazim; Hellenistic Judaism; Judaism in North America; Sephardim

Dibelius, Karl Friedrich Otto (1880–1967) German Lutheran churchman and ecumenical leader, born in Berlin. Suspended from church duties as general superintendent of the Kurmark following a 1933 sermon to Nazi leaders stating that 'the dictatorship of a totalitarian state is irreconcilable with God's will', he continued to support the Confessing Church, despite being forbidden to speak or publish. As Bishop of Berlin (1945–61), Chairman of the Council of the Evangelical Church in Germany (1949–61), and a president of the World Council of Churches (1954–61), he defended religious freedom in East Berlin and encouraged ecumenism. He wrote an autobiography, *In the Service of the Lord* in 1965. His theologian cousin, Martin Dibelius (1883–1947), pioneered the use of form criticism (*Formgeschichtliche*) in New Testament studies, as in *From Tradition to Gospel* (1934). ▷ Confessing Church; ecumenism; form criticism; Lutheranism; World Council of Churches

Didache (Greek 'teaching') The short title for 'The Teaching of the Lord through the Twelve Apostles', dated near the beginning of the 2nd century CE. It consists of a short manual of Christian moral teaching and church order, overlapping somewhat with the canonical Gospels, but also important for its description of early Christian ministry and sacramental practices. ▷ apostle; Christianity; Gospels, canonical

Di Deaeque (literally 'gods and goddesses') Roman religion had a complex gallery of gods and goddesses, the result of its very varied nature and structure. Each city had its own pantheon, with the number of divinities increasing at any time, although it involved a complicated legal process. Among the oldest Roman deities were Ceres (goddess of the earth), Juno (goddess of women), Jupiter (the sky-god, chief Roman god), Mars (god of war), Quirinus (god of the mass, later assimilated with Rome), Venus (goddess of love) and Vesta (goddess of Roman fire). Imports from the outside included Greek gods such as Apollo (god of the sun), and oriental deities such as Magna Mater (Cybele, the great mother-goddess of Anatolia), Isis (Egyptian goddess), and Mithra (the Persian god of light). Each divinity had its own image (most were anthropomorphic), function, way of acting and domain. Deities were attached to cities, districts, corporations and families, and might possess several homes (temples, altars, woods). In fact, to understand a Roman divinity, it is necessary to reconstruct not so much its mythic characteristics and history as the function of its cult within the overall system that comprised the cults of all the other divinities. Divinities were supposed to live both in the human world and in a world-system above it. They communicated with humans by inscribing messages in nature, by sending *prodigia*, or in some cases by even speaking directly with humans. ▷ auspicia; cult; prodigia; Roman religion

dietary laws Social or religious rules governing the consumption of or abstinence from certain food and drink. They may be applicable to a certain class only, eg priests, monks, or to all adherents of a religion. Believed to be divinely prescribed for the health or purity of a people, they may comprise a more or less total ban (eg the eating of pork at any time) or be restricted to certain days or periods (eg Lent in Christianity, Ramadan in Islam). Breach of these laws incurs divine disfavour and may carry severe penalties. ▷ kashrut

Digha Nikaya (Dīgha Nikāya) Part of the *Sutta Nikaya*, the discourses of the Buddha, which is one of the three sections of the Theravada Buddhist *tipitaka* or Pali Canon. It means a 'collection of long discourses', and consists of 34 discourses divided into three parts, which fill three volumes in the Pali Text Society edition. The first part deals with various ethical matters, and answers the false opinions of other sects; the second part contains two major discourses: on the death of the Buddha and on the 'foundations of mindfulness'; and the third part contains a code for lay Buddhists and a treatise on protective charms. The *Digha Nikaya* also contains other material that makes it popular among Buddhists, for example stories of the past lives of the Buddha. There is also a set of Sanskrit discourses in the *Dirghagama* of the Buddhist Sanskrit tradition that corresponds to the Dirgha Nikaya of the Pali tradition. ▷ parinirvana; Theravada Buddhism; tipitaka

din A Muslim concept meaning religion. The word is related to the term *dain*, meaning 'debt', and implies the practising of religion and the performing of religious duties out of indebtedness to God. Theologically it includes both faith and the putting into practice of the obligations of the shariah or religious law. As such it is sometimes contrasted with the secular realm of existence. ▷ religion; shariah

Dinka religion The Dinka are a cattle-herding Nilotic people of the southern Sudan. Like the neighbouring Nuer, they regard Spirit or Divinity (*nhialic*) as a single entity, sometimes to be thought of in universal terms as God, sometimes encountered in particular local manifestations or powers (*jok*, plural *jak*). These powers may cause punitive illness, inspire dreams, and possess diviners, thus conferring their insight and knowledge. There is a heirarchy of powers, the lowest being those associated with fetishes, which can be used by anyone (though it is dangerous to neglect the powers of fetishes in one's possession). Higher powers periodically possess diviners; those higher still maintain the inspiration of major prophets. A number of high powers (called by Godfrey Lienhardt 'free divinities') have names and widely-recognized manifestations and effects. All the contradictions of Dinka experience are concentrated in one of them, Macardit, whose actions invariably cause harm. Another set of powers are guardians of clans, represented by, but not identified with, particular animal species. Powers may be propitiated by animal sacrifice. The priestly masters of the fishing spear have important functions in intercession and sacrifice, for victory and rain, healing and protection; and they mediate in disputes. The deep bond between people and oxen finds many religious expressions. Like other south Sudan peoples, the Dinka have suffered much disruption in recent years, war having driven them from their homeland and their cattle. Many are now Christian. ▷ Nuer religion; Shilluk religion; totemism

Dionysiac religion Strictly, there was no 'Dionysiac religion', any more than there was the religion of any other single Greek god. However, most myths concerning him have a typical form which shows that he was felt to be in some ways an exception among the gods. The best known example (dramatized in Euripides' play *Bacchae*) tells how he came to Thebes, in disguise, in order to introduce his cult. Meeting with resistance, he drove the women of Thebes out to the mountains, where they performed ecstatic rites; the King of Thebes and leader of the resistance, Pentheus went out to fetch them home, but was hunted by the maddened women and torn to pieces by his own mother. Such 'Dionysiac resistance myths' reflect not a historical event but a perception of the god's own nature: the ecstasy that Dionysus embodies is alien to the normal life of the city (it comes from abroad), but necessary to it (those who resist it perish). The character of the actual Dionysiac festivals celebrated in various Greek cities varied greatly (some stressed wine, others ecstatic dancing by women); but at the level of the imagination 'Dionysiac religion' signified a necessary temporary madness. ▷ Apollonian religion; festivals, Greek; Greek religion; Thebes

Dionysius the Areopagite (c.500) Greek or Syrian churchman, one of the few Athenians converted by the apostle Paul (Acts 17.34). Tradition makes him the first Bishop of Athens and a martyr. The Greek writings bearing his name were written, not by him, but probably by an unknown Alexandrian of the early 6th century. They include the treatises *On the Heavenly and Ecclesiastical Hierarchies*, *On Divine Names*, *On Mystical*

Theology, and a series of ten *Epistles*, and had a great influence on the development of theology. ▷ martyr; theology

Dipankara (Dīpankara) The name of a previous Buddha whom Gautama Buddha had met in a past life. Gautama, who was then an ascetic called Sumedha, was inspired by Dipankara, whom he honoured, to work for Buddhahood. He became a disciple of Dipankara in this past life (described in one of the Jataka stories), and this led on to his becoming a bodhisattva committed to the search for full enlightenment. As a result of the inspiration of Dipankara, Gautama carried through his vow. He was born many different times and spent many lives in building up the qualities necessary for Buddhahood, and he met various other Buddhas, finally entering the Tusita heaven prior to being reborn on earth for the last time at Lumbini as the historical Buddha that we know. According to tradition Dipankara was the first of 24 Buddhas who are said to have predated Gautama Buddha, and he is described as being tremendously tall and very long-lived. ▷ bodhisattva; Gautama; Jataka; Lumbini

Dipavamsa (Dīpavaṃsa) A Pali chronicle or *vamsa* that narrates the Buddhist history of the island or *dipa* of Ceylon (now Sri Lanka) from its beginnings to the 4th century CE. Special emphasis is laid upon the entry of Buddhism into Ceylon. Another chronicle called the *Culavamsa* relates the history of Ceylon from about 300CE to the 19th century. Thus the two chronicles sum up the greater part of Sinhalese history as seen from the viewpoint of the Buddhist tradition. The Dipavamsa appears to have been composed during the century after the events it ends by describing, and it brings together the work of previous schools in order to relate its story. It is symbolic of the significance of Buddhism within the total history of Ceylon from its early days right up to present-day Sri Lanka. ▷ Sinhalese Buddhism; tipitaka

disciples (in early Christian Church) The followers of Jesus Christ in the Gospels, like those of John the Baptist and the Pharisees, are described as 'disciples'. A disciple learned from his master's teaching and way of life, expecting, in due course, to become a rabbi in his own right and to pass everything on to his own disciples. The Gospels portray Jesus as more active than traditional rabbis in two senses. He chose his first disciples (rather than attracting them), and he reinterpreted religious tradition (rather than merely passing it on) with a freedom that shocked the Pharisees. The Gospels sometimes equate 'disciples' with the inner group of 12 apostles, and sometimes use the term more broadly, as of the 70 or 72 sent out on mission (Luke 10). In the Book of Acts, the term 'disciples' is used of Christian believers in general. ▷ apostle; Jesus Christ

Disciples of Christ ▷ Churches of Christ

discursive meditation Silent mental (as opposed to vocal) prayer involving reflection on incidents in the life of Christ or other biblical themes, with the purpose of finding and adopting the will of God for one's life or on a particular issue. Of the many methods proposed, the best known and most influential are those of St Ignatius Loyola, *Spiritual Exercises* (1548), and St Frances de Sales (1567–1622) *Introduction to the Devout Life* (1608). Some hold that discursive meditation is a lower or preparatory form of prayer, preliminary to contemplation or non-discursive meditation. ▷ contemplation; Francis of Sales, St; Ignatius Loyola, St; prayer

disir ▷ fylgja

Dispensationalism A method of biblical interpretation pioneered by the leader of the Plymouth Brethren John Nelson Darby (1800–82). It was popularized by the American Congregationalist Cyrus Ingerson Scofield (1843–1921) in the *Scofield Reference Bible* (1909, rev. eds. 1917, 1967) and promoted by Lewis Sperry Chafer (1871–1952), founder of Dallas Theological Seminary, Texas. History is held to be divided into distinct periods or dispensations in which God works in a particular way. The present, sixth dispensation, the age of the Church, will end with the Second Coming of Christ. In this extreme form of premillennialism it is believed that an invisible 'secret rapture' of believers will be followed by a literal 1000-year kingdom of God on earth and the fulfilment of Old Testament prophecies of a restored Israel. ▷ kingdom of God; millenarianism

Dispersion ▷ Diaspora

ditthi (Sanskrit: dṛṣṭi) A word used in the early Buddhist tradition for a 'view' in the sense of an opinion that was usually wrong because it was based upon desire rather than insight, and was one-sided rather than balanced. A good example is the belief in a permanent self, either in the sense that the self will live eternally, or in the sense that the self, although permanent in life, will be annihilated in death. Other forms of wrong view included the false theories of other sects, and false views of human nature such as fatalism or materialism. The notion of ditthi was used less commonly in a more positive sense, for example in connection with the concept of 'right view' which was part of the eightfold path. This included insight into the laws of rebirth, ethical responsibility connected with karma and right action, and at a higher level insight into higher truths associated with awareness of the ultimate nature of things. ▷ anatman; atman; eightfold path; fatalism; samsara

Divali/Deepavali (Dīpāvali) The festival of the lights, an important Hindu festival celebrated throughout India in October/November and lasting for four to five days. The central deity of the celebrations is Lakshmi, goddess of wealth and good fortune, who is invited into the house. During the festival, houses are lit by oil lamps, and ornate patterns (*rangoli*), especially of lotuses, are drawn on the floor near the door. Presents are given to children and meals are shared with relatives. ▷ Hindu religious year; Lakshmi

divination A method used to gain information about people, phenomena or the future by means not amenable to normal investigation. It is present in all cultures, sometimes in implicit conflict with religion as in much of the history of the Christian tradition, at other times as part of popular religion as in the Delphi Oracle in Ancient Greece, the *I Ching* in China, and the oracles of Tibetan Buddhism. It can take an ascetic form in which case the diviner enters into a trance or a state of possession and then offers advice, or a non-ecstatic form in which case the diviner interprets through intuitive insight the sometimes unusual data that are put before him or her. Divination is usually religious, either because it gives spiritual distance in fraught communal situations by mediating between contesting forces by reference to a higher power, or because it gives meaning to events in personal lives by reference to transcendent concerns. It can have great consequences, as in Constantine's dream divination, which led to Christianity becoming the recognized religion of the Roman empire. Although dismissed in rational circles, it remains a strong element in primal religions around the world, and its importance is growing in the West where astrology and other methods of divination are increasing in popularity. ▷ astrology; Constantine I; Delphi, Oracle of; I Ching; mantike; Tibetan Buddhism

divination, African In primal societies it is less important to know what has caused a problem, and how, than to discover who has caused it, and why. It is not enough to look for the causes in the realm of nature (though it is recognized that this is one possible source). Instead one must look in the sphere of personal relations, those with one's neighbours, the ancestors, or the spirit world. Misfortune may be due to one's own or one's kin's wrongdoing or neglect, or to the malice of others, which may be expressed in witchcraft or sorcery. Knowing the cause allows proper action to be taken, such as confession, reparation, or self-protection. The diviner who assists in diagnosis has a vital role. He also helps people to make up their minds when faced with perplexing decisions.

There are two main methods of divination, and many peoples use both. Mediumistic divination offers direct access to the spirit world through the diviner, who enters a trance; in instrumental divination the diviner uses materials—perhaps sand, bones, or a tray or basket containing significant objects. Either form may be supported by a series of questions from the diviner, the answers to which provide a psychological map of the afflicted person's relationships and worries.

Another way of classifying systems of divination is to look at the source of the revelation. Thus 'agency' divination, whether by a spirit medium, or by bones or basket, is contrasted with 'wisdom' divination, which requires a comprehensive body of knowledge, normally expressed in myth. The former derives from spirits or lesser divinities, for the supreme being does not speak through mediums (Mwari is one of the rare exceptions). Wisdom divination, however, derives from God himself. Thus the Yoruba Ifa oracle uses 16 cowrie shells to represent the 16 sectors into which the world is divided. In one of these sectors the applicant's problem is outlined and answered, for all knowledge is hidden within this cosmic map, and is expressed in the myths attached to each sign that the cowries form (great diviners may know hundreds of verses for each of 256 signs). Wisdom divination gives the general directions of events, and thus enables the questioner to come to a decision. Wisdom oracle trays, however, sometimes carry the figure of the trickster divinity, the sign that things do not always turn out as planned. ▷ ancestors, African; Mwari; supreme beings; witchcraft and sorcery, African

divination, Ancient Near Eastern Practised throughout the Ancient Near East, divination took a wide variety of forms. The best evidence comes from Babylonia and Assyria, where thousands of individual omens were collected and catalogued on clay tablets by the diviners, who performed a vital function in society, since a favourable omen was required before almost any public or private activity could take place. The most important form of divination in Mesopotamia was extispicy: the examination of the entrails, especially the liver, of a sacrificed sheep for blemishes or abnormalities, from which predictions of future events were made. In contrast to extispicy, which was provoked by the diviner, other omens could be taken from unprovoked signs, such as the movements of animals or birds, the occurrence of abnormal births, and celestial phenomena, which were all collected in the omen texts. An interesting series of omens describes medical symptoms and prognoses for doctors to use. In the 1st millennium BCE astrological omens became very important, especially for the Assyrian kings. Babylonian forms of divination were influential outside Mesopotamia, reaching the peoples of Syria-Palestine and the Hittites in Asia Minor. Among the Hittites native divinatory practices included a highly developed science of the movements of birds and an obscure activity involving entities with symbolic names, which was the sphere of the village sorceresses, who were called simply 'Old Women'. ▷ Ancient Near Eastern religions; Assyrian religion; astrology; Babylonian religion; Hittite religion; magic, Ancient Near Eastern

divination, Roman Within Roman civilization divination developed because Romans believed that divinities could communicate with them by inscribing in nature a message to be deciphered (*auspicium*) or, when angry, by sending *prodigia*. Signs could be sent directly to a person (eg prophecies, dreams, appearance of spirits of the dead), or indirectly (where they might appear in the reading of lots, in the interpretation of the behaviour of animals, or of involuntary human acts, such as sneezing, in the reading of the entrails and internal organs of sacrificial animals, or in the study of weather-signs and astrology). The difficulties then consisted in defining the presence of signs and interpreting them. Divination played a central role in Roman society, politics and religion because the most important public actions and decisions could not be taken without first asking advice and requesting certain signs from divinities. The requests and interpretation were made by priests (magistrates) belonging to the college of augurs. Another college of priests (*quindecemviri sacris faciundis*) was in charge of consulting the *libri Sibyllini* (books of prophecies) to identify prodigia and to order the appropriate atonement. ▷ auspicia; prodigia; Roman religion; Sibylline Books

Divine Light Mission A new religious movement centred upon the work of Guru Maharaj Ji who was born in India in 1958. He moved to London in 1971 at the age of 13, and in the 1970s the Divine Light Mission grew quite quickly in the West. Guru Maharaj Ji is typical of the gurus of some Indian new religious movements who, like Swami Prabhupada of Hare Krishna and Maharishi Mahesh Yogi of Transcendental Meditation, have visited and consciously targeted the West, as opposed to others like Sathya Sai Baba, who has not been to the West. He was considered to be an embodiment of God, and his movement is centred upon four 'divine' methods of meditation which enable one to enter one's inner world and have an experience of Divine Harmony, Divine Light, Divine Nectar and the Divine Word. In its heyday the Divine Light Mission had thousands of members in the West as well as in India, living monastic or community lives in ashrams where they witnessed to their faith, meditated, and gave service to the community and the world. Another feature of the movement was the holding of large fairs in different parts of the world, where crowds would attend to have audience with Guru Maharaj Ji. In recent years disagreements among members of his family have weakened the influence of Guru Maharaj Ji and the Divine Light Mission. ▷ Hare Krishna movement; new religious movements in the West; Satya Sai Baba; transcendental meditation

divine names in Islam Islam has traditionally given 99 names to God. They are called 'the most beautiful names' according to Quran 7:179 ('to Him belong the most beautiful names'). Some of these names refer to the essence of God, such as Allah, the supreme name, which stands alone, and ar-Rahman, the merciful one, which is sometimes almost equated with Allah. Other names refer to qualities of God, such as *ar-Rahim*, the compassionate, and *al-Bari*, the producer. Another division is into the names of God that stress his beneficence, and those that stress his judgement and majesty. Most names of God are found in the Quran, others are derived from passages in the Quran, and yet others are traditional, and of non-Quranic derivation. The supreme name Allah was current in Arabia before the time of the Quran, but its meaning was transformed by the Quran. Typical examples of names of God are: *al-Haqq* (the Truth), *al-Ahad* (the One), *al-Hakam* (the Judge), *al-Quddus* (the Holy), *al-Kabir* (the Great), *al-Karim* (the Generous), *al-Wali* (the Protector), *al-Wadud* (the Loving). ▷ Allah; Quran

Diwali ▷ **Divali/Deepavali**

Docetism The belief, arising in early Christianity, that the natural body of Jesus Christ was only apparent (Greek *dokeo*, 'appear, seem') and not real, thereby stressing the divinity of Christ and denying any real physical suffering on his part. It was especially prevalent amongst 2nd-century gnostics, but was also perhaps a problem encountered in 2 John 7. ▷ Christology; Gnosticism

doctrine The official or orthodox teaching of a religion. This may be communicated by tradition, orally or in writing in the form of scripture, believed to be divinely inspired. A group or a single person may be invested with authority to declare doctrine in such a way that its acceptance is binding on all believers (eg general councils and popes in Roman Catholicism).

doctrine, Christian Christians believe in God, rather than in teachings about him. Their primary activity is prayer, worship, and finding the will of God for their lives through study of the Bible. Nevertheless, it has proved useful for instruction, apologetics, and evangelism to summarize the teachings of scripture and the Church's understanding of its implications in a thematic (the discipline of dogmatic or systematic theology) or chronological (historical theology) way.

Historical study of the development of doctrine shows how the Creeds and the decisions of the Councils arose out of specific practical contexts (such as the need to combat a particular heresy), and reveals how the understanding of the Church develops or changes. Thus the Roman Catholic Church, which holds that it has the authority to promulgate infallible dogmas that are binding on the faithful, makes a distinction between content and form, allowing for a developing understanding of what was always implicit. Churches of the Reformation (which valued tradition much less highly than scripture) usually restricted the term 'dogma' to the universally accepted decisions of the undivided Church of the first five centuries, and expressed their differing doctrines on other matters in subsidiary Confessions of Faith or Articles of Religion.

Christians hold that right belief (orthodoxy) and right practice (orthopraxy) go hand in hand. As a result, the tendency in all churches for doctrine to be studied and debated in the abstract by theologians or academics provokes one of two reactions: a call for a 'simple' or 'more biblical' faith, or for a change in theological method. The latter approach has been adopted by liberation theology, which demands that theological reflection begins, rather than ends, with commitment to the poor. Such 'contextualization' is also the basis of feminist theology. ▷ Council of the Church; creeds; feminist theology; infallibility; liberation theology

Dodd, Charles Harold (1884–1973) Welsh biblical scholar and Congregational pastor, born in Wrexham. He graduated from Oxford and served a Congregational church in Warwick. He returned to lecture at Oxford, was Professor of Theology at Manchester, then was elected to the Norris-Hulse Chair of Divinity at Cambridge (1936–49)—the first Nonconformist incumbent for nearly three centuries. In 1949 he became general director for the New English Bible translation. His own publications included *The Apostolic Preaching and Its Developments* (1936), *According to the Scriptures* (1952), and *Historical Tradition in the Fourth Gospel* (1963). ▷ Congregationalism; Nonconformists

Dogen (1200–53) Founder of the Soto school of Japanese Zen Buddhism, honoured as the greatest Zen figure in Japanese history. He was orphaned at seven, ordained at 13, and set out for China at the age of 23, where he achieved enlightenment under a Chan Master, and succession within the Soto school. He returned to Japan in 1227 and set up the first independent Japanese Zen temple at Koshohoringji. Dogen is venerated by all Japanese Buddhists as a bodhisattva. He was not exclusively Zen, but stressed the importance of simplicity and ordinary work in monastic practice generally. He emphasized the practice of zazen, sitting upright with legs crossed in simple meditation, and he believed that this enabled one to realize the Buddha nature which is the essence of all people and all things. He recommended the reading of scriptures (*sutras*), and the veneration of Buddha images, as well as the saying of koans that other Zen masters, such as Eisai, often advocated exclusively. He outlined his teachings in the *Shobogenzo, Treasury of the Knowledge* *of True Law*, in which he emphasized both scripture and faith in the Buddha, and also a gradual entry to enlightenment rather than the sudden enlightenment favoured by the other main Japanese school of Rinzai Zen. ▷ bodhisattva; Buddha image; Buddha nature; Chan; Eisai; koans; Rinzai; Soto; zazen; Zen Buddhism

Dome of the Rock A masterpiece of Islamic architecture completed in 691CE on Mount Moriah, Jerusalem. The shrine, which is built on an octagonal plan and surmounted by a gilded wooden cupola, encloses the holy rock where, according to tradition, Muhammad ascended to heaven and Abraham prepared to sacrifice Isaac. ▷ Abraham; Islam; Muhammad

domestic observances, Hindu The observant twice-born or high caste Hindu will perform a daily ritual (*puja*) to the household deity or deities, involving the circulation of the *arati* lamp and offering food to the deity which will be consumed by the family as *prasad* (food which has been blessed). The family shrine, perhaps no more than a simple image or picture, is usually located in the kitchen, the purest place in the house. Occasional rituals of the householder are the rites of passage (*samskaras*) which mark out a Hindu's life stages (ashramas). These include rites for birth, the first tonsure, a high caste boy's Vedic initiation or investiture of the sacred thread (*upanaya*), marriage and funerals. In Hindu literature, domestic observances were laid down in the *Grihya Sutras*, composed between the 8th and 4th centuries BCE.

domestic observances, Islamic This is the area where Muslim women come into their own, as the five pillars of Islam (the profession of faith, daily prayers, almsgiving, the fast of Ramadan and the pilgrimage to Mecca) are mainly a man's prerogative. The general atmosphere of the home—the upbringing of children, the health and well-being of the family, avoiding the evil eye, ritual purity, the preparation and eating of food, and hospitality—is an important part of the Islamic way of life that is superintended by women. In addition to this, individual and group observances held at home are open to the participation and even the leadership of women. They include readings from the Quran during the fast of Ramadan, special sermons, ritual dinners, religious observances associated with health and vows, and rites of passage held at home. In local areas special domestic observances may occur, for example in north-east Africa women may go to the home of a woman beset by a spirit or jinn and engage in ceremonies, including dancing, to get rid of the jinn. ▷ five pillars, Islamic; jinn; Quran; Ramadan; rites of passage; Islam, women in

Dominic, St (c.1170–1221) Spanish religious. In 1216 he founded the Order of Friars Preachers. Born in Calaruega in Old Castile, he studied at Palencia, acquiring such a name for piety and learning that in 1193 the Bishop of Osma made him a canon, and relied on his help to reform the whole chapter according to the Augustinian rule. He led a life of rigorous asceticism and devoted himself to missionary labours among Muslims and 'heretics'. In 1204 he accompanied his bishop on a political mission, and had to travel round the south of France three times. He undertook conversion of the Albigenses and travelled from place to place on foot, carrying St Paul's epistles, and preaching everywhere. He continued his labours for ten years, and gathered like-minded companions round him, for whom he founded the first house of his order at Toulouse. He also set up an asylum for women in danger from heretical influence, which developed into an order of nuns.

Events occurred during the Inquisition which left a deep stain on his memory and that of his order. Innocent III, incensed by the murder of his legate, Peter of Castelnau, called the barons of northern France, led by Simon de Montfort, to a crusade against the heretics; and Dominic became a consenting party to these cruelties. In 1215 he went to the fourth Lateran Council, and Innocent III promised approval of his new order on condition that it adopted an old rule. Dominic chose the rule of St Augustine, and next year the authorization was given by Honorius III. Dominic became 'Master of the Sacred Palace', an office which has continued to be hereditary in the order.

In 1220 the Dominicans, in imitation of their Franciscan brethren, adopted a poverty so rigid that not even the order as a corporation could hold houses or lands, and thus they forced themselves to become mendicants or beggars. Dominic died at Bologna. He had lived to see his order occupying 60 houses and divided into eight provinces. It had spread to England, where they were called Black Friars, because of their dress; to northern France, Italy, Spain and Austria. He was canonized in 1234 by his friend Gregory IX. His feast day is 4 August. ▷ Albigenses;

Augustinians; Dominicans; Innocent III; Inquisition; Lateran Councils; Paul, St

Dominicans A religious order, known officially as Ordo Praedicatorum (Latin 'Order of Preachers'), abbreviated OP; also known as the Friars Preachers, Black Friars, or Jacobins. It was founded by St Dominic in 1216 in Italy to provide defenders of the Roman Catholic faith. The order exercises individual and corporate poverty, but is devoted mainly to preaching and teaching. It has a fine record of learning (eg Thomas Aquinas, Albertus Magnus), and also of missionary activity, with houses in every part of the Christian world. There is also a second order (of nuns), and a third or tertiary order (of members not enclosed). ▷ Albertus Magnus, St; Aquinas, St Thomas; Dominic, St; monasticism; Roman Catholicism

Donatists African Christian schismatics named after Donatus (4th century), elected as rival to the Bishop of Carthage. The movement was rigorist and puritan, supported rebaptism, and declared invalid the sacraments celebrated by priests suspected of collaboration in times of persecution. It flourished in Africa in the 4th and 5th centuries, and despite condemnation by Augustine, the Roman emperor, and the Catholic Church (411), continued until the 7th–8th century. ▷ Augustine, St (of Hippo); heresy

doubt and belief Although doubt and belief are often regarded as opposites, doubt has often been seen as vacillation between belief and unbelief, or in a more positive sense as part of the creative process of true belief. Doubt can take various forms. It can imply openness of mind, as in Socrates. It can be a philosophical method, as in Augustine's statement 'if I doubt, I exist'. It can be an authentic part of faith, as in the Christian existentialism of Kierkegaard and his 'leap of faith'. Faith and belief are not necessarily equated, although in the Christian tradition with its emphasis upon theology and belief this has sometimes been the case. For example, the New Testament word *pistis* meant surrender to God and trust in God rather than belief as such, but in translation it veered in the direction of belief by being rendered in Latin as *credo* and then in English as 'I believe'. In most religious traditions the category of faith is deeper than that of belief in intellectual propositions. Doubt can more readily co-exist with faith than it can with belief. At the two extremes there are nihilism, doubt about anything and everything, and certainty, the inability to doubt anything at all. Most 'believers' take a midway position whereby philosophical certainty is not the sole criterion of their belief. Doubt can express humility, encourage tolerance, and denote mystery, and it can and often does coexist not only with faith but also with belief. ▷ existentialism, Christian; faith; Kierkegaard, Sören Aabye

Doukhobors, or **Dukhabors** A religious sect originating in Russia c.1740. It teaches that God is manifested in the human soul, which is eternal, and which at death passes into another body (metempsychosis). Frequently in conflict with the authorities, especially for refusing military service, the adherents were persecuted until 1898, when they were allowed to emigrate. Most settled in Canada. ▷ sect; soul

Dragon Boat Festival A Chinese festival, known as Tuan Yang Chien, that takes place on the fifth day of the fifth lunar month. It commemorates the death by drowning of a famous poet and politician Chu Yuan, who lived around 343–279BCE. He was depressed by the state of China during the chaotic period of the warring states, and by his dismissal by the ruler because of unjust slander, and committed a brave suicide in the cause of reform. According to tradition, Chinese dumplings were thrown in the sea in place of his body, and these dumplings are made and eaten as part of the festival. Boats are a feature of the festivities. They are hired by ordinary people, and taken out as venues for eating, drinking and music-making. In some places long and narrow dragon boats are made, which are up to 100 feet in length with a dragon's head at the front. They are used for races between crews of men sitting two abreast. In Hong Kong there is a famous international dragon boat competition between crews from various lands. After the races there is further use of boats to show off coloured lanterns by moonlight and to draw the festival to a peaceful end. ▷ festivals, Chinese

drama The conveying of a story by narrative dialogue and action, used in a religious setting to induce a sense of communion with a god or gods, as in the Ancient Greek festival honouring Dionysius. The use of drama is universal and dates back to Palaeolithic times. Drama may have originated from mimetic ritual where the principle of imitative magic, the idea that like will produce like, was involved. ▷ festivals

drama, Christian The Fathers of the early Church condemned plays because of their inextricable connection with pagan worship and the pursuit of pleasure. This problem disappeared with the Christianization of the Roman empire, and there are 10th-century records of dramatizations of the death and resurrection of Christ being performed in church. The Franciscans obtained permission in the 13th century to use nativity and other plays to communicate the Christian message. Mystery or miracle plays re-enacting biblical themes and legends of the saints, which were common in France, became popular in England in the 14th to 16th centuries. The Passion play at Oberammergau in Upper Bavaria has been performed almost every 10 years since 1634, to honour a vow made by the villagers in thanks for being spared the plague.

In Protestant countries religious drama was not prominent from the 16th to the 19th centuries. Some dramatists pointed out corruption and folly in the Church, others treated biblical subjects with farce and parody. General Puritan disapproval of the 'worldly' theatre and a movement to secular themes in drama reduced interest in religious issues. The 20th century has been equally secular, but there have been revivals of the medieval mystery plays, including new works such as Bernard Shaw's *St Joan* (1923/24), John Masefield's *The Coming of Christ* (1928), TS Eliot's *Murder in the Cathedral* (1935) and Dorothy Sayers' radio play *The Man Born to be King* (1943); and commercially successful if doctrinally unorthodox rock musicals like John Tebelak's *Godspell* (1971) and Andrew Lloyd Webber's *Jesus Christ Superstar* (1972). Professional and amateur Church groups employ modern acted parables, sketches and puppets in adult and children's religious education, while some churches, particularly those influenced by charismatic renewal, encourage dance in worship. ▷ literature, Christian

drama, Hindu This is seen as a religious practice in itself, seeking the liberation of both actors and audience. The theatre (often within temple precincts) is a sacred space. Hindu drama has a long history, rooted in Vedic rituals in which the creation, evolution and destruction of the universe was enacted. Traditionally, the first Indian dramatic theorist, the sage Bharata (c.2nd century BCE–2nd century CE), was permitted a viewing of a celestial drama in Indra's court along these lines, and was inspired to write a treatise on drama, the *Natya Shastra*, within which scholars have identified Aristotelian influences. Plots are usually based on the Epics and *Puranas*, especially the lives of Rama and Krishna, and are performed in a stylized fashion, using dance, music, song and mime. Costumes are ornate and full of symbolic import. Styles vary from region to region in India, but one of the most popular and, indeed, most sophisticated forms is the Kathakali dance drama from Kerala in South India. ▷ Indra; music, Hindu; Krishna; Puranas; Rama

Dravidians The people of South India and Sri Lanka who speak languages such as Tamil and Kanarese which derive from the Dravidian group of languages, as opposed to the languages of northern India derived from the Indo-European Sanskrit. Dravidian people tend to be darker skinned than North Indians and are the descendants of the indigenous Indian population before the Aryan incursions into India. The bhakti traditions of Hinduism in their more devotional manifestations originated amongst Dravidian people and many religious texts and poetry are written in Dravidian languages, particularly Tamil. ▷ bhakti; Tamil Hinduism

dreams and visions Subjective experiences occurring during sleep (dreams) or when waking or in a trance-like state (visions). In many religions, these may be interpreted as messages from God or the gods, or inspired prophecies concerning the future. Typical in the Judaeo-Christian tradition would be the example of Joseph (Genesis 37.5ff), Isaiah (Isaiah 6) and Peter (Acts 10.9ff).

dreams and visions, Christian These are rarer in biblical literature than in that of the surrounding cultures, and less prominent in the Old and New Testaments than in the Apocrypha and other intertestamental literature. Dreams and visions in the Old Testament generally fall in particular periods such as those of Joseph and Pharaoh, and Daniel and Nebuchadnezzar; or are linked with the call of prophets like Isaiah, Jeremiah, and Ezekiel. The dreams and visions 'seen' were often accompanied by a 'word of the Lord' which was 'heard', although apocalyptic literature in particular is not fully interpreted or is open to more than one interpretation. This is true of the Revelation to John in the New Testament. Other New Testament dreams or visions are associated with the birth of Christ and significant stages of the ministry of Peter and Paul in the early Church. Paul, however, considered visions of little consequence and not a matter for boasting (2 Corinthians 12). The spiritual dangers of accepting visions of demons or angels at face value were pointed out by St Anthony of Egypt and the Desert Fathers, and notable visionaries such as Julian of Norwich and Teresa of Ávila submitted their experiences of Christ and the Trinity to their spiritual superiors, believing (with the teaching of Paul and the Epistles of John) that any religious experience has to be judged for its agreement with Christian doctrine and its contribution to Christian charity or love. Some Christian sects or cults such as the Unification Church interpret the Bible on the basis of visions received by their founders. ▷ Desert Fathers; Julian of Norwich; prophecy, Jewish and Christian; Teresa of Ávila, St; Unification Church

Dreamtime, or **The Dreaming** ▷ **altjiranga**

Druids The name of an order of Celtic religious specialists known to have existed at least in Gaul and the British Isles. They fascinated Roman writers, who speak of their antiquity, prestige and impressive oral lore, which took, says one, 20 years to acquire. They came from the warrior aristocracy, and acted as arbitrators as well as priests, healers, seers and divines. The archaeological remains provide little that illuminates Celtic priesthood. As for post-classical literature, a Druid occurs as an opponent of Columba, the Irish Christian missionary in Scotland. In the Irish stories, which often reflect pre-Christian Celtic religion, there is little sign of anyone equivalent to the philosopher priest described by classical writers; only the figures of the wise man, soothsayer or shape-changer. Some modern scholars give credence to the classical writers and find links between the Druids and ancient Indian ideas and institutions. Others see them simply as shamans with conventional ritual roles. About the time of the Roman conquest the power of the Druids among the Western Celts was great; and if, as some suggest, they were establishing recognition of national, as distinct from local, Celtic divinities on the basis of such figures as Lug and Cernunnos, they would have formed a unifying force among the Celts. It was in the Roman interest to break any pan-Celtic factors, and it is not surprising that Druid power declined. Antiquaries of the 18th century produced a completely imaginary reconstruction of the Druids which has influenced various groups claiming to revive ancient British traditions. There is no evidence whatever, for instance, to connect the Celtic Druids with Stonehenge. ▷ Cernunnos; Columba, St; Lug; shamanism

Druid

Drummond, Henry (1851–97) Scottish evangelical theologian and biologist, born in Stirling. He studied at Edinburgh, and in 1877 became lecturer in natural science at the Free Church College, Glasgow, and professor in 1884. He travelled in the Rocky Mountains, Central Africa, Japan, and Australia. He attempted to reconcile Christianity and Darwinism in such works as *Natural Law of the Spiritual World* (1883), *The Ascent of Man* (1894), and *Tropical Africa* (1888). ▷ evangelicalism; Darwinism

Druze A religious faith which originated during the closing years of the Fatimid caliph al-Hakim (996–1021), whom some extremist Ismailis regarded as a manifestation of the Divinity. The Druze, who survive in parts of Jordan, Lebanon, and Syria, deviate considerably in belief and practice from the main Muslim body. They await the return from divine concealment of both al-Hakim and his disciple, Hamza ibn Ali. They assemble on Thursdays, instead of the usual Fridays, reject many of the prescriptions of the shariah, affirm monogamous marriage, and believe in the transmigration of souls. They number c.500000. ▷ Ismailis; shariah

dry paintings Sacred pictures ritually used by some Native American peoples of the southwest USA. Though often called sand paintings, sand provides only the background and in some paintings is not used at all. Sizes vary: some, a foot across, may be completed in an hour; others may take a dozen men a day's work. The pictures portray the holy beings of old, or symbols of the divine world; each painting relates to a particular myth and belongs to a particular stage of a ritual. Each is executed under the direction of the singer of the appropriate ritual, who has learned the picture by tradition. Conventions are strict (among the Navajo the much-loved figure of Changing Woman occurs only in Blessingway pictures). Preparation is a religious act, accompanied by prayer and song. The pictures increase the sense of participation with the holy beings in the rituals. In curing rituals the patient may be sat on the picture, and directed to touch various parts of the painted figures. At the end, the sufferer's family walks across the picture, carefully destroying it in the order it was made. They, too, have participated with the holy beings. ▷ Navajo religion; Pueblo religion

dualism In its religious sense, the doctrine of dualism states that there are two opposing forces or principles at work in creating and running the universe, namely good and evil. In its philosophical sense dualism embraces any theory which asserts the existence of two different kinds of thing, eg between temporal things and timeless forms. The most familiar philosophical dualism, held for example by Plato and Descartes, is between mind and matter. ▷ Descartes, René; Plato

duhkha (Pali: dukkha) One of the three chief characteristics of existence according to the teaching of the Buddha, commonly translated as 'suffering'. The other two are *anicca*, the notion of impermanence; and *anatman*, the notion that there is no such thing as a permanent and enduring self. In fact the three are bound up together, because suffering is said to follow from the desire to seek permanence in a world of flux, and from the desire to safeguard the self when such a thing does not really exist. Duhkha is built into the four noble truths of the Buddha: all life is suffering; suffering results from craving; suffering can be ended when craving is ended; and this can happen in practice by means of the eightfold path. 'Suffering' is not an ideal translation for duhkha in that duhkha includes not only trials and tribulations but also pleasant experiences and happinesses which, insofar as they are fleeting and beguiling, are also part of duhkha. It means rather unsatisfactoriness or dis-ease. All life is awry—apart from the good life to which we gain access through the dharma, and apart from the final goal of nirvana. ▷ anatman; ariya sacca; Buddha; dharma; eightfold path; nirvana; tanha

Dukhabors ▷ Doukhobors

Dumézil, Georges (1898–) French scholar of Indo-European thought and religion, born in Paris. He was exposed to the sociological ideas of Mauss and Durkheim, and became Professor of Indo-European Civilization in Paris. He revived Indo-European studies, created links with the more systematic and structural side of French thought, and enriched the field of comparative religion. Ranging far and wide through early Indo-European studies, including Greece, Rome, India, early Zoroastrianism, and Nordic religion, he brought out the threefold nature of Indo-European religion. He showed the links between certain kinds of gods, the social organization of human beings, and ideology or theology. Thus gods representing sovereignty are related on earth to the priestly class responsible for religion and sovereignty; warrior gods are related on earth to the warrior class responsible for military strength; and fertility gods are related on earth to the class of cultivators and herders responsible for sustenance and fertility. Although challenged in detail, Dumézil's tripartite theories have been widely influential. ▷ comparative religion; Roman religion; study of religion

Duns Scotus, John (c.1265–1308) Scottish scholastic philosopher who rivalled Aquinas as the greatest theologian of the middle ages but whose brief life is scantily documented. He was probably from Duns, Berwickshire; he became a Franciscan and was ordained priest in St Andrews Church, Northampton in 1291. He studied and taught at Oxford and Paris, probably also in Cambridge, and finally at Cologne where he died and was buried. His writings were mainly commentaries on the Bible, Aristotle and the Sentences of Peter Lombard and were left in various stages of completeness at his death. His associates collected and edited them (not always very responsibly), and the main works in the canon are now taken to be: The *Opus Pariense* (the Parisian Lectures, as recorded by a student), the *Opus Oxiense* (the Oxford lectures, also known as the *Ordinatio*, and probably revised by the author), the *Tractatus de Primo Principio* and the *Quaestiones Quodlibetales*.

His philosophy represents a strong reaction against both Aristotle and Aquinas. He propounded the primacy of the individual (in the dispute about universals), and the freedom of the individual will. He saw faith as the necessary foundation of Christian theology, but faith was for him exercised through an act of will and was practical, not speculative or theoretical. The Franciscans followed Scotus as the Dominicans did Thomas Aquinas; he was known by contemporaries as *Doctor Subtilis* for the refinement and penetration of his criticisms of Thomism, but in the Renaissance the Scotists were dubbed 'Dunses' (hence 'dunce') for their obstinacy and conservatism. More recently he has, however, been admired by figures as diverse as Charles Peirce, Martin Heidegger and Gerald Manley Hopkins, who found him 'of realty the rarest veinèd unraveller'. ▷ Aquinas, St Thomas; Aristotle; Heidegger, Martin; scholasticism; Thomism

Dunstan, St (c.909–988) Anglo-Saxon prelate, the son of a West Saxon noble, and Archbishop of Canterbury from 959. He was educated at Glastonbury abbey, and spent some time at the court of King Athelstan but was banished for practising unlawful arts. He took monastic vows and retired to Glastonbury where he devoted himself to studying. Recalled on the accession of Athelstan's brother King Edmund, he was appointed Abbot of Glastonbury (945). In this post he began to implement great reforms, turning Glastonbury into a centre of religious teaching. At the same time he became Edmund's treasurer and adviser, but on his death in 955 and the accession of Edwy, lost his influence. He fled to Flanders and Ghent where he first saw the strict Benedictine discipline which he was later to introduce into England. In 957 he was recalled by Edgar, who was now king of the country north of the Thames, and was created Bishop of Worcester and of London (959). In that year, on Edwy's death, Edgar became king of the entire country. One of his first acts was to appoint Dunstan Archbishop of Canterbury, and Dunstan's wise counsel greatly contributed to the peace and prosperity of Edgar's reign. With Oswald, Archbishop of York, Dunstan crowned Edgar at Bath in 973, a formal declaration of the unity of the kingdom. Dunstan strove to elevate the lives of the clergy and make them real teachers of the people in secular as well as religious matters. He made the payment of tithes by landowners obligatory, but did not entirely surrender the liberties of the Church to Rome. On Edgar's death he declared for Edward 'the Martyr', Edgar's elder son, and crowned him. On Edward's murder (978) the two archbishops crowned Æthelred, whose hostility ended Dunstan's political career. His feast day is 19 May. ▷ Benedictines; monasticism

Durga (Durgā) The mother goddess in her fierce or warrior aspect in Hinduism. Plagued by the buffalo-demon the gods asked the goddess for protection. She manifested herself in the form of Durga and after a fierce battle decapitated the demon. She is iconographically portrayed as being beautiful, riding a lion and killing the buffalo-demon with a trident. Most Hindu temples have a shrine to Durga and she is sometimes worshipped with blood-sacrifice. ▷ goddess worship

Durkheim, Émile (1858–1917) Pioneer French sociologist, generally regarded as one of the founders of the discipline. Educated at the Ećole Normale Supérieure, he taught at the University of Bordeaux from 1887 to 1902, and at the Sorbonne from 1902 to 1916. He was appointed to the first chair of sociology in France in 1913. Durkheim believed that sociology should be rigorously objective and scientific, and he developed a systematic sociological methodology based on the view that what he called 'social facts', that is, social phenomena, should be treated as 'things' to be explained solely by reference to other social facts, not in terms of any individual person's actions. This approach is presented in his methodological writings and is applied particularly in his study of suicide. Also central to his work is the idea that societies are held together by means of a 'conscience collective', powerful beliefs and sentiments that are shared in common by members of the society, and that exert a strong influence on individuals' behaviour. This is seen both in his study of the division of labour and in his analysis of the social basis of religion, which he regarded as having been created by society as a means of expressing its ideals and unifying itself. In addition to his contribution to sociology, Durkheim's writings have also been influential among anthropologists and historians. ▷ anthropology of religion; study of religion

Dusserah/Dasarah A Hindu festival occurring in October/November, celebrated particularly in Maharashtra. The festival commemorates a scene from the *Mahabharata* where the Pandus end their 13-year exile and retrieve their weapons which had been hidden in the hollows of trees. The festival involves the worship of the Shami trees in which these weapons were hidden. ▷ Mahabharata

Dutch Reformed Church The largest Protestant Church in Holland, stemming from the Calvinist Reformation in the 16th century. Its leaders and scholars have been influential in Dutch life, in former Dutch colonies, and also in Reformed theology. The Dutch Reformed Church in South Africa (totally separated from the Church in Holland) is the official Church of dominant white Afrikaans-speaking nationals, condemned in 1982 by the other Reformed Churches for justifying both theologically and practically the policy of apartheid. ▷ Calvinism; Protestantism; Reformed Churches

dying and rising gods The technical name given to deities who, according to myths associated with them, are said to have died and subsequently been resurrected. Such deities were invariably male and alleged to be found in agrarian societies around the Mediterranean, examples being Adonis (originally Semitic, known only through late Greek, Roman and Christian sources), Attis (Phrygia), Osiris (Egypt), Marduk (Babylon) and Tammuz (Asia Minor). Their dying and rising allegedly symbolized the annual cycle of vegetation of which they were personifications, and were said to form the basis of fertility cults and rituals. An additional explanation of their origin (offered by James G Frazer in *The Golden Bough*) hypothesized the killing of a sacred king after his fertility waned, which event became a myth of a dying god, followed by rejuvenation through rebirth or resurrection. In recent years, considerable doubt has been cast on the legitimacy of the category of 'dying and rising deities', evidence for such deities being based on late Greek, Roman and Christian texts, which in themselves are ambiguous. It has been suggested that interest in this category has been sustained by biblical scholars, concerned with the background to the Old and New Testaments and interested in the category of 'resurrection'. ▷ resurrection

E

Ea, or Enki A Mesopotamian god, who is believed to bring the sweet waters to make the earth fruitful. He helps human beings to survive by teaching them to plough the land, and is then revered as the source of creativity and wisdom. A myth in which Enki eats the plants in a paradise garden anticipates the story of Adam and Eve. ▷ Adam and Eve

early burial finds The earliest burial finds date back to the middle palaeolithic period around 75 000BCE. Important early finds include those at La Ferrassie and La Chapelle aux Saints in France, Teshik-Tash in the USSR, and Monte Circeo in Italy. The human skeletons discovered there and elsewhere often have their legs flexed or in crouched position, the head is usually to the east, the body is often lying on the right side, and tools and animal bones are frequently found in a place close by, possibly as burial gifts. Theories abound about the meaning of these finds, but the basic question is that of why human beings should bury their dead. It is clear that Neanderthal humans did bury corpses and that they had some comprehension of death and how to deal with it, namely through burial customs. Whether they had any comprehension of life in another world is not clear. There have also been other burial finds of bear skulls and animal bones in isolation from human remains. They may signify early animal sacrifices or hunting rituals. ▷ palaeolithic religion

Easter The chief festival of the Christian Church, commemorating the resurrection of Christ after his crucifixion. Observed in the Western Churches on a Sunday between 22 March and 25 April inclusive, depending on the date of the first full moon after the spring equinox; the Orthodox Church has a different method of calculating the date. The name Easter perhaps derives from Eostre, the name of an Anglo-Saxon goddess. Easter customs such as egg-rolling are probably of pagan origin. ▷ Christianity; Christian year

Eastern Orthodox Church ▷ Orthodox Church

Ebionites (literally 'poor men') A Judaeo-Christian sect of the early Christian era, opposed by Irenaeus in the late 2nd century. They were apparently ascetic, and continued to observe rigorously the Jewish Law. They also believed that Jesus was the Messiah, a virtuous man anointed by the Spirit, but not truly 'divine'. ▷ asceticism; Christology; Irenaeus, St

Ecclesiastes, Book of A biblical work, specifically attributed to 'The Preacher, the son of David, king of Jerusalem', who has traditionally been identified as Solomon, although the work is more usually now dated in the post-exilic period of Israel's history. It is largely philosophical in its reflections on the meaning of life, often declaring that 'all is vanity'. The title is derived from the Greek rendering of the Hebrew Koheleth: 'the preacher, one who speaks or teaches in an assembly'. ▷ Old Testament; Solomon

Ecclesiasticus, Book of (Latin 'The Church (Book)') Part of the Old Testament Apocrypha or Catholic deuterocanonical writings, originally attributed to a Jewish scribe c.180BCE, but later translated into Greek by his grandson; also called *The Wisdom of Jesus, the Son of Sirach*, or just *Sirach* or *Ben Sira*. It consists largely of collections of proverbs and exhortations; praises wisdom, attempting to link it with a Torah-centred way of life; and ends with a historical survey in praise of Israel's famous leaders. ▷ Apocrypha, Old Testament; Torah

Eck, Johann Mayer von (1486–1543) German Catholic theologian, born in Egg in Swabia. Professor of Theology at Ingolstadt (1510), he was the ruling spirit of that university until his death. He disputed with Luther at Leipzig in 1519, and wrote his *De Primatu Petri* and went to Rome in 1520, to return with the bull which declared Luther a heretic. He also disputed with Melanchthon at Worms (1540) and with Ratisbon at Worms (1541). ▷ Luther, Martin; Melanchthon; Roman Catholicism

Eckhart, Johannes, called Meister Eckhart (c.1260–1327) German mystic, born in Hochheim near Gotha. He entered the Dominican order, studied and taught in Paris, acted as Prior of Erfurt and as vicar of his order for Thuringia, was Dominican Provincial in Saxony, 1303–11, Vicar-General of Bohemia, 1307, and from 1312 preached at Strasbourg, Frankfurt and Cologne. Eckhart's teaching is a mystic pantheism, which influenced later religious mysticism and speculative philosophy. In 1325 he was accused of heresy by the Archbishop of Cologne, and two years after his death his writings were condemned by Pope John XXII. His extant works consist of Latin and German sermons and tractates. ▷ Dominicans; heresy; mysticism; pantheism

ecstasy (Greek *ek-stasis*, 'standing or being placed outside' or 'displaced') In religion this signifies the state of being outside the body or transcending oneself, a condition, often excited and frenzied or blissful, known in varying forms to nearly all religions. Typical is the state of the *shaman* or inspired priest of preliterate societies, who gains, in a trance or 'out-of-body' state, access to the spirit world, communicating with and receiving messages from spirits of the dead. Ecstasy is also a feature of prophetic experience (eg Saul in I Samuel 10.1–16), in which the prophet receives messages from God, and figures prominently in most forms of mysticism. In mystical experience, the subject transcends the body and the senses to achieve either communion or union (absorption or oneness) with the divine. The ecstatic state is almost always temporary.

Ecstasy played an important part among the adherents of the cult of Dionysos and of the mystery religions of the Graeco-Roman world (eg the cults of Adonis, Osiris, Mithra). It is testified to by the reports of mystics of, among others, the Judaeo-Christian, Islamic, Hindu and Buddhist traditions. Different religions offer different techniques for achieving ecstatic states: yoga (Hinduism), contemplation and asceticism (Christianity), orgiastic dancing (cult of Dionysos), and also flagellation, self-hypnosis, and deep-breathing. It can also be induced by drugs, as in the Peyote religion of Mexico and contemporary use of mescalin and LSD (lysergic acid diethylamide). Some commentators see the excitement and frenzy of large crowds, for example at football matches, as a secular expression of ecstasy. ▷ mysticism; peyote; psychedelic drugs; transcendence and immanence

ecumenism (Greek *oikoumene*, 'the inhabited world') A movement seeking visible unity of divided churches and denominations within Christianity. The 4th-century and 5th-century 'Ecumenical Councils' had claimed to represent the Church in the whole world. A

symbol of the ecumenical movement

dramatic increase of interest in ecumenism and the reuniting of Churches followed the Edinburgh Missionary Conference (1910), and led to the formation in 1948 of the World Council of Churches. Assemblies are held every seven years, the decisions of which guide but do not bind member Churches. The movement encourages dialogue between Churches of different denominations, unions where possible (as in the Churches of North and South India), joint acts of worship, and joint service in the community. ▷ Council of the Church; World Council of Churches

Edda (Old Norse, 'great-grandmother') The name of two separate collections of Old Norse literature. The *Elder Edda*, dating from the 9th century, consist of heroic and mythological poems; the later Edda were written (mainly in prose) in the early 13th century by the Icelandic poet Snorri Sturluson. ▷ Germanic religion; sagas

Eddy, Mary (Morse), née **Baker** (1821–1910) American founder of the Christian Science Church, born in Bow, New Hampshire and brought up as a Congregationalist. She was frequently ill as a young woman. After a brief first marriage (to George Glover, 1843–4), she was married a second time, in 1853, to Daniel Patterson (divorced in 1873). In the 1860s she tried all kinds of medication, but turned to faith-healing and in 1862 came under the influence of Phineas T Quimby (1802–66). While recovering from a severe fall in 1866 she turned to the Bible, and went on to develop a spiritual and metaphysical system she called Christian Science, explaining her beliefs in *Science and Health with Key to the Scriptures* (1875), which proclaimed the illusory nature of disease. She married Asa G Eddy in 1877, and in 1879 founded at Boston the Church of Christ, Scientist. Her church attracted great numbers of followers. She founded various publications, including the *Christian Science Journal* (1883), and the *Christian Science Monitor* (1908). ▷ Christian Science; Congregationalism

Eden, Garden of Biblical place associated with 'Paradise', where Adam and Eve lived prior to their sin and expulsion (Genesis 2, 3). 'Eden' may mean 'delight' (Hebrew) or simply and more probably 'a plain' (Sumerian). It is also used in Ezekiel as a symbol for the future restitution of Israel after the exile. ▷ Adam and Eve; Ezekiel, Book of

Edomites According to the Bible (Genesis 36), the descendants of Esau who settled in the mountainous area south of the Dead Sea to the Gulf of Aqabah; in Greek, *Idumeans*. They often appear as enemies of Israel, having been conquered by David, but retaking parts of Judah and becoming a kingdom in the 8th century BCE. They participated in the overthrow of Judah in 587BCE by the Babylonians, but were eventually conquered by John Hyrcanus in the late 2nd century BCE, forcing their integration into the Jewish people. Herod the Great was of Edomite descent. ▷ Bible; David; Esau; Judah, kingdom of

Edwards, Jonathan (1703–58) American philosopher and theologian, born in East Windsor, Connecticut, grandson of Solomon Stoddard. He was educated at Yale and succeeded his grandfather as minister of the Congregationalist Church at Northampton, Massachusetts (1727–50). Renowned for his powerful preaching and hardline Calvinism he helped inspire the revivalist movement known as the 'Great Awakening'. He was dismissed in 1750 for his overzealous orthodoxy and became instead a missionary to the Housatonnuck Indians at Stockbridge, Massachusetts, and eventually in 1757 became President of the College of New Jersey (now Princeton University). He is regarded as the greatest theologian of American puritanism, his main doctrinal work being the *Careful and Strict Enquiry into the Modern Prevailing Notions of that Freedom of the Will* (1754). ▷ Calvinism; Congregationalism; Great Awakening; Puritanism; Revivalism

eightfold path The fourth of Buddha's four noble truths, prescribing the way to enlightenment. It is also known as the middle path, since its prescriptions lay out a course that falls between sensuality and strict asceticism. The Path involves perfect understanding, perfect aspiration, perfect speech, perfect conduct, perfect means of livelihood, perfect endeavour, perfect mindfulness, and perfect contemplation. ▷ ariya sacca; Buddha

Eisai (1141–1215) Founder of Japanese Zen Buddhism, born in Japan. Ordained a monk while a boy, and trained at the famous Japanese Tendai monastery at Mount Hiei, he went to China twice and found enlightenment in the Linchu school of Chinese Chan Buddhism. He brought it back to Japan in 1191 as Rinzai Zen, which he saw as an important innovation both for Japanese Buddhism and for Japan itself. He built the first Rinzai temple at Hakata, and later advocated Rinzai Zen in Kyoto and Kamakura. He stressed the use of koans, paradoxical questions that can jerk the mind out of its usual patterns into enlightenment. He is recognized as the father of the Japanese tea-drinking culture. He emphasized sudden enlightenment rather than the gradual enlightenment that was later advocated by his pupil Dogen in the second Japanese Zen school of Soto Zen. His view of immediate enlightenment by sudden insight into the true nature of one's own experience and the surrounding world was attractive to the Kamakura leaders of his day, who recognized Zen as a separate school, and it eventually assumed more general importance in Japanese culture. ▷ Chan; Dogen; enlightenment; gradual/sudden enlightenment schools of Buddhism; koans; Rinzai; Soto; Tendai

El Canaanite high god. At ancient Ugarit El was head of the pantheon, king and father of the gods, called 'creator of created things'. His epithet 'Bull' emphasized his strength. His consort was the goddess Athirat (Asherah). In the mythological texts El is not active in battle, but presides over the divine assembly where important decisions are referred to him. He is portrayed as ancient, grey-bearded and wise. Nonetheless, one text portrays him with considerable sexual appetites and in non-Ugaritic sources he plays a more active and violent role. El is the common Semitic noun for god, and is used in this sense in the Hebrew Bible, although it occurs occasionally as a proper name, used as another name for Yahweh. ▷ Asherah; Canaanite religion; Ras Shamra texts; Ugarit; Yahweh

Elam The name given in antiquity to what is now south-west Iran. Its main city was Susa, and at its zenith in the 13th century

BCE it ruled an empire stretching from Babylonia in the west to Persepolis in the east. ▷ Babylon

Elamite religion From the middle of the 4th millennium BCE an urban civilization developed in Elam, north of the Persian Gulf and east of the River Tigris, with capitals at Susa and Anshan. A strong Elamite dynasty arose c.2000BCE; the Elamites were again powerful c.1300–1100BCE, but were subdued by the Assyrians in the 7th century. Data from the 3rd millennium show religion to have been centred on the powers possessed by goddesses, as evidenced by female figurines of clay and terracotta; this suggests that fertility was an important religious concept, as corroborated by images of bulls and rams on cylinder seals. The moon goddess appears to have been of special significance, and representations of her in procession connect her with trees, serpents and various animals. Temples were erected to honour the goddess, and in these animal sacrifices took place. ▷ Hittite religion; Hurrian religion; sacrifice; Sumerian religion

elder One who by reason of age or distinction is entrusted with shared authority and leadership in a community. 1 In the ancient biblical world, the elders of Israel exercised both religious and civil influence from the tribal period onwards; and city elders were active at a local level. Jewish synagogues were also governed by elders, but the title is reserved for scholars in the Mishnaic period. In the New Testament, elders were church officials (Greek *presbuteroi*, 'presbyters') with a collective authority for general oversight of a congregation, and are sometimes even called 'bishops' (Greek *episkopoi*; *Acts* 20.28, *Titus* 1.5–7) but not yet in the monarchical sense. ▷ bishop; Judaism; synagogue 2 In Reformed Churches, an officer ordained to 'rule' along with the minister (a 'teaching' elder). Elders exercise discipline, and oversee the life of a congregation and its individual members. ▷ Presbyterianism; Reformed Churches

election The choosing by the omnipotent and universal God for special favour, task or salvation of a particular people or individual. This concept is particularly prominent in Judaism, Christianity and Islam. In Judaism, the people of Israel are believed to be the 'chosen people' of Yahweh, by virtue of his convenants, especially with Abraham (Genesis 12) and Moses (Exodus 19). The election of Israel is not made because of any inherent merit in Israel, but purely out of God's love. By virtue of the covenant, however, Israel is obligated to worship and obey Yahweh by following specific moral and cultic principles. As the history of Israel progresses, suffering is recognized as a mark of their election. Certain individuals, priests and kings are understood to be elected by God for specific tasks and with specific responsibilities. In time, too, because of Israel's apostasy, election is concentrated on a 'remnant' who remain faithful. Election began to be seen as not only for the benefit of the elect, but for the benefit of all nations. Sometimes a more exclusive interpretation of election was made by schismatic Jewish groups, like the Qumran community.

Election figures strongly in Christianity through the identification of Jesus Christ as the elect one and on his followers in the Christian community, the Church, as the true Israel. Throughout the history of the Church, various groups have seen and declared themselves as exclusively 'the elect' of God (eg the Donatists of the 4th century CE and the Cathari in medieval Europe). At the time of the Protestant Reformation, the doctrine of election, and with it predestination, played a prominent part in the theology of John Calvin and subsequently of churches of the Reformed tradition. Election is also a concept known to Islam, where a covenantal relationship is recognized between Allah and believers. Specific individuals, including the Hebrew prophets and Jesus of Nazareth, as well as communities, are called chosen, culminating in the election of Muhammad and his community. Among the Sufis, election is particularly important for identifying those who have experienced the divine and received the gift of sainthood. ▷ Calvin, John; covenant; predestination; Sufism

Eliade, Mircea (1907–86) Romanian historian and philosopher of comparative religion, born in Bucharest. A student of Indian philosophy and Sanskrit at Calcutta University (1928–31) before becoming a lecturer in the history of religion and metaphysics at Bucharest from 1933 to 1939, he served in the diplomatic service during World War II, and later taught at the Sorbonne (1946–8) and Chicago University (1957–85). A pioneer in the systematic study of world religions, he published numerous books and papers, including *The Myth of the Eternal Return* (1949), *Patterns in Comparative Religion* (1958), Yoga: *Immortality and Freedom* (1958), *The Sacred and the Profane* (1959), *A History of Religious Ideas, I–III* (1978–85), and two volumes of autobiography (1982, 1988) covering the years

1907–60. He was editor-in-chief of *The Encyclopaedia of Religion* (1987), and wrote a number of novels, including *The Forbidden Forest* (1955). ▷ comparative religion; metaphysics

Elijah (9th century BCE) Hebrew prophet, whose activities are portrayed in four stories in 1 Kings 17–19, 21 and 2 Kings 1–2. He was prominent in opposing the worship of Baal in Israel under King Ahab and Jezebel, and by virtue of his loyalty to God was depicted as ascending directly into heaven. ▷ Ahab; Baal; Kings, Books of; prophet

Elisha (second half of 9th century BCE) Hebrew prophet in succession to Elijah; his activities are portrayed in 1 Kings 19 and 2 Kings 2–9, 13. He was active in Israel under several kings from Ahab to Jehoash, was credited with miraculous signs, counselled kings, and attempted to guide the nation against her external enemies, especially the Syrians. ▷ Ahab; Elijah; Kings, Books of; prophet

Elohim (Hebrew 'gods') A divine name for the God of Israel, the plural form here being purged of its polytheistic meaning, and used as a plural of majesty. There are over 2500 occurrences in the Hebrew Bible, making it one of the most common divine names therein, but it could still be applied to other gods, angels, or even figures such as Moses. ▷ God; Yahweh

emblems, Sikh Two emblems are especially popular and significant among Sikhs. The first is a symbol of God, Ik Oankar, which combines the figure one and the letter 'O' from the word 'Oankar'. It is found at the start of the *Mul Mantra*, one of the most important Sikh poems, and it signifies the unity of God. The second is an emblem of the Sikh community, the *Khalsa*, and is in effect a symbol of Sikhism itself. At the centre of this emblem is a double-edged sword; this sword is placed in the middle of a circle in the form of a steel quoit; on ether side of the circle is a Sikh ceremonial dagger (*kirpan*). The double-edged sword symbolizes the Sikh ideal of the soldier-saint, the circle represents the oneness of God and humanity, and the two ceremonial daggers refer to the balance of temporal and spiritual power. This emblem, called the *Khanda*, is worn on clothing, on the flags of Sikh temples, and on the palanquin in which the Sikh scripture, the *Guru Granth Sahib*, is kept. ▷ five Ks; Guru Granth Sahib; Khalsa; Mul Mantra

Sikh emblem denoting God and the Sikh community

Emerson, Ralph Waldo (1803–82) American poet and essayist, born in Boston of a long line of ministers. He graduated at Harvard in 1821, and after teaching at different places, became in 1829 pastor of the Second Church (Unitarian) in Boston, and married his first wife, Ellen Louisa Tucker (d.1832). In that year he preached views on the Lord's Supper which were disapproved by the majority of his congregation; this led him finally to resign his pulpit. In 1833 he went to Europe, and visited **Thomas Carlyle** at Craigenputtock, next year beginning that 38 years' correspondence which shows the two men with all their characteristics, different as optimist and pessimist, yet with many profound sympathies. In 1834 he removed to Concord. In 1835 he married his second wife, Lydia (Lidian) Jackson (1802–92). In 1836 he published a prose rhapsody entitled *Nature* which, like his earlier poems, was read by few, and understood by fewer still, but which contains the germs of many of his later essays and poems. It was followed by 'The American Scholar', an oration delivered at Harvard University. These two publications, the first in the series of his collected works, strike the keynote of his philosophical, poetical and moral teachings. The 'address before the Divinity Class, Cambridge, 1838', which follows them, defined his position in, or out of, the Church in which he had been a minister. A plea for the individual consciousness (as against all historical creeds, bibles, churches) for the soul of each man as the supreme judge in spiritual matters, it produced a great sensation, especially among the Unitarians, and much controversy followed in which Emerson took no part. In 1849 he revisited England to lecture on *Representative Men* (published in 1850). His *English Traits* appeared in 1856, *The Conduct of Life* in 1860, *Society and Solitude* in 1870, *Letters and Social Aims* in 1876. He appears as an idealist or transcendentalist in philosophy, a rationalist in religion, a bold advocate of spiritual independence, of intuition as a divine guidance, of instinct as a heaven-born impulse and of individualism in its fullest extent, making each life a kind of theocratic egoism. For him nature was a sphinx, covered with hieroglyphics, for which the spirit of man is to find the key.

emperor worship The Roman emperor was sometimes associated with divinities, or even directly deified. The precise form of worship varied according to time and place, and also according to whether the worshipped emperor was living or dead and whether the worship was part of public or private religion. Thus the eastern part of the empire, which had become accustomed to the phenomenon of divine kingship under Hellenized and Egyptian rulers, readily incorporated the cult of both a living and a deified emperor. In Italy, however, and especially in Rome, the early Roman emperors were worshipped only when dead, and in their lifetime only indirectly. For instance, it was through the association in Italy of his essence (*genius*) with divinities such as Roma and the Lares that Augustus could be worshipped during his life. At his death, he was formally made divine, and his cult officially instituted. Thus, the difference in worship between eastern and western provinces vanished with regard to a dead emperor. Not all emperors were deified: it was the Senate which decided whether or not to decree apotheosis to emperors. The development of emperor-worship in public religion created a new category of priests, incorporating both the high Roman élite and also freedmen seeking to acquire some political importance in their towns. ▷ kingship, sacred; Lares; Roman religion

empiricism A philosophical tradition which maintains that all or most significant knowledge is based on sense experience; it is usually contrasted with rationalism. Mathematical knowledge and language-competence provide difficult cases for empiricism. Some empiricists, such as Locke, claim that all concepts but not all propositions are empirical; the senses give the concept of twoness, and reason dictates that $2+2=4$. Some claim that mathematical truths are not 'significant'; others that they are just highly confirmed generalizations (Mill). Many allow that some patterns of reasoning are independent of experience. Some allow that there might be innate structures in the mind necessary to explain various human capacities, such as language-learning, but insist that the structures provide no evidence for rationalism. ▷ Locke, John; logical positivism; Mill, John Stuart; rationalism

emptiness A very important concept in Buddhism, especially within the Mahayana tradition. It is not the same as nihilism or nothingness, and in the history of the Buddhist tradition it has acquired a number of often interconnected meanings. In early Buddhist thought, it referred mainly to the emptiness or the fleeting nature of worldly existence, wherein everything, including pleasure, is impermanent and lacking in value of its own. In a more positive sense it could refer to the creative calm involved in disciplined meditation when it is empty of distractions, the clarity of insight techniques wherein things are seen to be empty of self and can therefore be seen 'as they are', and the unselfishness of the enlightened mind when it is empty of delusion, greed and hatred. Mahayana Buddhists finessed upon the meaning of emptiness. The Madhyamika school, founded by Nagarjuna at the end of the 2nd century CE, argued that everything is empty of substantial existence including language itself, and when we realize the emptiness, or openness, of the whole of life it can make us free truly to live. The Yogacara school, which arose in the 4th and 5th centuries, expressed this idea more positively. It spoke in terms of the Buddha nature or the Buddha mind, which is the original true mind within us, and defined emptiness as emptying oneself of all but the Buddha nature and the Buddha mind within. Finally the sense arose within Mahayana Buddhism that emptiness involved an application of wisdom and compassion to life, which although empty was not unreal, in such a way that one could live a free and relaxed life wherein one's understanding had been transformed. ▷ Buddha nature; Madhyamika; Mahayana Buddhism; Nagarjuna; wisdom; Yogacara

encyclical, papal Originally, a letter sent to all the churches in a particular area. The term is now restricted to official letters of instruction, usually doctrinal or pastoral in nature, issued by a pope to the whole Roman Catholic Church. ▷ Roman Catholicism

Encyclopaedists/Encyclopedists A collective term for the distinguished editors (Diderot and d'Alembert) and contributors (notably Voltaire, Montesquieu, Condorcet, Helvetius, and Rousseau) to the *Encyclopédie*, a major work of social and political reference published in France (1751–72), associated with the French Enlightenment.

Engels, Friedrich (1820–95) German socialist, a fellow-labourer with Marx and founder of 'scientific socialism', born in Barmen. From 1842 he lived mostly in England. Having gained experience from working in his father's cotton-factory in Manchester and established contacts with the Chartist movement, he wrote *Condition of the Working Classes in England in 1844* (1845). He first met Marx at Brussels in 1844 and collaborated with him on the Communist Manifesto (1848) and returned to Germany with his mentor in 1848–9 to work on the *Neue Rheinische Zeitung* and fight on the barricades at Baden during the unsuccessful revolution of that year. After Marx's death in 1883, Engels devoted the remaining years of his life to editing and translating Marx's writings, including the second (1885) and third (1894) volumes of the influential *Das Kapital*, which established the materialist interpretation of history. ▷ Marx, Karl; secular alternatives to religion

Enki ▷ Ea

enlightenment The notion of enlightenment is a common one in many religious traditions, denoting a coming to awareness and realization of the truth after being ignorant and unaware of it. It is especially important in the Buddhist tradition where the model of enlightenment is found in the Buddha's own experience under the Bo tree at Budh-Gaya in India in the 6th century BCE. Buddhist tradition recalls how he meditated systematically, and pierced various layers of existence with his spiritual eye, remembering previous births, unveiling the laws of rebirth, and realizing the four noble truths: life is suffering, suffering results from craving, suffering goes when craving goes, and this can be achieved in practice through the eightfold path. He became a Buddha, an enlightened one, in whom knowledge and experience crystallized, revealing to him the existential and theoretical meaning of life. Through enlightenment the Buddha attained provisional nirvana in life, and at his death he attained final nirvana. The early Buddhists followed his example and became saints or *arhats*. The Mahayana tradition viewed enlightenment slightly differently. For it wisdom (*prajna*) was the key to enlightenment rather than the four noble truths and becoming an arhat; enlightenment was awaking either gradually or suddenly to one's own Buddha nature, and experiencing a sense of bliss, freedom and purity. However, the Mahayana bodhisattva has aimed to achieve enlightenment, but he has postponed its final fruits (final nirvana after death) in favour of being reborn in the world in order to help others to achieve enlightenment, or in favour of living as a transcendent bodhisattva to give active help to all beings. ▷ ariya sacca; bodhi; bodhisattva; Buddha; Mahayana Buddhism; nirvana; prajna; suffering

Enlil, or **Ellil** Mesopotamian god of the wind and atmosphere, son of Anu the sky god, and patron deity of the city of Nippur. He was the most important god in the Sumerian pantheon, called 'father of the gods' and 'king of heaven and earth'. With Anu he ruled the divine assembly and granted kingship on earth, but had an ambivalent relationship with humans. His beneficent presence was the prerequisite for life and prosperity in the land, but as a storm god he could also be angry and hostile, and was responsible for the destruction of cities and temples and also the great flood. In the Old Babylonian period (18th–16th centuries BCE) and later, Enlil's importance diminished, many of his characteristics being taken over by the Babylonian national god Marduk, and by Asshur in Assyria. ▷ Asshur; Babylonian religion; Flood, the; kingship, Ancient Near Eastern; Marduk; Sumerian religion

ennead In Ancient Egypt, a group of nine deities. The earliest of these, the Great Ennead of Heliopolis, comprised the original creator god Atum (often identified with Re); his children Shu and Tefnut; their children Geb and Nut; and the fourth generation, the brothers Osiris and Seth, and their sisters Isis and Nephthys. In part it provided a divine genealogy for the pharaoh, who was thought of as Horus, the son of Osiris and Isis. The Heliopolitan ennead served as a model for others which developed at religious centres throughout Egypt. ▷ Atum; Heliopolis theology; Horus; Isis; Nephthys; Osiris; pharaoh; Seth

Ennin (792–864) The third patriarch of the great Buddhist monastery on Mount Hiei near Kyoto in Japan. He belonged to the Tendai school of Buddhism, and trained under Saicho, in whose time Tendai began to become an important force in Japanese religion. At the age of 46, he made a famous 10-year journey to Tang China, the details of which he recorded in his diaries. They provided a vivid and insightful account of Chinese Buddhism at a time just before the great persecution of 845 when it was at the height of its powers. After becoming chief priest of Tendai in Japan in 854, he introduced elements of Shingon esoteric Buddhism into Tendai, stressed the role of mandalas (symbolic circles), used anointing ceremonies, and sponsored the use of the *nembutsu*, calling upon the name of Amida Buddha. He thus strengthened the tendency, already begun by his teacher Saicho, to broaden Tendai into a wider synthesis of Japanese Buddhism. During the following century Tendai split into two groups, one of which followed Ennin's line of succession, while the other followed that of Enchin (814–91). ▷ mandala; nembutsu; Saicho; Shingon; Tendai

Enoch Biblical character, son of Jared, father of Methuselah. He was depicted as extraordinarily devout, and therefore as translated directly into heaven without dying (Genesis 5.24). In the Graeco-Roman era his name became attached to Jewish apocalyptic writings allegedly describing his visions and journeys through the heavens (1, 2, and 3 Enoch). ▷ apocalypse; Genesis, Book of; Methuselah; Pseudepigrapha

Ephesians, Letter to the New Testament writing attributed to Paul, but of disputed authorship, and with no specific addressees in the best manuscripts (which lack the words 'in Ephesus' in Ephesians 1.1); many similarities can be detected with the Letter to the Colossians. It sets out God's purposes in establishing the Church and uniting both Jews and Gentiles in it, and concludes with exhortations directed at the Church. ▷ Colossians, Letter to the; Gentiles; New Testament; Paul, St; Pauline Letters

Ephesus, early Christianity in A seaport and chief city of Roman Asia, whose temple of Artemis (the Greek name for the Roman goddess Diana) was Asia's biggest bank, as well as one of the seven wonders of the ancient world. Paul preached there briefly at the end of his second missionary journey, after his 18-month stay in Corinth. Later he returned to Ephesus and stayed there two years (Acts 18–19), consolidating work done by Apollos, Priscilla and Aquila during his absence. Paul's preaching, healing miracles, and casting out of evil spirits caused some Greeks to renounce publicly their practice of magic associated with the worship of Artemis. Others, chiefly silversmiths and other craftsmen connected with the honouring of the goddess who feared for the survival of their trade, joined a dramatic but unsuccessful public riot against Paul. When he said farewell to the Church leaders on his final journey to Jerusalem and captivity, Paul left a flourishing Christian community in Ephesus, which was to be commended some 40 years later in the Book of Revelation (Revelation 2) for resisting heresy and persecution and for persevering in the faith. The New Testament Epistle to the Ephesians (whose authorship by Paul and destination are debated by scholars, partly because of similarities to the Epistle to the Colossians) is a sustained statement of the doctrines of Christ and the Church and of Christian privileges and responsibilities.
Ephesus is the traditional location of the later ministry of the apostle John, and it was the venue of the third ecumenical Council of 431CE, which condemned Nestorianism. ▷ Council of the Church; John, St; Nestorians; Revelation, Book of

Ephraim, tribe of One of the 12 tribes of ancient Israel, said to be descended from Joseph's younger son, who was adopted and blessed by Jacob. It was apparently a powerful tribe in ancient Israel, whose territory included the central hill country of Palestine, stretching to Bethel in the south and almost to Shechem in the north. ▷ Israel, tribes of; Joseph, tribes of

epics Lengthy narratives in poetic form which may be acted, recited or sung, and of significance in particular religions or cultures. They may be written (like Virgil's *The Aeneid*, or *Beowulf*), or oral and unwritten. If the latter, they may undergo considerable variation and development in the course of time. Epics can combine religion, philosophy, mythology, history, folk tales, and stories of the gods and godesses. They generally tell of the feats and fates of heroes and heroines, human and divine, often with the aim, or at least the effect, of reinforcing particular religious and moral attitudes or worldviews. Of particular significance for Hinduism in India is the *Mahabharata*, originally oral but reduced to writing, like the other great epic, *Ramayana*, in Sanskrit. Heroes, whose earthly and spiritual journeys are immortalized and celebrated in epics, include Siegfried (of the *Niebelungenlied* in Germany), Qorqu (Turkish), Väinämöinen (in the Finnish epic, *Kalevala*) and Gilgamesh (Babylon). A common theme is the warrior hero's quest to gain or recover lost inheritance, facing various trials and opponents, human and demonic, on the way. The hero may be human, or divine, as in the case of Marduk who, in the Babylonian creation story, *Enuma elish*, eventually overcomes the tyrant goddess, Tiamat. There is generally a strong emphasis on the conflict between good and evil, and often on regeneration through sacrifice. ▷ scriptures

Epiphany A Christian festival (6 January) which commemorates the showing of the infant Jesus to the Magi (Matthew 2), the manifestation of Jesus's divinity at his baptism (Matthew 3), and his first miracle at Cana (John 2). Its eve is Twelfth Night. In some countries, gifts are exchanged at Epiphany rather than at Christmas. ▷ Christian year; Jesus Christ; Magi

episcopacy (Greek *episkopos*, 'bishop' or 'superintendent') A hierarchical (as opposed to consistorial) system of Church government, with bishops occupying the dominant role and authority. In the Roman Catholic, Orthodox, and Anglican communions, those consecrated bishops are the chief ecclesiastical officers of a diocese, normally with a cathedral as the mother church, and have the power to ordain priests and confirm baptized members of the Church. They are responsible for the general oversight of the clergy and the spiritual life of a diocese. They are often claimed to be the direct successors of the first 12 Apostles, but not in the Lutheran and other Reformation Churches which recognize the office of bishop. ▷ Anglican Communion; apostolic succession; bishop; Lutheranism; Orthodox Church; Roman Catholicism

Episcopal Church, Protestant The Anglican Church in the USA, formally established in 1784 after the War of Independence when Samuel Seabury (1729–86) was consecrated the first Bishop of Connecticut (by the bishops of the Episcopal Church of Scotland). It is an active missionary Church, especially in the Far East and South America. Traditionally, it has allowed more lay participation in the government of the Church than has the Church of England, and some bishops allow ordination of women as priests. ▷ Anglican Communion; episcopacy; Protestantism

Erasmus, Desiderius (c.1466–1536) Dutch humanist and scholar, one of the most influential Renaissance figures, born in Rotterdam. Educated by the Brethren of the Common Life at Deventer, he joined an Augustine monastery at Steyn near Gouda in 1487, and was ordained a priest in 1492. But he was already reacting against scholasticism and was drawn to the Humanists. He studied and taught in Paris, and later in most of the cultural centres in Europe, including Oxford (1499) and Cambridge (1509–14), where he was Professor of Divinity and of Greek. He travelled widely, writing, teaching and meeting Europe's foremost intellectuals (including John Colet and Thomas More, while in England), the very model of a cultivated and dedicated scholar. He published many popular, sometimes didactic works like *Adagia* (*Adages*, 1500, 1508), *Enchiridion Militis Christiani* (*Handbook of a Christian Soldier*, 1503), and the famous *Encomium Moriae* (*In Praise of Folly*, 1509). He also published scholarly editions of classical authors and the Church Fathers, and edited the Greek New Testament (1516). He became strongly critical of the pedantries and abuses of the Catholic Church and his *Colloquia familiaria* of 1518 helped prepare the way for Martin Luther and the Reformation; but he also came to oppose the dogmatic theology of the Reformers and specifically attacked Luther in *De Libero Arbitrio* (1523). Despite these controversies he enjoyed great fame and respect in his last years, which he spent in Basle. The story of his father's life forms the theme of Charles Reade's *The Cloister and the Hearth* (1861). ▷ Augustinians; humanism; Luther, Martin; More, Sir Thomas, St; Reformation; scholasticism

Erastianism An understanding of the Christian Church which gives the state the right to intervene in and control Church affairs. This tendency is associated with Thomas Erastus (1524–83), who, in 16th-century Heidelberg, had argued against Calvinists for the rights of the state in Church affairs, and against the Church's practice of excommunication. It is also evident in the teaching of the Anglican, Richard Hooker; and in the rights of the British Crown in electing bishops in the Church of England. ▷ Calvinism; Church of England; Hooker, Richard

Erastus, Thomas, properly **Liebler,** or **Lieber,** or **Lüber** (1524–83) Swiss theologian and physician, born in Swiss Baden. He studied theology at Basle, philosophy and medicine in Italy, and was appointed physician to the counts of Henneberg. Professor of Medicine at Heidelberg and physician to the Elector Palatine (1558), he became Professor of Ethics at Basle in 1580, and died there. Erastus was a skilful physician, and a vigorous writer against Paracelsus and witchcraft. In theology he was a follower of Zwingli, and represented his view of the Lord's Supper at Heidelberg in 1560 and Maulbronn in 1564. In England the name of Erastians was applied to the party that arose in the 17th century, denying the right of autonomy to the Church. John Lightfoot and John Selden were Erastians in this sense. ▷ Erastianism; Paracelsus; Zwingli, Huldreich

eretz Yisrael Hebrew term for the Land of Israel. It is found in the Bible but with no consistent meaning; it can signify the land inhabited by all Israelites (eg 1 Samuel 13.19) or that occupied only by the Northern Kingdom (eg 2 Kings 5.2). In post-biblical times eretz Yisrael became the general designation for the territory promised to the people of Israel (see Genesis 12.1 and Exodus 6.8). Since it was viewed as especially holy, much of biblical and rabbinic law was understood to apply only to those resident in it. However, despite the centrality and sanctity of the Land of Israel and God's special presence or *shekhinah* in Jerusalem, the destruction of the Temple in 70CE and decreasing numbers of Jews resident in eretz Yisrael led to the belief that the shekhinah was exiled along with the Jews throughout the world. Nonetheless, traditional Judaism has always looked forward to the eventual restoration of Jews to eretz Yisrael, as well as the return of the shekhinah, with the advent of the messianic era. Further, such traditional motifs, combined with the rise of modern nationalism, formed the basis for the development of Zionism. ▷ exile; Israel, State of; Kook, Abraham Isaac Hacohen; messianism; Zionism

Erigena, John Scotus (c.810–c.877) Irish philosopher and theologian, born in 'Scotia' (now Ireland), and also known as John the Scot, an enigmatic and singular figure who stands outside the mainstream of medieval thought. He taught at the Court of Charles II, the Bald, in France, then supported Hincmar in the predestination controversy, writing *De Praedestinatione* (851), which the Council of Valence condemned as *pultes Scotorum* (Irishman's porridge) and 'an invention of the devil'. He also translated into Latin and provided commentaries on the Greek writings of the theologians of the Eastern Church. His major work *De Divisione Naturae* (c.865) tried to fuse Christian and neo-platonic doctrines and to reconcile faith and reason, but his work was later condemned for its pantheistic tendencies and eventually placed on the Index by Gregory XIII in 1685. Tradition has it that, having become Abbot of Malmesbury, he was stabbed to death by his scholars with their pens 'for trying to make them think'. ▷ Christianity; neoplatonism; pantheism; predestination

Eriugena, Johannes Scotus ▷ Erigena, John Scotus

Esau Biblical character, the elder son of Isaac. He was depicted as his father's favourite son, but was deprived of Isaac's blessing and his birthright by his cunning brother Jacob (Genesis 27). The story was used to explain why Esau's descendants, the Edomites, were thereafter hostile to Jacob's descendants, the Israelites. ▷ Bible; Edomites; Isaac; Jacob

eschatology In Christianity the doctrine concerning the 'last things'—the final consummation of God's purposes in creation, and the final destiny of individual souls or spirits and of humanity in general. The expected imminent return of Christ to establish the kingdom of God was not realized, in early Christianity, which led to alternative, often symbolic, representations of the 'last things'. The notion is sometimes represented as a present spiritual condition rather than as a future cosmic event. Others believe that the kingdom of God has been inaugurated by the coming of Christ, and then give varying accounts of its future fulfilment. Some continue to adhere to the early belief in the literal 'second coming' of Christ. ▷ Adventists; Christianity; kingdom of God; Messiah; messianism; millenarianism; parousia

eschatology, Islamic The Islamic notion of the final days before the end of the world, and the final destiny of human beings. In the last days, the figures of Gog and Magog, interpreted allegorically as fire and flood, will lay the earth to waste. This will be followed by the reign of the Mahdi, the rightly-guided one, stressed by the Shiites, who will for a while restore justice and correct worship to the earth. However, before long this will be followed by the reign of the Antichrist, which will be a time of great tribulation. Jesus will then come and destroy the Antichrist in the final events of world history, and usher in the day of judgement when all will be weighed in the scales of judgement by God and consigned to paradise or hell. In some versions of Muslim eschatology Gog and Magog and the Antichrist are conflated, as are the Mahdi and Jesus, but the themes of a time of troubles, a millennium, and a final judgement are commonly present. ▷ Antichrist; judgement of the dead, Islamic view of; heaven and hell,

Islamic; Jesus Christ in Islam; Mahdi; millenarianism

Esdras, Books of 1 The First Book of Esdras, known also as 3 Esdras (in the Vulgate), part of the Old Testament Apocrypha; an appendix to the Catholic Bible. It reproduces much of 2 Chronicles 35–6, Ezra, and Nehem 7–8, covering two centuries from the reign of Josiah to Ezra's reforms after the exile, with an additional story about three young men of Darius' bodyguard. ▷ Apocrypha, Old Testament; Ezra; Josiah 2 The Second Book of Esdras, known also as 4 Esdras (in the Vulgate) or 4 Ezra, sometimes considered part of the Old Testament Apocrypha; also an appendix to the Catholic Bible. It depicts seven apocalyptic visions, ostensibly to Ezra (also called Salathiel), which address the problem of why God has permitted Israel's sufferings and the destruction facing the world. Dated probably late 1st century CE; chapters 1–2 and 15–16 may be two later Christian additions, today sometimes called 5 Ezra and 6 Ezra, respectively. ▷ Apocrypha, Old Testament; apocalypse; Ezra; Pseudepigrapha

esotericism A broad tradition within the history of religion which has stressed the importance of the spiritual and transcendental side as well as the outer side of religion. Derived from the Greek word *esoteros*, meaning 'inner', it has engaged with the inner knowledge or *gnosis* that is present in religion and leads to enlightenment or salvation. It gives entry to a higher level of religious understanding of myths, symbols and the sacred which is often not only conceptual but also existential. Present in the Hellenistic mystery religions and their offshoots in the Roman empire, it became an element within Christianity through the work of people such as Origen, Hildegaard of Bingen, Bonaventure and Dante but it began to decline within the Christian tradition with the early secularization process that began in the 14th century. It revived in the 16th century as a form of counter-culture through the work of Hermetism, Christian Kabbalah and Paracelsus. Since World War II the renewal of interest in Christian spirituality has led to an increasing awareness of the value of true Christian esotericism. Elsewhere in the West it is to be found in new religious currents such as theosophy, anthroposophy, the psychological work of Carl Jung, and the studies of thinkers of the perennial philosophy school such as René Guenon. ▷ anthroposophy; Bonaventure, St; Christian Kabbalah; Hermetica/Hermetism; Jung, Carl Gustav; mystery religions; new religious movements in the West; Origen; Paracelsus; theosophy

Esperanto An international language first invented in 1887 by the Pole Ludwig Lazarus Zamenhof in order to make global communication easier. A symbol of the desirability of worldwide linguistic union, it is encouraged by the Bahai religious tradition, which stresses the notion that as there is one God and one human race a universal language is also important. Zamenhof's *Fundamento de Esperanto* (1905) outlined the basic structure of the language: phonetic words, simple grammar, easy word endings, nouns without gender, only one definite article, regular verbs, and consistent suffixes. There are more than 30000 books in Esperanto, and there is an annual World Esperanto Congress, 50 national esperanto associations, and 22 international esperanto associations. It is estimated that there are over 100000 people in the world who speak Esperanto. Although it may well be the best attempt that has yet been made to construct an international language, its influence remains small compared to that of non-invented languages such as English. ▷ Bahaism

Essenes A Jewish sect renowned in antiquity for its asceticism, communistic life-style, and skill in predicting the future. The famous Dead Sea Scrolls are believed to have belonged to a local Essene community. ▷ Dead Sea Scrolls; Judaism; Qumran, community of

Esther, Book of A book of the Hebrew Bible/Old Testament, telling the popular story of how Esther, a cousin and foster daughter of the Jew, Mordecai, became the wife of the Persian king Ahasuerus (Xerxes I) and prevented the extermination of Jews by the order of Haman, a king's officer. The event is said to be the source of the Jewish feast of Purim. The **Additions to the Book of Esther** are several enhancements found in the Septuagint but not in the Hebrew Bible. They are part of the Old Testament Apocrypha, and appear as Esther 11–16 in the Catholic Bible. These chapters consist of Mordecai's dream and its interpretation, the prayers of Mordecai and Esther, and edicts issued by the king. They may supply a specifically religious perspective which the Book of Esther lacks. ▷ Mordecai; Old Testament; Purim; Septuagint

eternity Strictly, an attribute or quality of divine life which transcends time, not part of time, but related to it, not as past or future, but as present. In religions, the concept has particular significance in attempts to understand mystical experience, the nature of divine creativity and above all life after death (or participation of the dead in present life).

In the Christian and Islamic traditions, the influence of Plato, the neo-platonists and particularly Plotinus (3rd century CE) has been decisive in understanding eternity. For Plato, time is 'the passing image of eternity', which can be equated with the divine life. Because Mind is eternal, the individual soul can participate in eternity (hence the subsequent influence on mysticism). For Plotinus, eternity and time are to be treated together as twin poles, or two extremes of a continuum.

Eternity is not strictly timelessness on the one hand or endless duration on the other. It is best conceived qualitatively rather than quantitatively, intensively rather than extensively. It thus implies not that which is static, but something dynamic, full of life (eg 'eternal life' in St John's Gospel, John 17.3)

In Taoism, the classic *Tao Te Ching* begins: 'the Tao that can be spoken is not the eternal Tao' (*ch'ang tao*), thereby stressing transcendence. In Buddhism, eternity as *kalpa* (Sanksrit) or *kappa* (Pali) is an inconceivably long period of time, separable into different parts but endlessly repeating themselves. ▷ immortality; neo-platonism; Plotinus

ethical monotheism Term used to describe the system of belief which developed in Ancient Israel, where the exclusive worship of the god Yahweh led to his recognition as the only true god. Ethical monotheism is usually defined in contrast to philosophical monotheism, its concern being less with the numerical oneness of God than with a conscious commitment to worship one god alone. The faith found in the Hebrew Bible is more practical than theoretical; the existence of other gods is not denied, but they cannot be compared with Yahweh who is the only god effective on Israel's behalf. Only Yahweh deserves the people's allegiance since he is the one with whom they have a covenant relationship. The ethical dimensions to the nature of God are stressed in the law and prophets, both his inherent righteousness and the moral demands which that righteousness makes on his worshippers. ▷ monotheism; Yahweh

ethics in religion All religious traditions have a view of what is the correct way of life for both individuals and society. Although they differ in regard to particular applications they agree that ethics are relevant and necessary. Christians have stressed the general principles of love and service, but have not gone into great detail about how they should be applied. Jews in the *Torah* and Muslims in the Shariah have gone into greater detail about the legal minutiae of ethics, and felt that those details were important. Hindus have stressed the social ethics of the caste system, and together with Buddhists they have emphasized the importance of non-violence in regard to the natural world as well as to human beings. Jain monks have taken this to extremes by wearing a mask and carrying a broom to avoid killing insect life by swallowing it or treading on it. Some religions have laid greater stress on individual ethics, while others have emphasized social ethics. There has been general agreement that killing, stealing, lying, sexual misconduct, cruelty and gluttony are wrong. The circumstances of the modern world have brought ethical dilemmas to all religions in areas such as abortion, euthanasia, birth control, world economics, medicine, human rights, the role of women and divorce. Issues such as ecology, starvation in Africa and world poverty have led to increased dialogue between religions on the need for an ethic whereby religions can work together for global harmony. ▷ ahimsa; caste; Christian ethics; Greek religion and ethics; shariah; Torah

Ethiopian churches These are separatist African churches which have broken away from parent missionary bodies, and which seek to select those aspects of Christianity deemed appropriate to African cultural and social needs. They take their inspiration from the Donatist and Coptic churches, and have appeared in West, Central, and South Africa. Some have been apolitical, but many have become a focus for political discontent. ▷ Copts; Donatists

Eucharist (Greek *eucharistia*, 'thanksgiving') For most Christian denominations, a sacrament and the central act of worship, sometimes called the Mass (Roman Catholic), Holy Communion, or Lord's Supper (Protestant). It is based on the example of Jesus at the Last Supper, when he identified the bread which he broke and the wine which he poured with his body and blood (1 Corinthians 11.23–5; Matthew 26.26–8; Mark 14.22–4; Luke 22.17–20), and generally consists of the consecration of bread and wine by the priest or minister and distribution among the worshippers (communion).

Theological interpretations vary from the literal transformation of the elements into the body and blood of Christ, re-enacting his sacrifice on the Cross, through different interpretations such as transubstantiation and consubstantiation, to symbolism representing the real presence of Christ and a simple memorial meal. The Quakers (Society of Friends) rejected the sacrament because of its formality, but with the exception of them and the Salvation Army it is practised by all mainstream branches of Christianity. ▷ Christianity; consubstantiation; Jesus Christ; Last Supper; real presence; sacrament; Salvation Army; Friends, Society of; transubstantiation

Eusebius of Caesarea (c.264–340) Palestinian theologian and scholar, known as the Father of Church History, born probably in Palestine. He became Bishop of Caesarea about 313, and in the Council of Nicaea was the head of the semi-Arian or moderate party, which was averse to discussing the nature of the Trinity, and would have preferred the language of scripture to that of theology in speaking about the Godhead. His *Chronicon*, a history of the world to 325, is valuable as a source of extracts from lost works. His *Praeparatio Evangelica* is a collection of such statements in 'heathen' writings as support the evidences of Christianity; its complement is the *Demonstratio Evangelica* in 20 books, ten of which are extant, intended to convince the Jews of the truth of Christianity from their own scriptures. His great work, the *Ecclesiastical History*, is a record of the chief events in the Christian Church down to 324. Other works, all likewise in Greek, are his *De Martyribus Palestinae*, treatises against Hierocles and Marcellus, the *Theophania* (discovered in 1839), and a life of Constantine. ▷ Arius; Nicaea, Council of; Trinity

Evangelical Alliance A religious movement, founded in 1846—the formal expression of an international evangelical community embracing a variety of conservative evangelical churches and independent agencies. They are united by the common purpose of winning the world for Christ. ▷ evangelicalism; Jesus Christ

evangelicalism Since the Reformation, a term which has been applied to the Protestant Churches because of their principles of justification through faith alone (ie personal commitment), and the supreme authority accorded to Scripture (ie not to institutional figures of authority). The word comes from the Greek 'to announce the good news'. Subsequently it has been applied more narrowly to those Protestant Churches which emphasize intense personal conversion ('born-again Christianity') and commitment in their experience of justification and biblical authority. The term is not, however, limited to Protestant believers, but goes beyond denominational divisions.

Although commonly used to describe the revival of fundamentalism following World War II, evangelicalism was a feature throughout the history of the Christian Church, eg in the Apostolic Church, or in the medieval reform movements. With an emphasis on compassion and mission-work, the gospel being spread by active and enthusiastic evangelism, evangelicalism in the late 20th century has spread worldwide. Its outreach and subsequent forging of links between different branches of evangelicalism have been strengthened by gatherings such as the World Congress of Evangelism (1966) and the International Congress on World Evangelism (1974). ▷ fundamentalism; Graham, Billy; Protestantism; Reformation

Evangelical United Brethren Church A Christian denomination established in the USA in 1946 through the merger of the Church of the United Brethren in Christ and the Evangelical Church. Both Churches were similar in belief and practice, emphasizing the importance and authority of scripture, justification, and regeneration. In 1968 it merged with the Methodist Church to form the United Methodist Church. ▷ Christianity; evangelicalism; Methodism

evangelist (Greek *evangel*, 'good news') One who preaches the gospel of Jesus Christ. The New Testament suggests that some Christians have special gifts of evangelizing. Although evangelizing is now understood to be the task of the whole Church, the term has been more recently applied to popular preachers at missionary rallies. ▷ Graham, Billy; Jesus Christ; John, St; missions, Christian

Evans-Pritchard, Sir Edward Evan (1902–73) English social anthropologist, born in Crowbridge, Sussex. He studied history at Oxford, and succeeded his teacher Alfred Radcliffe-Brown to the chair of social anthropology (1946–70). He carried out fieldwork in East Africa in the 1920s and 1930s among the Azande and the Nuer, resulting in a number of classic monographs including *Witchcraft, Oracles and Magic among the Azande* (1937), *The Nuer* (1940) and *Nuer Religion* (1956). Though strongly influenced by the sociological theory of Émile Durkheim, he came to reject Radcliffe-Brown's view that social anthropology could be regarded as a natural science of society, choosing instead to emphasize its affinity with history, in that it required interpretation and translation rather than scientific explanation. His later work on religion was strongly coloured by his own experience of conversion to Catholicism. ▷ Durkheim, Émile; Radcliffe-Brown, Alfred Reginald

Eve ▷ Adam and Eve

evil That which works against the welfare of humankind or the purpose of a benevolent God. The most commonly recognized instances are pain in all its forms, as well as that which causes pain, and death itself as the denial and termination of life. The presence of evil is variously attributed to the sinfulness and ignorance of human beings, to the activity of the gods or malignant spirits or demons, or as a necessary correlative to good. In monotheistic religions in which a personal and omnipotent God is worshipped, there is much discussion as to whether evil is willed by God or merely permitted by him for some transcendent purpose. ▷ Angra Mainyu

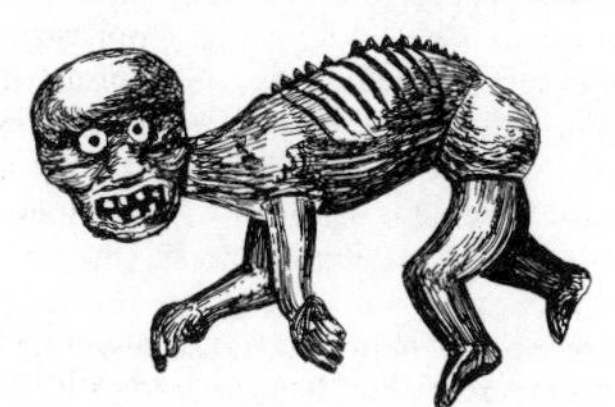

Inuit representation of evil

evil, Ancient Near Eastern concept of In Mesopotamia demons were held responsible for illness and played a major part in daily life. Among the most feared were the so-called 'Evil Seven' and the female demon Lamashtu. Incantation-priests, who were often called upon to perform exorcisms, used magical rites to drive them away. Demons were not to blame for all suffering, which might also be caused by black magic or as a result of the sin of the individual. No distinction was made between ritual and moral offences, and often a sufferer was unaware of his sin and had to use divination to determine which god he had offended and how. Mesopotamian attempts at theodicy suggest that the will of the gods is inscrutable, and humans should humbly submit to it, lamenting their sin and glorifying their god in order to renew his favour. ▷ Babylonian religion; divination, Ancient Near Eastern; magic, Ancient Near Eastern; theodicy

evil, Christian concept of The question of how so painful and problem-filled a world can be the creation of a good, loving and powerful God has taxed Christian imagination throughout the centuries. The most frequent response has been to blame our human exercise of free-will which, in disobeying God, wreaks havoc on his intentions for humankind and his environment. Sometimes, following Jewish and intertestamental speculation, the cause is attributed to an angelic or Satanic fall, which is responsible for human temptation. Before the evolutionary process was understood, it was sometimes assumed that there had once been a literal state of perfection, until Adam's disobedience brought about death, toil and pain. Twentieth-century attempts at theodicy (the vindication of God) tend either to exalt the moral responsibility we possess as free beings, but to concentrate on reversible evils, eg injustice, carelessness, greed, etc or to argue that such conditions as death and biological pain are indispensible to the world, and therefore not strictly evil. Some accounts, eg process theology, suggest that present evil is an acceptable provisional component of the situation because God's involvement with things takes the form of vulnerable mutuality rather than overriding managerial power. Others echo the medieval theme that the whole dynamic of our salvation is occasioned by the flawed character of our existence, and makes it ultimately worthwhile. ▷ process theology; Satan; suffering; theodicy

evil, Greek concept of In traditional Greek belief, 'all things come to man from the gods'; it follows, therefore, that the gods are the source of evil as well as of good. Sometimes particular evils are said to be sent as a punishment for an offence by an individual or by one of his ancestors; but at a more fundamental level the existence of evil is simply accepted as a part of the inscrutable will of the god Zeus. Myths told of a decline (but not a fall—man was not guilty) from a better time: in the Golden Age, men had lived free from disease and old age; or these evils only entered the world when they escaped from the famous box brought by the first woman, Pandora. A completely new element was introduced by the Orphic-Pythagorean movement (6th century BCE), which explained the suffering of individuals as a punishment for their crimes in a previous existence. This new interpretation was taken up by Plato in the 'myths' which he included in several dialogues. ▷ Greek religion; Orphic/Pythagorean movement; Plato

evolutionary humanism A form of humanism which holds that modern science and knowledge have emancipated people from bondage to supernaturalistic and dogmatic religion. In this view, the universe has no special human meaning or purpose. Humankind is part of an evolutionary process, and the application of science and human reason is its only resource in creating a more human world. ▷ Darwinism; freethought; humanism

exclusivism ▷ religious pluralism

exile In Jewish tradition, the concept of exile is used in two inter-related ways. It refers to the historical exile of Israel to Babylon and to the dispersion of the Jewish people between 70 and 1948. It also signifies separation from God and his land, from his Torah and the righteous life. Thus the Bible views the Babylonian Exile as a physical punishment for spiritual unfaithfulness and as a means of purification; the survivors experience both a literal return to the Holy Land and a spiritual return to God. After 70CE, a general sense of being in exile helped to maintain Jewish identity; by employing the theological category of exile, the Jewish situation could be seen as a time of trial and as an opportunity to be a force for good in the non-Jewish world. However, with the Enlightenment and resultant Jewish emancipation, the Diaspora's heightened sense of its exiled state declined, especially with the founding of the State of Israel in 1948. ▷ Diaspora Judaism; exodus theme; Israel, State of

existentialism A philosophical movement, closely associated with Kierkegaard, Sartre and Heidegger. Its most salient theses are that there is no ultimate purpose to the world; that persons find themselves in a world which is vaguely hostile; that persons choose and cannot avoid choosing their characters, goals and perspectives; that not to choose is to choose not to choose; and that truths about the world and our situation are revealed most clearly in moments of unfocused psychological anxiety or dread. ▷ Heidegger, Martin; Kierkegaard, Sören Aabye; Sartre, Jean Paul

existentialism, Christian A loose umbrella term for thinkers who offer theological answers to the philosophical questions raised by the existentialism of Sartre, Camus (1913–60) and others. There is no 'school' of Christian existentialism, only a shared conviction that the anxiety and absurdity of human life identified in secular existentialism is answered in the authentic existence of Jesus Christ, who made a perfect response to the call of God. The term 'Christian existentialism' has been applied to the works of the Roman Catholic philosophers Karl Theodore Jaspers (1883–1969) and Gabriel-Honoré Marcel (1889–1973), and to those of the theologian Karl Rahner. Protestant contributors to the dialogue include Kierkegaard, Barth (his early works), Bultmann, Tillich and Macquarrie. Existentialism's emphasis on freedom and choice is a significant element of the 'situation ethics' of Joseph Fletcher (1905–) and J A T Robinson. Critics of Christian existentialism argue that its welcome stress on individual commitment underplays the corporate element of Christianity that is recognized in theologies that understand the 'kingdom of God' to be a central concept. ▷ Barth, Karl; Bultmann, Rudolf Karl; Kierkegaard, Sören Aabye; kingdom of God; liberation theology; Macquarrie, John; political theology; Rahner, Karl; Robinson, John Arthur Thomas; Sartre, Jean-Paul; Social Gospel; Tillich, Paul Johannes

Exodus, Book of The second book of the Pentateuch in the Hebrew Bible/Old Testament. It narrates stories about the deliverance of the Jews from slavery in Egypt under the leadership of Moses, and about the giving of the Law to Israel through a revelation to Moses on Mount Sinai. It also provides instructions for building the wilderness tabernacle. ▷ Moses; Pentateuch; Sinai, Mount; Tabernacle; Ten Commandments

exodus theme Central to Judaism is the story of the exodus from Egypt, as recounted in Exodus 12, and celebrated every spring at the time of the Passover. Despite complex historical problems in reconstructing it, the theological significance of this event is fundamental, since it marks the formation of the people of Israel. The exodus theme is also associated with the end of the Babylonian Exile. Thus language in the second half of the book of Isaiah pictures the return to Palestine after punishment at the hand of Babylon as a new exodus, with travel through the wilderness and re-entry into the promised land (eg Isaiah 43.16–21). Similarly, after the destruction of Jerusalem in 70CE, Jews scattered throughout the world hoped for another exodus from the Diaspora and return to the

Holy Land with the advent of the messianic era. ▷ Diaspora Judaism; exile; Exodus, Book of; hagim; Passover

exorcism The act of compelling an evil spirit to leave a person, place or object by means of a command or ceremony. The term exorcism derives from the Greek *exorkōsis*, which literally means 'out-oath'. The practice of exorcism is ancient and worldwide and continues in many modern societies. Belief in a realm of malevolent spirits which can possess a place or person is a primal human fear deriving perhaps from a fear of the unknown or of the threatening powers of nature. Certainly most religious traditions have felt it necessary to develop rites and practices to deal with cases of possession by an evil spirit. The presence of evil spirits can be suspected for a variety of reasons. Often illness or pain is the most immediate reason for seeking the services of an exorcist. Possession may also involve hallucinations and delusions, the altering of the personality, even to the extent of the development of multiple personalities with accompanying voices.

The methods and practices of the exorcist vary between traditions. They may involve the use of elaborate formulae, spells and dances, which are derived from shamanistic practices. The exorcist himself may go into a trance-like state to gain contact with the spirit world. Alternatively a medium may act as a go-between between patient and healer. In Chinese and Japanese Buddhist practice chants and incantations drawn from sacred texts are recited. Herbs, incense and special diets may also feature in the cure. In Judaism, Islam and Christianity exorcism tends to be performed by means of words of command issued in the name and authority of God with a minimum of accompanying rites. ▷ demonology, biblical

extreme unction ▷ anointing the sick

Ezekiel, or **Ezechiel, Book of** A major prophetic work in the Hebrew Bible/Old Testament, attributed to Ezekiel, a 6th-century BCE priest amongst the Jews exiled in Babylonian territories after 597BCE. The prophecies in Chapters 1–24 warn of the impending destruction of Jerusalem (587BCE); Chapters 25–32 present oracles condemning foreign nations; and Chapters 33–48 promise hope for a restoration of Israel. The collection of these prophecies may have been the work of a later editor. ▷ Old Testament; prophet

Ezra (5th–4th century BCE) Religious leader who lived in Babylon during the reign of King Artaxerxes (I or II), who reorganized the Jewish community in Jerusalem, and renovated its religious cult. He may have brought part of the Mosaic law (the Pentateuch) with him; an Old Testament book bears his name, as well as the apocryphal works of 1 and 2 Esdras (the Greek equivalent of 'Ezra'). ▷ Apocrypha, Old Testament; Esdras, Books of; Ezra, Book of; Pentateuch

Ezra, Book of Part of the Hebrew Bible/Old Testament, and originally probably part of a historical work including Chronicles and Nehemiah. It describes stages in the return to Palestine of exiled Jews from 538BCE onwards, the attempts to rebuild the Temple and city of Jerusalem, and the story of Ezra's mission under Artaxerxes I or II to restore adherence to the Jewish law amongst Palestinian Jews. ▷ Chronicles/Esdras/Nehemiah, Book(s) of; Ezra; Old Testament

F

Fa Hsiang Tsung The Chinese form of Yogacara Buddhism which had been developed in India in the 4th and 5th centuries CE by Asanga and Vasubandhu. Literally meaning 'dharma characteristics', it emphasizes the crucial importance of consciousness to such an extent that it was also known as the 'Consciousness-Only' school. It was developed in China by a 7th-century Chinese pilgrim to India named Hsuan Tsang (596–664). He translated Vasubandhu's two great treatises on the *Establishment of the Consciousness-Only Doctrine* into Chinese. He argued that consciousness alone is real, and that the material world is the creation of consciousness. Thus the self and external objects, although they seem to be real, are not. One can realize this by means of wisdom (*prajna*), and one can attain insight into ultimate reality and enlightenment in this way. The Fa Hsiang school was influential in China during the middle part of the Tang dynasty, but it was deeply affected by the great persecution of the Buddhists in 845, from which it never really recovered, the Buddhist future in China after 845 lying with Chan and Pure Land. ▷ Asanga; Chan; Pure Land Buddhism; Yogacara

Fa Hsien (fl.late 4th century) Chinese Buddhist monk, born in Shansi. He was trained at Chang An, the western capital of China, and set out in 399 with six companions on an important pilgrimage to India. He visited various places associated with significant events in the life of the Buddha, as well as other sacred places in India, and wrote down descriptions of what he saw. These are important for reconstructing the state of the Buddhist tradition in 5th-century India, as well as being interesting travel journals in their own right. Fa Hsien arrived back in China in 414 having returned from India via Ceylon and Sumatra. In the 7th century other Buddhist pilgrims such as I Tsing and Hsuan Tsang followed in his footsteps, and their narratives indicate that the Buddhist tradition was less strong in India than it had been at the time of Fa Hsien's visit. When Fa Hsien was in India he collected and copied a number of Buddhist scriptures which, when he returned to China, were translated into Chinese. This helped to strengthen Chinese Buddhism at a time when Buddhism was beginning to decline in India, the land of its birth. ▷ Buddha; Mahayana Sutras

faith A term which describes the dispositional attitude of the believer towards the object of his belief. It is summed up in the words of St Paul, 'Now faith is the assurance of things hoped for, the conviction of things not seen' (Hebrews 11.1). Although this is a Christian definition it applies across the spectrum of world faiths. Christian faith has a variety of meanings. It can refer to The Faith, which is the body of truths comprising Catholic orthodoxy. According to Augustine faith is also an act of the will in which one assents to this set of doctrines. There is also a subjective element in faith which refers to the placing of one's trust wholly in God. Martin Luther's teaching on justification by faith emphasized this aspect of faith as a trusting in God for salvation. Faith is often contrasted with works but the Christian scriptures make it clear that faith without works is dead (James 2.17). Faith is not possible without the prior gracious activity of God and is the conviction of the believer that he or she is the object of God's faithful care. Faith is also central to Buddhist thought, where faith (*saddha*) is necessary to begin and persevere on the path of enlightenment. Faith is present in any wholesome consciousness and is one of the five cardinal virtues. The objects of faith are the Buddha, the dharma and the *sangha*. As in Christian thought, faith has three aspects: the intellectual, the devotional and the spiritual. Faith, variously defined as belief, trust, devotion and dependence is a universal feature of humankind's response to the presence of the divine in the midst of life. ▷ dharma; Luther, Martin; orthopraxy and orthodoxy; saddha; sangha

faith healing The alleviation of physical and mental ailments by the prayer of a healer relying on a higher source (usually, the power of God) working in response to faith. Known in several religions, the practice is now a major feature of Christian pentecostal and charismatic movements, often accompanied by the laying on of the healer's hands, usually in the context of worship. Critics assert that, even when apparently effective, it is difficult to ascribe healing to the action of the higher source, because so little is currently understood by medical science about the effects of psychological attitudes upon the body's biochemistry. ▷ charismatic movement; Pentacostalism; prayer

Fall, the A common theme in the myths, sagas and legends of many peoples and their religious traditions is the concept of a fall from an original state of paradise. This is portrayed as a golden age close to the beginning of time when men and gods communed with one another. The fall from this state results in the degradation of the original integrity of creation. Evil, suffering and death enter into the universe and man loses his innocence and the gift of immortality. The reasons given for the Fall vary between traditions. In some accounts the passage of time brings the waning of a golden era. In others the source of tension and disorder is located in disputes between the gods themselves. Most often the Fall is a result of human failings. This is the case in the biblical account in which Adam and Eve are expelled from the Garden of Eden for disobeying God (Genesis 3). As a result, sin enters the world and toil and pain mark the human condition. In the Christian development of this myth the whole of humanity is included in solidarity with Adam's disobedience. This explains the universality of the sinful condition of man and requires a second Adam (Christ) to redeem him (Romans 5.12f). The conviction underlying the biblical accounts of the Fall is that a sinful world is a distortion of God's purpose in creation and that God himself is acting to retrieve the situation. The concept of a fall seems to reflect man's need to explain the negativity he encounters at the heart of life by contrasting it with a mythical lost age of perfection. ▷ Adam and Eve; Eden, Garden of; golden age; original sin

falsafa The Muslim term for philosophy. Mainstream Islam has never fully accepted a strong philosophical element into its world-view, and although not lacking in great philosophers—such as Ibn Sina (Avicenna) and Ibn Rushd (Averroës)—it has viewed them as peripheral rather than central. The Quranic world-view was centred upon revelation rather than reason, and on Allah as existing rather than as provable. As Islam expanded into the Greek world and encountered philosophical influences such as the thought of Aristotle, Plato, and neo-platonism, orthodox Sunni Islam (exemplified in al-Ghazali) generally rejected their insights. It was left to less orthodox groups, such as the Mutazilites, the Twelver Shiites, and the Ismailis to investigate philosophy. However, the translations of Greek philosophers into Arabic, and rational trends such as philosophical proofs of the existence of God pursued by Avicenna and Averroës, fed into the theology of Western Christians such as Aquinas and had more influence there than within Islam. In general Islam has stressed practical behaviour (through the shariah) and theology (through *kalam*) more than philosophy. This scale of priorities has influenced Islamic self-understanding down the centuries, and remains relevant today. ▷ Allah; Aquinas, St Thomas; Averroës, Ibn Rushd; Avicenna; Ghazali, Abu Hamid Mohammed al-; Ismailis; kalam; Mutazilites; neo-platonism; Plato; shariah

Falwell, Jerry (1933–) American Baptist evangelist, born in Lynchburg, Virginia. He studied engineering at Lynchburg, but after a religious conversion graduated from Baptist Bible College, Springfield, Missouri, and in 1956 became pastor of Thomas Road Baptist Church, Lynchburg, which he founded. There he inaugurated the television 'Old-Time Gospel Hour', and founded Liberty Baptist College. In 1979 he founded Moral Majority Inc., forming a rallying point for conservative opinion in the 1980 and 1984 Presidential election campaigns. In 1982 an influential publication listed him among the 20 most prominent people in America. He wrote *Listen, America!* (1980), *The Fundamentalist Phenomenon* (1981), and *Wisdom for Living* (1984). ▷ Baptists; evangelicalism

fana (fanā') A term used by Sufis within the Islamic tradition, which literally means extinction, in the sense of loss of self. The peak of spirituality, according to some Sufi masters, ends in God, so that even fana itself is extinguished in the final union of the soul with Allah. The term fana is often associated with the term for purity (*safa*), keeping one's soul pure from worldly attachments, and with the term baqa, which means subsisting in God and 'dying' to the world. It is similar to the Buddhist notion of nirvana, except that the Muslim notion of fana is rooted in God and is not connected with the idea of reincarnation. It is also allied to the Christian and Jewish mystical notions of annihilating the human will before the will of God. ▷ Allah; mysticism; nirvana; soul; Sufism

fascism A term applied to a variety of vehemently nationalistic and authoritarian movements that reached the peak of their influence in the period 1930–45. The original fascist movement was founded by Mussolini in Italy (1921), and during the 1930s several such movements grew up in Europe, the most important being the German Nazi Party. The central ideas of fascism are a belief in the supremacy of the chosen national group over other races, and the need to subordinate society to the leadership of a dictator, who can pursue national aggrandisement without taking account of different interests. Fascism advocates the abolition of all institutions of democracy, the suppression of sources of opposition such as trade unions, and to varying degrees the mobilization of society under fascist leadership. Fascism is also strongly associated with militaristic and belligerent foreign policy stances. Since World War II its appeal has declined, although in some Latin American countries fascist-type governments have held office. ▷ Nazi Party; secular alternatives to religion

fasting The practice of abstaining from food or drink for religious purposes. This may be for a long or a short time. Different religions prescribe different fixed times for fasting (eg the 40 days of Lent in some denominations of Christianity; Yom Kippur or the Day of Atonement in Judaism; Ramadan in Islam). Fasting is often prescribed as preparation for special ceremonies, duties or activities, or as penance. It can also be practised as a form of political protest or social protest against the condition of prisoners, for example, or the plight of oppressed minorities. ▷ sawm

fasts, Jewish There are six fast-days in Jewish tradition. Four of these commemorate phases of the Babylonian devastation, three disallowing sustenance from dawn to dusk; on the fourth it is prohibited all day. The fifth, falling on Yom Yippur, is also a 24-hour fast, while the Fast of Esther lasts from dawn to dusk. The first fast occurs on 17 Tammuz, marking the breach of Jerusalem's walls by the Babylonians and Romans. The second is called Tishah beAv (literally '9 Av') and commemorates the destruction of the Temple by the Babylonians in 586BCE and by Rome in 70CE. A third fast on 3 Tishri, two days after the New Year or Rosh Hashanah, commemorates Gedaliah's assassination, recounted in 2 Kings 25.22–5. However, the most important fast, from sunset to sunset, is on Yom Kippur ('Day of Atonement') on 10 Tishri, the holiest day of the Jewish year. It is the culmination of 10 days of repentance and reflection starting with Rosh Hashanah. A fifth fast-day occurs on 10 Tevet, marking the beginning of the Babylonians' siege of Jerusalem in 587BCE. Finally, the Fast of Esther on 13 Adar is based on Esther 4.16. ▷ calendar, Jewish; hagim; Rosh Hashanah; Tishah beAv; Yom Kippur

fatalism A philosophical doctrine, attributed to the Stoics and others, which maintains that the future is as unalterable as the past; that what will be will be, no matter what a person may do to avert its happening. Fatalists are determinists, but not all versions of determinism entail fatalism. ▷ Stoicism

fatalism, Islamic The early Arab poets wrote about a fate that was decreed and destined for people, but they ascribed it as much to an impersonal force as to God, In the Quran human destiny is ascribed to the will of Allah. Fate lies in his decree (*qadar*) and stress is given to Allah's ordination of what will happen in human life. At the same time the Quran has a less pronounced emphasis upon human free will. Later theologians attempted to allow some scope to both points of view. It was asked whether, if God was just and required obedience he could at the same time decree fate and destiny. Also the Shiites argued that it was not the fate of Muslims to accept meekly the Sunni view of life. On the other hand, the Quran stance of attributing things to God's will was strengthened by the Sufi emphasis upon surrender to God's decrees. The general Islamic position came to be that human beings have an ability, within certain parameters, to acquire actions that are determined by God. However, at the grassroots level the notion of *kismet*, fate, is common among Muslims. ▷ predestination in Islam; Quran; Shiism; Sufism; Sunnis

Fathers of the Church A title usually applied to the leaders of the early Christian Church, recognized as teachers of truths of the faith. They were characterized by orthodoxy of doctrine and personal holiness, and were usually beatified. The study of their writings and thought is known as patristics. ▷ beatification; Christianity

Fatihah (Fātiḥah) The name of the section that opens the Quran. It is a central prayer of Islam, and has a ritual role similar to that of the Lord's Prayer within Christianity. Claiming to sum up the kernel of the Quran and the essence of the human relationship with Allah, it reads: 'In the name of God, the Merciful, the Compassionate. Praise to God, Lord of the Worlds, the Merciful, the Compassionate, King of the Day of Judgement. You alone we worship, you alone we beseech. Lead us in the straight path, the path of those upon whom is your grace, not of those upon whom is your wrath, nor of those who have gone astray'. Although the first section of the Quran to be revealed historically was Surah (chapter 96), the Fatihah was placed first, symbolizing its importance. It is recited at all Islamic ritual daily prayers, at weddings, funerals and other ceremonial occasions, and is also much used in Islamic extemporary prayer. One of the requirements of being a Muslim is to memorize the Fatihah in Arabic, together with a minimum of 12 other Quranic verses. ▷ Allah; Lord's Prayer; Quran

fatwa (fatwā) A legal opinion or decision given by a mufti or canon lawyer within the Muslim tradition. Individuals may regulate their lives and judges may decide cases in court as a result of fatwas given by competent authorities. These legal decisions are based upon past precedent rather than the individual brilliance of the lawyer; collections of decisions sometimes become significant as codes of precedent. As civil codes have become more prominent in Muslim states, fatwas have tended to concentrate on social matters such as marriage, divorce and inheritance. However, they can be applied more widely. They tend to be given according to the approach of one of the four legal schools within Islam. For example, in Turkey the Hanafi school was favoured and fatwas of Hanafi lawyers were given precedence. ▷ Hanafi; Islamic law schools; shariah

Faust, or **Faustus** Legendary German scholar of the early 16th century (derived from a historical magician of that name), who sold his soul to the devil in exchange for knowledge, magical power, and prolonged youth. His story inspired Marlowe's *Dr Faustus* (1592), literary works by Lessing (1784), Goethe (1808, 1832) and Thomas Mann (1947), and musical works including Gounod's opera *Faust* (1859).

feminist theology An increasingly prominent branch of theology, started within Christianity, which aims to reconstruct traditional theology in less exclusively male terms. In doing this the emphasis is placed on symbols, models and images which express the religious, social and psychological experience of women. Initially starting in the USA, the feminist critique of male-centred ideologies is now spreading beyond Christianity to other beliefs. Despite its title, this is not a divisive concept. It does not aim to exclude men, or to concentrate only on 'feminine' issues within the Bible or other sources. Instead, it is concerned with reinstating equality for all minority groups. ▷ Daly, Mary; theology; women in religion

Fénelon, François de Salinac de la Mothe (1651–1715) French prelate and writer, born in the château de Fénelon in Périgord. At 20 he entered the seminary of St Sulpice in Paris, and was ordained in 1675. After some time spent in parochial duties, he became director of an instittition for women converts to the catholic faith in 1678. Here he wrote *Traité de l'education des filles* (published in 1678), urging a more liberal education for women, and criticizing the coercion of Huguenot converts. At the revocation of the Edict of Nantes (1685) he was sent to preach among the Protestants of Poitou. From 1689 to 1699 he was tutor to Louis XIV's grandson, the young Duke of Burgundy, and as such he wrote the *Fables*, the *Dialogues of the Dead*, the *History of the Ancient Philosophers*, and *Adventures of Télémaque* (1699). He had been presented by the king to the abbey of St Valéry (1694). He had formed in 1687 the acquaintance of the celebrated quietist mystic, Madame Guyon, and, convinced of the unfairness of the outcry against her, he advised her to submit her book to Bossuet, who condemned it. Fénelon composed his own *Explication des Maximes des saints sur la vie intériure* in defence of certain of Madame Guyon's doctrines. A fierce controversy ensued, and in the end the pope condemned the *Maximes des saints*. Fénelon's *Télémaque* was considered by the king a disguised satire upon his court and from then on Fénelon was strictly restrained within his diocese. From this date he lived almost exclusively for his followers, but in the revised Jansenist dispute he engaged earnestly on the side of orthodoxy. He wrote extensively, and on many subjects. ▷ Jansenism; Protestantism; Roman Catholicism

feng shui A Chinese term, meaning literally 'wind and water', used in connection with making the correct decision as to where a building such as a house, temple or grave should be sited in order to ensure the best possible happiness of its occupants. Having first appeared during the Han dynasty (206 BCE–220CE), by the 12th century it had developed into the quasi-science of geomancy. It is based upon the notion that there are five basic elements: earth, fire, metal, water and wood, and two primary forces: yin and yang.

Natural features in the landscape such as hills and rivers are influenced by wind and water, and there is an interaction between these natural features, the five elements and yin and yang, which renders some places more auspicious than others. It is the duty of the geomancer to ponder these matters and to decide on the site where the cosmic currents are natural and right. Feng shui can either frustrate or benefit human beings and it is important that the forces of feng shui should be controlled for the well-being of humanity. It is a combination of divination, astrology, and an ability to relate the natural features of earth and sky to the requirements of man-made constructions and human beings themselves. ▷ yin and yang

Fenrir (the Fenriswolf) In Nordic stories Fenrir was the terrible offspring of Loki by a giantess. Immense, horrible and dangerous, he grew up to terrorize Asgard, the city of the gods. None could bind him, until the wisdom of Odin and the skill of dwarves forged a chain from impalpable things—root of mountain, beard of woman, noise of cat walking, breath of fish. This restrained him, but imposing this on Fenrir cost Tyr his hand. According to *Voluspa*, Fenrir breaks free at Ragnarok, and destroys Odin before being himself destroyed. Garm, the fierce hound at the gates of Hel, the underworld, probably represents the same figure. ▷ Loki; Odin; Ragnarok; Tyr, Tiwaz, Tu; Voluspa

Fenriswolf ▷ Fenrir

Ferrar, Nicholas (1592–1637) English Anglican clergyman and spiritual mystic, born in London. After studying medicine, and a brief period in politics, he became a deacon in the Church of England (1626). At Little Gidding in Huntingdonshire he founded a small religious community which engaged in constant services and perpetual prayer, while carrying out a range of crafts, such as bookbinding. It was broken up by the Puritans in 1647. He died at Little Gidding. ▷ Church of England; Puritanism

festival A day or set period of time which recalls and celebrates a significant event in the life of a community. Festivals often mark the seasons of the year and have an agricultural association. Festivals perform the function of binding communities together through shared ritual acts, usually involving sacred feasts from which the term festival literally derives.

festivals, Ancient Near Eastern In addition to the daily offerings in Ancient Near Eastern temples there were many festivals at which the gods were honoured by rejoicing, sacrifices, and libations. The early Mesopotamian city-states each had their own calendars, which became more standardized under the great empires, although local festivals remained significant. The sacred calendar was made up of regular lucky and unlucky days during the month as well as the major festivals of the gods, which could last several days. Important state festivals were normally performed by the king, whose role always involved religious duties. The most important of the Mesopotamian festivals was the New Year festival, known from Sumerian times (3rd millennium BCE) to the end of the Neo-Babylonian empire (6th century BCE). Information about Hittite festivals is fragmentary, although it appears that the most important of many was probably the spring *purulliyas* festival. Canaanite festivals appear to have followed the seasons of the agricultural year, and were influential in the development of the major Israelite feasts. ▷ Akitu; Canaanite religion; Hittite religion; New Year festivals, Ancient Near Eastern; temples, Ancient Near Eastern

festivals, Chinese These have been built into the pattern of Chinese folk religion. There was an attempt after 1949, and especially during the Cultural Revolution of 1966–76, to eliminate Chinese folk religion and most Chinese festivals from mainland China as being 'superstitious'. Since 1978, however, they have begun to revive on the mainland and have always remained strong in Taiwan and Hong Kong. New Year is an important time for Chinese festivals. Houses are cleaned and painted to expel the old and to welcome the new. Paper gods are burnt, especially the stove god, Tsao Chun, to whom offerings are made as he goes off to make his yearly report on the family to the Jade Emperor (Yu-Huang), and for whom firecrackers are set off on his return and reinstatement in the home. On New Year's Eve honours and offerings of food, incense and spirit money are given to the household ancestors and gods, and to earth and heaven. Later other offerings are made before the picture of the god of wealth in the hope of ensuring prosperity for the family during the coming year. At the start of spring there is a procession that often includes a paper spring ox to ensure a good ploughing and harvest. In the third month food and spirit money are offered to the *po* souls of the ancestors and to the god who protects them at the ancestral graves, which are repaired and renovated. In the seventh month there is a kind of all souls festival when offerings of food and drink are made and special prayers offered for souls who have died uncared for. Chinese festivals, although mainly connected with popular religion, also involve to some extent Buddhist and Taoist celebrations which spill over into folk religion. For example, the all souls festival involves Buddhists too, and the Buddha's birthday on the eighth day of the fourth month is remembered in Buddhist temples by Buddhists and others in special services that are the equivalent of festivals. ▷ Chinese pantheon; Chinese religion in Taiwan and Hong Kong (20th century); Chinese religion on the China mainland (20th century); Yu-Huang

festivals, Christian Christians observe Sundays as days of worship commemorating the resurrection of Jesus Christ, as well as the annual movable feast of Easter. Some Protestant churches recognize no other festivals. Churches that do celebrate Christmas as the nativity of Christ frequently deplore its commercialization in contemporary secular society, and some put more emphasis on the preceding season of Advent. Roman Catholic, Orthodox and Anglican churches celebrate other festivals connected with the life of Christ and the gift of the Holy Spirit at Pentecost. They also have liturgical calendars which require or permit the commemoration of the Virgin Mary, apostles, martyrs, saints or other notable Christians. Sundays and specified major festivals are 'days of obligation' for Roman Catholics, requiring attendance at Mass and avoidance of certain kinds of work. ▷ Christian year; Christmas; Easter; Pentecost; saint, Christian view of

festivals, Greek Greek festivals were extremely diverse. To take the most popular of the numerous Athenian festivals: The *Anthesteria* was a three-day festival of Dionysus, which centred around the broaching of the new wine; the *Panathenaea* was an occasion of civic display, with a great formal procession making its way through the heart of the city to the acropolis; at the *Apatouria*, new members were admitted to the kinship organizations known as phratiries; the *Thesmophoria* was a 'woman's rite', at which citizen women left their homes for three days and camped out in tents; the *Dionysia* was the dramatic festival at which the tragedies were first performed; and the *Eleusinian Mysteries* promised their initiates advantages in the afterlife. Another important type is represented by the *Brauronia*, a kind of 'initiation' of young girls, similar to those found in modern tribal societies. Festivals served, therefore, very different social functions. But they were all, in their different ways, bright spots within the dull round of the year. ▷ Dionysiac religion; Greek religion; Mysteria

fetish A word used with a confusingly wide range of meanings related to primal, and especially African, religion. Its origin is *feitiço* (simply 'a made thing') used by the Portuguese of the carved objects they saw West Africans wearing. It was then applied to images, in the sense of 'idol', under the false assumption that Africans worshipped 'made things'; and thence, still more misleadingly, to African or primal religions as a whole. The word could now perhaps be profitably abandoned; if used, it may conveniently be restricted to small, portable objects—charms, amulets, protective bundles of symbolic items often collectively called 'medicine'—seen as containing or mediating power which acts on behalf of the owner or user. Such items, though widely used, are not usually a focus of devotion, and belong rather to the margins of religion. They may be used for protection, revenge, healing, or to promote success, often having a function similar to that of insurance policies in other societies. As such, they may be employed by anyone; but since spiritual power involves danger and a tabu element, there are specialists in their preparation and use. Thus the *nganga* (a word widely used in Bantu languages for a doctor who can control dangerous forces) of the Kongo people of Zaire is the expert deployer of the *nkisi* bundles. The use of fetish for anti-social purposes constitutes sorcery. Destruction of fetish is a regular feature of Christian and other religious movements of reformation and revival in Africa and Melanesia. ▷ medicine bundles; tabu; witchcraft and sorcery, African

shrine fetish of the Bushoong people of Zaire

Feuerbach, Ludwig Andreas (1804–72) German philosopher, son of Paul Feuerbach, born in Landshut, Bavaria. He was a pupil of Hegel at Berlin but reacted against his idealism. His most famous work, *Das Wesen des Christentums* (1841), which was translated by Mary Ann Evans (George Eliot) as *The Essence of Christianity* (1854), attacked conventional Christianity and agreed that religion is 'the dream of the human mind', projecting on to an illusory God our own human ideals and nature. His naturalistic materialism was a strong influence on Marx and Engels. ▷ Engels, Friedrich; Hegel, Georg Wilhelm Friedrich; Marx, Karl; religion

Ficino, Marsilio (1433–99) Italian Platonist scholar, born in Florence. In 1463 he was appointed by Cosimo de' Medici (1389–1464) president of an academy for the diffusion of Platonic doctrines. Ordained at 40, he was made rector of two churches in Florence and canon of the cathedral. He retired to the country when the Medici were expelled from Florence in 1494. He was a major influence in the Renaissance revival of Platonism, and his own rather eclectic system was largely an attempt to reconcile Platonism with Christianity. ▷ Christianity; Platonism

fideism Any view which maintains that the principles of some area of inquiry cannot be established by reason, but must be accepted on faith. Fideism in religion may claim either that the basic tenets of religious belief go beyond what reason can establish or, more radically, that they contradict reason. ▷ religion

Filioque (Latin 'and from the Son') A dogmatic formula expressing the belief that in the operations of God, the Holy Trinity, the Holy Spirit 'proceeds' from the Son as well as from the Father. The term does not appear in the original Nicene-Constantinopolitan Creed, but was inserted by the Western Church, and insistence on its retention was a major source of tension and eventual breach between the Western (Roman Catholic) and Eastern (Orthodox) Churches in 1054. In the late 20th century attempts are being made by the World Council of Churches to reinterpret this doctrine in a sense acceptable to the Orthodox Church. ▷ God; Holy Spirit; Nicene Creed; Orthodox Church; Roman Catholicism; Trinity; World Council of Churches

fiqh The Muslim term for jurisprudence, which literally means knowledge, understanding or skill. In principle it applies to all aspects of life—civil, political and religious—but in practice it has dealt mainly with legal matters associated with the five pillars of Islam, ritual concerns, and social life. There are four main law schools within Sunni Islam that deal with fiqh: the Malikites, Shafiites, Hanafites and Hanbalites. In addition, the Kharijites and Shiites have their own schools. According to the Sunni schools of law, fiqh has four main sources. In order of importance these are the Quran, Muhammad's own sayings (Hadith), given independently of the Quran, analogical reasoning (*Qiyas*), and the consensus of the community (*ijma*). The different schools have their own separate basic treatises, but all are held to be equally valid, although particular schools may hold sway in different parts of the Muslim world. ▷ five pillars, Islamic; Hadith; ijma; Islamic law schools; Kharijites; Muhammad; Qiyas; Quran; Shiism

fire (Zoroastrian) Zoroastrians have been incorrectly described as 'fire-worshippers', an epithet whose implications they deeply resent. While Zoroastrian teaching certainly does not equate God with fire, it does regard fire, and other elements of the good creation, as divine. In the pre-Zoroastrian religion of the Iranians, Mithra, the divine lord of fire, was probably held to have set the world in motion, and the Zoroastrian concept of fire corresponds in many ways to the Western notion of energy: fire resides in men, animals and plants and enables them to move and grow. In the Zoroastrian tradition fire is particularly linked with Asha Vahishta, the Amesha Spenta representing Righteousness and right development. It is often addressed as 'Son of Ahura Mazda'. Ahura Mazda's pristine, ideal creation had 'the form of bright, white fire'. Fire was thus regarded, it seems, as a symbol on earth of the intangible pure sphere of the divine. In ancient times this symbolic function was fulfilled primarily by the hearth-fire, which the family fed by making small offerings to it, and which it faced when praying (the sun and moon being alternative directions for prayer). Later, with the adoption of a temple cult during the Achaemenian period, the temple-fire became an icon for the whole community, and in the course of time some of these fires enjoyed particular reverence: they were the object of pilgrimages, and played an important part in the national sentiments of the Iranians before the advent of Islam. Modern Zoroastrianism knows three categories of consecrated fire (as opposed to cooking fires, etc) namely, the very exalted *Atesh Bahram*, the somewhat lower-ranking *Atesh Adaran*, and lastly the *Atesh-e Dadgah*, which is simpler and less costly to maintain. ▷ Ahura Mazda; Amesha Spentas; Bundahishn; Zoroastrianism

firqa The notion of sect in the Muslim tradition. The Muslim community set up by Muhammad at Medina after the migration from Mecca in 622 was a united one. As Islam spread out of Arabia into the Middle Eastern world, it came into contact with Greek and other philosophies, and sects began to form. There was fierce debate over theological and practical questions such as whether the Quran was created or uncreated, and the seriousness of sin. For theological and/or political reasons, sects emerged. For example, the Kharijites arose in 657 and stressed that those who committed major sins forfeited salvation, and that faith without deeds was not real faith. In the 8th century the Mutazilites emphasized the importance of rational argument alongside revelation in the development of theology. More importantly, the Shiites emerged as the main rivals to the mainstream Sunnis, stressing the central role within Islam of Ali, the cousin and son-in-law of Muhammad. Within Shiism further sects arose, including the Ismailis, or Seveners, who stressed the role of their seven imams, in contrast to the twelve imams stressed by the mainline Shiites, who were also known as the Twelvers. Despite the existence of these and other sects, the Muslim community (*ummah*) has remained a basically united tradition. ▷ Ali; Ismailis; Kharijites; Muhammad; Mutazilites; Quran; Shiism; Sunnis; ummah

five divine presences, Islamic A metaphysical Islamic notion of the five different degrees of reality. According to the main version of this theory the five degrees are: absolute reality, the reality of a personal God, the reality of the world of angels, the reality of the subtle world, and the reality of the human world. Strongly influenced by neo-platonism, this notion of the five divine presences became important in Sufi thought, especially in the work of Ibn Arabi and his followers. They argued that this notion was not their own original discovery but an eternal truth that they had uncovered, and that a similar teaching was to be found in other religious traditions, especially Eastern ones. ▷ angels; Arabi, Ibn al-; God; neo-platonism; Sufism

five Ks (Pāñj Kakke) The five Sikh symbols which are worn by Sikhs who have been inducted into the *Khalsa* (community) founded by Guru Gobind Singh in 1699. Non-Khalsa Sikhs may also wear them by choice as external marks of being a Sikh. *Kes* is uncut hair, referring not only to hair on the head but also to hair on the rest of the body. The *Kangha* is a comb worn in the hair to keep the topknot of uncut hair under control. The turban which covers the comb and topknot, although not one of the five Ks, has become an emblem of Sikh identity. The *Kirpan* is a ceremonial sword or dagger with a curved blade that is worn as part of required dress. The *Kara* is a steel bangle worn on the right wrist which is not ornamental but functional and plain. The *Kachh* is a pair of shorts worn either as an outer garment or as an undergarment as part of Western dress. Symbolically the five Ks represent motivations to immediate readiness at a time of uncertainty and danger; functionally they are marks of Sikh identity. ▷ Gobind Singh, Guru; Khalsa; Rahit Maryada

five pillars, Islamic The five fundamentals of the Muslim tradition. They are as follows: affirming the *shahadah*, 'Allah is Allah and Muhammad is his prophet'; reciting the five daily prayers (*salat*); giving alms (*zakat*) as a kind of voluntary tax to help the poor; fasting (*sawm*) in the month of Ramadan; and going on pilgrimage (Hajj) to Mecca at least once. Although all five pillars are required of Muslims, reciting the shahadah and the five daily prayers are particularly important, while the fast of Ramadan and the performance of pilgrimage give unity to the whole Muslim world. Holy war (jihad) is occasionally called the sixth pillar of Islam. However, it is not prescribed and it is often internalized to symbolize an inward struggle for spiritual victory. Non-performance of four of the five pillars does not amount to a renunciation of Islam. However, all Muslims are expected to uphold the shahadah and not to repudiate the other four pillars. ▷ Allah; Hajj; Muhammad; Ramadan; salat; shahadah; zakat

five relationships, Confucian According to the Confucian tradition, five relationships are basic and universal in human society. These are the relations between ruler and minister, father and son, husband and wife, elder brother and younger brother, and friend and friend. These relations are established on the basis of a mutual moral obligation between the two parties in the relationship. However, except for the last relationship between friends, they are basically hierarchical and involve the superiority of one party over the other. The five relationships established by Confucius were disputed by Mo Tzu (c.470–391BCE), who argued that universal love, that could be offered equally to all people, was preferable. Mencius (c.371–289) defended Confucius's position, and wrote vigorously against what he felt was the unreality of Mo Tzu's position, in support of graded love. He said that it was necessary to start with five particular relationships and work towards a universal love for all from that beginning. Confucian society has traditionally stressed the five relationships and the hierarchy built into them and, in a modified sense, this remains the position today in a country such as Japan. ▷ Confucius; Mencius; Mo Tzu

Flood, the The idea of a primeval deluge destroying the world and all its inhabitants (apart from a faithful remnant favoured by God or the gods to survive) as a consequence of or punishment for human wrongdoing or sin. This is expressed in mythical form and is found in Hindu, Ancient Egyptian and Chinese religion as well as most notably in Judaism and Christianity in the story of Noah in Genesis 6 and the Babylonian *Epic of Gilgamesh*. ▷ Genesis, Book of; Gilgamesh Epic; Noah

flower arrangement in Japan An important art in Japan that is not only a matter of aesthetic beauty and technique but also implies a deeper spiritual motive. With roots in Zen Buddhism, it has an underlying symbolism and meaning that are connected with a psychological and spiritual discipline. To do flower arranging properly requires qualities of inward discipline, adaptability and self-denial that enable one to look away from oneself into the laws of the cosmos and at the same time to become more aware of the depths of one's own being. Flower arrangement begins with the arranger looking at flowers and consciously arranging them, but through practice and inward transformation it becomes more spontaneous, more creative and more pure. The ultimate aim is to embody the truth and the ultimate mystery naturally in the arrangement of flowers. The actual performance is secondary to the inner attitude that produces it and is produced by it. Underlying it is the 'principle of three': heaven, earth, and the world of humans, which are separate and yet one. Humans are midway between heaven and earth. In arranging the flowers of earth, they are channelling the spiritual nature of heaven and are bringing together the three principles. ▷ Zen Buddhism

Folk Islam Islam has retained or adopted a number of features of folk religion during its spread into different parts of the world. Folk Islam varies in different places, and often contradicts traditional Quranic monotheism, although this deviation is often tolerated by the local Muslim authorities and is often not even recognized as being unorthodox by the people concerned. A belief in spirits, or jinn, although present in the Quran, is heightened in Folk Islam so that guarding against assaults by jinn becomes an important matter in everyday life. Folk Islam stresses the role of saints who, with their holy power, or *barakah*, are influential aids in the 'battle of life'. For many Muslims visiting local saints' shrines, celebrating saints' holidays, or making a pilgrimage to an outstanding saint's tomb replaces the Hajj or pilgrimage to Mecca in practical importance. Protecting against the evil eye, the use of amulets and charms, the chanting of magical sayings, and the practice of divination are parts of Folk Islam at the local level. Rituals associated with the cycle of the seasons, and with rites of passage such as birth, marriage and death, have borrowed deeply from folk religion so that, for example, male and female circumcision are widely practised, although not recommended in the Quran, as is the shaving of part of a child's head, although prohibited by Muhammad. ▷ circumcision; divination; folk religion; Hajj; Muhammad; pilgrimage; saints in Islam

folk religion The term used to describe the beliefs, customs, practices and traditions of the peasant and rural societies of the world. Such beliefs and customs are usually passed on through tales, songs, popular art and myth. It is exceedingly difficult to specify exactly the content of any particular folk religion as it exists in a symbiotic relationship with the mainstream religious tradition of society as a whole. Attempts have been made to discern an original universal folk religion, based on the cycle of the agricultural year and utilizing such concepts as matriarchy, Mother goddesses and moon worship etc, but these are generally thought to have failed.

Folk religion often fuses the religious beliefs of a highly developed faith such as Buddhism with the ancient and primitive beliefs of the indigenous peoples. This happens in those societies where belief in the continued existence of an individual's soul beyond death is maintained, in contradiction of the clear teaching of Buddhist scriptures. Such developments have often led to folk religion being regarded as the religious practices of the masses over against the formalized beliefs of a literary élite. Whatever the truth of this, it is clear that the great and highly elaborate faiths such as Christianity, Islam and Buddhism are often understood at a popular level in ways which are quite contrary to official teachings. This would suggest that the continuation of folk religion testifies to the needs of people to distinguish between the sacred and the profane in ways which are appropriate and meaningful to them, even if this is incompatible with the official or majority faith of that particular society.

food and drink Of importance in religion in relation to the practice of fasting and in observance or breach of dietary regulations. Sometimes particular plants, vegetables or animals, and also the water from certain wells, acquire properties which give them a special religious significance. The offering of the right food is also of crucial importance in sacrifice.

food and drink, Sikh Except in the case of alcohol, which is banned to Sikhs, there are no absolute prohibitions in regard to food and drink following the instincts of Guru Nanak who is reported to have said 'only fools wrangle about eating or not eating meat'. (*Adi Granth* 1289). For him outward regulations were secondary and inner spirituality was primary. In practice it is unusual for Muslim halal meat to be eaten by Sikhs, and it is also unusual for beef to be eaten by them in deference to the Hindu reluctance to eat beef that is part of the North-Indian environment in which most Sikhs live. There is however no compulsion to be vegetarian, although a number of Sikhs follow vegetarian practice, and in Sikh gurdwaras only vegetarian food is served, to enable all visitors to participate. ▷ Adi Granth; gurdwara; Nanak

form criticism A method of analysing New Testament Gospel traditions, the early 20th-century representatives being Martin Dibelius (1883–1947) and Rudolf Bultmann, who were often critical of the historicity of these traditions. Individual stories and sayings in the Gospels are studied in isolation from their Gospel contexts, and in terms of the stereotyped forms of oral folklore, because it is believed that the sayings were originally transmitted individually and orally in the early Church before being strung together and given a context by the Gospel writers. ▷ biblical criticism; Bultmann, Rudolf Karl; Gospel criticism; Gospels, canonical

Forsyth, Peter Taylor (1848–1921) Scottish Congregational theologian and preacher, born in Aberdeen. As Principal of Hackney Theological College, Hampstead (1901–21), he championed a high doctrine of church, ministry, sacrament, and preaching in the Congregational Church. Influenced in his student days by Albrecht Ritschl at Göttingen, he rejected theological liberalism in the early 1880s, and came to a deep belief in God's holiness and the realities of sin and grace. His *The Cruciality of the Cross* (1909), *The Person and the Place of Jesus Christ* (1909), and *The Work of Christ* (1910), in some ways anticipating the neo-orthodoxy of Barth and Brunner, have enjoyed renewed popularity since World War II. ▷ Barth, Karl; Brunner, (Heinrich) Emil; Congregationalism; neo-orthodoxy; Ritschl, Albrecht

Fosdick, Harry Emerson (1878–1969) American Baptist minister, born in Buffalo, New York. Ordained in 1903, he was a professor at Union Theological Seminary, New York from 1915, and pastor of the interdenominational Riverside Church in New York from 1926 to 1946. An outstanding preacher, he was a leading 'modernist' in the controversy on fundamentalism in the 1920s. He wrote a number of popular books, including *The Second Mile* (1908), *A Faith for Tough Times* (1952) and *The Meaning of Being a Christian* (1964). ▷ Baptists; fundamentalism

Foucauld, Charles Eugène de, Vicomte (Brother Charles of Jesus) (1858–1916) French soldier, explorer, missionary-monk and mystic, born in Strasbourg. Achieving fame through his exploration of Morocco (1883–4), he returned to Catholicism in 1886 and embarked on a life-long spiritual journey. A Trappist in France and Syria, a hermit in Nazareth, a garrison priest at Beni-Abbès Algeria, and a nomadic hermit among the Tuareg around Tamanrasset, he felt called to imitate Christ in a life of personal poverty in small contemplative communities financed solely by their own manual labour. After his murder, his ideals survived in the foundation of the Little Brothers (1933) and Little Sisters (1939) of Jesus, now active worldwide. ▷ Jesus Christ; monasticism; mysticism; Roman Catholicism

Four Horsemen of the Apocalypse Symbolic biblical characters described in Revelation 6 (also Zechariah 6.1–7), where they signal the beginning of the messianic age. Each comes on a steed of different colour, symbolizing devastations associated with the world's end (black = famine; red = bloodshed, war; pale = pestilence, death), except for the white horse, which has a 'crown' and is sent 'to conquer'. ▷ Revelation, Book of

four noble truths ▷ **ariya sacca**

four purposes, Hindu There are four prescribed goals or purposes (*artha*) of life in orthodox Hinduism: dharma, the goal of duty with regard to one's class or caste and stage of life (*ashrama*); worldly success, status and profit (*artha*); the fulfilling of desire, especially sexual (*kama*); and liberation (*moksha*) from the cycle of transmigration (*samsara*). There has been some discussion in Hinduism as to which of these is the most important, but generally liberation is regarded as the highest, followed by dharma, artha and kama. Each of the first three goals has a body of Sanskrit literature, the *shastras*, associated with it. Thus there are *dharma-shastras* such as the *Laws of Manu*, concerned with social and ritual obligation; *artha-shastras* concerned with profit and political policy; and *kama-shastras* on desire, the most famous of which is the *Kama Sutra*. The goal of liberation, its interpretation and means of attainment, is the subject of many texts, such as the *Yoga Sutra*. ▷ dharma

four signs, Buddhist According to Buddhist tradition, the Buddha was brought up in wealth and security within his father's palace in India in the 6th century BCE, and even by the time he was married and had a child he had known little or nothing of the suffering of the world. However, he became convinced that there was more to life than what he had known at home, and he asked his charioteer to drive him out into the wider world where he saw the four signs that changed his life. They were a very old man, a sick and diseased man, a dead body being taken for cremation, and a wandering holy man dressed in a saffron robe. As a result of this experience the Buddha realized that suffering in the form of old age, infirmity and death was built into life, and he determined to leave his wife and child and the luxury of the palace to go out and seek the answer to the problem of suffering. He did this at first by becoming an ascetic, but later he abandoned this way, and under the Bo tree at Budh-Gaya in Bihar he had the experience of enlightenment whereby he found the cause and cure of the problem of suffering. ▷ ariya sacca; bodhi; Buddha; duhkha; enlightenment; peepul; Rahula

four stages, Hindu Along with the four purposes, the four stages of life are part of orthodox Hindu dharma ('law', 'duty' or 'religion'). There are four theoretical stages prescribed in Hindu law books, such as the *Laws of Manu*, for the high caste or 'twice-born' Hindu. The first is the student stage (*brahmacarya*) during which the student is celibate and studies the Veda with a teacher (*guru*) with whom he lives. During the second stage he gets married and becomes a householder (*grihastha*), bringing up a family, performing his caste duties, obtaining wealth (*artha*) and pursuing pleasure (*kama*). The third stage is that of the forest-dweller (*vanaprastha*), a stage in which a man would retire to the 'forest' with his wife to pursue religious and devotional practices. Last is the stage of renunciation (*sannyasa*) in which the Hindu's past life is transcended and he becomes a wandering holy man in search of liberation (*moksha*) from the cycle of reincarnation (*samsara*). Entry into this process is by the Vedic initiation rite (*upanaya*) at the age of about 12 and by the investiture of the sacred thread. Marriage marks the entrance to the second stage and the stage of renunciation is marked by a further rite in which the sacred thread might be burned and the renouncer perform his own funeral. Most Hindus remain householders and the forest-dweller stage can be reinterpreted to mean retirement from worldly concerns. ▷ dharma; four purposes, Hindu; guru; Manu; moksha; samsara

Fox, George (1624–91) English religious leader, and founder of the Society of Friends, or 'Quakers', born in Fenny Drayton, Leicestershire. Apprenticed to a Nottingham shoemaker, and a Puritan by upbringing, at the age of 19 he rebelled against the formalism of the established church, and the state's control of it. Bible in hand he wandered about the country, often interrupting services, especially when conducted by formalist 'professors'. The 'inner light' was the central idea of his teaching. He inveighed against sacerdotalism and formalism, and was equally vehement against social convention. Priests, lawyers and soldiers were all obnoxious to him; the Lord forbade him to put off his hat to any, high or low. He denounced amusements. In 1646 he had a divine revelation that inspired him to preach a gospel of brotherly love, and call his society the 'Friends of Truth'. His life is a record of insults, persecutions and imprisonments. In 1656, the year after he and his followers refused to take the oath of abjuration, they had so increased that nearly one thousand of them were in jail. He visited Wales and Scotland, and having married Margaret Fell, widow of a judge and one of his followers, went to Barbados, Jamaica, America, Holland, and Germany, latterly accompanied by William Penn, Robert Barclay, and other Quaker leaders. His preaching and writings were often turgid, incoherent and mystical, but as a writer he will be remembered by his *Journal* (1874). ▷

Friends, Society of; Penn, William; Puritanism

Franciscans Religious orders founded by St Francis of Assisi in the early 13th century, possibly in 1207, and given papal approval in 1209. St Francis set out a simple, strict rule, the main tenet of which was a vow of poverty (a condition that was to cause much conflict within the order, even before his death). He and his friars, with no personal possessions, travelled throughout Italy, preaching and working. They were so successful that within 10 years their numbers had risen to 5000. The first order, of Friars Minor, is now divided into three groups: the Observants (OFM), the Conventuals (OFMConv), and the Capuchins (OFMCap). These lead active lives preaching to the poor and needy. The second order is made up of nuns, known as the Poor Clares (PC). The third order is a lay fraternity. Together they constitute the largest religious order in the Roman Catholic Church, notable for missionary and social work. ▷ Capuchins; Francis of Assisi, St; monasticism; Roman Catholicism

Francis of Assisi, St, originally **Giovanni Bernadone** (1181–1226) Italian religious, founder of the Franciscan Order, born in Assisi, the son of a wealthy merchant. From his familiarity in his youth with the language of the troubadours, he acquired the name of *Il Francesco* ('the little Frenchman'). He was remarkable for his love of gaiety, of knightly exercises and ostentatious living. A serious illness was the first stage in his conversion, but in c.1205 he joined a military expedition. Halted by a dream, he returned and devoted himself to the care of the poor and the sick. In 1206 he was inspired to rebuild the ruined church of San Damiano. He renounced his patrimony, even his clothes, and lived as a hermit. His zeal became infectious and by 1210 he had a brotherhood of 11 for which he drew up a rule which was originally approved by Pope Innocent II. In 1212 he also founded the Poor Clares, a Franciscan order for women.

Like the older forms of monastic life, the Franciscan system is founded on chastity, poverty and obedience, with the emphasis on the second. He repudiated all idea of property, even in those things for personal use. The order increased rapidly in membership; at the first general assembly in 1219, 5000 members were present; 500 more were claimants for admission. Francis himself went to Egypt (1223) and preached in the presence of the sultan, who promised better treatment for his Christian prisoners, and for the Franciscan order the privilege they have since enjoyed as guardians of the Holy Sepulchre. It is after his return to Italy that his biographers place the legend of his receiving, while in an ecstasy of prayer, the marks (stigmata) of the wounds of Jesus Christ (1224). He was canonized by Pope Gregory IX in 1228, and in 1980 was designated patron saint of ecology. His works consist of letters, sermons, ascetic treatises, proverbs and hymns, including the well-known 'Canticle of the Sun'. His feast day is 4 October. ▷ Franciscans; monasticism; stigmata

Francis of Sales, St (1567–1622) French Roman Catholic prelate and devotional writer, born in the family chateau of Sales in Savoy. Educated by the Jesuits in Paris, he studied civil law at Padua, took orders, and became a distinguished preacher. He was successfully employed in a mission for the conversion of the Calvinistic population of Chablais, and in 1599 was appointed Bishop of Nicopolis. In 1602 in Paris he was invited to preach the Lent at the Louvre and his lectures had so much influence in converting several Huguenot nobles that the king offered him a French bishopric, which he declined. Soon afterwards, on the death of his colleague, he became sole bishop of Geneva. His administration of his diocese was exemplary. His *Introduction to a Devout Life* (1608), immediately a classic, was the first manual of piety addressed to those living in society. He established a congregation of nuns of the order of the Visitation under the direction of Madame de Chantal, with whom he kept up a correspondence over many years, and which was published in 1660. In 1665 he was canonized by Alexander VII.

Francis Xavier, St (1506–52) Spanish missionary, the 'Apostle of the Indies', born at his mother's castle of Xavero or Xavier near Sanguesa, in the Basque country. He was the youngest son of Juan de Jasso, Privy-Councillor to the King of Navarre. He studied, then lectured, at Paris, becoming acquainted with Ignatius Loyola with whom he founded the Jesuit Society (1534). Ordained priest in 1537, he lived in Rome in the service of the society, and was sent by John III of Portugal as a missionary to the Portuguese colonies of the East. He arrived at Goa in 1542 and worked with great energy and enthusiasm among the native population and the Europeans also. A year later he visited Travancore where he baptized 10000 natives. He then visited Malacca, the Banda Islands,

Amboyna, the Moluccas and Ceylon, where he converted the King of Kandy and many of his people. In 1548 he founded a mission in Japan which flourished for 100 years. In 1552 he returned to Goa to organize a mission to China, but the intrigues of the Portuguese merchants, and difficulties caused by the Governor of Malacca, wore out his strength and he died soon after reaching the island of Sanchian near Canton. He was buried, finally, in Goa and was canonized in 1622. His only literary remains are Letters (1631) and a Catechism, with some short ascetic treatises. His feast day is 3 December. ▷ Ignatius Loyola, St; Jesuits; missions, Christian

Frashokereti An Avestan word, usually translated as 'Renovation', in Pahlavi *Frashegird*. The term is used in the Zoroastrian tradition for the moment when evil has been eliminated from the world, ie the beginning of the final, ideal state, when the sun will stand still in mid-heaven and the dead will be resurrected. The way for Frashokereti is prepared by the Saoshyant, the final Saviour, who will make creation pure again, and it will be introduced by a final yasna ceremony performed by Ahura Mazda and the divinity Sraosha. The dead will rise up and the final judgement will take place. A stream of molten metal will flow like a river over the world; all people must pass through this stream, which will burn away any remaining sins, causing great distress to those who still have unexpiated sins, but none to the righteous. After this, all people will live in perfect peace and harmony in the world, together with Ahura Mazda and the divinities. ▷ Ahura Mazda; Avesta; Saoshyant; yasna; Zoroastrianism

fravashi In Zoroastrianism the fravashi is thought to be the part or aspect of the human soul which is pre-existent and eternal, and is capable of having dealings with humans on earth. The fravashis are represented as winged female beings. According to the Avesta they inhabit the air and can come to earth quickly to help their descendants; they strive to bring rain, promote procreation, and fight invisibly alongside men in battles. The fravashis of the ancestors come to their old dwelling place on earth on New Year's Eve; they are given offerings and are then bidden to depart. ▷ Avesta; soul; Zoroastrianism

Frazer, Sir James George (1854–1941) Scottish anthropologist and folklorist, born in Glasgow. He was educated at Larchfield Academy, Helensburgh, and Glasgow University, then at Trinity College, Cambridge, where he became a classics fellow. He studied law and was called to the English Bar in 1879, but never practised, and turned his attention to anthropology which, in combination with his classical studies, produced his monumental work, *The Golden Bough: A Study in Comparative Religion* (12 vols, 1890–1915), named after the golden bough in the sacred grove at Nemi, near Rome. His other anthropological works included *Totemism* (1884), *Totemism and Exogamy* (1911), *The Belief in Immortality and the Worship of the Dead* (1913–22), and *Magic and Religion* (1944). He also published an edition of Sallust (1884), and a translation of Pausanias's *Description of Greece* (1898). He was Professor of Social Anthropology at Liverpool (1907–8) and Cambridge (from 1908). ▷ comparative religion

freemasonry A movement claiming great antiquity, whose members are joined together in an association based on brotherly love, faith, and charity. The one essential qualification for membership is a belief in a supreme being. Non-political, open to men of any religion, freemasonry is known for its rituals and signs of recognition that date back to ancient religions and to the practices of the medieval craft guild of the stonemasons (in England). During the 17th century the masons' clubs, or lodges, began to be attended by gentlemen who had no connection with the trade. The Grand Lodge of England was founded in 1717, that of Ireland in 1725, and Scotland in 1736; freemasonry spread to the USA, the British colonies, and European countries. Freemasons are now mainly drawn from the professional middle classes. The organization regularly comes under attack for the secrecy with which it carries out its activities.

freethought A post-Reformation movement which rejected the control of any religious authority over reason in the examination of religious issues. The term was used by the 17th/18th-century deists, such as Anthony Collins (1676–1729). It is represented in the 19th century by the National Secularist Society (1866) and in the 20th century by the Secular Society. ▷ deism; humanism

free will ▷ **predestination**

Freud, Sigmund (1856–1939) Austrian neurologist and founder of psychoanalysis. Born in Freiburg, Moravia, of Jewish parentage, he studied medicine at Vienna and joined the staff of the Vienna General Hospital in 1882, specializing in neurology. He collaborated with the Austrian neurologist Joseph Breuer in the treatment of hysteria by the recall of painful experiences under hypnosis, then moved to Paris in 1885 to study under Jean Martin Charcot; it was there that he changed from neurology to psychopathology. Returning to Vienna he developed the technique of conversational 'free association' in place of hypnosis and refined psychoanalysis as a method of treatment. In 1895 he published, with Breuer, *Studien über Hysterie*, but two years later their friendship ended as a result of Freud's theories of infantile sexuality. Despite opposition from friends, patients and medical colleagues he developed his revolutionary thinking, and in 1900 published his seminal work, *Die Traumdeutung* (The Interpretation of Dreams), arguing that dreams, like neuroses, are disguised manifestations of repressed sexual desires. Appointed Extraordinary Professor of Neuropathology at the University of Vienna in 1902, he started weekly seminars in his home with kindred minds like Alfred Adler (the original 'Psychological Wednesday Society'), and produced further crucial works, *The Psychopathology of Everyday Life* (1904), and *Three Essays on the Theory of Sexuality* (1905), which met with intense and uncomprehending opposition. In 1908 these weekly meetings became the Vienna Psychoanalytical Society and, in 1910, the international Psychoanalytical Association, with Carl Jung as the first president. Both Adler (1911) and Jung (1913) broke with Freud to develop their own theories. Undeterred, Freud produced *Totem and Tabu* (1913), *Beyond the Pleasure Principle* (1919–20), and *Ego and Id* (1923), elaborating his theories of the division of the unconscious mind into the 'Id', the 'Ego', and the 'Super-Ego'. In 1927 he published a controversial view of religion, *The Future of an Illusion*. He was awarded the prestigious Goethe prize in 1930, and in 1933 published *Why War?*, written in collaboration with Albert Einstein. Under the Nazi régime psychoanalysis was banned, and in 1938, after the annexation of Austria, Freud was extricated from Vienna and brought to London with his family. He made his home in Hampstead, but died of cancer the following year. ▷ Jung, Carl Gustav; secular alternatives to religion

Frey ▷ Freya

Freya, or **Freyja** In Northern mythology, the goddess of love and beauty, especially first love. She and her brother Frey, the male fertility god, were the children of Niord and Skadi. To obtain the Brising necklace she betrayed her husband, Odur, and had to wander through the world looking for him. ▷ Germanic religion; mythology

friar A member of one of the mendicant ('begging') Christian religious orders founded in the Middle Ages. Unlike monks, they are not confined to a single monastery or abbey but are part of a tightly organized group, with members in many countries. In Britain they can be distinguished by the colour of their habits, hence the name Grey Friars being given to Franciscans, White Friars to Carmelites, and Black Friars to Dominicans. ▷ Augustinians; Carmelites; Dominicans; Franciscans

Friday Prayer in Islam (Ṣalāt al-jum'ah) Taking part in prayer (*salat*) five times daily is a fundamental responsibility for Muslims. The five daily prayers take place at sunrise, noon, late afternoon, sunset, and after dark. The Friday noon prayer is of special significance. It is performed in a large mosque in the presence of a congregation of 40 or more. During the Friday Prayer an imam or other competent preacher delivers an address lasting about 15 to 30 minutes. Attendance at the Friday Prayer is considered a duty for Muslim believers if they are free at that time, and business during this hour is forbidden, although it may be conducted at other times during the day. Friday is the Muslim day of assembly (*jumah*), although it is not a day of rest. However, in places like Saudi Arabia where Sunday is not a holiday, Thursday and Friday have in practice replaced the Western weekend. ▷ imam; mosque; salat

Friends, Society of A Christian sect with roots in radical Puritanism, founded by George Fox and others in mid 17th-century England, and formally organized in 1667; members are popularly known as Quakers, possibly because of Fox's injunction 'to quake at the word of the Lord'. Persecution led William Penn to establish a Quaker colony (Pennsylvania) in 1682. Belief in the 'inner light', a living contact with the divine Spirit, is the basis of its meetings for worship, where Friends gather in silence until moved by the Spirit to speak. Today most meetings have programmed orders of worship, though meetings based on silence (unprogrammed) still prevail in the UK and parts of the USA. They emphasize simplicity in all things, and are active reformers, promoting tolerance, justice, and peace as, for example, in the early 18th century, when they played a significant part in the abolition of slavery. Though pacifist they have done valiant work during wars and battles. ▷ Christianity; Fox, George; Holy Spirit; Penn, William

Frigg In Norse stories Frigg is the wife of Odin and loving mother of Balder; she is able to outwit the fates, and when necessary to manipulate her husband, on behalf of those she favoured. She seems once to have been important in Germanic religion; 'Friday' derives from Frija, the older form of her name. Her help was sought by women when desiring children and when in labour (Friday was long regarded in Germany as a lucky day for marriages). In Norse religion she seems overshadowed by the (quite distinct) Freya as the pre-eminent female divinity. ▷ Balder; Freya; Odin

frost giants In Norse literature the rivals of the divine Aesir. Just as one root of the world tree Yggdrasil passes through the divine realm, another passes through the giant world. Beneath it lies Mimir, the spring of wisdom, from which Odin derived his understanding. The giant and human races have a common origin; both ultimately derive from the body of the primal giant Ymir. Countless stories tell of competition in wits, skill and strength between gods and giants. Many of these feature Thor and his hammer. The Aesir cross a fiery bridge to reach the place where they meet in council; no frost giant is able to cross it. Loki's treachery to the Aesir is reflected in his connections with giants, and his monstrous children by a giantess. It is no surprise, then, that he and his brood join the giants and their allies against the gods at Ragnarok, where the giants also perish. Conflict among the powers of the other world is a regular component of Germanic religion. ▷ Aesir and Vanir; Loki; Odin; Ragnarok; Thor; Yggdrasil

Fuji, Mount, or **Fujiyama**, Japanese **Fujisan** The highest peak in Japan, in Chubu region, Central Honshu. A dormant volcano, it has been sacred since ancient times; until the Meiji Restoration of 1868 no woman was allowed to climb it. ▷ Japanese religion

fundamentalism A theological movement seeking to preserve what are thought to be the essential doctrines ('fundamentals') of the Christian faith, such as the virgin birth (Immaculate Conception) and Jesus Christ's resurrection. The term was originally used of the conservative US Protestant movement in the 1920s, characterized by a literal interpretation of the Bible, and revived to describe conservative Christian movements in the late 20th century. Its roots, however, lie in the 19th century when traditional assumptions about biblical truth were challenged by the concept of evolution and the development of biblical criticism. More generally, fundamentalism is any theological position opposed to liberalism. ▷ Bible; Immaculate Conception; resurrection

funerary practices The ritual burying or disposing of the dead which is an attested feature of human culture dating from Palaeolithic times. Although practices vary they seem to reflect a belief in some form of an afterlife. Funeral rites also function as expressions of sorrow and may be attempts to protect the living from the powers of the dead. ▷ cremation, Buddhist; dakhma; death ceremonies, Sikh

Meso-American funerary urn

funerary practices, Ancient Egyptian Many aspects of Egyptian funerary practice are related to a belief that life after death was very similar to this life, entered only if the body was properly preserved. This was achieved by mummifying the corpse. After embalming, the mummy was carried in procession to its tomb where the ritual of 'Opening the Mouth' was performed to restore life to the deceased. Offerings of food and drink were left in tombs for the sustenance of the dead, as well as furniture, games, and other possessions which they might want to use in the afterlife. Statues known as *ushabti* figures were left to perform agricultural tasks in the realm of Osiris. In some cases mortuary priests were paid to make daily offerings to ensure the survival of the dead; the wall paintings in tombs served the same purpose, if the regular offerings ceased. Tombs were often carefully designed to protect the mummy and funerary gifts from grave robbers. ▷ afterlife; Anubis; mummification; Osiris

funerary practices, Chinese The Chinese have traditionally buried their dead, and during the early Shang and Chou dynasties nobles and rulers often had possessions buried with them. Great care was taken with the preparation of the body, mourning, burial, and post-burial rituals, which are set out in their traditional form in the Confucian *Classic of Rites*. The body is usually prepared and left in the home for a number of days before the burial, at which Buddhist and Taoist priests often officiate. The elaboration of the ceremonies depends on the status of the person concerned within the family and on the status of the family within society. The aim is to enable the spirit (*shen*) of the departed person to traverse the underworld and arrive at the spirit tablet in the ancestral shrine of the family, or in some cases to arrive in heaven. The *po* soul is believed to reside in the grave and is given offerings of food and drink at periodic ceremonies to keep it content, while the ancestral shrine is periodically honoured to keep alive the memory of the deceased person.

funerary practices, Christian Burial of the dead is traditional, following Jewish and biblical custom. Christian influence caused the disappearance of cremation from the Roman Empire by the 5th century. When the practice re-emerged in urban Europe and North America in the late 19th century, it was forbidden to members of the Roman Catholic Church, on account of the opportunity taken by freethinkers to ridicule (as they thought) Christian belief in the resurrection of the body. The ban was relaxed in 1963, at a time of increasing concern that US funeral parlours were expensively hiding the reality of death. Many Christians today, understanding the doctrine of the resurrection of the body in terms of the preservation of the individual 'person' (a unity of 'body' and 'soul'), would choose between cremation and burial on practical rather than religious grounds. A religious service may be held in the home or at church, and at the cemetery or crematorium, reminding participants of the realities of death and judgement, expressing Christian hope in sharing in Christ's resurrection, and committing the departed to the love and mercy of God. ▷ resurrection; soul

fylgja (plural **fylgjur**) This Norse word stands for a person's 'fetch' or shadow-soul. Normally invisible, it is sometimes seen—often as a woman or as an animal—in dreams, or by those with second sight. The word may derive from the verb 'to accompany' or from the word for afterbirth, with care of which the shadow soul may be associated. A fylgja might be with a family over generations as a guardian spirit. Sometimes the word is used less concretely, for a person's inherent force (cf the Melanesian *mana*). In later Norse writings fylgjur is used interchangeably with *disir*, who were originally female guardian spirits of a family or place, worshipped, like the Celtic *matres*, with sacrifice. One story tells how the fylgjur or disir of one of Iceland's leading Christian families appeared, shortly before the conversion, and slew the eldest son. Recognizing that their day was passing, they took their portion while they could. ▷ guardian spirits; matres, matrones; Melanesian religion

G

Gabriel An angel named in both the Old and New Testaments, the only other named angel in the Bible being the archangel Michael (although seven archangels are named in the Jewish apocalyptic work 1 Enoch). Gabriel is said to have helped Daniel interpret visions (Daniel 8, 9). He is also recorded as foretelling the births of John the Baptist and of Jesus (Luke 1). ▷ angels; Annunciation; apocalypse; Bible; Daniel, Book of;

Gad One of the 12 tribes of ancient Israel, said to be descended from Jacob's seventh son (the first by Zilpah, Leah's maid). Its territory originally included the valley to the east of the Jordan River, bordered by the tribe of Manasseh in the north. ▷ Israel, tribes of; Jacob

Gahambars Six of the seven yearly festivals whose observance is obligatory for a Zoroastrian, the seventh being the New Year. The names of some of the Gahambars suggest that, in pre-Zoroastrian times, they were pastoral and farming festivals. In Zoroastrianism each of the seven obligatory festivals is dedicated to a member of the Heptad, ie to Ahura Mazda and to the Amesha Spentas. Formerly, Zoroastrian communities celebrated the Gahambars by attending a religious service, followed by a feast in which food that had been blessed in the ceremony was communally eaten. Every member of the congregation had to contribute to the expenses of the feast according to his means. In recent times the custom of celebrating the Gahambars communally has been widely given up by the Parsi community. ▷ Ahura Mazda; Amesha Spentas; Zoroastrianism

Galatians, Letter of Paul to the New Testament writing, widely accepted as genuinely from the apostle Paul to the churches in some part of Galatia in central Asia Minor. It is a strongly-worded letter arguing that non-Jewish converts to Christianity were no longer subject to Jewish practices and laws, and defending Paul's own mission on this basis. ▷ New Testament; Paul, St; Pauline Letters

Gampopa (sGam-po-pa) (1079–1153) Founder of the Kagyupa monastic order of Tibetan Buddhism. As a young man he studied Tibetan medicine. He married, but his wife died when he was in his twenties. As a consequence of his bereavement he became a monk, entering the Kadampa order and, having heard of a famous Tantric teacher called Milarepa, went in search of him. The *Blue Annals*, a 15th-century Tibetan history, describes how Gampopa met the wandering Tantric yogin Milarepa who instructed him in meditation, bestowing the teachings of tummo (gTum-mo, or yoga of inner heat) upon him. Gampopa returned to the monastic life, meditating constantly for three years, after which time he realized the 'suchness' (*tathata*) of all appearances. He then wandered and came to a place by a holy mountain called Gampo (hence his name) where he settled, gathering around him a number of followers. He combined the Tantric Mahamudra teachings of Milarepa, or the realization of transcendent knowledge, with the non-Tantric, monastic doctrines and discipline (*vinaya*) of the Kadampas, thus founding the Kagyupa order. Gampopa is famous for combining these 'two streams' of Tantric and non-Tantric teachings. The main Kagyupa sub-schools were founded by his disciples. ▷ Kadampa; Kagyupa; Milarepa; Tibetan religion

Gandhara A region in the north-west of ancient India, now in southern Afghanistan, that was important for the development of Buddhism and Buddhist art. It was ceded to the Indian ruler Chandragupta Maurya in the 4th century BCE, and became a frontier area on the trade routes connecting China, Central Asia and India with the Persian and Mediterranean regions. Thus the Buddhist art that developed there was influenced by classical Greek and Roman features as well as by elements derived from Iran and Central Asia. It was here (and also at Mathura further south) that images of the Buddha first appeared portraying him in an idealized human way. Under Kushana kings such as Kanishka Gandhara there developed a flowering Buddhist culture during the first three centuries CE, including many significant monastic centres such as Taksasila, and it was from this area that Buddhism spread along the trade routes from India into Central Asia and China. Gandhara nourished the vertical development of the stupa, for example in Kanishka's famous pagoda at Peshawar, and this probably had an influence upon the evolution of pagodas in Chinese Buddhism. Famous Mahayana scholars such as Asanga and Vasubandhu flourished in the Buddhist atmosphere of this region, which was, however, destined to decline due to the Hun invasions of the 5th century CE. ▷ Asanga; Buddha; Buddha image; Kanishka; Mahayana Buddhism; pagoda; stupa; Vasubandhu

Gandhi, Mohandas Karamchand, known as **Mahatma** ('Great Souled') (1869–1948) Indian nationalist and spiritual leader, born in Porbandar, Kathiawar. He studied law in London, and in 1893 he gave up a Bombay legal practice worth £5000 a year to live on £1 a week in South Africa, where he spent 21 years opposing discriminatory legislation against Indians. In 1909 he published *Hind Swaraj or Indian Home Rule*, outlining his ideas, particularly his hope for 'an exploitation-free society'. In 1914 he returned to India. While supporting the British in World War I, he took an increasing interest in the Home Rule movement (*Swaraj*), over which he soon obtained a personal dominance, becoming President of the Indian National Congress (1925). His civil disobedience campaign of 1920 resulted in violent disorders. From 1922 to 1924 he was in jail for conspiracy and in 1930 he led a 200-mile march to the sea to collect salt in symbolic defiance of the government monopoly. He was rearrested and on his release in 1931 negotiated a truce between Congress and the government and attended the London Round Table Conference on Indian constitutional reform. Back in India, he renewed the civil disobedience campaign and was arrested again—the pattern, along with his 'fasts unto death', of his political activity for the next six years. He assisted in the adoption of the constitutional compromise of 1937 under which Congress ministers accepted office in the new provincial legislatures.

When war broke out, Gandhi, convinced that only a free India could give Britain effective moral support, urged 'complete independence' more and more strongly. He described the Cripps proposal in 1942 for a constituent assembly with the promise of a new Constitution after the war as 'a post-dated cheque on a crashing bank'. In August 1942 he was arrested for concurring in civil disobedience action to obstruct the war effort, and was released in May 1944. In 1946 Gandhi negotiated with the British Cabinet Mission which recommended the new constitutional structure. In May 1947 he hailed Britain's decision to grant India independence as 'the noblest act of the British nation'. His last months were darkened by communal strife between Hindu and Muslim; but his fasts to shame the instigators helped to avert deeper tragedy. He was assassinated in Delhi by a Hindu fanatic, on 30 January 1948—ten days after a previous attempt on his life.

In his lifetime Mahatma Gandhi was venerated as a moral teacher, a reformer who sought an India as free from caste as from materialism, a dedicated patriot who gave the Swaraj movement a new quality. Critics, however, thought him the victim of a power of self-delusion which blinded him to the disaster and bloodshed his 'nonviolent' campaigns invoked. But in Asia particularly he has been regarded as a great influence for peace whose teaching had a message not only for India—of whose nationhood he became the almost mystical incarnation—but for the world. His publications include the autobiographical *The Story of My Experiment with Truth* (republished 1949). ▷ caste; Hinduism; Islam

Ganesha, (Gaṇeśa) or **Ganapati** The elephant-headed god of Hinduism. The name means 'Lord of hosts' (*gana*) ie of Shiva's retinue, and he is revered as the remover of obstacles, the Lord of beginnings, and the Lord of learning who broke off his tusk to write down the epic *Mahabharata*. His mount

Ganesha

is, somewhat incongruously, a rat. According to Hindu mythology, Ganesha has an elephant's head because his father Shiva, not recognizing his son, decapitated him as Ganesha protected his mother Parvati. Upon discovering his error Shiva replaced the head with that of an elephant. Ganesha is one of the five gods worshipped by the Smarta Brahmans and was an important Tantric deity. Indeed, for the Ganapatayas he was the supreme deity and an entire collection of tantras, now lost, were centred on him. ▷ Mahabharata; Parvati; Shiva

Ganga (Gaṅgā; Ganges) The holiest river for Hindus, rising in the Himalayas and spreading to a delta on the east coast. Although the entire river is regarded as auspicious, it is particularly purifying at the sacred city of Banaras and at the confluence with the Yamuna at Allahabad. Hindus go on pilgrimage to bathe in the Ganga, to purify themselves of karma and to immerse the ashes of their dead. The Ganga is venerated as a goddess who, in the mythology of the Puranas, descended to earth as a result of the austerity of the sage Bhagiratha. Her fall was broken by the matted hair of Shiva who then released her to fall to earth. ▷ Banaras; Puranas; Shiva

Gangesha (Gangeśa) (fl.c.1200) Founder of the New or Navya-Nyaya school of Hindu philosophy. Gangesha wrote on the four means of knowledge (*pramanas*) accepted by the Nyaya, namely perception (*pratyaksha*), inference (*anumana*), analogy (*upamana*) and verbal authority (*shabda*). He also developed a highly technical system of linguistic notation to specify the relationships between concepts, which is akin to modern Western symbolic logic. ▷ Nyaya

Gardiner, Stephen (c.1483–1555) English prelate, born in Bury St Edmunds, Suffolk. He studied at Cambridge, became Wolsey's secretary (1525), Bishop of Winchester (1531), and was sent to Rome to further Henry VIII's divorce (1527–33). He supported the royal supremacy, but opposed doctrinal reformation, and for this was imprisoned and deprived of his bishopric on Edward VI's accession. Released and restored by Mary in 1553, he became an arch-persecutor of Protestants. He died in London. ▷ Reformation; Wolsey, Thomas

Gaudapada (Gauḍapāda) (5th–6th century) Indian philosopher in the Vedanta tradition of Hinduism. Gaudapada espoused a monistic philosophy in his interpretation of the Upanishads. In his commentary on the *Mandukya Upanishad* he says that the appearance of diversity is illusion (*maya*) and only the non-dual (*advaita*) or one is ultimately real. This one, which is the self, is identified with the fourth state (*turya*) beyond the experiences of waking, dreaming and deep sleep. Ultimately, because of this non-duality there is no-one who is bound in the wheel of reincarnation (*samsara*) and no-one who is released. Buddhist influence, particularly of the Madhyamika school, can be discerned in these teachings and it has been suggested that Gaudapada himself was a Buddhist. He may have been Shankara's grand-teacher and certainly strongly influenced the latter's work. ▷ Advaita Vedanta; maya; Upanishads; Vedanta

Gautama, or Gotama (c.563–c.483BCE) Indian philosopher, born in Bihar. The founder of Nyaya, one of the six classical systems of Hindu philosophy, his *Nyaya Sutras* are principally concerned with ways of knowing and of reaching valid logical conclusions. Their claim that one can obtain real knowledge of the external world was disputed by Sriharsha and the Navya-nyaya school founded by Gangesha. ▷ Gangesha; Hinduism; Nyaya

Gehenna (Greek form of the Hebrew *Gehinnom*, 'Valley of Hinnom', a ravine south-west of Jerusalem) In c.7th century BCE, the site of cultic sacrifices of children to Baal by fire, condemned by Jeremiah (Jeremiah 19.4–6); later considered an entrance to the underworld. The name is metaphorically used in both Judaism and the New Testament as a place where the wicked would be tormented (usually by fire) after death (eg Mark 9.43). ▷ Baal; hell; Jeremiah, Book of; underworld

Gelugpa (d'Ge-lugs-pa) The principal monastic order of Tibetan Buddhism, sometimes known as the Yellow Hats in contrast to the Red Hats of the Nyingmapas. The Gelugpa order was founded by Tsongkapa (1357–1419), absorbing into it the oldest Tibetan order, the Kadampa, Indeed it was also called the New Kadampa. The Gelugpas, whose hierarch is the Dalai Lama, enjoyed enormous political power and privilege from the time of the fifth Dalai Lama, who became ruler of Tibet, to the Chinese invasion in 1951. He appointed a second dignitary, the Panchen Lama, though rivalries and diverse interests developed between the Panchen and Dalai lamas. The tradition emphasizes the monastic

Yellow Hat Lama or Gelugpa

discipline (*vinaya*), celibacy, not taking life, and abstention from intoxicants. Tantric teachings were therefore modified and accommodated within a celibate, monastic framework. The Gelugpas place great value on scholarship and intellectual endeavour, with formalized, public debates taking place between representatives of rival philosophical positions. The study of texts by the great Buddhist scholars such as Nagarjuna, Atisha, Chandrakirti, Dinnaga and Asanga are integral to the monks' training, especially for the 12-year *geshe* 'degree'. Philosophically the Gelugpas are Madhyamika, regarding all phenomena as empty of inherent existence. Gelugpa monastic institutions are now established in the West, for example the Manjushri Institute in Cumbria, England. ▷ Asanga; Atisha; Chandrakirti; Dalai Lama; Kadampa; Madhyamika; Nagarjuna; Nyingmapa; Panchen Lama; Tibetan religion; Tsongkapa

Gemara (Aramaic 'completion') A commentary on the Jewish Mishnah, which together with the Mishnah constitutes the Talmud. It consists largely of scholarly rabbinic discussions that interpret and extend the applications of legal teachings in Rabbi Judah's Mishnah. Distinct versions were produced in Palestine and Babylon. ▷ Judaism; Mishnah; Talmud

gender roles The growing realization of the importance of gender as a means of understanding power and symbolism in society has led to an increasing awareness of the ways in which religious traditions have dealt with the issue of gender. Broadly speaking there are two ways in which gender affects a person's status within a religious tradition. Firstly, there are the ways in which certain faiths and traditions preclude people of a certain gender from holding sacred offices. In Christianity, for example, the Catholic and Orthodox churches (and much of the Anglican communion) refuse to ordain women to the priesthood. Their reasons for doing so are specifically related to the issue of gender in that the priest is thought to be a representative of Christ, who was male, and cannot therefore be represented by a female.

The second way in which gender roles are seen to be important in religious practices is in the many examples of people assuming an altered sexuality in order to fulfil a religious function. *Shamans*, healers, priests and seers may dress in the clothes of the opposite sex and behave and act as members of it. Such cases of altered sexuality may be for only a limited time, but they may also be permanent alterations to the sexual behaviour of the individual. The desire to change sexuality is usually the result of a mystical experience and the belief is that such behaviour will enhance the spiritual power of the priest or shaman.

Studies of such changes of gender roles have suggested that gender is a much more socially created phenomenon than was previously thought. Certainly it is a more complicated issue than the basic issue of biological sex. The ways in which religious practices have found ways of subverting the social construction of gender suggest that differences in gender roles may produce an entirely different perception of reality. ▷ priesthood; women in religion

General Assembly The highest court, in Churches of Presbyterian order. It normally meets annually and comprises equal numbers of ministers and elders, elected by presbyteries in proportion to their size. It is presided over by a moderator, elected annually. ▷ elder; moderator; Presbyterianism; presbytery

Genesis, Book of The first book of the Hebrew Bible/Old Testament and of the Pentateuch, traditionally attributed to Moses, but considered by many modern scholars to be composed of several distinct traditions. It presents stories of the creation and of the beginnings of human history (Chapters 1–11), and then focuses on God's dealings with the people destined to become Israel, starting with Abraham and concluding with Jacob's sons. ▷ Abraham; Adam and Eve; creation myths; Enoch; Isaac; Jacob; Joseph; Moses; Noah; Old Testament; Pentateuch

Geneva Bible An English translation of the Bible, prepared and published in Geneva by Protestant exiles from England; it first appeared complete in 1560. It was notable for its small size and legible Roman type, for its notes, and for its verse divisions. It was especially popular in Scotland, and also in England until the Authorized Version. ▷ Authorized Version of the Bible; Bible

Gennep, Charles-Arnold Kurr van (1873–1957) French ethnographer and folklorist, born in Württemberg, Germany, of a Dutch father and French mother. He grew up in France, where his career was not primarily academic. He worked for the French government in various cultural organizations from 1903 to 1910, and again from 1919 to 1921. He also held brief academic appointments at Neuchâtel, Oxford and Cambridge. He became an energetic collector and publisher of folklore materials, including the *Manuel de Folklore Français Contemporaine* (1937–58). However he is principally known for his earlier work, *Les Rites de Passage* (1909), a comparative study of rituals marking transitions of social status. He discovered that such rituals have a regular tripartite structure, in which a stage of separation is followed by stages of transition and reincorporation. His other publications include *Religions, Mœurs et Légendes* (1908–14). ▷ rites of passage

Gentiles The term used to designate non-Jews, whether individuals or nations. In the Hebrew Bible the Gentiles or *goyim* include all peoples other than Israel, and are often viewed with some hostility due to their unacceptable religious beliefs and practices or aggressive stance towards Israel. In post-biblical Judaism the same usage continued but was broadened to include individuals as well as corporate nations. The designation of non-Jews as Gentiles reflects the biblical and Jewish idea of Israel being an elect nation. For the Bible and much ancient Jewish literature the corollary of this was the denial of any parallel status to other peoples. The assumption that other nations were invariably polytheistic and idolatrous, or else ill-disposed towards Jews and Judaism, explains this attitude. However, the rise of other monotheistic religions encouraged Jews to accept Christians and Muslims as worshippers of the same God, obliged to hold to monotheism and a basic morality rather than become Jews. As a development of this, many Jews in modern times accept that individuals and nations outside Israel also have an important part to play in the divine plan. ▷ conversion, Jewish; election

Germanic religion The name given to the pre-Christian religion of the people bounded by the Rhine, Vistula, and Danube rivers. Because of the early conversion of these peoples, evidence of their beliefs and rituals is scarce. What little is known comes largely from Roman accounts of varying reliability, missionaries, and archaeological finds. There was a pantheon of deities represented in human form, of whom four were particularly important during the Viking Age (9th–11th centuries CE). Odin (Germanic *Wodan*), father of the gods and ruler of Valhalla, was the god of poetry, wisdom and the dead. Thor (Germanic *Donar*), a sky-god, was the god of law and order. Frigg and Freya were fertility deities. The powers of nature were held to be magical, and were represented as sprites, elves, and trolls. Icelandic mythological poetry describes many of these supernatural beings. ▷ Edda; Freya; Hel; Loki; Odin; ship burial; Sutton Hoo ship burial; Thor; Valhalla; Vikings

Gesar (Ge-sar) Legendary King of Tibet, the hero of a Tibetan epic sung by wandering bards. The story tells how there was chaos in the world and how human beings, having no leader, implored the sky god to send them his son to create order. Gesar was born of the union of the sky god with the goddess of the watery sub-soil. As a child he was mischievous and possessed magical powers. His uncle, however, feeling threatened, banished Gesar and his mother. During his exile the young man's powers grew and he eventually gained the kingdom by winning a horse race. As king, Gesar defeated demons and other kings, bringing order to Tibet. He is said to have been the 26th incarnation of Avalokiteshvara. He is identified with the Dalai Lama (who is likewise an incarnation of Avalokiteshvara) and also with the Chinese warrior god Kuan Lin. Iconographically he is depicted in armour, riding a horse. Tradition maintains that he will one day return with his army from the mythic country of Shambala in the north. Some Zoroastrian influence on the legend is possible, and indeed the name Gesar, possibly being cognate with kaiser and caesar, suggests 'Western' influence. ▷ Avalokiteshvara; Dalai Lama

Gethsemane A place outside Jerusalem near the Mount of Olives where Jesus and his disciples went to pray immediately before his betrayal and arrest (Mark 14.32ff); described as a 'garden' in John 18.1. It is the scene of Jesus's agony over whether to accept martyrdom. ▷ Jesus Christ

Ghazali, Abu Hamid Mohammed al- (al-Ghazālī, Abū Ḥāmid Muḥhammad) (1058–1111) Muslim philosopher, theologian and jurist, born in Tus, Persia (near the modern Meshed). In 1091 he was appointed to the prestigious position of Professor of Philosophy at Nizamiyah College, Baghdad, where he exercised great academic and political influence; but in 1095 he suffered a spiritual crisis which led to a nervous breakdown and a speech impediment that prevented him from lecturing. He abandoned his position for the ascetic life of a mendicant Sufi (mystic), spending his time in meditation and spiritual exercises. Although he did teach again briefly he eventually retired to Tus to found a monastic community. His doctrines represent a reaction against Aristotelianism and an attempt to reconcile philosophy and Islamic dogma. A prolific author, his main works include: *The Intentions of the Philosophers*, *The Incoherence of the Philosophers*, *The Deliverance from Error* and the monumental *The Revival of the Religious Sciences*. ▷ Aristotle; Islam; mysticism; Sufism

Ghost Dance A religious movement of the 19th century affecting many Native American peoples. Around 1870, Tävibo, of the Nevada Paiute, prophesized an imminent cataclysm, a general resurrection, reunion with the departed ancestors, and a secure, happy future for the Indian peoples. These themes were revived with more effect in about 1888 by his son or kinsman Wovoka (d.1932). Wovoka, influenced by Christian teaching, preached the messianic return of Jesus, a strict ethical code, and peace with all, including whites; and he taught a circular shuffling dance, learned from a vision, which would effect reunion with the dead. By now the extinction of the buffalo by the whites had brought the Plains peoples to distress, and this message was heard eagerly east of the Rockies. The dance spread across the Plains peoples, causing terror to whites, who interpreted it as a war dance. It undoubtedly strengthened Sioux resistance in confrontations with whites. On the Plains the movement developed features unknown to Wovoka, formed a focus for the revival of old customs and gave a new religious significance to others (eg traditional games). The Sioux movement died with the defeat at Wounded Knee (1890); other peoples maintained the dance while modifying belief in the imminence of resurrection and reunion. ▷ Cheyenne religion; Sioux religion

giants ▷ frost giants

Gibb, Sir Hamilton Alexander Rosskeen (1895–1971) Scottish Arabic scholar, a key figure in the modern study of Islam. Educated at the Royal High School, Edinburgh, Edinburgh University and the University of London, he became a lecturer at London University in 1921, before being appointed Professor of Arabic there in 1930. In 1937 he became Professor of Arabic at Oxford University, and from 1955 to 1964 he held the same post at Harvard University. In honour of his services to scholarship he won honorary doctorates from Edinburgh and Harvard, became a Chevalier of the French Legion of Honour, and received a knighthood in 1954. Through his advocacy and his publications he pioneered the modern empathetic, yet academically rigorous, study of Islam and Arabic in both Great Britain and the USA. Among his many works, including ones which he edited, were: *The Arab Conquests in Central Asia* (1923), *Arabic Literature: An Introduction* (1926, 2nd ed 1963), *Studies in Contemporary Arabic Literature* (1926–35), *Whither Islam* (1932), *The Damascus Chronicle of the Crusades* (1932), *Modern Trends in Islam* (1947), and *Islamic Society and the West* (1950). He was especially interested in modern Islam, and understood the dilemmas within the Islamic tradition as it grappled with the problem of how to regain its vigour. This involved a conflict between being faithful to its own traditional insights and adjusting to the modern process of scientific and technological advance. By his example Gibb inspired a generation of Islamicists. ▷ Islamic modernism; study of religion

Gideons International An international organization, which began in Wisconsin in 1898 with the aim of spreading the Christian faith by the free distribution of copies of the Bible to public places, including hotel rooms, hospitals, and military bases. It is named after the biblical judge Gideon, who led Israel against the Midianites. ▷ Bible; Christianity; Midianites

Gilgamesh Epic A Babylonian epic poem, partially preserved in different versions, named after its hero, the Sumerian King Gilgamesh (3rd millennium BCE). It describes Gilgamesh's legendary adventures, and narrates a story of the Flood that has striking parallels with the biblical account. ▷ Babylonian religion; epics; Flood, the

Glemp, Jozef (1929–) Polish ecclesiastic. He became Bishop of Warmia in 1979 and succeeded Cardinal Stefan Wyszynski as Archbishop of Gniezno and Warsaw and Primate of Poland after the latter's death in 1981. A specialist in civil and canonical law, Glemp was a prominent figure during Poland's internal political unrest. He was made a cardinal early in 1983. ▷ Wyszynski, Stefan

glossolalia The practice of 'speaking in tongues'—uttering sounds whose meaning is unknown to the speaker, who is undergoing a religious experience. The phenomenon is closely related to xenoglossia, using a language that the speaker has never known or heard, a power ascribed to the Apostles during the first days of Christianity, as recounted in the Acts of the Apostles. No scientifically attested case of xenoglossia has come to light, but speaking in tongues is nonetheless widely practised by several Christian groups, such as Pentecostalists or charismatic Catholics, and interpreted among its practitioners as a supernatural sign of religious sincerity or conversion. ▷ apostle; charismatic movement; Pentecostalism; Roman Catholicism

Gnosticism (Greek *gnosis*, 'knowledge') A system of belief that flourished in 4th-century Christianity, but which may have had earlier, non-Christian roots, possibly stemming from a breakaway form of Judaism. Gnostics believed that they, rather than orthodox Christians, held the real truths taught by Christ about cosmic origins and the true destiny of the spirit within people, and that they alone would attain full salvation. Gnosticism was considered a heresy by the early Church Fathers, particularly for its appeal to secret traditions, its deprecatory view of the Creator God, and its docetic view of Christ (ie that Christ had only 'assumed' human form, and that his supposed crucifixion was merely a deception to fool the evil powers). ▷ Christianity; Docetism; Manichaeism; Nag Hammadi texts

Gobind Singh, Guru (Gobind Singh, Gurū) (1666–1708) Tenth and last of the Sikh gurus. He was the son of the ninth guru, Guru Tegh Bahadur, who was executed by the Mughals (1675) and during his time as guru there was constant armed struggle between the Sikhs and the Mughal empire. Four features characterized his rule. In 1699 he instituted the *Khalsa* as the foremost institution of the Sikh community. He gave it visible symbols, and thereafter the turban and the five Ks became outward signs of the Sikh Khalsa. Simultaneously the names of *Singh* (for men) and *Kaur* (for women) became commonly used among Sikhs. Singh means 'lion', and together with the five Ks it was symbolic of a second feature of his rule, namely a willingness to use force in the righteous cause of defence against aggression. He also stated that after his death the Sikh scripture, the *Adi Granth*, which became known as the *Guru Granth Sahib*, should become the visible Sikh guru, hence making himself the last in the line of human gurus. Finally he wrote a number of poems which were gathered, along with other poems, in the *Dasam Granth*, which became secondary to the *Guru Granth Sahib* as a canonical authority for the Sikhs. ▷ Adi Granth; Dasam Granth; five Ks; guru, Sikh; Mughal empire; Tegh Bahadur, Guru

God A supernatural being or power, the object of worship. In some world religions (eg Christianity, Judaism, Islam) there is one God only (monotheism), who is transcendent, all-powerful, and related to the cosmos as creator. In other religions (eg Hinduism, Classical Greek and Roman religions, and primitive religions) many gods may be recognized (polytheism), with individual gods having particular properties and powers. In the Judaeo-Christian tradition, God, though transcendent and invisible, is believed to have revealed himself in history through the life and response of the people Israel, and, in the Christian tradition, supremely and finally in the life, death, and resurrection of Jesus of Nazareth, the Christ, all as testified to in the scriptures of the Old and New Testaments. The conviction that Jesus stood in a unique relation to God led to the development in Christian thought of the Trinitarian understanding, whereby the one God is confessed as three persons (Father, Son, and Holy Spirit) of one substance.

In the mainstream Western tradition, influenced by Classical Greek philosophy as well as Christianity, God is conceived as 'being itself' or 'pure actuality' (St Thomas Aquinas), in whom there is no unactualized potentiality or becoming; as absolute, infinite, eternal, immutable, incomprehensible (ie unable to be comprehended by human thought), all-powerful (omnipotent), all-wise (omniscient), all-good (omni-benevolent), and everywhere present (omni-present). He is also said to be impassible, or incapable of suffering. The fact that the New Testament sums up its understanding of God as 'Love' (1 John 4.8), coupled with the apparent fact of evil in the world, has led to various modifications of this traditional Western conception. Thus God is sometimes understood as all-good but finite (and therefore unable to prevent evil); or as di-polar, ie in one aspect absolute and infinite but in another aspect, in so far as he relates to the cosmos, relative and finite (panentheism or process theology); or as comprising the whole of nature (pantheism). Corresponding to particular concepts of God are particular understandings of God's power in relation to human beings and the world of nature. These vary from absolute transcendence, such that God is reponsible for initiating the world process and laying down its laws, thereafter letting it run its course (deism), to total immanence, whereby God is understood as a power or spirit within the world motivating human beings. Orthodox Christianity seeks to preserve both the transcendence and immanence of God.

From the time of the ancient Greeks, philosophers have tried to prove the existence of God by reason alone (ie not by divine revelation), and of these attempts the 'ontological' arguments of St Anselm and Descartes, the 'Five Ways' of St Thomas Aquinas, and Kant's moral argument are among the more famous and abiding. While the general philosophical consensus seems now to be that none of these arguments is coercive, discussion in the 20th century of various aspects of individual arguments has continued unabated. Attempts to disprove the existence of God or to show concepts of God to be incoherent have been likewise generally unpersuasive. ▷ Anselm, St; Aquinas, St Thomas; Bible; Christianity; deism; Descartes, René; God, arguments for the existence of; Hinduism; Islam; Jesus Christ; Judaism; Kant, Immanuel; monotheism; pantheism; polytheism; process theology; religion; Trinity

God, arguments for the existence of These are not given in the scriptures of theistic religions: they assume God's existence. The Bible, for example, opens and closes with accounts of God's action in creation and re-creation. However, unless it is accepted that it does not matter if the assertions of revealed theology are contradictory to all human thought and experience, God's existence must be reasonable, even if not conclusively demonstrable.

In Western thought there are five main arguments: 1 the ontological argument (from *ontos*, Greek for 'being'), associated with St Anselm, holds that God exists by definition. 'That than which no greater can be conceived' must exist, unless (as critics maintain) it can be shown that existence is not a quality. 2 The cosmological argument, associated with St Thomas Aquinas, argues from existence to an origin different in kind, from causes to an uncaused first Cause. Critics assert that an infinite series of cause and effect would be equally plausible. 3 A variation on this is the teleological (from *telos*, Greek for 'end' or 'purpose') or design argument, associated with William Paley. This argues that just as the existence of a watch suggests that there must be an intelligent watchmaker, so the existence of the world suggests that there is an intelligent designer behind it. Critics point out that only certain parts of the world appear to be designed (an appearance that could be explained in evolutionary terms), and that the random or evil features of other parts raise questions about the power or moral qualities of any supposed designer. 4 An alternative to the above arguments, offered by Kant, is the moral argument. This claims that the universal existence of a sense of right and wrong suggests an ultimate personal moral source of both. The existence of God is also necessary in that he would bring a final judgement on humankind in which right was rewarded and wrong punished, so making sense of situations in present life where this does not happen. Critics argue that any hope of final judgement is beyond the concern of philosophy, and that life as it is suggests a moral source that is limited or arbitrary. 5 A final argument is the argument from religious experience. This maintains that claims to experiences of God from all kinds of people in every historical period are too varied and widespread to be reduced to wish-fulfilment and projection. Critics would ask for objective proof of subjective claims and also point out the difficulties of moving from a claim to have experienced God to proving a particular religion to be true.

All these arguments (in classical forms or modern reformulations) can be countered. But even if accepted, they make a limited contribution to a religious understanding of God where assertions that 'God is holy' and 'God is love' are far more central than the bare statement that 'God exists'. ▷ Anselm, St; Aquinas, St Thomas; Kant, Immanuel; Paley, William; projection theories of religion

God, Christian view of Christianity, like Judaism and Islam, holds that there is only one supreme being (theism), and rejects ideas of polytheism (the existence of many gods), pantheism (that creation and God are identical), and deism (God set creation in motion but no longer intervenes). But (unlike them) it also believes that God is Trinity: a unity of Father, Son and Holy Spirit.

In New Testament teaching, God is the holy God of the Old Testament, yet Jesus calls him 'Father' and, in the Lord's Prayer, teaches his disciples to do the same. Jesus also promises that when he leaves them he will send the Holy Spirit to confirm his teaching, continue making them holy and be with them permanently.

The relationship at the heart or inner being of God signified by the doctrine of the Trinity makes biblical statements such as 'God is love' more appropriate than some of the classical doctrinal statements that God is infinite, immutable (cannot be forced to change), impassible (cannot be made to suffer), omnipresent (all-present), omnipotent (all-powerful) and omniscient (all-knowing). Taken by themselves, such concepts paint a picture of an abstract God of philosophy, and not what Pascal described in 1654 as an experience of 'Certitude, certitude; feeling, joy, peace. God of Jesus Christ'. Theological statements about the nature of God need to be placed in a larger context (talk of an all-powerful and all-good God raises questions of evil and human freedom), and balanced by the language of the creeds ('We believe in [that is, trust] God...'), prayer ('We ask God...') and worship ('We praise God...'). ▷ God, arguments for the existence of; Creeds, Christian; deism; evil, Christian concept of; Holy Spirit; Lord's Prayer; Pascal, Blaise; prayer, Christian; Trinity; worship, Christian

goddess worship The worship of female deities. This, and the worship of female sacred images, has been practised from the earliest recorded times and still continues. Especially prominent in the Hindu, Buddhist and Shinto countries of Asia, goddesses were widely worshipped in Greece (eg Athena, Aphrodite) and Rome (eg Cybele). In Latin America, Indian goddesses have been transformed into images of the Virgin Mary (eg Virgin of Guadalupe). Frequently associated with fertility (agricultural and human) they have variously been experienced as mother/protectors of a community, symbols of national identity, mediators between human beings and male gods, and sources for healing.

goddess worship, Hindu Practised throughout India, especially in Assam and Bengal, the goddess (*devi*) is perceived in both gentle and ferocious forms. In her gentle and maternal forms she is the consort or female power (*shakti*) of a god, such as Lakshmi, the consort of Vishnu, and Parvati, the consort of Shiva, while in her ferocious form she stands alone as Durga, the slayer of the buffalo demon, and the terrible Kali who dances in the cremation grounds. Most Hindu temples have shrines dedicated to the goddess, often Durga, and in some temples she is the principal deity. An important member of the Hindu pantheon, the goddess is worshipped by orthodox Smarta Brahmans (along with Surya, Vishnu, Shiva and Ganesha). Exclusive devotees of the goddess are called Shaktas who mostly revere the Tantras of the goddess as their sacred texts. Worship of the goddess Kali involves blood-sacrifice and even human sacrifice has been prescribed and performed. The Shri Vidya tradition in South India worships the gentle Tripurasundari with vegetarian offerings, especially in the form of the *yantra*. At a village level, worship of local goddesses, perhaps represented as merely a painted stone, is very prevalent. In mythology, Shiva in his grief danced wildly with the corpse of his dead wife Sati. Vishnu, fearing the destruction of the universe, cut her body up with his discus, and the places where the parts of her corpse are thought to have fallen are regarded as pilgrimage centres (*pitha*). ▷ Durga; Hindu religious traditions; Kali; Lakshmi; Parvati

gods In polytheistic religions, spiritual or heavenly beings, capable of influencing events and people on earth and so worthy of human respect and worship. Individual gods, male and female, have particular functions, properties and concerns, the nature of which determines the appropriate type of worship required. They are generally grouped in hierarchies, with some more powerful and authoritative than others. Prayers and sacrifices may be offered to them to avert their anger, earn their favour or influence them in a particular direction.

Goeteia, Mageia Words used by Greeks to indicate religious practices which they considered abnormal and, usually, reprehensible. Mageia derives from *magos*, the Persian word for a religious expert: this semantic development reveals the very common tendency to treat foreign religious practices as disreputable 'magic'. The 'goetic' and 'magical' rites that early Greeks were said to have performed included calming the winds and raising the dead. Another widespread practice, spoken of by Plato with strong disapproval, was that of depositing a lead figurine representing an enemy, often pierced with nails, in a tomb or well, along with a tablet urging Hermes of the underworld to 'bind' the victim. In the post-classical period evidence for 'magical' practices of all kinds, including love magic, becomes abundant. ▷ Greek religion; magic; Plato; underworld

Gog and Magog Biblical names, applied in different ways to depict future foes of the people of God. Ezekiel 38.2–6 predicted that a ruler (Gog) of the land or people from 'the north' (Magog) would battle against Israel in the days before her restoration. Revelation 20.8 and rabbinic literature treat Gog and Magog as paired figures representing Satan in the final conflict against God's people. In British folklore the names are given to the survivors of a race of giants annihilated by Brutus, the founder of Britain. ▷ Bible; Satan; rabbi

Golden Age The notion of an idyllic time of happiness, harmony and prosperity, usually in the distant past. In primal religions it is the *illud tempus*, the original sacred time before history, which was the example of what life would be like in this world if it were fully real. For the three main monotheistic religions, the notion of the Garden of Eden has supplied material for the myth of the Golden Age, and at a more historical level Christians have sometimes looked back to the time when Jesus was on earth, and Muslims to the time of Muhammad and the four early caliphs, as historical approximations to the Golden Age. Hesiod's *Works and Days*, written in the 8th century BCE, outlines the Greek version of the Golden Age as a time when humans, nature and the gods lived in harmony, peace and paradise. From Greece and Rome came the notion of the cycle of the ages, wherein the Golden Age was followed by a process of decline in the Silver, Copper and Iron Ages. After this cycle, the return of the Golden Age began the process again; this idea of four great ages was taken up by Indian thought. The concept of a future Golden Age—either one recoverable from the past or a completely new age—has also been present in some religious traditions. It is partly bound up with the idea of a future millennium at the end of this age, to be introduced by a figure-to-come: the Jewish Messiah, the Second Coming of Christ, the Muslim Mahdi, Maitreya Buddha, or the Kalkin avatara of Vishnu. The Hindu story of Rama describes Ramarajya, the kingdom of Rama, where humans and nature lived in harmony, and Gandhi's vision of independent India was that it would be like Ramarajya. This notion of the re-establishment of the Golden Age in the present has been a common theme from the Roman emperors, through the Medicis at the time of the Renaissance, to Gandhi himself. ▷ avatara; Eden, Garden of; Gandhi, Mohandas Karamchand; Mahdi; Maitreya; Marx, Karl; Messiah; Rama; Vishnu

golden calf An idolatrous image of worship, fashioned by Aaron and the Israelites at Sinai (Exodus 32), and destroyed by Moses. Two such figures were apparently set up later under Jeroboam I, first king of the northern kingdom of Israel, in competition with the worship of God in Jerusalem (1 Kings 12). ▷ Aaron; Moses; Sinai, Mount

Golden Rule The name given today to the saying of Jesus about one's duty to others: 'Whatever things you wish that people would do to you, do also yourselves similarly to them' (Matthew 7.12; Luke 6.31). Similar sayings can be traced in earlier Jewish and Greek ethical teaching. ▷ Jesus Christ; Sermon on the Mount

Golden Temple ▷ Harimandir

Golgotha ▷ Calvary

Goliath Biblical character described (in 1 Samuel 17) as a giant from Gath in the Philistine army who entered into single combat with the young David and was slain by a stone from David's sling, resulting in Israel's victory. Some confusion exists over a similar name in 2 Samuel 21.19 (also 1 Chronicles 20.5). ▷ David; Samuel, Books of

Good, the At one level the concept of the Good relates to ethical and moral systems that have been emphasized by different religious traditions, but at a deeper level it refers to the notion of the Good as either residing in God or as being a given element in life itself. Although not all notions of God regard God as being good in himself, ethical monotheism centred in the Judaeo-Christian tradition has evolved the notion that God is intrinsically good, whether he creates or not. Plato reflected on the idea of the good being good in itself, as well as being good for human beings, and this kind of thinking was developed further by Christian thinkers such as Augustine and Aquinas who saw being and goodness as intimately related. Thus evil had no ultimate power of its own, and could be seen only in negative terms. Clearly religious and philosophical systems that were dualistic gave less significance to the Good than those that were not. More humanistic systems, such as those of Hobbes, Hume and Russell, were not willing to centre the Good upon God, nor could they agree on the common qualities of the Good in separation from God. It was left to Immanuel Kant to link religion with the practice of morality, and to argue that the Good makes demands that are unconditional. ▷ Aquinas, St Thomas; Augustine, St (of Hippo); ethical monotheism; Hume, David; Kant, Immanuel; Plato; Russell, Bertrand Arthur William

Gorakhnath, (Gorakhnāth) (11th century) Founder of the Nath or Natha Yoga tradition of Hinduism. Gorakhnath's teacher (*guru*) was Matsyendranath, one of the famous 84 Siddhas or Perfected Ones of Hindu and Buddhist Tantra. Gorakhnath was a celibate ascetic and is said to have possessed magical powers (*siddhi*), which he acquired through the practice of yoga. Hatha Yoga or the yoga of 'force' practised by the Nath yogins is said to have been developed by Gorakhnath and a number of texts on this subject are attributed to him, such as the *Goraksha-Shataka* and the *Siddha-Siddhanata Paddhati*. This latter text, important in the Nath tradition, develops the idea that the body, which is the locus of liberation, contains an esoteric anatomy of various psychic centres (*cakras*) linked together by channels (*nadis*), through which flows energy or subtle breath (prana). Hatha Yoga controls and perfects the body, awakening the latent power or Kundalini energy within the body, which results in liberation in life (*jivanmukti*). ▷ cakras; guru; Hatha Yoga; Kundalini; Nath Yogis; prana

Gosala (c.6th century BCE) A contemporary of the Buddha and the leader of the Ajivika order of ascetics. No Ajivika texts have survived and we know of Gosala's doctrines only through the texts of his opponents, the Buddhists and Jains. Gosala taught a doctrine of determinism (*niyati*), denying causation and maintaining that events occur in a predetermined sequence against which human effort is ineffective. A soul passes through a cycle of 8400000 great ages (*mahakalpas*) incarnating in various life-forms until liberation spontaneously occurs in a human body at the end of this cycle. Gosala's determinism denied the doctrine of karma and causation which is at the heart of Buddhist teachings. ▷ Ajivika; Buddha; Jainism

Gospel criticism The modern study of the New Testament Gospels with respect to their sources and relationships to one another (source criticism), the early history and forms of the individual traditions about Jesus that the Gospels contain (form criticism), the editorial and creative contributions of the Gospel writers (redaction criticism), and the significance of the larger structures of the Gospel stories (literary and structuralist criticism). ▷ biblical criticism; form criticism; Gospels, canonical

Gospels, apocryphal Several writings from the early Christian era which are often somewhat similar to the canonical gospels in title, form, or content, but which have not been widely accepted as canonical themselves. They include popular infancy stories about Jesus (eg Infancy Gospel of Thomas, Protoevangelium of James), apocryphal accounts of Jesus's final suffering (Gospel of Peter, Gospel of Nicodemus), gnostic collections of sayings and stories (Gospel of Thomas, Gospel of Philip), and Judaeo-Christian works (Gospel of the Hebrews). Many are known from citations in the early Church fathers or from recent Nag Hammadi discoveries. ▷ Apocrypha, New Testament; Christianity; Gnosticism; Gospels, canonical; Nag Hammadi texts

Gospels, canonical Four books of the New Testament, known as the Gospels according to Matthew, Mark, Luke, and John; called 'gospels' by the 2nd-century Church (Greek *euangelion*, 'good news'), but not itself a recognized genre in earlier Greek literature. Each portrays a perspective on the ministry and teaching of Jesus of Nazareth, concluding with the account of his arrest, crucifixion, and resurrection. Three of the four (Matthew, Mark, Luke) are sufficiently close in wording and order to suggest a close literary interrelationship, but the precise solution to this relationship is much debated (the synoptic problem). John's Gospel is different in character, and raises questions about whether its author knew the other Gospels at all, even though it is frequently dated as the latest because of the extent of theological reflection. None of the writings actually states its author's name. ▷ Gospels, apocryphal; Jesus Christ; John/Luke/Mark/Matthew, Gospel according to; synoptic gospels

Govinda, Anagarika, originally E L Hoffman (1898–) Buddhist writer, born of Bolivian and German parents. He eventually took the Buddhist name of Lama Anagarika Govinda. After studying archaeology, architecture and philosophy in Europe, he became an artist for a time, but having developed an interest in burial mounds, he went on to further this interest in Ceylon in 1928, and in studying Buddhist stupas he became attracted to Buddhism. He was ordained as an anagarika in Theravada Buddhism, and pursued various studies in Pali. However, in 1931 he came into contact with Tibetan Buddhism and a Tibetan guru Tomo Geshe Rinpoche in Darjeeling in India, and when his guru died he set up the Arya Maitreya Mandala as a Buddhist layman's movement in his memory. During the 1930s and 1940s Govinda furthered his studies of Buddhism in Ladakh, Sikkim and Tibet, and in 1947 and 1949 he made two important journeys into Tibet, visiting the legendary Mount Kailash and two lost cities in the upper Sutlej valley. He described these visits in *The Way of the White Clouds*, and he later wrote his main work, *Foundations of Tibetan Mysticism*, in which for the first time he opened up for the wider world what it was like to be a Tibetan Buddhist practitioner. His writing was clear, fluent and artistic, and he was influential in Buddhist circles in Germany and elsewhere in the West, paving the way for the teaching of Tibetan Buddhist leaders who came to the West in the wake of the Dalai Lama's flight from Tibet in 1959. ▷ Dalai Lama; stupa; Theravada Buddhism; Tibetan religion; tulku

grace 1 In Christianity, the free and unmerited assistance or favour or energy or saving presence of God in his dealings with humankind through Jesus Christ. The term has been understood in various ways, eg as prevenient (leading to sanctification), or actual (prompting good actions). Sacraments are recognized as a 'means of grace', but the manner of their operation and the extent to which humans co-operate has been a subject of controversy. 2 A form of praise and thanksgiving to God, said, or sung, before meals in many Christian countries. ▷ Jesus Christ; Reformation; sacrament; Trent, Council of

gradual/sudden enlightenment schools of Buddhism These divisions arose within the Chan school of Buddhism in China, and the Zen school of Buddhism in Japan. In China the school of gradual enlightenment became associated with Shen Hsiu (c.600–702CE), a pupil of the fifth Chan patriarch Hung Jen, whereas the school of sudden enlightenment became associated with another pupil of Hung Jen named Hui Neng (638–713). The gradual enlightenment school stressed the need to develop a pure mind in place of a false one, and to work carefully towards the point of enlightenment, whereas the sudden enlightenment school did not make the distinction between pure and false mind, and sought a sudden awareness of enlightenment even by rejecting the study of scriptures (*sutras*), the use of ritual, and the reverencing of Buddha images. This distinction was carried over into Japanese Zen Buddhism where Dogen (1200–53) and the Soto Zen (gradual) school recognized the role of the reading of sutras, the veneration of images, and especially the practice of *zazen*, sitting upright with legs crossed in simple meditation, whereas Eisai (1141–1215) and the Rinzai Zen school emphasized the use of koans, paradoxical questions that can jerk the mind out of normal patterns of thought into sudden enlightenment. ▷ Buddha image; Chan; Dogen; Eisai; Hui Neng; koans; Rinzai; Soto; zazen; Zen Buddhism

Graham, Billy (William Franklin) (1918–) American evangelist, born in Charlotte, North Carolina. After studying at Florida Bible Institute (now Trinity College), 1938–40, he was ordained a minister of the Southern Baptist Church (1940). In 1943 he graduated in anthropology from Wheaton College, Illinois, and in the same year married Ruth Bell. He made his first high-profile preaching crusade in Los Angeles in 1949 and has since conducted his crusades on all continents, and has preached in the USSR and other East European countries. Through his crusades and the subsidiary ministries of broadcasting, films and the printed word it is claimed that millions have been won to Christianity. A charismatic figure who has been the friend and counsellor of many in high office, including Richard Nixon, Graham has consistently emerged from investigative reporting as a person of high integrity, and his Billy Graham Evangelistic Association as a model of financial accountability. His books include *Peace with God* (1952), *World Aflame* (1965), and *Angels* (1975). ▷ Baptists; evangelist

Grail, Holy, or Sangreal In the Arthurian legends, the dish used by Christ at the Last Supper. Joseph of Arimathea brought it to Glastonbury. It appeared at Pentecost at King Arthur's table, and the knights set out to find it; this diversion of energy into unworldly matters may have led to the break-up of the Round Table. The grail may have features of Celtic magic cauldrons, but the cult of relics is a better clue to its origins. ▷ Arthur; Jesus Christ; Pentecost

Granth Sahib ▷ Adi Granth

Great Awakening A widespread 18th-century Christian revival movement in the American colonies, which reached its high point in the 1740s in New England. An offshoot of the Evangelical and Pietist/Quietist movements in Europe, it was centred mainly among Presbyterians, Baptists, Congregationalists, and the Dutch Reformed Church. A movement with Calvinistic tendencies, it caused division within these denominations. Jonathan Edwards and George Whitefield were among its leaders. A less emotional Second Great Awakening took place in the 1790s, leading to the foundation of mission societies and the establishment of various educational institutions. The increased freedom of individual thought and the growth of religious democracy brought about by the movement has been seen as a forerunner of the inspiration behind the American Revolution. ▷ Christianity; Edwards, Jonathan; Revivalism; Whitefield, George

Great Schism, the (1378–1415) The period when there were two rival popes, beginning with the election of Urban VI and Clement VII by rival factions of cardinals. In 1409 the Council of Pisa attempted to end the schism and elected Alexander V, but unity was only finally achieved by the election of Martin V by the Council of Constance in 1417. ▷ Council of the Church

Greek Orthodox Church The self-governing ('autocephalous') Orthodox Church of Greece. After the schism of 1054, the Orthodox Church in Greece remained under the patriarch of Constantinople, but was declared independent in 1833. The governing body is the Holy Synod, which comprises 67 metropolitan bishops, presided over by the archbishop of all Greece in the head see of Athens. In doctrine, it shares the beliefs of Orthodox Churches, and in worship uses the Byzantine liturgy. There is a strong monastic movement, still maintained in 150 monasteries. ▷ Christianity; liturgy; monasticism; Orthodox Church; patriarch

Greek Orthodox abbot

Greek religion The religion of the Ancient Greeks was polytheistic, as were earlier systems of belief in the Near East. The gods each had a sphere of influence (eg Poseidon over the sea) or an attachment to a locality (eg Athena at Athens); often both. Though mythologists try to systematize the relationships between the gods, it is unwise to take their tidying-up too seriously. It is doubtful whether the average Greek knew more than is contained in Homer. Besides the 12 major Olympian gods, there were later introductions of 'Oriental' deities, especially female, such as Cybele and Isis, who acquired great influence. The Homeric gods are very human in their passions and spiteful jealousies; the main difference is that they do not eat human food, and they do not die. They shade into a lower group of demi-gods and heroes, special people whose cults centred round their tombs. In the cults, ritual and sacrifice were important duties, in return for which the suppliant expected benefits. The system had to be seen to work, as in the case of the oracle at Delphi. In the 5th century the whole basis of religion was challenged by the Sophists, and the weakening of supernatural belief reinforced Greek humanism. Yet, at the same time, the Eleusinian and Orphic mystery cults began to grow; though highly secret, they were concerned with personal survival after death. Finally, after Alexander the Great had himself proclaimed as a god, the way was open to the ruler-cults of the Roman Empire. ▷ Homeric pantheon; Olympian pantheon; oracle; Roman religion

Greek religion and ethics Greek religion had no Ten Commandments and no sermons.

The gods of myth too, easy-going adulterers, scarcely provided moral 'role-models' in many spheres. Nonetheless, the gods oversaw various aspects of social relations such as the rules of burial and supplication. Above all, they were invoked in oaths; and oaths were taken in so many contexts in Greece that the gods were involved in most transactions where questions of justice arose. Philosophical critics of Greek religion found it morally inadequate, but the poet Sophocles was closer to popular assumptions in seeing religious belief as the foundation of social morality. ▷ Greek religion

Greek religion and philosophy In traditional belief, the gods often manifested their powers by breaking or distorting the order of nature: by sending an earthquake, for instance, as a 'sign' to man. Pre-Socratic philosophers insisted that there were no such exceptions to natural laws. This did not mean that they were atheists, indeed they often seem to have regarded natural principles as in some sense 'divine', an attitude most clearly expressed in the ideas of Anaxagoras (5th century BCE) that the regularity of the cosmic order is the work not of chance but of Mind. Traditionalists were, therefore, in part wrong to suspect philosophers, as a class, of impiety; it was, however, true that the 'god of the philosophers' was very different from that of mythology, as we see for instance from a famous attack by Xenophanes (c.500BCE) on anthropomorphism: 'if oxen and horses and lions had hands and were able to paint or sculpt like men, horses would paint the forms and shape the bodies of gods like horses', oxen like oxen's, each portraying the form they themselves have'. In reality, according to Xenophanes, God is a single, disembodied mind. ▷ Greek religion; pre-Socratic philosophy

Greek religious institutions In an important sense, there were no Greek religious institutions. There was no organized church; priests and priestesses received no training, normally only performed religious duties part-time, and did not form a coherent network that could propagate an orthodoxy or develop any important religious policy. The most influential religious institution was the Delphic oracle (states wishing to make amendments to their religious practices, for instance, regularly sought its sanction), but the veneration it drew attached to Apollo, the god who was believed to speak through it, not to the Delphic priesthood. No mortal could be said to exercise religious power. In another sense, Greek religious institutions were a subdivision of secular institutions. Religious decisions were taken by the same bodies that took political decisions (at Athens, by the democratic assembly); temples were paid for out of public funds; and priests were in effect state employees. 'Church' and 'state' were one. ▷ Greek religion

Green Corn Festival A major agricultural festival among the Amerindians of the north-east. The ceremony, lasting three or more days, was usually held in August with the ripening of the first corn, and took place in the Longhouse with prayers of thanksgiving, dancing, and a feast. ▷ Native American religions

Gregory I, the Great, St (c.540–604) Pope (590), a Father of the Church. Born in Rome, he was appointed Praetor of Rome by Justin II, but about 575 relinquished this office. He distributed his wealth among the poor and withdrew into a monastery at Rome, one of seven he had founded. It was while he was here that he saw one day some Anglo-Saxon youths in the slave-market, and was seized with a longing to convert their country to Christianity. He set out on his journey but Pope Benedict compelled him to return due to his popularity. Pelagius II sent Gregory as nuncio to Constantinople for aid against the Lombards. He stayed there three years, writing his *Moralia*, an exposition of Job. On the death of Pelagius Gregory was unanimously called by the clergy, senate, and people to succeed him. He tried to evade the dignity, but was forced to give in.

It is doubtful whether any pope has surpassed Gregory I as an administrator. The Roman Church is indebted to him for the complete organization of their public services and ritual and for the systematization of her sacred chants. The mission to England he entrusted to Augustine and the Gothic kingdom of Spain, long Arian, was reconciled with the Church. His zeal for the reformation of the Church was not inferior to his ardour for its growth. Towards 'heathens' and Jews he was most tolerant, and he used all his efforts to repress slave-dealing and to mitigate slavery. When Rome was threatened by the Lombards, he showed himself virtually a temporal sovereign; he rejected the assumption by John, Patriarch of Constantinople, of the title of ecumenical or universal bishop. In his writings the whole dogmatical system of the modern church is fully developed. He left homilies on Ezekiel and on the Gospels, the *Regula* (or *Cura Pastoralis*), and the *Sacramentarium* and *Antiphonarium*. In exegesis he is a fearless allegorist; his Letters and Dialogues abound with miraculous and legendary narratives. His feast day is 12 March. ▷ Augustine, St

Gregory VII, St, originally **Hildebrand** (c.1020–1085) Pope (1073), the great representative of the temporal claims of the medieval papacy. Born near Soana in Tuscany, his original name was Hildebrand. He passed his youth in Rome, in the monastery of St Maria. On the death of Gregory VI, whose chaplain he was, he is reported (doubtfully) to have spent some time at Cluny, from where he was recalled by the new and zealous Pope Leo IX, whom he accompanied to Rome in 1049, and who made him a cardinal. During the following four pontificates Hildebrand continued to exercise great influence and was himself elected pope three days after the death of Alexander II.

He addressed himself to amending the secularized condition of the Church. The feudal standing of the higher clergy, the claims of sovereigns upon temporalities, and the consequent temptation to simony were, he held, the cause of all the evils present in Europe. While he tried to enforce all the details of discipline, it was against investiture that his main efforts were directed. In 1074 he prohibited this practice, under pain of excommunication, and in 1075 he actually issued that sentence against several bishops and councillors of the empire. The emperor Henry IV, disregarding these menaces, was cited to Rome to answer for his conduct. Henry's sole reply was defiance and in a diet at Worms in 1076 he declared Gregory deposed. The pontiff retaliated by excommunication, which, unless removed by absolution in 12 months, involved (according also to imperial law) the forfeiture of all civil rights and deposition from every civil and political office. Henry's Saxon subjects, appealing over this law against him, compelled him to yield, and by a humiliating penance at Canossa in January 1077 he obtained absolution from the pope in person. But in 1080 Henry resumed hostilities, again declaring Gregory deposed, and appointed an antipope as Clement III. After a siege of three years, Henry took possession of Rome in 1084. However, just as Gregory was on the point of falling into his hands, Robert Guiscard, the Norman Duke of Apulia, entered the city, set Gregory free, and compelled Henry to return to Germany. But the wretched condition to which Rome was reduced obliged Gregory to withdraw ultimately to Salerno, where he died. His feast day is 25 May. ▷ antipope; papacy; Roman Catholicism

Gregory of Nazianzus, St (c.330–c.389) Greek prelate and theologian, born in Cappadocia. Educated at Caesarea, Alexandria and Athens, he became a close friend of Basil the Great, and was made bishop of Sasima, but withdrew to a life of religious study at Nazianzus near his birthplace. The emperor Theodosius I, the Great, made him patriarch of Constantinople (380), but he resigned from the post in 381. His theological works were largely concerned with upholding Nicene orthodoxy, and include discourses, letters and hymns.

Gregory of Nyssa (331–95) Christian theologian. By his brother St Basil the Great he was consecrated Bishop of Nyssa in Cappadocia about 371. During the persecution of the adherents of the Nicene Creed in the reign of Valens, Gregory was deposed, but on the death of Valens was welcomed back (378). He was present at the Council of Constantinople in 381, and was appointed to share in the oversight of the diocese of Pontus. He travelled to Arabia and Jerusalem to set in order the churches there, and was again at a synod in Constantinople in 394. His chief works are his *Twelve Books against Eunomius*, a treatise on the Trinity, several ascetic treatises, many sermons, 23 epistles, and his great *Cathechetical Oration* (1903). ▷ Basil, St; Nicene Creed

Grubb, Sir Kenneth George (1900–80) English missionary, ecumenist, and Anglican lay churchman, born in Oxton, Nottinghamshire. Following extensive research on religious and social conditions in South America in the 1930s and wartime service with the Ministry of Information, he became President of the Church Missionary Society (1944–69), Chairman of the Churches Committee on International Affairs (1946–68), and Chairman of the House of Laity in the Church Assembly (1959–70). Author of several studies on South America and successive editions of the *World Christian Handbook* (1949–68), he revealed his waspish assessments of himself and others in *A Layman Looks at the Church* (1964) and his autobiography *Crypts of Power* (1971). ▷ Anglican Communion; ecumenism

guardian spirits Belief in guardian spirits is widespread, being found from the South Pacific to Sub-Arctic Siberia. The term may refer either to beneficent, incorporeal beings or to embodied spirits possessing divine potency such as the *kami* of Japanese Shintoism. Both have the capacity to protect and preserve an individual's well-being, bringing luck, good-health, fertility, protection from

guardian spirit from the entrance to the Toshugu Shrine in Nikko, Japan

danger, spiritual power and the fulfilment of human desires. Guardian spirits are often associated with a specific place, traditionally dwelling in sacred places where shrines may be erected in their honour and religious rites performed. Alternatively they might be evoked through ecstatic shamanistic trances. Examples of the former include early Japanese religious rituals in which the spirits of sacred rocks, paddy-fields and the sea-shore were venerated and indigenous Javanese beliefs and rites concerning guardian spirits who oversee places such as caves, old wells and public buildings. As a consequence of the syncretism of Buddhism and Shintoism from the 9th century CE, some Shinto kami came to be regarded as guardians of the Buddha, and are sometimes referred to as bodhisattvas. Shamanistic activity on the other hand involves the religious practitioner or shaman making direct contact with the spirit world and evoking his/her personal guardian spirit helper through dreams and visions brought about by fasting and other austerities. The guardian spirit thus invoked is controlled by the shaman and assists him/her in the quest for spiritual power and the powers of healing. The best examples of this are from North American Indian culture in the idea of the vision quest, where a youth receives his own personal guardian spirit, usually in animal or bird form, who will then teach him and bestow power. Japanese folk religion acknowledges guardian spirits which speak through a shaman while she (Japanese shamanism is practised almost exclusively by women) is in a trance.

Guardian spirits are also found in other cultures and traditions. Early Icelandic literature, for example, speaks of a 'shape' (*fylgja*) which accompanied a man through the world: a kind of external soul, often in animal form. ▷ bodhisattva; Buddhism; fylgja; Japanese religions; kami; Native American religions; shamanism; Shinto; vision quest

guna (guṇa) A quality or modality in subjective, psychological conditions or objective cosmological states in Hindu philosophy, particularly Samkhya. There are three gunas: *sattva*, the quality of light and goodness, *rajas*, the quality of passion and energy, and *tamas*, the quality of darkness and inertia. According to Samkhya the gunas exist unmanifested and perfectly balanced in the primary substance or matter (*prakriti*) of the cosmos. When prakriti evolves, the gunas control the evolutes or categories (*tattvas*) from prakriti, of subjective experience and the objective universe. Thus different states of being, both subjectively and in the objective world, have different gunas predominating. A person, for example, can be of a sattvic, rajasic or tamasic disposition depending upon the predominant guna. Even food is classified according to this system, so, for example, garlic is rajasic or passionate and so avoided by Brahmans, whereas milk is sattvic. The gunas are associated with the colours white (sattva), red (rajas) and black (tamas). ▷ Samkhya

Gurdas, Bhai (Gurdās, Bhaī) (1551–1637) Early Sikh commentator and theologian, born in Goindwal in the Punjab, India. The nephew of the third Sikh guru, Guru Amar Das, he was an important interpreter of the sayings of the early Sikh gurus. He assisted the fifth guru, Guru Arjan, in compiling the Sikh scripture, the *Adi Granth*, and after the martyrdom of Guru Arjan and the detention of Guru Hargobind he was a key leader of the Sikh community during a difficult period. He wrote 39 passages, known as *vars*, that are venerated among Sikhs as an important source for understanding the historical and theological roots of the early Sikh tradition. Second to the canonical works of Sikh scripture, his writings are of deep significance among Sikhs, not only historically but for their own self-understanding. ▷ Adi Granth; Amar Das, Guru; Arjan, Guru; Hargobind, Guru

Gurdjieff, Georgei Ivanovitch (1874–1949) Spiritual leader, born in Alexandropol, Armenia. He became an unconventional teacher, feeding into many new currents of human potential thought during this century. He travelled in Central Asia and Tibet and taught in Russia before setting up an Institute for the Harmonious Development of Man at Fontainebleau, France, in 1922. He claimed to derive his teaching from hidden masters in Central Asia and was influenced by elements of Buddhism and Kabbalah. He aimed, through music, callisthenics and mystical philosophy, to guide his followers to higher levels of consciousness. He argued that most people are not truly alive, but act according to habit, and that the three things that guide them (thinking, feeling and moving) are out of harmony. This condition, resulting in underachievement and being 'asleep', can be changed by Gurdjieff's system of exercises and other practices that release the human potential that is available but untapped in everyone. He had an important associate in P D Ouspensky (1878–1947), and when he died his work was continued by such bodies as the Gurdjieff Foundation in New York. He has become a vibrant symbol in parts of the human potential movement and in elements of new age religion. ▷ Human Potential movement; new religious movements in the West

gurdwara (gurdwārā) (Sanskrit, 'guru's door') A Sikh temple, or any place where the scripture is installed. In addition to a worship area housing the scripture, it should include a hostel and a place for serving meals. ▷ Adi Granth; Sikhism

Gurmat A Sikh term, meaning 'the teachings of the Guru', often used by Sikhs as an equivalent for 'Sikhism'. Its scriptural source is the teachings of Guru Nanak and the other Sikh gurus, as found in the scripture, the *Guru Granth Sahib*. These teachings include the doctrines of God, of creation, of God's grace, of moral living, and of invoking the presence of God. Later tradition extended the orbit of the Gurmat to include Guru Gobind Singh's stress upon initiation into the Sikh *Khalsa*, with its external symbols such as the five Ks, and to include the rule of life found in the Code of Discipline, the *Rahit Maryada*. As a sort of synonym for Sikhism, Gurmat has become wider than 'teachings', and includes elements such as ethics, social involvement, and spirituality that are to be found in any model of religion. ▷ Adi Granth; five Ks; models of religion; Nanak; Rahit Maryada; Sikhism

Gurpurab Sikh festivals commemorating events associated with key happenings in the life of a Sikh guru. The three main ones are the birthday of the first guru, Guru Nanak (15 April), the birthday of the tenth guru, Guru Gobind Singh (22 December), and the martyrdom of the fifth guru, Guru Arjan (30 May). Others include the anniversary of the deaths of the sons of Guru Gobind Singh, and the anniversary of the installation of the *Adi Granth* in 1604. Other significant Sikh festivals include Baisakhi, Divali, and Hola Mahalla which are Hindu festivals adapted to Sikh usage. During these festivals (if they occur in a major Sikh centre) the scripture, the *Guru Granth Sahib*, is paraded ceremonially in an ordered procession, and afterwards it is read for 48 hours in an *Akhand Path* (uninterrupted reading). A shared meal, Langar, will often take place at the conclusion of a festival as a symbol of the importance attached to social matters in the Sikh tradition. ▷ Akhand Path; Arjan, Guru; Baisakhi; Divali/Deepavali; Gobind Singh, Guru; Guru Granth Sahib; Langar; Nanak

guru (gurū) A teacher of religious knowledge and/or the conveyor of spiritual power and liberation (*moksha*) in Hinduism. Hinduism does not have a centralized authority; instead religious knowledge and texts have been passed down orally through lines of transmission (*parampara*, *sampradaya*, *santana*) from guru to disciple. According to the Hindu theoretical model, a high caste ('twice-born') boy would learn the Veda from a guru for about 12 years, after his Vedic initiation (*upanaya*), before becoming a householder. In some Hindu traditions, such as Tantra, the guru is more than merely a teacher of texts, but is a *jivanmukti*, liberated whilst alive, and able to convey spiritual power (*siddhi*) and liberation to those whom he initiates. Such a teacher is a 'true' or *sat guru*, taking his disciples' karma upon himself and ensuring their liberation in this life or within a few lifetimes. In dualist traditions, such as the Hare Krishna movement, the guru is not identical with the absolute but still has the power to initiate through God's grace. In the Shaiva Siddhanta, Shiva temporarily takes possession of the guru for the purposes of initiation only. There are many gurus in India, treated with great reverence, such as Sai Baba, who have attracted a large following both in India and in the West. Indeed many lines of guru transmission are now carried on in the West. ▷ caste; Hare Krishna movement; jivanmukti; moksha; Shaiva Siddhanta; Veda

guru, Sikh (gurū) The notion of guru has been important for Sikhs in two ways. Firstly it represents the inner guiding voice and presence of God. Guru Nanak taught this basic truth and was taken to be a human channel for the Guruhood, and it was for this reason that he was given the title of Guru. The spirit and title of guru were inherited from Guru Nanak by nine successive gurus: Angad, Amar Das, Ram Das, Arjan, Hargobind, Hari Rai, Hari Krishna, Tegh Bahadur, and Gobind Singh. With the death of the tenth guru, Guru Gobind Singh, the succession of human gurus ended and the indwelling guru became present in the Sikh scripture, the *Adi Granth*, which became known as the *Guru Granth Sahib*, and secondarily in the Sikh community, the *Guru Panth*. The *Guru Granth Sahib* is treated as though it were a human guru. ▷ Adi Granth; Amar Das, Guru; Angad, Guru; Arjan, Guru; Gobind Singh, Guru; Guru Granth Sahib; Hargobind, Guru; Nanak; Tegh Bahadur, Guru

Guru Granth Sahib (Gurū Granth Sāhib) The main Sikh scripture and the key contemporary mediating symbol for the Sikh tradition. It became known by this name in 1708 when the death of Guru Gobind Singh, the tenth Sikh guru, signalled the end of the succession of personal gurus, but it was originally compiled as the *Adi Granth*, the First Book, by Guru Arjan in 1604. Its contents are the poems and hymns of Guru Arjan, of the four gurus who preceded him, and of Sant writers such as Kabir, Farid, Namdev, and Ravidas. Written in the Gurmukhi script in a form of early Hindi, it has a consistency of arrangement according to author, form, and metre. It is deeply revered as though it were a human guru by being taken from its resting place, carried in a procession to its canopy, installed there, and wafted with a ceremonial fan. Worshippers prostrate themselves in front of it, before returning it to rest. Installed in every Sikh temple as a focus of attention and authority, it is constantly referred to for advice, and is often read aloud, either in part or during an uninterrupted 48-hour reading called an *akhand path*. ▷ Adi Granth; akhand path; Arjan, Guru; Gobind Singh, Guru; Gurdwara; guru, Sikh; Kabir; Sant tradition

Gutiérrez, Gustavo (1928–) Peruvian liberation theologian, born in Lima. Abandoning medical studies for the Roman Catholic priesthood, he studied philosophy and psychology at Louvain (1951–5) and theology at Lyon (1955–9) before ordination in Lima, becoming Professor of Theology at the Catholic university there in 1960. His seminal and classic *A Theology of Liberation* (1971, English trans, 1973, revised 1988) is dedicated to 'doing' theology. This is defined as 'critical reflection on historical praxis', and is based on responding to the needs of the poor and oppressed rather than on imposing solutions from the outside. This has challenged supporters of the status quo in Latin America and practitioners of academic theology elsewhere. He explores the biblical and spiritual roots of liberation theology more deeply in *The Power of the Poor in History* (1984), *We Drink from Our Own Wells* (1984), and *On Job* (1987). ▷ liberation theology; Roman Catholicism

H

Habakkuk, or **Habacuc, Book of** One of the 12 so-called 'minor' prophetic books of the Hebrew Bible/Old Testament, attributed to the otherwise unknown prophet Habakkuk, possibly of the late 7th century BCE. It consists of two dialogues about why God allows the godless to 'surround' the righteous (Israel), with the response that 'the just shall live by his faith' (Habakkuk 2.4; Romans 1.17; Galatians 3.11). The final prayer celebrates God's coming in victory over his enemies. ▷ Old Testament; prophet

Hachiman An important *kami* (sacred power) within the Japanese Shinto tradition. He began as the kami of farmers and fishermen, and the first shrine built to him was at Usa on the west coast of Japan. Later he became associated with military matters and became known as the god of war. In addition to this, from the 8th century he was also known as a Buddhist bodhisattva, as the Shinto and Buddhist traditions grew closer together, eventually being seen as the protector of Buddhism. This was a precedent for the coming together of Shinto kami and Buddhist divinities in the syncretistic movement known as Ryobu Shinto. It is estimated that over a third of Shinto shrines are dedicated to Hachiman, who remains one of the most popular Shinto deities. ▷ bodhisattva; kami; Ryobu Shinto

Hades In Greek mythology the king of the Underworld, terrible but just. He was responsible for the seizure of Persephone. To the Greeks Hades was always a person, never a place, but by transference the Underworld—'the house of Hades'—became known by that name (which means 'the unseen'). It is located below the earth or in the Far West; there the feeble spirits of the dead continue to exist. ▷ Greek religion; underworld

Hadith (Ḥadīth) Islamic tradition on a variety of subjects, traced to the prophet Muhammad or one of his companions. It provides guidance for Muslims on all aspects of life, and is second in authority to the Quran. The teachings are prefaced by a chain of authorities through whom the tradition is said to have been transmitted and validated. ▷ Islam; Muhammad; Quran

Hadrian IV ▷ **Adrian IV**

Hagar Biblical character, the maid of Sarah (the wife of Abraham). Due to Sarah's barrenness, Abraham had a son Ishmael by Hagar (Genesis 16), but Hagar and her son were later expelled into the wilderness by Abraham after Isaac's birth (Genesis 21). ▷ Abraham; Bible; Isaac; Ishmael; Sarah

Haggadah (biblical) ▷ see **Aggadah**

Haggadah, or **Passover Haggadah** The title given to the liturgical text used during the *seder* or order of service for the eve of Passover; it consists of scriptural and other excerpts along with blessings and prayers. With the fall of Jerusalem in 70CE the focus of Passover celebrations shifted from the Temple to the home. Thus in traditional Jewish households the family sits around the table for the duration of the seder, including the Passover meal and recitation of the Haggadah. The Haggadah describes the slavery of the Israelites in Egypt and praises God for their redemption; it used to offer thanks for the gift of the promised land, but since 70CE this has been replaced by a petition for the advent of the final redemption. The Haggadah takes the form of a commentary on the summary of events in Deuteronomy 26.5–8, and responds to four set questions posed by the youngest present, beginning with 'How is this night different from all other nights?' Over the centuries many editions of the Haggadah have been produced, including some especially beautiful illuminated manuscripts from the 13th to 15th centuries. ▷ Aggadah; hagim; Passover; siddur; worship, Jewish

Haggai, Book of One of the 12 so-called 'minor' prophetic books of the Hebrew Bible/Old Testament, attributed to the prophet Haggai, a contemporary of Zechariah. Both supported the rebuilding of the Temple in Jerusalem in c.520BCE after the return from exile. It consists of exhortations to the governor and high priest in Judaea to pursue the rebuilding of the Temple, and to purify the Temple cult as preparations for God's new kingdom. ▷ Old Testament; Temple, Jerusalem; Zechariah, Book of

Hagia Sophia, or Santa Sophia A masterpiece of Byzantine architecture built (532–7) at Constantinople (now Istanbul). The lavishly-decorated, domed basilica was commissioned by Emperor Justinian I and designed by Anthemius of Tralles and Isidore of Miletus. The Ottoman Turks, who took Constantinople in 1453, converted it into a mosque. Since 1935 it has been a museum. ▷ art, Islamic; architecture, Islamic

hagim, or chagim The festivals or hagim (singular 'hag') in the Jewish year mark out times of religious significance. The three great pilgrim festivals are Pesach (or Passover), Shavuot (Weeks), and Sukkot (Tabernacles). The Bible stipulates that male Jews go to Jerusalem for ritual celebrations at these times, which were originally agicultural feasts. Pesach on 15–22 Nisan mixes two such occasions, but is also given a specifically historical-religious significance in commemorating God's redemption of Israel from Egypt. Until the destruction of the Temple in 70CE the slaughter of a lamb, eaten with bitter herbs and unleavened bread, was central. Since then the focus has shifted to the home and no lamb is consumed; an order of service or *seder* is centred on the family table incorporating the Haggadah (liturgical retelling of the exodus events). Seven weeks later comes Shavuot (literally 'weeks') or Pentecost on 6 Sivan. It became associated in post-biblical times with Moses's reception of Torah on Sinai (see Exodus 19.1). Thus the Ten Commandments (Exodus 20) and the Book of Ruth are read. Sukkot falls on 15–22 Tishri and retains more agricultural characteristics than Pesach and Shavuot. Families spend time in *sukkot* or booths, and palm branches with willow, myrtle and citrons are used in procession. Sukkot is connected with God's protection of the Israelites in the wilderness when they dwelt in booths (see Leviticus 23.43). Also, coming at the end of the harvest, it reminds the community of its dependence on God, and so Ecclesiastes is read.

Finally, two minor festivals should be mentioned. Hanukkah or Chanukkah ('dedication') on 25 Kislev celebrates Judas Maccabeus's restoration of the Temple in 164BCE (see 1 Maccabees 4.52–9). Similarly, Purim (literally 'lots') on 14 Adar commemorates Esther's victory over Haman, as recounted in the Book of Esther. ▷ calendar, Jewish; fasts, Jewish; Pentecost; Shavuot; Simkhat Torah; Sukkot

Haile Selassie (1891–1975) Emperor of Ethiopia from 1930, previously Prince Ras Tafari, son of Ras Makonnen. He led the revolution in 1916 against Lij Yasu and became regent and heir to the throne. He Westernized the institutions of his country. He settled in England after the Italian conquest of Abyssinia (1935–6), but in 1941 was restored after the liberation by British forces. In the early 1960s he played a crucial part in the establishment of the Organisation of African Unity (OAU). Opposition to his reign had existed since 1960, and the disastrous famine of 1973 led to economic chaos, industrial strikes and mutiny among the armed forces, and the emperor was deposed in 1974 in favour of the Crown Prince, though he was allowed to return to his palace at Addis Ababa. Accusations of corruption levelled against him and his family have not destroyed the unique prestige and reverence in which he is held by certain groups, notably the Rastafarians.

Hail Mary (Latin *Ave Maria*) A prayer to the Virgin Mary, also known as the Angelic Salutation, used devotionally since the 11th century in the Roman Catholic Church, and finally officially recognized in 1568. The first two parts are quotations from scripture (Luke 1.28, 42), the third part having been added later. In its Latin form it is often sung in Roman Catholic ceremonies, and has received many famous musical settings. ▷ Mary; liturgy; rosary

Hajj A formal pilgrimage to the holy city of Mecca during the Islamic month of Dhu-ul-Hijja. It is one of the five pillars of Islam. ▷ five pillars, Islamic; Islam; Mecca; pilgrimage

Halakhah The complete body of laws and decrees contained in the Talmudic and Rabbinic literature of Judaism, which governs religious or civil practice in the Jewish community. It is distinguished from the *Aggadah*, which is not concerned with religious law, and which includes such material as parables, fables, sagas, and prayers. Halakhah's origins are said to be the revelation to Moses on Mount Sinai. In more recent times rabbis have had to modify or adapt these laws to suit modern life. Reform Jews often ignore Halakhah's edicts. ▷ Judaism; midrash; Moses; Sinai, Mount; Talmud

Halevi, Jehuda (1075–1141) Spanish Jewish poet, philosopher and a prominent physician, born in Toledo. His experience of anti-Semitism in Cordoba led him to expound and celebrate the superiority of Judaism against Aristotle's philosophy, Christianity and Islam, in various highly-wrought prose and poetic works. He encouraged a vision of the Jewish people and the land of Israel which has endeared him to modern Zionists. His main philosophical work (in Arabic) is the *Book of the Khazars* (in full, the 'Book of Argument and Proof in Defence of the Despised Faith'), and there is a collection of his poems entitled *Diwan*, including *Zionide* ('Ode to Zion'), the most widely translated Hebrew poem of the middle ages. He reputedly died in Egypt on his way to Jerusalem. ▷ anti-Semitism; Aristotle; Christianity; Islam; Judaism; Zionism

Hallaj, al- (al-Ḥallāj, Ḥusayn ibn Manṣūr) (857–922) Muslim Sufi mystic, born in Tus, Persia. A cotton-carder by trade, he became well-known as a disentangler of consciences. He gained a reputation both as a saint and as a miracle-worker, and a book of poetry and a book of anecdotes have been attributed to him. He travelled widely in India, Persia and Turkestan, stressing the deep spiritual relationship that human beings can have with God. This bond is centred in love, entails suffering, and produces a deep joy. Some of his utterances seemed to remove the difference between human beings and God, a famous example being his statement 'I am the Truth', an affirmation which was considered heretical because it appeared to associate him with God. This was one reason for his brutal execution. He gained a reputation as the first Sufi martyr, as a saint, and as a poet among later Sufis. Some Christian scholars saw in his crucifixion echoes of Christ's death. ▷ Jesus Christ; Sufism

Hallowe'en A Christian and pagan festival, held on the evening of 31 October, when spirits of the dead are supposed to return to their former homes, and witches and demons are thought to be abroad at night. This was the last day of the Celtic and Anglo-Saxon year, and many Hallowe'en customs have their origin in pagan ceremonies. On Hallowe'en, children in some parts of the UK dress up, especially as witches or ghosts, and go from door to door offering short entertainments in return for presents; similarly, in the USA, children go around demanding 'trick or treat'—if no 'treat' or present is forthcoming, a trick or practical joke will be played on the householder.

Ham Biblical character, one of Noah's three sons, the brother of Shem and Japheth, and father of Canaan. He is described as helping Noah to build the ark, but after the Flood his son Canaan is cursed by God for Ham's apparent sin of having seen 'the nakedness of his father' Noah (Genesis 9.22). This curse may be an attempt to explain the later subjugation of the Canaanites to Israel as resulting from Canaanite sexual perversion. ▷ Bible; Canaan; Flood, the; Noah

Hammurabi (18th century BCE) Amorite King of Babylon (c.1792–1750BCE), best-known for his Code of Laws. He is also famous for his military conquests, which made Babylon the greatest power in Mesopotamia. ▷ Babylonian religion

Hanafi (Ḥanafī) An Islamic school of law founded by Abu Hanifah. It is a dominant legal force in India and in the area formerly dominated by the Turkish empire; today it has the largest following among the four Sunni schools of law within the Muslim world. The Hanafi school recognizes the other three Sunni schools as orthodox: the Hanbali school founded by ibn Hanbal (780–855), the Maliki school founded by Malik ibn Anas (716–95), and the Shafii school founded by al-Shafii (767–820). However, Muslims are expected to belong to one school and to adhere to its way. The Hanafi school has a more literal and formal method than the others, but it also allows for broad interpretations by its use of legal stratagems to circumvent the positive provisions of the law. ▷ Abu Hanifah; fiqh; Shafii, al-

hands in religion The importance of the hands in virtually every action which we perform has led to them becoming a universal symbol, with a plethora of associations, in every major religious tradition. In the scriptures of Judaism, Christianity and Islam the symbol of God's hand is used to depict God's power over his creation. God's hand stretches out to provide blessing and protection and to exercise judgement. In Hindu temples images of the deity have many arms and hands symbolizing power and competence. In Hindu teaching various parts of the hand are designated sacred to different forms of Vishnu.

Hands also feature prominently in the many acts of religious devotion. Hands are used in prayer and supplication, either outstretched or clasped. A priest may raise his hands over the congregation to bless them. In Hindu and Buddhist traditions the *mudras* are a series of ritual hand gestures which constitute a sacred hand language. Hands also function as transmitters of divine power. They are placed on an individual to bestow a blessing or to heal. In the Christian tradition the laying on of hands is used to consecrate and ordain people for service in the Church. Washing of the hands is an important symbol of cleansing from sin in many traditions, although due to the influence of the actions of Pilate, within Christian culture it has come to signify an abdication of responsibility (Matthew 27.24). To this day the raising of one's hand in allegiance, or the touching of a sacred object, signifies fidelity and truth. ▷ mudras; Vishnu

Handsome Lake (Ganioda'yo) (1735–1815) Amerindian prophet from Seneca. He had shared the demoralization of many Iroquois in contact with Western culture, and became an alcoholic. He had also known Christian (especially Quaker) influences. In 1799, during a dangerous illness, he had a vision of three messengers of the Great Spirit who healed him and called him to reform the life of his people. His remaining 15 years saw a great measure of reformation. He recalled his people to the 'old way', which he reinterpreted by means of Christian teaching. He remodelled traditional Iroquois dualism (based on the contrasting hero twins) by understanding it in terms of the conflict of God and the devil. His religion stressed prayer and devotion to the Great Spirit Haweniyo, accompanied by a strict moral code. Activities associated with the 'evil' twin Tawiskaron were banned as works of the devil (Haninseono) or diluted into purely social events. With less permanent success, he attacked the secret societies (which met at night, Tawiskaron's time). By transforming it, Handsome Lake enabled Iroquois traditional religion to survive; it is still served by preachers of his code. ▷ Iroquois religion

Hanukkah, or **Chanukah** An annual Jewish festival held in December (begins 25 Kislev), commemorating the rededication of the Temple at Jerusalem after the victory of Judas Maccabaeus over the Syrians in 165BCE (1st Book of Maccabees); also known as the Feast of Dedication or Feast of Lights (candles being lit on each of the eight days of the festival). ▷ Maccabees

Hanuman (Hanumān) The monkey-god of the Ramayana epic, who is the courageous and loyal supporter of Rama. A popular Hindu deity, he is represented as half-human and half-monkey. ▷ Hinduism; Rama; Ramayana

haoma The Avestan word means 'that which is pressed' and denoted a plant which was highly prized by the ancient Iranians. The identity of the original *haoma* plant is unknown, but like the plant now known in Iran as *hōm*, it may have been a species of ephedra. Its juice had a stimulating effect,

Hanuman

giving inspiration to poets and visionaries, and valour and strength to warriors. Haoma (Old Indian *Soma*) played an important role in the sacrificial ritual of the ancient Indians and Iranians: the preparation, consecration and ritual consumption of haoma juice are essential elements of the Zoroastrian *yasna* ritual, and the same was true of its Old Indian counterpart, the *yajña*. The ritual function of the plant led to the concept of a personalized divinity Haoma, invoked as a healer and protector, and to ward off drought and famine. ▷ Zoroastrianism

harae The ritual of purification used in Japanese Shinto. It is the most venerable of Shinto rituals, occurring first in the 8th-century Shinto chronicles, where the *kami* Izanagi purifies himself by washing in a river after entanglements with evil spirits. At the most basic level purification is used when entering a temple, by washing one's hands and rinsing one's mouth with water. It is also used by Shinto priests in their preparations and rituals. At the level of worship, each ritual begins with the priests purifying those who are present before they bow towards the kami, and before the door of the inner sanctuary is opened. Harae ceremonies are often conducted as exorcisms, at which evil spirits harmful to the community are dispelled and impurities connected with disasters, such as sorcery or death, are removed. Water is usually used, although in some circumstances salt or fire can also be used. The emphasis upon purity is important in Japan and can be seen today in wider matters, such as the use of damp cloths after meals and the emphasis on bathing. ▷ exorcism; kami; shrines, Shinto

Haramain This term refers to Mecca and Medina, the two sacred sites in Arabia where the Muslim tradition began. Non-Muslims are not allowed into these sacred zones, and it is forbidden to kill any creature there except in cases of urgent need. Mecca was a trading centre with an important shrine, the Kabah, which Muhammad purified when he returned to Mecca in 630. It had around it a *haram*, a sacred enclosure, which can only be entered at times of pilgrimage. Mecca with the Kabah and its other sacred places became the most important pilgrimage centre for Muslims. The Grand Mosque at Mecca is often called al-Haram, the Sacred. While taking part in the annual pilgrimage (Hajj) Muslims also visit Medina, which became Muhammad's base in 622, and remained the Muslim capital for over 30 years. It contains Muhammad's tomb and mosque which may, however, be visited at other times as well as during the pilgrimage. The Temple Mount at Jerusalem is the third sacred site for Muslims, although of less significance than Mecca and Medina. ▷ Black Stone; Hajj; Jerusalem in Islam; Mecca; Medina; Muhammad; pilgrimage

Hardy, Sir Alister (1896–1985) English zoologist and pioneer of research into religious experience, born in Nottingham and educated at Oxford University. After training and working as a zoologist, he became Professor of Zoology at University College, Hull (1928–42), Aberdeen University (1942–5), and Oxford University (1946–63). His scientific studies brought him a Zoological Society Scientific Medal in 1939, a Fellowship of the Royal Society in 1940, a Knighthood in 1957, the Pierre Lecomte de Nouy Prize in 1968, and Honorary Doctorates from Aberdeen, Hull and Southampton, and aroused in him an interest in religious experience as a human phenomenon. After giving the Gifford Lectures in Religion at Aberdeen University (1963–5), he founded the Religious Experience Research Unit at Manchester College, Oxford (1969), and was its first director (until 1976). His research showed that many people who might have no contact with institutional religion knew the reality of religious experience, and that the capacity for religious experience was an integral part of human nature. His books on religious topics included *The Divine Flame* (1966), *The Biology of God* (1975), and *The Spiritual Nature of Man* (1979). ▷ religious experience; spirituality

Hare Krishna movement A religious movement founded in the USA in 1965 by His Divine Grace A C Bhaktivedanta Swami Prabhupada as The International Society for Krishna Consciousness. The movement promotes human well-being by promoting consciousness of God based on the ancient Vedic texts of India. It is one of the best known of the new religious movements coming from the East, largely as a result of saffron-robed young people gathered in town centres chanting the *Maha mantra*, from which their popular name is derived. In their pursuit of spiritual advancement devotees practise vegetarianism, do not use intoxicants, do not gamble, and are celibate apart from procreation within marriage. ▷ Bhagavad Gita; Krishna

harem (ḥarīm) A private quarter for women in Muslim homes, which is secluded from the gaze of outsiders. Only certain categories of people are allowed access to the harem as listed in the Quran (24.31): 'tell the believing women...to draw their veils over their bosoms, and not to reveal their adornment save to their own husbands or fathers or husbands' fathers, or their sons or their husbands' sons, or their brothers or their brothers' sons or sisters' sons, or their women, or their slaves, or male attendants who lack vigour, and children who know naught of women's nakedness'. Harem literally means forbidden and is related to the word *haram* which means forbidden, restricted, or sacred. Whereas the harem is a forbidden area restricted to women, the *haramain* are the sacred sites at Mecca and Medina forbidden to non-Muslims. The harem is related to the notion of purdah, according to which Muslim women should be fully covered in public, but goes one stage further by forbidding women to be seen at all by strangers or by men other than close relations or eunuchs. ▷ haramain; Islam, women in; Quran; women in religion

Hargobind, Guru (Hargobind, Gurū) (1595–1644) Sixth of the 10 Sikh gurus, born in the Punjab, India, the only son of the fifth guru, Arjan. He became guru in 1606 at the age of 11 after his father's death (1605) in the custody of the Mughal emperor. Political circumstances moved him towards a more militant stance in regard to the Muslim Mughal empire, and he opposed Emperor Shah Jahan's policy of ending mixed marriages and of dismantling Hindu and Sikh worship places. He set up a centre in Kiratpur to which opposition to the Mughals could rally, and it appears that he officially sanctioned the first Sikh recourse to arms. His life was active rather than literary and unlike some of the other gurus he wrote very little. He built and repaired a number of temples and it appears likely that the term 'Gurdwara' was first used during his time as guru for Sikh places of worship. ▷ Arjan, Guru; gurdwara; Mughal Empire

Hari A name for Vishnu and also Krishna implying that he is the 'remover' (*hari*) of suffering. He is not a distinct deity from Vishnu and iconographically is depicted as identical to him, with conch, discus, lotus and mace. Hari sometimes occurs in conjunction with Hara, a name for Shiva in his aspect of 'remover' of life. Indeed the deity Hari-Hara is a representation of the supreme God as comprising two complementary halves. ▷ Shiva; Vishnu

Harijan Children of God (*Hari*). The term was coined by Gandhi to describe the untouchables, the lowest of the Hindu castes. The untouchables are so called because they are regarded as highly polluting by the higher castes, and they live in a condition of constant ritual impurity. Traditionally the untouchables live outside the village boundaries and are excluded from mainstream Hindu culture, including Vedic study, and they are excluded from many temples. Partly due to Gandhi's struggle for their rights, the Indian government has tried to improve the condition of these 'scheduled classes' through education, a programme which has met with resistance. ▷ Gandhi, Mohandas Karamchand; Hari

Harimandir, or **Golden Temple** The centre of the Sikh religion at Amritsar, Punjab, India. The temple dates from 1766 and stands in a sacred lake. It is faced with copper-gilt plates bearing inscriptions from the *Granth Sahib*, the holy book of the Sikhs, which is housed within. ▷ Amritsar; Guru Granth Sahib; Sikhism

Harnack, Adolf (Karl Gustav) von (1851–1930) German Protestant Church historian and theologian, born in Dorpat, son of the Lutheran dogmatic theologian Theodosius Harnack (1817–89). He was professor at Leipzig (1876), Giessen (1879), Marburg (1886), and Berlin (1889), where he also became keeper of the Royal (later State) Library (1905–21). His major writings include works on the history of dogma, on early Gospel traditions, and on a reconstruction of the essence of Jesus's teachings. From 1893 the orthodox suspected him of heresy on account of his criticism of the Apostles' Creed. ▷ Apostles' Creed; Jesus Christ; Protestantism; theology

Harris, William Wadé (?1865–1929) West-African prophet, who belonged to the Grebo people of Liberia. Baptized young, he served as a catechist and teacher of the Episcopal Church. Involved in a Grebo political movement, he was imprisoned (1910–11) and, while in prison, had a vision in which the archangel Gabriel commissioned him as a prophet of the new dispensation of Christ. On release he followed the visionary instructions as to dress (white robe and turban), took a bamboo cross, a bowl for baptizing, a calabash rattle and a King James Bible and began tours that took him across Liberia and Ivory Coast, into the Gold Coast and over to Sierra Leone. Everywhere he called on people to give up their fetishes (he regularly burned these), worship God, and obey God's commands (set out in short clear codes). He demonstrated the power of God and his own commission by healing, exorcism and battles with the spirits, and told his followers to await other messengers from God. His impact was greatest in Ivory Coast, where an estimated 200000 people responded. The French authorities, alarmed at a movement growing beyond their control, expelled him in 1914. Thereafter his work was mostly confined to Liberia, where he quarrelled with missionaries over polygamy. However, he endorsed the Methodist mission as the promised messengers in Ivory Coast; but he also ordained John Ahui as his successor there. In fact, Harris's work provided the foundation for most Catholic and Protestant work in Ivory Coast. The considerable Harrist Church, led by Ahui, has continued alongside them, an independent African prophet-healing church. Other preachers, some commissioned by Harris, others emulating him (notably Sampson Oppong and John Swatson in the Gold Coast) took his message into other areas with striking effect. ▷ African Independent churches

Hasan (al-Ḥasan ibn 'Alī ibn Abī Tālib) (625–70) The eldest son of Ali and Fatimah, the daughter of Muhammad, born in Medina. On Ali's assassination (661) Hasan succeeded him as fifth Muslim caliph. His caliphate lasted for only six months and he relinquished it voluntarily in an agreement with Muawiyah, who became the first caliph of the Umayyad dynasty. Hasan retired to Medina with money and pensions for himself and his brother Husayn. In the view of most Shiites he was the legitimate successor to Ali and therefore the second Shiite Imam after Ali, although some Shiites repudiated this claim since he had relinquished the caliphate. Hasan was well-known for his many marriages, which were in excess of 130. Despite his father's rebukes, his position as Muhammad's grandson enabled him to take this number of wives. ▷ Ali; caliphate; imam; Medina; Muhammad; Shiism; Umayyads

Hasidim, or **Chasidim**, also **Hasideans** (Hebrew 'faithful ones') Originally, those Jews in the 2nd century BCE who resisted Greek and pagan influences on Israel's religion and sought strict adherence to the Jewish law; they are probably ancestors of the Pharisees. They supported the early Maccabean revolt, but refused to fight for national independence once the legitimate high priesthood had been restored. In more recent times, it refers to extreme conservative Orthodox Jews who adhere to the principles of the 18th-century Hasidism movement. They do not wear modern clothes, and grow distinctive ear-locks of hair. They usually worship in small groups, separate from other Jews. ▷ Hasidism; Judaism; Maccabees; Pharisees

Hasidism A popular movement of Jewish mysticism, usually traced to a persecuted sect in the latter half of the 18th century in Poland, characterized by an ascetic pattern of life, strict observance of the commandments, and loud ecstatic forms of worship and prayer. It was originally opposed to rabbinic authority and traditional Jewish practices, stressing prayer rather than study of the Torah as the means of communicating with God, but as it spread through the Ukraine, Eastern Europe, and eventually Western Europe and America, it was finally accepted as a part of Orthodox Judaism. ▷ Judaism; Kabbalah; mysticism; rabbi; Torah

Hasmoneans ▷ Maccabees

Hatha Yoga The yoga of force (*hatha*) in Hinduism, Hatha Yoga was developed by the Nath yogis between the 9th and 11th centuries, though aspects of it are much older. The goal of the Hatha yogin is liberation in life (*jivanmukti*) through the purification of body and consciousness. By purifying the body the yogin hopes to create a divine body (*divya deha*) perfected or ripened in the fire of yoga, with which he will attain liberation (*moksha*). The main Sanskrit texts of the tradition are the *Hathayogapradipika* by Svatmarana Svamin (15th century) and earlier than this the *Gheranda Samhita* and the *Shiva Samhita*. These texts advocate the purification of the body through cleansing the stomach with a cloth which is swallowed (*dhauti*); intestinal cleansing through sucking water into the rectum (*basti*); cleaning the nose with threads (*neti*) and taking water through the nose and expelling it through the mouth (*kapala bhati*). Many bodily postures (*asanas*) are mentioned in these texts, among them the most famous is the lotus posture (*padmasana*). By stilling the body and breath through asana and breath control (*pranayama*), the mind can be stilled through concentration. These practices result in the awakening of Kundalini, the acquiring of magical powers (*siddhi*) and in eventual liberation. ▷ jivanmukti; Kundalini; moksha; Nath Yogis

Hathor Ancient Egyptian sky goddess, depicted as a cow or a woman with bovine features, a solar disc between her horns. Hathor was the goddess of love, dancing and joyful music, her special instrument being the sistrum rattle. As a mother goddess she featured in the royal imagery, frequently portrayed as a cow suckling the young pharaoh. At Thebes she was associated with the necropolis and worshipped as a mortuary deity. Her main cult centre was at Dendera in Upper Egypt, where a magnificent temple was built for her during the Graeco-Roman period. Here she was considered the consort of Horus, and her statue was taken annually to his temple at Edfu. In the New Kingdom (c.1567–1085BCE) and later, Hathor became increasingly identified with Isis. ▷ Horus; Isis; pharaoh; Thebes

Haumai The Sikh notion of human nature, corresponding to 'arrogance' or 'selfishness', and indicating the following of one's own will rather than the Word of God. The result of this attitude is rebirth, even when good actions have been performed from selfish intent. The Sikh aim of life is to live according to God's will (*Hukam*) and to overcome the tendency to live according to one's own inclinations. By remembering God, by invoking his presence, and by following his will, Haumai can be transcended. Nevertheless, it remains a bond preventing humans from escaping rebirth. God's Grace, God's Name, and God's Word are required to overcome its pull. ▷ Hukam; Sat Guru; Shabad

head cult (Celtic) Peoples in various parts of the world have venerated the human head as a source of power; ancient Celts did so to a remarkable degree. Classical writers and Roman inscriptions describe Celtic warriors collecting and solemnly dedicating the heads of the slain. Celtic sanctuaries, such as that at Roqueperteuse in France, not only carry carvings of heads, but display skulls in niches.

Severed heads are represented in metal (as in the famous Gundestrup bowl from Denmark), in stone (as in Celtic sites along Hadrian's Wall, where heads seem to have been removed from statues), and in Celtic inscriptions everywhere. Irish and Welsh folklore preserve traditions of heads speaking after death, and the Mabinogion tells of 'the entertaining of the noble head' of the hero Bendigheid Bran, which presided over his followers' feasts for 80 happy years. Though the full significance is now hard to interpret, the head was clearly associated with fertility and renewal; head cult and sacred springs belong together. The Bran story and other sources indicate a link with prosperity, security, prophecy and divine strength. ▷ Mabinogion

healing A major religious concern in the sense of overcoming physical ailments or disabilities, or more widely in removing sin or the effects of sin. This is primarily practised through prayer to God or, in polytheistic religions, to the appropriate god or gods, but may be accompanied by physical actions such as the laying on of hands, or by sacrifice. In some religions, healing is the particular province of a designated individual or class of individuals (priest, shaman, medicine-man).

Healthy-Happy-Holy Organization A new religious movement, also known as 3HO, that arose in Los Angeles in 1968. It combines Sikh doctrines and rigorous techniques derived from *Kundalini Yoga* which impose fairly heavy demands on potential Western followers. Even so, by 1973 it had ashrams in 80 locations, although even in its heyday in the 1970s it is estimated to have had only about 5000 members. It is the educational branch of the Sikh Dharma of the Western Hemisphere founded by Yogi Bhajan with the aim of servicing Sikhs from India and attracting Western followers into the Sikh tradition. Its members wear white clothes, both men and women wear turbans, and it is unusual in that it has an ordained ministry. Its outlook is positive, as the name suggests, and its aim is to enable people who join it to become good Sikhs by being healthy in body, happy in mind, and holy in living. ▷ Kundalini; new religious movements in the West

Heart Sutra (Sūtra) The shortest of the famous scriptures within the Mahayana Buddhist tradition known as the *Prajnaparamita Sutras*, the Perfection of Wisdom Scriptures. They emerged from the 1st century BCE onwards, and taught the key ideas of Mahayana Buddhism, such as the way of the bodhisattva and the doctrine of emptiness. The earliest of these scriptures has 8000 lines, and there are others with 25000 and 100000 lines. The *Diamond Cutter Sutra* has only 300 lines, and the *Heart Sutra* is shorter still. It gives the heart or core of the Mahayana teachings. It is read by Buddhists in Sanskrit or in Chinese, is recited in worship and in meditation, and is sometimes learnt by heart. At the beginning of the *Heart Sutra* wisdom is greeted as a beautiful woman: 'homage to the Perfection of Wisdom, the lovely, the holy', and at the end the teaching is summed up in a mantra or cryptic saying wherein wisdom and enlightenment are described as producing a bliss that is 'gone, gone, gone beyond, gone altogether beyond, o what an awakening, all hail!' ▷ bodhi; bodhisattva; Diamond Cutter Sutra; emptiness; enlightenment; Mahayana Buddhism; mantra; prajnaparamita

heaven In general, the dwelling-place of God and the angels, and in traditional Christianity the ultimate eternal destiny of the redeemed, there to reign with Christ in glory. In the Bible, it is usually conceived as high above the earth. In modern theology, the emphasis is more on the quality, transformation, or fulfilment of life, the fully-revealed presence of God, and the perfection of the divine-human relationship, than on a place. ▷ afterlife; angels; eschatology; God; paradise

heaven and hell, Islamic The Islamic heaven is usually symbolized as Paradise, and this often takes the form of a garden (*al-jannah*). This garden contains beautiful trees and flowers and fruits; it is enclosed and sheltered; and it repeats and extends the earthly Garden of Eden. However, it is also so wonderful that it is beyond the human imagination fully to conceive. Hell is a place of torment, often symbolized as a place of burning and fire. Physical pleasure and suffering are experienced in heaven and hell respectively, but mystical Islam sometimes sees them as the spiritual consequences of surrendering to God or denying God. Heaven and hell are taken to last for 'perpetuity', but not for 'eternity', which belongs to God alone. Intermediate stages and limbos are also possible after death, but receive much less attention than the more clear-cut judgement between heaven and hell given by God on the final day. ▷ Allah; judgement of the dead, Islamic view of; Paradise; jannah, al-

heaven and hell, Sikh Although the Sikh tradition accepts the theory of rebirth according to one's deeds, and this theory is often mentioned by Guru Nanak and the Sikh scripture, the *Guru Granth Sahib*, the main Sikh emphasis is upon this life and knowing God within it. Heaven is where God is present, where his praises are sung, where his saints live, and where everyday life is blessed; hell is where the opposite pertains. Liberation is possible in this life (*jivanmukti*). It hinges upon knowing God and his Name, and living his life in the world. Deeds are thus part of the spiritual life but they do not secure eternal life. Therefore although there is hell in this life in separation from God and unrighteous living, and there is rebirth according to one's deeds, the Sikh emphasis is not upon rebirth as such or upon heaven and hell in the afterlife, but upon becoming one with God in this life, and escaping hell here. ▷ Guru Granth Sahib; jivanmukti; karma; samsara

Hebrews, Letter to the A New Testament writing of unknown authorship and recipients, sometimes attributed to Paul, but this attribution widely doubted even from early times. It emphasizes how Jesus as Son of God is superior to the prophets, the angels, and Moses, and how Jesus acts as the perfect high priest in the heavenly sanctuary. Whether warning Jewish Christians not to return to Judaism, or challenging proto-gnostic heresies or Gentile cultic practices, the main instructions are against spiritual lethargy and falling back into sin. ▷ Jesus Christ; New Testament; Paul, St; Pauline Letters

Heenan, John Carmel (1905–75) Roman Catholic Archbishop of Westminster (1963–75), born in Ilford, Essex. Educated at Ushaw and the English College, Rome, he was ordained in 1930, became a parish priest in east London, and during World War II worked with the BBC, when he was known as the 'Radio Priest'. He was Bishop of Leeds (1951), and Archbishop of Liverpool (1957) and of Westminster (1963). A convinced ecumenist, he was created a cardinal in 1975. ▷ ecumenism; Roman Catholicism

Hegel, Georg Wilhelm Friedrich (1770–1831) German philosopher, the last and perhaps the most important of the great German idealist philosophers in the line from Kant, Fichte and Schelling. Born in Stuttgart, he studied theology at Tübingen, and was a tutor in Berne (1793) and Frankfurt-am-Main (1796); in 1801 he became a lecturer at Jena but his academic career was interrupted in 1806 by the closure of the university after Napoleon's victory over the city. He was temporarily a newspaper editor at Bamberg and then headmaster of the *gymnasium* at Nuremberg, 1808–16. He had published in 1807 his first great work *Phänomenologie des Geistes* (The Phenomenology of Mind), describing how the human mind has progressed from mere consciousness through self-consciousness, reason, spirit and religion to absolute knowledge. His second great work was *Wissenschaft der Logik* (Science of Logic, 2 vols, 1812 and 1816) in which he set out his famous dialectic, a triadic process whereby thesis generates antithesis and both are superseded by a higher synthesis which incorporates what is rational in them and rejects the irrational. This dialectical progression is not applied narrowly just to logical argument but to the evolution of ideas and to historical movements on the largest possible scale. The work gained him the chair at Heidelberg in 1816, and he resumed his university career and produced in 1817 a compendium of his entire system: *Encyclopädie der philosophischen Wissenschaften in Grundrisse* (Encyclopedia of the Philosophical Sciences, comprising logic, philosophy of nature and of mind). In 1818 he succeeded Fichte as professor in Berlin and remained there until his death from a cholera epidemic. His later works include the *Grundlinien der Philosophie des Rechts* (Philosophy of Right, 1821), which contains his political philosophy, and his important lectures on the history of philosophy, art and the philosophy of history. Hegel was a system-builder of the most ambitious and thorough kind, and though his philosophy is difficult and obscure it has been a great influence on such different groups as Marxists, Positivists, British Idealists, and Existentialists. In this century his importance declined after attacks by George Moore, Russell and the analytic philosophers, but he is now experiencing a modest revival of interest. ▷ existentialism, Christian; idealism; Kant, Immanuel; Marxism; philosophy; Russell, Bertrand Arthur William

hegira The migration of the prophet Muhammad from Mecca to Medina in 622. The departure marks the beginning of the Muslim era. ▷ Islam; Muhammad

Heidegger, Martin (1889–1976) German philosopher, born in Messkirch in Baden, the son of a Catholic sexton. He joined the Jesuits as a novice and went on to teach philosophy at Freiburg, where he did a dissertation on Duns Scotus. He became professor at Marburg (1923–8) and then succeeded Husserl as professor at Freiburg (1929–45), where he was appointed rector in 1933. In a notorious inaugural address he declared his support for Hitler. He was officially retired in 1945 but continued to be an influential teacher and lecturer. He succeeded Husserl as a leading figure in the phenomenological movement, but was also much influenced by Kierkegaard, and although he disclaimed the label of 'existentialist' he was a key influence on Sartre through his writings on the nature and predicament of human existence, the search for 'authenticity' and the distractions of Angst (dread). His major work is the highly original but almost unreadable *Sein und Zeit* (Being and Time, 1927), which presents a classification of the modes of 'Being' and an examination of the distinctively human mode of existence (*Dasein*) characterized by participation and involvement in the world of objects. His deliberate obscurity and riddling style partly account for his poor reception in the Anglo-Saxon world, but he is a continuing influence on continental European intellectuals. ▷ Duns Scotus, John; Husserl, Edmund Gustav Albrecht; Jesuits; Kierkegaard, Sören Aabye; Sartre, Jean-Paul

Heiler, Friedrich (1892–1967) German scholar of religion, born in Munich and educated at Munich University, where for two years he taught history and phenomenology of religion. He received a doctorate from Kiel University, and took up the chair of Comparative History of Religions and Philosophy of Religion at Marburg in 1922. He continued to teach at Marburg until his retirement in 1960, and he also taught for short periods at Greifswald, Chicago, and Munich. He presided over the International Congress for the History of Religions at Marburg in 1960. His monumental work, and the only one translated into English, was his book on prayer, *Prayer: A Study in the History and Psychology of Religion* (1932). This remains a seminal work on prayer as a universal phenomenon. Heiler believed that religion and the study of religion could be a reconciling factor in healing the divisions between churches and between religious traditions. He was interested in the theological side of the phenomenology of religion, and felt that religious truth was important as well as religious practices. He also felt that there was a basic unity underlying all religion. He worked for the integration of the historical and textual side of religion on the one hand, with the theological and philosophical explanations of religion on the other. He continued to be active in scholarship and ecumenical endeavour until his death. ▷ comparative religion; history of religion; prayer; psychology of religion; religionwissenschaft

Hel, or **Hela** In Norse mythology Hel was the youngest child of Loki; half her body was living human flesh, the other half decayed. She was assigned by Odin to rule Helheim (the underworld) and to receive the spirits of the dead who do not die in battle. ▷ Germanic religion; Loki; Valhalla; underworld

Heliopolis theology Situated south of the Nile delta, Heliopolis was the main cult centre of the sun god Re in Ancient Egypt. According to the theological system of its priests, it was here that the primeval hill rose out of the waters of Nun and the first god Atum appeared, who by procreation brought into being the elemental deities Shu (air) and his consort Tefnut (moisture). Their children were the earth god Geb and sky goddess Nut, and the non-elemental gods Osiris, Isis, Seth, and Nephthys were brought into the system as the children of Geb and Nut. These nine gods made up the Heliopolitan ennead. Geb, the first king, passed on his authority to his son Osiris, thus linking the cosmological scheme to the political system of the pharaohs, who were thought of as Osiris when they died, and his son Horus while they were alive. The influence of Heliopolis, at its height during the Old Kingdom (c.2686–2181BCE), waned during the 2nd millennium BCE, as the city of Thebes and its god Amun became dominant. ▷ Amun; Atum; ennead; Horus; Isis; Nephthys; Nun; Osiris; pharaoh; primeval hill; Re; Seth; Thebes

hell In traditional Christian thought, the eternal abode and place of torment of the damned. It developed out of Hebrew *sheol* and Greek *hades* as the place of the dead. Much contemporary Christian thought rejects the idea of vindictive punishment as incompatible with belief in a loving God. The emphasis acccordingly shifts from hell as a place of retribution to a state of being without God. Most religions have a concept of a place or condition which divides the good from the evil, or the living from the dead. Zoroastrianism, Judaism, Christianity and Islam all believe in hell as the place to which the damned are consigned after Judgement. Zoroastrianism and Islam envisage a bridge which the soul must cross to attain heaven. In Zoroastrianism the soul is weighed to see how good or evil it is. If evil, the bridge narrows and the soul tumbles into hell, a place of punishment, until the resurrection. In Islam, the damned fall from the bridge into a fiery crater where they suffer torments. Some Eastern concepts of hell are very different from Western, the idea of reincarnation making any period spent in hell relatively insignificant. ▷ eschatology; God; heaven and hell, Islamic; heaven and hell, Sikh; hells, Buddhist; Islam; Judaism; Satan; Zoroastrianism

Hellenistic Judaism Form(s) of Judaism from the Second Temple period (c.515BCE–70CE), influenced by Greek culture and language in the wake of Alexander the Great's imperial conquests. Hellenistic influence was strong among the Jewish Diaspora, but in Palestine there was reaction against it in the first half of the 2nd century BCE. Nonetheless, even Palestinian Judaism absorbed Hellenistic elements, as evident in Josephus's account of Jewish rulers after the Maccabees. Further afield, the *Book of Wisdom* (or *Wisdom of Solomon*) and the works of Philo of Alexandria, both Jewish writings from Egypt, exemplify deliberate attempts to marry Jewish and Greek traditions. The *Book of Wisdom*, for example, mixes Jewish Wisdom terminology (see Proverbs 8) with the Greek *Logos* idea. Philo gives the biblical commandments an allegorical significance, while maintaining that they ought also to be fulfilled literally. More subtle is the view that life after death applies only to the human soul, excluding any resurrection of the body. Such developments had a twofold aim: to encourage Jews in the Diaspora to remain faithful when attracted by Hellenistic culture, and to show non-Jews the essential reasonableness of Judaism. However, the rise of Rabbinic Judaism after 70CE meant that overtly Greek traits disappeared until their re-emergence in a different form during medieval times. ▷ Diaspora; Josephus, Flavius; Logos; Maimonides; Philo Judaeus; Wisdom of Solomon

Hellenists A group referred to in the Book of Acts (6.1, 9.29), contrasted with the 'Hebrews', and usually interpreted as Greek-speaking Jewish Christians who were critical of the Temple worship and who prepared for the Christian mission to non-Jews. St Stephen, the first Christian martyr, may have been one of them. Other interpretations of this group consider them Jews (not Christians) whose mother-tongue was Greek, or even non-Jews (Greeks). ▷ Acts of the Apostles; Christianity

hells, Buddhist In Buddhist cosmology hells are the lowest of six spheres of existence in the sensual world. Above them are the spheres of ghosts, animals, human beings, lower gods (*asuras*), and higher gods (*devas*). There are various hells, and in them for a period live beings who are suffering the effects of previous wicked deeds. Hell can be cold, dark or hot, and in each of them there are eight grades of severity. Buddhist hells are not occupied eternally but only for a period, and one can be reborn into one and out of one. To this extent they resemble the Roman Catholic notion of purgatory. ▷ asura; daevas; purgatory

Héloïse ▷ **Abelard, Peter**

henotheism A term which describes the attitude of those peoples who exclusively worship and follow one God, whilst also acknowledging that other gods exist and that they may be legitimately worshipped by other groups of people. As such the term has been used to describe Israel's attitude of faith from the earliest worship of Yahweh until the development of a pure monotheism was reached in the writings of Deutero-Isaiah in the 6th century BCE. The first commandment, 'I am the Lord your God, who brought you out of the land of Egypt, out of the house of bondage. You shall have no other gods before me' (Deuteronomy 5.6–7), represents a henotheistic attitude as it shows the absolute claim of Yahweh on the people of Israel within a polytheistic environment. There is considerable debate among scholars as to whether or not this term does justice to Israel's understanding that Yahweh was superior to all other gods. It is also now accepted that there is no clear progression from a primitive polytheism developing through henotheism to monotheism; instead, these concepts should be viewed as alternative perspectives within a richly varying rubric of religious traditions. ▷ Judaism; monotheism; polytheism

heresy False doctrine, or the formal denial of doctrine defined as part of the Catholic or universal faith. In the Christian Church in the 12th and 13th centuries the Inquisition was established to root out heresy, resulting in many trials and convictions. By the 20th century the Christian idea of heresy had been hugely modified, the ultimate sanction being excommunication. In Islam heresy is still punishable by death. Total heresy or the rejection of all faith is termed apostasy. ▷ Albigenses; Arius; Arminius, Jacobus; Donatists; Inquisition; Monophysites; Nestorians; Pelagius

Hermandszoon, Jakob ▷ **Arminius, Jacobus**

hermeneutics In religion, the theory of the interpretation and understanding of texts. Though its origins lie in ancient Greek philosophy, hermeneutics received fresh impetus in 18th-century discussions of the problems of biblical interpretation posed by the development of historical-critical method. Schleiermacher shifted attention from the formulation of rules of interpretation to the question of how it is possible to understand the written discourse of different cultures and ages. The discussion was carried further by Wilhelm Dilthey (1833–1911) and, in this century, by Heidegger and especially Hans-Georg Gadamer (1900–). During this time the discussion expanded to embrace all aspects of the understanding of texts and entered many fields, including literary theory, the social sciences, social philosophy, and aesthetics. ▷ biblical criticism; Heidegger, Martin; hermeneutics, Christian; Schleiermacher, Friedrich Ernst Daniel

hermeneutics, Christian In the Christian hermeneutical tradition, attention focuses on how to read Scripture. Implicit hermeneutics can be recognized, as well as explicit ones. For instance, the Church has often assumed that all Scripture is infallible, and therefore incapable of major disagreement, whereas critical scholarship presupposes that discrepancies may well indicate significant conflict. Similarly, read from a Marxist or feminist viewpoint, texts and contexts appear very differently. Or again, much early and medieval exegesis presumed that there was some vital allegorical meaning in all Scripture, whereas the Reformers deplored as distortion every departure from the 'plain sense'. There is heated debate between those who see interpretation as, in principle, attempting to reach objective truth, and those who think that a committed hermeneutic is indispensible and desirable when approaching any text or context, there being no neutral, objective reality. ▷ biblical criticism

Hermetica, Hermetism Traditions deriving from an Egyptian work in 18 treatises known as the *Corpus Hermeticum*, or *Hermetica*, which dates from the 2nd or 3rd centuries CE. A mystical philosophical text, it honours the Egyptian god Thoth who is identified with the Greek Hermes under the name of Trismegistus (Thrice-Greatest). The work proclaims a revelation that calls upon followers to repent of ignorance and wrongdoing, receive initiation, accept personal instruction in wisdom and right living, engage in ascetic self-discipline, focus on silent meditation, and finally enjoy a vision of Light and of God that gives rebirth into a sense of deep identity with God and the whole world. It reached Western Europe in the 15th century and was interpreted as being pre-Greek and pre-Christian and as preparing the way for Christ. It was thus acceptable to some Christians as a mystical and occult 'Christian' text which blended with neo-platonic and Christian Kabbalah ideas. When in 1614 scholarship proved it to be post-Christian its influence waned in Christian circles, but it has remained influential in areas of the West where magic, occultism, alchemy, unorthodox mysticism, and an interest in Ancient Egypt have remained strong. ▷ alchemy; Christian Kabbalah; magic; mysticism; neo-platonism; occult; Thoth

Herod, Antipas (22BCE–c.40CE) Ruler of Palestine in Roman times, son of Herod the Great, by whose will he was named tetrarch of Galilee and Peraea. He divorced his first wife in order to marry Herodias, the wife of his half-brother Philip–a union against which John the Baptist remonstrated at the cost of his life. It was when Herod Antipas was at Jerusalem for the Passover that Jesus was sent before him by Pilate for examination. In 39 he made a journey to Rome in the hope of obtaining from Caligula the title of king; he not only failed, but, through the intrigues of Herod Agrippa, was banished to Lugdunum (Lyon), where he died. ▷ John, St (the Baptist)

heroes, Greek Alongside the gods, the second important group of beings worshipped by the Greeks. The heroes in this cultic sense should be distinguished from the 'heroes' of myth and poetry, although there was considerable overlap between the two groups: many mythical heroes became cult figures, but cultic heroes could also be obscure local characters. A hero of cult was typically believed to be a dead mortal who somehow retained his powers and an influence over mortal life. The normal site for a hero-cult was therefore a tomb, but we also find figures with tell-tale names such as 'save-ship' or 'horse-disturber' who sound more like minor gods. The powers of heroes were very various. Most often, perhaps, they would help in battle (in accord with their own military interests while alive) send oracles, or heal, but their function as symbols of group identity was probably even more important than their specific powers. Cities, the subdivisions of the city known as 'tribes', and even villages, had their own distinctive heroes; it was largely participation in their cults that gave members of the relevant group a sense of common identity. ▷ cult; Greek religion

Herzl, Theodor (1860–1904) Zionist leader, born in Budapest. He graduated in law at Vienna, but wrote essays and plays until influenced by the Dreyfus trial (1894) and the anti-Semitism it aroused, which he reported for a Viennese newspaper. In the pamphlet *Judenstaat* (1896) he advocated the remedy in the formation of a Jewish state; he convened the first Zionist Congress at Basle (1897); and negotiated with the kaiser, Wilhelm I, Abd-ul-Hamid II, the Russian premier, Joseph Chamberlain and Baron Rothschild. ▷ anti-Semitism; Zionism

Heschel, Abraham Joshua (1907–72) American Jewish theologian, poet and academic, born in Warsaw. He studied in Berlin and taught in Frankfurt, but was forced to return to Poland by the Nazis along with all Polish Jews in October 1938. He escaped from Poland in 1939 and went to England, moving to the USA in 1941. From 1946 until his death he lectured on ethics and mysticism at Conservative Judaism's Jewish Theological Seminary in New York. He contributed academically in the areas of Rabbinic and Medieval Judaism, as well as Hasidism. His own theological writings were influenced by Hasidism and by elements of the Kabbalah. He was also a social activist, especially during the Civil Rights movement of the 1960s. His works include *God in Search of Man* (1956), *The Prophets* (1962) and *Who Is Man?* (1965). ▷ Conservative Judaism; Holocaust; Judaism in North America

hesychasm A term connected with the prayer practised by 'hesychasts', hermits or solitary monks (as opposed to 'cenobites', those who live in community). It can refer generally to the Orthodox traditions of inner prayer associated with St Maximus the Confessor (580–662) and St Symeon the New Theologian (949–1022), or more specifically to Nicephorus the Hesychast (late 13th century) and practitioners of the 'Jesus Prayer', or to the controversies about mystical awareness of God surrounding St Gregory Palamas. In the Jesus Prayer the repetition of 'Lord Jesus Christ, Son of God, have mercy on me' is accompanied by controlled breathing and posture and a focus on the heart or inner self. These traditions of mystical prayer were fostered by the monks of Mount Athos in the 14th century and revived from the late 18th century by publication of the *Philokalia* (1782, English trans 1951, 1979–), edited by St Macarius of Corinth (1731–1805) and St Nicodemus of the Holy Mountain (1749–1809). ▷ prayer; Palamas, Gregory

Hezekiah Biblical character, King of Judah in the late 8th century BCE (precise dating much disputed), renowned for his religious reforms, including the re-establishment of Temple worship in Jerusalem (2 Chronicles 29–32), and for his political attempts to obtain independence from Assyrian domination (2 Kings 18–20; Isaiah 36–9). ▷ Bible; Chronicles/Isaiah/Kings, Book(s) of

Hick, John Harwood (1922–) English theologian and philosopher of religion, born in Scarborough. During a long teaching career in the USA and Cambridge, followed by professorships in Birmingham (1967–82) and at Claremont Graduate School, California (1979–), Hick has produced several standard textbooks and anthologies in the philosophy of religion, as well as studies such as *Faith and Knowledge* (1966), *Evil and the God of Love* (1966), and *Death and Eternal Life* (1976). His concern with questions about the status of Christianity among the world religions, raised in *God and the Universe of Faiths* (1973) and *The Myth of God Incarnate* (1977), is developed in *Problems of Religious Pluralism* (1985) and the expanded Gifford lectures, *An Interpretation of Religion* (1989). He has also edited *The Myth of Christian Uniqueness* (1988), with Paul F Knitter, and *Three Faiths–One God, A Jewish, Christian, Muslim Encounter* (1989).

Hidden Imam (Imām) A notion not accepted by Sunni Muslims, but of crucial importance for Shiite Muslims, especially the Twelver Shiites. They consider that the twelfth imam, called Muhammad, who was said to have been born at Samarra in 869, disappeared in 873 at the age of four on the death of his father, the eleventh imam. He became the Hidden Imam who is considered to be invisible and still alive. He has exalted powers as 'Lord of the Age', and at the end of history he will come back as the Mahdi to bring justice and peace to the earth. According to Shiites he hears prayers and intercedes with God on behalf of humans, and he shows himself in a vision at the moment of death to those who are saved. Other Shiite groups in addition to the Twelvers, for example the Druze, claim to have similar hidden spiritual leaders. However, the notion of the Hidden (twelfth) Imam is of cardinal significance to the Twelvers. ▷ Druze; imam; Mahdi; Shiism; Sunnis; Twelvers

hieroglyphics

hieroglyphics The study of the symbols of Ancient Egyptian writing. The characters were originally pictograms, and were named hieroglyphs (from the Greek 'sacred carving') because of their frequent use in religious contexts, such as temple and tomb inscriptions. The symbols were usually written from right to left, and were developed to represent three kinds of information: some are ideograms, representing objects or concepts in the real world; others stand for a consonant or consonant sequence; and a third type has no phonetic value, but serves to disambiguate a hieroglyph with more than one meaning. ▷ Ancient Egyptian religion

hierophany A term, principally associated with the work of Mircea Eliade, meaning the manifestation of the sacred (from the Greek *hiero* 'sacred', and *phainein* 'to show'). The term is general and non-specific, applying to any appearance of the sacred in any particular object, whether it is sky, sun, stone or tree. A hierophany is recognized when the experience of the sacred through a particular item is recognized as the manifestation of some reality other than the mundane empirical reality of the world. Hierophanies are not limited to any specific culture or religious tradition. Virtually every aspect of the natural order and many human artifacts, and even individual men and women have acted as hierophanies at some time. However, the recognition of the sacred in an object such as a stone or a tree is itself sacred. One of the functions of the hierophany is to separate those objects that are sacred from those which remain profane. An important feature of a hierophany is that in manifesting the sacred through a particular object, the absolute limits itself in some way. In this sense every revealing of the absolute is also a veiling, for by appearing in a concrete particular, the absolutely sacred ceases to be absolute.

The concept of a hierophany makes no distinction between the relative value of the appearances of the sacred in the religious traditions of humankind. There can be no absolute manifestation of the sacred as every revealing shares in the necessary structure of also being a limitation of the absolute in some way. ▷ Eliade, Mircea; holy, idea of; sacred and profane

high priest Chief among the priests usually attached to a major temple or religious site; an office in Israel probably dating to pre-exilic times, but changing later when the high priest acquired civil as well as religious power. Normally it was a hereditary office held for life in Israel, and was ostensibly traced through the line of Aaron, Eleazar (his son), and Phinehas, but when Solomon appointed Zadok as high priest he began a line which continued until Maccabean times. The most important cultic duty of the high priest was entering the Holy of Holies in the Temple and making an offering on the Day of Atonement. ▷ Aaron; exile; Levites; priest; Solomon; Urim and Thummim; Yom Kippur; Zadokites

Hilal The crescent which has become a distinctive symbol of Islam. It was a decorative emblem in early Islamic aesthetics and architecture, and it subsequently appeared on the flags of the Mamluks in Egypt and the Ottomans in Turkey. Although it was viewed by outsiders as a quintessential symbol of Islam, notably by Western Christians who saw it as a kind of equivalent to the Christian cross, it was not until the 18th century that the Muslim world began to view it in the same light. The crescent and a star now feature on the flags of various Islamic countries. The Red Crescent has become well known as the Muslim equivalent of the Red Cross. ▷ cross; Ottoman Turks

Hildebrand ▷ **Gregory VII, St**

Hillel I, or **Hillel the Elder**, surnamed **Hababli** ('the Babylonian') or **Hazaken** (1st century BCE–1st century CE) One of the most respected Jewish teachers of his time, born (probably) in Babylonia, who immigrated to Palestine at about age 40. He founded a school of followers bearing his name which was frequently in debate with (and often presented more tolerant attitudes than) the contemporary followers of Shammai. Noted for his use of seven rules in expounding Scripture, his views were influential for later rabbinic Judaism. ▷ Judaism; Shammai

Hinayana Buddhism (Hīnayāna Buddhism) A Sanskrit term applied by Mahayana Buddhists to the 18 Buddhist schools other than their own. Insofar as the other 17 schools have since disappeared it tends to be equated with the sole remaining one, the Theravada school. It is in fact a derogatory term. *Yana* means vehicle, and Mahayana is therefore the 'great vehicle', and Hinayana the 'lesser vehicle'. Mahayana Buddhism sees its tradition as having a wider and more comprehensive scope and as being of greater appeal to more people, especially lay people, than its rivals. Needless to say Theravada Buddhism does not see itself as inferior to Mahayana. Moreover there is now a greater inclination throughout the Buddhist world towards genuine ecumenism. Nevertheless Theravada is sometimes described as Hinayana, especially in the West; this is incorrect since it implies a Mahayana perspective rather than a detached viewpoint. ▷ Mahayana Buddhism; Theravada Buddhism

Hincmar (c.806–882) French theologian, of the family of the Counts of Toulouse. Educated at the monastery of St Denis, he became Archbishop of Reims (845). He is remembered for his dispute with the Benedictine monk Gottschalk (d.868) on the issue of predestination. He also strenuously opposed Pope Adrian II's attempts to compel obedience in Imperial politics; and with equal firmness resisted the emperor's placing of unworthy favourites into benefices. ▷ predestination; theology

Hinduism The Western term for a religious tradition developed over several thousand years and intertwined with the history and social system of India. Hinduism does not trace its origins to a particular founder, has no prophets, no set creed, and no particular institutional structure. It emphasizes the right way of living (dharma) rather than a set of doctrines, and thus embraces diverse religious beliefs and practices. There are significant variations between different regions of India, and even from village to village. There are differences in the deities worshipped, the scriptures used, and the festivals observed. Hindus may be theists or non-theists, revere one or more gods or goddesses, or no god at all, and represent the ultimate in personal (eg Brahma) or impersonal (eg *Brahman*) terms.

Hindu trinity: Shiva, Vishnu and Brahma

Common to most forms of Hinduism is the idea of reincarnation or transmigration. The term *samsara* refers to the process of birth and rebirth continuing for life after life. The particular form and condition (pleasant or unpleasant) of rebirth is the result of karma, the law by which the consequences of actions within one life are carried over into the next and influence its character. The ultimate spiritual goal of Hindus is *moksha*, or release from the cycle of samsara. There is a rich and varied religious literature, and no specific text is regarded as uniquely authoritative. The earliest extant writings come from the Vedic period (c.1200–500BCE), and are known collectively as the Veda. Later (c.500BCE–500CE) came the religious law books (*dharma sutras* and *dharma shastras*) which codified the classes of society (varna) and the four stages of life (ashrama), and were the bases of the Indian caste system. To this were added the great epics, the Ramayana and the Mahabharata. The latter includes one of the most influential Hindu scriptures, the *Bhagavad Gita*.

There have been many developments in Hindu religious thought. In particular, Shankara (9th century CE) formulated the *advaita* (non-dual) position that the human soul and God are of the same substance. Ramanuja (12th century) established the system of *Vishishtadvaita* (differentiated non-duality) which, while accepting that the human soul and God are of the same essence, holds that the soul retains its self-consciousness and, therefore, remains in an eternal relationship with God. This provided the impetus for the later theistic schools of Hindu thought.

Brahma, Vishnu, and Shiva are the chief gods of Hinduism, and together form a triad (the *Trimurti*). There are numerous lesser deities, including the goddesses Maya and Lakshmi. Hinduism is concerned with the realization of religious values in every part of life, yet there is a great emphasis upon the performance of complex and demanding rituals under the supervision of Brahman priests and teachers. There are three categories of worship: temple, domestic, and congregational. Pilgrimage to local and regional sites is common, and there is an annual cycle of local, regional and all-Indian festivals. There are over 500 million Hindus. ▷ Advaita Vedanta; ashrama; atman; Bhagavad Gita; bhakti; Brahma; Brahman; dharma; Hinduism in South-East Asia; karma; Krishna; Lakshmi; linga; Mahabharata; mantra; moksha; Ramayana; samsara; Shankara; Shiva; Trimurti; Veda; Vishnu;

Hinduism, devotional attitudes and goals in Devotion (bhakti) to a particular deity expressed in ritual worship (*puja*) is the central religious act of the majority of Hindus. Devotional aspirations can vary from hopes of worldly success to liberation (*moksha*) from the cycle of transmigration (*samsara*) through God's grace. While the monist, such as an Advaitin, regards devotion to a personal Lord as a lower level of practice and understanding, the theist, such as a Krishna devotee, regards it as the highest. For the monist, only knowledge (*jnana*) of the non-dual absolute (*Brahman*) liberates, whereas for the theist liberation results from devotion to a personal God by his grace. ▷ Advaita Vedanta; bhakti; Brahman; Krishna; moksha; samsara; worship, Hindu

Hinduism, modern movements During the 19th century Hinduism underwent a 'renaissance' and its ideas and practices were reformulated in the light of Western rationalism. The founding father of this movement was Rammohun Roy who was influenced by Muslim writing as well as the Upanishads. He lived in Calcutta where he promoted religious and social reform, rejecting Hindu image worship and many social customs such as the tradition of sati or suttee, in which a widow would mount her deceased husband's funeral pyre. Roy maintained that the Upanishadic idea of the Absolute as having no qualities (*nirguna Brahman*) was the essential teaching of Hinduism. He founded the Brahmo Samaj in 1828 which promoted Hinduism as a rational religion which should be stripped of superstition and immoral practices. The Brahmo Samaj had an important effect on the development of modern India though it did not have popular appeal because of its intellectualism. The Arya Samaj founded in 1875 by Dayananda Sarasvati, like the Brahmo Samaj, promoted the reform of Hinduism, particularly rejecting image-worship in favour of a strict monotheism and promoting social reform such as the rejection of child marriage. The Arya Samaj became associated with Indian nationalism and Dayananda Sarasvati promoted Hindi as a national language. The association of Hinduism, in a fundamentalist form, with nationalist politics has continued today in India with the rise of Hindu nationalist parties such as the BJP. Gandhi emphasized the oneness of God or Truth and humanity and his *satyagraha* movement, which, in contrast to some other nationalist movements, emphasized the quality of non-violence (ahimsa) was instrumental in gaining India's independence. Gandhi is venerated throughout India and there are many institutions and societies based on Gandhian principles.

There have been other modern Hindu movements which have not had the political effect of movements such as the Arya Samaj, but which nevertheless have had wide popular appeal. These movements are usually focused on a specific guru. The Swaminarayan movement founded by Shree Sahajanand Swami or Swaminarayan (1781–1830) venerated as an incarnation of Narayana, a name for Vishnu, has had wide appeal in western India and also in East Africa until the expulsion of Asians from Uganda. Swaminarayan taught a form of the 'qualified non-dualism' of Ramanuja (12th century). There are other contemporary movements of wide popular appeal, such as the sect of the miracle-performing Sathya Sai Baba, the Siddha Yoga movement founded by Swami Muktananda and the Sikh influenced Radha Soami movements based at Beas in the Punjab and at Agra. The Hare Krishna tradition, founded in its present form by Bhaktivedanta Swami Prabhupada, which has had much success in the West, is also strong in India and accepted by Hindus. ▷ ahimsa; Arya Samaj; Brahmo Samaj; Sarasvati, Dayananda; Gandhi, Mohandas Karamchand; Hare Krishna movement; nirguna Brahman; Ramanuja; Rammohun Roy; Satya Sai Baba; Swaminarayan movement; Upanishads; Vishnu

Hinduism in South-East Asia The countries of South-East Asia had links with India from at least the early centuries CE and were collectively referred to in India as *suvarnabhumi*, the land of gold. Indian religions and cultural influences entered South-East Asia during the medieval period through trade routes and, probably more importantly, through Brahmans being invited to the courts of kings to serve as administrators, astrologers and advisers. A Sanskrit inscription from Indonesia of about 400CE testifies to this. Indeed, local kings adopted Indian ideas, rituals and iconography and Sanskrit became the court language, while many Sanskrit words were incorporated into popular speech. Although Buddhism became the major religious force in South-East Asia, especially through the influence of monks, there were nevertheless Hindu kingdoms and Hindu influence is seen today in religious rituals; in Thailand, for example, Brahman priests still conduct royal ceremonies. The most famous Hindu kingdom, which flourished from the 11th to 13th centuries, was that of the Khmer, the builders of the famous Angkor Wat, based in what is now Cambodia. Hinduism was adopted here partly because it seemed to sanction the Khmer idea of the God-king. The Khmer empire waned and in Thailand the Sukhothai kingdom developed, adopting Theravada Buddhism as the national religion. Hinduism, particularly Tantric Shaivism, also developed in Indonesia from Sumatra to Bali, where hymns to Shiva were composed. Indian art forms were adopted throughout South-East Asia as temple building in Java and Cambodia during the second half of the first millennium testifies. In Indonesia Hindu sculptures of deities have been found which are local imitations of styles of the Pallava (6th century) and Chola (11th–13th centuries) kingdoms of India. ▷ Buddhism; Hinduism; Shaivism; Theravada Buddhism

Hindu law Despite recent changes, the Indian legal system is still inextricably bound up with Hindu religiosity and the central concept of dharma. Dharma, or natural moral law, preserves the world order (*rita*), and from it derive the specific rules which bind all Hindus as well as, theoretically, Jains, Sikhs, and Hindu converts to Islam and Christianity (when they retain Hindu customs). Law is scripturally based and therefore has divine sanction. It is circumstantially interpreted within strict hermeneutical traditions, with reference to commentaries, general customs and in classical times, the decree of the king. The commentaries provide an enormous body of literature called the *dharmashastras* or *smriti* (literally, what has been remembered), some of which are attributed to the mythical figure Manu. Law enforcement has been vague and varies strikingly from region to region. Each Hindu's dharma is unique, making generalization difficult. Punishment and purification are for the purpose of righting the world order rather than being intended as a penalty or a deterrent. The Colonial period, especially under Lord Macauley, saw dramatic changes to the legal system, in which apparent inequalities, especially relating to caste, were modified, and a new codified Hindu law was written, based on precedents. Hindu law, in spite of the Colonial changes and the force of secularization, has influenced legal systems all over South-East Asia. ▷ dharma; Manu; rita; smriti

Hindu Mahasabha (Mahāsabhā) The 'great assembly' of orthodox Hinduism which occasionally meets to discuss matters of doctrine. Hinduism does not have a centralized authority and this assembly, which embraces many Hindu sects and ascetic orders, is Hinduism's nearest equivalent. The assembly meets, for example, during the Kumbha Mela pilgrimage, when many ascetic and monastic orders come together. In modern times the name Hindu Mahasabha has also been taken by an ultra-orthodox Hindu political party, a member of which assassinated Mahatma Gandhi in 1948. ▷ Kumbha Mela

Hindu religious traditions Hinduism comprises a number of great religious traditions. These can be categorized as being focused on one of the great Hindu deities such as Vishnu, Shiva and the goddess (Devi). These deities can be worshipped in an orthodox (Vedic) way or in a heterodox (Tantric) way which involves the transgression of orthodox norms. In orthodox traditions these deities might be worshipped along with others as manifestations of a supreme absolute (*Brahman*) or themselves be identified with the absolute theistic reality. Orthodox worshippers of Vishnu or Vaishnavas will accept the Veda as authoritative and *smriti* texts such as the *Bhagavad Gita* from the *Mahabharata* and the Vaishnava Puranas. Vaishnavas worship Vishnu either as himself or in one of his forms such as Narayana. He might also be worshipped in one of his incarnations (avataras) such as Krishna, Rama, or Narasimha. Krishna is a particularly popular deity and, while being regarded as an incarnation of Vishnu, is sometimes seen as the supreme deity in himself. In South India, the Shri Vaishnava tradition, one of the most important Vaishnava traditions, reveres the Veda but also the Tantric Agamas of the Pancaratra. The followers of Shiva or Shaivas might accept the authority of the Veda, but will also adhere to Shaiva Tantras as their textual sources of authority. For example, the Shaiva Siddhanta, while aligning itself with orthodoxy in accepting the *varnashrama-dharma* and the Veda, also accepts the Shaiva Agamas and Tantras. Other Shaiva groups, such as the Kapalikas, have rejected Vedic orthodoxy and accepted only the authority of the Tantras. Such groups might worship Shiva in his ferocious form as Bhairava or even worship the goddess Kali. Followers of the goddess can worship her as a young virgin (Kumari), in her maternal and benign forms as the spouse of Shiva or Vishnu, in her ferocious forms as Durga and Kali and even as an old crone (Kubjika). One of the most important traditions worshipping the Goddess in the South, particularly in the form of the *yantra*, is the Shri Vidya. ▷ avatara; Bhagavad Gita; Brahman; Durga; goddess worship, Hindu; Kali; Krishna; Mahabharata; Puranas; Rama; Shaiva Siddhanta; Shaivism; Shiva; Shri Vaishnavas; smriti; Tantric Hinduism; Vaishnavism; Veda; Vishnu; yantra

Hindu religious year The Hindu religious year contains many festivals, some of which are pan-Indian, others of which are celebrated only in a particular region. These festivals are based on the lunar calendar in which each month is divided into a 'light' (*shukra*) and 'dark' (*krishna*) fortnight. Although there are regional variations as to when each festival is celebrated, generally the first month, Chaitra (April) is marked by new year celebrations when people will put on new or clean clothes and draw patterns on a clean space in front of their doors. This month also contains festivals for the birth of Rama and Hanuman. The *Ratha Yatra* festival, during which the huge image of the deity Jagannatha is taken through the streets of Puri in a 'chariot' or cart, is held in Jaystha (June). During Shravan (July/August) is the festival of *Raksha Bandan* in which people exchange goodwill symbolized by wrist-bands. A month later the birth of Krishna (*Janamashtami*) is celebrated and also a puja to Ganesha. The month of Ashwin (October) is marked by *Navaratri*, the 'nine night' festival during which occurs Dusserah and the Durga puja. The most important Hindu festival held during Kartik (October/November) is *Divali*, the festival of the lights, which lasts for four or five days. It is sacred especially for business people as the main deity is Lakshmi, goddess of wealth. During the dark fortnight of Magh (February) the festival sacred to Shiva, the Mahashivaratri, is held. Devotees of Shiva might fast during this time. In the following month of Phalgun (February/March) is the last and probably most famous festival of Hinduism, namely Holi. This is a Spring festival sacred to Krishna in which bonfires are lit to mark the end of the old year, roles are reversed and people throw coloured water at each other. ▷ Divali/Deepavali; Durga; Dusserah; Ganesha; Hanuman; Janamashtami; Krishna; Lakshmi; Raksha Bandan; Rama; Shiva

history of religion This arose in the West in the 18th century and involves the use of historical criticism to interpret what happened in particular historical contexts. In terms of the study of religion this has involved painstaking work on individual traditions. This depends upon the availability of historical manuscripts and artefacts, which have been discovered in greater quantities this century. Out of the many historical facts and interpretations, the separate histories of independent religious traditions have been pieced together. Thus historical diffusion between cultures, and global correspondences avoiding historical diffusion, can be pondered—such as the significance of the simultaneous appearance during the Axial age of the 6th century BCE of the Ionian philosophers in Greece, the Hebrew prophets and the successors of Zoroaster in the Middle East, the Buddha, the Jain Mahavira and the Hindu Upanishads in India, and Confucius and the early currents of Taoism in China, as well as the simultaneous appearance in the 12th and 13th centuries CE of great religious syntheses in the work of Maimonides in Judaism, Aquinas and Bonaventure in Christianity, Chu Hsi in China, Ramanuja in Hindu India, and (slightly earlier) al-Ghazali in Islam. ▷ Aquinas, St Thomas; Ashoka; Axial Age; Bonaventure, St; Buddha; Chu Hsi; Confucius; Ghazali, Abu Hamid Mohammed al-; Mahavira; Maimonides; Ramanuja; study of religion; Upanishads; Zoroaster

Hittite religion Indo-European in origin, the Hittites had built an empire in Asia Minor by the mid 2nd millennium BCE, but from c.1200 they waned in the shadow of Assyria. The deciphering of cuneiform clay tablets discovered at Hattushah (Bogazköy in modern Turkey) has contributed much to knowledge about Hittite religion. Thus names of over 600 gods were found; although wiser and more powerful than humans, they were not omnipotent or omniscient and ate, drank, slept and had sexual intercourse like ordinary people. The pantheon was arranged hierarchically with different divinities having special spheres of influence; they required little from mortals whose relation to them was that of slave. However, offence against a deity constituted sin, for which punishment might be exacted and amends made. Hittite mythology included stories about struggles between gods and 'vanishing god' myths. In the latter natural disasters were explained through the disappearance of an enraged deity. The god had to be located, appeased and returned, and this was accomplished by oracular and ritual activity. At Hattushah Hittite temples were found, incorporating rooms for representative images of deities and for temple personnel. Hittite religious activities included prayer, sacrifice, and recitation of myths, while divine-human communication took place through oracles, prophet-like men and kings. Finally, there is some evidence for belief in an afterlife. ▷ Elamite religion; Hurrian religion; Sumerian religion

Holi The last festival of the Hindu calendar occurring towards the end of February. It is characterized by the reversal of normal codes of behaviour and a spirit of playfulness in which people throw coloured water and powder over each other. At a village level in some parts of India people might become intoxicated with *bhang*, a drink made with hemp, and bonfires are lit to symbolize the destruction of the old year. The festival is particularly associated with Krishna, the playful young god. ▷ Krishna

Holocaust The attempt by Nazi Germany systematically to destroy European Jews. From the inception of the Nazi regime in 1933 Jews were deprived of civil rights, persecuted, physically attacked, imprisoned, and murdered. With the gradual conquest of Europe by Germany, the death toll increased, and a meeting at Wannsee (Jan 1942) made plans for the so-called 'final solution'. Jews were herded into concentration camps, slave labour camps, and extermination camps. By the end of the war in 1945, more than six million Jews had been murdered out of a total Jewish population of eight million in those countries occupied by the Nazis. Of these the largest number, three million, were from Poland. Other minorities (gypsies, various religious sects, homosexuals) were also subject to Nazi atrocities, but the major genocide was against the Jewish people. ▷ Judaism; Nazi Party

holy, idea of Holiness, a religious category meaning the setting apart for a sacred purpose, is a common concept in the major religions of the world. A person, place or object may become holy in this sense by virtue of some special relationship which it has with the gods or a god. The term 'the idea of the holy' is drawn from a book with that title by Rudolf Otto (1896–1937), published in English in 1923. Otto analysed 'the holy' which he felt was a dimension peculiar to religious experience deriving from its contact with that which is 'numinous' or wholly other. For Otto the sense of the holy is the experience of that which is ultimately real, something which is mysterious, fascinating and awe-inspiring. This feeling of awe before 'the holy' is the characteristic human reaction common to all religious experience. The 'wholly other' quality of holiness gives rise to the distinction between the sacred and the profane. The profane is that which is for common and everyday use. The sacred is that which is imbued with the holy and which draws one into the realm of the holy. Therefore people, places and objects can be designated holy in as much as they recall and re-create the experience of the transcendent. According to Otto the idea that holiness means morally perfect or completely good is only a subsidiary feature of the term. However, in a faith such as Judaism the righteousness and holiness of Yahweh are inextricably intertwined. ▷ sacred and profane

Holy Ghost ▷ Holy Spirit

Holy of Holies The innermost and most sacred part of the Jewish tabernacle, and later of the Jerusalem Temple, cubic in shape, which contained the Ark of the Covenant. Only the High Priest was permitted to enter, and only once yearly on the Day of Atonement. ▷ Ark of the Covenant; day of judgement; Tabernacle; Temple, Jerusalem

Holy Orders ▷ Orders, Holy

Holy Shroud ▷ Turin Shroud

Holy Spirit A term used to denote the presence or power of God, often imbued with personal or quasi-personal characteristics; in Christian thought considered the third person of the Trinity, alongside the Father and the Son. Doctrinal differences exist, though, between Western churches which regard the Spirit as 'proceeding from' both the Father and the Son, and Eastern Christianity which accepts procession from the Father only. In the Bible the Spirit was often the vehicle of God's revelatory activity, inspiring the prophets, but it was also depicted as an agent in creation. In the New Testament, the Spirit is described as descending upon Jesus 'as a dove' at his baptism (Mark 1.10), as glorifying Jesus after his death (John 16.12–15), and even as 'the Spirit of Christ' in Romans 8.9. In Acts, the Church received the Spirit at Pentecost, from which time it continued to direct the Church's missionary activities. Paul not only considered the 'gifts of the Spirit' as empowering various ministries in the Church, but also as associated with the ecstatic practices of speaking in tongues and prophesying (1 Corinthians 12–14), which continue to feature prominently in Pentecostal churches. ▷ Christianity; glossolalia; God; Paul, St; Pentecostalism; Trinity

holy war, Jewish The concept of a holy war, declared, fought and won by Yahweh, god of Israel, originates in traditions of the god as a divine warrior which are found in the Hebrew Bible. In the Deuteronomic literature in particular a systematic ideology of holy war is laid out. In Joshua and Judges there are stories of Yahweh leading his people to victory in wars, mostly against the Canaanite occupants of the promised land. Deuteronomy gives regulations for the ritual accompanying such a war, culminating in the devotion of a captured city to Yahweh and consequent annihilation of all its inhabitants. That this practice was not limited to Israel is confirmed by an inscription of Mesha, King of Moab, who describes the devotion of captured Israelite cities to the Moabite god Chemosh. Although certain features of the holy war must have been present in early Israel, it is likely that the detailed institution seen in Deuteronomy is a later interpretation. In the 2nd century BCE the Maccabaean Revolt took on many of the characteristics of a holy war, directed as it was against pagan overlords. Holy war also features prominently in much of the apocalyptic literature, where the final battle takes on cosmic proportions. ▷ apocalypse; Old Testament

Homeric pantheon This concept was not recognized as such by the Greeks; it is a modern term for the gods who appear in the poetry of Homer (8th/7th century BCE). The most important are Zeus, 'father of gods and men', who is impartial in the Trojan War described by Homer; his wife Hera, daughter Athena, and brother Poseidon, who all favour the Greeks; his children Apollo, Artemis, Hephaestus and Leto also appear, as do lesser powers such as Iris, the demi-goddess Thetis, 'Sleep', and many others. The gods of the underworld, Hades and Persephone, are mentioned but do not participate in the action, while two gods of the highest cult importance, Demeter and Dionysus, are all but excluded. The gods in Homer live on Olympus, in the house of Zeus, where they often also assemble in council; in cult by contrast much more stress was laid on the association between particular gods and particular cities. The Homeric pantheon is therefore in important respects a poetic fiction: the historian Herodotus (c.430BCE) certainly exaggerated when he said that it was Homer and Hesiod (the other early mythological poet) who determined the names and powers and genealogies of the Greek gods. ▷ Greek religion; Olympian pantheon

Honen (1133–1212) The founder of the Jodo or Pure Land school of Buddhism in Japan. Born in Japan, he entered the great Tendai monastery at Mount Hiei as a boy, but after a period of seclusion and study at a nearby hermitage he emerged at the age of 43 to preach the Pure Land way. He stressed the importance of repeated calling upon the name of Amida Buddha in the *nembutsu*, on the principle that the mercy and grace of Amida Buddha provided the best way to rebirth into Amida's Pure Land and eventual nirvana. He distinguished between two Buddhist paths: one based on self-effort and disciplined activity relevant to an earlier age, the other based upon sincere faith in Amida Buddha relevant to his own age of decline. He was banished from Kyoto in 1207 for his Pure Land teachings, but influenced his great disciple Shinran, who established an even more radical form of Pure Land teaching in his Jodo Shinshu or True Pure Land. Today the Pure Land groups are more numerous in Japan than any other Japanese Buddhist school, and practices such as calling upon the name of Amida Buddha are widespread. ▷ Amida worship; jiriki/tariki; Jodo; Jodo Shinshu; nembutsu; Shinran; Tendai

Hooker, Richard (1554–1600) English theologian, born near Exeter. At an early age he showed a sharp intellect, and through his uncle, the antiquary John Hooker or Vowell (1525–1601), chamberlain of the city, was brought under the notice of John Jewel, Bishop of Salisbury, and sent to Corpus College, Oxford, where he became a fellow in 1577. In 1581 he took orders, and preached at Paul's Cross. He was led into a marriage with Joan Churchman, the shrewish unlovely daughter of his landlady in London, and in 1584 he became rector of Drayton-Beauchamp near Tring. Next year he obtained, through John Whitgift, the mastership of the Temple, against a strong effort made to promote the Temple reader Travers, a prominent Calvinist and Puritan. Travers' sermons soon became attacks upon the latitudinarianism of Hooker, and when Whitgift silenced Travers, the latter appealed to the Council with charges against Hooker's doctrine which Hooker answered in masterly fashion. But having been drawn into controversy against his inclination, he felt it his duty to set down the real basis of Church government and in order to achieve this he asked Whitgift to move him to a quieter living. In 1591 he accepted the living of Boscombe near Salisbury and became Subdean and Prebendary of Sarum. Here he finished four of the proposed eight books of the *Laws of Ecclesiastical Polity* (1594), the earliest great work of the kind in the English language. It is mainly to Hooker's work that Anglican theology owes its tone and direction. The fifth book appeared in 1597 and the last three posthumously (1648, 1662, 1648). He died in Bishopsbourne, near Canterbury, where he had lived since 1595. ▷ Anglican Communion

hope An orientation towards some future event which will radically transform the present order, which is found in most religious traditions. Judaism, for example, awaits its Messiah, Islam the return of the twelfth imam; and Christianity anticipates the second coming of Christ. Even a seemingly cyclical faith such as Buddhism awaits Metteya, the Buddha who is yet to come. What is hoped for depends upon the specific understanding of reality displayed by a particular faith and it can be an individual or a social hope which is held. In Buddhism the hoped-for goal is nirvana, a state of pure tranquillity, the ending of personal existence. In Christianity hope has traditionally taken the form of belief in a transformed personal existence in a new world order which is to be established by God. Recently, however, studies of biblical hope have rediscovered its profoundly social and communal character. The foundation of all hope is the liberating activity of God in history, particularly in the events of Israel's exodus from Egypt and the cross of Christ. Biblical thought, therefore, views history itself as moving forward to the future kingdom which God is working to establish. The realization that the anticipated future kingdom is present already in God's activity in the world, leads to dissatisfaction with the present order of things and becomes the basis of a liberating and transforming practice on the part of the Church. Hope is the religious expression of the fact that human beings find fulfilment by anticipating, projecting and realizing themselves in future acts. ▷ eschatology; imam; Messiah

Hopi religion The Hopi ('peaceful people') belong to the group of sedentary Native American peoples known as Pueblo. Their home creates an island in the midst of the Navajo reservation, formed by three mesas rising starkly out of the desert plain. Like other Pueblo peoples they see their appearance on earth (they believe themselves the original inhabitants of North America) as the result of emergence from another world. Unlike other Pueblo, they view the sun as the direct agent of creation, though the frequent Native American theme of the deities is represented in a pair of war gods. Hopi religion depends on ritual pattern, immense in its complexity. It reflects a sharp dualism between the upper and lower realms of the universe. Unlike the dualism of the forest-dwelling Iroquois, however, it is not a warlike opposition of ideas, persons and spheres, but a calendrical opposition of the seasons, necessary to maintain the life of the people; this is seen, for example, in the differing solstice ceremonies for delaying winter and hastening spring. The most widely-known ritual features the use of masked dancers who represent the *kachinas*, spirits of the dead and of nature. ▷ Iroquois religion; kachinas; Pueblo religion

Horeb, Mount ▷ Sinai, Mount

horoscope An important element in astrology which interprets the character and destiny of a person (and occasionally a larger group) according to the position of the planets, usually at the time of the person's birth. A horoscope is cast on the basis of information given by the person, and it is then interpreted according to systematic principles. The horoscope takes into account two main considerations: the circle of the 12 signs of the zodiac (Aries, Taurus, Gemini, Cancer, Leo, Virgo, Libra, Scorpio, Sagittarius, Capricorn, Aquarius, Pisces) as they are crossed by the sun, moon and planets at different periods; and a circle of 12 'houses' around which the circle of the zodiac turns, so to speak, each day. Casting a horoscope is a complicated procedure that depends upon getting data and times right. Relevant factors are the position of sun, moon, planets and signs of the zodiac; the 'aspects' of sun, moon and planets in

signs of the zodiac, used in casting horoscopes

relation to each other; and the position of sun, moon, planets and signs of the zodiac against the circle of 12 'houses'. Certain planets are thought to be allied with certain activities and human propensities (for example Venus with love); the 12 houses are thought to be connected with certain areas of life, for example the second house with money; and the 'aspects' are thought to be associated with helpful or unhelpful situations and possibilities. Horoscopes remain important in the East and are growing in popular significance in the West despite scientific sceptism. ▷ astrology; divination

Horus Ancient Egyptian sky god, represented as a falcon or falcon-headed man. He is a complex figure with many mythological associations. As a sky god, the sun and moon are his eyes and his wings stretch across the heavens. At Heliopolis he was associated with the morning aspect of the sun god Re and worshipped as Re-Harakhte. He was connected with the divinity of the pharaoh, who was seen as the 'living Horus'. In the royal ideology the king was often identified as son of Osiris (who represented his dead predecessor), and Horus was also worshipped as the son of Osiris and Isis. In the Osirian legends he was involved in a lengthy struggle against his uncle Seth, his father's murderer. As the infant son of Isis, reared by her in the delta marshes, he was popular in the Graeco-Roman period under the name Harpocrates, and was depicted as a child in his mother's arms. The Greeks identified him with Apollo. ▷ Isis; Osiris; pharaoh; Re; Seth

Hosea, or **Osee, Book of** The first of the 12 so-called 'minor' prophetic writings of the Hebrew Bible/Old Testament, attributed to the prophet Hosea, who was active in the northern kingdom of Israel c.750–725BCE, during a period of Assyrian military invasions. The work warns of judgement for Israel's defection to the Canaanite Baal cult, but affirms God's love in seeking to restore Israel. Many of these prophecies are presented as corresponding to Hosea's own experiences with his unfaithful wife Gomer. ▷ Baal; Old Testament; prophet

House Church Movement A description applied to a variety of denominational and non-denominational movements which seek to regain something of the life of the early Church. A distinction should perhaps be made between independent house churches (often organized on a Congregational pattern), which challenge the values of traditional churches, and traditional churches or denominations, that **1** have some fellowships that meet in private homes but retain links with the wider organization (such as house groups in Protestantism, and base communities in Latin American Catholicism), or **2** who meet in private because the state forbids or discourages public worship (as in China and North Korea). The House Church Movement in Britain and the USA includes groups of differing outlook. Some look to the discipleship or shepherding movement that has roots in a community in Fort Lauderdale, Florida; some describe themselves as 'restorationists' inspired by the example of the early Church in the New Testament; others emphasize kingdom of God theology. Historical precedent can be found in 16th-century radical groups such as the Anabaptists and Mennonites; the immediate forerunners of the post-1960 House Church Movement are the Irvingites (Catholic Apostolic Church) and the Brethren. ▷ Brethren (in Christ); Irving, Edward

hsuan hsueh (hsüan hsüeh) A Chinese term, meaning profound or mysterious learning, which refers to the new Taoism or neo-Taoism that emerged in China in the 3rd and 4th centuries CE. It was a metaphysical school of thought whose chief interpreters were Wang Pi (226–49), Ho Yen (d.249), and Kuo Hsiang (d.312). Although they emphasized certain elements of Taoist doctrine, they also gave great honour to Confucius, whom they hailed as the greatest sage. They reinterpreted the basic ideas of the original Taoist philosophical texts, the *Tao Te Ching* and the *Chiang Tzu*, and they asserted that there is a primordial Non-Being (*Wu*) which is the source of everything, and which is ultimate reality. However although this is the underlying unity behind all things, its function can only be realized through Being (*yu*). There is thus a distinction and a kind of dialectic between Non-Being and Being, and between source and function. This distinction was influential in developments that took place in later Taoism, neo-Confucianism, and Chinese Buddhism. ▷ Chinese Buddhism; Confucius; Chuang Tzu; neo-Confucianism; Taoism; Tao Te Ching

Hsun Tzu (c.300–c.230BCE) Chinese philosopher within the Confucian tradition. At the age of 50 he went to Chi in modern Shantung and became the best-known of a group of scholars working there. He later became a magistrate in Chu, and when he lost this position he continued teaching in Chu, where he died. He lived at roughly the same time as the great philospher Mencius (371–289) and they represent two different strands within the Confucian tradition: the natural and the idealistic. Hsun Tzu asserted that human nature is evil and that it must be restrained by education and by the law and order imposed by the state. His religion was pragmatic and naturalistic in that he believed in the importance of funeral rites and ancestor veneration, but downplayed the significance of heaven (*Tien*), ghosts and spirits. He had an interest in psychology, in reason and logic, and in the notion of progress. His stress upon discipline, moral authority and education had an influence upon the authoritarianism of the Chin dynasty (221–206BCE) and upon the firm control exercised by the Han dynasty (206BCE–220CE). After that, however, his significance waned and that of Mencius increased. The work that bears his name, the *Hsun Tzu*, has 32 chapters of essays on various topics, but as it was never designated a Confucian Classic, its influence was less than would otherwise have been the case. ▷ Confucian Canon; Mencius; Tien

huaca A Quechua word signifying 'holy' or 'numinous' and attached to objects or places, or to a sacred being or its representation. A natural feature (such as a rock or spring) or a building or a battlefield might be huaca by virtue of its association with a spirit or divinity or some past event. Mountains, especially the high Andes, had this numinous association in high degree; but any grave, temple or sanctuary was huaca. The concept was fully shared by the Inca, who adopted it into their system. The whole of Cuzco was one vast huaca. From its Temple of the Sun radiated 41 lines across the empire, each with its vital huaca. But the concept outlasted the Inca, and is still essential to Andean popular religion, now usually in a Christianized form. Even now the piles of stones (*apoceta*) to which the traveller makes his own addition with his prayer as he passes along a treacherous mountain track are still huaca. ▷ apu; Inca religion

Hua Yen A school of Chinese Buddhism which was developed by Fa Tsang (643–712CE). He adapted the thought of the Indian Mahayana scripture known as the *Avatamsaka Sutra* to Chinese conditions. This sutra was claimed to be the first discourse given by the Buddha after his enlightenment. He preached it to the bodhisattvas because it was too difficult for ordinary mortals to understand; ordinary people were taught a simpler version. Fa Tsang wrote the *Treatise on the Golden Lion* for the empress Wu and in it he gave a classical exposition of Hua Yen thought. It brought out the importance of Vairocana as the resplendent Buddha who contains all things, and it painted a vision of the interdependence and interpenetration of all things. Thus the coming into existence of any one thing involves the simultaneous existence of all other things so that the one and the many, the inward and the outward, and the whole and the part are bound up together. This gave a positive and Chinese slant to the basic Mahayana teaching of 'emptiness' so that it opened up new opportunities in China for the appreciation of harmony in nature and among human beings insofar as they are all part of Vairocana Buddha. ▷ Avatamsaka Sutra; bodhisattva; emptiness; Vairocana

Hubbard, Lafayette Ronald (1911–86) American scientologist and science-fiction writer, born in Tilden, Nebraska, and the inspiration behind the Church of Scientology. From the age of 16 he travelled extensively in the Far East before completing his education at Woodward Preparatory School and George Washington University. He became a professional writer of adventure stories, turning to science fiction in 1938, with such classics as *Slave of Sleep* (1939), *Fear* (1940), *Final Blackout* (1940), *Death's Deputy* (1940) and *Typewriter in the Sky* (1940). He served in the US navy during World War II, and in 1950 published *Dianetics: The Modern Science of Mental Health*, which claimed to be pioneering in its exploration of the human mind and its detailed description of how the mind works. This was followed by *Science of Survival* (1951), which formed the basis of the scientology philosophy. The first Church of Scientology was founded by a group of adherents in Los Angeles in 1954; in 1955 Hubbard became the Executive Director of the Founding Church Washington. From 1959 to 1966 he made his base in East Grinstead in England, resigning his position as Executive Director of the church in 1966. In 1982 he returned to science fiction with an epic best-seller, *Battlefield Earth: A Saga of the Year 3000*, followed by a ten-volume series under the composite title *Mission Earth* (1985–7). ▷ new religious movements in the West; scientology

Huddleston, (Ernest Urban) Trevor (1913–) English Anglican missionary, educated at Christ Church, Oxford, and ordained in 1937. He entered the Community of the Resurrection and in 1943 went to Johannesburg, where he ultimately became provincial of the order

(1949–55). From 1956 to 1958 he was novice-master of the community in Mirfield Yorkshire, and from 1958 to 1960 prior of its London House. From 1960 to 1968 he was Bishop of Masasi, Tanzania, then Bishop Suffragan of Stepney until 1978, and Bishop of Mauritius and Archbishop of the Indian Ocean (1978–83). He is distinguished by a passionate belief that the doctrine of the universal brotherhood of men in Christ should be universally applied. His book, *Naught for your Comfort* (1956), reflects this conviction in the light of his experiences in South Africa and its racial problems and policies. He also wrote *God's World* (1966) and *I Believe; Reflections on the Apostles' Creed* (1986). ▷ Anglican Communion; missions, Christian

Huehueteotl ▷ Ometeotl

huehuetlatolli ▷ calmecac

Hugh of St Victor (c.1096–1141) Victorine mystic and theologian. A native of Saxony, he joined the recently founded monastery of St Victor, Paris, in 1115, becoming prior and director of studies in 1133. His chief work, *On the Sacraments of the Christian Faith*, on the study of scripture, was complemented by several writings on the nature of prayer and its five stages: reading, meditation, prayer, growth in love, contemplation. Hugh's colleagues, who like him were dedicated to a monastic life balanced with scholarship, included the liturgist and poet Adam of St Victor (c.1110–1180) and the mystic Richard of St Victor (c.1123–1173). ▷ contemplation; discursive meditation; prayer

Hui Neng (628–713) Sixth patriarch of Chan (Zen) Buddhism in China, who was responsible for important developments in Chan Buddhism. He is traditionally portrayed as an ill-educated youth who went to work in the kitchens of the Yellow Plum monastery where the fifth patriarch Hung Jen lived. He had an experience of sudden enlightenment, and wrote a verse on the monastery wall containing the famous words 'the Buddha nature is always clear and pure; where is the room for dust?'. The fifth patriarch recognized Hui Neng's calibre, and he sent him to the south, where he founded the southern school of Chan, while the patriarch's other famous pupil, Shen Hsiu, became leader of the northern school of Chan. The *Platform Sutra*, the only sutra written in Chinese rather than in Sanskrit, is attributed to Hui Neng. In contrast to the northern school of Chan, Hui Neng taught that enlightenment is sudden not gradual, that long periods of quiet meditation and chanting of scriptures are unnecessary, and that one must wake up to one's own intrinsic purity and Buddha nature rather than make great efforts at purification in order to find them. The disputes between the two schools were settled at a council of 796CE, where the emperor decided in favour of Hui Neng's position. He was thus the key figure in determining the main historical development of Chan in China and of Zen in Japan. ▷ Buddha nature; Chan patriarchs; Zen Buddhism

Huirococha ▷ Viracocha

Huitzilopochtli Aztec god of the sun and of war. Human sacrifices were made before his image. He has been identified with the Toltec Quetzalcoatl, whom he replaced after the Aztec conquest. ▷ Aztec religion; human sacrifice, Meso-American; Quetzalcoatl

Huitzilopochtli

Hukam An important concept within the Sikh tradition, denoting the will of God. It was originally an Arab word meaning 'order' or 'command'. According to Sikhs, Hukam is the divine order. The human order stems from the divine order and the destiny of human beings is to follow God's Hukam and to live in harmony with his order and will. However humans often prefer to follow their own selfish will (*Haumai*), and they need to change from their own selfish ways and to respond to God's grace. Hukam stands for the will of God in the sense that God's will is not capricious but stable, compassionate and constant. The challenge for human beings is to submit to God's order and will, and to walk in the light of God's Hukam. Thus they will know God and find salvation (*mukti*).

humanism Historically, a movement that arose with the Italian Renaissance, in the writings of Ficino, Pico della Mirandola, and others, emphasizing the liberation of humanity from the thrall of the medieval Church and State. The movement continued with such thinkers as Erasmus and Thomas More. More generally, any position which stresses the importance of persons, typically in contrast with something else, such as God, inanimate nature, or totalitarian societies. ▷ Erasmus, Desiderius; More, Thomas; Pico della Mirandola

humankind, Christian view of Christianity holds that men and women are made in the image or spiritual likeness of God, and, as Augustine put it, they are restless until they find their rest in God. This image has been marred by sin, yet it can be remade through Christ. So, in the celebrated words of Irenaeus, 'The glory of God is man fully alive'. This potential, however, will be completely realized only in the heavenly kingdom of God, when evil and all the limitations of creaturely existence will be overcome. Meanwhile, the Church, faulty as it is because its members are still in the process of being made holy, by its display of the gifts and fruits of the Holy Spirit, gives some glimpses of the future reign of God.
The Christian view thus claims to be realistic, rather than over-optimistic (as with 19th-century belief in evolutionary 'progress') or over-pessimistic (as with 20th-century existentialism) about the state of humanity. In the name of the doctrine of the image of God it opposes everything in society that would dehumanize the individual, and by its understanding of the kingdom of God (which it prays may be known on earth, as it is in heaven), it argues that sin and salvation, along with specific ethical issues, are corporate and social, as well as individual concerns. Many Christians would also argue that the Church has to deal with individual and corporate sin in its own organization and structures, especially what some would perceive as the dehumanizing of women and minority groups such as the divorced or the disabled. ▷ afterlife, Christian concept of; atonement; Augustine, St; Church, Christian; Christian ethics; Irenaeus, St; kingdom of God; saint, Christian view of; salvation, Christian view of; sin; soul, Christian view of

humankind, Jewish view of Following the Book of Genesis 1.26–8, Jewish tradition views humans as formed in the image of God, giving them a special dignity within the created order. As such humankind has dominion over the earth but with it the responsibility to act as a faithful steward. However, such accountability implies free will, and Judaism maintains that people are free to act justly or wickedly, to trust God or reject him. That the latter option is often taken is not because human nature is inherently flawed but because everyone has been endowed with two inclinations—the *yetzer tov* ('good inclination') and the *yetzer ra* ('evil inclination')—which are in conflict. However, the yetzer ra was created by God and is essentially good. When harnessed properly it provides the impulse for activities like commerce, marriage and procreation; only when out of control does it lead to impiety. Nonetheless, in practice few, if any, are sinless. Therefore, central to the Jewish view of the human situation is *teshuvah* or repentance; any individual who has sinned may return to God and be forgiven without mediator or bribe. As for a final judgement, traditional Judaism developed belief in life after death, including a bodily resurrection, when rewards and punishments will be meted out according to God's mercy and justice. Although Judaism gives the Jewish people a special place within the divine scheme, it also affirms that God guides the overall destiny of humankind towards an ultimate good. ▷ Gentiles; Olam haBa; Judaism, women in

Human Potential movement A broad range of movements that attempt to enable people to attain a greater degree of self-awareness, self-development and self-mastery, and to maximize the human potential that is their birthright. Some are purely humanistic, some overtly religious, and some are a combination of both. Gurdjieff was an early symbolic figure in this movement which sprang to life in the 1960s, first in California and then elsewhere in the West. It can include many facets: counselling, psychotherapy, massage, vegetarianism, dance, music, martial arts, alternative medicine, visualization, yoga, Zen, meditation, Jung's thought, and so on. The therapies it recommends are varied, including, for example, rebirthing by re-experiencing one's own birth, Erhard Seminar Training (EST) centred upon weekends of emotional harangue and release, and encounter groups like the one at Esalen in California where frank and concerned sharing takes place. In these and in other ways it is thought that latent energies can be tapped and repressed feelings released. A variation of the human potential movement has been active in the church in the work of Christians such as Fulton Sheen, Norman Vincent Peale and Leslie Weatherhead. At a more unconventional religious level it has gathered up elements from mysticism, the occult, psychedelic drugs and eastern religions, and it is part of the recent development of new age religion. ▷ Gurdjieff, Georgei Ivanovitch; Jung, Carl Gustav; occult; psychedelic drugs; yoga; Zen Buddhism

human sacrifice, Israelite Although not common in the ancient Near East, the biblical polemic against human sacrifice (normally child sacrifice) suggests that it did occur to some extent in Ancient Israel. The stories of Abraham and Isaac and of Jepthah's daughter may reflect a time when child sacrifice was practised, but are probably better understood as folk tales. Nevertheless in the Bible there are many denunciations of the burning of children during the monarchical period. These sacrifices are sometimes to a god called Molech, and often at Topheth in the valley of the sons of Hinnom just south of Jerusalem. The practice is normally denounced in the context of Canaanite influence on Israel; thus among the other pagan practices they encouraged we hear that the Judaean kings Ahaz and Manasseh both burned their sons as offerings. The influence may be Phoenician, as we know of such child sacrifice among the Phoenicians. There may be a reference to a foundation sacrifice in I Kings 16 where we are told that Hiel of Bethel built Jericho 'at the cost of' one son for the foundations and another for the gates. ▷ Old Testament

human sacrifice, Meso-American Human sacrifice is an ancient institution in Central American civilizations. The central idea is maintenance of the cosmic order and the vegetation cycle by the supply of life-giving blood. In classical Mayan civilization, its use seems to have been restrained in comparison with later times, and the classical Maya did not engage in aggressive warfare. Under the warlike Toltec it developed greatly, and with a new rationale; Quetzalcoatl may have ordered religion without human sacrifice, but Tezcatlipoca, to whom the present age belonged, had reintroduced it. Under Aztec dominance, it increased exponentially; the gods had instituted warfare in order that the sun and other powers might be ritually fed from the blood of captives. When the great temple of Huitzilpochtli and Tlaloc at Tenochtitlan was dedicated in 1487, 20000 prisoners were sacrificed, and sacrifices consumed an estimated 50000 victims a year. The usual method was by tearing out the heart after the priest had stabbed with a stone knife; dismemberment followed the rolling of the body down the temple steps. Ritual cannibalism (only the upper classes participating) came to accompany sacrifices of this type. Certain types of sacrifice required beheading, combat, or shooting with arrows. At planting time, a slave was offered to Xipe Totec, the spring god; the priest put on the victim's flayed skin. In the dry season, children were slaughtered for Tlaloc, the rain god. The corn-cob goddess received a young girl, her head cut off like the cob from the stalk. The ripening warmth of Huehueotl, the fire god, was solicited by tearing the heart out of half-roasted prisoners. And the renewal of the calendar at the end of each 52-year cycle (*Toxiuhmolpilia*) involved removing the heart from a distinguished captive and lighting a fire in the cavity, following the ritual breaking of pots and dowsing of fires throughout the realm to mark the new era. The scale of human sacrifice in late Aztec times suggests a climate of acute fear and insecurity. ▷ Aztec religion; Maya religion; Quetzalcoatl; Tezcatlipoca; Toltec religion

Hume, (George) Basil (1923–) English Benedictine monk and cardinal, born in Newcastle-upon-Tyne. Educated at Ampleforth College, St Benet's Hall, Oxford, and Fribourg University, Switzerland, he was ordained a priest in 1950, and returned to Ampleforth College as senior modern language master two years later. From 1957 to 1963 he was Magister Scholarum of the English Benedictine Congregation, and in 1963 became Abbot of Ampleforth, where he remained until created Archbishop of Westminster and a cardinal in 1976. He published *Searching for God* (1977), *In Praise of Benedict* (1981), *To Be a Pilgrim* (1984), and *Towards a Civilization of Love* (1988). ▷ Benedictines; monasticism

Hume, David (1711–76) Scottish philosopher and historian, born in Edinburgh. His early years were unsettled: he studied but did not graduate at Edinburgh University; he took up law, but suffered from bouts of depression, and tried his hand instead at commerce as a counting-house clerk in Bristol. In 1734 he went to La Flèche in Anjou where he stayed for three years studying and working on his first and most important work, *A Treatise of*

Human Nature, which he had published anonymously in London (1739–40) when he returned to Scotland to stay on the family estate at Ninewells in Berwickshire (1739–45). The subtitle is 'An attempt to introduce the experimental method of reasoning into moral subjects' and the book is in many ways the culmination of the empiricist tradition from John Locke and George Berkeley, with major, and still influential, discussions of perception, causation, personal identity and what became known as 'the naturalistic fallacy' in ethics. In political theory he argued for the 'artificiality' of the principles of justice and political obligation, and challenged the rationalistic 'natural law' and 'social contract' theories of Thomas Hobbes, Richard Hooker, Locke and Rousseau. Hume was bitterly disappointed at the initial reception of the *Treatise* ('it fell dead-born from the press') and put out the more popular *Essays Moral and Political* (1741, 1742), which were immediately successful and helped gratify his literary ambitions.

His efforts to secure an independent income still proceeded by fits and starts: his atheism doomed his applications for the professorships of moral philosophy at Edinburgh (1744) and logic at Glasgow (1751); he became tutor for a year in 1745 to an insane nobleman, the Marquis of Annandale, then became secretary to General St Clair on an expedition to France in 1746 and secret missions to Vienna and Turin in 1748. In 1748 he published a simplified version of the *Treatise* entitled *An Enquiry concerning Human Understanding*; its translation was said to wake Immanuel Kant from his 'dogmatic slumbers' and provoked the Idealists to counter Hume's scepticism. The brilliant *Dialogues concerning Natural Religion* were written in 1750 but were prudently left unpublished until 1759. He became Keeper of the Advocates' Library in Edinburgh in 1752 and achieved real fame and recognition with his *Political Discourses* (1752) and his monumental *History of England* in five volumes (1754–62). From 1763 to 1765 he acted as secretary to the ambassador in Paris, and was received with great enthusiasm by the French court and literary society ('Here I feed on ambrosia, drink nothing but nectar, breathe incense only, and walk on flowers'). He returned to London in 1766 with Rousseau, whom he had befriended but who was later to provoke a bitter and famous quarrel with him, became Under-Secretary of State for the Northern Department in 1767, returning finally to Scotland in 1768 to settle in Edinburgh where he died and was widely mourned, the equal in intellectual reputation to his contemporary Adam Smith. He has been a dominant influence on empiricist philosophers of the 20th century. ▷ empiricism; idealism; Kant, Immanuel; Locke, John

Humphreys, (Travers) Christmas (1901–83) English Buddhist, born in London, the leading figure in British Buddhism for over half a century. In professional life he was a barrister at the Old Bailey, the central criminal court in London. Although educated at private school and Cambridge University and brought up as an Anglican, he was influenced by theosophy and the philosophy of Madame Blavatsky, and, with his future wife, he set up the Buddhist lodge in 1924 as an adjunct of the Theosophical Society. It remained this until 1943, when it became the Buddhist Society London, and then simply the Buddhist Society. Humphreys gradually shed some of his theosophy but even when he was the premier British Buddhist, his Buddhism retained a theosophical tinge. At first his interest was in Theravada Buddhism, but he later invited the well-known Zen Buddhist Daisetz Teitaro Suzuki to London, and became a personal exponent of Zen. He eventually encouraged not only Theravada and Zen but also Chinese, Japanese and Tibetan Buddhism to have a place within British Buddhism, which he foresaw as developing its own strain of the Buddhist tradition. A prolific writer, as a proselytizer, energizer and popularizer of Buddhism he was of key importance in influencing many other people, and in nurturing a Buddhist tradition in Great Britain that continued to grow until his death. ▷ Blavatsky, Helena Petrovna; Chinese Buddhism; Japanese Buddhism; Suzuki, Daisetz Teitaro; theosophy; Theravada Buddhism; Tibetan religion; Zen Buddhism

Hurrian religion An ancient, non-Semitic, non-Indo-European people, the Hurrians were present in northern Syria and northwest Mesopotamia by c.2300BCE. By the mid 2nd millennium the Hurrian kingdom of Mitanni had formed in northern Syria and Iraq. Hurrians may have been resident in Palestine by the mid 1st millennium, and many hold that the biblical Horites (eg Genesis 14) were Hurrians. As yet the Hurrian language is not fully understood and scholars rely on Hittite records for much of their data. The main Hurrian god was Teshub, weather god and King of Heaven, pictured with bull imagery and lightning; he had a consort Hebat and a son Sharruma. Other Hurrian gods included Sheri ('day'), Hurri ('night'). Kushukh (moon god) and Shimigi (sun god). According to

Hittite material, Teshub gained his position only after battling with divine relatives for heavenly supremacy. While there is evidence for an interest in bird sacrifice and magic, little is otherwise known about Hurrian religious practices. ▷ Elamite religion; Hittite religion

Husayn (al-Ḥusayn) (624–80) The second son of Ali and Fatimah, the daughter of Muhammad, born in Medina in Arabia. Husayn's story is a central element in the Shiite Muslim tradition. He lived in Medina during the rule of the first Umayyad caliph Muawiya, but on his death he retired to Mecca without swearing allegiance to Muawiya's son Yazid. As Muhammad's grandson he had claims to leadership of the Muslim community and he was persuaded to go to Kufah in Iraq in 680, having received promises of support. However, he and about 600 men were surrounded by an army of about 4000 at Karbala near Kufah, and having refused to surrender they were finally massacred. Husayn's death took place on the 10th Muharram (10th October), and this remains an anniversary of mourning for Shiite Muslims. His death is viewed as a sacrificial martyrdom by Shiites and the drama of Karbala is remembered in art, folklore, spirituality, and writing—and annually by frenzied and grief-stricken commemorative rituals in which devotees beat themselves in the streets. For Shiites Husayn was an imam in succession to his father Ali who mediated between humans and God. One of his sons survived, and the succession of the Imamate passed down among his successors until it is now lodged with the twelfth Hidden Imam. Karbala remains the most important shrine of the Shiite Twelvers. ▷ Ali; Hidden Imam; imam; Mecca; Medina; Muhammad; Shiism; Twelvers

Huss, or Hus, John (c.1369–1415) Bohemian religious reformer, born in Husinetz (of which Hus is a contraction) near Prachatitz, the son of a Bohemian peasant. In 1398, two years after taking his master's degree at Prague, he began to lecture there on theology. He had come under the influence of Wycliffe's writings, probably through Anne of Bohemia's retinue. In 1402 he was appointed rector of the university, and began to preach at the Bethlehem Chapel; in 1408 he was forbidden to exercise priestly functions within the diocese. In 1409 he was re-elected rector, but the archbishop commissioned an inquisitor to investigate the charges of heretical teaching against him. In connection with this, Pope Alexander V promulgated a bull condemning Wycliffe's teaching, ordered all his writings to be publicly burned, and forbade preaching in any except collegiate, parish and monastery churches. As Huss continued preaching, he was excommunicated (1411). Popular riots followed, and Huss, backed by the people, still maintained his position; nor did he give in even after the city was laid under papal interdict. But by 1413 matters had greatly changed, Huss having spoken out yet more boldly against the Church, resulting in some of his more influential supporters, including the university, falling away from him. On the advice of King Wenceslas of Bohemia he left Prague and found refuge at the castles of his supporters, for nearly all the nobles were on his side. He began writing his principal work, *De Ecclesia*, which, like many of his minor writings, contains numerous passages taken almost verbatim from Wycliffe.
About this time a general council was summoned to meet at Constance, and Huss was called upon to present himself before it. Provided with a 'safe conduct' guarantee from Emperor Sigismund, he reached Constance in November 1414. Three weeks later he was seized and thrown into prison. No precise charge had been lodged against him; but he had resumed preaching in Constance. The council condemned Wycliffe's writings in 1415 which did not bode well, and his own trial began in June 1416; but he was not permitted to speak freely in his own defence, nor allowed to have a defender. Called upon to recant unconditionally, and to pledge himself not to teach the doctrines that were put in accusation against him, Huss categorically refused, and was burned on 6 July. The rage of his followers in Bohemia led to the bloody Hussite wars, in which the two parties of Hussites under such leaders as Ziska and Podiebrad more than held their own in many battles with all the forces of the empire. They were not reduced till about the middle of the century. ▷ heresy; Wycliffe, John

Husserl, Edmund Gustav Albrecht (1859–1938) German philosopher, of Jewish origin, born in Prossnitz in the Austrian empire. He studied mathematics at Berlin (under Karl Weierstrass), psychology at Vienna (under Franz Brentano) and taught at Halle (1887), Göttingen (1901) and Freiburg (1916). He became founder and leader of the philosophical school of phenomenology. His *Logische Untersuchungen* (1900–1) defended philosophy as fundamentally an *a priori* discipline, unlike psychology, and in his *Ideen zu einer reinen Phänomenologie und phänomenologischen Philo-*

sophie (1913) he presented a programme for the systematic investigation of consciousness and its objects, which proceeded by 'bracketing off', or suspending belief in, the empirical world to gain an indubitable vantage-point in subjective consciousness. His approach greatly influenced philosophers in Germany and in the USA, particularly Heidegger, and helped give rise to Gestalt psychology. ▷ Heidegger, Martin

Hussites Followers of John Huss, who in the early 15th century constituted a movement for the reform of the Church in Bohemia (Czechoslovakia). They anticipated the Reformation by demanding the moral reform of the clergy, free preaching of the Word of God, and the availability of the Eucharist for all believers in both bread and wine. ▷ Eucharist; Huss, John; Reformation; Wycliffe, John

Hutchinson, Anne, née **Marbury** (c.1590–1643) English religious leader and American pioneer, the daughter of a Lincolnshire clergyman. In 1634 she emigrated with her husband to Boston, Massachusetts, where she lectured and denounced the Massachusetts clergy as being 'under the covenant of works, not of grace'. Tried for heresy and sedition, and banished, she, with some friends, acquired territory from the Narragansett Indians of Rhode Island, and set up a democracy (1638). After her husband's death (1642) she moved to a new settlement in what is now Pelham Bay in New York State, where she and all but one of her family of 15 were murdered by Indians.

Hutten, Ulrich von (1488–1523) German humanist, born in the castle of Steckelberg, uncle of Philip von Hutten. He was sent in 1499 to the neighbouring Benedictine monastery of Fulda, but his temper drove him to leave in 1504. He visited various universities, and then in 1512 went to Italy. Returning to Germany in 1517, and crowned poet laureate by the emperor Maximilian I, he entered the service of Albert, Archbishop of Mainz, and shared in the famous satires against the ignorance of the monks, the *Epistolae Obscurorum Virorum*. Eager to see Germany free from foreign and priestly domination, he took part in 1519, along with Franz von Sickingen, in the campaign of the Swabian League against Ulrich of Württemberg. He took on Luther's cause with his customary impetuosity and vehemence. A set of Dialogues (1520) containing a formal manifesto against Rome moved the pope to have him dismissed from the archbishop's service. He found shelter in Sickingen's castle of Ebernburg in the Palatinate, where he engaged in virulent polemics against the papal party to rouse the German emperor, nobles and people. His earliest work in German, *Aufwecker der teutschen Nation* (1520, 'The Rouser of the German Nation'), is a satiric poem. Driven to flee to Basle in 1522, he was coldly treated by Erasmus. He finally found a resting place through Zwingli's help, on the island of Ufnau in the Lake of Zürich, the exact location of which was discovered in 1958. ▷ Erasmus, Desiderius; humanism; Luther, Martin; Zwingli, Huldreich

Hutterian Brethren A Protestant denomination tracing its origins to the Moravian communities led by Jakob Hutter, who was martyred in 1536. Over 100 communities based on common ownership of property and separate schools exist today in the USA and Canada.

I

Iblis The Muslim name for the Devil, derived from the Greek word *diabolos*, hence the English word 'diabolical'. He was originally an angel but he refused God's command to bow down before Adam and was banished by God from heaven. He tempted Adam and Eve in the Garden of Eden, and the guilt for their fate lies with him and is not connected with any sense of original sin inherent in human beings. The Quran also sees Iblis as one of the jinn (subtle beings) who opposed the angels, and as head of the jinn he superintends hell until the final judgement. However, Quran 15.38 also suggests that Iblis will in some sense continue to serve God even in hell, and that he may finally be saved. Some Sufi thinkers have reflected on this side of Iblis's being and have seen in him a tragic element of misguided attractiveness. Most Muslims have seen him more negatively as the one who tempts human beings and attempts to lead them away from God. The *shahadah*, with its ringing affirmation that Allah is Allah and Muhammad is his prophet, is an antidote against the wiles of Iblis. ▷ Adam and Eve; Eden, Garden of; hell; Quran; Satan; shahadah; Sufism

Ibn al-Farid (Ibn al-Fāriḍ) (1182–1235) Muslim Sufi poet and thinker, born in Egypt. One of his most famous works was the mystical Wine Ode, *Khamriyyah*. This highlighted the tendency among Sufis to use wine as a symbol of calling upon the name of God, and to use drunkenness as a symbol of the ecstacy that results from a true knowledge of God. Similar sentiments are reflected in the well-known *Rubáiyát* of Omar Khayyam. For al-Farid, and Sufis in general, material elements point to deeper layers and levels of meaning. Thus in his Wine Ode the crescent represents a seeker after godly knowledge, the full moon represents the depths of knowledge to be found in a spiritual master, and a battle represents the war within oneself for spiritual mastery over one's own being. ▷ Omar Khayyám; Sufism

Ibn Hanbal (Ibn Ḥanbal, Ahmad) (780–855) Muslim, the originator of the Hanbalite school of Islamic law, born in Baghdad. Trained in Baghdad, he was a student of the outstanding legal thinker al-Shafii. He supported traditional Islamic learning and was opposed to the speculative theology of the Mutazilites who were backed by the Abbasid caliph al-Mamun. Ibn Hanbal's courage in opposing their notion that the Quran was a created and not an uncreated work led to his persecution, scourging and imprisonment. He was restored by a later caliph, al-Mutawakkil, having achieved a great reputation as a defender of the faith. His tomb in Baghdad became an object of veneration. His best-known work, the *Musnad*, is an important collection of the sayings of Muhammad (Hadith). The Hanbalite school of law established by his disciples stressed the centrality of the Quran and of the sayings and traditions of Muhammad as authorities for Islamic law. He was thus a traditionalist in the legal realm too, and his approach was eventually adopted by the puritan Wahhabi sect in 18th-century Arabia. ▷ caliphate; Hadith; Islamic law schools; Muhammad; Mutazilites; Quran; Shafii, al-; Wahhabis

Ibn Khaldun (Ibn Khaldūn, 'Abd al-Raḥmān ibn Muḥammad) (1332–1406) Arab philosopher, historian and politician, born in Tunis. He held various political positions in Spain but largely abandoned politics in 1375 and in 1382 went to Cairo where he became professor and a chief judge. His major work was a monumental history of the Arabs, *Kitab al-ibar* and the influential *Maqaddimah* ('Introduction to History') which outlined a cyclical theory of history by which nomadic peoples became civilized, attained a peak of culture, were then corrupted by their own success, and were in turn destroyed by another, more vigorous nomadic culture.

Ibn Taymiyyah (1263–1328) Muslim, a leading figure in what might be called the fundamentalist strand of Islam, born in Harran. He became a jurist in the Hanbalite school of law in Damascus, succeeding his father as professor of law; he then later taught in Cairo, where he was imprisoned for his literal interpretations of the Quran. He opposed various groups within Islam which did not understand the Quran literally, for example speculative philosophical theologians such as al-Ghazali, Sufis such as Ibn Arabi, who interpreted the Quran allegorically and symbolically, and other law schools which advocated consensus (*ijma*) or the use of legal stratagems. Rejecting innovations not found in the Quran or the traditions and sayings of Muhammad, he understood references in the Quran to parts of God's body in a literal fashion. In a famous sermon he argued that God came down from heaven to hear human prayers just as he himself descended the pulpit steps at the end of his sermon. Although regarded as being somewhat eccentric, he also became respected and after his death his tomb became a pilgrimage place. He stressed the role of the Muslim state in ordering law and discipline, and he was a forerunner of the 18th-century puritan Wahhabis of Arabia, and indirectly of some recent fundamentalist traits within Islam. ▷ Arabi Ibn al-; Hanbal Ibn; ijma; Quran; Sufism; Wahhabis

I Ching A Chinese work, known as the *Book of Changes*, which is one of the five classics of the Confucian Canon. Its early portions date back to around 1000BCE, and it began as a book of divination. Commentaries and additions known as the 'Ten Wings' later supplemented it, and it appears to have been written down in its present form by a Confucian editor in the 1st century CE. In addition to divination it included by this time the theory of the five elements (earth, fire, metal, water and wood), the notion of yin and yang, popular stories, historical legends and folk proverbs. It accepts that life is centred upon cosmic order, and yet cosmic order is subject to change and therefore human beings should learn to adapt to change in the best possible way. The *I Ching* contains the famous eight trigrams which symbolize the eight basic constituents of the universe, and the 64 hexagrams which symbolize the universal archetypes of human consciousness. It is assumed that there is a continuous chain of interaction and flux within the universe and that everything that occurs within it, whether within nature or humanity, is part of an integral whole and is capable of being understood through the medium of the *I Ching*. It has been the most influential of all the Confucian Classics. ▷ divination; Confucian Canon; yin and yang

ichthus An early Christian symbol which connects the letters of the Greek word for fish (*ichthus*) with the initial letters of the Greek confession of faith, 'Jesus Christ, Son of God, Saviour'. A symbol of Christ (the fish) and the newly baptized (little fishes, cf the disciples called to be 'fishers of men', in Matthew 4.19, Mark 1.17) in 2nd-century literature, the fish also appears in 4th- and 5th-century catacomb paintings as a symbol of the Eucharist. ▷ iconography; symbolism

icon (Greek *eikon*, 'image') A representation of Christ, the Virgin Mary, angels, saints, or even events of sacred history, used since the 5th century for veneration and an aid to devotion, particularly in the Greek and Russian Orthodox Churches. They are typically in Byzantine style, flat, and painted in oils on wood, often with an elaborately decorated gold or silver cover. They are believed to be the channel of blessing from God. ▷ art, Christian; iconoclasm; images

Russian icon

iconoclasm (Greek 'image breaking') The extreme rejection of the veneration of images. The practice was justified as an interpretation of the second of the Ten Commandments (Exodus 20.4), and was supported by the pope and the Roman emperor in the 8th century, and again by certain Reformers in the 16th century. ▷ icon; Reformation; Ten Commandments

iconography In religion, any representation of the divine or supernatural in visual form by way of portrait, statue or relief of some kind, icon being a Greek word meaning image.

Throughout the religious history of humankind there has been a widespread tendency to represent the divine order by means of visual imagery. Although early Christians made widespread use of images such as the cross and the fish, it was not until after the bitter iconoclast controversy that they were officially approved. The Eastern Orthodox and Roman Catholic churches accept the veneration of icons, arguing that worship is not directed to the image, but to the reality which it represents. Protestant churches, on the whole, rejected the use of images in worship, arguing that it was a form of idolatry. ▷ icon; iconoclasm; idolatry; images

iconography, Hindu Iconography is very important in Hinduism as images of deities are not merely representations of a higher power, but are usually regarded, once consecrated, as the deities themselves. The images of the gods, or *murtis* are the means whereby the invisible is made visible. Indeed, only through the visible can the invisible, eternal absolute (*Brahman*) be approached. Abhinavagupta (c.975–1025CE), a theologian of Kashmir Shaivism, says that a symbol (linga) has three levels: the gross physical level, which can be perceived through the physical senses, a subtle cosmic level, and an absolute level at which it is non-particularized and identical with the pure consciousness of Shiva. Icons of deities have traditionally been created by specific castes or guilds who follow precise rules for their construction. The sculptor (*sthapati*) would know the description of the deity from the *dhyana* or visual imagery sections of the texts, such as the *Brihat Samhita* (5th century CE), and know the purpose for which the image was intended. Each image usually displays the specific symbolic requirements of the deity, and the necessary number of faces, arms and so on. For example, Vishnu might be portrayed as having four arms, each holding one of his symbols: the conch, symbol of the five elements; the discus, symbol of the mind; the bow and lotus, symbols of the creative power of illusion (*maya*) and the moving universe; and the mace, symbol of spiritual knowledge. The attribution of symbolic meanings to various parts of an icon does, however, vary. Images are installed in the inner sanctum or 'womb room' (*garbha griha*) of temples, where they are consecrated, thus becoming divine. Some images are thought to be so sacred that only high castes can see them. Such images might on occasion be transported out of the temple for people to receive the deity's (ie icon's) darshan, for example the image of Jagadnatha at Puri, which is transported around the town during the *ratha yatra* festival. The images of deities will be treated as the deity and even woken in the morning bathed, dressed, fed and put to bed at night The deity can be expressed not only in an image, but also in sound as mantra, in abstract design as in *yantras* and mandalas and in gesture (*mudra*). ▷ Brahman; caste; darshan dhyana; Kashmir Shaivism; linga; mandala mantra; maya; Shiva; Vishnu; yantra

iconography and symbolism, Christian Theology and symbolism in Christianity are inextricably mixed. In a theological sense Christ is seen as the image or icon of the invisible God (Colossians 1.15) and the redeemer or restorer of the marred image of God in humankind that has been spoilt by sin. The supreme Christian icon in artistic terms is therefore the cross, traditionally portraying a cruficied figure of Christ suffering for the sins of the world. Some of those Protestants that do not reject crucifixes and crosses outright as idolatrous (rejecting the argument that there is a distinction between worship offered to God alone and veneration of things that symbolize God), prefer an empty cross in religious art or architecture to signify belief that the crucifixion was followed by the resurrection. Other well-known Christian symbols include the lamb (representing Christ as the suffering servant of Isaiah and the conquering Lamb of Revelation), the dove (representing the Holy Spirit), and the ichthus fish-symbol. ▷ art Christian; atonement; Holy Spirit; ichthus redemption; resurrection; sin

Id ('Īd) A general Muslim term for a festival used in particular for the two most important Islamic festivals. The first, Id al-Adha, the feast of the sacrifice, takes place at the end of the period of the Mecca pilgrimage, and commemorates the sacrifice by Abraham of a ram instead of his son, which event is held by Muslims to have taken place at Mina just outside Mecca. Muhammad began this festival during his second year at Medina, when it was not possible for the early Muslims to observe the pilgrimage in Mecca. The second festival, Id al-Fitr, the feast of breaking of fast, occurs at the end of the Ramadan Fast It is marked by the communal saying of the special Id prayer, and special alms are also given at that time. Both festivals are times of celebration, wearing new clothes, feasting and rejoicing, and the second festival is a time of public holiday within Islamic communities ▷ Abraham in Islam; fasting; Hajj; Husayn Mecca; Medina; pilgrimage; Ramadan

idealism In philosophy, the metaphysical thesis that the only things which really exist are minds and their contents. Berkeley maintained that 'to be is to be perceived or a perceiver'; physical objects are collections of ideas that exist only insofar as they are perceived by finite, human minds or by the infinite mind, God. Hegel claimed that even the minds of persons are mere fragments of the Absolute, an immaterial object that is not a person. ▷ Berkeley, George; Hegel, Georg Wilhelm Friedrich

ideology A term first coined by the philosopher Destutt de Tracy (1755–1836) to refer to the study of ideas; now typically used to describe any set of beliefs that support sectional interests. The prevailing ideologies in society are likely to reflect and justify interests of the dominant (class, political, or religious) groups. The term implies that ideological beliefs are in some way exaggerations or distortions of reality. Several individual uses of the term have emerged in different political theories (eg Marxism). ▷ religion; secular alternatives to religion

idolatry In Judaism, Christianity and Islam idolatry is the offering of worship, which is rightly due to God, to some person, place or object other than God. In its strictest etymological sense idolatry is the worship of images. The term idolatry comes from the Christian apologists of the 1st century, but the concept was one which they inherited from Judaism where the first two commandments explicitly forbid the worship of gods other than Yahweh and also the making of any kind of representation of the deity (Exodus 20.3–6). In this we see two possible forms of idolatry: the idolatrous worship of Yahweh through images, and the worship of other gods. The first is forbidden because of the danger of confusing the idol with God, who is beyond representation. The second is forbidden because of the emptiness of false gods and their idols.
The prohibition of idols was never completely successful, as is seen by the use of objects such as the teraphim (1 Samuel 19.13, 16), and also the prophetic attack on their continued existence (Isaiah 40.18–25). Christianity inherited the prohibition on idols from Judaism and exhibits the same degree of confusion over the use of images in worship. For example, the veneration of saints and images is attacked as a form of idolatry by the Protestant tradition. Catholic thought, however, insists upon a principle of mediation and rejects the charge that the use of a mediating agency to focus devotion is in itself idolatrous. ▷ icon; images

idols Images representing deities, widely used in the ancient world and still used in many faiths today. Idols and images are particularly prevalent in those areas which have been influenced by the Hindu and Buddhist faiths. Idols are consecrated to the god which they represent by a ceremony during which the god is worshipped. After this the idol's eyes are opened and the god is believed to inhabit the idol. This does not mean that the god cannot be found elsewhere, but rather marks a special association between idol and god, which means that the god can be guaranteed to be found there. Sophisticated believers argue that the idol is a visible representation of a spiritual power, but popular belief often attributes power to the idol itself. ▷ iconography; idolatry; images

idols, Islamic view of The age before the rise of Islam in Arabia is known among Muslims as the age of ignorance, when idols were worshipped. This idol-worship was condemned by the early Muslims as being wrong in the ringing tones of the monotheism of the shahadah, which stated that there was no God but Allah, and that Muhammad was his prophet. The main gods idolized in pre-Islamic Arabia were Hubal, the god of the moon, and the four goddesses al-Uzza, al-Lat, Manat and Wudd, although in all there were 360 idols erected in the Kabah in Mecca. Their main cults were centred upon rituals of sacrifice, and on processions that occurred at the times of great pilgrimages and fairs. With the triumph of Islam the idols were destroyed, but the Kabah, with its the Black Stone, was viewed as the 'holy house' and it remained as a sanctuary consecrated to God. It became the focus of the Hajj, the great annual Islamic pilgrimage to Mecca, which replaced the ancient fairs, like those of Mina and Ukaz, which had been centred upon the cults of idols. ▷ Allah; Black Stone; Hajj; Mecca; shahadah

Idumeans ▷ **Edomites**

Ifa ▷ **divination, African**

Ignatius Loyola, St, properly **Iñigo López de Recalde** (1491–1556) Spanish soldier and founder of the Jesuits. He was born at his ancestral castle of Loyola in the Basque province of Guipúzcoa. A page in the court of Ferdinand 'the Catholic', he then became a soldier. In the defence of Pampeluna he was severely wounded in the leg, which he had to have re-broken in order to be re-set. After this operation his convalescence was slow; and, his stock of romances exhausted, he turned to works on the lives of Jesus Christ and the saints. The result was a spiritual enthusiasm as intense as that by which he had hitherto been drawn to chivalry. Renouncing military life, he resolved to begin his new life by a pilgrimage to Jerusalem. In 1522 he set out on his pilgrimage, the first step of which was a voluntary engagement to serve the poor and sick in the hospital of Manresa. There his zeal and devotion attracted such notice that he withdrew to a cavern in the vicinity, where he pursued alone his course of self-prescribed austerity, until, utterly exhausted, he was carried back to the hospital. From Manresa he went to Rome, then proceeded on foot to Venice and there embarked for Cyprus and the Holy Land. He returned to Venice and Barcelona in 1524. He then resolved to prepare himself for the work of religious teaching, and at the age of 33 returned to the rudiments of grammar, followed up by courses at Alcalá, Salamanca and Paris.

In 1534 he founded, with St Francis Xavier and four other associates, the Society of Jesus. The original aim was limited to a pilgrimage to the Holy Land, and the conversion of the Infidels, but as access to the Holy Land was cut off by war with the Turks, the associates sought to meet the new wants engendered by the Reformation. Loyola went to Rome in 1539, and submitted to Pope Paul III the rule of the proposed order, and the vow by which the members bound themselves to go as missionaries to any country the pope might choose. The rule was approved in 1540, and the following year the association elected Loyola as its first general. From this time he resided in Rome. At Manresa he wrote the first draft of the *Spiritual Exercises*, a vital work in the training of Jesuits. He sent out missionaries to Japan, India and Brazil, and founded schools for training the young. He was beatified in 1609, and canonized in 1622. His feast day is 31 July. ▷ Francis Xavier, St; Jesuits; pilgrimage; Reformation

Ignatius (of Antioch), St (c.35–c.107) One of the apostolic Fathers, reputedly a disciple of St John, the second Bishop of Antioch. According to Eusebius, he died a martyr in Rome. The *Ignatian Epistles*, whose authenticity was long controversial, were written on his way to Rome after his arrest. They provide valuable information on the nature of the early Church. His feast day is 1 February. ▷ apostle; Eusebius of Ceasarea

ijma (ijmā‘) A term meaning ‘assembly’ which refers to one of the basic principles of Islamic law. It is the notion of establishing a consensus on a matter of law and is derived from a saying (hadith) of Muhammad: ‘my community will never be in agreement on error’. It relates especially to a consensus on an important matter of law agreed upon by leading religious authorities and teachers, but the way may be prepared for this by a consensus at grass-roots level. The three other sources for Islamic law are the Quran, the sayings and traditions of Muhammad (sunnah), and the principle of analogy (*Qiyas*) from preceding laws. The problem is that perfect consensus is not easy to attain and therefore in practice it usually implies the consensus of a majority rather than of all, and ijma has been a less important legal principle than the Quran and the sunnah. Two new doctrines that were absent in the Quran and sunnah but were established by ijma are the veneration of the saints and the sinlessness of the prophets. ▷ Hadith; Islamic law schools; Muhammad; Qiyas; Quran; sunnah

ijtihad (ijtihād) A term literally meaning ‘effort’, used in Islamic law. It comes from a saying (hadith) of Muhammad in which he advised a follower that the right criteria for administration were as follows: firstly the Quran, secondly the sunnah (the sayings and traditions of Muhammad), and thirdly ijtihad. It refers to personal efforts or original judgements which are not based upon precedents and laws. People with the authority to make such efforts or judgements were called *mujtahids*. The main mujtahids in the mainstream Sunni tradition were the four early caliphs who succeeded Muhammad, and the founders of the four schools of law. Since then the tendency in Sunni Islam has been to downplay ijtihad in favour of tradition, and to argue that the door of ijtihad is closed, although in practice this has never finally been the case. Among mainstream Shiite Muslims the situation is different and they recognize ijtihad as an ongoing necessity. In theory it is the function of their Hidden Imam, but in practice it belongs by delegation to religious leaders such as the ayatollahs in Iran. ▷ ayatollah; caliphate; Hadith; Hidden Imam; Islamic law schools; Muhammad; mujtahid; Quran; Shiism; Sunnis

Ikeda, Daisaku (1928–) Japanese buddhist, born in Omori, Tokyo, who became the third president of the Buddhist Soka Gakkai movement in 1960. He inherited a tradition that had grown rapidly in Japan since World War II, and continued his predecessor's penchant for fine organization, clear publication and planned growth. However, he also stressed the importance of pursuing world peace, and advocated a kind of Buddhist democratic socialism that took a middle course between capitalism and communism. He had strong educational ideals that combined modern knowledge and Buddhist insights, for example in his view that field theory in recent physics confirms Buddhist teaching on the inseparability of space and matter. He opposed the authority of the Nichiren priestly hierarchy in favour of the independent role of lay people guided by Nichiren's teachings as interpreted by Soka Gakkai. His writings include a biography of his predecessor Josei Toda, commentaries on Nichiren Shoshu scriptures, and the thoughts of Arnold Toynbee on religion. In addition to strengthening Soka Gakkai, especially among young people and internationally, Ikeda has also mellowed its approach and made it more acceptable to wider society. ▷ Japanese new religions; Nichiren Shoshu; Soka Gakkai

Illapa An important divinity among the Andean peoples, and under the Inca empire perhaps the most important in the pantheon after Viracocha and the sun god. He was the weather deity, the source of fertilizing rain, represented with a club and a sling (the signs of thunder), and shining garments (the sign of lightning). According to one myth, when earth people were crying for rain, he broke with a shot from his sling the pot in which the rains (from the Milky Way, the heavenly river) were stored. In post-Inca times Illapa has been fused with the much-invoked St James (Santiago). ▷ Christianity in Latin America; Inca religion; Viracocha

Illuminati A society of religious enthusiasts founded by Adam Weishaupt (1748–1830) in 1776 in Ingolstadt, Bavaria. It aimed to spread a new religion based on an enlightened reason that is in direct contact with the Divine Reason. As such it bypassed the jurisdiction of Church and State, and was against the Christian priesthood. It was also very democratic in its dreams of a coming world peace and a democratic world order. The Illuminati, who were a kind of secret society, were to be the initiating and creative factor in the coming new world. The organization of the order was based upon freemasonary and at one time became involved in it, but the Illuminati were later affected by schisms and were eventually dissolved. The general term Illuminism is applied to the notion of the direct illumination of the human mind by means of revelation or the inspired effect of human reason, and is used not only in connection with Weishaupt's Illuminati but also in connection with mystical groups such as the Alumbrados of 16th-century Spain, and the Illumines of 17th-century France, who both claimed direct inspiration from the Holy Spirit. ▷ freemasonry; Holy Spirit

images The use and veneration of images is a feature of almost all religions. However, it is difficult to be precise about their role and meaning, as the function and significance of images varies from faith to faith. In certain faiths, such as that practised in ancient Egypt, the image was believed to be indwelt by the cult god and was the object of toilet and feeding rituals. Chinese popular religion also regarded the image as being inhabited by the god it represented.

Images came to have a role in faiths which originally had no place for them. In Hinduism, for example, early Vedic religion did not use images and it was only gradually that they came to be in widespread use. According to tradition the god 'dwells' or is specially present in the image once it has been consecrated by a prescribed ritual. The god is not limited by his indwelling of the image and can be present elsewhere at the same time. Images can also be used to inspire devotion and veneration because of their apt depiction of, or close association with, some aspect of the divine. In Catholic Christianity images of Christ and the Virgin Mary are venerated, not because of any power which they as images possess, but as a representation of the object of worship. They are simply a means to inspire devotion.

The universality of images suggests that humankind has a need to put itself in touch with the divine in some tangible way. Certainly the appearance of images in originally anti-imagistic faiths such as Hinduism, Buddhism and Christianity and even their limited use in Judaism and Islam, the most profoundly aniconic of all faiths, suggests a deep need to symbolize the transcendent in a visible and material form. ▷ icon; idolatry

imam (Imām) A Muslim term meaning 'model' or 'example' which refers to three kinds of leaders within the Islamic community who have the same name but a different function. Firstly, it is used of a leader of prayer in a local community. He stands at the front of worshippers, who are organized in rows, and leads them in prayer, especially on Friday at the noonday prayers. He is knowledgeable in the Quran and respected, and may exercise the effective role of leadership in the local situation, although he is not formally ordained like a Christian minister. Secondly, it is a title given to the leaders of significant Muslim communities or schools. For example, the founders of the schools of Islamic law were called imams in this more exalted sense, and it is also an honorific title given to great scholars such as Ghazali or founders of great Sufi brotherhoods such as Shadhili. Thirdly, it has a special significance among Shiite Muslims. For them the imam is a unique intercessor who has exceptional spiritual authority and knowledge. They consider that God has designated a set of charismatic leaders as their imams in a line of succession running through Ali and his family. Since the disappearance of the twelfth imam, the Twelvers have said that the later imams have been concealed but that the final one will return as the Mahdi to set up a kingdom of justice and peace on the earth. Other Shiite groups give different details to the notion of the imam, but interpret it along the same lines of divine charisma. ▷ Ali; Friday Prayer; Ghazali, Abu Hamid Mohammed al-; Islamic law schools; Mahdi; Quran; salat; Shiism; Sufism; Twelvers

Imhotep (c.27th century BCE) Egyptian physician and adviser to King Zoser (3rd dynasty), probably the architect of the famous step-pyramid at Sakkara near Cairo. In time he came to be commemorated as a sage, and during the Saite period (500BCE) he was worshipped as the life-giving son of Ptah, god of Memphis. The Greeks identified him with Asclepius, because of his reputed knowledge of medicine. ▷ Ancient Egyptian religion; Ptah

Immaculate Conception The belief that the Virgin Mary from the moment of her conception was free from sin. After many centuries' history, this was promulgated as a dogma of the Roman Catholic Church by Pope Pius IX in 1854. It was always rejected by Protestants as unbiblical, and, since 1854, has been rejected by the Orthodox Church. ▷ Mary; Roman Catholicism

Immanuel, or **Emmanuel** (Hebrew 'God with us') In the Hebrew Bible, a name which appears only in Isaiah (7.14, 8.8), where the birth of a son of this name to a young woman is a sign to King Ahaz of Judah's security against her northern enemies. The text of Isaiah 7.14 is cited in Matthew 1.23 as a prophecy of the birth of Jesus the Messiah, one to be born of a young woman (or virgin), whose name is to be called Immanuel. ▷ Isaiah, Book of; Jesus Christ

immortality The belief in the continued existence of the individual beyond physical death is a widespread feature of religious faith. What constitutes continued existence and the content of that existence differs, however, from faith to faith.

The Ancient Egyptians believed in a resurrection of the physical body and consequently they preserved the body and provided food for the deceased. The cult of Osiris believed in a resurrection of the individual but also the facing of a day of judgement beyond death. The Ancient Greeks thought that all souls went to Hades, a subterranean place of the dead. Later it was felt that heroes went to paradise (*Elysion*).

Christianity inherited belief in a general resurrection of the dead from intertestamental Judaism, the Hebrews originally having no hope in a life beyond death. Christianity combined its belief in a resurrected body with the Platonic view of an immortal soul. In this scheme the soul survives physical death and awaits the bestowal of a resurrected body by a special divine act. There will be a final judgement where the ultimate destiny of the individual will be decided. Heaven will be the dwelling place of those who are saved, while hell awaits those who remain unforgiven.

Hindu and Buddhist teaching is characterized by the concept of reincarnation. In Hindu thought this means that upon death we are reborn in another life. This does not mean that the conscious individual is reborn but that the eternal spiritual reality of *jiva* is reborn. Finally the cycle of rebirth will end when the jiva attains enlightenment, transcends self-centredness and becomes one with atman, the universal self or *Brahman*. Buddhist thought is similar to this except that what is reborn in each life is not a continuous entity in the way that the jiva is, but rather

shou, a Chinese representation of the first stage of immortality

it is the stream of karma itself which is reborn. Eventually the deathless state of nirvana will be achieved. ▷ jiva, Jain; judgement of the dead; karma; nirvana; reincarnation; resurrection; soul

Inari The Shinto deity of rice, food and fertility. He is a very popular Japanese *kami* and his shrines are scattered around the countryside in Japan. His primary role is that of providing agricultural prosperity, but he is also recognized as being able to deliver wider benefits such as wealth and prosperity. Inari temples are unusual in that they are painted red, they contain long rows of sacred arches (*torii*), they have many statues featuring foxes, and they are characterized by a pear-shaped emblem. Inari shrines are commonly known as 'fox-shrines' because they have stone-fox images at their entrances, and the fox is regarded as Inari's servant and messenger. The main shrine built at Kyoto in 711 is known as Fushimi Inari, and is noted for its thousands of sacred arches within tunnels that cover the hill where it stands. ▷ kami; Shinto shrines

Inca religion The Inca were a Quechua (some have thought originally Aymara) people of the highlands around Cuzco. Between 1438 and 1493, under their great rulers Pachacuti and Topa, they established a single political and religious system covering most of modern Peru and Ecuador and much of Chile. It was this quite recently constructed empire that the Spanish encountered on their entry to South America. The religious aspect of the empire was based on the universal recognition of Viracocha, originally the Inca creator deity, as supreme being, and on the incorporation of all other divinities served by the Inca and by peoples of the empire into a defined, subordinate relationship to Viracocha. Most important of these was Inti, the sun god, from whom the Inca royal house was held to be descended, and whose consort was the moon goddess, Mamaquilla, who supervised the calendar, and thus the ritual year, for each month has its proper ceremonies. Next in importance was Illapa, the weather deity, and Pachamama, the earth mother. There were many star deities and other powers. The great gods of all the defeated states were brought into the central ritual at Cuzco where, from the Temple of the Sun (the sacred centre of the world), a ritual pattern covering and actively involving the whole empire was maintained. Only those of royal blood could serve there, and the high priest was always a brother of the emperor. Except on certain specified occasions, human sacrifice does not seem to have been an important feature. Religion, like all Inca life, was affected by the fundamental division of the people into upper and lower moieties, the upper led by the emperor, the lower by his consort. Priestly religion placed much stress on purity and confession of sins. The concerns of peasant religion with regard to fertility, healing and local cults were probably little disturbed by the Inca religious system and have outlasted it, remaining in popular religion in their Christianized forms. ▷ huaca; Illapa; Mamacocha; Pachacamac; Pachacuti; Pachamama

Incarnation (literally 'the putting on of flesh') The assumption of human shape or nature by a divinity. A term found in many religions, it is most widely associated with the Christian concept of the union between the divine and human natures in one person, Jesus Christ; this was expressed as the 'Word' of God becoming 'flesh' (John 1.14). In Hinduism the term refers to a life-spirit which is given a material form. ▷ avatara; Jesus Christ; Hinduism

incense A mixture of gums and spices which gives off a fragrant odour when burnt. It is widely used in many religious rites, and its smoke is often regarded as symbolic of prayer. Its use in Christianity cannot be traced before c.500. Its use in the Churches of the East is more widespread than in those of the West. ▷ religion

inclusivism ▷ religious pluralism

Index Librorum Prohibitorum (Latin 'index of forbidden books') A list of books which members of the Roman Catholic Church were forbidden to read. It originated with the Gelasian Decree (496), and was frequently revised, the last revision being published in 1948. Although the Roman Catholic Church still claims the right to prevent its members reading material harmful to their faith or morals, it was decided in 1966 to publish no further editions. ▷ Inquisition; Roman Catholicism

Indian philosophies Speculation about the nature of the world and human existence occurs in India from very early times with the composition of the Vedas (1200–800BCE). The beginnings of systematic thought occur in the Upanishads which lay the foundations for the later philosophical systems and provide some of the texts upon which philosophical commentaries were written. All philosophical systems are built on axioms or criteria of value. In Indian philosophies the highest value has been freedom or liberation (*moksha*) rather than an ethical absolute or good. There has also been a general tendency to accept the doctrine of rebirth or reincarnation and karma, although not all schools accepted these ideas. Indian philosophical traditions developed in specific schools through oral debates. The principle tenets of the schools were codified into short aphorisms (*sutras*) which were commented upon by later philosophers in the tradition. For example Badarayana's *Brahma Sutra* was commented upon by Shankara and Ramanuja, who reached different conclusions about it. Speculation upon the nature of language has been an important part of Indian philosophy, greatly enhanced by the early development of linguistics or Sanskrit grammar. One of the central concerns of Indian philosophies has been the nature of knowledge and its acquisition. Most schools agreed that authoritative words (*shabda*), perception, and inference were valid means of knowledge (*pramana*), though some schools, such as the materialists, only accepted perception. Indian philosophies have traditionally been divided into six orthodox systems (*astika*) and three heterodox systems (*nastika*). The six astika systems are: Samkhya, Yoga, Purva Mimamsa, Vedanta, Nyaya and Vaisheshika. These are usually linked together in three groups of two: Samkhya and Yoga, Mimamsa and Vedanta, and Nyaya and Vaisheshika. The nastika systems are materialism or scepticism, Buddhism and Jainism. Vedanta has been a pervasively influential school of philosophy, though equally important for Indian philosophy as a whole has been the development of logic in the Nyaya school. Through debate and the development of logic, arguments became increasingly sophisticated as can be seen from the Vedanta philosopher Shri Harsha (13th century). In Madhava's compendium of Indian philosophies (the *Sarvadarshanasamgraha*), he describes not only the orthodox systems listed above, but also other philosophical traditions such as the 'Recognition' school of Kashmir Shaivism and the dualism of Shaiva Siddhanta. Modern Indian philosophy has been strongly influenced by Western philosophy, both European phenomenology (for example in the work of K C Bhattacharya) and Anglo-American linguistic philosophy. ▷ Badarayana; Buddhism; Indian philosophy, six schools of; Jainism; Kashmir Shaivism; Mimamsa; Nyaya; Ramanuja; Samkhya; Shaiva Siddhanta; Shankara; Upanishads; Vaisheshika; Veda; Vedanta

Indo-Europeans A hypothetical prehistoric people or group of peoples, from whose language the so-called Indo-European languages are held to derive. Little is known with certainty of the religious beliefs of the Indo-Europeans. They probably worshipped a pantheon of gods and goddesses, and there is evidence to suggest that they had a strong tradition of composing religious poetry, traces of which survive in the ancient religions of the various peoples of Indo-European origin. Some scholars argue that much of the religion of this people can be reconstructed with considerable accuracy, while others doubt the value of such reconstructions; the question is still much debated. ▷ tripartite ideology

Indra In Hinduism, the Vedic king of the gods, to whom many of the prayers of the *Rig Veda* are addressed. A warlike figure, he was the god of rain, using thunder and lightning as his weapons, and gaining support from a special elixir and the help of other deities such as Vishnu. Also found in Jain and Buddhist mythology, he is the father of Arjuna, one of the central figures in the *Mahabharata*. His significance waned in later Hinduism, and his role was taken over by Brahma. ▷ Brahma; Hinduism; Mahabharata; Veda; Vishnu;

indulgences In Roman Catholicism, grants of remission of sin to the living, following repentance and forgiveness; also, to the dead in purgatory. They were based on the Church's treasury of merit, accumulated through the good works of Jesus Christ and the saints. Abuses in the Middle Ages, leading to the 'buying and selling' of places in heaven, finally occasioned Martin Luther's '95 Theses', which launched the Reformation. ▷ Jesus Christ; Luther, Martin; purgatory; Reformation; Roman Catholicism; sin

Indus Valley civilization Between 2500 and 1700BCE, before the incursion of Aryan tribes into India, an urban civilization flourished in the Indus Valley. The most important urban centres of this civilization which have been excavated are Mohenjodaro and Harrapa. This culture was perhaps akin to Mesopotamian civilizations with which there may have been trade links. The people of the Indus Valley were probably racially related to the Dravidian tribes as may have been their language. Little is known of the religion or social structures of these people and their language and script has not been deciphered. There are, however, hints which suggest that certain features of their religion continued into Hinduism, suggesting that Hinduism is a fusion of Aryan and non-Aryan elements. Terracotta figurines may relate to a goddess cult and the motifs on carved steatite seals may have been of religious significance. Most notable among these is a seal depicting a seated, possibly horned figure surrounded by animals. This has given rise to speculation that it represents a prototype of Shiva, the Lord of the Animals (Pashupati). Perhaps the most significant find is a bath complex at Mohenjo-daro with a large tank which was probably used for ritual bathing, an important feature of Hinduism which has continued to this day. ▷ Aryans; Dravidians; Hinduism; Shiva

infallibility In the Roman Catholic Church, the claim that statements on matters of faith or morals, made by a pope speaking *ex cathedra* ('from the throne'), or by a General Council if confirmed by the pope, are guaranteed the assistance of the Holy Spirit (ie are free from error). The claim is rejected by Protestants, for whom only God and the Word of God are infallible. ▷ Holy Spirit; Council of the Church; papacy; Protestantism; Roman Catholicism; Vatican Councils

initiation ▷ rites of passage

initiation, Christian The sacramental rites of baptism, confirmation and first communion or Eucharist that mark entrance to the full membership of the Christian Church. Originally a whole, initiation became separated in the West around the 5th and 6th centuries into three rites, with the administration of confirmation reserved to a bishop. The Eastern Church still links baptism, chrismation (anointing with holy oil) and communion. The Reformers treated confirmation as an adult confession of faith preceded by instruction through creed and catechism, while the Anabaptists took the same line with baptism and permitted only adults to be baptized (as do the Baptists). Those who support infant baptism argue from the Old Testament pattern of infant circumcision to membership of the 'new Israel' of the church, and stress that the objective grace of God given in baptism is independent of human capabilities. Similar arguments have led some churches in recent years to permit children to be admitted to communion before confirmation. ▷ Anabaptists; baptism; Baptists; catechism; confirmation; Creeds, Christian; Eucharist; rites of passage, Christian view of

Innocent III (1160–1216) Pope from 1198 to 1216, the greatest pope of this name. He was born Lotario de' Conti at Agnagni and succeeded Pope Celestine III. His pontificate is regarded as the culminating point of the temporal and spiritual supremacy of the Roman see; under the impulse of his zeal for the glory of the Church almost every state and kingdom was brought into subjection. He judged between rival emperors in Germany and had Otto IV deposed. He made Philip Augustus of France take back his wife. He laid England under an interdict and excommunicated King John for refusing to recognize Stephen Langton as Archbishop of Canterbury. John's submission made England and Ireland satellites of the Holy See. In his time the Latin conquest of Constantinople in the Fourth Crusade destroyed the pretensions of his Eastern rivals. He zealously repressed simony and other abuses of the time. He promoted the spiritual movement in which the Franciscan and Dominican orders had their origin. Under him the famous fourth Lateran Council was held in 1215. His works embrace sermons, a remarkable treatise on the *Misery of the Condition of Man*, a large number of letters, and perhaps the 'golden sequence' 'Veni, sancte Spiritus'. ▷ Dominicans; Franciscans; Roman Catholicism

Inquisition A tribunal for the prosecution of heresy, originally of the medieval Christian Church. The term comes from the Latin *inquirere* to 'inquire into', and signifies the idea that inquisitors were actively to hunt heresy. Pope Gregory IX (13th century) gave special responsibility to papal inquisitors to counter the threat to political and religious unity from heretical groups. The activities of the inquisitors were later characterized by extremes of torture and punishment, most notoriously in the case of the Spanish Inquisition, which survived until the 19th century. Among the original aims of the institution, however, was the intention to save misguided believers from the agony of hellfire, the pain inflicted by the inquisitors a pale imitation of the eternal punishment awaiting those who did not repent. ▷ heresy; Roman Catholicism

INRI The first letters of the Latin wording of the inscription placed on Jesus's cross at Pilate's command (John 19.19–20): *Iesus Nazarenus, Rex Iudaeorum* ('Jesus of Nazareth, the king of the Jews'). ▷ crucifixion; Jesus Christ; Pilate, Pontius

insan (insān) The notion of man within the Islamic tradition. Although stressing God and his nature more than human beings and human nature, Islam has a positive view of man. According to Islam, man in the form of Adam was created by God in his image to serve and praise him. Man is God's representative on earth. He is endowed with a spiritual component, or soul, which survives the body and returns to God. The Quran is less clear about whether man has free will or not, but although theory inclines towards predestination, in practical terms man is accorded a measure of free will. Mainstream Islam preserves a distance and a difference between the transcendent Allah and the created humanity. However, the Sufi tradition has maintained the doctrine of the perfect man (*al-Insan al-Kamil*), according to which man can attain not only a warm relationship with God but also communion or union with God. Although men and women are spiritually equal before God, and 'created of a single soul' (Quran 4.1), biologically and socially they are different and unequal. In practice the notion of insan has emphasized the role of men rather than women, although Islamic modernism has begun to redress the balance. ▷ Allah; predestination in Islam; khalq; Mara (Islamic); Quran; Ruh; Sufism; Islam, women in

intertestamental literature Jewish literature composed in the period between the close of the Hebrew Bible and the fall of Jerusalem in 70CE, which is close to the generally accepted date of the writing of the earliest Christian Gospel (Mark). It includes 1 Apocrypha: writings in the Greek Old Testament (the Septuagint or LXX), most of which are also included in the Latin Bible (the Vulgate) and the Roman Catholic canon, which are not found in the Hebrew Old Testament or the Protestant canon (though sometimes printed separately in Protestant Bibles); 2 Pseudepigrapha: writings attributed to, or composed in honour of, much earlier figures; 3 The Qumran literature (Dead Sea Scrolls) found since 1947, which shed light on sectarian Judaism; 4 The allegorical interpretations of the Pentateuch by the Hellenistic Jewish philosopher Philo Judaeus; and 5 The writings of the Jewish historian Josephus, especially his *Jewish War* (covering events up to 70CE) and *Jewish Antiquities*. ▷ Apocrypha; canon; Dead Sea Scrolls; Josephus, Flavius; Philo Judaeus; Pseudepigrapha; Vulgate

Inti ▷ **Inca religion**

intra-religious dialogue Relations between the world religions (like those between historically separated parts of the same religion) vary with the situation and motives of the participants, and may be friendly, hostile, or non-existent. Christianity and Islam are missionary religions, seeking adherents to their cause through evangelism (promoting their views as 'good news'). They also engage in apologetics (defence of their position) and polemics (attack on their opponents' standpoint). Hinduism is a more syncretistic religion, able to absorb elements of other religions, though it does contain fundamentalist elements as extreme as any that can be found in Christianity and Islam.

Persecution or cultural harassment may take place in regions where adherents of one religion are in a minority, and another religion is strong, perhaps supported by a religiously committed state. In this situation adherents of the predominant religion may see no need to engage in dialogue. On the other hand, if a state is actively atheistic, or in danger of allowing traditional values to be swamped by secularism or materialism, the religions of that region may come together in dialogue on matters of common concern such as religious freedom, social justice, or the values of family life. Dialogue may also take place on specifically religious and doctrinal issues, with the aim of eliminating ignorance and misconceptions. ▷ apologetics; Christianity, persecution of; Church and State; toleration

Iqbal, Sir Muhammad (1877–1938) Indian Islamic poet and philosopher, born in Sialkot (now in Pakistan). He taught philosophy at Lahore, studied law in England, and was knighted in 1923. He wrote poems in Urdu and Persian which are full of a compelling mysticism and nationalism which caused him to be regarded almost as a prophet by Muslims. His *Reconstruction of Religious Thought in Islam* (1934) was significant for its modernist assessment of Islam. ▷ mysticism

Irenaeus, St (c.130–c.200) Greek theologian, one of the Christian fathers of the Greek Church, born in Asia Minor. He was a pupil of Polycarp who had been a disciple of John the Apostle. He became a priest of the Graeco-Gaulish church of Lyon under Bishop Pothinus, after whose martyrdom in 177 he was elected to the see. Gregory of Tours says that Irenaeus met his death in the persecution under Severus in 202, but this has never been substantiated. Irenaeus was a successful missionary bishop, but he is chiefly remembered for his opposition to Gnosticism (especially the Valentinians), in criticism of which he wrote his invaluable work *Against Heresies*. A masterly expositor of Christian theology, he was also a key figure in the maintenance of contact between eastern and western sections of the Church. His feast day is 3 July. ▷ Fathers of the Church; Gnosticism; Polycarp; theology

Iroquois religion Five related peoples south of Lake Ontario, (the Seneca, Cayuga, Onondaga, Oneida and Mohawk), who were highly successful in agriculture and war, formed c.1570CE the Iroquois confederacy. Union was solidified by establishing cross-tribal clan brotherhoods. Iroquois religious thought is complex. The upper world is peopled by *ongwe*—archetypes or 'elder brothers' of the forms of life on earth, and their ultimate source. Myth, ritual, social organization and the calendar are dominated by a system of paired opposites. The complementary spheres of the light and the dark principles are represented by the twins, Oterongtongnia (Ioskeha), the culture hero, and Tawiskaron, the flint man, who is eventually destroyed by his brother. This pairing and opposition is reflected in seasonal festivals, the division of clans into two sections, and the times allocated for dances. The sacred building, the long house, (a model of the universe as so often found in North America) has no central pole, symbolizing the grasp of the supreme being; and *orenda*, the word which stands for supernatural power, is essentially impersonal. Both these features offer a contrast with the neighbouring Algonquin who give such prominence to the Great Spirit. However, Iroquois dualism was modified by the 19th-century reformer Handsome Lake, who transformed his people's religion by his stress on the supreme being, Haweniyo, 'the great voice' from heaven. By contrast Haninseono, the devil, lives on earth; and today is often particularly associated with the white-dominated 'modern' world. Iroquois healing rituals are famous for the masked medicine societies, the 'false faces'. ▷ Algonquin religion; culture hero; dualism; Handsome Lake; masks

Irving, Edward (1792–1834) Scottish clergyman and mystic, born in Annan. He studied at Edinburgh University, became a schoolmaster and in 1819 was appointed assistant to Thomas Chalmers in Glasgow. In 1822 he was asked to the Caledonian Church, Hatton Garden, London, where he enjoyed a phenomenal success as a preacher. In 1825 he began to announce the imminent second advent of Jesus Christ; this was followed up by the translation of *The Coming of the Messiah* (1827), supposedly written by a Christian Jew, but really by a Spanish Jesuit. By 1828, when his *Homilies on the Sacraments* appeared, he had begun to elaborate his views of the Incarnation, asserting Christ's oneness with the human race in all the attributes of humanity and he was charged with heresy for maintaining the sinfulness of Christ's nature. He was convicted of heresy by the London Presbytery in 1830, ejected from his new church in Regent's Square in 1832, and finally deposed in 1833. The majority of his congregation adhered to him, and a new communion, the Catholic Apostolic Church, was developed, commonly known as Irvingite, though Irving had little to do with its development. ▷ Chalmers, Thomas; heresy; incarnation; Jesus Christ

Isaac Biblical character, son of Abraham by Sarah, through whose line of descent God's promises to Abraham were seen to continue. He was nearly sacrificed by Abraham at God's command (Genesis 22). He fathered Esau and Jacob by his wife Rebecca, and was deceived into passing his blessing on to his younger son, Jacob. ▷ Abraham; Bible; Esau; Jacob

Isaiah, Hebrew **Jeshaiah** (8th century BCE) The first in order of the major Old Testament prophets, son of Amoz. A citizen of Jerusalem, he began to prophesy c.747BCE, and exercised his office until at least the close of the century. According to tradition he was martyred. ▷ Isaiah, Book of; prophet

Isaiah, or **Isaias, Book of** A major prophetic work in the Hebrew Bible/Old Testament, ostensibly from the prophet Isaiah, active in Judah and Jerusalem in the latter half of the 8th century BCE during a period of Assyrian threats. Many scholars doubt the unity of the contents, with Chapters 40–55 considered a much later exilic work looking forward to Judah's restoration and called Deutero-Isaiah ('Second Isaiah') and Chapters 56–66 either as part of Deutero-Isaiah or as a distinct Trito-Isaiah ('Third Isaiah'). ▷ exile; Isaiah; Micah, Book of; Old Testament

Isaias ▷ **Isaiah, Book of**

Ise shrines The most sacred Shinto shrine compound in Japan, comprising the inner shrine, dedicated to the sun goddess Amaterasu, and the outer shrine, dedicated to the grain goddess Toyouke. It is believed to contain a union of the deities of sky and earth, and it became and has remained a popular place of pilgrimage. This reputation was enhanced when Amaterasu became equated, in Ryobu Shinto, with the sun Buddha Vairocana, for Ise could then be seen as both a

Shinto and a Buddhist holy shrine. Most Japanese people hope to visit Ise once in a lifetime, and in this sense it is a kind of Japanese equivalent to Mecca. Ise, which is commonly known as the 'Grand Shrine of Ise', is situated in the Mie prefecture at a place of great beauty. Traditionally daughters of the emperor led worship at Ise, and the emperor himself also went periodically. Debate continues as to whether Ise is mainly an imperial shrine or a national shrine, the new situation following the demise of state Shinto in the wake of the defeat of Japan in World War II making that debate more poignant. An unusual aspect of the Ise shrines is that they are rebuilt every 20 years on alternative sites, their 'god-bodies' being transferred from site to site each time. ▷ Amaterasu; Kokutai Shinto; Mecca; Ryobu Shinto; Shinto shrines; Vairocana

Ishmael Biblical character, the son of Abraham by Hagar, his wife's maid; expelled into the desert with his mother from Abraham's household after the birth of Isaac. He is purported to have fathered 12 princes, and is considered the ancestor of the Bedouin tribes of the Palestinian deserts (the Ishmaelites). Muhammad considered Ishmael and Abraham as ancestors of the Arabs, and as associated with the construction of the Black Stone in Mecca. ▷ Abraham; Bible; Hagar; Isaac; Islam; Mecca

Ishtar Assyro-Babylonian goddess of love and war, known in Sumeria as Inanna. She became the principal goddess of the Babylonians and Assyrians. She existed in many local manifestations which could be called upon independently and as other goddesses became assimilated to her the word ishtar became a common noun for 'goddess'. Like Inanna she was identified with the morning and evening star, the planet Venus, and, as an astral deity, was linked with Sin, the moon god and Shamash, the sun god. A fertility goddess, she was patron of sexual love and protector of prostitutes, and was identified by the Greeks with Aphrodite. She was equally a goddess of war and was especially revered for this by the Assyrians, at the head of whose army she was believed to go. In the Sumerian myth Inanna travelled to the underworld to rescue her consort Dumuzi (Tammuz), an event commemorated in annual ceremonies. Ishtar was worshipped outside Mesopotamia by the Hittites and Hurrians, and shared many characteristics with her West Semitic counterpart Astarte. ▷ Assyrian religion; Astarte; Babylonian religion; Shamash

Ishvara (Īśvara) The personal deity or Lord in Hinduism. The idea of a personal deity who is the cause of the universe is first found in the *Shevtashvatara* Upanishad (4th–5th century BCE) where the Lord is also spoken of as Rudra or Shiva. These theistic trends are continued into the *Mahanarayana Upanishad* where the supreme deity is called Narayana, a name for Vishnu. In the *Bhagavad Gita*, Krishna reveals himself to Arjuna as the supreme, personal Lord and cause of all manifestation from whom the universe is created and who in the end destroys it. Patanjali, in his *Yoga Sutra*, introduces the idea of the Lord as a special kind of self (atman) among other selves and as an object of consciousness or experience in meditation. The Nyaya Vaisheshika school of Hindu philosophy maintained, against the Buddhists, that Ishvara was the first cause of the universe. This argument was presented by Udayana (1025–1100CE), a Nyaya philosopher who argued that the nature of the world is as an effect which must therefore demand a first cause. This cause is the Lord who, by means of his will (*iccha*), cognition (*jnana*) and effort (*prayatna*) moves the eternal atoms into the various combinations which comprise the universe. The Lord does this to enable the eternally distinct soul (atman) to experience the results of its past actions. Shankara in the Advaita Vedanta school argued that Ishvara was a lesser or lower understanding of the absolute, abstract and impersonal *Brahman* without qualities (*nirguna*). Ramanuja (12th century), on the other hand, argued against Shankara for a personal Lord as did Madhva (13th century) in presenting his dualist (*dvaita*) Vedanta. ▷ Advaita Vedanta; atman; Bhagavad Gita; Krishna; Madhva; Nyaya; Patanjali; Ramanuja; Shankara; Shiva; Upanishads; Vaisheshika; Vishnu; yoga

Isidore of Seville, St, or **Isidorus Hispalensis** (c.560–636) Spanish prelate and scholar, born in Seville or Carthagena. A Doctor of the Church, and the last of the Western Fathers of the Church, he succeeded his older brother, St Leander, as Archbishop of Seville c.600 and was considered the most learned man of his age. His episcopate was notable for the councils at Seville in 618 or 619, and at Toledo in 633, whose canons formed the basis of the constitutional law of Spain. He also collected all the decrees of councils and other Church laws before his time. A voluminous writer, he is best known for his vast encyclopedia of knowledge, *Etymologiae*, which was a standard work for scholars throughout the middle ages. He also wrote an introduction to the Old and New Testaments; a defence of Christianity against the Jews; three books of 'Sentences'; books on ecclesiastical offices and the monastic rule; and a history of the Goths, Vandals and Suevi. His feast day is 4 April. ▷ Council of the Church; Fathers of the Church

Isis Ancient Egyptian goddess, daughter of Geb and Nut, sister and wife of Osiris, mother of Horus. Isis is the ideal wife and mother, who found the scattered pieces of her murdered husband's body, embalmed and buried him, restoring his life by her power. She bore his son Horus and protected the growing child from Seth, her husband's murderer. As mother of Horus, who was embodied in the ruling pharaoh, she was associated in the royal ideology with the queen mother. Isis was also believed to be a great enchantress, taught her magical powers by Thoth. She is usually depicted as a woman with a throne (the hieroglyph of her name) as a head-dress. In the New Kingdom (c.1567–1085BCE) and later, she became identified with Hathor and wore the solar disc and cow's horns of that goddess. In Hellenistic and Roman times she was a central figure in mystery religions and the most enduring of all Egyptian deities; her temple on the island of Philae in Upper Egypt remained until the 6th century CE. ▷ ennead; Hathor; Horus; mystery religions; Osiris; pharaoh; Seth; Thoth

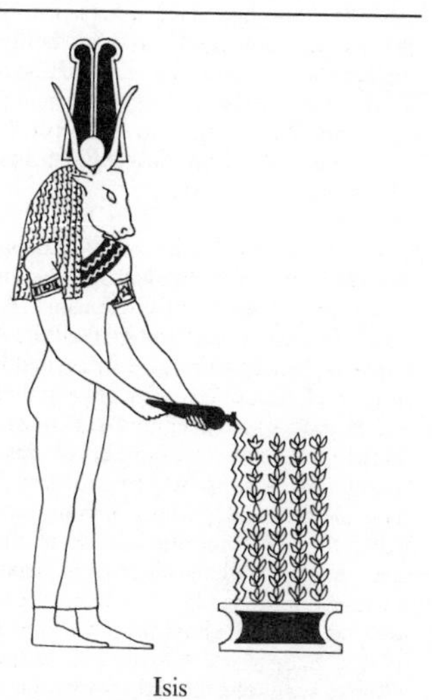

Isis

Islam The Arabic word for 'submission' to the will of God (Allah), the name of the religion originating in Arabia during the 7th century through the prophet Muhammad. Followers of Islam are known as Muslims, or Moslems, and their religion embraces every aspect of life. They believe that individuals, societies, and governments should all be obedient to the will of God as it is set forth in the Quran, which they regard as the Word of God revealed to his Messenger, Muhammad. The Quran teaches that God is one and has no partners. He is the Creator of all things, and holds absolute power over them. All persons should commit themselves to lives of grateful and praise-giving obedience to God, for on the Day of Resurrection they will be judged. Those who have obeyed God's commandments will dwell for ever in paradise, but those who have sinned against God and not repented will be condemned eternally to the fires of hell. Since the beginning of creation God has sent prophets, including Moses and Jesus, to provide the guidance necessary for the attainment of eternal reward, a succession culminating in the revelation to Muhammad of the perfect Word of God.

There are five essential religious duties known as the 'pillars of Islam'. **1** The *shahadah* (profession of faith) is the sincere recitation of the two-fold creed: 'There is no god but God' and 'Muhammad is the Messenger of God'. **2** The *salat* (formal prayer) must be performed at fixed hours five times a day while facing towards the holy city of Mecca. **3** Alms-giving through the payment of *zakat* ('purification') is regarded primarily as an act of worship, and is the duty of sharing one's wealth out of gratitude for God's favour, according to the uses laid down in the Quran. **4** There is a duty to fast (*saum*) during the month of Ramadan. **5** The Hajj or pilgrimage to Mecca is to be performed if at all possible at least once during one's lifetime. Shariah is the sacred law of Islam, and applies to all aspects of life, not just religious practices. It describes the Islamic way of life, and prescribes the way for a Muslim to fulfil the commands of God and reach heaven. There is an annual cycle of festivals, including Hegira, the beginning of the Islamic year, and Ramadan, the month in which Muslims fast during the hours of daylight. There is no organized priesthood, but great respect is accorded the Hashim family, descendants of Muhammad, and other publicly acknowledged holy men, scholars, and teachers, such as mullahs and ayatollahs.

There are two basic groups within Islam. Sunni Muslims are in the majority, and they recognize the first four caliphs as Muhammad's legitimate successors. The Shiites comprise the largest minority group, and regard the imam as the principal religious authority. There are a number of subsects, including the Ismailis (one group of which, the Nizaris, regard the Aga Khan as their imam), and the Wahhabis, a reform movement begun in the 18th century. There are over 700 million Muslims throughout the world. ▷ Allah; ayatollah; Black Muslims; day of judgement; five pillars, Islamic; Hajj; hegira; hell; imam; Islam, women in; Ismailis; Mecca; Muhammad; mullah; Muslim Brotherhood; Paradise; prophet; Quran; Quraysh; salat; Seveners; shahadah; Shiism; Sunnis; Wahhabis; zakat

Islam, slavery in Islam took for granted the institution of slavery which was common at the time of its emergence, with masters having sexual rights over female slaves. However, the Quran recommended compassion towards slaves, objected to their mistreatment, and also provided the possibility of their being freed. Gradually slavery became limited to the families of slaves and to people who were captured in war. Abu-Bakr, Muhammad's uncle, set a good example by ransoming slaves who had become Muslims and were persecuted for their faith by their owners. In medieval times slave bodyguards or soldiers such as the Mamluks in Egypt and the Janissaries in Ottoman Turkey were able to climb to positions of power. In recent times slavery has been abrogated in most Islamic areas, and in Saudi Arabia where the traditional shariah law remains, King Faisal abolished it by buying and freeing any existing slaves and ending the importation of new ones. ▷ Abu-Bakr; Muhammad; Quran; shariah; slavery

Islam, women in Although generalizations can be made about women in Islam, there are always exceptions, because Islam has become embodied in widely different cultures. For example, among the Berbers of North Africa women have a good deal of freedom compared with many other Islamic situations. Early Islam reformed the position of women in Arab society, placing restraints on divorce and polygamy and giving women some rights of inheritance and property. Theoretically Islam regards men and women as equal before God, and as 'created of a single soul' (Quran 4.1). However, they are not regarded as socially equal, and women are seen as having different roles from men. In law their testimony counted for less than that of a man, they needed men to act for them legally, and they had fewer property rights. In theory a woman can perform all Muslim rites, but except in women's mosques this rarely if ever happens in communal situations. The Quran called for modesty in female dress and in some Muslim societies this developed into full veiling from head to foot, and even strict seclusion in the home (purdah). However, in Sufi Islam women's branches and convents arose, and it was possible for female scholars and mystics such as Rabiah to write poetry that has become proverbial around the Muslim world. In modern Muslim states civil law has often freed women from restricting regulations and given them entry into professional and public life, as in the case, for example, of Benazir Bhutto in Pakistan. However, the shariah law remains more restrictive as far as women are concerned. ▷ marriage/divorce, Islamic; mosque; Quran; Rabiah; shariah; Sufism; veiling

Islamic dynasties Certain dynasties have been important within the history of the Muslim tradition. Muhammad was succeeded by the four 'rightly guided' caliphs who ruled from Medina (632–61) during the so-called golden age of Islam. From 661 to 750 the Umayyad caliphs ruled from Damascus, and from 750 to 1258 the Abbasid caliphs ruled from Baghdad. In practice the central authority of the caliphs declined after the 9th century, and provincial dynasties became significant in particular areas. These included the Fatimids in Syria, Egypt and North Africa (909–1171), the Seljuks in Iran and Iraq (1038–1194), and the Mamluks in Egypt and Syria from 1260. Later, four other dynasties attained unusual importance: the Ottoman Turks (1342–1924), especially after 1517 when their empire extended throughout the Middle East from Europe to the Persian Gulf; the Mughals (1526–1858) in India; and the Safavids (1501–1732) and the Qajars (1779–1925) in Persia. The caliphate held nominally by the Ottomans finally ended in 1924, although its effective power in the Muslim world had ended long before. During the 19th century much of the Islamic world came under the control of colonial powers, especially Britain and France. One exception was Arabia under the Saudi dynasty, which retains control there to this day. Elsewhere new and independent states have arisen in the Muslim world. ▷ Abbasids; caliphate; Medina; Mughal Empire; Muhammad; Ottoman Turks; Umayyads

Islamic law ▷ shariah

Islamic law schools Four law schools arose within Sunni Islam which agreed on matters of central importance and recognized each of the others as being orthodox. The first, the Hanifite, was named after Abu Hanifah (700–67), the founder of the Iraqi school, and is common in India, lower Egypt and western Asia. The second, the Malikite, was named after Malik ibn Anas (716–95), the founder of the Medina school, who was responsible for the first major Islamic law treatise; this school is common in north and west Africa and upper Egypt. The third, the Shafiite, was named after al-Shafii (767–820), the most powerful and influential thinker in early Islamic law; it is common in India, Indonesia, lower Egypt, Malaysia and Syria. The fourth, the Hanbalite, was named after ibn Hanbal (780–855), although established by his followers; common in Arabia, it is the most conservative and traditional of the law schools. There are also a number of Shiite law schools, the most important being the Jafari school of the Twelvers. The Zaydis and Kharijites also have their own school. The roots of Islamic law among the four Sunni schools are to be found in the Quran, the sayings and traditions of Muhammad (Hadith and sunnah), analogy (*Qiyas*), and popular consensus (*ijma*). A fifth principle, effort or *ijtihad*, involves the application of the four roots of law to particular cases. This is less stressed in Sunni circles but much stressed in Shiite circles. ▷ Abu Hanifah; Hadith; Hanafi; Ibn Hanbal; ijma; ijtihad; Qiyas; Quran; Shafii, al-; shariah; Shiism; sunnah; Sunnis

Islamic modernism A modern movement within the Islamic tradition which developed as a positive response to the scientific and technological power of Western science, the imperialism of Western nations, and the intellectual world-view lying behind Western power. It was also a response to the threat of Christianity, which was seen to be an integral part of the Western world-view. It aimed to reinterpret Islam in the light of the modern world so as to enable the Muslim tradition to adapt to the contemporary situation. Three of the most influential figures in this movement were al-Afghani (1838–97), whose activism and dynamism spread his radical modernism around the Muslim world, Muhammad Abduh (1849–1905), who was an influential educational reformer from his position as rector of al-Azhar University in Cairo and Grand Mufti of Egypt, and Sir Muhammad Iqbal (1873–1938), who was based in India and attempted to integrate the doctrines of the Quran with Bergson's Western notion of creative evolution. In their attempts to reinterpret the Quran in the context of the new conditions, and to create a synthesis of Muslim thought with the Western world-view, they were more successful in inspiring a new Muslim self-awareness than in creating a deep-rooted and progressive Islamic intellectual system. The initiative has passed to Islamic radical fundamentalism, although Islamic modernism is still active, albeit somewhat low-key. ▷ Abduh, Muhammad; Afghani, al-; Iqbal, Sir Muhammad; Quran

Islamic neo-fundamentalism The recent movement within Islam known as fundamentalism is better described as neo-fundamentalism. The 18th- and 19th-century puritan movements stemming from the work of al-Wahhab (1703–92) in Saudi Arabia are more accurately fundamentalist. Modern Islamic neo-fundamentalism is both a reaction to and an extension of Islamic modernism based on the reforms of men such as al-Afghani (1839–97), Muhammad Abduh (1845–1905) and Sir Muhammad Iqbal (1877–1938). It argues, in the writings of formative thinkers such as Mawlana Mawdudi (1903–79), that Islam is a total system including public as well as private matters. There is therefore such a thing as Islamic politics and Islamic economics as well as the duty to live in accord with the five pillars of Islam. Moreover, science and technology are also important for Islam. Nevertheless Western knowledge needs to be Islamicized, and modernization must be forwarded in an Islamic way and not in a Western way. Despite cultivating science and technology for pragmatic reasons, Islamic neo-fundamentalism is basically anti-Western and anti-modern. It reasserts some of the norms of traditional Islam such as the role of women, an emphasis on almsgiving, and the prohibition of bank interest. It is divided within itself in a number of ways: for example, it took a Shiite theocratic direction in the Iran of Ayatollah Khomeini, who argued that the priestly class must rule within Islam, whereas Colonel Gadafi in Libya stressed the will of the people as a key element in Islamic neo-fundamentalism. It is strengthened at grass-roots level by the support of many Muslim ulama who have become concerned at the increasing secularization of education and law in various parts of the Muslim world. ▷ Abduh, Muhammad; Afghani, al-; Iqbal, Sir Muhammad; Islamic modernism; Mawdudi; Shiism; ulama

Islamic worship The Islamic concept of worship is wider than that of formal worship in a mosque on Friday at noonday, or at a time of great celebration. In its widest sense it is submission to God ('Islam') in the whole of life. It finds general expression in the five pillars of Islam: saying the *shahadah*, the confession of faith, 'Allah is Allah and Muhammad is his prophet'; saying the five daily prayers, involving the whole of the body in prostrations, and the repeated recitation of the Fatihah, the opening part of the Quran, with its emphasis upon the praise and invocation of God, reliance on God, and living righteously; giving alms to help one's neighbour; engaging in the month-long fast of Ramadan, ending in the glorious Id festival; and sharing in the pilgrimage to Mecca. These five pillars, and the rituals built into them, shape a Muslim's life and worship. Private prayer (*dua*) is also important. Within Sufi Islam, the worship form known as *dhikr* involves repetitions of the names of God and other techniques which induce a state of trance and the ecstasy of fana. Shiite worship often takes an intense form centred upon the ritual remembrance of acts of suffering such as the death of Husayn at Karbala in 680. The individual body is regarded, so to speak, as one's own mosque, but outward mosque buildings are also important, especially for Friday mid-day prayers and for major festivals such as Id. Their architecture symbolizes the transcendent God, and within them the Quran is chanted and a sermon is heard, and the heart of the Muslim finds a wider venue for the praise of God. ▷ dhikr; fana; Fatihah; five pillars, Islamic; Husayn; Islam; Mecca; mosque; Quran; Ramadan; shahadah; Sufism

Islam in Africa After the death of Muhammad in 632, Islam spread rapidly along the north coast of Africa from Egypt in the east to Morocco in the west, making the southern part of the Mediterranean, which had once hosted the Christianity of St Augustine of Hippo, an Islamic shoreline. Islam eventually crossed the Sahara desert, through the work of Islamic traders and Sufi dervishes, into the southern Saharan region, and it moved into East Africa by sea in the search for black slaves and gold, as well as converts. North-east Africa maintained a Christian presence in the medieval period through the Christian kingdoms of Nubia and Ethiopia, and it was only in the modern epoch that Islam grew in influence there. During the expansion of African Islam southwards, the Sufi orders have played an important role, with their emphasis upon holy men, such as dervishes and *marabouts*, and pilgrimages to the tombs of local saints. In Black Africa, as opposed to Saharan Arab Africa, there has been more interaction between the incoming Islam and African primal religions with their indigenous traditions of medicine men, healing and ancestor worship, and there has been more accommodation to Christianity. Islamic reluctance to translate the Quran from Arabic into many African languages may have aided Christianity, with its policy of ready translation, to grow more rapidly in Black Africa, where it is dominant. ▷ ancestors, African; Augustine, St (of Hippo); Muhammad; Quran; Sufi orders

Islam in China Islam was first brought by Muslim traders to the region around what is now Canton in the 8th century CE. However, the main Muslim impact upon China came with the Mongol invasions and migrations from the 13th century onwards; as a result 7 per cent of China's people are now of Mongol extraction, and many of them are Muslims living in north-west China in the provinces that are now Inner Mongolia, Kensu, Sinkiang, Szechwan and Yunnan. They are commonly called Hui, and Chinese Islam is known as Hui Hui Chiao. Muslims have tended to be separate from the mainstream of Chinese people, who are Han by extraction, and they have coexisted with other traditions and recently with Chinese Marxism. Because of the unique position of Muslims it was possible to be both a Muslim and a member of the Communist Party. In its art and in other ways Islam has adapted to China both in the north-west and in large cities elsewhere where there are usually mosques. Islam has grown steadily in China by biological evangelism rather than by mission, and continues to do so today under the conditions of greater freedom pertaining since 1978. ▷ Marxism; Mongols; mosque

Islam in South Asia The strongest concentration of Muslims in the world is in South Asia, with especially high ratios in Afghanistan (100%), Bangladesh (80%) and Pakistan (97%), and with a significant minority in India (11%). Arab Muslims reached Sind in 711, and Mahmud of Ghazni (971–1030) made extensive raids into India, but it was not until the 13th century that Muslims settled in India in any numbers. The Mughal emperors (Babur 1483–1530, Humayun 1506–56, Akbar 1542–1605, Jahangir 1569–1627, Shah Jahan 1592–1666, Aurangzeb 1618–1707) established Islam as the dominant political force in India, and their reign continued in theory until the so-called Mutiny of 1857, by which time the British had already assumed effective power. Afghanistan was never really subdued by the British, and Pakistan achieved independence in 1947 and Bangladesh in 1971. Indian Islam had a strong mystical Sufi element built into it, as well as a smaller but significant strain of Shiism. Sufis had some success in acquiring converts through their own devotion and through disillusion in some quarters with the Hindu caste system. They fed into the Sant movement which was mainly devotional Hindu, and into the new Sikh tradition, and in Akbar's Cult of Divine Unity there was an extraordinary early attempt at religious synthesis. Sufi Orders such as the *Naqshbandiyyah* also built up a strong presence in India. Akbar's successors, notably Aurangzeb, reacted in the opposite direction towards Muslim exclusivism. This less eirenical trend continued in the new Islamic currents that arose from the work of Shah Wali Allah (1703–62), and it has been maintained by recent figures such as Mawlana Mawdudi, who reacted against Western modernism and campaigned for Pakistan to become an Islamic republic. However, Sir Muhammad Iqbal (1873–1938) was the main example of another trend in a more liberal and evolutionary direction. ▷ Akbar the Great; Iqbal, Sir Muhammad; Mawdudi; Mughal Empire; Naqshbandiyyah; Sufi orders; Sufism; Wali Allah, Shah

Islam in the West Islam has had a communal presence in Europe almost from the beginning of its history, and in recent times, especially since the end of World War II, it has grown in the West through immigration. Islam entered Spain in 711CE and remained a force there until the 'reconquest' of Spain, symbolized in the fall of Granada in 1492. The Muslim tradition entered Malta and Sicily soon after it had entered Spain; through the Mongol Tartars, who converted to Islam, it became and has remained embedded in southern Russia; and by the 16th century the Ottoman Turks had established Islam in most of the Balkan region. Islam remains a significant presence in Yugoslavia and Albania, and in the Caucasus and the Volga Basin of European Russia. Since World War II immigration of Muslims from the Arab world, Turkey and the Indian sub-continent into Britain, France, Germany and Holland has grown significantly, so that there are now more Muslims in the UK than there are members of the Free Churches put together. In the 19th century Muslims from India and Indonesia were accepted as indentured labour into the West Indies, and in the 20th century immigration into the USA and Canada has grown. There have been occasional conversions of Westerners to Islam, and in North America Black Muslims have been active among Afro-Americans through the work of Elijah Muhammad (1897–1975) and Malcolm X. ▷ Black Muslims; Malcolm X; Ottoman Turks

Ismailis (Ismā'īlīs) Adherents of a secret Islamic sect, one of the main branches of the Shiites; also known as the 'Seveners'. The sect developed from an underground movement (c.9th century), reaching political power in Egypt and North Africa in the 10th–12th centuries. It distinguished between inner and outer aspects of religion, was critical of Islamic law, and believed that in the eventual new age of the seventh imam, a kind of universal religion would emerge that was independent of the laws of all organized religions. Thus it welcomed adherents of other religions, but retained its own secret traditions and rites. ▷ imam; Islam; Shiism

Israel, State of Democratic republic in the Middle East founded in 1948 and bordering with Lebanon, Syria, Jordan, Egypt and the Mediterranean Sea. By 1990 it had a population of some 4614000, mostly Jewish but with a sizable Arab minority. Ultimate authority lies with the parliament or Knesset, consisting of 120 members elected by the populace for a four-year term. Although Zionist settlers began to arrive in the 1880s, when Palestine was under Ottoman rule, only in the 1930s and 1940s, against the background of Adolf Hitler's campaigns, did large numbers of Jewish immigrants enter Palestine during the British Mandate (which began in 1918). This increased the tension between Arabs and Jews so that the United nations voted to partition Palestine in 1947. However, on 14 May 1948 its founders announced the creation of the State of Israel (Hebrew *medinat Yisrael*), resulting in military conflict with surrounding countries in which Israeli forces were victorious. Further wars between Israel and its neighbours took place in 1967 and 1973; in the former, Israel captured land often referred to as the 'occupied territories': the Golan Heights, West Bank, East Jerusalem, and Gaza Strip. Thus, while the State of Israel has become a focus of hope for world Jewry after the Holocaust, the political situation in the region has not been stable. ▷ eretz Yisrael; exile; Israel, tribes of; Orthodox Judaism

Israel, tribes of In the Bible, a confederacy of 12 tribes generally traced to Jacob's 12 sons—six by Leah (Reuben, Simeon, Levi, Judah, Issachar, Zebulun), two by Rachel

(Joseph, Benjamin), two by Rachel's maid Bilhah (Dan, Naphtali), and two by Leah's maid Zilpah (Gad, Asher); the name Israel had been given to Jacob (Genesis 32.28) after the story of his wrestling with a divine being. During the settlement of Canaan and the Transjordan the tribes were allocated portions of land (Joshua 13–19); but the Levites, a priestly class, had no allocation and possibly were never a 'tribe' as such, and Joseph's 'tribe' was actually two tribes, traced to his two sons Ephraim and Manasseh (Genesis 48). The number of tribes was thereby maintained as 12. Once the monarchy was established in Israel (c.10th century BCE), the tribal confederation effectively ended, although it still played a role in Jewish religious thought. ▷ Asher/Benjamin/Dan/Gad/Issachar/Joseph/Judah/Naphtali/Reuben/Simeon/Zebulun, tribe(s) of; Levi

Issachar, tribe of One of the 12 tribes of ancient Israel, said to be descended from Issachar, one of Jacob's sons by his wife Leah. Its territory included the central plain of Jezreel between Mount Tabor and Mount Gilboa. ▷ Israel, tribes of

Izanagi no Mikoto and **Izanami no Mikoto** Respectively, a Japanese male and female god. In the creation myth these were the first beings who created islands in the water and the other gods. Izanami died when she gave birth to fire. Izanagi followed her to the land of the dead (*Yomi*), but she turned against him and pursued him. Finally he had to block the exit from Yomi with a large rock. Izanami then became the goddess of the underworld. ▷ creation myths; underworld

J

Jabneh, or Jamnia An ancient city on the coastal plain east of Jerusalem and south of modern Tel Aviv, referred to occasionally in writings of the biblical and Maccabean periods. It achieved special prominence in early Judaism after the fall of Jerusalem (70CE), when Rabban Johanan ben Zakkai asked the Roman Emperor for the city, and re-established the Sanhedrin council there for a time. Famous Jewish scholars gathered there to lay the foundations for the Mishnah and engage in study of the Torah. ▷ Akiva ben Joseph, Rabbi; Johanan ben Zakkai, Rabban; Judaism; Mishnah; Torah

Jacob Biblical character, son of Isaac, patriarch of the nation Israel. He supplanted his elder brother Esau, obtaining his father's special blessing and thus being seen as the inheritor of God's promises. He was re-named *Israel* (perhaps meaning 'God strives' or 'he who strives with God') after his struggle with a divine being. By his wives Leah and Rachel and their maids he fathered 12 sons, to whom Jewish tradition traced the 12 tribes of Israel. ▷ Bible; Esau; Isaac; Israel, tribes of; Rachel

Jacobins ▷ Dominicans

Jade Emperor ▷ Yu-Huang

Jahiliyyah (al-Jāhiliyyah) A Muslim term referring to the 'time of ignorance' preceding Muhammad's work and the revelation of Islam. Derived from the word *jahil*, meaning ignorant, it denotes the time of darkness and decline when the original monotheism revealed to Abraham fell away to be replaced by Arab paganism. According to Muslims, the rise of Islam restored true monotheism, brought enlightenment in place of ignorance, and established an ethical system based on divine law in place of decadence. The 'time of ignorance' had included the introduction of idols to Mecca. It had not been an era of complete paganism in that groups of Christians and Jews, and also mature spiritual individuals outside those groups, had retained an element of monotheism. Customs set up during the 'time of ignorance', such as influential fairs, times of truce to enable these fairs to flourish, and visits to sacred places such as the Kabah, with its Black Stone, in Mecca, were adopted by Islam in the new dispensation, especially in the form of the pilgrimage (Hajj) to Mecca. ▷ Abraham in Islam; Hajj; Mecca; monotheism; Muhammad; shariah

Jaimini (c.200BCE) Indian philosopher who founded the Mimamsa school and wrote the *Mimamsa-sutras* which are its basis. The sutras are commented upon by Shabara (c.200CE) and his commentary is used to elucidate the difficult, pithy statements of Jaimini. This in turn is commented upon by Prabhakara and Kumarila (8th century) who represent two main branches of the Mimamsa school. Mimamsa is exegesis of the Veda and Jaimini is especially concerned with understanding and interpreting dharma, which for him refers to Vedic injunctions about the sacrifice. Jaimini is concerned with the distinctions between ordinary (*laukika*) experience, ritual or Vedic experience and language. Ritual experience is quite distinct from ordinary experience, is non-reducible to it and provides knowledge. The idea of an unseen force or link (*apurva*) between sacrifice and its results is of central importance here and Jaimini identifies the Vedic sacrifice as the central cosmic act in relation to which human reality must be seen. ▷ Mimamsa; Veda

Jainism An indigenous religion and philosophy of India which regards Vardhamana Mahavira (599–527BCE), said to be the last *tirthankara*, as its founder, although its first proponent was possibly Parsva, a figure from about the 9th century BCE about whom very little is known. Springing from a reaction against the elitism of the Hindu caste system and the Hindu practice of sacrificing animals, Jainism bears some resemblance to Buddhist thinking. Jains do not believe in a creator god, but consider that salvation consists in conquering material existence through adherence to a strict ascetic discipline, thus freeing the soul from the working of karma for eternal all-knowing bliss. Liberation requires detachment from worldly existence, an essential part of which is the practice of ahimsa, non-injury to living beings. One of the central tenets of Jainism, this policy grew from the belief that since in reincarnation a person might come back in the form of an animal or insect, no living creature ought ever to be harmed. To

Jain believer, sweeping the ground before him and wearing a mask, both practices intended to prevent harm to any living creature

prevent even accidental damage to creatures, Jains may wear nose masks to prevent inhalation of insects, and sweep clear the ground ahead of them. Some do not wash for fear of killing body lice or other parasites. Mahatma Gandhi, though Hindu, was strongly influenced by the concept of ahimsa. The ascetic ideal is central to both monastic and lay Jainism, although final renunciation is possible only within the former. Because of their faith, Jains may not take employment in areas such as the manufacture or sale of weapons or alcohol. They number about three million. ▷ ahimsa; Gandhi, Mohandas Karamchand; karma; tirthankara

Jamaat-i-Islami (Jamā'at-i-Islāmī) A modern Islamic movement begun in India in 1941 by Mawlana Mawdudi. It is a conservative movement which claims that the Muslim law, the shariah, is supreme for Muslims and cannot be replaced. After the partition of India at the time of Indian independence, it grew in Pakistan and claimed that Pakistan should be a Muslim state governed by the shariah. It has fed into the recent rise of Islamic fundamentalism. It sees Islam as a system that can give set answers to the basic problems of humanity, and it argues that there is such a thing as Islamic politics, economics, and so on. It has lent itself to violence, for example in the Punjab riots of 1953 against the Ahmadiyyah movement (as a result of which Mawdudi spent two years in prison), but this is not its main aim. The coherence of its system of belief centred upon 'pure Islam', and the faith of its members has given it a significance beyond its numbers. ▷ Ahmadiyyah; Mawdudi; Shariah

James (son of Alphaeus), also known as **St James (the Less)** (1st century) One of the 12 apostles. He may be the James whose mother Mary is referred to at the crucifixion of Jesus. ▷ apostle; Jesus Christ

James, Letter of A New Testament writing, attributed to 'James', who was considered in early tradition to be James the brother of Jesus, but who today is often considered an unknown late 1st-century author, in view of the distance from Pauline theology and polemic in the writing. The letter's recipients are described only as 'the 12 tribes in the Dispersion'. It emphasizes a variety of ethical teachings, but was sometimes criticized (most notably by Luther) for lacking a distinctively Christian message and for its un-Pauline emphasis on 'works' rather than 'faith'. ▷ James, St ('brother of Jesus'); Luther, Martin; New Testament; Paul, St

James, St ('brother' of Jesus), known also as **St James (the Just)** (1st century) Listed with Joseph, Simon, and Judas (Matthew 13.55) as a 'brother' of Jesus of Nazareth, and identified as the foremost leader of the Christian community in Jerusalem (Galatians 1.19, 2.9; Acts 15.13). He is not included in lists of the disciples of Jesus, and should not be confused with James son of Alphaeus or James son of Zebedee, but did apparently witness the resurrected Christ (1 Corinthians 15.7), at which point he was converted. He showed Jewish sympathies over the question of whether Christians must adhere to the Jewish law. Most theologians consider him the author of the Epistle of James, although it has been ascribed to both others. The first of the Catholic Epistles, it was put by Eusebius of Caesarea among the list of controverted books (*Antilegomena*), and was finally declared canonical by the third Council of Carthage. According to Josephus, he was martyred by stoning (c.62). His feast day is 1 May. ▷ James, Letter of; Jesus Christ

James, St (son of Zebedee), also known as **St James (the Great)** (d.c.44) One of Jesus's

12 disciples, often listed with John (his brother) and Peter as part of an inner group closest to Jesus. They were among the first called by Jesus, and were with Jesus at his Transfiguration and at Gethsemane. He and his brother John were also called Boanerges ('sons of thunder'). According to Acts 12.2, he was martyred under Herod Agrippa I. Later legend suggests that his remains were miraculously spirited to Santiago de Compostela in Spain, which became a centre of medieval pilgrimage. His feast day is 25 July. ▷ apostle; disciples (in early Christian Church); Gethsemane; John, St (son of Zebedee)

James, William (1842–1910) American philosopher and psychologist, brother of the writer Henry James, born in New York. He graduated in medicine at Harvard, where he taught comparative anatomy from 1872, then philosophy from 1882, becoming professor in 1885 and changing his professorial title in 1889 from philosophy to psychology. In his *Principles of Psychology* (1890) he places psychology firmly on a physiological basis and represents the mind as an instrument for coping with the world. In philosophy he developed the pragmatist ideas of Charles Peirce and described himself as a 'radical empiricist': metaphysical disputes can be resolved or dissolved by examining the practical consequences of competing theories—beliefs are true if and because they work, not vice versa. He expounded these ideas most famously in *The Will to Believe* (1907) and *Pragmatism* (1907); and he treated ethics and religion in the same practical, non-dogmatic way, as in *The Varieties of Religious Experience* (1902), which comprises his Gifford Lectures delivered in Edinburgh, and *The Meaning of Truth* (1909). ▷ empiricism; ethics in religion; religion

Jamnia ▷ Jabneh

Janamashtami A Hindu festival celebrating the birth of Krishna, held on the eighth day of the dark fortnight of the month of Shravan (August). The festival is observed by most Hindus, not only Vaishnavas, and many will fast for 24 hours before the festival. The story of Krishna's birth might be told, how the evil King Kansa killed all the babies born to his sister Devaki because of a prophecy that one of her children would depose him. When pregnant with Krishna she and her husband Vasudeva were imprisoned. Upon the birth of Krishna, Vasudeva magically escaped from the prison with the baby, taking him across the river Yamuna to Yashoda who had just had a baby girl. He swopped Krishna for Yashoda's baby and returned to the prison. Kansa, upon discovering the child, killed her, but a voice from heaven told him that the baby was the deity Yogamaya, born solely to protect Krishna. Krishna eventually kills Kansa. ▷ Krishna

Janam Sakhis (Janam Sākhīs) The early Sikh accounts of the life and teaching of Guru Nanak, the first Sikh guru. They refer to his life as a child, his early adult residence in Sultanpur, his preaching, wonder-working, his travels within and beyond India, and his final teaching ministry in the exemplary community he set up in Kartarpur in the Punjab. Unlike the hymns and poems of the *Guru Granth Sahib*, the *Janam Sakhis* are in narrative story form, and are intended to spread the charisma and beneficence of Guru Nanak. Reinforcing his hymns, they have been used as 'gospels' to make his presence real. There are a number of *Janam Sakhis*, several of which have been handed down in manuscript form since the 17th century (the most used of these is a late version of the Bala tradition). Many Sikhs regard the *Janam Sakhis* as literal historical accounts of Guru Nanak's life; others regard them as reflecting the testimony and spirituality of the Sikhs who wrote them during the 100 years following his death. ▷ Guru Granth Sahib; Kartarpur; Mardana; Nanak; Punjab

jannah, al- A common Muslim notion of heaven. Al-jannah means a garden, and in the Quran a garden is the most popular allegory of paradise. It is interpreted as being an enclosed garden, surrounded by an enclosure and trees, and it forms an attractive symbol against the background of the desert environment in which Islam arose. The significance of the image is enhanced by the idyllic nature of the Garden of Eden, before the temptation of Adam and Eve, to which the name al-jannah is also given. Although the garden of paradise is seen to be beautiful, with flowers, trees and plants, its wonder cannot fully be imagined by human beings, for it is the place of God. As Quran 56.24–5 puts it, 'therein they shall hear no idle talk, no cause of sin, only the saying "Peace, Peace"'. ▷ Adam and Eve; Eden, Garden of; heaven; Quran

Jansen, Cornelius Otto (1585–1638) Dutch theologian, and founder of the Jansenist sect, born in Acquoi, near Leerdam in Holland. He studied at Utrecht, Louvain and Paris and became Professor of Theology at Bayonne and in 1630 at Louvain. In 1636 he was made

Bishop of Ypres. He died just as he had completed his great work, the *Augustinus* (4 vols, published in 1640), which sought to prove that the teaching of St Augustine against the Pelagians and semi-Pelagians on grace, free will and predestination was directly opposed to the teaching of the Jesuit schools. Jansen repudiated the ordinary Catholic dogma of the freedom of the will, and refused to admit merely sufficient grace, maintaining that interior grace is irresistible, and that Jesus Christ died for all. On its publication in 1640 the *Augustinus* caused a major outcry, especially by the Jesuits, and it was prohibited by a decree of the Inquisition in 1641. In the following year it was condemned by Urban VIII in the bull *In Eminenti*. Jansen was supported by Arnauld, Pascal and the Port-Royalists. The controversy raged in France for nearly a century, when a large number of Jansenists emigrated to the Netherlands. The Utrecht Jansenists are in doctrine and discipline strictly orthodox Roman Catholics, known by their countrymen as *Oude Roomsch* ('Old Roman'). ▷ Augustine, St (of Hippo); grace; Inquisition; Jansenism; Jesuits; Pelagius; predestination

Jansenism A heretical movement in the Roman Catholic Church in France and Holland in the 17th and 18th centuries. It followed the teaching of Cornelius Jansen, who adopted the theology of St Augustine, particularly on predestination, and promulgated a rigorous and ascetic way of life. Condemned in France, where its adherents included Antoine Arnauld and Blaise Pascal, it survived in Holland. ▷ Augustine, St (of Hippo); heresy; Jansen, Cornelius Otto; Pascal, Blaise; predestination; Roman Catholicism

Japanese Buddhism Buddhism entered Japan from Korea in either 538 or 552, but it made substantial advances through the work of Prince Shotoku. He built new Buddhist temples, introduced new Buddhist scriptures (*sutras*), and at the Japanese capital of Naro six Buddhist philosophical schools were created. Emperor Shomu virtually made Buddhism the Japanese state religion in 741. Its power at Nara increased to such an extent that Emperor Kammu moved the capital to Kyoto in 794 to counteract Nara Buddhism, and shortly afterwards sent emissaries to China who brought back Tendai and Shingon Buddhism to Japan. These new schools were syncretistic, and Buddhism became more popular as it assimilated Shinto elements in the Ryobu Shinto school, and as new movements were thrown up such as Pure Land,

Japanese buddhist temple, the Golden Pavilion in Kyoto

Zen, and Nichiren Buddhism. Pure Land stressed the possibility of rebirth in the paradise or Pure Land of Amida Buddha through faith in him; Zen stressed the possibility of gradual or sudden enlightenment in the here-and-now; and Nichiren was less tolerant and more exclusive in his stress upon the *Lotus Sutra*. Buddhism also became responsible for funeral rites at the local level in general worship. Since the Meiji restoration and the revival of Shinto from 1868 to 1945, life has been more difficult for the Buddhist tradition, but since World War II it has fragmented and flourished under the new conditions of religious freedom in Japan. ▷ Amida worship; Kammu; Nichiren Buddhism; Pure Land Buddhism; Ryobu Shinto; Shingon; Shomu; Shotoku; Tendai; Zen Buddhism

Japanese Buddhism, worship of buddhas and bodhisattvas Japan adopted the Mahayana tradition of Buddhism from Korea and China, and therefore incorporated Mahayana Buddhas and bodhisattvas into Japanese culture. The historical Buddha, known as Shaka in Japan, existed in image form by 606, but became less important subsequently. The Tendai school placed great emphasis upon Yakushi as a healing Buddha, and also upon Amida, who later became the key Buddha in Pure Land Buddhism. The Hosso school in Nara worshipped four Buddhas: Shaka, Yakushi, Amida, and Miroku (Maitreya), the last of whom became identified with the Buddhist prince Shotoku. In spite of this it was Amida who flourished in Japan, together with the sun Buddha Vairocana, who in Japan was known as Dainichi. The sun Buddha was surrounded in Shingon mandalas (symbolic circles) by other Buddhas, and he became identified with the cosmic body of the Buddha, the *dharmakaya*, which was seen as the reality behind all things. Among the bodhisattvas, Kannon, the goddess of mercy, who was the Japanese form of Kuan Yin, became popular as the giver of compassion; also popular is Jizo, who is seen as the guiding saint of children, pregnant mothers and travellers. ▷ Amida worship; bodhisattva; Buddha; dharmakaya; Kuan Yin; Mahayana Buddhism; Maitreya; mandala; Shingon; Shotoku; Tendai

Japanese new new religions The name given to new religious movements that have arisen recently in Japan. The unusual name is to distinguish them from the Japanese new religions which are no longer seen as particularly new, both in the sense that some of them date back before World War II and even to the 19th century, and in the sense that even since World War II they have gone through various stages of development and have become institutionalized. In the last 20 years novel religious movements have arisen such as *Agonshu* and *Sukyo Mahikari* (True-light Supra-Religious Organization). They are related to the occult boom and to some of the new age developments that are present in Japan, and Mahikari stresses the exorcism of evil spirits, the evangelization of neighbours and friends, mass leaflet publicity, and a belief in miraculous possibilities and mystical powers. As such these religions are not critical or reflective, but they are making a noticeable impact in Japan today. They illustrate the sociological principle that, while ecumenism may develop at one end of the religious spectrum, continuing novelty is the keynote at the other end and, as recent new religious movements 'settle down', even newer ones will take their place. ▷ Japanese new religions; new age religion; occult

members of the Soka Gakkai

Japanese new religions The Japanese term *shinko shukyo*, 'new religions', has been used to describe various new religious movements that have appeared in Japan in the last 200 years. Another term, 'new new religions', is often used to describe religious movements that have erupted in Japan since World War II. Some of the so-called new religions such as Konko-kyo and Tenri-kyo date back to the early 19th century and others, such as Rissho Koseikai and Soka Gakkai, arose between the two world wars. However, during World War II most of them were weakened because they were looked upon with disfavour by the nationalist government and state Shinto. After 1945 most new religions 'began again' in the new postwar atmosphere of religious freedom. In the immediate postwar years they grew locally and often stressed worldly benefits such as health, prosperity, family harmony, and wealth. Evangelism was important and in the 1960s this developed into the rise of mass movements among the new religions, some of which achieved national importance, for example the Soka Gakkai and its political wing Komeito. Rapid growth has led to the need for restructuring in recent times, with more emphasis being placed upon organization, self-improvement and development of character than on worldly benefits. Most new religions had a charismatic leader, offered solutions to immediate problems, practised faith-healing, appealed to individual faith, were syncretistic and emphasized exuberant proselytism. More recently some have begun to stress world peace, inter-religious dialogue, and even the unity of all religions. ▷ Japanese new new religions; Kokutai Shinto; Konko-kyo; Soka Gakkai; Tenri-kyo

Japanese religion Five traditions were important in the formation of Japanese religion up to the Nara period (710–84): the earliest Japanese indigenous tradition, the Shinto tradition, the Buddhist tradition, the Confucian tradition, and the religious Taoist tradition. They interacted with each other and, although they did not coalesce, they became inter-dependent within the totality of Japanese religion. After the Nara period, the earliest Japanese tradition and Shinto changed, but not by infusions from outside as they represented the indigenous religious soil of Japan. Buddhism was influenced by new currents from China which took a distinctive Japanese form in the Tendai, Shingon, Pure Land, Zen and Nichiren traditions. Neo-

Confucianism from China strengthened Confucianism, which gave a rationale and hierarchy to the Japanese state. Religious Taoism was deepened by its connection with imported elements of esoteric Buddhism. With the exception of the Nichiren and True Pure Land (*Jodo Shinshu*) traditions in Buddhism, and Christianity when it arrived, Japanese religion has been plural and tolerant. It has been possible for Japanese people at different times of their lives to take part in all of these traditions, rather than be channelled into one alone. Popular religion in a diffused form has also been important, especially since 1600 when the Tokugawa government (1600–1867) used Buddhism as an arm of government and the Meiji promoted Shinto as a state religion after 1868. Reciting the *nembutsu*, local festivals, local religious leaders, and elements of religious Taoism all flourished, and since 1945 various new religious movements began or re-emerged to increase the sense of vitality in Japanese religion. ▷ Japanese new religions; Kokutai Shinto; neo-Confucianism; Nichiren Buddhism; Pure Land Buddhism; Shingon; Taoism; Tendai; Zen Buddhism

Japheth Biblical character, one of the sons of Noah who survived the Flood, the brother of Shem and Ham. He is portrayed as the ancestor of peoples in the area of Asia Minor and the Aegean (Genesis 10). ▷ Bible; Flood, the; Noah

Japji (Japjī) A Sikh prayer-poem composed by Guru Nanak. Along with the *Mul Mantra* it was considered to be his first work, and it is placed with the *Mul Mantra* at the beginning of the Sikh scripture, the *Guru Granth Sahib*. Its place of precedence is accentuated by the fact that, unlike the other poems, it is given no musical accompaniment, thus underlining its importance for pesonal devotion and piety. It is to be both read and reflected upon. Devout Sikhs meditate upon it each morning, and it is also used in formal Sikh worship and rituals, for example in the ceremony of initiation into the Sikh community, known as the *Amritsanskar*. ▷ Adi Granth; amrit; initiation; Khalsa; Mul Mantra; Nanak; Shabad

Jat (Jāṭ) A farmer caste that is important in North India and especially in the Punjab. The Jats belong to different religious traditions, and may well be Hindus or Muslims, but they are especially significant as far as the Sikh tradition is concerned. They are well known for their warlike instincts, respect for family, and feeling for justice and equality. However at the same time they have a sense of their own social rank and destiny within the totality of the caste system in which they are placed. The talents of many of them have been placed in the service of the Sikh community. According to Indian tradition they emerged out of the locks of Shiva's hair, and this blends in with the Sikh tradition of keeping the hair long; so too do their martial instincts, their feeling for family and their respect for justice. ▷ caste; five Ks; jati; Shiva; varna

Jataka (Jātaka) Stories of the Buddha's previous births, contained in the Buddhist *Sutra* literature. ▷ Buddha; Buddhism

jati (jāti) Denoting 'caste' in Hinduism, this term is often confused with varna, the ancient 'class' system which has intermeshed with it. No conclusive theory exists as to the origins of the jati system and no reference to it is found before about 300CE. Although the jati system may have arisen out of the varna system, it could nevertheless have had an independent origin and been absorbed into the varna system later. As Hindu society developed, so did the complexity of Hindu social relationships, and tight social groups emerged based on occupation, or more specifically the degrees of purity involved in various occupations. These groups are the *jatis*. Within each varna are many jatis; even among the Brahmans there are said to be about 300 groups. Each member of a jati follows a hereditary profession and each jati keeps itself apart from the others to some degree. A caste is a well-defined group within, say, a few villages, who eat together and intermarry. Social relationships are organized between members of different families but within the same jati. Thus a weaver will marry into another weaver family, though outside of the caste within their village. Marriage outside of one's jati is generally forbidden. ▷ caste; varna

Jehovah Term used since the 11th century as a form of the Hebrew name for Israel's God 'Yahweh'. It is formed from a combination of the Latinized consonants of the Hebrew word *YHWH* (the name for God) with the vowels of the Hebrew word *Adonai* ('Master, Lord'), this combination being necessary to prevent correct utterance of the term YHWH, which was considered too holy to be spoken. ▷ Yahweh

Jehovah's Witnesses A millenarian movement organized in the USA in 1884 under

Charles Taze Russell (1852–1916) and expanded under the direction of Joseph Franklin Rutherford (1869–1942). They adopted the name Jehovah's Witnesses in 1931; previously they were called 'Millennial Dawnists' and 'International Bible Students'. They have their own translation of the Bible, which they interpret literally, and view themselves as entirely distinct from orthodox Christianity, claiming that their intent is to 'shock, rattle and unfrock' the traditional Church. Mistrustful of the claims of Protestant and Catholic Churches, whose ideology they see as false and deluding, they believe in the imminent second coming of Christ. They avoid worldly involvement, and refuse to obey any law which they see as a contradiction of the law of God—refusing, for example, to take oaths, enter military service, or receive blood transfusions. This pacifism led to severe jail sentences during World War I, although these were soon revoked, and meant that they were among the first in Germany to be put into Nazi concentration camps. They publish *The Watchtower* newspaper, meet in what are termed Kingdom Halls, and all 'witness' through regular house-to-house preaching. They number about one million. ▷ millenarianism

jen A Confucian term of central significance, meaning virtue, benevolence and humaneness. Before the time of Confucius it was relatively insignificant, but he magnified its meaning and usage in the *Analects* so that it became the primary virtue of the Confucian character, roughly equivalent to goodness or love. In this respect it is similar to the Greek term *agape* which was not of great significance in early Greece, but was magnified by the New Testament to mean love in its highest form. Jen is similar in meaning to agape, except that it is not related to God, and its social characteristics, such as courtesy, loyalty and public integrity, are emphasized. For Confucius jen was a transcendent quality that each person and humanity in general should aspire to but which was difficult to attain in all its fullness. The neo-Confucians, such as Chu Hsi, also brought out its role in nature, and indicated its role in the reciprocal relationship between nature, human beings and the Ultimate. ▷ Chu Hsi; Confucius; New Testament

Jenkins, David Edward (1925–) English theologian and prelate, born in Bromley, Kent. Appointed Bishop of Durham in 1984 amidst controversy over his interpretation of the Virgin Birth and the resurrection, his trilogy, *God, Miracle and the Church of England* (1987), *God, Politics and the Future* (1988), and *God, Jesus and Life in the Spirit* (1988), maintains the exploratory spirit of earlier books, which included *A Guide to the Debate About God* (1966), *The Glory of Man* (1967), *Living with Questions* (1969, revised as *Still Living with Questions*, 1990) and *The Contradiction of Christianity* (1976). A lecturer in Birmingham and Oxford before being appointed Director of *Humanum* Studies at the World Council of Churches, Geneva (1969–73), he was then Director of the William Temple Foundation, Manchester (1973–8) and Professor of Theology at Leeds (1979–84). ▷ immaculate conception; resurrection; World Council of Churches

Jeremiah, Letter of In the Roman Catholic Bible, Chapter 6 of the Book of Baruch; for Protestants, a separate work in the Old Testament Apocrypha. It is ostensibly a letter from the prophet Jeremiah to Jewish captives in Babylon (c.597BCE) warning them against idolatry. Today it is often considered to derive from the later Hellenistic period, possibly in Maccabean times. ▷ Apocrypha, Old Testament; Baruch; Jeremiah, Book of; Maccabees

Jeremiah, or **Jeremias, Book of** A major prophetic work of the Hebrew Bible/Old Testament, attributed to the prophet Jeremiah, who was active in Judah c.627–587BCE and who died apparently after fleeing to Egypt from Jerusalem. The work is notable for its record of the prophet's inner struggles, persecution, and despair. Warnings of disaster for Judah's immorality and idolatry are tempered only briefly by support for King Josiah's reforms; the warnings anticipate the fall of Jerusalem (587BCE) and the Babylonian Captivity of the Jews. The present book probably results from a complex history of transmission. ▷ Babylonian Captivity; Baruch; Josiah; Lamentations of Jeremiah; Old Testament

Jeremias ▷ **Jeremiah, Book of**

Jericho Oasis town in the Jerusalem governorate, the site of the world's earliest known town, which was continuously occupied from c.9000 to 1850BCE. It was the scene of famous siege during the Israelite conquest of Canaan, when it is said that the walls fell down at the shout of the army under Joshua. ▷ Israel, state of; Joshua, Book of

Jeroboam I (10th century BCE) First king of the divided kingdom of Israel. Solomon made him superintendent of the labours and taxes exacted from his tribe of Ephraim at the construction of the fortifications of Zion. The growing disaffection towards Solomon fostered his ambition, but he was obliged to flee to Egypt. After Solomon's death he headed the successful revolt of the northern tribes against Rehoboam, and, as their king, established idol shrines at Dan and Bethel to wean away his people from the pilgrimages to Jerusalem. He reigned 22 years. ▷ Solomon

Jerome, St, properly **Eusebius Sophronius Hieronymus** (c.342–420) Italian scholar and Latin Church father, born in Stridon. He studied Greek and Latin rhetoric and philosophy at Rome, where he was also baptized. In 370 he settled in Aquileia with his friend Rufinus, but then went to the East, and after a dangerous illness at Antioch retired between 374 and 378 to the desert of Chalcis. In 379, ordained priest at Antioch by St Paulinus of Nola, he went to Constantinople, and became intimate with Gregory Nazianzen. In 382 he went on a mission connected with the Meletian schism at Antioch to Rome, where he became secretary to Pope Damasus, and where he enjoyed great influence. In 385 he led a pilgrimage to the Holy Land, and settled in Bethlehem in 386. It was here that Jerome pursued or completed his great literary labours, in particular his Vulgate version of the Bible, the first Latin translation of the Bible from the Hebrew. He wrote biblical commentaries, and also fiery invectives against Jovinian, Vigilantius and the Pelagians, and even against Rufinus and St Augustine. St Jerome was the most learned and eloquent of the Latin Fathers. His feast day is 30 September. ▷ Augustine, St (of Hippo); Bible; Fathers of the Church

Jerusalem, early Located in the uplands of Judah, Jerusalem was inhabited from very early times, but does not figure as a major religious centre until c.1000BCE when David chose it as the capital of his united Israel, and installed the Ark of the Covenant there. His son Solomon went on to build a temple for Yahweh, and made Jerusalem the most important of the Israelite shrines. Under the divided monarchy which followed it remained the capital of Judah and seat of the Davidic dynasty. City and temple were destroyed by the invading Nebuchadnezzar in 587BCE, and much of the population exiled to Babylon. Among the exiles Jerusalem became a focus of both national and eschatological hopes, as can be seen in the prophecies of Ezekiel and Deutero-Isaiah. When some exiles returned and the temple was rebuilt, Jerusalem became part of a province within the Persian and then Seleucid Empires, with its administration chiefly in the hands of the temple hierarchy. After the Maccabaean Revolt Jerusalem was again for a time the centre of an independent Jewish state, but fell increasingly under the control of Rome. A major building programme was instituted by the Roman vassal King Herod the Great (37–4BCE), including a third building of the temple. This temple, along with the rest of the city, was destroyed in 70CE by the Romans after the Jewish rebellion; the city was sacked again in 135 following Bar Kokhbah's revolt, and Jews were banned from the area by the emperor Hadrian, who built his own pagan city, Aelia Capitolina, on the site. ▷ Ark of the Covenant; Bar Kokhbah; David; eschatology; Judah, kingdom of; Nebuchadnezzar; Solomon

Jerusalem, early Christian Church at The church that formed in Jerusalem shortly after the death and resurrection of Jesus Christ was soon scattered by the persecution of the Jewish authorities (including Saul of Tarsus, later to be the apostle Paul). The unforeseen result was the rapid spread of Christianity to centres such as Antioch where enthusiasm and initiative flourished, although questions of overall policy to Gentile converts were referred to a meeting of Christian leaders at Jerusalem. This 'Jerusalem Council' of c.49CE decided that Gentiles did not have to adopt circumcision and other Jewish practices in order to become Christians, thus preventing the church splitting into Jewish and Gentile factions at the beginning of its existence. The church in Jerusalem was weakened by the expulsion of all Jews from the city and further demoralized by the execution of its leader, James (the Just) the brother of Jesus, in 62. Christians left before the rebellion of 66. After the second rebellion of 132 Jerusalem was completely destroyed and rebuilt as a Roman city to which Jews had no access. Jerusalem and the holy places connected with the life of Jesus became a centre of Christian pilgrimage with the visit of Constantine's mother, St Helena, around 326, but the city passed into Muslim control in 638, after which the Dome of the Rock (Mosque of Omar) was erected on the Temple site. Jerusalem was in Christian hands during the Crusades (1099–1187) and for brief periods in the following century, but power and influence had long passed to the sees of Rome and Constantinople. ▷ Antioch, early Christianity in; Constantine I; Crusades; Rome, early Christian Church at

Jerusalem in Islam Jerusalem is the third great holy city of the Muslim tradition, surpassed in importance only by Mecca and Medina. During the early years of the history of the Muslim community, prayer was offered in the direction of Jerusalem, until during the Medina period the Kabah at Mecca became and has remained the focus of Islamic devotion. Jerusalem was important because it had figured prominently in the work of the earlier prophets, but above all because of Muhammad's traditional night journey with the angel Gabriel to the Dome of the Rock on Temple Mount, whence they ascended to the heavens. Jerusalem was occupied by Islamic forces during the caliphate of Umar (634–44), and since that time various Islamic buildings have been erected in it, including the famous mosque of Umar on Temple Mount. The present walls were built by a famous Ottoman Turkish Muslim, Sulayman the Magnificent. Jerusalem has remained a place of deep significance for Muslims down the ages, and this is one of the reasons why it is a bone of contention between Jews and Muslims now, and was between Christians and Muslims at the time of the Crusades. ▷ Crusades; Mecca; Medina; Night Journey of Muhammad; Ottoman Turks

Jesuits A male religious order, in full the Society of Jesus (SJ). Founded in 1540 by Ignatius Loyola, it is a non-contemplative order, demanding strict obedience, compliance with Ignatius' Spiritual Exercises, and special loyalty to the pope. Its aim is missionary in the broadest sense, ministering to society in many ways, especially in education, where it has founded several colleges and universities throughout the world. Jesuits have been leading apologists for the Roman Catholic Church, particularly at the time of the Counter-Reformation and, more recently, have had a great influence in modernizing the Church. ▷ Counter-Reformation; Ignatius Loyola; missions, Christian; papacy; Roman Catholicism

Jesus Christ, or **Jesus of Nazareth** (c.6–5 BCE–c.30CE) The central figure of the Christian faith, whose role as 'Son of God' and whose redemptive work are traditionally considered fundamental beliefs for adherents of Christianity; in Islam, as a prophet he is considered second only to Muhammad. 'Christ' became attached to the name 'Jesus' in Christian circles in view of the conviction that he was the Jewish Messiah ('Christ').

Jesus of Nazareth is described as the son of Mary and Joseph, and is credited with a miraculous conception by the Spirit of God in the Gospels of Matthew and Luke. He was apparently born in Bethlehem c.6–5BCE (before the death of Herod the Great in 4BCE), but began his ministry in Nazareth. After having been baptized by John in the Jordan (perhaps 28–29CE, Luke 3.1), he gathered a group of 12 close followers or disciples, the number perhaps being symbolic of the 12 tribes of Israel and indicative of an aim to reform the Jewish religion of his day.

The main records of his ministry are the New Testament Gospels, which show him proclaiming the coming of the kingdom of God, and in particular the acceptance of the oppressed and the poor into the kingdom. He was mainly active in the villages and countryside of Galilee rather than in towns and cities, and was credited in the Gospel records with many miraculous healings, exorcisms, and some 'nature' miracles, such as the calming of the storm. These records also depict conflicts with the Pharisees over his exercise of an independent 'prophetic' authority, and especially over his pronouncing forgiveness of sins; but his arrest by the Jewish priestly hierarchy appears to have resulted more directly from his action against the Temple in Jerusalem. The duration of his public ministry is uncertain, but it is from John's Gospel that one gets the impression of a three-year period of teaching. He was executed by crucifixion under the order of Pontius Pilate, the Roman procurator, perhaps because of the unrest Jesus's activities were causing. The date of death is uncertain, but is usually considered to be in 30. Accounts of his resurrection from the dead are preserved in the Gospels, Pauline writings, and Book of Acts; Acts and the Gospel of John also refer to his subsequent ascension into heaven.

The New Testament Gospels as sources for the life of Jesus have been subject to considerable historical questioning in modern biblical criticism, partly in view of the differences amongst the Gospel accounts themselves (with the differences between John's Gospel and the other three often casting doubt on the former). Form criticism has drawn attention to the influences affecting the Jesus-traditions in the period before the Gospels were written, and when traditions were being transmitted mainly in small units by word of mouth. Redaction criticism has, in addition, drawn attention to the creative role of the Gospel writers. Some scholars have been pessimistic about efforts to reconstruct the life of Jesus at all from Gospel sources, and have distinguished between the 'Jesus of history' and the 'Christ of faith', with only the latter being theologically significant for faith. More recent scholars have often attached greater importance to the historical Jesus for Christian faith, and in particular efforts have been made to present a credible hypothesis about the historical Jesus in terms of the social, political, and cultural situation in Judaism in the early 1st century. Limited references to Jesus can also be found in works of the Jewish historian Josephus and the Roman historians Tacitus and Suetonius. Other noncanonical Christian traditions circulated about Jesus, many of them late and probably spurious. ▷ Christianity; crucifixion; form criticism; Gospels, apocryphal/canonical; John, St (the Baptist); Josephus, Flavius; Mary; Messiah; Pharisees; Pilate, Pontius

Jesus Christ in Islam Jesus is held in high regard by the Muslim tradition. He is usually designated as Jesus the son of Mary (*Isa ibn Maryam*), and is seen as a great prophet second in importance only to Muhammad himself. According to the Quran, where he is mentioned 25 times, Jesus was born of a virgin, performed miracles, raised the dead, and restored monotheism by revealing the Gospel. However, contrary to Christian orthodoxy, Muslims believe that Jesus did not die upon the cross, was not divine, was not the Son of God, and was not part of the Trinity, which is seen as a contradiction of the unity of God. Therefore, although Muslims have a more positive view of Jesus than Christians have traditionally exercised towards Muhammad, they view him through the eyes of the Quran, not through the perspective of Christian theology. There is a tradition among Muslims that Jesus will come back before the final judgement, destroy the anti-Christ, and usher in the end of the age in a kind of second coming. This implies not that Jesus was resurrected from the dead, but that he did not really die at all and that he will return at the end of time. ▷ cross; Gospels, apocryphal; Mary; prophet; Quran; theology; Trinity

Jesus movement A Christian movement that arose in the USA during the 1960s, partly as a reaction to what were perceived to be the excesses of the hippy movement and the counter-culture. It was composed mainly of young people who were conservative evangelical Christians, and it used some of the high-profile methods of the counter-culture to proclaim what it called the Jesus Revolution. It expanded throughout North America and Europe in the 1970s, and became another element in the growth of conservative evangelical Christianity in the 1980s. Its followers, sometimes called the 'Jesus freaks', used car stickers, posters, balloons, T-shirts and various media outlets to spread the news of their rediscovery of Jesus and his message of love for all the world. It coalesced with charismatic renewal movements in various Christian churches, and it became involved with missionary groups such as Jews for Jesus which attempted to convert Jewish youngsters to Christianity. As an umbrella movement it also sprouted heterodox groups, such as the Children of God, which went beyond the bounds of what was deemed appropriate by Christians. The Children of God, founded by David Berg in 1968, were accused of using sex to effect conversions to the movement. ▷ charismatic movement; Children of God; evangelicalism; Jesus Christ; new religious movements in the West

Jewish languages Over the centuries Jews have spoken and written in as many languages as places they have inhabited. However, three stand out as particularly associated with Jews and Judaism: Hebrew, Aramaic, and Yiddish. Hebrew is the language of Judaism's formative documents, the Scriptures, as well as of the synagogue liturgy; even Reform Judaism, which historically has preferred services to be held in the vernacular, has experienced a revival of Hebrew since the founding of the State of Israel (1948). Further, some biblical and much post-biblical literature is in Aramaic, including material in the Talmuds and the Targums (paraphrases) of the Bible. More recently Yiddish has been the language of East European Jewry, being Germanic in character but employing Hebrew letters. However, the destruction of vast numbers of Ashkenazi Jews in the Holocaust, as well as the general encroachments of modern life upon all Jews since then, has led to serious erosion in the numbers speaking Yiddish towards the end of the 20th century. Mention should also be made of the considerable amount of Jewish Greek literature from the Second Temple period (c.515BCE–70CE), as well as a fair number of Arabic works by Jews under later Muslim rule. ▷ Holocaust; liturgy; Talmud; targum

jhana (jhāna; Sanskrit: dhyāna) An important term in Buddhist meditational techniques. It is related to the Sanskrit term *dhyana*, which means meditation, and in this sense the word passed into China as Chan and into Japan as Zen. Before jhana can be truly effective five hindrances must be overcome, namely sensual desire, ill-will, lethargy, worry, and fear of commitment. In order to overcome them the Buddhist meditator progresses through five mental states: concentrating on a single object, keeping the mind on that object, the emergence of joy, the emergence of contentment deeper than joy, and the rise of one-pointedness of mind whereby the mind is naturally and deeply concentrated on the object. These are sometimes known as jhana-factors. When they are complete then jhana in a fuller sense is obtained and it amounts to a form of trance. Even this can be deepened in a set of four jhanas, the fourth being a situation of deep peace and radiance. This is not equivalent to nirvana, and the jhanas are not ends in themselves but means to further ends, as in the case of the Buddha who went on from jhana to nirvana. ▷ bhavana; Buddha; Chan; dhyana; meditation; nirvana; Zen Buddhism

jihad (jíhād) (Arabic 'struggle') The term used in Islam for 'holy war'. According to the Quran, Muslims have a duty to oppose those who reject Islam, by armed struggle if necessary, and jihad has been invoked to justify both the expansion and defence of Islam. Islamic states pledged a jihad against Israel in the Mecca declaration of 1981, though not necessarily by military attack. ▷ Islam; Quran; Mecca

Jingi-kan A Japanese government agency, the Office of Divine Affairs, aimed at regulating religious and especially Shinto affairs in Japan. It had originally been set up after the Taika reform of 646 but was revivified in 1871, after the Meiji restoration of 1868, in order to regulate Shinto shrines. These were organized into different areas of jurisdiction at national, regional and local levels, the underlying presuppositions being that Shinto priests were actually government officials and that the emperor was the divine ruler of a Shinto state. Although a new Office was set up in 1877 to make allowances for Buddhism after that tradition had been persecuted between 1868 and 1872, its basic aim was to promote Shinto and to bring it under the wing of the state. This was later formalized in the setting up of state Shinto. After World War II a new era of religious freedom ensued, and Shinto became separated from the state, taking its place among the welter of religious movements in contemporary Japan. ▷ Kokutai Shinto; shrines, Shinto

jinja The name given to Japanese Shinto shrines. *Jin* means deity (or *kami*) and *ja* means dwelling place, so the jinja is the place where the Shinto deity or kami is enshrined. Originally there were probably no Shinto shrines as such, but there were sacred places around sacred objects such as stones or trees. Later, shrines were placed in compounds. At the entrance to the compound was a sacred arch (*torii*) through which one entered to gain access to the holy place, and where one could purify oneself by washing. Inside there would normally be a worship hall at the front of the compound and a kami hall at the back, and worship was directed from the worship hall to the kami hall, where a mirror or sword symbolized the presence of the kami. Eventually local shrines came to enshrine a specific local kami. Individual prayers would be offered at a shrine, but more commonly it was the venue for various traditional festivals, including New Year, spring and autumn festivals, and for special family festivals associated with birth, marriage, or a time of crisis. Here help and sustenance could be gained from the kami. From the Meiji restoration in 1868 to 1945 the term jinja was used for the shrines of state Shinto, whereas another term (*kyokai*) was used for the shrines of 'sect Shinto', but since 1945 and the collapse of state Shinto jinja have reverted to their original usage. ▷ kami; Kokutai Shinto; shrines, Shinto

jinn A class of spirits in Islamic mythology, formed of fire. They live mainly on the mountains of Káf, which encircle the world, assuming various shapes, sometimes as men of enormous size and portentious hideousness. ▷ Folk Islam

Jinnah, Mohammed Ali (1876–1948) Pakistani statesman, born in Karachi. He studied at Bombay and Lincoln's Inn, London, and was called to the Bar in 1897. He obtained a large practice in Bombay, in 1910 was elected to the Viceroy's legislative council and, already a member of the Indian National Congress, in 1913 joined the Indian Muslim League and as its president brought about peaceful co-existence between it and the Congress Party through the 'Lucknow Pact' (1916). Although he supported the efforts of Congress to boycott the Simon Commission (1928), he opposed Gandhi's civil disobedience policy and, resigning from the Congress Party, which he believed to be exclusively fostering Hindu interests, continued to advocate his '14 points' safeguarding Muslim minorities at the London Round Table Conference (1931). By 1940 he was strongly advocating separate statehood for the Muslims and he stubbornly resisted all British efforts, such as the Cripps mission (1942) and Gandhi's statesmanlike overtures (1944), to save Indian unity. Thus on 15 August 1947, the Dominion of Pakistan came into existence and Jinnah, *Quaid-i-Azam*

'Great Leader', became its first governor-general and had to contend with the consequences of the new political division, the refugee problem, the communal riots in Punjab and the fighting in Kashmir. ▷ Gandhi, Mohandas Karamchand; Islam

jiriki/tariki Terms used in Japanese Pure Land Buddhism to indicate 'self-effort' and 'other-effort' in attaining salvation. The distinction between the two is based upon the theory of decline in the history of the Buddhist tradition. According to the latter, in the earlier period of the teaching of the Buddhist dharma, self-effort (*jiriki*) had been appropriate, ie the ability of human beings to attain salvation by their own efforts through the study of doctrine, through ritual observance, and through meditational discipline. In the later period of the dharma, known as *mappo*, an easier method than self-effort was required, and this was to be found in other-effort (*tariki*), which involved putting one's faith in the grace of Amida Buddha by calling upon his name in the *nembutsu*, 'I put my faith in Amida Buddha'. By this means one could obtain rebirth into the paradise or Pure Land of Amida Buddha, the Buddha of infinite light and deep compassion, and from there one could eventually attain nirvana. Thus tariki represented the easy way of faith in the later age of Buddhism, whereas jiriki had represented the more difficult way of self-effort in the earlier age, nearer to the time of the Buddha himself. ▷ Amida worship; dharma; nembutsu; Pure Land Buddhism

jiva, Jain (jīva) A key category in Jain thought, meaning a soul. Jivas are eternal and immaterial. In ordinary life jivas, or souls, become associated with matter by means of deeds or karma. Karma clings to the soul and incarcerates it within a material body, and within worldly existence. The body and the world are alien to the soul's real nature, which is self-knowledge and bliss. However, until liberation from the round of rebirth occurs, the soul is destined to be reborn according to the karma of the being concerned, and these rebirths can be in all kinds of beings, not just humans. In order to achieve liberation asceticism is necessary. In the first place new karma must be stopped from clinging to the soul and weighing it down, and this is done by means of a life-style that is not bound to worldly activities; then previous karma must be removed from the soul by penance (*tapas*). The soul is then freed in life and has become itself again, separate from matter, and in a state of pure consciousness and bliss. In the case of the Mahavira and other Jain saints voluntary starvation was a method used to attain this end. When finally freed through death, the liberated soul ascends to the summit of the universe and remains there in bliss. ▷ cosmology (Jain); jivanmukti; karma, Jain; Mahavira; rebirth

jivanmukti (jīvan-mukti) A term used in Hindu and Jain thought to describe someone who is liberated in life. Although still alive, and living in the world, the person concerned has passed beyond the round of rebirths and, when he or she dies, will not be born again. The equivalent notion in Buddhism is the state of provisional nirvana which was acquired by the Buddha at his enlightenment but was not translated into final nirvana until his death 45 years later. The parallel notion in the Christian tradition would be a state of perfection in this life. In the Jain case, the notion has a literal sense. The *jiva*, or soul, is freed from the bondage of karma, which the Jains view as a subtle material substance which clings to the soul and weighs it down. By avoiding the accumulation of new karma by retreating from the world, and by burning away old karma through penance (*tapas*), the soul becomes freed from matter and from karma, and at death it will ascend to the summit of the universe and stay there for eternity. In the Hindu case, karma is viewed more psychologically as the continuing effects of one's deeds that continue over from one life to the next, and in the *Bhagavad Gita* the way of deeds is seen as a means to liberation provided that deeds are done without thought of reward and under God. Therefore a Hindu jivanmukti can still be active in the world and would not wish to engage in voluntary starvation as is the case with some Jain saints. ▷ Buddha; enlightenment; jiva, Jain; karma, Jain; Karma Yoga; nirvana; rebirth

Jnanesvar (Jñāneśvara) (13th century) The earliest of the Maratha saints. A poet-philosopher, his works include a commentary on the *Bhagavad Gita*. Although he was an Advaitin, bhakti influence is clearly apparent in his work. Unlike Shankara, who interpreted *Brahman* non-qualitatively, Jnanesvar posited that liberation was a continuum, pouring its light into the world, and the experience of this is to have one's own personality replaced by God's. ▷ bhakti; Bhagavad Gita; Brahman

Joachim of Floris, or Fiore (c.1135–1202) Italian mystic, born in Calabria. In 1177 he became Abbot of the Cistercian monastery of Corazzo and later founded a stricter order of monks, Ordo Florensis, at San Giovanni in Fiore, which was absorbed by the Cistercians in 1505. His mystical interpretation of history, based on historical parallels or 'concordances' between the history of the Jewish people and that of the Church, was grouped into three ages, each corresponding to a member of the Trinity, the last, that of the Spirit, which was to bring perfect liberty, to commence in 1260. This mystical historicism was widely accepted although condemned by the Lateran Council in 1215, but lost influence when its prophecies did not come to pass. ▷ Cistercians; Council of the Church; mysticism; Trinity

Joan of Arc, St (Jeanne d'Arc), known as **the Maid of Orléans** (c.1412–1431) French patriot and martyr, one of the most remarkable women of all time, the daughter of well-off peasants in Domrémy on the borders of Lorraine and Champagne. The English over-ran the area in 1421 and in 1424 withdrew. Joan received no formal education but had an argumentative nature and shrewd common sense. At the age of 13 she thought she heard the voices of St Michael, St Catherine and St Margaret bidding her rescue the Paris region from English domination. She persuaded the local commander, Robert de Baudricourt, after he had had her exorcised, to take her in 1429 across English-occupied territory to the dauphin (the future Charles VII) at Chinon. According to legend, she was called into a gathering of courtiers, among them the dauphin in disguise, and her success in identifying him at once was interpreted as divine confirmation of his previously doubted legitimacy and claims to the throne. She was equally successful in an ecclesiastical examination to which she was subjected in Poitiers and was consequently allowed to join the army assembled at Blois for the relief of Orléans.

Clad in a suit of white armour and flying her own standard, she entered Orléans with an advance guard on 29 April and by 8 May had forced the English to raise the siege and retire in June from the principal strongholds on the Loire. To put further heart into the French resistance she took the dauphin with an army of 12000 through English-held territory to be crowned Charles VII in Reims Cathedral. She then found it extremely difficult to persuade him to undertake further military exploits, especially the relief of Paris. At last she set out on her own to relieve Compiègne from the Burgundians, was captured in a sortie (1430) and sold to the English by John of Luxembourg for 10000 crowns.

She was put on trial (1431) for heresy and sorcery by an ecclesiastical court of the Inquisition, presided over by Pierre Cauchon, Bishop of Beauvais. Most of the available facts concerning Joan's life are those preserved in the records of the trial. She was found guilty, taken out to the churchyard of St Ouen on 24 May to be burnt, but at the last moment broke down and made a wild recantation. This she later abjured and suffered her martyrdom at the stake in the market place of Rouen on 30 May, faithful to her 'voices'. In 1456, in order to strengthen the validity of Charles VII's coronation, the trial was declared irregular. Belief in her divine mission made her flout military advice—in the end disastrously, but she rallied her countrymen, halted the English ascendancy in France for ever and was one of the first in history to die for a Christian-inspired concept of nationalism. In 1904 she was designated Venerable, declared Blessed in 1908 and finally canonized in 1920. Her feast day is 30 May. ▷ martyr

Joan of Arc

Job, Book of A major book of the wisdom literature of the Hebrew Bible/Old Testament, named after its hero and probably drawing on old popular traditions, but in its present form showing evidence of several additions. It is composed of narrative and speeches in which the poet tackles the question of the meaning of undeserved suffering and of faith; despite the advice of his friends, Job persists in his struggles until presented with the inscrutable majesty of God directly. ▷ Old Testament; prophet; theodicy; wisdom literature

Jodo A school of Pure Land Buddhism in Japan, founded by Honen in 1175. It stresses the mercy and power of Amida Buddha, the Buddha of infinite light and deep compassion, by whose grace one can be reborn into Amida's paradise or Pure Land, and from there one can eventually attain nirvana. Honen emphasized the practice of *nembutsu*, the repeated calling upon the name of Amida Buddha with sincere faith by saying 'I put my faith in Amida Buddha'. He claimed that this reliance on 'other-effort', ie on the grace of Amida Buddha, was easier and better in the later history of Buddhism than reliance on self-effort which had been more appropriate in earlier times. Honen's disciple Shinran (1173–1262) established an even more radical form of Pure Land in his Jodo Shinshu or True Pure Land School. Nowadays Pure Land is the most popular Japanese Buddhist way, and there are four main Pure Land schools, of which Jodo is the second largest. ▷ Amida worship; Honen; jiriki/tariki; Jodo Shinshu; nembutsu; nirvana; Shinran

Jodo Shinshu (Jōdo Shinshū) A Japanese Pure Land Buddhist school known as 'True Pure Land', founded by Shinran, the largest and most important school in the Japanese Buddhist tradition. Shinran took a more radical direction than Honen, who had founded the original Japanese Pure Land (*Jodo*) school in 1175. Honen had stressed the mercy and grace of Amida Buddha and the constant repetition of the *nembutsu* (calling upon the name of Amida Buddha) in order to gain rebirth into the paradise or Pure Land of Amida. Shinran stressed still more strongly the free grace of Amida, which remained available even when sin continued, on the principle that if Amida's grace was relevant to a good person it was even more relevant to a bad one. Shinran also discarded the monk's robes, and he married and led a secular life, thus bringing Pure Land Buddhism deeper into the everyday life of ordinary people. In contrast to Honen, who had been ready to use the nembutsu thousands of times a day, Shinran stated that even one recitation of the nembutsu, 'I put my faith in Amida Buddha', said with complete sincerity, would be sufficient for rebirth into Amida's Pure Land, and from there nirvana would follow. For Shinran faith in Amida Buddha alone implied the exclusion of other Buddhist and Shinto divinities. Jodo Shinshu was a radical form of Pure Land Buddhism that eclipsed other Pure Land and Buddhist groups in popularity. ▷ Amida worship; Honen; Jodo; nembutsu; nirvana; Shinran

Joel, Book of One of the 12 so-called 'minor' prophetic writings of the Hebrew Bible/Old Testament, attributed to Joel, of whom nothing is known, but who is today usually assigned to the post-exilic period (c.400–350BCE), a prophet with a strong interest in the priesthood and the Jerusalem Temple cult. It contains a notable reference to a locust plague, warning Judah of a devastating coming judgement and of the final 'Day of the Lord' when Israel's enemies will be destroyed. ▷ Old Testament; prophet; Temple, Jerusalem

Johanan ben Zakkai, Rabban (1st century) Prominent Jewish teacher and leader of the reformulation of Judaism after the fall of Jerusalem (70), who helped to found rabbinic Judaism. His early career was apparently in Galilee, although there are also traditions of his legal disputes with the Sadducees in Jerusalem before its fall. Afterwards he was instrumental in reconstituting the Sanhedrin council in Jabneh. ▷ Akiva ben Joseph; Jabneh; Judaism; rabbi; Sadducees

John, Gospel according to New Testament book, known also as the **Fourth Gospel**, distinct from the other three ('synoptic') gospels because of its unique theological reflections on Jesus as the Son of God and the divine Word come from God, and its records of Jesus's sayings and deeds. It is strictly anonymous, although chapter 21.24 associates it with 'the disciple whom Jesus loved', traditionally held to be John the son of Zebedee but often disputed today. ▷ Gospels, canonical; Jesus Christ; John, St (son of Zebedee); New Testament

John, Letters of Three relatively short New Testament writings, the latter two of which have the form of a letter addressed from 'the Elder', but the first of which lacks direct references to its writer or recipients. They were traditionally considered the work of the author of the Fourth Gospel, but today they are more usually assigned to a later stage of the 'Johannine community'. 1 and 2 John confront the problem of a schism within this Christian community, apparently over false teachings about the importance of Jesus's work on earth and the significance of sin for Christians. 3 John appears to be a private letter addressing problems with a local church leader called Diotrephes. ▷ John, Gospel according to; New Testament

John, St, byname **the Baptist** or **Baptizer** (1st century) Prophetic and ascetic figure referred to in the New Testament Gospels and in Josephus' *Antiquities*, the son of a priest named Zechariah; he was roughly contemporary with Jesus of Nazareth. A story of his birth to Elizabeth, cousin of Mary the mother of Jesus, is recorded in Luke 1. He baptized Jesus and others at the River Jordan, but his baptism seemed mainly to symbolize a warning of the coming judgement of God and the consequent need for repentance. He was executed by Herod Antipas, but the circumstances differ in the accounts of Josephus and the Gospels. He is treated in the New Testament as the forerunner of Christ, and sometimes as a returned Elijah (Matthew 11.13–14). His feast day is 24 June. ▷ Herod, Antipas; Jesus Christ; Josephus, Flavius; New Testament

John, St, or **John, son of Zebedee** (1st century) One of the 12 apostles, son of Zebedee, and the younger brother of James, a Galilean fisherman; one of the inner circle of disciples who were with Jesus at the Transfiguration and Gethsemane. Acts and Galatians also name him as one of the 'pillars' of the early Jerusalem Church. Some traditions represent him as having been slain by the Jews or Herod Agrippa I; but from the 2nd century he was said to have spent his closing years in Ephesus, dying there at an advanced age, after having written the Apocalypse, the Gospel, and the three Epistles which bear his name (although his authorship of these works has been disputed by modern scholars). His feast day is 27 December. ▷ apostle; disciples (in early Christian Church); James, St (son of Zebedee); Jesus Christ; John, Gospel according to; John, Letters of; Revelation, Book of

John XXIII, originally **Angelo Guiseppe Roncalli** (1881–1963) Pope (1958–63), born the son of a peasant in Sotto il Monte near Bergamo in northern Italy. Ordained in 1904, he served as sergeant in the medical corps and as chaplain in World War I, and subsequently as apostolic delegate to Bulgaria, Turkey and Greece. In 1944 he became the first Papal Nuncio to liberated France and championed the controversial system of worker-priests. Patriarch of Venice in 1953, he was elected pope in October 1958 on the twelfth ballot. He convened the 21st ecumenical council in order to seek unity between the various Christian sects and broke with tradition by leaving the Vatican for short visits to hospitals and prisons in Rome. In 1963 he issued the celebrated encyclical *Pacem in Terris* (Peace on Earth), advocating reconciliation between East and West. His diary was published in 1965 as *The Journal of a Soul*. ▷ ecumenism

John of Damascus, St, or **Chrysorrhoas** (c.676–c.754) Greek theologian and hymn writer of the Eastern Church. Born in Damascus he was carefully educated by the learned Italian monk Cosmas. He replied to the iconoclastic measures of Leo the Isaurian with two addresses in which he vigorously defended image worship. His later years were spent in the monastery of Mar Saba near Jerusalem. There, ordained a priest, he wrote his hymns, an encyclopedia of Christian theology (Fount of Wisdom), treatises against superstitions and Jacobite and Monophysite heretics, homilies, and *Barlaam and Joasaph*, now known to be a disguised version of the life of Buddha. His feast day is 4 December. ▷ iconoclasm

John of the Cross, St (1542–91) Spanish mystic and poet, born in Juan de Yepes y Álvarez in Fontiveros, Ávila. A Carmelite monk, in 1568 he founded with St Teresa of Ávila, the ascetic order of Discalced Carmelites. He accompanied St Teresa to Valladolid, where he lived an extremely ascetic life in a hovel until she appointed him to a convent in Ávila, where he was arrested by those hostile to monastic reform (1577) and imprisoned at Toledo. He escaped in 1578 and lived in illness at the monastery of Úbeda. He was canonized in 1726, and declared a Doctor of the Church in 1926. His poetry includes the intensely lyrical *Cántico espiritual* (Spiritual Cantide) and *Noche oscura del alma* (Dark Night of the Soul). His feast day is 29 June. ▷ Carmelites; mysticism; Teresa of Ávila, St

John Paul II, originally **Karol Jozef Wojtyla** (1920–) Polish Pope (1978–), born in Wadowice, the first non-Italian pope in 450 years. He was educated in Poland, ordained in 1946, and became Professor of Moral Theology at Lublin and Cracow. Archbishop and Metropolitan of Cracow (1964–78), he was created cardinal in 1967. Noted for his energy and analytical ability, his pontificate has seen many foreign visits, in which he has preached to huge audiences. In 1981 he survived an assassination attempt, when he was shot in St Peter's Square by a Turkish national, Mehmet Ali Agca, the motives for which have remained unclear. A champion of economic justice and an outspoken defender of the Church in communist countries, he has been uncompromising on moral issues. ▷ Christianity in Russia

Johnson, Hewlett, known as **the 'Red Dean'** (1874–1966) English prelate, born of a capitalist family in Macclesfield. Educated at Manchester and Oxford universities, he began life as an engineering apprentice, did welfare work in the Manchester slums and joined the Independent Labour party, resolving to become 'a missionary engineer'. He was ordained in 1905. In 1924 he became Dean of Manchester and from 1931 to 1963 was Dean of Canterbury. In 1938 he visited Russia and with the publication of *The Socialist Sixth of the World* began his years of praise for Sovietism. In 1951 he received the Stalin Peace Prize. Though he was not a member of the Communist Party, his untiring championship of the Communist states and Marxist policies involved him in continuous and vigorous controversy in Britain. His sobriquet was a self-bestowed title coined when, during the Spanish War, he said 'I saw red—you can call me red'. Other publications include *Christians and Communism* (1956) and the autobiographical *Searching for Light* (1968).

Jonah, or **Jonas, Book of** One of the 12 so-called 'minor' prophetic writings of the Hebrew Bible/Old Testament, unusual for its narrative about the reluctance of the prophet himself in preaching to the city of Nineveh. It includes the famous legend of Jonah's being swallowed by and saved from a 'great fish'. Although the story is set in the mid 8th century BCE, the work is probably post-exilic; it emphasizes Israel's role in addressing the heathen nations, and thus implicitly opposes Jewish exclusivism. ▷ Nineveh; Old Testament; prophet

Jonangpa A monastic tradition of Tibetan Buddhism, regarded as heretical by the Gelugpa tradition, and characterized by the doctrine that the essence or womb of enlightenment (*tathagatagarbha*) is an absolute reality. The tradition was founded by Shes-rab rGyal-tshan (1292–1361), flowering in the 14th century as a distinct monastic order. The Jonangpas were rejected by the Gelugpas, ostensibly on doctrinal grounds, though political reasons concerning the power of the Gelugpas played a role. The Jonangpas follow the mind-only (*cittamatra*) school of the Yogacara and the tathagatagarbha tradition. They maintain that in reality there is only pure consciousness, an unchanging absolute called the essence or womb of enlightenment or buddhahood (tathagatagarbha), which is also identified with the Truth Body (*dharmakaya*) of the Buddha. In contrast to the Gelugpas, the Jonangpas denied the emptiness (*shunyata*) of buddhahood; buddhahood is not 'self-empty', but only 'other empty', that is, empty of defilements or empty of everything other than itself. The influence of Hindu Kashmiri Shaiva doctrines is discernible in these ideas. Indeed Shes-rab's grand-teacher (his teacher's teacher) Candranatha, was from Kashmir. ▷ Buddha; Buddhism; emptiness; Gelugpa; Kashmir Shaivism; tathagata; Yogacara

Jonas ▷ **Jonah, Book of**

Jonathan (c.11th century BCE) Biblical character, the son and heir of Saul (the first King of Israel) and loyal friend of David. He is portrayed in 1 Samuel as a cunning soldier but he faces conflicting loyalties when he continues his friendship with David in spite of Saul's mounting hostility to David. David succeeds Saul as King of Israel, since Jonathan was killed in the battle of Gilboa against the Philistines. ▷ David; Old Testament; Saul

Jones, Bob (Robert Reynolds) (1883–1968) American evangelist, born in Dale County, Alabama. He conducted revival meetings from the age of 13, and was licensed by the Methodist Church to preach at the age of 15. Educated at Southern University, Greensboro, South Carolina, he began full-time evangelistic work in 1902, and is estimated to have preached more than 12000 'down-to-earth gospel messages'. In 1939 he left the Methodist Church, which he charged with theological liberalism, and broke also with other evangelists, notably Billy Graham, who displayed ecumenical tendencies. To further his brand of fundamentalism, in 1927 he founded Bob Jones University which from small beginnings in Florida eventually (1947) settled in Greenville, South Carolina with several thousand students. The school is known for its biblical theology, its Puritanical code which is binding on its students, and tends towards right-wing politics. He once drew unwelcome attention on himself by a pamphlet entitled *Is Segregation Scriptural?* to which he answered yes. ▷ evangelist; fundamentalism; Graham, Billy

Josaphat and **Barlaam** The names of two Christian saints whose story came into the Christian world from origins elsewhere. Josaphat was a prince of wealth and power who was persuaded to renounce his pomp by a hermit, Barlaam. He was baptized, left his throne, and went into the wilderness to seek spiritual truth as an ascetic. This story was derived from Muslim sources, but the Muslims had got it from the Manichees, and originally it went back to the Buddhists. It refers to Gautama—later the Buddha—who had renounced his family, palace and power to go out and seek an answer to the problem of suffering and to search for enlightenment. At that point he was a bodhisattva. In the Manichean story this becomes Bodisaf, in the Muslim story it becomes Yudasaf, and in the Latin Christian account it becomes Josaphat. Thus the Christian saint Josaphat can be traced back to the Buddha prior to his enlightenment. This extraordinary tale of the passing on of a story between different religions makes the point that religions are often far more interconnected than is first apparent. ▷ bodhisattva; Buddha

Joseph Biblical character and subject of many stories in Genesis 37–50; the eleventh son of Jacob, but the first by his wife Rachel. He is depicted as Jacob's favourite son (marked by the gift of a multicoloured coat) who was sold into slavery by his jealous brothers, yet who by prudence and wisdom rose from being a servant to high office in the pharaoh's court, with special responsibility for distributing grain supplies during a time of famine. Eventually he is portrayed as reconciled with his brothers, who come to Egypt to escape the famine. His sons, Ephraim and Manasseh, were blessed by Jacob, and became ancestors of two of the tribes of Israel. ▷ Ephraim/Manasseh, tribe of; Israel, tribes of; Jacob; Old Testament; pharaoh

Joseph, St (1st century BCE) Husband of the Virgin Mary, a carpenter in Nazareth, who last appears in the Gospel history when Jesus is 12 years old. He is never mentioned during Jesus's ministry, and must be assumed to have already died. His feast day is 19 March. ▷ Jesus Christ; Mary

Joseph, tribes of Although Joseph was the eleventh son of Jacob, his descendants were not usually described as 'the tribe of Joseph', one of the 12 tribes of Israel, but were represented by two tribes—Manasseh and Ephraim, Joseph's two sons who were blessed by Jacob (Genesis 48–9). It is uncertain whether a single 'tribe of Joseph' ever existed, since reference is often to 'the tribes of Joseph'. ▷ Ephraim/Manasseh, tribe of; Israel, tribes of; Jacob; Joseph; Old Testament

Josephus, Flavius (c.37–c.100) Jewish historian and soldier, born in Jerusalem. He was the son of a priest, while his mother was descended from the Asmonean princes. His ability in Hebrew and Greek literature soon drew public attention upon him, and he became conspicuous amongst the Pharisees, the national party, at 26 being chosen delegate to Nero in Rome. When the Jews rose in their last and fatal insurrection against the Romans (66), Josephus, as Governor of Galilee, displayed great valour and prudence; but the advance of Vespasian (67) made resistance hopeless, although he held out in Jotapata against a siege for 47 days. Josephus was kept in a sort of easy imprisonment for three years, and was present in the Roman army at the siege of Jerusalem by Titus (70). After this he appears to have resided in Rome. He survived Herod Agrippa II, who died in 100. His works are *History of the Jewish War*, written both in Hebrew and Greek (the Hebrew version is no longer extant); *Jewish Antiquities*, containing the history of his countrymen from the earliest times to the end of the reign of Nero; a treatise on the *Antiquity of the Jews*, against the Alexandrian Greek scholar Apion; and an *Autobiography* (37–90CE). ▷ Pharisees

Joshua, Hebrew **Yehoshua** In the Old Testament, the son of Nun, of the tribe of Ephraim, who during the 40 years' wanderings of the Israelites acted as 'minister' of Moses, and upon Moses's death was appointed to lead the people into Canaan. The Book of Joshua is named after him. ▷ Ephraim, tribe of; Joshua, Book of; Moses

Joshua, or **Josue, Book of** A book of the Hebrew Bible/Old Testament named after its main hero, Joshua (originally Hoshea, but renamed by Moses). It continues the stories of the Pentateuch, beginning with the death of Moses, and presents narratives of how Israel conquered the land west of the Jordan from the Canaanites after 40 years of wandering in the desert. It ends with the death of Joshua after the conquest and the apportionment of the land among the tribes of Israel. The author is anonymous, and the present form of the work seems to be composed of several distinct strands of tradition. ▷ Deuteronomistic History; Israel, tribes of; Old Testament; Pentateuch

Josiah (7th century BCE) Biblical character, King of Judah (c.639–609BCE), a favourite of the Deuteronomistic historians because of his religious reforms (2 Kings 22–3; 2 Chronicles 34–5), allegedly based on the discovery of 'the book of the law' in the eighteenth year of his reign. He is credited with destroying pagan cults and attempting to centralize worship in Jerusalem and the Temple. He died in battle against the Egyptians at Megiddo. ▷ Deuteronomistic History; Esdras/Jeremiah/Zephaniah, Book of; Old Testament

Josue ▷ Joshua, Book of

Jubilees, Book of An account purporting to be an extended revelation to Moses during his 40 days on Mount Sinai, a book of the Old Testament Pseudepigrapha, perhaps from the mid 2nd century BCE. Its name is derived from the division of time into 'jubilees' (49 years, representing 7 'weeks' of years), but it has also been called the Little Genesis or the Testament of Moses. It retells Genesis 1 to Exodus 12 (the Creation to the Passover), amplifying the account and emphasizing separation from non-Jews, loyalty to the Jewish religious law, and the importance of secret traditions for readers of its own times. ▷ Moses; Sinai, Mount; Pseudepigrapha

Judah, kingdom of An ancient Jewish state which incorporated the tribal areas of Judah and Benjamin, established when the united monarchy split into the kingdoms of Judah (in the south) and Israel (in the north) in the late 10th century BCE after the reign of Solomon. Each kingdom had separate kings, with Jerusalem being in the kingdom of Judah. Both Judah and Jerusalem fell to the Babylonians in 587BCE. ▷ Benjamin/Judah, tribe of; Israel, tribes of; Old Testament

Judah, tribe of One of the 12 tribes of ancient Israel, said to be descended from Jacob's fourth son by his wife Leah. Its territory originally extended south of Jerusalem, bounded on the west by the Mediterranean and on the east by the Dead Sea, but later it was restricted. ▷ Jacob; Judah, kingdom of; Israel, tribes of; Old Testament

Judaism The religion of the Jews, central to which is the belief in one God, the transcendent creator of the world who delivered the Israelites out of their bondage in Egypt, revealed his law (Torah) to them, and chose them to be a light to all humankind. The Hebrew Bible is the primary source of Judaism. Next in importance is the Talmud, which consists of the Mishnah (the codification of the oral Torah) and a collection of extensive early rabbinical commentary. Various later commentaries and the standard code of Jewish law and ritual (Halakhah) produced in the late Middle Ages have been important in shaping Jewish practice and thought.

However varied their communities, all Jews see themselves as members of a community

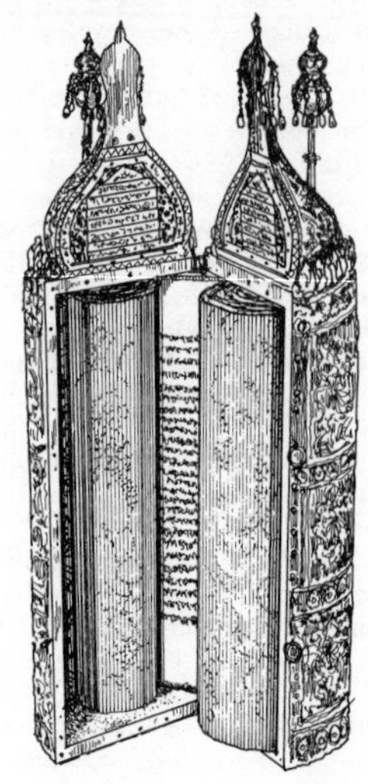

the scroll of the Torah in its tig case

whose origins lie in the patriarchal period. This past lives on in its rituals, and there is a marked preference for expressing beliefs and attitudes more through ritual than through abstract doctrine. The family is the basic unit of Jewish ritual, though the synagogue has come to play an increasingly important role. The Sabbath, which begins at sunset on Friday and ends at sunset on Saturday, is the central religious observance. The synagogue is the centre for community worship and study. Its main feature is the 'ark' (a cupboard) containing the hand-written scrolls of the Pentateuch. The rabbi is primarily a teacher and spiritual guide. There is an annual cycle of religious festivals and days of fasting. The first of these is Rosh Hashanah, New Year's Day; the holiest day in the Jewish year is Yom Kippur, the Day of Atonement. Other annual festivals include Hanukkah and Pesach, the family festival of Passover.

Modern Judaism is rooted in rabbinic Judaism, and its historical development has been diverse. Today most Jews are the descendants of either the Ashkenazim or the Sephardim, each with their marked cultural differences. There are also several religious branches of Judaism. Orthodox Judaism (19th century) seeks to preserve traditional Judaism. Reform Judaism (19th century) represents an attempt to interpret Judaism in the light of modern scholarship and knowledge—a process carried further by Liberal Judaism. Conservative Judaism attempts to modify orthodoxy through an emphasis on the positive historical elements of Jewish tradition. Anti-Semitic prejudice and periods of persecution have been a feature of the Christian culture of Europe, and increased with the rise of European nationalism, culminating in the Nazi Holocaust. Its effect has been incalculable, giving urgency to the Zionist movement for the creation of a Jewish homeland, and is pivotal in all relations between Jews and non-Jews today. There are now over 14 million Jews. ▷ anti-Semitism; Ashkenazim; Bible; Conservative Judaism; Diaspora; Halakhah; Hanukkah; Holocaust; Liberal Judaism; Mishnah; Orthodox Judaism; Pentateuch; Passover; philosophy, Jewish; rabbi; Reform Judaism; Rosh Hashanah; Sabbath; Sephardim; synagogue; Torah; worship, Jewish; Yom Kippur

Judaism, women in Although numerous 19th-century Jewish women rose to prominence, it was not until the 1960s/70s that the role of women within Judaism came to be debated seriously; this included the question of female rabbis. Responses were divided along denominational lines. Orthodoxy has maintained women's God-given role in the home, with a separate women's gallery in the synagogue. They must keep all 'thou shalt not' commandments but unlike men, and to lighten their domestic burden, are exempt from positive commands for specific times (eg dwelling in booths during Sukkot). Women's ordination makes little sense, therefore, but this is thought to reflect difference not inferiority. Reform Judaism has acknowledged that Jewish tradition discriminates against women, not least by their exclusion from public ritual. This has led, for example, to the introduction of a bat mitzvah ('daughter of the law') ceremony at 12 years, parallel to a boy's bar mitzvah ('son of the law') at 13 years; similar developments are now popular even within Orthodoxy. The first female Reform rabbi was ordained in 1972. Conservative Judaism tried to steer a course between Orthodoxy and Reform in this as in other areas. For instance, women were no longer separated from men in synagogues, although they could not be ordained. However, Conservative Judaism ordained its first female rabbi in 1985. ▷ menstruation, Jewish attitude to; Orthodox Judaism; Reform Judaism; women in religion

Judaism in Europe Europe has been home to Jews for around two millennia. There were Jews in Rome, for example, from the 2nd century BCE, and a community in Cologne as early as 321CE. During the Dark Ages their presence spread north and east into Poland, the Baltic and Ukraine, but it was from the 10th century that numbers increased, especially with the encouragement of urban Jewish settlement by European rulers for the stimulation of the economy. Thus despite sporadic violence and some social and religious resrictions, Jews flourished culturally and economically. However, by the end of the 11th century, when Jewish skills were less essential, the religious fervour of the crusades found expression in anti-Jewish sentiment, beginning a process which culminated in the expulsion of Jews from Spain in 1492. Soon afterwards urban Jews in various other places were confined to ghettos outside working times. With the Enlightenment new freedoms were experienced. Initially this encouraged assimilation, a problem that the Reform movement sought to tackle. At the same time many Jews emigrated to America as a result of continued anti-Semitism in the 19th century. This new type of prejudice, racial rather than specifically religious, ended in the Nazi Holocaust, devastating the Jewish population of Europe. Since then America has in many ways taken over from Europe as a vital force in world Jewry alongside Israel. ▷ anti-Semitism; Ashkenazim; Judaism in North America; Reform Judaism

Judaism in North America Jews first settled in North America in the mid 17th century, although the number was small until the 19th century. However, from the outset life there was different from that in Europe, with few restrictions based on religion, either before or after American independence (1776). Since Jews were able to integrate with their non-Jewish neighbours, no separate, autonomous, Jewish community was needed as it had been in Europe. There were individual Jewish congregations with synagogues, of course, but this paralleled Protestant and Catholic organization, and they were all part of a single community in which religious differentiation was more or less unimportant. As Jews began to flourish, others hearing of their success left Europe to join them. But it was emancipation and religious reform in Europe that saw a large increase in the number of American Jews in the 19th century, growing from 6000 in 1826 to some 150000 by the Civil War (1861), many of whom were from central Europe and of Reform disposition. However, persecution in Russia and East Europe from 1881 created vast numbers of new immigrants; some 2000000 came to America in subsequent decades, most of them orthodox. This accounts for the diversity within American Judaism, as well as the dominance of Orthodoxy and Conservatism. In addition, the growing confidence of North American Jews, based on their numbers as well as general religious tolerance, explains the support of many for the Zionist ideal and the State of Israel. By 1920 there were some 4500000 Jews in the USA, with some 2000000 in New York alone by the 1980s; in Canada there are around 300000 Jews. clearly the whole shape of world Jewry has thus been changed, with North American Jews now constituting a vital third force alongside European and Israeli Jewry. ▷ Conservative Judaism; Diaspora Judaism; Holy Land; Orthodox Judaism; Reform Judaism; Zionism

Judas Iscariot (1st century) One of the 12 disciples of Jesus, usually appearing last in the lists in the synoptic Gospels (Mark 3.19), identified as the one who betrayed Jesus for 30 pieces of silver by helping to arrange for his arrest at Gethsemane by the Jewish authorities (Mark 14.43–6). Other traditions indicate his role as treasurer (John 13.29) and his later repentance and suicide (Matthew 27.3–10, Acts 1.16–19). 'Iscariot' may mean 'man of Keriot', 'assassin', or 'man of falsehood'. ▷ apostle; disciples (in early Christian Church); Gethsemane; Gospels, canonical; Jesus Christ

Jude, Letter of A brief New Testament writing, considered one of the 'catholic' or 'general' letters, attributed to Jude the brother of James 'the Just' and thus of Jesus of Nazareth, but believed by many today to originate from very late in the 1st century. The work strongly warns an unspecified readership about false teachers, who are portrayed as immoral, intemperate, and divisive, and who perhaps represented libertine, gnostic views. The canonicity of the letter was long disputed in the early Church. ▷ Gnosticism; James, St ('brother of Jesus'); New Testament

Jude, St (1st century) One of the 12 apostles, probably the Judas who was one of the 'brethren of the Lord', the brother of James 'the Just'. A New Testament letter is named after him, but the authorship of the work is disputed. He is traditionally thought to have been martyred in Persia with St Simon. His feast day is 28 October (West), 19 June or 21 August (East). ▷ apostle; disciples (in early Christian Church); James, St ('brother of Jesus'); Jesus Christ; Jude, Letter of

judgement of the dead An idea first appearing in the Ancient Egyptian cult of Osiris. Here the deceased appears before Osiris and his heart is weighed against the feather of truth. If the deceased is declared justified he passes on to the Osirian underworld. If he fails he is eaten by the 'devourer of the dead'. The idea of a last day of judgement appeared in Israel in the 2nd century BCE. This judgement, however, is concerned with nations rather than individuals (Daniel 7). Israel is to be acquitted and the Gentile nations punished. Christianity inherited the concept through the preaching of Jesus himself who seems to have spoken of an apolcalyptic Son of Man who will come at the last day to judge the earth (Matthew 21.31–46). This idea was developed by the early Church which felt that Christ was the returning Son of Man who would judge the world. This judgement would take place at the end of time when the dead would rise to be consigned to heaven or hell, depending on whether or not their names

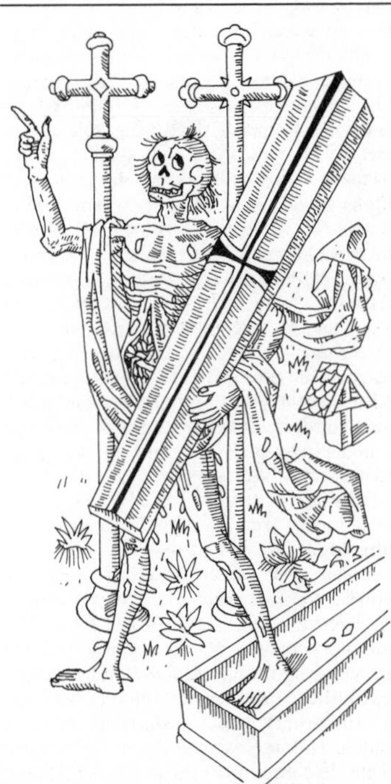

Christian representation of the raising of the dead on the day of judgement

were contained in the book of life. However, the delay in the second coming forced the Church to develop the concept of a particular judgement at the end of the individual's life. This individual judgement renders the final judgement unnecessary, but the image was too powerful to be eliminated from Christian thought. Islam, in accordance with its Judaeo-Christian heritage, shares the concept of a judgement of the dead by Allah at the end of time. ▷ Chinvat Bridge; eschatology; immortality; Osiris; resurrection

judgement of the dead, Islamic view of The Muslim view of the day of judgement and of resurrection, when the dead will rise and be weighed in the scales of God's judgement that will take account of all factors. Humans will be judged according to their conduct and belief, will be revealed for what they are, and as a result of the judgement will enter paradise or hell. The historical process will end on that day and the earth will cease to be. Many verses in the Quran speak about the day of judgement using vivid images and striking metaphors, and it remains a significant element in Muslim thinking today when in other traditions themes such as judgement and hell are emphasized less. ▷ eschatology, Islamic; heaven and hell, Islamic; Paradise; jannah, al-

Judges, Book of A book of the Hebrew Bible/Old Testament, with 'judges' referring to the tribal heroes (such as Deborah, Gideon, and Samson) whose acts of leadership are described. It relates to the unstable period between the initial conquest of Palestine by the Israelites and the establishment of the monarchy over Israel, and it attempts to draw moral lessons from the contrasting examples of good and bad leadership. Its stories probably underwent editing at several stages of Israel's history. ▷ Deuteronomistic History; Old Testament

Judith, Book of Book of the Old Testament Apocrypha (or deuterocanonical writings recognized by the Catholic Church), possibly dating from the Maccabean period (mid 2nd century BCE). It tells the story of how Judith, an attractive and pious Jewish widow, saved the city of Bethulia from siege by the Assyrian army (ostensibly c.6th century BCE) by beheading Holofernes, its general, in his tent once she had beguiled and intoxicated him. ▷ Apocrypha, Old Testament; Maccabees

Juggernaut (Jagannāth) (Sanskrit 'protector of the world') A Hindu deity equated with Vishnu. His temple is in Puri in East India, and is noted for its annual festival. ▷ Hinduism; Vishnu

Julian, or **Juliana of Norwich** (c.1342–after 1413) English mystic. Named possibly after the Norwich church outside which she became an anchoress at some stage of her life, Julian received a series of visions on 8 May 1373. Her account of these visions, written shortly afterwards, and meditations on their significance, made 20 years later (almost the only information we have about her) have survived in mid 15th- and mid 16th-century manuscript copies, published in modern versions as the *Showings* or *Revelations of Divine Love*. Her prayers, her assurance that everything is held in being by the love of God so 'all will be well', and her characterization of the Trinity as Father, Mother, and Lord, speak to many in search of a contemporary spirituality. ▷ mysticism; Trinity

Junayd, al- (al-Junayd, Abū'l-Qāsim ibn Muḥammad) (d.910) An outstanding Muslim mystic, important in the early history of the Sufis, whose birthdate and place of birth are unknown. He taught in Baghdad, and was a significant figure in the emergence of Sufi doctrine. His teachings were recorded by others, and he became famous as the exponent of 'sobriety' rather than 'intoxication' as the key to the mystic path. He saw mysticism as part of ordinary living; he felt that Sufis should be settled as householders rather than wander around as freelancers, and he considered that Sufi mysticism should be seen to be firmly rooted in Islamic orthodoxy. He was thus at variance with the so-called 'drunken Sufis' such as al-Bistami and his own disciple al-Hallaj, and he himself was a merchant with a shop in Baghdad. Like other Sufi leaders he referred to annihilation, effort, love and union as elements in the religious life. However, he said that human beings and the world are in no way identical with God, but exist through God, and he stressed witness to God and consciousness of God rather than being one with God. ▷ Bistami, al-; fana; Hallaj, al-; mysticism; Sufism

Jung, Carl Gustav (1875–1961) Swiss psychiatrist, born in Basle, the son of a Protestant minister. He studied medicine there and worked under Eugen Bleuler at the Burghölzli mental clinic in Zürich (1900–9). His early *Studies in Word Association* (1904–9, in which he coined the term 'complex') and *The Psychology of Dementia Praecox* (1906–7) led to his meeting Sigmund Freud in Vienna in

1907. He became Freud's leading collaborator and was elected President of the International Psychoanalytical Association (1910). His independent researches, making him increasingly critical of Freud's insistence on the psychosexual origins of the neuroses, which he published in *The Psychology of the Unconscious* (1911–12), caused a break in 1913. He then went on to develop his own school of 'analytical psychology'. He introduced the concepts of 'introvert' and 'extrovert' personalities, and developed the theory of the 'collective unconscious' with its archetypes of man's basic psychic nature. He held professorships at Zürich (1933–41) and Basle (1944–61). His other main works were: *On Psychic Energy* (1928), *Psychology and Religion* (1937), *Psychology and Alchemy* (1944), *Aion* (1951), *The Undiscovered Self* (1957) and his autobiographical *Memories, Dreams, Reflections* (1962). A man of wide interests and deep personal spirituality, he was seen as a religious leader by many and has also come to be viewed as the founder of a new humanism. ▷ Freud, Sigmund; humanism; secular alternatives to religion

Jüngel, Eberhard (1934–) German Protestant theologian, born in Magdeburg. A student in Naumberg, Berlin, Zürich and Basel, he lectured in East Berlin before becoming Professor of Systematic Theology in Zürich (1966–9), and then at Tübingen (1969–). He has written widely in German on the death of Jesus Christ and the doctrine of justification, on problems of religious language, and on natural theology. His works available in English include *Death* (1975), *The Doctrine of the Trinity* (1976), *God as the Mystery of the World* (1983), and *Theological Essays* (1987). ▷ Jesus Christ; justification; natural theology; Protestantism

Junrei The Japanese term for pilgrimage. Pilgrimages were of particular importance during the medieval period, although they still take place today. They linked key cities, such as the holy city of Kyoto and the southern capital of Nara, and incorporated various Buddhist and Shinto holy places, for example the two great Shinto shrines at Ise and Uji-Yamada. Times of peace such as the Ido period (1615–1868) were important for pilgrimages, and tours of Buddhist temples such as the Shingon temples originating from the work of Kukai and the temples associated with Kannon, the Japanese equivalent of Kuan Yin, became significant activities during that period. Pilgrimage was felt to be spiritually helpful, especially within the sphere of Buddhist spirituality, and physical benefits such as health cures were also expected and welcomed when they occurred. ▷ Ise shrines; Jingu; Kuan Yin; Shingon

Jupiter, or **Iuppiter** The chief Roman god, equivalent to the Greek Zeus, originally a sky-god with the attributes of thunder and the thunderbolt. He is sometimes given additional names (eg Jupiter Optimus Maximus). Roman generals visited his temple to honour him. ▷ Roman religion

justification In Christianity, to be made or declared right with God. Traditional Roman Catholic theology (following Augustine, Aquinas, and the Council of Trent) understands justification as a lifelong process of being made righteous, by grace imparted through the sacraments of baptism and penance. Protestant theology (following Luther and the Greek rather than the Latin terms in Paul's letters to the Romans and the Galatians) understands justification as a being declared or counted righteous for the sake of Christ. Salvation is by grace alone through faith alone in Christ alone. There is no way to earn merit (and so no need to fear being unable to do so), but justification (seen as a once-for-all renewal) is inseparable from sanctification or growth in holiness. The theme has been treated in modern theology by Ritschl, Barth, Kung, Reinhold Niebuhr, and Tillich. Ecumenical discussion has sought to clarify the terms of the Reformation debate and to ask whether justification is as central to Paul's theology as it was to Luther's experience. ▷ Luther, Martin; merit; Paul, St; Trent, Council of

Justin, St, known as **the Martyr** (c.100–c.165) Greek theologian, and one of the Fathers of the Church. Born in Sichem in Samaria, he was successively a Stoic and a Platonist; after his conversion to Christianity in Ephesus (c.130) he travelled about on foot defending its truths. At Rome between 150 and 160 he wrote the *Apologia* of Christianity addressed to the emperor Marcus Aurelius, followed by a second one, and a *Dialogue with Trypho*, defending Christianity against Judaism. He is said to have been martyred. His feast day is 14 April. ▷ Christianity; Fathers of the Church

K

Ka In Ancient Egypt, the life-force present in gods and humans, thought of as an almost independent entity. Present from birth, the Ka stayed with a person for his or her whole life, guiding and protecting its owner. After death it lived on in the tomb, sometimes called 'house of the Ka'. Here it required regular offerings of food and drink to sustain it, and could reside in the mummy or in a statue of the deceased. ▷ afterlife, Ancient Egyptian concept of; funerary practices, Ancient Egyptian; mummification

Kabbalah (Hebrew 'tradition') Jewish religious teachings originally transmitted orally, predominantly mystical in nature, and ostensibly consisting of secret doctrines. It developed along two lines—the 'practical', centring on prayer, meditation, and acts of piety; and the 'speculative' or 'theoretical', centring on the discovery of mysteries hidden in the Jewish Scriptures by special methods of interpretation. ▷ Judaism; mysticism; Zohar

Kabir (Kabīr) (15th century) A holy man in the Sant bhakti tradition of northern India. He was born into a weaver caste in Banaras who had converted *en masse* to Islam. Kabir advocated devotion to an absolute beyond qualities (*nirguna Brahman*) through the remembrance or repetition of God's name. The name (*nam*) or sound (*shabad*) of God perceived in meditation liberates the soul from illusion (*maya*) and the cycle of birth and death (*samsara*). Kabir combines the devotionalism of Vaishnava bhakti with the yoga of the Natha tradition. Three collections of Kabir's poetry have been preserved: the Eastern (the *Bijak*), the Rajasthani (the *Kabir Granthavali*) and the Punjabi poetry in the *Adi Granth*, the sacred scripture of Sikhism. His verses are often in 'upside down' or 'reversed' language (*ultavamsi*) which present the reader with a riddle to demonstrate that the absolute is beyond rational thought and language. ▷ Banaras; bhakti; maya; samsara; Sikhism; Vaishnavism

kachinas The Hopi word for spirits of the invisible forces of life: the spirits of nature (birds, plants, minerals, stars, clouds) and of the righteous dead. For half the year they live in the otherworld (into which those who have kept the laws emerge at death). At the winter solstice ceremony and the purification they return to the Hopi, symbolized by the appearance of carefully painted masked dancers at the rituals. The masked dancers became identified with the kachinas, and it is important that those who represent the spirits remain pure in thought and deed during the season. At midsummer, the kachinas depart for the otherworld. Dolls painted with the appropriate symbols are also called kachinas, but unlike the masks, these are not invested with power. The Zuñi, also a Pueblo people, have a similar institution, the spirit-powers and dance groups being known as koko. ▷ Hopi religion; Pueblo religion

Pueblo painting of the sun kachinas

Kadampa (bKa'-gdams-pa) The early monastic tradition of Tibetan Buddhism which provided the model for later monastic orders. The tradition was founded by Atisha (982–1054) who brought Buddhist teachings from India to Tibet, though the first monastery of the tradition was built by his disciple Dromten (or Brom-ston, 1008–64) at Reting in 1056. The Kadampas emphasized the gradual purification of the mind through developing morality centred on the monastic discipline (*vinaya*) and meditation, which results in insight into emptiness, the highest level of truth, and the development of compassion (*karuna*). Emptiness was identified with the thought of enlightenment (*bodhicitta*), from which flowed compassion for all beings. The Kadampa tradition contained Tantric teachings, though always within the constraints of a celibate, monastic discipline. Kadampa teachings are based upon Atisha's *The Lamp on the Path of Enlightenment* (*Bodhipathapradipa*), which integrates various Buddhist doctrines and practices into a gradual path. Although this is an important text, the emphasis of the Kadampas was undoubtedly on oral instruction from teacher (lama) to disciple. The Kadampas merged into the Gelugpa order founded by Tsongkapa. ▷ Atisha; emptiness; Gelugpa; karuna; lama; Tsongkapa

Kaddish (Aramaic 'holy') An ancient Jewish congregation prayer, mostly in Aramaic, which marks the closing parts of daily public worship, praising the name of God and seeking the coming of the kingdom of God. There are variations in its use, but it is mostly recited while standing and facing Jerusalem. It has affinities with the Christian formulation of the Lord's Prayer. ▷ Judaism; kingdom of God; Lord's Prayer; prayer

Kagawa, Toyohiko (1888–1960) Japanese Christian social reformer and evangelist. A convert to Christianity, he was educated at the Presbyterian College in Tokyo, and Princeton Theological Seminary in the USA. Returning to Japan, he became an evangelist and social worker in the slums of Kobe. He became a leader in the Japanese labour movement, helping found the Federation of Labour (1918) and Farmer's Union (1921). He helped to establish agricultural collectives. He founded the Anti-War League in 1928; after World War II he was a leader in the women's suffrage movement, and helped with the process of democratization. He wrote numerous books, including the autobiographical novel *Before the Dawn* (1920). ▷ evangelist

Kagyupa (bKa'brgyud-pa) A monastic tradition of Tibetan Buddhism founded by Gampopa, though retrospectively tracing its foundation to Marpa and thence to the wandering Tantric yogins or Siddhas of India. The Kagyupa combines the esoteric Tantric teachings of the Siddhas with the monastic discipline derived from the *Kadampas*. Among the Siddhas or 'Perfected Ones', the Kagyupa traces its origin to Tilopa who is said to have received teachings from Vajradhara, a manifestation of buddhahood. Tilopa initiated Naropa, who initiated Marpa, who passed the teachings on to Milarepa and thence to Gampopa. The Kagyupa emphasizes the doctrines and practices of Tantra and yoga, particularly the Mahamudra and the six yogas of Naropa. Mahamudra (the 'great seal') maintains that there is an ineffable, radiant consciousness outside time and space and beyond subject/object distinction, which is realized with the stopping of conceptualization. After Gampopa the Kagyupa split into six lineages, of which three survive today. The most important of these is the Karmapa, which is subdivided into the Red and Black Hat schools. Upon the death of the second karmapa (14th century), a child was recognized as his reincarnation and reared as his successor. This idea of succession through reincarnating lamas (*tulkus*) originated in the Kagyupa and was later adopted by other Tibetan orders, notably the Gelugpa. ▷ Gampopa; Gelugpa; Marpa; Milarepa; Naropa; siddhas; Tantra; tulku; yoga

Kahane, Meir, Rabbi (1932–90) Jewish leader, born in Brooklyn, New York. He was educated at New York University before graduating as a rabbi in 1957 at the orthodox rabbinical school in Brooklyn. He founded the Jewish Defence League in 1968, and became leader of the minority political Kach Party in Israel. An ardent campaigner against anti-Semitism, he worked for the rights of Soviet Jews within the USSR. He wished to keep Israel as a Jewish state founded on Jewish laws and denying rights to Arabs and Gentiles. Elected to the Israeli Parliament, the Knesset, in 1984, his somewhat violent right-wing views were repudiated by mainstream Jews in Israel and the USA, and in 1988 he was barred from re-election to the Knesset. His aggressive fundamentalism represented an extreme reaction to the Jewish experience of the Holocaust. He lived mainly in the USA and was shot in a New York hotel. ▷ anti-Semitism; Holocaust; Israel, State of; Orthodox Judaism

kalam (kalām) A Muslim term meaning 'speech' or 'dialectic' which came to refer to Islamic scholastic theology; theologians were referred to as the 'people of kalam'. Early Islam placed more emphasis upon the Quran, the sayings and traditions of Muhammad, and the building up of schools of law than it did upon theology. However, as the Muslim empire expanded and met with Greek and other systems of thought it became necessary to mount a rational defence of the Islamic intellectual position, to answer the doubts and questions increasingly being raised by Muslims, and to bolster their beliefs in a more systematic way. For example, the questions of free will and predestination, and of the importance or otherwise of sin, were significant issues in early Islamic debate. The Mutazilites, although perceived as somewhat unorthodox, were the first theological school to adopt a systematic application of reason to a broad spectrum of theological questions. The real founder of Muslim kalam was al-Ashari (873–935). His school and that of al-Maturidi (d.944) became the standard schools of Muslim theology. They worked out the orthodox Islamic theological position in opposition to the Mutazilites, the Hellenistic philosophers, and the literalist interpreters of the Quran. Later, al-Ghazali (1058–1111) worked out an even wider synthesis of theology, philosophy and mysticism that has done duty until recent times. Theology as such has never been as important in Islam as has been the case in Christianity, nor has it been as important as the law (shariah) within Islam itself. This remains the case today, as Islamic modernism stresses the need for dynamism and practical reform rather than systematic theology or kalam. ▷ Ashari, al-; predestination in Islam; Ghazali, Abu Hamid Mohammed al-; Islamic law schools; Islamic modernism; Mutazilites; philosophy, Islamic; Quran; shariah; sin, Islamic view of

Kali (Kālī) The Hindu goddess of destruction, who is also represented as the Great Mother, the giver of life. The consort of Shiva, she is sometimes depicted dancing on top of him. A fearsome character, she is generally represented as vicious and implacable, her four hands holding weapons, her body smeared with the blood of her victims. Among her adornments is a girdle made from severed hands. Representing the dark side of the goddess Devi, she is commmonly identified with Durga. ▷ Durga; Hinduism; Shiva

Kama (Kāma) The Hindu god of love, depicted as an attractive young man whose flower-arrows could induce love in those they pierced. He succeeded in making the ascetic god Shiva fall in love with and marry Parvati. Kama also refers to one of the four ends of life in Hindu tradition. In this view, the pursuit of love or pleasure, both sensual and aesthetic, is necessary for life, but should be regulated by considerations of dharma. Instruction and guidelines are given in the *Kama-Sutra*, a classic work of erotic technique, thought to have been written by the sage Vatsyayana. ▷ dharma; Hinduism; Parvati; Shiva

Kamakura A period in Japanese history dating from 1185 to 1333, especially important for the Buddhist tradition, when the capital of Japan was moved from Kyoto to Kamakura and a military dictatorship began. It was a time of decline for the Japanese court and nobility, as well as a time of feudal struggle and more general unrest. One consequence was that the Tendai and Shingon schools of Buddhism, which had achieved court patronage, began to decline in favour of new Buddhist movements that spoke more directly to the condition of the people. The Kamakura semi-turmoil was reflected in Buddhist theory. This viewed history in three stages: the ideal age of the Buddha when enlightenment was possible, a second age of decline, and a third age of degeneration when the former Buddhist ways were no longer relevant. Thus a better rebirth became a more realistic goal than nirvana. Three major Buddhist schools emerged in Kamakura times, which spoke to the real needs of the people in this new age. They were the Pure Land schools of Honen and Shinran, which stressed the aim of rebirth into Amida Buddha's paradise or Pure Land by saying with faith the *nembutsu*, 'I put my faith in Amida Buddha'; the Zen schools, Rinzai and Soto, which stressed the possibility of present enlightenment whether it be gradual or sudden; and the Nichiren schools, which stressed faith in the *Lotus Sutra* as a way to reform Buddhism and to revive Japan. ▷ Amida worship; Honen; Lotus Sutra; nembutsu; Nichiren Buddhism; nirvana; Rinzai; Shingon; Shinran; Soto; Tendai; Zen Buddhism

kami Objects of worship and sacred powers within the Japanese Shinto tradition. In the New Testament the word *theos* or god is translated in Japanese by the word kami, but the analogy with god is only approximate. Shinto in Japanese is known as the 'way of the kami', and they are central to an understanding of Shinto. Kami are present in awe-inspiring aspects of nature, for example Mount Fujiyama. They are mentioned in the early chronicles of Japan, the *Kojiki* and *Nihongi*, and two of them were responsible for making the islands of Japan. Their kami daughter, the sun goddess Amaterasu, was responsible for establishing the imperial line of Japan. Traditionally there are millions of kami; some are celestial beings who remain above the world and its concerns, whereas others are worldly kami who do have contact with people on earth. As Shinto and Buddhism grew closer together, kami were seen as protectors of Buddhas and bodhisattvas and, at the popular level, they sometimes became identified with them. Norinaga (1730–1801) made the first systematic attempt to define kami. He saw them as awe-inspiring, virtuous, extraordinary, and often intimately related to human beings, who are in fact descended from kami. Although omnipresent they are not all-powerful. Nevertheless, in scholarship and spiritual understanding, there is an increasing overlap between their sacredness and the notion of deity or gods. ▷ Amaterasu; bodhisattva; Buddha; New Testament; sacred mountains, Japanese; Shinto

Kammu (736–806) Early emperor of Japan, who had a deep influence upon Japanese religion after his enthronement in 781. By that time the Buddhist groups and temples in the capital Nara had acquired vast wealth and influence. To counteract this Kammu moved the capital elsewhere and built new cities, including Kyoto (794). His work changed the course of Buddhist history in Japan, and Japanese history in general, and Kyoto became Japan's premier holy city. He was responsible for sending Saicho to China in 804, resulting in the introduction of Tendai Buddhism into Japan, and he also sent Kukai to China in 805, thus bringing Shingon Buddhism into Japan; both schools were to become important in Japanese history. Although in the wake of Kammu's rule Buddhism had less political influence, it became more responsive to the needs of ordinary people, and at the local level it drew closer to the Shinto tradition. Head of the Confucian Academy in Japan, Kammu brought peace by ending the long war with the indigenous Ainu people of northern Japan. ▷ Kukai; Saicho; Shingon; Tendai

Kanada Traditionally the author of the *Vaisheshika sutra*. He is claimed, at least nominally, as the founder of the Vaisheshika school, one of the six systems of Hindu philosophy which eventually amalgamated with the Nyaya school. His dates are problematic. He is said to have lived during the 2nd century BCE, but according to some scholars, his *sutra* cannot be dated before the 2nd century CE. His name literally means 'atom-eater', in accordance with the school's atomic theories of reality. Devotional legends include an alternative name, Anluka (owl), referring to his practice of meditating all day and eating only at night. ▷ Nyaya; Vaisheshika

Kanishka (Kaniṣka) (1st–2nd century) Buddhist ruler of the Kushan empire in northwest India, whose dates are uncertain but who appears to have lived at the end of the 1st and the beginning of the 2nd century. He was important in the history of Buddhism, especially Mahayana Buddhism, and is reckoned to be on a par with other great Buddhist monarchs such as King Ashoka in India in the 3rd century BCE and Prince Shotoku in Japan (573–621). The Mahayana tradition records that Kanishka convened a Buddhist Council in either Kashmir or Jalandar in order to settle disputes about Buddhist doctrine, and this ranks in Mahayana eyes as the fourth Buddhist Council out of the six (or 10) that have ever been held. His kingdom lay astride part of the Silk Route that gave access from India into China, and during his rule Buddhists became more active in entering China. The fact that he was sympathetic to the Mahayana Buddhist tradition and built up a mainly Mahayana kingdom at a crucial geographical location had some influence on China's eventually adopting the Mahayana path, albeit only partially. It was in Kanishka's Kushan empire that Buddha images first began to appear, and it was here also that a 13-storied stupa was erected by Kanishka, and both Buddha images and pagodas similar to the Kushan stupa were to be features of later Chinese Buddhism. ▷ Ashoka; Buddha image; Buddhist Councils; Mahayana Buddhism; pagoda; stupa

Kanjur (bKa'-'gyur) One of the two parts of the Tibetan Buddhist canon, comprising texts translated from Sanskrit which are regarded as the word of the Buddha. The Kanjur, made up of over 100 volumes, comprises four broad categories of text: the *Vinaya*, the *Perfection of Wisdom* (*Prajnaparamita*) *Sutras*, other *Mahayana Sutras*, and Tantras. The Tantras are divided into Action (*kriya*) and Performance (*carya*) tantras concerned with ritual, yoga tantras concerned with visualization, and Supreme Yoga (*anuttarayoga*) tantras involving psychosexual symbolism. The second part of the Tibetan canon, the *Tanjur* (*bs Tan-'gyur*), contains over 200 volumes of commentary on the Kanjur and independent treatises on doctrine, ritual and iconography. The canon was systematized by Buston in the 14th century. ▷ Buddha; Buston; Mahayana Buddhism; prajnaparamita; vinaya-pitaka

Kant, Immanuel (1724–1804) German philosopher, one of the great figures in the history of Western thought. The son of a saddler, he was born in Königsberg, Prussia (now Kaliningrad), and stayed there all his life. He studied and then taught at the university, becoming Professor of Logic and Metaphysics in 1770. He lived a quiet, orderly life and local people were said to set their watches by the time of his daily walk. His early publications were in the natural sciences, particularly geophysics and astronomy, and in an essay on Newtonian cosmology (*Allgemeine Naturgeschichte und Theorie des Himmels*, 1755) he anticipated the nebular theory of Laplace and predicted the existence of the planet Uranus before its actual discovery by William Herschel in 1781. He published extensively, but his most important works were produced relatively late in his life: the *Kritik der reinen Vernunft* (Critique of Pure Reason, 1781), *Kritik der praktischen Vernunft* (Critique of Practical Reason, 1788), and *Kritik der Urteilskraft* (Critique of Judgement, 1790). The first of these is a philosophical classic, though a very difficult one, which he himself described as 'dry, obscure, contrary to all ordinary ideas, and prolix to boot'. In it he responds to Hume's empiricism and argues that the immediate objects of perception depend not only on our sensations but also on our perceptual equipment, which orders and structures those sensations into intelligible unities. He likened his conclusions to a Copernican revolution in philosophy, whereby some of the properties we observe in objects are due to the nature of the observer, rather than the objects themselves. There are basic concepts (or 'categories'), like cause and effect, which are not learnt from experience but constitute our basic conceptual apparatus for making sense of experience and the world. The second *Critique* deals with ethics, and his views are developed in the *Grundlagen zur Metaphysik der Sitten* (Groundwork to a Metaphysic of Morals, 1785) where he presents the famous Categorical Imperative, 'Act only on that maxim which you can at the same time will to become a universal law'. The third *Critique* deals with aesthetics or judgements of 'taste', for which he tries to provide an objective basis and which he connects with our ability to recognize 'purposiveness' in nature. He also wrote on political topics, and his *Perpetual Peace* (1795) advocates a world system of free states. Kant described his philosophy as 'transcendental' or 'critical' idealism, and he exerted an enormous influence on subsequent philosophy, especially the idealism of Fichte, Hegel and Schelling. ▷ secular alternatives to religion

Kapila An Upanishadic sage, reputedly the founder of the Samkhya school, one of the six orthodox systems of Indian philosophy. However, he greatly predates the Samkhya *sutras*, and thus his connection with the school is somewhat tenuous. His very existence seems to be little more than a collection of devotional legends. His name means 'red one', which is an epithet of the sun and of Vishnu, and he is mentioned in the *Mahabharata* as dramatically turning a band of impudent young warriors to ashes with a flash of his eye. Some scholars suggest that he gave his name to the Buddha's birthplace, the city of Kapilavastu. ▷ Buddha; Mahabharata; Samkhya; Upanishads

Kaplan, Mordecai Menahem (1881–1983) Founder of the Reconstructionist movement in Judaism, born in Lithuania. From the age of nine he lived in the USA. He was ordained as an Orthodox rabbi but, uncomfortable with traditional teachings, in 1909 he took up a post at Conservative Judaism's Jewish Theological Seminary in New York, with which he remained involved until his retirement in 1963. Although the creator and developer of Reconstructionism, he did not intend that his school of thought should become a new denomination; this took place under his successors. His major work is *Judaism as a Civilisation* (1934), but liturgical texts edited by him and others drew more attention. The *New Haggadah* (1941) and *Reconstructionist Prayer Book* (1945) attempted to combine modern ideals with ancient tradition but led to Kaplan's excommunication by the Union of Orthodox Rabbis (1945). Such pressures resulted in the formation of the Federation of Reconstructionist Congregations and a Reconstructionist Rabbinical College in 1968. These moves constituted the creation of a fourth denomination within Judaism. ▷ Conservative Judaism; Reconstructionist Judaism

Karah Prasad (Kaṛāh Prasād) Sacramentally blessed Sikh food (*Prasad*) prepared in an iron pan (*Karah*). It is given to those present at the end of important Sikh rituals and ceremonies, and is offered to all attenders irrespective of class, colour, creed, or position. Consisting of equal portions of clarified butter, wholemeal flour and sugar which are mixed to a firm consistency, it is blessed by the reading of verses from a sacred text, and touched by the worship leader with a ceremonial sword. These details are laid out in the *Rahit Maryda*, the Sikh Code of Discipline. It is given first to the person reading the Sikh scripture, the *Guru Granth Sahib*. Five helpings are then set out for especially faithful Sikhs, and finally it is distributed generally. The practice of *Langar*, taking food together in Sikh temples, is similar to Karah Prasad in terms of the principle of equality, but dissimilar in that it is not sacramental. The common partaking of food, whether blessed or not, is an important feature of the Sikh tradition. ▷ five Ks; gurdwara; Langar; Rahit Maryada

karma (Sanskrit 'action' or 'work') In Indian tradition the principle that a person's actions have consequences meriting reward or punishment. Karma is the moral law of cause and effect by which the sum of a person's actions is carried forward from one life to the next, leading to an improvement or deterioration in that person's fate.

karma, Jain The Jains have their own distinctive view of karma which is an important doctrine in their system. Both main schools of Jainism devote much attention to it in their sacred texts, and the Buddhists spend a lot of time refuting it. The Jains analyse in detail four elements of karma: its influx, bondage, duration and fruition. They claim, in opposition to the Hindus, that karma is a subtle kind of matter that attaches itself to the soul, the *jiva*. Thus the soul can expand, contract and become different, according to the weight of karma that lies upon it. All actions, whether good or otherwise, cause some karmic matter to attach to the soul, but evil actions produce a heavier karma that is more difficult to get rid of. Liberation from the round of rebirths occurs at two levels. By abandoning action it is possible to prevent further karma appearing, and by penance (*tapas*) centred upon a life of austerity it is possible to get rid of the karma already acquired. Thus absolute non-violence and voluntary starvation were features of the life of the Jain hero and effective founder, the Mahavira, and of a number of Jain saints. ▷ cosmology, Jain; jiva, Jain; jivanmukti; Mahavira

Karma Yoga The yoga of action; a path to liberation (*moksha*) through renouncing the results of action and offering those results to God. Along with *Jnana* and Bhakti, it is one of the yogas of the *Bhagavad Gita*, which advocates considering 'pleasure and pain, wealth and poverty, victory and defeat, as of equal worth' (*Bhagavad Gita* 2.38). Thus, the results of action are not the concern of the agent, but are completely resigned to God. Another emphasis within Karma Yoga is that of the proper execution of dharma. Generally, karma is said to dictate one's present status in life, one's occupation, and all associated duties or dharmas. Without making ethical evaluations, dharma and appropriate ashramas must be strictly observed. Thus, even those in socially unacceptable occupations, such as prostitution, should diligently fulfil their obligations (rendering all positive and negative fruits to God) in order to achieve a more advantageous rebirth or liberation. Karma Yoga also requires the perfection of the performance of religious rituals, another permutation of the theme of discipline and God-directed activity. ▷ Bhagavad Gita; bhakti; dharma; karma

Kartarpur (Kartārpur) A town important in the early history of the Sikh tradition. It was founded by Guru Nanak on the bank of the River Ravi in present-day Pakistan, where he retired with the aim of establishing an exemplary community for the growing Sikh fellowship. Reminiscent (on a smaller scale) of the ideal Hindu community Ramarajya (the kingdom of Rama), it gave Guru Nanak a centre of authority and a place to set up a patterned model of living. He rose before dawn, bathed, recited the *Japji*, established a pattern of daily work, and closed the day with preaching and hymns. It was in Kartarpur that Guru Nanak died. Another town of the same name was founded in 1596 near Jallandar in India by Guru Arjan, and the original Sikh scripture, the *Adi Granth*, is retained in a Sikh temple there. ▷ Adi Granth; Arjan, Guru; gurdwara; Janam Sakhis; Japji; Nanak

karuna (karuṇa) The notion of compassion within the Buddhist tradition. It is one of the four 'spiritual abidings' in Buddhism, the other three being equanimity, loving kindness, and sympathetic joy. However, it does not imply vicarious sacrifice, sentimental empathy, or vague pity. It is exercised to all other beings, and it is not emotional, but productive of action on behalf of others. It was the Buddha's compassion that led him to preach to others and to serve others. Mahayana Buddhism elevated the status of compassion to make it equal to wisdom, whereas Theravada Buddhism tended to give wisdom the higher place. In Mahayana Buddhism it can refer to the grace of a Buddha or bodhisattva whose intentions and acts are motivated by compassion. For example the bodhisattva Avalokiteshvara symbolizes compassion both in his Indian form and in the female form of Kuan Yin by which he became known in China. If one calls with sincerity and faith upon the name of Amidah Buddha, out of his compassion he will offer his saving grace to the one who calls. It is out of compassion that the bodhisattva vows that he will not accept nirvana but be reborn time and time again into the world until all other beings are released. By comparison with the notion of *anukampa*, which means human empathy, karuna has a wider and somewhat more technical meaning, and is also used meditationally as offering compassion to all beings. ▷ Amidah; anukampa; Avalokiteshvara; bodhisattva; Buddha; Kuan Yin; Mahayana Buddhism; nirvana; Theravada Buddhism; wisdom

Kashmir Shaivism (Kashmir Śaivism) A monistic tradition of Hinduism which developed from the 9th to the 12th centuries, centred in, but not confined to, Kashmir. Kashmir Shaivism maintains that there is only one reality, Shiva, who is pure consciousness and who manifests the manifold forms of the universe and the beings within it. This consciousness is a union of the male Shiva and his female energy or Shakti. Beings appear to be bound in transmigration (*samsara*), but can be freed from this illusion by recognizing their identity with Shiva. There were a number of Shaiva traditions in Kashmir, particularly the ritual systems of the Trika ('Threefold') and Krama ('Graded') with their own pantheons of deities based on the Shaiva Tantras, and the theological articulation of Shaiva monism in the Pratyabhijna ('Recognition') and Spanda ('Vibration') schools, expounded in the works of Abhinavagupta (c.950–100). There was also a thriving dualist tradition of Shaiva Siddhanta, but whereas this tradition accepted Vedic Hindu orthopraxy, the monistic tradition did not. Indeed the esoteric rituals of the Trika involved caste-free sexual intercourse in order to realize the identity of the practitioners in the rite with Shiva and Shakti. Other methods of realization are the descent of Shiva's grace (*shaktipata*); the shattering of thought by the upsurge of strong emotion; fixing the mind on a pure thought such as 'I am Shiva' until its truth is realized; and the repetition of mantras and ritual. A less esoteric form of Shaivism, the worship of Svacchandabhairava, a form of Shiva, can still be found in Kashmir. ▷ Shaiva Siddhanta; Shakti; samsara

kashrut A Hebrew noun describing the complex of laws governing consumption of food in Judaism; the related adjective is kosher (or kasher), meaning 'fit [for consumption]'. The basic rules, which were developed in post-biblical times, are found in Leviticus 11.1–47 and Deuteronomy 14.3–20; their purpose is to promote Israel's holiness. They apply mainly to animal products and may be summarized as follows. Firstly, only certain species may be eaten: four-legged animals with split hooves which chew the cud, fish with both scales and fins, and specified types of bird. Secondly, animals must be slaughtered by a trained shohet ('slaughterer') to ensure minimum suffering and drainage of the maximum amount of blood. Thirdly, carcasses for consumption must be free of blemishes and have certain parts removed. Finally, Deuteronomy 14.21 is understood to prohibit any mixing of milk and meat so that separate utensils must be employed for each.

In origin these laws probably stemmed from ancient taboos which are now obscure, and many Reform Jews no longer count them as significant. However, they are still observed by the orthodox, for whom they express the divine will and contribute to the sanctification of ordinary life. ▷ animal slaughter, Jewish; kosher; dietary laws; Orthodox Judaism

Keble, John (1792–1866) English churchman and religious poet, inspirer of the 'Oxford Movement', born in Fairford, Gloucestershire, near his father's living of Coln St Aldwins. At 15 he was elected a scholar at Corpus Christi College, Oxford, and in 1810 took a double first. In 1811 he was elected a fellow of Oriel and in 1812 won the Latin and English essay prizes. In 1815 he was ordained deacon, beginning active work as curate of East Leach, while continuing to live in Oxford, where he was college tutor (1818–23). In 1827 he published his first book of poems, *The Christian Year*. His theory of poetry, explained in the *British Critic* in 1838, was worked out at length in his Latin lectures delivered as Oxford Professor of Poetry (1831–41). Meanwhile Keble had gathered round him a small band of pupils, of whom the most striking was Hurrell Froude, and in this circle originated the Tractarian movement. In his sermon on national apostasy (1833) Keble gave the signal for action, and for the next eight years was engaged with Newman, Pusey, Isaac Williams and others in the issue of *Tracts for the Times*, brought to an end by Tract No. 90 in 1841. Keble had married in 1835, and had moved to the Hampshire living of Hursely, where he remained until his death. With Pusey he was the steadying influence which supported the party under the shock caused by Newman's conversion to Catholicism. Other works are a Life of Bishop Wilson, an edition of Richard Hooker, the *Lyra Innocentium* (1846), a poetical translation of the Psalter, *Letters of Spiri-*

tual Counsel (1870), 12 volumes of parochial sermons, and *Studia Sacra* (1877). Keble College, Oxford, was founded (1870) in his memory. ▷ Newman, John Henry; Oxford Movement

kehillah (plural **kehillot**) In Judaism the Hebrew name used for the autonomous Jewish community in Europe and Russia, also called the *kahal* (both meaning 'assembly'). Within the kehillot Jewish life was self-determined so that religious, judicial, educational and financial needs were locally organized, including the collection of government taxes. While small communities were run by a committee of trustees, larger ones had paid officials, including a rabbi; the main institutions of the kehillah were its synagogue and cemetery. The efficient and autonomous self-organization of the kehillot contributed much to the survival of Jewish communities in Europe during times of persecution. However, the situation changed dramatically in the modern period. Since each kehillah depended for its competent operation on a consensus within the community, as well as on the recognition of its leaders' authority, Jewish emancipation from the end of the 18th century led to its gradual disintegation. This took place first in central and western Europe and then in the east. It was caused by a number of factors which encroached upon traditional Jewish life in the aftermath of the Enlightenment: questioning of the tradition by the Reform movement, resulting assimilation and emigration, the rise of individualism, secularism and the modern nation-state, and Jewish involvement in government and commerce outwith the community. ▷ Judaism in Europe; Judaism in North America; Reform Judaism

Kempe, Margery, née **Brunham** (b.1364) English mystic, daughter of a mayor of Lynn. She was the wife of a burgess in Lynn and the mother of 14 children. After a period of insanity she experienced a conversion and undertook numerous pilgrimages. Between 1432 and 1436 she dictated her spiritual autobiography, *The Book of Margery Kempe*, which recounts her persecution by devils and men, repeated accusations of Lollardism, her copious weepings, and her journeys to Jerusalem and to Germany, and has been hailed as a classic. ▷ Lollards; mysticism; Wycliffe, John

Kempis, Thomas à (1379–1471) German religious writer, so called from his birthplace, Kempen. In 1400 he entered the Augustinian convent of Agnietenberg near Zwolle in the Netherlands, took holy orders in 1413, was chosen sub-prior in 1429, and died as superior. He wrote sermons, ascetical treatises, pious biographies, letters and hymns, and in particular the famous treatise *On the Following* [or *Imitation*] *of Christ*. Its theology is almost purely ascetical, and (excepting the fourth book, which is based on the doctrine of the real presence) the work has been used by Christians of all denominations. ▷ Augustinians; theology

kerygma (Greek 'proclamation', 'that which is announced', often referring to the content of a priestly or prophetic proclamation) In the New Testament it often refers to the apostles' announcement of the saving nature of Jesus's death and resurrection (1 Corinthians 15.3-5), so that Jesus becomes not just the proclaimer of salvation but that which is proclaimed.

Keshab Chandra Sen (1838–84) Hindu, a leading figure in the so-called 'Hindu Renaissance' in the 19th century. As leader of the reformist Brahmo Samaj movement he furthered the ideas of social reform begun by the group's previous leaders Rammohun Roy and Debendranath Tagore (1817–1905). Indeed, he was especially influenced by the latter, becoming a leading campaigner for social and religious change in India. His charismatic nature brought the movement national attention, underlining Roy's original aims of eradicating such institutions as caste and child marriage. However, Sen gradually began to move away from the ideas of his predecessors in that he wanted Brahmo Samaj to break out of its particularly Hindu mould. This, together with the fact that he married his daughter off at the age of 13, resulted in a series of schisms within the movement. Sen became increasingly interested in Christian ideas and formed the New Dispensation movement which was something of a synthesis of bhakti, Tantrism, and Christianity. After Sen's death his influence waned and the Brahmo Samaj was reunited under a general committee. His ideas were, however, important as they represented the views of a generation of Indians who were trying to reconcile their spirituality with the new ideas of science and rationality spreading from Europe. Sen recognized the possibility of a synthesis of the two, which later Indian thinkers were to stress in a less abstract way. ▷ bhakti; Brahmo Samaj; Rammohun Roy; Tantric Hinduism

Khadijah (Khadījah) (554–619) The first wife of Muhammad. During her lifetime she was his only wife. She was a wealthy widow when she met Muhammad, and she appointed him master of her caravans and later proposed marriage to him when he was 25 and she was 40. They had two sons who died in infancy and four daughters, one of whom, Fatimah, married Ali, who became a key figure in Shiite Islam. Khadijah was a great spiritual, psychological and material helpmate to Muhammad during the uncertain earlier years of his work, and she is revered by Muslims as the first believer and the first convert to Islam. She died in Mecca three years before the migration (Hegira) to Medina. Although Islam limited marriage to four wives at a time, a revelation in the Quran authorized more than four wives for Muhammad, and after the death of Khadijah he married 10 more times. ▷ Ali; hegira; Mecca; Medina; Muhammad; Quran; Shiism

Khalistan (Khālistān) The name of a separate state desired by some Sikhs. It means the land of the pure, or the land of the *Khalsa*. In aspiration it would cover the present Punjab state in India, supplemented by territory giving access to the sea and other areas occasionally ruled, in the past, by Sikh leaders such as Maharajah Ranjit Singh. In contemporary India the notion of an independent Sikh state of Khalistan separate from the country of India has been mooted by a minority of Sikhs as the end-result of their struggle for more home rule for the Sikhs and for the Punjab. At the time of the partition of India in 1946–7 the notion of Khalistan was raised, being envisaged as an area which, while not independent, would be dominated by Sikhs. Since the 1970s the ideas has been revived, this time envisaging a fully independent Sikh principality. ▷ Khalsa; Punjab; Ranjit Singh

khalq The notion of creation within the Muslim tradition. It is related to two main issues: the creation or otherwise of the Quran, and the creation of the world. After intense medieval debate on the createdness or otherwise of the Quran, the main view emphasized that it was uncreated in essence and was eternally pre-existent in God, but was created through revelation in its letters and sounds, ie in its written form and when chanted. The Quranic view of the creation of the world saw it as being created in six days by an eternal God out of nothing. Some later thinkers posited the notion of continuous creation: that God creates and sustains continuously rather than in one climactic act. Other later thinkers, influenced by Greek neo-platonism, saw creation as an emanation out of God whereby living beings reflect the divine essence. The Shiites finessed upon the notion of creation by suggesting that before the creation of the world there was a primordial creation of forms of light which eventually became channelled on earth in the form of Muhammad and the Shiite imams. ▷ Allah; imam; Muhammad; neo-platonism; revelation in Islam; Shiism

Khalsa (Khālsā) The Sikh community instituted by the tenth Sikh guru, Guru Gobind Singh, in Anandpur in 1699. Membership of the Khalsa is by means of an initiation ceremony (*Amritsanskar*) which includes scripture readings and the drinking and sprinkling of holy water (amrit). Initiates wear the five Ks and (in the case of men) a turban. Men add the name *Singh* (meaning lion) to their original name, and women add the name *Kaur* (meaning princess). Part of Guru Gobind Singh's motivation was to purify the Sikh tradition to prepare it for trials and to make it a vehicle for the mystical presence of God as guru. Another motive was to circumvent the increasingly corrupt and independent authority of the existing deputies in order to bring all Sikhs under Guru Gobind Singh's own authority. Members of the Khalsa promise to lead pure lives, and to follow the *Rahit Maryada*, the Sikh Code of Discipline. ▷ amrit; Gobind Singh, Guru; Rahit Maryada

Kharijites (Khārijites) Meaning literally 'the seceders', this was the name of an early Islamic sect that diverged from mainstream Islam, especially after 657. The Kharijites were opposed to the first Umayyad caliph Muawiyah, and supported Ali's army in opposition to him. However, they seceded from Ali's army in 659 and most of them were killed by Ali's troops. One of their number assassinated Ali in 661 in a mosque at Kufah, and this traumatic event had important consequences for later Shiite Islam. The Kharijites were a puritanical group who longed for the pristine purity of earliest Islam, and objected to the compromises involved in the wake of the spread of Islam around the Arab world. They argued that works were needed for salvation as well as faith, and that committing sin prejudiced the chance of salvation. They considered that the leader of Islam should be ethically upright and that the Muslim community should be a righteous people based on the Quran. They felt that it was justifiable to rebel against a sinful leader, and that inward conversion and commitment constituted a Muslim as well as outward profession.

They remained an aggressive force in early Islam in opposition to the caliphate, but gradually their violence subsided. Some small Kharijite communities survive today, especially among the moderate Ibadites in Oman, Algeria, Libya, Tunisia and Tanzania. ▷ Ali; caliphate; kalam; Quran; salvation; sin, Islamic view of

Khayyam, Omar ▷ Omar Khayyam

Khomeini, Ayatollah Ruhollah (1900–89) Iranian religious and political leader. A Shiite Muslim who was bitterly opposed to the pro-western régime of Shah of Persia Mohammed Reza Pahlavi, Khomeini was exiled to Turkey, Iraq and France from 1964. He returned to Iran amid great popular acclaim in 1979 after the collapse of the Shah's government, and became virtual head of state. Under his leadership Iran underwent a turbulent 'Islamic Revolution' in which a return was made to the strict observance of Muslim principles and traditions, many of which had been abandoned during the previous régime. In 1989 he provoked international controversy by publicly commanding the killing of Salman Rushdie, author of the novel *The Satanic Verses*. ▷ blasphemy; Islam; Shiism

khvarenah An important concept in Zoroastrianism, which is also worshipped as a divinity. Khvarenah may originally have been a force which brought fertility, growth, and perhaps general well-being; it was closely connected with light, sun, fire and water. In a Zoroastrian prayer it is said that khvarenah is distributed to the earth each morning by the *yazatas*, which indicates that it was expected to benefit everyone. The tradition also suggests, however, that kings had particularly close links with khvarenah, its presence or absence in a country depending upon the moral qualities of the ruler. The first person to possess khvarenah was the mythical King Yima, from whom khvarenah fled when he uttered a lie. In some of the Pahlavi books, khvarenah is closely associated with the concept of 'fulfilling one's proper role' (*khveshkarih*). The well-being which khvarenah was believed to bring, in other words, would only reach a country if social harmony and righteousness reigned there. The winged disc which many Zoroastrians now regard as a symbol of their faith may originally have been a representation of the khvarenah of the Achaemenian kings. ▷ Pahlavi; yazata; Zoroastrianism

kiddushin A part of the Jewish marriage ceremony which depicts the sacred character of marriage, when the bridegroom in front of two witnesses places the ring on the bride's finger and recites the vow: 'Behold, you are consecrated unto me by this ring according to the Law of Moses and Israel'. It is also the name of the Mishnaic and Talmudic tractates dealing with matrimonial matters. ▷ Judaism; Mishnah; Talmud

Kierkegaard, Sören Aabye (1813–55) Danish philosopher and religious thinker, regarded as one of the founders of existentialism. He was born in Copenhagen and read theology at the university there, though in fact he interested himself more in literature and philosophy. He periodically suffered emotional disturbances and anguish which his later writings sometimes reflect: he was particularly oppressed by his father's death in 1838 and by the burden of guilt he felt he had thereby inherited. He became engaged after leaving university in 1840, but after great heart-searching broke that off because he felt domestic responsibilities were incompatible with his personal mission from God to be a writer. His philosophy represents a strong reaction against the dominant German traditions of the day, and in particular against Hegel's system. Kierkegaard tried to reinstate the central importance of the individual and of the deliberate, significant choices each of us makes in forming our future selves. His philosophical works tend to be unorthodox and entertaining in a literary and determinedly unacademic style: *The Concept of Irony* (1841), *Either—Or* (2 vols, 1843), *Philosophical Fragments* (1844) and *Concluding Unscientific Postscript* (1846). He was also opposed to much in organized Christianity, again stressing the necessity for individual choice against prescribed dogma and ritual, in such works as *Fear and Trembling* (1843), *Works of Love* (1847), *Christian Discourses* (1848) and *The Sickness unto Death* (1849). He achieved real recognition only in this century and has been a great influence on such thinkers as Barth, Heidegger, Karl Jaspers and Buber. ▷ Barth, Karl; Buber, Martin; existentialism, Christian; Hegel, Georg Wilhelm Friedrich; Heidegger, Martin

King, Martin Luther, Jr (1929–68) American black clergyman and civil rights campaigner, born in Atlanta, Georgia. The son of a Baptist pastor, he studied systematic theology at Crozier Theological Seminary in Chester, Pennsylvania, and Boston University, and set

Martin Luther King

up the first black ministry at Montgomery, Alabama, in 1955. He came to national prominence as leader of the Alabama bus boycott (1955–6), and founded the Southern Christian Leadership Conference in 1957, which organized civil rights activities throughout the country. A brilliant orator, he galvanized the movement, based on the principle of non-violence, and led the great march on Washington in 1963, where he delivered his memorable 'I have a dream' speech. In 1964 he received an honorary doctorate from Yale, the Kennedy Peace Prize, and the Nobel Prize for Peace. He was assassinated in Memphis, Tennessee, while on a civil rights mission. His white assassin, James Earl Ray, was apprehended in London, and in 1969 was sentenced in Memphis to 99 years. King's widow, Coretta Scott King (1927–) has carried on his work through the Martin Luther King, Jr, Centre for Social Changes in Alabama. The third Monday in January is celebrated as Martin Luther King day in the USA.

kingdom of God, also **kingdom of heaven** A concept deriving from Jewish apocalyptic thought, acquiring central importance in the teaching of Jesus, and used by followers of both Judaism and Christianity with varying emphases. In Jewish apocalyptic writing it often expressed the hope for Jewish national restoration and the salvation of the people by a direct intervention of God. The imminent approach of the kingdom of God is, according to the Gospel of Mark (1.15), the chief theme of the message of Jesus Christ; its complete coming is still the prayer of Christians who use the prayer Jesus taught his disciples (the so-called Lord's Prayer, Matthew 6.9–13, Luke 11.2–4), 'Thy kingdom come, thy will be done, on earth as in heaven'. Thus Christians live between the promise (hinted at in Old Testament prophecy of a Messianic kingdom) and the fulfilment, and have interpreted the relation between church, society, and the kingdom of God in various ways down the centuries, as the classic study by H R Niebuhr, *Christ and Culture* (1951), notes. Notable historical examples of the possible options include the following. Monasticism, the Radical Reformers and some modern groups including the House Church movement, have identified the kingdom with a purified (sect-type) church; Pentecostal and charismatic groups have expected and sought healings and castings out of evil spirits as signs of the kingdom that featured in Jesus's ministry; Liberal Protestantism tended to equate the kingdom with the values of European civilization; the Social Gospel movement believed it could transform American society. Recent Roman Catholic theology sees the Church as a sacrament (sign and symbol) of the kingdom of God and the unity of humankind, with liberation theology proposing that the Church take an active role in forwarding the kingdom. ▷ House Church movement; Liberal Protestantism; liberation theology; monasticism; Niebuhr, Reinhold; political theology; sects, Christian; Social Gospel

Kings, Books of A pair of books of the Hebrew Bible/Old Testament, consisting of a compilation of stories about the kings and prophets of Judah and Israel from the enthronement of Solomon to the fall of the kingdom of Israel in c.721BCE and the final collapse of Judah and Jerusalem in c.587/6BCE. It is part of the Deuteronomistic History, probably once connected to the books of Samuel, and in some Catholic versions entitled 3 and 4 Kings. It is strongly critical of idolatry, apostasy, and religious fragmentation away from the Jerusalem Temple cult. ▷ Ahab; Deuteronomistic History; Elijah; Elisha; Old Testament; Samuel, Books of; Solomon; Temple, Jerusalem

kingship, Ancient Near Eastern In contrast to Egypt, Ancient Near Eastern kings were not normally thought of as divine, but were nonetheless the main link between the divine and human realms. In Ancient Mesopotamia kingship was said to have come from heaven; the king's position was given by the gods and his principal duty was to serve them. As mediators between gods and people kings had an important place in the cult and many religious obligations, including responsibility for the building and maintenance of temples; the Assyrian king, as high priest of Asshur, had a particularly pronounced cultic role. The kings were leaders of the national army and as 'shepherds' of their peoples were also concerned with the administration of justice and protection of the poor, widows and orphans. The king's success in war and peace was seen as a reflection of the favour of the gods. Similar patterns of kingship are to be seen in many of the states of Syria and Palestine, but precise information is limited. The Hittite kings also played an important role in the cult; although a king was not considered divine while alive, on his death he is described as 'becoming a god'; offerings were consequently made to the spirits of past kings. ▷ Asshur; kingship, sacred; pharaoh; temples, Ancient Near Eastern

kingship, sacred In ancient Israel the sacred character of the monarchy is shown by the fact that monarchs were anointed by Yahweh, usually through the medium of a prophet or priest (1 Samuel 10.1). Unlike other neighbouring rulers, the King of Israel was not thought to be divine or semi-divine, but ruled only as Yahweh's servant. The biblical model of monarchy influenced the medieval Christian concept of kingship. Here the king was held to rule by 'divine right', and this was upheld by the sacral nature of his consecration by the pope. This divinely appointed rule legitimized the hierarchical nature of society, as the king's rule was thought to mirror God's rule in heaven. ▷ kingship, Ancient Near Eastern

knowledge and ignorance Most religious traditions have stressed the importance of gaining knowledge and getting rid of ignorance. However, there are various levels of knowledge and ignorance. At one level, knowledge is knowledge of the concepts of revelation. Christianity, with its emphasis on theology, has highlighted this kind of knowledge, and it has defined heresy in terms of believing or not believing in certain key Christian concepts centred upon God the Trinity. Other religious traditions have also stressed concepts, for example the four noble truths of the Buddha, but at a second-order rather than primary level. For Islam and Judaism, heresy has been basically practical rather than conceptual. At another level, knowledge refers to philosophical knowledge applied to faith in order to explain, justify or defend it. The great Hindu philosophers such as Shankara and Ramanuja were also the 'theologians' who found it natural to apply philosophy to religion; the same applies to the great Buddhist thinkers. Christians incorporated Greek philosophy into their theology and generally felt that reason supported faith, but occasionally in the thought of a Luther or a Barth they have argued that philosophical reasoning and faith are separate, and that 'Athens has nothing to do with Jerusalem'. This has been the main viewpoint within Islam, whose great philosophers, Avicenna and Averroës, were mainly disregarded. At another level, knowledge has been seen to be deeper than concepts or philosophy. In some traditions it has been seen to be esoteric, as in Gnosticism, which traced the origin of the world to an act of ignorance, the removal of which, through Gnostic knowledge, was the aim of life. Finally, in most religions, religious knowledge has been seen to be more than intellectual, although it might be that as well. It has to do with experiential realization of the truth, as the Eastern traditions have stressed; it has to do with committing one's whole life to the truth, as the New Testament word *pistis* affirms; and it has to do with surrender and faith, as devotional religions generally have attested. ▷ ariya sacca; Averroës; Avicenna; Barth, Karl; Gnosticism; heresy; Jerusalem; Luther, Martin; Ramanuja; Shankara; Trinity

Knox, John (c.1513–1572) Scottish Protestant reformer, born in or near Haddington. He was educated there and probably at the University of St Andrews. From 1540 to 1543 he acted as notary in Haddington, and must till the latter year have been in Catholic orders. In 1544 he was acting as tutor to the sons of two families, by whom he was brought into contact with George Wishart, now full of zeal for the Lutheran reformation; from then on Knox identified with him. Wishart was burned by Cardinal David Beaton in March 1546, and Beaton was murdered in May. The cardinal's murderers held the castle of St Andrews, where Knox joined them with his pupils (1547). Here he was formally called to the ministry. A few months later the castle surrendered to the French and for 18 months Knox remained a prisoner on the French galleys. In February 1549, on the intercession of Edward VI, Knox regained his liberty, and for four years made his home in England. In 1551 he was appointed one of six chaplains to Edward VI, and in 1552 was offered, but refused, the bishopric of Rochester. Knox, with five others, was consulted by Cranmer regarding his forty-two articles, and largely on Knox's representation the thirty-eighth article was so couched as to commit the Church of England to the Genevan doctrine of the Eucharist. On Mary I's accession Knox fled to the continent, then ministered briefly to the English congregation at Frankfurt-am-Main. In Geneva he found a congregation of his own way of thinking, but he ventured into Scotland in September 1555, making preaching journeys to Kyle, Castle Campbell, etc, and returned to Geneva in July 1556. For the next two years he remained chiefly in Geneva, and was much influenced by Calvin. To 1558 belongs his *First Blast of the Trumpet against the Monstrous Regiment of Women*. In 1557 the advocates of reform in Scotland bound themselves to religious revolution by the *First Covenant*; and by 1558 they felt themselves strong enough to summon Knox to their aid. From May 1559 Knox, again in Scotland, was preaching at Perth and St Andrews. He gained these important towns to his cause, and by his labours in Edinburgh also won a strong party there. But the Reformers could not hold their ground against the regent, Mary of Guise, subsidized by France with money and soldiers. Mainly through the efforts of Knox, the assistance of England was obtained against the French invasion; and by the treaty of Leith and the death of the regent (1560) the insurgent party became masters of the country. Parliament ordered the ministers to draw up a *Confession of Faith* and Protestantism was established (1560). Now the ministers drew up the *First Book of Discipline* (1561), with its suggestions for the religious and educational organization of the country.

The return of Mary, Queen of Scots (August 1561) introduced new elements into the strife of parties; and during the six years of her reign Knox's attitude towards her was that of uncompromising antagonism. The celebration of mass in Holyrood Chapel first roused his wrath; and a sermon delivered by him in St Giles High Kirk led to the first of his famous interviews with Mary. He went so far as to alienate the most powerful noble of his own party–Lord James Stuart, afterwards the Regent Moray; but the marriage of Mary with Lord Darnley (1565) brought them together again. After the murder of David Rizzio he withdrew to Ayrshire, where he wrote part of his *History of the Reformation in Scotland*. The murder of Darnley, Mary's marriage with Bothwell, and her flight into England again threw the management of affairs into the hands of the Protestant party; and under Moray as regent the acts of 1560 in favour of the Reformed religion were duly ratified by the Estates. The assassination of Moray in 1570, and the formation of a strong party in favour of Mary, once more endangered the cause, and Knox removed to St Andrews for safety. In November 1572, at the induction of his successor, he made his last public appearance at St Giles. He was buried in the churchyard then attached to St Giles. His first wife, Marjory Bowes, died in 1560, leaving him two sons. By his second wife, Margaret Stewart, daughter of Lord Ochiltree, whom (then not above 16) he married in 1564, he had three daughters. Knox is the pre-eminent type of the religious Reformer—singleminded of purpose, and indifferent or hostile to every interest of life that did not advance his cause. The term fanatic is hardly applicable to one who combined in such degree the shrewdest worldly sense with ever-ready wit. His individuality, which is stamped on every page of his *History of the Reformation in Scotland*, renders his work unique.

koans A Japanese term used in Zen Buddhism for baffling exercises set by Zen Masters to enable their pupils to break out of normal patterns of thought into a sudden awareness of enlightenment. They had been developed by the Chan Masters of Tang China (618–906), and often took the form of illogical and unusual answers to slightly absurd questions that were later written down and gathered into collections. These collections were later developed in Japan and used to lead students to progressively deeper stages of realization. The school of Soto Zen founded by Dogen (1200–53) used koans sparingly, whereas the Rinzai Zen school founded by Eisai (1141–1215) used them more systematically. Examples of koans are as follows: Umman was asked 'What is the pure dharmakaya (cosmic body of the Buddha)?' He replied 'The blossoming hedge around the privy'. A monk asked Joshu 'What is the meaning of the coming of Bodhidharma to the West?' Joshu replied 'The cypress tree in the garden'. A monk asked Joshu 'Has a dog got Buddha nature?' Joshu answered 'Mu (nothing)'. ▷ Buddha nature; Chan; dharmakaya; Dogen; Eisai; Rinzai; Soto; Zen Buddhism

Kokutai Shinto (state Shinto) National structure Shinto in Japan, according to which the Japanese emperor is of divine origin. In the Shinto chronicles (the *Kojiki* and *Nihongi*, compiled in the 8th century CE) the imperial line is traced back to the sun goddess Amaterasu. The line of Japanese emperors is therefore seen as the continuation of the *kami* or divinities, and as such it cannot be broken. Ironically, the divinity of the Japanese emperors was renounced by Hirohito himself in 1945 at the end of World War II, but even so the Japanese imperial line still commands great respect, although it is no longer worshipped. Before that the emperor was both ruler and chief priest of the nation, and reverence for him was deepened by Confucian traditions of loyalty and hierarchy. During the medieval period of feudal rule by *shoguns* (generals), imperial power was theoretical only, but it was strengthened by the Meiji restoration of 1868 and the Imperial Rescript on Education of 1890. This advocated a national structure based upon emperor worship, whereby the Japanese nation was seen to be beloved of the gods and the Japanese emperor was seen to be, in some sense, the ruler of the universe. This became enshrined in state Shinto which ceased in 1945, together with the notion of the emperor's divinity. ▷ Amaterasu; kami; literature, Shinto

Konko-kyo (Konkō-kyō) One of the Japanese new religions founded in 1859 through the work of a humble farmer, Kawate Bunjiro (1814–83). His sayings were recorded and printed, after his death, in the Konko-kyo scripture, *Konko-kyokyoten*. After his death the movement was strengthened structurally in order to continue his work and headquarters were set up in his home town, which was renamed Konko. Spiritual leadership passed down in his family, and a second leader exercised executive oversight. Although nominally belonging to sect Shinto, the Konko-kyo divinity is not a Shinto *kami* but the monotheistic 'Parent God of the Universe', with whom a close relationship is possible through the mediation of Konko-kyo ministers. Women have played an important role in the movement as members and ministers. It has a good record of involvement in educational and social matters, and a deep concern for world peace. Its services include a liturgy and a sermon, and its two main festivals focus on the founder (who is honoured but not deified) and the Konko-kyo God. ▷ Japanese new religions; kami

Kook, Abraham Isaac Hacohen (1865–1935) Orthodox Jewish rabbi, mystic and Zionist, born in Latvia. He emigrated to Palestine in 1904, when he became rabbi of Jaffa. Enthusiastic for Jewish return to the Holy Land, he was appointed Chief Rabbi of Palestine in 1921. Although staunchly orthodox and no advocate of pluralism within Judaism, he supported the return of secular Jews to the Holy Land. He saw this as part of the divine plan prior to the advent of the Messiah; even if such non-religious Zionists were unaware of their role, the coming of the Messiah required a material basis in the land of Israel which they were preparing. Kook's views were influenced greatly by the teachings of the Kabbalah. In particular, he held that no real distinction exists between the sacred and the secular, especially since the Jewish mystic was to work towards *tiqqun* or 'restoration' of an original harmony within the universe as a whole. He also believed Palestine to be essentially holy and that, under its influence and with their task completed, secular Jews returning to the Holy Land would revert to Orthodox Judaism. ▷ Israel, State of; Kabbalah; Messiah; Orthodox Judaism; Zionism

Koran ▷ **Quran**

kosher Food fulfilling the requirements of Jewish Law, including the manner of preparation. In orthodox Judaism, only certain animals, which must be ritually slaughtered, may be eaten. ▷ food and drink; Judaism

Kraemer, Hendrik (1888–1965) Dutch theologian and scholar of religion, born in Amsterdam. He was educated at Deventer, Amsterdam, Rotterdam and Leiden, and obtained his PhD in 1921 for a study on a Javanese mystical text. He went as a missionary-scholar to what was then the Dutch East Indies from 1922 to 1928 and from 1930 to 1935, and in 1937 he took the chair in history and phenomenology of religion at Leiden University. He vacated this in 1947 to become Director until 1965 of the Ecumenical Institute of the World Council of Churches at Bossey in Switzerland. He became famous for his presentation at the International Missionary Congress at Tambaram in India in 1938 which was printed as *The Christian Message in a Non-Christian World*. This counteracted the liberal tendencies on the part of some Christians towards other religions, and reverted to the notion, derived partly from Karl Barth, that there is a radical discontinuity between Christ and other religions. He also wrote *Religion and the Christian Faith* (1956) and *World Cultures and World Religions* (1960). He argued that religions are not directly comparable because they revolve around different axes. Together with his interest in Christian missions and the ecumenical movement within the Christian churches, Kraemer also wrote on the topics of history and phenomenology of religion, in which he held his chair. He drew a distinction between Christianity as one of the world's religions and the revelation of God in Christ, and he agonized over the problem of whether and how one could combine an understanding of other religions and the normative values of theology. ▷ Barth, Karl; comparative religion; history of religion; theology of religion

Krishna (Kṛṣṇa) According to Hindu tradition, the eighth incarnation, in human form, of the deity Vishnu. A great hero and ruler, the story of his youthful amorous adventures is told in the *Mahabharata*, these exploits seen as symbolizing the intimacy between the devotee and God. His story reaches its climax when, disguised as a charioteer in an eve-of-battle dialogue with Arjuna, he delivers the great moral discourse of the *Bhagavad Gita*. ▷ avatara; Bhagavad Gita; bhakti; Hare Krishna movement; Hinduism; Mahabharata; Vishnu

Krishna

Krishnamurti, Jiddu (1895–1986) Indian theosophist, born in Madras. He was educated in England by Annie Besant, who in 1925 proclaimed him the Messiah. Later he dissolved The Order of the Star in the East (founded by Besant), and travelled the world teaching and advocating a way of life and thought unconditioned by the narrowness of nationality, race and religion. ▷ Besant, Annie; Messiah; theosophy

Kristensen, William Brede (1867–1953) Norwegian scholar of religion, born in Kristiansand. He was educated at the University of Oslo in theology, classics, Hebrew, Sanskrit and Egyptian and, after studies in Paris and London, he obtained his PhD from Oslo in 1896 for a thesis on the concept of life after death in ancient Egypt. He lectured at Oslo from 1897 to 1901, and from 1901 to 1937 he was Professor of the History of Religions at Leiden University in Holland. Some of his lectures at Leiden were translated into English in 1960 as *The Meaning of Religion*. This book and his earlier works were key factors in the growing importance of the new aproach known as the Phenomenology of Religion. Kristensen believed that religion and religions must be studied on their own terms. In a famous phrase he argued that 'the believer is right', and we must take the believer's viewpoint seriously. He was opposed to anthropological theories about the supposed evolution of religion, and was therefore less interested in the historical evolution of religion than in the study of religious texts and religious phenomena in their own setting, from their own standpoint, through their own symbolism. Kristensen's own particular researches into the ancient religions of Egypt, Greece, Mesopotamia, Persia and Rome provided him with the raw materials for his development of the Phenomenology of Religion. He asserted that the history, phenomenology and philosophy of religion complement one another. Philosophy investigates the essence of religion, history allows research into particular religions, and phenomenology groups different religious phenomena together so that they can be seen to be related, and so that philosophy can investigate their essence. ▷ anthropology of religion; history of religion

Kshatriyas (Kṣatriyas) Second to Brahmans in the varna (class) hierarchy as extolled in the *Rig Veda* (10.90: 11–12) which states that Kshatriyas are believed to come from the arms of *purusha*, the primal being. They are generally classified as a warrior class, although have also been variously described as kings, princes and tribal chiefs. The kshatrya class is identified with the warrior god Indra. ▷ Indra; purusha; varna

Kuan Yin A very popular Chinese Buddhist female bodhisattva, who in India had been the male bodhisattva Avalokiteshvara. She is the 'one who hears the cry of the world', and took over Avalokiteshvara's role of mercy and compassion, giving it, so to speak, a Chinese and a female slant. Kuan Yin is the protector of women, the giver of children, the patroness of sailors, and the compassionate goddess of mercy. She is often turned to by those who are in need, and is worshipped with gratitude and affection. She is present in image form in Pure Land and other Buddhist temples, in Taoist temples, and in temples built by the followers of Chinese folk religion. There are many popular stories about Kuan Yin, and many shrines have been set up in her honour. She is popular, too, in Korea and Japan, where she is known as Kannon. Various theories have been propounded to explain why, by the end of the 8th century, Kuan Yin had become primarily a female bodhisattva in China. None of them is fully adequate, and this is yet another example of how Indian Buddhism took on a different and unique character in China, Korea and Japan. ▷ Avalokiteshvara; bodhisattva; Chinese Buddhism; karuna; Pure Land Buddhism

Kukai (774–835) The founder of the Shingon school of Japanese Buddhism. In 921 he was given the posthumous title of Daishi (Great Master), and is commonly known as Kobo Daishi. He was trained in the doctrines of the Kegon school in the Japanese capital Nara, but in 805 he was sent to China by the emperor Kammu, and on his return he introduced Shingon doctrines into Japan and built the important Shingon temple on Mount Koya which became the headquarters of the school. Shingon had originated in the Tantric Buddhism of India and Tantric materials had been translated into Chinese in the 8th century, but no full-scale school was formed, and it was left to Kukai to form an independent school and to systematize the pantheistic mysticism of Shingon in the Japanese context. According to Kukai the world is the external form of Mahavairocana Buddha, the Great Sun Buddha, and all human beings have an inherent Buddha nature within themselves which they can realize through meditation. He stressed the importance of mandalas (symbolic representations of esoteric truth), mantras (sacred sayings), and fire and ordination rituals. He graded 10 religious forms, including Confucianism and Taoism, into 10 classes, culminating in Shingon where full Buddhahood could be achieved. He communicated an all-embracing mysticism which gave an esoteric flavour to Japanese Buddhism in general, and he is revered as being second only to Prince Shotoku among Japanese heroes and saints. ▷ Buddha nature; Kammu; mandala; mantra; Nanto Rokusho; Shingon; Shotoku Tantric Buddhism; Vairocana

Kumarajiva (Kumārajīva) (c.344–413) Bud dhist scholar, born at Kucha in Central Asi He had a formative influence upon Chines Buddhism, and ranks as one of the greate missionary translators the world has eve known. He was ordained as a monk aged 2 and in 383 was captured by a Chines expeditionary force which took him fro Kucha to the Liang court in China, where h learnt Chinese and continued his studies. I 401 he was taken to the Chinese capital Char An and, although technically under hous arrest, he was put in charge of what we woul call a research team in order to supervise th translation and editing of various Buddhi scriptures. He remained in China until h death in 413. He translated many importa texts, including the *Lotus Sutra*, the *Diamon Cutter Sutra*, the *Heart Sutra*, and the small *Pure Land Sutra*. He also made available ne Chinese editions of some of the great phil sophical works of Mahayana Buddhism, whic taught the important doctrine of emptines especially Nagarjuna's writings on Madhy mika. This resulted in a new critical awarene of Buddhism in China, and made Chine Buddhism attractive to intellectuals and the gentry. His correspondence with H Yuan provides a fascinating insight into th Buddhism of his day, especially into diffe ences between Buddhism in northern ar southern China. ▷ Diamond Cutter Sutr Lotus Sutra; Madhyamika; Mahayana Bu dhism; Nagarjuna; Pure Land Buddhism

Kumbha Mela A Hindu religious festiv held every 12 years at the confluence of t sacred rivers the Yamuna and the Ganges Allahabad. Up to 15 million people have be reported to attend the five-day festival, pa of which involves a procession of Hindu ho men or renouncers (*sannyasins*) into t Ganges. The naked Naga order of ascetics a the first in the procession, followed by saffro clad monks of the Dashanami order found by Shankara. Other orders and ordina Hindu pilgrims follow these to bathe in t purifying Ganges water. ▷ Ganga; Shanka

Kundalini (Kuṇḍalinī) In Hindu Tantra t female energy or power (*Shakti*) within t body, envisaged as a coiled snake. This ener lies dormant at the base of the subtle chann (*susumna nadi*) which traverses the body fro the region of the anus to the crown of t head. Once awakened through yoga practic such as breath control (*pranayama*), s moves up this central channel, piercing various centres (*cakras*) of spiritual power along the body's axis, until she unites with Shiva in the thousand petalled lotus at the crown of the head. The body is then filled with bliss and through continued practice the practitioner (*sadhaka*) is eventually liberated. As well as referring to the power within the body, Kundalini can also mean the cosmic force pervading the universe. ▷ cakra; Shakti; Shiva; Tantra; yoga

Küng, Hans (1928–) Swiss Roman Catholic theologian, born in Sursee, Lucerne. A professor at Tübingen (1960–), he has written extensively for fellow theologians and for lay people. His questioning of received interpretations of Catholic doctrine, as in *Justification* (1965), *The Church* (1967), and *Infallible? An Inquiry* (1971), and his presentations of the Christian faith, as in *On Being a Christian* (1977), *Does God Exist?* (1980), and *Eternal Life?* (1984), aroused controversy both in Germany and with the Vatican authorities, who withdrew his licence to teach as a Catholic theologian in 1979. He defended himself in *Why I am still a Christian* (1987). He has also written *The Incarnation of God* (1987), *Global Responsibility* (1991) and *Reforming the Church Today* (1991). ▷ Roman Catholicism

Kurds An Indo-European Iranian-speaking people who live in the Near East in a region they call Kurdistan which overlaps Turkey, Iran, Iraq, Syria and Armenia. They number about 10 million and have been Sunni Muslims since the 7th century CE. The best-known Kurd historically was Saladin, who fought the Muslim cause against the Christian Crusaders and founded the Ayyabid dynasty. The Kurds were formerly pastoral nomads who had some interest in agriculture, but since World War I they have increasingly gravitated to towns. Unable to set up an autonomous state, they have undergone various degrees of oppression, politically in Turkey, and religiously in Iran, especially since the Iranian revolution of 1979. In the aftermath of the Gulf War of 1990, their suppression in Iraq caused sympathy around the world. Sufi brotherhoods are significant within Kurdish Islam, including the Qadiriyyah, whose originator al-Qadir (1078–1166) was himself a Kurd, and the Naqshabandiyyah. Other less orthodox Muslim groups, such as the Yazidis, are also present among the Kurds. ▷ Naqshbandiyyah; Qadariyyah; Saladin; Sufism; sunnah

Kusinara (Kusinārā) A small town, now known as Kasia, in the Gorakhpur area of Uttar Pradesh in North India, one of the four holy places within the Buddhist tradition. It was here that the Buddha died and entered his final nirvana (*parinirvana*) as described in the Pali scriptures. The three other holy places are Lumbini where the Buddha was born, Bodhgaya where he experienced enlightenment, and Sarnath near Banaras where he preached his first sermon. Buddhist visitors from all over the world make special pilgrimages to these sacred places. According to tradition, the local tribal group known as the Mallas gave the Buddha elaborate funeral rites, and after his cremation some of his relics were placed in a stupa at Kusinara. Although a large monastic centre seems to have been built there, it was in decay by the 7th century CE when a Chinese pilgrim visited it. It is in the modern period that it has become better known again. ▷ Banaras; Buddha; Bodhgaya; Lumbini; nirvana; parinirvana; Sarnath; stupa; tipitaka

Kwakiutl An American Indian group living on the coast of British Columbia as fishermen and traders. They were famed for their woodwork, frequently painted in bright colours, including masks, totem poles, war canoes, whale-hunting vessels, and decorative boxes. Some art is still produced for the tourist trade. They also had elaborate dances and ceremonies, including the potlatch. ▷ Native American religions; potlatch

Kyrie eleison (Greek 'Lord, have mercy') An early Christian petition for divine mercy used in liturgical worship, dating back at least to the 4th century. It is widely used throughout both Eastern and Western Christianity, but in various forms. In the Roman Catholic Mass it may be part of a ninefold petition in which the Kyrie is recited three times, followed by a threefold variant *Christe eleison* ('Christ, have mercy') and then a final threefold Kyrie. It has been given a wide range of musical settings. ▷ Christianity; music, Christian; Mass; prayer

L

labarum Christian military standard, designed in the form of a cross, with a monogram composed of the Greek symbols for Christ's name, XP (*chi* and *rho*). It was first used as a symbol in the reign of Constantine I, who claimed that on the eve of his victory over Maxentius (312CE) he had seen a vision of the chi-rho emblem in the sky, with the words around it 'in this sign you shall conquer'. It became the official standard of the Roman Empire from 324. ▷ Constantine I; symbolism

Lactantius, Lucius Caelius or **Caecilius, Firmianus** (4th century) Christian apologist, brought up in North Africa. He settled as a teacher of rhetoric in Nicomedia in Bithynia, where he was converted probably by witnessing the constancy of the Christian martyrs under the persecution of Diocletian. About 313 he was invited to Gaul by Constantine to act as tutor to his son Crispus. His principal work is his *Divinarum Institutionum libri vii*, a systematic account of Christian attitudes to life. ▷ apologetics; Constantine I

Lakshmi (Lakṣmi) The Hindu goddess of prosperity and good luck, the consort of Vishnu, sometimes called 'the lotus-goddess'. She is associated with Divali, the autumn new year festival of lights, when people light lamps for her and leave their doors open to allow her to enter. ▷ Divali/Deepavali; Hinduism; Vishnu

lama (bla-ma) A spiritual teacher in Tibetan Buddhism; the word translates the Sanskrit term *guru*. The lama is treated with the highest respect as both the conveyor of a formal teaching and the conveyor of spiritual power to the disciple. Without initiation by a lama there can be no enlightenment, for the true lama is at one with the Buddha and gives access to buddhahood. Through initiation the disciple is empowered to read certain texts and to meditate upon the form of a deity or the lama himself, which leads to the realization that disciple, lama and deity are not distinct. Submission to the lama is a prerequisite for spiritual awakening, which means giving oneself wholly to the lama in body, speech and mind. There are many stories concerning the trials of faith a lama might put his disciples

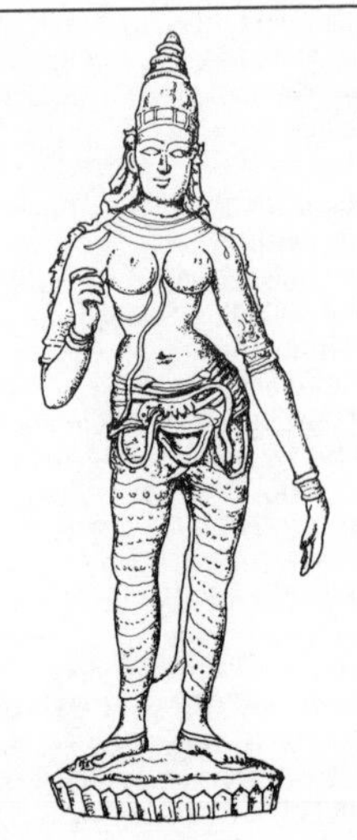

Lakshmi

through. For example, Milarepa had to perform exhausting, apparently pointless tasks for Marpa before he would initiate him. The oral instruction given by the lama is more important than the written text and should the line of transmission from lama to disciple become broken, then the text is rendered useless for the purposes of spiritual practice. Lamas are in different lineages and often became the heads of monastic communities; the Dalai Lama, for example, is head of the Gelugpa order. Some lineages are believed to be maintained by the lama reincarnating upon his death (*tulku*). ▷ Buddha; Dalai Lama; Gelugpa; guru; Marpa; Milarepa; tulku

Lamentations of Jeremiah A book of the Hebrew Bible/Old Testament, probably dated shortly after the Babylonian conquest of Jerusalem (c.587/6BCE), attributed in tradition to the prophet Jeremiah, but not of the same style as the Book of Jeremiah. It consists of five poems lamenting the destruction of Jerusalem, expressing the distress of its people, and petitioning God for its restoration. The first four poems are acrostics, with the stanzas beginning with successive letters of the Hebrew alphabet. ▷ Jeremiah, Book of; Old Testament

Land of Youth (Tir na n'Óc) The name of the Otherworld, the abode of supernatural beings in many Irish stories. Other names are Tir Tairngiri, the Land of Promise, and Mag Mell, the Delightful Plain. The beings we meet there neither age nor ail; the scenery, though lightly described, is invariably delightful, and it is never winter. Occasionally a human is invited or brought there. This involves a journey across the sea, or into a burial mound. Perhaps the Land of Youth gives us a glimpse of pre-Christian Celtic ideas of hopes of the afterlife; but it is significant that in the stories those humans who go there (for 'adventures' or 'visions', as they are called) always return to earth.

Lanfranc (c.1005–1089) Italian prelate and archbishop of Canterbury, born in Pavia. Educated for the law, about 1039 he founded a school at Avranches, in 1041 became a Benedictine at Bec, and in 1046 was chosen prior. He contended against Berengar of Tours in the controversy over transubstantiation. He at first condemned the marriage of William of Normandy (William I) with his cousin, but in 1059 went to Rome to procure the papal dispensation; and in 1062 William made him prior of St Stephen's Abbey at Caen, and in 1070 Archbishop of Canterbury. His chief writings are Commentaries on the Epistles of St Paul, a Treatise against Berengar's *De corpore et sanguine Domini* (1079), and Sermons. ▷ Benedictines

Lang, Andrew (1844–1912) Scottish man of letters, born in Selkirk, nephew of William Young Sellar. Educated at The Edinburgh Academy, Edinburgh, St Andrews, Glasgow and Balliol College, Oxford, he was a fellow of Merton College, Ocxford (1868–74), studying myth, ritual and totemism. He moved to London in 1875 to take up journalism, and became one of the most versatile and famous writers of his day. He specialized in mythology, and took part in a celebrated controversy with Friedrich Max Müller over the interpretation of folktales, arguing that folklore was the foundation of literary mythology. He wrote *Custom and Myth* (1884), *Myth, Ritual and Religion* (1887), *Modern Mythology* (1897) and *The Making of Religion* (1898). He wrote a *History of Scotland* (3 vols, 1899–1904) and a *History of English Literature* (1912), and published a number of fairy books which enjoyed great popularity. He also produced studies of many literary figures, including *Books and Bookmen* (1886) and *Letters to Dead Authors* (1886), a translation of Homer, and several volumes of verse. ▷ Müller, (Friedrich) Max; study of religion

Langar (Laṅgar) The practice of eating food together in Sikh temples. It was first instituted by Guru Nanak during his later ministry in Kartarpur as a means of fellowship and as a gesture against the Hindu caste system which restricted communal eating to certain caste groups. It is therefore symbolic of the Sikh striving for greater social equality. Langar often occurs after the end of Sikh services or rituals, but in major temples, especially in India, it can take place more frequently. The food, which is simple and vegetarian, can be offered, prepared and served by any Sikh; it is often given by families to mark special occasions. All visitors are welcome to participate in the meal. The term Langar refers both to the meal itself and to the kitchen where it is prepared. ▷ caste; gurdwara; Kartarpur; Nanak

Lankavatara Sutra (Laṅkāvatāra Sūtra) One of the nine main *Mahayana Sutras* which are the key scriptural texts of Mahayana Buddhism. It is somewhat disconnected in its organization, but gives an important if unsystematic summary of Mahayana Buddhist thought. Lankavatara means literally the 'descent into Ceylon', and the work contains conversations between the Buddha and Ravanna, the supposed Lord of Ceylon, and between the Buddha and the great bodhisattva Manjusri. It contains a critique of Hindu thought, but also acknowledges that there are important similarities between Hinduism and Mahayana Buddhism. It dates from around 300CE and was translated into Chinese in 420CE, after which it became important for China and Japan. According to tradition, Bodhidharma transmitted a Chinese translation of it around 520CE and viewed it as the most important scripture in Chan Buddhism. Hui Neng later praised the *Diamond Sutra* instead and gave it more significance in his Chan school of sudden enlightenment. The Lankavatara Sutra remained important for China and Japan, especially for its interpretation of the notion of the 'storehouse consciousness' (*alaya-vijnana*) and as a source for some of the doctrines of Yogacara and Chan Buddhism. ▷ alaya-vijnana; Bodhidharma; bodhisattva; Buddha; Chan; Diamond Cutter Sutra; Hui Neng; Mahayana Buddhism; Manjusri; Yogacara

Lao-Tzu (6th century BCE) Chinese philosopher and sage, literally 'the old master'. Little is known of his life but he is regarded as the inspiration for Taoism and for one of its principal works, the *Tao Te Ching* (The Way of Power), compiled some 300 years after his death, which teaches self-sufficiency, simplicity and detachment. Taoism venerates the 'feminine' qualities which promote longevity, equanimity and an instinctive unity with nature. ▷ Taoism; Tao Te Ching

Lao-Tzu

Lares Minor Roman deities. Normally associated with the household was the guardian of the hearth (*lar familiaris*), but there were also guardians of crossroads (*lares viales*) and of the State (*lares praestites*). ▷ Penates; Roman religion

Lascaux A small, richly-decorated Palaeolithic cave of c.15000BCE near Montignac, Dordogne, south-west France, renowned for its naturalistic mural paintings and engravings of animals—cows, bulls, horses, bison, ibex, musk-ox, and reindeer. Found by schoolboys in 1940 and opened to the public in 1947, it was closed permanently in 1963 when humidity changes threatened the paintings. A replica was opened nearby in 1984. ▷ art, Palaeolithic; prehistoric religion

Last Supper In the New Testament Gospels, the last meal of Jesus with his disciples on the eve of his arrest and crucifixion. In t
three synoptic gospels, this is considered
Passover meal, and is significant for Jesu
words over the bread and cup of wine, whe
he declares 'This is my body' and 'This
my blood of the covenant which is pour
out for many' (Mark 14.22–4). John's gosp
dates the meal before the Passover day, a
gives no record of these words. The event
commemorated in the early Church's ce
ebration of the Lord's Supper (1 Corinthia
11), and subsequently in the sacrament
Holy Communion. ▷ Eucharist; Gospe
canonical; Jesus Christ; Passover

Lateran Councils A series of Councils
the Church held at the Lateran Palace, Ron
between the 7th and 18th centuries. Th
held in 1123, 1139, 1179, and especially 12
are the most significant. The Fourth or Gr
Council defined the doctrine of the Euchar
('transubstantiation'), and represents the c
mination of medieval papal legislation.
Council of the Church; Eucharist; papa
transubstantiation

Latimer, Hugh (c.1485–1555) English Pr
estant martyr, born in Thurcaston, n
Leicester, the son of a yeoman. He was se
to Cambridge, in 1510 was elected a fell
of Clare College, and in 1522 was appoin
a university preacher. In 1524, for his E
thesis he delivered a philippic against M
anchthon, for he was, in his own words,
obstinate a papist as any in England'. N
year, however, through the influence of
preacher Thomas Bilney, he 'began to sm
the Word of God, forsaking the school doct
and such fooleries', and soon becoming no
as a zealous preacher of the reformed d
trines. One of the Cambridge divi
appointed to examine the lawfulness of Her
VIII's marriage to Catherine of Aragon,
declared on the king's side; and he was ma
chaplain to Anne Boleyn and rector of W
Kington in Wiltshire. In 1535 he was con
crated as Bishop of Worcester and at t
opening of Convocation in June 1536
preached two powerful sermons urging on
Reformation. Consequently falling out
favour at court he retired to his diocese, a
worked there in a continual round of 'teachi
preaching, exhoring, correcting a
reforming'. Twice during Henry's reign
was sent to the Tower (1539 and 1546),
the first occasion resigning his bishopric.
Edward VI's accession he declined to resu
his episcopal functions, but devoted hims
to preaching and practical works of benev
ence. Under Mary I he was examined

Oxford (1554), and committed to jail. In September 1555, with Ridley and Cranmer, he was found guilty of heresy, and the next month was burned with Ridley opposite Balliol College. ▷ Cranmer, Thomas; Melanchthon, Philip; Reformation; Ridley, Nicholas

Laubach, Frank Charles (1884–1970) American missionary and pioneer of adult basic education, born in Benton, Pennsylvania. Discovering that the Moro tribespeople of the Philippines (whom he had been sent to evangelize in 1915) were unable to read or write, he devised a simple way to combat illiteracy. His method and its application in Southern Asia, India, and Latin America are described in *India shall be Literate* (1940), *Teaching the World to Read* (1948), and *Thirty Years with the Silent Billion* (1961); and his spiritual motivation in *Letters by a Modern Mystic* (1937) and *Channels of Spiritual Power* (1955). ▷ missions, Christian

Laud, William (1573–1645) English prelate, and Archbishop of Canterbury, born in Reading, a well-to-do clothier's son. From Reading Free School he passed at 16 to St John's College, Oxford, becoming a fellow four years later. Ordained in 1601, he made himself obnoxious to the university authorities by his open antipathy to the dominant Puritanism; but his solid learning, his amazing industry, his administrative capacity, his sincere and unselfish churchmanship, soon won him friends and patrons. One of these was Charles Blount, Earl of Devonshire, whom in 1605 Laud married to the divorced Lady Rich (an offence that always was heavy on his conscience); another was Buckingham, to whom he became confessor in 1622.

Meanwhile he rose steadily from preferment to preferment: incumbent of five livings (1607–10), president of his old college and King's Chaplain (1611), Prebendary of Lincoln (1614), Archdeacon of Huntingdon (1615), Dean of Gloucester (1616), Prebendary of Westminster and Bishop of St Davids (1621), Bishop of Bath and Wells, Dean of the Chapel Royal, and a privy councillor (1626), Bishop of London (1628), Chancellor of Oxford (1630), and finally Archbishop of Canterbury (1633), in the very week that he received two offers of a cardinal's hat. Already, after the Duke of Buckingham's assassination, he had virtually become the first minister of the crown, one with the Earl of Strafford and Charles I in the triumvirate whose aim was absolutism in Church and State. Laud's task was to raise the Church of England to its rightful position as a branch of the Catholic Church, to root out Calvinism in England and Presbyterianism in Scotland. In England he drew up a list of 'Orthodox' and 'Puritan' ministers, whom he proceeded to separate by scolding, suspending and depriving. Freedom of worship was withdrawn from Walloon and French refugees; Englishmen abroad were forbidden to attend Calvinistic services; and at home 'gospel preaching', justification by faith, and Sabbatarianism were to be superseded by an elaborate ritual, by the doctrine of the real presence, celibacy and confession, and by the Book of Sports—changes rigorously enforced by the court of High Commission and the Star Chamber.

In Scotland, Laud's attempt (1635–7) to Anglicize the Church gave birth to the riot in St Giles's, Edinburgh; the riot led to the Covenant, the Covenant to the 'Bishops' war', and this to the meeting of the Long Parliament, which in 1640 impeached the archbishop of treason, and ten weeks later sent him to the Tower. He would not escape (Grotius urged him to do so); and at last, after a tedious and complicated trial before a handful of peers, in December 1644, he was voted 'guilty of endeavouring to subvert the laws, to overthrow the Protestant religion, and to act as an enemy to Parliament'. The judges declared that this was not treason; but under an unconstitutional ordinance of attainder, he was beheaded on Tower Hill. ▷ Calvinism; Presbyterianism; Puritanism; Roman Catholicism

Law, William (1686–1761) English churchman and writer, born in Kingscliffe, Northamptonshire, the son of a grocer. He entered Emmanuel College, Cambridge, in 1705, becoming a fellow in 1711. Unwilling to subscribe to the oath of allegiance to George I, he forfeited his fellowship. About 1727 he became tutor to the father of Edward Gibbon, and for ten years was 'the much-honoured friend and spiritual director of the whole family'. The elder Gibbon died in 1737, and three years later Law retired to Kingscliffe. About 1733 he had begun to study the work of Jakob Böhme, and most of his later books are expositions of his mysticism. Law won his first triumphs against controversy with his *Three Letters* (1717). His *Remarks on Mandeville's Fable of the Bees* (1723) is a masterpiece of caustic wit. Similarly admirable is the *Case of Reason* (1732), in answer to Tindal the Deist, but his most famous work remains the *Serious Call to a Devout and Holy Life* (1729), which profoundly influenced Samuel Johnson and the Wesleys. ▷ Böhme, Jakob; mysticism; Wesley, Charles; Wesley John

law and religion Although widely thought to be two discrete subject areas in contemporary society, this has not always been the case. The most obvious examples are Hebrew and Muslim societies, where observance of God's revealed law is itself a required religious act. However, in as much as a society's laws are connected with what the community believes to be of ultimate value, it is no surprise to find that law and religion have often been closely intertwined and that the concept of law has often been legitimized by association with the ultimate authority of the 'divine'. In the development of early Roman law, the priests (pontiffs) played a leading role. Both early Greek and Roman law concerned themselves with the regulation of religious ceremonies. Ecclesiastical and secular polity in the middle ages promoted the virtuous life, but canon law also allowed the obedient to be in communion with God. Today many laws relating to human rights issues stem from an original religious concern for the worth of the individual. ▷ fiqh; qadi; social morality

Lazarus New Testament character mentioned only in John's Gospel, depicted as the brother of Mary and Martha, and as the one whom Jesus raised from the dead by calling him to come forth from his tomb. The fame of this event led directly to the decision of the Jewish leaders to put Jesus to death (John 11, 12.9–11). A connection with the poor man Lazarus mentioned in the parable in Luke 16.19–31 is uncertain. ▷ Jesus Christ; John, Gospel according to

Le Clerc, Jean, or **Johannes Clericus** (1657–1736) Swiss theologian and biblical scholar, born in Geneva. A champion of Arminianism, in 1684 he became Professor of Philosophy in the Remonstrant seminary at Amsterdam. He wrote over 70 works and revealed what were then startling opinions on the authorship of the Pentateuch and on inspiration generally. His Bible commentaries were completed in 1731. Serial publications were *Bibliothèque universelle et historique* (25 vols, 1686–93), *Bibliothèque choisie* (28 vols, 1703–13), and *Bibliothèque ancienne et moderne* (29 vols, 1714–26). ▷ Arminius, Jacobus; Pentateuch

Leeuw, Gerhardus van der (1890–) Dutch scholar and minister of the Dutch Reform Church, born in The Hague. He was educated at Leiden University and took his doctorate in 1916, on the thesis topic 'Representations of the Gods in Ancient Egyptian Pyramid Texts'. In 1918 he was appointed to the new chair at Gröningen University and became involved in the development of the new approach known as the Phenomenology of Religion. Van der Leeuw was a man of wide interests. Outside the realm of scholarship he was an influential minister of the Dutch Reform Church, he was a fine musician, he was well-read in literature, and from 1945 to 1946 he was the Dutch Minister of Education. Academically he had deep interests in aesthetics, liturgy and theology, but his main contribution was to the phenomenology of religion, in which field he was a leading figure from the time of publication of his *Religion in Manifestation and Essence: A Study of Phenomenology* (Eng trans 1938). He advocated the use of *epochē*, putting one's views into brackets in order to understand the viewpoints of others; the use of *Einfühlung*, empathizing with others in order imaginatively to enter their religion and their worldview; and eidetic vision, classifying religious phenomena according to ideal types. Derived partly from Husserl's work on philosophical phenomenology, these views provided a framework for the further development of the phenomenology of religion. Van der Leeuw was able to see phenomenology as a preparation for and as separate from theology which, in its concern for the Ultimate Reality lying behind religious phenomena, brought more normative roles into play. ▷ Husserl, Edmund Gustav Albrecht; theology

Lefebvre, Marcel (1905–91) French schismatic Roman Catholic prelate, born in Tourcoing. He studied at the French Seminary in Rome and was ordained in 1929. In the 1930s he was a missionary in Gabon and became Archbishop of Dakar, Senegal (1948–62). As a clerical traditionalist he opposed the liberalizing liturgical and spiritual reforms of the Second Vatican Council (1962–5), and in 1970 formed the 'Priestly Cofraternity of Pius X' to oppose them. For his refusal to stop the ordination of priests at his headquarters in Switzerland without papal permission, he was suspended 'a divinis' in 1976 by Pope Paul VI. He defied the suspension and continued to ordain a further 216 priests before being formally excommunicated by Pope John Paul II in 1988, thus producing the first formal schism within the Roman Catholic Church since 1870. ▷ John Paul II; Roman Catholicism; Vatican Councils

left and right The notion that there is a difference between left and right, not only in physical but also in psychological terms, is common to most societies and religious traditions. It has been reinforced in recent times by scientific discoveries concerning the difference between the left and right sides of the brain. In general it is true to say that the right hand and foot have been regarded as primary and noble, and the left hand and foot have been regarded as secondary and inferior. By implication the right side has been seen as auspicious and superior, whereas the left side has been seen as inauspicious and debased. This classification fits into a wider structure of opposition between male and female, positive and negative, sacred and profane, and light and darkness. However, it also assumes a hierarchy wherein the right is part of a group of characteristics that are superior (male, positive, sacred, light), and the left is part of an inferior group (female, negative, profane, darkness). In Chinese thought, though, with its stress upon the complementariness of opposites known as yin and yang, things are different. Left and right are not opposed: they need each other, and find meaning in relation to each other, and in some Chinese situations the left side is a place of honour. Therefore context is important in determining the relationship between right and left, as are the religious symbols underlying each context. ▷ light and darkness; sacred and profane; yin and yang

Lenin (formerly **Ulyanov**), **Vladimir Ilyich** (1870–1924) Russian revolutionary, born into a middle-class family in Simbirsk (Ulyanov). He was educated at Kazan University and in 1892 began to practise law in Samara (Kuibyshev). In 1894, after five years' intensive study of Marx, he moved to St Petersburg, organizing the illegal 'Union for the Liberation of the Working Class'. Arrested for his opinions, he was exiled to Siberia for three years. During his Western exile, which began in 1900 in Switzerland, he edited the political newspaper *Iskra* (The Spark) and developed, with Georgi Plekhanov, an underground Social Democratic party, to assume leadership of the working classes in a revolution against Tsarism. His evolving ideas were set out in *What is to be done?* (1902), in which he advocated a professional core of party activists to spearhead the revolution. This suggestion was adopted by the party's majority, Bolshevik wing at the congress in London in 1903, but was opposed by the 'bourgeois reformism' Mensheviks (minority wing). Lenin returned to Russia in 1905, ascribing the failure of the rising of that year to lack of support for his own programme. He determined that when the time came Soviets (councils of workers, soldiers and peasants) should be the instruments of total revolution. Lenin left Russia in 1907 and spent the next decade strengthening the Bolsheviks against the Mensheviks, interpreting the gospel of Marx and Engels and organizing underground work in Russia. In April 1917, a few days after the deposition of Tsar Nicholas II, Lenin, with German connivance, made his fateful journey in a sealed train from Switzerland to Petrograd (formerly St Petersburg, later renamed Leningrad). He told his followers to prepare for the overthrow of the shaky provisional government and the remaking of Russia on a Soviet basis. In the October revolution the provisional government collapsed and the dominating Bolshevik 'rump' in the second Congress of Soviets declared that supreme power rested in them. Lenin inaugurated the 'dictatorship of the proletariat' with the formal dissolution of the Constituent Assembly. For three years he grappled with war and anarchy. In 1922 he began his 'new economic policy' of limited free enterprise to give Russia respite before entering the era of giant state planning. His health having been in progressive decline since an assassination attempt in 1918, he died in 1924, and his body was embalmed for veneration in a crystal casket in a mausoleum in Red Square, Moscow. He left a testament in which he proposed the removal of the ambitious Stalin from his post as Secretary of the Communist Party. Shrewd, dynamic, implacable, pedantic, opportunist, ice-cold in his economic reasoning, Lenin lived only for the furtherance of Marxism. Despite his faults, he was a charismatic figure and is still today revered in the Soviet Union as the nation's guiding force. ▷ communism; Marxism; Marxism-Leninism; secular alternatives to religion

Lenshina, Alice Mulenga (1920–78) African Christian prophetess who belonged to the Bemba people of Northern Rhodesia (now Zambia). In 1953, apparently dying, she had a vision of Christ. Recovering, she began to compose beautiful hymns in Bemba forms, and to preach personal repentance and a reformation of family life. By 1955 her movement had taken the shape of a new church, called Lumpa ('superior') and a campaign against witchcraft. In the late 1950s male leaders in the movement increasingly clashed with the colonial authorities, with the supporters of the United National Independence Party, and eventually with the Zambian government, resulting in bloodshed, emigration and drastic government action. Lenshina, no longer in charge, was either in detention, hiding or restriction from 1965 until her death. The movement united traditional Bemba values with a shift from ancestor veneration to the person of Christ (interpreted in traditional categories) and an emphasis on women's roles. ▷ African Independent churches; Jesus Christ

Lent In the Christian Church, the weeks before Easter, observed as a period of prayer, penance and abstinence in commemoration of Christ's 40-day fast in the wilderness (Matthew 4.2). In Western Churches Lent begins on Ash Wednesday; in Eastern Churches, it begins eight weeks before Easter. ▷ Ash Wednesday; Christian year; Easter

Leo I, St, the Great (c.390–461) Pope from 440, one of the most eminent of the Latin fathers, he is thought to have been born in Tuscany. He was the champion of orthodoxy in pronouncing against Eutyches who had refused to recognize the two natures of Christ, and was instrumental in convening in 451 the significant Council of Chalcedon in which his legates successfully pressed what has been called 'the Catholic doctrine of the Incarnation'. He stoutly resisted also the deviations of Manichaeans and Pelagians, persuaded threatening Huns (452) and Vandals (455) not to destroy Rome or its people, and consolidated the primacy of the Roman see. His feast day is 11 April. ▷ Council of the Church; Incarnation; Manichaeism; Pelagius

Levi Biblical character, the third son of Jacob by his wife Leah. It is debated whether his descendants ever formed one of the 12 tribes of Israel descended from Jacob's sons. Although they were called a tribe, no territory was apparently allocated to them (Joshua 13.14), and they seem to have been a kind of priestly class. Moses is later depicted as a descendant of Levi. ▷ Israel, tribes of; Jacob; Levites

Leviathan A rare Hebrew loan-word of uncertain derivation, apparently used to refer to a kind of sea or river monster (Psalms 104.26; also Isaiah 27.1; Psalms 74.14). In Job 41 it seems nearer a crocodile, but Ugaritic parallels suggest it may have been a mythical supernatural figure, a sea dragon, perhaps symbolic of chaos or evil. ▷ Old Testament

Lévi-Strauss, Claude (1908–) French structural anthropologist, born in Brussels and educated at Paris University. He taught in Sao Paolo and New York, did fieldwork in Brazil in the late 1930s, and became professor in Paris from 1959. His outstanding contribution to the modern doctrine of structuralism has had repercussions not only for the study of religion but for other disciplines too. He claims that the human mind contains a logical structure that is most clearly seen in the myths of primal religion. His analyses of myth, of primal religion, of the paradigm of language, of the innate logic of the human mind, and of the importance for religion and life of binary contrasts between opposites such as male and female, wet and dry, cooked and raw, sacred and profane, light and darkness, etc are brought out in such books as: *Structural Anthropology* (1958, Eng trans 1963), *Totemism* (1962, Eng trans 1963), *The Savage Mind* (1962, Eng trans 1966), and *The Raw and the Cooked* (1964, Eng trans 1969). His French theorizing contrasts with the more inductive fieldwork approach of British anthropologists of religion, with their concern for particular contexts, but his influence has been wider. ▷ anthropology of religion; dualism; Dumézil, Georges; totemism

Levites Descendants of the biblical character Levi (one of Jacob's sons), who apparently formed a class of auxiliary ministers dedicated to the care of the Tabernacle and eventually the Jerusalem Temple (Numbers 3.5–10). This role is distinct from that of the Aaronic priesthood itself, but the division between priest and Levite is blurred, and it is arguable that such distinctions arose only in later exilic times. ▷ Aaron; Levi; Leviticus, Book of; Zadokites

Leviticus, Book of A book of the Hebrew Bible/Old Testament, the third book of the Pentateuch, the English title referring to the priestly traditions of the Levites. It was probably compiled during the exile from earlier materials, despite the traditional attribution to Moses. It continues from the end of the Book of Exodus, and contains directions about offerings (Chapters 1–7), priesthood (8–10), purity laws (11–15), and the Day of Atonement (16), followed by a major section called the 'holiness code' (17–26) and an appendix (27). ▷ Levites; Old Testament; Pentateuch

Lévy-Bruhl, Lucien (1857–1939) French philosopher and sociologist, born and educated in Paris. He taught at schools in Poitiers, Amiens and Paris, but after gaining his doctorate in 1884 went on to become Professor of the History of Modern Philosophy at the Sorbonne, editing the *Revue Philosophique* from 1917. In 1925 he founded the Institut d'Ethnologie with Rivet and Mauss, but then retired in 1927 and spent much of the time up to his death travelling abroad. In addition to his studies in philosophy and the history of social thought, he became best known for his work on what he called the 'primitive' or 'archaic' mentality, which he contrasted with modern ways of thinking. He argued that for primal peoples 'the most important properties of the beings and objects they perceive are their occult powers, their mystic qualities', whereas for the modern mentality abstract thought is more important. Although his theories have been superceded, Lévy-Bruhl's was an important attempt to try to get inside primal religion and to see the world through primal eyes as a place where one could have a feeling of participation in and communion with mystical reality, and as a place where myths were creatively significant. His wish was to describe primal religion, not to judge it, feeling that the emotional and mystical elements in it were more important than the rational, but that all were significant to a rounded view of human nature. His main books on this theme were: *Primitive Mentality* (1923), *How Natives Think* (1926), *The 'Soul' of the Primitive* (1929) and *Primitives and the Supernatural* (1935). ▷ anthropology of religion; mysticism; mythology

Lewis C S (Clive Staples) (1898–1963) British academic, writer and Christian apologist, born in Belfast, the son of a solicitor. He taught at Oxford from 1925 to 1954, and was Professor of Medieval and Renaissance English at Cambridge from 1954. He published his first book *Dymer* (1926) under the name of 'Clive Hamilton'. It is a narrative poem in rhyme royal, at once satirical and idealistic, a flavour which characterizes most of his work. His medieval study, *Allegory of Love*, was awarded the Hawthornden Prize (1936). His widest-known book is *The Screwtape Letters* (1942). Other titles include *The Problem of Pain* (1940), *Beyond Personality* (1944), and *Mere Christianity* (1952); works of scientific fiction including *Out of the Silent Planet* (1938) and *Perelandra* (1943); and books for children chronicling the magic land of Narnia, of which *The Last Battle* was awarded the Carnegie Prize in 1957. His autobiography *Surprised by Joy* (1955) was an account of his conversion. He was briefly but happily married to Joy Davidman (1915–60). ▷ apologetics

lha and **dre** Gods and demons in Tibetan religion. They are supernatural powers which surround and pervade the human world and which need to be appeased and rendered submissive in Tibetan Buddhist rituals. The lha and dre dwell in wild places such as rivers and mountains, as well as occupying the home and even the body. Lha is the Tibetan translation of the Sanskrit *deva*, and they are sometimes assigned a high place in the Tibetan Buddhist cosmology, being contrasted with the *lu*, a translation of the Sanskrit *naga*, and demons below them. The Tibetan home contains various lhas protecting the outside and the inside. The body too contains lhas at various points—at the shoulders, under the arms, in the heart, and so on—which are evoked during rituals in which the body is seen to be divine. In meditation practice a lha is regarded more as a visualized form of energy expressing buddhahood. In Tibetan folk religion illness is regarded as the withdrawal of the soul (*bla*) from the body due to the intervention of a lha or dre. Once it has been determined which class of beings is responsible, the exorcist performs appropriate rituals to secure the return of the sick person's soul. ▷ Tibetan religion

Lhasa Capital of Tibet, situated in the valley plain of a tributary of the Tsang-po. King Srongtsan Gampo (ruled 627–50) built a palace at Lhasa, though it only became the capital with Ral-pa-can (815–38) for the duration of his reign. It became the centre of government again with the fifth Dalai Lama (1617–82) and has remained the political and religious centre of Tibet, though from 1951 to 1959 the government functioned under Chinese control and since then has been under direct Chinese control. Lhasa has been a place of pilgrimage for the Mahayana Buddhist world, containing the most famous Buddhist temple, the Jo-khang, with its image of Shakyamuni brought by Wen ch'eng, the Chinese wife of Srongtsan Gampo. The Potala Palace rising above the city was the official residence of the Dalai Lamas until 1959. ▷ Potala Palace; Tibetan religion

li A Chinese term meaning ritual. It also has a deeper significance in Confucian thought which makes it tantamount to ethics or even religion. The Book of Ritual (*Li Ching*) is one of the Five Classics of the Confucian Canon, and contains 46 chapters outlining the main rituals. These included official rituals relevant to the state and its leaders, communal and agricultural rituals relevant to neighbourhoods and harvests, and domestic rituals such as funeral rites relevant to family situations. The correct performance of rituals was seen to be important socially so that li came to mean, by implication, courtesy and 'good form'—doing what is necessary and appropriate to the situation. Thus a funeral was not just a matter to do with individual family grief, it was also a wider social concern. Indeed for Confucius, ritual was an outward expression of goodness (*jen*) and was equal in importance to inward spirituality. In later neo-Confucian thought, li also developed the technical meaning of a principle or universal transcending material force (*chi*). Although philosophically important, this meaning had less general significance. ▷ Confucian Canon; jen

Liberal Judaism, or **Progressive Judaism** Equivalent terms for Reform Judaism, one of four denominations within Judaism today, united under the World Union for Progressive Judaism (formed in 1926), yet incorporating much diversity in belief and practice. The Reform movement developed in Europe and then America during the 19th century, reconciling Judaism with modern life, but there was considerable variation in the extent of religious reform. In Germany the institutionalized movement was called Liberal Judaism; in the USA there flourished a radical Reform Judaism. However, in Britain early 19th-century Reform Judaism was rather conservative, and in order to be distinguished from it a radical Liberal Judaism developed at the start of the 20th century, which was similar to American Reform Judaism. The Liberal Jewish Synagogue was established in England by Claude Joseph Goldsmid Montefiore (1858–1938) in 1911. ▷ Mendelssohn, Moses; Reform Judaism

Liberal Protestantism A trend in mid 19th-century and early 20th-century continental Protestantism that sought contemporary expression of the essence of Christianity, unfettered by traditional dogma and biblical interpretation. Influenced by idealist philosophy and theologians like Schleiermacher, Ritschl, and Johann Georg Wilhelm Herrmann (1846–1922), it was exemplified in Adolf Harnack's (1851–1930) *What is Christianity?* (English trans. 1902) and defended as the highest European religion by Troeltsch. This school of thought had some influence on Anglican modernism in England and the Social Gospel movement in the USA. It declined when its underlying evolutionary optimism and tendency to identify culture with the kingdom of God were brought into question by World War I. It was replaced by neo-orthodoxy and, eventually, by Christian existentialism. ▷ Barth, Karl; Bushnell, Horace; existentialism, Christian; Fosdick, Harry Emerson; kingdom of God; neo-orthodoxy; Quest of the Historical Jesus; Ritschl, Albrecht; Schleiermacher, Friedrich Ernst Daniel; Social Gospel

liberation theology A style of theology originating in Latin America in the 1960s, and later becoming popular in many developing countries. Accepting a Marxist analysis of society, it stresses the role and mission of the Church to the poor and oppressed in society, of which Christ is understood as liberator. Oppression is defined in several ways: poverty and economic dependence, as in that of developing countries; persecution and discrimination, whether racial or political; and sexual prejudice against women. Its sympathy for revolutionary movements led to clashes with established secular and religious authorities. Since the 1970s interest in liberation theology has spread to many areas, such as Northern Ireland and South Africa. ▷ Jesus Christ; Marxism; theology

life A preoccupation with the goal and meaning of life is a feature of almost all the religious traditions of the world. The precise origin of life is variously understood but it is often regarded as being the product of a divine act and is consequently infused with purpose and value. Physical attributes such as breath and blood feature in many faiths as the basis of life, differentiating the animate from the inanimate. More recently life has been defined in terms of self-consciousness, the capacity for movement, purposeful activity etc.

In Judaism life is a gift of Yahweh and is therefore sacred. Life is to be lived in obedience to God for its fullest consummation. Disobedience is sin and a denial of God's purpose in creating man. In Rabbinic Judaism the preservation of life is the highest good before man. Christianity inherited this double aspect of life with and without God. Life without God is a life of sin and rebellion and is self-negating. Life with God is the new life in Christ which is a gracious gift of God. This life exists, not for itself, but in openness to God and in the service of its neighbour. The fulfilment of life in Christ is attained beyond this world in the world which is to come and which God will bring about.

Hindu thought on the purpose of life is characterized by the cycle of birth and rebirth. The goal of life is to achieve enlightenment and to end the cycle of life by realizing the ultimate identity between the human self and the universal self, *Brahman*. Buddhist teaching is similar except that life is marked by impermanence, suffering and non-selfhood. There

is no universal self and the object of life is to suppress desire and attain the state of changeless tranquillity (nirvana).
Recent Western philosophy has challenged the idea that life has purpose or value in any absolute sense, arguing that life is absurd and devoid of any final meaning. ▷ Brahman; eschatology; nirvana

light and darkness This is one of a number of contrasting forces that have been common in the history of religions, others being right and left, male and female, sacred and profane, and white and black. Light has generally been a symbol of life and immortality, and darkness a symbol of chaos and death. Many creation myths describe the emergence of light out of darkness, and many end-of-the-world myths foresee the final disappearance of light into darkness. In broad terms there have been three sets of relations between light and darkness within religious traditions. In Chinese yin and yang thought they were regarded as complementary, as needing each other, and as only understandable in terms of each other. In Zoroastrian thought, followed by monotheistic Jewish, Christian and Muslim thought, light was equated with the good creator God, Ahura Mazda, and darkness with the evil 'Satan' Angra Mainyu or Ahriman. In Gnostic-type thought there was an opposition between light, seen as spirit, and darkness, seen as matter, so that salvation was often viewed as liberation from the dark material world and body into the light of the spiritual world. Light in the form of candles or lamps piercing the darkness has been important in most religious traditions, in ordinary worship and also in festivals centred on light such as Christmas, the Jewish Hanukkah, and the Hindu Divali. Banaras, the Hindu holy city, is known as Kashi, the city of light; the Quran has its 'light verses'; and the Buddha is often portrayed with a halo of light. Darkness is sometimes seen as being helpful, as in the notion of the 'dark night of the soul' in the experience of the 16th-century Spanish mystic St John of the Cross, when union with God is attained by going through the 'dark nights' of the senses and of the spirit. ▷ Ahura Mazda; Banaras; Buddha; Christmas; creation myths; Hanukkah; John of the Cross, St; left and right; Quran; sacred and profane; yin and yang

lila (līlā) The 'sport' or 'play' of the gods in Hinduism, especially Vaishnavism. The term also refers to Vishnu's creation, maintenance and destruction of the universe; there is no reason for this other than God's play. The idea of lila is mythologically expressed with regard to Krishna as the cowherd (*gopala*) in Vrindaban, flirting and playing games with the cowgirls (*gopis*), especially Radha. Meditation upon Krishna's lila is a means of liberation or transformation to Krishna's heaven for some worshippers of Krishna. ▷ Krishna; Radha; Vaishnavism; Vishnu

Lilith, or **Lilit** Female demon in the Jewish tradition with diverse connotations. The word stems from the Sumerian *lil* ('wind'), not the Hebrew *laylah* ('night'). Nonetheless, Lilith was associated with the night-time, during which she purportedly set out to seduce men. She was also thought to harm infants and women in childbirth, and amulets were employed to ward her off. Isaiah 34.14 contains the only scriptural reference to Lilith, so that her identity and role were much developed in post-biblical times. Various traditions were conjoined in a medieval biblical commentary called *The Alphabet of ben Sira*, including belief in Lilith as the first woman. According to this, before Eve was formed from Adam's rib, God created Lilith from the dust of the earth and equal to Adam. But after quarrelling she deserted Adam and, as revenge for her punishment, resolved thereafter to slay children. Such beliefs, with associated protective customs, were not uncommon among East European Jewry even into the 19th century, but today they are considered to be outdated superstitions. However, in recent decades renewed interest in Lilith has viewed her as a symbolic representative of female vitality and autonomy. This is exemplified in the Jewish feminist magazine entitled *Lilith*, which began publication in 1976. ▷ demonology, biblical; sexuality; sexuality in religion; superstition

limbo In medieval Christian theology, the abode of souls excluded from the full blessedness of the divine vision, but not condemned to any other punishment. They included unbaptized infants and Old Testament prophets. ▷ Christianity; purgatory

linga (liṅga) The principal symbolic representation of the Hindu deity Shiva, a phallic emblem. The female equivalent is the *yoni*, the shaped image of the female genitalia. ▷ Hinduism; Shiva

Lingayats (Liṅgāyats) A sect of the Hindu tradition of Shaivism, founded in the 12th century by Basava, a Shaiva Brahman at the court of a king in Karnataka. The Lingayats or Virashaivas are characterized by the worship of Shiva in his 'phallic' form of the linga. This is worn around the neck and worshipped daily. The Lingayats were part of the wider devotional or bhakti movement which spread through South India in the early medieval period and then moved north. The medium of expression of the Lingayats has been free-verse poetry (*vacana*), written in Kanarese; particularly notable is the poetry of Basava himself, and of Allama Prabhu and Mahadevyakka. In her poetry Mahadevyakka writes of her longing for Shiva, her 'Lord white as jasmine', and scorns worldly love as impermanent and unsatisfying. The Lingayats rejected the authority of the Veda, rejected the caste system and rejected ritual as being irrelevant to salvation. Upon death the Lingayat believer goes straight to union with Shiva and so is buried, needing no orthodox funerary rites. Today there is a large community of Lingayats in Karnataka. ▷ caste; Shaivism; Shiva; Veda

litany A form of prayer used in public or private worship. Supplications or invocations are made by the priest or minister, to which the congregation replies with a fixed formula. ▷ liturgy; prayer

literature, Ancient Egyptian Ancient Egyptian religion had no canonical literature comparable to the Bible or Quran, being based on ritual rather than scripture. Nevertheless a wide and varied religious literature has survived, some on papyrus, and much in wall-inscriptions from temples and tombs. Perhaps most distinctive is the mortuary literature, spells interred with the dead to ensure their passage into the afterlife. These are found most notably in the Pyramid Texts, the Coffin Texts, and the Book of the Dead. A wide variety of other texts exist, including books of ritual for the divine cult, hymns, magical texts, theological works, and books of instruction or wisdom. ▷ afterlife, Ancient Egyptian concept of; temples, Ancient Egyptian; wisdom literature, Ancient Egyptian

literature, Ancient Near Eastern The first Ancient Near Eastern literature belonged to the Sumerians in Mesopotamia who invented the use of cuneiform writing, which their Semitic successors adapted. The many clay tablets which have survived provide the principal source for the study of Mesopotamian religion, and a rich and varied religious literature has been discovered. Myth and epic were important literary forms in Mesopotamia from Sumerian times. A number of Sumerian myths which have survived tell of the ordering of the world and the struggle between good and evil forces. The Babylonian epic literature includes the magnificent epic of Gilgamesh and the creation epic *Enuma Elish* , which was recited at the Akitu festival. Many hymns, laments, and prayers to the gods of the Mesopotamian pantheon have been discovered, some very beautiful. There is also a wisdom literature similar to that found in Israel and Egypt. The Assyrian king Asshurbanipal (7th century BCE) founded the first systematically gathered and organized library in the Ancient Near East, and the large proportion of omen texts which it contained reflects the Mesopotamian interest in divination. The most important archaeological find for the study of West Semitic religion has been the Ras Shamra texts at the site of ancient Ugarit. Other evidence of the literature of the Canaanites, Aramaeans or Phoenicians is very scarce, making the study of these cultures and their religions more difficult. ▷ cosmogony, Ancient Near Eastern; divination, Ancient Near Eastern; Gilgamesh Epic; Ras Shamra texts

literature, Christian The Bible contains many types of literature (epic drama, history, lyric poetry, story, biography, epistle, apocalypse) as well as the unique form of gospel, which focuses on the public ministry and last week in the earthly life of Jesus, at the expense of all the information modern readers require of a biography. Though uneven in literary quality in the original languages, the Bible has had a profound effect on European language and literature, particularly through Luther's German Bible (1534), the publication of which coincided with the media revolution of the printed book following Gutenberg's invention (1444) of movable type, and the English Authorized or King James Version of the Bible (1611). Leaving aside specifically religious works such as versions of the Bible, biblical commentaries, works of systematic and moral theology, and devotional and mystical writing, one is left with a great body of work of more than ecclesiastical interest. Augustine's *Confessions* (400) was the first spiritual autobiography (as well as a major work in philosophy); equally notable are the *Life* (1565) of Teresa of Ávila and the mystical poetry of John of the Cross (1542–91). The Italian language was brought to life by Dante's *Divina Commedia* (begun 1307), which combines biblical and classical themes. Much literature in English, from the fragmentary poetry of the 7th-century monk Caedmon to the *Four Quartets* (1944) of T S Eliot, can only be understood against a Christian background, whether it expounds aspects of faith, echoes biblical language, or charts the decline of belief. Any list of works in the first two categories would have to include William Langland's *Vision of Piers the Plowman* (c.1360–1400), the religious poetry of John Donne (1572–1631) and George Herbert, Milton's *Paradise Lost* (1667), Bunyan's *Pilgrim's Progress* (1679, 1684), and the poems of Gerard Manley Hopkins (1844–89).

The breakdown of an agreed world-view, which has been going on since the 18th century but has become increasingly obvious in 20th-century literature, has changed the way poets and novelists function. Some, like Graham Greene (1904–91), have an ambiguous relationship with traditional Christianity; others, like Iris Murdoch (1919–), who draws on the moral philosophy of Plato, look elsewhere for a consistent intellectual foundation. There are those, like Franz Kafka (1883–1924), Albert Camus (1913–60), and Jean-Paul Sartre, who reflect the individualism and heroism or despair of existentialism; and those (foreshadowed by the generally more explicitly Christian writings of George Macdonald, Charles Williams (1886–1945), C S Lewis and J R R Tolkien (1892–1973) who use the vehicles of myth and science fiction to construct new worlds in which to discuss issues previously evaluated in a Christian context. Detective stories also operate within a moral universe in which evil is punished and good vindicated. ▷ Augustine, St (of Hippo); Bunyan, John; drama, Christian; Lewis, C S; Luther, Martin; Macdonald, George; Sartre, Jean-Paul; Teresa of Ávila, St

literature, Jewish The foundational document of Judaism is the Hebrew Bible, produced over many centuries and frequently of uncertain date and authorship; the Torah is its most important section. However, numerous other works appeared in Second Temple times (c.515BCE–70CE), including many among the Apocrypha, Pseudepigrapha and Dead Sea Scrolls. With the Temple's destruction in 70CE and subsequent fixing of the canon, a law-code entitled the Mishnah was the next main piece of Jewish literature (c.200CE). This was further expanded in the Palestinian Talmud (c.400) and Babylonian Talmud (6th century), both of which consist of the Mishnah with halakhic and aggadic comment and elaboration. From the 6th century the Midrash Rabbah ('Great Midrash') evolved, commenting on the Torah and 'Five Scrolls' (Song of Songs, Ruth, Lamentations, Ecclesiastes, Esther).

The Middle Ages saw much literary production, including philosophical works by Maimonides (eg *Guide of the Perplexed*, 1190) and the kabbalistic text called the Zohar (c.1300). Halakhic and aggadic discussion continued in commentaries and law-codes by scholars like the 11th-century Rashi (an acronym for Rabbi Shimeon ben Isaac). In addition, various Responsa (essays answering halakhic questions) and a large body of poetic material were produced. From the 14th century a Yiddish literary corpus took shape in northern and eastern Europe, including a translation of the Bible (c.1676) for those whose Hebrew was poor.

Jewish emancipation encouraged the revival of Hebrew and production of a new Jewish literature in that language. Similarly, although some historical, geographical, and fictional works have been written by Jews, only in modern times have such genres come into their own. However, the question then becomes whether it is Jewish authorship or Jewish content (religious or secular) which defines Jewish literature. Two contemporary authors fulfilling both criteria are the American novelist Chaim Potok (1929–) and the Israeli writer Amos Oz (1939–); the former's works include *The Chosen* (1967), and the latter's *Mikha'el shelli* (1968; *My Michael*, 1972). ▷ Halakhah; Josephus, Flavius; Maimonides; Septuagint; Talmud; Zohar

literature, Shinto There are no Shinto works of philosophy and theology outlining the doctrines of Shinto in a systematic way. The two most important documents of early Shinto, that come closest to Shinto scripture, are the *Kojiki* (Records of Ancient Matters) written in 712, and the *Nihongi* (Chronicles of Japan) written in 720. They give an account of the early history of Japan up to 628 in the *Kojiki*, and up to 696 in the *Nihongi*. They also contain material about Shinto myths, shrines and worship in what is seen as the 'age of the gods'. They were compiled by the court élite to unify the nation under the emperor and to counteract the growing impact of Buddhism, and were influenced by Chinese thought. They outline the divine origin of Japan, her emperors and her people, and they stress the importance of the sacred powers (*kami*) that underlie the Japanese land and people. After the Meiji restoration in 1868, and up until 1945, these two chronicles were given greater prominence as the basis of what became state Shinto. They re-emphasized the interconnection between nationalism, respect for the emperor, and devotion to Shinto. Since the collapse of state Shinto in 1945 they have become less important, but they still remain the foundation literature of Shinto and the

Japanese people. ▷ kami; Kokutai Shinto; Shinto mythology; shrines, Shinto

liturgical movement A movement to reform the worship of the Christian Church by promoting more active participation by laity in the liturgy. Beginning in 19th-century France in the Roman Catholic Church, it became influential and effective in the mid 20th century in other Churches, often through the World Council of Churches and the ecumenical movement. ▷ ecumenism; liturgy; Roman Catholicism; World Council of Churches

liturgy (Greek *leitourgia*, 'duty' or 'service') The formal corporate worship of God by a Church. It includes words, music, actions, and symbolic aids, and in Christian form is derived from Jewish ritual. Liturgies exist in a wide variety of prescribed forms, reflecting the needs and attitudes of different religious communities. ▷ liturgical movement

Lloyd-Jones, David Martyn (1899–1981) Welsh preacher and writer, born in Newcastle Emlyn. He trained in medicine at London but in 1926 forsook a promising career in Harley Street to enter the Christian ministry. After 11 years in Aberavon he became colleague and successor to G Campbell Morgan at Westminster Chapel, London, and for 30 years made it virtually the heart of English Nonconformity, with his expository preaching based on Reformed theology. He had also an extensive ministry through correspondence, and among evangelical ministers who met regularly for fellowship at the chapel. His published works include *Truth Unchanged, Unchanging* (1951), *From Fear to Faith* (1953), *Conversions: Psychological and Spiritual* (1959), and *Studies in the Sermon on the Mount* (2 vols, 1959–60). ▷ evangelicalism; Nonconformists

Llull, Ramón ▷ Lully, Raymond

Locke, John (1632–1704) English philosopher, a formative influence on British empiricism and on theories of liberal democracy, born in Wrington, Somerset. Educated at Westminster School and Christ Church College, Oxford, he reacted against the prevailing scholasticism at Oxford and involved himself instead in experimental studies of medicine and science, making the acquaintance or Robert Boyle, John Wilkins and others. In 1667 he joined the household of Anthony Ashley Cooper, later first Earl of Shaftesbury, as his personal physician and became his adviser in scientific and political matters generally.

Through Ashley he made contact with the leading intellectual figures in London and was elected fellow of the Royal Society in 1668. When Ashley became Earl of Shaftesbury and Chancellor in 1672, Locke became Secretary to the Council of Trade and Plantations, but retired to France from 1675 to 1679, partly for reasons of health and perhaps partly from political prudence. In Paris he became acquainted with the circle of Gassendi and Arnauld. After Shaftesbury's fall and death in 1683 he felt threatened and fled to Holland where he joined the English supporters of William of Orange (the future William III) and remained until after the Glorious Revolution of 1688.

His *Two Treatises on Government* had been largely written earlier but were published, anonymously, in 1690. They constitute his reply to the patriarchal, Divine Right theory of Sir Robert Filmer and also to the absolutism of Hobbes. The *Treatises* present a social contract theory which embodies a defence of natural rights and a justification for constitutional law, the liberty of the individual and the rule of the majority. If the ruling body offends against natural law it must be deposed, and this sanctioning of rebellion had a powerful influence on the American and the French revolutions. Locke returned to England in 1689, declined an ambassadorship and became Commissioner of Appeals until 1704. His health then declined further and he spent his remaining years at Oates, Essex, at the home of Sir Francis and Lady Masham (the daughter of Ralph Cudworth).

His major philosophical work was the *Essay concerning Human Understanding*, published in 1690 though developed over some 20 years. The *Essay* is a systematic enquiry into the nature and scope of human reason, very much reflecting the scientific temper of the times in seeking to establish that 'all knowledge is founded on and ultimately derives from sense ...or sensation'. The work is regarded as the first and probably the most important statement of an empiricist theory of knowledge in the British tradition which led from Locke to Berkeley and Hume. His other main works were *A Letter concerning Toleration* (1689), *Some Thoughts concerning Education* (1693) and *The Reasonableness of Christianity* (1695), and are all characterized by the same tolerance, moderation and common sense. ▷ Berkeley, George; empiricism; Hume, David; scholasticism

logical positivism A philosophical movement beginning with the 'Vienna Circle' in the 1920s under the leadership of Moritz

Schlick and Rudolf Carnap. Positivism rejected traditional philosophy insofar as it did not possess scientific rigour; metaphysical, ethical, and religious pronouncements were branded as meaningless because their truth or falsity was unverifiable. ▷ philosophy

Logos The Greek word for 'word' or 'reason', applied in Hellenic Judaism to God's personified word or wisdom active in creation and in revelation, and in Christianity as a title of Jesus Christ. The Old Testament speaks of the word of God bringing creation to pass and communicating God's will through the law and the prophets. In the New Testament, the Prologue to John's Gospel (John 1.1–18) portrays Christ as the pre-existent Logos, active in creation and become incarnate as a human being. The 2nd-century Christian Apologists used the Logos concept as a means of communicating with their Greek contemporaries, but speculation about the relationship between Father and Logos sometimes led to the latter being considered secondary and subordinate. With the condemnation of Arianism and assertion of equality between the persons of the Godhead, 'Word of God' and 'Son of God' generally became interchangeable titles for Christ. ▷ Arius

Loisy, Alfred Firmin (1857–1940) French theologian, born in Ambrières, Haute-Marne. He was ordained priest in 1879 and in 1881 became Professor of Holy Scripture at the Institut Catholique, where by his lectures and writings he incurred the disfavour of the Church and was dismissed. In 1900 he was appointed lecturer at the Sorbonne, but resigned after his works on biblical criticism were condemned by Pope Pius X in 1903 as too advanced. These books, which proved him to be the founder of the modernist movement, were *L'Évangile et l'Église* (1902), *Quatrième Évangile* (1903) and *Autour d'un petit livre* (1903). For subsequent works of the same kind he was excommunicated in 1908. He was Professor of History of Religion in the Collège de France from 1909 to 1932. ▷ biblical criticism

lokapala (lokapāla) The guardians of the four directions in Buddhist and Hindu mythology. The four Buddhist lokapalas are mentioned in the early accounts of the Buddha's life. They were present at his birth, at his renunciation (when he left his palace to seek for the answer to the problem of suffering), and at his enlightenment under the Bo tree at Gaya in Bihar, India. Popular Buddhist deities in China, Japan and Tibet, they are usually portrayed as huge, well-armed, and in the process of trampling demons. The best known of them is Kubera, who is also a Hindu lokapala; the other three are well-known Vedic gods: Yama, Varuna and Indra. Portrayed in different colours (yellow, white, blue and red) they are depicted as being the King of the Gnomes, the King of the Snakes, the King of the Musicians, and the King of the Spirit-Beings known as *yaksas*. They are significant in popular religion as protector figures who are guardians of the north, south, east and west, and also of temples and other sacred places. ▷ Buddha; enlightenment; Indra

Lokayata (Lokāyata) An unorthodox (*nastika*) system of Hindu philosophy which teaches materialism; that the body is a combination of elements (as is all reality), and that the soul is a temporary manifestation springing from the particular configuration of elements that make up a person. When the body dies, so too does this provisional soul. Karma does not operate in this essentially materialistic system: knowledge comes only through sense experience, life after death is an untenable concept, and the caste system is reviled. The writings of this school are no longer extant. It flourished around the 1st century CE, and all we know of them is through the critiques of their opponents. Traditionally, the founder is said to have been Carvaka, whose dates are unknown. ▷ karma

Loki A frequently appearing figure among the Norse divinities. He is a companion of the Aesir, foster-brother of Odin, travelling companion of Thor. He is ingenious and full of tricks, which on occasion serve the gods well; but he is capricious, unreliable and treacherous. He causes Balder's death, begets the fell wolf Fenrir and, in one story, sets in train (by mischance rather than malevolence) the tragedy of the Ring of the Nibelungs. Traditions about Loki are ambiguous. In many he appears as a trickster figure, of the sort found in many polytheistic systems symbolizing chance and disorder. In some, he is a figure of entertainment, a sort of celestial Brer Rabbit. In others he is deeply evil and sinister, a type of Satan. In the Balder myth the gods bind him until the day of Ragnarok, and in the poem *Voluspa* he emerges, and falls, among the forces of evil there. There is no sign that regular worship was ever offered to him. ▷ Aesir and Vanir; Balder; Fenrir; Ragnarok; Voluspa

lokuttara (Sanskrit: lokottara) A technical term in Buddhist *Abhidharma* literature referring to a transcendent type of consciousness. This comes as a result of worthiness in ethical living and long practice in Buddhist meditation. Occurring first in a flash, the lokuttara consciousness changes the person who receives it, and makes him or her permanently into a saint or noble (*arya*). It is transcendent not in the sense of relating to a transcendent reality outside the human person, but in the sense of giving a direct awareness of unconditioned reality. There are four grades of saint in Theravada Buddhism: the one who 'enters the stream', the one who will be reborn once more, the one who will not be born again into this world, and the *arahat*. All these grades of saint partake of the lokuttara consciousness but with a deepening sense of vividness. ▷ Abhidharma; arahat; bhavana

Lollards A derisive term applied to the followers of the English theologian John Wycliffe (14th century). The movement, responsible for the translation of the Bible into the vernacular, was suppressed; however, it continued among the religiously enthusiastic but less literate sectors of society, who were generally anticlerical in attitude, and prepared the way for the Reformation in England. ▷ Bible; Reformation; Wycliffe, John

Lombard, Peter (c.1100–1164) Italian theologian, born near Novara in Lombardy. He studied in Bologna, at Reims, and (under Abelard) in Paris, and, after holding a Chair of Theology there, in 1159 became Bishop of Paris. He was generally styled *Magister Sententiarum* or the 'Master of Sentences', from his collection of sentences from Augustine and other Fathers on points of Christian doctrine, with objections and replies. The theological doctors of Paris in 1300 denounced some of his teachings as heretical; but his work was the standard textbook of Catholic theology down to the Reformation. ▷ Abelard, Peter; Augustine, St (of Hippo); Fathers of the Church; Reformation; Roman Catholicism

Lonergan, Bernard Joseph Francis (1904–85) Canadian Jesuit theologian and philosopher, born in Buckingham, Quebec. He entered the Society of Jesus in 1922. Professor of Systematic Theology at the Gregorian University, Rome, from 1954 to 1965, his main concern was to discover precisely how theology is done, following an analysis of the way human understanding in general proceeds. The findings of his massive and seminal studies on *Insight: A Study of Human Understanding* (1957), and *Method in Theology* (1972) are summarized in *Philosophy of God, and Theology* (1973) and *Understanding and Being* (1980). His other interests in theology and the history of ideas were explored in occasional papers, assembled in *Collection* (1967), *A Second Collection* (1974), and *A Third Collection* (1985). ▷ Jesuits

Lord's Prayer A popular prayer of Christian worship, derived from Matthew 6.9–13 and (in different form) Luke 11.2–4; also known as the **Pater Noster** ('Our Father'). It is a model for how Jesus's followers are to pray, consisting (in Matthew) of three petitions praising God and seeking his kingdom, followed by four petitions concerning the physical and spiritual needs of followers. The closing doxology ('For thine is the kingdom...') was apparently added later in Church tradition. ▷ Jesus Christ; Kaddish; prayer

Lot Biblical character, portrayed in Genesis as the nephew of Abraham who separated from him and settled in Canaan, near Sodom. Stories describe his rescue from the wickedness of that place by Abraham and two angels. Symbolic of backsliding, Lot's wife is described as looking back during this escape and being turned into 'a pillar of salt'. Lot was named also as the ancestor of the Moabites and Ammonites. ▷ Abraham; Old Testament; Sodom and Gomorrah

Lotus Sutra One of the most popular scriptures in Mahayana Buddhism, which became especially important in China and Japan. It is one of the *Mahayana Sutras* and was written in India around 200CE, being translated into Chinese by Kumarajiva at the beginning of the 5th century. It emphasizes the cosmic body of the Buddha which is equivalent to a kind of eternal and real Buddha of whom the historical Buddhas are merely manifestations. Through the *Lotus Sutra* and the eternal Buddha the way to Buddhahood is open to everyone. By use of the notion of skilful means, many ways are available whereby this progress to Buddhahood can occur. The Tien Tai school, founded in China by Hui Ssu (515–77), organized this into a five-tier theory of salvation. According to Tien Tai the *Lotus Sutra* was the key scripture and it made available the highest level of Buddhist understanding and salvation even though the other Buddhist traditions and sutras were authentic as well. The Tien Tai school was important in China in the 6th and 7th centuries CE, but its influence faded after the great persecution of the Buddhists in 845. It spread to Korea and Japan as Tendai, and in the 13th century

In Japan Nichiren elevated the *Lotus Sutra* to supremacy over all other scriptures and stressed the efficacy of the sincere and faithful prayer of praise to the *Lotus Sutra*. ▷ Buddha nature; dharmakaya; Kumarajiva; Mahayana Sutras; Nichiren Buddhism; skilful means; Tendai; Tien Tai

love A concept which has been and continues to be one of the most potent forces within the religious traditions of humankind. Love has been described as the most powerful force in the universe, binding all living things together. In the Christian tradition God himself is defined as love (1 John 4.16). Love is a multi-dimensional phenomenon, but it can be categorized under three broad headings. Firstly, there is erotic or sensual love. This type of love desires its object primarily for its own gratification and pleasure. Secondly, there is brotherly or friendly love. This is the love which is offered in affection to another human being, without thought of personal gain. Finally, there is divine love. This type of love is characterized by a self-giving, a bestowing of the divine upon the recipient, through grace.

In the Jewish and Christian traditions this third type of love is central. It is covenant love (*hesed*) where God binds himself in love to the people of Israel and desires that they should respond in love to him. In Christianity this covenant love reaches its fulfilment in the sending of Christ (John 3.16). The sacrificial character (*agape*) of divine love is revealed in the willingness of Christ to lay down his life for us (John 15.13). This love requires a response from us, namely that we should love God and our neighbours and this is seen to be the purpose of human life. Love is therefore both a gift from God and a task before God. The concept of a universal impartial love occurs in many traditions other than Christianity but reaches clearest expression there. (Mark 12.29–31). Love in this sense bestows value upon the individual and is an essential factor in the enabling, affirming character of human relationships. ▷ covenant; sacrifice

Loyola, Ignatius ▷ Ignatius Loyola, St

Lucifer ▷ Satan

Ludi In Roman religion numerous religious or votive games given in honour of divinities (especially Jupiter). The ritual could last several days and nights and was very expensive. There was a distinction between public (given by state) and private (offered by an individual) games. Public games were established by law and generally, like festivals, received a fixed calendar date. The seven annual games of the republic (which could include sacrifices and banquets) were increased to more than 100 during the Imperial period. A major event was the *Ludi Saeculares*, commemorating with games and sacrifices the end of a *saeculum* (c.100 years) and the beginning of a new one. Among private games, the most famous were funeral games (*Ludi funebres*), performed on the ninth day after death. Whether public or private, the nature of games differed and could be divided between those held in a circus or an amphitheatre (involving races, gladiatorial shows, the killing of animals) and those taking place in a theatre (ie scenic games such as plays, mimes, pantomimes and musical or athletic contests). Even though, during the Imperial period, entry to the games was not restricted only to Roman citizens, seats were reserved for certain individuals according to rank and status. ▷ Roman religion

Lug, Lugh, or **Lugus** In Irish mythology, the god of the sun, the divine leader of the Tuatha Dé Danann. A musician, wise-man and magician, he proved his abilities to the king of the Tuatha Dé Danann, who appointed him ruler for 13 days and entrusted him with the task of ridding the kingdom of the Formarians, evil spirits who occupied the country. Under Lug's organization sorcerers, druids, craftsmen and warriors were so efficiently deployed in battle that the enemy was defeated. ▷ Dagda, the

Luke, Gospel according to New Testament writing, one of the four canonical Gospels, and the first part of a two-fold narrative that includes the Book of Acts. It is anonymous, but traditionally considered the work of 'Luke', a Gentile convert, physician, and friend of Paul. The Gospel is noteworthy for its stories of the births of Jesus and John the Baptist (Luke 1–2), Jesus's promises to the poor and oppressed, the extensive so-called 'travel narrative' (Luke 9–19) containing many popular parables and sayings, and its special accounts of Jesus's passion and resurrection. ▷ Acts of the Apostles; Gospels, canonical; Luke, St; New Testament

Luke, St (1st century) New Testament evangelist, a Gentile Christian, perhaps 'the beloved physician' and companion of St Paul (Colossians 4.14, Philippians 24). Church tradition made him a native of Antioch in Syria, and a martyr. He is first named as author of the third Gospel in the 2nd century, and tradition has ever since ascribed to him both that work and the Acts of the Apostles. His feast day is 18 October. ▷ Acts of the Apostles; Luke, Gospel according to; Paul, St

Lull, Ramón ▷ Lully, Raymond

Lully, or **Llull** or **Lull, Raymond** or **Ramón** (c.1232–1315) Spanish theologian and mystic, known as, 'the enlightened doctor', born in Palma in Majorca. In his youth he served as a soldier and led a dissolute life, writing lyrical troubadour poetry, but from 1266 gave himself up to asceticism and resolved on a spiritual crusade for the conversion of the Muslims. To this end, after some years of study he produced his *Ars Magna*, the 'Lullian method', a mechanical aid to the acquisition of knowledge and the solution of all possible problems by a systematic manipulation of certain fundamental notions (the Aristotelian categories, etc). He also wrote a book against the Averroists, and in 1291 went to Tunis to confute and convert the Muslims, but was imprisoned and banished. After visiting Naples, Rome, Majorca, Cyprus and Armenia, he again sailed (1305) for Bugia (Bougie) in Algeria, and was again banished; at Paris he lectured against the principles of Averroës; and returning to Bugia, was stoned and died a few days afterwards. The Lullists combined religious mysticism with alchemy, but it has been disproved that Lully himself ever dabbled in alchemy. Apart from his *Ars Magna*, of his works *Llibre de Contemplació en Déuf* is masterly and he was the first to use a vernacular language for religious or philosophical writings. He also wrote impressive poetry. ▷ alchemy; asceticism; Averroës, Ibn Rushd; mysticism

Lumbini A place just over the border from India in Nepal where the Buddha was born in the 6th century BCE. It is one of four Buddhist holy places, the other three being Bodhgaya, where the Buddha had his great experience of enlightenment, Sarnath, where he preached his first sermon, and Kusinara, where he died. All four are important pilgrimage places for Buddhists from around the world. The great Indian emperor Ashoka set up a pillar in Lumbini around 249BCE in commemoration of his own visit, and in memory of the Buddha's birth. Later traditions suggest that it was also at Lumbini that the young Buddha came across examples of suffering that led him to renounce the luxury of his palace and to set out upon his life's quest for the answer to the problem of suffering. ▷ Ashoka; Bodhgaya; Buddha; duhkha; Sarnath

Lumpa Church ▷ Lenshina, Alice Mulenga

Lung Men Caves A set of caves near Loyang in China which contains around 100000 wall-paintings and statues of Buddhas and other Buddhist figures, ranging from minute figures to ones over 18 metres high. It is the third and most impressive set of Buddhist cave-temples in China. The earliest set had been started around 400CE at Tun-huang in north-west China, and the second one is at Datong, north of Loyang, near the Great Wall of China. They were authorized by the barbarian rulers from the Wei dynasty onwards who had invaded and captured north China. These rulers espoused Buddhism but their people knew little about it, and the Lung Men Caves offered visible teaching about the Buddhist tradition that told an immediate story to even the most illiterate peasant who came upon them. They also provide a visual history of the indigenization of Buddhism in China. They were completed in three stages: the first stage has Buddhas who are still recognizably Indian in their features, the second has Buddhas who have a combination of Indian and Chinese features, and the third has completely Chinese Buddhas. Many other Buddhist buildings were built by the Wei dynasty in Loyang, which became the capital of China in 494CE, but they have disappeared, whereas the Lung Men Caves remain. ▷ Buddha; Buddha image; Tun Huang

Luria, Isaac (1514–72) Jewish kabbalist or mystic, also known as the 'Ari' ('Lion'). He worked at Safed in Palestine, which, after the expulsion of the Jews from Spain in 1492, became the main centre of Jewish mysticism or kabbalah. He developed the ideas of the Zohar, a work purportedly written by Simeon ben Yohai, a 2nd-century CE Safed rabbi. Particularly interesting is Luria's notion of tzimtzum ('contraction') whereby God limited himself, thus creating a vacuum. Into this he injected light and mediatory kelim ('vessels') to form the created universe. Some of the vessels shattered, leading to turmoil and the uneven irradiation of light through the cosmos; the sin of the first human being resulted in further disharmony. Nonetheless good and evil are not irreconcilable opposites: the latter is fundamentally the absence of light. Therefore, in line with the Zohar, Luria held that man's role was to work towards the restoration of harmony through prayer, obedience to the commandments, and good deeds. To this end a strong soul might return to earth after death and enter a weaker person in order to sustain him. However, the harmonization process requires the advent of the Messiah for its completion. ▷ Kabbalah; Messiah; sefirah; Zohar

Luther, Martin (1483–1546) German religious reformer, and founder of the Reformation, born in Eisleben, the son of a miner. He went to school at Magdeburg and Eisenach, and entered the University of Erfurt in 1501, taking his degree in 1505. Before this, however, he was led to the study of the Scriptures, and spent three years in the Augustinian monastery at Erfurt. In 1507 he was ordained a priest, in 1508 he lectured on philosophy in the University of Wittenberg, in 1509 on the Scriptures, and as a preacher gained a still more powerful influence. On a mission to Rome in 1510–11 he was appalled by the conditions there, and after his return his career as a reformer began. Money was greatly needed in Rome; and its emissaries sought everywhere to raise funds by the sale of indulgences. Luther's indignation at the shameless traffic carried on by the Dominican Johann Tetzel became irrepressible. As Professor of Biblical Exegesis at Wittenberg (1512–46) he began to preach the doctrine of salvation by faith rather than works; and on 31 October 1517 he drew up a list of 95 theses on indulgences, denying to the pope all right to forgive sins, and nailed them on the church door at Wittenberg. Tetzel retreated from Saxony to Frankfurt an der Oder, where he published a set of counter-theses and burnt Luther's. The Wittenberg students retaliated by burning Tetzel's. In 1518 Luther was joined by Melanchthon.

The pope, Leo X, at first took little notice of the disturbance, but in 1518 summoned Luther to Rome to answer for his theses. His university and the elector interfered, and ineffective negotiations were undertaken by Cardinal Cajetan and by Miltitz, envoy of the pope to the Saxon court. Eck and Luther held a memorable disputation at Leipzig (1519). Luther meantime attacked the papal system as a whole more boldly. Erasmus and Hutten now joined in the conflict. In 1520 Luther published his famous address to the *Christian Nobles of Germany*, followed by a treatise *On the Babylonish Captivity of the Church of God*, both works which attacked also the doctrinal system of the Church of Rome. The papal bull containing 41 theses issued against him, he burned before a crowd of doctors, students, and citizens in Wittenberg. Germany was convulsed with excitement. Charles V had convened his first diet at Worms in 1521; an order was issued for the destruction of Luther's books, and he was summoned to appear before the diet. Finally he was put under the ban of the empire; on his return from Worms he was seized, at the instigation of the Elector of Saxony, and lodged (really for his own protection) in the Wartburg. During the year he spent here he translated the Scriptures and composed various treatises. Civil unrest called Luther back to Wittenberg in 1522; he rebuked the unruly elements, and made a stand against lawlessness on the one hand and tyranny on the other. In this year he published his acrimonious reply to Henry VIII on the seven sacraments. Estrangement had gradually sprung up between Erasmus and Luther, and there was an open breach in 1523, when Erasmus published *De Libero Arbitrio*, and Luther followed with *De Servo Arbitrio* (1525). In that year Luther married Katherine von Bora, one of nine nuns who had withdrawn from conventual life. In 1529 he engaged in his famous conference at Marburg with Zwingli and other Swiss theologians, obstinately maintaining his views as to the real (consubstantial) presence in the Eucharist. The drawing up of the Augsburg Confession, Melanchthon representing Luther, marks the culmination of the German Reformation (1530).

Luther died in Eisleben, and was buried at Wittenberg. Endowed with broad human sympathies, massive energy, affectionate simplicity, and rich, if sometimes coarse, humour, he was undoubtedly a spiritual genius. His intuitions of divine truth were bold, vivid and

Martin Luther

penetrating, if not philosophical and comprehensive; and he possessed the power of kindling other souls with the fire of his own convictions. His voluminous works include *Table-talk*, *Letters* and *Sermons*. His commentaries on Galatians and the Psalms are still read; and he was one of the great leaders of sacred song, his hymns having an enduring power. ▷ Augsburg Confession; Eck, Johann Mayer von; Erasmus, Desiderius; Eucharist; Melanchthon, Philip; papacy; Reformation; salvation; Zwingli, Huldreich

Lutheranism Churches derived from the Reformation of Martin Luther, and the doctrine which they share. Lutheran Churches originally flourished in Germany and Scandinavia, then in other parts of Europe; later they spread through immigration from Europe, in the USA, and through missionary activity in Africa and Asia. The doctrine is based on the Augsburg Confession (1530), the Apology (1531), Luther's two Catechisms, and the Formula of Concord (1577). It emphasizes justification by faith alone, the importance of scripture, and the priesthood of all believers. Three sacraments are recognized: baptism, Eucharist, and penance. The Lutheran World Federation, a free association of Lutheran Churches, was founded in 1947, and is the largest of the Protestant confessional families. ▷ Augsburg Confession; Luther, Martin; Reformation; Protestantism; sacrament

Lu Tsung A Chinese school of Buddhism which emphasizes the role of monks and monastic discipline. Founded by Tao Hsuan (596–667), it became known as the Chinese Vinaya school because it was based upon a concern for the organization and correct government of monasteries that are associated with the *vinaya-pitaka* of the Theravada *tipitaka* or Pali Canon. It also stressed a firm discipline and a clear morality, but was less concerned about doctrine and belief. Although never strong in its own right, it influenced the practice of more popular schools in Chinese Buddhism such as Chan and Pure Land. ▷ Chan; Pure Land Buddhism; Theravada Buddhism; tipitaka; vinaya-pitaka

Luwum, Janani (1922–77) Ugandan prelate, born in East Acholi, the son of poor Christians. He became a teacher after taking a missionary-run training course. Converted in 1948, he disturbed more quiescent Christians by his evangelical fervour. Ordained in the Anglican Church, he was theological college principal and Bishop of Northern Uganda, before election in 1974 as Archbishop of Uganda in a land where in 1971 Idi Amin had established a reign of terror. He spoke out fearlessly on behalf of victims and oppressed. At Amin's instigation (some say by his hand) the archbishop was shot dead, and Anglicans in Kampala were forbidden to hold a memorial service for him. ▷ Anglican Communion; evangelicalism

M

Maat, or **Mayet** In Ancient Egypt, the concept of the divine order of things established in the act of creation, which must constantly be renewed for the world to function properly. Maat is the essential food of the gods. In the human realm it is the particular responsibility of the pharaoh, who must uphold it in order to keep the kingdom unified and at peace. It is the basis of the law and of all ethical instruction and wisdom. This concept of order, truth and justice, vital for the running of Egyptian society, is personified as the goddess Maat, daughter of the sun god Re. In the Osirian hall of judgement she is fundamental as the standard against which the deceased's soul is balanced to determine his access to the afterlife. Maat is represented as a woman wearing a tall ostrich feather on her head, or, especially in scenes of judgement, as simply the feather. ▷ afterlife; Osiris; pharaoh; Re; wisdom literature

Mabinogion A collection of 11 Welsh stories (erroneously so named by its 19th-century translator, Lady Charlotte Guest) from the *White Book of Rhyddrch* and the *Red Book of Hergest*. The manuscripts are of the 14th century; parts of the text of the 11th and 10th centuries. They include, however, much older material, deriving from the Welsh bardic oral tradition. Like much early Irish literature this material gives hints about pre-Christian Celtic religion. Hero figures such as Bendigheid Bran almost certainly represent pre-Christian divinities. In their present form, however, the magnificent stories serve another purpose, and great caution is needed in using them as sources for the old religion.

Macarius, or **Makarios of Egypt** (c.300–390) Egyptian monk, known for his sanctity and miracles, and later (like his contemporary, Macarius of Alexandria), credited with numerous writings on the spiritual life. These letters, dialogues, collections of sayings, and homilies or sermons dealing with prayer and the work of the Holy Spirit are now held to have originated from Syria or northern Mesopotamia, and to date from the mid 4th century to the mid 5th century. ▷ hesychasm

Maccabees An important Jewish family, and those of its party (also known as the Hasmoneans) who initially resisted the influences of Greek culture on Israel and its religion during Syrian rule over Palestine. Judas Maccabeus (or ben Mattathias) led a revolt in 168BCE by attacking a Jewish apostate, and it was continued by his sons through a kind of guerrilla warfare. It resulted eventually in semi-independence from Syrian control, with Jonathan and Simon beginning a Hasmonean dynasty of high priestly rulers which lasted until the rise of Herod the Great under Roman patronage (c.37BCE). ▷ Hasidim; Maccabees, Books of the

Maccabees, or **Machabees, Books of the** Four writings, the first two being part of the Old Testament Apocrypha (or deuterocanonical works of the Roman Catholic canon) and the last two being assigned to the Old Testament Pseudepigrapha. 1 Maccabees is a historical narrative concerned with the victories of Judas Maccabeus and his family in 2nd-century BCE Palestine, leading eventually to Jewish semi-independence from Syrian control. 2 Maccabees roughly parallels 1 Maccabees 1–7, but is of less certain historical value. 3 Maccabees narrates stories of Jewish resistance before the Maccabean period, particularly in Egypt under Ptolemy IV Philopater (reigned 221–204BCE). 4 Maccabees presents vivid descriptions of tortures and martyrdoms during the early years of the Maccabean revolt, which were formulated to commend certain theological and philosophical ideals. ▷ Apocrypha, Old Testament; Maccabees; Pseudepigrapha

Macdonald, George (1824–1905) Scottish novelist, lecturer and poet, born in Huntly, Aberdeenshire, the son of a farmer. He was educated at King's College, Aberdeen, and Highbury Theological College. He became a Congregationalist pastor at Arundel, but his unorthodox views—primarily his belief in purgatory, and in a place in heaven for everyone, even animals—caused conflict with his parishioners, and finally brought his resignation. After the success of his first publication, the poem 'Within and Without' (1856), he turned to writing and lecturing, publishing the allegorical novel *Phantastes* (1858), which met with a cold reception. He followed this with a series of novels, including *David Elgin-*

brod (1863), *Robert Falconer* (1868), and *Lilith* (1895), confessing to use his books as his pulpit. He is now best known for his children's books, among them *At the Back of the North Wind* (1871), *The Princess and the Goblin* (1872) and *The Princess and Curdie* (1888), but his adult works have enjoyed a revival, especially among evangelical Christians. ▷ Congregationalism; evangelicalism

Machabees ▷ **Maccabees, Books of the**

Mackintosh, Hugh Ross (1870–1936) Scottish theologian, born in Paisley. Professor of Systematic Theology at New College, Edinburgh (1904–36), and Moderator of the General Assembly of the Church of Scotland (1932), he sought to spread understanding of developments in continental theology, which he had studied at Marburg. He helped produce translations of Albrecht Ritschl's *Justification and Reconciliation* and Schleiermacher's *The Christian Faith* (1821–2); his 1933 Croall lectures on trends from Schleiermacher to Barth, described by John Baillie as 'a fine mingling of generous appreciation with stern rebuke', were published posthumously as *Types of Modern Theology* (1937). Earlier books of note included *The Doctrine of the Person of Jesus Christ* (1912) and *The Christian Experience of Forgiveness* (1927). ▷ Barth, Karl; Schleiermacher, Friedrich Ernst Daniel

MacLeod, Baron George Fielden, of Fuinary (1895–1991) Scottish presbyterian clergyman, second son of Sir John MacLeod, 1st Baronet, a Glasgow MP. Educated at Winchester and Oriel College, Oxford, he won the MC and Croix de Guerre in World War I, and studied theology at Edinburgh, becoming minister of St Cuthbert's there (1926–30) and at Govan in Glasgow (1930–8). He founded the Iona Community, which set about restoring the ruined abbey on that historic island. The original dozen ministers and helpers soon grew in number and, working there every summer, renovated most of the monastic buildings. As Moderator of the General Assembly (1957–8) he created controversy by supporting the unpopular scheme to introduce bishops into the kirk in the interests of church unity. Well known as a writer and broadcaster, he was strongly left-wing, as his *Only One Way Left* (1956) testifies. He succeeded to the baronetcy in 1924, but preferred not to use the title. In 1967 he was created a life peer, as Baron MacLeod of Fuinary.

Macquarrie, John (1919–) Scottish theologian and philosopher of religion, born in Renfrew. A lecturer at Glasgow (1953–62), and professor at Union Theological Seminary, New York (1962–70), and at Oxford (1970–86), he has written extensively across the whole field of theology. While the influence of Bultmann and Tillich may be traced in *An Existentialist Theology* (1955) and *Principles of Christian Theology* (1966), his catholic interests may be discerned in *Paths in Spirituality* (1972), *In Search of Humanity* (1982), Gifford lectures *In Search of Deity* (1984), and *Theology, Church and Ministry* (1986). Students have also appreciated successive revisions of *Twentieth Century Religious Thought* (1963–88), and his editing of *A Dictionary of Christian Ethics* (1967), revised, with J F Childress, as *A New Dictionary of Christian Ethics* (1986). ▷ Bultmann, Rudolf Karl; Tillich, Paul Johannes

Madhva (13th century) Hindu Vaishnava theologian from South India who was a devotee of Krishna, as portrayed in the *Bhagavata Purana*. Along with Shankara and Ramanuja, Madhva is in the Vedanta tradition and wrote a commentary on the *Brahma Sutra*. However, in contrast to Shankara's monistic (*advaita*) philosophy, Madhva maintains a dualism (*dvaita*) between the soul and God and begins a 'dualist' school of Vedanta. Madhva maintains that there are three eternal and distinct realities: Brahman or Vishnu, souls and matter. Liberation (*moksha*) is the freeing of the soul from *samsara* through Vishnu's grace; yet even in liberation souls are distinct from Vishnu and from each other, inhabiting a world or heaven in which Vishnu dwells, in a spiritual body. He rejects the Advaita Vedanta idea that the world is illusion (*maya*), arguing that the differences are real between objects, between souls and objects, between one soul and another and between the soul and Vishnu. Madhva classifies beings into three categories, those who shall be saved through Vishnu's grace, those who are destined to wander through samsara eternally, and those who are destined for damnation. There is possibly some Christian influence on these doctrines. Madhva accepted the authority of the Veda and believed that the Veda is eternal. ▷ Advaita Vedanta; Bhagavata Purana; Brahman; Krishna; moksha; samsara; Vaishnavism; Veda; Vishnu

Madhyamika An important school of Mahayana Buddhist philosophy founded by a South-Indian monk named Nagarjuna (c.150–250). It is also known as the 'emptiness teaching' because its main notion is that of emptiness. Murti has described it as the central philosophy of Buddhism and a middle way between the Hindu concept of the atman (self) and the *Abhidharma* position of Buddhism. According to Madhyamika everything is empty in three senses: there is an inherent nature of things, all things operate according to dependent origination, and although things may 'exist' at the conventional level of truth, at the ultimate level they are empty. Only by realizing the emptiness (*shunyata*) of all existing forms is it possible to make sense of the everyday life of change and of the ultimate goal of enlightenment. Thus the reality of the self, or of any sort of god, or even of the dharmas of the Abhidharma, is ruled out, yet there is an ultimate truth in nirvana which is unconditioned and beyond words, and realizable through wisdom (*prajna*). Historically in the 5th and 6th centuries CE Madhyamika split into two schools, the Prasangika and the Svatantrika, and in the 8th century it became syncretized with *Yogacara* ideas. It was in this latter form that it passed over into Tibet, where it became dominant. ▷ Abhidharma; atman; bhavana; dharma; emptiness; Mahayana Buddhism; Nagarjuna; nirvana; prajna; Yogacara

madrasah The name for an Islamic institute of higher education. Attendance at it usually presupposed a knowledge of the Quran committed to memory. It was a place of residence including a courtyard, a prayer hall, and student accommodation, and was often attached to a mosque where instruction was given. Although centred upon religious education—the Quran, the sayings and traditions of Muhammad, Quranic interpretation, Islamic theology and Muslim law—it could also include a wider curriculum, for example the liberal arts, mathematics, literature, history, music, medicine and agronomy. The madrasah teacher gave his students certificates which in turn enabled them to teach. The main Muslim madrasahs offered a blueprint for later Western universities with their wearing of black gowns, their notions of graduate and undergraduate studies, their chairs and their scholarships. Famous madrasahs included a 9th-century one in Baghdad founded by Caliph al-Mamun, al-Azhar in Cairo founded in 972, and the Nizamiyya in Baghdad, founded in 1065, where al-Ghazali was a professor. In the last century madrasahs have sometimes been supplemented or replaced by colleges and universities with a more Western-style curriculum and teaching system. ▷ Azhar, al-; Ghazali, Abu Hamid Mohammed al-; Hadith; Islamic law schools; kalam; mosque; Quran

magen David Hexagram or six-pointed star, also called the 'star of David'. A very ancient symbol, it has been used by many cultures for decoration and as a sign of good luck. It was also used in magic as an amulet and named 'seal of Solomon'. However, the title magen David ('shield of David') prevailed among Jews, and was first found in the 14th century, perhaps reflecting a belief that King David's shield pictured a hexagram. Although already in Jewish books and coats of arms (it was used by Jews from Second Temple times—c.515BCE–70CE), the magen David became particularly associated with Jewry in the 17th and 18th centuries (for example, it marked the boundaries of Vienna's Jewish quarter from 1656), but it was not until the 19th century that it was used widely by Jews as a symbol parallel to the cross in Christianity. Its general acceptance as a Jewish symbol is shown by its appearance in anti-Semitic propaganda from this time, culminating in the star-shaped yellow badge forced upon Jews by the Nazi Third Reich. Nonetheless, 19th-century Zionism adopted it, and the magen David remains on the Israeli flag. ▷ anti-Semitism; menorah; symbolism; Zionism

Magi A group of unspecified number guided by a mysterious star (Matthew 2.1–12), who came from 'the East' and presented gifts to the infant Jesus in Bethlehem, after inquiring of his whereabouts from Herod. Origen suggests they were three because of the three gifts of gold, frankincense, and myrrh. Tertullian deduced that they were kings. Later Christian tradition named them as Gaspar, Melchior, and Balthasar. ▷ Jesus Christ; Matthew, Gospel according to; Origen; Tertullian

magic A ritual activity aimed at producing effects in the world by means of supernatural rather than causal means. It is present in every society, including the West, and ranges from the magic of popular folk-religion to complex magical systems. However, it has not thrown up elaborate theological frameworks to explain its workings, even though it does overlap with religion. It usually deals with concrete problems such as healing, seeking revenge, finding lost valuables, avoiding calamity, and finding out misdoers. It implies that there is a connection between what happens in one realm of life and what happens in another, so that if an action is performed symbolically in one realm it will have conse-

Siberian sorceress

quences in the other realm. Thus in black magic a pin stuck in an effigy of a person aims to affect the live person the effigy represents. Much academic theory has been applied to magic: did it precede religion? does it work automatically whereas religion does not? is it a substitute in primal societies for science? is it a method of social control? does it require faith for it to work? and so on. It is clear that magic does have links with religion and that it takes seriously the supra-logical elements in the human mind. It remains a factor among primal religions, and since the mid 19th century there has been a small-scale revival of magic in the West associated with the Hermetic Order of the Golden Dawn founded in 1888, and the work of individuals such as Aleister Crowley. ▷ Crowley, (Edward) Aleister; divination; neo-paganism; witchcraft

magic, Ancient Egyptian Magic was an important part of Egyptian life. Personified as Hike, it was the mysterious power possessed by gods and pharaoh. It was accessible to magicians, who could manifest it through word and action, using principles normally linked with 'sympathetic' magic. The spoken and written word had a creative force, and the knowledge of names could be used to gain control over objects and people. There was also magical power in images; the statues and pictures in Egyptian tombs were not just decorative but were believed to come to life for the benefit of the deceased. Amulets and talismans were used throughout Egyptian society to ward off all sorts of evil, and magic played an important part in medicine. Magic was used in particular for the benefit of the dead and dominated funerary rites. Egyptian mortuary literature consisted of spells, such as those found in the Book of the Dead, to guide the deceased safely into the afterlife. Two deities, Thoth and Isis, were believed to possess special magical knowledge and power. ▷ afterlife, Ancient Egyptian concept of; funerary practices, Ancient Egyptian; literature, Ancient Egyptian; pharaoh

magic, Ancient Near Eastern Many Ancient Near Eastern texts describe magic rituals and practices designed to ward off evil from demons or harmful spells, to avoid the consequences of omens, to inflict evil on enemies, and to bring success in all areas of life. In Mesopotamia demons were held responsible for illness and incantation-priests regularly performed exorcisms; in some cases a ritual substitution took place, where a sacrificial animal was offered in place of the sick man. In the case of illness magical rites were often combined with medical or surgical practices. Among the Hittites magicians practised at all levels of society, from the village sorceresses ('Old Women') to the priests in the gods' temples. Magic was not always used beneficially, and Babylonian and Hittite law codes recognize black magic as a serious crime. ▷ evil, Ancient Near Eastern concept of

Mahabharata (Mahābhārata) The sacred book of the Hindus, its 110000 couplets making it the longest epic in the world. Dating back to the first millennium BCE, it was orally transmitted and not printed until the 19th century. The central plot concerns the conflict between the *Kurus* (spirits of evil) and *Pandus* (spirits of good). ▷ Hinduism; Ramayana

Mahabodhi Society (Mahābodhi Society) A Buddhist society set up in 1891 in Ceylon (now Sri Lanka) by Anagarika Dharmapala. Its formation was occasioned by Dharmapala's visit to Bodhgaya in India, the site where the Buddha had experienced his enlightenment (*bodhi*). He found it neglected and in the hands of a Hindu owner, and the aim of the Mahabodhi Society was to restore the site at Bodhgaya to some sort of order and to Buddhist oversight, and to revive Buddhism in India, the land of its birth. The first aim of restoring Bodhgaya to Buddhist hands was eventually achieved in 1949, and the second aim has also been successful, as Buddhism continues to grow in independent India. Branches of the Mahabodhi Society were set up at various places around India such as Sarnath, Delhi, Bombay, Madras, Lucknow, and Ajmer, as well as in Ceylon, and Buddhist Studies were revived in a number of Indian universities. In addition to this, through the *Maha Bodhi Journal* and in other ways the Society has quickened an interest in Buddhism in the Western world. ▷ Bodhgaya; bodhi; Dharmapala, Anagarika; Sarnath

Maharishi (Sanskrit, 'great sage') The Hindu title for a guru or spiritual leader. In the West, the teaching of Transcendental Meditation by the Maharishi Mahesh Yogi is well known. ▷ guru; transcendental meditation

Maharishi Mahesh Yogi (1911–) Hindu yogi and founder of the Transcendental Meditation movement. Maharishi Mahesh Yogi was a physics graduate of Allahabad University who then went to study under a spiritual master Guru Dev (1869–1953). Guru Dev taught a meditation technique which Maharishi brought to the West in 1958. This technique, known as Transcendental Meditation or TM, involves the repetition of a personal mantra which calms the mind and allows the practitioner eventually to attain refined and 'transcendental' states of consciousness, which are the source of creativity. Maharishi outlines seven levels of consciousness, the highest of which is the enlightened state. Through practising TM the practitioner is also said to be able to develop supernormal abilities or *siddhis*. The underlying philosophy of TM is Vedanta, though Maharishi claims that the technique can be used independently of any reference to Hindu ideas. Transcendental Meditation and organizations associated with it, such as the Maharishi Corporate Development International and the Maharishi International University, also aim to reduce world poverty, promote health and create world peace. During the 1960s the Maharishi became a popular figure due to the involvement of the pop group, the Beatles, with his meditation technique. His ideas enjoyed a revival in Britain with the formation in 1992 of the Natural Law Party. ▷ Transcendental Meditation; Vedanta

Mahasanghika (Mahāsāṅghika) An important branch within early Buddhism meaning literally 'those of the great assembly' (*mahasangha*). They had a broader and more democratic approach than other branches such as the Theravada, which were more conservative and held more closely to the doctrines and traditions of the elders. They introduced a new viewpoint concerning the person of the Buddha, conceived new ways of realizing enlightenment, and practised what amounted to a kind of devotion to the Buddha. The Mahasanghikas themselves divided into a number of separate schools and it is very probable, though difficult to prove, that they paved the way for the rise of Mahayana Buddhism. ▷ bodhi; Buddha; enlightenment; Mahayana Buddhism; sangha; Theravada Buddhism

Mahashivratri (Mahāśivarātri) The yearly Shiva festival, usually held on the thirteenth night of the dark half of the month of Magha (January–February). The thirteenth night of the dark half of every month is sacred to Shiva, but on this particular date devotions to the deity reach a climax. Mahashivratri literally means 'great night of Shiva'. The night is preceded by strict fasting, followed by an all-night vigil involving linga worship and other related ceremonies. The next day is full of feasting and rejoicing, and fairs are held on the river banks. It is considered especially auspicious to enter into the celebrations on this day. ▷ linga; Shiva

Mahavamsa, (Mahāvaṃsa) The 'great chronicle' which sets out the Buddhist history of Ceylon. It begins with the Buddha himself and early Indian Buddhism, and shows how Buddhism was introduced to Ceylon and how it grew there up to the time of King Mahasena in the 4th century CE. The traditional author is Mahanama, who is reckoned to have written the *Mahavamsa* in the early 6th century CE. The great chronicle covers material similar to that in the *Dipavamsa*, which is also a narrative of the early Buddhist history of Ceylon. However, it is more comprehensive, and takes the form of an epic poem; as such it ranks with significant epics in other religious traditions. It is supplemented by the *Culavamsa*, which takes the story of the Buddhist history of Ceylon from 302CE to the 19th century. The existence of these chronicles shows how important the Buddhist tradition has been in the history of Sri Lanka. The *Mahavamsa* is also an important historical source for the story of Buddhism in early India and Ceylon. ▷ Buddha; Culavamsa; Dipavamsa

Mahavastu (Mahāvastu) A Buddhist text, meaning literally the 'great account', which is an account of the life of the Buddha up to the time when his first disciples were converted. It emanates from a sub-sect of the

Mahasanghikas, and was probably written over a period of time centring on the beginning of the Common Era. It introduces a lot of information about the previous births of the Buddha. It also goes in a different direction from the Theravada view of the Buddha in that it stresses the Buddha's role as a purveyor of marvels. It sees the Buddha as being transcendent even before his Buddahood, and as an omniscient being who condescends to live in the world so that his life-events are all full of special significance. It also enlarges upon the theme of the bodhisattva, and describes the 10 stages that occur in the career of a bodhisattva. In some ways the Mahavastu foreshadows Mahayana ideas, but it also includes passages from Mahayana scriptures and must therefore still have been in the process of being finished when the Mahayana tradition arose in the 1st century CE. ▷ bodhisattva; Buddha; Jataka; Mahasanghika; Mahayana Buddhism; Theravada Buddhism

Mahavira (Mahāvīra) (c.540–468BCE) The title given by the Jain tradition to its effective founder. It means 'great hero' and was added to his own name of Vardhamana in the same way that his contemporary, the Buddha, had the title Buddha added to his own name of Gautama. The Mahavira, like the Buddha, was from the warrior caste; also like him he lived in the lower Ganges area of India and gave up the life of a householder to explore the meaning of life. At the age of 30 he left home to wander in the forest, talking to other philosophers and engaging in austerities to the extent of giving his clothes away and pulling out his hair. For 12 years he fasted and underwent penances in order to free his soul from entanglement with worldly activity, and by the age of 42 he had gained enlightenment, become a *jaina* ('one who had overcome'), and had begun to teach others. A group of followers formed around him, and his sayings, sermons and travel stories are preserved in the Jain scriptures. He is seen by Jains as the 24th and last in a succession of spiritual leaders known as *tirthankaras* ('ford-makers') who have lived in this cosmic age. Apart from him the others are lost to history. They are not viewed as divine, but as outstanding persons who have attained liberation in life and passed on its meaning and possibility to others. ▷ Buddha; cosmology, Jain; enlightenment; jiva, Jain; jivanmukti; karma, Jain; tirthankara

Mahayana Buddhism (Mahāyanā) (Sanskrit 'greater vehicle') The form of Buddhism commonly practised in China, Tibet, Mongolia, Nepal, Korea, and Japan. It dates from about the 1st century CE, when it arose as a more liberal development within Buddhism in Northern India. Emphasizing various forms of popular devotion based on its theory of the bodhisattvas, it believes that the aim of life is not to become perfect (a 'perfected saint') but to postpone this stage in order to help others towards enlightenment. In Mahayana the prime emotion is compassion, ranked equal to wisdom as a means of achieving enlightenment. The aim for followers is to become bodhisattvas and finally Buddhas. Different schools of Mahayana include Zen Buddhism, Nichiren Buddhism and Pure Land Buddhism, each of which lays emphasis on a different method of attaining spiritual perfection. ▷ bodhisattva; Buddhism

Mahayana Sutras (Mahāyāna Sūtras) The sacred texts of the Mahayana Buddhist tradition. The Mahayana tradition arose around the 1st century CE; it emphasized the importance of the supramundane Buddha as opposed to the historical Buddha; the compassionate bodhisattva who was willing to be reborn repeatedly for the sake of suffering humanity as opposed to the Theravada saint (*arahat*), who was more concerned with his own spiritual advancement; and the philosophy of emptiness and the universal salvation it opened up for everybody. These principles were enshrined within the *Mahayana Sutras*, a set of scriptures brought into being by the new Mahayana groups in India from their beginnings until the 6th century CE. They were seen as fulfilling the earlier suttas of the *tipitaka* or Pali Canon, which were regarded as preparation for the deeper teaching of the *Mahayana Sutras*. They were also seen as teachings of the still-existing Buddha, produced by wisdom and inspired by meditation, that had been kept hidden until the world was ready to receive them. They were written in Sanskrit, and some, such as the *Lotus Sutra*, *Diamond Sutra*, *Heart Sutra*, *Lankavatara Sutra* and *Pure Land Sutra*, are very well known. When translated into Chinese and Tibetan they had a deep influence upon those lands. ▷ arahat; bodhisattva; Buddha; Diamond Cutter Sutra; emptiness; Lankavatara Sutra; Lotus Sutra; Pure Land Buddhism; tipitaka

Mahdi (al-Mahdī) (Arabic, 'divinely guided one') The name given by Sunni Muslims to those who periodically revitalize the Muslim community. Sunnis look forward to a time before the Last Day when a Mahdi will appear and establish a reign of justice on earth. Shiites identify the Mahdi with the expected reappearance of the Hidden Imam. Many Muslim leaders have claimed the title, such as Muhammad Ahmed, who established a theocratic state in the Sudan in 1882. His great-grandson, Sadiq al-Mahdi, became Prime Minister of the Sudan in 1986. ▷ imam; Islam; Shiism; Sunnis

Maimonides, properly **Moses ben Maimon** (1135–1204) Jewish philosopher, and the foremost figure of medieval Judaism. Born in Cordoba, Spain (then under Moorish rule), he studied medicine and Greek philosophy, and settled eventually in Cairo about 1165 where he became physician to Saladin, sultan of Egypt, and head of the Jewish community. He wrote a Hebrew commentary on the Mishnah (Jewish code of law), but his other main writings are in Arabic. His greatest work is the *Guide to the Perplexed* (1190), which tries to harmonize the thought of Aristotle and Judaism. He was a very great influence on a range of philosophers and traditions, Jewish, Muslim and Christian. ▷ Aristotle; Judaism; Mishnah

Maitreya The name of the Buddha who is to come. This has distant analogies with the notion of the one who is to come in other religions such as the Jewish Messiah, the Second Coming of Christ, the Muslim Mahdi, and the Hindu incarnation or avatara of Vishnu who is to come. According to the Buddhist theory of history there have been past Buddhas, there was the Buddha of the present age who lived in India in the 6th century BCE, and there is the future Buddha Maitreya. He lives at present in the Tusita heaven, waiting for the time of his birth into this world. Maitreya means 'the kind one', and in Mahayana Buddhism he is revered as a bodhisattva who gives present help as an encourager to the faithful, to the departed, and to Buddhist masters who become discouraged. It is possible through deep meditation to gain access to the Tusita heaven and the presence of Maitreya. He has been known among all Buddhists in different Buddhist traditions from a very early period, and occasionally in parts of the Buddhist world the notion of his future coming has been a focus for Messianic-type movements. ▷ avatara; Mahayana Buddhism; Mahdi; Messiah; messianism; Vishnu

mala (mālā) An Indian term for a garland or wreath, often given to visitors or honoured guests as a mark of respect. In religious terms it often takes the form of a rosary which can be used as a help in meditation and prayer. In this sense it is a necklace of beads or knots which differ in make according to religious tradition. For example the rosary used by devotees of Vishnu is made up of *tulsi* beads, whereas the Sikh mala uses wool made into knots. Certain numbers are held to be important: for example, Sikh malas have 108 knots or 29 knots. Among some Hindu groups malas are held to have sacred powers and to be protective charms, but true devotees in all traditions see them not as ends in themselves but as aids towards a more effective worship of and communion with God. ▷ rosary; Vishnu

Malachi, or **Malachias, Book of** The last of the 12 so-called 'minor' prophetic writings of the Hebrew Bible/Old Testament; probably anonymous, since 'Malachi' in Hebrew means 'my messenger'; possibly the work of a 'cult prophet' in view of the strong criticism of priestly neglect of cultic requirements. Usually dated c.510–460BCE, in the period before the reforms of Ezra and Nehemiah, it stresses the need for faithfulness to the covenant with Yahweh, the need for fidelity in marriage, and the threat of a coming day of judgement. ▷ Old Testament; prophet; Yahweh

malaikah (malā'ikah) The notion of angels in the Islamic tradition. They are celestial beings created by God, who live in a celestial world commonly known as heaven. Four archangels stand at their head: Mikal (Michael); Jibril (Gabriel), who brought the revelation of the Quran to Muhammad; Israfil, who will blow the last trumpet at the end of time; and Izrail, the angel of death. Although angels, and especially archangels, are reckoned to be closer to God and higher than human beings, they are not considered to be higher than God's prophets, who were sent as messengers of humanity, nor do they have free will or the ability truly to know God as humans have. One of the angels, Iblis (or Satan), rebelled against God by refusing God's request that the angels should bow down to Adam, and it was Iblis who tempted Adam and Eve in the Garden of Eden. He thus became a fallen angel and was reduced to the state of a jinn, a subtle being. ▷ Adam and Eve; angels; Eden, Garden of; Gabriel; Iblis; jinn prophets in Islam; Quran

Malalasekara, Gunapala Pujasena (1899–1973) Buddhist, founder of the World Fellowship of Buddhists who had a deep influence upon the life of his homeland. Born in Punadura, Ceylon, he was educated in Colombo and London, and from 1942 to 1959 he held the Chair of Pali and Buddhist Studies at the University of Ceylon, expanding the Faculty of Oriental Studies during that period. From 1957 to 1967 he had ambassadorial responsibilities in the Soviet Union, Canada, the United Nations and the UK, and from 1967 to 1972 chaired the National Council of Higher Education in Sri Lanka. He wrote a number of books on Pali and Buddhism, and was the chief editor of the monumental *Encyclopaedia of Buddhism* which was begun in 1956. For 25 years he was President of the All-Ceylon Buddhist Congress, and he was Founder President of the World Fellowship of Buddhists from 1950 to 1958. This helped to unify Buddhists from Theravada and Mahayana schools around the world, to organize them to work for peace and social involvement on a world scale, and to give them a voice in world affairs. It fed into the 2500th anniversary of the founding of the Buddhist tradition (1956) and made Buddhism into a recognized world religion and world force. ▷ Buddhism; Mahayana Buddhism; Sinhalese Buddhism; Theravada Buddhism

Malcolm X (Malcolm Little) (1925–65) American black nationalist leader, born in Omaha, Nebraska, the son of a radical Baptist minister. He was brought up in Lansing, Michigan, and Boston. He was imprisoned for burglary in 1946 and in 1952, and while still in jail was converted to the Black Muslim sect led by Elijah Muhammad. On his release in 1953 he assumed the name Malcolm X and travelled the country promoting the sect. An opponent of the integrationist movement, he pressed for black separatism and advocated the use of violence in self-defence. In 1964, following a trip to Mecca, his views changed and he founded the Organization of Afro-American Unity, which blended elements of orthodox Islam, African socialism, anti-colonialism and racial solidarity. A factional feud ensued, culiminating in Malcolm X's assassination by Black Muslim enemies during a rally in Harlem in 1965. ▷ Black Muslims

Malebranche, Nicolas (1638–1715) French philosopher, born in Paris. He studied theology and joined the Catholic community of Oratorians in 1660, but was drawn to philosophy, particularly by Descartes' works. His own major work is *De la recherche de la verité* (1674), which espouses Descartes' dualism of mind and body but explains all causal interaction between them by a theory of 'occasionalism' (divine intervention, governing our bodily movements and all physical events), and argues as a corollary that 'we see all things in God' since external objects cannot act directly upon us. His other works include *Traité de la morale* (1684) and *Entretiens sur la métaphysique et la religion* (1688). ▷ Descartes, René; Oratorians

Malinowski, Bronislaw (1884–1942) Polish-born British anthropologist, born in Cracow, a founder of modern social anthropology. He studied physics and mathematics at the Jagellonian University, and went on to study psychology under Wilhelm Max Wundt at Leipzig, and sociology under Edvard Westermarck at London. In 1914 he left on a research assignment to Australia, but with the outbreak of war was partially confined to the Trobriand Islands, off the eastern tip of New Guinea. Returning to London in 1920, he was appointed in 1927 to the first chair in social anthropology at the London School of Economics. In 1938 he moved to the USA, where he taught at Yale University and undertook field research in Mexico. Malinowski is remembered as the originator of modern methods of ethnographic fieldwork, involving long periods of intensive participant observation. His works on the Trobriand Islanders, especially *Argonauts of the Western Pacific* (1922) and *Coral Gardens and their Magic* (2 vols, 1935), set new standards for ethnographic description that were emulated by his many students. His better-known writings on the Trobriands include *Crime and Custom in Savage Society* (1926) and *Sex and Repression in Savage Society* (1927). Malinowski was also a strong advocate of the theory of functionalism, as set out in *A Scientific Theory of Culture* (1944), according to which social and cultural institutions exist to satisfy basic human physiological and psychological needs.

Mamacocha Literally 'mother of waters', the sea goddess of the coastal Quechua of Peru. Naturally her goodwill was important to fisher folk and among marine peoples she held something of the importance of Pachacamac for the farming community. Other water sources were related to her (springs, for instance, were her 'daughters'). Under the Inca empire her worship was adopted into the imperial religious system. ▷ Inca religion; Pachacamac

Manasseh, Prayer of Short, eloquent writing of the Old Testament Pseudepigrapha (but often considered part of the Apocrypha even though not clearly in the Septuagint), ostensibly the work of Manasseh, a notoriously wicked king of Judah (c.687–642BCE), expressing his personal confession of sin and petition for pardon. Most scholars date the work from the 2nd century BCE to the 1st century CE, considering it a late elaboration based on parts of 2 Chronicles 33. ▷ Apocrypha, Old Testament; Pseudepigrapha; Septuagint

Manasseh, tribe of One of the 12 tribes of ancient Israel, said to be descended from Joseph's elder son, who with Ephraim was adopted by Jacob to share in his blessing (Genesis 48–9). Perhaps originally it was a half tribe. Its territory in central Palestine extended on both sides of the Jordan River, located between the tribes of Ephraim and Issachar in the west. ▷ Ephraim/Israel/Issachar/Joseph, tribe(s) of

Mandaeans A small Gnostic sect in Iran and Iraq who believe that the spiritual soul will be freed from its imprisonment in the evil material world by the redeemer, Manda d'Hayye ('the knowledge of life'). ▷ Gnosticism; sect; soul

mandala (maṇḍala) (literally 'circle') A mandala represents a complex geometric design which is used in Hindu and Buddhist rituals to represent the entire universe. Although mandalas initially appeared in Tantric writings, it is generally believed that they existed earlier than this. Those who have achieved the necessary levels of concentration are able to construct mandalas in their mind. Indeed, the mandala is believed to be a powerful centre of psychic energy, which is rendered distinct from the profane realm by a number of devices in its construction. To ensure this, particular rites are carried out during the drawing of a mandala, including the chanting of mantras. The visualization of mandalas, therefore, is believed to enable the devotee to tap into this power. A more specialized version is a *yantra* ('instrument' or 'engine') which is also used in Tantric worship, with each god or goddess being represented by their own yantra. Like mandalas, yantras are full of power and symbolism. ▷ mantra; Tantra; yantra

Mani (216–c.277) Prophet, and founder of the Manichaean religion, born in northern Babylonia to parents of Iranian descent. His father, Patteg, became a convert to an ascetic sect, known as 'those who wash themselves' (*almughtasila*), and Mani was brought up among this sect. Tradition has it that he received his first revelation as a boy, possibly in 228, from a spirit he describes as 'the Twin'. Around 240 the Twin appeared to him again, urging him to preach what he had learned. Mani first preached his faith to his immediate family, and then set out on a journey to the north-western part of the Indian subcontinent, where he apparently made many converts. He returned to Iran early in the reign of King Shahbuhr I (241–72). There he became a member of the king's court, and was allowed to preach in Persia, Parthia and adjacent lands. He wrote a compendium of his teachings, the *Shahbuhragan*, for King Shahbuhr, and converted one of the king's brothers, Mihrshah, King of Mesene. During this period he sent missions to many places, including Egypt and north-eastern parts of Iran. By the time of Shahbuhr's death, Manichaeism was felt to be a serious threat to Zoroastrianism in Iran. From the time of his return to Iran in the 240s, Mani's great adversary had been the Zoroastrian high priest Kirder, who eventually had Mani put in prison, where he died. ▷ Manichaeism; Zoroastrianism

Manichaeism, or **Manichaeanism** A religious sect founded by the prophet Manes (or Mani) (c.216–276), who began teaching in Persia in 240. His teaching was based on a primeval conflict between the realms of light and darkness, in which the material world represents an invasion of the realm of light by the powers of darkness. The purpose of religion is to release the particles of light imprisoned in matter, and Buddha, the prophets, Jesus, and finally Manes have been sent to help in this task. Release involved adherence to a strict ascetic regimen. The Zoroastrians condemned the sect and executed Manes, but it spread rapidly in the West, surviving until the 10th century. ▷ asceticism; Augustine, St (of Hippo); Buddha; Jesus Christ; prophet; Zoroastrianism

Manitou A word used by the Algonquin people of North America as a general designation of the spirit world. It may be translated as 'the supernatural' or 'the mysterious'. According to the context, it may be used of the spirits encountered in the vision quests of the higher powers of nature, or of the supreme being. The latter is sometimes referred to as Kitshi Manitou, 'the Great Spirit', sometimes simply as 'Manitou', 'the Spirit'. ▷ Algonquin religion; vision quest

Manjusri (Mañjuśrī) An important bodhisattva in Mahayana Buddhism who symbolizes insight and wisdom (*prajna*). He does not appear in the *tipitaka* or in the early Mahayana works, but after the 3rd century CE he is present in important scriptures such as the *Lankavatara Sutra* and the *Lotus Sutra*. He became popular in China, where one of the five great mountains, Mount Wutai, became associated with him (it is still important today, with over 30 Buddhist temples being open on its highest slopes). Manjusri is portrayed in Buddhist art as having a five-pointed tiara on his head, a sword of knowledge in one hand, and a book symbolizing wisdom in the other. He is concerned to help all beings to obtain release from the round of rebirths, he appears to his followers in visions and dreams, and he lives in different Buddha-fields. Very wise rulers have sometimes been considered to be incarnations of him. As the bodhisattva of wisdom, Manjusri's counterpart is Avalokiteshvara, the bodhisattva of compassion; the two qualities are seen to be equal in Mahayana Buddhism. ▷ Avalokiteshvara; bodhisattva; Lankavatara Sutra; Lotus Sutra; Mahayana Buddhism; tipitaka

mantike The Greek term for divination, a fundamental element in Greek religion. It took very different forms. There were fixed oracles, such as Apollo's at Delphi (even at these, the techniques employed varied greatly), and there were also 'portable' forms of divination, such as consultation of the entrails of sacrificial animals. Greeks used mantike not in order to peer into the future, but to seek the 'advice' of the gods about particular decisions that had to be made: whether to marry, for instance, or undertake a trading expedition, or go to war. At a different level, divination underpinned the whole structure of Greek religion: since there were no inspired or sacred books, it was only through divination that knowledge of the will of the gods could be acquired. ▷ Delphi; Delphi, Oracle of; divination; Greek religion; oracle

mantra (literally 'sacred utterance') This represents the prescribed formulae or words of power which are present in all Hindu rituals, their correct recitation being vital to the efficacy of such rites. Its length can vary from a single syllable, such as *om*, to a full-length hymn. The notion of the mantra lies in the belief that there are magical properties inherent in sound, and as such mantras do not have to convey actual meaning to the worshipper. To orthodox Hindus valid mantras come only from the Vedas—that is the *shruti* texts which are regarded as direct revelation—and as such are believed to put the adherent in touch with eternal reality, the mantra conveying its essence. Indeed, the properties believed to be inherent in mantras are such that no one is permitted to perform them unless they have received the correct initiation (*diksha*). A mantra only gains its power when passed from the guru to the *sishya* (pupil) in this process of initiation. For orthodox Hindus this is only available to members of the 'twice-born' classes.

In Hindu Tantrism, the notion of the mantra was developed further. The idea of initiation is still present, although in Tantra it is the guru, not the mantra itself, that holds the power. Unlike orthodox or vedic Hinduism, in Tantra the possession of mantras is open to all.

Mantras are the equivalent in sound of the visual mandalas and *yantras*. Mantras are used in ritual by Tantrics to deify themselves by ascribing them to certain parts of the body. Moreover, it is believed that each deity has both a visual and a sonic form. Mantras play a part in personal salvation as it is believed that their recitation can generate the necessary compassion from the supreme God for the adherent to escape from the cycle of rebirth (*samsara*). ▷ mandala; Om; samsara; shruti; Tantra

Manu, Laws of Manu is a mythical figure, variously represented as the progenitor of man and the father of all moral and social law. To him are attributed some of Hinduism's great legal works, called the *Manusmriti*, which consist (as extant) of 2685 verses in 12 books. These texts provide the first systematization of Hindu law and are held as absolutely binding. Generally they provide divine sanction for the caste system and a theoretical framework for the juridical interpretation of the *Brahmanas* and Vedas, as well as elucidating the dharma of kingship. ▷ Brahmanas and Aranyakas; dharma; Kshatriyas; Veda

Maoism Specifically, the thought of Mao Zedong (Tse-tung), and more broadly a revolutionary ideology based on Marxism-Leninism adapted to Chinese conditions. Maoism shifted the focus of revolutionary struggle from the urban workers or proletariat to the countryside and the peasantry. There were three main elements: strict Leninist principles of organization, Chinese tradition, and armed struggle as a form of revolutionary activity. Mao gained political power in 1949 through a peasant army, his slogan being 'Political power grows through the barrel of a gun'. While there were attempts to take account of the views of the masses, the Chinese Communist Party was organized along strict centralist, hierarchical lines, and increasingly became a vehicle for a personal dictatorship. In domestic terms Mao pursued a radical and far-reaching attempt to transform traditional Chinese society and its economy, using thought reform, indoctrination, and the psychological transformation of the masses. Maoism was regarded in the 1960s at the height of the Cultural Revolution as a highly radical form of Marxism-Leninism that was distinct from the bureaucratic repression of the Soviet Union, and had a strong appeal among the New Left. Since Mao Zedong's death, his use of the masses for political purposes, his economic reforms, and his conception of political power have been increasingly criticized inside and outside China as seriously misguided and too rigid. ▷ Mao Zedong; Marxism-Leninism; secular alternatives to religion

Maori religion The Maori are a Polynesian people who, because of long isolation, developed their own civilization while retaining the general features of an East Polynesian world view. This includes a power-packed universe, in which all, or at least all the well-born, shared in *mana*, the most powerful chiefs and leaders partaking of it in high degree. This mana was fenced round with a system of *tapu* (*tabu*) or ritual prohibitions, which regulated daily life. But mana extends beyond human relations into a universe of spiritual beings. This universe has two spheres. Te Rangi is the sphere of sky, heaven, day and light; Te Po the sphere of night, dark, the underworld. The two spheres are always in tension, but they are complementary rather than opposed, and creative forces arise from their relationships. It is an open universe, in constant evolution, a stream of processes and events. The forces in the spiritual universe are *atua*, a word with a wide range of meaning. Knowledge of the atua in myth was the subject of an expert tradition, carefully passed down to suitable candidates, but no concern of the general population. For most people, active religion was essentially the proper observance of tapu: there were no temples. Even among specialists (*tohunga*) there was a wide range of status. Low grade atua need only low grade tohunga. Only the lower atua have mediums who give knowledge in trance. The highest knowledge is passed to the worthy in the shape of myth, and the highest tohunga are prophets who deliver their oracles in short song form (*karakia*). The majority of Maori became Christians in the 19th century, giving rise to modifications in the tapu system and a series of new religious movements. ▷ atua; tabu

Mao Zedong (Mao Tse-tung) (1893–1976) Chinese Communist leader, first Chairman (1949) of the People's Republic, born in the village of Shaoshan in Hunan province, the son of a peasant farmer. Educated at Changsha, he went in 1918 to the University of Peking (Beijing), where as a library assistant he studied the works of Marx and others and helped found the Chinese Communist party (CCP) in 1921.

Seeing the need to adapt communism to Chinese conditions, seeking a rural, rather than urban-based, revolution, he set up a Communist 'people's republic' (soviet) at Jiangxi in South-East China between 1931 and 1934. The soviet defied the attacks of Chiang Kai-shek's forces until 1934, when Mao and his followers were obliged to uproot themselves and undertake an arduous and circuitous 'Long March' (1934–6) to Shaanxi province in North-West China. During this march, Mao was elected CCP chairman at the Zunyi conference of February 1935. At the new headquarters of Yanan he set about formulating a unique Communist philosophy which stressed the importance of ideology, re-education and 'rectification', and, in 1939, he married his third wife, Jiang Qing. By employing the tactic of mobile, rural-based guerrilla warfare, Mao's Communists successfully resisted the Japanese between 1937 and 1945, and on their collapse issued forth to shatter the Nationalist régime of Chiang Kai-shek and proclaim the People's Republic of China in Beijing in 1949.

Mao resigned the chairmanship of the Republic in 1959, but remained chairman of the CCP's politburo until his death. During the early 1960s an ideological rift developed between Mao and Khrushchev, with Mao opposing the latter's policy of peaceful co-existence with the West and the USSR's volte-face during the Cuban missile crisis (1962). This developed into a formal split in 1962 when the USSR supplied fighter aircraft to India during the brief Sino-Indian border war of that year. Domestically Mao's influence waned during the early 1960s as a result of the failure of the 1958–60 'Great Leap Forward', the experiment of rapid agricultural and industrial advance through the establishment of giant communes. However, the 'Great Helmsman' re-established his dominance during the 1966–9 'Cultural Revolution', a 'rectification' campaign directed against liberal, 'revisionist' forces. Concerned with the anarchic 'Red Guard' excesses, he then, working closely with Zhou Enlai, his premier, oversaw a period of reconstruction from 1970. During his final years, however, when beset by deteriorating health, his political grip weakened.

Mao's writings and thoughts, set out in *New Democracy* (1940) and, most popularly, in his *Little Red Book*, dominated the functioning of the People's Republic between 1949 and 1976. He stressed the need for reducing rural-urban differences and for 'perpetual revolution' to prevent the emergence of new élites. Overseas, Mao, after precipitating the Sino-Soviet split of 1960–2, became a firm advocate of a non-aligned 'Third World' strategy. Since 1978, the new Chinese leadership of Deng Xiaoping has begun to re-interpret Maoism and has criticized its policy excesses. However, many of Mao's ideas remain influential in contemporary China. ▷ Maoism; Marx, Karl; Marxism; Marxism-Leninism; secular alternatives to religion

Mara (Māra) (Buddhist) The notion of the tempter or the evil one in Buddhist thought. Although vaguely analogous to the concept of the devil elsewhere, Mara has no ultimate reality or ontological significance. He appeared to the Buddha at the time of his quest for enlightenment in a series of temptations that have a distant resemblance to the temptations of Christ. The Buddha was tempted by Mara to put his bodily comforts and sensual desires first, and to follow the path of rituals. He overcame these temptations by putting ethical and spiritual priorities first and by committing himself to his chosen path. After his enlightenment, he was tempted to keep his tremendous experience to himself and not to preach it to others, and he was also tempted to return to the ascetic life instead of following the way of service and spiritual insight. Again he overcame the temptations of Mara. Belief in Mara provided a link from the popular belief in demons to a more sophisticated way of understanding the possible difficulties in the way of gaining a true insight into the nature of things. It became, so to speak, a psychological help, and the Buddha's spiritual victory over Mara was an exemplary model for strengthening the faith of the early Buddhist community. ▷ bodhi; Buddha; enlightenment; Satan; temptation

Mara (Mar'a) (Islamic) The Muslim Arabic word for woman. Early Islam gave women greater rights than they had had before, and there is some evidence that their situation declined under the Abbasid caliphs (750–1258) before beginning to revive in modern times. According to classical Islam men and women were spiritually equal before God, but were not socially or legally equal. Due partly to the rise, in parts of the Muslim world, of the veiling of women, and of the custom of living in harems, they took little part in public affairs, and exercised their main influence on family life behind the scenes. Islamic modernism in recent times has reinterpreted the Quranic teaching on women's roles and has introduced Western notions of individual freedom, human rights and natural justice to the debate about women's rights. During this century secular laws in various Muslim states have increased the possibilities open to women. Even in earlier centuries the situation differed in different parts of the Islamic world—for example, among the Berbers of North Africa women have traditionally known a good measure of social freedom. ▷ Abbasids; Allah; harem; Islamic modernism; Quran; veiling

Marcionism The teaching of the Gnostic Marcion (d.c.160), holding that Christianity had no connection with Judaism and that the God revealed in the Old Testament was quite unlike the God of the New Testament. He held that the Old Testament was not a Christian book and that the New Testament should be purified of Jewish elements. On this basis Marcion compiled the first known canon of scripture, which he limited to a shortened version of Luke and 10 edited epistles of Paul. The term 'marcionism' is also applied more generally to denote deliberate or benign neglect of the Old Testament in the Christian Church. ▷ canon

Mardana (Mardāna) (1459–1534) A lifelong companion of the first Sikh guru, Guru Nanak, who, like him, was born in the village of Talwandi in the Punjab, India. A 'low-caste' Muslim, his skills lay in providing music at festivals and ritual occasions. Able to offer musical accompaniment to the poems and spiritual presentations of the guru, he became a useful adjunct, and together they travelled for over 20 years around India (and according to tradition around the world) before returning to the Punjab and settling down in Kartarpur to set up an exemplary community. The friendship of the Muslim Mardana with Guru Nanak symbolized the guru's desire to bridge the gap between different religions and social classes. ▷ Kartarpur; Nanak; Punjab

Marduk Ancient Babylonian national god. Originally patron of the city of Babylon, Marduk later became the supreme god of the

Marduk

Babylonian pantheon, taking over many of the functions of Enlil. Like Enlil he was sometimes called Bel ('lord'). He was also a god of magic associated with Ea, and was frequently appealed to in incantations for healing the sick. He takes the principal part in the Babylonian creation epic *Enuma Elish*, which describes his victory over the primal chaos waters personified by the dragon Tiamat, and his subsequent elevation to kingship over the gods. An agricultural aspect of his nature is indicated by his symbol, the hoe or spade. His consort was called Sarpanitum and his son, the god Nabu of Borsippa near Babylon, was patron of writing and scribal wisdom. Marduk was popular even when Babylon was in decline and was honoured in Assyrian and Persian royal inscriptions. ▷ Akitu; Babylonian religion; cosmogony, Ancient Near Eastern; Ea; Enlil; Tiamat

Marett, Robert Ranulph (1866–1943) British anthropologist, born in Jersey. He studied classics and philosophy at Balliol College, Oxford and German philosophy at Berlin. He was admitted to the Bar in Jersey in 1891 but he had already developed an interest in anthropology and, after becoming a fellow of Exeter College, Oxford in 1891, he progressively pursued this line of enquiry. He obtained his doctorate in 1909 and in 1910 he became Reader in Anthropology at Oxford, where he founded the Department of Anthropology. He also became rector of Exeter College in 1928, and after his retirement he continued as rector until his death. He wrote a number of influential books, including *The Threshold of Religion* (1909), *The Birth of Humility* (1910), *Anthropology* (1912), *Psychology and Folklore* (1920), *Man in the Making* (1928), *The Raw Material of Religion* (1929), *Faith, Hope and Charity in Primitive Religion* (1932), *Sacraments of Simple Folk* (1933), *Head, Heart and Hands in Human Evolution* (1935), and *Tylor* (1936). Marett became famous for his theory of pre-animism or dynamism in which he went beyond Tylor's theory of animism and Frazer's theory of magic. He argued that religion begins with a sense of awe in the face of a religious force that is felt and experienced rather than thought about and reasoned out. Thus religion starts with a supernatural stage, and before long Marett was using the Melanesian term *mana* as a useful word to describe the religious force at work. His work influenced anthropological theory and also the work of Otto and Van der Leeuw. ▷ anthropology of religion; Frazer, Sir James George; Otto, Rudolf; Tylor, Sir Edward Burnet; Leeuw, Gerhardus Van der

Mari The most important city on the middle Euphrates in the third and second millennia BCE until its destruction c.1759BCE by the Babylonians. It was the centre of a vast trading network in north-west Mesopotamia. Since 1933, c.20000 cuneiform tablets dating from c.18th century BCE have been discovered, providing a great deal of information about the period. Although no mention is made of any actual biblical character or place, several offer interesting parallels to practices in the patriarchal period of Israel's history.

Maria Legio (Legion of Mary Church) An African Independent church originating among the Kenya Luo of southern Nyanza, in the Catholic diocese of Kisii. The leaders, recipients of visions, were Simeo Ondeto, later called 'Holy Father' and a 20-year-old married woman, Gaudencia Aoko, who had been traumatized by the death of her children. The movement owed its shape to Catholic devotional societies and has continued the use of crucifixes and rosaries as well as adopting a hierarchical system with bishops and a cardinal. After its public emergence in 1963, however, it became strongly anti-Roman, adopted Protestant features in the use of the Bible and women's ministry, and the common features of African Independent churches as regards prophecy and healing. The movement is probably the largest African secession from the Catholic Church and one of the few large-scale prophetic movements to arise after 1960 (it was estimated to have 90000 initial members). ▷ African Independent churches

Mark, Gospel according to The second book of the New Testament canon, the shortest of the four gospels, and argued by many scholars also to be the earliest; although anonymous it has been traditionally attributed to John Mark. Because it contains less teaching material than the other Gospels, it places relatively greater emphasis on Jesus's passion, and draws attention to the mystery of his role and activities. It is noteworthy also for its abrupt beginning (compared with the other Gospels) and for disputes concerning the original ending of the Gospel. ▷ Gospels, canonical; Mark, St; New Testament

Mark, St (1st century) New Testament evangelist, more fully, 'John, whose surname was Mark', traditionally the author of the second canonical Gospel. Mark accompanied St Paul and Barnabas on their first missionary journey, but left them at Perga. He was later reconciled with Paul, and, according to tradition, was the 'disciple and interpreter' of Peter in Rome. He is also said to have gone to Alexandria as preacher. In medieval art Mark is symbolized by the lion. His feast day is 25 April. ▷ evangelist; New Testament; Paul, St; Peter, St

Maronite Church A Christian community originating in Syria in the 7th century, claiming origin from St Maro (died 407). Condemned for its Monothelite beliefs in 680, the Church survived in Syria and elsewhere, and since 1182 has been in communion with the Roman Catholic Church.

Marpa (Mar-pa) (1012–96) Tibetan holy man, to whom the founding of the Kagyupa order was retrospectively attributed. A layman, not a monk, he learned Sanskrit from Drogmi (992–1072, the founder of the Sakyapa order) at Myung-lung monastery, and then travelled to India where he studied Buddhist teachings for 16 years. He became a disciple of the siddha Naropa from whom he received the teachings of the six yogas. He also received Mahamudra meditation teachings from another master (guru/lama) before returning to Tibet. There he took up the life of a married householder, passing on the teachings he had received for a substantial fee. Among his disciples the most famous was Milarepa. Marpa is regarded as a siddha and as having magical powers. ▷ guru; Kagyupa; lama; Milarepa; Naropa; siddhas

marrano The name given to Spanish Jews whose conversion to Christianity was mistrusted. Encouraged by a spirit of toleration, Jewish culture and religion flourished in Spain during the 13th and 14th centuries; but when, in the 1390s, Jews supported the losing side in a civil war, anti-Jewish violence flared up. As a result, large numbers of Jews, including many of their leaders, became Christians through fear. Some of these *conversos* were given important jobs in both State and Church, including participation in public debates with those who remained true to Jewish belief and practice. However, despite initial acceptance many Christians began to suspect that conversos were remaining secret Jews. Thus anti-converso violence broke out in the mid 1400s, and the converts were dubbed marranos from the Spanish word for 'swine'. When the Spanish Inquisition was established (1480) to investigate all forms of heresy, those marranos accused of remaining Jewish did not fare well; many thousands were burned alive in subsequent decades. Hatred also continued to be directed towards those who had remained faithful to Judaism, and in 1492 a decree was issued expelling all such Jews from Spain. That summer some 100000–150000 Jews left Spain to settle in other parts of Europe and North Africa. ▷ Diaspora Judaism; Judaism in Europe; Nahmanides

marriage/divorce The union of men and women in marriage is a universal cultural institution, although the forms and functions of the marriage relationship differ from society to society. For either sex marriage may involve more than one partner. In many cultures an adult is not considered complete if he or she is not married. Divorce is the act by which a marriage is dissolved. The degree to which divorce is prohibited in a society is determined by its understanding of the nature of marriage.

marriage/divorce, Christian In the Christian view marriage is an honourable estate, ordained by God (Genesis 1 and 2) and blessed by Jesus Christ (John 2), that exists for fellowship, companionship, and the procreation of children. It involves lifelong faithfulness between one man and one woman (monogamy) until they are parted by death. Divorce—allowed for the sole reason of unchastity by Jesus Christ in Matthew's Gospel (Matthew 19.3,9) but not in Mark's (Mark 10.2–12; see Luke 16.18)—is allowed, in certain circumstances, by some churches. Roman Catholicism, which holds marriage to be a sacrament and indissoluble, has legal (nullity) procedures for declaring apparent marriages never to have taken place.

Views in Anglican and Protestant churches on the remarriage of divorced persons are divided. Some would forbid it in the interests of maintaining a firm stand against secular trends; others would take a more pastoral approach and examine each case on its own merits, seeking to avoid the criticism that the Church was appearing to make divorce the only unforgivable sin, and stressing the interests of the particular individuals concerned. Others again would take one approach on this issue with lay people and apply higher standards to the clergy as exemplars of the Christian life.

Marriage, in the view of the apostle Paul (1 Corinthians 7), may sometimes be forgone in order to serve God unfettered by the responsibilities of family life. This is the case with monasticism and the unmarried priesthood of the Roman Catholic Church (where it is compulsory). Luther and the Reformers dismissed the idea that the unmarried state was superior (a view linked with negative attitudes to sex) or that priests, monks and nuns were called to reach higher standards than other Christians. In their view each Christian had to be faithful to his or her call or vocation, whether it was to be in the married state or not. ▷ rites of passage, Christian view of; Christianity and sex

marriage/divorce, Islamic Marriages are arranged in most parts of the Islamic world. They are effected by a contract, and confirmed by a bride dowry and by the bride's consent given in the presence of witnesses. The venue of marriage may often not be a mosque but a private house or a judge's office. The Fatihah (the opening part of the Quran) is recited at the ceremony, and is sometimes followed by a wedding procession, and usually by a reception and feast. Divorce occurs in Islam in three ways: through the repudiation of the wife by the husband, which is legal at the end of three months; through the consent of husband and wife; and through judicial dissolution of the marriage by a court on the request of the wife on grounds of apostasy, madness, etc. In recent times in various lands civil laws have attempted to give more protection than the Muslim shariah courts to women, who can be divorced by a single repudiation on the husband's part. Another recent complication is that Muslim men can legally marry non-Muslim women, but not vice versa, and when Muslim women marry outside Islam according to civil law, this may not be acceptable in Muslim law. ▷ Fatihah; Quran; shariah

marriage/divorce, Jewish Traditionally, marriage is greatly esteemed in Judaism and celibacy is rare. It has three purposes: procreation, fellowship, and maintenance of family life. Around these aims the rabbis formulated regulations based on Leviticus 18 and 20. Several are noteworthy as peculiarly Jewish, eg the law of the agunah. This prohibits remarriage of a woman whose husband is missing without proof of his death. In contrast, divorce has always been permitted within Judaism, although discouraged. A *get* (certificate of divorce) must be issued by a rabbinical court, and in modern times a civil dissolution is also required. The tradition maintains that both partners in marriage should be Jewish and has, from the Middle Ages, insisted on monogamy.

The Jewish marriage service contains two elements which at one time took place a year apart. The ceremony, which must avoid certain points in the Jewish calendar (eg a Shabbat or holy day), is held under a huppah (canopy) either in the synagogue or outdoors. The first part of the service, qiddushin (consecration), renders the marriage legal by the giving of vows and a ring, as well as recitation of special blessings. Then the ketuvah (marriage contract) is read out, originally intended to guarantee a sum of money to the wife upon divorce or bereavement. The second part of the ceremony, nissuin (nuptials), involves further blessings and praise of God as the creator of marital bliss. Finally, the groom smashes a glass in remembrance of Jerusalem and its destruction (see Psalms 137.5–6), and then the celebrations begin. In the period when nissuin was a separate service this was the time for consummation to take place.

In Jewish tradition sexual intercourse is considered a gift from God, although forbidden during menstruation (Leviticus 18.19). However, such laws, including that of the agunah, have been relaxed or discarded by the Reform movement as inessential to Judaism; there is also a greater tolerance of mixed marriages. Further, affirming the validity of different ways of life, Reform Judaism has recently sought to integrate single and homosexual people into the Jewish community. ▷ Judaism, women in; menstruation, Jewish attitude to; Orthodox Judaism

Mars The Roman god of war, second only to Jupiter. The month of March is named after him. His mythology is borrowed from Ares, though various annual ceremonies at

Rome indicate that he was originally an agricultural deity who guarded the fields. ▷ Ares; Roman religion

Martineau, James (1805–1900) English Unitarian theologian, born in Norwich, brother of Harriet Martineau. Educated at the grammar school there and under Dr Lant Carpenter at Bristol, he became a Unitarian minister at Dublin and Liverpool until 1841, when he was appointed Professor of Mental and Moral Philosophy at Manchester New College. He left for London in 1857, after the New College had been transferred there, becoming also a pastor in Little Portland Street Chapel. He was later principal of the London college (1869–85). One of the profoundest thinkers and most effective writers of his day, his works include *Endeavours after the Christian Life* (1843–7), *A Study of Spinoza* (1882), *Types of Ethical Theory* (1885), *A Study of Religion* (1888), and *The Seat of Authority in Religion* (1890). ▷ Unitarians

Marty, Martin Emil (1928–) American Church historian, born in West Point, Nebraska. He had an extensive theological training before taking a PhD at Chicago University. Ordained in the Lutheran Church in 1952, he ministered in Illinois, then was appointed Professor of the History of Modern Christianity at Chicago in 1963. A versatile scholar, he was also one of the editors of the liberal *Christian Century* (1956–85), and a well-received lecturer in Roman Catholic and moderate evangelical circles. Among his many books are *A Short History of Christianity* (1959), *Second Chance for American Protestants* (1963), *Righteous Empire* (1970), *Health and Medicine in the Lutheran Tradition* (1983), and *Protestantism in the United States* (1985). ▷ Lutheranism

martyr Literally a witness, from the Greek *martus* meaning 'witness'. The Christian sense of the term originally applied to those apostles who were eye-witnesses to the life and death of Christ. However, as the Church underwent persecution by the Roman authorities, the term was applied to those who witnessed for their faith by undergoing suffering and death. The Islamic use of the term martyr is similar. A martyr is someone who is killed in a holy war (jihad) against unbelievers. In many faiths martyrs are revered, occupying a high place in heaven and acting as heroic figures of inspiration for the faithful. ▷ apostle; jihad; Christianity, persecution of

martyr, Sikh The Sikh tradition began through the ministry of Guru Nanak (1469–1539) in the Punjab in India, and his aim was to spread religious harmony, work for peace, and offer spiritual liberation to all people. Due to the changing situation within the Mughal Empire the Sikhs found themselves subject to severe persecution, and in these circumstances martyrdom became inevitable and significant. The first exemplary martyr was the fifth guru, Guru Arjan (1563–1606), who had lived at peace under Akbar. When Jehangir succeeded Akbar in 1605, Guru Arjan was arrested, and he died in Mughal hands. The ninth guru, Guru Tegh Bahadur (1621–75), was also killed by the Mughals. Numerous other Sikhs died in Mughal times and later rather than abjure their faith. They are known as *shaheeds* and are honoured within the Sikh tradition. As the *Guru Granth Sahib* 698 puts it, 'they attain glory both here and hereafter'. ▷ Arjan, Guru; Guru Granth Sahib; Mughal empire; Nanak; Tegh Bahadur, Guru

Marx, Karl (1818–83) German social, political and economic theorist, the inspiration of modern, international communism. He was born and brought up in Trier in a Jewish family which the father converted to Protestantism to escape anti-Semitism. He studied at the universities of Bonn (1835–6) and Berlin (1836–41), where he associated with the radical followers of Hegel, 'the young Hegelians', who were concerned particularly with the critique of religion. His own doctoral dissertation was on 'The Difference between the Philosophies of Nature in Democritus and Epicurus'. In 1842 he worked as a journalist and then editor of the liberal Cologne paper *Rheinische Zeitung*, but in 1843 the paper was suppressed by the government (which it regularly and virulently attacked) and Marx emigrated to Paris where he became a communist and first stated his belief that the proletariat must itself be the agent of revolutionary change in society. He wrote here his first long critique of capitalism, usually called *Economic and Philosophical Manuscripts of 1844* (not published until 1932), which develops the important Marxist notion of the alienation of man under capitalism. He also began in Paris his lifelong friendship with Friedrich Engels. Under political pressure he moved on to Brussels in 1845, and in collaboration with Engels wrote the posthumously published *German Ideology*, a full statement of his materialist conception of history, and the famous *Communist Manifesto* (1848), a masterpiece of political propaganda which ends with the celebrated rallying-cry 'The workers have nothing to lose but their chains. They have a world to win. Workers of all lands, unite!' After the 1848 revolution in Paris he returned to Cologne as editor of the radical *Neue Rheinische Zeitung*, but when that folded in 1849 he temporarily abandoned his political activism and took refuge with his family in London. They lived in some poverty, but in the reading room of the British Museum he began the researches which led to the publication of his major works of economic and political analysis: *Grundrisse der Kritik der politischen Ökonomie* (1857–8, published in Moscow 1939–41), *Zur Kritik der politischen Ökonomie* (1859), and most notably *Das Kapital* (Volume 1, 1867). This last was his magnum opus (two further volumes were added in 1884 and 1894) and one of the most influential works of the 19th century. In it he develops his mature doctrines of the theory of surplus value, class conflict and the exploitation of the working class, and predicted the supersession of capitalism by socialism and the ultimate 'withering away' of the state as the classless society of communism was achieved. The role of the communist was to ease the birth-pangs of this historical evolution: 'Philosophers have previously tried to explain the world, our task is to change it'. Marx was supported in his research over these years by his collaborator, Engels, and he eked out his income by journalistic work from 1825 to 1862 as European correspondent for the *New York Daily Tribune*. He later revived his political involvement and was a leading figure in the First International (Working-men's Association) from 1864 until its effective demise in 1872 when the anarchist followers of Mikhail Bakunin split off. The last decade of his life was marked by increasing ill-health. On his death he was buried in Highgate cemetery, London. Many of his specific predictions and doctrines have been falsified by history, and 'Marxism' has been shown in practice often to have abhorrent social and political implications; but his general theories still exert an enormous influence on social science, and the secular adherents of 'Marxism' have often outnumbered the followers of almost any other religious or political creed. ▷ anti-Semitism; Hegel, Georg Wilhelm Friedrich; Protestantism; Marxism; secular alternatives to religion

Marxism The body of social and political thought informed by the writings of Karl Marx. It is essentially a critical analysis of capitalist society, contending that such societies are subject to crises which create the conditions for proletarian revolutions and the transformation to socialism. Much of Marx's writing, especially *Das Kapital*, was concerned with the economic dynamics of capitalist societies, seeing the state as an instrument of class rule supporting private capital and suppressing the masses. Because of private capital's need to earn profits or extract surplus value, wages have to be kept to a subsistence minimum. This produces economic contradictions, because it restricts the purchasing power of workers to consume the goods produced. Capitalism is, therefore, inherently unstable, being subject to crises of booms and slumps. Marx's view was that these crises would become increasingly worse, and eventually lead to revolution, whereby the working class would seize the state and establish a dictatorship of the proletariat, productive power would be in public hands, and class differences would disappear (socialism). This classless society would eventually lead to the withering away of the state, producing a communist society. Marxism has sought to popularize and extend this method of analysis to contemporary conditions. In particular, Western Marxism has examined the impact of state intervention in smoothing out the crises of capitalism and establishing a legitimacy for the existing capitalist order through its control over education and the media. In non-industrialized societies Marxism has been adapted to account for revolution in countries where there is no extensive development of capitalism, in contrast to Marx's view of history. It is generally recognized that Marx's writings regarding the transformation to socialism and the nature of socialism lacked detail. In consequence, Marxism has adopted a wide range of interpretations. ▷ dialectical materialism; Marx, Karl; secular alternatives to religion

Marxism-Leninism A distinct variant of Marxism formulated by Lenin, who prior to the Bolshevik revolution argued for direct rule by workers and peasants, and advocated direct democracy through the soviets (councils). In practice, the Bolshevik revolution did not produce a democratic republic, but gave a 'leading and directing' role to the party, seen as the vanguard of a working class which had insufficient political consciousness to forge a revolution; such a well-organized and disciplined party, operating according to the principles of democratic centralism, would be able to exploit the revolutionary situation. Leninist principles of a revolutionary vanguard have become the central tenet of all communist parties. All are organized according to the idea of democratic centralism which affords the leadership, on the grounds of their revolutionary insight, the right to dictate party policy, to select party officials from above, and to discipline dissenting party members. Lenin modified Marx's theory of historical materialism, contending that revolutionary opportunities should be seized when they arose, and not when the social and economic conditions of capitalist crisis leading to proletarian revolution existed. He also developed a theory of imperialism which held that it was the last stage of a decaying capitalism. This was used to justify revolution in feudal Russia, because it was an imperial power, and since then to justify communist intervention in underdeveloped countries as part of the struggle between socialism and imperialism. ▷ communism; Lenin, Vladmir Ilyich; Maoism; Marxism; secular alternatives to religion

Mary, also entitled **Our Lady** or **the Blessed Virgin Mary** (d.c.63) Mother of Jesus Christ. In the New Testament she is most prominent in the stories of Jesus's birth (Matthew and Luke) where the conception of Jesus is said to be 'of the Holy Spirit' (Matthew 1.18), and she is described as betrothed to Joseph. She only occasionally appears in Jesus's ministry, but in John 19.25 she is at the Cross and is committed to the care of one of the disciples. According to the Acts of the Apostles, she remained in Jerusalem during the early years of the Church, and a tradition places her tomb in Jerusalem. She has become a subject of devotion in her own right, especially in Roman Catholic doctrine and worship, and apocryphal traditions were attached to her in works such as the Gospel of Mary and Gospel of the Birth of Mary. The belief that her body was taken up into heaven is celebrated in the festival of the Assumption, defined as Roman Catholic dogma in 1950. Her Immaculate Conception has been a dogma since 1854. Belief in the apparitions of the Virgin at Lourdes, Fatima, and in several other places attracts many thousands of pilgrims each year. In Roman Catholic and Orthodox Christianity, she holds a special place as an intermediary between humankind and God. ▷ Assumption; cross; Immaculate Conception; Jesus Christ; New Testament; Orthodox Church; Roman Catholicism

Mary Magdalene New Testament character; Magdalene possibly means 'of Magdala', in Galilee. Luke 8.2 reports that Jesus exorcized seven evil spirits from her; thereafter she appears only in the narratives of Jesus's passion and resurrection where, seemingly with other women, she appears at the Cross and later at the empty tomb. John 20 relates a private encounter with the resurrected Jesus (Matthew 28.9). Her identification with Mary the sister of Martha (John 11–12) is very tenuous. ▷ Cross; Jesus Christ; New Testament

Mascall, Eric Lionel (1905–) English Anglo-Catholic theologian, and author. He read mathematics for four years at Cambridge with the intention of making his career as an applied mathematician. An interest in philosophy led him to theology, however, and he was ordained priest in 1932. After a few years in parish work he became sub-warden of Lincoln Theological College where he remained for eight years. From 1946 to 1962 he was tutor in theology and university lecturer in the philosophy of religion at Christ Church, Oxford, and (1962–73) Professor of Historical Theology at London University. His books *He Who Is* (1943) and *Existence and Analogy* (1949) have acquired the role of textbooks on natural theology. His other works include *Christian Theology and Natural Science* (Oxford Bampton Lectures, 1956) on the relations of theology and science, the ecumenical *The Recovery of Unity* (1958), *The Christian Universe* (1966), *Nature and Supernature* (1976), *Whatever Happened to the Human Mind* (1980), *Theology and the Gospel of Christ* (2nd ed 1984) and *The Triune God* (1986). ▷ Anglo-Catholicism; theology

masks A form of disguise usually worn over the face to disguise the identity of the wearer. Masks feature in many religious rituals throughout the world and possess a rich variety of meanings. The term mask can be widened to cover any headpiece, or depiction

Amerindian mask

of a face, irrespective of whether or not it is worn over the face.

Masoretes, or Massoretes (Hebrew 'transmitters of tradition') Jewish scholars considered responsible for preserving traditions regarding the text of the Hebrew Bible, and especially for creating a system of vowel signs to reflect the pronunciation of the Hebrew consonantal text in their day. The resulting vocalized text (c.9th–10th century) was known as the Masoretic Text, the basis for the text of the Hebrew Bible normally used today. ▷ Old Testament

Mass (Latin *missa*, from *missio* 'dismissal') The sacrament of the Eucharist (Holy Communion) in the Roman Catholic Church and some other churches. Bread and wine are consecrated by a priest, and the elements (usually bread alone) distributed among the faithful. According to the doctrine of the Council of Trent (counteracting the teaching of the 16th-century Reformers) the bread and wine become the body and blood of Christ (transubstantiation), and the sacrament is to be understood as a divine, propitiatory sacrifice. Masses perform different functions in the life of the Church, eg a Requiem Mass for the dead, a Nuptial Mass for a marriage. ▷ music, Christian; Eucharist; Jesus Christ; Roman Catholicism; sacrament; transubstantiation

materialism The metaphysical view that everything is composed exclusively of physical constituents located in space and time. Materialists thus deny the existence of such abstract entities as numbers and sets, and claim that mental phenomena can be accounted for without positing the existence of anything non-physical. ▷ dialectical materialism; idealism

Mather, Cotton (1663–1728) American clergyman, born in Boston, son of Increase Mather. After graduating at Harvard he became a colleague to his father at the Second Church, Boston, and succeeded him in 1723. He published 382 books, and his *Memorable Providences relating to Witchcraft and Possessions* (1685) did much to fan the cruel fury of the New Englanders. During the Salem witchcraft mania (1692–3) he wrote his *Wonders of the Invisible World* (1692), but with hindsight disapproved. He supported smallpox inoculation and other progressive ideas. His *Magnalia Christi Americana* (1702) contains a mass of material for the church history of New England. Other major works include *Curiosa Americana* (1712–24) and *Christian Philosopher* (1721). ▷ Mather, Increase; Salem, witches of; witchcraft

Mather, Increase (1639–1723) American theologian, born in Dorchester, Massachusetts, the eldest son of an English Nonconformist minister who emigrated in 1635. He graduated at Harvard in 1656, and again at Trinity College, Dublin, in 1658. His first charge was Great Torrington in Devon; but in 1661, finding it impossible to conform, he returned to America, and from 1664 till his death was pastor of the Second Church, Boston, and from 1681 also President of Harvard. He published no fewer than 136 separate works, including *Remarkable Providences* (1684) and a *History of the War with the Indians* (1676). Sent to England in 1689 to lay colonial grievances before the king, he obtained a new charter from William III. He was less of an alarmist about witchcraft than his son, Cotton Mather, and his *Cases of Conscience Concerning Witchcraft* (1693) helped to cool the heated imaginations of the colonists. ▷ Mather, Cotton; Nonconformists; witchcraft

matres, matrones The mother goddess was clearly a vital component of Celtic devotion; in Celtic lands the symbolism of female powers abounds in sculptures and inscriptions. In Gaul and Britain goddesses are often represented in groups of three, frequently accompanied by symbols of fertility and plenty—children, trees, fruit, the cornucopia sign. Sometimes they appear to be placed as local guardians or protectors. A number from Romanized areas carry the Latin title 'matres', or sometimes 'matrones' (the mothers, the matrons). It can harldly be accidental that in the Irish stories which reflect Celtic pre-Christian religion at several removes, goddesses also often belong to triads. The Morrigan ('the great queen') is one of three war goddesses; Brigit, clearly associated with fertility, is one of the three sisters; three goddesses guard the territory of Ireland. In the stories, however, the triadic goddesses usually appear singly. ▷ goddess worship

matsuri Ceremonies and festivals that take place in the Japanese Shinto tradition. There are five different kinds of matsuri: agricultural festivals related to harvests and the cycle of the seasons; national ceremonies formerly observed by the emperor in public but now held in private after the demise of state Shinto; festivals to ward off calamities such as the Gion festival in July, which dates back to a plague in 876; fertility festivals of one sort or another, and local ceremonies that focus upon local *kami*. During Shinto ceremonies the presence of the kami is invoked; priests purify the worshippers; they all bow towards the kami; the door of the inner worship-hall is opened; and offerings are given, prayers are said, and music is played. In addition to general festivals, family ceremonies, such as the ritual of marriage, are increasingly being celebrated in Shinto temples. ▷ kami; Kokutai Shinto; shrines, Shinto

Matthew, Gospel according to The first work of the New Testament canon; one of the four canonical Gospels, until this century widely thought to have been the earliest Gospel written. Although anonymous, 2nd-century traditions assign it to the apostle and former tax-collector, Matthew. It is noteworthy for its story of the Magi at Jesus's birth, its wealth of moral instruction (as in the Sermon on the Mount), and its emphasis on Jesus as the fulfilment of the Old Testament expectations. ▷ disciples (in early Christian Church); Gospels, canonical; Matthew, St; New Testament; Magi; Sermon on the Mount

Matthew, St (1st century) One of the 12 apostles, a tax gatherer before becoming a disciple of Jesus, identified with Levi in Mark 2.14 and Luke 5.27. According to tradition he was the author of the first Gospel, a missionary to the Hebrews, and suffered martyrdom, but nothing is known with certainty about his life. His feast day is 21 September (West) or 16 November (East). ▷ apostle; disciples (in early Christian Church); Jesus Christ; Levi; Matthew, Gospel according to

Maurice, (John) Frederick Denison (1805–72) English theologian and writer, born in Normanston near Lowestoft, the son of a Unitarian minister. He studied at Trinity College and Trinity Hall, Cambridge, but as a Dissenter left in 1827 without a degree, and began a literary career in London. He wrote a novel, *Eustace Conway*, and for a time edited the *Athenaeum*. Influenced by Coleridge, he took orders in the Church of England, became Chaplain to Guy's Hospital (1837) and to Lincoln's Inn (1841–60); in 1840 he became Professor of Literature at King's College, London, where he was Professor of Theology 1846–53. From 1866 he was Professor of Moral Philosophy at Cambridge. The publication in 1853 of his *Theological Essays*, dealing with atonement and eternal life, lost him his professorship of theology. His books include *Moral and Metaphysical Philosophy*, *The Conscience*, and *Social Morality*. Maurice strenuously controverted Mansel's views on our knowledge of God, and denounced as false any political economy founded on selfishness and not on the universe. With Thomas Hughes and Charles Kingsley he founded the Christian socialism movement. He was also the founder and first principal of the Working Man's College (1854) and of the Queen's College for Women.

Mawdudi (al-Mawdūdī, Mawlānā Abū-l-Alā) (1903–79) Traditional Islamic reformer who founded the influential Jamaat-i-Islami in 1941 in what is now Pakistan. He was a journalist who edited a monthly journal, *Tarjumanu-l-Quran*, from 1932 in Hyderabad in the Deccan, from 1938 to 1947 in Pathankot, and then from 1947 in Lahore in the new country of Pakistan. He was influenced in his views by the Muslim Brethren, founded in Ismailia Egypt in 1927 by Hasan al-Banna to maintain and strengthen Islam. Mawdudi felt that the Quran upheld scientific knowledge and he wanted to forge the new Pakistan on Islamic and Quranic principles. He worked for economic improvement and promoted social service and charitable agencies, wishing Islam to return to the fundamental principles of the Quran and the shariah (Muslim law), and to reconstruct itself on the foundations of traditional Islam. After the 1953 Punjab riots involving attacks on the Ahmadiyyah movement Mawdudi was imprisoned for two years. In his many pamphlets and books, especially his six-volume commentary on the Quran, *Tafhim al-Quran*, he claimed that Islam is a system that offers answers to the world's problems and that there is, for instance, such a thing as Islamic politics and Islamic economics. Apart from his influence upon Pakistan and the Jamaat-i-Islami, he has given theoretical justification to some of the elements in recent Islamic fundamentalism. ▷ Ahmadiyyah; Jamaat-i-Islami; Quran; shariah

maya (māyā) An important concept in Indian thought that is commonly but not altogether accurately translated as 'illusion'. Its original meaning related to the creating and transforming power of a Vedic god, and this was extended in some Hindu Upanishads and in the *Bhagavad Gita*. The world was seen to be an emanation of divine energy, or maya, which was both attractive and mysterious. In some Hindu devotional schools maya was sometimes seen as a goddess, either in her own right or as a female consort of the male gods Shiva and Vishnu, by means of whom the world appears. The mother of the Buddha was also called Maya, and she was an extremely worthy woman who at the time of her conception dreamed of being pierced by a bodhisattva in the form of a white elephant. However, in the Advaita Vedanta system made famous by the Hindu philosopher Shankara, maya is seen in a more negative sense as being illusion. According to Shankara, the world is not a hallucination, it is not unreal, and it is not imaginary. But we mistake the nature of the world because of maya and because of our ignorance. We think that it is a separate thing, but it is not, it is part of Brahman, ultimate reality. We think it is like a snake on a path, but it is really like a rope. Later Vedanta thinkers such as Ramanuja reacted against Shankara and gave a more positive interpretation to maya, as have recent thinkers such as Radhakrishnan. They agree that the world is mysterious, that it is derived from God, and that it is fleeting; yet is is also real and historical and attractive—in Ramanuja's phrase, it is the body of God dynamically rather than illusorily produced by maya. ▷ Advaita Vedanta; Bhagavad Gita; bodhisattva; Brahman; Buddha; Radhakrishnan, Sir Sarvepalli; Ramanuja; Shankara; Shiva; Upanishads; Vishnu

Mayan figure of death

Maya religion The Maya people form an ethnic block in Guatemala, Western Honduras and southern Mexico including Yucatan. In an area of rain forest and a limestone plateau there developed between c.300 and 900CE the most remarkable of all the American civilizations. By 900CE, probably through a combination of military pressure and climatic change, the temple cities were reverting to forest, and when the Spaniards reached the area they met a culture long past its glory. Classical Mayan civilization is remarkable for its religious and priestly orientation. This corn-growing community built great temples on the top of stepped pyramids—no doubt representing, like the Sumerian ziggurats, the cosmic mountain—and developed mathematics, writing and deep learning. Mayan civilization could only have operated through the co-operation of priest and peasant. There is little sign of strong central authority. Local priest-kings appear as the community's leaders, and local development, allied to priestly creativity, may explain some of the inconsistencies or divergences suggested by the sources. Mayan religion was directed to securing the fertility needed by corn-growers. The priesthood developed great skill in mathematics and astronomy, gaining a basis for weather forecasting as well as producing a calendar more accurate than the Gregorian. (In effect there were two calendars, one for the solar and one for the sacred year; time was divided into cycles of 52 solar or 73 sacred years; history was reckoned as beginning in 3113BCE and expected to end in 2011CE.) The universe had 13 higher and nine lower levels, and religious thought was centred on a conflict between the upper, life-giving powers (the divinities responsible for fertility) and the lower, death-bringing agents of drought, war and famine. The struggle was symbolized in the ritual ball game, played on a court reflecting the assumed shape of the universe. The chief upper deity, the many-faceted Itzamna, is associated with sky and sun, and infuses the breath of life into humanity. Other important figures are the long-nosed rain god Chac, the corn god Ah Mun (who seems to have received human sacrifices at the season's end to ensure the next crop), the monkey-faced Xamen Ek, pole star god and guide of merchants, and the sinister Cizin, the death god. ▷ Aztec religion; ball game; Toltec religion

May Day A modern festival of hope, centred in many places upon Labour Day, but having much earlier roots. To the early Celts it was the feast of Beltane in honour of the sun god

Beli. To the Romans it was the festival of the mother-goddess Maia, goddess of nature and growth, after whom the month of May is named. In modern cities it is Labour Day, which honours the dignity of workers. Until recently, in communist countries, May Day processions were occasions to exalt the achievements of Marxism. This festival has remained more strongly pagan than others such as Christmas, which have been incorporated into Christianity. It gathers up natural and secular themes such as sunrise, the advent of summer, growth in nature, and Robert Owen's vision in 1833 of a millennium in the future, beginning on May Day, when there would be no more poverty, injustice or cruelty but people would work and live together in harmony and friendship. ▷ Christmas; Marxism

Mbiti, John Samuel (1931–) African theologian, born in Kenya. Teaching theology and comparative religion at Makere University College, Uganda, before becoming Director of the World Council of Churches Ecumenical Institute, Bossey, Switzerland (1972–80), he now teaches Christianity and African religions at Berne University and is a pastor in Burgdorf, Switzerland. His books, which include *African Religions and Philosophy* (1969), *Concepts of God in Africa* (1970), *New Testament Eschatology in an African Background* (1970), *The Prayers of African Religion* (1975), and *Bible and Theology in African Christianity* (1987), maintain that the African is naturally religious and that the Christian message should be seen as a fulfilment of traditional African beliefs rather than a rejection of them. ▷ African religions; comparative religion; theology; World Council of Churches

McPherson, Aimée Semple, neé Kennedy (1890–1944) Canadian-born American Pentecostal evangelist, born near Ingersoll, Ontario, into a Salvation Army family. In 1908 she married a Pentecostal missionary, Robert Semple, but was soon widowed when her husband died in China in 1910. She returned to North America with her daughter and subsequently embarked on an evangelistic career. She married again, in 1912 (to Harold McPherson, divorced 1921), and a third marriage, in 1931, also ended in divorce. Flamboyant and imaginative, she was hugely successful as an evangelist. In 1918 she founded the Foursquare Gospel Movement in Los Angeles, and for nearly two decades she conducted a preaching and healing ministry in the Angelus Temple, Los Angeles, which cost her followers $1.5 million to construct. She had her own radio station, Bible school, magazine, and social service work. Considerable controversy surrounded her: continuous embroilment in legal suits against her; a bizarre and unexplained five-week disappearance in 1926 (she claimed to have been kidnapped). Even her death raised questions; authorities differ on whether it was the result of a heart attack or of an overdose of barbiturates. Her books include *This is That* (1923), *In the Service of the King* (1927) and *Give Me My Own God* (1936). ▷ evangelist; Pentecostalism; Salvation Army

Mecca Islamic holy city in Mecca province, Saudi Arabia. The birthplace of Muhammad, it is the site of the Kabah, which houses the holy Black Stone. It is the chief shrine of Muslim pilgrimage. Between 1.5 and 2 million pilgrims visit Mecca annually. ▷ Islam; Muhammad

medicine bundle A pouch or bag, commonly leather, containing the sacred objects proper to the personal guardian spirit received through the vision quest of the Native American peoples. Among peoples using medicine lodge initiation, the bundle is given in the context of the lodge. With the bundle there frequently belongs a particular spirit song, to be sung when opening the bundle to establish contact with the guardian spirit in time of need. Increasingly situations developed where medicine bundles, with the songs, were transferred by inheritance or even by sale (or reciprocal gift), a practice said to be stimulated in the north by the fur trade. This in turn has sometimes led to communal or clan possession of what were formerly personal possessions. ▷ medicine lodge; vision quest

medicine in religion In primal religions there is a close relationship between illness and the way it is treated and religion. Most illnesses are seen as being influenced by ghosts, gods, spirits, witches or other forces, and as needing healing intervention by a traditional doctor, medicine man, or shaman. African Independent Churches and new religious movements often stress the importance of healing and the psychosomatic side of illness, and the contribution that can be made by alternative medicine is being increasingly recognized in the West. Healers have also been important in China, India and Japan. Their origins were often traced back to divine founders such as the Japanese sun goddess Amaterasu, and the three god-emperors in China. Their arts were influenced by religious factors such as ancestor veneration in China, the search for immortality in Taoism, the concept of reincarnation in Hinduism and Buddhism, and the notion of ritual defilement in various parts of the East. In Tibet medicine became a predominantly religious concern and was carried on in monasteries. In the Ancient Near East there were no strict divisions between religion, magic and medicine. Modern Western medicine traces its oath back to the Greek physician Hippocrates, and medicine has been a favoured occupation in the Christian, Jewish and Muslim traditions with their positive view of the created world of matter and the body, and of charitable activity. Since the scientific revolution of the 17th century, and especially since the 19th century, medicine has become more secular in the West and more neutral or opposed as far as religion is concerned. Until recently it has been opposed to alternative therapies used by various religious groups outside the orbit of Western scientific medicine. More recently there has been a greater willingness to see inter-connections between medicine and religion, a greater emphasis on holistic health and medicine, and a more constructive dialogue on such matters as the ethics of life-support systems, organ transplants, genetic engineering, abortion and euthanasia. ▷ African Independent churches; Amaterasu; ancestor, Chinese; immortality; medicine man; reincarnation; witchcraft

medicine lodge A term best applied to the buildings (and associated ceremonies) used by the secret medicine societies of Native American peoples. The best known example is the Midewiwin ('mystic doings society') of the Ojibwa Algonquin, which has four grades of membership, the fourth attained by very few. Collectively the society holds the combined traditional lore of the people, including the herbal pharmacopoeia, the techniques of healing, and the background of myth on which both ritual and healing depend. Entrance at each grade requires a fee and a period—this can last years—of instruction by a member of that grade. Initiation involves a ritual death and rebirth. The medicine bundles of all the members are used to effect the rebirth symbolism; the new graduate thereafter receives his own medicine bundle and accompanying spirit song. The symbolism of the lodge itself represents the universe and the acknowledgement of Kitshi Manitou, the Great Spirit. ▷ Algonquin religion; medicine bundle

Medina, Arabic Madinah An Islamic holy city in Medina province, Saudi Arabia, the second most important holy city of Islam (after Mecca), containing the tomb of Muhammad, who sought refuge here after his flight from Mecca. ▷ Islam; Muhammad

meditation Devout and continuous reflection on a particular religious theme, practised in many religions and serving a variety of aims, such as deepening spiritual insight, or achieving union with the divine will. Some religions hold that disciplined breathing, posture, and ordering of thoughts deepen meditation. ▷ religion

megalithic religion Megalithic religion is associated mainly with the megaliths, or large stones, used in neolithic Western Europe to build temples, tombs and other structures over the 3000-year period between the 5th and 2nd millennia BCE. There are four main types of megalithic structures: stone-slab temple buildings (found especially in Malta), the floor shape of which resembles that of a standing or seated goddess; burial chambers, including court tombs, gallery graves, passage graves, and dolmens (upright stones supporting a horizontal stone slab); single menhirs, or upright stones, which may be up to six metres high and sculpted to represent a deity; and standing stones, in rows or rings, such as Stonehenge. In all there are roughly 50000 megalithic structures across Britain, France, northern Germany, Portugal, southern Sweden and Spain. Different theories have been used to interpret these structures, including the notions that they were connected with death rituals, initiation rituals, belief in an earth goddess who was also mother of the dead, and belief in a lunar goddess. Megaliths are also found in the Indo-Pacific region, for example at Nias off Sumatra, Bali, Tahiti, the Gilbert Islands and Oceania. They appear to have served as tombs to the power of chiefs, shrines for ancestral spirits or gods, and sighting-stones for navigation. Other theories which suggest that European megaliths were astronomical observatories, or that Indo-Pacific megaliths were stepping-stones in prehistoric migrations are more speculative. ▷ goddess worship; neolithic religion; Stonehenge

Meher Baba (Meher Bābā) (1894–1969) Leader of a new religious movement, born at Poona in India to Zoroastrian parents of Iranian origin, but initiated by a Muslim woman saint as a Sufi master. His followers came to look upon him as an avatara, an incarnation of God, and his name, 'Meher Baba', means the Father of Love. Sometimes called 'Baba-lovers', his disciples believe that through love and trust in Meher Baba they can receive self-fulfilment and enlightenment. He journeyed much around Europe and the USA and had a powerful influence upon a number of prominent people, including film stars and titled persons. From 1925 until his death he kept a vow of silence and made contact with followers and visitors by means of gestures and letters arranged on a board. He and his followers had a concern for insane holy men in India and devised a means of helping them. ▷ avatara; new religious movements in the West; Sufism

Meiji Restoration (1868) An important point in Japanese history, when the last Shogun was overthrown in a short civil war, and the position of the emperor (Meiji, the title of Mutsuhito, who ruled until 1912) was restored to symbolic importance. Powerful new leaders set about making Japan into an industrial state. The four hereditary classes of Tokugawa Japan were abolished and new technology and technical experts were brought from the West. ▷ Japanese religion

Meiji Shrine An important pilgrimage centre in Tokyo. The shrine was completed in 1920 and dedicated to Emperor Meiji. The present building is a reconstruction of the original which was destroyed in World War II. ▷ Japanese religion

Melanchthon, (Greek for original surname, **Schwarzerd**, 'black earth') **Philip** (1497–1560) German Protestant reformer, born in Bretten in the Palatinate. He was appointed Professor of Greek at Wittenberg in 1516 and became Luther's fellow-worker. His *Loci Communes* (1521) is the first great Protestant work on dogmatic theology. The Augsburg Confession (1530) was composed by him. After Luther's death he succeeded to the leadership of the German Reformation movement but lost the confidence of some Protestants by concessions to the Catholics; while the zealous Lutherans were displeased at his approximation to the doctrine of Calvin on the Lord's Supper. His conditional consent to the introduction of the stringent Augsburg Interim (1549) in Saxony led to painful controversies. ▷ Augsburg Confession; Calvin, John; Luther, Martin; Protestantism; Reformation

Melanesian religion Melanesia includes many peoples diverse in origin and language, on large islands and small, and many who have for centuries lived in a restricted universe of small groups in mountain valleys. There is naturally a wide range of myth, ritual and practice among Melanesians, but there are various recurrent themes. God is rarely prominent in accounts of Melanesian religion, though the great power in the universe is often identified with the sky, and 'feeding the sky' is the name of the sole major sacrificial rite of one people. A common theme in cosmology is that of the release of the sea, a primal catastrophe (often provoked by an act of human greed or folly) that has separated people ever since. Another is the story of two brothers. At first co-operating, they become estranged. One was cleverer than the other, or one cheated the other; eventually they separated and one brother left for the otherworld. This otherworld is sometimes conceived as above, sometimes below.

If we put these themes together, and bearing in mind the fragile world of most Melanesian peoples, where disharmony can spell destruction, it is not surprising to find another set of themes about the end time. One day the peoples will be united, the lost brother and his kin return, and the deep human longing 'to eat together in one place' be fulfilled. These myths of the end time at first seemed to explain the arrival of the whites; subsequent relations with whites gave a new twist to the myth of the two brothers. Christian preaching about the Fall, the kingdom of God, and the return of Christ found echoes in these stories and sometimes assisted reinterpretation of them, shown in various new religious movements, including those in which 'cargo' is prominent. ▷ cargo; creation myths

Memphite Theology The city of Memphis in Lower Egypt was the pharaoh's capital during the 3rd millennium BCE. Its local god Ptah achieved considerable importance and his priests developed a distinctive theology, best preserved in a late copy from the 25th Dynasty (c.700BCE). In this document, known as the Memphite Theology, Ptah is responsible for the creation of the world by his word, unlike the theology of Heliopolis where creation was by procreation. By forming a concept in his heart and uttering it with his tongue, he brought into being the world and the gods, including the Heliopolitan ennead. The Memphite Theology is noteworthy for its degree of abstraction in comparison with other Ancient Egyptian cosmogonies. ▷ Atum; cosmogony; creation myths; ennead; Heliopolis theology; Ptah

Mencius (Meng Tzu) (c.371–c.289BCE) Confucian philosopher, born in what is the modern province of Shantung in China. He is regarded as the second greatest Confucian after Confucius himself, and his career was similar to that of his predecessor. Like Confucius he was a teacher and he too served as an official in the state of Chi from 319 to 312 without outstanding success. He also travelled extensively attempting to persuade rulers to initiate reforms and to end the period of warring states. Mencius asserted that human nature was originally good and in this respect he differed from his near-contemporary Hsun Tzu, who asserted the opposite. Mencius taught that the basic Confucian virtues of humaneness (*jen*) and righteousness (*i*) were innate and could be uncovered by inward contemplation and moral endeavour. Rulers should rule ethically in accordance with the will of heaven (*Tien*) so that society and the individuals in it could realize their true potential. Mencius opposed Mo Tzu's stress on universal love by saying that it was unrealistic, and what was needed was graded love focused on family, friends, workmates and neighbours. Only then could one extend one's love to include the whole world. His sayings are collected in the *Book of Mencius* which became one of the Four Books designated by Chu Hsi (1130–1200CE) as set texts for the Chinese civil service exams. He died around 289BCE having had a profound influence on Chinese thought. ▷ Chu Hsi; Confucian Canon; Confucius; Hsun Tzu; jen; Mo Tzu; Tien

Mendelssohn, Moses (1729–86) German Jewish philosopher and biblical scholar, born in Dessau, grandfather of Felix Mendelssohn. He studied in Berlin and went on to become the partner to a silk manufacturer. He is an important figure in the history of Jewish philosophy and in the Enlightenment, and his main works reflect his commitment both to Judaism and rationalism: *Phädon* (1767) is an argument for the immortality of the soul, based on Plato's *Phaedo*; *Jerusalem* (1783) advocates Judaism as the religion of reason; *Morgenstunden* (1785) argues for the rationality of belief in the existence of God. ▷ Judaism; Plato; rationalism

Mendicant Orders (Latin *mendicare*, 'to beg') Religious Orders in which friars were not permitted to hold property, either personally or in common. Such Orders were able to survive only through the charity of others. ▷ Augustinians; Carmelites; Dominicans; Franciscans; monasticism; Orders, Holy

Mennonites Dutch and Swiss Anabaptists who later called themselves Mennonites after one of their Dutch leaders, Menno Simons. They adhere to the Confession of Dordrecht (1632), baptize on confession of faith, are pacifists, refuse to hold civic office, and follow the teachings of the New Testament. Most of their one million adherents live in the USA. ▷ Anabaptists; Simons, Menno

menorah A candlestick of seven branches, with three curving upwards on each side of a central shaft, an ancient symbol of Judaism, and the official symbol of the modern State of Israel. In the Bible, it was originally part of the furnishings of the Tabernacle in the wilderness, and eventually of the Jerusalem Temple. The Hanukkah candleholder has eight arms, and in many synagogues the arms number other than seven, so as to avoid direct imitation of that in the Temple (forbidden in the Talmud). ▷ Judaism; Tabernacle; Temple, Jerusalem

menstruation The periodic discharge of blood from the womb, widely regarded in many cultures as a polluting act second only in its severity to contact with a dead person. The result of such beliefs is that menstruating women are often excluded from religious acts and indeed, in some cases, women as an entire gender may be forbidden to play a role in religious rites. In many tribal cultures a young woman is frequently required to leave home until ritual purification renders her clean. Menstruating women are believed to pose great dangers to men and innumerable bans are placed upon them. In Islamic societies a menstruating woman is excused from the obligatory daily prayers and is required to clean herself ritually before resuming daily worship. The *Kharajis* Muslims, however, teach that menstruating women should still pray and fast. ▷ Kharijites; menstruation, Jewish attitude to; women in religion

menstruation, Jewish attitude to Traditionally, the education of Jewish women, apart from basic literacy skills, covered only what was thought necessary to become a good wife and mother: the laws of kashrut, observance of the sabbaths and festivals, and regulations concerning menstruation. The latter, based on Leviticus 15.19–24 and 18.19, are found in the Mishnah tractate called Niddah (literally 'uncleanness' but particularly connoting menstrual impurity) and are further developed in the Talmud. In short, a woman may have no contact with her spouse during menstruation, nor for seven subsequent days, during which she must inspect herself for signs of blood. After this she must immerse herself in a ritual bath or miqveh, upon which sexual relations may be resumed. These laws are still followed by the Orthodox, but the Reform movement does not consider such ritual matters as essential. ▷ kashrut; miqveh; Talmud; Judaism, women in

merit The Roman Catholic doctrine that the performance of good deeds deserves a reward from God. By co-operating with divine grace, more grace, eternal life and blessedness may be obtained. Believers (especially the saints) may also do more than is required for their own salvation, performing 'works of supererogation' which attract extra reward that is added to the Church's 'treasury of merit'. This can be drawn on through indulgences to help others who lack merit. This doctrine was rejected by the Reformers, who insisted on justification by grace through faith in Christ's merits alone. In response to the accusation that to reject the idea of merit was to suggest that moral behaviour was irrelevant (antinomianism) and to overlook the fact that most people need the incentive of rewards and punishments (as seemed to be offered in the Bible), they argued that good deeds were the fruit rather than the cause of justification. To say that no one has merit before God is not the same as saying that all human deeds are equally worthless. ▷ justification; Reformation

Merkavah Mysticism That part of the Kabbalah or Jewish mysticism centred on the *maaseh merkavah* or Divine Throne-chariot described in Ezekiel 1. This throne-chariot became associated with esoteric speculation about the nature of God and the heavenly realms, the secrets of which would be revealed to individuals who succeeded in entering those realms or *hekhalot* ('[heavenly] halls'). This could be accomplished in an ecstatic trance-like state, attained through ascetic practices, ablutions and reciting the names of God. Once access was gained, the mystic hoped to be found worthy of receiving a vision of the maaseh merkavah and insight into the future or the workings of heaven. The resultant body of doctrines is found in the main writings of Merkavah Mysticism, known as Hekhalot literature because of the Heavenly Halls from which a revelation of the throne-chariot was sought. Similar to Merkavah Mysticism's nature and aims is another part of the Kabbalah, which focused on the *masseh bereshit* or 'act of creation' found in Genesis 1. However, in talmudic and early medieval times such traditions appear to have been confined to the ranks of the initiated élite; this was to guard against misunderstanding and any resultant heretical developments. ▷ Ezekiel, Book of; Kabbalah; Talmud

Merlin In the Arthurian legends, a good wizard or sage whose magic was used to help King Arthur. He was the son of an incubus and a mortal woman, and therefore indestructible; but he was finally entrapped by Vivien, the Lady of the Lake, and bound under a rock for ever. He was famous for his prophecies. ▷ Arthur

Merton, Thomas (1915–68) American Cistercian monk, born in Prades, France, of New Zealand and American parentage. He studied and taught English at Columbia, but in 1938 he became a convert to Roman Catholicism and in 1941 joined the Trappist order at Our Lady of Gethsemane Abbey, Kentucky. His best-selling autobiography, *The Seven Storey Mountain* (1946), prompted many to become monks, but Merton himself was to discover intense tensions between his hermitic inclinations and community living. However, ways were found for him to follow his vocation free *for* the world rather than free *from* it (cf *Contemplation in a World of Action*, 1971), keeping up a voluminous correspondence and writing many books, ranging from personal journals and poetry to social criticism. His growing interest in Eastern spirituality led him to attend a conference in Bangkok. He died there, accidentally electrocuted by a faulty fan. ▷ Cistercians; Roman Catholicism; Trappists

Meru, Mount The mythical centre of the universe in Hindu cosmology. Some sources say that it is made of pure gold, that it is 160000 leagues high and that it towers above all the heavenly *lokas*. Others say the lokas are situated on its slopes. It is the centre of four continents and oceans, and a gigantic *jambu* (rose apple) tree grows on its slopes, overshadowing at least one of these continents (*Jambudvipa*), on which its ripe fruit drops, forming the Jambu River in which flows the water of immortality. More mundane, it is often situated in the Himalayas at the rise of the Ganges, or in the Pamirs. This theory would strengthen the argument that the myth originated in Iran, as has been suggested by some scholars. ▷ Hinduism

Mesmer, Franz Anton (1734–1815) Austrian physician and founder of mesmerism, born near Constance. He studied medicine at Vienna, and about 1772 claimed that there exists a power, which he called 'magnetism', that could be used to cure diseases. In 1778

he went to Paris, where he created a sensation; but in 1785 a learned commission reported unfavourably, and he retired into obscurity in Switzerland. He died at Meersburg.

Messiah (Hebrew 'anointed one') In Jewish writings from c.2nd century BCE onwards, one who would help deliver Israel from its enemies, aid in its restoration, and establish a worldwide kingdom. Many different representations of this figure can be discovered in early Judaism and Christianity. In Christian thought, the role is interpreted as fulfilled in Jesus of Nazareth: 'Christ' is derived from the Greek rendering of the Hebrew word for 'messiah'. ▷ Christianity; David; Jesus Christ; Judaism; messianism

messianism Jewish movements expressing the hope for a new and perfected age. Jewish Orthodoxy reflects this through traditional beliefs in the coming of a personal Messiah who would re-establish the Temple in Jerusalem and from there rule over a redeemed world. Reformed Judaism anticipates the world's perfection by the example of Judaism in human achievements such as social reforms and justice, though is still concerned with preserving the identity of the Jewish race within existing states. In contrast, Zionism places emphasis on the physical restoration of the Jewish state in Palestine and the return of exiled Jews there. ▷ Judaism; Messiah; Temple, Jerusalem; Zionism

metaphysics The branch of philosophy which deals with questions about what sorts of things exist (ontology) and how they are related. The term, which originally meant 'after physics', was used by Hellenistic philosophers to name a collection of Aristotle's texts; it then came to acquire the sense 'beyond physics'. Monists claim that only one sort of thing really exists; some monists are materialists, others are idealists. Pluralists claim that two or more sorts of things ultimately exist; the most familiar variety is a dualism of matter and mind. ▷ Aristotle; dualism; idealism; materialism; monism; ontology; pluralism; predestination

Methodism A Christian denomination founded in 1739 by John Wesley as an evangelical movement within the Church of England, becoming a separate body in 1795. The movement spread rapidly as he travelled the country on horseback and sent other evangelical leaders to the American colonies, where the movement flourished. In the 19th century doctrinal disputes caused divisions both in Britain and the USA. These were healed in Britain in 1932, and partially so in the USA, with the uniting of the three main bodies of Methodists. The principal doctrines of the Church are laid down in Wesley's sermons, his notes on the New Testament, and his Articles of Religion. According to him, 'A Methodist is one who lives according to the method laid down in the Bible'. The basic principles of Methodism involve an emphasis on the importance of the Holy Spirit and a close personal relationship with God in a believer's life; a strong belief in the historical doctrines of Christianity, which nevertheless leaves room for a degree of doctrinal nonconformity among members; and a simplicity and egalitarianism of worship, in which ministers and lay people work in partnership. There is also a devout concern for the welfare of the poor and unfortunate. There are 25 million Methodists worldwide. ▷ Church of England; evangelicalism; Holy Spirit; Wesley, John

Methodius, St ▷ Cyril, St

Methuselah The eighth and longest-lived of the Hebrew patriarchs, who lived before the Flood. His supposed 969 years makes him the paragon of longevity. ▷ Flood, the; patriarch

metta (mettā) The notion of loving kindness in the Buddhist tradition. It is one of the four moral attitudes and universal virtues that are stressed by Buddhists, the other three being compassion (*karuna*), sympathetic joy (*mudita*), and equanimity (*upekkha*). They were creatively summarized especially by the great Theravada monk-scholar Buddhaghosa, and Buddhists were encouraged to build up these four virtues in such a way that they could be extended to all beings everywhere. Metta is built into meditational disciplines. It is unemotional, non-possessive, inclusive, and concerned for the benefit of others. It can be beamed out on others, and can affect others, as in the story told about the Buddha in which he diverts the charge of an elephant by beaming metta towards it. Within the sphere of the four moral attitudes, the key virtue is equanimity. Loving kindness takes on a calm, unselfish, balanced and yet effective air by reason of its association with equanimity. ▷ Buddha; Buddhaghosa; karuna; Theravada Buddhism; upekkha

Mevlevis An Islamic Sufi order found mainly in Turkey, and founded by the great Sufi poet and thinker Rumi (1207–73). The

Mevlevis have become well known as the 'whirling dervishes' because of their practice of whirling to the music of flutes, drums and chants in order to deepen their spirituality. The whirling is graceful and ritualistic, and consists of four movements that last for about an hour. It is deeply symbolic, representing the dance of creation from God and back to God, and the encounter (*muqabalah*) of the soul with itself, with others, and with God who is the One. The *pir*, or spiritual master, is important among the Mevlevis, and he appears among the dancers at the climax of the dance. The founder, Rumi, is also important, and a number of Mevlevis claim to have a spiritual experience of him. They were banned in Turkey in 1928 along with other Sufi orders, but have since reappeared there, and are also present in the West, as well as in Syria, Egypt and in other ex-Ottoman states. ▷ music, Islamic; Ottoman Turks; Rumi; Sufism

mezuzah (plural **mezuzot**) A cylindrical box placed on the doorposts of Jewish houses, containing Deuteronomy 6.4–9 and 11.13–21. The first of these passages is part of the Shema, and both prescribe the writing of the words of Torah on the doorposts (mezuzot) of the home. The aim is to remind Israelites of their obligation to fulfil God's commandments. Traditionally, therefore, a mezuzah is placed on the right-hand post of the main door and living-room door of a Jewish household. In early Israelite times the practice may originally have been intended to ward off evil spirits, but this is not the case for the biblical injunction as it now stands. ▷ mitzvah; Shema; tefillin; Torah

mezuzah

Micah, or **Micheas, Book of** One of the 12 so-called 'minor' prophetic books of the Hebrew Bible/Old Testament, attributed to the prophet Micah of Moresheth-gath (in the hill country of Judah), a contemporary of Isaiah in Judah and active in the late 8th century BCE. The work is noted for its attack on social injustices against the poorer classes, as well as for predicting the punishment of Samaria and Jerusalem because of the sins of their people. Some parts of the work may be of later date (6th–5th century BCE). ▷ Isaiah, Book of; Old Testament; prophet

Micheas ▷ **Micah, Book of**

Middle Way A name sometimes given to the Buddhist tradition which is derived from the teaching of the Buddha. He took a middle way between the practical extremes of a life of luxury in his palace and a life of asceticism—both of which he tried and abandoned; and he took a middle way between the philosophical extremes of eternalism and nihilism. He taught that the middle way brought vision and knowledge, and caused calm, enlightenment and nirvana. The eightfold path—right understanding, right thought, right speech, right action, right livelihood, right effort, right mindfulness and right concentration—is the middle way of Buddhist practice. Philosophically the middle way was related to the concept of dependent origination, and it is also connected to the Madhyamika school of Mahayana Buddhist philosophy. Madhyamika means 'middle way', and Nagarjuna's formative verses, the *Madhyamika-karika*, are the 'Verses of the Middle Way'. ▷ dependent origination; dharma; eightfold path; Madhyamika; Mahayana Buddhism; Nagarjuna; nirvana

Midewiwin ▷ **medicine lodge**

Midianites An ancient semi-nomadic people dwelling in the desert area of the Transjordan; in Genesis 25, reputedly descended from the offspring (Midian) of one of Abraham's concubines (Keturah). Later they are portrayed as enticing the Israelites into idolatry, but are overcome by Gideon (Judges 6–8). They were noted for their use of camels in raids. ▷ Abraham; Judges, Book of

midrash In general terms, teaching linked to a running exposition of scriptural texts, especially found in rabbinic literature. The scriptural interpretation is often a relatively free explanation of the text's meaning, based on attaching significance to single words, grammatical forms, or similarities with passages elsewhere so as to make the text relevant to a wide range of questions of rabbinic interest. The term can also apply to the genre of rabbinic writings which consists of such interpretations. ▷ Judaism; rabbi

Mihrab (Miḥrāb) A niche in the wall of a mosque that indicates the direction of Mecca, and hence the direction towards which Muslims offer their daily prayers. It was first used at a mosque at Quba just outside Medina in 709, and the earliest surviving one is at the Dome of the Rock in Jerusalem. Mihrabs provided Islamic craftsmen with the opportunity to indulge their artistic creativity with alabaster, gold, marble, mosaics and semi-precious stones, notably at the mosque at Cordoba in Spain. The mihrab is often constructed acoustically in a way that makes the voice of the leader of worship echo back to the worshippers. It highlights the importance of Mecca as a sacred place and the importance of *salat*, the five daily prayers, in the life of a Muslim. The mihrab is a symbol of the 'cave' which is a token of worship and inwardness; hence it is also a symbol of the heart where one exercises inward spirituality. ▷ art, Islamic; Jerusalem; Mecca; Medina; mosque; salat

miko A term denoting female shamans in the Japanese Shinto tradition. They were virgins who entered the service of the Shinto gods, the *kami*, and assisted in worship at the shrines of the Shinto tradition. Part of their duty was to engage in sacred dances and in order to fulfil this service they underwent a strict discipline of training, celibacy, and preparation. Some of them also developed shamanic gifts of mediumship whereby they were able to enter into a possessed state, to contact the spirits, and to mediate between them and interested persons. The miko were recruited from carefully chosen families; in the early Shinto tradition they were sometimes related to the Emperor of Japan. During the later medieval period female shamans increasingly exercised their gifts of mediumship and divination outside the Shinto temples in the wider community. ▷ divination; kami; shamanism; Shinto; shrines, Shinto

Milarepa (Mi-la-ras-pa) (1052–1135) Tantric yogin, poet and lama in the Kagyupa tradition of Tibetan Buddhism. He is a very popular saint who composed songs of his experiences (in the Indian *doha* tradition) and who is attributed with the writing of an autobiography. His father died when he was young and his uncle and aunt cheated his family of their inheritance. Driven by revenge and encouraged by his mother Milarepa destroyed his relatives and their family through black magic. Feeling remorse for this and other evil deeds and fearing the karmic consequences of his actions, Milarepa went in search of spiritual enlightenment. He found lama Marpa, who rebuked him and repeatedly refused to initiate him, putting him through various ordeals designed both as tests of faith and as expiations for his past actions. At Marpa's instruction, Milarepa repeatedly built and dismantled a number of towers, making himself ill in the process and coming near to despair. With the support and care of Marpa's wife, however, Milarepa eventually gained initiation from Marpa, from whom he received the six yogas of Naropa. He spent the remainder of his life meditating in caves and passing on his teachings to Gampopa. ▷ Buddhism; Gampopa; Kagyupa; karma; lama; Marpa; Naropa

Milinda An ancient Graeco-Indian king, usually thought to be King Menander, who lived at Sagala in what is now Pakistan, and became famous within the Buddhist tradition. He came to a monk called Nagasena with a set of questions and perplexities which were then answered by Nagasena. The exchange was written down in Sanskrit at the beginning of the Common Era in the *Milindapanha*, the 'Questions of Milinda'. This was soon translated into Pali, and it became important in the Theravada Buddhist tradition. It summarizes the past lives of Milinda and Nagasena, and then deals with the basic doctrinal and moral questions raised by Milinda. They include the idea of karma or deeds, the notion of rebirth, the nature of personhood, and how to fulfil and achieve ultimate success in perfecting the goal of life. It also includes some technical discussions of Buddhist doctrine that were probably added later to the original core. ▷ karma; rebirth; Theravada Buddhism

Mill, John Stuart (1806–73) English philosopher and social reformer, one of the major intellectual figures of the 19th century and a leading exponent of the British empiricist and utilitarian traditions. Born in London, son of the Scottish philosopher James Mill, his father was wholly responsible for his remarkable and rigorous education. He was taught Greek at the age of three, Latin and arithmetic at eight, logic at 12, and political economy at 13. He was shielded from association with other boys of his age and his only recreation was a daily walk with his father, who, as they walked, conducted oral examinations. After a visit to France in 1820 he broadened his studies into history, law and philosophy and in 1823 began a career under his father at the India Office, where he advanced to become head of his department, before retiring in 1858 on the dissolution of the East India Co. His forced education gave him an advantage, as he put it, of a quarter of a century over his contemporaries, and he began enthusiastically to fulfil the ambitions his father had designed for him of becoming leader and prophet of the Benthamite utilitarian movement. He began publishing in the newspaper *The Traveller* in 1822; he helped form the Utilitarian Society, which met for reading and discussion in Jeremy Bentham's house (1823–26); he was a major contributor to the *Westminster Review* and a regular performer in the London Debating Society; he corresponded with Carlyle and met Maurice and Sterling; he espoused Malthusian doctrines and was arrested in 1824 for distributing birth control literature to the poor in London. But in 1826 he underwent a mental crisis which he describes in his famous *Autobiography* (1873) and which was the unsurprising consequence of his precocious but emotionally restricted development. For a while he was in 'a dull state of nerves', but the depression passed and he recovered, with his sympathies broadened and his intellectual position importantly modified, as his reviews of Tennyson (1835), Carlyle (1837), Bentham (1838) and Coleridge (1840) indicate. He effectively 'humanized' utilitarianism by recognizing differences in the quality as well as the quantity of pleasures and by thus restoring the importance of cultural and idealistic values. He published his major work, *A System of Logic*, in 1843; it ran through many editions, established his philosophical reputation, and greatly influenced John Venn, John Neville Keynes, Friedrich Frege and Bertrand Russell, particularly in its treatment of induction.

In 1830 he had met Harriet Taylor, bluestocking wife of a wealthy London merchant, and after a long, intense but apparently chaste romance he married her in 1851, two years after her husband's death. She took an active interest in his writing and though he undoubtedly exaggerated her role in the *Autobiography*, she helped him draft the brilliant essay *On Liberty* (1859), the most popular of all his works, which eloquently defines and defends the freedoms of the individual against social and political control. Harriet died in 1858, but her views on the marriage contract and the status of women helped inspire *The Subjection of Women* (1869), which provoked great antagonism. His other main works include *Principles of Political Economy* (1848), *Considerations on Representative Government* (1861), *Utilitarianism* (1863), *Examination of Sir William Hamilton's Philosophy* (1865), *Auguste Comte and Positivism* (1873) and *Three Essays on Religion* (1874). He remained politically active in later life and was elected to Parliament in 1865, campaigning for women's suffrage and generally supporting the Advanced Liberals. In 1872 he became godfather, 'in a secular sense', to Lord Amberley's second son, Bertrand Russell. His last years were spent in France and he died in Avignon.
▷ empiricism; utilitarianism

millenarianism The belief held by some Christians that there will be a thousand-year (millennium) reign of the saints, either before or immediately after the return of Christ. The belief is usually based on an interpretation of Revelation 20. 1–7. The main body of Christians has not endorsed millenarianism, but it had its advocates from the earliest years of Christianity, and in the 19th century there was a renewal of apocalyptical and millennial ideas, such as the Plymouth Brethren and the Adventists. In recent decades the term has been used more broadly by social scientists, referring to any religious group looking forward to a sudden and early transformation of the world. Such movements tend to arise in periods of great social change or during social crises, and usually aim to advance a suppressed social group, as in the Melanesian cargo cults. ▷ Adventists; Anabaptists; apocalypse; cargo; Plymouth Brethren

Mimamsa (Mīmāṃsā) One of the six schools of orthodox Hindu philosophy. Mimamsa or *Purva Mimamsa* refers to a tradition founded by Jaimini (c.200BCE) who wrote the *Mimamsa Sutras*. Mimamsa is a school of philosophy concerned with critical enquiry into the sacred texts of the Veda. Shabara (c.400CE) wrote a commentary on Jaimini's *sutras* and these are further explained by two thinkers, Kumarila and Prabhakara (7th century) who created two sub-divisions of the school. The Mimamsa claims that the Veda is primarily concerned with action and interprets it as a series of injunctions. Purva Mimamsa is distinct from Vedanta (or *Uttara Mimamsa*) and yoga, which stress knowledge and contemplation. The Mimamsa analyses language and maintains that language exists independently of human speech which manifests it, and that the meaning of the word is an intrinsic property of that word.

minaret ▷ architecture, Islamic

Mindszenty, Jozsef, Cardinal (1892–1975) Hungarian Roman Catholic prelate, born in Mindszent, Vas. Primate of Hungary (1945) and created cardinal (1946), he became internationally known in 1948 when he was arrested and charged with treason by the communist government in Budapest. He was sentenced to life imprisonment in 1949. Temporarily released in the wake of the 1956 uprising, he was granted asylum in the American legation at Budapest where he remained as a voluntary prisoner until 1971, when he went to Rome. There he criticized the Vatican's policy towards Hungary, and was asked by Pope Paul VI to resign his primacy. He settled in Vienna, where he spent his last years in a Hungarian religious community. His memoirs were published in 1974. ▷ Roman Catholicism

ministry, Christian Fundamentally, this is humble service by all Christians to their neighbours, following the example and teaching of Jesus Christ. Official ministries in the church, usually recognized by the rite of ordination, are derived from this, and are closely related to the form of church organization (episcopacy, presbyterianism, or independency) concerned. Following the fairly fluid organization of the New Testament church, in which ministry was chiefly a matter of the exercise of varied gifts and functions, rather than status, a three-fold ministry of bishops, priests and deacons emerged and became the norm in Roman Catholicism, the Orthodox Church, and Anglicanism.

The Reformers rejected the Catholic view of apostolic succession through ordination by bishops in unbroken succession to Peter. They also could not accept the necessity for a celibate priesthood, or the belief that the priest uniquely represented Christ in offering the sacrifice of the Mass (an important aspect of the Roman Catholic argument against the ordination of women) and in being able to absolve from sin through the sacrament of penance. Instead, they understood apostolic succession in terms of faithfulness to the apostles' teaching, gave ministers a preaching, teaching and pastoral role, and sought to return to New Testament patterns of mutual service and the 'priesthood of all believers'.

The Roman Catholic Church ordains only unmarried men. Orthodox priests may marry before ordination, but if they do they cannot become bishops. Some Protestant (and a few Anglican) churches today allow women to be ordained as well as men. Many churches, of all traditions, now see the clergy more as enablers of the laity, helping them to fulfil their own ministries in the workaday world. Most clergy minister to congregations that meet together for Sunday worship. Some, like industrial chaplains, minister to people in their weekday place of work. Churches that have traditionally depended on full-time salaried clergy with lengthy theological training have experimented with other models of lay and ordained ministry, including ecumenical and team ministries that make better use of buildings and human resources. ▷ Church organization; Orders, Holy; penance; Christianity, women in

ministry, holy The special office or function in a Church of a person (a minister) ordained or appointed to exercise liturgical, pastoral, and administrative duties. The basic notion is one of service, generally to God and humankind, applied to the Church as a whole or to any part of it. ▷ Christianity; Orders, Holy; priest

Minoan religion Religious belief and ritual action in Minoan Crete (3000–1000BCE) were aimed at the protection, continuance and increase in the human and animal populations and the usable products of the whole environment. To achieve this, contact or communion with the divinity was sought at many different kinds of sacred site. There were shrines on the summits and slopes of mountains, caves with revered stalactites, stalagmites and pools of water, and open air shrines in the courts of palaces and lesser buildings, while inside were shrine rooms with bench, raised altar and low tables for offerings, dark crypts with pillars and subterranean chambers. These crypts and chambers appear to be the built equivalents of sacred caves. Two symbolic objects recur among the shrine sites: the double axe incised on stone or in sheet bronze set up on a pole, and a pair of stone horns (stylized bulls' horns).

The divinity was summoned by invocation, gesture, sound, dance and offerings, and became present in a shrine, sometimes within a rounded stone, pillar, tree or eight-shaped shield. Offerings were of many kinds, votive statuettes of humans, or of parts of humans healed or to be healed, and of animals being particularly common. Sacrificial offerings of animals and, occasionally, human beings were made.

The finest technical skills and artistic senses were frequently employed in making equipment for shrines, especially pouring vessels (*rhytons*) of many forms (such as bulls' heads)

and materials (rare imported stones, faience, delicate painted pottery, precious metals). Another, highly important type of evidence for ritual action is the frozen picture in the form of scenes carved in relief on stone vessels, engraved on the bezels of small gold rings and on sealstones, and on painted murals. Inscriptions on stone vessels remain undeciphered, although repeated syllabic signs may indicate titles or invocatory formulae. On the fundamental question of who was worshipped, expert views remain divided. There is evidence for a powerful female divinity, for at least one male divinity and probably for lesser female divinities. Certain names for female divinities in use in Greco-Roman times are likely to be Minoan survivals, such as Diktynna, Ariadne and Eileithyia, while Rhea, who gave birth to Zeus in Crete, seems in substance if not in name to be the later outcome of a powerful Minoan goddess. ▷ Greek religion; Mycenaean religion

miqveh, or **mikveh** (plural **miqvaot**) A ritual bath or pool of water used in Judaism to restore ritual purity to persons or objects through immersion. Its use in post-biblical times is based on stipulations in Leviticus 15 and Numbers 19 and 31.19–24. The uncleanness concerned may be contracted from corpses, various defiling objects, and bodily discharges; it appears to have been envisaged as some kind of gaseous substance. However, the impurity is spiritual not hygienic (though it became customary to wash before using the miqveh) and may, but need not, entail sinful action. After the destruction of the Jerusalem Temple in 70CE, the purificatory requirements of the priests and of Jews wishing to enter the Temple were removed. Since then the miqveh has been associated mainly with menstruation and conversion. The Mishnah tractate Miqvaot deals with the complex regulations concerning the building and operation of the miqveh. Essentially it covers the materials to be employed, the minimum amount of water required for an effective miqveh, and the appropriate sources of water for filling it. Orthodox Jews continue to make use of miqvaot, but Reform Judaism has tended to discard such practices. ▷ conversion; menstruation, Jewish attitude to; Mishnah

Mira Bai (Mīrā Bāī) (c.1498–1546) Bhakti poet and mystic, devoted to Krishna. She was born a Rajput princess, and was duly married to a prince before she was 20. However, even then she had already surrendered herself to Krishna and neglected her husband as a result. Mira Bai constantly had to fight against the traditional roles ascribed to women in society, the crisis coming on the death of her husband when her father-in-law insisted that she become a sati. She escaped to a community of bhakti devotees who supported her, eventually becoming a wandering ascetic attached to a temple in the holy city of Dwarka. Mira Bai's poetry reflects her deep love for Krishna, especially in her use of the romantic symbolism of the 'mystical marriage' between herself and her Lord. In common with other mystics Mira Bai often expresses her devotion in two contrasting ways. Firstly, in describing Krishna's beauty and the blissful experience of being in his presence; and secondly in expressing the deep pain of separation from Krishna. Mira Bai is unusual in that she cannot be placed in any particular category, her notion of Krishna encompassing both his mythological and transcendent natures. As a result she is able to identify herself with him on the personal level and by seeing herself as being absorbed in him. Indeed, it is this that helps to explain her wide appeal. ▷ bhakti; Krishna; sati

miracles Actions, happenings or events exceeding the known powers of nature and attributed to a supernatural cause. A constant feature of the religious traditions of the world, they often function as signs which testify to the divine approval of the message which is being proclaimed. However, many faiths, including Christianity, Islam and Sikhism, show an ambivalent attitude towards miracles by warning against the seeking of signs. The Quran, for example, attributes no miracles to Muhammad but portrays him as someone who is content to point to God's action in nature. Islamic tradition, however, attributes many miracles to Muhammad. Within Sikhism, at the level of folk religion there are a number of Sikhs who believe in miracles, and miracles are to be found in the *janam sakhis*, the life stories of Guru Nanak. Basically, however, miracles are rejected by the Sikh gurus and responsible Sikh opinion. There are three main reasons for this: they are seen as devices to attract the gullible; the true miracle is not miraculous displays but God himself, whose Name and Word and Guruship are true; and God's *Hukam*, or will, is stable, consistent and constant, therefore divine interventions to change that will are whimsical and meaningless. ▷ Hukam; Janam Sakhis; Muhammad; Nam; Nanak; Quran

miracles, Christian Miracles were not unusual in biblical times, but as they could be performed by both true and false prophets they were not in themselves proofs of religious truth. In Western society since the 18th century, rationalism, deism (the belief that God set the universe in motion but does not intervene in its workings) and belief in a closed universe of fixed natural laws have ruled out the possibility of miracles. At best, so-called miracles (if not misreported) could be the result of occasional operations of natural laws not yet understood. Some theologians, like Bultmann, have dismissed the miracles recorded in the New Testament, especially those involving the casting out of evil spirits, as deriving from an outmoded pre-scientific world-view that needs to be 'demythologized'. However, the development of quantum physics has suggested to some that a closed universe is an equally outmoded or incomplete scientific view of reality.

Miracles performed by Jesus, the disciples, and Paul in the New Testament are not presented as 'wonders' (unusual occurrences that might breach known laws of nature), but as 'signs' (occurrences, possibly but not necessarily unusual, that make those involved more aware of God and his power or kingdom). This factor led the philosopher Ian Thomas Ramsey to describe them as 'disclosure situations'. Supreme among such events would be the resurrection of Jesus, the truth of which, according to Paul (1 Corinthians 15), is the basis of all Christian belief. The view, held by some Protestants, that miracles ended with the death of the apostles is challenged both by Roman Catholicism, which traditionally requires evidence of miraculous intervention by persons being considered for canonization as saints, and expects healings at holy places like Lourdes; and by Pentecostal and charismatic groups, which believe that the power of the Holy Spirit recorded in the early Church in the Book of Acts is still demonstrated today. ▷ Bultmann, Rudolf Karl; charismatic movement; deism; demonology, biblical; demythologizing; kingdom of God; Pentecostalism; Ramsey, Ian Thomas; resurrection

Mirandola ▷ Pico della Mirandola

Miriam (15th–13th century BCE) Sister of Moses and Aaron in the Hebrew Bible, usually identified with the unnamed sister who watched Moses put into the Nile in a basket, and who found his mother as a wetnurse for him when he was rescued by Pharaoh's daughter (Exodus 2). She is given the title of 'prophetess' when she leads the women of Israel in singing and dancing after the crossing of the Red Sea (Exodus 15). Later she and Aaron are depicted as challenging the exclusive right of Moses to speak in the name of Yahweh, and for this arrogance she is struck temporarily with leprosy (Numbers 12). She is remembered by later biblical tradition both for her leprosy and as a leader of the people together with Moses and Aaron. Traditions about Miriam and her prophecy are expanded in the Rabbinic literature; she is said to have prophesied Moses's birth and his future as a redeemer. ▷ Aaron; Moses; Yahweh

Mishnah (Hebrew 'repetition', referring to the practice of learning by repetition) An important written collection of rabbinic laws, supplementary to the legislation in Jewish Scriptures. A compilation of oral laws set down over a period of about 200 years, it is classified under six main headings (*sedarim*): Seeds (agricultural tithes), Set Feasts, Women, Damages, Holiness (offerings), and Purities. Although the Mishnah's general arrangement can be traced to Rabbi Akiva (c.120CE), its final editing was due to Rabbi Judah the Prince (c.200). Critical studies of the Mishnah were compiled into a work known as Gemara. This was joined to the Mishnah, forming the Talmud. ▷ Akiva ben Joseph; Gemara; Halakhah; Judaism; Talmud; Torah

Missal The liturgical book of the Roman Catholic Church, containing liturgies for the celebration of Mass throughout the year. It includes all the prayers, biblical readings, ceremonial, and singing directions. ▷ liturgy; Mass; Roman Catholicism

mission Missionary activity is primarily a feature of Buddhism, Christianity and Islam, the three world faiths which most obviously seek to win new adherents to their cause. Other faiths such as Judaism and Hinduism may occasionally proselytize but they are not truly missionary faiths. Missionary faiths are characterized by the possession of a unique revelation or universal truth, which transcends a particular historical situation and which compels them to take their vision to people everywhere. For example, the Christian message of salvation through Christ and the Buddhist doctrine of enlightenment demand transmission because of their universal application.

Missionary activity can take many forms. Buddhist monks took many centuries to spread their message from India throughout Asia to China, Tibet and Mongolia. From 400BCE to the 16th century CE Buddhist teaching was transmitted by wandering monks using trade routes. Islamic missionary activity, however, followed closely the path of Arab conquests in the early middle ages. So successful was this activity that it displaced Buddhism from its Indian birthplace for many centuries. Missionary activity has been a permanent feature of Christianity since its earliest inception. Quickly spreading to become the official religion of the Roman Empire in the 4th century CE, Christianity survived the collapse of the empire and established itself throughout Western Europe. The next major phase of Christian missionary activity took place in the wake of the expansion of European power into South America and Africa. Today missions are aware of the dangers of exporting culture rather than faith and the establishment of locally-led indigenous churches worshipping in terms drawn from local culture is the norm.

missions, Christian The promotion of Christian faith among non-Christian people. Missionary activity has been a permanent feature of Christianity, particularly in the Roman Catholic and Protestant Churches. In the past, it was often associated with the expansion of European or American power, but modern missions recognize the importance of establishing indigenous churches, with worship expressed in terms of local culture. ▷ Christianity; Paul, St

Mithra, or **Mithras** A god worshipped in the early Roman Empire, of Persian origin, and identified with the sun. The cult was predominantly military, and restricted to males; it was practised in caves, and involved baptism. Other resemblances to Christianity include Mithras's miraculous birth and his adoration by shepherds. The main story was of his fight with the bull, which he conquers and sacrifices. ▷ baptism; Roman religion

Mithraism A mystery cult which became prominent in Roman society in the early centuries of the Christian era. The cult appears to have been popular throughout the Roman Empire, and *mithraea*, the places where members gathered, have been found as far from Rome as Britain and Germany. No sacred texts of the cult are known, and its beliefs and tenets therefore have to be inferred from relatively few references in classical literature, and from material remains such as reliefs and statues. The scene which is most often portrayed, and which was evidently felt to be highly significant, is that of the god Mithra killing a bull. Astrological beliefs also played an important part in the world view of the Mithraists, and the cult knew a hierarchical pattern of grades of initiation. Since Mithra is an Iranian god, until a few decades ago scholars generally assumed that the cult had Iranian origins. Since then, many have preferred to regard Mithraism as a purely Roman phenomenon, dismissing its early origins as irrelevant, except in so far as the Mithraists themselves claimed Iranian origins for their beliefs. Recent developments in the study of ancient Iranian religions, however, suggest a direct link between Mithraism and the pre-Zoroastrian religion of the Western Iranians. ▷ cult; Mithra; Zoroastrianism

mitre, or **miter** (Greek *mitra*, 'turban') The liturgical headwear of a bishop of the Western Christian Church. It takes the form of a shield-shaped, high, stiff hat, representing the 'helmet of salvation'. ▷ bishop; liturgy; vestments

mitzvah (plural **mitzvot**) Hebrew word meaning 'commandment'. In Judaism a mitzvah is a particular commandment concerning individual or communal conduct or ritual. Accordingly the rabbis counted 613 mitzvot in the Torah, of which 248 are positive and 365 negative. However, this does not take into account those commandments no longer applicable in post-biblical times, nor the elaboration to which others were subjected. There are mitzvot covering every sphere of human behaviour. The resultant system of law, referred to as the Halakhah, may be viewed as central to traditional Judaism; it is both open-ended (allowing new rulings to be made in changed circumstances) and obligatory for individual and community alike (since it is revealed by God). Despite this, Judaism is not narrowly legalistic as has often been maintained, since the Torah is regarded as God's original blueprint for the universe. Thus adherence to the mitzvot brings life and harmony to the individual, the community and the cosmos. For this reason, the mitzvot, though obligatory, can be carried out in a spirit of devotion and joy. ▷ Aggadah; Halakhah; Kabbalah; Torah

Moabite Stone An inscribed basalt slab, discovered in 1868 and subsequently broken up, which describes the successful revolt of Mesha, King of Moab, against the Israelites during the reign of Ahab (7th century BCE) or possibly of his son Jehoram (2 Kings 1.1). It is also important for the linguistic and historical light cast on the Hebrew biblical narratives. ▷ Ahab; Old Testament

Moabite Stone

models of religion Models of religion provide a means of understanding and comparing individual religious traditions. A well-known model is that of Ninian Smart. He sees religion as a seven-dimensional organism, typically containing doctrines, myths, ethical teachings, rituals, social institutions and aesthetic representations, and animated by religious experiences of various kinds. Lying behind these seven dimensions is the history of the religion concerned, although the dimensions are, in effect, pegs which provide a framework within which the religion can be defined and subsequently compared with others. Michael Pye offers another model centred upon the four aspects of religious action, religious groups, religious states of mind, and religious concepts, which are subdivided into various sub-themes and comparisons. Smart uses his model to show that secular alternatives to religion, such as Marxism, humanism and nationalism, are functional equivalents to religion. By putting a notion of transcendence and a mediating focus at the beginning of the model (God in Christ, Allah in the Quran, Yahweh in the *Torah*, Brahman in the atman or a Hindu god, and nirvana in the Buddha or the Dharma), and a notion of faith or intentionality at the end of the model, it is possible to make it more substantive and yet keep it flexible and relevant to the study of religion. ▷ Allah; atman; Brahman; Buddha; dharma; humanism; Jesus Christ; Marxism; nirvana; Quran; secular alternatives to religion; Smart, Ninian; study of religion; Torah; Yahweh

moderator A person who presides over Presbyterian Church courts, such as the kirk session, presbytery, synod, or General Assembly. In Reformed Churches generally, the term is applied to the chairman of official Church gatherings. ▷ Presbyterianism; Reformed Churches

Modimo, or **Morimo, Molimo** or **Mlimo** The word used for God by the Sotho-Tswana and several other Bantu peoples of Southern Africa. Early 19th-century missionaries preaching the Christian God were assured by Tswana speakers that his Tswana name was Modimo. The same missionaries noted that, while people used the name constantly, they were little interested in the idea of creation. The meaning of the word is uncertain, though some have linked it with the root 'to penetrate, to permeate'. Grammatically the word belongs to a class of non-personal beings, implying 'it' rather then 'he', but it is also used as a title of honour for great men. Its regular plural *badimo* has a totally distinct meaning, that of the spirits of the dead collectively, of the lower divinities, of evil spirits, none of them being categories to which Modimo belongs. A modern Tswana scholar deduces from the traditional evidence that Modimo is: one; supreme; owner and master of all; invisible and intangible; mother; associated with the sky; the root and source of all; the enabler. Since Modimo is the source of all, all things and persons are related in him.

moksha (mokṣa) Liberation from transmigration (*samsara*) in Hinduism. Moksha is the ultimate, though perhaps far distant, goal of Hindus. Through performing meritorious deeds and fulfilling one's caste obligations (*svadharma*), a Hindu might hope to be reborn in circumstances conducive to attaining *moksha*, perhaps by becoming a renouncer and practising yoga. Generally speaking moksha is regarded as freedom from all sorrow, a state of bliss (*ananda*) and higher awareness beyond desire. However, different Hindu traditions understand moksha in different ways: as being attained by one's own efforts, or by the grace of a personal God, or by a mixture of both effort and grace. The nature of liberation is also variously understood. For example, the Advaita Vedanta regards moksha as the merging of the self (*atman*) into the absolute (*Brahman*) as a drop merges into the ocean without a ripple, whereas in Shaiva Siddhanta it is the soul's becoming equal, but not identical, with Shiva. In contrast, some Vaishnavas see moksha as being with Krishna in one of his heavens in a specific form. On the whole Hinduism maintains that there are many different ways to attain liberation: for example, the *Bhagavad Gita* mentions devotion (*Bhakti Yoga*), knowledge (*Jnana Yoga*) and action (*Karma Yoga*). The various spiritual practices of Hinduism aspire to liberation in life (*jivanmukti*), though some traditions, such as the Shaiva Siddhanta, have maintained that liberation will occur at death (*videhamukti*) by means of initiation (*diksha*) and by following a set of prescribed ritual obligations. ▷ Advaita Vedanta; Bhagavad Gita; bhakti; jivanmukti; Karma Yoga; Shaiva Siddhanta; samsara; yoga

Molina, Luis de (1535–1600) Spanish Jesuit theologian, born in Cuenca. He studied at Coimbra and was Professor of Theology at Évora for 20 years. His principal writings are a commentary on the *Summa* of Aquinas (1593); a treatise, *De Justitia et Jure* (1592); and the celebrated treatise on grace and free will, *Concordia Liberi Arbitrii cum Gratiae Donis* (1588). Molina asserts that predestination to eternal happiness or punishment is consequent on God's foreknowledge of the free determination of man's will. This view was assailed as a revival of Pelagianism, and hence arose the dispute between Molinists and Thomists. A papal decree in 1607 permitted both opinions; and Molinism has been taught by the Jesuits. ▷ Jesuits; Pelagius; Thomism

Moltmann, Jürgen (1926–) German Reformed theologian, born in Hamburg. A professor at Wuppertal (1958–63), Bonn (1963–7), and Tübingen (1967–), he is best known for his influential trilogy, *Theology of Hope* (1967), *The Crucified God* (1974), and *The Church in the Power of the Spirit* (1977); and also for *The Trinity and the Kingdom of God* (1981), the Gifford Lectures *God in Creation* (1985), *The Way of Jesus Christ* (1990). Probably the most significant Protestant theologian of the 20th century since Karl Barth, Moltmann's espousal of a theology of hope marked a reaction against the individualistic existential approach of Rudolf Bultmann, and a revival in Protestant theology of concern for the social nature of Christian faith in the modern world. His other books include *Hope and Planning* (1971), *On Human Dignity* (1984), and *Creating a Just Future* (1989). ▷ Barth, Karl; Bultmann, Rudolf Karl; Protestantism

monasticism A form of religious life found in both Christianity (mostly in Roman Catholic and Orthodox circles) and Buddhism, emphasizing the perfection of the individual either through a solitary ascetic existence or more often through life in a consecrated community. In Christianity the movement is often traced back to Antony and Pachomius of Egypt (late 3rd century). Although initially a lay movement, it soon became dominated by clergy, and was often marked by voluntary poverty and a life of devotion and worship. The most significant early monastic legislation was the rule of Benedict, which became a standard in Western Christianity. In the Middle Ages monks were increasingly involved in scholarly research and copying manuscripts. In the 13th century several new orders emerged, known as friars or mendicant orders, which combined monastic life with missionary preaching to those outside. Periods of decline and reform followed from the 14th century to the 16th century. ▷ Augustinians; Benedictines; Buddhism; Capuchins; Carmelites; Carthusians; Christianity; Cistercians; Dominicans; Franciscans; Mendicant Orders; Passionists; Taizé

Mongols The general name applied to the tribes of central Asia and south Siberia who effected the violent collapse of the Abbasid Empire before converting to Islam. United under Genghis Khan in 1206, they conquered China under his grandson Kublai, who ruled as first emperor of the Yan dynasty (1271–1368). ▷ Abbasids

monism A term coined by the German philosopher Christian Wolff (1679–1754) to refer to philosophical systems of thought which emphasize the oneness and unity of all reality. This is not to say that there is one monist school of philosophy, but rather it is an umbrella term which describes a number of different thinkers with a similar understanding of reality. There is agreement only on the oneness of ultimate reality but no agreed definition of what that unity is, whether it is 'being' itself, or idea, soul, substance or material reality. Monist philosophies occur in both Eastern and Western traditions. Plotinus (204–70) taught that ultimate reality is the One, which is absolute and transcendent, beyond description and known and percieved only through mystical experience. The One is the unity which underlies all individual and particular things. Sankara, an Indian philosopher of the 9th century, developed a monist understanding of the *Brahman* or Absolute, based on the ancient Hindu scriptures. Sankara taught that everything that we perceive as individual and particular—objects, people, thoughts, even gods—are real only in the sense that they are one with Brahman. Similar monist theories have been suggested by Benedict Spinoza (1632–77), who argued that the world is a manifestation of God within his own essential unity. Process theology may be the most recent monist philosophy as it argues that there is one ultimate reality relating itself to everything that is taking place in the universe. ▷ dualism; process theology; Spinoza, Baruch

Monophysites (Greek 'one nature') Adherents to the doctrine that Christ did not have two natures after his Incarnation—one human and one divine—but rather had only one nature, which was effectively divine since the divine apparently dominated the human. This view grew out of controversies over the nature and person of Christ which raged from the 4th to 6th centuries, associated especially with Eutyches (c.378–454, head of a monastery in Constantinople), and condemned by Pope Leo (449) and the Council of Chalcedon (451); yet variant forms continued to arise in subsequent centuries, especially influencing Coptic, Syrian, and Armenian churches. ▷ Christology; heresy

monotheism The belief that only one God exists. It developed within the Jewish faith, and remains a feature of Judaism, Christianity, and Islam. It is opposed to both polytheism and pantheism. Christian belief in the Trinity is thought by Muslims and Jews to deny monotheism. ▷ Christianity; God; Judaism; Islam; pantheism; polytheism

Montanism A popular Christian movement derived from Montanus of Phrygia (c.170) and two women, Prisca and Maximilla, whose ecstatic prophecies and literal expectation of the imminent end of the world won a wide following of churches in Asia Minor. Its austere ethical and spiritual ideals were opposed by the Catholic Church, which defended the importance of the institutional ministry and apostolic tradition. ▷ Christianity; prophet

Moody, Dwight Lyman (1837–99) American evangelist, born in Northfield, Massachusetts. He was a shoe salesman in Boston and in 1856 went to Chicago, where he gave up his job to engage in missionary work, and organized the North Market Sabbath School. In 1870 he was joined by Ira David Sankey (1840–1908), who was born in Edinburgh, Pennsylvania. In 1873 and 1883 they visited Great Britain as evangelists, Moody preaching and Sankey singing; afterwards they worked together in America. They published the *Sankey and Moody Hymn Book* (1873) and *Gospel Hymns* (1875). In 1899 he founded the Moody Bible Institute in Chicago. ▷ evangelist

Moon, Sun Myung (1920–) Korean religious leader, born in Pyungan Buk-do. In his main book, *The Divine Principle* (1952), he claimed that at the age of 16 he had a vision of Christ which told him that he was to complete Christ's work in the world. He began preaching in 1946 and two years later was imprisoned by the North Koreans. Escaping to South Korea in 1950, in 1954 he founded the Holy Spirit Association for the Unification of World Christianity, otherwise known as the Unification Church. This spread to Japan but was not successful in the West until the late 1960s, when it began to grow significantly in the USA. Moon has lived in the USA since the early 1970s. From the Unification Church headquarters at Tarrytown, New York, and their seminary at Barrytown, New York, he has spearheaded the life of the Church, establishing worldwide business operations, and educational conferences. He and his wife are revered by Unification Church followers (popularly known as Moonies) as the ideal family, and mass weddings have become an important ritual in the Church's life. *The Divine Principle* is a reinterpretation of the Bible, including additional revelations, and Christ is interpreted as having achieved spiritual but not physical salvation for the world. The present age is recognized as being of great significance and Moon himself is seen by his followers as a Messiah figure. His movement has been accused by the anti-cult movement of brainwashing and breaking up families, but his opponents in turn have been accused of illegally kidnapping Moonies and of forcible deprogramming. Moon's church is a fascinating example of a new religious movement of Christian origins, arising in Asia with global aspirations, that has grown and changed rapidly. Its total membership is estimated at about a quarter of a million. ▷ Anti-Cult movement; Jesus Christ; Messiah; new religious movements in the West; salvation; Unification Church

Moonies ▷ **Unification Church**

Moral Rearmament A movement founded by Frank Buchman in 1938 to deepen the spirituality and morality of Christians. It succeeded the 'Oxford Group Movement' (founded 1921), and the original individualistic and pietistic emphasis was expanded to include political and social concerns. At the heart of the movement is Buchman's belief in the importance of four 'absolute' qualities of life: absolute purity, absolute unselfishness, absolute honesty and absolute love. ▷ Buchman, Frank; Christianity; Pietism

moral theology A theological discipline concerned with ethical questions considered from a specifically Christian perspective. Its sources include scripture, tradition, and philosophy. In Roman Catholic teaching, it deals traditionally with God as the goal of human life, and provides instruction on spirituality and the means of grace. It is often divided into foundational and special moral theology, the former dealing with such topics as scriptural ethics, Christian anthropology, freedom, responsibility, and sin; the latter dealing with particular areas of social and political morality. Since the Second Vatican Council, it has become increasingly ecumenical, and is concerned with issues such as peace, justice, and bioethics. ▷ Christianity; ecumenism; ethics in religion; Roman Catholicism; theology; Vatican Councils

Moravian Brethren, or **Unitas Fratrum** A Protestant body descended from an association of Brethren formed in Bohemia in 1457. Holding evangelical beliefs, they stressed a Christ-centred, non-violent philosophy. They attached considerable importance to the place of hymns in worship and in 1501 printed the first Protestant hymn-book. Driven out of Bohemia in 1722 by persecution, they re-formed in Saxony under the title 'Moravian' rather than the earlier 'Bohemian' Brethren. They spread over Europe, where they were influenced by Pietism. In 1734 the Moravian Church was established in North America, where most members live today. Pioneers in missionary activity, they were especially keen to reach under-privileged societies such as the Innuit (Eskimos) and American Indians. Until 1793, when the Baptist Missionary Society was formed, they had more missionaries 'in the field' than the rest of the Protestant Church. ▷ missions, Christian; Pietism; Protestantism

Mordecai Biblical hero, described in the Book of Esther as a Jew in exile in Persia (c.5th century BCE) who cared for his orphaned cousin Esther and gained the favour of King Xerxes after uncovering a plot against him. He used his subsequent influence to protect Jews from an edict issued against them. The event is commemorated by the annual Jewish feast of Purim. ▷ Esther, Book of; Old Testament

More, Henry (1614–87) English philosopher and theologian, a leading figure in the circle of 'Cambridge Platonists'. Born in Grantham, Lincolnshire, his father being 'a gentleman of fair estate and fortune', he was educated at Eton and Christ's College, Cambridge, where he remained all his life. He devoted himself entirely to study, despite the turbulent political times in which he lived, and developed a particular affinity for Plato, Plotinus and Descartes, the last of whom he corresponded with enthusiastically at first, though his admiration for him later waned as his interest in occultism and mysticism grew. He was, however, generally concerned in his philosophy to demonstrate the compatibility of reason and faith. He wrote in both prose and verse and his main works were: *Philosophical Poems* (1647), *An Antidote against Atheism* (1653), *The Immortality of the Soul* (1659), *Enchiridion Ethicum* (1666) and *Divine Dialogues* (1668). ▷ Descartes, René; Plato; Plotinus

More, Sir Thomas, St (1478–1535) English statesman and scholar, born in London, the son of a judge. Educated at Oxford under John Colet and Thomas Linacre, he completed his legal studies at New Inn and Lincoln's Inn, and was for three years reader in Furnival's Inn, and spent the next four years in the Charterhouse in 'devotion and prayer'. During the last years of Henry VII he became Under-Sheriff of London and Member of Parliament. Introduced to Henry VIII through Wolsey, he became Master of Requests (1514), Treasurer of the Exchequer (1521), and Chancellor of the Duchy of Lancaster (1525). He was Speaker of the House of Commons, and was sent on missions to France to Francis I and Charles V. On the fall of Wolsey in 1529, More, against his own strongest wish, was appointed Lord Chancellor. In this office he displayed a primitive virtue and simplicity. The one stain on his character as judge is the harshness of his sentences for religious opinions. He sympathized with Colet and Erasmus in their desire for a more rational theology and for radical reform in the manners of the clergy, but like them also he had no promptings to break with the historic church. He saw with displeasure the successive steps which led Henry to the final schism from Rome. In 1532 he resigned the chancellorship. In 1534 Henry was declared head of the English Church; and More's steadfast refusal to recognize any other head of the Church than the pope led to his sentence for high treason after a harsh imprisonment of over a year. Still refusing to recant, he was beheaded. More was twice married; his daughter Margaret, the wife of his biographer William Roper, was distinguished for her high character, her accomplishments, and her pious devotion to her father. By his Latin *Utopia* (1516, English trans 1556), More takes his place with the most eminent humanists of the Renaissance. His *History of King Richard III* (1513) 'begins modern English historical writing of distinction'. Erasmus indicates a man of a winning rather than an imposing personality. He was canonized in 1935. His feast day is 9 July. ▷ Erasmus; humanism; Wolsey, Thomas

Morisco The name given to those Spanish Muslims and their descendants who accepted Christian baptism. They were expelled from Spain in 1609. ▷ Christianity; Islam

Mormons The name given to religious sects that base their beliefs on *The Book of Mormon*. The largest of these sects, with over four million followers (most of whom live in America), is headquartered in Salt Lake City, Utah—'The Church of Jesus Christ of Latter-Day Saints'. A religious movement based on the visionary experiences of Joseph Smith, who founded it in 1830 at Fayette, New York. Smith claimed to have been led to the *Book of Mormon*, inscribed on golden plates and buried 1000 years before on a hill near Palmyra, New York. An account of an ancient American people to whom Jesus Christ appeared after his ascension, it teaches Christ's future establishment of the New Jerusalem in America. Along with other works by Smith, Mormons take their doctrine from the King James Version of the Bible. Mormonism diverges widely from Christian doctrine. Mormons believe that the trinity are three separate beings, Heavenly Father and Jesus Christ (who have physical bodies) and the Holy Ghost (who is a spiritual being). Mormons believe humans are literally God's children, that God was once like them, and that they can become gods and that many others have achieved godhood. Mormons hold that humans existed before birth in spirit form with God, and that in this pre-birth state Satan rebelled against God and was cast out of heaven. Some Mormons believe that faithfulness in their pre-birth state determines race and other human characteristics. After death most people will be sent to a heavenly kingdom. Christ's Incarnation is seen to be unique only because he was the first. Followers believe in the coming of a millennium when Christ will rule over the world from Jerusalem and Independence, Missouri. Mormons consider that the Christian Church had abandoned its principles until 1830, when it was restored under Joseph Smith, becoming the only true church. ▷ Jesus Christ; Smith, Joseph

Mosaic Law ▷ Torah

Moses, Hebrew *Môsheh* (15th–13th century BCE) Old Testament Hebrew prophet and lawgiver. According to the Pentateuch he led the people of Israel out of Egypt by way of Sinai, Kadesh and Moab (where he died) towards the Promised Land. On Mount Sinai he was given the Ten Commandments by Yahweh (Jehovah). As a child in Egypt he was saved from the slaughter of all male Jewish children by being hidden in bulrushes in the Nile, where he was found and brought up by one of Pharaoh's daughters. ▷ Pentateuch; Sinai, Mount; Ten Commandments; Yahweh

Moses ben Maimon ▷ Maimonides

Moslem ▷ Muslim

mosque A building in which Muslims meet for prayer, worship, education, and social intercourse. The word is taken from the Arabic term *masjid*, which means a place of prostration. The area around the Kabah in Mecca was called a masjid before Muhammad's time, and Abu-Bakr (the first caliph after the death of Muhammad) built a place of prayer next to his house in Mecca during Muhammad's early ministry. The first mosque as such was built by Muhammad at Quba in Medina. The style of mosques varies according to culture; for example, Chinese mosques often have Chinese aesthetic characteristics. However, in all mosques there is normally a place of worship where the worshippers assemble in rows behind their imam or prayer leader when he leads the ritual prayers. There is a mihrab, or niche, which indicates the direction of Mecca, there is a pulpit from which the Friday sermon is delivered, and there is often a stand upon which the Quran rests. There is also a courtyard containing facilities for washing, since ablutions are necessary before the performance of prayer. In addition there is often a minaret (or minarets) that the muezzin can ascend in order to give the call to prayer. Some of the great mosques of Islam, for example Cairo, Cordoba, Isfahan and Istanbul, are superb examples of architecture and artistic adornment. Although most daily prayers can be said anywhere, the Friday noonday prayer takes place whenever possible in a mosque in the presence of a congregation. ▷ Abu-Bakr; Islamic art; Friday Prayer in Islam; imam; Mecca; Medina; Mihrab; salat

mother goddesses ▷ matres, matrones

Mo Tzu (c.470–391BCE) Chinese philosopher, whose life spanned the period between the death of Confucius in 479 and the birth of Mencius around 371. He differed from them and founded a Moist movement that lasted until the time of the Han dynasty (206BCE). His best-known theory was that of universal love, and it is being revived in some quarters now, as being relevant to the global situation into which we are moving. He argued that universal love for all was in accord with the will of heaven and was to the benefit of human beings in that it would devalue offensive war and create better human relations. Mencius retorted that one should begin at home with filial piety and 'graded love' before trying to love equally the families, parents and countries of others, and this remained the Confucian position. Mo Tzu was a utilitarian who weighed up the merit of various courses of action on the basis of whether they would increase in practice the health and prosperity of humankind. He condemned ceremonies, music and elaborate rituals such as funerals, arguing that they did not promote righteousness and were against the will of heaven, which he deeply respected. He believed in an ordered state where there was, as he put it, 'agreement with the superior', but he saw the state as a defensive rather than an aggressive organ of power. ▷ Confucius; five relationships, Confucian; Mencius; Tien

Mount of Olives ▷ Olives, Mount of

Mount Sinai ▷ Sinai, Mount

mudras Symbolic gestures, especially gestures of the hands, used in classical Indian dance, in Hindu and Tantric rituals, and in Hindu and Buddhist iconography. In the Buddhist context the word refers especially to the hand-gestures made by the Buddha. These are profoundly symbolic, and tell a vivid story to Buddhist devotees as they gaze at a Buddha image. Five mudras are of outstanding importance: the Buddha raises his right hand as a symbol of calming fear; he forms a wheel with his hands as a symbol of his teaching; he puts his hands together facing upwards as a symbol of meditation; he points his hand to the earth to call it as a witness; and he holds out his hand to offer gifts to the world. Classical Indian dance uses hundreds of mudras in standard yet beautiful miming gestures. It is common in popular Indian worship to touch six parts of the body with appropriate gestures. Mudras are used in various forms of Hindu worship, and they can be used in Tantric meditation to evoke and therefore form the intention of attaining a higher state of consciousness. ▷ bhavana; Buddha; Buddha image; Tantra; Tantric Buddhism; Tantric Hinduism

muezzin In Islam, an official of the mosque who issues the call to prayer to the faithful. The name means 'announcer'. ▷ Islam

Mughal or **Mogul Empire** An important Indian Muslim state (1526–1857), founded by Babur (1526–30). It temporarily declined under Humayun (1530–40), who lost control to the Afghan chieftain Sher Shah (1540–5). His son, Akbar the Great, defeated the Afghan challenge at Panipat (1556) and extended the empire to include territory between Afghanistan and Deccan. This was a period of religious freedom, in which a policy of conciliation was pursued with the Rajput states. Akbar was succeeded by Jehangir (1605–27) and Shah Jehan (1627–58). Its last great emperor was Aurangzeb (1658–1707), who extended the limits of the empire further south; however, religious bigotry alienated non-Muslim supporters and undermined the empire's unity. The Empire disintegrated under Maratha and British pressure. By the mid 18th century it ruled only a small area around Delhi. Its last emperor, Bahadur Shah II (1837–57) was exiled by the British to Rangoon after the 1857 uprising. ▷ Akbar the Great

Muhammad (Muḥammad), or **Mohammed** (c.570–c.632) Arab prophet, and founder of Islam, born in Mecca. He was the son of Abdallah, a poor merchant of the powerful tribe of Quaraysh, hereditary guardians of the shrine in Mecca. Orphaned at six, he was brought up by his grandfather and uncle, Abu Talib, who trained him to be a merchant. At the age of 24 he entered the service of a rich widow, Khadijah (c.595–619), whom he eventually married. They had six children, including their daughters Fatimah and Umm Kulthum, who married Uthman, the third caliph. While continuing as a trader, Muhammad became increasingly drawn to religious contemplation. Soon after 600 (the traditional date is c.610) he began to receive revelations of the word of Allah, the one and only God. This Quran (Koran), or 'reading', commanded that the numerous idols of the shrine should be destroyed and that the rich should give to the poor.

This simple message attracted some support but provoked a great deal of hostility from those who felt their interests threatened. When his wife and uncle died, Muhammad was reduced to poverty, but began making a few converts amongst pilgrims to Mecca from the town of Yathrib, an agricultural community to the north. By 622 the position of Muhammad and his small band of devoted followers had become untenable, but they were saved by an invitation from the people of Yathrib, who wanted Muhammad to come and arbitrate in the feuds that racked their community. He migrated there, and this migration, the Hegira, marks the beginning of the Muslim era. The name of the town was changed to Medina, 'the city of the prophet'.

The most important act in the first year of the Hegira was Muhammad's permission to go to war with the enemies of Islam—especially the Meccans—in the name of God. In December 623 his Muslims defeated a Meccan force, but he was severely wounded at a battle at Ohod (January 625). In 627 he repelled a Meccan siege of Medina. By 629 he was able to take control of Mecca, which recognized him as chief and prophet. By 630 he had control over all Arabia. In March 632 he undertook his last pilgrimage to Mecca, and there on Mount Arafat fixed for all time the ceremonies of the pilgrimage. He fell ill soon after his return and died on 8 June in the home of the favourite of his nine wives, Aishah, daughter of one of his first followers, Abu-Bakr. His tomb in the mosque at Medina is venerated throughout Islam. ▷ Abu-Bakr; Islam; Mecca; pilgrimage; Quran

Muharram The first month of the Muslim year; also used as the name of a religious celebration, especially among Shiite Muslims, held at that time in commemoration of the death of Husain, grandson of Muhammad, with processions in which the faithful beat their breasts or whip themselves. ▷ Muhammad; Islam; Shiism

mujtahid A man who exercises personal interpretation of the shariah or Muslim divine law. Shiism allows such interpretations, while Sunnism has usually refused them. ▷ Islam; shariah; Shiism; Sunnis

mullah (Arabic 'master') In Islam, a scholar, teacher, or man of religious piety and learning. It is also a title of respect given to those performing duties related to Islamic Law. ▷ Islam; shariah

Müller, (Friedrich) Max (1823–1900) German-born British philologist and orientalist, born in Dessau, where his father, the poet Wilhelm Müller (1794–1827), was ducal librarian. He studied at Dessau, Leipzig and Berlin, and took up the then novel subject of Sanskrit and its kindred sciences of philology and religion. In Paris, under Eugène Burnouf, he began to prepare an edition of the *Rig Veda*, the sacred hymns of the Hindus; he came to England in 1846 to examine the MSS, and the East India Company commissioned him (1847) to edit and publish it at their expense (1849–74). He was appointed Taylorian Professor of Modern Languages at Oxford (1854) and Professor of Comparative Philology (1868 onwards), a subject he did more than anyone else to promote in Britain. Among his most popular works were *Lectures on the Science of Language* (1861–4), *Auld Lang Syne* (1898), and *My Indian Friends* (1898), and he edited the *Sacred Books of the East* (51 vols, 1879–1910). ▷ Sanskrit; Veda

Mul Mantra (Mūl Mantra) An important Sikh theological poem composed by the first Sikh guru, Guru Nanak. Together with the equally significant *Japji*, it is considered to be his earliest composition, and they are placed together at the beginning of the Sikh scripture, the *Guru Granth Sahib*. The *Mul Mantra* contains the kernel of Sikh theology in its assertion that God is one and true; He is the creator and sustainer of all things and He is immanent in all things; He is beyond time and rebirth; He is beyond the emotions of fear and enmity; yet He is self-manifesting, and is known through the grace of the Guru. Unlike Hindu mantras the *Mul Mantra* is not secret but is open to all and is formally taught and interpreted in connection with Sikh initiation (*Amritsanskar*). Its importance is heightened by its being placed, in shortened form, at the head of each section of the *Guru*

Granth Sahib. ▷ amrit; Guru Granth Sahab; Japji; Khalsa; mantra; Nanak

Mulungu, or **Murungu, Mlungu, Mluku, Mungu** or **Mngu** One of the most widespread names of God in East and Central Africa, found from the Lower Zambesi to Lake Victoria. Despite the fact that it occurs in many languages, the meaning is obscure. Generally speaking it stands for God the creator, associated with sky, rain and thunder. In most languages it has no plural, on the ground that Mulungu is one; all other spirit beings are of a different class. But examples can be found of languages where its plural stands for ancestral spirits, as well as the use of the word not as a name but as an impersonal term for the supernatural as a whole. A 19th-century observer of the Ngoni understood it as the corporate representation of all the spirits of the departed. Bible translations in at least 25 languages use it as the name of God.

mummification The process of embalming used in Ancient Egypt, where survival after death depended on the preservation of the corpse in a recognizable form. The soft internal organs and brain were removed to deter decomposition and the flesh dehydrated using natron, then treated with oils and resins. The body was padded out and wrapped in linen bandages, under which amulets were inserted. The mummy was put in its coffin wearing a mask with the deceased's features, and the whole process was highly ritualized. In the late period cheaper mummies used only bitumen as a preservative. Many sacred animals were also mummified for burial. ▷ afterlife; animal cults; Anubis; funerary practices, Ancient Egyptian

Münzer, Thomas (c.1489–1525) German religious reformer and Anabaptist, born in Stolberg. He studied theology, and in 1520 began to preach at Zwickau. His socialism and mystical doctrines soon brought him into collision with the authorities. After preaching widely, in 1525 he was elected pastor of the Anabaptists of Mülhausen, where his communistic ideas soon aroused the whole country. He joined the Peasants' Revolt of 1524–5, but was defeated at Frankenhausen, and executed a few days later. ▷ Anabaptists

Murti ▷ iconography, Hindu

music, Ancient Near Eastern Music was important from a very early period in the religious life of Ancient Mesopotamia and Egypt, where it accompanied the daily temple ritual, the great festivals, and also funerary rites. The Sumerians believed that its sounds were pleasing to the gods, and it is clear that families of professional musicians were active among the personnel of temples. Much of the temple music involved the singing of hymns and psalms, often accompanied. The musical instruments which were used are known from illustrations, reliefs and models. Some instruments have been preserved intact, such as the famous Ur lyre which has a bull-shaped soundbox. Harps and lyres predominate, but a variety of other stringed, wind, brass and percussion instruments were also used in both Mesopotamia and Egypt. The instrument most characteristic of Egyptian religion was the sistrum rattle, a symbol of the goddess Hathor. Systems of musical notation were developed in the Ancient Near East, but examples of these have proved difficult to decipher, and reconstructions are largely speculative. ▷ festivals, Ancient Near Eastern; Hathor; temples, Ancient Near Eastern

music, Christian The early Christians used the Psalms of the Old Testament in worship and sang songs and hymns. St Ambrose (c.339–397) is considered the father of Latin hymnody, while the traditional music of the Roman Catholic Church, the so-called Gregorian chant or plainsong, chiefly dates from the 10th century. Palestrina (c.1525–1594), the most distinguished composer of the Renaissance, developed the motet. The Reformation period is noted for Luther's chorales and Calvin's metrical psalms; the next century for the cantatas, chorales, and *St Matthew Passion* (1729) of J S Bach (1685–1750), and

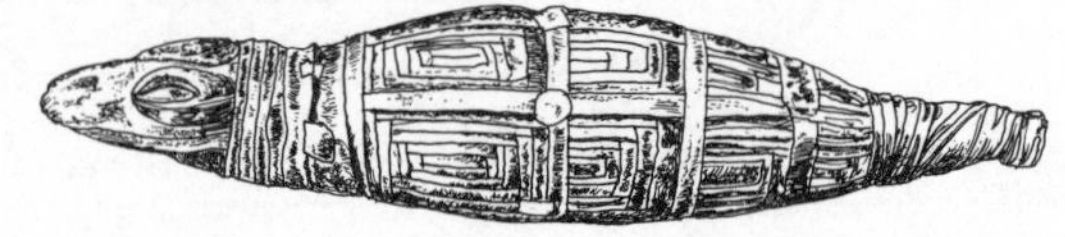

mummified crocodile

the cantatas and oratorios, especially the *Messiah* (1742) of Handel (1685–1759). In Britain metrical psalms became popular in worship, but were eventually overtaken in England by hymns. Many of the compositions of Isaac Watts (1674–1748), Charles (1707–88) and John Wesley (1703–91), are still found in current hymnals. The mid 17th century saw the widespread destruction of church organs (which had been used in parish churches since the 13th century) by the Puritans, but after the Restoration they were reintroduced and a golden age of Baroque organ music followed. In the 20th century, the classical sacred music tradition has continued largely unchanged, with few sustained attempts at expression in modern idiom, apart from the works of the French composer and organist Olivier Messiaen (1908–). There has, however, been an explosion of popular sacred music, from the revivalist songs of Dwight Moody (1837–99) and Ira David Sankey (1840–1908) to 1960s and 1970s folk masses, rock and youth musicals, songs of charismatic renewal and songs that can be accompanied on guitars or sung unaccompanied (like the chants from the ecumenical community of Taizé). Black Gospel music and hymns and tunes from Africa have also had some influence. While much of this varied material has proved ephemeral, some has been incorporated in new hymnals, and is often used in small singing groups that meet in private homes, as well as in more formal worship in church buildings.

music, Hebrew Bible Music played a part in the secular and sacred life of ancient Israel from earliest times, but the systematic organization of religious music probably did not begin until the age of David and Solomon (10th century BCE), when the Jerusalem Temple was planned and built. King David himself is portrayed as a proficient musician and composer of psalms. The Books of Chronicles provide information about the families of Levitical singers who were responsible for the temple music; these were a group of highly trained professionals following the pattern of Ancient Mesopotamia. The Book of Psalms contains examples of the kind of hymns, prayers, lamentations, and thanksgivings sung in the temple, and it is likely that they were accompanied by a variety of musical instruments: lyre and harp, pipes and flute, and a range of percussion instruments. The shophar or ram's horn was blown as a signal both in the cult and in times of war. It is almost impossible to reconstruct the sound of Israelite music; although the psalm superscriptions include musical instructions these are largely inaccessible to the modern reader. It is likely that the music of the temple influenced the development of later Jewish and Christian plainsong and chant. ▷ Chronicles, Books of; David; Levites; Psalms, Book of; Solomon

music, Hindu Music plays an integral role in Hinduism, from mantras, the sonic representatives of power in the universe, through Vedic chants, devotional songs (*bhajan*), music and song as accompaniment to the dramatization of the Epics and *Puranas*, to the complex classical genre, the *raga*, many of which were written and performed as devotion to particular deities. Music has a specifically religious connotation, since the world is created and maintained by vibration, and involvement in music is seen as a path to liberation (*ganamarga*, 'song-way'). Devotional songs can either be directed towards a personal god, such as those of the saint Tyagaraja (1767–1847) dedicated to Rama, or those of Mira Bai (1403–70) dedicated to Krishna; or they can be a religious expression of *nirguna Brahman*, such as those of Kabir. ▷ Kabir; Krishna; mantra; Mira Bai; nirguna brahman

music, Islamic Along with most other forms of aesthetic endeavour, music has been less important in mainstream Islam than in most other religious traditions. However, the chanting of the Quran and of the call to prayer have been developed to a high degree as forms of musical expression. In some of the Sufi orders music, in the sense of dancing, flute-playing, and the singing or chanting of vernacular hymns, has been much more developed. The main Sufi liturgy, know as *dhikr*, is based on the continued chanting of the names of God to the accompaniment of music. The so-called whirling dervishes of the Mevlevi order make great use of Turkish songs, of the reed flute with its symbolic plaintive cry for God, and of their four-point dance wherein they ritually enact the encounter of the soul with God. Among Sufis music is seen as a means of achieving spiritual ecstasy and bringing the soul into intimate awareness of God. ▷ Islamic art; Call to Prayer; dervish; dhikr; Mevlevis; Quran; Sufism

music, Jewish Although the Bible witnesses to various types of folk music and to music associated with magic and prophecy, music is chiefly connected with worship in the Temple at Jerusalem. It was performed by a class of professional musicians, the Levites, and was both vocal and instrumental. However, after the destruction of the Temple in 70CE attitudes changed. To mourn the Temple's loss musical instruments were banned from synagogues; their employment came to be viewed as a distraction, and some even considered them satanic in origin. This meant that Judaism developed an adaptable semi-oral tradition of cantillation in which the liturgy, including the Hebrew text of the Bible, was chanted. However, with Jewish emancipation from the late 18th century onwards the situation altered again, so that the Reform movement adopted musical instruments and choirs at synagogue services after the pattern of Christian worship. Further, from this time there arose individual Jewish composers and musicians in a modern sense, eg, Felix Mendelssohn (1809–47), Jewish-born grandson of Moses Mendelssohn. More recent figures include Leonard Bernstein (1918–90) and Aaron Copland (1900–91). However, the question then arises of whether Jewish music is defined by the Jewishness of the composer or by the employment of traditional Jewish sounds. ▷ art, Jewish; cantor; Mendelssohn, Moses; worship, Jewish

Muslim A follower of the Islamic tradition—literally, one who has 'surrendered' to God, from the Arabic word *aslama*, 'to surrender'. The associated word Islam, meaning surrender or submission, has become the name for the Muslim tradition. This is one of the rare cases where the name of a religion has arisen within the tradition itself, rather than being given by outsiders: the Christians were called Christians, *Christianoi*, in Antioch; the Hindus were called Hindus by the Muslims; and the Shinto in Japan were given that name by the Chinese. The word Muslim assumes that the initiative is with God. The Muslim has surrendered and submitted to God, and is resigned to do the will of God, therefore it is God who acts and the Muslim who follows. There is discussion among Muslims at the moment about the tension between the notion of Islam as a dynamic, historical and self-conscious religious tradition, and the notion of Muslims as those who are surrendered to a sovereign God. A great compiler of the sayings (Hadith) of Muhammad was also called Muslim (Abu-l-Husayn Muslim 816–73), and his two collections of Hadith are ranked as two of the most important within the Islamic tradition. ▷ Allah; Hadith; Islam

Muslim Brotherhood An Islamic movement, founded in Egypt in 1928 by an Egyptian schoolteacher, Hasan al-Banna, its original goal being the reform of Islamic society by eliminating Western influences and other decadent accretions. Subsequently, it became more radical, and its goal of a theocratic Islamic state found support in many other Sunni countries. ▷ Islam; Sunnis

Mutazilites (Mu'tazilites) An important school of thought within early Islam which was significant for the development of Muslim theology as a science (*kalam*), and was especially important in the 8th and 9th centuries. They were influenced by rationalist currents emanating from the Greek world-view, and introduced philosophical notions into Islam that were not altogether compatible with the Quran. Their stress was upon reason, free will, upon the Quran as created, and on God's attributes as being one with his essence. The orthodox Muslim position later inspired by al-Ashari (873–935) veered more towards revelation, determinism, the Quran as uncreated, and the notion that God's attributes were *in* his essence but were *not* his essence. Politically the Mutazilites took a middle position between the Sunnis and Shiites by virtue of their philosophical principle of the importance of 'a position between two positions'. In practice they became a formative influence upon Shiite theology, especially that of the Twelvers. Although a temporary force within Islamic history, they were important for their philosophical insight, their theological finesse, and their attempts at intellectual mediation which fed into the evolution of Islamic philosophy and theology. ▷ Ashari, al-; predestination in Islam; kalam; Quran; rationalism; Shiism; Sunnis; Twelvers

Mwari The name of God among the Shona people of Zimbabwe and one of the names among the Venda of Transvaal. Amongst the northern Shona he is acknowledged as creator, but is not thought of as often intervening directly in human life except to punish major breaches of the order he established, eg incest. Normal religious activity is directed to the *midzimu* or ancestral spirits, who indeed may be appropriate intercessors with Mwari when necessary (though he is less likely to be interested in personal than national concerns). Among the southern Shona, however, especially the Kalanga and Karanga, Mwari is the centre of a major cult, and has an oracle where he speaks directly. His home is in the Matopo Hills, where his caves are, and his presence is sometimes shown there by fire. The cult is esoteric, with its own priesthood versed in its secrets, and the oracle is consulted over a wide area, not only by Shona and Venda people but by Ndebele and others. Such a cult of the supreme being, where he speaks through a priesthood, is unusual in Africa. Mwari is often used as the name of the

Christian God, but some groups, anxious to distinguish God from the oracle, reject this.

Mycenaean religion Information about Mycenaean Greek religion comes from three principal sources. First, in the early Mycenaean period (1600–1400BCE) cult scenes engraved on gold rings, of local manufacture or imported from Crete, are a rich source of information about ritual actions at altars and before a seated female divinity. Dance rituals, offerings of flowers, pulling or shaking a tree, and the eight-shaped shield are all comparable with Minoan scenes. The problem is whether these Minoan-derived rituals were understood and practised by the Mycenaeans who owned the rings displaying the rituals, or whether the rings were simply decorative. The number of such scenes on rings on the mainland suggests at least some degree of actual religious practice. Likewise the one known major early Mycenaean religious site on the mainland, the hill sanctuary of the later Apollo Maleatas above Epidauros, has clear links with Minoan mountain shrines. The contemporary temple on the Cycladic island of Kea had at least 32 (and perhaps over 80) female statues of Minoan form but unparalleled in size in Crete, and whose divine status is not certain. Secondly, a series of shrines from the later Mycenaean period (1400–1200BCE), within and beside the citadel walls of Mycenae and Tiryns and at Phylakope on Melos, are for the most part different from Minoan shrines. Their location suggests that protection of the citadel was a primary purpose. Statuettes of one or more female divinities stood on benches or stands in these shrines, or were in store. Stylized votive statuettes were present in some numbers at Tiryns; offerings of beads were *in situ* at Mycenae. At the latter site models of coiled snakes probably represent desired protection and well-being of households and buildings. Within palaces wall paintings of richly dressed women in procession and holding offerings indicate ritual action at palatial level. Finally, the Mycenaean Greek (Linear B) tablets from Pylos, Thebes, Mycenae and from the period of Mycenaean control at Knossos list over 20 divinities by name, a clear polytheism. Several, such as Zeus, Hera, Poseidon and Hermes, show that Greek religion was already well developed in the 14th and 13th centuries BCE. ▷ Greek religion; Minoan religion

Mysteria The cult of the Mysteries at Eleusis was a cult of the Athenian state, but one which, very unusually, was open, on payment of a fee, to all Greeks. The Mysteries honoured Demeter, goddess of corn, and her daughter Persephone, goddess of the underworld. The content of the rites was a well-kept secret, but we do know that the large crowds who underwent initiation (a process that took several days) were promised a better lot in the afterlife. Little is known about other mystery-cults of the classical period in Greece. In the later Graeco-Roman period, 'Mysteries' of various kinds proliferated; these, it seems, often promised to improve the initiate's lot in this life as much as in the next. ▷ Greek religion; underworld

mysteries, Eastern Orthodox The rites in the *Euchologion* liturgical book, which combines what the Western Church distinguishes as sacraments and occasional offices or sacramentals. The chief mysteries are baptism, chrismation (an anointing with holy oil akin to confirmation, though not a separate service from baptism as in the West), confession, Eucharist, marriage, *euchelaion* (prayer for the sick, corresponding to extreme unction), and ordination. The other mysteries include monastic profession, funeral and memorial services, and various rites of blessing. ▷ baptism; confirmation; Eucharist; marriage/divorce, Christian; Orders, Holy; sacrament

mystery religions Religious cults of the Graeco-Roman world, full admission to which was restricted to those who had gone through certain secret initiation rites or mysteries. The most famous were those of Demeter at Eleusis in Greece, but the cults of Dionysus, Isis, and Mithra also involved initiation into mysteries. ▷ Greek religion; Roman religion

mysticism The spiritual quest for the most direct experience of God, or—in non-religious terms—a hidden wisdom. The need for such a search is partly explained in Tagore's belief that 'man has a feeling that he is truly represented in something which exceeds himself'. Characteristically, mysticism concentrates on prayer, meditation, contemplation, and fasting, so as to produce the attitude necessary for what is believed to be a direct encounter with God. Christian mysticism tends to focus on the person and sufferings of Christ, attempting to move beyond image and word to the immediate presence of God. In contrast with other forms of mysticism, Christian mystics reject the idea, common in some other religions, of the absorption of the individual into the divine, and retain the distinction between the individual believer and God. Mysticism takes its place in religion alongside the devotional aspect of worship, although many argue as to the relative merits of each. ▷ God; meditation; prayer; religion; Tagore, Sir Rabindranath

mythology The traditional stories of a people, often orally transmitted. They usually tell of unbelievable things in a deliberate manner, so that a 'myth' can mean both 'an untrue story', and 'a story containing religious truth'. The subject-matter of myths is either the gods and their relations with human or other beings, or complex explanations of physical phenomena. Until recently mythology implied Greek mythology, which is distinct in its concentration on stories of heroes and heroines, and its avoidance of the bizarre episodes in contemporary Near Eastern myths. Greek mythology was largely derived from Homer; it referred to a specific historical period (before the Trojan War), and it was, to a certain extent, rationalized and beautified by later writers. The use of this mythology by Elizabethan and Romantic poets indicates a wish to break out of narrowly Christian patterns of behaviour. Some writers (such as Blake and Yeats) created mythical systems of their own by synthesizing disparate materials. Recent scholarship has been either folklorist or structuralist, finding unexpected parallels in myths from widely different sources, and showing their function in determining social behaviour. ▷ Blake, William; demythologizing; Greek religion; Mythos

Mythos No 'myths' are so familiar as those of Greece; yet for once the Greeks did not have a word for it. Mythos originally means simply 'word, speech, story'. In the 5th century BCE, a distinction between mythos—fanciful or unreliable speech—and *logos*—rational, well-founded speech—begins to appear; but in this sense *mythoi* are tall stories in general, not 'myths' in our sense. The Greeks, therefore, had no myths; what they had were 'stories about gods and heroes' (as they might have said) which later came to be seen as 'myths'. ▷ Greek religion

N

nabi (nabī) An Islamic term for prophet. The Muslim tradition refers to two kinds of prophet: the *rasul*, or messenger, who brings a new kind of revelation to the world; and the nabi, who is a prophet within an existing tradition. The line of rasuls, or messengers, is seen to be more significant than the nabis, and includes Adam, Seth, Noah, Abraham, Ishmael, Moses, Lot, Jesus and Muhammad. The nabis are more numerous—Islamic tradition mentions 124000—and they bring good news to their contemporaries, but also warning about the judgement to come if people do not mend their ways. The Quran includes a number of native Arabian prophets, other prophets taken from the Hebrew Bible, and others such as John the Baptist and Jesus from the Christian New Testament. Muhammad is seen as the fulfilment of the prophets, and the Quran is considered to be the fulfilment of earlier scriptures. Muhammad is also seen as the last of the prophets; hence later 'prophets', such as Bahaullah (1817–97) of the Bahai tradition, and Mirza Ghulam Ahmad (1835–1908) of the Ahmadiyyah tradition, are viewed as inauthentic within traditional Islam. ▷ Abraham in Islam; Adam and Eve; Ahmadiyyah; Bahaism; Bahaullah; Jesus Christ in Islam; John, St (the Baptist); Muhammad; New Testament; prophet; Quran; Revelation, in Islam

Nagarjuna (Nāgārjuna) (c.150–c.250) Indian Buddhist monk-philosopher. He was the founder of the Madhyamika or Middle Path school of Buddhism. ▷ Buddhism; Madhyamika

Nag Hammadi texts A library of religious texts recorded in Coptic and discovered in 1945 in Egypt near the town of Nag Hammadi. It consists of some 12 books containing 52 tractates, the scriptures of the Christian Gnostic movement in Egypt, although some works are neither openly 'Gnostic' or 'Christian' but are rather of a philosophical or Jewish character. It is valuable evidence for this early form of 'heretical' Christianity, and contains many previously unknown works. ▷ Christianity; Copts; Gnosticism

Nahmanides, or **Nachmanides** (1195–1270) The Latinized name of the Spanish Jewish scholar and mystic, otherwise known as Rabbi Moses ben Nahman (or Ramban for short). He was an expert in the Bible and Talmud, whose work had a great impact on the Jews of Spain and Provence. This influence continued up to the expulsion of the Jews from Spain in 1492 and, less markedly, thereafter. Indeed, as one of numerous important medieval commentators, Nahmanides' text still appears in rabbinic editions of the Bible. In his commentary on the Torah Nahmanides stressed the importance of both the plain meaning of the text and its deeper, typological and mystical meanings. Accordingly, he maintained that every word of the Pentateuch was of spiritual significance; he even argued that at base it is made up of the secret names of God. However, the fact that he was a respected talmudic scholar and halakhist helped Nahmanides in the task of promulgating the wide acceptance of mysticism. Holding that the Kabbalah was of the essence of Jewish faith, he convinced many throughout Spain of its compatibility with traditional Rabbinic Judaism. Nahmanides spent the last years of his life in Palestine, revitalizing the Jerusalem community and becoming head of the Jews in Acre. ▷ Halakkah; Kabbalah; Nahman of Bratslav; Torah

Nahman, or **Nachman of Bratslav** (1772–1810) Lithuanian Hasidic rabbi, great-grandson of Baal Shem Tov, who founded Hasidism; not to be confused with the 13th-century Spanish kabbalist Nahmanides. After spending some time in Palestine, where he had a transforming mystical experience, he returned to Lithuania, proclaiming himself to be the tzaddiq (normally the spiritual leader of a particular hasidic group, thought of as perfectly righteous) of his whole generation. Influenced by Lurianic Kabbalah, he stressed the search for truth as the means of salvation for Israel and the world. Nonetheless he was rejected by the hasidic establishment. In 1802 he moved to the Lithuanian town of Bratslav, heading a band of Hasidim and composing works which were written down by a disciple. In these he communicated through imaginative stories the contrast between the heavenly, ideal world and the earthly, human sphere. Although Nahman had messianic pretensions, both for himself and his son, he attributed his rejection by his contemporaries to their unpreparedness for the messianic era. However, distressed by the deaths of his son and wife, he himself also fell ill and died. ▷ Baal Schem Tov; Hasidism; Kabbalah; Luria, Isaac

Nahum, Book of One of the 12 so-called 'minor' prophetic writings of the Hebrew Bible/Old Testament, attributed to a prophet named Nahum, about whom little else is known. The oracle vigorously announces the imminent downfall of Assyria and the destruction of Nineveh (612BCE), which is interpreted as the Lord's judgement upon its wickedness and as good news for Judah. It was perhaps intended to encourage Judean stirrings for independence from the occupying power. ▷ Nineveh; Old Testament; prophet

Nalanda (Nālandā) A town in the state of Bihar in India that is important in the history of the Buddhist tradition. Some of the Buddha's discourses took place there, and it is especially famous as the site of the outstanding Buddhist monastic university which was active for about 800 hundred years from the 5th to the 12th centuries. Beginning in the 5th century CE the Gupta kings built monasteries there, and eventually the whole campus was surrounded by a wall and became a monastic university. In its heyday scholars enrolled from all over the Buddhist world. Entrance exams were strict, and the curriculum included general studies in grammar, logic, medicine and other subjects, as well as religious studies in Mahayana philosophy which became its major specialization. It has been suggested that one reason for the decline of Buddhism in India was the great reputation of monastic universities such as Nalanda, which drew monks away from the villages where their example was needed. Nalanda eventually declined as well. Its great library was burnt in the 10th century, and the Muslim invasions two centuries later sounded its death-knell. ▷ Buddha; Mahayana Buddhism; philosophy; sutta-pitaka

Nam (Nām) A Sikh Punjabi term meaning 'name'. Denoting the Name of God, it is a crucial term in Sikh theology. It is often used as a kind of synonym for the being and nature of God, and the phrase 'Sat Nam', the True Name, is frequently used for God. While Nam is manifest everywhere, it is better known through experience, rather than intellectually. Hence a meditation technique known as *Nam Simran*, remembering the Name, is important. This can take three forms. It can involve disciplined and systematic meditation of the Nam, which deepens one's spirituality and climaxes in bliss, *sahaj*. It can also involve Nam Japan, the repetition of a set phrase or mantra which may be Sat Nam itself; a rosary may be used as an aid in this. It can also involve the singing of hymns as part of a daily spiritual discipline. Meditating on, repeating, and chanting the Name of God are common in various religions, including the Sant tradition that fed into Hinduism, but the Sikhs gave it a new slant and a new significance as an expression of all that God is. ▷ Akal Purukh; Nam Simran; rosary; Sahaj; Sant tradition

Namdhari (Nāmdhāri) A Sikh reform movement which arose in the 19th century. Its originator was Baba Balak Singh (1799–1861) and it grew under his successor Baba Ram Singh. It aimed to reform moral backsliding in the Sikh community, particularly drug and alcohol abuse, the eating of meat, caste, excessive marriage expenses, and the treatment of widows. In 1872 the British transported Baba Ram Singh to Rangoon in Burma for fomenting aggression aimed at reinstating Sikh rule in the Punjab; however, Namdharis consider that he is still alive and will come back to lead them. They also believe that the tenth Sikh guru, Guru Gobind Singh, did not die in 1798 but lived until 1812 to bestow Guruhood on Baba Balak Singh. Wearing white turbans distinctively laid flat across the forehead, they follow a reformed code of behaviour associated with Baba Balak Singh, and in their prayers they use a rosary of wool which includes 108 knots. ▷ Gobind Singh, Guru; Nirankar; Nirmalas; Udasi

names of prophet, Islamic Muhammad has been given many names by Muslims during the evolution of their tradition. Al-Jazuli mentions 200 names of the prophet in his *Dalail al-Khayrat*, and others have given further names to Muhammad. The name Muhammad means 'he who is glorified' and according to custom every time he is mentioned, either by name or by title, the phrase 'peace be upon him' is added. Many of his names are honorific, and others summarize his work. Obvious examples are as follows: servant of God, most beautiful of God's creation, bringer of good tidings, abode of wisdom, soul of the prophets, the rightly-guided, the chosen, the messenger, the holy spirit, he of the night ascent, intercessor for sinners, the legislator, the fount of blessings. According to Muslims he is mentioned in Genesis 49.1–10 under the name Shiloh. Muhammad is considered by Muslims to be the greatest man who ever lived, yet not divine, and this is reflected in his names. Although they heap respect upon him, they do not deify him. This is one reason why the title Muhammadan formerly given to Muslims is considered inappropriate, as it seems to confer divinity upon the name of Muhammad. ▷ Genesis, Book of; Muhammad; prophet; Shiloh

Nam Simran (Nām Simraṇ) A term that is important in Sikh spirituality. It means literally 'remembering the Name of God', and is equivalent to prayer and meditation. At one level it is keeping God in mind and invoking his presence at all times. At a more concrete level it involves three things: a disciplined and systematic meditation on the name and nature of God so that one grows into harmony with God and attains his bliss (*sahaj*); a repetition of the name of God, if necessary with the help of a rosary, so that God's Name becomes part of one's nature; and singing the praises of God in hymns and chants from the Sikh scripture, the *Guru Granth Sahib*. Although *Nam Simran* is mainly to do with individual spirituality, it can also be used in groups. However, although discipline and set times of prayer are recommended, the gurus are careful to stress the ultimate aim of mystical union with God as being the point of *Nam Simran* rather than particular techniques for attaining it. ▷ Guru Granth Sahib; mala; Nam; Sahaj

Nanak (Nānak), known as **Guru Nanak** (1469–1539) Indian religious leader, and founder of Sikhism, born near Lahore. A Hindu by birth and belief, he travelled widely to Hindu and Muslim centres in search of spiritual truth. He settled in Kartarpur, in the Punjab, where he attracted many followers. His doctrine, set out later in the *Adi-Granth*, sought a fusion of Brahmanism and Islam on the grounds that both were monotheistic, although his own ideas leaned rather towards pantheism. ▷ Adi Granth; Brahmanism; Islam; pantheism; Sikhism

Nanto Rokusho The six Buddhist schools in the Japanese capital of Nara during the early history of Buddhism in Japan. The six schools were Jojitsu, Sanron, Kusha, Hosso, Kegon and Ritsu, and they were at first not separate sects but merely overlapping philosophical schools. The first two disappeared, and the third school, Kusha, was amalgamated into the fourth, the Hosso school. Hosso, Kegon and Ritsu developed into separate sects of Japanese Buddhism, and they remain so

Guru Nanak

today, with a number of temples and followers. They originated in India, but came to Japan via China, and then became rooted on Japanese soil. Hosso was the Japanese version of the Yogacara school; Kegon was based on the Garland (*Avatamsaka*) Sutra; and Ritsu emphasized the rules and disciplines of Buddhist monasticism. Although these three sects survived after the emperor Kammu had moved his capital away from Nara following his enthronement in 781CE, they became less influential, and the Buddhist future lay with the Tendai, Shingon, Zen and Pure Land schools that were introduced and flourished later. ▷ Avatamsaka Sutra; Kammu; Pure Land Buddhism; Shingon; Tendai; Yogacara; Zen Buddhism

naojote The Parsi word for the initiation ceremony of a child. Iranian Zoroastrians call the ceremony *sedra-pushun*, 'putting on the *sudreh*', the sacred shirt. The sudreh and the *kusti*, or sacred cord, are the outward signs of adherence to the Zoroastrian faith, and the moment when the priest makes the child put these on is the culminating part of the ceremony. Before the actual naojote the child is made to take a ritually prescribed bath, and during the ceremony itself he or she recites a few prayers which have been learned by heart. The naojote must be performed by a priest, but need not take place in a fire-temple. After the ceremony, a festive meal is usually held for a large gathering of relatives and friends of the family. ▷ rites of passage; Zoroastrianism

Naomi (Hebrew 'my delight') Biblical character, described in the stories of the Book of Ruth as the mother of Ruth and Orpah. After Naomi was widowed, she returned from Moab to Bethlehem with her daughter, and attempted to arrange the marriage of Ruth with Boaz, one of the secondary kinsmen of Naomi's deceased husband. The offspring of this union was said to be the grandfather of David. ▷ David; Old Testament; Ruth, Book of

Naphtali, tribe of One of the 12 tribes of ancient Israel, said to be descended from Naphtali, Jacob's second son by Bilhah (Rachel's maid). Its tribal territory was in North Palestine, immediately west of the Sea of Galilee and upper Jordan River. The tribe is described in the Book of Judges as consisting of courageous warriors. ▷ Jacob; Israel, tribes of; Old Testament

Naqshbandiyyah An important Muslim Sufi order founded by Naqshband of Bukhara (1317–89). This order stresses silence as a significant element in living spirituality, and emphasizes the spiritual disciplines of concentration and recollection as ways to God. As part of this general approach the Naqshbandis invoke God within the heart by silent invocation (*dhikr*), rather than by means of the more normal invocation through the use of ritual speech. This happens at the subtle centre of a person in an inner sanctuary which is the spiritual heart. It involves an existential spiritual awareness rather than a rational or spoken one. There are parallels to this spirituality of inward invocation in other religions, eg in the Jewish Hesychastic prayer of the heart and in Hindu yogic practices. The order became important in the Caucasus, Central Asia and India. Imam Shamil (1797–1871), who led the Daghestan Muslims against the Russian conquests in the Caucasus, was a Naqshbandi, as was Shah Wali Allah of Delhi, who succeeded his father as local leader of the order in 1719, and worked to revive and refashion Indian Islam in the light of his Sufic principles. ▷ dhikr; hesychasm; Sufism; Wali Allah, Shah; yoga

Nara The first capital of Japan (710) and the centre of Japanese Buddhism. It has the oldest temple complex in Japan, and the oldest wooden buildings in the world. ▷ Buddhism

Naropa (Nāropa) (956–1040) Indian Tantric yogin or siddha whose teachings entered Tibet via his disciple Marpa. Born in Bengal of royal parentage, he went to study in Kashmir at the age of 11. On returning to Bengal as a young man he married, but the marriage was eventually dissolved by mutual agreement. He became the abbot of Nalanda Buddhist University, a post he held for eight years before resigning as a result of a vision. In this vision the goddess Vajravarahi, as an old woman, revealed to him that his guru was Tilopa. Naropa set off on an arduous search and, upon finding Tilopa, stayed with him for 12 years until Tilopa's death. During this time, through meditation and the guru's grace, Naropa attained liberation (nirvana). Naropa's teachings are formulated in the doctrine of the six yogas. These are: **1** the yoga of inner heat (*gTum-mo*), which is the awakening of the goddess Candali within the body, and which produces great bodily heat; **2** the yoga of the illusory body, aimed at realizing that the body and its world are mind-produced; **3** the yoga of the dream state; **4** the yoga of the clear light, realizing or entering the absolute light of emptiness; **5** the yoga of the intermediate state (*bardo*); and **6** the yoga of transferring consciousness at death to another body. ▷ bardo; emptiness; guru; Marpa; Nalanda; nirvana; siddhas; Tilopa

Nasr, Seyyed Hossein (1933–) Iranian scholar of religion, born in Teheran. His early education was in Shiite Iran, and his later degrees are from the Massachusetts Institute of Technology and Harvard. Returning to Iran in 1958, he lectured on Islamic science and philosophy, and increasingly on Islam in general and Sufi mysticism in particular, achieving high office at Teheran University. He now lectures in Islamics at George Washington University, Washington DC. His books focus upon Islam in general, upon Sufi mysticism, Iranian culture, and upon the plight of Western culture, including a prophetic ecological work, *Man and Nature, The Spiritual Crisis of Modern Man* (1968). He is an exponent of the perennial philosophy that while religions are outwardly different at the level of doctrines, rituals and scriptures, inwardly they converge at the level of spirituality. He has been influential in encouraging the publication of various classics of spirituality from Western and Eastern religions, and was the first non-Judaeo Christian Eastern scholar to give the famous Gifford Lectures in Religion at Edinburgh University. ▷ perennial philosophy; Shiism; spirituality; Sufism; study of religion

Nastika ▷ Indian philosophies; Buddhism; Jainism

Nataraja (Nātarāja) One of the names of the Hindu deity, Shiva. As the Lord of the Dance he dances the creation of the universe. ▷ Hinduism; Shiva

Nataraja

Nathan (11th–10th century BCE) Biblical prophet, associated with the court of King David, who appears in three incidents. When David considers building a temple for Yahweh in Jerusalem it is Nathan whom he consults; it is Nathan who receives from Yahweh the prophecy that the task must be left to his son, and who goes on to prophesy the establishment and continuance of the Davidic dynasty (2 Samuel 7). To the Deuteronomistic editors of the books of Samuel this prophecy of temple and dynasty is the high point of David's reign. Later Nathan reproves David for his immoral behaviour in having Uriah the Hittite killed in order to take his wife Bathsheba (2 Samuel 11.12). In David's old age the prophet is portrayed as active in the palace intrigue leading to the designation of Solomon as David's heir and, with Zadok the priest, is reponsible for his anointing as king (1 Kings 1). ▷ David; Solomon; Yahweh

Nathanael (Hebrew 'God has given') New Testament character appearing only in John 1.45–51, 21.2. He is said to have been brought to Jesus by Philip, and is one of the first to confess Jesus as 'Son of God, King of Israel'. He does not appear by this name in any list of disciples in the synoptic Gospels, however; possibly he was not one of the 12 or even a historical individual at all, despite some attempts to identify him with Bartholomew or Matthew in the synoptic lists of the 12 disciples. ▷ apostle; Jesus Christ; John, Gospel according to; Philip, St

Nath Yogis (Nāth Yogis) A yoga tradition of Hinduism originating in the medieval period and tracing its origins to the legendary Matsyendranath and his disciple Gorakhnath (c.1200CE). The Naths are also called the *Kanphatas* ('split-ear'), because during their initiation ceremony the ear lobes are split and large earrings placed in them. Nath Yoga philosophy is influenced by Tantric Buddhism and Shaivism. It aims at liberation in life (*jivanmukti*), which is the realization of one's innate (*sahaja*) identity with the absolute, attained in a body made perfect (siddha) or divine (*divya*) in the 'fire' of yoga. The Naths practise Hatha Yoga and attempt to awaken the force of Kundalini hidden within the body. Thus they accept the idea of an esoteric anatomy of various subtle centres (*cakras*) along which energy (prana) flows, which can be harnessed for spiritual enlightenment. The most important texts of the Sanskrit Naths which have come down to us are the *Siddhasiddhanta Paddhati*, which deals with the perfection of the body and the realization of the universe within it, and the *Hathayogapradipika* and *Gheranda Samhita*, which are texts on yoga. There are still a number of Nath Yoga monastic orders in India. ▷ Buddhism; cakras; Gorakhnath; Hatha Yoga; jivanmukti; Kundalini; prana; Shaivism; Tantric Hinduism

National Council of the Churches of Christ in the USA An association of Protestant, Eastern Orthodox, and National Catholic Churches formed in 1950 in the USA. Affiliated to the World Council of Churches, it is committed to the principle of manifesting the oneness of the Church of Christ. ▷ Christianity; World Council of Churches

Native American Church An indigenous 19th-century religious movement among North American Indians, combining native religion with certain elements of Christianity. It was formally founded in 1918. Its main ritual centres on the sacramental and curative use of the non-narcotic hallucinogen mescaline, derived from the peyote plant. ▷ Native American religions

Native American religions 'Native American' is the term now used for the indigenous peoples of North America. It covers a wide range of language and ethnic origin, from the Inuit of the Arctic across the continent to peoples whose affinities are with those of Meso America. Habitat is equally diverse: tundra, sub-Arctic hunting grounds with marginal agriculture, forest, open plains, the cool wet North-West Pacific coast, the southern maize belt, the hot lands bordering the desert. The picture is further complicated by migration over vast distances, with consequent changes in lifestyle. Thus the Navajo, once probably part of an Athapascan hunting culture of the North-West, are now cultivators in the South-West, while the Wind River Shoshoni, belonging to the Uto-Aztec complex of Meso America, live as far north as Wyoming. These migrations frequently involve religious changes since religion is inevitably influenced by the community's way of life. The (generally traumatic) competition of Native American peoples with the expanding white population led to further dislocation and, by the extinction of the Plains buffalo, an enforced change of lifestyle. The white impact stimulated other religious changes by reaction (eg the Ghost Dance) and others by interaction with Christianity.

Native American concepts of God vary widely. The sub-Arctic Algonquin revere the Great Spirit, Manitou; the Sioux have a wider category of the sacred, *wakan*, which appears to oscillate between the supreme being and other manifestations of the sacred; the Iroquois had a thorough dualism of opposed cosmic principles which the reformer Handsome Lake reinterpreted as the opposition of God and the devil; while in the elaborate mythology and ritual of the Pueblo peoples the supreme being plays only a distant part. Most Native American religious systems recognize a culture hero who is responsible for establishing the community's conditions of life. A common feature, as in Melanesian religions, is that the culture hero has a twin, reflecting polarity in the organization of life. Most hunting peoples have a mythic figure who is Master of the Animals, the guardian of the supply on which the community depends. Ritual patterns naturally vary greatly, especially between agricultural and hunting peoples, but a recurrent feature is the construction of a symbolic representation of the universe in a particular locality, since the rites help to maintain the universe and keep its sustaining processes in repair. The northern peoples also had the vision quest, with its personal search for power and its requirements of purity and discipline, and the (possibly related) institution of shamanic healing.

The breakdown and demoralization of Native American society under white impact has produced movements of protest, revival and reform, harking back to ancestral custom, but often employing themes from Christianity (as Handsome Lake did) or new institutions (as the Native American Church has done with peyote). Recent assertions of Native American identity and dignity have tended to stress the Native American religious inheritance as a whole, and traditional spirituality, rather than reconstructing the belief systems of particular peoples. ▷ Algonquin religion; Black Elk; calumet; Cheyenne religion; dry paintings; Ghost Dance; Handsome Lake; Hopi religion; kachinas; Manitou; medicine bundle; medicine lodge; Navajo religion; peyote; Pueblo religion; shaking tent; shamanism; Sun Dance; supreme beings; sweat lodge; vision quest; windigo

Inuit-Aleut representation of a caribou spirit

Nativity, the The story of the miraculous birth of Jesus of Nazareth to Mary, the accompanying events of which are variously described in the opening chapters of the Gospels of Matthew and Luke. Although the year of Jesus's birth is unknown, it is usually fixed at c.6BCE, two years before the death of Herod the Great (Matthew 2.1, 16–20). The observance of the birth, the festival of Christmas, has been celebrated throughout most of Christendom since the 4th/5th century on 25 December. ▷ Christmas; Jesus Christ; Mary; New Testament

nats The concept of hostile spirits within the Burmese religious tradition. At one level they are seen as guardian spirits, of whom 37, headed by a king, have traditionally been very important; at another level they are seen as being potentially malevolent and must therefore be propitiated. They are not worshipped, but rather placated with gifts and offerings. At the cult level they are served by mediums who dance for them at rituals and celebrations and offer representative gifts to them. They are similar in many ways to the *yakkhas* of the Buddhist *tipitaka* or Pali Canon, semi-divine spirits who may be morally neutral but are more often seen to be hostile to human beings. ▷ tipitaka

natural religion The notion that there is a natural religious response to the world, or a religiousness that is a natural human endowment. At the time of the 18th-century Enlightenment natural religion stood for religious beliefs that were supposedly held by all human beings, and were accessible to human reason, as opposed to supernatural beliefs in concepts such as miracles, providence and eternal life. Natural religion contrasts with positive religions in the sense of separate religious traditions. They have their own specific communities, rituals, ethics, social involvement, scriptures, doctrines, aesthetics and spirituality. Although religious traditions may not be in conflict with one another, neither are they 'natural', being the products of particular social, historical and spiritual forces. There is an even sharper contrast between natural religion and revealed religion, which is based on the notion that religion is revealed by some external authority such as God. According to this view natural religion exists in all religions and, while there can be dialogue at the philosophical level between religions, little discussion is possible at the theological level because the sources of revelation differ. From the viewpoint of revealed religion, natural religion, if it is thought to be possible at all, can only be viewed as something which is second best, or alternatively as a preparation for revealed religion itself. ▷ enlightenment; God; revelation

natural theology Medieval Catholicism crystallized a distinction between natural theology (deemed to deal with those aspects of faith discoverable by common reason) and revealed theology (which needed special divine self-disclosure). It was argued that such truths as the existence of God, the immortality of the soul, and the major dictates of ethics were engraved on the human heart and mind in creation, whereas doctrines such as the Trinity, the character of atonement, or the ethics of self-sacrifice required attention to the specific revelation in Christ. Debate continues as to the possibility and limits of natural theology. In general, Catholic and Anglican traditions, relatively trustful of human reason, still urge an argued defence of the faith. Since the Reformation, Protestant traditions, often asserting the corruption of our natural reason at the Fall, tend to suspect any theology not grounded in Scriptural revelation. New challenges come, for example, from inter-faith dialogue, from feminism and from radical activists, each claiming that the natural theology tradition merely reflects an outmoded, male, cerebral, Western style, highly unnatural to other cultures, and itself parochial. The basic underlying question is whether everyone has natural access to the reality of God, in thought, religious instinct or ethical intuition, or whether some have privileged access. ▷ apologetics; Fall, the; feminist theology; theism

Navajo religion The Navajo are the most numerous Native American people. Originally an Athapascan sub-Arctic hunting people, whose religion was shamanistic and directed to the maintenance of the animal supply, they migrated south, perhaps seven centuries ago, and are now based in Arizona. Change of habitat led to agriculture, sheep rearing and, since the 1960s, mineral extraction. These changes have affected Navajo religion, as have the influence of their Pueblo neighbours (who had already determined the sacred significance of the local landscape) and of whites (Kit Carson's war leading to mass imprisonment and the reduction of the homeland, 1864–8, and the 1930s sheep culls).

Navajo cosmology is complex. Creation results from a process of upward emergence through several worlds. It involves First Man (creator of First Boy and First Girl, whose names are Full Life and Happiness) and Coyote (a trickster who brings about death and secures the balance of opposites in the world). Changing Woman, daughter of First Boy and First Girl, represents the earth, and the processes producing orderly life cycle and harmony. By her husband the sun, she is mother of hero twins who slay the worst monsters and make earth habitable. Since emergence into the present world and the departure of these holy beings, the function of religion is to maintain the full life and happiness symbolized by First Boy and First Girl. This involves rituals which re-enact the great myths, notably Blessingway, the original ceremony performed at creation, and Holyway, which repairs breaches of harmony. Their effectiveness is related to the fact that all beings, animate or inanimate, have 'wind souls' (*diyin dine'e*) which are not subject to decay. Ritual, properly performed, relates this inner essence to the outward form, and controls it for good. Since rituals require punctilious accuracy, they involve specialist singers with capacious memories. The sweat lodge is an important institution. ▷ peyote; Pueblo religion; sweat lodge

Nazianzen ▷ Gregory of Nazianzus, St

Nazi Party A German political party which originated as the German Worker's Party, founded in 1919 to protest against the German surrender of 1918 and the Treaty of Versailles, and renamed the *Nationalsozialistische Deutsche Arbeiterpartei* (National Socialist German Worker's Party, or Nazi Party) in 1920. Adolf Hitler became the party's leader the following year. Its ideology was extremely nationalist, imperialist, and racist, maintaining that the world was divided into a hierarchy of races: Aryans, of whom Germans were the purest example, were the supreme culture-bearing race, while the Jews were the lowest. It was also contended that the Jews were intent on world conquest through infesting the Aryan race. This set of ideas was set out by Hitler in *Mein Kampf* (1925). It was not until the 1930s that the Nazi Party gained a position of significant support: in 1932 with 37.3 per cent of the vote they became the largest party in the Reichstag. Support came from people of all backgrounds, but was most prominent among Protestants, the middle class, and the young. In 1933 Hitler was appointed Chancellor in a coalition government, a position from which he, aided by the party, was able to build up a personal dictatorship, through legal measures, terror, and propaganda. Once in power, the Nazis ruthlessly crushed opposition, indoctrinated the public with their ideas, engaged in extensive rearmament, and in the late 1930s invaded Austria, the Sudetenland, and the rest of Czechoslovakia, which according to the ideology was necessary for obtaining land for the 'master race'. During World War II, their actions included slave labour, plunder, and mass extermination. Nazism as a political ideology is now viewed very much as the expression of extreme inhumanity, fanatical nationalism, and the logic of nihilism. ▷ fascism; secular alternatives to religion

Nazirites (Hebrew 'separated ones', 'dedicated ones') Holy men in ancient Israel who took a special vow (in later times normally only for a fixed period) to separate themselves from others. Numbers 6 describes this vow as prohibiting the cutting of their hair, the consumption of grapes or grape products, and the contact with corpses (even of close relatives). The biblical stories about Samson and Samuel may reflect such practices, and vows of this kind are attested also in New Testament times (Acts 21.23–4) and rabbinic Judaism, but not in medieval Judaism. ▷ Judaism; Numbers, Book of; Samson; Samuel

Nebuchadnezzar, or **Nebuchadrezzar** (c.630–562BCE) King of Babylon (605–562BCE), the son of Nabopolassar, founder of the New Babylonian Empire, and the most famous King of Babylon. Under him, Babylonian civilization reached its height, and its empire extended as far as the Mediterranean. In the West, he is remembered chiefly for his deportation of the Jews to Babylonia (586BCE). ▷ Babylon

Nehemiah, Book of A book of the Hebrew Bible/Old Testament, originally joined to the Book of Ezra, and probably also to 1 and 2 Chronicles. This historical writing was named after a Jewish official of the king of Persia, Nehemiah, who apparently led a return to Judea by Jewish exiles in Persia. He had two periods of governorship in Judea during the reign of Artaxerxes I (465–424BCE) or possibly Artaxerxes II (404–359BCE). There is some chronological confusion in the work, because of the presence of some sections which appear to belong to the Book of Ezra. ▷ Ezra, Book of; Old Testament

Neill, Stephen Charles (1900–84) Scottish missionary and theologian of mission, born in Edinburgh. From 1924 he worked in south India as an evangelist, theological teacher, and latterly as Anglican Bishop of Tinnevelly (Tirunelveli). He became deeply concerned with producing Tamil Christian literature and promoting Church union. Returning to Europe in 1944 he maintained his ecumenical interests through working with the World Council of Churches and lecturing in Hamburg, Nairobi, and elsewhere. Author of many books, his *Anglicanism* (1958), *Interpretation of the New Testament* (1962), and *History of Christian Missions* (1964) remain classics in their fields, as does the *History of the Ecumenical Movement* (1954, edited with Ruth Rouse). ▷ ecumenism; World Council of Churches

nembutsu The practice found in Japanese Pure Land Buddhism of repeating the name of Amida Buddha. It originated in China but was given the name nembutsu in Japan, and it means 'I put my faith in Amida Buddha'. By means of this practice and the faith in the grace of Amida Buddha underlying it one can obtain rebirth in the paradise or Pure Land of Amida Buddha and from there one can obtain nirvana. Nembutsu entered Japan significantly through the Tendai school from 805 onwards, but it became popular through the Pure Land school (*Jodo*) founded by Honen in 1175, and the True Pure Land school (*Jodo Shinshu*) founded by Shinran. Honen placed more emphasis upon constant repetition of the nembutsu, whereas for Shinran the faith underlying it was important and one saying of the nembutsu offered with absolute sincerity and faith would bring rebirth in Amida's Pure Land. The practice of saying the nembutsu passed beyond the confines of Pure Land Buddhism into Japanese Buddhism in general as a way of asking for spiritual help, and it is often recited when it is clear that death is not far away, in the hope of attaining rebirth in Amida Buddha's Pure Land. ▷ Amida worship; Honen; Jodo; Jodo Shinshu; nirvana; Pure Land Buddhism; Shinran; Tendai

neo-Confucianism The new Confucianism that emerged during the Sung dynasty in China (960–1126CE). After the collapse of the Han dynasty (206BCE–220CE), which had been a Confucian empire, the Taoist and Buddhist traditions grew much stronger. Neo-Confucianism was a reinterpretation and a reassertion of Confucian values which also assimilated some elements from Taoism and Buddhism. Its influence was strongest in China from the Sung dynasty to the beginning of this century. Among the early neo-Confucians Chuo Tun I (1017–73) was important with his influential work *Explanation of the Diagram of the Supreme Ultimate*. According to this, everything in the world, including human characteristics, is generated from the Supreme Ultimate (*Tai Chi*) or Ultimate Non-Being (*Wu-Chi*); by living in harmony with them inward calm and outward peace can be achieved. Two main schools emerged which centred upon the brilliant intellectual synthesis of Chu Hsi (1130–1200) in his school of Principle, and upon the more idealist synthesis of Wang Yang Ming (1472–1529) in his school of Mind. Chu Hsi reorganized the Confucian Canon to include the *Analects of Confucius*, the *Book of Mencius*, the *Doctrine of the Mean*, and the *Great Learning*; these became the basis of the Chinese civil service exams from 1313 to 1905. Althugh some Confucian scholars of the Manchu period (1644–1912) wished to return to Confucius himself, the synthesis of Confucianism and neo-Confucianism remained the key element in Chinese thought and society. ▷ Chu Hsi; Confucian Canon; Tai Chi; Wang Yang-Ming

Neo-Hinduism A term covering a variety of modern movements which have arisen within Hinduism since the 'Hindu renaissance' of the 19th century. Neo-Hinduism seems to be mainly an urban development, associated with the educated classes who regard Hinduism as compatible with science, or believe, more specifically, that science corroborates the Vedas. More fundamentalist movements associated with the less educated classes might also be subsumed under the general heading of Neo-Hinduism. These politically conservative groups have become an important force in the religious and political life of India. This can be seen in the Hindu-Muslim conflict over the mosque on the alleged site of Rama's birth at Ayodhya. ▷ Hinduism, modern movements; Rama

neolithic religion This refers to the religious ideas and practices connected with the neolithic civilizations that flourished in the world between 8000 and 3000BCE. The neolithic revolution was centred upon the rise of agriculture, the domestication of animals and plants, the invention of pottery, and the growth of settled communities, and included a focus upon the sanctity of nature, the cycle of the seasons, and mother goddesses. Among the nine neolithic civilizations discovered—those in the Near East, south-eastern Europe, north-western Europe, Malaya, northern China, Japan, northern Africa, the Nile Valley, and middle America—most is known about those in Asia Minor and south-eastern Europe. Because of the large areas and long time-span involved it is difficult to generalize about neolithic religion. In addition to the factors mentioned above, also important in particular regions were ancestor cults, fertility rites, religious centres (such as Lepenski Vir in the Danube region: 7000 to 6500BCE, and Catal Huyuk in Anatolia: 6300 to 5400BCE), burial ceremonies, household gods, megalithic monuments, and rock and pottery art. A definitive summary of neolithic religion as a whole remains to be done, and it may be that it will only be possible to summarize the separate religions of the nine regions. However, it appears likely that in neolithic times there was an increasingly intimate relationship between human beings, the earth they were learning to harness, and the transcendent powers they felt to reside in both. This ecological feel for nature was similar to that of American Indians. ▷ early burial finds; megalithic religion

neo-orthodoxy A reaction against the optimism of pre-World War I Liberal Protestantism, neo-orthodoxy reasserted Reformation principles of sin, grace and faith, and located theology in the Church rather than the university. Not an organized movement, neo-orthodoxy's alternative titles of 'dialectical' and 'crisis' theology refer more particularly to Barth's *Romans* (1919, rewritten for second edition 1922) and other early writings. These, inspired by Kierkegaard, Luther and Dostoyevsky, denied the liberal method of arguing from experience to God (here Barth disagreed with Brunner, who saw a limited place for natural theology), asserting that human language can only speak about God indirectly, in apparent paradoxes. Yet God reveals in Christ a message of judgement or 'crisis' (from the Greek *krisis*, 'judgement'). This dynamic revelation in Christ and the preaching about him was developed in Barth's later works, including the monumental *Church Dogmatics* (1932–59, English trans. 1956–77), thus gaining neo-orthodoxy a third alternative title of 'kerygmatic' theology (from the Greek kerygma, 'gospel'). This description could also be applied to the theology of Bultmann and Friedrich Gogarten (1887–1967), which developed towards Christian existentialism. The theology of the Niebuhr brothers is also described as neo-orthodox. ▷ Barth, Karl; Brunner, (Heinrich) Emil; Bultmann, Rudolf Karl; existentialism, Christian; Kierkegaard, Sören Aabye; Luther, Martin; Niebuhr, Helmut Richard; Niebuhr, Reinhold

neo-paganism The name often given to a modern form of witchcraft practised in the contemporary West. It was inspired by the work of Gerald Gardner (1884–1964) who used his experience in Asia as a British civil servant to investigate Asian magic and religion and to combine elements from them in the new witchcraft that he evolved. Neo-paganism was an amalgam of Eastern magic and religion, Western magic, freemasonry, goddess worship, and elements derived from the work of Aleister Crowley. It began in Britain in the 1950s, spread to the USA in the 1960s and since then has reached continental Europe and Africa. It is essentially a kind of nature religion based upon worship of the Mother Goddess. Many covens of neo-pagan witches have been formed and meet semi-secretly. Their aim is to recover and revalorize the ancient neo-paganism of Europe before the advent of Christianity; there is also a growing sense of ecological concern and a 'feel' for God as female. As neo-paganism has spread into new countries and cultures it has thrown up new rituals and magical techniques; at the same time it is moving from an interest in changing the world for one's own sake to an interest in changing oneself for the sake of the world. ▷ freemasonry; goddess worship; magic; witchcraft

neo-platonism A school of philosophy founded by Plotinus (205–70), lasting into the 7th century, which attempted to combine doctrines of Plato, Aristotle, and the Pythagoreans. Basic to Plotinus's philosophy is The One, whence emanate Intelligence (which contains the Platonic ideas) and Soul (which includes individual souls). ▷ Aristotle; Plato; Plotinus

neo-Thomism A philosophical movement in the late 19th century and 20th century which sought to revive interest in the thought of St Thomas Aquinas. 'Thomism' was declared the official theology of the Roman Catholic Church in 1879, and neo-Thomism (and the natural theology associated with it) remains an important feature of Roman Catholic and some Anglican thought. ▷ Aquinas, St Thomas; Roman Catholicism; theology

Nephthys Ancient Egyptian goddess, the daughter of Geb and Nut, and member of the Heliopolitan ennead, sometimes believed to be the mother of Anubis. Nephthys was the wife of Seth, but in the Osirian mythology normally appears on the side of Osiris. She helped Isis prepare Osiris's body for burial and they both mourned him in the form of kites. They are often depicted as mourners at either end of a bier or coffin. Nephthys is portrayed as a woman with the hieroglyph of her name as a head-dress, but she appears not to have been worshipped except in connection with Isis, and had no cult centre in Ancient Egypt. ▷ Anubis; ennead; Isis; Osiris; Seth

Nergal Mesopotamian god of the underworld, at first a solar deity capable of killing enormous numbers of people in the heat of the summer sun. Although some inscriptions refer to him as a benefactor Nergal was feared and respected as a god of mass destruction and pestilence, and absorbed the personality of Erra, god of plague. He was most important as god of the dead, and myths describe how he forced Ereshkigal, the original goddess of the underworld, to share her power with him. His city was Cutha in central Babylonia, which could be used as a name for the abode of the dead. In Syria and Palestine Nergal was identified with the god Reshef. ▷ afterlife, Ancient Near Eastern concept of; Reshef; underworld

Nestorians Followers of Nestorius, Bishop of Constantinople (d.c.451), who is alleged to have taught the doctrine, later declared heretical, of two persons (one human, one divine) as well as two natures in the incarnate Christ. They formed a separate Church which survived in parts of Persia as the Assyrian Church and, in India, as the Christians of St Thomas. ▷ Christians of St Thomas; Christology; heresy; Nestorius

Nestorius (d.451) Syrian ecclesiastic, a native of Germanicia in northern Syria. As a priest he became so eminent for his zeal, ascetic life, and eloquence that he was selected as Patriarch of Constantinople (428). The presbyter Anastasius having denied that the Virgin Mary could be truly called the Mother of God, Nestorius warmly defended him; and so emphasized the distinction of the divine and human natures that antagonists accused him of holding, that there were two persons in Christ. A controversy ensued, and at a general council in Ephesus in 431 Nestorius was deposed. He was confined in a monastery near Constantinople, was banished to Petra in Arabia, and died after confinement in the Greater Oasis in Upper Egypt and elsewhere. ▷ heresy; Nestorians

new age religion Although this movement has become increasingly prominent recently, it remains difficult to summarize because of its individualistic, flexible, free and disorganized nature. Insofar as it is suspicious of dogmas, institutions and establishments, it has not built up a strong religious organization of its own. It is a network of varied movements and ideas that are weakly linked, and has a vague worldview. It takes seriously the fact that the year 2000 will soon be here, and it seeks to discover and practise new religious paradigms that will be relevant to the new millennium. It has an intellectual affinity with new scientific theories such as Fritjof Capra's view in *The Tao of Physics* that sub-atomic physics is akin to eastern mysticism, David Bohm's theory of implicate order in the universe, Rupert Sheldrake's biological theory of formative causation, James Lovelock's Gaia hypothesis that the earth is a living organism, Teilhard de Chardin's view of creative evolution, and the systems theory in science which stresses the inter-relationship between different areas of knowledge. New age religion has an emphasis upon ecology, women's rights, and the need to balance the rational and the intuitive. It emphasizes healing in the widest sense, and opens up the human potential that is latent in everyone. It proclaims the power of the inner voice to guide through meditation and spiritual experience in relation to a God who is immanent as well as transcendent. It borrows from other religions, for example from the spirituality of Hinduism, Buddhism, Sufi Islam and the American Indians, but it is not a branch of them, nor is it a new religious movement, because unlike them it does not have a strong leader or a close-knit organization. Some of its practitioners use astrology, sacred geometry, reincarnation theories, and crystals, and some of them claim to channel spirits (for example Alice Bailey channelled the Tibetan Master D K, Jane Roberts the spirit Seth, J Z Knight the spirit Ramatha, and Jack Pursel the spirit Lazaris). New age religion has inherited and adapted some of the insights of theosophy and anthroposophy, but it is wider than them in thought and influence, and cannot be circumscribed by the unusual recent theories of Shirley Maclaine or David Icke. ▷ anthroposophy; new religious movements in the West; spirituality; theosophy

New Church Also known as the Church of the New Jerusalem, founded by Emanuel Swedenborg, and popularly known as the Swedenborgian Church. Swedenborg was a Swedish scientist who in 1743 began to undergo deep spiritual experiences which he erected into a system of ideas that formed the basis of New Church's theology. He stressed the reality of the spiritual world that is held within the outward physical world. Thus there is a spiritual meaning to the outward words of the Bible, and a spiritual meaning to the outward world itself whereby the heat and light of the sun are equivalent to the love and wisdom of God. The opening up of this inner world of spiritual meaning is effected by Jesus Christ through the New Church. The aim of life is to develop one's inner spiritual world by repentance, good living, inner awareness, and loving God, thus leading to a life in heaven as an angel among a series of grades of angels. Swedenborg claimed to converse with angels and held the angelic world of heaven to be important and real. So also is hell, which we can create for ourselves and which continues after death. There are still a few Swedenborgians and Swedenborgian churches in Britain and the USA. ▷ angels; Bible; heaven; hell; Jesus Christ; Swedenborg, Emmanuel

New English Bible An English translation of the Bible from the original languages undertaken by an interdenominational committee of scholars under the auspices of the University Presses of Cambridge and Oxford from 1948. The first edition of the New Testament was completed in 1961, and the first complete Bible was produced in 1970. The goal was to present the text in good English literary idiom rather than in 'biblical English', and to reflect the results of recent biblical scholarship. It was substantially revised in 1989 under the title of the *Revised English Bible*. ▷ Bible

New Fire ceremony ▷ calendar, Meso-American; human sacrifice, Meso-American

New Jerusalem, Church of the, known also as the **New Church** A religious sect based on the teachings of the Swedish scientist and seer, Emmanuel Swedenborg, who believed he had direct contact with the spiritual world through visionary experiences. There he saw that a first dispensation of the Christian Church had ended and a new one was beginning, the 'New Jerusalem'. His first church was organized in London in 1783. ▷ spiritualism; Swedenborg, Emmanuel; theosophy

Newman, John Henry (1801–90) English prelate and theologian, born in London, brother of Francis William Newman. His father was a banker; his mother, a moderate Calvinist, deeply influenced his early religious views. He went up to Trinity College, Oxford, in 1817, and in 1822, in spite of taking a second class degree, he was elected a fellow of Oriel College, and here he formed his close intimacy with Edward Pusey and Richard Hurrell Froude. In 1824 he was ordained, in 1828 became vicar of St Mary's, Oxford and in 1830 broke definitely with Evangelicalism. His first book, *The Arians of the Fourth Century* (1833), argued that Arianism was a Judaizing heresy which sprang up in Antioch. In 1832–3 Newman accompanied Hurrell Froude and his father on a Mediterranean tour, when many of the poems in *Lyra Apostolica* (1834) were written and also 'Lead, kindly Light'. He was present at Keble's Oxford Assize sermon on National Apostasy (July 1833), which he regarded as the beginning of the Tractarian movement ('Oxford Movement'). He threw himself enthusiastically into the *Tracts for the Times*, composing a number of them himself. Tract 90 (1841) was the most famous of the tracts. Newman contended that the intention of the Thirty-nine Articles was Catholic in spirit, and that they were aimed at the supremacy of the pope and the popular abuses of Catholic practice, and not at Catholic doctrine. But Tract 90 provoked an explosion which was the end of the Tractarian movement, and brought on the conversion to Catholicism of those of the Tractarians who were most logical as well as most earnest. Newman struggled for two years longer to think his position tenable, but in 1843 resigned the vicarage of St Mary's, which he had held since 1828, and retired to Littlemore. The magnificent sermon on 'Development in Christian Doctrine' was the last which he preached in the university pulpit.

In October 1845 he invited the Passionist Father Dominic to his house at Littlemore in order that he might be received into the Roman Catholic Church. He went to Rome for a year and a half, where he joined the Oratorians and became a priest, and on his return in 1847 he established an Oratorian branch in England at Edgbaston, Birmingham; here he did a great deal of hard work, devoting himself to the sufferers from cholera in 1849 with the utmost zeal. The lectures on *Anglican Difficulties* (1850) drew public attention to Newman's great power of irony and the delicacy of his literary style, and were followed by his lectures on *Catholicism in England* (1851) and *The Idea of a University* (1852) while he was rector of Dublin Catholic University (1851–8). His long series of Oxford sermons contains some of the finest ever preached from an Anglican pulpit, and his Roman Catholic volumes—*Sermons Addressed to Mixed Congregations* (1849) and *Sermons on Various Occasions* (1857)—though less remarkable for their pathos, are even fuller of fine rhetoric.

In 1864 a casual remark by Charles Kingsley in *Macmillan's Magazine* on the indifference of the Roman Church to the virtue of truthfulness, an indifference which he asserted that Dr Newman approved, led to a correspondence which resulted in the publication that year of the remarkable *Apologia pro Vita Sua*. In 1865 he wrote a poem of singular beauty, 'The Dream of Gerontius', republished in *Verses on Various Occasions* (1874). In 1870 he published his *Grammar of Assent*, on the philosophy of faith. In the controversies which led to the Vatican Council, Newman sided with the Inopportunists. He was at this time in vehement opposition to the Ultramontanes under Henry Manning and William George Ward, and the bitterness between the two parties ran very high. Leo XIII, anxious to show his sympathy with the moderates, in 1879 summoned Newman to Rome to receive the cardinal's hat. ▷ Calvinism; evangelicalism; Oratorians; Oxford Movement; Pusey,

Edward Bouverie; Roman Catholicism; Thirty-nine Articles; Ultramontanism; Vatican Councils

new religious movements in the West There are new religious movements throughout the world, but they have received most attention in the West because of their unusual nature. It is important to remember that the major religions, including Christianity, were once new and unusual religious movements. New religious movements came to public attention in the 1960s, attracting adverse publicity through the mass suicide connected with the People's Temple at Jonestown in 1975 and the reactions of the Anti-Cult movement. Recently, their wide diversity and individual characteristics have been recognized and there has been a greater readiness to understand them in their own terms. Most of them are composed of reasonably affluent young people. Their membership is constantly changing, they are fairly small and they make a ready appeal at a time of great change. They are more common in the English-speaking world, and often have a charismatic leader. Some of them are revivals of old traditions; the Hare Krishna movement, for example, can be traced back to the 16th-century Hindu devotional leader Chaitanya, and neo-paganism goes back to pre-Christian nature and goddess worship. Some have Christian origins, such as the Unification Church, the Children of God, the Jonestown Movement, and Way International; some have Indian origins, such as Ananda Marg, Brahma Kumaris, Divine Light Mission, Hare Krishna, Meher Baba, Rajneesh meditation, 3HO, and Transcendental Meditation. Some have a more secular orientation aimed at increasing human potential, such as Scientology, the Gurdjieff movement and Synanon; others overlap with new age religion, which is not necessarily classed as a new religious movement. Some of them have utopian ideas about perfecting the world while others, such as the Brahma Kumaris, foresee the end of this world before a new dawn can happen. Some have a committed core group plus less committed members, others require a full commitment from all their members. They are seen in some quarters as an example of the secularization of religion; more commonly they are seen as illustrations of the fact that human beings are 'religious animals' who, if not satisfied with orthodox outlets for religion, will find other outlets to satisfy their religious sensibility. ▷ Ananda Marg; Anti-Cult movement; Brahma Kumaris/Raja Yoga movement; Chaitanya movement; Children of God; Divine Light Mission; Gurdjieff; Hare Krishna movement; Healthy-Happy-Holy Organization; Meher Baba; new age religion; People's Temple; Rajneesh meditation; scientology; Synanon; transcendental meditation; Unification Church; Way International

New Testament Along with the Old Testament, the sacred literature of Christianity. It is called 'New Testament' because its writings are believed to represent a new covenant of God with his people, centred on the person and work of Jesus Christ, as distinct from the old covenant with Israel which is described in the 'Old Testament'. The 27 New Testament writings were originally composed in Greek, mainly in the 1st century, unlike the Old Testament writings which are primarily in Hebrew and from earlier centuries. The New Testament writings are usually grouped as follows: four Gospels (Matthew, Mark, Luke, John), the Acts of the Apostles, 13 letters attributed to Paul (Romans; 1 and 2 Corinthians; Galatians; Ephesians; Philippians; Colossians; 1 and 2 Thessalonians; 1 and 2 Timothy; Titus; Philemon), the Letter to the Hebrews, seven General or 'Catholic' letters (James; 1 and 2 Peter; 1, 2 and 3 John; Jude) and the Book of Revelation. This corpus largely achieved recognition in the Christian Church by the end of the 2nd century, but a few works continued to be contested in later centuries. ▷ Acts of the Apostles; Apocrypha, New Testament; Bible; covenant; Gospels, canonical; Hebrews, Letter to the; James/John/Jude/Peter, Letter(s) of; Jesus Christ; Pauline Letters; Revelation, Book of

New Year festivals, Ancient Near Eastern In some parts of the Ancient Near East the New Year began in the spring, at the beginning of the growing season; in other calendars it fell in the autumn when rains ended the drought of summer. The most important festival of the Mesopotamian year, it is known from 3rd-millennium Sumer to the later Babylonian period (6th century BCE). Sumerian New Year festivals involved processions and sacrifice, the celebration of a sacred marriage and the determination of a good destiny for the king for the next year. The New Year festival at Babylon in the 1st millennium was known as the Akitu festival and took place in the spring. New Year festivals in Assyria and elsewhere followed a similar pattern, although there could be considerable local differences. The Hittite *purulliyas* festival in the spring may have been a New Year festival. Evidence from the Ras Shamra texts suggests that the Canaanite New Year was celebrated in the autumn, as in

Ancient Israel. ▷ Akitu; festivals, Ancient Near Eastern; Ras Shamra texts; sacred marriage, Ancient Near Eastern

Nganga A term widely used among the Bantu peoples of Africa, referring to one who can heal people and control evil forces. The powers of the Nganga vary considerably from group to group, and include divination, expertise against witchcraft, and functioning as a medium. ▷ Bantu religion; fetish; witchcraft and sorcery, African

nibbana ▷ nirvana

Nicaea, Council of 1 (325) The first ecumenical Council of the Church, called by Emperor Constantine to settle the doctrinal dispute between the Arians and the Orthodox on the person of Christ. ▷ Arius; Christology; Council of the Church **2** (787) A Council of the Church called to deal with the question of the veneration of images. ▷ iconoclasm

Nicene Creed An expanded formal statement of Christian belief, based on the creed of the first Council of Nicaea (325). This is still publicly recited as part of the Eucharistic liturgies of the Orthodox and Roman Catholic Churches, as well as many Protestant Churches. ▷ Christianity; Eucharist; liturgy; Nicaea, Council of

Nichiren Buddhism A sect founded by the Japanese Buddhist reformer Nichiren (1222–82), sometimes called the Lotus sect, because of his claim that the *Lotus Sutra* contained the ultimate truth. He attacked other forms of Buddhism, and called the nation to convert to true Buddhism. There are almost 40 subsects today. ▷ Buddhism; Soka Gakkai

Nichiren Shoshu (Nichiren Shōshū) The most important of the Nichiren Buddhist sects in Japan today, which arose from the work of Nichiren. Together with the Bahais and the Mormons it currently has one of the largest memberships in the world among new religious movements outside the major world religions. Nichiren took his vows in 1237, studied with the Tendai school up to 1242, and inaugurated the Nichiren movement in 1253 when he adopted the mantra (sacred verse), paying homage to the supremacy of the *Lotus Sutra*. He spent the rest of his life aggressively presenting this position, and Nichiren Shoshu and other Nichiren movements have followed him in this untypical Buddhist exclusivism. Nichiren Shoshu stresses three main teachings: that the hidden truth of the *Lotus Sutra* affirming that the Buddha exists from all eternity is superior to the truth of any other sect or religion; that the *Lotus Sutra* is the only relevant scripture in the later period of Buddhist history and the repetition of a mantra stressing the *Lotus Sutra* can bring salvation; and that the teaching of Nichiren is the final truth and Nichiren Shoshu is intended to be the national religion of Japan and ultimately of the world. Nichiren Shoshu emphasizes the true succession from Nichiren as going through Nikko (1246–1333), that Nichiren himself is in some way the Buddha, and that 'three great secrets' are contained in the truths mentioned above. ▷ Bahaism; Buddha; Lotus Sutra; Mormons; Nichiren Buddhism; Tendai

Nicholas of Cusa (1401–64) German philosopher, scientist and churchman, born in Cues, Trier. He studied at Heidelberg (1416) and Padua (1417–23), received a doctorate in canon law, and was ordained about 1430. He was active at the Council of Basle in 1432, supporting in his *De concordantia catholica* (1433) the 'conciliarists' who advocated the supremacy of Church councils against the pope; but he later switched allegiance to the papal party, undertook various papal missions as a diplomat, and was created cardinal in 1448. His main philosophical work is *De docta ignorantia* (1440), which emphasizes the limitations of human knowledge but at the same time argues that faith, science, theology and philosophy all pursue convergent though different paths towards the ultimately unattainable goal of absolute reality. He also wrote on mathematics and cosmology and anticipated Copernicus in his non-geocentric theories. ▷ Council of the Church

nidanas (nidānas) The 12 links in the chain of the Buddhist notion of dependent origination. Being interdependent, these links condition, and are conditioned by, the other links in the chain. The 12 links are: spiritual ignorance; constructing activities; consciousness; mind and body; the six sense-bases; sensory stimulation; feeling; craving; grasping; existence; birth; and ageing and death. Thus the ultimate root of the twelfth link, ageing and dying, lies in the first link, spiritual ignorance. Moreover, after death the effects of spiritual ignorance and constructing activities carry over, resulting eventually in another birth—and death—and another birth. In addition to spiritual ignorance another weak point in the chain is the eighth link, namely craving (*tanha*). This is singled out as being the basic cause of suffering (*duhkha*) in the second of the four noble truths. Indeed all the 12 links are behind the basic problem of suffering, and the end of suffering will come when there is an end of spiritual ignorance, craving, and the other links of the chain. When this is achieved, there will be no rebirths and nirvana will be attained. ▷ ariya sacca; dependent origination; duhkha; nirvana; tanha

Niebuhr, Helmut Richard (1894–1962) American theologian, born in Wright City, Missouri, brother of Reinhold Niebuhr. He taught at Yale University from 1931, becoming Professor of Theology and Christian Ethics and Director of Graduate Studies. Like his brother, he had enormous influence on generations of students. His classic study *The Meaning of Revelation* (1941) was followed by *Christ and Culture* (1951), *Radical Monotheism and Western Culture* (1960), and *The Responsible Self* (1963): a series of books advocating critical reflection on the relation between faith and moral action and a quest for a Christian transformation of society. Niebuhr's concern that ministers be adequately trained for this task was reflected in his direction of a survey of American Protestant theological education (1954–6). ▷ Niebuhr, Reinhold

Niebuhr, Reinhold (1892–1971) American theologian, born in Wright City, Missouri, brother of Helmut Niebuhr. Educated at Elmhurst (Illinois) College, Eden Theological Seminary and Yale Divinity School, he became an evangelical pastor in working-class Detroit (1915–28) and Professor of Christian Ethics in the Union Theological Seminary, New York, from 1928 to 1960. An advocate of Christian Realism, he wrote *Moral Man and Immoral Society* (1932), *The Nature and Destiny of Man* (2 vols, 1941–3), *Faith and History* (1949), *The Irony of American History* (1952), *Structure of Nations and Empires* (1959) and many other books. ▷ evangelicalism; Niebuhr, Helmut Richard

Niemöller, Martin (1892–1984) German Lutheran pastor and outspoken opponent of Hitler, born in Lippstadt, Westphalia. He rose from midshipman to become one of Germany's ace submarine commanders in World War I, studied theology, was ordained in 1924 and became pastor at Berlin-Dahlem in 1931. Summoned with other Protestant Church leaders to meet Hitler, who wished to get their co-operation for the Nazi régime, Niemöller declared that he, like Hitler, also had a responsibility for the German people, given by God, which he could not permit Hitler to take away from him. His house was ransacked by the Gestapo and, continuing openly to preach against Hitler, he was arrested and confined from 1937 to 1945 in Sachsenhausen and Dachau concentration camps. Acclaimed by the Allies as one of the few 'good Germans' at the end of the war, he caused great astonishment when it was discovered that he had in 1941 volunteered in vain to serve again in the German navy, despite his opposition to Hitler. His explanation was that he had a duty to 'give unto Caesar what is Caesar's'. In 1945 he was responsible for the 'Declaration of Guilt' by the German churches for not opposing Hitler more strenuously. On the other hand he loudly condemned the abuses of the de-Nazification courts. He vigorously opposed German rearmament and the nuclear arms race. Federal Germany he described as 'begotten in Rome and born in Washington'. From 1947 to 1964 he was Church President of the Evangelical Church in Hesse and Nassau. In 1961 he became President of the World Council of Churches. He wrote *Vom U-Boot zur Kanzel* (1934, 'From U-Boat to the Pulpit'), and collections of his sermons were published in 1935, 1939, 1946, and 1956, particularly *Six Dachau Sermons* (1946, trans 1959). ▷ Barmen Declaration; Lutheranism; Nazi Party

Nietzsche, Friedrich Wilhelm (1844–1900) German philosopher, scholar and writer, though really unclassifiable by conventional labels. He was born in Röcken, Saxony, son of a Lutheran pastor (who died in 1849), and proved himself a brilliant classical student at the school at Schulpforta and at the universities of Bonn and Leipzig. He was appointed Professor of Classical Philology at the University of Basle at the age of 24 and became a Swiss citizen, serving briefly as a medical orderly in 1870 in the Franco-Prussian war but returning to the university in poor health. His first book, *Die Geburt der Tragödie* (1872, 'The Birth of Tragedy'), with its celebrated comparison between 'Dionysian' and 'Apollonian' values, was dedicated to Richard Wagner, who had become a friend and whose operas he regarded as the true successors to Greek tragedy. But he broke violently with Wagner in 1876, nominally at least because he thought the Christian convictions expressed in *Parsifal* 'mere playacting' and political expediency. In 1878 he was forced to resign his university position after worsening bouts of his psychosomatic illnesses and he spent most of the next ten years at various resorts in France, Italy and Switzerland, writing and trying to recover his 'shattered health'. But in 1889 he had a complete mental and physical breakdown, a collapse that was probably syphilitic in origin, and he was nursed for the next 12 years, first by his mother at Naumberg, then by his sister Elizabeth at Weimar. He never recovered his sanity.

In the 16 years from 1872 he had produced a stream of brilliant, unconventional works, often aphoristic or poetical in form, which have secured him an enormous, if sometimes cultish, influence in modern intellectual history. The best known writings are: *Unzeitgemässe Betrachtungen* (1873–6, 'Untimely Meditations'), *Die Fröliche Wissenschaft* (1882, 'The Joyous Science'), *Also Sprach Zarathustra* (1883–92, 'Thus Spake Zarathustra'), *Jenseits von Gut und Böse* (1886, 'Beyond Good and Evil'), *Zur genealogie der Moral* (1887, 'On the Genealogy of Morals'), and *Ecce Homo* (his autobiography, completed in 1888 but withheld by his sister and not published till 1908). One cannot derive systematic 'theories' from these often highly-wrought literary works but the characteristic themes are: the vehement repudiation of Christian and liberal ethics, the detestation of democratic ideals, the celebration of the *Übermensch* (superman) who can create and impose his own law, the death of God, and the life-affirming 'will to power'. His reputation suffered when his views were taken up in a simple-minded and perverted form by the German Nazis, but he is now regarded as a major, though very individual, influence on many strands of 20th-century thought, including existentialism and psychoanalysis, and on figures as various as Heidegger, Yeats, and Foucault. ▷ existentialism; existentialism, Christian; Heidegger, Martin

Night Journey of Muhammad A famous event in the life of Muhammad, which is said to have occurred at an unknown date before the migration from Mecca to Medina in 622. It is hinted at in Quran 17.1, and was embellished by later traditions. It included a journey with the Angel Gabriel on a winged horse from Mecca to Jerusalem where, with Abraham, Moses, Jesus and others, the prophet prayed in the temple of Solomon. Muhammad then ascended with Gabriel from Jerusalem through the seven heavens to God's presence, on the way encountering various prophets in their spiritual form. He was commanded by God to tell Muslims to pray 50 times a day, although this was later reduced to five times daily. When Muhammad recounted elements of his night journey to others in Mecca he was ridiculed, but Abu-Bakr and the Muslim companions believed him, and were convinced of the authenticity of his mission. There has been inconclusive discussion as to whether the night journey was supposed to be a vision or a real event. It became extremely important for Muslim thought and devotion, for Persian miniature paintings, as a foretaste for later Muslims of their own ascent to heaven, as a symbol for Sufis of their own spiritual journey, and for Dante in his cosmology of heaven. ▷ Abraham; Abu-Bakr; art, Islamic; Gabriel; hegira; Jesus Christ in Islam; Mecca; Medina; Muhammad; Quran; salat; Sufism; Sunnah

Nihangs A group of militant Sikhs, distinguished by their uniform which consists of blue robes with yellow sashes, blue turbans, and steel weapons. They served valiantly in the forces of the tenth guru, Guru Gobind Singh, and in the 18th century they formed horseback units to harass Mughal and Afghan forces in the Punjab. Later they became associated with the Akali movement to free Sikh gurdwaras (temples) from Hindu control. Nihang means 'carefree', and the Nihangs lead a relatively unmaterialistic life in their desire to serve the Sikh cause. Organizing themselves into an 'army' they live in encampments, have few belongings, and travel round the Punjab, often on horseback. Their religious life includes sustained periods of hymn singing, and the 'sacramental' eating of *bhang*, a form of cannabis. ▷ Akali Dal; Gobind Singh, Guru; gurdwara; Mughal empire; Punjab

Nile The regular annual flood of the River Nile was fundamental in the development of Egyptian civilization, providing the fertile soil which allows cultivation in the Nile Valley. The river's rise was celebrated every year as a major festival, and the Ancient Egyptians personified the Nile, and particularly its inundation, as the god Hapi. He was portrayed as a bearded man with female breasts and blue or green skin, often carrying tables laden with food as a symbol of fertility. ▷ Ancient Egyptian religion

Niles, Daniel Thambyrajah (1908–70) Tamil Methodist and ecumenical leader and evangelist, born near Jaffna. A fourth-generation Tamil Christian he became increasingly involved in the developing ecumenical movement. The youngest delegate at the 1938 International Missionary Council Tambaram Conference, he was appointed a president of the World Council of Churches after Uppsala (1968), and at the time of his death was Chairman of the East Asian Christian Conference and President of the Methodist Church in Ceylon. He wrote 45 hymns for the *EACC Hymnal* (1963), and these, along with the posthumous *A Testament of Faith* (1972), convey the spirit of his many books. ▷ ecumenism; evangelist; Methodism; World Council of Churches

Nilotic religion ▷ African religions; Dinka religion; Nuer religion; Shilluk religion

Nimbarka (Nimbārka) (12th century) A Hindu theologian who developed the 'difference-in-identity' (*Bhedabheda* or *Dvaitadvaita*) system of philosophy. This is a doctrine similar to that of Ramanuja, stating that the Lord, souls and the world are identical (ie they share the same ontological ground) yet that they are also distinct. Nimbarka advocated devotion (bhakti) or surrender (*prapatti*) to Krishna and his consort Radha as the means of liberation (*moksha*). ▷ Krishna; moksha; Radha; Ramanuja

Nimrod In the Table of Nations (Genesis 10), purportedly the son of Cush and great-grandson of Noah. He was a legendary warrior and hunter, and allegedly one of the first to rule over a great empire after the Flood, becoming King of Babylon and southern Mesopotamia as well as of Assyria, where he is said to have founded Nineveh. In some rabbinic traditions he was also considered the builder of the Tower of Babel (Genesis 11), but it is uncertain whether he was a historical individual at all. ▷ Babel, Tower of; Flood, the; Nineveh; Noah

ninety-five theses A series of points of academic debate with the pope, posted by Martin Luther on the castle door at Wittenberg in 1517. They attacked many practices of the Church, including indulgences and papal powers. This act is generally regarded as initiating the Reformation. ▷ indulgences; Luther, Martin; papacy; Protestantism; Reformation

Nineveh One of the most important cities of ancient Assyria, located east of the Tigris, and the site of royal residences from c.11th century BCE. It was founded in prehistoric times, although some biblical legends associate its origin with Nimrod, and the temple of Ishtar is noted there in the Code of Hammurabi. It was at its height of importance in the 8th–7th century BCE under Sennacherib, but fell in 612BCE to the Medes and Persians. Its royal libraries, containing thousands of clay tablets, are one of the best surviving sources of ancient Mesopotamian history. ▷ Assyrian religion; Hammurabi; Ishtar

Nippur The religious centre of the Sumerians, where their kings were crowned and perhaps also buried. It was never a political capital, but the seat of the god, Enlil, the head of the Sumerian pantheon. ▷ Enlil; Sumerian religion

Nirankar (Niraṅkār) A Sikh epithet for God as the 'One who is Unchanging and Formless'. In this concept God cannot descend to earth in the form of an avatara as Vaishnava Hinduism suggests, or through incarnation as Christianity suggests; nor can the 10 Sikh gurus be seen as 'God-men', important as they are for the Sikh tradition. In addition, God is a spiritual reality beyond the scope of sexual metaphors or human imagery. However, the term 'Nanak Nirankari' is sometimes applied to Guru Nanak in the sense that he blended in and partook of the One who is Unchanging and Formless. Moreover, a Sikh reform movement inspired by Dayal Das (d.1855) called themselves Nirankaris rather than Sikhs. Emphasizing the formless nature of God, they removed images from Sikh temples, and stressed the centrality of the Sikh scripture, the *Guru Granth Sahib*, in Sikh ceremonies. Their focus is upon spirituality rather than what they perceive as the somewhat aggressive institutionalism of the *Khalsa*. They have their own guru and their own headquarters in Chandigarh, and are perceived as a form of fringe sect within the Sikh tradition. ▷ avatara; guru, Sikh; Incarnation; Khalsa; Nanak; Vaishnavism

nirguna Brahman (nirguṇa Brahman) The aspect of *Brahman* first distinguished in the Upanishads, in contrast to *saguna Brahman*. It literally means Brahman 'without qualities', and those who follow this doctrine are exhorted to see through the ignorance (*avidya*) that shapes the perceived world, because of *maya* (illusion), in order to realize their oneness with Brahman, the universal soul. These ideas were developed by Shankara. He too distinguishes the two aspects of Brahman. However, he sees Ishvara (God), the saguna Brahman (Brahman 'with qualities'), as essentially being nirguna Brahman, and therefore indivisible from the essential oneness which is all pervading. This notion of Ishvara being 'merely' part of a whole was a problem for many. However, it was most effectively reinterpreted by Ramanuja, whose 'qualified monism' regarded the level below Brahman as real, while at the same time subscribing to the notion of nirguna Brahman at another level. Sarvepalli Radhakrishnan attempted to reconcile the views of Sankara and Ramanuja, arriving at a position close to that of Sankara, except that he saw the empirical world as being real. He explained this by seeing four levels of reality: Brahman, Ishvara, the 'World-Spirit', and the World. None of these should be seen as separate from the others. ▷ Brahman; Ishvara; maya; Radhakrishnan, Sir Sarvepalli; Ramanuja; Shankara; Upanishads

Nirmalas (Nirmalās) A Sikh ascetic movement deriving its name from the word 'nirmal' which means 'without blemish'. It began with five men who went to study, at the behest of the tenth Sikh guru, Guru Gobind Singh, at the Hindu holy city of Banaras (Varanasi). They established schools of instruction within the Sikh tradition, but showing the influence of their contact with Hindu ideas. Wearing the robes worn by Hindu ascetics, they observe Hindu birth and death ceremonies, and their main centre is at another Hindu holy city, Hardwar. Historically they have served as Sikh missionaries and as priests in Sikh temples, and it appears that they introduced the double-edged sword (*Khanda*) as a significant emblem within Sikhism. ▷ Banaras; Gobind Singh, Guru

nirvana, or **nibbana** (nirvāṇa; nibbāṇa) A term used in Indian religion, especially in Buddhism, to denote a state of deep inner freedom. It has traditionally been interpreted in the West as meaning annihilation and extinction, but this is inaccurate. It originated from the verb *nibbati*, 'to cool by blowing', and referred to someone like the Buddha who was cooled from the fires of delusion, greed and hate, and freed into a state of non-attachment, purity and tranquillity. This was the achievement of the Buddha and the Buddhist saints and the aspiration of the Buddhist tradition. After his enlightenment the Buddha attained provisional nirvana, nirvana in life. But he lived on to preach and serve for many more years until the time of his death, which gave him his final nirvana (*parinirvana*). Early Buddhism did not speculate too much upon the meaning of nirvana after death, and felt that the question was unhelpful if not unanswerable, albeit it did not signify heaven or annihilation. In the later Mahayana schools of philosophy nirvana became related to concepts of an unconditioned reality such as emptiness (*shunyata*), and the cosmic body of the Buddha (*dharmakaya*). Mahayana thought also emphasized the bodhisattva ideal according to which the bodhisattva reaches the verge of final nirvana but postpones it out of compassion for others and is continually reborn into the world so that others too can know nirvana. In any event nirvana is not nothingness, but is creative and positive. ▷ bodhisattva; Buddha; dharma; dharmakaya; emptiness; Mahayana Buddhism; parinirvana

Nitnem The Sikh daily rule of prayer which is observed three times a day by devout Sikhs: in the morning, at sunset, and before sleeping. In the morning the *Japji* of Guru Nanak, and the *Jap* and 10 poems of Guru Gobind Singh are read and meditated on. At sunset the same procedure is applied to the *Rahiras*, which contains nine hymns of Guru Nanak, Guru Amar Das, and Guru Arjan. Before sleeping, the *Sohila*, which contains five hymns by the same three gurus, becomes the source of reading and meditation. All these compositions, and a formal set of petitions called the Ardas, are gathered together in a book known as the *Nitnem*. Like the Sikh scripture, the *Guru Granth Sahib*, it is treated reverently by being wrapped in a white cloth when not in use and by being touched only by freshly washed hands. ▷ Amar Das, Guru; Arjan, Guru; Gobind Singh, Guru; Guru Granth Sahib; Japji; Nanak

Niwano, Nikkyo (1906–) Leader of a new religious movement, the Rissho Koseikai. Born in Tokamachi in Japan he had an early interest in divination and faith-healing and, from 1935 to 1938, he became a member of the Reiyukai Kyodan, a Nichiren-type Buddhist movement, which stressed the *Lotus Sutra* and intensive group-counselling. Together with Mrs Nyoko Naganuma, Niwano split off from that movement for doctrinal reasons and because of its links with the militaristic government, and together they founded Rissho Koseikai in 1938. It grew rapidly until in 1975 its membership was over four million. Its early emphases with regard to the insecure situation of postwar Japan were on immediate benefits, escape from suffering, finding a purpose in life, and belonging to a caring community. After Mrs Naganuma's death in 1957, Niwano increasingly stressed Rissho Koseikai's Buddhist world-view by emphasizing the Buddha's four noble truths and the bodhisattva ideal of compassion for all. Niwano continued the emphasis on intensive group-counselling from his earlier background, and in recent times he has given more energy to the search for international peace and inter-religious co-operation through the International Institute for the Study of Religions in the Rissho Koseikai grounds in Tokyo. Like Soka Gakkai, Niwano has recommended the teaching of Nichiren and the *Lotus Sutra*, but his movement is more ecumenical and liberal than that of its famous rival. ▷ ariya sacca; bodhisattva; Buddha; Lotus Sutra; Reiyukai Kyodan; Soka Gakkai

nkisi ▷ fetish

Noah Biblical character, depicted as the son of Lamech; a 'righteous man' who was given divine instruction to build an ark in which he, his immediate family, and a selection of animals were saved from a widespread flood over the earth (Genesis 6–9). In the Table of Nations (Genesis 10), Noah's sons (Japheth, Ham, and Shem) are depicted as the ancestors of all the nations on earth. A similar flood legend was told of a Babylonian character, Utanapishtim, in the Gilgamesh Epic. ▷ Flood, the; Genesis, Book of; Gilgamesh Epic

nominalism Any metaphysical theory which claims that only individual things exist; there are no universals such as properties. Thus 'red'in 'this rose is red' either refers to nothing, or simply names this rose again, or refers to the individual patch of redness on this rose. ▷ metaphysics; realism

Nonconformists Originally, those Protestants in England and Wales in the 17th century who dissented from the principles of the Church of England. It has subsequently been applied to such denominations as Baptists, Congregationalists, and Methodists, and generally refers to Christians who refuse to conform to the doctrine and practice of an established or national Church. ▷ Christianity; Church of England

non-theistic religions Those religions in which the belief in a single divine personal being actively related to but distinct from the divinely created world is either not part of its structure of beliefs (eg Buddhism) or is permissible but not required (eg Hinduism). ▷ religion; theism

North India, Church of A Church established in Nagpur in 1970 by the union of six different, originally missionary churches in India, including the Anglicans, United Church of North India, Methodists, Baptists, Brethren, and Disciples of Christ. Its constitution combines episcopal and conciliar government. ▷ Christianity; ecumenism; episcopacy

Nostradamus, or Michel de Notredame (1503–66) French physician and astrologer, born in St Rémy in Provence. He became a doctor of medicine in 1529, and practised in Agen, Lyon, and other places. He set himself up as a prophet about 1547. His *Centuries* of predictions in rhymed quatrains (two collections, 1555–8), expressed generally in obscure and enigmatical terms, brought their author a great reputation. Charles IX on his accession appointed him physician-in-ordinary. ▷ astrology

Nuer religion The Nuer, a Nilotic cattle-herding people in the southern Sudan, reflect a world view with similarities to that of the Old Testament. The fundamental concept is *Kwoth*, translated as Spirit. In many contexts this word stands for God; other manifestations of Kwoth are modes or localized refractions of God's activity. God is father of all, the creator of the world from nothing, the source of custom, the decider of destinies. Prayer is addressed to him constantly.

Nuer recognize 'spirits from above' and 'spirits from below'. The former include spirits of the air (more important for some people, families and sectors than others) and *colwic*, certain persons now transfused into spirit (signalized, for example, by being struck by lightning). Spirits from below include the totemic spirits of particular clans, native spirits and spirits of fetish objects. There is some evidence that the Nuer formerly recognized only God and the colwic spirits, the other manifestations of Kwoth being adopted from neighbouring peoples. Ancestors play a limited role, fetish a minor, witchcraft and magic a minimal one. Ideas of ritual purity are almost absent. Kwoth punishes sin—wilful breach of his laws—with open punishment. Spirit can be both a source of help and of danger, and sacrifice, sincerely offered, turns Kwoth away.

Nuer depend on their cattle. At initiation to manhood, the ox seals the new relationship with God, family and ancestors; and the ox is the prime sacrificial animal. There is a 'priesthood of the earth' with important though limited functions. Prophets began to appear in the colonial period. ▷ Dinka religion; totemism

Numa, calendar of Numa Pompilius (8th–7th century BCE), the second King of Rome, is held responsible for a major reform of the calendar. Previously the calendar contained 10 months. Numa added 2 months and fixed the dates of festivals. According to Livy, the insertion of the intercalary months was caused by the problem of coincidence between the cycle of the moon and the cycle of the sun. Thus, with the adding of months, the calendar agreed with the solar year at the end of 19 years. Although this statement appears in other sources such as Cicero, it proves neither the existence of the legendary king, nor that he created a new calendar. The tradition could derive from the fact that Numa was considered the founder of the Roman year of 355 days. It is, in effect, very difficult to calculate cycles of years and to determine actual dates of events before the reform of the calendar by Julius Caesar.

Numbers, Book of A book of the Hebrew Bible/Old Testament, the fourth book of the Pentateuch; entitled in the Hebrew text 'In the Wilderness' or 'And He Spoke', but called 'Numbers' in Greek tradition because of the census of the tribes recorded in the first chapters. It describes the wilderness wanderings of Israel after the Exodus, starting with the preparations for leaving Sinai, and including the journeys to Kadesh-barnea and to the Transjordan prior to the entry into Canaan. Moses is the dominant character in the narrative, but there is also much ritual and legal material (often assigned to the priestly source). ▷ Israel, tribes of; Moses; Old Testament; Pentateuch

Numen A complex concept in Roman religion, which has no proper equivalent today. Etymologically it means a nod, but to explain and understand the term properly it is important to know the history of the word. Up to the time of the emperor Augustus, *numen* was only used with the genitive of the name of a deity, an entity or a collectivity, and signified the expression of a specific will. From Augustan writers onwards, three other meanings were added **1** it acted as a synonym for a particular god or goddess in poetry; **2** it constituted the divine force (the power that controls events and activities) of gods and goddesses, and their divine nature (eg the divine element of a deified person); **3** it expressed a superhuman force, the mysterious in the unseen world. Thus it is impossible to understand numen as a divine presence before the existence of deities—a thesis developed by the modern school of predeism and primitivism. ▷ Roman religion

numerology The notion that there is a mystical and religious meaning in numbers. This is sometimes linked with sacred geometry, which attributes cosmic significance to the numerological proportions of buildings such as the temple in Jerusalem and the pyramids of Egypt. However, it is more often linked to numbers proper; the number seven, for example, is taken to be of deep esoteric significance. In the West it dates back to Pythagoras who felt that number was the key to the universe and that certain qualities were intrinsic to certain numbers. Numerology was also a feature of the Bible's early commentators, and continued to be of interest to biblical interpreters until the Enlightenment and modern critical study of the Bible rationalized it away. Jewish Kabbalah mysticism, ancient Near Eastern religions (especially in Babylon and Egypt), and the Hindu, Buddhist and Chinese religious traditions have all attributed their own patterns of sacredness to numbers, and numerology appears to have been a universal phenomenon among numerate peoples. ▷ Bible; Kabbalah; Pythagoras

nun A member of a religious order of women living under vows of poverty, chastity, and obedience. The term includes women living in enclosed convents, as well as sisters devoted to service of the sick or poor. ▷ monasticism; Orders, Holy; Ursulines

Nun, or **Nu** In Ancient Egypt, the primeval waters out of which the first god arose in the act of creation. As the original source of everything, Nun is personified as 'father of the gods' and portrayed as a bearded man waist deep in water, but he is less important than the gods that followed him. Nun is not the substance from which the world or gods were made, but continues to exist as the waters surrounding the earth, out of which

17th-century nun

the sun rises each morning. ▷ Atum; creation myths; Heliopolis theology

Nyaya (nyāya) One of the six orthodox (*astika*) schools of Indian philosophy which became amalgamated with the Vaisheshika. Nyaya is primarily concerned with methodology and reason (ie how to do philosophy) and develops a system of logic. The system was founded by Gautama, who wrote the *Nyaya Sutras* (1st century CE, though tradition maintains that Gautama lived in the 3rd century BCE). This work was commented on by Vatsyayana (4th century CE). Nyaya develops a form of argument or syllogism with five parts. For example, 'there is fire on the mountain because there is smoke; as in a kitchen, but unlike a lake'. Here the first element is the mountain; the second element is the thing which is to be proved, namely fire on it; the third element is the reason for the fire; the fourth element is a positive example of such an instance, namely a kitchen; and the last element is a negative example, namely a lake (in which fire does not occur). Nyaya-Vaisheshika became a theistic system: Udayana (1025–1100) developed arguments for the existence of God (*Ishvara*), particularly a cosmological argument that the nature of the world is an effect, therefore it must have a first cause. Udayana also argues that a conscious agent, namely Ishvara, arranges atoms into the various combinations which make up the world and arranges for souls to experience the result of their past actions (karma). In the 13th century a new school of Nyaya (*Navya-Nyaya*), founded by Gangesha, developed a system of linguistic notation to specify the relations between concepts. ▷ Gangesha; Ishvara; karma; Vaisheshika

Nyingmapa (rNying-ma-pa) The 'old order' (*rNying-ma*) of Tibetan Buddhism, tracing its origin to the siddha Padmasambhava (8th century), who was regarded as the 'second Buddha'. The Nyingmapa tradition originates in the first diffusion of Buddhism to Tibet during the 8th and 9th centuries from India and Central Asia. With the second diffusion of Buddhism from India from the 10th century onwards, the Nyingmapas became a distinct order emphasizing practice over scholarly pursuits. The Nyingmapas accepted the Buddhist canon while retaining their own old Tantras whose authenticity had been rejected by Buston. They also maintained a tradition of discovering hidden texts or 'treasures' (*gterma*) concealed by Padmasambhava, foreseeing a time of persecution for Buddhism. Buddhist teachings are ordered by the Nyingmapas into nine vehicles divided into three groups of three. The first group, for those of low intellectual and spiritual ability, comprises the Hinayana way of the disciples or 'hearers' (*shravaka-yana*), the way of the solitary Buddhas (*pratyekabuddha-yana*) and the way of the bodhisattvas. The second group, for those of medium ability, comprises the teachings of the three lower classes of Tantra, namely kriya, carya and yoga, while the highest teachings comprise the three classes of Tantra known as *mahayoga*, *anuyoga* and *atiyoga*. The esoteric teachings of the atiyoga or *Dzogchen* (*rdzog-chen*) are characteristic of the Nyingmapas. Dzogchen or 'Great Perfection' teachings maintain that there is an absolute, self-existent, luminous reality, identified with the Buddha Samantabhadra, beyond *samsara* and nirvana. To be liberated from the wheel of reincarnation is to dissolve into this light. These ideas were heretical to the Madhyamika teachings of later Tibetan Buddhism. The Nyingmapas have much in common with the Bonpos, such as married priests, older Tantras rejected by later traditions, and the Dzogchen teachings. ▷ bodhisattva; Buddha; Buddhism; Buston; Hinayana Buddhism; Madhyamika; nirvana; Padmasambhava; pratyeka Buddha; samsara; siddha; Tantra

Nzambi A name for God in wide use throughout West Central Africa. Nzambi is creator and master of the world, but apparently withdrew from earth because of human crimes. ▷ African religions; God

O

Obadiah, Book of One of the 12 so-called 'minor' prophetic writings of the Hebrew Bible/Old Testament, and the shortest book of the Hebrew Bible; named after the otherwise unknown prophet, whose name means 'Servant of God'; sometimes called *Book of Abdias*. The work may have originated soon after the fall of Jerusalem in 587/6BCE, but it is not always seen as a unified composition deriving from one time. It prophesies the fall of Edom in retribution for taking sides against Jerusalem, and predicts judgement on the nations and the restoration of Israel on the final day of the Lord. ▷ Edomites; Old Testament; prophet

obedience The act by which an individual or group carries out the will of a recognized authority. There are varying degrees of obedience, ranging from the external or lawful obedience of a command to the willing obedience to a superior authority which the individual consents to follow.

The exercise of proper obedience finds a place in most faiths, particularly in Judaism and Islam where obedience to the decalogue and submission to Allah constitute the heart of faith. Generally speaking, absolute obedience is due only to God, whereas obedience to human authorities and institutions is derived from their divine sanction and is limited by the claims of conscience. Nevertheless, obedience is necessary for the orderly functioning of society and institutions and monastic orders and organizations have traditionally required vows of obedience from their adherents. This is true of both Buddhism and Christianity. In Christianity the clearest chain of authority is that enjoined by canon law outlining the obedience that is required of a priest to a bishop and bishop to the pope. Non-episcopal churches normally demand obedience to the courts and synods of a church. Hindus too are obliged to obey the laws of Manu and also their personal spiritual teacher. The practice of obedience is often a prerequisite of spiritual progress. However, problems can develop when obedience to a higher principle conflicts with the clear instruction of a faith or institution. The Christian rejection of Jewish ritualism and the Buddhist abandonment of strict Hindu codes of conduct are examples of such conflicts. ▷ authority, Christian; Manu, Laws of

obi A blend of African witchcraft and certain elements of Christianity, practised in the West Indies. ▷ African religions; Christianity; witchcraft

occult A word literally meaning 'hidden' that is used in a vague way to cover a number of groups who are concerned with the supernatural but do not belong to any of the major religious traditions. Thus a number of new religious movements, and some elements of new age religion, are regarded as occult. There is often a sense that the occult is for the spiritual élite rather than for the masses, and that knowledge of the occult should be kept guarded, but it is difficult to be precise because the word is used in such an indistinct way. As a result groups as diverse as Swedenborg's New Church, spiritualism, theosophy, magic, witchcraft, satanism, and Tantric Buddhism are often described as occult. It is sometimes also a pejorative term to describe groups that

occult image combining various hermetic symbols

orthodox religion does not commend. In the term 'occult sciences', it is used to denote extra-sensory perception and paranormal phenomena such as telepathy, clairvoyance, ghosts, poltergeists, precognition and so on. ▷ magic; new age religion; New Church; psychic powers; Satanism; spiritualism; Tantric Buddhism; Theosophical Society; witchcraft

Ochino, Bernardino (1487–1564) Italian Protestant reformer, born in Siena. He joined the Franciscans, but in 1534 moved to the Capuchins, becoming vicar-general of the order after four years. In 1542 he was summoned to Rome to answer for evangelical tendencies, but fled to Calvin in Geneva. In 1545 he became preacher to the Italians in Augsburg. Cranmer invited him to England, where he was pastor to the Italian exiles and a prebend in Canterbury. At Mary I's accession (1553) he fled to Switzerland, and ministered to the Italian exiles in Zürich for ten years. The publication of *Thirty Dialogues*, one of which the Calvinists said contained a defence of polygamy, led to his being banished. Ochino fled to Poland, but was not permitted to stay there and died at Slavkow in Moravia. ▷ Calvin, John; Cranmer, Thomas; Protestantism

Ockham, William of (c.1285–c.1349) English philosopher, theologian and political writer, born in Ockham, Surrey. He entered the Franciscan order young, studied theology at Oxford as an 'inceptor' (beginner), but never obtained a higher degree or a teaching chair because of his controversial views, and left technically still an undergraduate—hence his nickname 'the Venerable Inceptor'. He was summoned to Avignon by Pope John XXII to answer charges of heresy, and became centrally involved in the dispute about Franciscan poverty, which the pope had denounced on doctrinal grounds. He was forced to flee to Bavaria in 1328, was excommunicated, and stayed under the protection of Emperor Louis of Bavaria until 1347. He died in Munich, probably of the Black Death. He published many works on logic while at Oxford and Avignon, particularly the *Summa Logicae*, *Quodlibeta Septem* and commentaries on the *Sentences* of Peter Lombard and on Aristotle; and also several important political treatises in the period 1333–47, generally directed against the papal claims to civil authority and including the *Dialogus de potestate Papae et Imperatoris* and the *Opus nonaginta dierum*. His best-known philosophical contributions are his successful defence of nominalism against realism, and his deployment in theology of 'Ockham's razor', a rule of ontological economy to the effect that 'entities are not to be multiplied beyond necessity'. He was perhaps the most influential of later medieval philosophers. ▷ Franciscans

Odin In Norse mythology, the All-Father, the god of poetry and the dead; also known as *Woden* (English) or *Wotan* (German). He gave one eye to the Giant Mimir in exchange for wisdom. He rides the eight-legged horse Sleipnir, and keeps two ravens to bring him news. Often he wanders the world as a hooded one-eyed old man. ▷ Germanic religion; Valhalla

Office, Divine or **Holy** In the pre-Reformation Western Church and in the Roman Catholic Church, prayers which must be said by priests and devotees every day, originally at fixed hours. The practice dates from early monasticism, and derives from Jewish tradition. ▷ breviary; Benedict of Nursia, St; monasticism

Olam haBa A Hebrew phrase, normally translated as 'the world to come'. Traditional Judaism allows considerable diversity in conceptions of the afterlife, since speculations about it belong to Aggadah not Halakhah. Thus whilst rabbis of early talmudic literature equated the Olam haBa with the Messianic Era, later writers viewed this era as an intermediate stage between this and the world to come. Nonetheless, all would agree with the Mishnah's statement: 'This world is like a vestibule before the world to come: prepare thyself in the vestibule that thou mayest enter into the banqueting hall' (Avot 4.16). The best preparation is the study and practice of God's commandments. In the Hereafter, the righteous will contemplate God's Shekinah and continue Torah study, but food, drink, business and procreation will be unnecessary. As for who would gain access to Olam haBa, the prevailing view again appears in the Mishnah: 'All Israelites have a share in the world to come' (Sanhedrin 10:1); only relatively few would be excluded through heresy. Further, many accepted that Gentiles who were monotheists and adhered to a basic morality would also gain entrance. In modern times some have questioned these traditional ideas. American Reform Judaism, for example, accepted belief in an immortal soul but rejected ancient belief in the resurrection of the dead. More radical Jews would question the existence of any personal afterlife altogether. ▷ afterlife; Aggadah; messianism; Reform Judaism; Shekinah

Old Believers Russian Orthodox traditionalists who rejected the reforms instituted in 1666. Although persecuted, they survived, established their own hierarchy in 1848, and were recognized by the state in 1881. ▷ Russian Orthodox Church

Old Catholics A group of Churches separated at various times from the Roman Catholic Church, including the Church of Utrecht (separated 1724), and German, Austrian, and Swiss Catholics who refused to accept papal infallibility (1870); it also includes some former Poles and Croats in North America. They are united by their adherence to the Declaration of Utrecht (1889) and enjoy intercommunion with Anglicans. ▷ Anglican Communion; infallibility; Roman Catholicism

Old Testament The sacred literature of Judaism, in which the corpus of writings is known simply as the Jewish Scriptures or Hebrew Bible, or even sometimes the Torah; it was also adopted by Christians as part of their sacred writings, and they began to call it the 'Old Testament' as distinct from the Christian writings that constitute the 'New Testament'. The canon of the Jewish religious community, which was fixed c.100CE, was arranged into three parts—the Law, the Prophets, and the Writings—although the precise arrangement and divisions of the books have varied through the centuries. The Law consists of the five books of the Pentateuch (Genesis, Exodus, Leviticus, Numbers, Deuteronomy). The Prophets have been divided since about the 8th century CE into the former and latter prophets: the former prophets consist of the narratives (presumed written by prophets) found in Joshua, Judges, Samuel, and Kings, and the latter prophets consist of Isaiah, Jeremiah, Ezekiel, and the Book of the Twelve Prophets (Hosea, Joel, Amos, Obadiah, Jonah, Micah, Nahum, Habakkuk, Zephaniah, Haggai, Zechariah, Malachi). The Writings contain all remaining works: Psalms, Proverbs, Job, Song of Songs (also known as the Song of Solomon or Canticles), Ruth, Lamentations, Ecclesiastes, Esther, Daniel, Ezra-Nehemiah, and Chronicles.

All the books of the Hebrew Bible appear in the versions of the Old Testament used by Protestant Churches today, but have been divided so as to number 39 in total. Roman Catholic versions of the Old Testament, however, accept 46 works, the additions not appearing in the Hebrew Bible but being found in Greek versions and the Latin Vulgate. These extra works are considered part of the Old Testament Apocrypha by Protestants. ▷ Apocrypha, Old Testament; Bible; Christianity; Judaism; Lamentations of Jeremiah; New Testament; Pentateuch; Pseudepigrapha; Song of Solomon; Torah; Amos / Chronicles / Daniel / Deuteronomy / Ecclesiastes / Esther /Exodus / Ezra / Genesis / Habbakuk / Haggai / Hosea / Isaiah / Jeremiah / Job / Joel / Jonah / Joshua / Judges / Kings / Leviticus / Malachi / Micah / Nahum / Nehemiah / Numbers / Obadiah / Proverbs / Psalms / Ruth / Samuel / Shephariah, Book(s) of

Olives, Mount of, or **Mount Olivet** A rocky outcrop overlooking the Old City of Jerusalem across the Kidron Valley, a site of sanctuaries during the reigns of David and Solomon, and a traditional Jewish burial ground. In Jesus's ministry this marks the location of his discourse about the coming of the end of the age (Mark 13). It is also near the site of the Garden of Gethsemane where Jesus was arrested, and the supposed location of the ascension of the risen Jesus (Acts 1.6–12). ▷ ascension; David; Gethsemane; Jesus Christ; Solomon

Olmec religion Olmec is the name of a people found in historic times in southern Mexico near the Gulf coast. Their name is often given to the earliest of Meso-American civilizations which emerged in this area and lasted perhaps from c.1200 to 400BCE. Some prefer the name La Venta civilization, after the most notable archaeological site, since its builders may have originated outside the Olmec religion. La Venta has many features of later American civilizations: pyramids,

Olmec head

massive buildings, writing, a numerical calendar, even traces of the ball game. Its religion can only be deduced from monuments which it is natural to interpret in the light of similar features in the later civilizations. Stone altars and an abundance of jade votive offerings suggest a developed system of worship, and a columned burial chamber has been held to suggest a rule of priest-kings. There are many representations of a part-human, part-animal figure, usually read as a jaguar. Its face appears even on the altars, which have themselves been seen as representing a jaguar's jaws. The jaguar-divinity motif, frequent in later civilizations, here may have represented the rain god. Some, however, have read the human/animal figure as representing another feature of later civilizations, the great earth serpent. There is no evidence of fully personified deities. The description 'the Olmec face' has been given to figures with thick nose, swollen upper lip and down-turned mouth. Representations of another physical type, taller, thinner, narrow-nosed, have given rise to the idea of two ethnic groups, rulers and ruled, 'jaguar people' and 'serpent people'. ▷ Aztec religion; Maya religion; Toltec religion

Olympian pantheon There was no official classification of gods in Greece (no mortal had the religious authority to provide such a thing). One cannot, therefore, draw up an authoritative list of Greek gods or of members of the Olympian pantheon. A distinction was often drawn between gods 'of heaven' (*ouranioi*) and 'of earth' (*chthonioi*), and it was the former group who tended to be called 'Olympian' (from association with Zeus's lofty home on Mount Olympus). But even this distinction was not absolute, since Zeus, for instance, the Olympian *par excellence*, was also worshipped as Zeus 'under the earth' (*katachthonios*). From the 6th century BCE we find a tendency, perhaps under oriental influence, to worship a group of Twelve Gods: but the less important members of the list varied from city to city, and even a state which had a cult of the Twelve Gods worshipped many minor divine figures besides. One can, however, identify certain major gods who were honoured in virtually every Greek state: Zeus, Hera, Poseidon, Apollo, Artemis, Demeter, Dionysus, Persephone, and Hermes. ▷ Chthonian religion; Greek religion

Om A mystical and sacred monosyllable in Hindu tradition, the sound of which was believed to have a divine power. It was used at the beginning and end of prayers, as a mantra for meditation, and as an invocation

the sacred symbol Om

itself. In the Upanishads it is mentioned as the primary sound syllable. ▷ Hinduism; mantra; meditation; Upanishads

Omar, or **Umar** (c.581–644) The second Muslim caliph. He was father of one of Muhammad's wives, and succeeded Abu-Bakr in 634. With the help of his generals he built up an empire comprising Persia, Syria and all North Africa. He was assassinated in Medina by a Persian slave. ▷ Islam; Muhammad

Omar Khayyam, or **Umar Khayyam** (c.1048–c.1122) Persian poet, mathematician and astronomer, born in Nishapur. His father was a tent-maker, hence his surname. He was well educated, particularly in the sciences and philosophy, in his home town and in Balkh. Later he went to Samarkand where he completed a seminal work on algebra. Consequently he was invited by Seljuq sultan Malik-Shah to make the necessary astronomical observations for the reform of the calendar, and collaborated on an observatory in Isfahan. When his patron died in 1092 he made a pilgrimage to Mecca, on his return from which he served at the court as an astrologer. In his own country and time he was known for his scientific achievements but in the English-speaking world he is indelibly associated with the collection of *robáīyát*, or quatrains, attributed to him. As a poet he had attracted little attention until Edward Fitzgerald translated and arranged the fugitive pieces into *The Rubáiyát of Omar Khayyám*, first published anonymously in 1859. Replete with memorable sayings, they have been translated into all the world's major languages and have influenced Western ideas about Persian poetry. Though some questioned their authorship, it has been established that at least 250 *robāīyát* were the work of Omar. ▷ astrology

Ometeotl The divinity most readily identifiable in Aztec religion as the supreme being. The name means 'God of dualities'. Ometeotl is androgynous, combining male and female characteristics, and thus contains the potential of all creation. Ometeotl's four children (produced by internal coupling) include Quetzalcoatl and Tezcatlipoca, who carry out the creative functions more directly. Dwelling in the highest of the heavenly levels, Ometeotl receives no direct worship (though there is evidence of invocation in emergency). Forms of description include 'Our father, our mother', 'dual lord-lady' and 'the old, old god' (Huehueteotl), although this title also belongs to the fire god, Xiuhtecuhtli. ▷ Aztec religion; Quetzalcoatl; Tezcatlipoca

ontological argument An argument for God's existence, allegedly based on logic alone, presented by St Anselm, Descartes, and others. According to Anselm, God is the being than which nothing greater can be conceived. If God did not exist something greater than he could be conceived; therefore God must exist. ▷ Anselm, St; Descartes, René; God, arguments for the existence of

ontology In metaphysics, the investigation of what sorts of things exist most fundamentally. For example, a materialist ontology claims that matter is the only fundamentally existing thing, so that anything else alleged to exist must either not really exist or be accounted for in exclusively materialistic terms. ▷ metaphysics; monism; pluralism

Ophir A land of unknown location, mentioned in the Bible as famous for its resources of gold; 1 Kings 9–10, 22 suggests that it was reached from Palestine by ship, so it is variously placed in Arabia, India, or East Africa. Solomon is said to have sent a fleet there from Ezion-Geber, but the fame of the 'gold of Ophir' is known also from archaeological inscriptions. ▷ Bible; Solomon

Oppong, Sampson ▷ Harris, William Wadé

Opus Dei (Latin 'work of God') 1 The title of a Roman Catholic society, founded in 1928, to promote the exercise of Christian virtues by individuals in secular society. In some countries and at certain periods (eg Spain in the mid 20th century) it acquired a measure of political power. ▷ Roman Catholicism 2 A term formerly used by the Benedictines, referring to the divine office, to express the duty of prayer. ▷ Benedictines; prayer

oracle Divine prophetic declarations about unknown or future events, or the places (such as Delphi) or inspired individuals (such as the sibyls) through which such communications occur. In ancient Greek stories these revelations were usually given in response to questions put to the gods. In biblical traditions, however, oracles are sometimes distinguished from 'prophecies', in that the latter are unsolicited, although the Old Testament also testifies to interrogations of the divine being. Sometimes oracles were not expressed as verbal messages, but were associated with casting lots or other methods of the divination of signs. ▷ Delphi; God; prophet

oracle bones Inscribed shoulder blades of pig, ox, and sheep (later tortoise shells) used for divination by the Shang monarchs of Anyang, North China, c.1850–1030BCE. The patterns of cracks made by hot brands applied to the bones were read as guidance from royal ancestors, this information being recorded alongside, using an ideographic script of 3000 characters—the earliest-known Chinese writing. Since 1928 c.200000 bones have been recovered.

oral tradition The verbal transmission of myths, legends, sagas and stories within a religious tradition, which bind a community together by creating a shared understanding of the nature of reality. Often these traditions will describe the cosmic order, the coming into existence of a particular people, and contain some reference to a future goal. Such traditions generally pre-date the formalizing of tradition in written form, but it would be false to suggest that oral accounts need necessarily be less reliable than their written counterparts. Recent studies suggest that a sharp division between the relative value of the two forms of tradition is untenable. Once it was felt that written documents were necessary for the development of complex bodies of doctrine. However, recent studies have suggested that sophisticated systems of belief are possible in non-literate societies. Form criticism of the biblical stories of creation and also of the Gospels was originally conceived as an attempt to trace the content and situation of the material before it was written down. The existence of various accounts of the same

incident, and the repetition of formulaic passages introducing certain stories, helped to identify the original oral content and form of a particular passage.
In Islamic thought the existence of oral tradition is explicitly recognized in the legitimation of the body of teaching, supplementary to the Quran, which was written down following the death of Muhammad. The criterion of authenticity was the existence of a chain of oral tradition comprising individuals contemporaneous with one another and in direct communication with each other. ▷ Quran

Oratorians 1 A community of priests, followers of St Philip of Neri, living together without vows, and devoted to prayer, preaching, and attractive services of worship. They still flourish in many countries, including Italy, France, and England where they were introduced by Cardinal Newman. ▷ Neri, St Philip; Newman, John Henry; prayer **2** Priests of the French Oratory, or Oratory of Jesus Christ, founded in 1611 and re-established in 1852. This community is noted for educating priests and furthering popular devotion. ▷ priest

Orders, Holy Grades of ministry in Orthodox, Roman Catholic, and Anglican Churches. Major Orders consist of ordained ministers, bishops, priests, and deacons (and, in the Western Church, subdeacons). Minor Orders include, in the Western Church, lectors, porters, exorcists, acolytes; in the Eastern Church, subdeacons. Major Orders constitute the hierarchy of the Church, to be distinguished from the laity. A distinction is also drawn between First Orders (fully professed men), Second Orders (fully professed women), and Third Orders (those affiliated usually to one of the Mendicant Orders). A member of a Third Order (a 'Tertiary') may live in a religious community, or in the everyday world. ▷ bishop; Church of England; deacon; Mendicant Orders; Orthodox Church; priest; Roman Catholicism

Origen (c.185–c.254) Christian scholar and teacher, the most learned and original of the early Church fathers, born probably in Alexandria, the son of a Christian martyr. He studied in the catechetical school in Alexandria, where he made a thorough study of Plato, the later Platonists and Pythagoreans, and the Stoics, under the Neoplatonist Ammonius. He was head of the school in Alexandria for 20 years (c.211–232), and composed there the chief of his dogmatic treatises, and began his great works of textual and exegetical criticism. During a visit to Palestine in 216 the bishops of Jerusalem and Caesarea employed him to lecture in the churches, and in 230 they consecrated him presbyter without referring to his own bishop. An Alexandrian synod deprived him of the office of presbyter. The churches of Palestine, Phoenicia, Arabia and Achaea declined to concur in this sentence; and Origen, settling in Caesarea in Palestine, founded a school of literature, philosophy and theology. In the last 20 years of his life he travelled widely. In the persecution under Decius in Tyre he was cruelly tortured and there he died.
His exegetical writings extended over nearly the whole of the Old and New Testaments, and included *Scholia*, *Homilies* and *Commentaries*. Of the *Homilies* only a small part has been preserved in the original, although much has been saved in the Latin translations by Rufinus and Jerome; but, unfortunately, the translators tampered with them. Of the *Commentaries* a number of books on Matthew and John are extant in Greek. His gigantic *Hexapla*, the foundation of the textual criticism of the Scriptures, is mostly lost. His *Eight Books against Celsus*, preserved entire in Greek, constitute the greatest of early Christian apologies. The speculative theology of the *Peri Archon* is extant mostly in the garbled translation of Rufinus. Two books on *The Resurrection* and ten books of *Stromata* are lost. The eclectic philosophy of Origen bears a Neoplatonist and Stoical stamp in which the idea of the proceeding of all spirits from God, their fall, redemption and return to God, is the key to the development of the world; at the centre of this is the incarnation of the Logos. All scripture admits of a threefold interpretation—literal, psychical or ethical, and pneumatic or allegorical. ▷ Alexandria, Catechetical School of; apologetics; Fathers of the Church; neo-platonism; Stoicism

original sin The traditional Christian doctrine that, by virtue of the Fall, every human being inherits a 'flawed' or 'tainted' nature in need of regeneration and with a disposition to sinful conduct. There have been various interpretations of the Fall and humanity's sinful condition, ranging from the literal to various symbolic accounts. ▷ Christianity; Fall, the; grace; sin

origin of religion The way in which religious manifestations first arose in the world, and from which later religious forms developed. Early anthropologists accepted the theory of evolution and assumed that it was possible to trace the origins of religion from later religious forms. Different anthropologists had different theories of the origin of religion. For Frazer it was magic, for Tylor it was animism, for de Brosses it was fetishism, for Marett it was pre-animism, for Schmidt it was original monotheism, and for others it was polytheism. It has now become clear that reliable historical evidence of the origin of religion cannot be obtained, and that theories must remain unproven. Evidence from prehistory such as ritually treated skulls, burial sites, cave paintings and megalithic stones reveals nothing about the origin of religion; neither does research into present-day Eskimos, Bushmen, Pygmies, or Aborigines, and nor do myths about the creation of the world. However, although of little value in elucidating the origin of religion, anthropological theories and creation myths have been shown to be of relevance to rich foundation myths such as that of the Garden of Eden. ▷ anthropology of religion; creation myths; Eden, Garden of; Frazer, Sir James George; Marett, Robert Ranulph; megalithic religion; neolithic religion; palaeolithic religion; Tylor, Sir Edward Burnet

Orpheus A legendary Greek poet from Thrace, able to charm beasts and even stones with the music of his lyre. In this way he obtained the release of his wife Eurydice from Hades. He was killed by the maenads, and his head, still singing, floated to Lesbos. ▷ Hades

Orphic/Pythagorean movement Pythagoras was a philosopher of the late 6th/early 5th centuries BCE who set up a school in Italy; 'Orphism' is a term derived from poems falsely ascribed to the mythical singer Orpheus, probably composed in fact in the 6th century BCE. Pythagoreanism and Orphism are therefore distinct; but they have enough in common for 'orphic/pythagorean' to be a useful description for a set of religious ideas of wholly untraditional type that appeared in Greece in the second half the 6th century BCE. The essence of this unorthodox religious mood is an ascetic, other-worldly orientation: the self is seen as a stranger or exile within the body. Pythagoras taught the transmigration of souls (and consequently the necessity of vegetarianism); Orphic poetry seems to have described a primal crime through which all humankind became guilty, and now requires to seek 'purification' through ritual; in both cases, the fate of the soul after death has become a central concern. ▷ afterlife, Greek concept of; evil, Greek concept of; Greek religion; Pythagoras; soul

Orthodox Church, or **Eastern Orthodox Church** A communion of self-governing Churches recognizing the honorary primacy of the Patriarch of Constantinople and confessing the doctrine of the seven Ecumenical Councils (from Nicaea I, 327, to Nicaea II, 787). It includes the patriarchates of Alexandria, Antioch, Constantinople, and Jerusalem, and the Churches of Russia, Bulgaria, Cyprus, Serbia, Georgia, Romania, Greece, Poland, Albania, and Czechoslovakia. It developed historically from the Eastern Roman or Byzantine Empire. In doctrine it is strongly trinitarian, and in practice stresses the mystery and importance of the sacraments, of which it recognizes seven. Episcopal in government, the highest authority is the Ecumenical Council. ▷ Council of the Church; episcopacy; Greek Orthodox Church; Russian Orthodox Church; patriarch; sacrament; Trinity

Orthodox Judaism One of the four denominations within Judaism today. It maintains that the Torah, both written and oral, was revealed by God to Moses, constitutes an inexhaustible and self-consistent unity, and relates with binding authority to every aspect of a Jew's life. The ways in which it is applied vary depending on the halakhic authorities followed and local custom. However, there are considerable divergencies within Orthodoxy. Some, for example, choose to cut themselves off from the outside world, while others seek to be part of it, believing Judaism to be an influence for good in the world at large; there are also numerous postions between these. Such distinctions render Orthodoxy a modern, albeit traditionally based, phenomenon in that it must acknowledge the existence of non-orthodox Jews and itself constitutes one set of responses to the enlightenment and Jewish emancipation. This can be illustrated by attitudes to the State of Israel. The most traditional do not acknowledge the largely secular State as valid since its establishment should be left to God and his Messiah. Some support the State of Israel, arguing that it paves the way for the messianic era, whilst others take a neutral position. Despite such differences, Orthodoxy in its various forms has been gaining ground within Judaism in recent years. ▷ Halakhah; Israel, State of; Reform Judaism; Torah

orthopraxy and orthodoxy Terms meaning right practice and right belief respectively. Orthopraxy has not been a familiar term in

Western religious discourse for some time due to the stress upon the correctness of doctrine in Western culture. However, in faiths such as Hinduism, Judaism and Islam correct practice, in the form of the carrying out of ritual obligations and the obeying of divine commands, is as important as correctness of belief. Here religious faith is a way of life rather than a system of belief. Orthopraxy has come to the fore in recent Christian political theology, where the stress is upon praxis or doing the will of God. It is argued that Christian truth and knowledge of God are gained by following the praxis of Jesus and not by detached contemplation of religious truths.
Nevertheless most faiths have found it necessary to test the assent of the individual to fundamental beliefs of the faith. Disputes over differing interpretations require a means of settlement. In Christianity appeal is made to Church Councils, scripture, creeds and papal authority as a means of legitimizing positions. Catholics and Protestants agree on the need for an absolute authority, but whereas Protestants argue that scripture is the sole authority, Catholics accord an equal role to the pronouncements of popes and Church Councils. Buddhists too have resorted to councils to settle disputes on monastic discipline and the canon of Buddhist scriptures. Monastic orders traditionally act as preservers of the pure teaching of the Buddha. In Hinduism the Brahmans are preservers of ancient wisdom and ritual. Increasingly in all traditions orthodoxy is challenged by cross-cultural communications, creating simultaneously loss of faith and the revival of fundamentalist forms of all faiths. ▷ Brahman; Council of the Church; creeds, Christian; papacy

Osee ▷ **Hosea, Book of**

Osiris Ancient Egyptian god of the dead and of vegetation. The son of Geb and Nut, and member of the Heliopolitan ennead, he was one of the most important and popular deities in Ancient Egypt, and the subject of a considerable mythology. When he received the kingship from his father Geb, his jealous brother Seth tricked and murdered him. His body was found by his sister-wife Isis who, helped by Nephthys and Anubis, mourned him and saw to his embalming and burial. By this she restored his life, and Osiris became King of the Dead. As such he was identified from an early date with the dead pharaoh, and his son Horus with the reigning successor. From the Middle Kingdom (c.2133–1786BCE) commoners were also identified with Osiris when they died, and he became the supreme funerary deity. He was also a fertility god, his death and resurrection representing the cyclical growth, death and rebirth of vegetation. He was worshipped throughout Egypt, with his main cult centre at Abydos, which became a place of pilgrimage. Osiris is normally depicted as a man in mummy wrappings, his hands holding the royal crook and flail and wearing the *atef* crown—the white crown of Upper Egypt, with a red feather on either side. ▷ afterlife, Ancient Egyptian concept of; Anubis; ennead; Heliopolis theology; Horus; Isis; Nephthys; pharaoh; pilgrimage; Seth

Otto, Rudolf (1869–1937) German Protestant theologian and philosopher, born in Peine, Hanover. A professor at Göttingen and Breslau before settling at Marburg in 1917, he was prompted by Kant, Schleiermacher, and several journeys he made to the East to study non-Christian religions, to define religion in a new way. In *Das Heilige* (1917, trans *The Idea of the Holy*, 1923) he describes religious experience as a non-rational but objective sense of the 'numinous', a *mysterium tremendum et fascinans* inspiring both awe and a promise of exaltation and bliss. His other books include *India's Religion of Grace and Christianity* (1930), *The Philosophy of Religion* and *Religious Essays* (1931), and *Mysticism East and West* (1932). ▷ Kant, Immanuel; Protestantism; religion; Schleiermacher, Friedrich Ernst Daniel

Ottoman Turks An important Muslim dynasty (1342–1924) that had its centre in Turkey but expanded as far west as Hungary, as far east as the Persian Gulf, as far north as Azerbaijan, and as far south as Egypt and North Africa. Their early progress was impeded by the depredations of Tamerlane (1336–1405), and in their later years their decline in the face of the rise of the West led to Turkey's becoming known as the 'sick man of Europe'. Their time of greatness began with the conquest of Constantinople from the Christians in 1453—they renamed the city Istanbul. They claimed the succession to the caliphate from the Abbasids after they had conquered Egypt in 1517, and this honour was later ceded to them in practice by the Muslim world. The institution of the caliphate as defender and symbol of Islamic orthodoxy remained with the Ottomans until their dynasty ended in 1924, since when Islam has lacked the symbolic leadership of the caliphate. The great Ottoman era occurred under Süleyman, the Magnificent (1494–1566), who superintended military advance, administrative and social progress, and artistic creativity. Although the Ottomans besieged Vienna as late as 1683, their effective strength declined after their loss of the sea battle of Lepanto in 1571, and their growing weakness before the advance of the West was mirrored by the increasing internal inertia within the Muslim tradition itself. ▷ Abbasids; caliphate; Islamic dynasties; Süleyman, the Magnificent

Our Lady ▷ Mary

Oxford Movement A movement within the Church of England, beginning in 1833 at Oxford, which sought the revival of high doctrine and ceremonial; also known as Tractarianism. Initiated by 'tracts' written by Keble, Newman, and Pusey, it opposed liberal tendencies in the Church and certain Reformation emphases. It led to Anglo-Catholicism and ritualism, and has remained influential in certain quarters of Anglicanism. ▷ Anglo-Catholicism; Church of England; Keble, John; Moral Rearmament; Newman, John Henry; Pusey, Edward Bouverie

P

Pachacamac Literally 'world-maker', a Quechua divinity of the central coastal regions of Peru, who had an important shrine near Lima, much sought after for its oracle. By 1000CE it was the centre of a complex of smaller shrines along the coast and mountain area, thought of as 'wives' or 'children' of Pachacamac. So widely recognized was the cult that not even the zeal of the Inca emperors Pachacuti and Topa could subject it as fully to the Inca religious system as those of other recognized divinities. Under the Inca empire Pachacamac was worshipped with the sun god and eventually identified with Viracocha. The incidence of violence and human sacrifice was reduced in the process. ▷ Pachacuti; Taqui Onqoy; Viracocha

Pachacuti The title of Cusi Inca Yupanqui, creator of the Inca empire. The son of Inca Viracocha, 8th emperor, who had claimed a vision of the deity Viracocha, Pachacuti came to throne in 1438 and abdicated in favour of his son Topa Inca Yupanqui in 1471. Between them Pachacuti and Topa built an empire extending from modern Ecuador to central Chile, and established across it a distinctive politico-religious system. This effectively installed the Inca people as the empire's nobility, and the Inca traditional religion as imperial religion, while incorporating the cults of the conquered peoples in a subordinate role. By tradition, the Inca royal house was descended from the sun god, Inti. Pachacuti had a vision of Inti at a crossroads in his early career but, like his father, claimed the patronage of the creator divinity Viracocha. He declared him the supreme being, exalted above the nature divinities and all the local centres of worship. Cuzco, his capital, was not only the political but also the religious focus of the empire, forming the apex of a carefully constructed pyramid of ritual activity in which each district of the empire played a part. ▷ Inca religion; Viracocha

Pachamama A title, meaning earth mother, given to a subterranean mother goddess by various Andean peoples, and incorporated into the religious system of the Inca empire. Outstanding features of the terrain, such as rocks, were reminders of her presence or activity. Taking care of the plants during their time in the earth, she was important to peasant life; she seems also to have had llamas and other herds in her care (metal symbols of alpacas were buried in pasture land). She was also mother of the dead, landworkers (unlike the nobility) being expected to go below earth at death. Caves and natural openings, entrances to her kingdom, were obvious places for reverent acknowledgement of Pachamama. ▷ goddess worship

Padmasambhava (8th century) Tantric siddha, instrumental in introducing Buddhism to Tibet. He is regarded by the Nyingmapa order as their founder and looked upon as the 'second Buddha'. His life story is imbued with legend. Padmasambhava, meaning 'lotus-born', is said to have emerged as a boy from a lotus in the river Indus, and his spiritual father is said to have been the Buddha Amitabha. As a youth he studied various systems of philosophy and practices, developing magical powers (*siddhi*) and being initiated by Tantric goddesses or *dakini's*, including Vajravarahi, from whom he gained vast spiritual knowledge. Having defeated demonic powers he is said to have reached the highest perfection (*mahamudra*). The Tibetan King Trisong Detsen (740–98) had invited the scholar Shantarakshita to Tibet, where he disseminated Buddhism and inspired the founding of the first Buddhist monastery at Samye (*bSamyas*). The king then invited Padmasambhava to exorcise the local demons and gods who resisted the teachings (dharma). He did so, making them protectors of the dharma, a story which illustrates how Buddhism incorporated local Tibetan traditions. The two figures of Shantarakshita and Padmasambhava exemplify two strands of Buddhism in Tibet, the one centred on the celibate, monastic discipline, the other centred on the Tantric traditions of magical power (siddhi) and exorcism. ▷ Buddha; Buddhism; dharma; Nyingmapa; siddhas

pagoda A Buddhist shrine or memorial-building that is often used as a venue for Buddhist worship. Its origins lie in the Indian stupas, which were burial mounds covered by a dome in which the ashes of the Buddha were placed. As monks began to reside at these holy places, and as these stupas spread

Japanese pagoda

along the trade routes to China, their style evolved dramatically until they became pagodas with many-storeyed sides and peaked roofs. The Chinese pagoda, which emerged in the 3rd century CE, was probably influenced by King Kanishka's great 13-storeyed stupa at Peshawar, and by the design of Chinese wooden watchtowers. As pagodas proliferated across Korea, Japan and South-East Asia they adapted in style to the cultural setting in which they were located. One of the oldest still standing is a 6th-century CE stone pagoda at Honan in China; the largest known pagoda, at Tingchou in China, is 360 feet high. They are usually made of brick, are often octagonal, and are traditionally viewed as symbols of happiness for their neighbourhood. They are sometimes built as acts of devotion, and can be interpreted symbolically as sacred miniatures of the Buddhist cosmos compressed into a building. ▷ Buddha; Kanishka; stupa

Pahlavi A term originally meaning 'Parthian', and now commonly used for the form of Middle Persian which is written in the so-called Pahlavi script. This script derives from the Aramaic alphabet; in Achaemenian times scribes were Aramaeans who wrote in their own language. In time these were replaced by Iranians, who at first continued to write Aramaic but evidently thought in Old or Middle Persian. Gradually they began to write Persian words and verb-endings, whilst retaining many Aramaic words as ideograms (so that the proper way of writing shah, 'king', was the Aramaic form *MLK'*). This led to a highly complex system of writing, which was probably extensively used only by professional scribes. Texts written in Pahlavi script include the Sasanian inscriptions, and the Zoroastrian Pahlavi books. Most of the latter are based on old oral traditions, but were written down in their final form in the 9th and 10th centuries. The majority of these works are religious in character; some of them are based on the Pahlavi translation and exegesis of the *Avesta*, the *Zand*. ▷ Avesta

Paisley, Ian Richard Kyle (1926–) Northern Ireland clergyman and politician, founder of the Free Presbyterian Church of Ulster, born in Northern Ireland. Ordained by his Baptist minister father in 1946, he began his own denomination in 1951, and by 1985 his Free Presbyterian Church had some 10750 members, with Paisley himself as minister of its largest congregation, in Belfast. He became increasingly involved in politics, and (with one brief self-imposed break) has been a Westminster MP since 1970, and leads his own Democratic Unionist party. He is also a Member of the European Parliament, in which he staged a well-publicized one-man protest against the pope as guest speaker in 1988. Strongly pro-British and strenously opposed to the unification of Ireland, he is a rousing orator who inspires both fanatical devotion and deep distrust. Roman Catholic constituents nonetheless have given credit to his impartiality in carrying out routine constituency tasks on their behalf. ▷ Presbyterianism

palaeolithic religion This term refers to the religion of early human beings up to the neolithic period, which began around 8000BCE. Palaeolithic civilization focused upon hunting and gathering, whereas the neolithic revolution switched attention to agriculture and settled communities. Evidence of palaeolithic religion relies upon the interpretation of four kinds of artefacts: human skull remains, burial finds, cave paintings, and female figurines. Early skull remains, such as that of Peking Man (*Sinanthropus Pekinensis*), dating back about half a million years, show evidence of the ritual treatment of skulls. Early burial finds, such as those at La Ferrassie and La Chapelle aux Saints in France, Teshik-Tash in the USSR, and Monte Circeo in Italy dating back to 70000BCE onwards, show bodies lying on the right side, with heads facing the east, legs flexed or in a crouching position, and tools or animal bones lying nearby, possibly as burial gifts. This seems to indicate a comprehension of death and how to deal with it ritually. Cave paintings in places such as Lascaux in France and Altamira in Spain are clearly not art for art's sake and have religious connotations. They portray mainly animals, or humans with animal attributes that seem to be masked dancers, sorcerers, or human-animal figures. They have been interpreted in terms of sympathetic magic, shamanism, hunting rituals, and even deities, but such interpretations are not exact. Female figurines, such as the Venus of Willendorf in Austria, focus on areas of the body, namely the stomach and breasts, which can be taken to represent pregnancy, birth and nurture. They appear to be associated with fertility and possibly with the notion of mother goddesses. We are at the mercy of the evidence we have, but partly at stake is the question of whether, and in what way, early humans were religious. Although the evidence is open to varied interpretation it is possible to argue a case that religion in a general sense has been with us more or less from the beginning, and that human beings are in some sense 'religious animals'. ▷ early burial finds; neolithic religion; shamanism; Venus of Willendorf

Palamas, Gregory (1296–1359) Orthodox mystic and defender of hesychasm against the criticisms of Baalaam the Calabrian (c.1290–1348). This controversy over the nature of God and methods of prayer arose over the question of whether or not God could be directly experienced in this life. Palamas argued that God was both unknowable and knowable, he could not be experienced in his essence (inner being), but he could in his energies (effects). In this sense believers could experience the same divine light as the disciples did at Jesus's transfiguration. Palamas's views eventually prevailed (1351). He was canonized in 1368. ▷ hesychasm; Transfiguration

Paley, William (1743–1805) English theologian, born in Peterborough. He was fellow and tutor of Christ's College, Cambridge (1768–76), and became Archdeacon of Carlisle (1782) and Subdean of Lincoln (1795). He published *Principles of Moral and Political Philosophy* (1785), expounding a form of utilitarianism. In 1790 he produced his most original work, *Horae Paulinae*, the aim of which is to prove the improbability of the hypothesis that the New Testament is a cunningly devised fable. It was followed in 1794 by his famous *Evidences of Christianity*. Perhaps the most widely popular of all his works is *Natural Theology, or Evidences of the Existence and Attributes of the Deity* (1802). ▷ New Testament; utilitarianism

Pali Canon ▷ tipitaka

pancasila (pañcasīla) The moral code of the Buddhist tradition is known as *sila*, and the pancasila are the five moral precepts that are central to Buddhist ethical practice. Morality is the first of three stages on the Buddhist way, and therefore following the five moral precepts is the beginning of the Buddhist path. They are: not harming other living beings; not stealing what belongs to others; avoiding undue sensuality; desisting from wrong and harmful speech; and abjuring drugs, alcohol and other substances that hinder consciousness. The five moral precepts are recited by lay Buddhists during worship as obligations they accept for themselves. On Buddhist holy days some lay Buddhists vow to abstain from sex as well as to observe three more moral precepts: not eating after noon; not going to entertainments or wearing adornments; and not sleeping on luxurious beds. Buddhist monks add one more precept to these in their own moral code, namely not to handle gold or silver. The pancasila—avoiding injuring, stealing, lust, untruth and harmful drugs and drink—are generally common to most religious traditions, as are the additions of other precepts for zealous laymen and for monks. ▷ ethics in religion; sila

Panchen Lama Spiritual leader and teacher in Tibetan Buddhism, second in importance to the Dalai Lama, and said to be the reincarnation of the Buddha Amitabha. The late Panchen Lama (1938–89), the tenth reincarnation, became the ward of the Chinese in his childhood, and some Tibetans disputed his status. ▷ Dalai Lama; Tibetan religion

panentheism The concept that God and the universe are one, but that God is, at the same time, greater than the universe—in other words, that the world is in God, but that he also exists beyond the world. This is distinct from pantheism, which sees God and the universe as absolutely identical. Some philosophers have expressed this idea by analogy to the human body, ie that one is dependent on one's body for most experiences, but can also transcend it. ▷ pantheism; theism

Panikkar, Raimundo (1918–) Spanish ecumenical and global scholar of religion, born in Barcelona. The son of a Hindu father and

Spanish Roman Catholic mother, he was brought up in a Hindu-Catholic environment. Educated in Spain, Germany and Italy, he took doctorates in philosophy, science and theology, and became a Roman Catholic priest. At Banaras Hindu University, Harvard (1967–71), and Santa Barbara, California (1971–), he has made significant contributions to universalization theology (*The Unknown Christ of Hinduism*, 1964), Christian theology (*Christianity and World Religions*, 1969), comparative spirituality (*The Trinity and World Religions*, 1970), inter-religious dialogue (*The Intra-Religious Dialogue*, 1978), Hindu studies (*The Vedic Experience*, 1979), futurology (*From Alienation to Atoneness*), and myth and hermeneutics (*Myth, Faith and Hermeneutics*, 1978). His scholarship is multi-disciplinary, inter-religious, and global in scope, and his personal background and wide-ranging mind make his studies of religion exciting and relevant to an emerging global world. His thought combines philosophy, theology, hermeneutics, comparative religion and global issues into an integral whole. It also contains the seeds for a potentially new and more universal Christian theology. ▷ comparative religion; study of religion; theological attitudes; theology of religion

Panini (Pāṇini) (350–250BCE) The first Sanskrit grammarian. Little is known about his life but devotional legends include the story that he was a slow learner as a child, but by the grace of Shiva or Vishnu became a great scholar at Taxila University, and his status rose sufficiently for him to become the friend of one of the Nanda Emperors. His masterpiece, the *Ashtadhyayi*, standardized classical Sanskrit, and in it he introduced a theoretical framework for the laws of euphonic combination (*sandhi*) and reduced many words to root forms, from which, using grammatic conventions, the language is created. His treatise was the earliest grammar in any language and anticipates many developments of modern linguistics, such as context-sensitive rules. Indeed, the development of linguistics in the West has been influenced by Panini's grammar.

pan-Islamicism The idea that because all Muslims share the same religious identity it would be helpful for them to unite and work together politically on a global scale. In modern times al-Afghani and Muhammad Abduh advocated pan-Islamicism as a way for Muslims to combat Western imperialism. The notion of pan-Islamicism seemed especially helpful to Muslim communities on the fringes of the Islamic heartlands that felt threatened by the West. The Khilafat Movement in India (1918–24) was another facet of pan-Islamic endeavour. When the Ottoman Caliphate was abolished in 1924 and Turkey became a secular state, Islam lost the unifying force of a figure-head; when Muslim states later gained independence, rivalries arose among them. Nevertheless the ideal of pan-Islamicism remains, based partly on a yearning for the golden age of Muhammad and the four early caliphs, which is seen as having been a time of unity, and partly on the desire to think and act collectively as Muslims throughout the world. ▷ Abduh, Muhammad; Afghani, al-; caliphate; Muhammad; Ottoman Turks

Pannenberg, Wolfhart (1928–) German Lutheran theologian, born in Stettin (now Poland). Professor of Systematic Theology at Wuppertal, Mainz, and Munich (1968–), his best-known work is *Jesus—God and Man* (1964, trans 1968), which opposes Bultmann's programme of demythologization with the claim that revelation and history *are* significant theological categories and that the resurrection of Jesus is the pivot on which everything turns. His other works, including *Basic Questions in Theology, I-III* (1970–3), *Theology and the Philosophy of Science* (1976), and *Anthropology in Theological Perspective* (1985), defend the place of reason in theology. He has also written on ethics, spirituality, the Church and secularization. ▷ Bultmann, Rudolf Karl; Lutheranism; resurrection

Panth A Sanskrit word meaning 'path', used to describe religious communities in India which follow particular teachers or beliefs. It was applied to groups such as the Kabir-Panthis who followed the way of *kabir*, while the early Sikh movement was called the Nanak-Panth because it followed the way of Guru Nanak, the first Sikh guru. In time the word 'Nanak' was dropped and the Sikh community became known as the Panth. This is still the favoured title. A local congregation (as opposed to the whole community) is known as a *Sangat*, each Sangat functioning as a branch of the total Sikh Panth. ▷ Kabir; Nanak; Sangat

pantheism The belief that God and the universe are ultimately identical. It may equate the world with God or deny the reality of the world, maintaining that only the divine is real and that sense experience is illusory. It is a characteristic feature of Hinduism and certain schools of Buddhism. ▷ Buddhism; God; Hinduism; Spinoza, Baruch

papacy The title 'pope' (Latin *papa*, Greek *papas*, 'father'), originally given to any bishop, became restricted to the Bishop of Rome with the rise of that see's importance. As Head or Supreme Pontiff of the Roman Catholic Church, he is elected by a conclave of the College of Cardinals, his authority deriving from the belief that he represents Christ in direct apostolic succession from the Apostle Peter, said to be the first Bishop of Rome. After the decline of the ancient churches of the Eastern Roman Empire, resulting from the spread of Islam, the pope in Rome became the centre of the Christian Church, and enjoyed considerable political power as the temporal sovereign of the extensive papal states in Europe (now restricted to the Vatican City in Rome).

The papal claim to infallibility was formalized at the First Vatican Council in 1870. The pope's claim to be 'vicar of Christ' on earth and head of the whole Christian Church was rejected by the churches of the East in 1054, and by Anglicanism and Protestant churches at the Reformation. Papal authority over the church in France was regularly questioned between the 13th and 18th centuries. Uniate Churches of the East are in communion with Rome, but maintain their own order and practice. Some Anglo-Catholics, and some supporters of ecumenism, would allow the pope a modified authority of honour, but not jurisdiction, as a centre of unity of the world church, with a status similar to that enjoyed by the Archbishop of Canterbury in the Anglican Communion. ▷ Anglican Communion; Anglo-Catholicism; apostle; apostolic succession; ecumenism; infallibility; Roman Catholicism; Uniate Churches; Vatican Councils

parable A metaphor in narrative form (although sometimes considered a simile) with the purpose not so much of imparting propositional truths or general moral lessons as challenging the perspective of the hearer. In the Bible, parables are frequently used by Jesus in his preaching about the kingdom of God, and include well-known stories about the Good Samaritan, the Prodigal Son, the Sower, and many others. These parables were often subjected to allegorical interpretation by the Church fathers. ▷ Jesus Christ; kingdom of God; New Testament

Paracelsus (1493–1541) A name coined for himself by **Theophrastus Bombastus von Hohenheim**, a German alchemist and physician, born in Einsieden, Switzerland: the name meant 'beyond Celsus' (the Roman physician Aulus Cornelius Celsus). He studied alchemy and chemistry at Basel University, and then learned about metals and minerals and mining diseases at the mines in the Tirol. He wandered through Europe, Russia and the Middle East (1510–24), amassing a vast store of erudition, and learning the practice of medicine. In 1526 he became town physician in Basel and lectured at the university (in German, not Latin), but was driven out in 1528 and finally settled in Salzburg in 1541. Despite his obsession with alchemy, he nonetheless made new chemical compounds, and coined the word 'alkahest', apparently from Arabic, for the hypothetical universal solvent sought by alchemists. He encouraged research, observation and experiment, and revolutionized medical methods. He was the first to describe silicosis, and to connect goitre with minerals found in drinking water. He improved pharmacy and therapeutics, and established the role of chemistry in medicine.

Paradise A term, probably of Persian origin, referring to a walled garden or park; in the Bible, it is applied variously to the Garden of Eden (Genesis 2–3, in the Septuagint only) and to forests, but only later to a blessed, future heavenly state and place of bliss (2 Corinthians 12.4; Revelation 2.7). In ancient and modern thought paradise has been visualized not only as gardens, but also as mountains and islands. ▷ afterlife; Bible; Eden, Garden of; heaven; jannah, al-

Paralipomenon ▷ **Chronicles, Books of**

paramita (pāramitā) The notion of perfection in Mahayana Buddhism, referring to mental qualities developed to the highest degree by saints or bodhisattvas. There are various lists of these mental qualities that are developed to perfection, but the main list includes six: giving, morality, acceptance, strength, meditation, and wisdom. Thus there is 'perfection of giving', 'perfection of wisdom', and so on. Of special importance is the perfection of wisdom (*prajna-paramita*), and the scriptures of that name, the *Prajna-paramita Sutras*, are very important in Mahayana Buddhism. The perfection of wisdom is sometimes singled out as being the key paramita, with the other five being more functional and related to skilful means. They are all seen as tendencies that are built up and perfected over many births, not only by Mahayana saints (bodhisattvas) but also by Theravada saints (*arahats*). ▷ arahat; bodhisattva; Mahayana Buddhism; prajna; Theravada Buddhism; wisdom

paranormal Beyond the bounds of what can be explained in terms of currently-held scientific knowledge. Thus, to describe an event as paranormal requires that all other possible explanations for the event, based on known principles, be ruled out. However, the use of the term does not imply that the eventual explanation, as science discovers more about allegedly paranormal events, will be non-physical; it allows for the possibility that new discoveries in physics may account for events which are now classified as paranormal. This is in contrast with the term supernatural, which implies a non-physical explanation for events that lie forever beyond natural laws.

parinirvana, or **parinibbana** (parinirvāṇa; parinibbāna) This refers to the complete or final nirvana obtained by a Buddhist. It is possible to attain living nirvana while one is still alive, in which case parinirvana happens when one finally dies. This was the case with the Buddha, who obtained provisional nirvana at the time of his enlightenment, but then embarked upon a long ministry; it was only at the end of his life that his parinirvana ensued and with it the end of all rebirths. The climax and end of the Buddha's life are described in the longest discourse in the *tipitaka* or Pali Canon, the *Mahaparinibbana Sutta*. The place where he died, Kusinara near the Nepal border with India, is one of the four holy places of the Buddhist tradition and a place of pilgrimage for many Buddhists from around the world. It was here that the Buddha was cremated, his ashes stored, and stupas built to commemorate his death and his attainment of final nirvana. ▷ bhavana; Buddha; Kusinara; nirvana; stupa; tipitaka

Parker, Matthew (1504–75) English prelate, and the second Anglican Archbishop of Canterbury, born in Norwich. He became chaplain to Queen Anne Boleyn (1535), Dean of a college at Stoke in Suffolk, a Royal Chaplain, Canon of Ely, Master of Corpus Christi College, Cambridge (1544), Vice-Chancellor (1545) and Dean of Lincoln. He married, and was deprived of his preferments by Queen Mary I. Under Elizabeth I he was consecrated Archbishop of Canterbury (1559). The ritual was not the Roman one; but the scandalous fable that he was informally consecrated in an inn called the Nag's Head originated in Catholic circles 40 years later. The new primate strove to bring about more general conformity. The Thirty-nine Articles of Anglican doctrine, as revised by him, were passed by convocation in 1562; and his 'Advertisements' for the regulation of service, and measures of repression, perhaps forced upon him by the queen, provoked great opposition in the growing Puritan party. Parker originated the revised translation of the Scriptures known as the Bishops' Bible (1572). He edited works by Aelfric, Gildas, Asser, Matthew Paris, Sir Francis Walsingham and Giraldus Cambrensis, was an indefatigable collector of books, and maintained printers, transcribers and engravers. His *De Antiquitate Britannicae Ecclesiae* (1572) is said to be the first privately printed English book. ▷ Anglican Communion; Puritanism; Thirty-nine Articles

parousia (Greek 'coming', 'arrival', 'presence') In Christian thought, normally the future return or 'second coming' of Christ, which will be marked by a heavenly appearance, God's judgement of all humanity, and the resurrection of the dead. Belief in the imminence of Christ's return is particularly prominent in Paul's letters. Protracted delay of the event eventually led to some reformulation of the belief, although some Christian movements continue to await the literal fulfilment of this predicted event and the signs associated with it. ▷ Christianity; eschatology; Jesus Christ; Paul, St

Parrinder, Geoffrey (1910–) English scholar of religion. Ordained into the Methodist ministry, he spent 20 years teaching in West Africa and studying African religions. In *West African Religion* (1949), he gave an overview of the chief principles of African religion. On returning to Britain to teach comparative religion at King's College, London, he extended his overview method to comparative themes embracing all the world's religions: themes such as religious teachings, scriptures, worship, witchcraft, incarnation, mysticism, and sex. Having selected a theme, he traced it through each religion without attempting evaluation or judgement. This pioneering thematic approach became a new way of comparing religions. By following a pattern on each theme, usually from classical Europe, the Bible, the Quran, Indian scriptures, and Chinese classics, he has enriched and extended the field of comparative religion. He held a personal chair at London University from 1970 to 1977, and has published extensively, his works including *The World's Living Religions* (1965) and *Sex in the World's Religions* (1980). ▷ African religions; comparative religion; history of religion; study of religion

Parseeism The religion of the descendants of the ancient Zoroastrians, who fled Persia after its conquest and settled in India in the 8th century CE. They live mainly in the region around Bombay, and preach a rule of life conforming to the purity of Ahura Mazda. Originally agriculturalists, they turned to commerce and industry under British colonial rule, adopting British customs such as the education of girls, and ending their practice of child marriage. They also adapted to the Hindu environment by reducing the extent of their blood sacrifices. Believers are not bound to go through rituals to prove their faith, but are expected to show this in their daily way of life. ▷ Ahura Mazda; Zoroastrianism

Parsi religious reforms These began in the course of the 19th century, owing in part to the greater economic prosperity of the Parsis and to the spread of Western education, but especially to the confrontation of the traditional Parsi community with Western religious concepts and values. The attack on Zoroastrian doctrine made by the Scottish missionary, John Wilson, affected the Parsis very strongly. In his writings Wilson stated that Parsi doctrine was dualist in character and that, as it fell short of his ideal of monotheism, it was 'monstrous and supremely unreasonable'. The Parsis naturally rejected these arguments. However, they had long understood their religion as one that preached simple, practical goodness, and in the ensuing discussion it became clear that their knowledge of the more theoretical aspects of their faith had eroded over the centuries, so that even learned priests were no longer able effectively to rebut attacks made by Western theologians. As a result the priestly classes suffered a significant loss of prestige and authority. This, together with the spread of Western-style education, led many Parsis to look for a new interpretation of their religion, rejecting many aspects of traditional Zoroastrianism. These tendencies were strengthened by their contacts with the German philologist Martin Haug, who taught in Puna for a time in the 1860s. Haug had discovered that, of all the texts which make up the Avesta, only the *Gathas* represent the actual words of the Prophet Zoroaster, and he declared that a ritualistic approach to religion was not part of the message of the Gathas. As a result, the Parsi community came to be divided between the 'traditionalists', who held fast to the form of Zoroastrianism adhered to by their ancestors, and various groups of 'reformists', who wished to return to what they believed to be a purer form of their faith. Zoroastrian modernism has many forms, but most reformists believe that Zoroaster taught a pure monotheism, unencumbered by rituals. Rejecting the charge of dualism, they stress that the Evil Spirit holds the same position in Zoroastrianism as the devil in Christianity and other monotheistic religions. Many reformists seek to rediscover the spiritual truths and values of the faith, which they hold to be more important than the rituals and observances which characterize traditional Zoroastrianism. ▷ Avesta; dualism; monotheism; Satan; Zoroastrianism

Parvati (Pārvatī) One of the most important goddesses of Hindu mythology and literary tradition. As the goddess daughter of the Himalayas, she is associated with all mountains; indeed, her name means 'mountain'. She is known primarily as the gentle and benign consort of the god Shiva and many popular tales are told about them. One of these tells how Shiva initially spurned Parvati because of her dark colour, perhaps indicating that Parvati has a non-Aryan origin, so she practised rigorous asceticism (*tapas*) which made her body glow. This attracted Shiva who, in order to test her loyalty, assumed the form of a dwarf. The dwarf proceeded to vilify Shiva, whereupon Parvati defended him, thus demonstrating her love and fidelity. Shiva is a deity of contrasts possessing both ascetic and erotic aspects. As his wife, Parvati fulfils

Parvati

a specific role by channelling Shiva's spiritual and sexual energy, which he accumulates by his ascetic practice, into the world for the benefit of all. In popular devotional representation, Shiva and Parvati are shown embracing or as a family unit in the Himalayas with their two sons, the elephant-headed Ganesha and the six-headed Skanda. ▷ Ganesha; Shiva; tapas

Pascal, Blaise (1623–62) French mathematician, physicist, theologian and man of letters, born in Clermont-Ferrand, the son of the local president of the court of exchequer. Following the death of his mother the family moved to Paris (1630), where his father, a considerable mathematician, personally undertook his children's education. Blaise was not allowed to begin a subject until his father thought he could easily master it. Consequently it was discovered that the 11-year-old boy had worked out for himself in secret the first 23 propositions of Euclid, calling straight lines 'bars' and circles 'rounds'. Inspired by the work of Girard Desargues, at 16 he published an essay on conics which Descartes refused to believe was the work of a teenager. It contains his famous theorem on a hexagram inscribed in a conic. Father and son collaborated in experiments to confirm Evangelista Torricelli's theory, that nature does not, after all, abhor a vacuum. These experiments consisted in carrying up the Puy de Dôme two glass tubes containing mercury, inverted in a bath of mercury, and noting the fall of the mercury columns with increased altitude. This led on to the invention of the barometer, the hydraulic press and syringe. In 1647, he patented a calculating machine, later simplified by Gottfried Leibniz, which Blaise had built to assist his father in his accounts. In 1651 Pascal's father died, and his sister, Jacqueline, entered the Jansenist convent at Port-Royal. Blaise divided his time between mathematics and socializing in Paris. His correspondence with Pierre de Fermat in 1654 laid the foundations of probability theory.

Then, according to a note found sewn into his clothes, just before midnight on 23 November 1654, he had the first of two revelations, and he came to see that his religious attitude had been too intellectual and remote. He joined his sister in her retreat at Port-Royal, gave up mathematics and society almost completely and joined battle for the Jansenists against the Jesuits of the Sorbonne who had publicly denounced Antoine Arnauld, the Jansenist theologian and mathematician, as a heretic. In 18 brilliant anonymous pamphlets, the *Lettres provinciales* (1656–7), Pascal attacked the Jesuits' meaningless jargon, casuistry and moral laxity. This early prose masterpiece in the French language, the model for Voltaire, failed to save Arnauld, but undermined for ever Jesuit authority and prestige, while Pascal's papers on the area of the cycloid (1669) heralded the invention of the integral calculus. Notes for a case book of Christian truths were discovered after his death, and published as *Pensées* in 1669. The groundwork for Pascal's intended Christian apology, they contain profound insights into religious truths coupled, however, with scepticism of rationalist thought and theology. Their style owes much to Montaigne and Pierre Charron. ▷ Jansenism; Jesuits

Passionists A religious order, founded in Italy in 1720 by St Paul of the Cross; properly known as the Congregation of the Barefooted Clerics of the Most Holy Cross and Passion of our Lord Jesus Christ. With houses in Europe and the USA, their declared objective is to maintain the memory of Christ's sufferings and death. ▷ Jesus Christ; monasticism

passion narrative That part of the story of Jesus in the canonical Gospels which presents the record of his last days in Jerusalem: his last supper with the disciples, his betrayal by Judas, his arrest and appearances before the authorities, and his crucifixion and burial. Each Gospel has such a narrative of the passion (meaning 'suffering') near its close, but differences of detail have been the subject of much scholarly discussion. ▷ crucifixion; Gethsemane; Gospels, canonical; Jesus Christ; Last Supper

passion play A religious drama originating in the medieval period, focusing upon the suffering, death and resurrection of Jesus Christ. Originally based on extracts from the gospels, particularly the passion narratives, such plays gradually came to include poetical sections on wider biblical themes, often recited in the vernacular. By the 16th century many plays had degenerated into anti-clerical farces and consequently many were forbidden by the authorities. The most famous surviving passion play is that staged at Oberammergau in Bavaria. Performed every 10 years since 1634CE, it is produced entirely by the villagers themselves. ▷ drama

passion play, Islamic The passion play is an important event in the Muslim Shiite tradition. It commemorates the death at Karbala in 680 of Husayn, the son of Ali, who was himself the son-in-law and cousin of Muhammad. It re-enacts in a poignant fashion the tragic and gruesome events connected with the death in battle of Husayn, and is performed in the Shiite world, especially in Iran and the Indian sub-continent, around the anniversary of the original death on the 10th of Muharram. There is great emotion and grief on the part of Shiites during the dramatic presentation of what is regarded as Husayn's martyrdom. It is a sad and sorrowful time for Shiites, who remember not only Husayn's death but also the guilt of their own tradition in failing to prevent it. To this extent there is some resemblance to Christian passion plays, and the theme of suffering has become a comparative topic in some Christian and Muslim scholarship in recent years. ▷ Ali; Husayn; Muhammad; Shiism

Passover An annual Jewish festival, occurring in March or April (15–22 Nisan), commemorating the exodus of the Israelites from Egypt. It is named from God's passing over the houses of the Israelites when he killed the first-born children of the Egyptians (Exodus 13); also known as Pesach. ▷ Judaism

Pastoral Letters, or **Pastoral Epistles** Three New Testament writings—the First and Second Letters to Timothy and the Letter to Titus—so named since about the 18th century because they purport to give Paul's advice to his colleagues Timothy and Titus about Church leadership. Their direct authorship by Paul, however, is now widely doubted on grounds of vocabulary, theology, and setting. ▷ New Testament; Paul, St; Pauline Letters

Patanjali (Patañjali) (2nd century) The author of the *Yoga Sutras* and founder of the Yoga school of philosophy. Patanjali probably codified ideas and systems of yoga which were present in Hinduism, combining these systems with the philosophy of Samkhya, which provides the metaphysical presupposition of his text. For Patanjali liberation (*moksha*) is the 'isolation' (*kaivalya*) or separation of the self (atman) from its entanglement in matter (*prakriti*). This is done through the practice of yoga. Hence, like Samkhya, yoga philosophy is dualistic, maintaining an eternal distinction between the soul and matter. This 'isolation' is the gradual purification of consciousness (*citta*) or the detachment of the mind from worldly attachments and desires. Indeed, Patanjali defines yoga as 'the cessation of mental fluctuations' (*cittavritti-nirodha*). This stilling of the mind leads to concentrated states of higher consciousness or absorptions (*samadhi*), eventually leading to the highest samadhi in which consciousness or the 'seer' (*drashtri*) is purified of all sensory input and mundane mental activity. A difference between Samkhya and Patanjali's yoga is that Samkhya is an atheistic system, whereas Patanjali introduces the idea of God or the Lord (*Ishvara*) as an object of concentration. Patanjali's system of yoga has eight branches or limbs (*ashtanga*), also called 'royal' (*raja*, ie 'the best') yoga, namely moral restraint (*yama*), purity (*niyama*), posture (*asana*), breath control (*pranayama*), sense-withdrawal (*pratyahara*) and three degrees of concentration or mental absorption (*dharana*, *dhyana* and *samadhi*). ▷ atman; dhyana; Ishvara; moksha; prakriti; samadhi; Samkhya; yoga; Yoga Darshana

Pater Noster ▷ **Lord's Prayer**

Patimokkha (pāṭimokkha: Sanskrit: prātimokṣa) The code of rules guiding Buddhist monks and nuns. It is part of the first section of the Buddhist scriptures, known as the *tipitaka* or Pali Canon, which deals with monastic discipline (*vinaya-pitaka*), and it organizes the rules in relation to the seriousness of the infringement concerned. On the days of the new and full moons, local assemblies of Theravada monks hold a ceremony in which they recite the whole of the Patimokkha. In the tipitaka 227 rules for monks are laid out according to eight categories. The four deepest offences in relation to monastic order are murder, theft, sexual activity, and spiritual arrogance, and they warrant the removal of the offender from the order. Different schools use different versions of the code, and in most versions there are fewer rules for monks than for nuns, who are viewed as being in some respects subordinate to the monks. ▷ monasticism; tipitaka; vinaya-pitaka

Patit A Sikh who has seriously offended against the Sikh Code of Discipline (*Rahit Maryada*) or lapsed from the faith. Literally meaning 'fallen', it refers particularly to those who have been initiated into the Sikh *Khalsa* but have fallen from their vows, for example by cutting their hair or smoking, and who are therefore expelled. Minor offences can be repaired by a fine or a penance, but major misdemeanours render the offender patit or 'apostate'. To be readmitted after becoming patit confession must be made and a second initiation undergone. Sometimes the word is also used in a general sense for conspicuous

Sikh miscreants, although strictly speaking it applies only to those who have taken initiation into the Khalsa and reneged on it. ▷ Khalsa; Rahit Maryada

patriarch 1 The head of a family or tribe. In biblical literature it is usually applied either to the 10 purported ancestors of the human race prior to the Flood (Genesis 5), or more commonly to Abraham, Isaac, Jacob, and Jacob's 12 sons (Genesis 12–50). The 12 tribes of Israel are traced to the 12 sons of Jacob. ▷ Bible; Flood, the; Israel, tribes of 2 An ecclesiastical title used since about the 6th century for the bishops of the five important ecclesiastical centres of the early Christian Church: Alexandria, Antioch, Constantinople, Jerusalem, and Rome. These bishops exercised influence and jurisdiction over the churches in the areas surrounding their cities. ▷ bishop; Christianity

Patrick, St (5th century) The apostle and patron saint of Ireland, born perhaps in South Wales, less probably at Boulogne-sur-Mer, or Kilpatrick near Dumbarton. His father was a Romano-British deacon named Calpurnius. His own Celtic name or nickname was Succat. According to legend he was seized by pirates in his sixteenth year, carried off to Ireland and sold to an Antrim chief called Milchu. After six years he escaped, and, probably after a second captivity, went to France, where he became a monk, first at Tours and afterwards at Lérins. He was consecrated a bishop at 45, and in 432 it is thought he was sent by Pope Celestine I as a missionary to Ireland. He landed at Wicklow; from there he sailed north to convert his old master Milchu. In Down he converted another chief, Dichu. At Tara in Meath he preached to the King of Tara, Laoghaire. From there he proceeded to Croagh-Patrick in Mayo, to Ulster, and as far as Cashel in the south. He addressed himself first to the chiefs, and made use of the spirit of clanship to spread his teaching. After 20 years spent in missionary labours, he fixed his see at Armagh (454). He died at Saul (Saul-Patrick, from *Sabhal*, 'barn'), the spot which Dichu had given him on his arrival, and was very probably buried at Armagh. The only certainly authentic literary remains of the saint (both in very rude Latin) are his spiritual autobiography 'Confession', and a letter addressed to Coroticus, a British chieftain who had carried off some Irish Christians as slaves. His feast day is 17 March. ▷ apostle

patristics ▷ **Fathers of the Church**

Paul, St, also known as **Saul of Tarsus** (d.c.64/68) Apostle to the Gentiles and important theologian of the early Christian Church, born of Jewish parents in Tarsus, Cilicia. He apparently trained as a rabbi in Jerusalem, becoming a fervent Pharisee and persecutor of Christians. On his way to Damascus (c.34–5), he was converted to Christianity by a vision of Christ, and after several months in Nabatea began to preach the Christian message and undertake missionary journeys, first in Cyprus, Antioch of Pisidia, Iconium, Lystra, and Derbe. Around 48–51 he had to address an apostolic conference in Jerusalem on the disputed issue of how Gentiles and Jews were to be admitted to the Church (Galatians 2.1–10; Acts 15.1–21), and a form of resolution was apparently reached which allowed him to continue his mission to the Gentiles, although a later dispute with Peter did arise in Antioch.

The precise chronology of his missionary activities is confused, but other journeys took Paul, with Silvanus (Silas), to Asia Minor and through Galatia and Phrygia to Macedonia and Achaia, where in Corinth he was especially successful. An extensive mission was also undertaken in Ephesus, amid many difficulties, leading eventually to a final visit to Macedonia and Corinth. On his return to Jerusalem, he was apparently imprisoned for two years, following disturbances against him by the Jews. He was transferred to Caesarea and to Rome after appealing to Caesar. According to later tradition, he was executed by Nero (although some traditions suggest that he was released and went to Spain). Thirteen New Testament letters are traditionally attributed to him, as well as some extra-canonical works. His feast day is 29 June. ▷ Acts of the Apostles; Christianity; disciples (in early Christian Church); Gentiles; New Testament; Pauline Letters

Pauline Letters, or **Pauline Epistles** A set of New Testament writings ascribed to the apostle Paul, usually numbering 13, excluding the letter to the Hebrews which rightly does not claim Pauline authorship. Modern scholars are confident of Paul's authorship in only seven cases (Romans; 1 and 2 Corinthians; Galatians; Philippians; 1 Thessalonians; Philemon), and debate the authenticity of 2 Thessalonians, Colossians, Ephesians, and the Pastoral Letters. The widely accepted writings were actual letters to specific churches and situations in areas where Paul had a pastoral or missionary interest, and were not general systematic treatises. ▷ Colossians/ Corinthians / Ephesians / Galatians / Philemon/Philippians/Romans/Thessalonians, Letters to the; New Testament; Pastoral Letters; Paul, St

peace Absence or cessation of war; tranquillity of mind or conscience. In religious belief the ultimate source of peace is God and only when communities and individuals sustain a proper relationship with him can they attain peace. In many religions a distinction is made between the earthly peace possible in this world and a final, eschatological peace. In the Old Testament the basic meaning of peace (*shalom*) is wholeness, completeness and well-being, states which come about through the right relationship with Yahweh (Isaiah 18.18), who is himself peace (Judges 6.24). Attempts to achieve peace without reference to Yahweh are doomed to failure (cf Jeremiah 6.24). The Old Testament also looks forward to an eschatological peace (Ezekiel 34.25–30; 37.26–8; Isaiah 11.6–9; 32.15–20) and to the coming of the Prince of Peace (Isaiah 9.5–6).
Peace is a major feature of Christ's redemptive work. He blesses the peacemakers (Matthew 5.9) and urges human beings to be at peace with each other (Matthew 9.50). Christ himself is 'our peace' (Ephesians 2.11) and in and through him we have peace (John 16.33; Romans 5.1; Colossians 1.20; of Acts 10.36). On departing this world he leaves his peace with his disciples (John 11.27). Similarly, Paul urges Christians to pursue peace (Romans 11.19; of 2 Timothy 2.22; Hebrews 12.14) and describes God as the 'God of peace' (Romans 15.33; 16.20). Peace is also connected with the Holy Spirit (Galatians 5.22; Romans 8.6; 11.17; Ephesians 4.3). The 'peace' is now a common feature in much church liturgy, often accompanied by the shaking of hands, hugging or the exchanging of a kiss.
In Islam peace is understood as one of the attributes of God (Quran 59.23) and, since Muhammad, has been employed as a Muslim greeting. In Islamic liturgy the confession of faith is preceded by a prayer for peace on the faithful. ▷ Jesus Christ; Muhammad; Sahaj; Yahweh

Peale, Norman Vincent (1898–) American Christian Reformed pastor and writer, born in Bowersville, Ohio, the son of a physician and pastor. Educated at Ohio Wesleyan University and Boston University, he was ordained as a Methodist Episcopal minister in 1922 and held three pastorates before beginning his long ministry at Marble Collegiate Reformed Church, New York City (1932–84). He established a psychiatric clinic, the American Foundation of Religion and Psychiatry, next door to his church. He wrote the bestseller, *The Power of Positive Thinking* (1952), and was much in demand as a lecturer on public affairs. His other works include *The Tough-Minded Optimist* (1962), *Jesus of Nazareth* (1966), and *Power of the Positive Factor* (1987). ▷ Reformed Churches

peepul (also called **pipal** or **bo-tree**) A species of strangler fig, native to South-East Asia, and regarded as sacred in India.

Pelagianism ▷ **Pelagius**

Pelagius (c.360–c.420) British monk and heretic, of either British or Irish origin, his name being a Greek translation of the Celtic *Morgan* ('sea-born'). He never took orders, and settled in Rome about 400. There he wrote *On the Trinity, On Testimonies* and *On the Pauline Epistles*, and persuaded Celestius, an Irish Scot, to his views. About 409 the two withdrew to Africa, and Pelagius made a pilgrimage to Jerusalem. Celestius, having sought ordination in Carthage, had his doctrines examined and condemned; and in 415 Pelagius too was accused of heresy before the synod of Jerusalem. The Pelagian heresy rejected the doctrine of original sin and predestination, insisting on free will and man's innate capacity to do good. The impeachment failed, but a new synod of Carthage in 416 condemned both Pelagius and Celestius; ultimately Pope Zosimus adopted the canons of the African Council, and Pelagius was banished from Rome in 418. The Pelagian sect was soon extinguished, but Pelagianism and Semi-Pelagianism often troubled the church. ▷ heresy

penance (Latin *poena*, 'punishment') Both the inner turning to God in sorrow for sin, and the outward discipline of the Church in order to reinforce repentance by prayer, confession, fasting, and good works. In the Orthodox and Roman Catholic Churches, penance is a sacrament. ▷ confession; fasting; God; sacrament

penance, Christian One of the seven sacraments of the Roman Catholic Church (and the Eastern churches), concerned with turning to God or public returning to the Church after post-baptismal sin. It involves acts of contrition (sorrow for sin) and confession of the circumstances to a priest, satisfaction (making amends or carrying out prescribed acts of atonement), and receiving absolution (God's forgiveness pronounced by a priest).

A priest's power to absolve sin was derived from the authority given by Jesus to the apostles (see Matthew 16.19, 18.18; John 20.23) and Paul's instructions to the church at Corinth (1 Corinthians 5.1–13); 2 Corinthians 2.5–11). Support for the idea of a sacrament of penance was also given in medieval times by the Latin translation of the New Testament, which reads *poenitentia* (penance) where the Greek has *metanoia* (repentance).

By the 3rd century the discipline of penance was available only once in a lifetime, so the practice of deathbed repentance arose. A later development was the commutation of severe and lengthy penances such as pilgrimages into money payments and the purchase of indulgences. The Reformers denied that penance was a sacrament instituted by Christ, and rejected satisfaction along with the doctrines of merit and indulgences, but they retained confession and absolution (though not limiting them to the priesthood). Lutheran and Anglican churches practise general public confession and permit private confession to a minister or priest. Roman Catholicism since Vatican II has taken a more pastoral and congregation-oriented approach to what is now called the 'Reconciliation of the Penitent'. ▷ indulgences; merit; pilgrimage, Christian; sacrament; Vatican Councils

Penates In Roman religion the guardians of the storeroom. 'Lares and Penates' were the household gods. The *Penates publici* were the 'luck' of the Roman state, originally brought by Aeneas from Troy and kept at Lavinium. ▷ Lares; Roman religion

penitential psalms A set of seven Old Testament psalms—Psalms 6, 32, 38, 51 (Miserere), 102, 130 (De Profundis) and 143, although differently numbered in the Vulgate and many Catholic versions—which have been used in Christian liturgy since at least the early Middle Ages, when they were regularly recited on Fridays during Lent. They are mainly laments, although not all are directly concerned with repentance of sin. ▷ liturgy; Old Testament; Psalms, Book of

Penn, William (1644–1718) English Quaker reformer and colonialist, founder of Pennsylvania, born in London, the son of Admiral Sir William Penn (1621–70). He was sent down from Christ Church College, Oxford, for refusing to conform to the restored Anglican Church, and his father sent him to the Continent, in the hope that the gaiety of French life would alter the bent of his mind. He returned a polished man of the world, having seen brief naval service in the Dutch war. He studied law at Lincoln's Inn for a year, and in 1666 his father dispatched him to look after his estates in Cork. There he attended Quaker meetings, and was imprisoned. He returned to England a convinced Quaker. In 1668 he was thrown into the Tower for writing *Sandy Foundation Shaken*, in which he attacked the ordinary doctrines of the Trinity.

While in prison he wrote the most popular of his books, *No Cross, No Crown*, and *Innocency with her Open Face*, a vindication of himself that contributed to his liberation, obtained through the intervention of his father's friend, the Duke of York (the future James VII and II). In September 1670 he was again imprisoned for preaching; and in 1671 he was sent to Newgate for six months. He took advantage of the Indulgence for making preaching tours, championing religious tolerance, and visited Holland and Germany for the advancement of Quakerism. Meanwhile, as one of the Quaker trustees of the American province of West Jersey, he had drawn up the settlers' celebrated 'Concessions and Agreements' charter. In 1681 he obtained from the Crown, in lieu of his father's claim upon it, a grant of territory in North America, called 'Pensilvania' in honour of the old admiral, with the intention of establishing a home for his co-religionists.

Penn with his emigrants sailed for the Delaware in 1682, and in November held his famous interview with the Indians on the site of Philadelphia. He planned the city of Philadelphia, and for two years governed the colony wisely, with full tolerance for all that was not regarded as wicked by Puritanism (card-playing and play-going, however, being strictly forbidden as 'evil sports and games'). He returned to England (1684–99) to exert himself in favour of his persecuted brethren at home. His influence with James VII and II and his belief in his good intentions were curiously strong. Through his exertions, in 1686 all persons imprisoned on account of their religious opinions (including 1200 Quakers) were released.

After the accession of William III, Penn was repeatedly accused of treasonable adherence to the deposed king, but was finally acquitted in 1693. In 1699 he paid a second visit to Pennsylvania, where his constitution had proved unworkable and had to be much altered. He did something to mitigate the evils of slavery, but held black slaves himself. He departed for England in 1701. His last years were embittered by disputes about boundaries, etc; he was even thrown into the Fleet

Street debtors' prison for nine months in 1708. He was twice married, and wrote over 40 works and pamphlets. ▷ Puritanism; Friends, Society of; Trinity

Pentateuch The five Books of Moses in the Hebrew Bible/Old Testament, comprising Genesis, Exodus, Leviticus, Numbers, and Deuteronomy; also called by Jews the Torah. Although attributed to Moses since ancient times, the works as a whole are believed by modern scholars to be composed of several discrete strands of traditions from various periods (such as an early Judean source 'J'; a northern Israelite source 'E'; a priestly source 'P', perhaps from exilic times; and a source 'D' responsible for most of Deuteronomy). Together they trace Israel's origins from the earliest times, through the patriarchs, to the Exodus and Sinai periods prior to the entry to Canaan; they also contain much cultic and legal instruction. ▷ Moses; Old Testament; patriarch 1; Torah

Pentecost 1 The Jewish feast of Shavuot. 2 A festival day in the Christian calendar, some 50 days after the death and resurrection of Jesus (seven weeks after Easter Sunday), commemorating the event in Acts 2 when the Holy Spirit was said to have come upon Jesus's apostles in Jerusalem, enabling them to 'speak in other tongues' to those present. In Acts 2.1 this occurred on the Jewish feast of Pentecost. In the English Church, this day is sometimes called 'Whitsunday'. The term Pentecost may also be used for the entire period between Easter Sunday and Pentecost Sunday. ▷ Christianity; glossolalia; Holy Spirit; Shavuot; Pentecostalism

Pentecostal Churches ▷ Pentecostalism

Pentecostalism A modern Christian renewal movement inspired by the descent of the Holy Spirit experienced by the Apostles at the first Christian Pentecost (Acts 2). It is marked by the reappearance of speaking in tongues, prophecy, and healing. The movement began in 1901 in Topeka, Kansas, USA, and became organized in 1905 in Los Angeles. Rejected by their own churches, new churches were established, commonly called 'Pentecostal', and since then their missionary zeal has reached every part of the world. Pentecostal churches are characterized by a literal interpretation of the Bible, informal worship during which there is enthusiastic singing and spontaneous exclamations of praise and thanksgiving, and the exercise of the gifts of the Holy Spirit. There are over 22 million Pentecostals worldwide. Since the 1960s Pentecostalism (usually referred to as 'charismatic renewal') has appeared within the established Protestant, Roman Catholic, and Greek Orthodox Churches. ▷ charismatic movement; Christianity; faith healing; glossolalia; Holy Spirit; Pentecost

People's Temple A notorious new religious movement founded by a charismatic figure, the Reverend Jim Jones, in 1953. It was unusual among new religious movements in that most of its members were black and from a humble background. It moved to California in 1965 and grew in numbers, attracting the attention of some liberal whites and prominent people through its social involvement and radical politics. However, it moved its operations to Guyana, where the People's Temple was set up in a colony named Jonestown. Problems arose in the colony due to Jones's autocratic leadership, and news of this filtered back to America. A US Congressman named Lee Ryan was sent out to investigate the allegations of ill-treatment and unusual practices at Jonestown. He was murdered and shortly afterwards, in November 1978, over 900 of the People's Temple, men, women and children, committed collective suicide in Jonestown. This tragedy brought new religious movements to the attention of the world in an unfortunate way, and for a while there was a tendency for all new religious movements to be seen in the light of the People's Temple. Nowadays, due partly to an increased understanding of the differences and realities of new religious movements and partly to the excesses of the anti-cult movement's denigration of them, there is a more balanced perspective. ▷ Anti-Cult movement; new religious movements in the West

perennial philosophy During this century, and especially since World War II, a loosely-knit group of scholars has formed which owes a general allegiance to the school of thought known as *philosophia perennis* or the perennial philosophy. Amongst its members are Seyyed Hossein Nasr, Ananda Coomaraswamy, and Huston Smith. The group would concur with Aldous Huxley's statement in *The Perennial Philosophy* (1945) that this philosophy comprises 'the metaphysic that recognises a divine Reality substantial to the world of things and lives and minds; the psychology that finds in the soul something similar to, or even identical with, divine Reality; the ethic that places man's final end in the knowledge of the immanent and transcendent Ground of all being.' The perennial philosophy agrees that religious traditions are different in outward matters such as institutions, rituals, scriptures and doctrines. It claims, however, that on the level of spirituality religions converge. Thus, although outwardly they are varied and unique, with their own stamp and historical tradition, inwardly there is a basic spiritual unity of all the religions. Not all scholars or believers accept that there is an essential unity of religious traditions at their spiritual core. However, the perennial philosophy has served to highlight the importance of inner spirituality by contrast with what it would consider to be the more superficial elements of outward religious belonging. ▷ mysticism; Nasr, Seyyed Hossein; spirituality; study of religion

Pesach ▷ **Passover**

Peter, Letters of New Testament writings attributed to the apostle Peter, although both are widely considered by modern scholars to be pseudonymous. The first letter claims to be written from 'Babylon' (possibly a cipher for Rome) to Christians in Asia Minor, encouraging them to stand fast amidst persecution, and reminding them of their Christian vows and obligations. It has been variously dated between the Neronian persecution of 64CE and the Domitian persecution c.95CE. The second, shorter letter yields no direct references to its situation, but appears to oppose teachers who deny the second coming of Christ and espouse gnostic-tending doctrines. It is sometimes dated in the first half of the 2nd century, and its canonical status was at times disputed in the early Church. ▷ Gnosticism; New Testament; Peter, St

Peter, St (1st century) One of the 12 apostles of Jesus, originally named Simeon or Simon bar Jona ('son of Jonah'), a fisherman living in Capernaum during the public ministry of Jesus, but renamed by Jesus as Cephas or Peter (meaning 'rock') in view of his leadership amongst the disciples. In the Gospels he is often the spokesman for the other disciples, and leader of the inner group which accompanied Jesus at the Transfiguration and Gethsemane. Immediately after Jesus's resurrection and ascension, Peter appears also as the leader of the Christian community in Jerusalem; later he may have engaged in missionary work outside Palestine, certainly visiting Antioch, but little is directly known of these activities. Tradition says that he was impaled or crucified with his head downward in Rome; his presence in Rome was in fact uncertain, but he is regarded by the Roman Catholic Church as the first Bishop of Rome. Two New Testament letters bear his name, but the authenticity of both is often disputed; other apocryphal writings also exist in his name, such as the Acts of Peter and the Apocalypse of Peter. His feast day is 29 June. ▷ Acts of the Apostles; apostle; disciples (early Christian); Jesus Christ; Peter, Letters of

Peter Lombard ▷ **Lombard, Peter**

Pettazzoni, Raffaele (1883–1959) Italian scholar of religion, born in San Giovanni Persiceto. He was educated at Bologna, where from 1914 to 1923 he was Professor of the History of Religions. He was subsequently appointed to the same position at Rome (1923–53). Pettazzoni was President of the International Association for the History of Religions from 1954, presiding over its Rome congress in 1955. He had a deep influence upon the development of the study of religion in Italy and internationally. His work on comparative religion included an epoch-making essay comparing the spread of Christianity in Europe with the spread of Buddhism throughout the Far East; he also wrote on the place of the history of religion within religious studies in general (*Essays in the History of Religion*, 1954). In *The All-Knowing God. Researches into Early Religion and Culture* (1956), he insisted that early monotheism was neither an evolution from polytheism nor an original premonition of later monotheism, but was unique in its own right. ▷ comparative religion; monotheism; Schmidt, Wilhelm

peyote A hallucinogenic drug from the cactus *lophophora williamsii*, now in religious use among many native American peoples. The plant grows in the Rio Grande Valley and southwards, and originally formed part of an elaborate but localized cult in Mexico. In the late 19th century its use spread northwards; it is now to be found among peoples of the southwest (between 25 and 50 per cent of Navajo were estimated to be participants by the 1960s), across the Plains peoples and among some woodland and Basin peoples. Its use was accompanied by a religious revival which stressed Native American tradition while incorporating some Christian features. This has been given institutional form in the Native American Church, which in some states of the USA provides the only legal way of taking peyote. Peyotism offers spiritual healing and confidence, and has helped combat the common fear of witchcraft, and has had some success in curing alcoholism. It revives ancient Native American traditions (eg the vision quest) without the effort and expense of the traditional ceremonies. Enhancing Native American identity, it also accommodates aspects of modern life and of Christianity. It tends, however, to strengthen pan-Indian, rather than tribal identity, and the visions it offers do not involve the preparation or the self-sacrifice of the old rites—features which have brought opposition from traditionalists. ▷ ecstacy; Navajo religion

Pfleiderer, Otto (1839–1908) German Protestant theologian, born in Stetten in Württemberg. He studied at Tübingen (1857–61), became pastor at Heilbronn in 1868, in 1870 Professor of Theology at Jena, and in 1875 at Berlin. In New Testament criticism Pfleiderer belonged to the critical school which grew out of the impulse given by Ferdinand Baur (1792–1860), and was an independent thinker, suggestive and profoundly learned. His works include *Primitive Christianity* (14 vols, trans 1906–11), *The Influence of the Apostle Paul on Christianity* (Hibbert Lectures, 1885) and *The Philosophy of Religion* (Gifford Lectures, 1894). ▷ biblical criticism; Protestantism

pharaoh The title applied to the god-kings of Ancient Egypt from the New Kingdom (c.1500BCE) onwards. Pharaohs were the chief mediators between their mortal subjects and the gods, and after death were believed to become gods themselves, as their mummified forms show; all have the attributes of the god Osiris—plaited beard, crook, and flail. ▷ Ancient Egyptian religion; Osiris

Pharisees An influential minority group within Palestinian Judaism before 70CE, mainly consisting of laymen; possibly originating out of the Hasidim who opposed the political aspirations of John Hyrcanus I (c.2nd century BCE). They were noted for their separation from the common people, and for their punctilious observance of written and oral laws regarding ritual purity, cleansings, and food laws, assuming even the obligations placed upon priests. In the New Testament Gospels, they are often portrayed as the opponents of Jesus. After the fall of Jerusalem in 70, it was from Pharisaic circles that the rabbinic movement arose. ▷ Hasidim; Jesus Christ; Judaism; rabbi; Sadducees

Philemon, Letter to The shortest of Paul's letters, usually accepted as genuinely from the apostle to an individual Christian named Philemon, whose runaway slave Onesimus had been converted by Paul in prison. Paul asks Philemon to forgive and receive Onesimus as a fellow Christian, and not to seek punishment under Roman law. It dates perhaps from the late 50s to the early 60s. ▷ New Testament; Paul, St; Pauline Letters

Philip, St (1st century) One of the disciples of Jesus, listed among the 12 in Mark 3.14 and Acts 1, but especially prominent in John's Gospel, where he is said to come from Bethsaida in Galilee, leads Nathanael to Jesus (1.43), is present at the feeding of the 5000 (6.1) and brings 'the Greeks' to Jesus (12.21). His later career is unknown, but traditions suggest he was martyred on a cross. He is probably not to be confused with Philip 'the Evangelist' (Acts 6.5). His feast day is 1 May (West) or 14 November (East). ▷ apostle; crucifixion; disciples (in early Christian church); Jesus Christ; John, Gospel according to

Philippians, Letter to the New Testament writing, widely accepted as genuinely from the apostle Paul to a Christian community that he had founded earlier at Philippi in Macedonia, although the unity of the work has been debated. Writing while imprisoned (? mid 50s CE), Paul thanks them for a gift sent to him, apprises them of his situation and difficulties, warns them of sectarian teaching, but generally displays a warm regard for their commitment. ▷ New Testament; Paul, St; Pauline Letters

Philistine religion The Philistines were the ancient warlike inhabitants of the coastal area of the South East Mediterranean between present day Jaffa and Egypt. They originally migrated with the Sea Peoples in the 13th and 12th centuries BCE, probably from the Mycenaean world. They were constantly at odds with the Israelites of the hinterland, a struggle epitomized by the stories of Samson and of David and Goliath. Whatever their original religious beliefs they appear to have taken over substantial elements of the indigenous Canaanite religion. Information is sparse but a limited picture of Philistine religion can be gleaned from the Hebrew Bible and some archaeological evidence. According to the Bible the chief god of the Philistines was Dagon, who had temples at Gaza and Ashdod. Also worshipped were Baalzebub and the goddess Astarte. The Semitic names of these deities suggest that the Philistines adopted local Canaanite traditions. Some Aegean influence is apparent in the 'Ashdoda' figurines, which have the form of a chair or throne on which female characteristics have been moulded. Excavations of Philistine temples have shown a fusion of both Aegean and Canaanite features, but little is known about the sacrificial practices of these temples or about the personal beliefs of the Philistines. ▷ Astarte; Canaanite religion; Dagan; David; Israel, tribes of; Samson; temples, Ancient Near Eastern

Phillips, John Bertram (1906–82) English Bible translator, writer and broadcaster, born in Barnes. He was made famous by *Letters to Young Churches* (1947), translations of St Paul's epistles begun in 1941 to encourage his church youth club, and in due course by the complete *New Testament in Modern English* (1958). He wrote a dozen best-sellers, including *Your God is Too Small* (1952), *A Man Called Jesus* (1959), and *Ring of Truth: A Translator's Testimony* (1967). Few were aware of his continuous battle against depression from 1961, until the posthumous publication of his autobiography, *The Price of Success* (1984), and letters to others in similar situations (*The Wounded Healer*, 1984).

Philo Judaeus (1st century) Hellenistic Jewish philosopher, born in Alexandria, where he was a leading member of the Jewish community. A prolific author, he sought to effect a synthesis between Greek philosophy and Jewish scripture, and greatly influenced subsequent Greek Christian theologians like Clement and Origen. In c.40CE he headed a deputation to the mad Emperor Caligula to plead with him on behalf of Jews who refused to worship him, as he records in the *De Legatione*. Most of his other works consist of allegorical interpretations of the Pentateuch, many of which survive in the original Greek. ▷ Clement of Alexandria, St; Hellenistic Judaism; Origen; Pentateuch

philosophy (literally the love of wisdom) Philosophy deals with some of the most general questions about the universe and our place in it. Is the world entirely physical in its composition and processes? Is there any purpose to it? Can we know anything for certain? Are we free? Are there any absolute values? Philosophy differs from science, in that its questions cannot be answered empirically or by experiment, and from religion, in that its purpose is entirely intellectual, and allows no role for faith or revelation.

Philosophy tends to proceed by an informal but rigorous process of conceptual analysis and argument. Philosophers have also questioned the nature of their own enterprise: what philosophy is or should be, is itself a philosophical issue. The major branches of philosophy are metaphysics, the inquiry into the most general features, relations, and processes of reality; epistemology, the investigation of the possibility, types, and sources of knowledge; ethics, the study of the types, sources, and justification of moral values and principles; and logic, the analysis of correct and incorrect reasoning. Philosophical issues can arise concerning other areas of inquiry, for example, in art, law, religion, and science; the issues tend to be ramifications of one or more of the four major branches. Western philosophy began with the Presocratics in the 6th century BCE in the Greek-speaking region around the Aegean Sea and southern Italy. Ancient philosophers such as Plato and Aristotle probed virtually every area of knowledge; there was as yet no distinction between philosophy and science. As Christianity became an important social force in Europe and North Africa (2nd –5th centuries), apologists such as St Augustine began to synthesize ancient philosophy with the Christian world-view, a process that continued throughout the Middle Ages.

With the scientific revolution of the 16th and 17th centuries, the physical sciences began to separate from philosophy, and philosophers such as Descartes, Locke, and Leibniz began to assess the philosophical implications of the new scientific results. In the 19th century and early 20th century, psychology established itself as a discipline distinct from philosophy. This process of continued separation of disciplines from philosophy raises the question whether philosophy has a subject-matter proper to itself. The perennial nature of the questions mentioned above suggests that it does; moreover, as new subject matters emerge, new philosophical issues typically arise with respect to them. Two contemporary examples are hermeneutics, conceived most generally as the study of the interpretation of such meaning-laden phenomena as language, works of art, and social practices; and cognitive science, the investigation of how the results of neurophysiology, psychology, linguistics, and computer simulation shed light on the workings of the mind. ▷ Aristotle; Augustine, St (of Hippo); Descartes, René; ethics in religion; falsafa; hermeneutics; Locke, John; metaphysics; Plato; secular alternatives to religion

philosophy, Islamic Philosophy has not been a dominant motif in the Muslim tradition. The Quran was essentially concerned with God's revelation to human beings through the medium of Muhammad. Muhammad's conscious mind and human reason were not seen to be an element in that revelation, and the rapid advance of early Islam meant that the Quranic Arabic world-view spread quickly and triumphantly and did not have to accommodate other world-views unless this was desirable. The Greek philosophical world-view with which it came into contact stressed reason rather than revelation, scripture as a created rather than an uncreated phenomenon, heaven and hell as psychological states rather than real places, free will rather than determinism, and God as Being rather than as having separate qualities. Great Muslim philosophers wrestled with these matters, ranging from the Mutazilites of the 8th century CE to the great Ibn Sina (Avicenna) and Ibn Rushd (Averroës). However, their thought was not integrated into mainstream Islam and they remained at the periphery. Al-Ghazali introduced the classical synthesis of the competing themes of earlier Islam, but he refuted the possibility of philosophy achieving real truth and certainty in his *Refutation of the Philosophers*, and he reduced philosophy to a secondary helpmate for theology. It was left to Sufi thinkers such as Ibn Arabi to develop a more metaphysical philosophy derived from Plato rather than from Aristotle (who had influenced Avicenna and Averroës), and although this metaphysical philosophy did not deeply influence Islam, it was important for Islamic mysticism. ▷ Arabi, ibn al-; Aristotle; Averroës, Ibn Hamid Mohammed; Avicenna; falsafa; predestination in Islam; Ghazali, al-; Muhammad; Plato; Quran; revelation; Sufism

philosophy, Jewish Jewish philosophical endeavour has assumed numerous forms and emphases depending on its time and place of origin. However, it is convenient to think of three periods in Jewish philosophy: that in the Second Temple period (c.515BCE–70CE), Jewish thought in the Middle Ages, and philosophical enquiry undertaken in modern times. During the Second Temple period Jews encountered Greek philosophy with varying responses: some resisted the absorption of its ideas, while others tried to marry Jewish and Hellenistic modes of thought. The latter predominated in the Diaspora as exemplified in the works of Philo of Alexandria. However, the rise of Rabbinic Judaism after the destruction of the Temple in 70CE brought the removal of overt Greek traits from Judaism until medieval times. During the Middle Ages the rediscovery of ancient texts renewed interest in Greek philosophy, at first in Islam and then in Judaism and Christianity. This led Jewish scholars to justify and expound their religion on rational grounds, as seen in the work of Maimonides. Modern Jewish philosophy is especially diverse but has sought to come to terms with several factors: the rise of secular philosophy, Christianity as Europe's dominant faith, and Jewish identity after emancipation. These issues are dealt with by philosophers such as Baruch Spinoza, Moses Mendelssohn and Martin Buber. In addition to these are those whose Jewishness or Jewish origin may be less perceptible in their work, eg Wittgenstein. ▷ Buber, Martin; Diaspora Judaism; Hellenistic Judaism; Maimonides; Mendelssohn, Moses; Philo Judaeus; Spinoza, Baruch; Wittgenstein, Ludwig Josef Johann

Phoenicia The narrow strip in the eastern Mediterranean between the mountains of Lebanon and the sea, where the cities of Arad, Byblos, Sidon, and Tyre were located. It derived its name from the Phoenicians; descendants of the Canaanites, they were the dominant people of the area from the end of the second millennium BCE, and this was their base first for trading all over the Mediterranean and then, from the 8th century BCE, for establishing trading posts and colonies in the western Mediterranean, such as Leptis Magna and Carthage in North Africa. From here came their most important contribution to Western culture—the alphabet. ▷ Canaan

Phoenician religion The religion of the Phoenicians was in many ways continuous with earlier Canaanite religion, but had its own emphases and developments. There was no strictly set pantheon, and a multitude of local cults were important, the chief gods of cities often being fertility deities. The chief god of Tyre was Melqart, and because of Tyre's supremacy was widely worshipped throughout Phoenicia and beyond. The Sidonian god of health and healing, Eshmun, was later identified by the Greeks with Asklepios. The dying and rising god Adonis was worshipped at the shrine of Aphka at the source of the river Nahr Ibrahim, which turned red in the spring, marking the beginning of annual mourning rites. The most popular goddess was Astarte, goddess of love and war, who was known as Tanit in Carthage and the western colonies. Egyptian influence on Phoenician religion was strong and led to the worship of Bes and Osiris; a number of Mesopotamian deities were also honoured. Local influences upon the Phoenician colonies in Carthage and the western Mediterranean can also be seen. The gods were worshipped by a sacrificial cult in open-air sanctuaries

Phoenician deity

and temples. There is evidence from Carthage of the sacrifice and ritual immolation of small children; thousands of urns containing their remains have been found in a precinct sacred to Tanit. Phoenician burials contained numerous domestic and ritual objects, which would suggest a belief in the afterlife, though it is difficult to be more specific about this, or about other personal beliefs of the Phoenicians. ▷ afterlife, Ancient Near Eastern; Astarte; Canaanite religion; human sacrifice, Israelite; Osiris; temples, Ancient Near Eastern

Photius (c.820–891) Byzantine prelate, and Patriarch of Constantinople. On the deposition of Ignatius from the patriarchate of Constantinople for correcting the vices of the emperor Michael, Photius, a soldier and courtier, was hurried through all the stages of holy orders, and installed in his stead. In 862, however, Pope Nicholas I called a council at Rome which declared Photius' election invalid, excommunicated him, and reinstated Ignatius. Supported by the emperor, Photius assembled a council at Constantinople in 867, which condemned many points of doctrine and discipline of the Western Church as heretical, excommunicated Nicholas, and withdrew from the communion of Rome. Under the emperor Basilius, in 867 Photius was banished to Cyprus and Ignatius reinstated. In 869 the eighth general council, at which Pope Adrian II's legates presided, assembled at Constantinople; Photius was again excommunicated, and the intercommunion of the churches restored. Yet, on the death of Ignatius, Photius was reappointed. In 879 he assembled a new council at Constantinople, renewed the charges against the Western Church, and erased the *filioque* from the creed. Photius was finally deprived, and exiled to Armenia by Leo, son of Basilius, in 886. His main surviving works are *Myriobiblon* or *Bibliotheca*, a summary review of 280 works which Photius had read, and many of which are lost; a *Lexicon*; the *Nomocanon*, a collection of the acts and decrees of the councils and ecclesiastical laws of the emperors; and a collection of letters. ▷ Council of the Church; patriarch

Pico della Mirandola, Giovanni, Comte (1463–94) Italian philosopher and humanist, born in Mirandola, Ferrara. He studied in Italy and France, and settled later in Florence, where he came under the influence of Marsilio Ficino. In 1486 in Rome he wrote his *Conclusiones*, offering to dispute his 900 theses on logic, ethics, theology, mathematics and the Kabbalah against all-comers, but the debate was forbidden by the pope (Innocent VIII) on the grounds that many of the theses were heretical, and he suffered persecution until Pope Alexander VI finally absolved him in 1493. He wrote various Latin epistles and elegies, a series of florid Italian sonnets, *Heptaplus* (1490, a mystical interpretation of the Genesis creation myth), and some important philosophical works including *De ente et uno* (1492, an attempt to reconcile Platonic and Aristotelian ontological doctrines) and *De hominis dignitate oratio* (1486, on freewill). ▷ humanism

Pietism Originally, a movement within Lutheranism in the 17th and 18th centuries stressing good works, Bible study, and holiness in Christian life. It was a reaction against rigid Protestant dogmatism, and influenced other groups, such as Moravians, Methodists, and Evangelicals. ▷ Lutheranism; Methodism; Moravian Brethren

Pilate, Pontius, properly **Pontius Pilatus** (1st century) Roman appointed by Tiberius in c.26 as prefect of Judea, having charge of the state and the occupying military forces, but subordinate to the legate of Syria. Although based in Caesarea, he also resided in Jerusalem, and was noted for his order to execute Jesus of Nazareth by crucifixion at the prompting of the Jewish authorities. He caused unrest by his use of Temple funds to build an aqueduct, by his temporary location of Roman standards in Jerusalem, and by his slaughter of Samaritans in 36 (for which he was recalled). ▷ Annas; Jesus Christ

pilgrimage A journey to a sacred place made for religious reasons. It is undertaken in order to gain a greater sense of closeness to the sacred or as a means of affirming one's faith. Pilgrimage is made to sites associated with the founders of particular religions, such as, for example, Jerusalem and Mecca, or to places where important religious events have taken place. ▷ shrines

pilgrimage, Christian Journeys to holy places in order to obtain divine help, give thanks, fulfil vows or obtain forgiveness by doing penance are not required in Christianity, but they have been undertaken at least since St Helena, mother of the emperor Constantine, visited Jerusalem in 326. Pilgrimages to the Holy Land, Rome, and local shrines associated with Mary or the saints were highly organized in medieval Europe. The motive and piety of participants varied, as can be seen from Chaucer's *Canterbury Tales* (1386). Not all would be making a spiritual pilgrimage of detachment from worldly concerns to seek the presence of Christ, as advocated by Chaucer's contemporary, Walter Hilton (d.1396), in *The Scale of Perfection*, and in much other Christian spirituality from Gregory the Great to John Bunyan's *Pilgrim's Progress* (1678) and the anonymous Russian *The Way of a Pilgrim* (1884, Eng trans. 1960). The Reformation criticism of indulgences, fictional relics and other abuses of pilgrimage reduced the practice, but it survived, increasing in Victorian times with the advent of the railways and package tours. The 19th and 20th centuries have seen a revival of devotion to Mary at places like Lourdes (France), Fatima (Portugal) and Medujigore (Yugoslavia). Modern Protestant and ecumenical centres of spiritual if not geographical pilgrimage include the island of Iona (Scotland), once the resting place of the bones of St Columba and now the home of the Iona Community, and Taizé (France), home of the Taizé Community. ▷ Bunyan, John; Columba, St; Constantine I; Gregory I, the Great, St; indulgences; MacLeod, Baron George Fielden, of Fuinary; Mary; penance; Roger of Taizé, Brother; saint, Christian view of

pilgrimage, Sikh Sikhs have a somewhat ambivalent attitude towards pilgrimage. Guru Nanak and the other Sikh gurus reacted against what they felt was an unhealthy stress by contemporary Hindus on sacred cities, sacred rivers, and pilgrimage to sacred places. As Guru Nanak typically put it in the *Adi Granth* (687), 'there is no place of pilgrimage like the guru who alone is the pool of compassion and contentment'. However, the city of Amritsar, and the Golden Temple in Amritsar, have become de facto places of pilgrimage for Sikhs from around the world. In addition to this, as a kind of negative inducement, the third guru, Guru Amar Das, set up a bathing place in Goindeval as an incentive for Sikhs not to visit the Hindu pilgrimage centre of Hardwar. ▷ Adi Granth; Amar Das, Guru; Amritsar; guru; Nanak

Pilgrim Fathers The English religious dissenters who established Plymouth Colony in America in 1620, after crossing the Atlantic aboard the *Mayflower*; 102 sailed, and one was born at sea. They originally came from Lincolnshire, but had spent an extended period in the Netherlands before migrating to America.

pillars of Islam ▷ five pillars, Islamic

pipal ▷ peepul

pipe, sacred ▷ calumet

Pius IX, named **Giovanni Maria Mastai Ferretti** (1792–1878) Pope from 1846, born in Sinigaglia, Italy. He took deacon's orders in 1818, in 1827 was made Archbishop of Spoleto, and in 1832 Bishop of Imola. In 1840 he became a cardinal, and was elected pope on the death of Gregory XVI. He entered at once on a course of reforms. He granted an amnesty to all political prisoners and exiles, removed most of the disabilities of the Jews, authorized railways, projected a council of state, and in March 1848 published his *Statuto Fondamentale*, a scheme for the temporal government of the papal states by two chambers, one nominated by the pope, the other (with the power of taxation) elected by the people.

At first the new pope was the idol of the populace. But the revolutionary fever of 1848 spread too fast for a reforming pope, and his refusal to wage war on the Austrians finally forfeited the affections of the Romans. In 1848 his first minister, Count Pelegrino Rossi, was murdered, and two days later a mob assembled in the square of the Quirinal. The pope escaped to Gaeta, and a republic was proclaimed in Rome. In April 1849 a French expedition was sent to Civita Vecchia; in July General Oudinot took Rome after a siege of

30 days; and henceforward the papal government was re-established.

Pius IX proved an unyielding conservative and Ultramontane, closely allied with the Jesuits. The war of the French and Sardinians against Austria in 1859 and the popular vote of 1860 incorporated a great part of papal territory with the Sardinian (Italian) kingdom; but Pius always refused to recognize the fact. He re-established the hierarchy in England, sanctioned a Catholic University in Ireland, and condemned the Queen's Colleges. He concluded a reactionary concordat with Austria. By the bull *Ineffabilis Deus* (1854) he decreed the Immaculate Conception; his famous encyclical *Quanta Cura* and the *Syllabus of Errors*, appeared in 1864. The Vatican Council (1869–79) proclaimed the infallibility of the pope. For the previous ten years the pope's temporal power had only been maintained by the French garrison; on its withdrawal in 1870 the soldiers of Victor Emmanuel II entered Rome. For the rest of his days the pope lived as a voluntary 'prisoner' within the Vatican. ▷ Immaculate Conception; Ultramontanism

Plato (c.428–c.348BCE) Greek philosopher, indisputably one of the most important philosophers of all time and so enormously influential that Whitehead was able to characterize the subsequent history of Western philosophy as a series of 'footnotes to Plato'. He was the pupil (or at least the associate) of Socrates and the teacher of Aristotle, and this trio were the great figures in ancient philosophy. Plato was probably born in Athens, of a distinguished aristocratic family, but little is known of his early life. Any youthful political ambitions must have withered when his friend and mentor, Socrates, was condemned to death in 399BCE by the restored democracy in Athens. Plato immortalized the story of Socrates' trial and last days in three of his dialogues: the *Apology*, the *Crito* and the *Phaedo*, all of which reflect vividly his profound affection and respect for Socrates. After the execution he and other disciples of Socrates took temporary refuge at Megara with the philosopher Euclides, and Plato himself then travelled widely in Greece, Egypt, the Greek cities in southern Italy (where he no doubt encountered Pythagoreans) and Sicily (where he made friends with Dion, brother-in-law of Dionysius I, the ruler of Syracuse). He returned to Athens in c.387BCE to found the Academy, which became a famous centre for philosophical, mathematical and scientific research, and over which he presided for the rest of his life. He visited Sicily again in 367BCE, at Dion's request, to try and train Dionysius II to become a philosopher-statesman, but despite a second visit in 361–360, which placed him in some personal danger, the attempt failed completely.

His corpus of writings consists of some 30 philosophical dialogues and a series of *Letters*, of which the Seventh is the most important (biographically and philosophically) and only the Seventh and Eighth are likely to be genuine. The dialogues are conventionally divided into three groups—early, middle and late—though the exact relative chronology of individual dialogues is a vexed and probably insoluble problem of scholarship. The early Socratic dialogues have Socrates as the principal character, usually portrayed interrogating his unfortunate interlocutors about the definition of different moral virtues (piety in the *Euthyphro*, courage in the *Laches*, and so on); their initially confident assertions are shown to be confused and contradictory and all parties end up sharing Socrates' professed perplexity. The middle dialogues show the character 'Socrates' expressing more positive, systematic views, which are taken to be Plato's own. This group includes the most dramatic and literary of the dialogues, the *Symposium*, *Gorgias*, *Phaedo*, and *Republic*, and presents such famous Platonic doctrines as the theory of knowledge as recollection, the immortality of the soul, the tripartite division of the soul, and above all the theory of forms (or 'ideas') which contrasts the transient, material world of 'particulars' (objects merely of perception, opinion and belief) with the timeless, unchanging world of universals or forms (the true objects of knowledge). The *Republic* also describes Plato's celebrated political utopia, ruled by philosopher-kings who have mastered the discipline of 'dialectic' and studied the hierarchy of the forms, including its apex, the form of the Good. The details of this visionary state—the rigid class structure of workers, soldiers and rulers, the education of the rulers (both men and women), their communism of property and of family, their totalitarian powers—have been variously idealized, attacked, misinterpreted and imitated in subsequent political theory and literature, but the *Republic* remains one of the most compelling and influential works in the history of philosophy. The third group of 'late' dialogues is generally less literary in form and represents a series of sustained and highly sophisticated criticisms of the metaphysical and logical assumptions of Plato's doctrines of the middle period. The *Parmenides*, *Theaetetus* and *Sophist* in particular have attracted the interest of contemporary analytical philosophers and contain some of Plato's most demanding and original work.

Taken as a whole, his philosophy has had a pervasive and incalculable influence on almost every period and tradition, rivalled only by that of his greatest pupil Aristotle, which was its principal competitor for much of the Hellenistic period, the middle ages and the Renaissance. ▷ Aristotle; Socrates; Whitehead, Alfred North

Platonism Any philosophical position which includes many of the central features of Plato's philosophy. These include a belief in a transcendent realm of abstract, perfect entities; the inferiority of the physical world; the power of reason to know these perfect entities; and bodily separability and the immortality of the soul. ▷ neo-platonism; Plato

play in religion Although religion is essentially serious, play has been an important element within many traditions, finding expression in different ways. In some worldviews, for example in Hinduism, play is a facet of the world process itself. The world is a play (*lila*) of forces arising out of the play of God. Religious festivals also contain an element of play in the sense of rejoicing, celebration and festivity. Sometimes the play element reverses the normal everyday roles in life, so that in the European carnival the spirit of licence precedes the coming of Lent, and in the Hindu Krishna Lila, caste positions are overturned for the day. Within religious ritual, play may occur, but it is defined within more rigid limits. Ritual plays occur in many traditions within boundaries laid down by the occasion, ranging from the passion plays of Christianity and Shiite Islam commemorating the suffering of Christ and Husayn, to the open-air nightly presentation of the story of the Hindu deity, Rama, in the Rama Lila. Here the element of imagination and makebelieve still occurs, but it is adapted to a serious and even poignant purpose. In various religions the ability to 'become a child' in spiritual attitudes is treasured, so that religious commitment combines a sense of seriousness with a sense of play. ▷ Husayn; Jesus Christ; Krishna; lila; passion play; Rama

Plotinus (c.205–270) Neoplatonist philosopher, probably born in Egypt of Roman parentage, though his education and intellectual background was Greek. He studied in Alexandria (under Ammonius Saccas), and in Persia, and in 244 settled in Rome where he became a popular lecturer, advocating asceticism and the contemplative life, though he seemed to live in some style himself. At the age of 60 he tried to found in Campania a 'Platonopolis' modelled on Plato's utopian *Republic*, but the emperor Gallienus in the end put a stop to it. His prolific writings, produced between 253 and 270, were posthumously edited and arranged by his pupil Porphyry into six 'groups of nine books' (or *Enneads*). They established the foundations of neo-platonism as a philosophical system, combining Platonic with Pythagorean, Aristotelian and Stoic doctrines. He greatly influenced early Christian theology, and neoplatonism was the dominant philosophy in Europe for a millennium, establishing a link between ancient and medieval thought. ▷ Aristotle; asceticism; neo-platonism; Plato; Stoicism

pluralism Any metaphysical theory which is committed to the ultimate existence of two or more kinds of things. For example, mindbody dualists, such as Descartes, are pluralists. ▷ Descartes, René; dualism; metaphysics; monism

Plymouth Brethren A religious sect founded by a group of Christian evangelicals in 1829 in Dublin, Ireland. It spread to England, where in 1832 a meeting was established in Plymouth. Millenarian in outlook, the sect is characterized by a simplicity of belief, practice, and style of life based on the New Testament. By 1848 it had split into the 'Open' and the 'Exclusive' Brethren. ▷ Christianity; evangelicalism; millenarianism

polemics, Islamic/Christian Islamic/Christian polemics have been partly theological. Whereas the Quran accepted Jesus as a prophet second only to Muhammad, the Christian community did not accept Muhammad as a prophet. Moreover, Islam, while accepting the virgin birth, miracles and resurrection of Jesus, did not accept his divinity or crucifixion, and looked upon the doctrine of the trinity as implying the existence of three gods. Furthermore, the Muslim tradition considered that the Christians had distorted their own Bible, which required the Quran to correct and fulfil it, whereas the Christians considered the Quran to be heretical and misguided. Theological polemics along these lines have been present to a greater or lesser extent throughout Islamic/Christian interchanges. Communally the Muslims regarded the Christians as a 'people of the Book', and allowed Christians whose territories they conquered to keep their religion on payment of a poll-tax. Matters worsened at the time of the Crusades, when theological polemics became intertwined with war, and Muslim opinion hardened against Christians living in the Muslim world, who were put under greater pressure to convert to Islam. In the modern situation, as the West became stronger externally, and the Islamic world became weaker internally, Islam saw the Western world as being 'Christian', and Western powers underestimated the 'Islamic' nature of the Islamic political world so that Islamic/Christian polemics combined political and religious issues. However, there has also recently been an increase in Islamic/Christian dialogue which aims to increase mutual understanding and to enable the two traditions to work together in building a unified world. ▷ Bible; crucifixion; Crusades; Immaculate Conception; Jesus Christ in Islam; Muhammad; polemics, Islamic/Jewish; Quran; resurrection; Trinity;

polemics, Islamic/Jewish Although sharing a belief in a monotheistic and unincarnate God, Muslims and Jews have differed on other matters. The Muslims foresaw co-operation with Jews on the basis of Quran 3.64—'O people of the Book! Let us come together on a platform that is common between us, that we shall serve naught save God'—but, conversely, felt that the Jews had distorted their own scriptures and the teaching of their own prophets, so that the Quran was needed to correct and fulfil the insights of the Jewish Bible and the Jewish prophets. The Jews, however, refused to accept the Islamic view of their Bible and their prophets, and of the role of Muhammad, and they were driven out of Medina by Muhammad, and out of Arabia by Caliph Umar. Nevertheless, as a 'people of the Book' they were able to keep their own religion and culture in the rest of the Muslim world, and a great scholar such as Moses Maimonides was able to write on Jewish matters and to advise Jews from his vantage-point as a physician in the court of a Muslim sultan in Egypt. Relations between Jews and Muslims remained reasonably amicable compared with Islamic/Christian polemics until the foundation of the state of Israel in 1948 and the Palestinian question arising from it. This has vast political overtones, but it also includes religious polemic over Jerusalem, which is regarded as a holy city by both Jews and Muslims. Islamic/Jewish dialogue has arisen in an unassuming yet expanding way between liberal Muslims and Jews in some academic and religious quarters, and it can be expected to grow quietly. Deeper dialogue and real meeting await the resolution of the Middle Eastern crisis. ▷ Bible; Israel, State of; Jerusalem; Maimonides; Medina; Muhammad; polemics, Islamic/Christian; prophets in Islam; Quran

political theology A German Protestant movement that emerged in the 1960s, popularized by Johann Baptist Metz (1936–), Dorethee Soelle (1929–) and Moltmann. It moved away from denominational, apolitical or individualistic theology to concentrate on the social and political implications of Christian faith. Many concerns of European political theology (the relation between faith and action, peace and justice, suffering, solidarity, democratic socialism) are taken up more widely in feminist theology, liberation theology, and other theologies emerging from the third world. ▷ feminist theology; liberation theology; Moltmann, Jürgen; Protestantism

Polycarp (c.69–c.155) Greek Christian martyr, and one of the 'Apostolic Fathers'. He was Bishop of Smyrna during the earlier half of the 2nd century. He bridges the little-known period between the age of his master, the Apostle John, and that of his own disciple Irenaeus. His parentage was probably Christian. Ephesus had become the new home of the faith, and there Polycarp was 'taught by apostles', John above all, and 'lived in familiar intercourse with many who had seen Christ'. He was intimate with Papias and Ignatius. At the close of his life Polycarp visited Rome to discuss the vexed question of the time for keeping the Easter festival; he then returned to Smyrna, only to win the martyr's crown in a persecution which broke out during a great pagan festival. The fire, it was said, arched itself about the martyr, and he had to be killed with a dagger. The graphic *Letter of the Smyrnaeans* tells the story of the martyrdom. The only writing of Polycarp extant is the *Epistle to the Philippians*, incomplete in the original Greek, but complete in a Latin translation. Somewhat commonplace in itself, it is of great value for questions of the canon, the origin of the Roman Church, and the Ignatian epistles. ▷ Fathers of the Church; Ignatius (of Antioch), St; Irenaeus, St; John, St; martyr

Polynesian religion ▷ **Maori religion**

polytheism The belief in or worship of many gods, characteristic not only of primitive religions but also of the religions of classical Greece and Rome. It is an attempt, contrasting with monotheism, to acknowledge a divine presence in the world. ▷ monotheism; pantheism

Poor Clares ▷ Franciscans

pope ▷ papacy

popular religion A generic term employed to describe the unorthodox, non-institutional beliefs, rites and practices that accompany mainstream religions. Despite its name, it is not a religion in the normal sense of the term, since it lacks the usual features of a religion such as creeds, liturgy, priesthood, etc. Instead, it is a fusion of a variety of traditional, pagan, and superstitious beliefs with concepts and beliefs drawn from mainstream religion.
Popular religion is closely related to the class structure of a society. Orthodox and official religion has for the most part been the province of the intellectual, cultural and class élites of a society. Official religion has only been superficially adhered to by the lower classes, however, and has often been imposed upon them from above. The result is that traditional pagan and supersititous beliefs are retained, though disguised with a thin veneer of the official religion. It is this that constitutes popular religion.
In the 19th and earlier 20th centuries popular religion was treated negatively and often understood as an inferior form of religion. In the latter part of the 20th century, however, popular religion has come to be interpreted in a more favourable light. It is now understood that the fusion of mainstream religious beliefs and concepts with cultural factors and traditional beliefs derived from the society into which the mainstream religion is introduced is essential if a religion is to gain a place in society.

positivism Any philosophical position which maintains that all genuine knowledge is acquired by science, and denies the validity of metaphysical speculation. Positivism flourished in the latter half of the 19th century; its elements can be found in such diverse thinkers as Comte, the English utilitarians, Herbert Spencer, and Ernst Mach. ▷ Comte, Auguste; logical positivism; utilitarianism

postures and gestures Postures and gestures are universal among humans, and indeed among animals, and are especially important in religion. For example, in the five daily prayers within Islam there is a set cycle of postures and gestures, including standing, bowing, prostrating and sitting, together with gestures of the head, hands, arms and feet. Kneeling in religion often denotes adoration, humility and prayer; prostration is a posture of deep submission; sitting (for example in the lotus position) is often used in meditation; standing is a gesture of respect; and dancing is significant in many rituals, for example the American Indian rain dance and the whirling dance of the Mevlevi Muslim dervishes. Gestures of the hands are of great importance: in greeting, blessing, praying, baptizing, ordaining—and in the *mudras* (hand gestures) in Indian dance and iconography, for example in the five mudras of the Buddha found in Buddha images which tell an immediate story to a Buddhist. It is common to find that the use of the right hand or foot is regarded as clean and auspicious and the use of the left hand or foot as unclean and inauspicious. Ritual kissing of objects, such as the Black Stone at Mecca by Muslims or of a crucifix by Roman Catholics, is also common. Whereas posture and gesture sometimes unify, as in Islam, they can also divide, as is the case between Orthodox and Catholic Christians, who make the sign of the cross in a different way. ▷ Buddha image; cross; left and right; Mecca; meditation; Mevlevis; mudras; prayer

Potala Palace An imposing 13-storey stronghold constructed in the 17th century on a rocky outcrop near Lhasa, Tibet. Once the religious and political centre of Tibet, the complex includes the Red Palace (former seat of the Dalai Lamas) as well as many halls, chapels, and prisons. ▷ Dalai Lama; Lhasa; Tibetan religion

potlatch Amerindian feast celebrating an important event, or following personal humiliation, at which the host gives away his wealth (slaves, blankets, canoes, etc), or destroys it in front of the guests. People receiving wealth in this way would later give their own potlatches, ensuring circulation of some of the property. It was a common practice among North American Indians of the Northwest Pacific coast. ▷ Native American religions
See illustration on p 410

Potter, Philip (1921–) West Indian ecumenical leader, born in Roseau, Dominica. After studying law and pastoring a Methodist church in Haiti, he became Secretary of the Youth Department of the World Council of Churches in 1954. Appointed Methodist Missionary Society (London) Field Secretary for Africa and the West Indies (1960–8) and Chairman of the World Student Christian Federation (1960–7), he was promoted Director of World Mission and Evangelism (1967–

potlatch figure

72) and then General Secretary (1972–84) of the World Council of Churches. His aim has been described as one of keeping the ecumenical movement theologically faithful and socially credible, as he discusses in *Life in All its Fullness* (1981). ▷ ecumenism; Methodism; World Council of Churches

prajna (prajñā) A Sanskrit Buddhist term meaning 'wisdom' that is very important in the Buddhist world-view. It has a deeper meaning than mere knowledge or belief, and refers to a direct and intuitive understanding of the truth. It is one of three divisions into which the eight parts of the Buddhist path can be placed, the other two being morality and mental discipline. According to this division prajna includes right intentions and right views. Wisdom involves seeing through the superficiality and artificiality of life to realize its impermanence (*anicca*), its suffering (*duhkha*), and its wrong view that there is such a thing as a permanent self (*anatman*). Mahayana Buddhists accused Theravada Buddhists of overstressing wisdom at the expense of compassion, and they gave a balanced emphasis to both wisdom and compassion. However, one set of Mahayana scriptures, the *Prajnaparamita Sutras*, stressed the 'perfection of wisdom' as being of supreme importance, and while Mahayana Buddhists did enhance the role of compassion they also exalted wisdom. ▷ anatman; duhkha; eightfold path; karuna; Mahayana Buddhism; prajnaparamita; sila; Theravada Buddhism

prajnaparamita (prajñāpāramitā) A Buddhist term meaning the perfection of wisdom. It is used for a set of Mahayana Buddhist scriptures known as the *Prajnaparamita Sutras*. They were begun in the 1st century BCE and continued to be extended for about 1000 years in Sanskrit, Chinese and Tibetan. Their basic message is that reality transcends all existing forms, and concepts of the mind, and can only be known by intuitive wisdom (*prajna*). Some of the scriptures are very well known, including the Perfection of Wisdom Sutra, the Heart Sutra, and the Diamond-Cutter Sutra. The great Mahayana Buddhist philosophers Nagarjuna, Asanga and Vasubandhu wrote commentaries on some of the scriptures, which were significant for some of the developments of Buddhism in China and Tibet. ▷ Asanga; Mahayana Buddhism; Nagarjuna; paramita; prajna; Vasubandhu

prakriti (prakṛti) A term in Hinduism meaning 'matter' or 'nature' and used in the Samkhya school. It occurs in the Samkhya Karikas (c.350–550), though its origins can be traced back before this to the Veda, particularly the Upanishads. The Samkhya school divided existence into 25 categories (*tattvas*), of which all but consciousness or the 'soul' derive from prakriti. *Purusha* is seen as being wholly distinct from prakriti, which is totally permeated by the three *gunas* (qualities) of *sattva* (lightness), which is identified with purity and goodness, *rajas* (energy or power), which is the active element which produces karma, and *tamas* (darkness), which is the hindering element. Prakriti is sometimes identified with *maya*. ▷ guna; maya; purusha; Samkhya; Upanishads; yoga

Pralaya The period at the end of the *kaliyuga*, the degenerate age, which is spoken of in the *Puranas* and other classical Indian literature. It translates as doomsday in eschatological thought, although the process takes hundreds of thousands of years. The sun sets the worlds (celestial, terrestrial and the underworld) on fire, and when they are totally consumed a huge deluge ensues and the universe turns once again into the ocean of chaos from which it was born in the first place. It is the period in which Brahma sleeps dreamlessly until his next awakening, which will initiate the next cycle of four *yugas*, a process which will continue interminably. ▷ Brahma; Puranas; yugas

prana (prāṇa) A term in Hinduism, particularly used in yoga, variously translated as 'breath', 'respiration', 'vitality', 'strength', 'wind' and 'energy'. Prana can be understood on a number of levels or in several senses. Two of the most important understandings are **1** as *Brahman*, the universal absolute; and **2** as the life-force or creative source of energy which is thought to pervade and vibrate through the universe. In Indian thought breath has great significance, indeed it is personified in the *Atharva Veda* and has a hymn addressed to it. The idea of prana was particularly developed in yoga, where it denotes respiration, the drawing of the life-force into the body, and also refers to five forms of prana which circulate through and maintain the subtle body. There is an intimate connection between prana and consciousness in yoga, the two being mutually supporting. To calm the breath is therefore to calm the mind and vice versa. This belief has led to the development of special breathing practices (*pranayama*), the fourth 'limb' of Patanjali's yoga, whereby the involuntary process of breathing is brought under the control of the will. ▷ Brahman; Patanjali; yoga

pratyeka Buddha (Pali: pacceka Buddha) A Sanskrit Buddhist term referring to a single or isolated Buddha who achieves enlightenment alone, then continues to live a private life rather than going out to teach others. This Theravada Buddhist notion of the solitary Buddha, together with the view of a saint as an *arahat* concerned with his own salvation, was contrasted by the Mahayana Buddhists with their ideal of the bodhisattva who has compassion for others and voluntarily abjures the immediate hope of nirvana in order to be reborn for the sake of helping others. This narrower view of Buddhahood and salvation was one of the reasons why the Mahayana school designated other schools such as Theravada as Hinayana, the lesser way. ▷ arahat; bodhisattva; Buddha; Hinayana Buddhism; Mahayana Buddhism; nirvana; Theravada Buddhism

prayer As humans are uniquely the creatures of language, it is natural that the deepest expression of their religious feeling, in all religious traditions, should be through the verbal medium of prayer. Prayer can take many forms and fulfil many needs. Primitive forms of prayer indicate that they may have been intended to function like incantations

Amerindian feather prayer sticks

and spells. Prayer may be an obligatory act, as in the Islamic faith, or it may be voluntary. It can be spontaneous and extemporary, or formal and stylized as in liturgical prayer. It can be individual or communal, vocal or silent (although silent prayer is more akin to meditation). Prayer is the heartfelt response of the individual to the object of his or her faith, encompassing everything from worship and adoration to thanksgiving, confession and supplication. ▷ Amidah; Call to Prayer; Hail Mary; Kaddish; kiddushin; litany; liturgy; Lord's Prayer; meditation; Nitnem; qiblah; salat; Shema

prayer, Christian Christian prayer is prayer to God the Trinity: to the Father, through the Son, by the Holy Spirit. It may include elements of adoration, confession, intercession, petition, or thanksgiving, following the pattern of the so-called 'Lord's Prayer' which Jesus taught his disciples (Matthew 6.9–15), Luke 11.2–4) and other biblical examples of prayer, especially those found in the New Testament epistles and the Old Testament psalms. Use is also made of the prayers of saints and spiritual writers. Posture in prayer varies. Some traditions teach kneeling, some standing, some sitting. The 'Jesus Prayer' in hesychasm advocates a seated position focused on the heart or inner self, with controlled breathing. Forms and types of prayer also vary. Both private and public worship may employ liturgical or set prayer in which use is made of printed, or previously composed prayers, and non-liturgical or extempore prayer which is to some degree impromptu. One can also distinguish between vocal and non-vocal (or mental) prayer, and between meditation and contemplation. ▷ spirituality, Christian; contemplation; discursive meditation; hesychasm

prayer wheel An aid to piety especially important in Tibetan Buddhism, although it is also found among other groups such as the Mongols of Central Asia and the followers of the Bon religion. There are different varieties of prayer wheel, but they usually take the form of a cylinder which has an important verse inscribed on its outside surface, and inside contains a scroll upon which various prayers are written. The prayer wheel is rotated by hand in a clockwise direction and this activates the prayers and makes them effective. This method of devotion presupposes the importance of written sacred texts and the power that is to be gained by revolving them in a wheel. Until recently vehicles with wheels were not common in Tibet because of the sacredness attached to prayer wheels. In addition to smaller hand-operated prayer wheels there have also been much larger ones, some of them containing mini-libraries whose rotation confers great merit upon the persons or groups which activate them. Wind and water, and in recent times electricity, have been used to turn prayer wheels. The most famous verse or mantra used in Tibet is 'Om Manipadme Hum', and turning this prayer in a prayer wheel not only evokes the compassion of the bodhisattva Avalokiteshvara but also beams out the prayer into the world. ▷ Avalokiteshvara; mantra; Tibetan religion

preaching The public proclamation of a religion with reference to the religious texts upon which that religion is based. It is this adherence to a prescribed text that distinguishes preaching from other forms of religious discourse. Preaching has two basic functions. Firstly, it reinforces the congregation's acceptance and understanding of their religion. The preacher shows how the principles and mythologies of the religion shed light upon the lives of the congregation and the world in which they live. The intention is to deepen the faith of the listeners and to enable them to live in the world according to the principles of their religion. Secondly, preaching has a missionary function. It aims at proclaiming the religion to the non-believers outside the congregation in the hope of winning their allegiance. Common to most religions where preaching is practised is the idea that it is not so much the preacher who speaks as God. Thus the Christian preacher, for example, is only a vehicle for expressing the Word of God. He does not preach in his own name or propagate his own ideas but proclaims the salvation that God has brought about in Christ. ▷ worship

predestination In Christian theology, the doctrine that the ultimate salvation or damnation of each human individual has been ordained beforehand. A source of endless dispute, the doctrine has been interpreted in many ways. It was first fully articulated by Augustine during his controversy with the Pelagians, who upheld the doctrine of free will. The Protestant Reformers Luther and Calvin defended the doctrine, though in varying degrees. Jacobus Arminius rejected the Calvinist view of predestination, and argued that the divine sovereignty was compatible with human free will. In Islam the concept of predestination, as outlined in the Quran, takes the form of believing that the outcome of human actions is predetermined, and that the time of a person's death is preordained. It is considered useless to try to avoid what God has already decreed will happen. However, although the outcome of events is predetermined, individual acts themselves are not. ▷ Arminianism; Arminius, Jacobus; Augustine, St (of Hippo); Calvin, John; Calvinism; predestination in Islam; Luther, Martin; Lutheranism; Pelagius

predestination in Islam There is evidence for both free will and predestination in the Quran and the traditions of Islam. While human life is predestined in the sense that nothing can ultimately oppose God's will, human beings have to make choices and take decisions that involve an element of free will. The question became urgent during the Umayyad period (661–750), when the Qadariyyah offered a staunch defence of free will against predestination, and the Mutazilites argued that God could not predestine both good and evil and at the same time be seen as a just God. Al-Ashari reacted in favour of predestination in his theory that human beings 'acquire' acts which originate in God, and his position has generally been adopted by Muslims. Nevertheless, although the divine will ordains all things, humans have the freedom to accept God and surrender to Him, or to reject God and face the consequences. ▷ Ashari, al-; kalam; Mutazilites; Qadariyyah; Umayyads

prehistoric religion By definition prehistoric religion is difficult to summarize as the evidence for it is not written down, but is sparse, scattered, and open to different interpretations. Skull finds from Palaeolithic times, for example that of *Sinanthropus Pekinensis*, Peking Man, dating back half a million years, indicate some sort of ritual treatment of skulls by early humans. Burial remains from various continents, dating back 50000 years, show that burial, with its religious overtones, was a practice among early human beings. From about 35000BCE aesthetic artefacts become more evident, for example religious cave-paintings at places such as Lascaux in France and Altamira in Spain, with their suggestions among other things of fertility rituals; also evident are female figurines, such as the Venus of Willendorf, suggesting regard for mother goddesses. In neolithic times from 10000BCE the fertility and goddess themes become stronger as the rise of agriculture increased the relevance of a religion adapted to nature, to the cycle of the seasons, and to nurture in general. Finally, there is evidence of the rise of shrines in places like Malta; of the appearance of megalithic monuments around Europe at places such as Stonehenge; and of the emergence of rock-art and other artefacts suggesting shamanism. It is becoming clear from the evidence derived from every continent and from the Pacific Islands that there was not just one prehistoric religion but many. ▷ early burial finds; megalithic religion; neolithic religion; palaeolithic religion; shamanism; Venus of Willendorf

presbyter ▷ **elder**

Presbyterianism The conciliar form of Church government of the Reformed Churches, deriving from the Reformation led by John Calvin in Geneva and John Knox in Scotland. Government is by courts at local congregational (eg kirk session), regional (presbytery), and national (General Assembly) levels. Elders (ordained laymen) as well as ministers play a leading part in all courts. Through emigration and missionary activity from Scotland, Ireland, and England, Presbyterianism has spread world-wide. The World Presbyterian Alliance was formed in 1878, to be succeeded in 1970 by the World Alliance of Reformed Churches. ▷ Calvin, John; elder; General Assembly; Knox, John; presbytery 3; Reformation; Reformed Churches

presbytery 1 The east part of the chancel of a church, behind the choir. 2 The traditional name for the dwelling-house of priests in the Roman Catholic Church. ▷ priest; Roman Catholicism 3 In Presbyterianism, a church court composed of equal numbers of elders and ministers, presided over by a moderator, and overseeing a geographical grouping of congregations. ▷ elder; moderator; Presbyterianism

pre-Socratic philosophy The 'pre-Socratic' philosophers is the collective name for a succession of early Greek thinkers who provided non-mythical answers to the question of the origins and nature of the universe. The tradition began with Thales of Miletus (early 6th century BCE), and continued to the end of the 5th century; it is called 'pre-Socratic' because Socrates (late 5th century BCE) temporarily turned philosophy in a new direction, towards ethics and away from the 'scientific' problems tackled by the pre-Socratics. ▷ cosmology, Greek; Greek religion; Greek religion and philosophy; Socrates; Theogonies, Greek

priest The person authorized within a religion to carry out rituals for other believers. In Christianity the term derives from the Old Testament sacrificial system, and developed in the New Testament with Jesus Christ as great High Priest, a mediator between humankind and God. In the Christian Church formal priesthood did not emerge until c.200 and later, reaching its peak in the middle ages before the Reformation. Now, mainly in Roman Catholic and Orthodox usage, it refers to an ordained officer authorized to administer the sacraments, in particular the Eucharist (the sacrifice of the Mass). ▷ Eucharist; Jesus Christ; Mass; Old Testament; Orders, Holy; Reformation; sacrament

priesthood The Christian concept of priesthood derives from the Hebrew scriptures where the Levites and Zadokites act as a professional priestly class, responsible for cultic sacrifice. In Christian theology, before the 3rd century CE, the term priest was not applied to anyone other than Christ, who is perceived as the great high-priest. Since then the function of the priest has been to represent the people before God and to act on their behalf. The language of temple sacrifice has forged a close link between priest and Eucharist, the priest offering the sacrifice of the Mass and dispensing grace to the people. The Protestant tradition rejected this view of priest and Mass, and recognized the priesthood of all believers. In hierarchical churches the priesthood forms a second tier of ministry, falling between bishops and deacons, priests being authorized to administer the sacraments. ▷ cult; Eucharist; Levites; Mass; sacrament

priesthood, Meso-American The great Meso-American civilizations were religiously oriented, and the priesthood was crucial to their direction. A rich mathematical, astronomical and literary legacy was left by classical Maya civilization. Through the institution of the *calmecac* school the traditions were carried on through Aztec times, and indeed their intellectual and artistic elements were developed (painting is a major aspect of Aztec tradition). Even for the militaristic Aztec the king was above all *tlatoani* (chief speaker) of the divine being (Huitzilopochtli), whom he represented. Priests (*teopixque*) were normally recruited from the upper class (though there seem to have been exceptions) and served in war. Personal discipline could be intense, with asceticism, regular bloodletting and self-torture. The Spaniards were amazed that such technological and intellectual achievements went hand in hand with matted hair, blackened face, mutilated features, and the stench of human blood. ▷ calendar, Meso-American; calmecac

primate The most senior bishop of a given area; for example, in the Church of England the Archbishop of Canterbury is primate of All England. Originally, the name applied to the metropolitan of a province, and then to the patriarch. ▷ bishop; Church of England; patriarch 2

primeval hill In Ancient Egyptian cosmogonies the first act of creation was the emergence of a hill or island from the primeval waters of Nun. This belief probably originated at Heliopolis, where the first god Atum was believed to have come into being on this hill and was sometimes said to have been it himself. The priests of Heliopolis believed their sanctuary to be located on this primordial mound, thought to be the centre of the earth. Other cult centres like Memphis and Hermopolis similarly claimed to be the location of the primeval hill and emphasized the activity of their own local gods in creation. ▷ Atum; cosmogony; creation myths; Heliopolis theology; Memphite theology; Nun; temples, Ancient Egyptian

process theology A theological system based on the dynamic view of God and reality in the philosophy of A N Whitehead and Charles Hartshorne (1897–). To be real is to change: God is seen as being 'in process', directly related to creation and affected by its development. He suffers and understands, and is continually seeking to bring his creatures' potential to fulfilment (an evolutionary view shared with the philosopher Henri Bergson (1859–1941) and Teilhard de Chardin). This panentheism (everything is 'in' God, but God is more than the universe) contrasts with traditional concepts of theism (God is separate from his creation) and pantheism (God and the universe are identical). ▷ panentheism; pantheism; Teilhard de Chardin, Pierre; theism; Whitehead, Alfred North

prodigia Signs sent by the divinities indicating that the peace treaty (*pax deorum*) between gods and Romans had been broken or was about to be broken. A *prodigium* was easy to recognise because it was an 'extraordinary event', like a meteor, earthquake, volcanic eruption, a rain of blood, weeping statue, monstrous child, or a sacrificial animal without a heart. The Roman state had a recognized procedure for dealing with prodigia. Firstly, the Senate decided whether to deal with it by itself or to entrust it to the college of priests (*pontifices*). Secondly, the exact nature of the prodigium had to be defined in order to know which divinity was angry and why. Usually, the identifications were made by Etruscan experts (*heruspices*). In difficult cases, the Sybilline Books or even the Delphic oracle were consulted by the college of priests in charge of them—the *quindecemviri sacris faciundis*. Thirdly, the ritual of expiation (*procuratio*) required to conciliate the divinities was identified and declared in an edict. Finally, the expiation was made (normally by means of prayers or blood-sacrifices) under the supervision of the consuls. ▷ Delphi, oracle of; Roman religion; Sibylline Books

Progressive Judaism ▷ Liberal Judaism

projection theories of religion The belief that religion in general, or a particular form of it, is nothing more than a projection of human wishes is as old as religion itself. Examples are found in Buddhism, Greek philosophy, the Old Testament, and early Christian theology. In modern Western thought, projection theories derive from the work of Feuerbach, Nietzsche, and the psychoanalyst Sigmund Freud (1856–1939); theories of a less individual and more corporate kind are associated with Marx and the sociologist Émile Durkheim (1858–1917). Critics of projection theories would maintain that they are only partial explanations. It may well be that one's image of God is related to one's early experience of one's parents and need for security (Freud), or that religion is a powerful instrument of social control (Marx and Durkheim). It is also the case that religion can transform personality, question any sense of personal security and make demands that challenge rather than reinforce the social status quo. ▷ Feuerbach, Ludwig Andreas; liberation theology; Marx, Karl; Nietzsche, Friedrich Wilhelm; political theology; Social Gospel

prophecy The foretelling of future events through divine inspiration or the delivering of a divine message to a contemporary situation. Ancient practices such as augury and the consulting of oracles were a primitive form of prophecy. The Islamic faith has two words for prophets, *rasul* meaning messenger and *nabi* meaning prophet. The messenger has a higher status than the prophet, as he delivers a message to a special community, with scripture containing a law, whereas a prophet proclaims a message only. Every messenger is a prophet but not vice versa. Islamic tradition includes among the messengers figures such as Abraham, Noah, Moses and Jesus. Prophets include Enoch, David, Solomon, and Elijah. ▷ nabi; oracle

prophecy, Jewish and Christian Old Testament prophecy, whether recorded in historical books like Samuel and Kings or in the prophetical books named after individual prophets, may be seen both as a foretelling and a forthtelling. It predicts what God will do, not on an arbitrary whim, but on the basis of his already-revealed character and will. The prophets reminded the kings, religious authorities or the Jewish community as a whole of the law of God and what would follow if it was disobeyed. Their prophecies of an eventual restoration through a messianic or Christ figure have been read by Christians as predictions about Jesus; a point emphasized by the many references to the fulfilment of prophecy in the Gospel of Matthew, and symbolized by the appearance of Moses (chief representative of the Torah or law) and Elijah (chief representative of the prophets) with Christ on the mount of transfiguration. The New Testament church included prophets, but their exact function is unclear. It would seem that they gave messages of encouragement and comfort (1 Corinthians 14.3) in particular situations, but not teaching of permanent and universal significance that would become accepted as scripture, like that of the Old Testament prophets. (The one exception is the Book of Revelation, though is is usually classifed as apocalyptic rather than prophetic literature, because it deals with eschatology, the end of all things.) Both the Old and New Testament recognize the possibility of false prophecy, and insist that a prophet's word has to be tested against the accepted teaching of Moses or Jesus. ▷ apocalypse; eschatology; Revelation, Book of; Transfiguration

prophet One who is inspired to reveal a message from a divine being; an important figure in many religious traditions, sometimes with cultic functions, but sometimes a lone figure opposing the established cult or social order (eg Jeremiah, Amos, and Hosea in the Old Testament). Although their messages may acquire an enduring relevance, they usually address a specific situation or problem. In Islam Muhammad is seen as the greatest and last of God's prophets, Jesus Christ being the second most important. In the New Testament prophets are listed after apostles in Paul's lists of Christian ministries (1 Corinthians 12.28f; Ephesians 4.11), but the problem of false prophets is also of concern in some works (Matthew 7.15; 1 John 4.1). ▷ God; Jesus Christ; Muhammad; New Testament; Old Testament; oracle

prophets in Islam A number of prophets are important in the Muslim tradition, and the most significant among them are Jesus and above all Muhammad, who is seen to be the seal of the prophets. There are two kinds of prophet within Islam. The *nabi* exercises a mission within the framework of an existing religious tradition in order to renew it by bringing to it either glad tidings or a warning of the wrath to come if things do not improve. The *rasul*, on the other hand, is a messenger whose work inaugurates a new religious movement or a major new revelatory insight that transcends the insularity of a particular tradition. Included in this second category of prophet are Adam, Noah, Abraham, Moses, Jesus and Muhammad. Neither Jews nor Christians, however, regard Muhammad as a prophet (except by 'interpretation' and dialogue). Muslims consider that the message of the Jewish prophets and Jesus became distorted by their followers, and that Muhammad came to renew and fulfil their work. Insofar as there are taken to be no prophets after Muhammad, later prophetic figures within the Muslim world, such as Bahaullah (1812–92), the effective founder of the Bahais, and Mirza Ghulam Ahmad (1835–1908), the founder of the Ahmadiyyahs, are not looked upon with favour by the Muslim tradition. ▷ Abraham in Islam; Adam and Eve; Ahmadiyyah; Bahaism; Bahaullah; Jesus Christ in Islam; Moses; Muhammad; nabi; Noah

Protestantism The generic term for expressions of Christian faith originating from the Reformation as a protest against Roman Catholicism. The word derives from *protestari*, which means not just to protest but also to avow or confess. Protestants wished to return to the early Church's style of faith, which they felt had been lost under Catholic practices. Common characteristics include the authority of scripture, justification by faith alone (ie that those who believe in Christ and the Gospel are deemed righteous, regardless of personal merit), and the priesthood of all believers, in which each believer is able to hear confession of sin, this no longer being the domain only of the clergy. The original groupings were those who followed Luther, Calvin, and Zwingli, and the term now embraces most non-Roman Catholic or non-Orthodox denominations. ▷ Anabaptists; Baptists; Calvin, John; Calvinism; Church of Scotland; Congregationalism; Dutch Reformed Church; Episcopal Church, Protestant; Luther, Martin; Lutheranism; Nonconformists; Orthodox Church; Presbyterianism; Reformation; Roman Catholicism; Unitarians; Zwingli, Huldreich

Proverbs, Book of A book of the Hebrew Bible/Old Testament, attributed in the opening title to Solomon, but probably consisting of collected wisdom traditions from several centuries. It contains several sub-collections: Chapters 1–9 include poems about personified Wisdom, and moral admonitions of a father to his son; Chapters 10–29 present sets of individual sayings on virtues and vices with little thematic arrangement, similar to Egyptian wisdom instructions; Chapters 30–1 are two appendices, ending with a poem about the virtuous wife. ▷ Old Testament; Solomon

providence The belief that all things are ultimately ordered and governed by God towards a purpose. Some form of this belief features in Judaism, Islam, and Christianity, and is implied in the belief in the trustworthiness, goodness, and power of God. Human free will is not generally denied, it being claimed that God either overrules it or works through it. ▷ Christianity; God; Islam; Judaism

Providence Industrial Mission A Black missionary initiative in Nyasaland (now Malawi), established in 1900 by John Chilembwe, the first convert of a radical Baptist missionary, Joseph Booth. Chilembwe was educated at a Black college in the USA and the mission was supported and assisted by Black Americans. The 'industrial' aspect, which included broad-based education and agricultural plantations, was intended to demonstrate the potential of a self-reliant and self-sufficient Christian community. Chilembwe increasingly came into conflict with Europeans, and especially with the European-owned estates. In 1914 he opposed the recruitment of Africans for military purposes. In 1915 he led a rising against the British and was killed. The secret disposal of his body assisted the growth of a powerful myth of the martyr's eventual triumphant return. Though often cited as an example of 'Ethiopianism', Chilembwe made no religious innovations; he remained a simple Baptist, taking his politics and his religion undiluted from the Bible. The Providence Industrial Mission was reconstituted in 1926 by one of his converts, Daniel Malikebu (d.1978); its recent history has been complicated by its relations with the National Baptist Convention of the USA. ▷ African Independent churches

Psalms, Book of A book of the Hebrew Bible/Old Testament, designated *tehillim* (Hebrew 'songs'), but the name 'Psalms' deriving from the Greek translation; also known as the Psalter. It consists of 150 hymns or poems of various types, including songs of thanksgiving, individual and community laments, wisdom poetry, and royal and enthronement songs. Many of the poems have individual titles and attributions, and the collection represents material from several centuries, brought together in its present form probably in the post-exilic period. The Psalter is regularly used in Jewish and Christian worship, its hymns admired for the religious insights of their composers. It was the most important type of medieval illustrated book. ▷ Old Testament; worship

Psalter ▷ **Psalms, Book of**

Pseudepigrapha An ancient Jewish (and sometimes Christian) body of literature which is not part of the Jewish Scriptures or of major Christian versions of the Old Testament or the Apocrypha, but which is similar to the Old Testament in character, in that its works claim to present a divine message, derived from Old Testament characters or ideas. Strictly the term means works 'written under a false name', but this does not adequately distinguish this literature from the Old Testament or the Apocrypha. This large collection of writings spans roughly the period 200BCE–200CE, although it was first collected by Johannes Fabricius (1668–1736). It includes apocalypses (eg 1 Enoch, 4 Ezra), testaments (eg Testaments of the 12 Patriarchs), wisdom literature, prayers and psalms (eg Prayer of Manasseh, Psalms of Solomon), and additions to Old Testament stories (eg Life of Adam and Eve). ▷ Apocrypha, Old Testament; Bible; Jubilees, Book of; Judaism; Maccabees, Books of the; Old Testament; Manasseh, Prayer of; Solomon, Psalms of; testament literature

psychedelic drugs The word 'psychedelic' refers to a state of intensified imagination and perception brought about by ecstasy. When drugs are used to achieve this state they are known as psychedelic drugs. They include hashish, also known as marijuana, derived from hemp which, when smoked, leads to intoxication and eventually hallucination; LSD (lysergic acid diethylamide), which gives extreme stimulation to a portion of the brain so that ordinary phenomena are transformed into dazzling colour and beauty, time is overridden, and opposites seem to merge (eg good and evil); mescalin, from the peyote cactus, which was used by Aldous Huxley in a search for mystical experience, and is used sacramentally in the Native American Church; and opium, derived from the poppy, which can produce spiritual experiences. Psychedelic drugs have been used by many religions, from Vedic Hinduism down to the present-day American Indian traditions, to induce religious experience. There has also been the awareness that they can sometimes have harmful effects, and that they can be merely an aid to mystical experience and not a substitute for it. ▷ mysticism; Native American Church; new religious movements in the West; peyote

psychic powers Special psychic talents present in gifted persons within various religious traditions, and also to some extent in non-religious individuals. They include extra-sensory perception: having a telepathic awareness of the thoughts of others, a precognition of future events, a clairvoyant ability to see beyond the range of the eyes, and a clairaudient ability to hear beyond the range of the ears. At a more visible and spectacular level they may also include the skills of levitating the body from the ground, and of moving objects around without actually touching them (psychokinesis). The mystical strands of most religious traditions claim that such psychic powers are often available to people skilled in meditation. However, there is also the tradition current among spiritual adepts that true spirituality is not manifested in displays of extraordinary powers but in living ordinary life in an extraordinary way. Modern movements that have stressed psychic powers include the New Church of Emanuel Swedenborg, the Mesmerism school of Franz Anton Mesmer, the Spiritualism of Andrew Jackson Davis (1826–1920), the Theosophical Society of Madame Blavatsky and Colonel Olcott (1826–1920), and more recently some elements of new age religion. ▷ Blavatsky, Helena Petrovna; Mesmer, Franz Anton; new age religion; New Church; spiritualism; Swedenborg, Emmanuel; Theosophical Society

psychology of religion One of the three social sciences of religion along with the anthropology and sociology of religion. Unlike the latter two, which focus on society, the psychology of religion typically centres upon the individual and his or her religious experience. One of the main classics in the field was William James's *Varieties of Religious Experience* (1902), in which he describes the religion of the healthy-minded and the sick soul, the religion of the once-born and the twice-born, and the psychological basis of prayer, meditation, mysticism, conversion and spiritual fruitfulness. Around the same time Freud was beginning to develop his depth psychology based on the interpretation of dreams and intensive counselling, in which he emphasized the importance of childhood sexual experiences and the notion that religion was illusion and projection. The psychiatrist Carl Jung broke with Freud and stressed the psychological reality of religion with its myths, symbols and archetypes, and its access to the spiritual treasures of the collective unconscious. More recent work in the psychology of religion has centred upon questionnaires about how religious different people or institutions are, and upon analysis of what is mature religious faith, what are the spiritual potentialities of human nature, and what are the stages of religious development in children and adults. The psychology of religion has suffered because it has been an important element in neither religion nor psychology, with the consequence that it has sometimes been subordinated to ecclesiastical ends and, at other times, as in the work of some of Freud's disciples, it has been reduced to psychology. However, there is some recent evidence that the psychology of religion is beginning to gain more prominence as a pursuit in its own right. ▷ anthropology of religion; Freud, Sigmund; James, William; Jung, Carl Gustav; social sciences of religion; sociology of religion

Ptah Ancient Egyptian god, the local god of Memphis in Lower Egypt. His worship

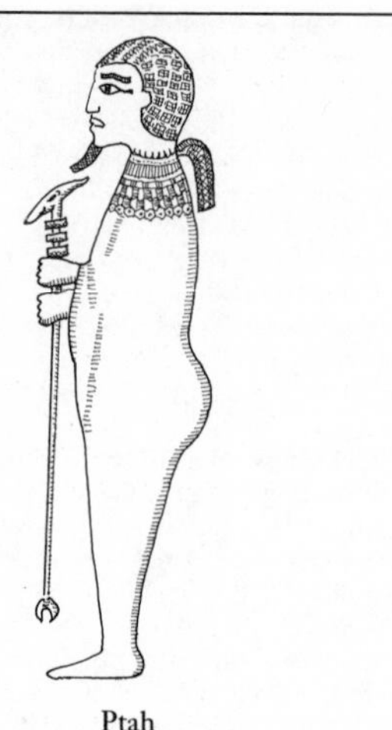

Ptah

increased along with the city's political importance as royal capital during the Old Kingdom (c.2686–2181BCE). The Memphite Theology describes his creation of the world through heart and tongue, but ordinary people thought of him in a less sophisticated way as patron god of artisans, craftsmen and artists. With his consort Sekhmet and son Nefertum he was worshipped as one of the 'Memphite Triad', and was also connected with Apis the sacred bull of Memphis. In the late period he was often associated with the funerary gods Osiris and Sokar. Ptah is depicted in human form, normally with a bald head and beard, dressed in mummy wrappings. The name Egypt arose from a misunderstanding of the Egyptian *hut-ka-ptah*, which means 'the mansion of Ptah'. The historian Herodotus equated him with Hephaistos. ▷ Apis; Memphite Theology; Osiris

pudgala A Buddhist term meaning 'person' which was applied to the Pudgalavadins, a Buddhist sect which emerged in India in the 3rd century BCE. They attempted to answer questions raised by the Buddhist no-self (*anatman*) theory of what endured from one life to another if there was no self, and of what was the justice of vast differences in rebirths if there was no self doing good or bad deeds. Their originator, Vatsiputra, argued that something did pass on across the rebirths and that this was the pudgala or person. He also argued that the Buddha had used the term pudgala. The other Buddhist sects replied that the Buddha had not used the term in a real sense, and that to introduce it amounted to bringing back the notion of self (atman) which was anathema to basic Buddhist thought. As late as the 7th century CE the Pudgalavadins were recorded by a Chinese pilgrim as forming a quarter of the total of the Indian monks, but they later declined, and very few of their writings remain. ▷ anatman; atman; karma; punna; rebirth; samsara

Pueblo religion Pueblo is a generic term for the Native American agricultural peoples indigenous to the southwest USA, notably Arizona and New Mexico, and includes the Acoma, Sia, Hopi and Zuñi. They belong to quite different linguistic families, but have common cultural features, such as adobe houses and the successful cultivation of maize, despite the fragile environment. Apart from a bruising rising against the Spanish in 1680, their lifestyle has been essentially peaceful. Their religious patterns are also diverse, and most are immensely complex. Recurrent features include a belief (which they have conveyed to alien incomers such as the Navajo) in the emergence of the people from another world to their present home. Cracks in the terrain are venerated as possible places through which the people arrived, or by which souls pass elsewhere. The supreme being plays little part in these or other myths. Creation is the function of a pair of beings and the key figures of the spirit world are the pillars of the agricultural cycle—sun father, earth mother, corn deities. To these should be added in the case of the Hopi and the Zuñi ancestral figures and other spirit powers (kachinas, koko). But, complex as it is, myth is subordinate to still more complex ritual, vital to the partnership of spirit beings and humans needed to maintain the brittle environment. Different officials, societies, dance groups and sectors of the community have specific, interlocking ritual functions, from observing the exact time of solstice to the performance of a masked representation of the ancestors. The ritual pattern reflects the calendar, summer dances contrasting dramatically with winter dances, and the totality representing the world and the cycle of life. ▷ Hopi religion; kachinas; Navajo religion

Punjab (Puñjāb) A territory in the north-west of the sub-continent of India, covering the present Indian state of the Punjab, and stretching over into what is now Pakistan. It means the 'land of the five rivers', namely the Beas, Chenab, Jhelum, Ravi, and Sutlej. The Sikh tradition began there, and has maintained its heartland in that area. Guru Nanak was born in Talwandi in the Punjab, and finally retired to the area, to Kartarpur, where he set up an exemplary community. The other Sikh gurus centred their work there, Guru Ram Das founding the town of Amritsar which, with its Golden Temple (Harimandir) and Akal Takht, has become a headquarters of the Sikh tradition. The Sikh scriptures are written in the Gurmukhi Punjabi script, most Sikhs are Punjabi by origin, and their preferred language at home and at worship is usually Punjabi. In the present Indian state of the Punjab Sikhs are in a slight majority. However, through emigration and conversion, Sikhs are spreading into various parts of the world and Sikhism is becoming a world religion with emotional roots in the Punjab. ▷ Amritsar; guru, Sikh; Harimandir; Kartarpur; Nanak; Ram Das, Guru

punna (puñña; Sanskrit: puṇya) The important notion of merit in the Buddhist tradition. By means of acquiring merit one can obtain a better rebirth in the next life. This requires living in such a way that one's deeds (karma) are fruitful and productive of merit. There are three main kinds of merit: the giving of gifts, the living of a moral life, and the practice of meditation. The first two are normally more appropriate for lay folk, the third for monks. The ultimate aim of Buddhism is to follow the four noble truths and the eightfold path in such a way that one attains enlightenment, nirvana, and the cessation of rebirths. At the popular level the lower aim of producing merit to improve one's earthly lot by means of better rebirths tends to be followed in practice. ▷ ariya sacca; bhavana; eightfold path; karma; meditation; nirvana; rebirth; sila

Puranas (Purāṇas) In Indian tradition, a set of sacred compositions dating from the Gupta period (c.4th century CE onwards), dealing with the mythology of Hinduism and covering subjects such as festivals, caste obligations and pilgrim sites. There are 18 main Puranas, each exalting one of the Hindu trio of gods, Vishnu, Shiva and Brahma. They are very important in popular Hinduism, the most popular being the *Bhagavata-Purana*, which relates Krishna's early life, and has had a huge impact on Indian religious belief. ▷ Hinduism; Krishna

Pure Land Buddhism A school of Buddhism founded, it is said, by the Chinese monk, Hui Yuan (334–417) and one of the commonest forms of Mahayana Buddhism. It is characterized by devotion to the bodhisattva Amitabha, who rules over a 'pure land'. The goal of those devoted to Amitabha and the pure land is to be reborn there, and attain enlightenment. The school also spread to Japan, where it split from the main sect and formed a separate school. ▷ bodhisattva; Buddhism; Mahayana Buddhism

purgatory In Roman Catholic and some Orthodox teaching, the place and state in which the souls of the dead suffer for their sins before being admitted to heaven. Those in purgatory may be assisted by the prayers of the faithful on earth. ▷ heaven; Orthodox Church; prayer; Roman Catholicism; sin

purification The removal of polluting and defiling elements held to impede an individual or group's relationship with God. Pollution may occur for a number of reasons. Firstly, there is accidental pollution. This comes about through unintentional contact with things held to be unclean such as the dead, certain foods, etc, as well as with such involuntary and unavoidable products of human existence as blood, vomit, faeces, and urine. Secondly, there is intentional, deliberate pollution. This comes about when an individual violates the accepted religious or social norms of a society. Such acts threaten the strict boundaries that exist within a society and between the sacred and the profane. If no action is taken, they undermine the very structure of that society and jeopardize its relationship with the Divine.

To overcome the disruption caused by pollution, whether deliberate or accidental, and to re-establish proper relations between the individual, society and God, the community lays down a series of rites of purification. These vary according to the severity of the pollution and the status of the person responsible for it. Thus, for example, more stringent acts of purification are demanded from priests because they come into greater contact with the Divine. In some religions these rites of purification may take the form of certain concrete physical acts, such as ritual bathing, self-mortification, etc. This is particularly so in those cultures where pollution is understood primarily as a material, perhaps semi-magical phenomenon. In other religions, such as Christianity, emphasis is placed upon repentance, conversion and the cultivation of personal holiness. ▷ rituals

Purim The Jewish Feast of Lots, celebrated on 14 Adar (about 1 March), commemorating the deliverance of the Jews from a plot to have them massacred, as related in the Book of Esther. ▷ anti-Semitism; Esther, Book of; Judaism

Puritanism The belief that further reformation was required in the Church of England under Elizabeth I and the Stuarts. It arose in the 1560s out of dissatisfaction with the 'popish elements', such as surplices, which had been retained by the Elizabethan religious settlement. It was not always a coherent, organized movement; rather, a diverse body of opinions and personalities, which occasionally came together. It included the anti-episcopal Presbyterian movement of John Field (1545–88) and Thomas Cartwright (1535–1603) in the 1570s and 1580s; the separatist churches that left England for Holland and America from 1590 to 1640; the 'presbyterian', 'independent', and more radical groups which emerged during the Civil War and interregnum; and the nonconformist sects persecuted by the Cavalier Parliament's 'Clarendon Code' under Charles II. ▷ Church of England; Nonconformists; Reformation

purusha (puruṣa) Literally 'person', although it has had a number of different meanings in Hindu thought. It originally represented the 'primal being' as described in the *Rig Veda*, by which the notion of varna was legitimized. The notion of purusha was developed in the Upanishads. It was linked with the concepts of atman and *Brahman*, with atman taking the idea of the individual self and Brahman that of the universal self—although they were essentially seen as being one. In Samkhya philosophy purusha becomes the individual experience or soul entangled in matter (*prakriti*) from which it must free itself. ▷ atman; Brahman; prakriti; Samkhya; Veda

Pusey, Edward Bouverie (1800–82) English theologian, and leader of the 'Oxford Movement', born in Pusey, Berkshire. His father, the youngest son of the first Viscount Folkestone, had assumed the name Pusey when he inherited the Pusey estates. Edward was educated at Eton and Christ Church, Oxford, in 1823 was elected a fellow of Oriel College, Oxford, and from 1825 to 1827 lived in Germany and acquainted himself with German theological teaching. In 1828 he was ordained deacon and priest and appointed Regius Professor of Hebrew at Oxford, a position which he retained until his death.

His first work was an essay on the causes of rationalism in recent German theology, which was criticized as being itself rationalistic. The aim of his life was to prevent the spread of rationalism in England. Hence, when in 1833 Newman began the issue of the *Tracts for the Times*, Pusey very soon joined him; and they, with Keble, were the leaders of the movement. They endeavoured to make the Church live again before the eyes and minds of men as it had lived in times past. With this aim Pusey wrote his contributions to the *Tracts*, especially those on baptism and the Holy Eucharist, and in 1836 began the *Oxford Library of the Fathers*, to which his chief contributions were translations of Augustine's *Confessions* and works of Tertullian.

In 1843 Pusey was suspended for two years from preaching in Oxford for a university sermon on the Holy Eucharist; at the first opportunity he reiterated his teaching, and this time was left alone. But before his suspension was over Newman, with several of his leading disciples, had joined the Roman communion. With Keble, Pusey at once set himself to reassure those who were distressed by this development. But soon another band of distinguished men, including Archdeacon (Cardinal) Manning and Archdeacon Wilberforce, departed to the Roman Church. Pusey loyally laboured on. His numerous writings during this period include a letter on the practice of confession (1850) and *A Letter to the Bishop of London* (1851), a general defence of his position. *The Doctrine of the Real Presence* (1856–7), and the series of three *Eirenicons* (1865–9), clear the way for reunion between the Church of England and that of Rome. The reform of Oxford University, which destroyed the intimate bond between the university and the Church, greatly occupied Pusey's mind. His evidence before the commission, his remarkable pamphlet on *Collegiate and Professorial Teaching*, and his assiduous work on the Hebdomadal Council are proofs of the interest he took in the university.

By 1860 the tide had turned. The teaching for which the Tractarians had laboured was beginning to be recognized. But the fruits of the intolerance and persecution of which Oxford had been the scene were also ripening into religious indifference and rationalism. Against such teaching Pusey contended for the rest of his life. In private life Pusey was an ascetic, deeply religious man of warm affection, widely known for his gentleness, sincerity and humility, and was constantly sought as a spiritual guide by persons of every station. He spent large sums in helping to provide churches in East London and Leeds, and in founding sisterhoods. He married in 1828 and his only son, Philip Edward (1830–

80), predeceased him. ▷ Church of England; Eucharist; Keble, John Henry; Newman, John; Oxford Movement; rationalism; Roman Catholicism

pyramid An architectural structure with a triangular, square, or polygonal base, with triangular sides meeting in a single point. In Egyptian architecture, it is a sepulchral stone monument with a square base. In Pre-Columbian architecture, it is an artificial hill with a flat top. The phrase 'the Pyramids' usually refers to the Fourth Dynasty pyramids of the Giza plateau on the south-west outskirts of modern Cairo. The Great Pyramid of Cheops (c.2589–2566BCE) is 146 m/480 ft high, 230 m/755 ft square, and 2352000 cu m/27688000 cu ft in volume, made up of 2.5 million limestone blocks each of 2.5 tonnes. ▷ art, Ancient Egyptian; architecture, Ancient Egyptian; Ancient Egyptian religion

Pythagoras (6th century BCE) Greek philosopher, sage and mathematician, born in Samos. About 530BCE he settled in Crotona, a Greek colony in southern Italy, where he established a religious community of some kind. He may later have moved to Megapontum, after persecution. He wrote nothing, and his whole life is shrouded in myth and legend. Pythagoreanism was first a way of life rather than a philosophy, emphasizing moral asceticism and purification, and associated with doctrines of the transmigration of souls, the kinship of all living things and various ritual rules of abstinence (most famously, 'do not eat beans'). He is also associated with mathematical discoveries involving the chief musical intervals, the relations of numbers, the theorem which bears his name, and with more fundamental beliefs about the understanding and representation of the world of nature through numbers. The equilateral triangle of ten dots, the tetractys of the decad, itself became an object of religious veneration, referred to in the Pythagorean oath 'Nay, by him that gave us the tetractys which contains the fount and root of ever-flowing nature'. It is impossible to disentangle Pythagoras' own views from the later accretions of mysticism and neo-platonism, but he had a profound influence on Plato and later philosophers, astronomers and mathematicians. ▷ mysticism; neo-platonism; Plato

Egyptian step pyramid at Saqqarah

Q

Qadariyyah A school of early Muslim thinkers (sometimes also known as the Qadaris) who, during the first Muslim century, stressed the concept of free will, in contrast to the Jabariyyah, who emphasized predestination. In fact the word *qadar* means 'power', 'will' or 'capacity'. 'Capacity' implies limitation and therefore destiny. Thus the word used by the Qadariyyah to stress free will could also be used in the opposite sense of destiny, hence predestination. This school was succeeded by the Mutazilites, to whom the name Qadariyyah was sometimes somewhat inaccurately given. Nevertheless the original Qadariyyah remain a forceful reminder that there is still a vibrant strain of free-will thinking within Islam. ▷ Ashari, al-; predestination in Islam; Mutazilites; Sufis

qadi (qāḍi) A Muslim judge in a shariah court (which dispenses traditional Islamic law). He should be a male (women are not eligible) of fine character and of sound learning. He should also be free of offices and commitments that might impede his impartial execution of justice. In theory the qadi was responsible for both civil and criminal law, but in practice he became mainly restricted to civil law, dealing with family law and inheritance, marriage and divorce, widows and orphans, and other charitable causes. Where the shariah prescribed a punishment laid down by God, the qadi was responsible for seeing that such a punishment was applied. Although there was theoretically no appeal against a qadi's decision, most Muslim states introduced an appeal system. In fact, the state has taken over the administration of criminal justice in many Muslim areas, and in countries such as Egypt the shariah courts have been abolished. The qadi was supposed only to apply past precedents and not his own judgement. In reality, however, the judges introduced small modifications, and the shariah did not remain completely static. Recently the possible enhancement of the role of shariah courts and the role of the qadis has been more widely discussed, but the relationship between shariah law and state law remains unclear. ▷ shariah

Qadiriyyah (Qādiriyyah) A Muslim Sufi order set up in Baghdad by Abd al-Qadir al-Jilani (1077–1166). He became venerated as a saint among Muslims, and the Qadiriyyah continued to revere his memory. He is said to have promised that he would 'ride on a charger' to help those who called upon him in spiritual need. The Qadiriyyah was the first structured Sufi *tariqah* (rule of life) to emerge in Islamic history; it was followed by several others such as the *Suhrawardiyyah*, the *Mawlawiyyah*, and the *Sanusiyyah*, all of which look back to a particular founder as their inspiration. The order has members throughout the world, from India to Morocco. In parts of the Arab world it has incorporated elements of folk Sufism. ▷ Muhammad; Naqshbandiyya; Sanusis; Sufi orders; Suhrawardi; tariqah

qiblah The direction Muslims face when taking part in their daily prayers. During the first two years of the Muslim community's existence in Medina (622–4), the temple in Jerusalem was the qiblah, but it was replaced in 624 by Mecca. This was symbolic of a desire on the part of early Islam to stress its own Arab identity and its independence from the Jewish tradition. The Black Stone in the Kabah at Mecca is the actual qiblah, and in all mosques there is a prayer niche or direction finder (mihrab) that locates the direction of the Kabah for worshippers. When it is impossible to know where Mecca is, Quran 2.115 is helpful: 'To God belong the East and West and wheresoever you turn, there is the face of God'. Despite this general truth, the focus on the qiblah and the importance of daily prayers in Islam concentrate the attention upon the centrality of Mecca as the supreme sacred place for Muslims. ▷ Black Stone; Mecca; Medina; Mihrab; Quran

Qiyama The notion of resurrection in Islam, which is to be followed by the final judgement. Bodies will be raised from the earth and reunited with their souls. God will judge them by weighing up their deeds. Only Muhammad and (in later popular Islam) various local saints are able to intercede on behalf of a person. Souls will cross the narrow bridge that spans hell and either drop into it or cross over into the bliss of paradise. Some Muslims suggested that there was also an earlier judgement of souls at death, after which they returned to the tomb to await the final resurrection. According to Muslims the cross of Christ was an appearance only, and he passed immediately into an invisible state from which he will return before the resurrection and final judgement in order to destroy the anti-Christ and usher in the final events that mark the end of the age. ▷ afterlife; Antichrist; hell; Jesus Christ; Muhammad; Paradise; resurrection

Qiyas (Qiyās) The principle of analogy, which forms the third basis of authority within Muslim law (shariah). The first source of authority is the Quran. The second source is Muhammad's conscious sayings, the Hadith. Qiyas is the third source, used in circumstances not covered by the Quran and Muhammad's sayings. By analogical reasoning it attempts to work out how the principles of the first two sources would operate in the new context. Where there is still doubt, a fourth source of authority, the popular consensus of the community (*ijma*), comes into play. Al-Shafii played a leading role in emphasizing the importance of analogy within Islamic law. ▷ Allah; fiqh; Hadith; ijma; Quran; Shafii, al-

Qoheleth ▷ **Ecclesiastes, Book of**

Quakers ▷ **Friends, Society of**

Quesnel, Pasquier (1634–1719) French Jansenist theologian, born in Paris. He studied at the Sorbonne, and in 1662 became director of the Paris Oratory, where he wrote *Nouveau Testament en français avec des réflexions morales* (1687–94, New Testament in French with Thoughts on Morality). Having refused to condemn Jansenism in 1684, he fled to Brussels. Hostility to his work led to his imprisonment (1703), but he escaped to Amsterdam, where he died. ▷ Jansenism

Quest of the Historical Jesus The attempt in Liberal Protestantism to write lives of Jesus separating the historical 'facts' embedded in the Gospels from the faith claims of the Church. The movement was named after the title of the English translation (1910) of the famous book by Albert Schweitzer, *Von Reimarus zu Wrede* (1906), rewritten as *Geschichte der Leben-Jesu Forschung* (1913). He judged the liberal effort a failure for not realizing that it created a congenial Jesus at the expense of denying key aspects of his eschatological message. The title 'New Quest of the Historical Jesus' has also been used of biblical scholars such as Günter Bornkamm (1905–), Ernst Käsemann (1906–) and James M Robinson (1924–), who argue for a larger historical core to the Gospels than the form-critical approach of Bultmann would allow. ▷ biblical criticism; Bultmann, Rudolf Karl; Schweitzer, Albert

Quetzalcoatl A recurring figure in Meso-American religion, Quetzalcoatl is in some contexts a historical figure, the culture hero of the Toltec, in others a sky deity and creator, in others the Aztec high priest. He is represented as a feathered serpent, as his name implies (the quetzal bird has a distinctive blue-green plumage). As culture hero, originally named Ce Acatl, he is associated with a golden age in the city of Tollan (Tula) where he invented the calendar, developed all the arts, and set the norms for legislation and religion (the latter without human sacrifice). Conflict with his brother Tezcatlipoca led to his departure from Tollan and the beginning of troubles; but in due time he will return. As a divine figure he is one of the four children of Ometeotl, 'the god of dualities'. A creator figure (active both in the original creation and subsequent re-creations), a sustainer (he introduced agriculture), a redeemer (he vanquished the lord of the dead), he is also guardian of the mysteries (and hence patron of priesthood). He is identified with the morning star (Venus). The Toltec took his worship to their new centre at Chichen Itza, where it gained a new lease of life among the post-classical Maya under the translated name Kukulcan. The Aztec adopted it enthusiastically, though in time they merged some of Quetzalcoatl's characteristics with those of their own god Huitzilopochtli, and offered him human sacrifices. The theme of opposition between Quetzalcoatl and Tezcatlipoca is constant and was no doubt represented in ritual. The arrival of the Spaniards in

Quetzalcoatl

Mexico was at first interpreted as the return of Quetzalcoatl and his hosts. ▷ Aztec religion; Maya religion; Ometeotl; Tezcatlipoca; Tollan; Toltec religion

Quietism In a general sense, the belief that God works only in a person whose being is completely passive or quiet, and that religious believers should withdraw from concern with the world. In Christian thought the term is applied to trends in the Middle Ages (which were condemned by the Flemish mystic Ruysbroeck), and more commonly to the 17th-century controversies involving the Spanish priest Miguel de Molinos (1628–96), who was condemned in 1687 by Pope Innocent XI; and the 'semi-quietism' of the French nun Madam de Guyon (1648–1717) and Archbishop Fénelon, which was condemned in 1699 by Pope Innocent XII. ▷ Fénelon, François de Salignac de la Mothe; Ruysbroeck, Jan van

Qumran, community of (c.2nd century BCE–1st century CE) An exclusive Jewish sect, located near the north-west corner of the Dead Sea, apparently closely related to the Essene sect mentioned by Josephus. They opposed the Hasmonean highpriesthood of the 2nd century BCE, and considered themselves alone to be the true Israel awaiting God's new kingdom, being kept pure by their strict practices of legal observance and community discipline. They were destroyed during the Jewish revolt of 66–70CE, but many of their writings were discovered in 1947 as part of the Dead Sea Scrolls. ▷ Dead Sea Scrolls; Essenes; Josephus, Flavius; Judaism; Teacher of Righteousness

Quran (Qur'ān) The sacred book of Islam. It is held to be the direct word of God, inscribed in heaven and revealed piecemeal to the prophet Muhammad by the angel Gabriel over a period of 20 years as a message for all humanity. It superseded earlier Jewish and Christian scriptures, which, in the eyes of Muslims, had become imperfect. The first revelation began in 610 when Muhammad was meditating in the cave of Hira outside Mecca. In its present form it dates from the caliphate of Uthman (644–56). The text itself is regarded as sacred, and Muslims should be ritually pure before touching it. Imitation of its literary style is seen as sacrilegious. Considered the highest authority on all legal and religious matters, its pronouncements are commonly regarded as infallible.

Roughly the same extent as the New Testament, it is divided into 114 unequal chapters (surahs), generally arranged according to length. For the daily reading given during Ramadan, however, it is divided into 30 sections. Largely written in the voice of God, who talks as 'we', it is less concerned with narrative flow than with being instructive. The earliest surahs focus on God as creator, on God's oneness and greatness, the need to obey him and help one another, the role of Muhammad as the messenger warning of God's wrath if he is not heeded, and the importance of Islam in God's working out of history. Later surahs contain more communal, legal and social material concerning family, marriage and other social and ethical matters relating to the growing community. These prescriptions form the basis of the shariah, Islamic law.

The Quran is poetry rather than prose, and is chanted for devotional and liturgical purposes in haunting ways according to different conventions. Although past Muslim scholars questioned whether it could be meaningfully translated, it has now been translated into all major languages. Quranic schools, in which the text is memorized, are still common in various parts of the Muslim world. The main source of doctrine and law in Islam, it has the meaning for a Muslim that the Torah has for a Jew, or Christ has for a Christian. ▷ Allah; Commentaries on the Quran; Fatihah; Islam; Muhammad; Ramadan; shariah; Uthman

Quraysh The premier tribe in Mecca into which Muhammad was born and out of which Islam arose. It had come to Mecca in the pre-Islamic period and settled there by force under an ancestor of Muhammad named Qusayy. Mecca's importance as a trading city, and the cultic prestige of its famous Black Stone in the Kabah, gave it great significance; as a consequence the Quraysh became powerful and affluent. The clans living nearest to the Black Stone were known as the Quraysh of the Hollow, whereas the less important tribes, living further away, were known as the Quraysh of the Outskirts. When Muhammad began to preach, the Muslim message appeared to question the vested interests of the Quraysh, and it was partly to escape their depredations that he went on the flight (hegira) to Medina. Mecca and the Quraysh eventually became Muslim and all the early Arab caliphs were from the Quraysh tribe. Even so, the rise of Islam and economic factors led to the demise of the Quraysh as a trading tribe. ▷ caliphate; hegira; Mecca; Medina; Muhammad

R

rabban ▷ rabbi

rabbi (Hebrew 'my lord' or 'my master/teacher') In Judaism after 70CE a title for accredited Jewish teachers or sages, who often exercised judicial functions too; prior to 70 it was used less technically as a form of respectful address, as presumably in the New Testament Gospels. The teachings of these early sages are preserved in the Mishnah, the Talmud, and many other forms of rabbinic literature. Rabban is a superior form of the title, used in the Mishnah for four early scholars: Gamaliel the Elder, Johanan ben Zakkai, Gamaliel II, and Simeon ben Gamaliel II. Today rabbis also have pastoral functions and a role in worship, much like ministers or clergy of other faiths. ▷ Judaism; Mishnah; synagogue; Talmud

Rabiah (Rābi'ah al-'Adawiyyah) (713–801) Muslim saint, born in Basra into a poor family. Stolen as a child, she became a slave, but was freed because of her evident saintliness. She attracted a circle of followers, lived an ascetic life, wrote pithy mystical sayings (some of which have become proverbial among Muslims), and performed miracles. While stressing the oneness and greatness of God, she nevertheless felt that the soul could be united with God. Purification was important in order to achieve this, and so was love. She believed that God should be loved for his own sake, not for fear of punishment or for hope of reward. Only God was real so that although God's creatures were not equal to him, neither were they independent of him, and their birthright was intimacy with God. Rabiah is acknowledged among Sufis in particular, as well as among Muslims in general, as a mystic, an ascetic example, and a saint. ▷ Allah; love; purification; Sufism

Rachel Biblical character, daughter of Laban and wife of Jacob, mother of Joseph and Benjamin. According to Genesis 29, Jacob worked 14 years to earn Rachel as his wife, after having once been tricked into taking her elder sister Leah. At first, Rachel was said to be barren, but later she died when giving birth to her second son Benjamin. ▷ Jacob; Joseph; Old Testament

Radcliffe-Brown, Alfred Reginald (1881–1955) English social anthropologist, born in Birmingham. After studying at Cambridge, he carried out field research in the Andaman islands (1906–8) and Australia (1910–11), which served as a basis for his later works on *The Andaman Islanders* (1922) and *The Social Organization of Australian Tribes* (1930–1). After moving to South Africa in 1920 he became Professor of Anthropology at Cape Town, but in 1926 returned to Australia to take up the chair in anthropology at Sydney. He was subsequently professor at Chicago and Oxford. Along with Bronislaw Malinowski, Radcliffe-Brown was the principal architect of modern social anthropology, but despite his early fieldwork his major contribution was more theoretical than ethnographic. Greatly influenced by the sociology of Émile Durkheim, he regarded social anthropology as the comparative study of 'primitive' societies, whose aim was to establish generalizations about the forms and functioning of social structures. According to his structural-functional theory, institutions serve to maintain the total social order of which they are parts, as organs of the body maintain the whole body. His concern throughout was to emulate the methods of natural science, and he attacked the 'pseudo-historical' conjectures of many of his predecessors. He also distinguished social anthropology sharply from ethnology, which he saw as a descriptive rather than a theoretical enterprise. His *Structure and Function in Primitive Society* (1952) contains all the essentials of his theoretical programme. ▷ Durkheim, Émile; Malinowski, Bronislaw

Radha (Rādhā) A goddess in Hindu mythology, the favourite *gopi* ('cowgirl') of Krishna. Radha's nature contrasts with that of other Hindu goddesses in that she does not possess fierce or gentle aspects, such as those of Kali or Parvati, nor does she personify the mother goddess. Although she is sometimes the object of worship, she has never attained real independent status, but rather is worshipped solely in relation to her lover, the god Krishna, who was also her childhood companion in Vrindaban. Radha was the daughter of Krishna's adoptive father and was his favourite gopi. A married woman herself, she left her husband, family and all social obligations, drawn by her intense desire to be with Krishna. The love of Krishna and Radha, their separations and longings, their agonies and joyous fulfilments, are vividly described by Jayadeva, a 12th-century Bengali poet, in his lyrical love poem the *Gitagovinda*. The union of Radha and Krishna may be interpreted on many levels. Although the poetic words of love evoke images of erotic possession, Radha is not only revered as the earthly beloved of Krishna, but also as his eternal consort, being one half of the divine reality. The intensity, steadfastness and depth of Radha's love represents the heights of human passion and also symbolizes the religious ideal of selfless devotion to God. Similarly Krishna's devotion to Radha is taken to be symbolic of God's love for the soul. From the 15th and 16th centuries Vaishnava mystics developed this theme of love, particularly Chaitanya, who even at times dressed as Radha. Present-day devotees worship Radha and Krishna through their images and attend performances at which the love story of Radha and Krishna is reenacted by professional singers and dancers. ▷ Chaitanya; Krishna

Radhakrishnan, Sir Sarvepalli (1888–1975) Indian philosopher and statesman, born in Tiruttani, Madras. He was educated at Madras Christian College, before becoming professor at the universities of Mysore, Calcutta and Oxford. At Oxford he gave the Upton lectures at Manchester College in 1926 and 1929, and in 1936 became Spalding Professor of Eastern Religions and Ethics. He also lectured abroad, in America in 1926 and 1944 and in China in 1944. From 1931 to 1939 he attended the League of Nations at Geneva as a member of the Committee of Intellectual Cooperation. In 1946 he was chief Indian delegate to Unesco, becoming Chairman of Unesco in 1949. A member of the Indian Assembly in 1947, he was appointed first Indian ambassador to Russia in 1949, Vice-President of India from 1952 to 1962, and President from 1962 to 1967. He was awarded the OM in 1963. He wrote many scholarly philosophic works including *Indian Philosophy* (1927), his Hibbert lectures of 1929 published as *An Idealist View of Life* (1932), which is often thought to be his greatest work, and *Eastern Religion and Western Thought* (2nd ed 1939).

Radhasoami (Rādhāsoāmi) A religious movement that began in Agra in North India in 1861, and which arose mainly out of the Sikh tradition, but is now separate from it. It was founded by Shiv Dayal (1818–78) and the name signifies the union between Radha, symbolizing the soul, and Soami, symbolizing God. It aims to unite the soul with God through the help of the gurus of the Radhasoami tradition. After Shiv Dayal's death the movement split, with one centre continuing in Agra under a line of gurus, and the other more active group arising in Beas in the Punjab in 1891 under Jaimal Singh (1839–1933). Its concepts include: commitment to God through a living guru (the present one being Charan Singh), living the married life of a householder, moral discipline through giving up alcohol, drugs and meat, and mental/spiritual discipline by tapping into the inner currents and vibrations of God through yoga and meditation. The Beas Radhasoamis now have a large town in the Punjab as their headquarters, and their worldwide followers number well over two million, including members from other religions. They have departed from the Sikh tradition by stressing their own gurus rather than the *Guru Granth Sahib*, by initiating their own members, and by conceptualizing a more complex notion of God, the universe, and the nature of spirituality. ▷ guru; Guru Granth Sahib; Radha; yoga

Radin, Paul (1883–1959) Polish-born American anthropologist of religion, born in Lodz, but taken to the USA as a child and brought up in New York. He studied in New York, Berlin and Munich, receiving his doctorate from Columbia University in 1911. He worked as an ethnologist engaged in field research at various locations from 1910 onwards (the Winnebago Indians being a favourite topic), and he taught at various American universities, including Brandeis, until his death. His works include *The Ritual and Significance of the Winnebago Medicine Dance* (1911), *Monotheism among Primitive Peoples* (1924), *Primitive Man as Philosopher* (1927), *The Method and Theory of Ethnology* (1933), *Primitive Religion: its Nature and Origin* (1937), *Winnebago Culture as Described by Themselves* (1949), *The World of Primitive Man* (1953), and *The Trickster* (1956). Radin contended that there are degrees of religious-mindedness among different groups in different communities. The more religious-minded are in a minority, they are often artists or philosophers, and they usually become the religious leaders of the community. He thus showed that primal religions are not all of a type as had previously been thought, but contain varieties of religious thought and imagination within their communities. He had a psychological theory for the rise of religion. He viewed it as a compensation for insecurity, especially economic insecurity, and felt that there was a neurotic force at work in the lives of the religious élite. Religion is therefore a rational attempt on the part of the élite to deal with and compensate for the tribulations of life. However, although everyone is spontaneously religious at times of crisis, the religious are those who are spontaneously religious on numerous other occasions as well. ▷ anthropology of religion; psychology of religion

Ragnarok In Norse mythology, the final battle between the gods and the monstrous forces hostile to them. Though gods and monsters die, a new world will arise. ▷ Germanic religion

Rahit Maryada (Rahit Maryādā) The Sikh Code of Discipline, accepted in 1945 as a set of comprehensive regulations for the Sikh community, the *Khalsa*, and providing a unifying source of good practice. Traditionally it is thought to have originated with the tenth guru, Guru Gobind Singh, when he founded the Khalsa in 1699. The first recorded code appeared half a century later, and others evolved during the period 1750–1850, incorporating new features which reflected the growing importance of the Jat caste in Sikh life and the implications of opposition to Islam. From 1931 to 1945 the Sikh Elective Council, the Shiromani Gurdwara Parbandhak Committee, worked on an authorized version which was accepted in 1945 and issued in 1950. Outlining regulations for Sikh temples, it not only sets out Sikh ritual procedures, but lays down guidelines for the conduct of individual Sikhs, thus defining standards for the Sikh tradition at both institutional and personal levels. For example, it requires Khalsa Sikhs to wear the five Ks and to abstain from adultery, smoking, haircutting, and eating meat killed by Muslim methods. ▷ five Ks; Gobind Singh, Guru; Jat; Khalsa

Rahner, Karl (1904–84) German Roman Catholic theologian, born in Freiburg. He joined the Society of Jesus in 1922 and was ordained a priest in 1932. He was much influenced by transcendental Thomism. He began his teaching career in Innsbruck in 1937. Here, and later at Munich and Münster, his lectures and writings maintained a dialogue between traditional dogma and contemporary existential questions, based on the principle that grace is already present in human nature. As a prolific writer, editor, and adviser to the Vatican Council II, he has probably been the most influential Catholic theologian of the 20th century. The substance of his magisterial *Theological Investigations* (1961–81) is laid out in *Foundations of Christian Faith* (1978) and *The Practice of Faith* (1985). A man of prayer and deep love for God, his mystical beliefs may be glimpsed in his *Prayers for a Lifetime* (1984) and the autobiographical interviews *I Remember* (1985). ▷ existentialism; mysticism; Roman Catholicism; Thomism; Vatican Councils

Rahula (Rāhula) The name of the son of Gautama Buddha. According to the tradition of the Pali texts he was born in Kapilavatthu to his mother Yasodhara at the time when the Buddha heard the call to leave home and renounce the world in order to search for the answer to the problem of suffering and to seek enlightenment. Hence the meaning of the name given to his son: Rahula stands for 'bond' or 'hindrance'. The Buddha later went back to Kapilavatthu when Rahula was a child, and Rahula was ordained as a Buddhist novice monk. The *tipitaka* or Pali Canon suggests that the Buddha taught Rahula much, that some of the birth stories (Jataka) and discourses (*sutta*) of the Buddha were told to his son, that Rahula died before his father did, and that he was the author of some of the verses of the *Theragatta*. ▷ Buddha; Gautama; Jataka; sutta-pitaka; tipitaka

Raja Ram Mohan Rai ▷ **Rammohun Roy**

Rajneesh meditation Bhagwan Rajneesh is an Indian religious leader who founded a new religious movement with centres in Poona and elsewhere in India. This movement has made as much impact on the West as on India, and its membership at one time was mainly Western. The Rajneesh Foundation was unusual in that it came straight from India to Europe without the mediation of the USA, and it was only later that it transferred its main operations to New Jersey and Oregon. In the 1970s many Rajneesh meditation centres sprang up in the West to study his teachings and to practise the 'loving meditation' taught by him. Committed followers, sometimes known as the 'orange people', wore orange robes. Like other new religious movements of eastern origin centred on exalted masters such as Meher Baba and Mutananda, Rajneesh meditation involved an intense devotional relationship between devotees and Bhagwan Rajneesh himself. Internal differences have recently lessened the significance of Rajneesh and his meditational movement. ▷ Meher Baba; new religious movements in the West

Raksha Bandan On the full moon of Shravan (August–September) twice-born Hindus have silk threads (*rakshas*) tied to their wrists in a festival called Raksha Bandan, now most common in northern India. The practice has several interpretations. The threads are tied by priests, or more commonly by friends or female relations, especially sisters, on one level to celebrate the bonds between friends and relations, on another in remembrance of the ceremony of the Sacred Thread. That women generally tie the rakshas is significant. The practice takes place at the end of the agricultural year, at harvest, a time when fecundity is vital.

Rama (Rāma) A Hindu god who is an incarnation (avatara) of Vishnu and the hero of the epic *Ramayana*. In the *Ramayana* Rama is a hero who defeats the demon Ravana and wins back his abducted wife Sita. Rama becomes deified and is regarded as a king and upholder of ethical duty (dharma). During the medieval period in India Rama became especially popular in the Hindi-speaking north and his wife Sita was worshipped alongside him as his power of illusion (*maya*). Not only did the name Rama refer to the Hindu deity and hero of the epic, but came to be used by the holy men of the Sant tradition, such as Kabir, to refer to the absolute without qualities (*nirguna Brahman*). In religious art Rama is often depicted following the *Ramayana*, accompanied by Sita and his brother Balarama as they wander in the forest. Hanuman the monkey accompanies Rama as the model devotee. ▷ avatara; dharma; Hanuman; Kabir; maya; Ramayana; Vishnu

Ramadan (Ramaḍān) The ninth month of the Muslim year, observed as a month of fasting during which Muslims abstain from eating and drinking between sunrise and sunset; the Ramadan fast is one of the five 'pillars', or basic duties, of Islam. ▷ five pillars, Islamic; Islam

Ramakrishna Paramahamsa (Rāmakrishna Paramahamsa), originally **Gadadhar Chatterjee** (1836–86) Indian mystic, born in the Hooghly district of Bengal. A priest at Dakshineswar Kali Temple, near Calcutta, he took instruction from several gurus of different schools in his spiritual search, finally coming to believe in self-realization and God-realization, and that all religions were different paths to the same goal. His simple but effective re-telling of traditional stories, and personal charisma, attracted the interest of Calcutta intellectuals, including Swami Vivekananda, who became Ramakrishna's spiritual heir. ▷ guru; mysticism; Vivekananda, Swami

Ramana Maharishi (Rāmana Maharshi) (1879–1950) South Indian sage, born in Tirukuli, Madurai district. Attracted to the holy mountain Arunachala (at Tiruvannamalai, about 100 miles south-west of Madras) in 1896 at the age of 17, following a religious experience, he remained there until his death. Much of the time he lived in caves on the mountain and avoided publicity, but he later allowed devotees to establish an ashram at Villupuram, at the foot of the mountain. His philosophy of seeking self-knowledge through integration of the personality in the 'cave of the heart' became known to Westerners through the books of Paul Brunton as well as his own *Collected Works* (1969), *Forty Verses on Reality* (1978) and other anthologies. ▷ ashram

Ramananda (Rāmānanda) (c.1360–1470) Vaishnava *sannyasin*, born in Allahabad, who was at one time fifth in succession to Ramanuja, the great reformer and devotional theist. However, his relationship with Ramanuja's school was by no means harmonious. As a wandering ascetic he had, according to the school, made himself ritually impure, and, much to his disappointment he was ostracized. He eventually left and founded his own order of Rama bhakti. He wrote and spoke in vernacular Hindi, mainly operating from Banaras. He preached against caste, claiming that all people are equal in the sight of God. His order still survives (his disciples and followers are known as Ramanandins), and the devotional spirit he engendered still inspires Hindus. His teachings are akin to the sant bhakti tradition of northern India. Amongst his followers was Mira Bai, the great female poet-saint and Kabir, the poor weaver turned poet. He is even said to have influenced the writings of Guru Nanak, the founder of Sikhism. Thus in some respects Ramananda provided a source for trans-religious communication on the Indian subcontinent in the 15th century. ▷ Banaras; bhakti; Kabir; Mira Bai; Nanak; Ramanuja; Sikhism; Vaishnavism

Ramanuja (Rāmānuja)(11th–12th century) Tamil Brahman philosopher, born near Madras, South India. Dateable biographical information within a century of his death is not available, but his position in Indian thought is unassailable. Rejecting Sankara's *Advaita* or non-dualistic Vedanta for *Visishtadvaita* (which held that the soul was united with a personal god rather than absorbed into the Absolute) he prepared the way for the bhakti or devotional strain of Hinduism that was taken up by Madhva, Nimbarka, Vallabha and Chaitanya. ▷ Advaita Vedanta; bhakti; Brahman; Chaitanya; Hinduism; Madhva; Vedanta

Ramayana (Rāmāyaṇa) An epic poem of Hinduism written in Sanskrit and attributed to the poet Valmiki. The poem cannot be dated with accuracy, though probably was composed between the 2nd century BCE and the 2nd century CE. The story concerns the exile of Rama, accompanied by his wife Sita and brother Balarama, to the forest; the abduction to Sri Lanka of Sita by the demon Ravana; and the war against Ravana to win her back. Dasharatha the King of Ayodhya, Rama's father, has promised a boon to his wife Kaikeya, Rama's stepmother. She asks that her son Bharata be made king and Rama be exiled for 14 years. Although upset, Dasharatha keeps his promise and exiles Rama making Bharata king, and shortly after dies of a broken heart. The significance of this is that although the people of Ayodhya would prefer Rama to be king, righteousness and good moral conduct (dharma) must be upheld at all costs. Whilst Rama and Balarama are hunting in the forest, Sita is stolen away by the demon king Ravana and taken to Sri Lanka. Rama, with the help of a monkey army, particularly the monkey general Hanuman, rescues her and defeats Ravana. Some scholars have thought that this defeat represents the gradual Aryan domination of the south. After his exile Rama becomes king, but people begin to question Sita's chastity while she was imprisoned by Ravana. Rama knows that she remained chaste, but nevertheless banishes her from the kingdom. In traditional Hindu eyes this is a further example of Rama's selfless and exemplary conduct as king and upholder of dharma. ▷ Rama; Valmiki

Ram Das, Guru (Rām Dās, Gurū) (1534–81) Fourth of the 10 gurus, born in the Punjab, India. He was the son-in-law of the third guru, Guru Amar Das, and became guru in 1574. As founder of Amritsar as a Sikh centre he encouraged Sikhs to gather there for the Baisakhi and Divali festivals; the city's importance was bolstered later by the building of the Golden Temple (Harimandir). When he died he conferred the Guruship upon his youngest son Arjan, and it remained in his succession until 1708 when it passed from the tenth guru, Guru Gobind Singh, to the Sikh scripture, the *Guru Granth Sahib*. Important as an author, Guru Ram Das wrote a wedding hymn that is used in Sikh wedding ceremonies; 679 of his compositions are included in the *Guru Granth Sahib*. ▷ Amar Das, Guru; Amritsar; Baisakhi; Divali/Deepavali; Gobind Singh, Guru; Guru Granth Sahib; guru, Sikh; Harimandir

Rammohun Roy (Rāmmohun Roy), or **Raja Ram Mohan Rai** (1774–1833) Indian religious reformer, born in Burdwan, Bengal, of high Brahman ancestry. Early on he came to question his ancestral faith, and studied Buddhism in Tibet. Revenue collector for some years in Rangpur, in 1811 he succeeded to affluence on his brother's death. He published various works in Persian, Arabic and Sanskrit, with the aim of uprooting idolatry; and he helped in the abolition of sati (suttee). He issued an English abridgment of the Vedanta, giving a digest of the Veda. In 1820 he published *The Precepts of Jesus*, accepting the morality preached by Christ, but rejecting His deity and miracles; and he wrote other pamphlets hostile both to Hinduism and to Christian Trinitarianism. In 1828 he began the Brahmo Samaj association, and in 1830 the Emperor of Delhi bestowed on him the title of raja. In 1831 he visited England, where he gave invaluable evidence before the Board of Control on the condition of India. ▷ Brahman; Brahmo Samaj; sati; Veda

Ramsey, Ian Thomas (1915–72) English prelate, theologian and philosopher of religion, born in Kearsley, near Bolton. Having taught at Cambridge from 1941 and become a professor at Oxford in 1951, he was appointed Bishop of Durham in 1966. He was respected both as a diocesan bishop and for his intellectual contribution to the Church of England's Board for Social Responsibility, Doctrine Commission, and the committee on religious education that produced *The Fourth R* (1970). His enthusiasm for new causes left him relatively little time to develop his philosophical work on language about God and the understanding of religious experiences as 'disclosure' situations, as in *Models and Mystery* (1964) and *Models for Divine Activity* (1973). ▷ Church of England

Ranji A sky-father in the creation stories of New Zealand Maori religion. He and the earth mother Papa are the creators of gods and human beings. ▷ creation myths; Pacific religions

Ranjit Singh (Rañjit Singh) (1780–1839) Sikh leader, known as the 'Lion of the Punjab'. At the age of 12 he succeeded his father, a Sikh chief, as ruler of Lahore, and directed all his energies to founding a kingdom which would unite all the Sikh provinces. With the help of an army trained by Western soldiers, including generals Ventura and Allard, he became the most powerful ruler in India. He was a firm ally of the British, the boundary between their territories having been amicably agreed as the river Sutlej. In 1813 he procured from an Afghan prince, as the price of assistance in war, the Koh-i-noor diamond. ▷ Sikhism

Rasputin, Grigoriy Efimovich (?1871–1916) Russian peasant and mystic, self-styled 'strannik', or holy man, born in Pokrovskoye in Tobolsk province. In 1904 he left his village and devoted himself to religion. In St Petersburg from 1905, his apparent ability to ease the bleeding of the haemophiliac crown prince gave him a magnetic influence over the empress Alexandra and her husband, Nicholas II. Much disliked for his ignorance and immorality, he extended his malign influence over the court and government, until he was assassinated at the Yusupov Palace by a party of noblemen led by the Grand Duke Dimitry Pavlovich and Prince Yusupov. ▷ mysticism

Ras Shamra texts Some 350 texts, inscribed on tablets, found 1928–60 on the site of ancient Ugarit in north-west Syria, many written in a previously unknown cuneiform script now described as 'Ugaritic', and others in Babylonian. The texts include several epics, with stories about the Canaanite gods El, Baal, Astarte, and Asherah. Dated c.1400BCE, they are important not only for descriptions of pre-Israelite Canaanite religious practices and ideas, but also for light shed on practices recorded in the Hebrew Bible. ▷ Baal; Bible; Canaanite religion; Old Testament; Ugarit

Rastafarianism A religious movement from the West Indies. It derives largely from the thought of Jamaican political activist Marcus Garvey (1887–1940), who advocated a return to Africa as a means of solving the problems of Black oppression. When Haile Selassie was crowned Emperor of Ethiopia in 1930, he came to be viewed as the Messiah, with Ethiopia seen as the promised land. Rastafarians follow strict taboos governing what they may eat (eg no pork, milk, coffee); ganja (marijuana) is held to be a sacrament. They usually wear their hair in long dreadlocks, and they cultivate a distinctive form of speech. ▷ Haile Selassie

Rastafarians

Ratana movement ▷ **Christianity in Australasia**

rationalism A philosophical tradition which maintains that knowledge is independent of sense experience; it is usually contrasted with empiricism. Versions of it flourished with Descartes, Spinoza, and Leibniz, who maintained that all of science is a deductive system, patterned after Euclidean geometry, and reflecting the fact that there is no contingency in nature. The axioms are that ideas within us innately hold objective truth (for example, that God exists), and that a cause must be adequate to its effect. Rationalism was rejected by the empiricists, Locke, Berkeley, and Hume. The innateness of some ideas has been urged recently by Chomsky to account for language acquisition; it is not clear that this is inconsistent with empiricism. ▷ empiricism

Ravidas (Ravidās) (1414–1526) A member of the Sant tradition that arose out of devotional Hinduism, who was born in Banaras, the Hindu holy city. Like his Sant colleagues such as Namdev and Kabir, Ravidas stressed the importance of deep devotion to a monotheistic God, rejected ritualism, caste and institutional Hinduism, and was influenced in his mystical spirituality by currents from the Nath Yoga tradition and Sufi Islam as well as devotional Hinduism. He described himself as a cobbler (a *chaman*), and as an outcaste; 41 of his hymns are included in the Sikh scripture, the *Guru Granth Sahib*. In the late 19th century a number of members of the cobbler caste to which Ravidas had belonged attempted to better themselves by aligning with the Sikh tradition. This did not succeed, and during this century they have set up their own temples in the Punjab and in Banaras which acknowledge the Sikh scripture, the *Guru Granth Sahib*, and the 10 Sikh gurus, but also stress the teaching of 'Guru Ravidas' and celebrate Ravidas's birthday in February/March. They are now a new religious movement attempting to interpret the teaching of Ravidas in the contemporary situation. ▷ Banaras; Guru Granth Sahib; guru, Sikh; Kabir; Sufism

Re (also **Ra, Phra**) Ancient Egyptian sun god of Heliopolis. At an early stage he was identified with the creator god Atum who emerged from Nun at the beginning of time. As the sun, he was thought of as a youth in the morning, mature by noon, and an old man by the evening. Every day Re crossed the sky in his solar boat, and at night as a ram-headed god he sailed through the underworld. He was accompanied on these journeys by companions, including Maat and Thoth, who defended Re against various adversaries, most notably the evil serpent Apophis. Associated with Horus as Re-Harakhte, he was often represented as a falcon-headed man with the sun disc encircled by a uraeus on his head. He became the protective deity of the Old Kingdom pharaohs and principal state deity; the pharaoh was 'son of Re' and even an incarnation of the sun god. With the rise of the Theban god Amun in the Middle and New Kingdoms, the sun god was not displaced, but the two gods coalesced into the supreme Amun-Re. ▷ Amun; Atum; Heliopolis theology; Horus; Maat; pharaoh; Thebes; Thoth; underworld; uraeus

realism 1 The philosophical doctrine, held by Aristotle, Descartes, Locke, and others, that whatever exists has its character independently of its being perceived by human or divine minds; it is opposed to verificationism and some versions of idealism and phenomenalism. 2 A theory about universals, held by Plato, which maintains that properties such as redness exist outside the mind; it is opposed to nominalism and conceptualism. 3 The philosophical thesis that scientific theories aim or should aim to depict the way the physical world really is; it is opposed to instrumentalism. ▷ idealism; nominalism

real presence The belief that the body and blood of Christ are actually present in the bread and wine at communion (Eucharist/Mass). The nature of Christ's presence became the subject of great controversy at the Reformation. ▷ consubstantiation; Eucharist; Jesus Christ; Reformation; transubstantiation

rebirth The notion, especially prominent in Indian religion, that one is born not just once but many times in a succession of lives according to one's deeds (karma). If one's deeds are good the next birth will be more favourable; if they are not good, the next birth will be less favourable. The ultimate aim of life within this world view is to escape from the round of rebirths into the salvation and release of *moksha* or nirvana. The notion of rebirth, absent from the early parts of the Hindu Veda, emerged in the Upanishads and later Hindu and Buddhist scriptures. It implied that one life was not enough to work out one's total destiny, and also implied a just solution to the age-old problem of suffering: one is reborn justly according to what one has done and how one has lived. Hindus and Buddhists differ in that the Hindus believe that there is a permanent self (atman) that is reborn, whereas the Buddhists deny the notion of the self while retaining a belief in rebirth. ▷ atman; karma; moksha; nirvana; samsara; suffering; Upanishads; Veda

Reconstructionist Judaism A movement founded by Mordecai Kaplan, emphasizing Judaism as an evolving religious civilization. Kaplan did not intend to start a new denomination, so the synagogues that joined the Reconstructionist Federation of Congregations (from 1955) remained members of the Conservative or Reform denominations.

Kaplan argued that Judaism includes all aspects of Jewish culture, not merely the narrowly religious. Thus Reconstructionist Judaism mixes religion, philosophy and sociology, influenced by two main factors of the modern situation: increased knowledge about the natural world, and the rise of democratic nationalism with its stress on individualism. These render impossible any theory of supernatural theism or Torah as immutable divine revelation. According to Kaplan Judaism exists for the Jewish people. Jewish religion has to do with a people's search for meaning, constituting its salvation; belief in God relates to a sense of dependence on the powers of the universe. This allows for change which is not incompatible with continuity; Kaplan therefore found no problem in reconstructing Jewish theology and practice, including the omission of inappropriate elements from the liturgy (eg the notion of Israel's special election). After Kaplan's retirement (1963) the movement formed itself into a fully-fledged denomination. This included the founding of the Reconstructionist Rabbinical College in Philadelphia in 1968. ▷ Conservative Judaism; Kaplan, Mordecai Menahem; Reform Judaism; Torah

rector In the Church of England, the parish priest receiving full tithe rents; in other Anglican churches, generally a parish priest. In Roman Catholicism the term denotes the priest in charge of a religious house, college, or school. ▷ Church of England; priest; Roman Catholicism

Red and Yellow Hats A term referring to the monks of the Nyingmapa order of Tibetan Buddhism, who wear red hats, and to those of the Gelugpa order, who wear yellow hats. In Tibetan monasticism hats indicate degrees of status and function. For example, in the Nyingmapa or 'red hat' tradition, the head covering in the style of Padmasambhava is reserved for the highest lamas. Other styles are worn by monks who have undertaken a certain course of study, or on specific occasions, eg during a discourse or when explaining a text. Red Hats are not exclusive to the Nyingmapas, but are also worn by the Kagyupas, though the Karmapa lineage of this order is famous for its Black Hat lamas. ▷ Buddhism; Gelugpa; Kagyupa; Nyingmapa; Padmasambhava

redemption The belief that through the work of Jesus Christ humanity is enabled to be released from a state of sin to a state of grace with God. The term was originally applied to the purchase of the liberty of a slave. ▷ atonement; grace; Jesus Christ; sin

Red Sea A term used since antiquity to translate the Hebrew *yam suph* which most probably means 'sea of reeds'. In the biblical Exodus story it is the name of the body of water which Yahweh miraculously parted to allow the Israelites to cross over as they were fleeing Pharaoh's army. The water then flowed back to drown the Egyptians. The crossing was seen as the turning point in Israel's fortunes and the end of the bondage in Egypt. Attempts to locate this water have, like attempts to trace the whole of the exodus route, produced various results, none of which is fully satisfactory. In the New Testament and Christian tradition the crossing is considered as prefiguring baptism, and has also gained prominence with the emphasis given to the exodus story by modern liberation theologians. ▷ liberation theology

reductionism Any attempt to claim that the phenomena of one theory can be accounted for by another theory. Some philosophers claim that psychology and/or biology reduce to physics. Logicism is the thesis that mathematics reduces to logic. Some phenomenalists maintain that physical objects reduce to sense data. ▷ philosophy

Reformation The Protestant reform movements in the Christian Church, inspired by and derived from Martin Luther, John Calvin, and others in 16th-century Europe. A complex phenomenon, various factors are common to all reforms: a biblical revival and translation of the Word of God into the vernacular; an improvement in the intellectual and moral standards of the clergy; emphasis on the sovereignty of God; and insistence that faith and scriptures are at the centre of the Christian message. Non-religious factors aiding the spread of the Reformation included the invention of the printing press; the political, social and economic uncertainties of the age; and a general feeling of revival caused by the Renaissance.

In Germany, Luther's 'ninety-five theses' (1517) questioned the authority of the Church and led to his excommunication. The Lutheran Church then spread rapidly, in Switzerland under Zwingli and later under Calvin, neither of whom allowed any form of worship or devotion not explicitly warranted by scripture. The authority of scripture, the cornerstone of the Reformation, required a degree of ecclesiastical authority (and power) to justify and maintain it. The doctrine of the priesthood of all believers and the importance placed on preaching the Word of God led to an educated clergy, and decentralized church communities were better able to prevent abuse of ecclesiastical privilege. In England, Henry VIII declared that the king was the supreme head of the English Church, and appropriated Church property; in 1549 the Book of Common Prayer, embodying Reformation doctrine, was published, and under Elizabeth I a strong anti-papal stance was taken. In Scotland, under the influence of Calvin and the leadership of John Knox, the Presbyterian Church of Scotland was established in 1560, and remains the national Church. The Reformation also took root as Lutheran and Reformed Churches in France, Scandinavia, Czechoslovakia, Hungary, Romania, and Poland. ▷ Book of Common Prayer; Calvin, John; Christianity; Church of England; Church of Scotland; Knox, John; Luther, Martin; ninety-five theses; Protestantism; Reformed Churches; Zwingli, Huldreich

Reformed Churches Churches deriving from Calvin's Reformation in 16th-century Geneva, adopting a conciliar or presbyterian form of Church government. They are now worldwide in extent, with most being members of the World Alliance of Reformed Churches. ▷ Calvin, John; elder; Presbyterianism; Reformation; Reformed Church in America

Reformed Church in America A Christian denomination established in 1628 with the organization of the Collegiate Church for the early Dutch Reformed settlers. It gained its independence in 1770, was incorporated as the Reformed Protestant Church in 1819, and adopted its current name in 1867. In 1784 it established the New Brunswick Theological Seminary, the oldest Protestant seminary in the USA. ▷ Protestantism; Reformed Churches

Reform Judaism A movement beginning in early 19th-century Germany for the reform of Jewish worship, ritual, and beliefs in the light of modern scholarship and knowledge. It is based on the belief that since many Jewish practices were not directly revealed by God, these need not be followed if they do not fit into modern life. Instead, greater emphasis is placed on the ethical teachings of the prophets than on ritual law, and reason and experience are primary in the assessment of belief. Thus it challenged the Orthodox faith in the absolute authority of the Bible and other rabbinic works. Worshippers were not obliged to wear prayer shawls or cover their heads, men and women could sit together during services, work was allowed on the Sabbath, and dietary laws were relaxed. Reform Jews are now united in the World Union for Progressive Judaism. ▷ Judaism; Mendelssohn, Moses

Reimarus, Hermann Samuel (1694–1768) German theologian and philosopher, born in Hamburg, where he became a teacher of oriental languages from 1727. His first book was published quite late in life, at the age of 60, and was a moderate defence of natural religion entitled *Abhandlungen von den vornehmsten Wahrheiten der natürlichen Religion* (1754, 'Treatises on the Principal Truths of Natural Religion'). But he went on to write a far more radical attack on Revelation, a series of rationalistic essays rejecting altogether the accounts of miracles in the Gospels and the supernatural origins of Christianity. These were published posthumously, and only in part, by Gotthold Lessing, who claimed they were fragments from an anonymous manuscript found in the Wolfenbüttel Library, Brunswick, where Lessing was librarian. The work was described as *Wolfenbüttler Fragmente eines Ungenannten* (1774–7); it caused something of a sensation on publication, and was very influential in later German theology. ▷ Christianity; natural religion; Revelation

reincarnation The belief that following death, some aspect of the self or soul can be reborn in a new body (human or animal), a process which may be repeated many times. This belief is fundamental to many Eastern religions, such as Hinduism and Buddhism, and is also found in more modern Western belief systems such as theosophy. Alleged past-life regressions, where a hypnotized person appears to 'remember' past lives, have recently fuelled Western interest in reincarnation, although such cases may only represent the person trying to meet the implied demands of the hypnotist. ▷ afterlife; Buddhism; Hinduism; theosophy

reincarnation, Jewish concept of There is no evidence for Jewish belief in reincarnation apart from that found among Jewish mystics of the medieval period. When Josephus (1st century) mentions the holy bodies into which the righteous enter, he is probably referring to resurrection. In contrast, medieval kabbalists accepted the notion of reincarnation or transmigration of souls as early as the *Sefer Bahir*. But even in these circles there was considerable difference of opinion. Reincarnation (Hebrew *gilgul*) was considered by some as a severe punishment for sexual transgression which nonetheless provided the offender with a second chance. Another interpretation, based on Job 33.29, held that a soul commonly passed into three bodies in addition to its original in order to atone for sin. Others claimed that even the righteous were indefinitely reincarnated for the benefit of the cosmos. However, such ideas were strongly opposed by the majority of medieval Jewish philosophers. ▷ Kabbalah; Maimonides; reincarnatiion; Sefer Bahir

Reiyukai Kyodan (Reiyūkai Kyodan) A movement within the Nichiren tradition of Japanese Buddhism, set up in 1925 by Kubo Kakutaro (1890–1944). It counts as one of the many new religious movements in Japan, but is unusual in that it was not bound by government decrees or by the power of state Shinto during the era 1925 to 1945. This is because, having begun as a lay movement stressing ancestral rites and a return to traditional values, it adopted state Shinto-type teachings in the prewar and war periods. However, divisions arose within it, the most notable being the defections in 1938 that led to the rise of Rissho Koseikai, and this did fall foul of the state. Kuba Kakutaro was succeeded in 1945 by his sister-in-law Kotani Kimi (1901–71) and although the movement did not advance under her, it did engage in important social service programmes. Under the later leadership of Kubo Tsuginari, the founder's son, there has been renewal, modernization, and the rise of a flourishing youth wing; innovations have included a journal entitled *Inner Trip*, and a training centre. ▷ Nichiren Buddhism; Rissho Koseikai; Shinto

relativism Any philosophical position which maintains that there are truths and values, but denies that they are absolute. Epistemological relativism, first defended by Protagoras, asserts that all truth is necessarily relative; 'is true' is always elliptical for 'is true for x', where x might be an individual, society, or conceptual framework. Ethical relativism, held by the anthropologist Ruth Benedict (1887–1948) and others, comprises three doctrines, often confused: cultural relativism, the anthropological hypothesis that different societies have fundamentally different views about values; normative relativism, the thesis that there are no absolute values valid for all societies; and metaethical subjectivism, the doctrine that there can be no objective decision procedures for resolving value disputes. ▷ philosophy

relics Material remains (eg bones, skin) of, or objects which have been in contact with, a saint or person worthy of special religious attention. In many religions, and in the Roman Catholic and Orthodox Churches, these are objects of veneration, and the churches in which they are housed places of pilgrimage. ▷ Orthodox Church; Roman Catholicism

Scottish reliquary from c.750 CE

relics, Buddhist Relics of the Buddha and Buddhist saints have become a significant feature in the Buddhist tradition. Early Buddhist stupas arose as buildings in which relics of the Buddha, and occasionally of Buddhist saints, were enshrined. According to the Buddhist tradition, there are prestigious Buddhist buildings still existing that contain relics of the Buddha, for example the Temple of the Sacred Tooth at Candy in Sri Lanka, where the Buddha's tooth is said to be kept, and the Shwe Dagon Pagoda at Rangoon in Burma, where some of the Buddha's hairs are said to be kept. The Buddha's alms bowl is said to have been present variously in India, Sri Lanka, China and Persia. In the custom of revering relics of the human body the Buddhist tradition has resemblances to the reverence paid to Christian and Muslim relics, but it has diverged from Hindu and Jain practice in India. ▷ Buddha; stupa

religion A concept which has been used to denote: **1** the class of all religions; **2** the common essence or pattern of all supposedly genuine religious phenomena; **3** the transcendent or 'this-worldly' ideal of which any actual religion is as an imperfect manifestation; and **4** human religiousness as a form of life which may or may not be expressed in systems of belief and practice. These usages suffer from a tendency to be evaluative, to presuppose a commitment of some sort, or are so general as to provide little specific guidance. What is clear is that no single definition will suffice to encompass the varied sets of traditions, practices, and ideas which constitute different religions. Some religions involve the belief in and worship of a god or gods, but this is not true of all. Christianity, Islam, and Judaism are theistic religions, while Buddhism does not require a belief in gods, and where it does occur, the gods are not considered important. There are theories of religion which construe it as wholly a human phenomenon, without any supernatural or transcendent origin and point of reference, while others argue that some such reference is the essence of the matter. Several other viewpoints exist, and there are often boundary disputes regarding the application of the concept. For example, debate continues as to whether Confucianism is properly to be considered a religion; and some writers argue that Marxism is in important respects a religion. ▷ Buddhism; Christianity; comparative religion; Confucianism; God; Islam; Judaism; Marxism; origin of religion; theology; theology of religion; women in religion

Religionswissenschaft The German term for the study of religion, meaning literally the 'science of religion'. It includes the history of religion, the phenomenology of religion and comparative studies of religion, but is normally distinguished from theology and philosophy of religion on the one hand, and from the social sciences of religion on the other. However, the term that is used for Religionswissenschaft in the Anglo-Saxon world, Religious Studies, sometimes does include the social sciences of religion and in some cirumstances may include the philosophy of religion and even the theology of religion also, according to how theology is defined. In the past the history of religion has stressed studies of particular religions according to the historical method, but has more recently begun to think in more universal terms of how to conceptualize the global history of religion. The phenomenology of religion has emphasized the notions of *epoché* (putting one's convictions and presuppositions to one side in order to understand others) and *Einfühlung* (empathizing with the world view of others) as fundamental approaches to the study of religion. It has also engaged in the comparison of religion through the method of typology, as in the work of van der Leeuw and Eliade. However, other methods of comparing religions in an unbiased way have also arisen, for example through the use of models and through the comparison of themes such as rituals, scriptures, ethics, religious communities, sex in religion, witchcraft, doctrines, mysticism, devotional attitudes and incarnation. The assumption of Religionswissenschaft is that the study of religion includes in principle the study of all religions past and present, and that it involves the use of different methods and approaches to such study. Present discussion includes reflection about whether or not philosophy, theology, and the social sciences (anthropology, psychology and sociology) should be used in Religionswissenschaft, and if so, to what extent and whether it is a field of studies without a systematic base or a discipline with its own inbuilt agenda. ▷ anthropology of religion; comparative religion; Eliade, Mircea; Leeuw, Gerhardus van der; philosophy of religion; psychology of religion; social sciences of religion; sociology of religion; theology of religion; typology

religious communities In every religious tradition there is a notion of religious community. In Christianity it is the Church with its various branches: Orthodox, Roman Catholic and Protestant; in Islam it is the ummah, with its Sunni and Shiite branches, which often has a close relationship to wider society and politics; in Buddhism it is the sangha, with its Theravada and Mahayana branches, which has historically stressed the role of monks; in Judaism there are the modern Orthodox, Reformed and Conservative communities within the wider whole which also emphasizes ethnic factors; and in Hinduism, within the original social framework of the caste system, there are religious communities (*sampradayas*) centred upon the main deities Shiva, Vishnu, Rama, Krishna, the goddess Devi and so on. However, at a local level there are many particular forms of religious community. Some are naturally part of society: religious cults based on family, kinship, local associations, race, and nation. Others are specially founded religious communities such as secret societies, mystery religions, circles of disciples that gather round a charismatic leader, religious brotherhoods, ecclesiastical-type bodies, protesting bodies in wider religious communities, and independent sects or cults. Others are based upon occupation, rank or status, such as religions of the warrior, merchant, or peasant. Others arise out of the work of an authoritative religious leader: a founder, reformer, prophet, seer, magician, diviner, saint, priest, contemplative, or charismatic. Religious communities assume that religion has a social dimension that requires people to come together rather than be spiritually alone. They also have different relationships to the state, ranging from virtual identity in Shinto Japan, Zoroastrian Sassanid Persia and Byzantine Christianity, to radical separation in secret and mystery religions, with many gradations in between. ▷ caste; Conservative Judaism; Krishna; Mahayana Buddhism; Orthodox Church; Orthodox Judaism; Protestantism; Rama; Reformed Judaism; Roman Catholicism; sangha; Shiism; Shinto; Shiva; Sunnis; Theravada Buddhism; ummah; Vishnu

religious education Originally taking the form of religious instruction into the Christian faith, religious education has increasingly come to mean the attempt to understand the nature and function of all religions within their historical and cultural settings. This change was necessitated by the increasingly multi-faith character of Western society and the decline of the Christian faith. In those

European countries where there is a statutory requirement for religious education, the comparative study of religion is commonplace. In other countries, such as New Zealand, religious education is covered within subjects devoted to understanding the culture of the indigenous inhabitants of the Pacific islands. In the USA religious instruction is not allowed in schools although teaching about religion is theoretically permissible.

religious education, Christian Christianity, like Judaism, sees the home as the prime focus of religious education, developing and supporting formal instruction in church by catechism, creed and sermon. Medieval mystery plays, stained glass and wall paintings, and hymns in the vernacular languages were also educational aids for the illiterate. The coincidence of the Protestant Reformation with the development of printing and the production of Bibles in the vernacular (rather than Latin) was of no small importance to its success, and provided a religious motive for establishing schools. The modern Sunday school movement, originally offering religious and general education to children who spent the rest of the week working, began in England in 1780 with the pioneering efforts of Gloucester publisher and philanthropist Robert Raikes (1735–1811), and in the USA in 1785 in Oak Grove, Virginia.

In Britain, secular education was largely in the hands of the churches until the late 19th century. Under subsequent legislation (1870) state-supported schools in England and Wales could offer non-denominational Christian religious instruction, which became compulsory (along with a daily act of Christian worship) under the 1944 Education Act. This had to follow locally formulated Agreed Syllabuses, which by the time of the 1988 Education Reform Act were concerned with religious 'education' (rather than 'instruction') and included the study of religions other than Christianity. Roman Catholic, Anglican and other schools funded jointly by the state and religious bodies are permitted to follow their own programmes of religious education, a privilege that some state schools in predominantly Muslim areas wish to be accorded to themselves. In Scotland, current legislation regarding religious education dates from the Education (Scotland) Act of 1872. The legislation is generally open and permissive, which has allowed for freedom of conscience and variation in practice without breaching the statutory provision. Unlike England and Wales, however, this legislation did not provide teachers with an opt-out conscience clause. Today's developments make religious and moral education one of the main five areas of Scottish primary curriculum, and one of the eight modes in the secondary curriculum. From age five, the curriculum includes study of a range of major religions, although Christianity is the main religion studied. Religious and moral education is particularly concerned with the development of the child for a plural society and world and so also includes study of non-religious stances for living. This is most apparent in the later stages where Humanism, Marxism and science are specifically identified as challenges to Christianity.

Teaching 'about religion' is permitted in American public schools, but the ban on prayer and devotional reading of the Bible and conservative reaction to early 20th-century state bans on teaching 'creationism' (which opposes the biblical account of the creation with evolutionary theory) has led to a parallel development of private Christian schools and colleges. Sunday schools in the USA have church-based programmes of religious education for adults as well as children and young people.

religious experience Religious experience can be defined in a narrow way as inward spiritual experience, or in a wider way as experience of all the elements in religion. The term was made popular in the West by William James in his *Varieties of Religious Experience* of 1902, where he defines religion as 'the feelings, acts and experiences of individual men in their solitude, so far as they apprehend themselves to stand in relation to whatever they may consider the divine'. The individual experience, James implies, is difficult to describe because it has to be put into words, and what we read about are not religious experiences as such, but expressions of religious experience. One view states that all religious experience in this 'mystical' sense is the same, but we have to use words to describe it and so it seems to be different. Another view states that different religions have different religious experiences, because the different words and symbols brought to the experiences make them different. Zaehner claims that there are four types of religious experience that may be present in the same religion or in different religions: the experience of being one with the world, the experience of being one with one's own real self in separation from the world, the experience of oneness with God and the world, and the experience of loving union with God. Religious experience in the wider sense of experiencing all the elements of religion goes beyond the realms of inward spirituality. In the Hindu *Bhagavad Gita* it can take four forms which are reasonably typical: doing one's duty in the world under God, without thought of reward; loving god in faith, surrender and trust; using religious ritual as a way of experiencing truth; and, through meditation, realizing spiritual inwardness. Religious experience can involve one or indeed all of these ways. The focus then is not just on inward spirituality but on a more holistic religious experience that involves the religious community, the wider community and sacred texts as well. ▷ Bhagavad Gita; James, William; mysticism; spirituality; Zaehner, Robert Charles

religious orders, Christian Members of a religion who are linked by a rule of life and promises or vows which demand more than is required of believers in general. Biblical examples include Samson and other Nazirites and John the Baptist. The Essenes or Qumran covenanters followed a stricter standard than contemporary Judaism. The Desert Fathers took a similar approach when Christianity became the official religion of the Roman empire. Monks are also found in Buddhism and in pre- and post-Christian Hinduism.

In Western Christianity monks (male religious) and nuns (female religious) generally make vows of poverty, chastity and obedience which are designed to free them from the distractions of the world in order to serve God and the world better. They may live alone or in community. Their originally unremarkable form of dress, in remaining virtually unchanged for centuries, now acts as a symbol of difference similar to that signified by radical Protestant groups such as the Amish. Besides making vows, monks and nuns also follow a rule of life which is usually associated with an early monastic pioneer or reformer and biased towards a 'contemplative' life of prayer (as with the Cistercians), or towards an 'active' life of service (Franciscans), preaching (Dominicans), or teaching and missions (Jesuits). Some groups, such as the Third Order of St Francis, adopt vows or promises and rules of life or spiritual disciplines that can be followed in family and secular situations.

The Reformation rejected the abuses of medieval monasticism and the idea that there was one standard for Christians who entered religious orders and a lower standard for the rest. Luther substituted the doctrine of vocation by which every Christian is called to serve God in his or her own particular circumstances. Religious orders were revived in the Anglican Church in the 19th century. The 20th century has seen the founding of the Protestant Taizé Community, devoted to promoting unity in the churches and reconciliation in society, and the ecumenical Iona Community, whose members and associates share a rule of prayer and working for justice and peace. ▷ Amish; Cistercians; Desert Fathers; Dominicans; Essenes; Franciscans; Jesuits; MacLeod, Baron George Fielden, of Fuinary; monasticism; Qumran, community of; Roger of Taizé, Brother

religious pluralism The acceptance of religions outside one's own religious tradition as having truth and validity. Its meaning is best understood by comparing it with two alternative approaches to comparative religion, namely exclusivism and inclusivism. Exclusivism is the belief that a particular religion is in sole possession of the truth and the means of salvation. This was the dominant position in the Christian Church until the end of the 19th century and is expressed in the doctrine *extra ecclesiam nulla calus* (there is no salvation outside the Church). Inclusivism is the belief that all human beings, regardless of religious affiliation, participate in the benefits of Christ's salvific work. Other religions are regarded as lower levels on humankind's quest for God. This is the position adopted by Roman Catholicism since the Second Vatican Council (1962–5) and finds expression in Karl Rahner's suggestion that genuinely committed adherents of other religions are 'anonymous Christians'. Although inclusivism treats other religions with greater respect, it still presumes the superiority of its own religious tradition and it is from the basis of this superiority that other religions are treated.

Religious pluralism takes the inclusivist position a stage further. Alternative religions are no longer understood as receiving their validity through their relationship to a particular faith such as Christianity, but as possessing validity and truth in their own right. These religions are understood as different cultural reflections or expressions of the same divine reality and as such constitute legitimate ways to God. An important modern representative of this position and a thinker who has attempted to work out a philosophy of religious pluralism is John Hick. ▷ comparative religion; Hick, John Harwood; Rahner, Karl

Remonstrants Christians adhering to the Calvinistic doctrine of Jacobus Arminius (17th-century Holland), whose followers were also known as Arminians. They were named after the 'Remonstrance', a statement of Arminian teaching dating from 1610. Small in number, they were influential among Baptists, and in Methodism and Calvinism. ▷ Arminius, Jacobus; Baptists; Calvinism; Methodism

Renan, (Joseph) Ernest (1823–92) French philologist and historian, born in Tréguier in Brittany. Trained for the Church, he abandoned traditional faith after studying Hebrew and Greek biblical criticism. In 1850 he started work at the Bibliothèque Nationale, and published *Averroès et l'Averroïsme* (1852), *Histoire générale des langues sémitiques* (1854), and *Études d'histoire religieuse* (1856). His appointment as Professor of Hebrew at the Collège de France in 1861 was not confirmed (until 1870) by the clerical party, especially after the appearance of his controversial *La Vie de Jésus* (1863), which undermined the supernatural aspects of Christ's life and his teachings. It was the first of a monumental series on the history of the origins of Christianity, which also included books on the Apostles (1866), St Paul (1869) and Marcus Aurelius (1882). Among his other works were books on Job (1858) and Ecclesiastes (1882), and an *Histoire du peuple d'Israël* (1887–94). ▷ biblical criticism; Jesus Christ

renunciation The practice of denying oneself food, sleep, sexual intercourse or worldly goods for a religious reason. This is a widespread phenomenon and the notion of self-control and discipline involved in such acts is often regarded as an essential prerequisite of spiritual growth. The practice of renunciation is often linked to a low estimation of the physical world and in particular the human body. Both Buddhism and Christianity have had strong ascetical tendencies, as both have inclined to be world-denying faiths. The true disciple, in order to proceed, has to rid himself of worldly concerns. Renunciation in the form of abstinence for a set period of time has been a disciplinary measure imposed by the Church. ▷ asceticism; celibacy

renunciation, Buddhist Renunciation is a common feature in many religious traditions whereby lesser things are renounced for higher gain, material benefits for spiritual reward, and present luxuries for future saintliness. The Christian Lent and the Muslim fast of Ramadan are recurring examples of temporary practical renunciation. The Buddhist tradition has exemplified the theme of renunciation in the great renunciation of the Buddha himself. According to Buddhists, the Buddha was brought up in a pleasant and wealthy home with access to luxuries. Then in quick succession he saw examples of worldly suffering: a very old man, a diseased person, a dead body, and a saffron-robed ascetic. He was married with a child named Rahula (the bond) but he resolved to leave home, wife and child, and to become an ascetic in order to find an answer to the problem of suffering. He renounced his family for the sake of all beings, although he went back later after he had become the Buddha, the enlightened one, and taught his family, ordaining his son as a monk. The Buddha's renunciation was a symbolic example and precedent for later Buddhists who became monks and nuns. Today they still renounce worldly life and receive alms from lay Buddhists; when monks are ordained, their heads are shaved as a symbol of renouncing worldly vanity. Monks and nuns renounce 10 things in their moral code: harming others, stealing, sex, lying, drugs and alcohol, eating after noon, entertainments, rich clothes, luxurious beds, and handling silver or gold. Lay Buddhists renounce the first five moral prohibitions mentioned above as the first step along the deeper Buddhist path. ▷ almsgiving, Buddhist; Buddha; Lent; Rahula; Ramadan; sila; suffering

repentance In general terms, an intense feeling of remorse at past actions or at not having performed good actions, and the resolution to embark upon a new life in which the failures of the past are put aside and a moral renewal is undertaken. In a religious context repentance is understood as a turning back to God. The individual repents of his previous life, which has disregarded God, ignored his commandments, etc, and resolves to embark upon a life that is centred on God. Repentance can also be understood as the removal of those barriers that impede a person's relationship with God, thereby enabling God's grace and forgiveness to flow freely to the repentant sinner. Repentance thus consists of a double movement: a movement away from sin and a movement towards God.

The concept of repentance plays an important role in most religions. Thus in the Old Testament the prophets urge the people of Israel to 'return' to Yahweh. Similarly, the earliest recorded words of Christ's mission are to call the people to repentance in the face of the imminent arrival of the kingdom of God (Mark 1.15). Islam stresses God's compassion and merciful nature and holds out the possibility of forgiveness if the sinner repents, turns to the truth and carries out good works (Quran 6.54; 12.25–6).

Most religions also make a distinction between interior and exterior repentance. Interior repentance describes the personal remorse of the sinner and his commitment to self-improvement. Exterior repentance refers to the various penitential acts prescribed by a religion as an outward expression of an individual's repentance. Such penitential acts can vary from wearing sackcloth and ashes to the confession of sins. ▷ kingdom of God

requiem (Latin 'rest') In the Roman Catholic Church, a Mass for the dead. It comes from the first words of the introit, *Requiem aeternam dona eis Domine* ('Give them eternal rest, O Lord'). Requiems are performed at funerals, on anniversaries of a person's death, and on All Souls' Day (2 November). They are intended to help the dead in their journey through purgatory. ▷ music, Christian; liturgy; Mass; purgatory

Reshef, or **Resheph** Ancient West Semitic god of plague and the underworld, known from Ugarit, Phoenicia, and other parts of the Ancient Near East. At Ugarit he appears regularly on offering lists, and in one of the epic texts is responsible for the plague which destroys several princes. As a god of mass destruction he was identified with the Mesopotamian Nergal and later with Apollo. Reshef became popular in Egypt during the 18th Dynasty (16th–14th century BCE). He is represented in Egyptian sculpture as a warrior god wielding axe and shield, and wearing a tall pointed head-dress with gazelle horns. ▷ Ancient Near Eastern religions; Canaanite religion; Nergal; Phoenician religion; Ugarit

resurrection A form of re-animation of a person after death, the belief in which can be traced to late biblical Judaism and early Christianity. The nature of the new corporeality, the timing of the transformation, and the matter of whether all people would be raised from the dead or only the 'just' have been variously expressed in Jewish and Christian literature, but the emphasis on some form of revival of the body after death is distinct from many views about the immortality of the soul. Christian faith affirms the resurrection of Jesus Christ in particular, signifying God's vindication of Jesus. ▷ afterlife; Christianity; eschatology; immortality; Jesus Christ; Judaism; Qiyama; reincarnation; soul

Reuben, tribe of One of the 12 tribes of ancient Israel, portrayed as descended from Jacob's first son by Leah. Reuben is also said to have encouraged his brothers to cast Joseph into a pit, rather than to kill him. The tribe's territory included the region east of the Dead Sea and south of Gad. ▷ Israel, tribes of; Jacob; Old Testament

revelation In religion the term used to refer to disclosures offered by God or from the divine as distinguished from those attained by the human processes of observation, experiment and reason. ▷ Bible; God; Quran

Revelation, Book of or **The Apocalypse of St John** The last book in the New Testament, whose author is named as 'John', an exile on the island of Patmos (1.9), although scholars differ about his precise identity, and parts of the Eastern Church were slow to accept the work as canonical. Chapters 1–3 are letters of exhortation to seven churches in Asia Minor, but Chapters 4–22 consist of symbolic visions about future tribulations and judgements marking the End times and the return of Christ. It may have been an attempt to offer hope to a church facing persecution in the early 90s. ▷ apocalypse; eschatology; New Testament

revelation, in Islam According to Islam the Quran is the direct revelation of God to the world through the channel of Muhammad. It is *wahy*, inspired by a divine source, namely God, and it is *tanzil*, sent down from heaven by God. Thus Muhammad's conscious mind is considered not to have intervened in the transmission of the Quran, whereas his sayings, the Hadith, are considered to be his own utterances and, although authoritative, they are not in the same revelatory category as the Quran. By contrast, the Christian Gospels, except for the words of Jesus himself, are seen by Muslims to be the narrations of the Gospel writers and therefore not fully revelation. According to this view, the Christian Bible is more equivalent to the Hadith of Muhammad. However, the Quran for Muslims is equivalent to Christ for Christians (but not for Muslims), that is to say they are viewed by their respective traditions as the direct revelation of God. According to Muhammad the Quran was revealed in two ways: by the angel Gabriel to Muhammad as one person to another, or like the painful ringing of a bell penetrating his heart. ▷ Gospels, canonical; Hadith; Jesus Christ in Islam; Muhammad; Quran

Revised English Bible ▷ New English Bible

revival and renewal Religious traditions are in a continuous process of development.

When that development becomes rigid and fixed this often leads to a desire for revival of the essentials that seem to have become fossilized or lost, and for renewal that will enable the tradition to have a more vibrant message for the present. Although revival and renewal have been continuing factors in most religions, they have been especially prominent in Christianity and, recently, in primal religions. They may result in the revitalization of the tradition concerned, or in the creation of new religious movements that leave the parent body and become a separate religion or church. The alternative to revival and renewal is not to respond to the need for change and to retreat into a shell, in which case the result may be the reduction or recession of the tradition, its absorption into another tradition, or its restatement in terms of another tradition. Revival often takes the form of a creative restoration of tradition, as in the recent revitalization movements among the American Indians, Australian Aborigines, Orthodox Jews, Buddhists, Muslims and Hindus, and evangelical Christians. Renewal is usually more adventurous than the desire merely to restore the past, and often involves reform, adjustment to present needs, and appropriation of new and even radical ideas so that the tradition does not merely revive but goes forward prophetically. Recent examples include the work of the Dalai Lama in Buddhism, or Gandhi in Hinduism, Vatican II within Christianity, and a general willingness to take more seriously new and pressing global issues such as ecology. ▷ Dalai Lama; evangelicalism; Gandhi, Mohandas Karamchand; new religious movements in the West; Vatican Councils

Revivalism In the 18th century several apparently spontaneous outbreaks of a mass awareness of a need for God, like that recorded at Pentecost (Acts 2) occurred, revitalizing churches in England, Wales and America. Similar awakenings in Wales, South America, India, Africa, China, and South Korea have taken place in the 20th century. The effects of the Great Awakening of 1740 were studied by the American theologian Jonathan Edwards. The conditions under which revivals took place were analysed and then promoted by 19th- and 20th-century American revivalists such as Charles Grandison Finney (1792–1875), Dwight Moody, Billy Sunday (1862–1935), and Billy Graham. Seeking and expecting revival is also the normal approach of the Salvation Army, and pentecostal and charismatic renewal groups. ▷ Edwards, Jonathan; Graham, Billy; Moody, Dwight Lyman; Pentecostalism; Salvation Army

Ricci, Matteo (1552–1610) Italian missionary, founder of the Jesuit missions in China, born in Macerata. He studied at Rome, and lived in Nanking and in Peking. He so mastered Chinese as to write dialogues which received high commendation from the Chinese literati, and he met with extraordinary success as a missionary, although his methods aroused much controversy. ▷ Jesuits; missions, Christian

Ridley, Nicholas (c.1500–1555) English Protestant martyr, born in Unthank Hall near Haltwhistle. He was elected in 1524 a fellow of Pembroke College, Cambridge, studied at Paris and Louvain (1527–30), and became proctor at Cambridge in 1534, domestic chaplain to Cranmer and Henry VIII, Master of Pembroke in 1540, Canon, first of Canterbury, then of Westminster, Rector of Soham, and in 1547 Bishop of Rochester. An ardent and outspoken reformer, he was in 1550, on the deprivation of Edmund Bonner, Bishop of London, made his successor. In this high position he distinguished himself by his moderation, learning and munificence, and assisted Cranmer in the preparation of the Thirty-nine Articles. On the death of Edward VI he denounced Mary I and Elizabeth as illegitimate, and espoused the cause of Lady Jane Grey; on Mary's accession he was stripped of his dignities and sent to the Tower. In 1554 he was tried at Oxford, with Latimer and Cranmer, by a Committee of Convocation; all three were judged obstinate heretics and condemned. Ridley lay in jail for 18 months, and after a second trial was burnt, along with Latimer, in front of Balliol College, Oxford. ▷ Cranmer, Thomas; heresy; Latimer, Hugh; Thirty-nine Articles

Ridvan Garden (Riḍvān Garden) A garden situated on the outskirts of Baghdad, a place of great significance to Bahais. Its original name was the Najibiyya garden, but it was changed to the Garden of Ridvan, meaning 'Paradise', because of the importance attached to the 12 days spent there by Bahaullah in 1863, when he declared himself to be a manifestation of God. It was here too that he forbade jihad, holy war, as well as announcing that no further manifestation of God would appear for another thousand years. Ridvan Garden is therefore important for Bahais as the place where Bahaullah first claimed that he was the promised one of all religions, that his message was for all humans, and that a new time in human history had begun. ▷ Babis; Bahaism; Bahaullah

Rime (ris-med) A 19th-century religious movement in Tibet, which attempted to heal the rifts between the different monastic orders and present a unified, non-sectarian form of Buddhism. The movement regarded differences between the traditions as being of less importance than the shared features of common texts and teachings, which were recognized by all schools. Although it was drawn from all four important monastic orders, the main proponents of this movement were Nyingmapas. ▷ Buddhism; Nyingmapa

Ringatu ▷ **Christianity in Australasia**

Rinzai One of the two main branches of Japanese Zen Buddhism. It originated in the Lin Chi school of Chan Buddhism in China, and was brought by Eisai from China to Japan in 1191. Rinzai received the support of the shoguns and appealed mainly to the aristocracy, striking up an alliance with the samurai and Japanese national concerns. It stressed the importance of sudden enlightenment and advocated unusual means of achieving it, such as shouts, slaps, and the use of koans. Rinzai used collections of koans systematically in its temples, and downplayed the reading of scriptures (*sutras*) and the veneration of Buddha images in favour of seeking the Buddha nature directly through the use of koans and practical living. Dogen, who introduced the second Zen sect, Soto, from China to Japan in 1227, stressed the way of gradual enlightenment through the reading of sutras, the veneration of Buddha images, occasional koans, and *zazen*, sitting upright with legs crossed in simple meditation. Soto became more popular than Rinzai Zen, but the latter flourished during the medieval Kamakura period, and one of its masters, Hakuin (1685–1768), introduced reforms that paved the way for modern Zen. ▷ Buddha image; Buddha nature; Chan; Dogen; Eisai; gradual/sudden enlightenment schools of Buddhism; koans; Soto; Zen Buddhism

Rissho Koseikai (Risshō Kōseikai) A new religious movement within the Nichiren tradition of Japanese Buddhism, founded in 1938 by Nikkyo Niwano. It separated from the Reiyukai Kyodan (founded in 1926) which had become accommodated to State Shinto and the government policies of the prewar period, and it suffered from harassment in its early years. After World War II it became one of the fastest growing new religious movements in Japan. Its basis lay in the teachings of Nichiren and his stress upon the *Lotus Sutra*, but in its early history it accommodated Japanese folk religion at a time of insecurity in order to enable people to find immediate solutions to pressing problems, a sense of meaning in life, and membership of a caring community. Thus faith-healing, divination, counselling, shamanism, and the charisma of its founder were important factors in its early success. It has since become more obviously Buddhist in its approach, with a fresh emphasis upon the bodhisattva ideal of compassion and the four noble truths, although it continues to emphasize the possibility of immediate happiness and benefits in life and its own role as a community. Among important recent elements have been its fellowship groups where about 12 people meet, often daily, for mutual counsel, and its stress upon world peace and the need for deep inter-religious dialogue. ▷ ariya sacca; bodhisattva; Kokutai Shinto; Lotus Sutra; Nichiren Buddhism; Niwano, Nikkyo; Reiyukai Kyodan; shamanism

rita (ṛta) (literally, 'cosmic order') This represents the cosmic laws and forces by which all things are maintained. Rita can be seen as a universal truth which predates even the Vedic gods, and is said to provide them with their power. It can, in some ways, be seen as the antecedent of dharma, especially in its universal aspect and in its relation to karma. Thus humans, and even the gods, obey the laws of rita. It was the god Varuna who is said to have produced rita, although he should be seen as a guardian rather than a creator. Rita, therefore, provided explanations for the occurrence of natural phenomena, being an impersonal source of these in terms of both creation and maintenance of the universe. It was believed that humans could gain access to this power through the correct performance of the rituals outlined in the Vedas. Indeed, it was believed that if these rituals were not carried out, then the cosmic order would collapse. ▷ dharma; karma; Veda

rites, Greek The most important rite of Greek religion, deployed on almost every possible occasion, was animal sacrifice. The act of killing was invariably accompanied by a prayer beseeching blessings for the sacrificer and his group; and the meat was normally then divided and eaten. Often the sacrifice was preceded by a procession, perhaps accompanied by singing, to the sacred place. Another basic form of worship was dancing by choirs, often in competition with one another. ▷ festivals, Greek; Greek religion; sacrifice

rites, Islamic Islamic rites in the wider sense include the rituals connected with the five pillars of Islam, namely saying the profession of faith, the shahadah, 'Allah is Allah, and Muhammad is his prophet'; saying the five daily prayers; engaging in almsgiving to help the poor; sharing in the Fast of Ramadan; and going at least once in a lifetime on the pilgrimage to Mecca. In a narrower sense they include rituals that take place in a mosque, especially the Friday noonday prayers when a sermon is delivered, and also celebrations of great festivals such as Id. In a more exact sense they focus on the various rites of passage: birth, naming, circumcision, puberty, marriage, pregnancy, parenthood and death. There are wide local variations in these rites of passage. It is significant that they do not have to take place in a mosque, although for some of them in certain circumstances this can be the case. Ultimately Muslim rites are related to submission to God ('Islam') and to social observance rather than to ritual duties for their own sake. ▷ five pillars, Islamic; Hajj; Id; Islam; mosque; Muhammad; Ramadan; rites of passage; shahadah

rites of passage Those ritual acts which govern and set out the correct procedure to be observed at all major events of life. They mark the transition and initiation of the individual into a new social and religious standing. The great transitional points of life—birth, puberty, marriage and death—are the primary areas where rites of passage occur. The function of the rite is to preserve harmonious relationships within the social order by inculcating a society's rules and values into those who are about to become its fully-fledged members. The forms of rite which are observed are numerous, including baptism, circumcision, tooth filing, elaborate wedding rituals and funerary practices. ▷ baptism; circumcision; funerary practices; naojote; rituals; sacrament

rites of passage, Christian view of Christian churches and individual congregations vary in their attitude to requests to provide religious services for the occasions of birth, marriage, and death. Some, principally from a state or national church background, count all citizens as at least potential believers and rites of passage as evangelistic opportunities, and offer Christian baptism, marriage, and burial to all who ask. Others, including churches that sociologists would class as 'sects', but also some of the 'church' type who feel a need to witness against the pressures or assumptions of secular society, offer Christian rites for those willing to undergo a course of instruction and make a commitment of faith, and alternative services of blessing or commemoration for those who cannot undertake this. Views on controversial issues such as the remarriage of divorced persons in church are divided on theological and pastoral grounds. ▷ baptism; funerary practices; initiation, Christian; marriage/divorce, Christian; sects, Christian

Ritschl, Albrecht (1822–89) German Protestant theologian, born in Berlin, cousin of Friedrich Wilhelm Ritschl. He became Professor of Theology at Bonn (1851), and Göttingen (1864). His principal work is on the doctrine of justification and reconciliation (1870–4). Other works were on Christian perfection (1874), conscience (1876), pietism (1880–6), theology and metaphysics (1881). The distinguishing feature of the Ritschlian theology is the prominence it gives to the practical, ethical, social side of Christianity. ▷ Christianity; Protestantism

rituals Ritual behaviour, in the sense of prescribed action repeated from time to time in a systematic way, is a common part of human life, which has been especially important in religion. Religious rituals vary between religions, but tend to take four main forms. Rites of passage are used at the key transition stages of life: birth, initiation and/or puberty, marriage, and death. Worship rituals are performed in churches, mosques, synagogues, temples, pagodas and so on according to certain patterns, and sometimes on particular days (for example Sunday is especially important for Christians, Saturday for Jews, and Friday lunchtime for Muslims). Festive rituals are common in most religions and often celebrate the birthdays of key figures, such as Jesus, Muhammad, Krishna, Rama, Buddha and Bahaullah, or key events and seasons. In some religions sacramental rituals are important, and these are sometimes related to rites of passage, such as in the Orthodox and Roman Catholic baptism, initiation, marriage and funeral services, but also to matters of religious importance such as ordination, confession and the Eucharist (at which the death of Christ is ritually remembered and celebrated). The term ritual is often used together with the term myth, because the ritual that is enacted is often connected with a particular myth or significant story. ▷ festivals; mythology; rites of passage; sacrament; worship

rituals, Roman Roman religion was a ritualistic religion based not on one sacred text delivering a revelation but on cult practice. Roman rituals (composed of prayers, songs, processions, sacrifices, feasts, games and festivals) were governed by many rules fixed by tradition, which needed to be observed in order to maintain the peace treaty between gods and Romans. Public rituals were inscribed on Roman calendars as days of *nefas* (days reserved to the gods), meaning that no business could be conducted on those days, since each citizen had to participate in the rituals. In fact, the degree of involvement of Romans in public rituals differed according to gender (it was mainly a male task) and status (the actual performer or ruler of a public ritual was a magistrate or a priest, while most Romans were passive observers). So, performing a ritual such as an animal sacrifice showed the social division of labour in a ritual: while a magistrate or priest led the procession, read prayers, and poured incense and wine on sacrificial altars located in front of temples, the more menial work of killing and the shedding of blood was marked out as the work of slaves. In private religion it was the responsibility of the head of the household to choose and to perform the rituals to family gods. ▷ prodigia; Roman religion

ritual slaughter The killing of animals or human beings for religious purposes. The grounds for ritual slaughter may vary considerably from culture to culture. There appear, however, to be three different reasons for this practice. Firstly, ritual slaughter may be carried out in order to provide a deceased king or nobleman with companions and servants in the next world. Secondly, ritual slaughter may be performed as a sacrificial offering to gods or other supernatural beings. This practice stems from primitive man's equation of blood with life. In slaughtering a sacrificial victim the sacrificer is liberating a life-giving force, thereby restoring or renewing the life of his community and its relationship with the supernatural world. As the life-principle, blood is also employed to seal pacts between the divine and human worlds. This can be seen in Exodus 24.6–8 where Moses throws half of the blood of slaughtered oxen on to the people and the other half on to the altar in order to ratify the covenant between Israel and Yahweh. Slaughtered sacrificial victims are also capable of atoning for the sins of the community. Sin is transferred from the community to the sacrificial victim, usually an animal but in some cultures a sacral king or chief, which is then slaughtered in the place of the community. This idea has, of course, been taken up and refined by the Christian Church in interpreting Christ's death. Christ is understood as freely laying down his life in the place of humankind in order to atone for our sins and re-establish our relationship with God. Thirdly, ritual slaughter may be carried out as part of the re-enactment of a mythical pact. In some cultures it is held that the world has come about through the primeval slaughtering of a god. Ritual slaughter is an act of remembering or re-enacting this primal act by killing a representative of the slaughtered god. ▷ human sacrifice, Israelite; human sacrifice, Meso-American; sacrifice

Aztec sacrificial knife

ritual slaughter, Islamic Within Muslim tradition, animals must be killed by ritual slaughter in order to be *halal* (acceptable) food. The only two exceptions to this are the killing of game animals by means of a gun or by a dog (in which case the 'slaughter formula' is still used), or dire necessity, in which case animals killed by Christians or Jews can be eaten. However, normally only a Muslim can engage in ritual slaughter. In preparation for it the formula 'In the Name of God, God is most great' is used, and in the actual slaughter the throat is cut with one stroke. The whole operation is preceded by forming the intention to engage in ritual slaughter, and if the animal in question is intended for a sacrificial feast such as Id, this and other relevant details are set out when the intention to kill is originally formed. As blood is forbidden as part of food in Islam, any blood must be drained from the dead animal before it can be consumed. ▷ Id

Roberts, (Granville) Oral (1918–) American evangelist and faith healer, born in Ada, Oklahoma, the son of a Pentecostal preacher and a half-Creole mother. He was ordained at 18 in the Pentecostal Holiness Church. Flamboyant and enterprising, he gained a reputation for faith-healing, and when he founded Oral Roberts University in Tulsa in 1967 the state governor attended and Roman Catholics and Jews were among its backers. By 1978 it had 3800 students and assets of about $150 million. Roberts has a weekly national TV programme, a radio station, and a mass circulation monthly magazine. His writings include *If You Need Healing, Do These Things* (1947), *The Miracle Book* (1972), and *Don't Give Up* (1980). ▷ evangelist; Pentecostalism

Robinson, John Arthur Thomas (1919–83) English Anglican prelate and theologian, born in Canterbury. He was educated at Cambridge where he lectured before appointment as Bishop of Woolwich (1959–69). In 1963 he published *Honest to God*, which he described as an attempt to explain the Christian faith to modern man. It scandalized the conservatives, became a bestseller, and blocked his chances of further ecclesiastical advancement. He also made weighty—and more orthodox—contributions to biblical studies in other volumes, including *Jesus and His Coming* (1957), *The Human Face of God* (1973), and *Redating the New Testament* (1976). ▷ Anglican Communion

Roger of Taizé, Brother, originally **Roger Louis Schutz-Marsauche** (1915–) Swiss founder of the Taizé Community, born in Provence, the son of a Protestant pastor. In 1940 he went to Taizé, a French hamlet between Cluny and Citeaux, to establish a community devoted to reconciliation and peace in Church and society. Since Easter 1949, when the first seven brothers took their vows, this vision has attracted thousands of pilgrims, especially young people drawn by the distinctive worship in the Church of Reconciliation, which was built in 1962. His publications include *The Dynamic of the Provisional* (1965), *Violent for Peace* (1968), and several volumes of extracts from his journal. ▷ Taizé

Rolle of Hampole, Richard (c.1290–1349) English hermit, mystic and poet, born in Thornton, Yorkshire. He studied at Oxford, but at 19 became a hermit, first at Dalton and then at Hampole, near Doncaster. He wrote lyrics, meditations and religious works in Latin and English, and translated and expounded the Psalms in prose.

Roman Catholicism The doctrine, worship, and life of the Roman Catholic Church. A direct line of succession is claimed from the earliest Christian communities, centring on the city of Rome, where St Peter (claimed as the first Bishop of Rome) was martyred and St Paul witnessed. After the conversion of the emperor Constantine, Roman bishops acquired something of the authority and power of the emperor. Surviving the fall of Rome in the 5th century, the Church was the only effective agency of civilization in Europe, and after the 11th-century schism with the Byzantine or Eastern Church it was the dominant force in the Western world, the Holy Roman Empire. The Protestant Reformation of the 16th century inspired revival, and the need to restate doctrine in an unambiguous form and to purge the church and clergy of abuses and corruption was recognized. The most dramatic reforms were enacted by the two Vatican Councils of the 19th and 20th centuries. The Second Vatican Council signalled a new era, with a new ecumenical spirit pervading the Church. Although the doctrines of the faith remained largely untouched, there was a new openness to other Christian denominations—indeed, to other world religions. Great emphasis was placed on the Church as the 'people of God', with the laity being given a much more active part in liturgy (eg the Mass being said in the vernacular instead of Latin).

Doctrine is declared by the pope, or by a General Council with the approval of the pope, and is summarized in the Nicene Creed. Scripture is authoritative, and authoritatively interpreted by the *magisterium* or teaching office of the Church. The tradition of the Church is accepted as authoritative, special importance being attributed to the early church Fathers and to the medieval scholastics, notably St Thomas Aquinas. Principal doctrines are similar to those of mainstream Protestant and Orthodox Churches—God as Trinity, creation, redemption, the person and work of Jesus Christ and the place of the Holy Spirit—the chief doctrinal differences being the role of the Church in salvation, and its sacramental theology. Modern liturgies reflect a cross-section of historical inheritance, cultural environment, and social factors. Ancient traditional practices such as the veneration of the Virgin Mary and the saints, or the Stations of the Cross, are still regarded as valuable aids to devotion. At the other extreme, Roman Catholic priests in South America, preaching liberation theology, have assumed a political role, for which they have been rebuked by Rome.

The hierarchy of the Church includes cardinals, bishops, priests, and several minor orders. Many religious orders, male and female, exist within the Church. The vast and complex organization of the Church is controlled by the Vatican, an independent state in Rome which, under the direction of the pope, implements Church policy, and administers property and finance. In predominantly Catholic countries, the Church maintains a degree of political influence, and extends canon law into the realm of civil law, notably on moral issues (eg birth control). ▷ Aquinas, St Thomas; Bible; bishop; cardinal; Constantine I; Council of the Church; Counter-Reformation; ecumenism; God; Holy Spirit; Jesus Christ; liberation theology; liturgy; Mary; Mass; Nicene Creed; papacy; Paul, St; Peter, St; priest; sacrament; salvation; Stations of the Cross; theology; Trinity; Vatican Councils

Roman Curia (Latin *curia*, 'court') An organization in the Vatican (Rome) which administers the affairs of the Roman Catholic Church under the authority of the pope. It is comprised of congregations (administrative), tribunals (judicial), and offices (ministerial), all as defined in canon law. ▷ papacy; Roman Catholicism

Roman religion The first Romans were farmers and lived in a world full of *numen*, a powerful spiritual force behind appearances waiting to be revealed, and *genius*, the spirit of an ancestor, or a locality. Etruscan and Italic deities were absorbed, and a priestly college was established, presided over by the *pontifex maximus*. By Cicero's time the diversity of cults had been organized into uniformity throughout most of Italy. Augustus took the title of *pontifex* for himself, and reaffirmed the ancient worship. The Romans believed that all peoples worshipped the same gods under different names (eg Mercury = Hermes), and so had no difficulty in absorbing Greek mythology, having nothing comparable themselves. After Augustus' death the worship of the emperor became a religious duty, but increasingly exotic foreign cults flourished. When Constantine accepted Christianity in 312, the ancient Roman religion became 'paganism', ie the practices of country people. ▷ Constantine I; Greek religion

Romans, Letter to the A New Testament book, often considered the most significant of the works of the apostle Paul. Although Paul did not establish the Church in Rome, he wrote to it (perhaps c.55–8) to present his understanding of salvation for both Gentiles and Jews, and to warn against libertine and legalistic interpretations of the Christian message. Chapters 1–8 set out his understanding of justification and salvation; Chapters 9–11 address the problem of Israel's unbelief; Chapters 12–16 deal with Christian living and community relationships. ▷ New Testament; Paul, St

Rome, early Christian Church at Paul's Epistle to the Romans, written in 57CE, probably while he was at Corinth on his third missionary journey, shows that he was addressing a large church that was mostly, but not entirely, Gentile in origin. He had not visited Rome at that point, but knew quite a number of the Christians by name. It is not known how Christianity reached Rome—it may have happened through the conversion of Roman Jews who were present in Jerusalem at the first Pentecost in 30CE (Acts 2.10).

After Paul exercised his rights as a Roman citizen to appeal to Caesar to judge the case brought against him by the Jewish authorities, he was under house-arrest in Rome (59–61 or 61–3), before his final imprisonment and execution in 64 or 68. The apostle Peter is also said to have been martyred in Rome. Nero (65) was the first of many Roman emperors to persecute the Church, until the conversion of Constantine (312) made Christianity a tolerated and favoured religion. With the rise of the ecclesiastical influence of the church in Rome came the assertion that the apostle Peter was its first bishop, and the claim of Roman Catholicism that this proved that subsequent bishops of Rome (popes) had unique authority over the whole Christian church through apostolic succession. ▷ apostolic succession; biblical history; papacy; Paul, St; Peter, St; Roman Catholicism; Romans, Letter to the

Romero y Galdames, Oscar Arnulfo (1917–80) Salvadorean Roman Catholic prelate, born in Ciudad Barrios. Ordained in 1942, and generally conservative in outlook, he was made bishop in 1970 and (to the dismay of progressives) archbishop in 1977. However, acts of political violence and repression of the poor made his public utterances and actions more outspoken. After thousands had died in a brutal state persecution the archbishop himself was murdered while preaching, one year after he was nominated for the Nobel Peace Prize by a large number of American and British parliamentarians. Some of his 'Thoughts' appeared in translation (by James Brockman) as *The Church Is All of You* (1984). ▷ Roman Catholicism

rosary A form of religious meditation, found in several religions, in which a sequence of prayers is recited using a string of beads or a knotted cord, each bead or knot representing one prayer in the sequence. In Christianity it most commonly refers to the Rosary of the Blessed Virgin Mary, one of the most popular of Roman Catholic devotions. This is a sequence of one Our Father, 10 Hail Marys, and one Glory Be to the Father (a decade), repeated 15 times (in the full version) or five times (in the more commonly used shorter version), each decade being associated with a particular 'mystery' or meditation on an aspect of the life of Christ or the Virgin Mary. It probably dates from the 13th century. ▷ Jesus Christ; Mary; meditation; Roman Catholicism

Rosenzweig, Franz (1886–1929) German theologian, born in Kassel into a Jewish family. He first studied medicine, then switched to modern history and philosophy and did his doctoral dissertation on Hegel's political philosophy. But he came to react against Hegel and German idealism in favour of an existential approach that emphasized the experience and interests of the individual. He was on the point of converting from Judaism to Christianity, but a critical religious experience in 1913 caused him to reaffirm his Jewishness and devote the rest of his life to the study and practice of Judaism. His major work was *Der Stern der Erlösung* ('The Star of Redemption'), begun while on active service in World War I and published in 1921. From 1922 he suffered progressive paralysis, but still collaborated with Martin Buber from 1925 on a new German translation of the Hebrew Bible, and after his death exercised a profound influence on Jewish religious thought. ▷ Buber, Martin; existentialism; Hegel, Georg Wilhelm Friedrich; idealism; Judaism

Rosh Hashanah The Jewish New Year (1 Tishri), which falls in September or October. During the New Year's Day service, a ram's horn is blown as a call to repentance and spiritual renewal. ▷ Judaism

Rosicrucianism An esoteric movement which spread across Europe in the early 17th century. In 1614–15 two pamphlets appeared in Germany and were attributed to Christian Rosenkreutz (1378–1484), who claimed to possess occult powers based on scientific and alchemical knowledge he had brought from the East. He founded the Order of the Rosy Cross, and the pamphlets invited men of learning to join. No trace of the Order has been found, but many occult organizations claim Rosicrucian origins. ▷ alchemy; mysticism; occult

Ruether, Rosemary Radford (1936–) American theologian, born in Minneapolis. Professor of Applied Theology at Garrett-Evangelical theological seminary, Evanston, she has written extensively on women and theological issues. Her books, analysing the effects of male bias in official Church theology and seeking to affirm the feminine dimension of religion and the importance of women's experience, include *New Woman/New Earth* (1975), *Mary: The Feminine Face of the Church* (1979), *Sexism and God-Talk* (1983), and *Women—Church* (1985). ▷ feminist theology

Ruh (Rūḥ) The Arabic word for 'spirit' as conceived in the Muslim tradition. It was sometimes contrasted with *nafs*, meaning 'self' or 'soul'. The inference was that ruh was the higher perfected spirit within human beings, whereas nafs was the lower passionate soul. According to Suhrawardi the spirit was the source of good, the soul was the source of evil, and they were in conflict. For Muslims the spirit is everlasting; at death it goes to heaven for preliminary judgement before returning to the tomb to await the final judgement. The spirits of certain notable people, such as prophets and martyrs, go straight to heaven at death rather than having to await final judgement. Ruh in a person is part of the essence of God; it is that faculty which makes humans higher than animals and even higher than angels. The name Ruh Allah (Spirit of God) is given to Jesus in the Quran (4.169). ▷ Allah; Jesus Christ; judgement of the dead, Islamic view of; martyrs; prophets; Suhrawardi

Rumi (Jalāl ad-Din ar-Rūmī) (1207–73) Muslim mystic, born in Bulkh, Persia. He and his family were eventually invited by the Sultan of Rum to live at Iconium (present-day Konya) in Turkey (his name came from this association). He became a religious teacher and poet, and was influenced mystically by Tabrizi, who had a deep spiritual effect upon him. Rumi founded the Mevlevi Sufi order in Iconium, which has become celebrated for the music and dancing of its 'whirling dervishes'. He was in Baghdad in 1258 just before it was sacked by the Mongols, and the spiritual response of his writings to that trauma is sometimes compared to St Augustine's response to the sack of Rome by the Huns in 410. His six-volume *Mathnawi* is the best-known of his works. Containing stories and poetry of exceptional spiritual excellence and insight, it has become a treasure-house of Persian literature and Sufi mysticism. He remained a major influence upon Sufism in particular and the non-Arab Muslim world in general, and his followers sometimes claim to have a present experience of his nearness. In some ways he was unorthodox, for example in his belief in rebirth and in his universalism, which encompassed religions other than Islam. Yet his stress upon the spiritual eye being more important than the body, and upon heavenly models being more important than earthly forms continues to influence the Muslim consciousness. His tomb in Konya is still a place of pilgrimage. ▷ Augustine, St (of Hippo); dervish; Mevlevis; Mongols; Sufism

Russell, Bertrand Arthur William, 3rd Earl Russell (1872–1970) Welsh philosopher, mathematician, prolific author and controversial public figure throughout his long and extraordinarily active life. He was born in Trelleck, Gwent; his parents died when he was very young and he was brought up by his grandmother, the widow of Lord John Russell, the Liberal prime minister and 1st Earl. He was educated privately and at Trinity College, Cambridge, where he took first-class honours in mathematics and philosophy. He graduated in 1894, was briefly British Embassy attaché in Paris, and became a fellow of Trinity in 1895, shortly after his marriage to Alys Pearsall Smith. A visit to Berlin led to his first book, *German Social Democracy* (1896), and he was thus launched on an amazingly long, wide-ranging and fertile intellectual career.

His most original contributions to mathematical logic and philosophy are generally agreed to belong to the period before World War I, as expounded for example in *The Principles of Mathematics* (1903), which argues that the whole of mathematics could be derived from logic, and the monumental *Principia Mathematica* (with Alfred North Whitehead, 1910–13), which worked out this programme in a fully developed formal system and stands as a landmark in the history of logic and mathematics. Russell's famous 'theory of types' and his 'theory of descriptions' belong to this same period. Wittgenstein came to Cambridge to study under him from 1912 to 1913 and began the work that led to the *Tractatus Logico-philosophicus* (1922), for the English version of which Russell wrote an introduction. Russell wrote his first genuinely popular work in 1912, *The Problems of Philosophy*, which can still be read as a brilliantly stimulating introduction to the subject. Politics became his dominant concern during World War I and his active pacifism caused the loss of his Trinity fellowship in 1916 and his imprisonment in 1918, during the course of which he wrote his *Introduction to Mathematical Philosophy* (1919). He had now to make a living by lecturing and journalism, and became a celebrated controversialist. He visited the USSR, where he met Lenin, Trotsky and Gorky, which sobered his early enthusiasm for communism and led to the critical *Theory and Practice of Bolshevism* (1919). He also taught in Peking from 1920 to 1921. In 1921 he married his second wife, Dora Black, and with her founded (in 1927) and ran a progressive school near Petersfield; he set out his educational views in *On Education* (1926) and *Education and the Social Order* (1932). In 1931 he succeeded his elder brother, John, 2nd Earl Russell, as 3rd Earl Russell. His second divorce (1934) and marriage to Patricia Spence (1936) helped to make controversial his book *Marriage and Morals* (1932); and his lectureship at City College, New York, was terminated in 1940 after complaints that he was an 'enemy of religion and morality', though he later won substantial damages for wrongful dismissal. The rise of fascism led him to renounce his pacifism in 1939; his fellowship at Trinity was restored in 1944, and he returned to England after the war to be honoured with an OM, and to give the first BBC Reith Lectures in 1949.

He was awarded the Nobel Prize for Literature in 1950. He had meanwhile continued publishing important philosophical work, mainly on epistemology, in such books as *The Analysis of Mind* (1921), *An Enquiry into Meaning and Truth* (1940) and *Human Knowledge: Its Scope and Limits* (1948), and in 1945 published the best-selling *History of Western Philosophy*. He also published a stream of popular and provocative works on social, moral and religious questions, some of the more celebrated essays later being collected in *Why I am not a Christian* (1957). After

1949 he became increasingly preoccupied with the cause of nuclear disarmament, taking a leading role in CND and later the Committee of 100, and engaging in a remarkable correspondence with various world leaders. In 1961 he was again imprisoned, with his fourth and final wife, Edith Finch, for his part in a sit-down demonstration in Whitehall. His last years were spent in North Wales, and he retained to the end his lucidity, independence of mind and humour. His last major publications were three volumes of *Autobiography* (1967–9). ▷ fascism; Whitehead, Alfred North; Wittgenstein, Ludwig Josef Johann

Russian Orthodox Church A Church originating from missionary activity of the see of Constantinople of the Orthodox Church, with a community organized in Kiev in the 9th century. In 988 Christianity was declared the official faith; in the 14th century Moscow became the see of the metropolitan; and in the 15th century the Church declared itself autonomous. It existed in a state of tension with the emperor, and after the Revolution of 1917 was separated from the state and suffered persecution. Gaining some recognition as a result of its support of the authorities in World War II, it was largely controlled by government agencies. It reflected the Byzantine or Greek tradition until the 19th century, when a new translation of the Bible was approved, and in the 20th century there was some revival of interest on the part of the intelligentsia, conscious of the role the Church had played in Russian art and culture. The contemporary Russian Church retains fidelity in doctrine and liturgy to its Orthodox inheritance, but is also developing its national character. ▷ Bible; Christianity; liturgy; Old Believers; Orthodox Church

Ruth, Book of A book of the Hebrew Bible/Old Testament, presenting a popular story ostensibly set in the time of Israel's tribal judges, but named after its central character, Ruth. Ruth's mother, Naomi, arranges a levirate marriage of Ruth to Boaz, the rich kinsman of Naomi's deceased husband, upon their return to Judah from Moab; Ruth became the mother of Obed, grandfather of David. Usually dated c.5th–4th century BCE, it is significant for its liberal attitudes to non-Israelites and mixed marriages, since Ruth was a Moabitess. ▷ David; Naomi; Old Testament

Ruysbroeck, Jan van (1293–1381) Flemish Catholic mystic, born in Ruysbroeck near Brussels. Ordained priest at 24, he was Vicar of St Gudule's, Brussels. He left in 1343 to found a monastery at Groenendael, of which he later became prior. His spirituality, expressed in *The Kingdom of the Lovers of God* and other works, simplified in the *Adornment of the Spiritual Marriage* (also known as *The Spiritual Espousals*), links the school of Rhineland mysticism (Eckhart, Heinrich Suso (c.1295–1366), and Tauler) and the *Devotio Moderna* of Geert de Groote (1340–84), the *Brethren of the Common Life*, and *The Imitation of Christ* of Thomas à Kempis. ▷ Eckhart, Johannes; Kempis, Thomas à; Tauler, Johann

Ryobu Shinto A syncretistic movement within Japan that brought together Shinto and Buddhist elements in 'dual-aspect' Shinto. It is said to have been influenced by the thought of Gyogi (670–749) and Kukai (774–835), and in it Shinto accepted the Shingon Buddhist idea that the world can be seen through two mandalas or world-pictures that bring together seemingly different things on the pattern of Taoist teaching that there is a harmony between opposites (yin and yang). Thus Shinto *kami* (sacred powers) and Buddhist deities could be co-ordinated, and at the great Ise temple Amaterasu the Shinto sun goddess became equated with Vairocana the sun Buddha as the deities featured in its inner and outer shrines. As Buddhist temples spread around the Japanese countryside, joint Shinto-Buddhist buildings served by joint priesthoods sometimes came into being, and Shinto ethical and philosophical insights were deepened by their contact with Buddhism. In 1868 Ryobu Shinto was proscribed because its syncretism was deemed unworthy of true Shinto, and the differences between Shinto and Buddhism were stressed. Since World War II the co-operative motif stressed by Ryobu Shinto has re-emerged in Shinto, Buddhism, and elements of some of the new Japanese religions. ▷ Amaterasu; Ise shrines; kami; Kukai; mandala; Japanese new religions; Shingon; Shinto; Vairocana; yin and yang

S

Sabbath, or **Shabbat** (Hebrew 'cessation', 'rest') The seventh day of the week, which in Jewish belief is designated a day of rest and cessation from labour, beginning just before sunset on Fridays and lasting until nightfall on Saturday, when candles are lit to signify the end of a holy time. The laws of Sabbath observance derive from a short ban found in the Pentateuch (Exodus 20.8–11; 31.12–17) and from God's own rest in the Genesis creation account. Rabbinic regulations specify 39 forbidden activities, which are then further elaborated, but in more liberal Reform Judaism the Sabbath is mainly a day of worship. ▷ Judaism; Pentateuch; rabbi; Reform Judaism

Sacerdotes Roman priests. The concept of a priest within Roman religion was different from that of a Christian priest: no training, no personal belief and engagement, and no full-time occupation were needed. To define priests in Rome is difficult since their recruitment, organization, duty and duration of service differed. Most priests were male, a famous exception being the Vestal Virgins. Public priesthoods could be held collectively or restricted to an individual (eg the *flamines* who were attached to one precise god). The four main groups were the college of *pontifices* (in charge of keeping liturgic tradition), the college of augurs (who took and deciphered *auspicia*), the college of 10, later 15 men (the *quindecemviri sacris faciundis* who guarded and consulted the Sybilline Books after a *prodigium*), and the college of seven men (the *septemviri epulones* in charge of public games and their associated sacrifices). The main function of public priests was to act on request as expert advisers. Priests could be patricians or plebeians, but most of the famous priesthoods were held by senators as part of their political career. In private religion the functions and role of a priest were assumed by the *paterfamilias* (head of the household). ▷ auspicia; prodigia; Roman religion; Vestal Virgins

Sach-Khand The highest stage of spiritual ascent in Sikh mysticism. Translated as the 'realm of truth', it is the fifth and final stage of spiritual attainment, the realm of bliss and harmony, wherein a believer passes beyond rebirth and attains union with God at the culmination of a spiritual journey. This stage is reached by a pattern of disciplined meditation and worship, and by leading a moral life in the everyday world. It constitutes an experience which is difficult to express in words. This notion of Sach-Khand was stressed by the first Sikh guru, Guru Nanak, and it remains a traditional Sikh concept. More popularly it has come to mean the Abode of the Formless One, a kind of heaven to which one goes after death. ▷ Akal Purukh; Nam; Nanak; Sat Guru

sacrament A Christian rite understood as an outward and visible sign of an internal and spiritual grace. Orthodox and Roman Catholic Churches recognize seven sacraments: baptism, confirmation, the Eucharist (Mass), penance, extreme unction, holy orders (ordination), and matrimony. Protestant Churches recognize only baptism and the Eucharist (Communion) as sacraments. ▷ anointing the sick; baptism; confirmation; Eucharist; Orthodox Church; penance; Protestantism; Roman Catholicism

sacred and profane Religion is often defined in terms of the sacred as distinct from the profane. The words come from the Latin *sacrum*, meaning a sacred place belonging to a god, and *profanum*, meaning the place in front of a temple. In this sense some buildings are set apart as sacred, and what lies outside them belongs to the profane world. In a wider sense the notion of the sacred has to some extent been identified with what is religious, and the notion of the profane with what is not religious. The sacred has been seen in terms of that which was separate, holy, awesome, remote and other. Rudolf Otto aligned the idea of the holy to the idea of the sacred as that which was numinous, awesome and reducible to reason. However, as Mircea Eliade points out, the sacred is revealed in the profane, and anything that humans have ever handled, come in contact with, or loved can reveal the sacred. If the sacred is seen as that which is worshipped and worthy of respect, as that which reveals 'being' and has real meaning, then modern Western humanity's sacred is the material—in other words, it is the profane. The problem for

Westerners, according to Eliade, is to recapture a sense of the sacred as separate from, although revealed in, the profane. ▷ Eliade, Mircea; Otto, Rudolf

sacred dance Dance carried out as part of religious ritual. In many primitive societies dance occupies the place reserved for prayer and worship in the major religions. Rites of passage and major events in the life of the community can also be marked by dancing.
The origins of sacred dance are shrouded in the mists of time and it is difficult, perhaps impossible, to establish with certainty why this form of worship should have developed. It may be that it originated as a result of primitive peoples' desire to imitate the movement of the supernatural beings they believed to permeate and control the natural world. Many primitive societies claim that they were taught their sacred dances by their gods. Other sacred dances seem to have arisen as a conscious effort to imitate the movements of an animal held in particular reverence by a community. Thus the Plains Indians in the USA perform a 'buffalo dance' in which they imitate buffaloes and recreate the stages of a buffalo-hunt. In Islam sacred dance was practised above all by the Sufis, who aimed to induce a state of religious ecstasy by means of wild, energetic dancing. Dance played a central role in their worship with each movement representing a spiritual truth. Sacred dance has for the most part been a peripheral phenomenon in Christianity. However, in the 20th century there has been a revival of this form of worship and some churches, particularly those influenced by the charismatic movement, have introduced them as part of their divine worship. ▷ rituals

sacred geometry The notion that there is some sort of correlation between geometry and the sacred buildings and texts of various religious traditions. For example, cubic dimensions are present in sacred buildings such as the Greek altar at Delphi, the chapel of the Egyptian goddess Leto at Buto, the Holy of Holies in the temple of Solomon, the Sumerian ark, and the Vedic fire altar. The Black Stone at Mecca, which is sacred to Muslims, is housed in the Kabah, which means literally 'cube'. In early times the artefacts of neolithic religion were decorated with geometrical designs that seemed to identify order and aesthetics with a sense of the sacred. A musical geometry was at the heart of Plato's maths, and Chinese and Greek cosmology relied on the insights of tonal geometry. For example 64 and 108 are important, and there are 64 hexagrams in the significant Chinese text, the *I Ching*, and 108 beads in Buddhist rosaries. Euclid's *Elements* transformed geometry into a more rational system which was influential in the rise of modern science. Scientific insights from Einstein onwards have weakened the apparent certainty of Euclid's rational geometry, and rekindled an interest in the sacred geometry built into more recent religious structures such as Christian cathedrals, as well as into the notion of aesthetic symmetry that is present in complementary ways in geometry and religion. ▷ cathedral; cosmology; Delphi; I Ching; Mecca; neolithic religion; Plato; rosary; Solomon

sacred marriage (or **hieros gamos**), **Ancient Near Eastern** In Ancient Mesopotamia there is evidence for the practice of sacred marriage from Sumerian times (3rd millennium BCE). This was normally a ritual union between the king and the goddess of the city, who was represented by her priestess or by one of the king's wives, and helped establish the king's rule and ensure the fertility of the land. A prototype can be found in the Sumerian myth of the divine lovers Dumuzi and Inanna (the Babylonian Tammuz and Ishtar). Sacred marriage was part of Sumerian New Year festivals and probably also of the Akitu festival at Babylon. Evidence for the practice outside Mesopotamia is more fragmentary, although there are good grounds for believing it was part of Canaanite ritual. Ritual sexual intercourse served by analogy to strengthen the powers of nature and fertility and can also be seen in the widespread practice of cultic prostitution which was so condemned by the authors of the Hebrew Bible. ▷ Akitu; Ishtar; kingship, Ancient Near Eastern; New Year festivals, Ancient Near Eastern

sacred mountains, Japanese During the course of human history various natural phenomena have been deemed to be sacred by different peoples. In Japan, mountains have been vested with sacredness by the people in general and by some groups in particular. Reasons for this include the Japanese love for natural beauty, and the idea that mountains take humans up towards heaven, and bring the *kami* down towards earth. In addition to a natural reverence for mountains in Japan, there is a particular reverence for special mountains. The main sacred mountain is Mount Fuji, which was especially revered by a Shinto group who worshipped the Great Deity of Mount Fuji (*Sengen Daishin*). Similarly, Mount Ontake was revered by another

Mount Fuji, sacred mountain of Japan

Shinto group who worshipped the Great Deity of Mount Ontake (*Ontake Okami*). Other sacred mountains too have their own kami. An interesting aspect of Japanese mountain veneration has been the climbing of mountains for religious reasons. Mountain ascetics known as *yamabushi* climbed mountains in medieval times for spiritual reward and power, and a religious movement known as Shugendo formed around them. Pilgrims still climb mountains such as Fuji for religious reasons, aiming to arrive at the top by sunrise, where they worship at the Shinto shrine. Some still wear the traditional white robe and straw sandals and carry a staff on their two-day pilgrimage. ▷ kami; pilgrimage; shrines, Shinto; Shugendo

sacrifice The renunciation of something of value and its transferral to a supernatural being or power. Although usually understood as the slaughter of animals or even human beings ('blood offerings'), sacrifice is a broad term and encompasses a variety of ways of presenting offerings to the Divine. Thus in some societies, particularly in food-gathering and in some agricultural societies, so-called 'bloodless offerings' such as crops, milk, cakes and even items of clothing, weapons, jewellery and money were offered up to the deity. In the higher religions sacrifice has increasingly come to be understood as the human being's self-giving and self-abnegating commitment to God. Asceticism, fasting, celibacy, renunciation of possessions, etc, have come to be understood as the highest forms of sacrifice. The purpose of sacrifice is to establish or maintain good relations with the supernatural world. This is necessary so that the community continues to receive those blessings upon which it is dependent for its survival. To achieve this, three forms of sacrifice may be practised. Firstly, sacrifices may be made in order to bribe the deity to bestow his blessings upon the sacrificer. Secondly, sacrifices may be performed as thanksgiving for what the sacrificer has received. Thirdly, sacrifices may be carried out to atone for breaches that have come about in the community's relationship with the Divine. Natural disasters such as famine and plague, military defeat, and so on, are regarded as indications that the community has fallen out of favour with the supernatural world. In such cases, the sin of the community is often transferred onto a 'scapegoat', which is offered as an atoning sacrifice in the community's place. The Christian doctrine of atonement can be understood as a sophisticated form of this type of sacrifice. For Christians Christ's death on the cross constitutes the ultimate and perfect sacrifice that redeems humankind from its sins and makes redundant all other forms of sacrifice. ▷ haoma; human sacrifice, Israelite; human sacrifice, Meso-American; ritual slaughter; sacrifice, Ancient Israelite

sacrifice, Ancient Israelite From earliest times to the destruction of the third temple in 70CE, sacrifice played a central part in the worship of Ancient Israel. Only certain ritually clean domestic animals could be killed; their blood, thought of as the seat of life, was splashed or smeared on the altar, then all or part of the carcass was burned as an offering to Yahweh. Cereal offerings of flour or cakes were also burned on the altar. Two types of animal sacrifice predominated, the burnt offering or holocaust in which a whole animal was burned on the altar, and the peace offering where only the blood and suet of the animal were burned, the meat being divided between the priest and the owner for food. An elaborate ritual for sacrifice was developed, especially in the post-exilic period, which is found in the book of Leviticus. Here there are detailed regulations for all kinds of sacrifice, including daily temple sacrifices, public and private sacrifices, guilt offerings and sin offerings. The sacrificial cult was centred on the Jerusalem Temple from the time of Josiah (late 7th century BCE) onwards, and ceased when the temple was finally destroyed; the synagogue worship of the Jewish communities in Palestine and the diaspora did not involve sacrifice. ▷ human sacrifice, Israelite; Yahweh

sadaqah (ṣaḍaqah) A Muslim word meaning at one level the voluntary giving of alms to those in need, and at another level a certain view of truth (from *sadaqa* 'to speak truth' or 'to be true'). At the first level it refers in a general sense to deeds of kindness, and in a particular sense to the giving of grain or money to the needy at the time of the Id festival which occurs at the end of the fast of Ramadan. It is different from *zakah*, which is the structured and required giving of alms, and which is one of the five pillars of Islam. At the second level it expands into the more general meaning of 'truth' in a personal rather than a philosophical sense. It does not signify propositional truth whereby certain verbally stated propositions are held to be true or false; rather it signifies personal truth in the sense of being true and living righteously, and is a facet of character rather than merely an attribute of mind or of philosophical accuracy. ▷ almsgiving; five pillars, Islamic; Id; Ramadan; truth

saddha (saddhā; Sanskrit: sraddhā) The Buddhist notion of faith or trust. It is important at the beginning of the Buddhist way as a kind of provisional acceptance of the truth of Buddhism prior to it being verified experientially. It is also an important factor on the path and can be seen formally in three ways: as devotion, as spiritual energy, and as belief. In the Theravada tradition it tends to be subordinated to wisdom, whereas in the Mahayana tradition it is equal to wisdom. The objects of Buddhist faith are mainly the three refuges: the Buddha, the teaching (dharma) of the Buddha, and the Buddhist community or sangha. However, faith is not centred upon belief or authority as such: it is not meaningful until it is personally apprehended. ▷ Buddha; dharma; faith; prajna; sangha; Theravada Buddhism; wisdom

Sadducees A major party within Judaism (c.2nd century BCE–70CE), the name probably deriving from the priest Zadok, whose descendants held priestly office from Solomon's time. They were mainly aristocrats, associated with the Jerusalem priesthood (with the high priest from among their number), and influential in Israel's political and economic life. Josephus suggests that they differed from the Pharisees by their denials of the legal force of oral traditions, of bodily resurrection, and of divine determinism. ▷ Josephus, Flavius; Judaism; Pharisees; Solomon; Zadokites

sadhu A wandering ascetic or holy man in Hinduism. Sadhus are renouncers who have dedicated themselves completely to a god of the Hindu pantheon, and are revered, especially those who practise asceticism (*tapas*). They are often initiated as children, but adult conversions to sadhuism are common. They have few possessions and are clothed either in saffron or are naked (*naga sadhus*) and are smeared in ashes as a symbol of penance. There are some female sadhus, and some sadhus are allowed to marry, although usually they are celibate. Sadhu adepts are thought to have magical powers or *siddhis*, and can perform all kinds of superhuman and psychic acts, and often make a living doing so. The great festival, Kumbha Mela, sees the congregation of sadhus from all over India providing an overwhelming show of religious austerities. Ritual suicide sometimes occurs as sadhus are said to know the correct time to die, and in Hindu social terms are ritually dead anyway. Generally, sadhus are pacificist, but some are militaristic, being regarded as defenders of the faith. Sadhu sorcerers and black magicians are greatly feared. ▷ Kumbha Mela; tapas

sagas A body of Icelandic literature, mostly of the 12th and 13th centuries CE, some dealing with the lives of kings of Norway, others with various Icelandic families and other distinguished people in the Norse world. Contrary to former belief, they are literary compositions—and some of the greatest of medieval times—not just oral recitals in written form. They come from Christian times, and must be used with caution, though not necessarily scepticism, as regards their accounts of pre-Christian religion in the north. The sagas tell us something about pre-Christian religious practices and attitudes, but they do not give us the insight into myths and ideas that we find in Snorri Sturluson's *Edda* (also composed in Christian times, but using early material) and in *Voluspa* and other old Norse poetry. ▷ Edda; Sturluson, Snorri; Voluspa

Sahaj A term used in a number of Indian religions, meaning bliss, peace, and spiritual harmony. It is especially important in the Sikh tradition, where it indicates a state of spiritual joy attained in life at the climax of a spiritual journey. This journey, which goes through five stages, results in a sense of union with God. A concept similar to the Hindu notion of *jivanmukti* (ie being 'released' while still alive), it involves total God-centredness and a continual practice of the presence of God. This state is attained by means of disciplined meditation, worship, and ethical living centred upon the Name and Will and Word of God, and is associated with the Realm of Truth (*Sach-Khand*), the highest stage of spiritual ascent. Although having passed beyond the cycle of birth and rebirth, one who knows sahaj—which amounts to salvation—is still alive and physically present on earth. ▷ jivanmukti; Sach-Khand

Sahajayana (Sahajayāna) One of the four main forms of Tantric Buddhism which developed as a later and separate school within the Mahayana Buddhist tradition. The first Tantric form (*Mantrayana*) stressed the use of mantras, mystical sayings which are given by a guru to a pupil on his initiation and are repeated regularly. The second Tantric form (*Vajrayana*) stressed the visualization of transcendent Buddhas and bodhisattvas by means of mandalas, circular maps of the transcendent world. The third Tantric form (*Kalacakrayana*) developed as a kind of spiritual astrology centred on the Primal Buddha named Kalacakra. Sahajayana, which arose in the 8th century CE in eastern India, was the fourth form. It stated that it was wrong to consider worldly existence and liberation (*samsara* and nirvana) as different. They are twinned (*sahaja*) and are within each other. It reacted against the use of mantras, external observances and systematic thought, and stressed the role of insight in gaining liberation. In life-style it tended towards spontaneity and reacted against the Buddhist establishment, accepting women and sexuality as being natural and on the level of the sacred, so that sexual union could be incorporated in the sphere of enlightenment. In and after the 8th century CE, Sahajayana mystics such as Saraha in his *Dohakosa* spread their ideas in their mystical poems, and Sahajayana Buddhism lingered on in eastern India after it had disappeared elsewhere in the land where Buddhism was born. ▷ Adi-Buddha; Mahayana Buddhism; mandala; mantra; nirvana; samsara; Tantric Buddhism; vipassana

Saicho (767–822) Founder of the Tendai school of Japanese Buddhism. In 866 he was given the posthumous title of Daishi (Great Master), and is commonly known as Dengyo Daishi. He took his vows in 786, and in 804 was sent by the emperor Kammu to China, where he studied the Tien Tai teachings of Chinese Buddhism. He brought these teachings back to Japan as Tendai in 805, and it became a unifying factor in Japanese Buddhism. He expounded the Lotus Sutra, and stressed the importance of everyone realizing the Buddha nature that is already part of each individual's own consciousness. Saicho had influence in the Japanese court; he built an important monastery on Mount Hiei just outside Kyoto, he built the first Lotus Sutra meditation hall in 812, and he introduced elements of esoteric Shingon Buddhism into Tendai. Thus Tendai Buddhism under Saicho was already a broad synthesis, and it is perhaps no accident that three important but different schools of Japanese Buddhism—the Pure Land, Zen, and Nichiren traditions—arose from Tendai origins. ▷ Buddha nature; Kammu; Lotus Sutra; Nichiren Buddhism; Pure Land Buddhism; Shingon; Tendai; Tien Tai; Zen Buddhism

saint In Roman Catholic and Orthodox teaching, a man or woman recognized as being in heaven because of special qualities. In the New Testament, all Christian believers are referred to as saints, but in the 2nd century, veneration of saints (often martyrs) began, and individual saints were eventually looked to for intercession and devotion. The practice of veneration was forbidden by 16th-century Reformers, but continued in the Orthodox and Roman Catholic Churches. An elaborate procedure is required before canonization may proceed. In Buddhism, a saint is anyone who has lived a pure and holy life, such as a bodhisattva or *arahat*. ▷ arahat; bodhisattva; canonization; martyr; Orthodox Church; Reformation; Roman Catholicism; saints in Islam

saint, Christian view of In biblical thought, holiness applies primarily to God and secondarily to the people he calls to be like him. The Jews were called to be the holy people of God, and the early Christians saw themselves as the new Israel, likewise called to be holy. Consequently, the apostle Paul addresses all the recipients of his epistles as saints, however far short they had fallen from their vocation. In his understanding, they were made holy both by their call and by the Holy Spirit working in them, a process of transformation that would be completed only in the afterlife. However, by the 2nd century, respect for outstanding living Christians had become veneration for the dead martyrs, and by the 4th century 'confessors and virgins' were honoured along with them. Prayers for the saints to intercede on behalf of the living arose from the belief that there was an unbroken 'communion of saints' of earth and heaven.

From the 11th and 12th centuries the Roman Catholic Church developed a formal procedure for canonizing or giving universal recognition to Christians thought to deserve the description 'saint'. Their lives are examined for evidence of supernatural sanctity and heroic Christian virtues such as joy, and for miracles performed during their lifetime or invoked through prayer for their aid. This legal process usually takes many decades, though exceptions have occurred: St Therèse of Lisieux was canonized in 1925 and the Auschwitz martyr St Maximilian Kolbe (1894–1941) was beatified in 1971. Those who have been canonized may be invoked in public prayer, have services offered in their honour (especially on their festival days), have church buildings dedicated to them, and have their relics honoured. In Christian art they are conventionally depicted as surrounded by heavenly light.

Following the medieval explosion of veneration of the saints, and the abuses of bogus relics, legendary miracles, and the sale of indulgences, the Reformation churches rejected the idea of individual saints other than the New Testament apostles, and dismissed much of the devotion to the Virgin Mary. There is no Protestant alternative to canonization for recognizing sainthood, but some churches of the Anglican Communion have liturgical calendars that include optional commemorations of noteworthy post-Reformation Christians. ▷ afterlife, Christian concept of; beatification; canonization

saint, Islamic view of The cult of saints is common in the Muslim world even though it is often suspect in orthodox circles. There are three levels of saints in Islam: popularly there is an invisible hierarchy of saints that has cosmic significance; secondly the wali, or friends of God, are important in line with Quran 10.63—'Lo, the friends of God, there is no fear upon them, neither do they grieve'; and thirdly there is the 'saint', who is purified or blessed (*tahir*) and ranks lower than the 'friend of God'. The tombs of saints are found in various parts of the Muslim world, especially in places influenced by Sufism, and symbolically saints and their tombs are considered to be a bridge between heaven and earth. Conservative movements such as the Qahhabis of Arabia frown upon saints and cults of saints for reasons similar to those used by Protestant Christians in regard to Roman Catholic saints: namely, that there is direct access to God, who does not require the mediation of saints. ▷ Quran; saint; Sufism; Wahhabis

sainthood A state of holiness resulting from an individual's pre-eminent expression of the principles of his religion. In the New Testament, all Christian believers are described as saints. From the 2nd century, however, the term was restricted to martyrs and, with the end of persecution, to ascetics. Because of the saint's embodiment of the principles of his or her religion, he or she is both a model and an object of veneration for ordinary believers. ▷ clergy; martyr; priesthood

Sakyapa (Sa-skya-pa) A monastic order of Tibetan Buddhism, founded by Drogmi (992–1072). Along with other Tibetans, Drogmi travelled to India in search of religious teachings, spending eight years at the monastery of Vikramashila. He studied the Vinaya, Prajnaparamita and Tantra, and translated the *Hevajra Tantra* into Tibetan. On returning to Tibet he founded a monastery in 1043, though it was his disciple Konchog Gyalpo who founded the monastery at Sakya (Saskya) in 1073, from where the tradition takes its name. Along with other orders the Sakyapa share the teachings of a gradual path, though also sharing a common root with the Kagyupas in the teachings of the wandering Tantric siddhas. An offshoot of the Sakyapa, the Jonangpa, was considered to be heretical by the Gelugpas. The tradition has emphasized scholarship and produced exegetical works and historical accounts of Buddhism. The famous *Blue Annals*, a history of Tibetan Buddhism, was written in the 15th century by a member of the order. During its history the Sakyapa had been engaged in power struggles with other orders, particularly the Gelugpa. In the 13th century the order became very powerful, when Sakyapa abbots were appointed regents of Tibet by the Mongol rulers of China, though the order's power declined with the demise of the Mongol dynasty. ▷ Buddhism; Gelugpa; Jonangpa; Kagyupa; prajnaparamita; siddhas; vinayapitaka

Saladin (Salāh al-Dīn al-Ayyūbī) (1137–93) Sultan of Egypt and Syria and founder of a dynasty, born in Takrit, on the Tigris, of which his father Ayyub, a Kurd, was governor under the Seljuks. He entered the service of Nur al-Din, Emir of Syria, held command in the expeditions to Egypt (1167–8), and was made grand vizier of the Fatimid caliph, whom in 1171 he overthrew, constituting himself sovereign of Egypt. On Nur al-Din's death (1174) he further proclaimed himself Sultan of Egypt and Syria, reduced Mesopotamia, and received the homage of the Seljuk princes of Asia Minor. His remaining years were occupied in wars with the Christians and in the consolidation of his extensive dominions. In 1187 he defeated King Guy of Jerusalem and a united Christian army at Hattin near Tiberias, and then captured Jerusalem and almost every fortified place on the Syrian coast. A great army of crusaders, headed by the kings of France and England, captured Acre in 1191, Richard Coeur-de-Lion defeated Saladin, took Caesarea and Jaffa, and obtained a three years' treaty. Saladin died in Damascus. His wise administration left traces for centuries in citadels, roads and canals. His opponents recognized his chivalry, good faith, piety, justice and greatness of soul. ▷ Crusades, Islamic view of

salat (salāt) The ritual daily prayer that is one of the five pillars of Islam. It consists of a series of movements and recitations that are repeated, and it is thus more an act of worship than an exercise in spontaneous private prayer. It is performed five times daily: in the morning, at noon, in the late afternoon, at sunset, and after dark. It may be performed alone, but preferably it takes place in groups, and it is offered in the direction of Mecca. In Muslim countries the melodious 'call to prayer' alerts people to the correct times to pray. Shoes are removed at the place of prayer, and a person should be ritually pure before praying. The Friday noonday prayer is especially important, it is preceded by a sermon, and it takes place in a mosque in the presence of a congregation. The salat is said in the sacred Arabic language, and it is symbolic in its words and its prostrations of glad submission to the one God. ▷ Allah; five pillars, Islamic; Mecca; mosque

Salem, witches of A notable US example of the 17th-century 'witch crazes' prevalent in continental Europe, which took place in Salem, Massachusetts, in 1692. Three people were accused originally, but with mounting hysteria the number grew to 30. Nineteen were hanged after trials that were officially condemned as unjust four years later. Sociologists consider the origin or motivating force of this incident to have been religious interpretations of the social tensions in a church and community that was deeply divided over the appointment of a new minister and over family and neighbourhood problems. ▷ witchcraft

Sales, St Francis of ▷ Francis of Sales, St

Salome (1st century) The traditional name of the daughter of Herodias. Mark 6.17–28 relates that she danced before her stepfather Herod Antipas and was offered a reward. At her mother's instigation, she was given the head of John the Baptist. The incident is not recorded in the historical account by Josephus, however. ▷ John the Baptist; Josephus, Flavius

salutations, Sikh Sikhs generally greet one another by putting their hands together, bowing slightly, and saying the words *Sat Sri Akal*, 'Truth is eternal'. Within the fellowship of the Sikh temple, the gurdwara, there is often a formal salutation at the beginning and end of an address which proclaims 'The Khalsa are the chosen of God! Victory belongs to God!' Within the fellowship of the Sikh assembly another common salutation is offered by the leader who cries *Jo bole so nihal*, 'Blessed is the one who cries', and the community responds with the personal greeting mentioned above, now used as an acclamation: *Sat Sri Akal*, 'Truth is eternal'. These Sikh salutations are now more formal and demonstrative than the normal North-Indian greeting of putting the hands together and saying *Namaste* or *Namaskar*. ▷ gurdwara; Khalsa

salvation The deliverance of humankind by religious means from sin or evil, the restoration of human beings to their true state, and the attainment of eternal blessedness. In theistic religions salvation comes about through God's intervention to heal broken and sinful humankind and to provide it with eternal life. In Buddhism salvation means escaping from the cycle of birth and rebirth and attaining nirvana. ▷ enlightenment; healing; nirvana; soteriology

salvation, Christian view of There are various views in Christian theology of what constitutes our ultimate well-being, the healing of the human condition, and the establishing of God's intention for creation. For Eastern Orthodox traditions, the core of salvation lies in the linking of divine and human lives made irreversible in Christ. In Western traditions, both Catholic and Protestant, the main emphasis has been on overcoming the alienation created between God and humankind by sin. Christ, the agent of this reconciliation, is understood to have reversed this estrangement once and for all by his willing identification with sinful humanity, and by his self-offering on the cross, in which it is believed he healed for all time the dislocation and distance between God and the world. Much classical debate in this area has concentrated on the question of how, precisely, Christ's death on the cross affects the God/

world relationship, as penalty, example, substitution and so on. There have been recurrent arguments as to whether all or only some will be saved, and whether people make any contribution to their own salvation or simply receive it as a gift. Major differences of emphasis exist as to whether salvation is primarily about the transformation of this world, restored by the impact of God to a place of justice, peace and responsible community, or whether it is primarily about the well-being of the individual before God in another life and condition of existence beyond death. ▷ afterlife; atonement; Pelagius; universalism

Salvation Army A non-sectarian Christian organization founded in the East End of London by William Booth in 1865, dedicated to minister to the poor and needy. It retains a military-style structure and evangelical atmosphere, and its members, both men and women, wear distinctive uniform. It is now established in over 80 countries. ▷ Booth, William; Christianity; evangelicalism

Salvation Army member

samadhi (samādhi) The notion of deep mental concentration found in Indian religions. In the classical Hindu Yoga of Patanjali it is the last and highest of eight steps within the discipline of yoga. It is an intense state of meditational achievement amounting to trance when one achieves the goal of going beyond the activity of thought into an awareness of being. In the Buddhist tradition it is used in two senses. At the general level it is the element of meditation or concentration that is one of the three parts of the Buddhist way, the other two being ethical living (*sila*) and wisdom (*prajna*). At the narrower level it is similar to the one-pointedness of mind amounting to trance that is the culmination of Hindu yoga. However it is a means to an end rather than an end in itself, and it is preliminary to the ultimate goal of enlightenment and nirvana. In the Jain tradition samadhi is a general term for meditation, and in this tradition it is more closely related to asceticism and non-violence than elsewhere. ▷ ahimsa; bhavana; meditation; nirvana; Patanjali; prajna; sila; yoga

Samaritans A sect of Jewish origin, living in Samaria, the northern territory of Israel, who apparently were not deported in the Assyrian conquest of c.721BCE and who were in tension with the Jews of Judea during the rebuilding of Jerusalem after the return from exile and well into New Testament times. Jews criticized them for their mixed ancestry, their building of a rival temple on Mount Gerizim, and their schism from true Judaism. A small remnant survives today. ▷ Judaism; Temple, Jerusalem

samatha A key form of Buddhist meditation which stresses the attainment of inner calmness. It is achieved by overcoming the five 'hindrances': greed, anger, lethargy, guilt and doubt. There are many varieties of training in calm meditation, but they all stress the importance of building up alertness and deep contentment. The four *jhanas* (meditations in a technical sense) are also encouraged as a way of raising consciousness. This may result in both a higher state of consciousness including calmness, contentment and joy, and extra-sensory awareness of one sort or another. There has been much debate among Buddhist meditators about the relationship between 'calm meditation' and 'insight meditation', and some would suggest that, insofar as the fruits of calm meditation are not necessarily permanent and can be lost, insight meditation is a fulfilment of calm meditation. Others would feel that they are more equal and complementary, and that they can be synthesized. ▷ bhavana; meditation; vipassana

sambhogakaya (sambhogakāya) The blissful or heavenly body of the Buddha, and one of the three bodies of the Buddha according to Mahayana Buddhist thought. The other two are the historical body (*nirmanakaya*), and the cosmic body (*dharmakaya*). These three aspects of the Buddha nature are related to each other, and at the level of sambhogakaya the Buddha appears as a celestial figure with a body of bliss. This is the body that is seen by celestial beings, and it is also the body 'enjoyed' by the Buddha himself. It is a glorious kind of body manifested to non-mortals and to the Buddha himself, symbolizing his power and glory in the celestial realm. The key to Buddhahood lies in the cosmic body of the Buddha which is not apparent or available directly to celestial beings or humans, hence the manifestations of his body in other forms suitable to their state. The notion of the three bodies of the Buddha (*trikaya*), including the blissful body, was systematized by Asanga and his successors in India from the 4th century CE. ▷ Asanga; Buddha; Dharmakaya; Mahayana Buddhism; trikaya

Samhain One of the Celtic quarterly feasts. It was celebrated on 1 November to mark the beginning of winter when, it was believed, the way to the 'other world' was opened and the dead could return to communicate with the living. There are many tales of mysterious happenings at Samhain.

Samkhya (Sāṃkhya) One of the six orthodox schools of Hindu philosophy. Samkhya ('enumeration') is a dualist system of philosophy which maintains an eternal distinction between matter or nature (*prakriti*) and the soul or individual spirit (*purusha*, literally 'person'). Samkhya is an enumeration of the principles (*tattvas*) underlying the universe. It posits 25 tattvas, the non-material purusha and 24 material principles. This is an emanationist cosmology in which the lower tattvas are generated from the higher. These levels are also psychological states and functions. Thus, from matter (prakriti) evolves 'intellect' or 'higher mind' (*buddhi*), which in turn generates the ego or sense of 'I' (*ahamkara*). From this evolve the mind (*manas*) and, subjectively, the five senses (hearing, touching, seeing, tasting and smelling) and the five capacities of action (speech, handling, walking, evacuation and reproduction). From ahamkara also evolve, objectively, the five subtle elements (the objects of the senses, namely sound, touch, colour, taste and smell), from which in turn evolve the five gross elements (space, air, fire, water and earth). At prakriti three qualities (*gunas*) are generated, namely 'lightness' (*sattva*), 'passion' (*rajas*) and 'inertia' or 'darkness' (*tamas*), which govern the lower evolutes. Samkhya is an atheistic system and maintains that liberation (*moksha*) is the freeing of the soul from entanglement in matter. The Samkhya system provides the metaphysics behind yoga and is influential in later Hindu philosophy, finding its way into the *Bhagavad Gita*, and being elaborated in Tantra. The principles of the system are laid down in Ishvarakrishna's *Samkhya Karikas* (5th century CE). ▷ gunas; Indian philosophies; Indian philosophy, six schools of; prakriti; purusha

samnyasa (saṃnyāsa) 'Renunciation of the world', one of the most important developments in Hinduism as a necessary way to gain *moksha* (liberation). In Hinduism samnyasa represents the fourth stage of life which orthodox Hindus would have to live according to their dharma, the other three stages being: *brahmacarin* (celibate student), *grhastha* (householder), and *vanaprastha* (forest-dweller).

The principle characteristics of the life of a samnyasin (renouncer) are similar for all Hindu groups, namely breaking all formal ties with society in order to seek liberation from rebirth (*samsara*). Consequently samnyasins are homeless, wandering constantly (except during the rainy season), and either dressed in an ochre robe or naked. They do not work, but beg for anything they need, and also practise celibacy.

Only 'twice-born' Hindus can technically become renouncers once they have paid the three debts which are incurred at birth, namely, the study of the Vedas, sacrifice, and procreation, which are paid to the sages, the gods and the ancestors of the individual. The initiation rite into renunciation is seen as a ritual death. During this the renouncers perform their final sacrifice, burn their sacred thread, and free themselves of all their possessions. They then internalize the sacred fires by breathing in the smoke. Some even perform their own funeral. They are then free to wander as ascetics without attachment to the world. ▷ dharma; moksha; samsara; Veda; worship, Hindu

samsara (saṃsāra) The cycle of birth, death and rebirth maintained by karma, in Hinduism, Buddhism and Jainism. Samsara can be seen in relation to *moksha*, the latter being liberation from the former. In Hinduism the soul is bound to samsara through a series of rebirths, each one being dictated by the karma inherited from previous lives. The type of karma which is incurred depends on how true each individual is to his or her dharma. As well as the universal dharma there is also the dharma by which the adherent must live according to the *jati* (caste) into which he or she has been born. This, therefore, lays out the ritual and ethical laws which must be obeyed if good karma is to be accrued and a favourable rebirth gained. Consequently the adherent hopes that such action will eventually lead to moksha, ie release from samsara. ▷ dharma; jati; karma; moksha; rebirth

Samson (?c.11th century BCE) Legendary hero of the tribe of Dan, purportedly the last of Israel's tribal leaders ('judges') prior to Samuel and the establishment of the monarchy under Saul. Stories in Judges 13–16 tell of his great strength, his battles against the Philistines, his 20-year rule, and his fatal infatuation with Delilah. When she cut his hair, breaking his Nazirite vow, he lost his strength, and was held by the Philistines until his hair grew back and he pulled down their temple upon them. ▷ Dan, tribe of; Delilah; Judges, Book of

Samuel (11th century BCE) (Hebrew, probably 'name of God') In the Hebrew Bible/ Old Testament, the last of the judges and first of the prophets, son of Elkanah and his wife Hannah; an Ephraimite who was dedicated to the priesthood as a child by a Nazirite vow. After the defeat of Israel and loss of the Ark of the Covenant to the Philistines, Samuel tried to keep the tribal confederation together, moving in a circuit among Israel's shrines. He presided, apparently reluctantly, over Saul's election as the first king of Israel, but later criticized Saul for assuming priestly prerogatives and disobeying divine instructions given to him. Samuel finally anointed David as Saul's successor, rather than Saul's own son, Jonathan. ▷ Ark of the Covenant; David; Jonathan; prophet; Samuel, Books of; Saul

Samuel, Books of Two books of the Old Testament, which were one in the Hebrew Bible and probably were also once combined with Kings; also called 1 and 2 Kings in some Catholic versions. They present a narrative of Israel's history from the time of the prophet Samuel and Israel's first king Saul (1 Samuel) to the story of David's accession and reign (2 Samuel). They are probably a compilation from several, partially-overlapping sources, with a late editing after the Exile. ▷ David; Deuteronomistic History; Kings, Books of; Old Testament; Samuel; Saul

samurai A Japanese warrior. Tokugawa Japan (1603–1868) had four hereditary classes: samurai, farmers, craftsmen, and merchants. (Outcasts were not part of this system.) Only samurai were allowed weapons, and they carried two swords. They had to serve their daimyo masters loyally and follow the warrior's code, bushido; in return they received lodging and income. They are often regarded as heroic figures. ▷ bushido; Meiji Restoration

San Chiao (three Chinese ways) An expression used in Chinese religion to refer to the three ways of China: the Confucian, the Taoist and the Buddhist. Although being very different paths, they are also complementary, thus all three could be followed at the same time. The Confucian way, beginning with Confucius in the 6th century BCE, stressed a good education, social virtues, outward observance of rituals, ethical conduct, courtesy, activism and the character of a gentleman. The Taoist way, expressed in the *Tao Te Ching* and the *Chuang Tzu* from the 4th century BCE, stressed spontaneity, living in accord with nature, following the 'flow of things', inward mysticism, creative inaction and the feminine virtues. Like the Chinese concept of yin and yang, although the Confucian and Taoist ways were opposite they complemented one another and worked in harmony. Mahayana Buddhism grew in China from the 1st to the 6th century CE, and it added a philosophical curiosity, an organized community (the *sangha*), a concern for the afterlife, and a monastic system that stressed meditation. From the time of the Sung dynasty (980–1279) the three ways became more closely connected at the level of grassroots religion. Although they remained separate, ordinary people were able to engage in them all to suit the different needs of their lives, and they fed into one another by interborrowing and sharing ideas. ▷ Chuang Tzu; Confucius; Mahayana Buddhism; Tao Te Ching

sand paintings ▷ **dry paintings**

Sangat (Saṅgat) A Sikh concept, derived from Hinduism, denoting a fellowship or company, and referring especially to the congregation of a Sikh temple or to a local Sikh community. This stress upon fellowship, which is sometimes known as the 'company of the saints', is important for the Sikh tradition, which considers it odd to think in terms of a solitary Sikh. The early Sikh gurus established Sangats and relied upon them as a means of sustenance and mission. The term used for the Sikh community in general is the Sikh Panth, whereas the Sangat is a local branch of the wider community. Individual spirituality is important within the Sikh tradition but it is practised within the context of the Sangat as a worshipping congregation and as a company socially involved in the well-being of society. ▷ guru, Sikh; Panth

sangha (saṅgha) The community of *bhikkus*—those who have formally committed themselves to pursuing the Buddhist way of life and to living in accord with the set of rules known as the *Patimokkha*. It began with the first disciples of Buddha, and remains influential and widespread today. ▷ Buddhism

Sanhedrin (Greek 'council', also called by Josephus the *gerousia*, Greek 'senate') A Jewish council of elders meeting in Jerusalem, which during the Graeco-Roman period acquired internal administrative and judicial functions over Palestinian Jews, despite foreign domination. Convened by the high priest, its membership numbered 71, although local courts with this designation outside Jerusalem had fewer members (usually 23 or just three) and more limited jurisdiction. After the fall of Jerusalem in 70CE, the Jerusalem Sanhedrin was effectively replaced by a new court of sages in Jabneh. ▷ Jabneh; Judaism

Sankey, Ira David ▷ **Moody, Dwight Lyman**

Sanskrit The name given to the early forms of Indo-Aryan, c.1000BCE, in which the sacred Hindu texts known as the Vedas were written. Their grammatical form and pronunciation have been scrupulously preserved as a matter of religious observance. Sanskrit proved to be the key to the reconstruction of Indo-European in the 19th century. ▷ Veda

Sant tradition A group of devotional religious teachers who had an important influence in North India from the 15th to 17th centuries. Although traditionally linked to a prominent Hindu devotional figure named Ramananda, whose historical details are unclear, they were in fact influenced by three groups: Hindus devoted to Vishnu, the Nath Yoga tradition, and Sufi Islam. They stressed monotheism and devotion to God, but not through incarnations (avataras). They wrote deeply expressive hymns in vernacular languages other than Sanskrit. They rejected caste, ritualism, images, and institutional Hinduism, and were sometimes of low caste. Some of them, such as Namdev (fl.c.1270), Ravidas, Kabir and of course Guru Nanak, had some of their hymns included in the Sikh scripture, the *Adi Granth*. They emphasized a deep, rich and mystical devotion based on trust and faith in God, that was open to all of whatever rank or status, as being the key to salvation (*mukti*). Although not linked in a formal school, indeed without really knowing one another, they exercised a wide influence at grass-roots level as well as in a more sophisticated way on Islam and Hinduism, and especially upon the Sikh tradition which was a manifestation of their spirit. ▷ avatara; Guru Granth Sahib; Kabir; Nanak; Ramananda; Ravidas; Sufism; Vishnu; yoga

Sanusis (Sanūsīs) A Muslim political-cum-religious organization widely found in Libya and also present in the Sudan. The first Sanusi lodge was founded in Mecca by an Algerian named al-Sanusi (1791–1859), who called himself the Great Sanusi, and the movement combined puritan fundamentalism with Sufi mystical ideas. The founder moved from Arabia to Cyrenaica in Libya, and after his death the Sanusis were expanded by his sons, especially Sayyid Muhammad al-Mahdi, who established hundreds of Sanusi lodges before his death in 1902. His son became King Muhammad Idris of Libya; the monarchy was later overthrown in 1969 by a coup headed by Colonel Gaddafi. The Sanusis were similar to the Wahhabis in Arabia in that they were a reforming puritanical movement that ensured that their strong religious ideals had political backing. ▷ Mecca; Sufism; Wahhabis

Saoshyant An Avestan word meaning 'One who will bring Benefit' or 'Saviour'. Passages in the Gathas where Zoroaster himself refers to this concept suggest a sense of immediacy. Many scholars therefore believe that, initially at least, Zoroaster used the word for a person or group of people who would restore the world to a pristine state of purity within or shortly after his lifetime. In post-Gathic (and possibly late Gathic) Zoroastrianism, however, expectations of the appearance of a Saviour came to be projected into the remoter future. The Saoshyant, who would appear just before the end of time and bring about the final battle between good and evil, was probably thought to be in some way connected with Zoroaster himself. A legend thus evolved that he would be born from a virgin who had bathed in Lake Kansaoya, where Zoroaster's semen is held to be preserved. In the later Zoroastrian tradition legends about the Saoshyant became more complex, postulating three such figures, each born from the prophet's seed, who would appear at the end of each of the three millennia of the period of Mixture, at a time when the world was entirely dominated by evil. The last of these, the Saoshyant proper, would usher in Frashokereti. ▷ Bundahishn; Frashokereti; Zoroaster; Zoroastrianism

Sarah, or **Sarai** (Hebrew 'princess') Biblical character, wife and half-sister of Abraham, who is portrayed (Genesis 12–23) as having accompanied him from Ur to Canaan. On account of her beauty she posed as Abraham's sister before Pharaoh in Egypt and Abimelech in Gerar, since their desire for her may have endangered her husband's life. Long barren, she is said to have eventually given birth to Isaac in her old age as God promised. Allegedly she died at age 127 in Kiriath-arba. ▷ Abraham; Hagar; Isaac; Old Testament

Sarnath (Sārnāth) The deer park six miles outside the holy city of Banaras in Uttar Pradesh in North India where the Buddha preached his first sermon. After his enlightenment at Bodhgaya he went to Sarnath and met five ascetics whom he had known earlier when he had himself experimented unsuccessfully with the ascetic way. He uttered his first discourse to them, or 'turned the wheel of the dharma' as the Buddhist tradition would put it. He preached to them about the middle way, the four noble truths and the eightfold path, features that became the basic elements of his teaching and the essence of the Buddhist way. From the time of Ashoka in the 3rd century BCE to the Muslim invasions of the 11th century CE Sarnath was one of the four main Buddhist pilgrimage centres with a monastic university and various stupas and monasteries. During this century it has revived and is again a great pilgrimage centre. The original 150-foot-high stupa and the stump of Ashoka's pillar remain, and a modern temple and Buddhist centre have been set up at the place where the Buddha preached his first sermon. Also at Sarnath there is a modern Jain temple dedicated to the eleventh great Jain teacher (*tirthankara*), Sri Amsanatha, who is said to have lived and died at that site. ▷ ariya sacca; Ashoka; Banaras; Buddha; dharma; eightfold path; Middle Way; stupa; tirthankara

Sartre, Jean-Paul (1905–80) French philosopher, dramatist and novelist, born in Paris. He studied at the Sorbonne with Simone de Beauvoir and taught philosophy at Le Havre, Paris and Berlin (1934–5). He joined the French army in 1939, was a prisoner of war in Germany (1941), and after his release became an active member of the Resistance in Paris. In 1945 he emerged as the leading light of the left-wing, left-bank intellectual life of Paris, but he eventually broke with the Communists. In 1946, with Simone de Beauvoir, he founded and edited the avant-garde monthly *Les Temps Modernes*. A disciple of Heidegger, he developed his own characteristic existentialist doctrines, derived from an early anarchistic tendency, which found full expression in his autobiographical novel *La Nausée* (1938) and in *Le Mur* (1938), a collection of short stories. The Nazi occupation provided the grim background to such plays as *Les Mouches*, a modern version of the Orestes theme, and *Huis clos* (both 1943). *Les Mains sales* (1952), filmed as *Crime Passionel*, movingly portrayed the tragic consequences of a choice to join an extremist party. He became the most prominent exponent of atheistic existentialism. His doctrines are outlined in *L'Existentialisme est un humanisme* (1946, trans 1948) and fully worked out in *L'Être et le néant* (1943, trans as 'Being and Nothingness', 1957). Other notable works include the novels which comprise *Les Chemins de la liberté* (1945–9), the play *Les Séquestrés d'Altona* (1959), and a study of Flaubert, *L'Idiot de la famille* (1971). In 1964 he was awarded, but declined to accept, the Nobel Prize for Literature. In the late 1960s he became closely involved in opposition to American policies in Vietnam, and expressed support for the student rebellion in 1968. ▷ atheism; existentialism; Heidegger, Martin

Sarvastivada (Sarvāstivāda) The doctrinal system held by an early Indian school of Buddhism called the Sarvastivadins. They differed from other schools such as the Theravada over whether past and future mental events (dharmas) are real as well as present ones. Their opponents denied this and they affirmed it. Their very name suggests their viewpoint that everything (*sarva*)—past, present and future—exists (*asti*). Their persistence and growth occasioned the calling by King Ashoka of the third Buddhist Council at Pataliputra in the 3rd century BCE to discuss their views. By contrast with the Theravada school they used the Sanskrit rather than the Pali language. Although they were lumped together with the Theravada school by the Mahayana tradition as part of the derogatively named Hinayana (lesser vehicle), they can be seen as more adventurous than the Theravada tradition, as well as being a kind of bridge to Mahayana Buddhism itself. ▷ Ashoka; Buddhist Councils; dharma; Hinayana Buddhism; Mahayana Buddhism; Theravada Budhism

Satan A fallen angel held to be the personification and instigator of evil. The term is derived from the Hebrew verb 'satan', which means 'to oppose'. The Septuagint translation of 'satan' as 'diaboloc' gave rise to the term 'devil'. Both terms are usually employed synonymously. Satan is the personification of the evil and negative qualities of humankind. He is understood as a tempter, deceiver and liar, as the cause of immoral feelings and actions, and as having the power of death and destruction over the bodies and souls of human beings. In Jewish literature Satan resided along with other demonic and negative powers in the lower atmosphere. Christianity has regarded hell, a place of fiery torment beneath the earth, as Satan's dwelling place.

The term Satan first appears in the Old Testament, where it initially means 'adversary' or 'opponent' and can be used both of human beings (I Samuel 24.4; II Samuel 19.22; I Kings 11.14, 23; Psalms 109.6) and angels (Zachariah 3.1–2; Job 1–2). In the latter case, the term describes a function similar to that of prosecutor in a court of law. Towards the end of the Old Testament period and particularly during the intercanonical period 'Satan' came to be more closely identified with evil. This development was probably due to the influence of Persian dualism. In the New Testament the identification of Satan with evil is continued and strengthened. Satan is understood as being opposed to Christ and is seen as a source of temptation (Matthew 4.1–11; Mark 1.12–13; Luke 4.1–13). There is also some speculation concerning Satan's origins (2 Peter 2.4; Jude 6; Revelation 12.7–9) and discussion of his ultimate eschatological defeat (2 Corinthians 2.11; Revelation 20.2, 7–10), which has begun with Christ's death and resurrection.

Many other religions have a similar concept of personified evil. Thus in the Quran we find the concepts of 'Shaytan' and 'Iblic'. These two concepts cover most of the meanings contained in the Judaeo-Christian concept of Satan. The chief differences are that Satan is accused of opposing divine revelation (22.52) and that the cause of his fall is his refusal to bow down before Adam (2.34). A similar personification of evil is also to be found in Buddhism in the form of 'Mara'. This being possesses many of Satan's qualities but differs in not being a fallen angel. ▷ hell; Iblis; Mara (Buddhist)

Satanic Verses This refers to two or three verses that were introduced into surah 53 of the Quran but were later cut out on the grounds that they were satanic and therefore not properly a part of the Quran. The key passage states: 'Have you considered al-Lat and al-Uzza and Manat, the third, the other? These are the intermediaries exalted, whose intercession is to be hoped for.' This reference to three local goddesses as intermediaries was clearly contrary to the spirit and the letter of Muslim monotheism. In September 1988 a novel entitled *The Satanic Verses*, written by Salman Rushdie, was published in Britain, winning the Whitbread Prize. Interpreted literally by many Muslims, it caused a furore in the Islamic community which viewed it as containing gratuitous insults to Islam, for example in its use of the word *Mahound*, which had been a medieval demonization of Muhammad. This raised a number of questions, such as what is blasphemy; should laws against blasphemy be applied to all religions in Great Britain, not just Christianity; do novelists have an unfettered right of free speech; is the Quran open to any criticism; and can Muslims repudiate their faith? In the end a fatwa was issued by Ayatollah Khomeini condemning Rushdie to death for blasphemy, and the author was forced into hiding, where he remains. ▷ ayatollah; blasphemy; fatwa; monotheism; Muhammad; Quran; surah

Satanism The worship of Satan or other figures of demonology. It may include the perversion of religious rituals (eg the black Mass), the practice of witchcraft, and other practices associated with the occult. The Christian Church often accused those who did not conform to Christian tenets of being Satanists. The Albigensians, for example, were thought to have Satanists among their members, while from the later middle ages witchcraft and Satanism were considered synonymous. There was a revival of Satanism in the 19th century, and instances of it are still to be found. ▷ black Mass; Crowley, (Edward) Aleister; Devil; heresy; occult; witchcraft

Sat Guru (Sat Gurū) A Sikh term for God as the 'True Guru'. Other important Sikh names for God are the Timeless One (*Akal Purukh*), which is theologically significant, and Wonderful Lord (*Wahiguru*), which is popularly favoured. However, God is often described as Sat Guru by the first Sikh guru, Guru Nanak, in the Sikh scripture, the *Guru Granth Sahib*, and it remains an important designation for God. For Guru Nanak the notion of Sat Guru indicated the inner voice or inner presence of God, and because he and the other Sikh gurus so obviously knew and were known by this Sat Guru they were themselves given the title of 'Guru'. However, they were not seen as divine or regarded as avataras (incarnations) of God but were viewed as human channels of the divine guru. After the death of the tenth guru, Guru Gobind Singh, the function of channelling the Sat Guru was taken over by the Sikh scripture, the *Adi Granth*, which was given the name *Guru Granth Sahab*. ▷ Adi Granth; Akal Purukh; Guru Granth Sahib; Gobind Singh, Guru; guru, Sikh; Nanak; Nirankar

sati (satī), or **suttee** A form of suicide in which a widow climbs on to her husband's funeral pyre. In orthodox Hinduism the woman has no right to wear her own sacred thread and after her husband's death she would therefore become marginalized by society. It would, in that case, often seem to be preferable for the widow to immolate herself so that she might attain heavenly bliss with her husband. The act of sati is also seen as being one of purification for both the husband and wife. Although sati was supposedly a voluntary act, there is little doubt that in some communities the widow was more or less expected to carry it out.

satori A Japanese word meaning enlightenment and the realization of the Buddha nature. Its origin lies in the enlightenment of the Buddha himself at Bodhgaya in India in the 6th century BCE, but in Japan it became particularly associated with Zen Buddhism. It came to mean the experience of awakening to one's own real nature and of realizing the Buddha mind within. This was achieved by a combination of seated meditation (*zazen*), counselling with Zen Masters, and the use of koans (paradoxical sayings) that lead to a realization of one's own nature. This initial experience of satori may be followed by other experiences which, although similar, build up a depth of maturity in the spiritual life. The Rinzai school, founded by Eisai in 1191, stressed the role of koans in achieving satori, whereas the Soto Zen school, founded by Degen in 1227, stressed zazen as the key. The experience itself is basically mystical and cannot be put into words. However, a Zen scholar summed it up under eight headings: irrationality, intuitive insight, authority, affirmation, transcendence, impersonality, exaltation and momentariness. ▷ bodhi; Buddha nature; Dogen; Eisai; koans; peepul; Rinzai; Soto; Suzuki, Daisetz Teitaro

satsang A Sikh term meaning a congregation or a local assembly within the Sikh tradition. In the hymns of the Sikh gurus contained within the Sikh scripture, the *Guru Granth Sahib*, it was used for the Sikh community as a whole, but nowadays the term *panth* is used for the Sikh tradition as a whole and satsang is used for a local manifestation of it. Satsang also refers not only to the outward community of the local congregation but to the fellowship that ought to characterize the community. It thus combines the notion of fellowship in the sense of intimacy and fellowship in the sense of a communal body of people. ▷ Guru Granth Sahib; guru, Sikh; panth

Satya Sai Baba (1926–) Guru and wonder-worker, one of the most popular living Indian holy men. In contrast to many modern gurus he has never brought his teaching to the West and remains with his sizeable following in India. After a trance-like religious experience at the age of 14, he declared himself a reincarnation of Sai Baba of Shirdi and began to preach. He is dedicated to the propagation of an eclectic form of Hinduism, advocating a bhakti-style devotion along with a certain level of religious discipline, including abstinence from alcohol, drugs and meat, and the study of the scriptures. Virtue, too, is a central theme in his teachings. He claims his miracles, which have attracted a popular following, are simply intended to facilitate the spread of his teachings. ▷ bhakti

Saul Old Testament king, the first to be elected by the Israelites. He conquered the Philistines, Ammonites, and Amalekites, became jealous of David, his son-in-law, and was ultimately at feud with the priestly class. At length Samuel secretly anointed David king. Saul fell in battle with the Philistines on Mount Gilboa. ▷ David; Old Testament; Samuel

Saul of Tarsus ▷ **Paul, St**

Sautrantika (Sautrāntika) A school of Buddhist philosophy dating from the 1st century CE. It wished to return to the Buddha's discourses (*sutras*) as being the key to Buddhist teaching, and rejected the later *Abhidharma* as being an addition to—and in a sense a deviation from—the basic doctrines of Buddhism. According to them the Buddha's *sutras* were the end (*anta*) of his teaching, hence their name: Sutra-anta-ka. They wished to jump back behind later accretions to the original discourses of the Buddha. However they did this in a subtle and not in a fundamentalist way. They also talked about there being an ongoing existence of a subtle consciousness that progresses from one life to another, and goes on to nirvana. This was an attempt, similar to that of the *Pudgalavadins*, to explain how, if there is no permanent self (atman), it is possible to talk meaningfully about rebirth. Their concepts appear to have had some influence upon the later *Yogacara* 'Consciousness' school of Mahayana Buddhism, although they did not survive as a separate school. ▷ Abhidharma; atman; Mahayana Buddhism; nirvana; rebirth; Yogacara

Savonarola, Girolamo (1452–98) Italian religious and political reformer, born of a noble family in Ferrara. In 1474 he entered the Dominican order at Bologna. He seems to have preached in 1482 in Florence, but this was a failure. In a convent at Brescia his zeal won attention, and in 1489 he was recalled to Florence. His second appearance in the pulpit of San Marco—on the sinfulness and apostasy of the time—was a great popular triumph; and by some he was hailed as an nspired prophet. Under Lorenzo de' Medici, he Magnificent, art and literature had felt he humanist revival of the 15th century, whose spirit was utterly at variance with Savonarola's conception of spirituality and Christian morality. To the adherents of the Medici therefore, Savonarola early became an object of suspicion, but until the death of Lorenzo (1492) his relations with the Church were at least not antagonistic; and when, in 493, a reform of the Dominican order in Tuscany was proposed under his auspices, it was approved by the pope, and Savonarola was named the first vicar-general. But at this stage his preaching began to point plainly to political revolution as the divinely-ordained means for the regeneration of religion and morality, and he predicted the advent of the French under Charles VIII, whom he soon fterwards welcomed to Florence. However, he French were shortly compelled to leave Florence, and a republic was established, of which Savonarola became the guiding spirit, is party ('the Weepers') being completely in he ascendant.

At this point 'the puritan of Catholicism' isplayed his extraordinary genius and the xtravagance of his theories. The Republic of Florence was to be a Christian commonwealth, f which God was the sole sovereign, and His Gospel the law; the most stringent enactments were made for the repression of vice and frivolity; gambling was prohibited; the vanities f dress were restrained by sumptuary laws. ven the vainest flocked to the public square fling down their costliest ornaments, and avonarola's followers made a huge 'bonfire f vanities'.

Meanwhile his rigorism and his claim to the ft of prophecy led to his being cited in 1495 to answer a charge of heresy in Rome, and on his failing to appear he was forbidden to preach. Savonarola disregarded the order, but his difficulties in Florence increased. The new system proved impracticable and although the conspiracy for the recall of the Medici failed, and five of the conspirators were executed, this very rigour hastened the reaction. In 1497 came a sentence of excommunication from Rome; and thus precluded from administering the sacred offices, Savonarola zealously tended the sick monks during the plague. A second 'bonfire of vanities' in 1498 led to riots; and at the new elections the Medici party came into power. Savonarola was again ordered to desist from preaching, and was fiercely denounced by a Franciscan preacher, Francesco da Puglia. Dominicans and Franciscans appealed to the interposition of divine providence by the ordeal of fire, between da Puglia and a Franciscan. But in the month the trial was due to have taken place (April 1498) difficulties and debates arose, destroying Savonarola's prestige and producing a complete revulsion of public feeling. He was brought to trial for falsely claiming to have seen visions and uttered prophecies, for religious error, and for sedition. Under torture he made avowals which he afterwards withdrew. He was declared guilty and the sentence was confirmed by Rome.

On 23 May 1498, this extraordinary man and two Dominican disciples were hanged and burned, still professing their adherence to the Catholic Church. In morals and religion, not in theology, Savonarola may be regarded as a forerunner of the Reformation. His works are mainly sermons, theological treatises, the chief *The Triumph of the Cross*, an apology of orthodox Catholicism, some poems, and a discourse on the government of Florence. ▷ Dominicans; heresy; Reformation; Roman Catholicism

Sawm (Ṣawm) The notion of fasting within Islam, associated especially with the Fast of Ramadan. Fasting was encouraged by Muhammad as a method of spiritual discipline; however, it was undertaken so seriously by the early Muslims in Medina that Muhammad had to modify its severity. There are various other fast days within Islam in addition to the Fast of Ramadan, and fasting may be embarked upon as a spiritual regimen, or as a penance or reparation for some omission. The Fast of Ramadan is one of the five pillars of Islam, and it takes place during the ninth month of the Muslim calendar. Eating and drinking are prohibited, unless there are special circumstances, between sunrise and sunset. This is a tremendous discipline, especially in places where the temperature becomes very hot during the day, and it gives unity to Muslims throughout the world because they know they are all sharing the Fast together. It represents a sacrifice, a limitation upon indulgence, and a kind of purification; it is also a moral symbol of the need to empathize with the sufferings of the hungry throughout the world. ▷ fasting; five pillars, Islamic; Medina; Muhammad; penance; purification; Ramadan

scapegoat In ancient Jewish ritual (Leviticus 16), on the Day of Atonement and after the sacrifices of a bull and a goat as sin-offerings, a second goat (the 'scapegoat') was released into the wilderness 'to Azazel', possibly a desert demon, symbolizing how the people's sins were removed. The high priest cast lots to determine the respective fates of the two goats. Today the term is more generally applied to one who takes the blame for another. ▷ Yom Kippur

scarab The dung beetle, symbolic in Ancient Egypt of resurrection and immortality. Amulets and stamp seals were often made in the shape of the beetle and worn either in pendants or rings. ▷ immortality; resurrection

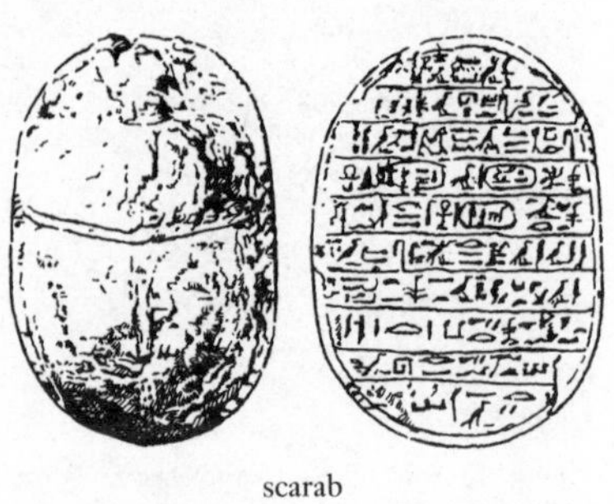

scarab

scepticism, or **skepticism** A philosophical tradition which casts doubt on the possibility of human knowledge. An extreme version, held by the followers of Pyrrho of Elis, maintains that one is never in a position to have justified beliefs about anything, including the truth of scepticism. Less extreme versions are directed at particular sources of knowledge, such as perception, memory, or reason. ▷ philosophy

Schillebeeckx, Edward Cornelis Florentius Alfons (1914–) Belgian Dominican theologian, born in Antwerp. Professor of Dogmatics and the History of Theology at Nijmegen in the Netherlands from 1958 to 1983, his publications have ranged widely across the whole field of theology, from sacraments (*Christ the Sacrament*, 1963), to the presentation of the gospel in contemporary society (*Jesus in our Western Culture*, 1987). Like Hans Küng, he has attracted Vatican investigations for questioning received interpretations of doctrine and church order, as in *The Church with a Human Face* (1985) replacing *Ministry* (1981); and *Jesus* (1979), *Christ* (1980), and *Church* (1990). He has also published sermons (*God Among Us*, 1983, and *For the Sake of the Gospel*, 1989), and autobiographical interviews, *God is New Each Moment* (1983). ▷ Dominicans; Küng, Hans

Schimmel, Annemarie (1922–) German scholar of Islam. She gained a doctorate in Islamic Studies from Berlin University (1941) and a doctorate in the history of religion from Marburg University (1951). She taught at Marburg from 1946, became Professor of the History of Religions at Ankara in 1954, Professor of Islamics at Bonn in 1961, and professor of Indo-Muslim Culture at Harvard in 1970. Her numerous awards include the Friedrich-Ruckert medal for outstanding translations, the Golden Hammar-Purgstall medal from Graz Austria, the Sitari-i Quaid-i Azam and Hilal-i Imtiaz from Pakistan, and the Order of Merit First Class from Germany in 1981. She has honorary doctorates from Hyderabad, Islamabad and Peshawar, and was President of the International Association for the History of Religion from 1980 to 1990. Her numerous publications include works in Arabic, English, German and Turkish, and prominent among them are translations into German of the works of the great Muslim writers Rumi and Iqbal. Among her books are *As Through A Veil: Mystical Poetry in Islam* (1982), and *Calligraphy and Islamic Culture* (1984). In addition to her particular studies, Professor Schimmel has through her frequent travels between Bonn, Harvard and the Islamic world, increased understanding within the field of Religious Studies between different continents and different religions. ▷ history of religions; Iqbal, Sir Muhammad; Rumi; Sufism

schism (Greek *schisma*, 'separation') Deliberate separation from the Christian Church on matters of Church order or discipline rather than doctrine, as with 3rd-century Novatianism and 4th-century Donatism. These movements were stricter than the

Church at large, refusing to re-admit to fellowship believers who had lapsed from the faith under persecution. Roman Catholic theology has traditionally treated the Orthodox Church and the churches of the Reformation as schismatic in the sense of their being out of communion with the papacy and so outside the true Church. The problem has more recently been seen as one of internal divisions in the one Church of Christ, rather than a matter of external separation from it. ▷ Great Schism, the

Schleiermacher, Friedrich Ernst Daniel (1768–1834) German theologian and philosopher, born in Breslau in Lower Silesia. He was brought up in the Moravian faith but became intellectually disillusioned with its dogmatism and studied philosophy and theology at the University of Halle. In 1796 he became a clergyman at the Charité, a Berlin hospital, and joined the literary and intellectual circles associated with figures like Friedrich and August von Schlegel and Karl Wilhelm von Humboldt. He became professor at Halle (1804–6) and Berlin (1810), and had a significant role in the union of the Lutheran and Reformed Churches in Prussia in 1817. His works include *Reden über die Religion* (1799), *Monologen* (1800), a translation of Plato (started in collaboration with Schlegel, 1804–10), his major treatise *Der Christliche Glaube* (1821–2), and an influential, posthumous life of Jesus. He was much involved in German romanticism and the critique of traditional and Kantian religious and moral philosophy. He defends a view of religious liberalism and an understanding of Christianity rooted in historical tradition, and is now regarded by many as the founder of modern Protestant theology. ▷ Kant, Immanuel; Protestantism; theology

Schmidt, Wilhelm (1868–1954) German priest and ethnologist, born in Hörde, Westphalia. He joined the Society of the Divine Word Missionary order (SVD) in 1883 and was ordained a priest in 1892. After studying oriental languages at Berlin University (1893–5), he became professor in the St Gabriel Mission Seminary at Mödling, where he remained until 1938. He also taught at Vienna and Fribourg. His interest in ethnology stemmed from the observations of the SVD missionaries, and from the influence of the ethnologist Fritz Graebner. He sought to develop and refine Graebner's system of 'Kulturkreise' or trait clusters, proposing a theory of devolution to counter that of cultural evolution. In 1906 he founded the journal *Anthropos*.

scholasticism Philosophical speculation as it developed in cathedral schools in western Europe between the 12th and 14th centuries. It is characterized by its use of philosophy in the service of Christianity, its use of ancient authorities such as Aristotle and St Augustine, and its dialectical method. ▷ Aristotle; Augustine, St (of Hippo); philosophy

Scholem, Gershon (1897–1982) German Jewish historian, born in Berlin. Scholem became a Zionist and emigrated to Palestine in 1923. Having already studied the Kabbalah, he taught Jewish mysticism at Jerusalem's Hebrew University from its opening in 1925, and remained there until his retirement in 1965. His works include *Major Trends in Jewish Mysticism* (1961) and *The Messianic Idea in Judaism and other Essays in Jewish Sprirituality* (1971). One abiding effect of his work is that the Kabbalah now occupies a central position in the academic discipline of Jewish studies. Prior to this it had been largely ignored, viewed as peripheral and secondary when compared with the legal and rationalist traditions within Judaism. In contrast, Scholem maintained that mystical elements belong to the later stages of any religion's development. Thus, since the task of mysticism is one of revitalization, its importance for Judaism's survival over the centuries should not be underestimated. However, Scholem also argued that, since the Kabbalah was dependent on Gnosticism, it was a source not only of renewal but also of danger, as demonstrated in the movement surrounding Shabbatai Tzvi. Although not a mystic himself, Scholem believed that the Kabbalah has continued to exercise its influence upon Jewish history in modern times, including on the Zionist movement. ▷ Gnosticism; Kabbalah; Shabbatai Tsvi; Zionism

Schweitzer, Albert (1875–1965) Alsatian medical missionary, theologian, musician and philosopher, born in Kaysersberg in Alsace, and one of the noblest figures of the 20th century. He was brought up in Günsbach in the Münster valley, where he attended the local *realgymnasium*, learnt the organ eventually under Widor in Paris, studied theology and philosophy at Strasbourg, Paris and Berlin, and in 1896 made his famous decision that he would live for science and art until he was 30 and then devote his life to serving humanity. In 1899 he obtained his doctorate on Kant's philosophy of religion, became

curate at St Nicholas Church, Strasbourg, in 1902 *privat-dozent* at the university, and in 1903 principal of the theological college. In 1905 he published his authoritative study, *J S Bach, le musicien-poète* (1905), translated by Ernest Newman (1911), followed in 1906 by a notable essay on organ-design. Schweitzer was all for the preservation of old organs, many of which he considered had a better tone than modern factory-built ones. The same year appeared the enlargement of his theological thesis (1901), *Von Reimarus zu Wrede*, re-issued in 1913 as *Geschichte der Leben-Jesu Forschung*, (The Quest of the Historical Jesus, trans 1910), a thoroughgoing demolition of Liberal theology which marked a revolution in New Testament criticism. His Pauline studies *Geschichte der Paulinischen Forschung* (1911, trans 1912) and *Die Mystik des Apostels Paulus* (1930, trans 1931) were intended as companion volumes to these.
True to his vow, despite his international reputation as musicologist, theologian and organist, he began to study medicine (1905), resigned as principal of the theological college (1906) and, duly qualified (1913), went off with his newly-married wife to set up a hospital to fight leprosy and sleeping sickness at Lambaréné, a deserted mission station on the Ogowe river in the heart of French Equatorial Africa. Except for his internment by the French (1917–18) as a German and periodic visits to Europe to raise funds for his mission by organ recitals, he made his self-built hospital the centre of his paternalistic service to Africans, in a spirit 'not of benevolence but of atonement'. His newly discovered ethical principle 'reverence for life' was fully worked out in relation to the defects of European civilization in *Verfall und Wiederaufbau der Kultur* (1923), (The Decay and Restoration of Civilization, trans 1923) and philosophically in *Kultur und Ethik* (1923, trans 1923). He was Hibbert lecturer at Oxford and London (1934) and Gifford lecturer at Edinburgh (1934–5). He was awarded the Nobel Prize for Peace (1952). His other works include *On the Edge of the Primeval Forest* (trans 1922), *More from the Primeval Forest* (trans 1931), *Out of My Life and Thought* (1931; postscript 1949), and *From My African Notebook* (1938). ▷ Quest of the Historical Jesus

scientism A term applied to science when it tends to become an all-embracing ideology that attempts to deal with areas of life outside its own parameters of measurement, prediction and control. When it embraces matters to do with awe, imagination, beauty, goodness and truth, and is viewed as having answers to the problems of heartache, suffering and mortality, science is said to have slipped into scientism, the suggestion being that it has over-reached its proper concerns and become a quasi-religion. New trends in the philosophy of science have questioned some of the scientistic assumptions of positivism, namely: there is an external world that can be fully explained in scientific language; that language stands in a one-to-one relationship to the facts; the facts can be fully discovered by observation and experiment; scientific observation and experiment are based upon what our senses can reveal; scientific theories are built up by the accumulation of more data; these theories are objective and not reliant on personal predilections; and the scientific knowledge that results is proven knowledge of the world as it objectively is. Recent scientific thinking about subatomic physics, systems theory, chaos theory and so on has suggested that scientific truth is more complex, subtle, multi-faceted and integral than this, and that the old certainties of scientism were too simple. The way is opened up for the insights of science and religion to be seen as complementary. ▷ secular alternatives to religion

scientology A movement on the fringe of Christianity, developed in the USA by L Ron Hubbard in the 1950s, which strives to open the mind of adherents to all great truths and to self-determination. Jesus is seen as one of several important teachers. The Church's scientific and religious claims have given rise to much controversy, as have its methods of financial management, and in the 1980s it defended several lawsuits in the USA. Nevertheless it has a wide following. ▷ Christianity; Hubbard, Lafayette Ronald; new religious movements in the West

scribe In post-exilic and pre-rabbinic Judaism, a class of experts on the Jewish law (the *sopherim*). Although Ezra was both a priest and a scribe, a class of lay Torah scholars eventually arose, who not only preserved and interpreted biblical laws, but by New Testament times were also involved with courts of justice. Most were Pharisees. They were also attested in Judaism outside of Palestine. ▷ Ezra; Judaism; Pharisees; rabbi; Torah

scriptures A term taken from the Latin *scriptura*, meaning writing, which refers to a written work that is held to be authoritative by a religious tradition. Insofar as they have oral rather than written traditions, primal religions do not have scriptures and their oral myths are for them the functional equivalent of scriptures. Scriptures are usually bound up with other elements in a religious tradition: they are often used in rituals, give a guide to ethics, are the basis for doctrines, are important for spirituality, and are significant to the life of the community. Although originating from revelation, defined in different ways, scriptures are designated as such by religious communities, and this process of setting up a canon of scripture can take hundreds of years, as with the Christian Bible, or a short time, as with the Quran. Either way, the scripture is handed down in oral form before it is finally written down. Once it is finalized in written form it cannot be modified in any way. However, a sacred text such as the *Bhagavad Gita* in Hinduism, which is not part of the original Veda, is as important as the Veda in practice; the same applies to the Jewish Talmud, which supplemented the Jewish Bible. Occasionally the same scripture is authoritative for more than one tradition, for example the Jewish Bible is the Christian Old Testament, and the Theravada Buddhist *tipitaka* or Pali Canon is recognized as a preparatory scripture by the Mahayana Buddhists. The interpretation of scripture is the work of a class of scholars or priests; the fact that religious believers throughout history have generally been illiterate has meant that they may have been denied direct access to scripture, especially as it has often been written in a sacred language such as Hebrew, Greek, Pali, Sanskrit or Arabic. In modern times the translation of scripture has assumed increasing importance in all religious traditions in spite of qualms as to whether the holy language should be 'tampered with'. ▷ Bhagavad Gita; canon; models of religion; Old Testament; Quran; revelation; Talmud; tipitaka; Veda

sect A separately organized group, usually religious, which rejects established religious or political authorities, and claims to adhere to the authentic elements of the wider tradition from which it has separated itself. It is distinctive and exclusive, claiming to possess true belief, correct ritual, and warranted standards of conduct. Membership is voluntary, but the sect accepts or rejects persons on the basis of some test of worthiness, and membership takes precedence over all other allegiances. ▷ religion

sects, Christian The term 'sect' may be applied theologically or sociologically. In the first sense it refers to Christian groups that have partly broken with orthodox belief (or Church order and practice, as with 'schism'), as opposed to 'cults' that are deemed to have completely broken away. In the second sense, a distinction is made between 'sect', 'church', and 'cult' or 'mysticism' (as in Troeltsch), or between 'sect', 'church', and 'denomination' (as in H R Niebuhr). In both sociological uses a contrast is intended between more-or-less automatic membership of the Church by everyone (as in medieval Catholicism), or membership by the majority of a particular social class of the same denomination (as with Anglicanism and other established churches), and voluntary membership of a (usually smaller) sect on the basis of a particular view of religion and society judged to be the 'truth'. Sects may arise on the basis of fresh interpretations of the Bible (Jehovah's Witnesses), additional written or psychic revelations (Mormons, Christian Science, Seventh Day Adventists, Unification Church), or they may treat the Bible as of quite secondary value. Their varied aims and attitudes resist easy classification. Theological and popular use of the terms 'sect' and 'cult' with negative or derogatory overtones has encouraged the adoption of the more neutral term 'new religious movements'. ▷ Christian Science; Jehovah's Witnesses; Mormons; Niebuhr, Helmut Richard; schism; Seventh Day Adventists; Troeltsch, Ernst Peter Wilhelm

sects, Sikh Although there are no sects within the Sikh tradition in the way that there are churches within the Christian tradition, there are distinct Sikh groups that differ from one another. The main division in the Sikh tradition is between Sikhs who have taken formal initiation into the Sikh *Khalsa* founded by Guru Gobind Singh in 1699 and follow its code of discipline, including the wearing of the five Ks (bangle, comb, shorts, sword, uncut hair), and those who have not. The latter are not a sect but are, so to speak, freelance rather than organized Sikhs. In recent times this has crystallized into the division between those who accept the revised Code of Conduct, the *Rahit Maryada*, accepted in 1945 after 14 years' preparatory work by the Shroman Gurdwara Parbandhak Committee, and those who do not. Within those who accept the Code of Conduct there is a further division between Sikhs who become actively involved in committed Sikh movements, such as the Sikh Sabha, founded in 1873, or the Akali Dal Party, and those who do not. Four heterodox Sikh groups can be distinguished from the Sikhs mentioned above. The ascetic Udasi order was founded by Guru Nanak's son, Babra Sri Chand (c.1494–1612), but is now basically Hindu rather than Sikh. Another ascetic order, the Nirmalas, originated from five men sent by Guru Gobind Singh to study in Banaras, but their movement too became close to Hinduism. In more recent times the Nirankaris, founded by Baba Dayal (1783–1855), attempted to return to the pure spirituality of Guru Nanak and move away from the martial emphases of later times, but as they have their own line of living gurus they are viewed with suspicion by many Sikhs. The same is true of the Namdharis, who followed Balak Singh (1797–1862), Ram Singh (1816–85) and presently Satguru Jagjit Singh, and in spite of their rigour they are viewed as being somewhat unorthodox. ▷ Akali Dal; five Ks; Gobind Singh, Guru; Khalsa; Nanak; Namdhari; Nirankar; Nirmalas; Udasi

secular alternatives to religion During the evolution of the modern Western world with its more secular emphases, various secular alternatives to religion have arisen. They may be substitutes for, rivals of, or complementary to the traditional religions. They include nationalism, Marxism, scientific positivism, Freudian depth psychology, utilitarianism, and secular humanism. Extreme nationalism in the form of Nazism was responsible for World War II, and it remains a force as many new nations have become independent and as ethnic groups strive to establish their own position. Like religion, nationalism has its own community, rituals, ethics, doctrines, sacred texts, aesthetics, and even spirituality. So to a greater or lesser degree do other secular alternatives to religion. Marxism until recently held sway in many lands, and Marx's and Mao's writings were treated as sacred texts, and 'faith' and 'conversion' were part of communism. Scientific positivism has faith in science and its possibilities for the betterment of the world. Freudianism with its faith in psychoanalysis; depth humanism, often deriving from Carl Jung's work, with its faith in human potential; utilitarianism, which for John Stuart Mill functioned as a sect; and secular humanism, seen in figures such as Bertrand Russell, who combined social involvement and radical protest with his agnostic views—all these have functioned as alternatives to religion. However, although they have often mounted an attack upon religion as being against the state, 'the opium of the people', projection, illiberal, and so on, in practice there has often been a fusion of elements of a religion and a secular alternative as in liberation theology, Christian humanism, civil religion, etc. ▷ civil religion; Freud, Sigmund; Human Potential movement; Jung, Carl Gustav; liberation theology; Marxism; Mill, John Stuart; Russell, Bertrand Arthur William; scientism; secularism; secularization

secular Christianity A mid 20th-century theology which acknowledged the secularization of Western civilization and sought to present a 'religionless' Christianity, with the emphasis on human freedom and responsibility, and divine transcendence understood historically rather than metaphysically. ▷ Bonhoeffer, Dietrich; Christianity; 'death of God' theology

secularism In Western theory, secularism is viewed as an ideology which supports the absolute authority of secular bodies to regulate the life of society, and which is opposed to religious belief. It is an alternative worldview which functions as an equivalent to religion, with its own secular orthodoxy. As such it is different from secularization, which is taken to be a neutral process whereby society and culture are delivered from religious tutelage and control, but which is not anti-religious in intent. However, in the multi-religious situation of India, secularism has a different meaning. It refers not to the absence of religion but to a political and social order wherein no one religion is preferred to the others, but all are given equal respect by the state. Secularism in the West, by contrast, has its own functional equivalents to religious institutions, rituals, ethics, scriptures, doctrines, and even spirituality: the difference from religion is that secularism in the West has its ultimate point of reference in the world and not beyond it in supernatural categories. It can take different and sometimes opposing forms such as Marxism, Freudianism, nationalism, utilitarianism, secular humanism, and scientific positivism. ▷ humanism; Marxism; scientism; secular alternatives to religion; secularization

secularization The process of change whereby authority passes from a religious source to a secular source, and whereby areas of life formerly under religious control, such as education and medicine, come under secular domination. It is a process that is not necessarily opposed to the best interests of religion, indeed secular theologians such as van Leeuwe have welcomed it as an agent of the Christian Gospel in freeing human beings from injustice and discrimination. It is different from secularism, which is an ideology encouraging unbelief. Some social scientists have argued that the process of secularization is irreversible. However the Islamic revolution, the rise of new religious movements and new age religion, and the collapse of communism in many parts of the world do not support this view. Moreover, in various cultures there appears to be a resurgence of interest in spirituality which suggests a growth of spiritualization as well as secularization. Another question is whether—if there is a trend towards secularization—it happens in a uniform way, or varies according to culture. If it does vary, it need not be seen as equivalent to westernization, but there can be such trends as Islamic, Buddhist and Hindu secularization with their own unique characteristics. ▷ Marxism; new age religion; new religious movements in the West; secular alternatives to religion; secularism; spirituality; theological attitudes

Sefer Bahir A short kabbalistic work originating in southern France towards the end of the 12th century. Its title appears to be based on Job 37.21, 'And now men cannot look on the light when it is bright [*bahir*] in the skies'. Written in Hebrew and Aramaic and probably based on earlier material, it purports to be a collection of early rabbinic sayings, but unfortunately it is not possible to ascertain its precise authorship. The Sefer Bahir contains general discussion as well as midrashic comment on biblical material. It is haphazardly arranged but is nonetheless of interest, since it is the first known piece of kabbalistic literature to treat the Bible as a systematic guide to heavenly as well as earthly matters; the question of divine attributes is also central. As a result the Sefer Bahir became influential among Spanish Jewish mystics until the appearance of the Zohar at the beginning of the 14th century. ▷ Kabbalah; sefirah; Zohar

sefirah (plural **sefirot**) A term used in the Kabbalah or Jewish mysticism to denote 10 of the 32 principles or paths by which God created the universe. They are described in the *sefer yetzirah* ('Book of Creation'), a work from talmudic times concerned with the origin and nature of the universe. The 32 paths are the letters of the Hebrew alphabet, combined with 10 sefirot, all of which are non-material. Since God created the world by his word (eg Genesis 1.3; Psalms 33.6), his articulation of the letters brought matter into being. The sefirot are: air, water, fire, north, south, east, west, height, depth, and the Spirit of God.

In the more developed mysticism of the Zohar (c.1300) the sefirot are attributes of God, active in the cosmos and renamed as follows: Crown, Wisdom, Understanding; Love, Strength, Beauty; Victory, Splendour, Foundation, and Kingdom. The first represents God's initial will to create and the last his harmonizing presence throughout creation; the others stand for God's cognitive and moral centrality in the universe. However, each sefirah is united to the rest and intimately connects to every facet of the cosmos. In particular, the sefirot relate to aspects of the human soul and body, so that prayers and deeds affect the whole created order. For this reason Israel was given the Torah, so that through obedience to its *mitzvot* the original harmony lost through Adam's sin might be restored. ▷ cosmogony, Jewish; Kabbalah; mitzvah; Torah; Zohar

Segundo, Juan Luis (1925–) Uruguayan Jesuit liberation theologian, born in Montevideo. After studying in Argentina and Europe he became Director of the Pedro Fabbro Institute of socio-religious research in Montevideo. Though critical of the methodology of some liberation theologians in *The Liberation of Theology* (1976), he defended them against Vatican criticisms in *Theology and the Church* (1986). He advocates employing a 'hermeneutical circle', in which reflection on reality prompts a questioning of prevailing ideological and theological assumptions that govern the received way of interpreting scripture leads to new understanding. His own multivolume exposition of liberation theology is entitled *Jesus of Nazareth Yesterday and Today* (5 vols, 1984–8). ▷ hermeneutics; Jesuits; liberation theology

Seljuks A Turkish dynasty belonging to a group of tribes known as the Oghuz, whose ancestor, Seljük, converted to Sunni Islam in Transoxania in the late 10th century. In the 1040s his grandsons, Tüghrül-Beg (c.990–1063) and Chagri-Beg (c.990–1060) conquered most of Persia, dividing up their conquests between them. In 1055 Tüghrül-Beg and his troops entered Baghdad, freeing the Abbasid caliph from the tutelage of the Shiite Buyids and receiving from him the title of 'sultan' which legitimized his position as the real ruler over most of the caliphate. He was succeeded by Chagri-Beg's son Alp-Arslan, who united the family domains; under him and his son Malik-Shah (1055–92), sultan from 1072, the Great Seljuk empire attained its greatest extent, incorporating Persia, Iraq, Syria, and Anatolia. The basis of Seljuk power was their regular army of Turkish mamluk slaves, frequently augmented by nomadic Turkmen tribesmen, and the Persian administrative system which they took over. However,

in accordance with the Seljuk tradition of joint rule, Malik-Shah divided up the empire among his family, a development which coincided with the arrival of the First Crusade. The loss of Syria to the Franks at the beginning of the 12th century was accompanied by the factual independence of many of the Turkmen leaders and even of the *atabegs*, provincial governors who were in theory regents for infant Seljuks.
The most enduring of the various Seljuk successor states was the sultanate of Rum in Anatolia, established by Alp-Arslan's cousin Süleyman (d.1084) and his son Kilij-Arslan I (d.1107) on territory won from the Byzantine ('Roman') empire. Thereafter the sultanate, based on Iconium (Konya), fell under the domination of the Danishmends, a rival Turkmem emirate in northern Anatolia, a situation reversed in the 1140s by Masud (d.1155), whose son Kilij-Arslan II (d.1192) won a decisive victory over the Byzantine emperor Manuel Comnenus at Myrioke phalon (1176). After the reign of Kay-Qubad (d.1237), who ruled from 1220, the sultanate gradually crumbled under Mongol pressure, to be finally destroyed in 1308. ▷ caliphate; Crusades

Separatists A Christian group founded in England by Robert Browne in 1580, and exiled to Holland. They were critical of the 'impure' national Church, and sought to model their Church on the New Testament. Their influence was felt in Congregationalism. ▷ Browne, Robert; Congregationalism; New Testament

Sephardim Descendants of Jews who lived in Spain and Portugal before 1492, but who were then expelled for not accepting Christianity, and became refugees in North Africa, Turkey and Italy. Subsequently they migrated to Northern Europe and the Americas, where during the 16th and 17th centuries they kept distinct from other Jews (especially those from Central Europe), considering themselves innately and culturally superior. They preserved their own rituals, customs, dialect (Ladino), and pronunciation of Hebrew. ▷ Diaspora; Judaism

Septuagint A translation into Greek of the Hebrew Bible, obtaining its name (meaning 'translation of the 70') from a legend in the *Letter of Aristeas* (2nd century BCE) about its composition as the work of 72 scholars, six from each of the twelve tribes of Israel. The translation was begun c.3rd century BCE to meet the need of Greek-speaking Jews in the Diaspora, but work progressed by several stages over about a century. It has a different order of books from that in the Hebrew canon, and contains some works not in that canon. When it was adopted by Christians as their preferred version of the Old Testament it lost favour among the Jews. ▷ Apocrypha, Old Testament; Bible; Diaspora; Old Testament

seraphim Heavenly beings mentioned in Jewish Scriptures only in the vision in Isaiah 6, where they are described as having six wings and being stationed above the throne of God, chanting refrains announcing the holiness of God. The origin of the term is uncertain. They are similar to the cherubim in Ezekiel 1. ▷ cherubim; God

Serapis A compound deity, combining the names and aspects of two Egyptian gods, Osiris and Apis, to which were further added features of major Greek gods, such as Zeus and Dionysus. The god was introduced to Alexandria by Ptolemy I in an attempt to unite Greeks and Egyptians in common worship. ▷ Apis; Greek religion; Osiris; Roman religion

sermon An address or homily, part of Christian worship, usually on a biblical text or theme. As 'the preaching of the Word of God' it is particularly stressed in Reformed worship. ▷ Christianity; Reformed Churches

Sermon on the Mount or **Plain** A collection of Jesus's ethical teaching, depicted in Matthew 5–7 as preached on a mountain early in Jesus's ministry, but in Luke 6.20–49 as on a 'plain'. Matthew's version is longer, and contains the Beatitudes, teaching about true adherence to God's law, instruction on love of enemies, the Lord's Prayer, admonitions about material anxieties, the Golden Rule, and exhortations to observe what is taught. ▷ Beatitudes; ethics; Golden Rule; Jesus Christ; Lord's Prayer

Servetus, Michael (1511–53) Spanish theologian and physician, born in Tudela. He worked largely in France and Switzerland. In *De Trinitatis Erroribus* (1531) and *Christianismi Restitutio* (1553) he denied the Trinity and the divinity of Jesus; he escaped the Inquisition but was burnt by Calvin in Geneva for heresy. He lectured on geography and astronomy, practised medicine at Charlien and Vienna (1538–53), and discovered the pulmonary circulation of the blood. ▷ Calvin, John; heresy; Inquisition; Trinity

Seth (also **Set, Sutekh**) Ancient Egyptian god of evil, darkness, the desert. Son of Geb and Nut, brother of Osiris, and husband of Nephthys, he acquired his evil character from his role in the Osirian legends. Jealous of his brother's rule over the earth, Seth tricked and murdered Osiris, then persecuted his widow Isis and young son Horus. Later he was involved in a great struggle with Horus, who sought to avenge his father's murder. Seth is normally represented as a man with the head of his cult animal, an unidentifiable creature with square-topped pricked ears and an arrow-like tail. Not always considered evil, he was worshipped in prehistoric times, and again by the Ramessid pharaohs (1320–1085BCE). His cult centre was at Ombos in Upper Egypt, and Seth was called 'Lord of Upper Egypt'. He was sometimes thought to be the son of Re and his defender in the solar boat. He was considered the god of foreigners and was worshipped, as Sutekh, by the Hyksos invaders (17th–16th century BCE), who identified him with Baal. ▷ Baal; ennead; Horus; Isis; Nephthys; Osiris

Seton, St Elizabeth Ann, née Bayley (1774–1821) American Catholic, the first native-born saint of the USA. Born into New York upper-class society, she married at 19 into a wealthy trading family, and in 1797 founded the Society for the Relief of Poor Widows with Small Children. In 1803 she herself was left a widowed mother of five. She was converted to Catholicism from Episcopalianism, took vows, founded a Catholic elementary school in Baltimore, and in 1809 founded the USA's first religious order, the Sisters of Charity. She was beatified by Pope John XXIII in 1963, and canonized in 1975. Her feast day is 4 January. ▷ canonization; Roman Catholicism

seven deadly sins The fundamental vices thought, in Christian tradition, to underlie all sinful actions. They are pride, covetousness, lust, envy, gluttony, anger, and sloth. ▷ Christianity; sin

Seveners (Ismaʿīlis) A sect within Shiite Islam that broke off from the mainstream body at the end of the 8th century. This sect claimed that Ismail, the eldest son of the sixth Shiite imam, should properly have been designated the seventh imam, hence the name Seveners. The position was complicated by the fact that Ismail died in 762, before his father, and according to the main Shiite branch, the Twelvers, the true succession came down through Ismail's brother. The Seveners developed a distinctive interpretation of the Quran and of Islam which aimed to bring out internal meanings, hidden truths and esoteric insights. For example, they stressed the mystical nature of the number seven, outlined a distinct cosmology, built up a speculative theology, and developed the notion of the supernatural nature of the Shiite imams. They gained political importance with the setting up of the Fatamid dynasty in Egypt and Syria (909–1171). In the 12th and 13th centuries a group of them gained notoriety as the Assassins. The Seveners survive today, their best-known offshoots being the branch centred upon the Aga Khan, and the Druzes of the Lebanon. ▷ Assassins; Druze; imam; Quran; Shiism; Twelvers

Seventh Day Adventists A section of the American Adventist movement of 1831 that stemmed from the preaching of William Miller (1782–1849). When Miller's prophecies that Christ would return to earth in 1843 or 1844 were disappointed, many left the movement. Some, agreeing with Ellen G White (1827–1915) that a spiritual change had taken place in heaven in 1844, also accepted the vision she had received about the importance of the fourth of the Ten Commandments (about honouring the Sabbath), and formed the Seventh Day Adventists. This group, officially founded in 1863, holds Ellen White's many other visions and prophecies in high regard, worships on Saturdays rather than Sundays, and observes other Old Testament requirements. It practises adult baptism by total immersion and teaches abstinence from alcohol and tobacco. It has its own publishing houses, schools and colleges, and a worldwide missionary programme. ▷ Adventists

sexuality in religion Sexuality has often been said to have religious significance, and three main attitudes have been adopted towards it. A positive attitude is seen in fertility rituals and ritual orgies where sex is considered natural and helpful to society and human well-being. A more negative attitude is found in many ascetic traditions, where methods of sexual self-control are often outlined and stressed, and sexual intercourse is frowned upon. Thirdly, sexuality can be seen as a way for the individual to gain spiritual advancement and to approach spiritual perfection. An example of this appears in Tantric Buddhism and Hinduism where ritual sexual intercourse (*maithuna*) is the culmination of a set of yogic pracices whereby sex is made sacred and is seen as an aid to spiritual growth. In most religious traditions sex within marriage has been permitted but sex outside marriage questioned. In some traditions, such as Gnosticism, sexuality was seen in two opposing ways. For those Gnostics who saw the material world as evil and the spiritual world as good, sexuality was to be avoided as part of the fallen material world; but for others it could be indulged in wantonly as being of no consequence in a sinful world. ▷ Christianity, sex and; Gnosticism; Tantric Buddhism; Tantric Hinduism

Shabad (Śabad) A Sikh term meaning 'Word', referring both to the divine revelation of God's Word, and to the words of the Sikh scripture, the *Guru Granth Sahib*. The first Sikh guru, Guru Nanak, saw the Word as a medium through which God's message was communicated to the world. Guru Nanak's communications and interpretations of Shabad were seen to have peculiar potency, and his hymns came to be viewed as Shabad in their own right. The same honour was given to the hymns of the later gurus, while hymns included in the *Guru Granth Sahib*, by writers other than the Sikh gurus, were also given the same consideration. Thus eventually Shabad became a general designation for all the hymns in the *Guru Granth Sahib*. ▷ Adi Granth; Guru Granth Sahib; Nanak

Shabbat ▷ Sabbath

Shabbatai Tsvi (1626–76) Jewish mystic and messianic pretender, born in Smyrna at a time of messianic expectation among many Jews. After a traditional upbringing, study of the *Zohar*, and a number of years spent travelling, he joined a group of mystics in Cairo. Moving to Gaza he met Nathan Benjamin Levi (1644–80), who believed Shabbatai to be the Messiah. This claim was made public in 1665, and Jews in the Diaspora were urged to repent and prepare themselves for the messianic era. Shabbatai returned to Smyrna, where he was rejected by some; others had visions of him crowned upon a messianic throne. While in Istanbul in 1666 he was imprisoned, with the result that Jews from far and wide made pigrimage to see him. However, when a Polish kabbalist called Nehemiah ha-Kohen decried him to the Turkish authorities, Shabbatai had to choose between death and conversion to Islam. When he opted for the latter, his apostasy came as a great shock to the majority of his supporters, although some attempted to justify it from rabbinic or kabbalistic tradition. In 1672, Shabbatai was banished to Albania, where he died. ▷ Diaspora Judaism; Hasidim; Kabbalah; messianism; Zohar

Shabuot(h) ▷ Shavuot

Shafii, al- (al-Shāfiʿī, Muḥammad ibn Idrīs) (767–820) The inspirer of the Shafiite school of law within Islam, born in Palestine. Raised in Mecca, he studied with Malik ibn Anas in Medina, lived in Baghdad and Mecca, and died in Egypt, where his tomb has remained a place of pilgrimage. He belonged to the Quraysh tribe and was therefore distantly related to Muhammad. In his *Rasala*, written towards the end of his life, he laid the systematic foundations for much of Islamic law. He argued that the four roots of Muslim jurisprudence were firstly the Quran itself, secondly the traditions and sayings of Muhammad, and thirdly and fourthly analogical reasoning (*Qiyas*) and the consensus of the community (*ijma*). This approach was adopted by the other law schools within Islam, although they each gave their own particular slant to al-Shafii's system. The Shafiite school has been mainly influential in East Africa, parts of Arabia, and South East Asia, although al-Shafii himself has been well regarded throughout the Islamic world from an early date. ▷ fiqh; ijma; Islamic law schools; Mecca; Medina; Qiyas; Quran; Quraysh; shariah

shah The Persian word for 'king'. Claims that the concept of sacral kingship is rooted in Zoroastrian doctrine, and is thus an essential part of Iranian culture, have been made, either implicitly or explicitly, by some Iranian dynasties from the Achaemenians (559–323BCE) until the recent Pahlavis. It is true that the notion that the khvarenah of the virtuous king is essential for the well-being of the country has its roots in ancient Iranian thought, though such ideas have usually been particularly prominent at times when they served the interests of a powerful dynasty. The inscriptions of the Achaemenians clearly imply that they claimed to have come to power with God's help, in order to establish harmony and order. Such ideas were developed further in Sasanian times (226–7th century), when it was said that 'kingship is based on religion, and religion on kingship'. Very similar ideas are occasionally found in Islamic Persian literature. ▷ khvarenah; kingship, sacred; Pahlavi; Zoroastrianism

shahadah (shahādah) The basic testimony and creed of Islam: 'I perceive (and bear witness) that there is no God except Allah and I perceive (and bear witness) that Muhammad is the messenger of God'. This affirmation is central to Islam and is the first and most important of its five pillars. It acts as a confession of faith, because, when it is sincerely affirmed in Arabic, it becomes a sign of being a Muslim. Repeated daily by Muslims at the five daily prayers and also on various other occasions, it combines two meanings derived from the verb *shahida*, namely perceiving the truth and testifying to the truth that one has perceived. This may involve not only living out the truth but also dying for the truth, and the term *shahid* means a martyr. It symbolizes the centrality of Allah in Muslim thinking and living and, for Muslims, the centrality of Muhammad as the key prophet of God. ▷ Allah; creeds; five pillars, Islamic; martyr; Muhammad

Shahrastani (Shahrastānī, Abū-l-Fatḥ Muḥammad ibn ʻAbd al-Karīm) (1076–1153) Muslim scholar of religion, born in Shahrastan, Khorasan. He studied law and theology, and wrote *The Limits of Prowess in Theology*, *The Productions of the Philosophers*, and *The Book of Religions and Systems of Thought*. The last work is especially remarkable in that, although he wrote from an Islamic viewpoint, he offered penetrating insights into various different religious traditions, as well as supplying much information about them. He had four grades: religions based on a revealed book (Christianity, Islam, Judaism); those that had an approximation to a revealed book (the Magians and Manichaeans); those that followed laws and judgements without the aid of a revealed book (the Sabians, ie Hellenistic 'pagans'); and those without a revealed book and without firm laws (worshippers of idols and stars). He also dealt with the Buddhists, Gnostics, Hindus, Pythagoreans, and the Zurvanite form of Zoroastrianism, as well as with the various sects of Islam. Within the limits of his context he was able to be reasonably objective, and he ranks as one of the first historians of religion, and one of the first comparative religionists. ▷ Buddhism; Christianity; Gnosticism; Hellenists; Hinduism; Judaism; Manichaeism; Pythagoras; theology; Zoroastrianism; Zurvan

Shaiva Siddhanta (Śaiva Siddhānta) A tradition of Shaivism which developed initially in Kashmir from the 9th century and by the 11th century had been transplanted to South India. As opposed to Kashmir Shaivism, Shaiva Siddhanta is a theistic or dualistic tradition in which Shiva, the supreme Lord (*pati*), is eternally distinct from the particular soul, the 'beast' (*pashu*), and from the universe or 'bond' (*pasha*). Liberation (*moksha*) is the soul's release from transmigration (*samsara*) in which it realizes its equality, but not identity, with Shiva. The Kashmir tradition of Shaiva Siddhanta is based on the 'dualist' revelatory texts called the Tantras and Agamas, which advocate the worship of Shiva in the form of Sadasiva, though they also accepted the Veda as revelation. In the South, the Shaiva Siddhanta merged with the Devotionalism (bhakti) of the Tamil poet-mystics, the Nayanars, and the tradition's sacred scriptures there include, along with the dualist Tantras and Agamas, Tamil poetry such as the *Sacred Sayings* (*Tiruvacagar*) of the famous poet Manikkavacagar (9th century). A text summarizing Shaiva Siddhanta theology is Meykandadeva's *Shivajnanabodha* (c.1200) in which he outlines the doctrine of the three realities (God, souls and the universe) and the soul's dependence upon God or Shiva. For the Shaiva Siddhanta liberation is achieved, with Shiva's grace, by initiation (*diksha*) and the performance of daily rituals in the morning, at midday and evening. These eradicate the substance of pollution (*mala*) covering the soul and, if performed regularly, the Shaiva Siddhantin will be liberated at death. Ardent devotion (bhakti) to Shiva can also result in liberation. ▷ Kashmir Shaivism; bhakti; moksha; samsara

Shaivism A major tradition in Hinduism, focused on the deity Shiva. Shaivism embraces a variety of theologies and practices, though it has tended to be more ascetic than the other great Hindu tradition, Vaishnavism, emphasizing yoga, asceticism (*tapas*) and renunciation (*sannyaṣa*). The tradition is very ancient in India: hymns to Shiva or Rudra are found in the Vedas and worship of Shiva possibly stretches back as far as the Indus Valley civilization, where a seal has been found of a figure reminiscent of Shiva. Within the general category of Shaivism a number of traditions can be subsumed, some of which developed in the context of the householder's way of life, others of which were developed by ascetics living in cremation grounds. These ascetics, such as the Pashupatas and the more extreme Kapalikas or their modern equivalents the Aghoris, sought liberation (*moksha*) through yoga, smearing themselves with ashes and imitating Shiva in his wild, ascetic aspect. Shaiva Siddhanta and Kashmir Shaivism adapted some of the sectarian aspects of Shaivism to the householder's lifestyle, though these two traditions are very different, Shaiva Siddhanta maintaining a strict dualism between the soul and Shiva, who is the absolute, and Kashmir Shaivism maintaining that the soul and Shiva are identical. The emphasis on knowledge (*jnana*) of Shiva in Kashmir

Shaivism contrasts with the emphasis on ritual action of the Shaiva Siddhanta and with the devotion (bhakti) of the Lingayats. Orthodox brahmanical Shaivas will revere the Veda and maintain the rules of Vedic ritual purity, while others will revere the heterodox Shaiva Tantras and go against purity prohibitions as part of their religious practices. Shiva is worshipped in most Hindu temples, particularly as the linga, the 'phallic' form of Shiva representing Shiva's creative force in union with his female energy or shakti. Shaivas can be distinguished from Vaishnavas be three horizontal marks painted on the forehead. ▷ bhakti; Indus Valley civilization; Kashmir Shaivism; Lingayats; Shiva; tapas

Shakers The popular name for members of the United Society for Believers in Christ's Second Appearing, founded in England under the leadership of Ann Lee (1736–84), a psychic visionary, who led them to America in 1774. They believe that Christ has appeared with Ann Lee. They are communitarian and pacifist, and their ecstatic dancing gave rise to their popular name. Their acceptance of strict celibacy has led to their virtual disappearance. ▷ Christianity; millenarianism

shaking tent, or **spirit lodge** A form of séance held by shamans in some Arctic cultures and among the Algonquin and some of their Plains neighbours. In the Algonquin form it takes place at night in a dark lodge or around a structure made from thick posts driven into the ground and covered with birch wood, to which bells and animal hooves are attached. The shaman's trance is accompanied by violent shaking of this solid structure, ringing and knocking from the bells and hooves, showers of sparks and strange animal noises. The spirits having thus demonstrated their presence, the shaman announces the answers of the spirits to the questions previously posed by those attending and claims the spirits' help in healing. A practice which at one time seemed to be declining among Native American peoples, it has shown signs of revival in modern times. ▷ Algonquin religion; shamanism

Shakti (Śakti) The female energy or power of the Hindu god Shiva. While Shiva is regarded as passive consciousness his consort, Shakti, is the power whereby he performs the five acts of the creation, maintenance and destruction of the universe, bestowing grace on devotees and concealing himself from them. Shakti is personified in Shiva's wives, such as Parvati, in orthodox texts but is particularly important in the heterodox texts called Tantras. In the Shaiva Siddhanta tradition, Shakti remains a purely abstract power of Shiva, but in Kashmir Shaivism and other Tantric traditions, she is personified in various gentle or ferocious forms. Indeed Shakti becomes more important in religious practice than Shiva in many Tantric traditions. For example, a form of the ferocious Kali who is emaciated, eyes rolling with intoxication, garlanded with severed male heads, is the focus of esoteric worship in Kashmir Shaiva traditions, transcending the male deity Sadashiva on whose corpse she dances. In the Shri Vidya tradition Shakti takes the gentle form of the beautiful Tripurasundari as the focus of worship. In Hindu Tantra Shakti is not only a cosmic power, but also a power within the body in the form of Kundalini who, once awakened through yoga, causes liberation (*moksha*). ▷ Kashmir Shaivism; Kundalini; moksha; Shaiva Siddhanta

shamanism The word shaman is used with a variety of meanings. Loosely (and misleadingly), it is used to denote any medicine man, diviner or magician, or anyone who uses possession or ecstasy. A more precise definition derives from the original use of the word by the Tungus people of Siberia. The Tungus shaman searches for the souls of sick people, and heals them (since sickness is

shaman from the Tungus people

caused by 'soul loss'), brings the souls of sacrificed animals to heaven, conducting them there personally, and leads the souls of those that die away from the area of the corpse (where they may annoy or endanger the living). These feats are done in ecstasy, conditioned by the beating of a drum (which also plays a part in the shaman's flights to the Other World). In ecstasy, he performs feats of strength, speaks in animal or bird language, and is attended by spirits, recognizable by strange voices or by remarkable phenomena—the shaking tent, a rope in the sky, fire of no obvious origin. His dress has animals painted on it, and he wears a cap and mask. The same or closely similar features are found among all the Siberian peoples, of whatever ethnic group, amongst the pre-Christian Lapps and amongst the Inuit (Eskimo) from Greenland to Alaska (where the shaman is called *angakok*), and amongst the Plains Indians of North America. Besides this circumpolar band of shamanism, similar institutions occur in Tierra del Fuego and among some Australian Aboriginal peoples; it is also found in Korea and, to a lesser degree, in some of the forest peoples of South East Asia. Echoes of the practice occur elsewhere, including Africa, although it is often less important than it is in Siberian religion, where it forms the centre of religious activity. There, and in other circumpolar religions, the shaman's help is vital to the community; in others he is simply a valuable adjunct, especially in healing. The shaman is often 'called' to his vocation by the spirits in the form of an illness that will not yield until he obeys. In Tibet, shamanism has been fused with other influences in a unique synthesis. ▷ shaman

Shamash Assyro-Babylonian sun god, known to the Sumerians by the name Utu. He travelled across the sky in a chariot by day and through the underworld by night. As he crossed the heavens he dispelled all darkness, giving light and life (*shamash* is the common Semitic word for 'sun'), and is praised for this in numerous hymns. His great importance was as god of justice, since on his daily journey he saw all the deeds of men. He was responsible for judgement and the punishment of sin, and is often depicted carrying a rod and a ring, symbols of straightness and completeness. Shamash had cult centres at Larsa in southern Mesopotamia and Sippar in the north. ▷ afterlife, Ancient Near Eastern concept of; Babylonian religion; Sumerian religion

Shambala In Tibetan Buddhism a mythical kingdom to the north of Tibet. The Tibetan canon describes the country as surrounded by mountains. At the centre is a city containing the king's palace and a garden which contains the wheel of time (*kalacakra*) mandala. The first king of Shambala was Sucandra, an incarnation of the bodhisattva Vajrapani, who was to be succeeded by 25 kings, each reigning for 100 years. The last king will ride out from Shambala, destroy the Muslims and usher in a new golden age of Buddhism. This messianic figure is sometimes identified with the legendary King Gesar. The Shambala legend is associated with the kalacakra tradition and may be modelled on an actual place to the north of India where Buddhism encountered Islam. ▷ bodhisattva; Buddhism; Gesar; Islam; mandala

Shammai (c.1st century BCE–1st century CE) Jewish scholar and Pharisaic leader, apparently a native of Jerusalem, head of a famous school of Torah scholars, whose interpretation of the Law was often in conflict with the equally famous school led by Hillel. Relatively little is known of Shammai himself, except that his legal judgements were often considered severe and literalistic, compared to Hillel's. Both are often referred to in the Mishnah. ▷ Hillel I; Judaism; Mishnah; Pharisees; Torah

Shang Ti A Chinese term meaning the 'Lord on High', which is one of the nearest approximations in Chinese to a synonym of the word 'God'. Shang Ti was the main deity during the Shang dynasty (1523–1027BCE). He was conceived in personal and anthropomorphic terms but was not seen as a creator God. His role was to control the cosmic round of the seasons; he was responsible for defending and protecting the Shang people; and he was the object of worship in the state religion centred on the sacrifices offered to him by the emperor. From the time of the Chou dynasty (1027 onwards) Shang Ti became assimilated into the more impersonal notion of heaven (*Tien*). When Christians wished to translate the word 'God' into Chinese, Protestants used the term Shang Ti and Roman Catholics used the term *Tien Chu* (Lord of Heaven). ▷ God; Tai Chi; Tien

Shankara (Śaṅkara) (788–820) Brahman from South India, often regarded as the greatest Indian philosopher who expounded the doctrine of Advaita Vedanta. Shankara was born in Kerala to a Nambuthiri Brahman family. His father died when he was a child and he was reared by his mother. Whilst still a child Shankara wished to become a world renouncer (*sannyasin*) but his mother forbade it. One day however, according to his biographies, an alligator caught Shankara in the river. He called out to his mother for permission to take renunciation and, thinking he was about to die, she conceded. The alligator, of course, released him and he became a renouncer. Finding a guru Shankara was taught the tradition of Vedanta and on the advice of his guru went to Varanasi. There, or in the Himalayas, he composed commentaries on various Upanishads, on the *Bhagavad Gita*, on the *Brahma Sutra* and an independent work the *Upadeshasahasri*. In these texts he expounded his philosophy of non-dualism (*advaita*), that the self (atman) is identical with the absolute (*Brahman*). This is known from statements in the sacred scriptures, such as 'I am Brahman' (*aham brahmasmi*), and from the experience of liberation in life (*jivanmukti*). Shankara founded a monastic order, the Dashanamis, and is said to have travelled to the four corners of India, the 'conquest of the directions' (*digvijaya*), founding four monasteries. These monastic traditions have continued unbroken to the present day. Shankara is also attributed with various devotional works such as the *Saundaryalahari* to the Goddess. ▷ Advaita Vedanta; Bhagavad Gita; guru; Upanishads

Shantideva (Śāntideva) (late 7th/early 8th century) One of the most popular writers in the Mahayana Buddhist tradition. He appears to have succeeded his father as King of Saurastra in India. However, he renounced his throne and became a monk as a result of a dream in which the bodhisattva Manjusri appeared to him. Two of his works are especially important. One of them (the *Siksa Samuccaya*) is a compendium of the doctrines of Mahayana Buddhism, especially the Madhyamika doctrines. It contains quotations from the main Mahayana Sutras, most of which are now lost in their original form. Another work (the *Bodhicaryavatara*) contains an excellent summary of the metaphysics of the important Madhyamika system. It reveals deep spiritual insight as well as philosophical power, and has been compared to the *Imitation of Christ* by St Thomas à Kempis. It stresses devotion to the Buddhas and bodhisattvas, and recommends confession of one's shortcomings before them as important elements in a mature spirituality. On both spiritual and intellectual grounds, Shantideva is an important Buddhist thinker. ▷ bodhisattva; Buddha; Kempis, Thomas à; Madhyamika; Mahayana Sutras; Manjusri

shariah (shari'ah) A Muslim term for the way ordained by God for human beings, much of which is to be found in practical terms in the canon law of Islam. It is similar to the Hindu term dharma. Much recent Muslim usage has focused upon the shariah as traditional Muslim law as opposed to Western secular law. This law is found in the Quran and the sunnah (the sayings and acts of Muhammad), and has been elaborated by the four orthodox schools of law, the Shafii, Hanbali, Hanafi and Maliki, and also by the Shiite schools of law. The four sources of orthodox law are: the Quran, the sayings and acts of Muhammad, the principle of analogy (*qiyas*), and the consensus of the Muslim community (*ijma*). Another source, *ijtihad* or meaningful interpretation, has been downplayed in modern times by the orthodox schools but emphasized by the Shiites. According to the shariah, acts are divided into five categories: obligatory, recommended, neutral, disapproved and prohibited. In theory the shariah covers the whole of life, but in practice it has recently become limited to matters concerned with family and religious practice. Outside Saudi Arabia and some Gulf countries shariah law is no longer dominant, and it has been superseded or balanced by Western codes. The recent rise of Islamic radicalism and the desire for less secular forms of politics have led to the call in parts of the Muslim world for a return to the shariah law. The influence of local religious leaders, the *ulama*, has given an impetus to this call. However, there is also the sense that shariah in essence is more than just jurisprudence (*fiqh*); it is God's ideal as a total way of life for human beings, transcending as well as including law. ▷ Allah; dharma; fiqh; Hanafi; Ibn Hanbal; ijma; ijtihad; Islamic law schools; Qiyas; Shafii, al-; sunnah; ulama

shastras (literally precepts or rules) Shastras are bodies of literature, often in verse, which form treatises or commentaries on *sutras*. Within Hinduism the most important shastras are those pertaining to the three types of obligation which fall to Hindus: dharma, *artha* and *kama*. The *dharmashastras* (c.200BCE–100CE), some of which are attributed to Manu, deal with the duties to be performed in the various *ashramas*, or stages of life, duties relevant to specific castes, and penances prescribed for particular transgressions. The *arthashastras* (c.400BCE–400CE), only discovered this century, deal with politics and the well-being of the nation (the goal of *artha* being, for the individual Hindu, the practical provision for oneself and one's home and family). The *kamashastras*, corresponding in some detail with the *arthashastras*, provide instructions on living life to the fullest within the restraints of caste. They are particularly concerned with sexual pleasure (kama), as the *kama sutra* testifies. ▷ dharma; four purposes, Hindu

Shavuot, or **Shabuot(h)** The Jewish Feast of Weeks, observed in May or June (6 Sivan) in commemoration of God's giving of the Law to Moses on Mount Sinai (Exodus 19); it is also known as Pentecost. ▷ Moses; Pentecost

Shay The concept of fate or destiny in Ancient Egypt, a term meaning 'that which is decreed', and personified as a deity. His fate was attached to each man from the moment of his birth, determining the length of his life and manner of death, and appearing after death in the hall of judgement. Shay could also determine good and bad fortune during his life, but was not completely unalterable; a man's destiny could be changed by his own actions or the influence of a deity. ▷ afterlife, Ancient Egyptian concept of

shaykh A Muslim title meaning literally an elder, a man over 50 years of age. It can be used generally as a title for the head of a village or town, for the head of a whole tribe, or for a person of quality and authority in political or spiritual matters, and especially for a person versed in matters of deep learning. In a particular sense it refers to the spiritual master of a Sufi order, and in India and Iran the equivalent title of *Pir* is used. Within Sufism different shaykhs have different functions: to initiate into a Sufi order; to provide effective teaching concerning the spiritual path; and to convey spiritual realization through spiritual charisma and example. Within Sufi orders the shaykh is usually the head of the community, and he will often be able to trace his spiritual ancestry back to the founder of the order. In his role as spiritual director the shaykh expects to be obeyed; at this level his role is similar to that of a guru in Hinduism. ▷ guru; Sufism

Shaykhism A movement within Shiite Islam that became significant within Iran at the beginning of the 19th century and paved the way for the Babi and Bahai traditions. Its initial inspiration was Shaykh Ahmad al-Ahsai (1753–1826), who was active in Iran from 1806 to 1822. During the time of his successor, Sayyid Kazim Rashti, it developed into a distinct sect and gained a number of followers. The two leaders stressed their intimate relationship with the Shiite Hidden Imam, and their followers claimed that they were a 'Fourth Support' to the foundations of true Islam because they were agents of grace between the Hidden Imam and his followers. Outward observances were now subordinate to 'inner truth', and these believers were the proclaimers of this new age of inner realities. They also had unusual views on eschatology, making the movement even more suspect in orthodox eyes. When Sayyid Kazim Rashti died without appointing a successor (1844), a gap was created in the development of the movement, and out of this situation the Babi tradition arose through the work of the Bab (1819–50). Later, the Bahai tradition grew out of the Babi community. ▷ Bab, the; Babis; Bahaism; eschatology; imam; Shiism

Shechem Israelite city some 40 miles north of Jerusalem, in the pass between Mount Ebal and Mount Gerizim. Archaeological evidence and early Egyptian texts suggest that Shechem was an important city during the period of the Hebrew patriarchs, and the traditions of the book of Genesis tell of both Abraham and Jacob erecting altars there. Shechem also figures importantly in the traditions about Israel's entry into Canaan, being the place where, after the conquest, Joshua established a covenant which bound the tribes of Israel to Yahweh their god and to one another as a tribal league (Joshua 24). It was not a prominent religious site during the period of the monarchy, although Solomon's son Rehoboam went there to be confirmed as king by an assembly of the northern tribes. When he was rejected, the usurper Jeroboam I was made king by the assembly and used Shechem as his capital for a time. The city was destroyed by the Assyrian invasion of 724–721BCE. It was rebuilt c.350BCE as the main religious centre of the Samaritans, who had a temple on Mount Gerizim to rival the one in Jerusalem, but was again destroyed at the end of the 2nd century BCE. ▷ Abraham; covenant; Jacob; Joshua; Samaritans

Sheen, Fulton John (1895–1979) American Roman Catholic prelate and broadcaster, born in El Paso, Illinois, the son of a farmer. He graduated from the Catholic University of America, then took a PhD at Louvain, Belgium. Ordained in 1919, he returned to the Catholic University to teach philosophy (1926–59) before becoming National Director of the Society for the Propagation of the Faith. Meanwhile he had gained a reputation as a broadcaster on the 'Catholic Hour' which was heard worldwide (1930–52), and he gained an even larger hearing with the TV programme *Life is Worth Living* (1952–65). He was auxiliary Bishop of New York (1951–65) and Bishop of Rochester (1966–9), then retired as titular archbishop. His many writings include *Peace of Soul* (1949), *Those Mysterious Priests* (1974) and *The Electronic Christian* (1979). ▷ Roman Catholicism

Shekinah (Hebrew 'dwelling', 'residence') God's special 'presence' with his people, Israel; in rabbinic works, his immanence, often associated with particular locations where he consecrated a place or object, as with the burning bush at Sinai or the Tabernacle in the wilderness. The motifs of light and glory are frequently linked with it. Some later Jewish philosophers considered it a created entity or intermediary figure distinct from God. ▷ God; rabbi; Tabernacle

Shem Biblical character, the eldest son of Noah, the brother of Ham and Japheth. He is said to have escaped the Flood with his father and brothers, and to have lived 600 years. His descendants are listed in Genesis 10, where he is depicted as the legendary father of 'Semitic' peoples, meant to include the Hebrews. ▷ Flood, the; Genesis, Book of; Noah

Shema (Hebrew 'hear') A well-known ancient Jewish prayer, traced at least to the 2nd century BCE, incorporating the words of Deuteronomy 6.4–9, 11.13–21 and Numbers 15.37–41, and beginning 'Hear, O Israel: The Lord our God, the Lord is one'. It introduces the Jewish morning and evening prayers, preceding the Amidah and itself preceded by two benedictions. It may be recited in any language and affirms belief in the oneness of God. ▷ Amidah; Judaism; mezuzah; tefillin

Sheol The most common word in the Hebrew Bible for the abode of the dead. In common with most ancient Near Eastern conceptions of the afterlife, Sheol is seen as a subterranean place where the dead are gathered in a shadowy existence. Occurring mainly in poetry, the word is not carefully defined, but we can build up a general picture of Sheol as a gloomy place of darkness, dust and silence, from which there is no return; its characteristics seem defined by contrast with human activity in the world of the living, and its inhabitants are remote from God, even if not entirely beyond his reach. For most of the Old Testament period all the dead, good and bad, go down to Sheol, whereas in later Judaism Sheol is replaced by Gehenna, a fiery hell where the wicked are punished for their sins. In biblical poetry Sheol is often used figuratively to describe a situation of extreme danger or suffering. ▷ afterlife; hell

Shepherd of Hermas A popular 2nd-century Christian work purportedly by Hermas, a Roman slave who was freed and became a merchant. The work is divided into visions, mandates, and similitudes (or parables), and is called 'The Shepherd' after the angel of repentance who appears in one of the visions. Its strong moral earnestness and stress on the need for penitence after baptism appealed to parts of the early Church, which for a time considered it 'inspired', but ultimately distinguished it from the New Testament canon. ▷ baptism; canon 1; Christianity

Sheppard, David Stuart (1929–) English Anglican prelate, and former Test cricketer, born in Reigate, Surrey. He graduated at Cambridge and worked in London's East End as Warden of the Mayflower Family Centre, Canning Town (1957–69). He was Bishop of Woolwich before becoming Bishop of Liverpool in 1975. There his profound social concern, the remarkable rapport in which he and Archbishop Derek Warlock (1920–), his Roman Catholic counterpart, work together (see their book, *Better Together*, 1988), and perhaps also his past record as former England and Sussex cricket captain, have made a lasting impact on the city. He has written *Parson's Pitch* (1964), *Built as a City* (1974), and *Bias to the Poor* (1983). ▷ Anglican Communion

Shiism (Shī'ism) One of the two main branches within the Muslim tradition, the other—much more numerous—one being the Sunni community. Shiism refers back to Ali, the cousin and son-in-law of Muhammad, as its original hero, and the word 'shia' originally meant the 'partisans' of Ali. The Shiite tradition contains less than 20 per cent of the Islamic population, and is mainly present in Iran, Iraq and the Indian sub-continent, although there are pockets too in East Africa, East Arabia, the Lebanon, Syria and Turkey. However, the Iranian revolution inspired by Ayatollah Khomeini in Iran has given it a prominence far in excess of its numerical strength. It accepts Ali and his descendants as the authentic imams within the Muslim tradition; it has developed its own system of law and theology; it has given a more provisional authority to governments than the Sunnis (hence the greater possibility of overthrowing the Shah of Iran in 1978–9); and it has highlighted the problem of suffering as a theme in Islam through its poignant dwelling on the death of Ali's son Husayn at Karbala in 680. It has split into different branches, including the Twelvers who recognize 12 imams, the Fivers who recognize five imams, and the Ismailis whose leader is the Aga Khan. Shiism became established in Iran with the rise of the Safavid dynasty in the 16th century, and its main centre has remained there. ▷ Ali; ayatollah; Husayn; imam; Ismailis; Muhammad; Sunnis; Twelvers

Shilluk religion The Shilluk are a Nilotic people of the South Sudan, living on the west bank of the Nile. Their religious system differs from those of their Dinka and Nuer neighbours, and is sometimes used as one of the models of African religion. It has two poles. One is Juok, which may in many contexts be translated as 'God', but may be manifested in various other spirit forms. Juok is creator, and the one on whom all ultimately depends. His preference accounts for the varying overlordship exercised by outsiders—Turks, Europeans, Arabs—in the area. But Juok is not directly worshipped. Religious activity centres on the culture hero Nyikang, who derives his ancestry from sky, river and earth, the three components of the local environment. The national myths describe his journey to the present homeland, his separation from the founders of the other Nilotic peoples, and his establishment of the kingdom by cunning and ruthless belligerence. From his clan comes each new Shilluk king (*reth*), who in his installation is identified with Nyikang. In this sense, kingship is sacral, though this has never inhibited criticism or rejection of a king. It is through Nyikang (and subsequent kings) that Juok is approached; indeed the language used sometimes identifies Nyikang with God. ▷ Dinka religion; Nuer religion

Shiloh The site of an ancient city in Central Palestine about 14 km/9 miles north of Bethel; it was noted as the central sanctuary of the tribes of Israel during the conquest and settlement of Palestine under the tribal judges. It also sheltered the Ark of the Covenant, and was thus a strong unifying force amongst the tribes. It was destroyed c.1050BCE, when the Ark was captured by the Philistines, and the priesthood then moved to Nob. ▷ Ark of the Covenant; Judaism; Philistine religion

Shingon The Japanese school of esoteric and mystical Buddhism, introduced from China into Japan by Kukai in 806. His *Jewel Key to the Store of Mysteries* (*Hizoboyaku*) in three volumes is a key text, in which he describes the spirituality of Shingon as the climax of spiritual attainment which fulfils nine other spiritual paths found in Buddhism and elsewhere. Mandalas (symbolic world-pictures) and other forms of sculpture and painting became important in Shingon, as was its stress upon Vairocana Buddha, the Buddha of infinite light, as the source of everything that exists and as the one through whom Buddhahood and the Buddha nature can be found in this world. It is assumed in the school that the esoteric truth of Shingon is deeper than, and the fulfilment of, the outward teachings of the historical Buddha. Rituals such as a fire ritual and an ordination ritual using water, the use of mantras (sacred sayings), and *mudras* (gestures) became part of Shingon practice. Today there are over 40 Shingon schools in Japan, in addition to which elements taken from Shingon have passed into various other schools of Japanese Buddhism. ▷ Buddha nature; Kukai; mandala; mantra; mudras; Vairocana

Shinran (1173–1263) Founder of the Japanese Buddhist Pure Land school known as Jodo Shinshu (True Pure Land). He developed in a more radical direction the work of his teacher Honen (1133–1212), who founded the original Jodo (Pure Land) sect in Japan. Shinran began by studying Tendai Buddhism on Mount Hiei just outside Kyoto, but he left to be with Honen, and through him came to emphasize the *nembutsu*, invoking the mercy and grace of Amida Buddha by using the phrase 'I put my faith in Amida Buddha'. In contrast to Honen he stressed the importance of the faith underlying the nembutsu rather then mere repetition of it, to the extent that if it could be said only once with absolute sincerity it would achieve for the sayer rebirth in the paradise or Pure Land of Amida Buddha. Shinran innovated by ending the celibacy of priests, and by stressing that Amida's grace was available to all, however sinful, on the premise that if it could be received by a good man how much more could it be received by a bad man. He stressed the 'other-power' or free grace of Amida rather than self-effort as being the appropriate means of salvation in the third degenerate phase of Buddhist history that pertained in his day. He simplified Pure Land and related it more closely to the lives of the ordinary people, so that his True Pure Land school eventually became the largest Pure Land group in Japan. ▷ Amida worship; Honen;

jiriki/tariki; Jodo; Jodo Shinshu; nembutsu; Pure Land Buddhism; Tendai

Shinto The indigenous religion of Japan, so named in the 8th century to distinguish it from Buddhism, from which it subsequently incorporated many features. It emerged from the nature-worship of Japanese folk religions, and this is reflected in ceremonies appealing to the mysterious powers of nature (*kami*) for benevolent treatment and protection. By the 8th century divine origins were ascribed to the imperial family, the emperor believed to be descended from the sun god, and in time became the basis for State Shintoism and its loyalty and obedience to the emperor. In the 19th century it was divided into Shrine (*jinga*) Shinto and Sectarian (*kyoho*) Shinto, with the former regarded as a 'state cult' and the latter officially recognized as a religion but ineligible for state support. In 1945, State Shinto lost its official status and now worship is a private affair, although it remains a significant part of Japanese life. ▷ Buddhism; Japanese religion; jinja; Kokutai Shinto

Shinto mythology The basic myths of Japanese Shinto are contained in the *Kojiki* written in 712 and the *Nihongi* written in 720. They outline the original creation of the cosmos out of chaos in the shape of an egg which then separated. During the mythological age of the gods that supervened the world and its *kamis* or divinities came into being. A succession of seven generations of divinities resulted in the marriage of a male *kami Izanagi* and a female *kami Izanami*, who together created the terrestrial world with its water, mountains and other natural elements. They also created the Japanese islands as a special feature. From Izanagi and Izanami descended the sun goddess Amaterasu, who in turn gave birth to the imperial line of Japan. The basic Shinto myths thus summarize the divine origin of Japan, her emperors and her people, and emphasize the significance of the divinities or kami that underlie the Japanese land and people. ▷ Amaterasu; creation myths; literature, Shinto; kami

ship burial Long before the Viking era, and over many centuries, Germanic peoples used ships as burial places. These ranged from fine vessels laden with treasures, such as must have borne the East Anglian king at Sutton Hoo, to modest rowing boats containing very basic goods, found in Iceland. The ship was often placed inside a funeral mound. Generally only fragments and nails, or the impress of a boat's shape, have survived until today, but whole ships have been found in good condition, especially in Norway. Sometimes ships were burned, or cremated bodies were placed in buried ships; while in the Anglo-Saxon poem *Beowulf*, a boat bearing a dead king and his treasures is sent out to sea. The practice suggests belief in a journey of the soul to the other world (in an Icelandic story 'death shoes' are tied on a corpse, implying a land journey). But there may be other factors behind the custom, too, such as, perhaps, a link with the Vanir, the deities of fertility and plenty. Freyr owned 'the best ships', and Njord, his father, was god of ships. ▷ Aesir and Vanir; Freya; Sutton Hoo

shirk A Muslim term meaning 'association' in the sense of associating anything with God. It is the fundamental sin in Islam. Insofar as God is one, absolute, perfect and complete, nothing can be added to him or set beside him. To associate anything with God, to commit *shirk*, is the one sin that cannot be forgiven: 'God forgives not that anything should be associated with him' (Quran 4.116). Shirk is the opposite of *tawhid*, the notion of the unity of God. It is also in opposition to 'Islam', which means literally 'surrender to God', and the touchstone of the Muslim faith is found in the affirmation of the *shahadah*: 'Allah is Allah and Muhammad is his prophet'. Shirk is sometimes used in connection with paganism in the sense of idolatry: pagans are termed 'the associaters'; it is sometimes used in connection with polytheism; it occasionally refers to atheism, not recognizing God at all; and it sometimes refers to the condition of being in opposition to God (rather than associating something else with God). In any case it is seen as the most fundamental error and basic sin that human beings can commit. It has analogies with the Christian notion of heresy. ▷ atheism; heresy; idolatry; Islam; polytheism; Quran; shahadah; tawhid

Shiva (Śiva) One of the three principal deities of the Hindu triad (*Trimurti*)—a god of contrasting features: creation and destruction, good and evil, fertility and asceticism. He is the original Lord of the Dance (*Nataraja*) and his principal symbolic representation is a phallic emblem denoting procreation. He is often depicted holding weapons and having three eyes, the third of which not only allows him inward vision but can destroy whoever it looks out on. ▷ Durga; Hinduism; Kali; linga; Nataraja; Parvati; Trimurti

shofar, or **shophar** A Hebrew term for a ram's horn, blown as a musical instrument;

it is mentioned in the Bible as to be sounded particularly at the Jewish New Year (Rosh Hashanah) and at the close of the Day of Atonement (Yom Kippur), but also used at war or for announcing important events. In modern times in Israel it has also been blown on Friday afternoons to announce the Sabbath. ▷ Judaism; Rosh Hashanah; Sabbath; Yom Kippur

Shoghi Effendi (Shoghi Effendi Rabbani) (1897–1957) The eldest grandson of Abdul-Baha, who had succeeded his father Bahaullah as leader of the Bahai movement in 1892. Shoghi Effendi succeeded Abdul-Baha as Bahai leader in 1921 while he was still a student at Oxford, and his successful leadership built up the Bahai tradition to the point where, at his death, it was poised to become a world religion rather than merely a new religious movement. He developed the Bahai Administrative Order on the basis of Local and National Spiritual Assemblies and in 1951 he set up the International Bahai Council. This was a forerunner of the Universal House of Justice which, formed in 1962, assumed leadership of the Bahai community in succession to three human leaders. Shoghi Effendi had an important teaching role through his translations into English of the works of his predecessors and through his own writings. He interpreted and formalized Bahai doctrine in the form that largely holds sway today. *God Passes By* (1944) and various volumes of letters were his most significant publications. ▷ Abdul-Baha; Bahaullah; Bahaism

Shomu (699–756) Japanese emperor who was responsible for the spread of Buddhist tradition in Japan. After becoming emperor in 727, he authorized the increased use of scripture readings from the Buddhist sutras, an increase in the number of Buddha images made, the building of many more seven-storied pagodas, and the spread of new convents and monasteries throughout China. He was mindful of the material benefits offered by the Buddhist tradition, eg to counteract the smallpox plague of 737, but he was even more mindful of its spiritual advantages, and abdicated in 749 to give himself more time for Buddhist pursuits. He built the huge Todai-ji temple at Nara with its famous bronze Buddha image; his collection of Buddhist and other objects is still on display in the Todai-ji compound. He ranks with Shotoku and Kammu among Japanese emperors who have had an important influence upon the Buddhist tradition in that land. ▷ Buddha image; Kammu; pagoda; Shotoku

Shotoku (Shōtoku) (573–621) Japanese prince who was of crucial importance in the introduction of the Buddhist tradition into Japan. He was prince regent for his aunt from 594 until his death, and during that period he helped to give new strength to the fledgling Japanese nation by importing important Confucian and Buddhist elements from Chinese culture and balancing them with Shinto. He is credited with having set up Japan's first constitution in 604; this included 17 points, one of which was respect for the Buddha. He had a personal Buddhist faith as well as seeing Buddhism as a cultural force in the new Japan; he welcomed Buddhist priests from Korea, received and studied Buddhist scriptures (*sutras*), and built Buddhist temples such as the Horyu-ji temple near his own palace. He had no preference for any particular Buddhist sect, and was impressed by what he saw as the Buddhist universalism of the Lotus Sutra. His fame as a Buddhist 'saint' arose after his death, and in Fujiwara Kanesuke's *Biography of Crown Prince Shotoku* written in 917 he is credited with various miracles, gifts and predictions, and is seen as an earthly manifestation of the bodhisattva Avalokiteshvara. Later Buddhist schools were able to increase their credibility by claiming links with Shotoku's teachings, and he has become a primary Buddhist hero in Japanese eyes. ▷ Avalokiteshvara; bodhisattva; Japanese Buddhism; Lotus Sutra

shrines A sacred place held to be imbued with spiritual power and religious significance. Shrines are often regarded as points where the divine world touches the secular world.

Torii, entrance to a Shinto shrine

They are usually established at locations intimately connected with important events and persons in a religion. Thus Mecca is an important shrine for Muslims because it was here that Muhammad's mission was centred. Similarly, the events of Jesus's life are commemorated by numerous shrines throughout Israel. In primitive societies shrines may be established at locations connected with the society's ancestors or with their burial sites. Sometimes it is claimed that a particular god himself founded the shrine. Shrines play an important role in religious life. They act as a focus for the religious feelings of a community and enable people to draw on and immerse themselves in their religious and social traditions. Shrines may therefore play a significant part in binding people together into a community.

The importance of shrines has led to the development of pilgrimage. To visit a shrine, particularly if this is at great cost to the pilgrim, is an important religious act. It is an affirmation of one's faith and may impart various religious advantages to the pilgrim. Shrines may also be places of healing. Many shrines are believed to possess the power to heal or transform the human being such as that at Lourdes (France), where, through its connection with the Virgin Mary, its waters are believed to possess miraculous powers. ▷ pilgrimage; temples

shrines, Shinto Japanese Shinto shrines are of different sizes and shapes. At the smallest level there are the shrines found in homes that are often 'god-shelves' (*kamidana*), containing *kami* on the shelves. They are found in the rooms of many houses and also in places like shops. As well as these there are portable shrines called *mikoshi* that are kept in temples and taken outside at times of processions. Shinto shrines in the more obvious sense were probably originally sacred areas set up around sacred objects, such as trees, and eventually fixed buildings were constructed in the Japanese countryside, often in groves of trees. Larger Shinto shrines usually have a compound, an entrance arch or *torii* where hands are washed and mouths are rinsed, a worship hall in which priests conduct worship, and a kami hall towards which worship is directed and in which symbols of the kami, such as a sword or mirror, are placed. Great shrines, such as the one dedicated to the sun goddess Amaterasu at Ise, achieved national importance. As Shinto drew closer to Buddhism, Shinto shrines were influenced by Buddhist elements but, after the Meiji restoration of 1868, shrine Shinto came into being under the control of the Japanese government to deal with shrines as state institutions. After the collapse of state Shinto in 1945 these shrines reverted to non-governmental and independent religious control. ▷ Amaterasu; Ise shrines; kami; Kokutai Shinto; miko

Shri Vaishnavas (Śrī Vaiṣṇavas) A tradition believed to have originated some time around the 9th or 10th centuries CE, in what is now the Indian state of Tamil Nadu—although its roots can be traced back to as early as the 6th century CE. As its name suggests the school reveres Vishnu, along with his consort Shri (Lakshmi), and is one of the principal Vaishnava schools. The Tamil philosopher, poet and theologian Yamuna is generally credited with founding the tradition, but it was Ramanuja who, more than any other, gave the movement philosophical credibility.

Central to the Shri Vaishnavite tradition are the temple ceremonies, as well as a good deal of home worship, in which Tamil hymns are recited. These were credited to the 12 *Alvars*, many of whom have had mythological stories attached to them. Conversely, the teachers (*acaryas*) of the tradition are given much more precise biographies, and it is from these that the tradition can be traced. Liberation is achieved by devotion (bhakti) and surrender to Shri and Vishnu who ultimately rescue their devotees by divine grace and lead them to union with *Brahman*.

The literature of the tradition, because of the fusion of Vedic and bhaktic ideas, is composed of a majority of Sanskrit texts with a significant minority of Tamil texts. This, in part, contributed towards a gradual schism in the movement between the *Vatakalai* ('northern culture') and *Tenkalai* ('southern culture'). ▷ bhakti; Brahman; Lakshmi; prakriti; Ramanuja; Tamil Buddhism; Vaishnavism; Vishnu; Yamuna

shruti (śruti) (literally 'what is heard') This encompasses the Hindu literature that is believed to have been revealed, which includes all Vedic scripture and the Upanishads. These scriptures are said always to have existed, and are believed to have been 'heard' by *rishis* (sages) who wrote them down without altering them in any way. This is because the words in the shruti texts are not only said to be eternal in meaning, but also in form. As a result their transmission is said to be infallible. ▷ smriti; Vedas; Upanishads

Shudras (Śūdras) The lowest varna (class) in Hinduism, largely made up of the non-

Aryan peoples who inhabited northern India before the Aryan invasion. They were generally classified as servants or slaves. Although not directly identified with any deity, they are mentioned in the *Rig Veda* (10.90: 11–12) which states that they emanated from the feet of the primal being, *purusha*. As shudras do not belong to one of the 'twice-born' varnas, they—according to orthodox Hinduism—are not able to receive initiation (*diksha*), and so cannot receive mantras or read the Vedas. ▷ purusha; varna; Vedas

Shugendo A Japanese religious movement known as 'mountain religion' which developed during the Heian period (794–1185). It arose out of the activities of mountain ascetics known as *yamabushi*, the first of whom is said to date back to the 6th century. They climbed sacred mountains to gain spiritual power, to engage in exorcism, and to train themselves to minister the will of the *kami* (deities) to the local people. They combined the characteristics of different elements of Japanese religion: Shinto kami located on sacred mountains, local Buddhas and bodhisattvas, and the charms and practices of religious Taoism. A 9th-century priest named Shobu helped to spread Shugendo, whose legendary founder combined Buddhist asceticism on a Shinto sacred mountain with some Chinese Taoist practices. The Shugendo groups became associated with esoteric Shingon Buddhism and, when it began to decline, it was Shugendo practitioners who passed on some of its charms and practices to the people, thereby helping to spread Buddhism in north Japan. Shugendo was proscribed in 1873 as being inimical to true Shinto. However, Shugendo yamabushi ministers still operate in the contemporary world. ▷ bodhisattva; Buddha; exorcism; kami; Taoism, Japanese; sacred mountains, Japanese; Shingon

Shulhan Arukh, or **Shulchan Aruch** Jewish law code, first published in Venice in 1565 and compiled by the mystic Joseph Karo (1488–1575). After Jewish displacement during the 15th century, most notably the expulsion of the Jews from Spain in 1492, the confusion that resulted necessitated a compendium of Jewish law. Karo, who himself left Spain, lived in Turkey and then settled in Safed in Palestine, met this need in a work called *Beit Yosef* ('House of Joseph') and in the shorter, more useful, *Shulhan Arukh* ('Set Table'). In this he claimed to be instructed by a heavenly Maggid (guide). He systematized Jewish law, taking works by three important predecessors as a basis and following the majority opinion on halakhic matters. However, since he was concerned primarily with Spanish law and custom, the *Shulhan Arukh* was revised by Moses Isserles (c.1520–1572), who took into account the traditions of East European Jewry; this made it useful for Jews everywhere for years to come. ▷ Ashkenazim; Halakhah; Luria, Isaac; Sephardim

shunyatavada (sūnyatāvāda) A form of Mahayana Buddhist philosophy that focuses upon the notion of emptiness, *shunyata*. The inspiration for the school arose from the original *Mahayana Sutras*, but teaching about emptiness in a systematic form emerged in the writing of the great monk-philosopher Nagarjuna in the 2nd century CE. He founded the Madhyamika school and it became closely linked with shunyatavada. Essentially this viewpoint repeated and placed great emphasis upon the Buddha's rejection of all speculative views. Reality could not be summed up in a parcel of concepts. Rigid beliefs or conceptual views are empty, and what is needed is an experiential insight into emptiness. This can be obtained by 'insight meditation' which can provide the possibility of penetrating to a transcendent awareness of the reality of emptiness by 'letting go' and going beyond mental or sense objects. It is necessary to pass from the conventional everyday level of truth to the higher level of truth in order to gain true insight into emptiness. Emptiness is thus not nihilism or unreality, but implies a deep renewal of the understanding and consciousness. The shunyatavada developed in India through the work of thinkers such as Chandrakirti, and it became a sect in China and Japan and a central force in Tibetan Buddhism. ▷ Buddha; Chandrakirti; emptiness; Mahayana Buddhism; Nagarjuna; vipassana

Sibylline Books In imperial Rome, a collection of prophetic utterances kept in the Temple of Palatine Apollo, and consulted in times of public calamity to learn how to divert the gods' displeasure. It was purchased, according to legend, by Tarquinius Superbus from the Sibyl of Cumae. ▷ divination, Roman; Roman religion

siddhas The name given to saints, or perfected ones, in the Tantric Buddhist tradition. They exemplified important features of Tantric Buddhism by their stress upon meditation, personal realization, lay spirituality, the guru-pupil chord, and the importance of both householders and wandering ascetics. They came to prominence from the 8th to the 12th centuries CE in India, and they came from low as well as high-caste backgrounds. Their stories tend to follow a set structure: they are ordinary humans who feel an unresolved call; this is resolved when they meet a Tantric teacher and find individual awakening; they begin intensive study with their guru; and eventually they find enlightenment in this life. As the equivalent of Mahayana Buddhist bodhisattvas, they offer great compassion to all beings and they are also able to engage in miraculous practices such as Saraha's walking on water. After death they remain available in a celestial realm, and in Tibet some of them appear as incarnate *tulkus* or lamas. There is a list of 84 of the greatest siddhas, and they are grouped into seven lineages by the Tibetan writer Taranatha. They wrote many Tantric works, and were important disseminators of Tantric Buddhism from India to Tibet, South-East Asia, and China (whence Tantric Buddhism went to Japan). The four great Tibetan schools date themselves back to Indian siddhas. The siddhas combined a stress on formless meditation, Tantric worship, involvement in the world, and unconventional spirituality, and are a unique form of Buddhist sainthood. ▷ bodhisattva; guru; lama; Mahayana Buddhism; Tantric Buddhism; Tibetan religion; tulku

siddur (plural **siddurim**) Jewish prayer book(s) used in worship on weekdays and Sabbaths. Only from the 9th century CE did a semi-standardized text take shape, when the Babylonian authorities sought to harmonize Jewish practice world-wide. The *seder* ('order') of the 9th-century sage Rav Amram was especially influential; even when Europe became the centre of things Jewish from the 10th century, Amram's work shaped the form of both Ashkenazi and Sefardi siddurim. At this stage, the siddur included the orders for all services; as services became increasingly long and complicated it became necessary to introduce a separate *mahzor* for the major festivals and a special Haggadah for Passover. Thus from the 13th century the siddur covered only weekdays and Sabbaths. The siddur text was never completely standardized, although the advent of printing encouraged harmonization. However, the Reform movement brought changes. From the end of the 18th century some Jews attempted to reconcile Judaism and modernity in terms of both practice and belief. This touched on the siddur. For example, Reform Judaism removed from its services references to Israel's election, hope for the Temple's restoration and a return to Palestine. Although many such alterations have since been reversed, each of the the various denominations within modern Judaism currently has its own siddur. ▷ Reform Judaism; worship, Jewish

sigalovada (sigālovāda) The name of a famous piece of teaching given by the Buddha which is found in the *Sigalavada Sutta* in the *tipitaka* or Pali Canon. Sigala was a young householder of Rajagaha who worshipped the four directions of the compass. The Buddha instructed him in a better form of worship by pointing out that he had social and ethical obligations in the direction of six sets of people: parents, teachers, family, friends, workmates, and religious teachers. In the process of teaching Sigala the Buddha gave a comprehensive summary of the social duties of lay Buddhists in regard to the six basic human relationships: between parents and children, teachers and pupils, husband and wife, sets of friends, employer and employee, and monk and layman. According to the Pali tradition Sigala, who was a Brahman, became a disciple of the Buddha. The discourse that bears his name gives a full account of the obligations of a householder, and has similarities to the five relationships that are central to the Chinese Confucian tradition. ▷ Buddha; ethics in religion; five relationships, Confucian; sila; tipitaka

Sikh history The Sikh tradition began with the work of Guru Nanak, who wrote beautiful devotional hymns, set out the early Sikh doctrines, and gathered disciples around him. He was succeeded by nine other human gurus, the last of whom was Guru Gobind Singh. During their leadership the community was built up, the Sikh sacred city of Amritsar was founded, the Sikh scripture the *Adi Granth* was compiled, and skirmishes took place with the Mughal empire which began to persecute the Sikhs. The final guru, Guru Gobind Singh, founded the Sikh order, the *Khalsa*, which gave the Sikh community its distinctive outward identity including the five Ks (bangle, comb, shorts, sword, and uncut hair) and the name *Singh*. After the tenth guru's death in 1708 the Sikh scripture, which then became known as the *Guru Granth Sahib*, succeeded him as the supreme authority of the Sikh tradition. His death also coincided with outright rebellion against the Mughals, and guerrilla warfare continued until the collapse of Mughal authority in the mid 18th century. At the end of that century Ranjit Singh united the Sikhs and became Maharajah of the Punjab, ruling until his death in 1839. However, when the British annexed the Punjab in

1849 there was a period of internal weakness in the Sikh tradition. This was alleviated by the rise in 1873 of the Singh Sabha, which opposed militant Christianity and Hinduism by setting up schools, colleges and a programme of literature, and gave a lead in the later founding of the Akali Dal movement to regain control of the Sikh gurdwaras from Hindu hands. Since the late 19th century, and especially since World War II, the Sikh tradition has become a world religion through emigration to Europe, North America, East Africa, Australasia, and other countries in Asia. In India there has been a struggle for increased Sikh influence in their native Punjab. ▷ Adi Granth; Akali Dal; Amritsar; five Ks; gurdwara; Gobind Singh, Guru; Guru Granth Sahib; Khalsa; Nanak; Punjab; Sikh religion worldwide; Singh

Sikhism A religion founded by Guru Nanak (1469–1539) in the Punjab area of North India and combining elements from Hinduism and Islam. Nanak believed that in both these religions the truth about God was obscured by ritual. He believed that one would come close to God through meditation and devotion rather than by ceremonies and religious ritual. Under his leadership and that of his nine successors Sikhism prospered. It is called a religion of the gurus, and seeks union with God through worship and service. God is the true guru, and his divine word has come to humanity through the 10 historical gurus. The line ended in 1708, since when the Sikh community is called guru. The *Adi Granth*, their sacred scripture, is also called a guru. The Sikh understanding of life is closely related to Punjab identity. ▷ Adi Granth; Amar Das, Guru; Angad, Guru; Arjan, Guru; five Ks; Gobind Singh, Guru; guru; Hargobind, Guru; khalistan; Khalsa; Nanak; Nihangs; Punjab; Rahit Maryada; Ram Das, Guru; religion; Sikh history; Tegh Bahadur, Guru

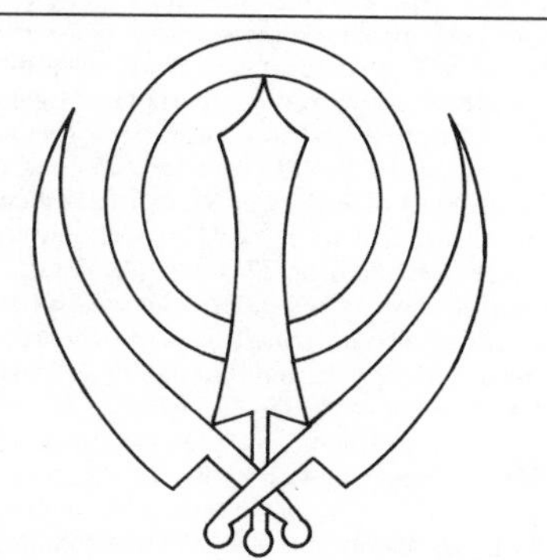

Khalsa, symbol of the Sikh community

Sikh languages Insofar as the Sikh homeland is the Punjab of India, the Punjabi language and its Gurmukhi script are of deep importance to Sikhs. The life stories of Guru Nanak, known as the *janam sakhis*, were written in Punjabi. The Sikh scripture, the *Adi Granth*, had a slightly more complex linguistic background. Vernacular Indian languages were arising at the time it was written and replacing Sanskrit in popular affection. However they were developing and changing themselves, like European languages at the time. Thus, in the *Adi Granth*, some Punjabi is used, as is some popular Hindi, which was the devotional language of the writers of the Sant movement, some of whose works are included in the *Adi Granth*. In the later secondary Sikh scripture, the *Dasam Granth*, the Braj language of Mathura (connected with the Krishna stories) was used, albeit in the Punjabi Gurmukhi script. In spite of this dallying with other languages in the two Sikh scriptures, in the late 18th century, and again in the 1980s, there has been a return to Punjabi language and culture, which is taken by Sikhs as defining Sikhism. A problem with this is that the Sikh tradition has now become a world religion, and this concentration on Punjabi may pose some questions for Sikhs born outside India who have little access to the Punjabi language. ▷ Adi Granth; Dasam Granth; Janam Sakhis; Krishna; Nanak; Punjab; Sant tradition

Sikh modern reform movements (Singh Sabhas) Throughout Sikh history there have been a variety of reform movements. In modern times the Singh Sabha movement has been especially important. It arose in response to the apparent diminishment of the Sikh community in 1849 under the British Raj. Singh Sabhas developed in Amritsar in 1873 and Lahore in 1879 and later in other Sikh areas. Their aim was to restore essential Sikh tenets and practices through books and pamphlets, public meetings, educational reforms and renewed religious assemblies. After splits between the two main Singh Sabhas, and their reunification in the Khalsa Diwan of 1902, a more radical movement arose, aimed at recovering control of the Sikh temples, the gurdwaras, from the Hindu priests who officiated in them. This led to the Akali movement, which began a programme of vigorous persuasion in 1920. This resulted in the successful transfer of the Sikh gurdwaras into the control of the Shiromani Gurdwara Parbandhak Committee, which was a Sikh organization. The Akali Dal became and remains a Sikh political party in the Punjab of India. ▷ Akali Dal; Amritsar; gurdwara; Punjab

Sikh religion worldwide The 'homeland' of the Sikhs is the Punjab of India, and although the Sikh tradition has recently become a world religion most Sikhs still have family or contacts in the Punjab, where about 15 million Sikhs now live. Thus there remains an emotional attachment to the culture, language and soil of the Punjab, even though some Sikhs in today's world may never have visited their sacred turf. The first significant exodus from the Punjab came after it was annexed by the British in 1849. Sikhs settled as traders in parts of India adjoining the Punjab, and as members of the British army they went to, and began small settlements in, Hong Kong and Singapore, from where they went on to Fiji, Australia and New Zealand. Others went to East Africa to work on the railways, and a few others went to North America. Significant Sikh dispersion began after World War II. When African countries became independent many Sikhs emigrated to the UK, other Commonwealth countries, or North America, countries where the English language was spoken. The main motive was the desire to find work and send money back to relatives. There are about 300000 Sikhs living in Britain, the largest concentration outside India, and small groups of Sikhs have also gone in new directions, especially to European countries, even though English is not the spoken language. Although there is not a strong missionary emphasis within the Sikh community, a trickle of Western converts have become Sikhs through the work of such organizations as the Sikh Dharma of the Western Hemisphere, founded by Yogi Bhajan in 1971, and its better-known educational offshoot 3HO (Happy, Healthy, Holy Organization). ▷ Happy-Healthy-Holy Organization; Punjab

sila (sīla) The Buddhist term for ethics and morality. One element in Buddhist morality is the observation of five negative ethical precepts (*panca-sila*), namely not to injure any living being, not to steal, not to engage in undue sensuality, not to speak unworthily, and not to partake of strong drink or drugs. A slightly more positive view of sila is given in the three ethical items built into the eightfold path: to engage in right speech, to engage in right action, and to engage in the right means of making a living. In the eightfold path the three items on morality are preceded by two items concerned with faith, and succeeded by three items concerned with meditation; faith, morality and meditation are seen to be integral parts of the full Buddhist life. Ten ethical precepts are binding upon monks as opposed to lay folk, although the laity if they want to be ethically zealous can take up three more moral precepts in addition to the five mentioned above. In practice generosity of giving by the laity is ethically valued, including giving to the monks. ▷ bhavana; eightfold path; ethics in religion; saddha

Simeon, tribe of One of the 12 tribes of ancient Israel, purportedly descended from Jacob's second son by Leah. Its territory was in the southern extremity of Palestine, south of Judah, into which it seems to have been nearly absorbed. ▷ Israel, tribes of; Jacob; Old Testament

Simeon Stylites, St (387–459) The earliest of the Christian ascetic 'pillar' saints. After living nine years in a Syrian monastery without leaving his cell, he became revered as a miracle-worker. To separate himself from the people, c.420 he established himself on top of a pillar about 20 m/70 ft high at Telanessa, near Antioch, where he spent the rest of his life preaching to crowds. He had many imitators, known as stylites. His feast day is 5 January (West) or 1 September (East). ▷ asceticism; Christianity

Simkhat (or **Simchat**) **Torah** The day in the Jewish year on which the cycle of synagogal Torah readings comes to an end and immediately recommences. The Torah is divided into weekly portions so that it is completed in the space of one year, along with the set prophetic readings or Haftarot (singular Haftarah). Simkhat Torah (literally 'rejoicing in the Torah') falls on 23 Tishri, immediately after the Festival of Sukkot (Tabernacles), for Jews in the Diaspora; Jews in Israel celebrate it on 22 Tishri. As the name implies, the day is one of festivity, and the Torah scrolls are paraded around the synagogue with singing and dancing. ▷ calendar, Jewish; hagim; worship, Jewish

Simon Peter ▷ Peter, St

Simons, Menno (1496–1561) Dutch Anabaptist leader, founder of the Mennonites. He was born in Witmarsum, Friesland, and ministered as a Catholic priest in Pingjum and

Witmarsum until, having read Luther, he renounced Catholicism for non-militant Anabaptism in 1536. A 25-year itinerant ministry followed, in which he organized Anabaptist groups in the Netherlands, the Rhineland, and Danish Holstein. He was persecuted by both Catholics and Protestants. ▷ Mennonites

sin Rebellion against and alienation from God. What are popularly regarded as 'sins', ie greed, hate, cruelty, lying, and especially sensuality, are consequences of the primary sin of turning away from God and his commandments. The distinction between sin and crime is that the former always involves offence against God, whereas the latter is simply a violation of civil law. Sin is a factor in many religions, though it is represented in a wide variety of ways. The Hebrew Bible, for example, represents sin as a constant element in the experience of Israel. ▷ evil; Fall, the; original sin; sexuality

sin, Christian view of Christianity accepts the Jewish belief that all humanity is flawed (original sin) and falls short of the will of God, but finds the Old Testament system of sacrifice unsatisfactory. Although most individual sins against God and one's neighbour can be forgiven, the basic problem of a tendency to sin remains. The remedy of a 'new covenant' written 'on the heart', which was promised by the prophet Jeremiah (Jeremiah 31), and the 'suffering Servant of the Lord' who will deal with sin, promised by the prophet Isaiah (Isaiah 52–3), are seen by Christians to be fulfilled in Jesus Christ. The precise way that the death of Christ (John 3.14–16) makes believers justified or right with God has been a matter of debate since earliest times. Theologians have also discussed the way to deal with sins committed after baptism, the relationship between sin and free will, and degrees of responsibility for sin. Liberation theology speaks of structural or institutional sin in Church and society as well as of personal sin. The link between sin and sex in the popular mind has some basis in a strand of thinking that goes back to Augustine, but the overall Christian view is much wider: everything that causes human beings to fall short of the glory of God and the demands of love is sin. ▷ atonement; Augustine, St (of Hippo); Christianity, sex and; humankind, Christian view of; indulgences; justification; liberation theology; merit; original sin; Pelagius; penance; salvation, Christian view of; seven deadly sins

sin, Islamic view of The notion of original sin is absent from Islam. The fault for the fall of Adam and Eve in the Garden of Eden is traced back to Satan rather then to Adam, who is in any case not viewed as a representative human being as he is in Christianity. Muslims view sin under two different headings. It is seen firstly as a fault or shortcoming (*dhanb*), which happens inadvertently rather than by malice aforethought; Adam's and Eve's fall is seen in this light. At a deeper level, sin is seen as wilful transgression (*ithm*), which is a matter of intention rather than accident. Thus wilful sin (ithm) includes inadvertent sin (dhanb), but accidental sin does not include intentional sin. Muslims share the doctrine of the sinlessness of the prophets, and Shiite Muslims include their own imams within this doctrine. Thus the prophets of Islam and the Shiite imams may sin inadvertently, but they do not sin intentionally. Even intentional sin can be overcome by repentance and accepting God's forgiveness, and although unbelief (*kufr*) is the most basic sin of all, even this can be overcome by conversion to the truth (*tawbah*). As Ibn Ata Allah put it: 'there is no minor sin when his [God's] justice confronts you; there is no major sin when his grace confronts you'. In early Islam the Kharijites had held a radical view of the enormity of sin and it was in dialogue with this view that orthodox Islamic theology developed the more tolerant view that became the Muslim norm. ▷ Adam and Eve; dhanb; Eden, Garden of; imam; Shiism

Sinai, Mount A mountain of uncertain location, traditionally placed among the granite mountains of the South Sinai peninsula, but sometimes located in Arabia east of the Gulf of Aqabah; it is also called Horeb in the Hebrew Bible. According to the Book of Exodus this is where God revealed himself to Moses, and made a covenant with Israel by giving Moses the Ten Commandments on tablets of stone. ▷ covenant; Moses; Ten Commandments

Singh (Siṅgh) A Sikh name meaning 'lion', used by all male members of the Sikh community, the *Khalsa*, and many other 'freelance' Sikhs, in place of or in addition to their own names. It was given to all Sikhs when the Khalsa was set up at the Baisakhi festival of 1699 by Guru Gobind Singh in an attempt to unite the Sikh community in the face of danger from the Mughal Empire. It was also given to replace other names that stressed particular castes or kinship groups that the Sikhs wished to leave behind in their desire to become a more universal community. The name Singh Sabha was given to a new Sikh association set up in Amritsar in another time of crisis (1873) to react against Christian attempts to convert Sikhs. In 1877 the Arya Samaj began to try to convert Sikhs to Hinduism, and this gave a further impetus to the Singh Sabha. It developed schools, colleges and literature, and later gave a lead to the foundation of the Akali political party and the movement to regain control of Sikh gurdwaras from Hindu hands. The name Singh at an individual or group level denotes courage and steadfastness. ▷ Akali Dal; Arya Samaj; Baisakhi; Gobind Singh, Guru; Khalsa; Mughal Empire

Sinhalese Buddhism According to Buddhist tradition, Buddhism spread significantly into Ceylon as a result of the missionary efforts stimulated by the Indian emperor Ashoka in the 3rd century BCE. The *Dipavamsa* and the *Culavamsa* purport to give the story of the Buddhist tradition in Ceylon from the time of the Buddha to the 4th century CE, and from the 4th to the 19th century CE. Although good historical sources are sparse, it is clear that Buddhism in its Theravada form was a significant force in Sinhalese life, and it was when Buddhaghosa went to Ceylon from India around 430CE that he became the great authority for Theravada Buddhism. There was an alliance between the monarchy, the Buddhist sangha, and the laity, which made Theravada the implicit national religion of the island. During medieval times Tamil-speaking Hindus entered Ceylon, and during the time of the British Raj, Western Christians and missionaries entered too. Three main modern trends can be discerned. Sinhalese Buddhism was influenced by local deva cults and traditional rituals so that it took an indigenous form. It also spearheaded a nationalistic reaction against foreign domination and Christian proselytism. It was also influenced by Protestant Christianity, by Western movements such as theosophy, and by the Western world view. There was an attempt to reform Buddhism so that it became more rational, more historically minded, more scientific, more socially involved, and more modern. However, at the village level Buddhism continued to stress merit-making activities rather than reason or liberation, and at the political level Buddhism became uncharacteristically aggressive in its confrontation with Tamil separatism. ▷ Ashoka; Buddhaghosa; Buddhism in South-East Asia; Dipavamsa; sangha; Theravada Buddhism

Sion ▷ Zion

Sioux religion The term 'Sioux' has two applications. The narrow one is to the alliance of 'the Seven Fire Places', known to the French as the Teton and Oglala Sioux, and together as the Dakota (now increasingly rendered Lakota). The wider definition takes in the Omaha, Osage, Ponca, Crow, Winnebago and other members of the Siouan language family. White competition forced the Sioux from forest dwelling and corn growing to plains hunting and then to reservations, processes inducing religious change. Among the southern Sioux the word *Wakonda* represents both the supreme being and manifestations of supernatural power more generally. For the Dakota, *wakan* stands for supernatural power; *Wakan Tanka* is the Great Spirit (eventually identified with the Christian God). The sun and other great powers of nature are also *wakan*; so are more localized spirits. The accepted (but not necessarily original) account of the origin of Lakota religion speaks of the bringing of the Sacred Pipe by the White Buffalo Woman, and devotional smoking retains important religious and social functions. The enforced move to the plains brought the Sun Dance, with its agonizing disciplines and ritual representation of death and rebirth. Painful discipline appears in other institutions: the sweat lodge, the vision quest, the strenuous initiation of the medicine man (*wakan wicasa*). The Ghost Dance movement affected the Sioux especially, culminating in the tragedy of Wounded Knee in 1890, when they were massacred by US troops. ▷ Black Elk, calumet; Ghost Dance; medicine lodge; Sun Dance; sweat lodge; vision quest

Sitra Ahra, or **Sitra Achra** The domain in which evil operates, according to traditions in the Kabbalah or Jewish mysticism. Because they conceive the world to be essentially good, Jewish mystics have sought to explain the existence of evil. Thus, the disturbance of an original universal harmony, either by some cosmic degeneration and/or the sin of Adam, resulted in corruption. But the detail of this picture varies. The Sefer Bahir, for example, holds that evil originated with the 10 sefirot or attributes of God active in creation. One of them, the attribute of power or judgement, when disturbed from proper integration with its counterpart, the attribute of love or compassion, overflowed so as to form the sitra ahra (literally 'the other side'), the source of evil and demons. Although the sitra ahra is not part of the divine realm, its connection to one of the divine attributes must mean that even death and evil have a positive origin. Another view, found in the Zohar, posits that evil has its origin in the remnants of former worlds that were destroyed. ▷ Kabbalah; Sefer Bahir; sefirah; Zohar

skandhas A Buddhist term referring to the five constituent elements that make up a person. There is no 'self' lying behind the constituent elements like a motor giving them life. The notion of the 'self' is a meaningless conventional label which does not refer to anything that really exists. All that exist are the five skandhas, which are: physical form, feelings, perceptions, volitions, and consciousness. These are the five factors that constitute what is outwardly called a person, and the ultimate aim of the Buddhist way is to go beyond the superficial and false notion that there is a permanent self holding together the skandhas. They are impermanent (*anicca*), unsatisfactory (*duhkha*), and empty of self (*anatman*). Nevertheless, the five skandhas do relate together as a collection of functioning aggregates to form a 'person', just as the parts of a chariot relate together functionally to form a chariot, but there is no transcendent 'self' or 'chariot'. ▷ anatman; dependent origination; duhkha

skilful means A Buddhist term referring to the ability of the Buddha and Buddhist teachers to adapt their teaching to the particular context in which they found themselves. This meant taking into account the temperament and level of understanding of the people addressed, and selecting a different story or doctrine from a general body of teaching to speak to particular circumstances. The later Mahayana tradition deepened the notion of skilful means (*upaya-kaushalya*) in a subtle way even to the extent of countenancing compassionate tricks if they would further spiritual advance. A 7th-century writer, Shantideva, wrote that a bodhisattva was even justified in doing a deed that would lead to hell if it would truly help someone else. The Mahayana thinkers therefore gave deep flexibility to the notion of skilful means while at the same time trying to avoid excess by stressing compassion, meditation and the working-out of the process of karma (deeds). This notion may be one of the reasons why the Buddhist tradition was able to adapt to vastly different cultures as it spread from India across South-East Asia. ▷ bhavana; bodhisattva; Buddha; karma; karuna; Mahayana Buddhism

Skobtsova, Maria (1891–1945) Russian Orthodox nun, born in Riga. She early identified herself with the Social Revolutionaries when a student in St Petersburg, where she was the first woman to enrol at the Ecclesiastical Academy. Bolshevik excesses having disillusioned her, she was among those who escaped to France. She began work with the Russian Orthodox Student Christian Movement which administered also to refugees, and in 1932, despite having had two divorces, became a nun. Unconventional and radical, she worked among society's cast-offs, whom she fed and housed. Nazi measures against the Jews in wartime Paris provided a new challenge. She was arrested and sent to Ravensbrück concentration camp in 1943, where she brought Christian light and hope despite appalling conditions. She was gassed on the eve of Easter, 1945, reportedly going voluntarily in order to help her companions to die. ▷ Nazi Party; Russian Orthodox Church

slavery The ownership of one person by another. In the Old Testament slavery was taken for granted as part of the social order and a series of laws was developed regulating the treatment of slaves. In the New Testament there is no outright condemnation of slavery, although it can be argued that Christ's teaching as a whole is an implicit criticism of the institution.

Slavic religion An animistic religion, with themes from hunting, fishing, and agriculture, common to Slavic regions, being practised certainly up to the 14th century, with traces surviving into the 20th century. Local deities and supreme gods were worshipped, but there were no temple centres or any organized priestly caste. ▷ animism

Slessor, Mary (1848–1915) Scottish missionary, born in Aberdeen. She worked as a mill girl in Dundee from childhood but, conceiving a burning ambition to become a missionary, got herself accepted by the United Presbyterian Church for teaching in Calabar, Nigeria (1876), where she spent many years of devoted work among the natives. She was known among the natives as 'Great Mother'. ▷ Presbyterianism *See illustration on p 490*

Smart, Ninian (1927–) British scholar of religion, educated at Glasgow Academy and Oxford University. He became interested in non-Western religion through service in the British Intelligence Corps (1945–8). He taught philosophy at University College of Wales, Aberystwyth (1952–5), history and

Mary Slessor

philosophy of religion at University of London, King's College (1956–61), theology at Birmingham University (1961–6), and became Professor of Religious Studies at Lancaster University (1969–72) and University of California, Santa Barbara (1972–), where he is Chairman of the Department of Religion. His diverse interests include religious education in schools, television as a medium for religious studies, a whole range of areas in the study of religion, and secular worldviews such as Marxism and humanism, as part of the remit of 'religious studies'. An influential figure, his publications include *The Religious Experience of Mankind* (1969), *The Phenomenon of Religion* (1973) and *Beyond Ideology* (1981). This work was particularly important for outlining his notion that a religion is a 'six-dimensional organism, typically containing doctrines, myths, ethical teachings, rituals, and social institutions, and animated by religious experiences of various kinds', an approach which has gained currency in academic and popular circles. One of his concerns is to differentiate between theology, which he sees as relatively value-laden, and the study of religion, which he sees as relatively value-free. Nevertheless, empathy and a concern for understanding others are an important aspect of the study of religion. ▷ comparative religion; history of religion; humanism; Marxism; models of religion; Religionswissenschaft; study of religion

Smith, Joseph (1805–44) American religious leader, regarded as the founder of the Mormons, born in Sharon, Vermont. He received his first 'call' as a prophet at Manchester, New York, in 1820. In 1823 an angel told him of a hidden gospel on golden plates, with two stones which should help to translate it from the 'Reformed Egyptian'; and on the night of 22 September 1827, the sacred records were delivered into his hands by an angel. The *Book of Mormon* (1830) contains a postulated history of America from its colonization at the time of the confusion of tongues to the 5th century of the Christian era, and is said to have been written by a prophet named Mormon. In 1830, the new 'Church of Jesus Christ of Latter-Day Saints' was founded in Fayette, New York, and despite ridicule and hostility, and sometimes open violence, it rapidly gained converts. In 1831 it established its headquarters at Kirtland, Ohio, and built Zion in Missouri. Events culminated in 1838 in a general uprising in Missouri against the Mormons; and Smith was often arrested. In 1840 the Church moved to Illinois, near Commerce, where they founded the community of Nauvoo, and within three years the Mormons in Illinois numbered 20000. It is widely agreed that at this time Joseph Smith started practising polygamy ('spiritual wives'). However, Smith's wife and other Mormons who did not migrate west, deny that he was involved in polygamy and proved their case in the courts. Joseph Smith was imprisoned, with his brother Hyrum, awaiting trial, but on 27 June 1844, 150–200 disguised men broke into Carthage jail and shot them dead. Thereafter most of the Mormons continued their westward migration, to Utah, under Brigham Young. ▷ Mormons; Young, Brigham

Smith, Wilfred Cantwell (1916–) Canadian historian of religion, born in Toronto, and educated at Toronto, Cambridge and Princeton universities. His years spent in Lahore (1941–9) gave him personal and academic contact with Muslims which he continued in Canada by founding the McGill Insitute of Islamic Studies in 1951, further widening his interest as Director of the Harvard Center for the Study of World Religions (1964–73). In a series of books, notably *The Meaning and End of Religion* (1964), he revolutionized the study of religion and remains a doyen among religious studies scholars. An ordained clergyman of the United Church of Canada, his contribution has been primarily academic in deepening an awareness of 'religion' among secular academics. By his stress upon persons, his concern to understand the world view of others, his notion that religious truth involves faith as well as concepts, his awareness of the world community, his stress upon transcendence, his emphasis on inter-religious dialogue and discussion, and his sense that the study of religion is a crucial part of human knowledge, he has switched attention away from religions as 'objects', to the faith of persons encompassed within religious traditions, and to the God or transcendence that lies behind all religious traditions. ▷ comparative religion; history of religion; study of religion; theology of religion

Smith, William Robertson (1846–94) Scottish theologian and orientalist, born in Keig, Aberdeenshire. He studied at Aberdeen, Edinburgh, Bonn and Göttingen, and in 1870 became Professor of Hebrew and Old Testament Exegesis in the Free Church College, Aberdeen. His *Encyclopaedia Britannica* article 'Bible' (1875) was strongly attacked for heterodoxy, but he was acquitted of heresy (1880). He was deprived of his professorship (1881) for another article on 'Hebrew Language and Literature'. In 1883 he became Lord Almoner's Professor of Arabic at Cambridge, in 1886 university librarian and in 1889 Adams Professor of Arabic. He became co-editor and chief editor (1887) of the *Encyclopaedia Britannica*. His chief works are *The Old Testament in the Jewish Church* (1881), *The Prophets of Israel* (1882), and *The Religion of the Semites* (1889).

smriti (smṛti) (literally 'what is remembered') This represents that mass of Hindu literature that does not come under the category of *shruti* ('what is heard') or Vedic revelation. Smriti literature is seen as historical and of human authorship, while shruti is timeless revelation. Indeed, the former would often affirm the authority of the latter. Smriti texts were often the tangible results of the oral tradition in Hinduism, as well as underpinning mythological conceptions. As a result such literature is able to command some of the authority accredited to shruti texts, although it can never claim to be completely flawless because of the nature of its transmission. ▷ shruti; Veda

Social Gospel An early 20th-century movement in the USA concerned with the application of Christian principles to the social and political order in the service of the kingdom of God. Among its most prominent leaders were Washington Gladden (1836–1918), Walter Rauschenbusch (1861–1918), and Shailer Matthews (1863–1941). ▷ Christianity; kingdom of God

socialism A wide-ranging political doctrine which first emerged in Europe during industrialization in the 18th century. Most socialists would agree that social and economic relationships play a major part in determining human possibilities, and that the unequal ownership of property under capitalism creates an unequal and conflictive society. The removal of private property or some means of counterbalancing its power, it is held, will produce a more equal society where individuals enjoy greater freedom and are able to realize their potential more fully. A socialist society will thus be more co-operative and fraternal. Possibly the major division within socialism is between those who believe that to bring it about revolution is necessary, and those who believe change can be achieved through reforms within the confines of democratic politics. There are also differences of opinion as to how far capitalist production needs to be eradicated to bring about a socialist society. ▷ Maoism; Marxism; Marxism-Leninism; secular alternatives to religion

social morality Laws, rules and standards of behaviour designed to enable members of a society to live together harmoniously. Without social morality the behaviour of individuals could not be regulated and society could not exist. Violation of social morality is met either with criminal proceedings or, in the case of non-criminal offences, social disapproval. ▷ civil religion; law and religion

social sciences of religion Anthropology, psychology and sociology are the three social sciences involved in the study of religion. They are part of the total study of religion in the field of Religious Studies, but are sometimes distinguished from theology and the philosophy of religion on the one hand, and *Religionswissenschaft* (centred on the history of religion), the phenomenology of religion and the comparative study of religion on the other. The anthropology of religion has concentrated on the religion of primal societies, and in its early days was dominated by the theory of religious evolution and the search for the origin of religion. For Frazer the origin of religion was magic, for Tylor it was animism, for Marett it was pre-animism, for Schmidt it was original monotheism, and for others it was totemism, fetishism, or polytheism. Anthropology has recently abandoned sweeping theories (except in the binary notions of Lévi-Strauss) and concentrated on field studies of particular tribes, or the analysis of myth, ritual and symbol. The psychology of religion concentrated upon the religious experience of individuals in the work of scholars such as William James in his *Varieties of Religious Experience* (1902). Depth psychology opened up the theory of the unconscious mind in the work of Freud, who saw religion as illusion and projection, and in the work of Jung, who saw religious archetypes and symbols as being 'real' and part of the collective unconscious of the human race. The sociology of religion found its leading exponents in Durkheim, who stressed the social functions of religion as a stabilizing element in society, and Weber, who saw the potential of the dynamic and prophetic element in religion for changing society, as in his classic study of religion and the rise of capitalism. Recently sociologists have examined the process of secularization, including the apparently diminished role of religion in society, the notion of civil religion, and the differences between religious groups such as churches, denominations, sects and cults. While anthropologists have concentrated mainly on small-scale primal societies, sociologists on modern Western societies, and psychologists on individuals, their work can be seen as complementary, although insofar as their allegiance is to their own discipline, the question has to be asked as to whether they are reducing religion as a whole to its social science components. ▷ anthropology of religion; Durkheim, Émile; Frazer, Sir James George; Freud, Sigmund; history of religion; James, William; Jung, Carl Gustav; Lévi-Strauss, Claude; Marett, Robert Ranulph; origins of religion; psychology of religion; Schmidt, Wilhelm; secularization; sociology of religion; theology of religion; Tylor, Sir Edward Burnet; Weber, Max

Socinianism A 16th-century Protestant rationalist movement co-founded by Laelius Socinus and his nephew Faustus. It questioned traditional Christian teaching on sin and salvation, and on the person and work of Jesus Christ, laying stress on his exemplary and inspirational life. Jesus was human, not divine. He revealed God but was given a share in his power only at the Resurrection and Ascension. This anti-Trinitarian view (enshrined in the Racovian Catechism of 1605) influenced 17th- and 18th-century Anglican Latitudinarianism, the Cambridge Platonists, and the early Unitarians. ▷ Socinus, Faustus; Socinus, Laelius; Trinity; Unitarians

Socinus, Faustus, or **Fausto Paulo Sozini** (1539–1604) Italian Protestant reformer, nephew of Lælius Socinus, born in Siena. A co-founder with his uncle of Socinianism, he studied theology at Basel, where he developed his uncle's anti-Trinitarian doctrines, arguing that Luther and Calvin had not gone far enough, and that human reason alone was the only solid basis of Protestantism. Later he became secretary to Duke Orsini in Florence (1563–75). In 1578, on the publication of his *De Jesu Christo Servatore*, he narrowly escaped assassination, and moved to Poland, where he became leader of an anti-Trinitarian branch of the Reformed Church in Cracow. At the synod of Bresz in 1588 he argued against all the chief Christian dogmas—the divinity of Christ, propitiatory sacrifice, original sin, human depravity, the doctrine of necessity, and justification by faith. Denounced by the Inquisition in 1590, his possessions were confiscated. Destitute, he sought refuge in the village of Luclawice, where he died. ▷ Calvin, John; Inquisition; Luther, Martin; Protestantism; Reformed Churches; Socinianism; Socinus, Laelius

Socinus, Laelius, or **Lelio Francesco Maria Sozini** (1525–62) Italian Protestant reformer and co-founder of the doctrine of Socinianism, born in Siena. A lawyer by training, he turned to Biblical research and settled in Zürich in 1548. He travelled widely, meeting leading Protestant reformers like Calvin and Melanchthon, and developed an anti-Trinitarian doctrine that tried to reconcile Christianity with humanism, which profoundly influenced his nephew, Faustus Socinus. ▷ Protestantism; Socinianism; Socinus, Faustus

sociology of religion One of the three social sciences of religion, along with the anthropology and the psychology of religion. In contrast with the psychology of religion it focuses upon society rather than the individual, and in contrast with the anthropology of religion it analyzes modern Western societies rather than small-scale primal societies. The two great names in the early sociology of religion were Émile Durkheim (1858–1917) and Max Weber (1864–1920). Durkheim's functional approach stressed the importance of religion as a factor in the health and stability of society. There is also evidence of what Berger was later to call methodological atheism—God was irrelevant to the sociology of religion, which was interested in religious institutions and not in the God who might lie behind them. Weber was more dynamic and positive about religion, seeing its prophetic side as an instrument for change in his classical study of religion and the rise of capitalism. Joachim Wach (1898–1955) analysed in detail the various kinds of religious institutions: religious groups based on family, kinship, sex and age that are naturally part of society; religiously founded groups such as secret and mystery religions, charismatic religions, churches, denominations and sects; religious groups emerging out of rank, occupation or status such as religion of the warrior, the merchant and the peasant; religious groups influenced by individuals—founders, prophets, seers, reformers, saints, contemplatives; and religious groups in their relation to the state, ranging from those virtually identical like the Japanese Shinto to those radically opposed such as mystery religions. Recent sociology of religion has centred upon analysis of the process of secularization and whether it involves a real or seeming decline of religion, and upon analysis of different religious groups, whether they be churches, denominations, sects and cults within Christianity, or the wider classifications of groups in religion generally. ▷ anthropology of religion; Durkheim, Émile; mystery religions; psychology of religion; secularization; Shinto; social sciences of religion; sociology of religion; Wach, Joachim; Weber, Max

Socrates (469–399BCE) Greek philosopher, born in Athens, where he spent his whole life. He wrote nothing, founded no school and had no sect of disciples, but along with Plato and Aristotle is one of the three great figures in ancient philosophy. His pivotal influence was such that all earlier Greek philosophy is classified as 'preSocratic', and he was responsible for the decisive shift of philosophical interest from speculations about the natural world and cosmology to ethics and conceptual analysis. What little we know of his life and personality has to be gleaned, and interpreted, from three very different and each rather biased sources. Aristophanes the comic playwright caricatured him in his play *The Clouds* as a professional sophist of the kind he actually seems to have opposed and exposed. Xenophon was an admirer, but a soldier not a philosopher, and presents him as the sort of practical commonplace figure he was himself. Plato was by far his most brilliant associate and pupil and is the best and main source. He gives an unforgettable, dramatized portrait in such dialogues as the *Apology*, *Crito* and *Phaedo*, which describe Socrates' trial, last days and death; in later dialogues he makes Socrates the mouthpiece for what were undoubtedly Plato's own opinions.

Socrates was apparently ugly, snub-nosed, with a paunch and a shrewish wife, Xanthippe. He took part as a good citizen in three military campaigns at Potidaea (432–429BCE), Delium (424BCE) and Amphipolis (422BCE), and distinguished himself by his bravery, remarkable physical endurance and indifference to fatigue, climate and alcohol. He otherwise held aloof from politics, guided by his 'voice' which impelled him to philosophy and to the examination of conventional moral attitudes and assumptions with his fellow citizens and with the notable politicians, poets and gurus of the day. He represented himself as just the midwife for the opinions of others, and gave that as the reason for the Delphic Oracle's pronouncement that he was the wisest man alive. The 'Socratic method' was to ask for definitions of familiar concepts like justice, courage and piety, to elicit contradictions in the responses of his unfortunate interlocutors, and thus to demonstrate their ignorance, which he claimed ironically to share, and the need for a deeper and more honest analysis. This unpopular activity no doubt contributed to the demands for his conviction for 'impiety' and 'corrupting the youth', and he was tried at the age of 70; he rejected the option of merely paying a fine, declined a later opportunity to escape from prison, and was sentenced to die by drinking hemlock. ▷ Aristotle; Plato

Söderblom, Nathan (1866–1931) Swedish churchman, born in Trönö near Söderhamm. Educated at Uppsala, he was ordained in 1893 and was Lutheran minister of the Swedish Church in Paris, and later Professor of History of Religion at Uppsala (1901) and Leipzig (1912). In 1914 he was appointed Archbishop of Uppsala and Primate of the Swedish Lutheran Church. A leader in the ecumenical movement, he wrote several works on comparative religion and was the principal promoter of the Life and Work movement, whose aims were to bring Christian principles to bear within society as a whole. He was awarded the 1930 Nobel Prize for Peace. ▷ comparative religion; ecumenism; Lutheranism

Sodom and Gomorrah Two of five 'cities of the plain' in ancient Palestine, perhaps now submerged under the south end of the Dead Sea or located to the south-east of the Dead Sea. In Genesis 18–19 they were legendary for their wickedness, especially their sexual perversity. The stories tell how Lot and his family were warned to flee from their home in Sodom just before the city was destroyed by 'brimstone and fire' as a divine judgement. ▷ Genesis, Book of; Lot

Soka Gakkai A new religious movement in Japanese Buddhism that has grown rapidly since its foundation in 1937 by Tsunesaburo

Makiguchi. It is part of the Nichiren Buddhist tradition, associated with the exclusivistic and nationalistic teaching of Nichiren (1222–82), based upon the *Lotus Sutra*. It has placed great emphasis upon lay participation, which has had political consequences, following the movement's entry into politics through the Komeito or Clean Government Party. At first Soka Gakkai was harassed for refusing to conform to the Shinto wartime government, and Makiguchi died in prison. From 1945 to 1960 there was tremendous growth under the leadership of Josei Toda, especially in large cities. The movement's message that Buddhahood is within the grasp of all, that happiness is a key human possibility, that salvation is available through reciting the mantra known as the *daimoku*, and that this age is the age of salvation, made it attractive in postwar Japan. Its strong organization, based on 'family units' and the achievement of worldly goals such as profit, beauty and goodness were also important in its popularity. From 1960 under Daisaku Ikeda it became less frenetic, more political, and more international in its desire to spread the message of Nichiren to the world. ▷ Ikeda, Daisaku; Japanese new religions; Lotus Sutra; mantra; Nichiren Buddhism

Sol Invictus A cult which appeared in the Roman world around the middle of the 2nd century CE). Literally, the unconquered and unconquerable sun. The adjective *invictus* allowed identification with a Syrian god, thus distinguishing him from a native Roman god, named *Sol Indiges*. The introduction of his cult in Roman religion was helped by syncretism (by association with Apollo who had himself integrated aspects of Helios, the Greek sun) and by imperial attempts to develop his worship. The emperor Elagabalus (ruled 218–22CE), as priest and incarnation of the sun god of Emesa, tried to introduce the cult in Rome, endowing it with the same status as that of Jupiter, but it ceased upon his murder. A second attempt was made by the Roman emperor Aurelian (ruled 270–75CE) whose mother was priestess of a similar oriental sun cult. ▷ Roman religion; syncretism

Solomon (10th century BCE) King of Israel, the second son of David and Bathsheba. His outwardly splendid reign (described in 1 Kings 1–11 and 2 Chronicles 1–10) saw the expansion of the kingdom and the building of the great Temple in Jerusalem. But high taxation and alliances with heathen courts bred discontent which later brought the disruption of the kingdom under his son Rehoboam. Solomon was credited wit extraordinary wisdom, and became a legendary figure in Judaism, so that his name becam attached to several biblical and extra-canonica writings. ▷ David; Proverbs, Book of; Solomon, Psalms of; Song of Solomon; Wisdor of Solomon

Solomon, Psalms of A book of the Ol Testament Pseudepigrapha, consisting of 1 psalms, probably written c.1st century BCE i response to the Roman occupation of Jerusalem. It expresses hopes for a Jewish state fre of foreign domination, brought about by messianic deliverer. It is traditionally considered the work of a Pharisee (but this i now uncertain), and is significant for it expression of Jewish messianic expectation at this time. ▷ messianism; Pharisees; Pseud epigrapha; Solomon

Soloviev, Vladimir (1853–1900) Russia philosopher, theologian and poet, born i Moscow, son of the historian Sergei Mikhailovitch Soloviev. He proposed a universal Christianity which would unite the Catholic an Orthodox Churches, and attempted a synthesis of religious philosophy with science His main works were *The Crisis of Wester Philosophy* (1875), *The Philosophical Principle of Integral Knowledge* (1877), *Russia and th Universal Church* (1889) and *The Justificatio of the Good* (1898). ▷ Christianity; Orthodo Church; Roman Catholicism

Soma A deity in Vedic Hinduism, recorde in the *Rig Veda*, and also a plant or th substance derived from it. This plant probabl contained hallucinogenic properties and ma have been the fly agaric mushroom (*amanit muscaria*) which is used in shamanism although there is some debate about this When the Aryans entered India, they brough with them rituals which involved sacrifice an the consuming of *soma*, which assured th taker of immortality, giving him a perceptio of immense personal power. Soma is praise in the *Rig Veda* as a god associated with Agn at the level of the earth (*bhu*, as opposed t being a deity of the atmosphere or sky) an as an intoxicating drink. The *Rig Ved* describes the elaborate process of preparin the soma drink, which was pressed by stone into wooden bowls and filtered through wooden sieve to produce a tawny-coloure liquid. The Vedic sages or *rishis* are inspire by soma, though increasingly soma is replace by 'substitutes' during rituals, perhaps indicating that the Aryans moved away from th source of the soma plant. ▷ Aryans; shamanism; Veda

Song of Solomon, Song of Songs, or **Canticles** A book of the Hebrew Bible/Old Testament, probably a collection of love songs, although sometimes considered a single poem or drama. The absence of explicit religious content, and the presence of erotic allusions, caused some 2nd-century rabbis to question its canonical status, but allegorical religious interpretation made it acceptable in most Christian and Jewish circles. Although the poems may be quite ancient, on linguistic grounds the collection is usually dated c.3rd century BCE. ▷ Old Testament; rabbi; Solomon

Song of the Three Young Men Part of the Old Testament Apocrypha, or in Catholic versions an extension of the Book of Daniel inserted between what would be 3.23 and 24 in other texts. It is one of several additions to Daniel found in Greek and Latin versions, but not in Hebrew. It tells of three Jewish captives in Babylon—Shadrach, Meshach and Abednego—who are cast into a fiery furnace for refusing to worship an idol, but emerge unscathed. It presents a hymn of thanksgiving and praise that is today known as the *Benedicite* in Catholic worship. Its date is uncertain, but is often put c.2nd–1st century BCE. ▷ Apocrypha, Old Testament; Azariah, Prayer of; Babylon; Daniel, Book of

Son of Man A term found in Jewish and Christian literature, most strikingly in the New Testament Gospels as a frequent self-designation by Jesus. The term's significance is debated: in Aramaic it is an idiomatic reference to 'man' in general, and possibly also a circumlocution for 'I'; in Daniel 7 it seems to depict the righteous ones who are exalted at the end of the age and given dominion; in 1 Enoch 48 it apparently describes a heavenly messianic figure who will exercise judgement in the End times. ▷ eschatology; Jesus Christ; Messiah

sopherim ▷ scribe

Sophonias ▷ Zephaniah, Book of

soteriology The doctrine of salvation. The basic principle underlying all soteriologies is that human beings are in a defective condition from which they need to be rescued. Soteriology is the examination of this condition and the provision of the means for overcoming it and restoring the human being to wholeness. The form a soteriology takes will depend on two factors.

Firstly, it will be determined by the understanding of the human condition. If, for example, the human condition is understood as sin, a soteriology will be developed that concentrates on methods of removing this sin. If, on the other hand, the human condition is understood to be one of ignorance, a soteriology will be developed which conceives of salvation in terms of knowledge and enlightenment.

Secondly, the form a soteriology takes will be determined by what is understood as the highest principle or ultimate value in a religion, such as God, *Brahman*, nirvana, etc. In the theistic religions salvation tends to be conceived in terms of a relationship with a personal God. This relationship, which is understood as communion or union with God, is brought about by the gracious activity of the deity, which is often undertaken by a saviour figure. This emphasis on the initiative of God allows the development of doctrines of atonement, redemption, mediation, etc. In the non-theistic religions, however, salvation is not understood in terms of an intervention on God's part to heal the sinful condition of the human being, but as an escape from the human condition in general and the limitations this places upon human beings. The emphasis here, therefore, is on acquiring the knowledge and developing the techniques whereby the individual may achieve this. ▷ enlightenment; healing; salvation

Soto (Sōtō) A school of Japanese Zen Buddhism. It was introduced into Japan by Dogen in 1227 after a journey to China where Soto had been known as Tsao-tung. Dogen lived in Kyoto and wrote for the new Soto school his *General Teaching for Seated Meditation*. Seated meditation, or *zazen*, became a key ingredient of Soto, and it consisted of sitting upright with legs crossed and engaging in deep meditation. In another work, the *Shobo Genzo*, Dogen stressed a combination of zazen, daily labour, discipline and koans as the way to discover the Buddha nature within, and to come to a true realization of one's own self and the world around. As a method of self-control Soto became a useful aid to the lesser samurai and peasant farmers. It diverged from the other main Japanese Zen school, Rinzai, which had been introduced from China by Eisai in 1191. Rinzai had stressed sudden enlightenment and the use of koans, paradoxical questions for jerking the mind out of its normal patterns into a sudden awareness of the truth. Soto stressed gradual enlightenment, and a combination of methods including koans, but relying mainly on the silent illumination of seated meditation, zazen, which goes through five stages, ending in the realization of the individual's oneness with reality. Soto is an important element in Japanese Buddhism, and is more popular than Rinzai Zen, having increased its influence by incorporating Pure Land funeral practices into its approach. ▷ Buddha nature; Dogen; Eisai; gradual/sudden enlightenment schools of Buddhism; Japanese Buddhism; koans; Rinzai; zazen

soul The seat of the personality, the life-force that animates living beings, a synonym for 'self' or 'mind'. The concept derives from Plato, for whom it was a metaphysical entity, ultimately incorruptible and eternal. In religious thought the soul is often regarded as a divine or immortal element imprisoned in the human body. At death the soul is liberated from the body and continues to exist in disembodied form or is reincarnated in a new body. ▷ afterlife; immortality; transmigration

soul, Christian view of The early Christian Fathers assumed that the body and soul were separate. The view that the soul was pre-existent and immortal was dismissed as a Platonic and Gnostic heresy, leaving a choice between the theory that the soul was transmitted through procreation (traducianism, which was consistent with Augustinian and Reformed views of original sin), and the idea that God created each new human soul afresh (creationism). Thomas Aquinas held that the soul was made for the body, but could exist temporarily apart from it, between death and the general resurrection.

Religious talk of 'body', 'soul' and 'spirit' or of spiritual care of the 'soul' alone is not an adequate reflection of biblical language that equates 'living being' and 'soul' and understands the doctrine of the resurrection of the body not as the reassembly of organic matter but as the preservation of personal identity. In the language of the apostle Paul (1 Corinithians 15) there will be resurrection to a 'spiritual body' that is as appropriate to the afterlife as the 'physical body' is for this. ▷ afterlife, Christian concept of; Aquinas, St Thomas; humankind, Christian view of; original sin; resurrection

soul, Hindu view of The soul (atman) is a central concept in all branches of Hinduism, except perhaps the unorthodox Lokayata school which provided a critique for it. Definitions of its nature and role differ overwhelmingly amongst scriptural sources, and again in the different schools, teachings and individual beliefs. The earliest meaning of atman was 'breath', and from this derive current yogic practices which involve the control of breath (prana), seen as a central, animating life-force (*jiva*). Early Vedic death rituals were based on belief in a transmaterial person who, at the death of the physical body, would be reborn in one of the *lokas* or afterlifes. The Samkhya *darshana* also stresses a duality between matter (*prakriti*) and a non-physical soul or spirit (*purusha*).

The development of Upanishadic thought saw, to a certain extent, the abandonment of this dualism and, although different scriptures have different emphases, the general trend amongst the forest-dwelling ascetics who wrote the Upanishads was towards a belief in a transpersonal, universal soul or *paramatman*, with which the individual atman is identical, and from which all differentiation proceeds, into which everything ultimately merges, and which is both all-pervading and transcendent. This theory was given shape as *nirguna Brahman*, or impersonal absolute reality without qualities, and it was towards a realization of this that religious practice was directed.

This theme has perpetuated throughout history, reaching a high point with the writings of the great Advaita Vedanta philosopher, Shankara. It has also developed further. Based on the idea that Brahman is all-pervading, it is believed that the many gods of the Hindu pantheon cannot be aberrations, but are representatives of Brahman (*saguna Brahman*—Brahman with qualities), as there is nothing, including matter, that is not Brahman. This provides a rationale for such branches of Hinduism as bhakti, in which the soul is seen as provisionally separate from God, but in imminent union with him through the medium of love and devotion. In Hindu eschatology, the ever-transmigrating soul will remain in limbo during the period known as the night of Brahma (cf *yugas*) and will once again take up the karmic yoke at the start of the next world cycle. On one level this is just another permutation of the doctrine of samsara, and it is from this that the Hindu seeks to release his or her soul, whether that soul is interpreted monistically or dualistically. ▷ Advaita Vedanta; bhakti; Brahma; Lokayata; nirguna Brahman; prakriti; prana; purusha; Samkhya; Shankara; Upanishads; yugas

soul, Islamic view of There are two Muslim Arabic words for soul. The word for the independent soul is *nafs*, which is equivalent to the Greek word *psyche*. It is sometimes seen to stand for the soul in an unregenerate state which requires to be altered so that it can, through conscience and amendment of life, become a soul at peace. The word for the non-independent element in the soul is *ruh*, sometimes translated as 'spirit', and equivalent to the Greek word *nous*. It is the element that gives human beings a deep spiritual dignity, elevating them above animals and, to some extent, above the angels. In the sentiments of the Sufi mystics soul, in the sense of ruh, is the centre of being within any human life, and is continuous with Being in the sense of God. The Quran, in fact, applies the phrase 'the spirit of God' (*Ruh Allah*) to Jesus. Thus the notions of nafs and ruh combine the lower and the higher, the human and divine, sides of what is known as the soul. ▷ Quran; Ruh; spirit; Sufism

South India, Church of A Church inaugurated in 1947 in Madras, India, from the merger of Anglicans, Methodists, and United Churches. It reflected a common desire for missionary and social work as well as worship, and tries in its organization to preserve the traditions of each of its constituent traditions. It is governed by a General Synod, with bishops, presbyters, and deacons, and significant lay participation. ▷ Anglican Communion; ecumenism; Methodism; missions, Christian

Spencer, Herbert (1820–1903) English philosopher, born in Derby. He had a varied career as a railway engineer, teacher, journalist and sub-editor at *The Economist* (1848–53) before devoting himself entirely to writing and study. His particular interest was in evolutionary theory which he expounded in *Principles of Psychology* in 1855, four years before Darwin's *The Origin of Species*, which Spencer regarded as welcome scientific evidence for his own *a priori* speculations and a special application of them. He also applied his evolutionary theories to ethics and sociology and became an advocate of 'social Darwinism', the view that societies naturally evolve in competition for resources and that the 'survival of the fittest' is therefore morally justified. He announced in 1860 a *System of Synthetic Philosophy*, a series of volumes which were to comprehend metaphysics, ethics, biology, psychology, and sociology, and nine of these appeared between 1862 and 1893. He viewed philosophy itself as the science of the sciences, distinguished by its generality and unifying function. His other works include *Social Statics* (1851), *Education* (1861), *The Man Versus the State* (1884) and *Autobiography* (1904). ▷ Darwin, Charles Robert

sphinx In ancient Greece a mythological monster with a human head and a recumbent animal body (usually a lion's); sometimes it was winged and had female breasts. Originating in the east, probably Egypt, it is found throughout the Levant and eastern Mediterranean. ▷ Greek religion

Spinoza, Baruch, or **Benedictus, de** (1632–77) Dutch philosopher, born in Amsterdam into a Jewish emigré family that had fled from Portugal to escape Catholic persecution. His deep interests in optics and the new astronomy and his radical ideas in theology and philosophy led to his expulsion from the Jewish community for heresy in 1656. He became the leader of a small philosophical circle and made a living grinding and polishing lenses, moving in 1660 to Rijnsburg near Leiden, where he wrote his 'Short Treatise on God, Man and His Well-Being' (about 1662), the *Tractatus de Intellectus Emendatione* (1662, 'Treatise on the Correction of the Understanding') and most of his geometrical version of Descartes' *Principia Philosophiae*, which was published in 1663 (the only book published in his lifetime with his name on the title page), and which marks the point at which Spinoza moved decisively beyond Descartes' influence. He moved in 1663 to Voorburg near The Hague and in 1670 to The Hague itself. The *Tractatus Theologico-Politicus* was published anonymously in 1670 and aroused great interest but was banned in 1674 for its controversial views on the Bible and Christian theology. He advocated a strictly historical approach to the interpretation of biblical sources and argued that complete freedom of philosophical and scientific speculation was consistent with what was really important in the Bible—the moral and practical doctrines, not the factual beliefs assumed or expressed. He had sent Leibniz his tract on optics in 1671, and Leibniz came to The Hague to visit him in 1676. But Spinoza was by then in an advanced stage of consumption, aggravated by the glass-dust in his lungs from his lense-grinding work, and he died the next year in Amsterdam, leaving no heir and few possessions.

His major work was the *Ethics*, which was published posthumously in 1677. As the Latin title (*Ethica Ordine Geometrico Demonstrata*) suggests, this was a complete, deductive metaphysical system, intended to be a proof of what is good for human beings, derived with mathematical certainty from axioms, theorems and definitions. He rejects the Cartesian dualism of mind and matter in favour of a God who is identified with the ultimate substance of the world—infinite, logically necessary and absolute— which has mind and matter as two of his attributes. Spinoza's God is thus not a personal creator, but more a pantheistic nature, the ultimate explanation of why everything must exist and happen exactly as it does. His work was first condemned as atheistical and subversive, but his reputation was restored by literary critics like Lessing, Goethe and Coleridge and later by professional philosophers, and he is now regarded, along with Descartes and Leibniz, as one of the great rationalist thinkers of the 18th century. ▷ Bible; Descartes, René; pantheism; rationalism

spirit 1 A concept common to many religions and philosophies, Eastern as well as Western, primitive as well as mature, and consequently with a profusion of meanings. Generally conceived as a non-physical, non-material power which energizes and affects life in the cosmos (sometimes for ill as well as for good), it is a principle of life, related to and associated with the soul or mind in contrast to the body or matter. In Western culture, 'spirit' has a long philosophical tradition stemming from Greek thought, as that which surpasses the human yet remains an essential element of humanity. In Hegel, it becomes synonymous with Being or the Absolute. In the Judaeo-Christian tradition, it is power proceeding from God, at work in creation and in the preservation of the cosmos. In Christianity, the Holy Spirit is both one of the 'persons' (along with the Father and the Son) of the triune God and immanent, abiding, personal power, enabling response to God and the upbuilding of the Christian community. 2 A non-material body or being, either 'uncreated' or the emanence from a departed human. Such spirits are believed to exert influence on the physical world, either for good or evil. Consequently they are often a focus of worship and/or propitiation. Lesser spirits, such as angels and jinns, are revered alongside the major spirits who are termed gods. ▷ ancestor worship; angels; God; guardian spirits; jinn; shamanism; soul; Trinity

Chinese talisman, used for contacting the spirit world

Spiritism ▷ **Afro-Brazilian religions**

spirit lodge ▷ **shaking tent**

spirit possession The invasion and control of a person by a spirit, demon or god. Spirit possession is characterized by a change of personality and behaviour on the part of the possessed. In some societies illness is regarded as a form of spirit possession. The New Testament records many instances of Jesus freeing individuals from spirit possession. ▷ devils; exorcism

spiritual discipline Voluntary submission to a teacher, teachings, or set of religious rules in order to achieve a higher spiritual state. To subject oneself to spiritual discipline is to undertake a series of activities aimed at enabling one to express more fully a particular religious ideology. This may involve subjecting both body and mind to a severe regimen whereby those elements believed to impede the disciple's progress towards his spiritual goal are removed or suppressed. Thus many religions advocate poverty, fasting, chastity, self-mortification, and seclusion as means of bringing body and mind under the control of the spirit. In addition to this, some religions recommend certain techniques such as yoga, chanting or controlled breathing as a means of progressing towards spiritual enlightenment. Many religions have developed codes to enable disciples to sustain and remain under spiritual discipline. Buddhist spiritual life was organized by the Vinaja, a set of rules regulating spiritual discipline. Christian examples of codes of spiritual discipline are the Rule of St Benedict and the Spiritual Exercises of St Ignatius Loyola. ▷ Benedictines; celibacy; fasting; Ignatius Loyola, St; obedience; renunciation

spiritualism An organized religion which believes that spirits of the deceased survive bodily death and communicate with the living, usually via a medium by means of messages, or apparently paranormal physical effects. While many different cultures, past and present, believe in spiritism (the ability of spirits of the deceased to communicate with the living), spiritualism is primarily a Western religion, most commonly found in North America and in Europe, from the mid 1800s. It attempts to distinguish itself from other spiritist beliefs by taking a 'scientific' approach; spiritualists query whether communicating spirits are who they claim to be by posing questions which could only be answered by the spirit of the deceased and by the person asking the question. Spiritualists believe in God, and feel that through communications with the deceased they may come to understand better the laws of God. They welcome members from different religious faiths. Spiritualism is frequently criticized for having at least some members who use trickery to produce its phenomena. ▷ paranormal

spirituality The experiential side of religion, as opposed to outward beliefs, practices and institutions, which deals with the inner spiritual depths of a person. Spirituality has been present in all religious traditions, including Kabbalah Judaism, Sufi Islam, the yoga traditions within Hinduism, the meditational disciplines within Buddhism, and some strands of Christianity. It has been revived in recent years after a period of seeming decline in the West, and the 70 volumes of the *Classics of Western Spirituality* is an example of its present vitality. Some scholars have suggested that spirituality does not differ greatly between religions; others, such as Scholem, have argued that each religion has a very different spirituality. Zaehner has claimed that there are four types of spirituality within and between religions: loving union with a personal God; a sense of oneness with the Absolute and the world; a sense of merging with the world, and a sense of being separate from the world and becoming one with one's real self. Cousins has offered a historical interpretation of global spirituality. He suggests that the spirituality of early humans was mythic, cosmic and ritualistic, and that they felt at one with nature and the tribe. But in the Axial Age of the 6th century BCE there arose the possibility of an individual spirituality that was self-reflective, speculative, analytical and separate from nature and the tribe. He suggests that we are now living in the second Axial age, in which a new spirituality is emerging that is recovering a spiritual consciousness of nature. Whether this is the case or not, it appears that a new spirituality which integrates the material, the humane and the translucent—nature, humans and God—is beginning to emerge in the conditions of our time. ▷ Axial Age; Kabbalah; religious experience; Scholem, Gershon; Sufism; yoga; Zaehner, Robert Charles

spirituality, Christian A convenient if somewhat vague modern umbrella term for the age-old concern to integrate prayer, life and thought that has been traditionally the concern of ascetical and mystical theology and the subject-matter of devotional books. This attention to the integration of religion and life is to be distinguished from any one-sided concept of 'spirituality' which separates the two, results in pietism or sentimentality, or focuses on abnormal religious experiences. Christian mystics hold that prayer is to be tested not by its effect on the person who prays, but by its influence on their behaviour and the quality of their love for their neighbour. This common thread may be found in all traditions of Christian spirituality: from Jesus Christ and Paul to the Desert Fathers, from Teresa of Ávila to Jeremy Taylor, Charles de Foucauld and Thomas Merton. ▷ contemplation; Desert Fathers; Foucauld, Charles Eugène, Vicomte de; hesychasm; Jesus Christ; Merton, Thomas; Paul, St; Quietism; Taylor, Jeremy; Teresa of Ávila, St

Spurgeon, Charles Haddon (1834–92) English Baptist preacher, born in Kelvedon, Essex. In 1854 he became pastor of the New Park Street Chapel, London. The Metropolitan Tabernacle, seating 6000, was erected for him in 1859–61 and provided him with a pulpit until his death (it burnt down in 1898). In 1887 he withdrew from the Baptist Union because no action was taken against persons charged with fundamental errors. Apart from 50 volumes of sermons, he wrote collections of pithy sayings such as *John Ploughman's Talk* (1869) and many other works. ▷ Baptists

Srongtsan Gampo (Srong-btsan sgam-po) (7th century) King of Tibet (627–50), during whose reign Buddhism became established. He succeeded to the throne following the assassination of his father in 627, and set out on a programme of expansion and military conquest. Realizing that Buddhism brought with it cultural and educational advantages from India, he encouraged its development. Among his wives were a Chinese princess Wen Ch'eng and a Nepalese princess, both of whom were Buddhists. Srongtsan had the Jokhang temple at Lhasa built for Wen Ch'eng, who installed in it an image of the Buddha brought from China. Although probably not a Buddhist himself, adhering instead to the pre-Buddhist ancestor cult of divine kings, Srongtsan is nevertheless regarded as a manifestation of Avalokiteshvara, and his two wives as manifestations of Tara in her green and white forms. Srongtsan's reign allowed the permanent establishment of Buddhism in Tibet and marked the beginning of its first diffusion, an expansion which continued to the reign of Langdarma (838–42). ▷ Avalokiteshvara; Buddha; Buddhism; Lhasa; Tara

Ssu Ma Chien (Ssu-ma Ch'ien) (c.135–93BCE) Chinese historian, who wrote a synthesis of Chinese history around 100BCE in the *Historical Legends* (*Shih-chi*). This carried on the work of his own father, and brought together previous work in the historical field to provide a model for a series of histories of China that continued to be written right up to modern times. One of China's greatest historians, Ssu Ma Chien used oral traditions, written texts, archive material, and contemporary persons to summarize the history of China from the Chou period to his own day, and he wrote it in a superb literary style. It provides evidence for the history of religion from 841 to 100BCE. It is divided into three parts: the annals of the sovereign, biographies, and treatises, the last of which are especially important for religion. It is a symbol of the importance of history in Chinese culture compared with cultures such as that of India, about whose early history very little is known. ▷ Tien

Star of Bethlehem A star mentioned in Matthew 2.1–12, depicted as heralding Jesus's birth and guiding Magi from the East to the birthplace in Bethlehem. Although sometimes considered a comet (Halley's comet c.11BCE), a supernova, or a conjunction of Jupiter and Saturn in the constellation Pisces (c.7BC), it is doubtful that these can explain the sustained presence or movement that is described. Legends about the births of Mithridates and Alexander Severus also allege the presence of special stars. ▷ Jesus Christ; Magi

Star of David ▷ magen David

star worship The practice in a number of civilizations of seeing the sun, moon, planets and stars as divine, and of offering worship to them. Although linked to astrology it is also separate, since for astrology the sun, moon, planets and stars are cosmic indicators but not divine in themselves. Many religions have seen the sky as a symbol of transcendence, sacredness and constancy in contrast to the unpredictability of the natural world. The heavenly bodies in the sky partake of the sky's beauty and mystery, and they are seen as influencing directly the earth's times and tides; thus they evoke worship. There is a subtle difference between worship of star gods (and especially sun gods) and worship of the stars themselves. For example in republican Rome a cult of the sun, Sol, arose but this was transformed in the Roman empire into worship of Mithra and of the Roman emperor as sun gods. Star worship was also present in ancient Mesopotamia and in Mayan Central America, and it may well have been a factor in prehistoric megalithic civilizations such as the one represented at Stonehenge. Although not equated with astrology and astronomy it helped to give rise to them. ▷ astrology; megalithic religion; Mithra; Stonehenge; sun

Stations of the Cross A popular form of devotion in the Roman Catholic and some Anglican Churches. It consists of meditating on a series of 14 pictures or carvings recalling the passion of Christ from his condemnation to his burial. ▷ Jesus Christ; Roman Catholicism

Steiner, Rudolph (1861–1925) Austrian social philosopher, born in Kraljevíc, the founder of anthroposophy, a spiritual doctrine still influential in Europe and America. He studied science and mathematics, and edited Goethe's scientific papers in Weimar from 1889 to 1896. He was much influenced by Annie Besant and the Theosophists, but went on to found his own Anthroposophical Society in 1912 and established at Dornach near Basle his Goetheanum, a 'school of spiritual science'. He aimed to restore by training the innate human capacity for spiritual perception, which had become dulled by the material preoccupations of the modern world. His work helped inspire many other, still flourishing, educational and therapeutic enterprises, usually emphasizing the importance of activities centred on art, myth, drama and eurhythmy. He founded his first school in 1919, the first of more than 70 Rudolf Steiner schools now operating. His main publications were *The Philosophy of Freedom* (1894), *The Philosophy of Spiritual Activity* (1894), *Occult Science: an Outline* (1913) and *Story of my Life* (1924). ▷ anthroposophy; Besant, Annie; theosophy

Stewart, James Stuart (1896–1990) Scottish preacher and devotional writer, born in Dundee. A Church of Scotland parish minister before becoming Professor of New Testament at New College, Edinburgh (1947–66), he was Moderator of the General Assembly of the Church of Scotland (1963–4). He was joint-editor of the 1928 English translation of Schleiermacher's *The Christian Faith*, wrote popular books on Jesus, Paul, and the art of preaching, lectured widely in Britain and overseas, and published several volumes of sermons, including *The Gates of New Life* (1937), *River of Life* (1972), and *King for Ever* (1974). ▷ Church of Scotland; moderator

stigmata Marks or wounds appearing on the human body, similar to those of the crucified Jesus. They may be temporary (related to ecstasy or revelation) or permanent, and are alleged to be a sign of miraculous participation in Christ's suffering. ▷ cross; crucifixion; ecstacy; Jesus Christ; revelation

Stoicism A philosophical movement which flourished in Greece and Rome (300BCE–180CE), founded by Zeno of Citium. It included such figures as Seneca, Epictetus, and Marcus Aurelius. Stoicism emphasized that all people are equally part of a law-governed physical nature; the ideal life is one of unperturbedness and duty to the dictates of this natural order. ▷ Zeno of Citium

stone circles Circular or near circular rings of prehistoric standing stones, found particularly in Britain and Ireland, dating from the Late Neolithic and Early Bronze Ages. About 900 examples survive, some as much as 400m/1300 feet in diameter. They most probably functioned as temples in which celestial events, the passing of the seasons, and the fertility of the land and people could be celebrated. ▷ prehistoric religion; Stonehenge

Stonehenge A prehistoric sanctuary near Amesbury, southern England. In use from c.3100 to 1100BCE, it was constructed in three phases: c.2800BCE, a low bank and ditch of earth about 110 m/360 ft in diameter; c.2100BCE, a double ring of 80 pillars of South Wales bluestone, apparently dismantled before completion; and c.2000BCE, the surviving monument, a 30 m/100 ft diameter lintelled circle and inner horseshoe of 80 dressed sarsen (sandstone) blocks, each weighing 20–50 tonnes. Alignment on the midsummer sunrise/midwinter sunset implies prehistoric use for seasonal festivals, but the association with the Druids dates only from 1905, and has no historical basis. ▷ stone circles

Stott, John Robert Walmsley (1921–) English Anglican clergyman and writer, born in London. He graduated at Cambridge, and had a remarkable ministry at All Souls', Langham Place (in the heart of London's West End) as curate and then rector (1945–75). Widely acknowledged as a leading spokesman for Anglican Evangelicals, he has also had an effective ministry worldwide as conference speaker, especially among students, and has been a royal chaplain since 1959. He was Director of the London Institute for Contemporary Christianity (1982–6) and later its president. His many books include *Basic Christianity* (1958), *Fundamentalism and Evangelism* (1959), *Our Guilty Silence* (1967), *Christian Counter-Culture* (1978), *Issues facing Christians Today* (1984), *The Cross of Christ* (1986), and *Essentials* (1988), a dialogue with David L Edwards. ▷ Anglican Communion; evangelicalism

Stonehenge

Strauss, David Friedrich (1808–74) German theologian, born in Ludwigsburg in Württemberg. He studied for the Church at Tübingen, where in 1832 he became *repetent* in the theological seminary, lecturing also on philosophy in the university as a disciple of Hegel. In his *Leben Jesu* (1835, trans by George Eliot, 1846) he sought to prove the gospel history to be a collection of myths, and by an analytical dissection of each separate narrative to detect a nucleus of historical truth free from every trace of supernaturalism. The book marks an epoch in New Testament criticism and raised a storm of controversy. Strauss, dismissed from his post at Tübingen, in 1839 was called to be Professor of Dogmatics and Church History at Zürich; but the appointment provoked such opposition that it had to be dropped. His second great work followed, *Die Christliche Glaubenslehre*, a review of Christian dogma (1840–1). A new *Leben Jesu* (1864, trans as *Life of Jesus*, 1865), attempts to reconstruct a positive life of Jesus. In *Der alte und der neue Glaube* (1872, trans as *The Old Faith and the New*, 1873) Strauss endeavoured to prove that Christianity as a system of religious belief is dead, and that a new faith must be built up out of art and the scientific knowledge of nature. He also wrote several biographies, notably that of Ulrich von Hutten (trans 1874), and lectures on Voltaire (1870). He separated from his wife, the opera singer Agnese Schebest (1813–70). ▷ biblical criticism; Christianity; Hegel, Georg Wilhelm Friedrich

study of religion The study of religion as a phenomenon made a tentative start in ancient Greece but has emerged with new significance in the modern West since the mid 19th century CE. It involves the study of all religions—primal, dead, minor and major living religions, and new religious movements—using various methods. As such it has detached itself from Christian theology (although this is included as a component) and from the reductionist elements within the social sciences, but has retained the anthropology, psychology and sociology of religion. Underlying it are the two phenomenological assumptions of *epochē* (putting one's convictions into brackets in order to understand others) and *Einfühlung* (empathizing with the worldview of others). In addition to historical studies of particular religions, it looks at religions comparatively, according to Max Müller's principle that 'he who knows one religion knows no religion'. Concerned with involving many non-Western scholars, it seeks to become a global study, and attempts to engage in what Eliade called creative hermeneutics whereby it can act as a catalyst within modern scholarship. ▷ anthropology of religion; Eliade, Mircea; history of religion; Müller, (Friedrich) Max; psychology of religion; social sciences of religion; sociology of religion; theology of religion

stupa (stūpa) An Indian cairn or mound, originally constructed over the ashes of an emperor or some other great person, such as the Buddha. Later they were used to house the ashes of Buddhist monks and holy relics. ▷ Buddhism; pagoda; relics

Sturluson, Snorri (1179–1241) Icelandic historian, poet and chieftain, the outstanding man of letters of medieval Scandinavia. He was born at Hvammur in western Iceland and fostered at Oddi, the home of the powerful chieftain, Jón Loptsson. He amassed wealth and property, including the estate of Borg (former home of his ancestor, the saga hero Egill Skallagrimsson) and Reykholt, where he lived much of his life, and rapidly rose to prominence in national life, becoming law-speaker (president) of the Althing (parliament) for the first time in 1215. It was a time of great civil unrest in Iceland (the so-called Sturlung Age), with warring factions in the Icelandic republic jockeying for power, aided and abetted by King Haakon IV Haakonsson ('the Old') of Norway. Eventually, Snorri was assassinated at the king's behest at his home at Reykholt. As an author, Snorri Sturluson towers over his contemporaries. He wrote *Heimskringla*, a monumental prose history of the kings of Norway down to the year 1177, and compiled a prose account of Norse mythology in his *Prose* (or *Younger*) *Edda*, which is also a handbook of poesy illustrated with his own poetry. He is also believed to have written *Egils saga*, a prose biographical history of his ancestor, Egill Skallagrimsson.

Stylites, Simeon ▷ Simeon Stylites

Subud A new religious movement founded by Muhammad Subuh, who was born in Java, Indonesia, in 1901. In 1925 he had a vivid spiritual experience, involving the sensation of light descending on him, and by 1933 he was teaching the doctrines of the new Subud movement in Java. The word Subud derives from three Sanskrit terms: *sujisa* (ethical conduct), *bodhi* (enlightenment), and dharma (the cosmic way). Subud stresses the importance of a psychic ritual experience named *latihan*, which involves various outward sensations such as dancing, groaning, laughing and sobbing. The aim of latihan is to worship God and obtain purification by surrendering one's will to God. There is group participation in this experience at Subud meetings. In 1956 Subuh went to the Gurdjieff Centre at Coombe Springs in Britain and was seen by some followers of Gurdjieff as the one who would fulfil the work of their master. During his month-long visit, over 400 people experienced latihan. After a quiet period during the 1960s, the movement became more active in the late 1970s and groups were set up in different parts of the world. Although of Islamic origin, Subud is separate from Islam. ▷ bodhi; dharma; Gurdjieff, Georgei Ivanovitch

suffering The experience of physical or mental pain, loss and distress. Suffering occupies an important but ambiguous position in religious thought. It is both the factor that prompts human beings to reflect on religious questions, such as the meaning and purpose of life, and one of the most significant reasons for disillusionment with and rejection of religion. In non-theistic religions suffering is accepted as a brute fact and emphasis placed not so much on finding an explanation for suffering, but on developing practical techniques and methods for eliminating it. Thus in Buddhism and Hinduism suffering is ascribed to an individual's failure to fulfil the moral law (dharma) in a previous incarnation. To avoid suffering the individual must strive for two goals. On the one hand, he should strive to fulfil the moral law in order to secure a superior position in his next incarnation. On the other hand, he should strive to free himself from the whole cycle of birth and rebirth and thereby escape from the suffering that is an intrinsic feature of existence.

The problem of suffering becomes most acute in the theistic religions, where the problem is that of relating suffering to belief in the goodness of God. This means that theistic religions are confronted not only with the problem of devising practical means of dealing with suffering, but also with finding an explanation for it which protects the justice and goodness of God. Numerous theories have been advanced to deal with this problem. A common argument, particularly in early Judaism, is to interpret suffering as punishment for sin (Proverbs 22.8; Isaiah 3.10f). This, however, as the Book of Job makes clear, fails to account for innocent suffering. Another common theory is to interpret suffering in educative terms. Suffering is understood as an educative process by which the soul is moulded and refined (Proverbs 3.12; Jeremiah 11.4; Isaiah 48.10; Romans 5.3f; Hebrews 12.3–13; James 1.2–4; cf Quran 2.150ff). In later Judaism (cf Isaiah 53) and particularly in Christianity, the doctrine of vicarious suffering was developed. That is, an individual was understood as suffering on behalf of others, of taking upon himself and atoning for the sins of his fellow human beings. Thus Christians draw strength to face suffering through their belief that God in the person of Jesus Christ has entered into and participates in human suffering. Another important development in the attempt to deal with the phenomenon of suffering, in particular with the phenomenon of innocent suffering, was the introduction of the concept of an afterlife in which the virtuous are rewarded and the evil punished. The problem of suffering thus leads to such concepts as immortality and the Last Judgement. ▷ afterlife; atonement; evil; samsara

Sufi institutions Sufism is the mystical wing of Islam, and it began to be institutionalized at an early date, when Sufis formed communities with a residential centre where they could live together and engage in educational work. Sufi centres were often established by means of charitable trusts (*waqf*), and they developed their own way of life. They stressed the importance of an inward search for God as being complementary to the outward ordinance of the shariah or law. In practice they emphasized the liturgical ritual of *dhikr*, which involved the remembrance of God, chanting the names of God, and realizing the presence of God, often using aids such as music, a rosary, dancing, and systematic breathing exercises. Sufi institutions also stressed outward virtues such as humility and care for one's neighbour. They later became formalized in Sufi orders known as *tariqahs*. Although they had a concern for mission, they viewed jihad mainly as an inward struggle to overcome the unreality in oneself, rather than as an outward struggle against human enemies. ▷ dhikr; jihad; mysticism; shariah; Sufi orders; tariqah; waqf

Sufi orders The Sufi institutions of the early days of Islam evolved by the 12th century into formal Sufi orders known as *tariqahs*. They were led by a spiritually gifted leader known as a *shaykh*, and they included full members (who might or might not be married) and lay adherents. The main orders subdivided until hundreds of them came into being. Although their main purpose was to increase mystical awareness of God, they also performed an important missionary function, especially on the fringes of the Muslim world in places such as Central Asia, India, the Sudan and West Africa. At one extreme their doctrine was elevated, esoteric and contemplative; at the other, more popular extreme they sometimes produced *fakirs*—grass-roots magicians who might have psychic powers and indulge in unusual phenomena such as trance dancing and glass-eating. At their apogee in the medieval period the Sufi orders strengthened the sense of community among Sunni Muslims and met their emotional and devotional needs by stressing the central importance of realizing the presence of God and having an inner knowledge of God. Important orders include the following: the Qadiriyyah, deriving from al-Qadir (1077–1166) and active from India to Morocco; the Mevlevis, deriving from Mevlana Rumi (1207–73) and active in the Turkish world; the Naqshbandiyyah, deriving from Naqshband (1317–89) and active in the Caucasus and Central Asia; and the Bektashi, active in the regions of the Ottoman empire. ▷ Bektashi; Mevlevis; mysticism; Naqshbandiyyah; Qadariyyah; Rumi; shaykh; Sufi institutions; tariqah

Sufism An Islamic mystical movement which represented a move away from the legalistic approach in Islam to a more personal relationship with God. The word comes from *suf* ('wool'), because the early story-tellers from whom Sufism evolved wore woollen garments. Sufis aim to lose themselves in the ultimate reality of the Divinity by constant repetition of the *dhikr* or 'mentioning (of God)'. ▷ dhikr; Islam

Suhrawardi (Suhrawardī, shiḥāb ad-Dīn Yaḥyā) (1154–91) Founder of the 'illuminationist' school of philosophy in Islam, born in Persia. His greatest work was *The Book of Illuminationist Wisdom* (*Kitab Hikmat al-Ishraq*) in which he argued that wisdom and supra-rational realization must be part of philosophy. He combined a number of elements in his thinking, including Hellenistic insights, Hermetism, Orphic ideas, and Zoroastrian notions of angels, as well as concepts from Muslim Sufi and Shiite thought. His school, known as the Ishraqi School, was centred upon intellectual mysticism and had a significant impact upon Iran up to modern times. Suhrawardi lived and worked mainly in Aleppo; while there he was imprisoned by Saladin's officials on suspicion of heresy, and was eventually put to death. For this reason he is sometimes called the murdered Suhrawardi, Suhrawardi maqtul. ▷ Hellenists; Hermetica, Hermetism; Saladin; Shiism; Sufism; Zoroastrianism

Sukkot, or **Sukkoth** or **Succoth** The Jewish Feast of Tabernacles or Booths celebrated in September or October (15–21 Tishri) as a festival of thanksgiving. 'Booths' or light temporary shelters are constructed in homes or gardens and in synagogues, in memory of the huts or tents used by the Israelites in the desert after leaving Egypt (Exodus 13). ▷ Judaism

Süleyman, the Magnificent (1494–1566) Ottoman emperor, son of Selim I, the greatest of the Ottoman sultans. He succeeded his father in 1520 at a time when the empire was militarily strong both on land and at sea, while he himself was an experienced soldier and administrator. Known in the West as 'the Magnificent', he was known to his own people as *Kanuni*, the 'Law Giver'. He instituted a programme of internal reforms, aimed at securing higher standards of justice and administration and ensuring freedom of religion throughout the empire. He extended the bounds of the empire, both to the east and west; he captured Belgrade in 1521 and Rhodes in 1522. In 1529 he unsuccessfully besieged Vienna. He conquered Mesopotamia from the Persians and annexed much of Hungary to the empire. Under Barbarossa the Ottoman fleet was able to establish Ottoman naval supremacy in the eastern Mediterranean and Aegean while also challenging the Portuguese in the East. The constant campaigning led Süleyman to withdraw increasingly from the active direction of government at home a tendency which, continued by his successors, fatally weakened the empire in the long term. Nevertheless during his reign Ottoman power abroad and Ottoman institutions and culture at home reached the peak of their achievement.

Sumer The name given to the part of Lower Mesopotamia between Babylon and the Persian Gulf. It is the place where the world's first urban civilization evolved; among the greatest of Sumerian city-states were Eridu, Ur, and Uruk. Surviving art forms date from c.2500BCE, and include the stone statues of Gudea and many coloured bas-reliefs. ▷ art, Babylonian; architecture, Sumerian and Assyrian; Ur

Sumerian religion Each of the Sumerian city-states had its own local deities; these were organized into a pantheon of many hundred of gods who represented cosmic and natural forces. Most important were the four creative and cosmic deities: An, the sky-god; Enlil, god of the atmosphere; Enki, god of the waters; and the earth goddess Ninhursag. The three astral deities, Nanna, the moon god, Utu, the sun god, and Inanna, goddess of the planet Venus, were also highly honoured. The pantheon was conceived as an assembly, with An and later Enlil at its head. Sumerian mythology shows that the gods were conceived as very human in form and behaviour, their principal advantages being immortality and supernatural power. Extensive temple complexes were the focus of Sumerian cities, and were dwelling places where the gods' needs for food, clothing and shelter were supplied by a large staff of priests. The kings had a sacral role and were prominent in cult and festivals. Human beings were created only for serving the gods, and although a person might have a personal deity who would help him or her through the difficulties of life, the Sumerians were pessimistic about the prospect of any improvement of the human condition after death. Sumerian religion provided the basic pattern for the remarkably continuous Mesopotamian religious tradition, and was largely adopted and developed by the Babylonians, Assyrians, and others who later were the dominant powers in the region. ▷ afterlife, Ancient Near Eastern concept of; Ancient Near Eastern religions; Assyrian religion; Babylonian religion; cosmogony, Ancient Near Eastern; cosmology, Ancient Near Eastern; Ea; Enlil; festivals, Ancient Near Eastern; Ishtar; literature, Ancient Near Eastern; Shamash

sun The nearest star to the earth and the source of light, warmth and ultimately life itself. Sun worship was practised in Ancient Egypt, Greece, Rome, and Meso-America. A common feature in such religions is the portrayal of the sun as the heroic conqueror of darkness. Even in those religions and cultures where sun worship is not practised, the sun is often an important religious symbol. Thus in many cultures sunset represents death whereas sunrise portrays birth and life.

Sun Dance An annual summer ritual of the North American Plains, supported, with regional variations, by peoples of different ethnic and language groups. Vernacular titles translate as 'dance for renewal of life', 'dance watching the sun', and 'thirst dance'. Originally it was probably a thanksgiving rite to the supreme being for the supply of plants and animals, and especially the buffalo, on which life depended. It developed other aspects, acting variously as a source of power, insight and spiritual achievement for those capable of the necessary discipline and sacrifice; as a means of initiation; as a focus of group renewal. Essential elements include the building of a lodge, a process which re-enacts creation, for the lodge is a working model of the universe. At its heart is a great pole—the axis of the world, the tree or pillar which is rooted in earth and stretches to heaven. For the period of the dance this not merely represents, but becomes the centre of the universe; for the ritual has cosmic effects. Pariticipants undergo days of strict purification (the sweat lodge may play a part here) and are painted with rich symbolism. The ritual itself proclaims death and rebirth. The strain on the volunteer dancers—agonizing thirst, steady gazing at the sun—is severe. The dance movements are dignified; the drumbeat compelling; the corporate involvement sustaining. The dance has traditionally involved vows and self-offering; at one time those men who had so vowed attached their bodies by hooks and skewers to the cosmic tree, swinging from it until the muscles tore them free; women offered flesh cut from themselves. ▷ Cheyenne religion; Sioux religion; sweat lodge

Sunday The day of the week set aside by the Christian religion for divine worship, mainly in commemoration of Christ's resurrection. As early as New Testament times it replaced the Jewish Sabbath, when Paul and the Christians of Troas gathered on the first day of the week to 'break bread' (Acts 20), and it is called 'the Lord's day' (Rev 1). In 1971 the UK ratified the recommendation of the International Standardization Organization that Monday replace Sunday as the first day of the week. ▷ Christianity; Sabbath

Sunday School Classes for the religious education of children in Protestant churches, usually linked to worship services. They derive from the Sunday charity school, instituted in London in 1780 for the basic education of children of the poor. ▷ Protestantism

sun god ▷ **Inca religion**

sunnah An important Muslim term meaning 'custom' or 'usage' which is applied especially to the custom and usage of Muhammad himself as found in his sayings (Hadith) and deeds. Thus the sunnah was an important complement to the Quran as a source of authority within Islam. According to Muslims the Quran was revealed directly by God through Muhammad as a channel, but it was complemented, confirmed and interpreted by the sayings and deeds exercised consciously by Muhammad and recorded in the sunnah. The Quran and the sunnah became the main sources for Sunni Islamic law (shariah), and when further sources were needed analogy and the consensus of the community came into play. In some matters the sunnah extended the Quran significantly, for example in recommending five daily prayers instead of three, and in recommending how they should be performed. Also, in some respects Muhammad's example could not be taken literally, for example in his having 11 wives rather than four. Mainstream Islam became known as Sunni, or orthodox, Islam in that it recognized the important role of the four early caliphs who succeeded Muhammad and helped to formulate the sunnah rather than giving precedence to Muhammad's son-in-law Ali and his Shiite successors, and in that it recognized the authority of the four Sunni schools of law. Over 80 per cent of Muslims are Sunnis, the remainder being mainly Shiites, who give special reverence to Ali, his family, and the Shiite imams who followed them. ▷ Ali; caliphate; Hadith; ijma; imam; Islamic law schools; Muhammad; Qiyas; Shiism; Sunnis

Sunnis (Sunnīs) Members of an Islamic religious movement representing 'orthodoxy' in Islam, comprising about 80 per cent of all Muslims. They recognize the first four caliphs as following the right course (*rashidun*), and base their sunnah ('path' of the prophet Muhammad) upon the Quran and the Hadith or 'traditions' of the prophet. They are organized into four legal schools which all enjoy equal standing. The other major Islamic group is made up of Shiites. ▷ Hadith; Islam; Quran; Shiism

supernatural ▷ paranormal

superstition Beliefs regarded by reasonable and educated people to be irrational and unfounded. The term is usually employed pejoratively to reject rival beliefs as illegitimate and invalid. Firstly, it is often employed by the adherents of one religion to describe other religions. One's own religion is regarded as the true religion, whereas rival religions are rejected as false, irrational and even demonic. Thus the Romans rejected Christianity as superstitious, a charge which Christianity in turn levelled at the religion of the Romans and later at other religions with which it came into contact. Secondly, the term may be employed to refer to excessive adherence to certain aspects of one's own religion. This view was advanced by Thomas Aquinas, who wrote that 'superstition is a vice opposed to the virtue of religion by excess' (*Summa Theologica* 2a2ae, 92, I). This charge was levelled by the 16th-century humanists and protestant reformers at what they regarded as Catholicism's excessive adherence to external ceremonial forms. Thirdly, the term may be applied to certain popular beliefs and traditions such as avoidance of walking under ladders, belief in charms and talismans, fear of the number 13, etc. Fourthly, in the modern age 'superstition' has come to be defined not in relation to religion but to science. That is, beliefs are considered superstitious if the arguments and evidence upon which they are based are not valid or verifiable according to scientific criteria. ▷ folk religion; popular religion

supreme beings Transcendent, omnipotent, omnipresent, omniscient, primordial creator gods. Their activity is often restricted to creation, the running of the world being delegated to lesser deities. Consequently supreme beings are remote from the world and its affairs, a fact which finds expression in their being described as 'sky gods' and in the belief that they dwell in or beyond the sky. Because of their remoteness they usually occupy an insignificant place in religious worship, where they are replaced by lesser but more active deities. ▷ cosmogony; creation myths

surah (sūrah) A Muslim term referring to a chapter of the Quran. There are 114 chapters in the Quran, and in each surah there are a number of verses which are called *ayat*, meaning 'signs'. The Quran is organized according to the length of the surahs so that the longer ones precede the shorter ones. Thus, although some surahs were revealed to Muhammad in Mecca and others were revealed later in Medina, they are written down according to length rather than according to the sequence of revelation. For purposes of reading and recitation the 114 surahs of the Quran are divided into 30 sections of about equal length. The chapters are given different names according to a prominent word within them, for example the 'cow surah'; or according to Arabic letters that are given at the head of each chapter. Muslims believe that the surahs of the Quran were divinely revealed by God to Muhammad. The Arabic language in which they were revealed is sacred to Islam, and the poetic prose of the Quran is not easy to translate. There is a contrast here to the verses of the Bible which are not sacred linguistically and have been translated into every known language. ▷ Bible; Mecca; Medina; Muhammad; Quran

Surya (Sūrya) The sun god in Hindu mythology. He was the son of Indra, the pre-eminent god of the *Rig Veda*. ▷ Hinduism; Veda

Susanna, Story of A book of the Old Testament Apocrypha, or Chapter 13 of the Book of Daniel in Catholic versions of the Bible. An addition to the Book of Daniel of uncertain date or provenance, it tells of how the beautiful Jewess Susanna is wrongfully accused in Babylon of adultery and is condemned to death, but is rescued by Daniel. The artful narrative commends lessons of Jewish morality and faith in God. ▷ Apocrypha, Old Testament; Daniel, Book of

suttanta (suttānta; Sanskrit: sautrāntika) A Pali term referring to the substantial discourses on the *sutta-pitaka*, found in the second part of the Buddhist scriptures known as the *tipitaka* or Pali Canon. A monk who memorized these discourses was called a *suttantika*, and his role was different from that of a monk who memorized the monastic discipline in the first part of the tipitaka (the *vinaya-pitaka*), and different again from that of a monk who taught the analytical system of doctrine found in the *Abhidharma*, which was the third part of the tipitaka. The *suttanta* were discourses of the Buddha relevant to particular contexts and to the specific needs of actual people which could be added to and interpreted, whereas the Abhidharma was fuller, more objective and more universal. It worked back from general categories of thought to particular events, whereas the suttanta worked from specific situations and historical sequences to wider principles. Because of the possibility of applying it more generally and more scientifically, the abhidharma approach acquired a good reputation by contrast with that of the suttanta. However, the suttanta approach retained its appeal, especially in Theravada Buddhism. The Sanskrit version of this term, *Sautrantika*, was the name given to an early school of Buddhism that reacted against the Abhidharma teaching in favour of returning to the discourses of the Buddha as the key to Buddhist teaching. ▷ Abhidharma; Sautrantika; sutta-pitaka; tipitaka; vinaya-pitaka

sutta-pitaka (sutta piṭaka; Sanskrit: sūtra-piṭaka) The second of the three parts of the *tipitaka* or Pali Canon which contains the discourses of the Buddha. The first part of the tipitaka focuses on monastic discipline, and the third part centres on a systematic arrangement of Buddhist doctrine. Each discourse included in the *sutta-pitaka* has a particular setting, deals with a particular topic or set of topics, and follows a particular thread (the meaning of the word *sutra*). In addition to the discourses, the *sutta-pitaka* also contains some slightly different yet important material such as the birth stories of the Buddha (Jataka), and the popular short piece known as the *Dharmapada*. Its style is popular, including allegories, illustrations, parables and repetitions, and it is basically a vehicle for apologetic and teaching on behalf of the Buddhist way. There are five main sections (*nikayas*) of the Buddha's discourses in the tipitaka. It is likely that they were originally separate pieces and traditions that were preserved and transmitted in separate areas or monasteries before being brought together. The best-known commentary on the *sutta-pitaka* was written by the great Theravada scholar Buddhaghosa in the 5th century CE. The Mahayana tradition accepted the tipitaka, including the *sutta-pitaka* as a kind of preliminary scripture that was, so to speak, fulfilled by its own *Mahayana Sutras*, and in its own version of the *sutta-pitaka* there were four sections called *agamas* that were roughly parallel to the first four sections of the *sutta-pitaka* in the tipitaka. ▷ Abhidharma; Buddhaghosa; Dharmapada; Jataka; Mahayana Buddhism; Theravada Buddhism; tipitaka; vinaya-pitaka

suttee ▷ sati

Sutton Hoo ship burial The grave of an Anglo-Saxon king, probably Raedwald of East Anglia (d.624/5), discovered beneath a barrow on the River Deben near Woodbridge, eastern England, in 1939. Near the middle of the ship in a 40-oar open rowing boat stood a wooden burial chamber containing silver plate, gold jewellery, coins, weapons, and domestic equipment (now in the British Museum). It is the richest single archaeological find ever made in Britain, and offers an insight into religious symbolism in Britain before its conversion to Christianity. ▷ ship burial

Suzuki, Daisetz Teitaro (1870–1966) Buddhist scholar and leader, born into a Samurai family in northern Japan. Educated at school in Ishikawa, he became an English teacher in a Japanese village, where he was given the title Daisetz, meaning 'great humility', as a symbol of Zen enlightenment. His career falls into three parts. Up to the mid 1920s he presented and defended Buddhism in the West, and reformulated it in the East; up to 1949 he translated and commented on Buddhist texts from India, Japan and China; from 1949 to 1966 he continued to reinterpret Buddhism worldwide, but also represented Buddhist views on various contemporary issues, especially in the USA, where he was hugely influential. His first major work, *Outlines of Mahayana Buddhism*, appeared in 1907 and was succeeded by 20 others in both English and Japanese. Although interested in Buddhism in general his main concern was for Mahayana Buddhism, especially Zen and Pure Land. Fascinated by the theme of mysticism, he examined this comparatively in *Mysticism: Christian and Buddhist* (1957). As well as for this, he is remembered for his researches into and renewal of Zen Buddhism. In *An Introduction to Zen* (1961) he wrote 'Zen professes itself to be the spirit of Buddhism, but in fact it is the spirit of all religions and philosophies. When Zen is thoroughly understood, absolute peace of mind is attained, and a man lives as he ought to live'. He saw Zen and Buddhism not only as objects of study but also as means of personal fulfilment, and was important in Japan and the West not merely as an outstanding scholar but also as an experiential advocate of the Buddhist way. ▷ enlightenment; Mahayana Buddhism; mysticism; Pure Land Buddhism; Zen Buddhism

Swaminarayan movement A revivalist Hindu mission, founded by Shri Sahajanand Swami or Swami Narayan in the 19th century. It spread throughout India, particularly in Gujarat, and even reached Indian communities in East Africa. Since the expulsion of Asians from Uganda, Swami Narayan temples have been established in Britain and the USA. Swami Narayan travelled around India, advocating purity of living, non-violence (ahimsa) and teaching a form of the qualified non-dualism (*vishisthtadvaita*) of Ramanuja. ▷ ahimsa; Ramanuja

swastika A symbol consisting of a cross with its four arms bent at right angles, either clockwise or anti-clockwise. Found in ancient Hindu, Mexican, Buddhist, and other traditions, possibly representing the sun, it is now politically and culturally tainted, since its appropriation by the Nazi Party as its official emblem. The name derives from the Sanskrit 'svasti + ka', meaning a mystical cross used to denote good luck. ▷ Nazi Party; symbolism

sweat lodge A means of purification employed by a wide range of Native American peoples. Its basic action involves pouring cold water on hot stones within an enclosed structure made for the purpose; the four elements of earth, air, fire and water thus all act in the purification. It may be used as a preparation for personal prayer or other religious activity. Before the Sun Dance or other major rituals a substantial lodge may be established, following a prescribed pattern, and, like the Sun Dance lodge, acting as a representation of the universe. Among the Navajo and other southern peoples the sweatbath is a regular social and recreative activity (largely a male one). Nonetheless the atmosphere, as caught in the songs used in the sweatbath, remains ritual. ▷ Navajo religion; Sun Dance

Swedenborg, Emmanuel, originally **Swedberg** (1688–1772) Swedish mystic and scientist, born in Stockholm. Educated at Uppsala, he travelled in Europe, and on his return was appointed assessor in the college of mines. He wrote books on algebra, navigation, astronomy, and chemistry, and in 1734 published his monumental *Opera Philosophica et Mineralia* (Philosophical and Logical Works), a mixture of metallurgy and metaphysical speculation on the creation of the world. Curious dreams convinced him that he had direct access to the spiritual world. He communicated his spiritual explorations in *Heavenly Arcana* (1749–56), and spent the rest of his life in Amsterdam, Stockholm, and London, expounding his doctrines in such works as *The New Jerusalem* (1758). His followers (known as Swedenborgians) formed the Church of the New Jerusalem. ▷ New Jerusalem, Church of the; mysticism

Swedenborgian Church ▷ New Church

symbolism The use of symbols. A symbol is a sign which opens up or makes transparent insights and truths that were previously hidden. Symbolism plays an important role in religion. Religious symbols allow the believer to encounter the sacred. The success and survival of a religion may be said to be dependent upon the ability of its symbols to open up new dimensions of religious experience for its adherents. ▷ emblems, Sikh; five Ks; uraeus

Trimurti, Hindu symbol of the cosmic functions of the Supreme Beings

Symeon the New Theologian (949–1022) Orthodox theologian, ranked second only to St Gregory of Nazianzus. Intended for a political career, Symeon became a monk at 27, some years after a vision of divine light. His mysticism, based on this experience, echoes that of the hesychasts, and his spirituality of personal awareness of Christ and the Spirit, movingly expressed in his 'Hymns of Divine Love', resembles that of the 'Spiritual Homilies' attributed to Macarius. Symeon was abbot of the monastery of St Mamas, Constantinople, for about 25 years and spent his retirement as a hermit. ▷ Gregory of Nazianzus, St; hesychasm

synagogue (Greek 'congregation' or 'meeting') The local Jewish institution for instruction in the Torah and worship, but not infringing on the ritual or sacrificial roles of the Jerusalem priesthood. It was the local religious focal point of individual Jewish communities, both in Palestine and in cities of the Diaspora. Congregations were usually governed by a body of elders, who exercised certain disciplinary functions. While the term synagogue applied to the congregation, eventually it was also used of the buildings in which the people met, and in great cities such as Alexandria these could be quite elaborate. After the destruction of Jerusalem and the Temple in 70CE, the institution of the synagogue gained even greater importance as the major religious institution in Jewish life. Rabbis became leaders of synagogues in this later period. In Orthodox synagogues, men and women have traditionally separated; but in non-Orthodox synagogues, they now sit together. ▷ Diaspora; elder 1; Judaism; rabbi; Torah

Synanon A type of new religious movement founded in California in 1958 by Charles Dederich. It aimed to heal addicts afflicted by alcohol and drugs, but evolved from this into an encounter-group movement which sought to increase the human potential of its members. It encouraged set-piece dramas where members of groups could express great emotion between themselves and criticize themselves and one another. However, the aim was that in ordinary life they would be able to act in a happy and contented way. The Synanon Corporation emerged out of the work of the group, and it became and remains very rich. ▷ Human Potential movement; new religious movements in the West

syncretism The merging of different religions or religious traditions, or the absorption of foreign elements into a particular religion. The term is often employed negatively to refer to the contamination of one religion by another. Israel's adoption of certain elements of Canaanite religion and early Christianity's fusion with Hellenistic thought-forms can be regarded as examples of syncretism. ▷ religious pluralism; toleration

syncretism, Roman A Greek word defining the phenomenon of fusion in ancient religion. The Romans were not consciously aware of this concept, since it is connected with the contrast of attitudes between ancient Roman religion (tolerance towards foreign gods) and monotheism (intolerance), which only arose later. Instead of looking for differences between Roman and foreign deities, the Romans sought similarities. When Caesar wrote about the deities of Gaul, he regularly gave them the names of Roman gods. In Roman religion, fusion appeared both in rituals and in the nature of divinities. Foreign rituals and cults were assimilated with those already existing in Roman religion, and the nature and function of divinities increased with the addition of new aspects (eg the assimilation of Greek divinities gave Roman deities a mythology). The nature and function of the two syncretized deities did not necessarily have to be similar. Consequently Roman religion was never static. A second stage of syncretism occurred with the growth in power of the foreign divinities invited to Rome under their native names, such as Isis and Mithras. ▷ Isis; Mithra; Roman religion

synoptic gospels A term applied to three New Testament Gospels (Matthew, Mark, Luke), so called because of the striking amount of common material that they contain.

Most of Mark's Gospel, for example, is reproduced in Matthew and Luke, and the correspondence often extends to the order of passages and wording, although differences also exist. The precise way in which the works are interrelated is known as the 'synoptic problem', for which many competing solutions have been offered. John's Gospel presents a strikingly different portrayal of Jesus. ▷ Gospels, canonical

Syrian Christianity Christianity came to Syria before the conversion of Paul, and Antioch became an important centre of Christian mission and study, particularly after the fall of Jerusalem in 70CE. Syrian Christianity is responsible for much important surviving early Christian literature, including the *Peshitta* or Syriac Bible (second only in value to the Greek and Latin versions), a commentary on the earliest harmony of the Gospels, and the Gnostic *Odes of Solomon* and *Acts of Thomas*. Controversies over the nature of Christ lead to the 5th and 6th-century formation of the Nestorian East Syrian (Assyrian or Chaldean) Church and the Monophysite (Jacobite) Church. Further fragmentation resulted with the emergence of several Catholic Uniate Churches in the 12th and 16th to 18th centuries. Jacobite influence also extended outside Syria to South India in the 17th century, where there is still a Syrian Orthodox Church and the associated reformed Mar Thoma Church. The Christian population of modern Syria increased between World War I and World War II with the immigration of Armenians from Turkey and Iraq, but has subsequently fallen through emigration. Most Christians in Syria today are Greek Orthodox. ▷ Antioch, early Christianity in; Armenia, Christianity in; Uniate churches

T

Tabari, Abu Jafar Mohammed Ben Jarir-al- (839–923) Arab historian, born in Persia. He spent most of his life in Baghdad. He travelled in the Middle East, and in Arabic wrote invaluable Muslim annals, most notably *History of the Prophets and Kings*. He is also known for his *Qur'ān Commentary*.

Tabernacle A movable sanctuary or tent; in early Israelite religion, the shelter for the Ark of the Covenant during the desert wanderings and conquest of Canaan, eventually replaced by Solomon's Temple. Elaborate instructions for its construction and furnishing are given in the Book of Exodus, but many consider these to derive from a later priestly source. ▷ Ark of the Covenant; Holy of Holies; Temple, Jerusalem

tabu, tapu or **taboo** A Polynesian word for a prohibition or restriction related to the sacred. Since many other religious systems have prohibitions of some sort, the word has passed into general use for ritual prohibition, and has become further diluted by use in contexts where there is no reference to the sacred. Tabu can be seen as similar to the notices on power stations: 'danger—high voltage', and is intended to limit casual or unthinking approaches to the holy. It was particularly important in the Polynesian religious system. In a universe packed with power (*mana*), tabu (in New Zealand tapu) indicated the areas of safety in behaviour. Chiefs and ritual specialists (*tohunga*) were particularly fenced round. The head was especially sacred (touching a chief's head was immensely dangerous). When in his ritual state, a tohunga could not even feed himself; young virgins had to assist him. Ritual prohibitions also help to prevent mana diminishing, or communities being destroyed by carelessness or by the indiscriminate application of power. Tapu trees, or tapu days for fishing, may act as a conservation mechanism. In Melanesia, where similar concepts exist, the word *tambu* is found. ▷ Maori religion

tafsir (tafsīr) A Muslim term meaning explanation, or elucidation, but referring especially to a commentary on the Quran. It aims to provide background information and commentary on the Quran rather than analysis of the essence or inner interpretation of the text. This more mystical kind of explanation is achieved by another kind of commentary known as *tawil*. The symbolical and allegorical approach of tawil is seen to be complementary to the more outward and external approach of *tafsir*, although in the eyes of some more orthodox Muslims tawil engenders more suspicion. The earliest tafsir commentator on the Quran was Abd Allah ibn al-Abbas, the nephew of Muhammad. He was influenced by the approach of the Jewish *haggadah* writers to which he was introduced by Jewish converts to Islam. His 'Ocean of Knowledge' (*Bahr al-Ilm*) was important for later commentators such as al-Tabari (839–923) and al-Baydawi (d.1291). ▷ Muhammad; Quran

Tagore, Sir Rabindranath (1861–1941) Indian poet and philosopher, born in Calcutta, the son of a wealthy Hindu religious reformer, Debendranath Tagore (1817–1905). He studied law in England (1878–80) and for 17 years managed his family estates at Shileida, where he collected the legends and tales he later used in his work. His first book was a volume of poetry, *A Poet's Tale* (1878), written when he was 17, followed by a novel, *Karuna*, and a drama, *The Tragedy of Rudachandra*. In 1901 he founded near Bolpur the Santiniketan, a communal school to blend Eastern and Western philosophical and educational systems, which developed into Visva-Bharati University. He received the Nobel Prize for Literature in 1913, the first Asiatic to do so, and was knighted in 1915—an honour which he resigned in 1919 as a protest against British policy in the Punjab. He was openly critical of Mahatma Gandhi's non-cooperation as well as of the Government attitude in Bengal. His major works include *Binodini* (1902, the first truly modern novel by an Indian writer), *The Crescent Moon* (1913, poems about childhood), *Gitanjali* (1912, a volume of spiritual verse), *Chitra* (1914, his first and finest play), *The Religion of Man* (1931) and *Farewell My Friend* (1940). Among his memoirs are *My Reminiscences* (1917). ▷ Gandhi, Mohandas Karamchand; Punjab

Taharah (Ṭaharāh) A Muslim term which literally means purification. It refers to the state of ritual purity that is a requirement before Muslims can touch the Quran, or engage in daily prayers or other ritual acts. There are two forms of purification. The major one (*ghusl*) occurs after sexual intercourse and menstruation, whereas the minor one (*wudu*) occurs before daily prayers and ritual activities of other kinds. Purification is usually obtained by ablutions involving water, but if water is absent other materials such as sand may be used. There are also spiritual implications to purification, and outward ablutions are symbolic of spiritual purity within the inner person. ▷ Quran; salat

Tai Chi (T'ai Chi) The Chinese notion of the Great Ultimate which is the underlying cause of everything. In the third appendix to the *I Ching* it is the One through which the Tao manifests itself and then engenders the yin and the yang which combine to produce the phenomenal world. For the Taoist tradition in China, the *Tai Chi* was the unity that underlies all things. It is inactive but by its inaction it enables everything to be accomplished. The term was deepened by the neo-Confucian tradition. Chou Tun I (1017–77) wrote an important work, *Explanation of the Diagram of the Great Ultimate* (*Tai Chi Tu*), and in it he claimed that everything in the world including human characteristics is generated from the Great Ultimate. It is the transcendent first cause from which all else follows. It contains the underlying principle (*li*) which derives from the Great Ultimate and is analogous to the Tao. Along with *Shang Ti* and *Tien*, Tai Chi is the nearest thing to an equivalent to God in Chinese thought. ▷ I Ching; li; Shang Ti; Taoism; Tien; yin and yang

Taiping Rebellion (1851–65) A rebellion that spread all over South China, led by Hong Xiuquan (1822–64), a Hakka from Guangdong. Its programme, which aimed at ushering in a 'Heavenly Kingdom of Great Peace' (*Taiping tianguo*) was a mixture of religion and political reform. The rebels took Nanjing (Nanking) in 1853 and made it their capital, but internal strife, foreign intervention, and the Qing forces under Zeng Guofan (1811–72) eventually brought the downfall of the movement.

Tai Shan (T'ai Shan) A sacred mountain in the Shantung province of China which has been a holy place for Chinese popular religion from the time of the Shang dynasty (1523–1027BCE). From 110BCE to 1000CE it was one of the places where imperial sacrifices could be offered. Tai Shan is the abode of a popular Chinese god, the 'Great Divine Ruler of the Eastern Peak'. As the guardian of the Jade Emperor (Yu-Huang), the supreme god in the hierarchy of Chinese popular religion, the Great Divine Ruler of the Eastern Peak can determine how long a person will live, and what will happen to that person at their death. He is therefore a major god at the popular level, and his own prestige and that of mount Tai Shan interact to their mutual benefit. ▷ Chinese pantheon

Taizé An ecumenical community founded near Lyon, France, by members of the French Reformed Church in 1940. Members observe a rule similar to most monastic orders, but dress as laymen. Their aim is the promotion of Christian unity, particularly between Protestants and Catholics. They provide a popular retreat and mission to the young. ▷ ecumenism; monasticism; Reformed Churches; Roman Catholicism

Taj Mahal Literally the 'crown palace', this Islamic monument is recognized as one of the finest buildings ever erected. It was built at Agra in India between 1632 and 1647 by the Mughal emperor Shah Jahan (1592–1666) as a mausoleum for his wife Mumtaz Mahal. It is an integrated monument of great beauty, executed in white marble and semi-precious stones, centred upon an impressive centrepiece 250 feet high which contains the mausoleum itself. Although having an obvious functional purpose, it is full of religious symbolism. The four approaches to it, and the four gardens enclosed within it, symbolize the gardens of paradise and the four divine rivers. Its general structure and spiritual milieu owe much to ideas developed within Islamic Sufi thought, and the central building and the matched buildings around it symbolize God's own abode within the realm of paradise. ▷ Mughal Empire; Paradise; Sufism

Takht A Sikh term meaning 'throne' which signifies a seat of temporal authority within the Sikh tradition. Of the five takhts the first and most important, the Akal Takht, was established in 1609 by Guru Hargobind opposite the Golden Temple (Harimandir) in Amritsar. Three other takhts associated with Guru Gobind Singh were designated later at Anandpur in the Punjab, Patna in Bihar, and Namded in Maharashtra, and in 1966 a fifth was declared at Bahinda in the Punjab. In Guru Hargobind's time the Sikh religious leader had achieved a temporal as well as a spiritual role, and the takht became a symbol of his temporal function. Leaders of the takhts, named jathedars, are appointed for life by the Sikh Elective Board, the Shiromani Gurdwara Parbandhak Committee. Their function is administrative and potentially political rather than spiritual.The takht's task has been to debate and proclaim important decisions affecting the Sikh community, to safeguard their practice, and occasionally to pronounce on doctrinal and political matters. At crucial junctures it is thought desirable for the leader of the Akal Takht at Amritsar to call together a representative *Khalsa*, drawing upon the views of the whole Sikh community before a decision is made. ▷ Amritsar; Gobind Singh, Guru; Harimandir; Hargobind, Guru; Khalsa

Talmud (Hebrew 'study') An authoritative, influential compilation of rabbinic traditions and discussions about Jewish life and law. After the Mishnah of Rabbi Judah was compiled (c.200CE) it became itself an object of study by Jewish scholars in Palestine and Babylon; their commentary on it (the Gemara), together with the Mishnah, constitutes the Talmud, of which there were two versions: the Jerusalem or Palestinian Talmud (c.4th century) and the longer Babylonian Talmud (c.500). Outlining a precise judicial system and laying down precepts on areas such as worship, social welfare, diet and hygiene, it also covers subjects like magic, dream analysis and theology. ▷ Gemara; Judaism; Mishnah; rabbi; Torah

Tamil Hinduism While Hinduism is often associated with North India, particularly the 'homeland of the Aryans' (*Aryavarta*) in the Ganges plain, there have nevertheless been thriving traditions of Hinduism in the Tamil-speaking south, particularly in the Kaveri basin. Hindu culture thrived under the Hindu kingdoms which existed in South India; for example, the Chola dynasties (9th–13th centuries CE), which produced beautiful bronzes of Hindu deities. The medium *par excellence* of Tamil culture has been poetry, most notably the two styles of heroic war poetry (*puram*) and love poetry (*akam*). Indeed, poetry modelled on the akam style became the medium for the expression of Tamil devotionalism or bhakti, whose more emotional and ecstatic forms originated in the south around the 6th century CE. The Tamil bhakti poets tended to play down the caste system, reject the brahmanical monopoly on religion and emphasize liberation (*moksha*) through selfless devotion rather than knowledge (*jnana*): the God of the Tamil poets was personal rather than an abstract force, and an intense personal relationship between the devotee and God was emphasized. This bhakti movement tended to be either Shaiva or Vaishnava, the devotees worshipping local forms of Shiva or Vishnu and their families. Murukan was the deity identified with Shiva and with Shiva's son Skanda, while Vishnu was worshipped as Tirumal. The Shaiva and Vaishnava Tamil traditions were expressed in the poetry of the Nayanmars and Alvars respectively. Their works became sanctified and included in the canons of religious texts of those traditions. For example, the *Tiruvaymoli* of Nammalvar is regarded as the 'Tamil Veda' and sung alongside the orthodox Sanskrit Veda by devotees. The poetry of the Shaiva Nayanmars was similarly incorporated into the Sanskrit canon of the Shaiva Siddhanta. Although devotional in character, Tamil Hinduism produced high-ranking theologians, particularly Ramanuja, a theologian and leader of the Shri Vaishnava community. His pupil Pillan wrote a commentary, largely in Tamil, on the *Tiruvaymoli*. The Tantric-inspired Tamil *Cittars* (Sanskrit 'Siddhas') developed the practice of Hatha Yoga and wrote poetry expressing their desire for a perfected body through yoga. Devotion to Shiva and Vishnu is expressed in temple worship, particularly at the Shaiva and Vaishnava centres of Cidambaram and Shri Rangam. ▷ Alvar; Ganga; moksha; Ramanuja; Shaiva Siddhanta; Shaivism; Shiva; Shri Vaishnavas; siddha; Vaishnavism; Veda; Vishnu

Tangeroa ▷ atua

tanha (tanhā; Sanskrit: trishna: tṛṣṇa) The notion of craving in Buddhist thought. Craving, or desire, is a primary element in human behaviour, but is also one of the main reasons why humans are bound to this world of suffering, and destined to be reborn into it, until release from the round of rebirths and the peace of nirvana are achieved. Craving is central to the second and third noble truths preached by the Buddha, which state that the cause of suffering (*duhkha*) is craving, which must be eliminated in order that suffering may be ended. Craving is the eighth of the 12 links in the chain of dependent origination, and, together with the first link, spiritual ignorance, is one of the two weak links in the chain. Both of them must be eroded by ethical discipline and meditation, and destroyed by the development of wisdom. Tanha is often linked with greed and passion, but is associated more widely with craving for the psychological gratification of the six senses of sight, hearing, smell, tasting, feeling, and thinking.

In his first sermon the Buddha distinguished between three kinds of craving: craving for sensual desires, craving for the continuing existence of the self, and craving to avoid unpleasant circumstances. Tanha literally means 'thirst'—for satisfaction in the present without thought for long-term priorities and consequences. ▷ ariya sacca; Buddha; dependent origination; duhkha; nirvana; rebirth

tanka (thang ka) Painted scroll or temple banner of Tibetan Buddhism. These scrolls, which hang in temples and monasteries, depict Buddhas, lamas, various deities and mandalas, which are painted on a cotton or sometimes silk base. The images themselves are often taken from religious scriptures such as the *Lotus Sutra*, or depict mandalas described in different tantras. Tankas are revered as sacred, and there are precise instructions concerning their painting. They play an important role in meditation, in that the forms they depict are internalized in visualization practices. Indeed, some tankas are revealed only to those who have the necessary initiation. ▷ Buddha; lama; Lotus Sutra; mandala

Tannaim (Aramaic 'teachers', 'transmitters of oral tradition') Early sages and teachers of Judaism (mainly 10–220CE) who were instrumental in the emerging rabbinic movement by their study of the Jewish Law (Torah) and formulation of the nucleus of the Mishnah and Midrashim. Followers of Hillel and Shammai are often considered the first Tannaim. ▷ Hillel I; Judaism; midrash; Mishnah; rabbi; Shammai; Torah

Tantra (literally 'looms') A type of Hindu or Buddhist ritual text, and the practice of its instruction. Similar in some ways to the *Puranas*, the Tantras are Sanskrit texts, dating from about the 7th century CE. They may include treatises describing spells, magical formulae, mantras, meditative practices, and rituals to be performed. The practice of Tantra requires instruction by a guru. ▷ Buddhism; guru; Hinduism; mantra; Puranas; Tantric Hinduism

Tantric Buddhism A later form of Buddhism arising out of developments in the Mahayana Buddhist tradition and developing its own form and momentum, especially in Tibet. The tantras themselves are ritual texts that were said to have been originally transmitted by the Buddha and to have been passed on secretly until the 5th and 6th centuries CE, when they emerged in India and were developed by 84 Tantric saints or siddhas, including such figures as Saraha and Naropa. The tantras encourage the evocation of various gods, the pursuit of magical powers, the use of sacred chants known as mantras, the use of bodily gestures known as *mudras*, the use of mystical verses known as mandalas, and various forms of meditation and yoga. The role of the guru (usually standing in an unbroken line of succession) is important in Tantric Buddhism. He motivates and empowers the follower to embark on meditation, transmits the relevant texts, and teaches the correct method of imbibing and practising the relevant teaching and discipline. The Tantric stress is upon the present and everyday rather than upon nirvana as a future goal. There has been an overlap between Hindu and Buddhist tantrism, and both have included an orthodox 'right-hand' form and a less conventional 'left-hand' form that was willing to make ritual use of forbidden articles such as fish, meat, aphrodisiacs, liquor, and sexual union. Tantric Buddhism died out in India, but was taken to Tibet by Padmasambhava and others, becoming dominant there, especially in its more orthodox form. ▷ Buddha; guru; mandala; mantra; mudras; Naropa; nirvana; Padmasambhava; Tibetan religion

Tantric Hinduism Although notoriously difficult to define, Tantra might generally be said to be an unorthodox form of Hinduism concerned with acquiring spiritual power (*siddhi*) and liberation in life (*jivanmukti*), through the realization of one's essential or innate divinity. Other general features are that it regards the body as a microcosm of the cosmos, it uses sacred formulae or mantras in its rituals and it emphasizes *Shakti*, the dynamic female power or energy. This energy is contrasted with Shiva, the passive, masculine consciousness which, without the energy of Shakti, is powerless. The male-female cosmic polarity is recapitulated in male and female bodies and even within each body. These ideas are spoken of in a large group of texts called Tantras, Tantric Hinduism's revealed scriptural authority in contrast to the orthodox Veda. These texts usually take the form of a dialogue between Shiva and Shakti and are concerned with cosmology, initiation, mantras, ritual and yoga. In Tantric ritual it is said that only a god can worship a god, so the practitioner (*sadhaka*) is purified and divinized by mantras. Indeed, the mantras are regarded as identical with the deities of the various Tantric pantheons who are visualized. These deities are themselves manifestations of an absolute power, sometimes regarded as

Shiva, sometimes regarded as the goddess (such as Kali). Some Tantric rites involve caste-free sexual intercourse in order to harness sexual energy for a spiritual end, to offer sexual substances to the deity and to gain power through breaking orthodox taboos. Indeed the rite of the 'five Ms' or the ritual use of wine (*madya*), meat (*mamsa*), fish (*matsya*), parched-grain (*mudra*) and sexual intercourse (*maithuna*), has made Tantra notorious in orthodox Hindu eyes. Tantric Yoga involves awakening Kundalini, who rises up the body through the various centres (*cakras*) to unite with Shiva at the crown of the head, filling the body with bliss and spiritual knowledge. Although Tantric texts can only be dated to about the 7th century CE, elements of Tantric Hinduism are very ancient and a tradition of ascetics living in cremation grounds, from where Tantrism develops, goes back at least to the time of the Buddha. Tantric traditions developed in all major branches of Hinduism, most notably Kashmir Shaivism and the Pancharatra of Vaishnavism, though erotic rites tend to be absent here. ▷ Buddha; cakras; Hinduism; jivanmukti; Kali; Kashmir Shaivism; Kundalini; mantra; Shaivism; Shakti; Shiva; Tantra; Vaishnavism; Veda; yoga

Tao chia The Chinese school of Taoist philosophy. This philosophical Taoism is found most centrally in the *Tao Te Ching* and the *Chuang Tzu* which are its key texts (around 4th century BCE), and to a lesser extent in the *Lieh Tzu* and *Huai Nan Tzu*. These texts were commented on by a succession of scholars, especially by the new Taoists, or neo-Taoists, from the 3rd century CE onwards. The key figures in this movement were Wang Pi (226–49), Hon Yen (d.249) and Kuo Hsiang (d.312). Philosophical Taoism was different from religious Taoism, which arose as a sect at the end of the Han dynasty (23–220CE). It was concerned with alchemy, the search for immortality, hygiene, healing, and pantheons. Although they are not completely divorced, philosophical and religious Taoism are better treated as separate movements. ▷ alchemy; Chinese pantheon; Chuang Tzu; Taoism; Tao Te Ching

Taoism A translation of the Chinese terms for 'the school of the tao' and the 'Taoist religion', both of which have had a huge influence on Chinese thought and history. The former refers to the philosophy of the classical Taoist texts of no earlier than the 4th–3rd century BCE: The *Lao Tzu* or *Tao Te ching* (thought to have been written by the sage Lao-Tzu), *The Chuang Tzu*, and *The Lieh Tzu Tao* or 'the way' are central in both Confucianism and Taoism, with the former stressing the tao of humanity, and the latter the tao of nature, harmony with which ensures appropriate conduct. Expressions of mystical thought, these texts are concerned with the political order and practical life of the individual. Taoist religion developed later, in about the 2nd century CE, incorporating alchemy, divination, magic and, particularly, the importance of the balancing powers of yin and yang. With Buddhism and Confucianism it is one of the main religions in China. ▷ Confucianism; Lao-Tzu; mysticism; yin and yang

Tao Te Ching An important Chinese philosophical text which together with the *Chuang Tzu* is the key to philosophical Taoism. It is traditionally ascribed to Lao Tzu, who is said to have been a contemporary of Confucius in the 6th century BCE. However, its authorship is uncertain, and it probably dates from the 4th century BCE. The sayings of the *Tao Te Ching*, compressed into 5250 words, are cryptic and therefore open to different interpretations. It was written at the time of warring states in China, to help rulers to rule better according to the principle that creative inaction (*wu-wei*) is better than frenetic activity. It advocates naturalness and spontaneity and the idea of yielding ground in order to advance. Central to it is the notion of the Tao which cannot be named but is the source of all that is and the unchanging principle behind the universe. The secret of life is to live in accordance with the Tao which 'never acts, yet nothing is left undone' (37). The Tao is the effortless and spontaneous 'Way' to be followed by rulers and by all the people so that they may rule others, rule themselves, and live in harmony with one another and with nature. This teaching was complementary to the activism, moral endeavour, ritual involvement, educational discipline and five relationships stressed by the Confucians. Although in seeming opposition, they were able to live side by side in China according to the principle of the harmony of opposites (yin and yang). ▷ Chuang Tzu; five relationships, Confucian; Taoism

tapas Asceticism or the 'heat' created by asceticism in Hinduism. Many Hindu holy men (sadhus) or renouncers practise tapas in order to create spiritual power (*siddhi*) and eventually to attain liberation (*moksha*). The idea of tapas occurs in the *Rig Veda* where it is identified with the sacrifice and associated with Agni, the fire god. With the Upanishads tapas becomes internalized as an inner power, which can be created through yoga and ascetic practices, and which leads to liberation. Tapas is prescribed in the Hindu Law books, such as the *Laws of Manu*, as part of the fourth or renouncer's stage of life (*ashrama*). During this stage, the ascetic must beg for food, wander homeless and be celibate. More extreme asceticism can be found, such as vowing silence; vowing not to lie down for 12 years (the body rests by the ascetic leaning on a 'hammock'); holding an arm or both arms above the head until locked in that position; or sitting in the heat of the day between burning fires. ▷ Agni; ashrama; Manu; moksha; sadhu; Upanishads; Veda

Taqui Onqoy A Quechua religious movement in south central Peru in the 1560s and early 1570s. It mobilized resistance to the Spanish a generation after the conquest. 'Taqui' indicates a traditional song or dance, associated with pre-Christian festivals. 'Onqoy' suggests the June festival associated with both the star-group Pleiades and with the driving out of illnesses. The movement vigorously rejected Christianity (though its leaders took the names of John the Baptist and other saints) and called for a return to ancestral ways. It asserted some 60 or more *huacas*, including Pachamacac and ancient deities bearing the local names of Tiahuanaco and Titicaca. These deities, who rode on the wind, possessed their followers in trance, demanded moral purity and observances of days, fasts and ceremonies and offered eventual victory. Though seen, then and later, as an Inca revolt, Taqui Onqoy ignored the Inca deities Viracocha and the sun god; nor was possession a normal part of Inca religion. Rather the movement was a reassertion of the old primal religion in a form revitalized by contact with Christianity, one in which local and pan-Andean deities return, not to the destroyed shrines, but to the bodies of their followers. ▷ Inca religion; Pachacamac; Viracocha

Tara (Tārā) A female deity within the Tantric Buddhist tradition. She is known as the Saviouress, and is especially popular in Tibet, where she appears in different forms, one of which is the patron goddess of that country. She is very compassionate, and two of her forms are said to have been born out of two tears shed by the bodhisattva of compassion, Avalokiteshvara, when he viewed the horrors of hell. She has her own mantra, or sacred phrase, which is said to sum up her essence. At the popular level Tara is viewed as an external goddess, but at the deeper level she is regarded as a force or consciousness latent within the believer's own mind that can be visualized and developed to spiritual advantage. She is represented in image form in various temples, particularly in Nepal and Tibet. ▷ Avalokiteshvara; bodhisattva; mantra; Tantric Buddhism; Tibetan religion

targum (Hebrew 'translation') An Aramaic translation of the Hebrew Scriptures or parts thereof, probably originally composed orally (c.1st century BCE) when the Torah was read aloud in the synagogues, since most Jews of the time understood Aramaic rather than Hebrew, but then written in the rabbinic period. The translations sometimes betray early rabbinic ideology. Best known is the *Targum Onkelos*. ▷ Bible; Judaism; Old Testament; rabbi; Torah

tariqah (ṭarīqah) A Muslim term meaning 'path' or 'way' which is used in three different senses: to refer to the true Muslim path; to refer to Sufism in general; and to refer to various specific Sufi paths or brotherhoods. The first sense of religion as a way or a straight path is common to various religious traditions: for example, the early Christians were called followers of the way, and the Tao of the Taoist tradition means 'the Way'. The first chapter of the Quran refers to the true Muslim as one who follows the straight path or tariqah, as opposed to infidels who deviate from it. Secondly, tariqah is a generic term referring to Sufism as the path leading from the outer truth of the law to the inner truth of mystical realization. As such it draws together the doctrines and methods of the Sufi tradition in general as representing a means of going from the world to God, and from God back into the world. Thirdly, from the 12th and 13th centuries, independent Sufi brotherhoods called tariqahs came into being, which often developed from the work of a renowned *shaykh*. In all, hundreds of tariqahs came into being, although they all trace their authority back via a chain of transmission that includes a shaykh and Muhammad's companions, going back to the prophet Muhammad himself. The first specific Sufi tariqah to emerge was the Qadiriyyah, through the work of Abd al-Qadir al-Jilani (1077–1166), and many others have emerged since, including the Bektashi, Mevlevis and Naqshbandiyyah. ▷ Bektashi; Mevlevis; Naqshbandiyyah; Qadiriyyah; Quran; shaykh; Sufi institutions; Sufi orders; Tao Te Ching

Tarot A set of cards that are used as a medium of divination. They emerged about

Tarot cards

1440 in Italy as playing cards but were given a Hermetic interpretation by Gebelin in 1781 and from then on were used more commonly for divination. A L Constant (1810–75), also known as Eliphus Levi, gave Tarot cards a Kabbalistic interpretation, derived from the Jewish Kabbalah, and this method of interpretation is now used in most divination sessions. A Tarot pack has 78 cards, including 56 cards in four suits (wands, pentacles, cups, and swords) of 14 each, plus 22 other freelance trumps (major arcana cards) which feature deeply symbolic pictures. Divination is based upon the sequence of the cards, the interpretation of the major arcana cards, and clairvoyance resulting in an insight into the character and destiny of the person concerned. Ostensibly there are usually four main reasons for consulting Tarot cards: money, a life-crisis, love, and family matters. However, at a deeper level they contain an arcane or mysterious element that is often important to their practitioners and constitutes for them a series of interlocking occult mysteries. ▷ divination; Kabbalah; occult

tathagata (tathāgata) A Buddhist term meaning 'the one who has thus gone', ie, one who has gone along and completed the way to enlightenment. It was often used by the Buddha in relation to himself and indicated that he had apprehended reality or 'suchness' (*tathata*), and that he had attained wisdom. Tathagata is also sometimes used as a kind of equivalent to nirvana, and refers to a condition that transcends death. In a famous comment the Buddha said that the state of a tathagata after death was neither 'is', nor 'is not', nor 'both is and is not', nor 'neither is nor is not'. In other words it cannot be described in ordinary language, yet the truth of the reality it refers to cannot be disregarded, and it is seen in the experience and teaching of the Buddha. Buddhaghosa, the great Theravada commentator, gave eight separate interpretations of it in his famous commentary on the 'great discourse' in the *tipitaka* or Pali Canon, thus indicating both its difficulty and its importance. The Mahayana tradition used the notion of the *tathagata-garbha* to refer to a kind of Buddha potential within all beings, and it became associated with the idea of the Buddha nature that is present in all humans. ▷ Buddha; Buddhaghosa: Mahayana Buddhism; nirvana; tathata; Theravada Buddhism; tipitaka

tathata (tathatā) The notion of 'suchness' or reality in Mahayana Buddhist thought. It involves seeing things as they are, and experiencing the absolute in the relative. The Buddha was an example of one who had achieved suchness, and it is related to equivalent terms such as emptiness and nirvana. It transcends logical analysis, is beyond duality, and is obtained through wisdom (*prajna*). It is important in Zen Buddhism in the sense of finding and experiencing enlightenment in everyday situations of ordinary life, and in the sense of waking up to the Buddha nature within through the practicalities of life such as the hewing of wood and the drawing of water. It is a less common term in Mahayana Buddhist thought than emptiness (*shunyata*), although is has a slightly more positive meaning. As with other attempts to express reality in Buddhist thought, it defies conceptual expression, and the point is to realize it rather than merely talk about it. ▷ Buddha; emptiness; Mahayana Buddhism; nirvana; tathagata; Zen Buddhism

Tatian (2nd century) Syrian Christian thinker. He became a pupil of the martyr Justin at Rome and was converted to Christianity by him. After Justin's death in c.165 he was estranged from the Catholic Church and returned to Syria c.172 where he established, or was at least closely associated with, an ascetic religious community of Encratites, which fostered a heretical combination of Christianity and Stoicism. Only two of his many writings survive: the *Oratio ad Graecos* ('Speech to the Greeks') is a denunciation of the intellectualism of Greek culture and the corruption of its moral and religious values, which he compares unfavourably with the 'barbarian philosophy' of Christianity; the *Diatessaron* (literally 'Out of Four') is a patchwork version of the four gospels arranged as a continuous narrative, which in its Syriac version was used as a text in the Syrian Church for centuries. ▷ Christianity; Justin, St; Roman Catholicism; Stoicism

Tauler, Johann (c.1300–1361) German mystic and preacher, born in Strasbourg. He became a Dominican c.1318. Driven from Strasbourg by a feud between the city and his order, he settled at the age of 24 in Basle and associated with the devout 'Friends of God', having before then been a disciple of Meister Eckhart. His fame as a preacher spread far and wide, and he became the centre of the quickened religious life in the middle Rhine valley. ▷ Dominicans; Eckhart, Johannes; mysticism

tawhid (tawḥīd) The notion of the unity of God within Islam. It is central to the Islamic tradition, and acceptance of the absolute oneness of God is the touchstone of the Muslim faith. It is enshrined in the statement of faith, the *shahadah*, 'There is no god but God, and Muhammad is his prophet'. However, it can be interpreted in different ways. At one level it denotes opposition to idolatry, and to polytheism, and to any view of God that seems to compromise his unqualified oneness (like the Christian view of the Trinity seen through Muslim eyes). At another level it can be understood exclusively or inclusively. The exclusive view exemplified in the Wahhabis stresses that God is God, and he is not reflected in the created world (except the Quran), which therefore lacks sacredness. The world is material reality only and it lacks divine quality. The inclusive view argues that there is nothing, the world included, outside God—'there is no God *except* Allah'; this has been the dominant view. The Sufis have moved in a more spiritual direction. For them, tawhid must be internalized so that any sentiment or imagination that withdraws from God should be abandoned. At the deepest level of all, as seen in Ibn Arabi's *Treatise on Oneness*, there is annihilation (*fana*) of everything but God from the human unconscious as well as conscious awareness. ▷ Allah; fana; Arabi, Ibn al-; Muhammad; Quran; shahadah; Sufism; Wahhabis

Taylor, Jeremy (1613–67) English theologian, the third son of a Cambridge barber. He entered Caius College, Cambridge and became a fellow of All Souls College, Oxford (1636), chaplain to Archbishop Laud, and in 1638 Rector of Uppingham. *The Sacred Order and Offices of Episcopacy* (1642) gained him his DD. During the Civil War he is said to have accompanied the royal army as chaplain, and was taken prisoner at Cardigan Castle (1645). After the downfall of the cause he sought shelter in Wales, kept a school, and found a patron in the Earl of Carbery, then living at Golden Grove, Llandilo, immortalized in the title of Taylor's still popular manual of devotion (1655).

During the last 13 years (1647–60) of Taylor's enforced seclusion appeared all his great works, some of them the most enduring monuments of sacred eloquence in the English language. The first was *The Liberty of Prophesying* (1646), a noble and comprehensive plea for toleration and freedom of opinion. *The Life of Christ, or the Great Exemplar* (1649) is an arrangement of the facts in historical order, interspersed with prayers and discourses. *The Rule and Exercises of Holy Living* (1650) and *The Rule and Exercises of Holy Dying* (1651) together form the choicest classic of English devotion. The *52 Sermons* (1651–3), with the discourses in the *Life of Christ* and many passages in the *Holy Living and Dying*, contain the richest examples of their author's characteristic expressiveness. The more formal treatises were *An Apology for Authorised and Set Forms of Liturgy* (1646); *Clerus Dominio* (1651, 'On the Ministerial Office'); *The Real Presence in the Blessed Sacrament* (1654); *Unum Necessarium* (1655, 'On Repentance', which brought on him the charge of Pelagianism); *The Worthy Communicant* (1660); *The Rite of Confirmation* (1663); *The Dissuasive from Popery* (1664); and the famous *Ductor Dubitantium* (1660), the most learned and subtle of all his works, intended as a handbook of Christian casuistry and ethics.

During the Civil War Taylor was thrice imprisoned, once for the preface to *The Golden Grove* (1655); the last time in the Tower for an 'idolatrous' print of Christ in the attitude of prayer in his *Collection of Offices* (1658). In 1658 he was given a lectureship at Lisburn, at the Restoration the bishopric of Down and Connor, with the following year the administration of Dromore; he also became Vice-Chancellor of Dublin University and a member of the Irish Privy Council. In his first visitation (in spite of his *Liberty of Prophesying*) he ejected 36 Presbyterian ministers, but neither severity nor gentleness could prevail to force a form of religion upon an unwilling people. His works were published in 1820–2 (rev. 1847–54). ▷ Pelagius; toleration

Teacher of Righteousness The religious leader and founder of the Qumran community, probably in the mid 2nd century BCE; apparently a Zadokite priest who opposed the Hasmoneans, assuming the role of Jewish high priest, and who led his followers into exile near the Dead Sea. His identity is otherwise unknown, but this title is applied to him in the Damascus Document and various Qumran commentaries, because of his role in guiding the community in their interpretation of the Torah. ▷ Maccabees; Qumran, community of; Torah; Zadokites

tefillin Two black leather boxes worn by adult male Jews when they attend weekday morning services. The boxes, also called phylacteries, are tied to the left arm and the forehead and contain the four passages from the Hebrew Bible which instruct Jews to 'bind the words of God between your eyes and upon your arm', to remind them of God and of the commandments of the law. They are not worn by Reform Jews, who interpret the biblical passages metaphorically. ▷ Amidah; Judaism; Reform Judaism; Shema

Tegh Bahadur, Guru (Tegh Bahādur, Gurū) (1621–75) Ninth of the 10 Sikh gurus, born in the Punjab, India. He became Guru in 1665 at a time when the Mughal emperors were pursuing aggressive Muslim policies in North India, and his name, which means 'brave sword', symbolizes his heroic opposition to Emperor Aurangzeb's forces. When arrested, he refused the offer of a reprieve from death if he converted to Islam. He was executed in Delhi, and is venerated among Sikhs as a martyr. His policy of opposition to the Mughals was followed by his son Guru Gobind Singh. A prolific author, 116 of his poems are included in the Sikh scripture, the *Guru Granth Sahib*. In his earlier years he engaged in social welfare schemes on behalf of the hungry, hence his original nickname Degh Bahadur ('Brave Cooking-Pot'). ▷ Gobind Singh, Guru; Guru Granth Sahib; guru, Sikh; Mughal Empire; Punjab

Teilhard de Chardin, Pierre (1881–1955) French Jesuit theologian, palaeontologist, and philosopher, the son of an Auvergne landowner. He was educated at a Jesuit school, lectured in pure science at the Jesuit College in Cairo, was ordained a priest in 1911, and in 1918 became Professor of Geology at the Institut Catholique in Paris. Between 1923 and 1946 he undertook palaeontological expeditions in China, (where he helped to discover Peking Man in 1929) and later in central Asia, but increasingly his researches did not conform to Jesuit orthodoxy and he was forbidden by his religious superiors to teach and publish, and in 1948 was not allowed to stand for a professorship at the Sorbonne in succession to the Abbé Breuil. Nevertheless, his work in Cenozoic geology and palaeontology became known and he was awarded academic distinctions, including the Legion of Honour (1946). From 1951 he lived in the USA and worked at the Wenner-Gren Foundation for Anthropological Research in New York. Posthumously published, his philosophical speculations, based on his scientific work, trace the evolution of animate matter to two basic principles: nonfinality and complexification. By the concept of *involution* he explains why *homo sapiens* is the only species which, in spreading over the globe, has resisted intense division into further species. This leads on to transcendental speculations, which allow him original, if theologically unorthodox, proofs for the existence of God. This work, *The Phenomenon of Man* (1955), is complementary to *Le Milieu divin* (1957). ▷ Jesuits; Peking Man

teleological argument Known as the 'argument from design', this theory states that the existence of God can be deduced from the evidence of design in the creation and working of the world. This argument is criticized by David Hume who claimed that at best the evidence suggested a finite designer or designers, and not necessarily God. ▷ God, arguments for the existence of; Hume, David

teleological ethics Any normative ethical theory which takes the goodness or badness of the consequences of an action as fundamental in determining whether it is right or wrong. Teleologists also typically provide a theory about what sorts of things are in fact good. They claim that an action is right if it produces at least as much goodness as any alternative. Egoists such as Thomas Hobbes maintain that one ought to produce maximum goodness for oneself. Utilitarians such as J S Mill insist that the right action must produce maximum goodness on balance for everyone affected, even if that requires choosing less goodness for oneself. ▷ deontological ethics; Mill, John Stuart; utilitarianism

temenos A Greek term which etymologically denotes an area cut off (*temno* meaning 'I cut') from ordinary use. In Homer we find royal temenē, but by the classical period the only proprietors of temenē were gods. At its simplest, a temenos might be a small area of land with an altar in the middle; a grander temenos might contain a temple, in front of which the altar stood, and perhaps a sacred grove. On the largest scale, the whole area of such elaborate sanctuaries as that of Zeus at Olympia was a temenos. ▷ Greek religion

templa Although a *templum* might have included what we call a temple, technically it had another meaning: it indicated a sacred space that was 'inaugurated'(defined by an augur) either in the sky or on the ground. A templum in the sky was marked off with imaginary lines which divided it into four regions according to cardinal points and was used for taking auspices—for instance, observation of the flights of birds. On the ground, the space might either be marked off with imaginary lines or with physical delimitations such as walls. A templum on the ground might also be used for augury, but terrestial templa could also designate buildings, and thus have other functions. For example, since political and legislative decisions could only be made within a templum, the senate house was itself a templum, but this also meant that such decisions could take place in the temple of a divinity. A templum in the restricted sense of a deity's territory included a temple (*aedes*) and, in front of it, an altar around which cults and rituals were performed. ▷ auspicia

Temple, Jerusalem The central shrine of Jewish worship and its priesthood since its establishment under Solomon. It was first destroyed by Nebuchadnezzar in c.587BCE, but rebuilt later in the 6th century BCE after the return from exile. Extended on an elaborate scale by Herod the Great, beginning c.20BCE, it was barely renewed before its destruction under Titus during the Jewish revolt of 70CE. Still unrestored today, its site is now partly occupied by the Muslim mosque, the Dome of the Rock, built in the late 7th century. ▷ Dome of the Rock; Holy of Holies; Judaism; Solomon; Tabernacle

Temple, William (1881–1944) English prelate, and Archbishop of Canterbury, born in Exeter, son of Frederick Temple. He was educated at Rugby and Oxford, where he became a fellow of Queen's College (1904–10). He took orders in 1908, was headmaster of Repton School (1910–14) and became a canon of Westminster in 1919. In 1921 he became Bishop of Manchester, in 1929 Archbishop of York and in 1942 Archbishop of Canterbury. With interests as broad as his humanity he united solid learning and great administrative ability. As primate he was one of the greatest moral forces of his time. An outspoken advocate of social reform, he made his main task the application to current problems of his conception of the Christian philosophy of life, crusading against usury, slums, dishonesty, and the aberrations of the profit motive. Temple's leadership was also seen in his chairmanship of the Doctrinal Commission of the Church of England and in his work for the Ecumenical Movement of Christian Union. His publications include *Church and Nation* (1915), *Christianity and the State* (1928) and *Christianity and the Social Order* (1942). ▷ Church of England; ecumenism

temples Buildings sacred to a god or where a god is believed to reside. Temples usually contain an inner sanctum in which an image of the god is kept. This is the most holy part of the temple. Most temples may only be entered by the priests, although they too may be prohibited from entering the inner sanctum. ▷ pilgrimage; shrines; worship

temples, Ancient Egyptian Temples in Ancient Egypt, called 'the house of god', were where the gods' statues were housed and where they were believed to dwell. The earliest temples were simple reed enclosures, but these developed into the magnificent stone structures of the New Kingdom (c.1567–1085BCE) which remained the model up to the Graeco-Roman period. The walled temple compound was laid out along an axis, with an open court then colonnaded hall leading up towards the inner sanctuary where the statue was kept. The floor level of the sanctuary was raised to symbolize the primeval hill, and the room kept dark to increase the sense of mystery. Here the daily ritual took place, where the priest would cleanse, clothe, decorate, and feed the image, fulfilling divine needs seen in very human terms. The priests served on behalf of the king, who was portrayed on the walls making offerings. On festival days the statue was carried out to the court for the public to see. The temples of the gods should be distinguished from mortuary temples where offerings were made to the dead to provide for them in the afterlife. ▷ afterlife; primeval hill

temples, Ancient Near Eastern Primarily conceived as a dwelling place for the god rather than a place for worshippers to congregate, Ancient Near Eastern temples took different forms in different places and periods. In early Mesopotamia each city had a temple for its own god or gods, whose presence ensured prosperity for the city. King and temple were the two principal state institutions, and large temple complexes were important economic units, having their own fields and workers who provided food for the god and for the temple staff. The temple itself was dominated by its ziggurat, the large stepped tower which was the tallest building in the city. At the foot of the ziggurat was the cella. Here the god's image was kept, usually in the form of a richly ornamented wooden statue. A large and specialized staff of priests cared for the god with daily washing, clothing and feeding. Outside the shrine was a large court where the public assembled on festival days. The building and upkeep of temples formed a large part of the religious responsibilities of Mesopotamian kings. Among the Hittites and West Semitic peoples the gods were worshipped not only in elaborately built temples, but also in open air shrines and sacred places which must have resembled the 'high places' of the Hebrew Bible. ▷ festivals, Ancient Near Eastern; kingship, Ancient Near Eastern; ziggurat

Templo Mayor Literally 'the great temple', this denotes the Aztec shrine at Tenochtitlan, dedicated to the war-god Huitzilopochtli and the rain-god Tlaloc. Its double sanctuary rises above a pyramid base with two sets of steps. It was the scene of human sacrifice on a massive scale. ▷ Aztec religion; human sacrifice, Meso-American

temptation Attraction to an object or activity regarded as detrimental to the human being's moral state or relationship with God. The term 'temptation' can refer to the object or activity itself, to the state of being tempted, or the act of tempting. Temptation is in itself not evil, but is a natural occurrence arising from the nature and structure of human existence and the gift of freedom. Temptation becomes a sin, however, when instead of resisting it and choosing the good, the human being freely chooses what is wrong (cf Genesis 3).

In the Bible the term 'temptation' is employed in several different ways. In some passages disobedience, lack of trust, and hostility towards the divine will are all understood as tempting God (Exodus 17.2, 7; Deuteronomy 6.16; Psalms 95.9; I Corinthians 10.9; Hebrews 3.8f; Matthew 4.7; Acts 5.9, 15.10). More usually, however, the term is employed to describe the powers that may endanger his relationship with God, his spiritual welfare, and securing of salvation. This is the motive behind Christ's warnings and prayers that we might not be led into such temptations (Matthew 6.13; Luke 11.4; Mark 14.38). Temptation also plays an important role in Christ's mission. His temptations by Satan were aimed at undermining his understanding of himself as a suffering Messiah (Matthew 4.11; Luke 4.1–13; cf Mark 1.12f; Matthew 16.23). Similar tests of vocation were undergone by the Buddha and Zoroaster.

Ten Commandments, or **Decalogue** The fundamental laws of the Jews. In the Bible, they are said to have been given to Moses on Mount Sinai. They describe the general religious and moral requirements for the Jewish people, and set the terms of God's covenant with them, although often phrased as universal principles. Slightly variant forms of the 'ethical' decalogue are found in Exodus 20 and Deuteronomy 5, but a 'cultic' variant appears in Exodus 34.14–26 (covering major Jewish feasts and offerings). A further tradition declares that God inscribed them on two tablets of stone which were then deposited in the Ark of the Covenant (Deuteronomy 9). The well-known 'ethical' decalogue contains the commands: 1 that the God of Israel shall be acknowledged as one and unique; 2 worship of images is prohibited; **3** misuse of the Lord's name is prohibited; **4** the Sabbath must be observed; **5** one's parents must be honoured; **6–10** murder, adultery, theft, false testimony, and desiring one's neighbours goods are prohibited. This numbering varies, however, in some Jewish and Christian circles. ▷ Ark of the Covenant; covenant; God; Sinai, Mount; Torah

Tendai A Japanese Buddhist school, named after Tien Tai mountain in China, and the Tien Tai school of Chinese Buddhism that arose there. Tendai was brought to Japan by Saicho in 805. He introduced it into his Enryakuji temple on Mount Hiei near Kyoto, which had replaced Nara as the capital of Japan, and Tendai became a key element in the new developments in Japanese Buddhism after that date. The foundation of Saicho's teaching was to be found in the *Lotus Sutra* and his view that all forms of life rank equally in attaining Buddhahood, but he established Tendai on a broad basis which included elements of mystical Shingon Buddhism taught by his contemporary Kukai. His construction of a Lotus Sutra hall in 812 was a significant step in the development of reverence to Amida Buddha and the rise of Pure Land sects, while he also set in train the tendency to introduce elements of Shinto into Buddhism, and a generation after his death Zen-type meditation was also present in Tendai. During the Kamakura period (1185–1333) other popular branches of Buddhism arose within Tendai, which was based upon sound ethical principles, systematic meditational disciplines, and a sense that the Buddha nature is present in all persons. It became almost too broad, and more particular sects, including the important Pure Land, Zen and Nichiren traditions, had their origins in Tendai. Although still present in Japan it is less important than the three above-mentioned sects and the Japanese new religions. ▷ Amida worship; Buddha nature: Kamakura; Kukai; Lotus Sutra; Nichiren Buddhism; Pure Land Buddhism; Saicho; Shingon; Tien Tai; Zen Buddhism

Ten Lost Tribes of Israel Ten tribes of Israel taken captive by Assyria in 721BCE and merged (hence 'lost') with the Assyrians. They are alleged by British Israelites to be the ancestors of the British and American peoples, but this theory is largely discredited. ▷ Israel, tribes of

Tenri-kyo (Tenri-kyō) A Japanese new religion with Shinto associations, set up in 1838. Its prehistory lies in the work of a female peasant Kino (1756–1826), who felt inspired by God to preach his love and universal salvation for all people on the basis of her own experience. Her work was followed up by the real foundress of Tenri-kyo, Nakayama Miki (1798–1887), who in 1838 had an experience of trance and faith-healing powers through the Lord of Heaven (*Tenri-O-no-mikoto*), which led her to sell her property and serve the Lord of Heaven. By 1863 Tenri-kyo had come into being and Miki was then joined by Master Iburi, who is considered to be the movement's co-founder. Prior to World War II Tenri-kyo was registered as a Shinto sect, but since 1945 it has distanced itself from Shinto and has grown rapidly. Its impressive headquarters are at Tenri, where creation is said to have taken place, and its leaders are all descendants of the foundress. God is seen as the creator and sustainer of all things, human beings having life as a form of stewardship for God. There is a belief in reincarnation, but the main emphasis is upon overcoming the evils or 'dusts' built up in life, in order to achieve happiness and prosperity in this world and to work for humanity through education, healing, orphanages, poverty centres and other forms of social involvement, so that all life can be bettered and the whole world converted to God. ▷ Japanese new religions; Shinto

teopixque ▷ **calmecac; priesthood, Meso-American**

Teresa of Ávila, St (1515–82) Spanish mystic and saint, born of a noble family in Ávila in Old Castile. In 1533 she entered a Carmelite convent there. About 1555 her religious exercises reached an extraordinary height of asceticism; she was favoured with ecstasies, and the fame of her sanctity spread far and wide. She obtained permission from the Holy See in 1562 to remove to a humble house in Ávila, where she founded the Convent of St Joseph to re-establish the ancient Carmelite rule, with additional observances. In 1567 the General of the Carmelite Order urged on her the duty of extending her reforms; in 1579 the Carmelites of the stricter observance were united into a distinct association; and within her own lifetime 17 convents of women and 16 of men accepted her reforms. She was canonized in 1622. The most famous of her many works are her autobiography, *The Way of Perfection*, and *The Book of the Foundations* (1565), which describes the journeys she made and the convents she founded or reformed; and *The Interior Castle* (trans

1852). Her feast day is 15 October. ▷ Carmelites; ecstacy; monasticism; mysticism

Teresa of Calcutta, Mother (Agnes Gonxha Bojaxhiu) (1910–) Roman Catholic nun and missionary to India, born in Yugoslavia of Albanian parents. She lived in Skopje as a child. She went to India in 1928, where she joined the Sisters of Loretto (an Irish order in India) and taught at a convent school in Calcutta, taking her final vows in 1937. She became principal of the school, but in 1948 left the convent to work alone in the slums. She went to Paris for some medical training before opening her first school for destitute children in Calcutta. She was gradually joined by other nuns and her House for the Dying was opened in 1952. Her sisterhood, the Order of the Missionaries of Charity (started in 1950), became a pontifical congregation in 1956. In 1957 she started work with lepers. The congregation now has about 2000 sisters in 200 branch houses in several countries. In 1971 she was awarded the Pope John XXIII Peace Prize. She was awarded the Nobel Prize for Peace in 1979. ▷ Roman Catholicism

Mother Teresa

Tertullian, properly **Quintus Septimius Florens Tertullianus** (c.160–c.220) Carthaginian theologian, one of the Fathers of the Latin Church, born in Carthage, and known as the 'Father of Latin theology'. He was brought up in Carthage, then lived for some time in Rome, where he was converted to Christianity (c.196) and then returned to Carthage. That he was married is suggested by his two books *Ad Uxorem*, in which he argues against second marriages. His opposition to worldliness in the Church culminated in his becoming a leader of the Montanist sect about 207. He had the heart of a Christian with the intellect of an advocate. His style is vivid, vigorous and concise, abounding in harsh and obscure expressions, abrupt turns and impetuous transitions, with here and there bursts of glowing eloquence. He was the creator of ecclesiastical Latinity, and many of his sentences have become proverbial, eg 'The blood of the martyrs is the seed of the church' and 'The unity of heretics is schism'. His works are divided into three classes: **1** controversial writings against 'heathens' and Jews, as in *Apologeticum*, *Ad Nationes* and *Adversus Judaeos*; **2** against heretics, as in *De Praescriptione Haereticorum*, *Adversus Valentinianos*, *De Anima*, *De Carne Christi* (against Docetism), *De Resurrectione Carnis*, *Adversus Marcionem* and *Adversus Praxean*; **3** practical and ascetic treatises, in which can be traced his increasing hostility to the Church and his adoption of Montanist views. Hence the division of these treatises into Pre-Montanist and Montanist, of which *De Virginibus Velandis* marks the transitional stage. Tertullian had a greater influence on the Latin Church than any theologian between Paul and Augustine. His Montanism, indeed, prevented its direct exercise, but Cyprian, as interpreter, gave currency to his views. ▷ Augustine, St (of Hippo); Cyprian, St; Fathers of the Church; Montanism; Paul, St

testament literature A loose genre of writings found in the Old Testament Pseudepigrapha, stemming from post-exilic times, which purportedly gives the last words or 'testaments' of significant figures from Israel's history. Although often ethical in nature, testaments also include visions of the future. In their present form some may reflect Christian and not just Jewish interests. Most notable are the *Testaments of the 12 Patriarchs*, the *Testament of Moses*, the *Testament of Adam*, and the *Testament of Job*. ▷ Pseudepigrapha

Tetoinnan ▷ Aztec religion

Tetragrammaton ▷ Yahweh

Tetzel, Johann (c.1465–1519) German monk, born in Pirna, Saxony. He became a Dominican in 1489, and was appointed in 1516 to preach an indulgence in favour of contributors to the building fund of St Peter's in Rome. This he did with great ostentation, thereby provoking the Wittenberg theses of Luther, and his own reply, 122 theses (written for him by Conrad Wimpina), bringing him criticism from the papal delegate for literary extravagence. ▷ Dominicans; indulgences; Luther, Martin; Reformation

Tezcatlipoca Literally 'the smoking mirror', this was originally the city-god of Texcoco, one of the most prominent Aztec deities. Adopted from the Toltec, by whose account the deity, using an obsidian mirror, ejected Quetzalcoatl from Tolla (and restored human sacrifice), Tezcatlipoca is regularly presented as the adversary and polar opposite of Quetzalcoatl. He represents the divine creative energy, but the 'dark' side of divinity, the powers of night and the underworld. The dualistic principle so often at work in Aztec religion, however, brought about a combination of opposites; the twin gods were necessary for worship and the ritual year. In each case language appropriate to the supreme being is used in certain contexts. Because of the smoking mirror, Tezcatlipoca was associated with divination, and an obsidian mirror said to be his was carefully preserved in five blankets. In other contexts, Tezcatlipoca was the reigning sun god. ▷ Aztec religion; human sacrifice, Meso-American; Quetzalcoatl; Toltec religion

Thebes 1 Capital of Ancient Egypt during the Middle and New Kingdoms, situated on the Nile where Luxor now stands. Its local god Amun became the supreme state god, and Thebes was especially pre-eminent during the New Kingdom (c.1567–1085BCE). On the east bank of the river stand the temples of Karnak and Luxor, the great temple of Amun at Karnak being the largest of all Egyptian temples. On the west bank is the necropolis, containing the mortuary temples of the pharaohs, and further to the west the Valley of the Kings where many of the New Kingdom pharaohs were buried in rock-hewn tombs, among them Tutankhamen. Thebes was a tourist attraction as early as Roman times. ▷ Amun; funerary practices, Ancient Egyptian; temples, Ancient Egyptian; Tutankhamen 2 In Ancient Greece, the most powerful city-state in Boeotia. Although prominent in Greek legend (the Oedipus cycle is based there), in historical times it was rarely able to rival Athens and Sparta. Only under the brilliant Epaminondas in the 370s BCE did it succeed briefly in being the leading power in Greece. ▷ Greek religion

theism Belief in a single divine being, transcendent and personal, who created the world and who, although involved with and related to the creation, is distinct from it. This creator is intelligent, powerful, and moral, and can act through his creation for the good of humankind. As a personal being he can also reveal himself to humans. Theism is a feature of Jewish, Islamic and Christian faith, and is contrasted with both deism and pantheism. As a philosophical tradition it started with Plato, and has been developed since by philosophers such as Aquinas and Kant. ▷ agnosticism; Aquinas, St Thomas; atheism; deism; God; Kant, Immanuel; pantheism

theism, Jewish As in other monotheistic faiths, in Judaism God possesses certain attributes: he is unlimited by space and time, omniscient, omnipotent, immaterial, both transcendent and immanent, righteous and holy. However, traditional Judaism focuses on orthopraxis more than orthodoxy, seeking to direct conduct rather than belief. All theological speculation, including that concerning the nature of the Deity, belongs to Aggadah, while the Halakhah is authoritative; exceptions to this are affirmation of God's existence and his unity, both of which constitute two of the 613 mitzvot. Nevertheless, the place of God in the spiritual life of the Jew is more central than this might suggest. Thus one common description of God is taken from Exodus 34.6–7a, stressing divine grace and mercy. The characteristics of the Deity in this passage, with the careful exclusion of the second half of verse 7, came to be known as the Thirteen Attributes of God. In a different list, the medieval philosopher Maimonides set out 13 principles of faith which, though not constituting a binding creed, are still used today. As well as monotheism, they stress the trustworthiness of the Torah, Moses as the greatest of the prophets, and the certainty of the advent of the Messiah and resurrection of the dead. In modern times, Reconstructionist Judaism has moved away from any supernatural theism, while many secular Jews, with a strong Jewish identity, would nonetheless not subscribe to theistic belief. ▷ Aggadah; Halakhah; Maimonides; mitzvah; Reconstructionist Judaism; Torah

theodicy The defence and vindication of God, defined as both omnipotent and good in the light of evil in the world. The term was first used by Gottfried Leibniz in 1710. ▷ God

Theodore of Mopsuestia (c.350–428) Greek theologian, born in Antioch. He studied with St John Chrysostom under the Greek Sophist Libarines, then became first a monk, then a deacon there, and in 392 Bishop of Mopsuestia in Cilicia. The teacher of Nestorius, he was, perhaps, the real founder of Nestorianism. He wrote commentaries on almost all the books of Scripture, of which remain, in the Greek, only that on the Minor Prophets; in Latin translations, those on the Epistles of Paul besides many fragments. As an exegete he eschews the allegorical method, adopts the literal meaning, considers the historical and literary circumstances, and assumes varying degrees of inspiration. Already suspected of leaning towards the 'Pelagians', as he was, when the Nestorian controversy broke out, he was attacked over his polemical writings, which were condemned by Justinian (544). The fifth ecumenical council (553) confirmed the condemnation. ▷ Chrysostom, St John; Council of the Church; Nestorians; Pelagius

Theodosius I, the Great (c.346–395) Roman Emperor, son of Theodosius the Elder. He was born in Cauca in north-west Spain. He served with distinction until his father's execution induced him to retire (376), but was recalled by Gratianus to become his colleague and emperor in the East (379). He campaigned against the Goths, first from Thessalonica, then from Constantinople, but eventually allowed them to settle within the Roman Empire (382). He secured peace with the Persian Sassanids by partitioning Armenia with them (c.386). When the usurper Magnus Maximus killed Gratianus in 383, Theodosius at first recognized him, but when in 387 Maximus expelled Valentinian II from Italy, Theodosius marched west and defeated and killed Maximus at Aquileia (388). For some years Theodosius lived at Milan in friendship with St Ambrose who had great influence over him. In 390, when the Governor of Thessalonica was lynched by a circus mob, Theodosius invited the citizens into the circus, and had 7000 of them massacred. Ambrose excommunicated Theodosius for eight months until he had done public penance. In 392 Valentinian II was murdered, and in 394 Theodosius marched against the Franks and their puppet emperor Eugenius. He defeated Eugenius, and for the remaining four months of his life ruled as sole Roman emperor. A pious and intolerant Christian, he summoned in 381 a council at Constantinople to affirm the Nicene Creed, pursued heretics and 'pagans', and eventually in 391 ordered the closing of all temples and banned all forms of pagan cult. ▷ Ambrose, St; Nicene Creed

Theogonies, Greek The earliest Greek accounts of the origins of the universe took the form of Theogonies, or 'Births of Gods'. The most famous and influential Theogony was that of Hesiod (8th or 7th century BCE), who described, perhaps partly under Oriental influence, how the first god Ouranos, Heaven, was castrated and overthrown by his son Kronos, who was overthrown in turn by the final ruler of the universe, Zeus; the many divine marriages and births at each of these stages are also recounted. Since some gods (such as 'Ocean' or 'Earth') were also parts of the world, a Theogony was also in part an account of the history of the universe: the castration of Ouranos, husband of Earth, for instance, is a mythical way of describing the separation of the two spheres. ▷ creation myths; Greek religion

theological attitudes There are basically seven theological attitudes that one religious tradition can adopt towards other traditions. They range from exclusivism at one end of the spectrum to relativism at the other. Although they have been worked out in more detail in Christianity, which has taken theology as a discipline more seriously than others, they are intrinsically present in all religions. Exclusivism argues that one's own position is exclusively right and the position of others is exclusively wrong. It may stress the role of beliefs as the touchstone of exclusive truth, or the role of a privileged community as the sole guardian of truth as in the phrase 'outside the church there is no salvation'. Discontinuity theology claims (as in the thought of Karl Barth within Christianity) that there is a discontinuity between 'revelation', which is God's revealing of himself to humans, and 'religion', which is the human search for God. Secularization theology and spiritualization theology contend, respectively, that what is needed is more secularization or more spiritualization, and that the religions that provide these have an advantage. Fulfilment theology is a favourite stance in many religions: the notion that all religions have truth and goodness and spirituality, but that one's own tradition has them in fuller measure. It therefore follows that the partial truth present in all religions will eventually be fulfilled in the fullness of truth. This position has been further refined in the recent theology of Roman Catholic thinkers such as Raimundo Panikkar and Karl Rahner, and other thinkers elsewhere, in universalization theology, whereby one's own position is universalized to include everyone else. Dialogue theology concentrates upon understanding between religions, but has developed a theological position of its own. Relativism argues that religions are relative with regard to culture, truth (Christ is the truth for one person, Krishna for another, the Buddha for another, etc), and goal (they are separate but equal paths to the same ultimate goal). Theological attitudes, even eirenical ones, assume a position within one religion from which standpoint all other traditions are viewed. New departures within the theology of religion are attempting to conceptualize a world theology that will be universal rather than particular. ▷ Barth, Karl; Buddha; Jesus Christ; Krishna; Rahner, Karl; theology of religion

theology (Greek *theologia*) Literally the science of the divine, or of discourse about God. By the 2nd century CE it was a term used largely of Christian teaching about God. However, it need not be restricted to the Christian faith and embraces generally the subjects of God and humankind, salvation, and the end of the world/afterlife (eschatology). In Christianity it is understood as the systematic critical clarification of the historical beliefs of the Church. It has been divided into natural theology, ie that which can be known about God from nature or by reason alone, and revealed theology, that which can only be known through the self-disclosure of God. ▷ Christianity; eschatology; God; Heliopolis theology; Memphite Theology; natural theology; revelation; tripartite ideology

theology of religion On one level this can be seen as the theological attitudes adopted between religions, ranging from exclusivism at one end of the spectrum to relativism at the other. In the wider and more appropriate sense it is the name of a new enterprise which attempts to bring into being a global theology of religion, and which tries to conceptualize theological categories that are applicable to all the religions of the world and not just to one. It begins at the global level and works back to the particular, rather than starting from particular theologies that tend to divide and then trying to overcome their individuality. Examples are to be found in the work of Wilfred Cantwell Smith, John Hick and Raimondo Panikkar. Smith and Hick start with the notions of 'God' and 'human beings' as given. According to them religious traditions provide a means by which human beings can move from self-centredness to God-centredness. Thus religious traditions themselves are another element in the theology of religion, as is 'faith', which enables humans to move from self-centredness to God-centredness. Hick argues that God can be seen as either a personal or an impersonal absolute. However, the assumption is that God, who is ineffable, is in some sense One, and also that human beings are essentially one the world over. While some religious traditions would not accept this argument, Hick would claim that they have not made the 'Copernican revolution' from thinking in terms of a particular theology of one religion to a general theology incorporating all religions. ▷ Hick, John Harwood; Panikkar, Raimundo; Smith, Wilfred Cantwell; study of religion; theological attitudes

theosis Sometimes translated in English as 'deification', this is the term in Greek Orthodox theology for the end point in the process of sanctification, in which the believer is a participant in the communion of the holy Trinity. Although there were certain signals of pre-eminent holiness in the ascetic traditions of Greek monasticism (eg indifference to heat, cold or hunger, radiance of countenance), theosis was seen as the destiny of the whole Christian community, the ultimate consequence of the Incarnation for the Church. Protestantism, Judaism and Islam have been hesitant about this account of final blessedness, fearing that it blurs the distinction between God and creation, and lends itself to pantheist interpretations. Apart from the mystical traditions, the language of beatific vision has more usually implied a distance between the worshipping believer and God. The Eastern Orthodox vision, however, is arguably not one which levels out the distinction between God and man, as if man progressed to being God. Rather it is the corollary of an understanding of grace in which God's generosity in the sharing of his proper joy is so ungrudging that he invites the believer not only to behold it but to taste it, so to speak, from inside. ▷ beatification; Greek Orthodox Church; Incarnation; pantheism

Theosophical Society An institution founded in 1875 in New York by Madame Helena Blavatsy and Colonel Henry Steel Olcott (1832–1907). Its aim was to further the cause of world harmony, to study comparative religion and especially the religions of India, and to investigate the spiritual element in human beings and the world. In 1877 it moved to India and its headquarters remain in Adyar, Madras. When Madame Blavatsky died effective leadership of the movement passed to Annie Besant, and in its first 50 years it was important beyond its numbers in spreading ideas from Eastern religion to the West, and for rekindling interest in Hinduism and Buddhism in India. Theosophical theory is based mainly on Madame Blavatsky's work as expanded by later writers and is derived partly from Buddhist and Hindu sources. It states that there is an esoteric unity of all religions and that this is grounded in theosophy. Meditation is important, and the spiritual development of individuals is (or can be) guided by a secret set of Masters living in Tibet. Theosophy states that we all reincarnate many times, according to our deeds, and the aim of life is that we should achieve our real self and our full potential by aligning ourselves to the divine will of the universal Spirit. The universe has seven planes and we have seven bodies, and both the universe and we are evolving towards a spiritual destiny. Although still present in many countries theosophy is not as strong as it was, partly due to the defection of Jiddu Krishnamurti, who was being groomed by Annie Besant to be the new 'World Teacher'. It has, however, influenced other movements, including elements in new age religion. ▷ Besant, Annie; Krishnamurti, Jiddu; new age religion

theosophy Any system of philosophical or theological thought based on the direct and immediate experience of the divine. It has been used to describe any developed system of mystical thought and practice, and especially the principles of the Theosophical Society founded in 1875 by Madame Blavatsky and H S Olcott (1832–1907) in New York. ▷ Blavatsky, Helena Petrovna

Theravada Buddhism (Theravāda) The form of Buddhism commonly found in South Asia (Sri Lanka, Burma, Thailand, Cambodia, and Laos). Its doctrines remain essentially as they were in the 3rd century BCE. Using the *tipitaka* or Pali Canon as their main source of scripture, Theravadas interpret the Buddha's teachings in a conservative manner and, while worshipping Buddha, do not revere other figures. Theravada is generally distinguished from the later Mahayana Buddhism in its rejection of the theory of bodhisattvas. The ultimate goal for a Theravada is to become a 'perfected saint' or *arhat*. They do not believe, however, that lay believers can attain true enlightenment. This is only possible by entering religious orders. Even then they consider it almost impossible for anyone to become a Buddha. ▷ arhat; bodhisattva; Buddha; Buddhism; Mahayana Buddhism; tipitaka

Theresa, Mother ▷ Teresa of Calcutta, Mother

Thessalonians, Letters to the New Testament writings of Paul to the church he founded in the capital of the Roman province of Macedonia, although his authorship of the second letter is disputed. In the first letter (perhaps c.50CE), he defends his earlier ministry in Thessalonica against Jewish propaganda, appears gratified at their perseverance despite persecution, and instructs them about ethical matters and Christ's second coming. The second letter is similar, but emphasizes the persecution of the community, and tries to dampen a fanaticism based on the belief that the Day of the Lord had already arrived, leading to idleness. ▷ New Testament; Paul, St; Pauline Letters; parousia

Thielicke, Helmut (1908–86) German Lutheran theologian and preacher, born in Barmen. He was dismissed from his post at Heidelburg for criticizing the Nazis, and in 1944 contributed to a draft declaration on Church-State relations for use by a revolutionary government in the event of a successful plot against Hitler. He was appointed Professor of Theology at Hamburg after World War II, becoming Dean of Theology (1954) and university rector (1960), retiring in 1974. A prolific author, best-known perhaps for *The Waiting Father* (1960) and other volumes of sermons, he published substantial studies in theology and ethics, including *The Evangelical Faith* (1974–82), *Theological Ethics* (1951–64, abridged trans 1966–9), *The Ethics of Sex* (1964) and *Living with Death* (1983), though these appeared in Engish much later than his devotional works. ▷ Lutheranism; Nazi Party

Thirty-nine Articles A set of doctrinal formulations for the Church of England, issued after several earlier efforts under Elizabeth I in 1563 (but without Article 29 about 'eating the body', in order to appease the Romanists), and finally adopted as a whole by the Convocation of 1571. They do not comprise a creed, but rather a general Anglican view on a series of contentious matters in order to maintain the unity of the Anglican churches and Anglican Communion. Some articles are ambiguous in wording, but they are generally opposed to both extreme Romanist and extreme Anabaptist views. They concern matters such as the presence of Christ in the Eucharist, the authority of Scriptures and the Councils, and the doctrine of predestination. Church of England clergy have been required since 1865 to affirm these principles in general terms. ▷ Anabaptists; Anglican Communion; Church of England; Eucharist; predestination; Roman Catholicism

Thomas, St (1st century) An apostle of Jesus, listed as one of the 12 disciples in the

Gospels, but most prominent in John's Gospel where he is also called Didymus ('the Twin'), and where he is portrayed as doubting the resurrection until he touches the wounds of the risen Christ (John 20). Early church traditions describe him subsequently as a missionary to the Parthians or a martyr in India. Many later apocryphal works bear his name, such as the Gospel of Thomas, Acts of Thomas, and Apocalypse of Thomas. He is the patron saint of Portugal. His feast day is 21 December. ▷ apostle; disciples (in early Christian church); Jesus Christ

Thomas à Becket ▷ Becket, St Thomas à

Thomas à Kempis ▷ Kempis, Thomas à

Thomas Aquinas, St ▷ Aquinas, St Thomas

Thomism In Christian philosophical theology, the name given to the doctrines of Thomas Aquinas, and to later schools claiming descent from him. ▷ Aquinas, St Thomas; Christianity

Thor In Norse mythology, the god of Thunder, son of Odin and Frigga; also known as the Hurler. His hammer is called Miolnir. In the stories, much is made of his appetite for food and drink. He is the strongest of the gods, and protects them. At Ragnarok he will fight with the Midgard-Serpent, kill it, and then die. ▷ Germanic religion; Odin; Ragnarok

Thoth Ancient Egyptian god of the moon and wisdom. As the moon god Thoth was the lord of reckoning and responsible for the calculation of time. He invented writing and was the patron of scribes. Because of his power over words and time Thoth was also associated with magic and medicine. He was one of Re's companions on the solar boat and responsible for its protection. In the Osirian legends Thoth looked after Isis and the young Horus, and mediated in the quarrel between Horus and Seth. In the Osirian hall of judgement Thoth records the result of the weighing of the deceased's heart against Maat. He is normally represented as an ibis-headed man or as a baboon, these being his sacred animals. Many mummified ibises and baboons were found in cemeteries at Thebes and at Hermopolis, Thoth's major cult centre. ▷ afterlife, Ancient Egyptian; Horus; Isis; mummification; Re; Seth; Thebes

Thoth

Thousand and One Nights A collection of popular stories of many different kinds which became popular in 9th-century Islamic Baghdad when it was the capital of the Abbasid caliphs. Many of the stories were adapted from India—from the Hindu ethical tales of the *Hitopadesha*, or from the Buddhist Jataka stories. The background lay in the cruelty of king Shahryar, who married and killed a succession of women in response to having been betrayed by women. He was finally charmed and cured by his latest wife Shahrazad, who kept him occupied for a thousand and one nights with a succession of fascinating tales. In the process they bore three children and his pain and heartlessness were ended. The tales passed from their Indian language and form into Persian, were translated into Arabic in 9th-century Baghdad, and later took on their classical Muslim and Arabic form in Mamluk Egypt. Their translation into French in the 18th century led to their popularity in the West. Many of the tales have a spiritual moral in that they describe the soul's journey through life, the attempts of magicians and others to beguile the soul with trivial illusions, and the need to free the soul into immortality. ▷ Abbasids; Jataka

three fires, Buddhist The Three Fires—greed, hatred and delusion—are the three root evils within the Buddhist tradition. They are the key reasons why people are tied to the round of rebirths and are unable to see things as they truly are. Greed is linked to craving (*tanha*), which is mentioned in the second noble truth of the Buddha as being a prime cause of suffering. Hatred is the opposite of the four Buddhist qualities of equanimity, loving kindness, compassion, and sympathetic joy. It prevents true ethical insight—the beginning of the Buddhist way—from arising. Delusion is akin to ignorance, which involves ignorance of the four noble truths but also ignorance at a deeper level thus binding a person to continual rebirth, to unhelpful karma (deeds), and to wrong views. In order to go along the Buddhist path towards nirvana, it is essential that these three fires are 'blown out'; 'blown out' is one meaning of the word nirvana. ▷ ariya sacca; duhkha; karma; nirvana; rebirth; tanha

three jewels (tri-ratna) A Buddhist term that refers to the three main features of the Buddhist tradition, namely the Buddha, the teaching of the Buddha (dharma), and the Buddhist community (*sangha*). The basic Buddhist formula and a basic chant in Buddhist devotion involve giving acknowledgement to the centrality of these Three Jewels in the Buddhist way of life. They are also known as the three refuges according to the commitment made by a Buddhist when he or she says: 'I go for refuge to the Buddha...to the dharma...and to the sangha'. The three are interlinked and interdependent, and are regarded as the touchstones of being a Buddhist, that is to say giving allegiance to and affirmation of the Buddha and his teaching as continued and extended by the Buddhist sangha. According to the Buddha those who trust in the Three Jewels have already put their hand to the plough, 'entered the stream', and set out along the path to enlightenment. There are different levels of interpretation of the Three Jewels according to tradition and personal predilection, but all are acknowledged to be central. ▷ Buddha; dharma; sangha

three marks A term of crucial importance to the Buddhist tradition, signifying the 'Three Marks' that are built into all existence. According to Buddhism, all things and beings are impermanent (*anicca*), are characterized by suffering (*duhkha*), and have no selfhood or substance (*anatman*). With the exception of nirvana, impermanence and change are built into everything; because this is so, everything is unsatisfactory; and insofar as this is the case it is futile to think that there is a permanent and unchanging self at the heart of what is fleeting and in flux. Although the notion of suffering is at the heart of the four noble truths taught by the Buddha, the three marks of impermanence, suffering and no-self belong together and interact to permeate everything. The aim of life is to gain enlightenment, to obtain nirvana, and to achieve release from this changing world of rebirth, unsatisfactoriness and false egoism. This cannot happen unless insight is gained into the impermanence and lack of substance that are built into the changing world, the fluctuating pleasures of the world, and the sense of self that binds us to the world. Thus an insightful understanding of the Three Marks is a precondition for spiritual advance and release. ▷ anatman; anicca; ariya sacca; duhkha; nirvana

three refuges A Buddhist notion summed up in the important formula: 'I go for refuge to the Buddha...to the dharma...and to the sangha'. It highlights the importance of these three elements within the Buddhist tradition: the Buddha himself; the teaching, or dharma, that he uncovered when he lived in India in the 6th century BCE; and the Buddhist community, the *sangha*, which he founded. The three refuges are also known as the three jewels (*tri-ratna*). The actual chanting of the above formula is an important act of Buddhist devotion. To gain a mature understanding of the meaning of the three refuges is, however, a more complex matter, as the Buddha, the dharma and the sangha can be understood at a number of different levels according to different Buddhist traditions and one's own depth of personal comprehension. There are also different ways of looking at their interrelationship: for example, the Buddha can be seen as the teacher and embodiment of dharma, which is then continued in the life of the Buddhist community. Ultimately it is not just a matter of taking refuge in three outward things, but of taking refuge in them deep within oneself. ▷ Buddha; dharma; sangha; three jewels

Thummim ▷ **Urim and Thummim**

Thunderbird, or **Skyamsen** A totem figure in north-western Amerindian religion. Lightning flashes from its eye and it feeds on killer whales. The chief of the Thunderbirds was Golden Eagle (Keneun). ▷ Native American religions *See illustration on p 530*

Tiamat The personification of the primeval salt waters in the Ancient Babylonian creation epic. As the first act of creation Tiamat and her consort Apsu, who represents the fresh waters, mingle and give birth to generations of gods. When the god Ea kills Apsu, Tiamat

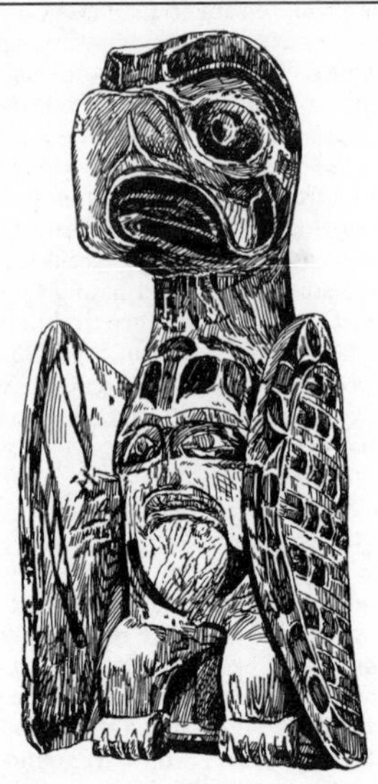

Thunderbird

plans revenge, creating an army of terrible monsters to fight with her and destroy her offspring. Marduk alone of all the gods stands up to her and defeats her, then splits her body in two and uses it to roof the sky and construct the various elements of the universe. ▷ cosmogony, Ancient Near Eastern; creation myths; Ea; Marduk

Tibetan religion There have been two principal religious traditions in Tibet, namely Buddhism and Bon, though the latter can also be regarded as a form of Buddhism. Mahayana Buddhism entered Tibet from India and China during the 7th century CE when Tibet emerged as an expanding political power under King Srongtsan Gampo. The transmission of Buddhism to Tibet in its orthodox Mahayana and Vajrayana or Tantric forms came mainly through missionaries invited from India during the 8th century. These include Shantarakshita, the founder of the first Buddhist monastery at Samye, who taught the monastic discipline (*vinaya*) and doctrines based on the *Mahayana Sutras*; Padmasambhava, regarded as a siddha and instructor in the Tantras; and Atisha, a great Buddhist scholar who founded the Kadampa monastic order.

The popular Buddhism of Tibet has emphasized the appeasement of malevolent deities, pilgrimages and the accumulation of merit. Apart from this folk religion there are four Buddhist orders, the Nyingmapa, the Kagyupa, the Sakyapa and the Gelugpa. These orders represent different lineages of teachers and teachings, often based on different scriptures. The texts which comprise the Buddhist canon were translated into Tibetan from Sanskrit mainly in the 8th century, when a standardized technical dictionary of Sanskrit-Tibetan terms was produced. The canon is divided into the Kanjur, which includes the word of the Buddha, and the Tanjur, comprising commentaries on the Kanjur as well as independent works.

Doctrinally Tibetan Buddhism accepts the general Mahayana teachings concerning the bodhisattva's gradual path to buddhahood or emptiness, which is to realize the non-distinction of the phenomenal world of rebirth (*samsara*) with the absolute truth of nirvana. The monastic emphasis is upon the development of Buddhist virtues (*shila*), meditation involving visualizations, ritual and the development of wisdom.

After the Chinese invasion, during the cultural revolution, Buddhism was severely repressed and few monasteries remain, though in the 1980s there was a revival of Buddhism in Tibet. Following the Dalai Lama's fleeing to India in 1959, Tibetan Buddhism has been established and consolidated in the West. ▷ Atisha; bodhisattva; Bon, Bon po; Buddha; Dalai Lama; emptiness; Gelugpa; Kadampa; Kagyupa; Kanjur; Mahayana Buddhism; merit; nirvana; Nyingmapa; Padmasambhava; rebirth; Sakyapa; siddhas; Srongtsan; Tantra; Tantric Buddhism; vinaya-pitaka

Tien (T'ien) A Chinese term usually translated as 'heaven', which corresponds to the notion of providence or God in an impersonal sense. It refers to the supreme being or supreme principle controlling the universe. In Shang China (1523–1027BCE) *Shang Ti* was used for the Lord on High, and it was only with the coming of the Chou dynasty in 1027 that *Tien* emerged and became important. It had a more abstract sense than Shang Ti, and gradually assimilated Shang Ti into itself as an overall term for 'God'. Confucius paid respect to heaven, and the will of heaven. The notion of the mandate of heaven also became significant as a supreme moral authority, requiring morality from an emperor for his dynasty to survive and flourish. Tien was worshipped by Chinese rulers from the Chou dynasty onwards, and the worship was enacted on an altar under the open sky. Tien is sometimes used in the sense of fate or destiny.

At the level of popular religion Tien is worshipped as the Jade Emperor who is the supreme deity in the popular Chinese pantheon. ▷ Chinese pantheon; Confucius; Shang Ti

Tien Tai (T'ien T'ai) A school of Chinese Buddhism which stresses the role of the *Lotus Sutra*, one of the key scriptures of the Mahayana Buddhist tradition. It was founded by Hui Ssu (515–77) and Chih I (538–97), and was influenced by their interpretations of the *Lotus Sutra*. It is named after Mount Tien Tai in China, to which Chih I went in later life and where, on the basis of his lectures, there were written the 'three great works' of the school: *Profound Meaning of the Lotus Sutra*, *Commentary on the Lotus Sutra*, and *Great Concentration and Insight*. Basic to Tien Tai thought is the notion of the threefold truth (empty, temporary, and middle): all things are empty of self because they depend on other causes; all things are temporary because they are produced by other causes; and all things are middle, both temporary and empty, because they are temporary yet exist at the same time. The implication of this theory is that things are both distinct and part of a whole. All beings, though distinct, share the same Buddha nature, and will attain Buddhahood eventually. Tien Tai tolerantly recognized all schools of Buddhism, but divided Buddhism into five periods leading up to the *Lotus Sutra* as the crown of Buddhism. After the great persecution of the Buddhists in 845 Tien Tai declined in China, but became important in Korea and Japan as Tendai. ▷ Buddha nature; Lotus Sutra; Mahayana Buddhism; Tendai

Tillich, Paul Johannes (1886–1965) German-born American Protestant theologian and philosopher, born in Starzeddel, Brandenburg. He became a Lutheran pastor (1912) and served as military chaplain in the German army in World War I, a traumatic experience which led him to take an active political interest in social reconstruction. He taught at Berlin (1919–24), and held professorships in theology at Marburg (1924–5), Dresden (1925–8), Leipzig (1928–9) and in philosophy at Frankfurt (1929–33). He was an early critic of Hitler and the Nazis and in 1933 was barred from German universities, the first non-Jewish academic 'to be so honoured', as he put it. He emigrated to the USA, and taught at the Union Theological Seminary in New York (1933–55), Harvard Divinity School (1955–62) and Chicago Divinity School (1962–5), becoming a naturalized US citizen in 1940. His influence on the development of theology in this century has been very substantial and is characterized by an attempt to mediate between traditional Christian culture and beliefs and the secular orientation of modern society. His main work is *Systematic Theology* (3 vols, 1951–63), which combines elements from existentialism and depth-psychology, as well as from the ontological tradition in Christian thought. He explains faith as a matter of 'ultimate concern' with a reality transcending finite existence rather than a belief in a personal God, and this has led to oversimplified accusations of atheism or crypto-atheism. His popular works like *The Courage to Be* (1952) and *Dynamics of Faith* (1957) have reached very large general readerships. ▷ Lutheranism; Nazi Party; Protestantism; theology

Tilopa (10th century) Indian siddha, the guru of Naropa, revered by the Kagyupa lineage of Tibetan Buddhism. Tilopa is regarded as an enlightened master or siddha, one who has attained buddhahood through the path of Tantra. He passed on to Naropa the teaching of the six yogas and the Mahamudra or 'Great Perfection' teachings concerning the non-dual nature of reality. ▷ Buddhism; guru; Kagyupa; Naropa; siddhas

Timothy, Letters to Two of the Pastoral Letters in the New Testament, for which Pauline authorship is often disputed today. Both letters are purportedly addressed to Paul's close companion Timothy (Acts 16.1, Thessalonians 3.2), but mostly concern questions of church order and discipline, and problems with false teachers who seemingly were spreading gnostic and Jewish speculations. The second letter, however, does make several references to Paul's personal experiences and circumstances. ▷ Gnosticism; New Testament; Pastoral Letters; Pauline Letters

Tindale, William ▷ **Tyndale, William**

tipitaka or **Pali Canon** (tipiṭaka; Sanskrit: tripiṭaka) Meaning literally the three parts or 'baskets', these are the most complete and earliest collection of scriptures in the Buddhist tradition. The tipitaka is recognized as authoritative by Theravada Buddhists in Sri Lanka, Thailand, Burma, Cambodia and Laos. Its three baskets are: the monastic discipline of the Buddhist tradition in the *vinaya-pitaka*; the discourses of the Buddha in the *sutta-pitaka*; and the systematic analysis of the doctrines of Buddhism in the *abhidharma-pitaka*. According to Buddhist tradition the bringing together of the tipitaka began as early as the council of Rajagaha, which was called after the death of the Buddha. It is traditionally claimed that the first two baskets—the monastic discipline and the Buddha's teachings—were gathered together and recited at that first Buddhist council. By the time of the third council called by King Ashoka at Pataliputra around 252BCE the verbal canon of the tipitaka was complete, including the abhidharma section. However it was not until the 1st century BCE that it was written down in Pali in Ceylon. Other tipitakas were also written by other schools in Sanskrit, containing the same three baskets but a somewhat different set of contents. They now survive mainly in Chinese and Tibetan translations. The Mahayana tradition accepts the tipitaka, but sees it as a preparation for its own Mahayana Sutras which, so to speak, fulfil the three baskets of the Pali Canon. ▷ Abhidharma; Ashoka; Buddha; Buddhist Councils; Mahayana Sutras; sutta-pitaka; Theravada Buddhism; vinaya-pitaka

Tir na ńOc ▷ **Land of youth**

tirthankara (Tírthankara)(Sanskrit, 'fordmaker') A title used by Jains of the 24 great heroes of their tradition who, by their teaching and example, taught them the way to cross the stream from the bondage of physical existence to freedom from rebirth. They are also called *Jina*, 'conqueror', from which Jains take their name. ▷ Jainism

Tishah beAv The day in the Jewish year on which the destruction of the Temple in Jerusalem under Nebuchadnezzar (586BCE) and again by the Romans (70CE) purportedly took place. The most solemn day in the calendar, Tishah beAv (literally '[day] nine in [the month of] Av') remembers these events and is the culmination of three weeks of severity. For 24 hours, from sunset to sunset, no food may be consumed, and the book of Lamentations is read in the synagogue. In view of what it commemorates, 9 Av in later times was associated with other calamities in Jewish history, especially the expulsion of the Jews from Spain in 1492. ▷ fasts, Jewish; hagim; calendar, Jewish

tithes Offerings of a proportion (literally 'the 10th part') of one's property or produce to God, often given to the priesthood of temples; customary among peoples since ancient times. In Jewish Law, instructions regarding tithes were listed in Leviticus 27, and were subsequently elaborated in the Talmud. Taxes of this description were used to support Christian clergy in Europe from medieval times, and in England from the 10th century, until greater secularization after the Reformation brought increased opposition. Civil tithes were replaced in England by a rent charge in 1836, and even this was abolished in 1936. ▷ Church of England; Reformation; Talmud

Titus, Letter to One of the Pastoral Letters in the New Testament, for which Pauline authorship is usually disputed today. The letter addresses problems of church order and false (gnostic?) teachers, with specific instructions about the importance of sound doctrine, the selection of elders and bishops, family and social relationships, and submission to rulers and authorities. ▷ Gnosticism; New Testament; Pastoral Letters; Pauline Letters

Titus, St (1st century) In the New Testament, a Gentile companion of the apostle Paul, not mentioned in Acts, but referred to in Galatians 2 and 2 Corinthians 8.6. Ecclesiastical tradition makes him the first bishop of Crete. The purported Letter of Paul to Titus gives advice on the way the churches there should be organized. His feast day is 6 February (West) or 23 August (East). ▷ Gentiles; New Testament; Paul, St; Titus, Letter to

Tlaloc The Aztec god of rain, to whom children were sacrificed in time of drought. The features of his face are formed of serpents, representing lightning. ▷ Aztec religion; sacrifice

tlamatinime ▷ **calmecac**

Tlatoani ▷ **Aztec religion; priesthood, Meso-American**

Tobit, or **Tobias, Book of** A book of the Old Testament Apocrypha, or deuterocanonical book in Catholic Bibles; named after its hero, Tobit, written perhaps c.3rd–2nd century BCE by an unknown author. This popular legend is set in 8th-century BCE Nineveh, from where Tobit's son (Tobias) is sent to Media, accompanied by the angel Raphael, to reclaim money deposited there by his father. He also learns magic formulae to heal his father's blindness and to exorcize a demon from his future wife, Sarah. The characters exemplify aspects of Jewish piety. ▷ Apocrypha, Old Testament; Judaism

Tohunga ▷ **Maori religion**

toleration Permission to hold beliefs of which the ruling class or the majority in a society disapproves. With regard to religion this means tolerating unorthodox religious beliefs and allowing freedom of worship. Toleration has often been absent in the great monotheistic religions, which have tended to regard non-orthodox beliefs as idolatry, heresy or apostasy. Pantheistic religions are more tolerant by virtue of their ability to expand the pantheon to incorporate new deities. In many societies religious liberty is now regarded as a fundamental human right. ▷ religious pluralism

toleration, Christian The close relations between Church and State that have existed during much of Christianity's history have often made dissent from religious belief appear unpatriotic or treasonable, and persecution a moral good. Growth in religious toleration from the 17th century onwards can be attributed to several factors. The Reformation had fragmented Europe religiously and socially, preparing the way for the realization that there was no longer one worldview or concept of truth. The rationalism of the 18th century found conflicting religious views superstitious or irrelevant, in comparison with the universal truths of reason: the arts of government, politics and economics could develop independent of religious beliefs. If the 19th century was the era in which different varieties of Christian belief were accepted in much of Europe, the 20th century has been the period of recognizing the religious and cultural values of the non-European religions. The persistence of anti-Semitism in Germany, Russia and elsewhere has shown how ingrained religious intolerance can be, but a measure of international acceptance of religious freedom has been enshrined in the United Nations Universal Declaration of Human Rights 1948 (article 18) and the Declaration on Intolerance of 1981. ▷ anti-Semitism; Church and State; Holocaust; Christianity, persecution of

Tollan The name of the original Toltec city of which Quetzalcoatl was the city god. It is probably to be identified with Tula in the Valley of Mexico, where the god's feathered serpent image is to be found. Tollan probably flourished in the 9th to 11th centuries CE. Its main importance, however, is mythological. The Aztec took over the idea of the reign of Quetzalcoatl (from whom both Aztec and Toltec believed their rulers to be descended) in Tollan as a golden age, a lost paradise which one day will return. Tollan thus stands not only for a historical site but also for the ideal metropolis. This may explain why the name became attached to various locations, including Cholollan (Tolan Cholollan Tlachihualteptel) which, when the Spaniards arrived, was the great religious pilgrimage centre of Mexico. ▷ Aztec religion; Quetzalcoatl; Toltec religion

Toltec religion The Toltec are a Nahuatl-speaking people of uncertain origin, who established their rule over parts of Yucatan at the time when classical Maya culture was decaying. Their culture hero, Ce Acatl, belonged to the city of Tollan (Tula) in the Valley of Mexico; the principal Toltec centre in Yucatan is at Chichen Itza. According to Aztec records, the 10 kings of the Toltec ruled from 980 to 1168CE. Thus they are transitional between the Maya of the classical period and the Aztec dominance. They seem to have preserved the outlines of the Mayan religious system, and probably to a large extent the Mayan priesthood, but in a modified and coarsened form. Priestly rule was replaced by that of a warrior caste, war gods took some precedence over gods of fertility in the orientation of worship, and human sacrifice increased very considerably. Besides the regular sacrifice of human victims, drought or other emergency required rites at the cenote (a giant natural well) where jade, precious metals, and live humans were thrown into the abyss. Ce Acatl is said to have taken the name Kukulcan, which is simply the Maya translation of Quetzalcoatl, the feathered serpent. ▷ Aztec religion; human sacrifice, Meso-American; Maya religion; Quetzalcoatl; Tollan

tonalpohualli ▷ calendar, Meso-American

Torah (Hebrew 'instruction') The Jewish Law, most narrowly considered the Priestly Code found in the Pentateuch and said to have been given to Moses by God. The term was also often applied to the Pentateuch as a whole; and as the importance of the Prophets and Writings grew, it was sometimes used to describe them all as divinely revealed instructions and traditions. This written Torah was eventually supplemented in Pharisaic and rabbinic tradition by the Oral Torah, not a fixed revelation but an elucidation and application of the Written Torah by sages of various periods. ▷ Judaism; Mishnah; Old Testament; Pentateuch; Pharisees; rabbi

Torquemada, Tomas de (1420–98) Spanish Dominican monk, and first Inquisitor-General of Spain, born in Valladolid, the nephew of a cardinal. He entered the Dominican order and became prior at Segovia. Chaplain to

Ferdinand and Isabella from 1474, he persuaded them to ask the pope to sanction the institution of the 'Holy Office' of the Inquisition, with himself as Inquisitor-General from 1483. In this office he displayed pitiless cruelty. He was responsible for the expulsion of the Jews from Spain in 1492. ▷ Dominicans; Inquisition

Torrance, Thomas Forsyth (1913–) Scottish theologian, born of missionary parents in Chengtu, Szechwan, western China. He was Professor of Dogmatics at New College, Edinburgh (1952–79), Moderator of the Church of Scotland General Assembly (1976–7), and winner of the Templeton Prize (1978). Drawing on the Greek Fathers and Karl Barth, he holds that while much recent theology mirrors an outdated model of detached and objective scientific investigation, post-Einsteinian science is open-ended, reponding to the reality it encounters. Theology, therefore, should abandon its preconceptions and do the same, both in relation to science and in the quest for an acceptable ecumenical theology. His views have been expounded in many books, including *Theological Science* (1969), *Theology in Reconciliation* (1975), *Divine and Contingent Order* (1981), and *The Trinitarian Faith* (1988). ▷ Barth, Karl; ecumenism; moderator; theology

Tosefta, or **Tosephta** (Aramaic 'supplement') A large collection of rabbinic, extra-Mishnaic traditions and discussions which expand and supplement the teachings of the Mishnah, but are usually considered of lesser authority. The material is arranged topically, with headings similar to those of the Mishnah. In its present form it was perhaps compiled c.4th–5th-century CE, but some of the traditions were much earlier. ▷ Mishnah; rabbi; Talmud

Toshogu Shrine A sacred site in Japan where the early Tokogawa generals are buried. The Tokogawa period from 1600 to 1867 gave Japan law and order after earlier periods of instability, and the Toshogu shrine was started in 1634 at Nikko in honour of Tokugawa Ieyasu (1542–1616). It is a place of natural beauty near Mount Nantai and Lake Chuzenji. It includes a Shinto shrine, which commemorates the early Tokugawas in a kind of ancestor veneration, but it also has a huge Tendai Buddhist temple. This became associated with mountain worship, religious mountain climbing and various rituals and activities of religious merit. After the Meiji restoration, the Toshogu shrine site declined in importance because of the shift in state attention from Buddhism to Shinto, but it still remains a viable concern. ▷ sacred mountains, Japanese; shrines, Shinto; Tendai

totemism The practices and concepts surrounding the belief in a mystical or kin-type relationship between humans and nature. Derived from the Algonquin tribe's word ototeman, which denotes a brother-sister blood tie, totemism is a common feature in tribal societies, where natural objects and creatures are imbued with a soul and with supernatural powers. A totem is an object which serves to represent a particular society or person, and from which all members of that society are thought to descend. Thus this unites the group while also providing it with a 'guardian spirit'. This spirit might be viewed as a protector or helper, and held, at the same time, in awe and venerated. Generally there is a rule against killing, eating or touching the totem, and there are a variety of rituals, reinforcing its significance and powers. Totem poles are one form of representing a group's guardian spirit.

Tournier, Paul (1898–1986) Swiss physician and writer on the integration of psychology and Christianity, born in Geneva, the son of

totem pole

a pastor, Louis Tournier. He spent his whole professional life as a general practitioner in private practice in Geneva. Discovering religious faith through contact with the Oxford Group in 1932, he realized the need to treat his patients as whole human beings. *A Doctor's Casebook in the Light of the Bible* (1954) and *The Meaning of Persons* (1957) were followed by more than a dozen other best-selling books, including *The Strong and the Weak* (1963) and *Learning to Grow Old* (1972). *A Listening Ear: Fifty Years as a Doctor of the Whole Person* (1986) collects his occasional autobiographical reflections. ▷ Oxford Movement

Toxiuhmolpilia ▷ calendar, Meso-American; human sacrifice, Meso-American

Tractarianism ▷ Oxford Movement

Tracy, David (1939–) American theologian, born in Yonkers, New York. A professor of theology at Chicago University Divinity School, he has explored questions of hermeneutics: the problems of theological communication in modern pluralistic society where addressing the Church, the academic world and society in general is a difficult task requiring imagination, sensitivity and learning from the arts of conversation. Drawing on the thought of Tillich, Lonergan, Gadamer and others, he develops these themes in *Blessed Rage for Order* (1975), *The Analogical Imagination* (1980), and *Plurality and Ambiguity* (1986). ▷ hermeneutics; Lonergan, Bernard Joseph Francis; Tillich, Paul Johannes

transcendence and immanence Terms describing the manner in which God is related to the world. Transcendence indicates that God cannot be identified with the world but is infinitely above and beyond it. This is often expressed by saying that God is 'wholly other'. This basic definition can be refined by distinguishing between different forms of transcendence. Firstly, God is ontologically transcendent. This means that God is a self-contained reality that is not dependent on anything else for its existence. Ontological transcendence also describes the nature of God's being, which, unlike that of his creation, is eternal and infinite. Secondly, God is epistemologically transcendent. That is, God's essential nature remains incomprehensible to humankind. Our minds are simply incapable of grasping the Divine Essence. Epistemological transcendence is expressed theologically in terms of holiness, mystery and incomprehensibility.
Immanence denotes God's indwelling and omnipresence in the world. Since the world is utterly dependent on God, his constant presence is a necessity for its continued existence. Both transcendence and immance must be held in conjunction if theological problems are not to arise. If transcendence is emphasized at the expense of immanence, God is in danger of becoming so distant from his creation that he ceases to be of any relevance to humankind. Similarly, if immanence is too heavily emphasized, there is a danger of degenerating into pantheism. A viable theology must establish an equilibrium between the two poles of transendence and immanence.

transcendental meditation, or TM A meditation technique, based in part on Hindu meditation. Rediscovered this century by Guru Dev, it came to prominence through Maharishi Mahesh Yogi, who had spent 13 years in seclusion with Guru Dev. On Dev's death (1958) he began to travel across the world, teaching TM. It has been widely practised in the West since the 1960s, when he 'converted' the Beatles and others, such as Jane Fonda. Its practitioners are taught to meditate for 20 minutes twice a day as a means of reducing stress, achieving relaxation and gaining self-understanding. The ultimate goal is 'god-realization'. Officially known as the World Plan Executive Council, the movement has established a university in Iowa, and runs a variety of organizations, each aimed at spreading TM to different sectors of society. ▷ new religious movements in the West

Transfiguration An incident in Christianity in which the appearance of Jesus Christ changed in front of the apostles Peter, James and John. 'His face shone like the sun, and his clothes became as white as the light' (Matthew 17.2; see Mar 19, Luke 9, 2 Peter 1.16–18). With Jesus on the mountain appeared Moses and Elijah, the chief representatives of Old Testament law and prophecy. They were accompanied by a voice from a cloud which echoed the message of divine approval given at Jesus's baptism (Matthew 3.17). The incident was understood as a revelation of the glory of the Son of God and as a confirmation that Jesus's mission lay through the suffering and death about which he had recently been teaching the disciples (Matthew 16). In later Orthodox theology, particularly that of St Gregory Palamas and the hesychasts, a parallel was drawn between the transfiguration of Christ and the transformation of human nature. The light on the mountain was understood as God's divine energy, which the disciples were able to 'see' spiritually as well as physically. In the liturgical year, the feast of the Transfiguration is observed on 6 August. ▷ Christian year; Palamas, Gregory; hesychasm; Jesus Christ

transmigration The process by which the soul, spirit, or some other seat of personality, vacates the body it has been occupying and enters another body or object. Transmigration is also known as rebirth or reincarnation (especially in the Eastern religions), metempsychosis, metensomatosis, and palingenesis. In the Western world the concept first appears in the Greek religious sect known as Orphism (7th century BCE). It was then taken up by Pythagoras and his followers (6th century BCE), before being passed on to Plato. Through Plato the concept of transmigration went on to influence neo-platonism, gnosticism and ultimately medieval thought. In the Western religions in general, however, the concept has been rejected. In Christianity the idea has been held to be incompatible with belief in resurrection of the body and with the doctrine that the soul comes into existence at the moment of conception.

In the Eastern religions transmigration constitutes one of the foundations of religious belief. Indian religions subscribe to the doctrine of samsara, the wheel of birth and death, according to which life is an eternal cycle of birth, suffering and death. The position the soul occupies in a given existence is determined by its behaviour in a previous existence. Those who have lived evil, irreligious lives will be reincarnated at a lower position in the hierarchy of being, in some beliefs even as insects, vermin or vegetables. Those who have lived good lives will be born into wealthy or higher caste families. The goal of both Buddhism and Hinduism is to escape from this endless cycle of reincarnation. For the Hindu this comes about when the self discovers its common ground in *Brahman*, the principle of true reality. For the Buddhist the goal is nirvana, the cessation of desire and the extinction of consciousness. ▷ immortality; nirvana; soul

transubstantiation The Roman Catholic doctrine of the Eucharist (Mass), affirming the belief that the bread and wine used in the sacrament are converted into the body and blood of Christ, who is therefore truly present. The doctrine, rejected by 16th-century Reformers, was reaffirmed by the Council of Trent. ▷ consubstantiation; Counter-Reformation; Eucharist; Mass; Roman Catholicism; Trent, Council of

Trappists The popular name of the Cistercians of the More Strict Observance, centred on the monastery of La Trappe, France, until 1892. The Order continues throughout the world, devoted to divine office, and noted for its austerity (eg perpetual silence, and abstention from meat, fish, and eggs). ▷ Cistercians; monasticism

Trent, Council of (1545–63) A Council of the Roman Catholic Church, held in Trento, Italy. It was called to combat Protestantism and to reform the discipline of the Church and as such spear-headed the Counter-Reformation by clarifying many points of doctrine and practice. ▷ Council of the Church; Counter-Reformation; Protestantism; Roman Catholicism

tribes of Israel ▷ **Israel, tribes of**

trikaya (trikāya) The notion of the three (*tri*) bodies (*kaya*) of the Buddha developed in Mahayana Buddhism to express the fullness of the Buddha nature. Early Buddhism had put more emphasis upon the historical Buddha. The Mahayana tradition had a wider view of the Buddha, which saw his body or nature as having three levels: the *nirmanakaya* or assumed body, at the worldly and historical level relevant to human beings; the *sambhogakaya*, or bliss body, at the celestial level relevant to celestial beings; and the *dharmakaya*, or cosmic body, at the highest level which represented, as it were, the essence of the Buddha nature. According to this view there have been, and will be, a number of historical manifestations of the Buddha in cosmic history. There are also a number of heavenly Buddhas and bodhisattvas, such as Amitabha, residing in Pure Lands at the celestial level to whom devotion can be given. Although at the conventional level of truth the earthly and heavenly bodies of the Buddha are real, at the ultimate level of truth they are symbolic and not truly real. The real nature of the Buddha resides in the dharmakaya, in his cosmic body, which is self-existent. In Mahayana thought therefore the emphasis switched from the historical Gautama Buddha to the three bodies, especially the cosmic body, of the Buddha. This theory of the trikaya became systematized in the 4th century CE by the *Yogacara* school within Mahayana Buddhism. ▷ bodhisattva; Buddha; Buddha nature; dharmakaya; Mahayana

Buddhism; Pure Land Buddhism; sambhogakaya; Yogacara

Trimurti (Trimūrti) (Sanskrit, 'having three forms') The Hindu triad, manifesting the cosmic functions of the Supreme Being, as represented by Brahma, Vishnu, and Shiva. Brahma is the balance between the opposing principles of preservation and destruction, symbolized by Vishnu and Shiva respectively. ▷ Brahma; Hinduism; Shiva; Vishnu

Trinity A distinctively Christian doctrine that God exists in three persons, Father, Son, and Holy Spirit. The unity of God is maintained by insisting that the three persons or modes of existence of God are of one substance. The doctrine arose in the early Church because strictly monotheistic Jews nevertheless affirmed the divinity of Christ (the Son) and the presence of God in the Church through the Holy Spirit. The functions of the persons of the Trinity, and the relationship between them, has been the subject of much controversy (eg the split between Eastern and Western Churches on the *Filioque* clause), but the trinitarian concept is reflected in most Christian worship. ▷ Christianity; Filioque; God; Holy Spirit; Jesus Christ

tripartite ideology A system of beliefs which, according to some scholars, was held by the ancient Indo-Europeans, and by the peoples who descended from them. The theory that the tripartite ideology was at the heart of Indo-European religious beliefs was put forward by the French scholar Georges Dumézil, whose first works appeared in the 1920s. Dumézil argued that in all religions of Indo-European origin, the gods who make up the pantheon have functions which fall into three distinct categories: those of a king or priest (the 'first function'), of warriors (the 'second function'), or a nourishing role, like husbandmen (the 'third function'). Dumézil stressed the 'functional' similarities between gods from different Indo-European cultures, suggesting that such divine figures had a common Indo-European origin. The theory has ardent supporters, as well as vehement opponents. ▷ Dumézil, Georges; Indo-Europeans

Troeltsch, Ernst Peter Wilhelm (1865–1923) German Protestant theologian of the history-of-religions school, born in Haunstetten, near Augsburg. He studied at Erlangen, Berlin and Göttingen, and taught in Bonn, Heidelberg and Berlin. A philosopher of history concerned with historical relativism and the effects of culture, he is best known for *The Absoluteness of Christianity and the History of Religion* (1902), which defended Christianity in relative terms as the supreme religion for European culture. His other great work, *The Social Teaching of the Christian Churches* (1912, English trans. 1931), an exploration of Church-state relationships and social ethics, influenced the development of the sociology of religion. ▷ Church and State; sects, Christian

Trotskyism A development of Marxist thought by the Russian revolutionary Leon Trotsky (1879–1940). Essentially a theory of permanent revolution, Trotskyism stressed the internationalism of socialism, avoided co-existence, and encouraged revolutionary movements abroad; this conflicted with the ideas of Joseph Stalin (1879–1953), who advocated 'socialism in one country'. Trotskyism has since inspired other extreme left-wing revolutionary movements but they are factionally divided, and have little support outside some Western capitalist states. ▷ communism; Marxism-Leninism; secular alternatives to religion

Trueblood, (David) Elton (1900–) American Quaker scholar, born in Pleasantville, Iowa. He had a comprehensive education, including a Harvard PhD, before teaching philosophy at various institutions, notably at Earlham College (1946–54). He retained his link there as professor-at-large after his appointment in 1954 as Chief of Religious Information at the United States Information Agency. His books include *The Yoke of Christ* (1958), *The Company of the Committed* (1961), *The People Called Quakers* (1966), and *The Validity of the Christian Mission* (1972). ▷ Friends, Society of

truth A distinction should be made between epistemological, ontological/metaphysical and existential truth. Epistemological truth is the correspondence between a proposition, judgement or concept, and the reality these purport to describe. If a statement accurately reflects or expresses this reality it constitutes a true statement. As Kant puts it, truth is 'the conformity of our concepts with the object'. Ontological/metaphysical truth is knowledge of the underlying reality of things. This form of truth is often linked with the concepts of goodness or being and is regarded as eternal, absolute, and immutable. Existential truth is a quality of existence. If a human being's existence corresponds to what it truly is or should be, then he is in the truth.

Religious thought has been concerned primarily with ontological and existential truth, although epistemological truth is by no means absent. The individual is in the truth when he sustains a relationship to God and expresses this in his personal existence. Thus in the Old Testament the expressions 'to walk in the truth' and 'to do the truth' mean to live in faithful adherence to God's will. In the New Testament, although 'truth' retains many of its traditional meanings, it now comes to refer first and foremost to Christ, the salvation he brings, and what he reveals about God. Christ is the way, the truth and the life (John 14.6). ▷ faith

Tsongkapa (Tsong-kha-pa) (1357–1419) Reformer of Tibetan Buddhism and founder of the Gelugpa order, a scholar and Madhyamika commentator. He was born in eastern Tibet, took novitiate vows at seven years of age and became a fully ordained monk at the age of 25. He studied Mahayana philosophy, Tantra and medicine at various monasteries, including Sakya, Jonang and Lhasa. As he became famous for his scholarship, he attracted a group of disciples who formed a new sect, the Gelugpas, which were a revitalized form of the Kadampas and which were to become the most powerful monastic order in Tibet. Tsongkapa strictly adhered to the monastic discipline (*vinaya*) and stressed the requirement of celibacy and abstinence, thereby opposing the Tantric sexual yoga practised by some orders. The first monastery was founded at Ganden in 1409; Drepung and Sera were founded (1416 and 1419) by Tsongkapa's disciples. He also instituted a new year festival at the Jokhang temple in Lhasa. Philosophically he was a Madhyamika, whose teachings were formulated through the study of Atisha, Nagarjuna, Dharmakirti and Dinnaga. His most famous work, the *Lam rim chen mo* or 'Great Exposition of the Gradual Path', is a commentary on Atisha's *Bodhipathapradipa*. Tsongkapa consistently maintained a Madhyamika position, attaching great importance to logic and insight into emptiness through analysis. ▷ Atisha; Buddhism; emptiness; Gelugpa; Lhasa; Madhyamika; Mahayana Buddhism; Nagarjuna; vinaya-pitaka

Tuatha Dé Danann A race of wise beings who came to Ireland c.1500BCE, and became the ancient gods of the Irish; the name means 'the people of the goddess Danu'. They were conquered by the Milesians, and retreated into tumuli near the River Boyne. ▷ Dagda, the; Lug

Tula ▷ Tollan

tulku (sprul sku) An incarnate lama in Tibetan Buddhism. He is usually the abbot of a monastery, on whose death he reincarnates in the world to take up his monastic office once again. After the death of a tulku a search is made for a child, who then undergoes various tests. If he recognizes possessions belonging to the previous lama, the child will be reared as the new tulku. The idea of the tulku as an incarnation in an unbroken chain originated in the Karmapa branch of the Kagyupa tradition, when lama Dusum Khyenpa (Dusgrum mkhyen-pa, 1110–93) predicted his future reincarnation. The Kagyupa tradition developed several important lineages of tulkus, though the idea was adopted by other orders as well. The most famous lineage is that of the dalai lamas, each being an incarnation of the previous lama as well as a manifestation of the bodhisattva Avalokiteshvara. Rather than an unbroken succession, the Nyingmapas have the slightly different idea that the disciples of Padmasambhava reincarnate at times considered by them to be appropriate. Tulkus, referred to by the respectful title 'Rimpoche', are treated with great reverence. Following the Tibetan diaspora the tulku tradition has continued and there are now tulkus born in the West. ▷ Avalokiteshvara; bodhisattva; Buddhism; Dalai Lama; Kagyupa; lama; Nyingmapa; Padmasambhava

Tulsidas (Tulsīdās) (1532–1623) Indian Hindu devotional poet, born in Eastern India. Traditionally believed to have lived for 120 years, the time allotted to a sinless human being, he wrote more than a dozen works. His best-known is *Rāmacaritamānas* ('The Holy Lake of Rama's Deeds'), an immensely popular Eastern Hindi version of the *Rāmāyana* epic, which he began in 1574. His bhakti or devotional approach, concern for moral conduct, and idea of salvation through Rama incarnated as absolute knowledge and love, suggest a Nestorian Christian influence on his work. ▷ bhakti; Hinduism: Nestorians

Tung Chung Shu (176–104BCE) Chinese Confucian writer who lived during the Han dynasty. He was one of the principal architects of Han Confucianism which gave intellectual backbone to the Han empire. This was an amalgam of different elements drawn from the Confucian Classics, Taoism, the doctrine of the Five Elements, and the yin and yang theory. Tung Chung Shu founded a new school of exegesis on the basis of these elements, which inaugurated a renewal of the

Confucian tradition in a wider synthesis. This strengthened the authority of the Han emperors, who were seen to hold the mandate of heaven (*Tien*) and to be responsible for total order in their empire which was bolstered by Confucianism. Tung Chung Shu's renewal of the Confucian tradition was one of a number of such renewals, the most important of which was the later neo-Confucian movement which emerged during the Sung dynasty (960–1126). ▷ Confucian Canon; neo-Confucianism; Tien; yin and yang

Tun Huang An oasis in north-western China, on the Silk Route from India to China, which became an important Buddhist centre for a thousand years. It is famous for its cave-temples and grottoes that were begun in 366CE and continued to be built until the end of the Yuan dynasty in 1368. The sculptures and murals contained in them reveal fascinating developments in Buddhist art in China from the Indian-type figures of the early period to the fully Chinese figures of the later age. At its apogee Tun Huang had a thousand grottoes full of wall paintings and sculptures; it provides an intriguing picture not only of Buddhist but also of Chinese religious and social history. Equally important is the collection of Chinese and Tibetan manuscripts, accidentally discovered at Tun Huang in 1900, which reveal the early history of Buddhism in Tibet. They record the role played by two Tibetan kings, Srongsten Gampa and Trisong Detsun, in helping Buddhism to become important in Tibet, and the role played by Padmasambhava as an early Indian Buddhist missionary to Tibet. They also show that significant elements in later Tibetan Buddhism such as the notion of *bardo* (an intermediate stage between death and the next rebirth) and Tantric doctrines were already present around 800CE. ▷ bardo; Buddha image; Tantric Buddhism; Tibetan religion

turban A well-known symbol of Sikh identity. Although it is not one of the five Ks prescribed for Sikhs belonging to the *Khalsa*, in practice most Sikh men wear it, and this custom is recommended in the Sikh Code of Discipline. Although the early Sikh gurus are pictured as wearing turbans, they only became widely used by the general Sikh community during the time of the tenth Sikh guru, Guru Gobind Singh, for whom they represented distinguishing marks of identity and signs of courage. Members of the Akali Dal party sometimes wear blue turbans; Namdharis wear white turbans tied flat over the forehead; and those who sympathize with the idea of an independent Sikh state of Khalistan sometimes wear orange turbans. However, in India turbans are not worn by Sikhs only, so identification by colour can never be absolutely certain. ▷ Akali Dal; five Ks; Gobind Singh, Guru; Khalsa; Namdhari; Rahit Maryada

Turin Shroud A relic, alleged to be the burial-sheet of Jesus Christ, known since the 14th century, and preserved in the Cathedral in Turin since 1578. It portrays an image (clearer when shown using a photographic negative) of the front and back of a man's body, with markings that seem to correspond to the stigmata of Jesus. Controversy over its authenticity resulted in the use of independent radiocarbon-dating tests by three research centres in 1988, using a tiny piece of the fabric. The results indicated that the shroud was made long after the time of Christ. The question of how the body image was produced remains open. ▷ Jesus Christ; relics; stigmata

Tutankhamen (c.1370–1352BCE) Egyptian pharaoh of the 18th dynasty (1361–1352), the undistinguished son-in-law of the heretic pharaoh, Akhenaton. He came to the throne at the age of 12 and died at the age of 18; he is famous only for his magnificent tomb at Thebes, which was discovered intact in 1922 by Lord Carnarvon and Howard Carter. ▷ Akhenaton; pharaoh; Thebes

Tutu, Desmond Mpilo (1931–) Black South African Anglican prelate, born in Klerksdorp, the son of a primary-school headmaster. He studied theology at the University of South Africa and London University. After briefly working as a schoolteacher he became an Anglican parish priest (1960) and rapidly rose to become Bishop of Lesotho (1977), Secretary-General of the South African Council of Churches (1979), the first black Bishop of Johannesburg (1984) and Archbishop of Cape Town (1986). A fierce critic of the apartheid system, he has repeatedly risked imprisonment for his advocacy of the imposition of punitive sanctions against South Africa by the international community. He has also, however, condemned the use of violence by opponents of apartheid, seeking instead a peaceful, negotiated reconciliation between the black and white communities. He was awarded the Nobel Prize for Peace in 1984. ▷ Anglican Communion

Twelve, the ▷ apostle

Twelvers The most important branch within Shiite Islam. They give special prominence and reverence to 12 imams, the first three of whom are Ali, the son-in-law of Muhammad, and Ali's two sons Hasan and Husayn. The Twelvers claim that the twelfth imam, who mysteriously disappeared in the 9th century, is still alive as the Hidden Imam, and that he will return at the end of the age to sum up history as the Mahdi. They are the dominant Muslim group in Iran where, since the Iranian Revolution of 1978/9 under Ayatollah Khomeini, they have wielded significant power; they are the largest Muslim group in Iraq, and they are also present in the Lebanon, Syria, Pakistan, eastern Arabia, and some Gulf states. In all they number less than 15 per cent of Muslims, compared with 80 per cent who are Sunnis. The Twelvers have developed their own body of law and their own theology; they differ mainly from the Sunnis in not recognizing the authority of the four early caliphs or the four Sunni law schools, but in giving spiritual authority to Ali and his successors. For example, the Twelver version of Muhammad's famous night journey to heaven makes Muhammad share his spiritual status in that journey with Ali and his 11 descendants, whereas the Sunni version does not mention the 12 at all. The Twelvers have highlighted the theme of suffering in Islam by stressing the death of Ali's son Husayn at Karbala in 680, an event commemorated in a passion play that is performed every year at Muharram on the anniversary of his death. ▷ Ali; caliphate; Hasan; Husayn; imam; Islamic law schools; Mahdi; Muhammad; Night Journey of Muhammad; passion play, Islamic; Shiism; sunnah

Tylor, Sir Edward Burnet (1832–1917) English anthropologist, born in Camberwell, London. He travelled with Henry Christy to Mexico and published *Ahahuac*, an account of his journey, in 1861. His first major anthropological study, *Researches into the Early History of Mankind*, appeared in 1865, and in 1871 he published his monumental *Primitive Culture* (2 vols). In this work he sought to show that human culture, above all in its religious aspect, is governed by definite laws of evolutionary development, such that the beliefs and practices of primitive nations may be taken to represent earlier stages in the progress of humankind. After the appearance of Darwin's *The Descent of Man* (1871) he veered towards the view that cultural variation may be due to racial differences in mental endowment, a view reflected in his general introductory work *Anthropology* (1881). Tylor is widely regarded as the founder of the systematic study of human culture, and his definition of culture is still current today. Though he never obtained a university degree, he became one of the leading professional anthropologists of his time. He was Keeper of the University Museum at Oxford and from 1896 to 1909 the first Professor of Anthropology at Oxford University. ▷ Darwin, Charles Robert

Tyndale, Tindale, or **Hutchins, William** (c.1494–1536) English translator of the Bible, born probably in Slymbridge in Gloucestershire. He was educated at Magdalen Hall, Oxford (1510–15). After a spell at Cambridge he became chaplain and tutor in a household at Little Sodbury. His sympathy with the New Learning aroused suspicion however, and, already a competent Greek scholar, in 1523 he went to London. Bishop Tunstall having refused support for his translation of the Bible, he went in 1524 to Hamburg, to Wittenberg, where he visited Luther, and in 1525 to Cologne, where he began that year the printing of his English New Testament. This had not proceeded beyond the gospels of Matthew and Mark when the intrigues of Cochlaeus forced Tyndale to flee to Worms, where Peter Schoeffer printed for him 3000 New Testaments in small octavo. The translation owed much to Luther and Erasmus, much to Tyndale's own scholarship and literary skill. Tunstall and William Warham denounced the book; hundreds of copies were burned; but it made its way. In 1527 Tyndale moved to Marburg to the protection of Philip the Magnanimous; in 1529 he was shipwrecked on the way to Hamburg, where he met Coverdale; in 1531 he went to Antwerp. It was there probably, (ostensibly at Marburg), that his *Pentateuch* (1530–31) was published: a work in which the marginal glosses, almost all original, contain violent attacks on the pope and the bishops. Here he leans heavily on Luther. In 1531 appeared his version of *Jonah*, with a prologue. An unauthorized revision of Tyndale's New Testament was made at Antwerp in August 1534, and in November Tyndale himself issued there a revised version. One copy of his works was struck off on vellum for presentation to Anne Boleyn, under whose favour, apparently, a reprint of Tyndale's revised New Testament was printed in 1536 by T Godfray, the first volume of Holy Scripture printed in England. Tyndale revised his Testament in 1535, this time without the marginal notes. The emissaries of Henry VIII had often tried to run him to ground; at last in 1535 he was arrested in Antwerp through the treachery of Henry Philips, a Roman Catholic zealot, and imprisoned in the Castle of Vilvorde, tried there (1536), and on 6 October strangled and burned. His other original works were *The Parable of the Wicked Mammon* (1528); *The Obedience of a Christian Man*, his most elaborate book (1528); and *Practyse of Prelates* (1530), a pungent polemic. His *Works* were published in 1573. ▷ Bible; Coverdale, Miles; Erasmus, Desiderius; Luther, Martin; New Testament

typology There are three forms of typology in the field of religion. In the study of the Christian Bible it is a way of interpreting scripture by tracing a type from one part of the Bible to another, for example the Messiah in relation to Jesus Christ. In the study of religion, typology is a way of classifying religions according to type. For example some religions are founded (Buddhism), others are not (Hinduism); some religions are living, others are dead (Egyptian religion); some religions are primal (tribal religions), others are world religions; some are major living religions (Christianity, Judaism, Islam, Buddhism, Hinduism), others are minor living religions (the Sikhs, Bahais, Taoists, Shinto); some are new religious movements, others are long-established; some are prophetic (the Zoroastrian, Jewish, Christian and Muslim traditions), others are mystical (Buddhism, Hinduism, Taoism). A third kind of typology is that found in the phenomenology of religion where types of religious phenomena are classified together. For example Eliade brings together various typologies which he calls hierophanies—structures which manifest the sacred. He looks at hierophanies of the sky, the sun, the moon, water, stones, the earth, vegetation and farming, as well as sacred time, sacred places, myths and symbols. Classifying religions according to type is a way of showing the *differences* between religions; classifying religious phenomena according to typology is a way of showing the *similarities* between religious structures. ▷ Eliade, Mircea; Jesus Christ; Messiah; Religionswissenschaft; study of religion

Tyr, Tiwaz, Tu Names of a deity widely worshipped in Germanic religion and at one time evidently regarded as one of the chief divinities. The Romans thought him the German equivalent of their own war-god Mars. Tuesday (Tiwaz-day) bears his name; as the French word for Tuesday (*mardi*) recalls, that was Mars' day. Other sources link Tyr with justice, order, courage and magic runes. The later Scandinavians seem to have given him less prominence than the Germans. The best-known Norse story about Tyr tells how he sacrificed a hand to bind the evil wolf Fenrir. ▷ Fenrir; Mars

tzitzit According to Numbers 15.37–41 the Israelite is to fix a tassel ('tzitzit') onto each corner of his garment as a reminder of God's commandments. In post-biblical times Jews fulfilled this obligation literally, but when the traditional rectangular garment of the East ceased to be used, the injunction was fulfilled by wearing a prayer-shawl or *tallit*. This, with its fringes and tasselled corners, is still worn by men at morning prayer and on some fast days, including Yom Kippur. However, in order to obey the commandment continually, some Orthodox Jews wear a small tallit as an undergarment with its tassels protruding. ▷ fasts, Jewish; hagim; calendar, Jewish; mezuzah; tefillin

U

Uchimura Kanzo (1861–1930) Japanese Christian, founder of the Mukyokai ('no church church') non-denominational movement. Converted in 1876 while a student at Sapporo agricultural school, under the influence of the American agriculturalist William Smith Clark (1826–86), Uchimura became leader of an independent Japanese church, the first of many that rejected the denominational differences and divisions imported by Protestant missionaries. After some time as a schoolteacher, Uchimura devoted his life to lecturing and writing on biblical themes. Stress on Bible study remains a distinguishing feature of the Mukyokai movement (currently consisting of some 600 groups), which has no clergy, buildings, or organization.

Udasi (Udāsī) A Sikh term with two different connotations. It refers firstly to the journeys of the first Sikh guru, Guru Nanak, during his travelling ministry, when he preached through India, and possibly in other parts of the world. It also refers to an order of ascetics set up by the eldest son of Guru Nanak, Baba Sri Chand. The Udasis have established centres, known as akharas, at various places in India, especially in the north, but they are more recognizably Hindu than Sikh, using Sanskrit rather than the Punjabi language, and installing Hindu images in their temples. ▷ Nanak; Nirankar; Nirmalas; Punjab; Sanskrit

Uganda Martyrs A group of 22 African youths, converted to Roman Catholicism, who were killed for their faith in Uganda between 1885 and 1887. Canonized in 1964, they were among many Christians put to death in that period of persecution. ▷ canonization; martyr; Roman Catholicism

Ugarit A flourishing Canaanite city on the coast of North Syria opposite Cyprus, which in the late Bronze Age (c.1450–1200BCE) enjoyed wide contacts with the Egyptians, Hittites, and Mycenaeans. It was destroyed by the Sea Peoples c.1200BCE. ▷ Hittite religion; Mycenaean religion

ulama (ulamā) The term for religious scholars and authorities within the Islamic world. During the early development of the Muslim tradition, direction was sought by leaders from scholars skilled in Arabic, the Quran, Islamic law, and the sayings of Muhammad. Rulers looked for guidance to the *ulama*, but gradually they became institutionalized so that they developed into a kind of professional class, albeit without formal ordination as in the case of Christian ministers. They became arbiters of law, and a bulwark of Islamic society as the caliphate became less powerful, and as they began to receive better training in the developing Muslim colleges their confidence grew. Later dynasties such as the Mughals and Ottomans tried to control and regulate them, but they became a middle force between rulers and people. In the Shiite Muslim world, especially among the Twelvers and in Iran, the ulama became powerful, attracted strong personal followings, had the authority to make legal decisions, and were able to act with more political independence than in the orthodox Sunni world. This is exemplified in the role of the ulama in recent Iranian history, and in the persons of powerful ayatollahs such as Khomeini. ▷ ayatollah; caliphate; Hadith; Islamic law schools; madrasah; Mughal Empire; Muhammad; Ottoman Turks; Quran; Shiism; Sunnis; Twelvers

Ulfilas, or **Wulfila** (c.311–383) Gothic translator of the Bible. Consecrated a missionary bishop to his fellow countrymen by Eusebius of Nicomedia in 341, after seven years' labour he was forced to migrate with his converts across the Danube. He devised the Gothic alphabet, and carried out the first translation of the Bible into a Germanic language. ▷ Bible

Ultramontanism (literally 'beyond the mountains') A movement, deriving from France, asserting the centralization of the authority and power of the Roman Catholic Church in Rome and the pope. It gained impetus after the French Revolution (1789), and reached its high point with the First Vatican Council (1870) and the declaration of papal infallibility. ▷ infallibility; papacy; Roman Catholicism; Vatican Councils

Umar Khayyam ▷ **Omar Khayyam**

Umayyads ('Umayyads) An Arab dynasty belonging to the Quraysh tribe of Mecca, caliphs from 661 to 750. The founder of the dynasty was Muawiya I, born Abi Sufyan (c.605–680), Governor of Syria, who led opposition to the caliph Ali in demanding vengeance for his kinsman Uthman and was accepted as caliph by the majority of the Muslim community on Ali's death. He established his capital at Damascus (661). The caliphate, previously elective, became a hereditary monarchy with the succession of his son Yazid (683), who defeated the first of several Shiite revolts at the battle of Karbala in which Ali's son al-Husayn was killed (680). On the death of Yazid's son Muawiya II in 683, the caliphate passed to a collateral branch of the family in the person of Marwan I, born al-Hakam (c.623–685). Abd al-Malik (c.646–705) carried out lasting reforms, substituting Arabic for the pre-Conquest languages as the medium of administration and introducing a Muslim coinage. The reign of al-Walid I (c.670–715), caliph from 705, saw the conquest of Transoxania, North Africa, and the overthrow of the Visigothic kingdom in Spain by the general Tariq, an advance not halted by the Christian West until 732. Abd al-Malik and his sons were also great patrons of architecture, responsible for the Dome of the Rock in Jerusalem and the Great Mosque of Damascus as well as numerous palaces and hunting-lodges. After the reign of Hisham (691–743), the tenth caliph, Umayyad rule was progressively weakened by struggles over the succession, exacerbated by tribal rivalries among the Arabs, provincial resentment at the dominance of Syria and discontent among many of the non-Arabic converts to Islam. In 750 Marwan II al-Himar (c.692–750) was overthrown by a revolution led by the Abbasids and later killed. One of the few Umayyads to escape the ensuing massacre of the entire family was a grandson of Hisham, Abd er-Rahman I, who in 756 established himself as Emir of Muslim Spain (*al-Andalus*) with his capital at Cordoba, where the Umayyads continued to rule until 1031. ▷ caliphate; Dome of the Rock; Shiism

Umbanda ▷ **Afro-Brazilian religions**

ummah A term used by Muslims to denote the Islamic community, or people, or 'nation'. It refers ideally to the totality of Islam transcending ethnic and political considerations, and includes both the Sunni and Shiite branches. The development of regional rulers during the decline of the Abbasid caliphate, the rise of medieval dynasties such as the Mughals and the Ottomans, and the recent emergence of Islamic nation-states has seemed to diminish the appeal and validity of the ummah as a universal category. Nevertheless it persists as an ideal. In origin the Arabs had priority within the ummah in that Muhammad was seen to be the prophet to the Arab 'nation', and caliph Umar (634–44) confirmed Arab priority in the ummah register that he established. However, as Islam spread it became more non-Arab, and now far more Muslims live outside the Arab world than within it. Although there are rivalries between Islamic states today, there remains a sense of the ummah as a religious solidarity uniting Muslims in the face of challenges from the West, secularism, materialism, and other threats to traditional Islam. ▷ Abbasids; Mughal Empire; Muhammad; Ottoman Turks; secularism; Shiism; Sunnis

Underhill, Evelyn (1875–1941) English poet and mystic, born in Wolverhampton. She was educated at King's College, London. In 1907 she married Herbert Stuart Moore, a barrister, and in 1921 became lecturer on the philosophy of religion at Manchester College, Oxford. A friend and disciple of Hügel, she found her way intellectually from agnosticism to Christianity, wrote numerous books on mysticism, including *The Life of the Spirit* (1922), volumes of verse and four novels. Her *Mysticism* (1911) became a standard work. ▷ agnosticism; Christianity; mysticism

underworld A region situated beneath the earth, inhabited by the souls of the dead. In the earliest strata of religious tradition there seems to have been little differentiation between heaven and hell. All the departed, irrespective of merit, were consigned to the underworld. In pre-exilic Israel the dead were consigned to Sheol, a land of darkness where they eked out a shadowy existence cut off from Yahweh's presence (Psalms 39.12–13; 88.9–12; 115.17–18; Isaiah 38.18–19). Similar ideas can be found in Greek and Roman thought. According to Homer, the souls of the deceased descend to Hades, a huge subterranean cavern, where they flutter around like shadows or dreams (cf Odyssey 11.207).
As religious thought developed, however, the underworld came increasingly to be regarded as a place of punishment for the wicked. Corresponding to this, the concept of heaven was developed as the abode of the righteous and pious. The theory developed that an individual's behaviour in this life determined whether he would be consigned after death to heaven or hell. We find such ideas

developing in later, particularly post-exilic, Judaism. Thus in the Ethiopic Apocalypse of Enoch (22.9–13), Sheol is divided into separate regions for the righteous and the unrighteous. In Christianity this development was continued and refined still further. Sheol and Hades were assimilated into the concept of hell, a place of fiery torment where sinners were punished for their earthly misdeeds. Christianity also developed the concept of purgatory to cater for those who were not so wicked that they had to be consigned to everlasting damnation, nor so virtuous that they could be translated immediately to heaven. Purgatory is temporary and finite punishment for sin aimed at purifying the soul to make it worthy of dwelling in the Divine Presence.

In the modern period there has been considerable discomfort with the concept of hell as being incompatible with the concept of a loving God. There is thus a tendency to interpret hell in psychological terms (cf Sartre's statement that 'hell is other people') or to argue that oblivion rather than eternal torment awaits the wicked. ▷ afterlife; immortality; judgement of the dead; soul

Uniate churches More properly Eastern or Greek Catholic churches in communion with Rome that retain their own language, rites, and canon law, allowing, for example, clerical marriage and communion (Eucharist) in both kinds (ie both bread and wine). There are five major rites: Byzantine (including the Ukrainians who make up half of all Uniate Christians), Antiochine, Alexandrian, Chaldaean, and Armenian. Uniate churches arose during attempts to heal the division between the Eastern and Western Church and have usually been in a minority, often oppressed in their own territories by larger Orthodox churches and, more recently, by Islamic and atheistic states. ▷ Eucharist

Unification Church A religious movement founded by the Reverend Sun Myung Moon in 1954 in Korea, known popularly as the 'Moonies'. Combining elements of Taoism and Christianity, its teachings are based on Moon's book *Divine Principle*, which contains a special interpretation of the Bible, and on revelations he is said to have received from God. The purpose of creation was to establish a perfect family, but the Fall frustrated its realization until its fulfilment in Reverend and Mrs Moon. Now is the time for a sinless messiah to return to earth and bring the kingdom of heaven. Some see Moon as this messiah, although he has not proclaimed himself as such. The movement's most important ritual is the mass weddings conducted by Moon, at which as many as 8000 couples have been married at a time. There is weekly rededication of commitment to the Church. It has extensive commercial interests, and some of its activities have generated public hostility, bringing accusations of brain-washing and the deliberate severance of new believers from their families. ▷ Fall, the; kingdom of God; Messiah; Moon, Sun Myung; new religious movements in the West; religion

Unitarians A religious group which, although in many ways akin to Christianity, rejects the doctrines of the Trinity and the divinity of Christ. As an organized group it dates back to the Anabaptists at the time of the Reformation. ▷ Anabaptists; Jesus Christ; Reformation; Trinity

United Church of Christ A Christian denomination formed in the USA in 1961 (after 20 years of negotiations) by the union of the Congregational and Christian Churches with the Evangelical and Reformed Church. Envisaged as an ecumenical Protestant Church, it allows for variation in local organization and in the interpretation of doctrine, but continues to reflect its Reformed theological background. ▷ Congregationalism; ecumenism; Reformed Churches

universalism The religious belief that all people will be saved. It implies rejection of the traditional Christian belief in hell. A feature of much contemporary Protestant theology, it is motivated by moral doubts concerning eternal punishment, and by a recognition of the validity of other non-Christian world faiths. ▷ Christianity; hell; predestination; Protestantism

Unleavened Bread, Feast of ▷ Passover

Upanishads (Upaniṣads) Literally 'to sit beneath'—implying a group of students sitting at the feet of a teacher. These are Sanskrit writings which underpin much Hindu philosophy. Although there are in excess of 100 writings which bear the name Upanishads, classically there are 13 principal ones, written between the 8th and 4th centuries BCE. They are often also referred to as the Vedanta ('end of the Vedas') and are therefore defined as being *shruti*, with the remaining ones being *smriti*. Although their teaching is not homogenous, there are, nevertheless, a number of speculations which are common to many of them. Possibly the most important of these is

the idea of an eternal and underlying essence common to the whole universe, which the earliest Upanishads term atman or *Brahman*. Conversely there are certain theistic Upanishads which attribute these terms to a deity, who is often associated with one of the gods or goddesses of the Hindu pantheon.
Despite such differences, however, it could be said that the Upanishads do represent a significant development of the Vedas in that they contain much that is esoteric and mystical. They show a significant shift towards the internalization and spiritualization of many concepts, and as a result much of the Vedic tradition is demythologized, with the many gods being reduced to a single concept, be it monistic or theistic. Vedic ritual is also radically reinterpreted. No longer can *moksha* be gained solely by action. Instead the devotee must overcome ignorance (*avidya*) by gaining knowledge (*jnana*) of the true nature of the universe that is veiled from the individual by illusion (*maya*). ▷ atman; Brahman; maya; moksha; shruti; smriti; Veda

upekkha A Buddhist term for equanimity. It is one of the four universal virtues in Buddhist thought, the other three being loving kindness (*metta*), compassion (*karuna*), and sympathetic joy (*mudita*). They are held to be universal because they can be built up in such a way as to embrace all beings throughout the world. The key virtue of the four is equanimity. The other three, if seen in isolation, can become too emotional and subjective, and need the stabilizing power of equanimity to become truly universal and unselfish. Thus Buddhist loving kindness has a somewhat calm and unemotional nature compared with love in some other religious traditions. Buddhists would claim that it is the underlying quality of equanimity that gives loving kindess, compassion and sympathetic joy their true power and impact, and that equanimity is the basic posture of life that best fits in with the four noble truths taught by the Buddha. ▷ ariya sacca; Buddha; karuna; love

uposatha A Buddhist term referring to Buddhist holy days that occur four times a month according to the phases of the moon. There is therefore a similarity between the uposatha and the Western notion of the Sabbath. On two of these holy days there is a recitation of the Patimokkha, the code of monastic law, by local assemblies of monks. These recitals have become a focus of unity for Buddhist monks throughout the world. The uposatha days are also important for lay Buddhists. Keen lay devotees, known as *upasakas*, observe eight moral precepts on these holy days instead of the normal five. They are also times of lay celebration when lay Buddhists visit the local monastery to share in devotions before a Buddha image, to listen to recitations from the scriptures, and to hear a sermon delivered by a monk. They are observed with especial regularity in Sri Lanka, where they are public holidays, and also in some other parts of South-East Asia; in some countries special religious broadcasts are made on uposatha days. There are also annual Buddhist holy days, such as Vaisakha which recalls three of the great events of the Buddha's life, although the term uposatha is used especially of the monthly holy days. ▷ Buddha; Buddha image; Patimokkha; Sabbath; Vaisakha

Ur An ancient Sumerian city-state lying to the south east of Babylon. The early home of the Jewish patriarch Abraham, it was at its zenith in the third millennium BCE, when twice it became the capital of Sumer. Destroyed by Elam c.2000BCE, the city recovered but never attained its former greatness. It was finally abandoned in the 4th century BCE. ▷ Abraham; Elam; Sumer

uraeus In Ancient Egyptian art and mythology, the cobra. Regarded as a symbol of royalty and power, it was normally depicted rearing, with hood inflated. It was used to represent the separable and independent left eye of Re, the sun god, which he placed on his forehead as a sign of its dominion over the world. In this form it appeared first on the forehead of Re, then on the crowns of Upper and Lower Egypt and the head-dresses of pharaohs, a sign of their majesty and descent from the sun god. The uraeus symbol also appears on the brows of other deities and

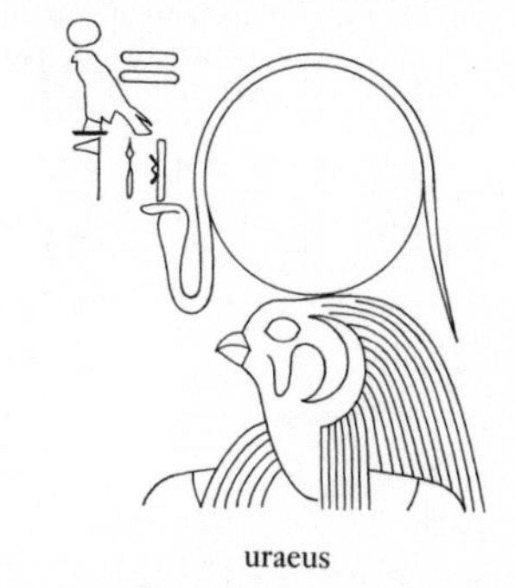
uraeus

especially coiled around the sun-disc of Re. ▷ pharaoh; Re

Urim and **Thummim** Objects of uncertain description, kept in the breastplate and vestments of the Israelite high priest. They were apparently used to discern God's answer to 'yes'-or-'no' questions put to him, and served either as gemstones catching the light (if *urim* means 'lights') or as flat markers used in casting lots (if *urim* means 'curse' and *thummim* means 'perfect'). ▷ Judaism; oracle

urna (ūrṇā) A word, usually translated as 'beauty spot', which refers to a spot in the middle of the forehead that is taken to be one of the 32 marks of a great man such as the Buddha. As the *tipitaka* or Pali Canon puts it, 'in the space between his eyebrows he has hair growing which is white with the sheen of soft cotton'. In practice, in various kinds of Buddha images the urna is usually a small circular mark between the eybrows of the Buddha. It is linked to the notion of the 'third eye' or the 'wisdom eye' by means of which the Buddha was able to have a deep perception into the heart of things. The urna is not present in all images of the Buddha, being absent, for example, in Sri Lanka Buddhas, but elsewhere it is common as symbolizing his attribute of wisdom. ▷ Buddha; Buddha image; Sinhalese Buddhism; tipitaka; wisdom

Ursula, St (4th century) Legendary saint and martyr, especially honoured in Cologne, where she is said to have been slain with 11 000 virgins by a horde of Huns on her journey home from a pilgrimage to Rome. She became the patron saint of many educational institutes, particularly the teaching order of the Ursulines. Her feast day is 21 October. ▷ Christianity; martyr; Ursulines

Ursulines A Roman Catholic order, established with the then unique aim of educating girls exclusively. The principal and oldest congregation was founded in 1535 by St Angela Merici as the Company of St Ursula, after the legendary 4th-century saint and martyr St Ursula. It was later recognized as a monastic order. Quickly spreading worldwide, in 1900 the various Ursuline convents were united by the pope through the Roman Union of the Order of St Ursula. Its main aims remain charitable work and the teaching of Christian doctrine. ▷ nun; Roman Catholicism

Uthman ('Uthmān) (d.656) Fourth caliph. He was elected in succession to Omar, in preference to Ali (644). He established a commission of scholars who collected the revelations of Muhammad to produce the definitive version of the Quran. However, Uthman's administration was badly organized, and disagreements concerning the division of the gains made in the Muslim conquests gave rise to increasing social tensions, culminating in a revolt in which he was killed. ▷ Ali; caliphate; Muhammad; Omar Khayyám; Quran

utilitarianism A teleological ethical theory which maintains that one ought always to act so as to maximize welfare. Act utilitarians such as Jeremy Bentham enjoin us always to choose that action, of the available alternatives, which will produce the most welfare on balance for all people affected. Rule utilitarians (David Hume, at times) enjoin us to follow those rules, general conformity to which would produce more welfare than alternative rules. An act utilitarian would claim that one ought not to keep a promise if keeping it would be harmful, whereas a rule utilitarian might claim that the promise should be kept because keeping it conforms to a rule, general conformity to which is maximally valuable. ▷ Hume, David; teleological ethics

Utopia (Greek 'nowhere') A name for a fictional republic, invented by Sir Thomas More in *Utopia* (1516); hence, any imaginary (and by implication, unattainable) ideal state. Later works include Samuel Butler's *Erewhon* (= Nowhere) (1872); William Morris's *News from Nowhere* (1891); and Aldous Huxley's *Island* (1962). The term dystopia refers to the reverse, a nightmare state such as that depicted in George Orwell's *Nineteen Eighty Four* (1948). ▷ More, Sir Thomas, St

V

Vaibhashika (Vaibhāṣika) An early school of Buddhism that emerged within a wider sect called the *Sarvastivadins*, which stressed the logical analysis of Buddhist doctrines known as the *Abhidharma*. At a Buddhist council convened by King Kanishka around 100CE in what is now Kashmir the authenticity of their views was discussed. Around this time a Great Commentary (*vibhasa*) was written on a key part of the Abhidharma; the Vaibhashikas took their name from this commentary, and were regarded as the orthodox interpreters of the Sarvastivada position. They argued that the constituent elements of reality known as dharmas have a continuity whereby they move from a future state to a present active state to a past state, and in all this they do not change their inner nature. They were criticized by another group called the *Sautrantikas*, who stressed the authority of the discourses of the Buddha as having priority over the Abhidharma, which came later. The Indian philosopher Vasubandhu (c.5th century CE) summarized the Vaibhashika position in this controversy in his great *abhidharmakosa*, which became important for China and Tibet as well. The Vaibhashikas were also criticized by the later Mahayana tradition for giving too much substance to the constituent elements of reality, whereas the Mahayana school argued that they too were 'empty'. Nevertheless, their general viewpoint underlay some of the elements in the Mahayana position. ▷ Abhidharma; dharma; Kanishka; Mahayana Buddhism; Sarvastivada; Sautrantika; Vasubandhu

Vairocana The name of the sun Buddha who is omnipresent and radiates great light, and is important in Tibetan and Japanese Buddhism. In Japan he became associated with the Shinto sun goddess Amaterasu, and was jointly worshipped with her at the great Ise shrine. Vairocana was a key figure in Japanese Shingon Buddhism, and his origins were more Indian than Chinese. Known in Japan as Dainichi, he is at the centre of the Indian *Mahavairocana Sutra*, where he is considered to be the source of the whole cosmos, including human beings. In the cosmos there are six basic elements which are paired off into dualities, and these are formed artistically into mandalas, or symbolic world-

Vairocana

pictures, in which Vairocana plays a central part. Thus Vairocana became an important object of meditation in Shingon and Tibetan Buddhism. He also became associated in some quarters with the cosmic body of the Buddha, the *dharmakaya*, which is seen as the ultimate reality. He is thus the source of the higher esoteric truth in Buddhism, and yet he gathers together other realities as well in the architectonic unity of Vairocana. ▷ Adi-Buddha; Amaterasu; dharmakaya; Ise shrines; mandala; Shingon; Tibetan religion

Vaisakha (Vaísākha; Pali: Vesākha) The name of a month in the Indian calendar, corresponding to the period mid April to mid May, which is the occasion of the greatest Buddhist festival, which is also known as Vesak. It commemorates three of the key events in the life of the Buddha; his birth at Lumbini, his enlightenment at Bodhgaya, and his death at Kusinara. This is the most widely celebrated of all the Buddhist festivals. Although Buddhist monasteries are at the centre of the celebrations, it is also important for layfolk and for whole neighbourhoods throughout the Buddhist world. Houses are lit up, fairs are set up, food is shared, processions are held, Buddhist shrines are walked around, and lessons are read and sermons given on the three milestones in the life of the Buddha remembered at this time. From the King of Thailand in the royal palace at Bangkok to the local abbot of a monastery in a tiny village in Sri Lanka there is rejoicing as the main incidents in the life of the Buddha are remembered with thankfulness and praise. ▷ Buddha; Bodhgaya; Kusinara; Lumbini

Vaisheshika (Vaiśeṣika) One of the six orthodox (*astika*) schools of Indian philosophy which became amalgamated with the Nyaya. While Nyaya in itself was concerned with logic and valid reasoning, the Vaisheshika was concerned with physics and provided much of the content for the merged schools. The foundation text of the school is Kanada's *Vaisheshika Sutra* (1st century CE) which presents an atomic theory of nature. That is, nature is made up of atoms which combine to form 'molecules' of the five elements: earth, water, air, fire and ether (*akasha*). These elements are particular (*vishesha*), possessing specific characteristics which distinguish them from each other and from non-material substances, such as souls and time. There was some debate as to whether the Lord (*Ishvara*), who arranges the atoms, was a distinct category. The *Vaisheshika Sutra* classifies the totality of appearances into six categories (*padarthas*), namely: substance, quality, action, universality, particularity and inherence. Knowledge of these categories will result in release or liberation (*moksha*). While resembling certain features of modern Western science, this was a system of speculative philosophy and not a scientific theory established through experiments. It was, however, concerned with establishing its ideas through reason and logical argument. ▷ Indian philosophies; Ishvara; moksha; Nyaya

Vaishnavism (Vaiṣṇavism) A major tradition in Hinduism, focused on the deity Vishnu and his incarnations (avataras), especially Krishna and Rama. Vaishnavism has tended to be less ascetic than Shaivism, emphasizing worship (*puja*) of a personal God (Vishnu, Rama or Krishna), selfless devotion (bhakti) and salvation or liberation (*moksha*) through God's grace. Hymns to Vishnu are found in the Veda, though theistic worship of Vishnu does not develop until much later in the 5th or 4th centuries BCE. Vaishnavism is a fusion of the cult of Narayana, who became identified with Vishnu, and the Bhagavata cult of Krishna, who is an incarnation of Vishnu. The Narayana cult is expressed in the *Mahanarayana Upanishad* (5th–4th centuries BCE) as well as sections of the epic, the *Mahabharata*, while the Bhagavatas produced the slightly younger *Bhagavad Gita*. The cult of Krishna developed into a tradition which centres on Krishna Gopala, a young cowherd in Vrindaban, playing and having love affairs with the cowgirls (*gopis*), especially Radha. The *Harivamsha* (1st–3rd centuries CE) presents a complete mythological account of Krishna's life, the 'erotic' aspect of which is developed in the *Bhagavata Purana* (11th century) and later Vaishnava poetry such as Jayadeva's *Gitagovinda*. This Krishna Gopala tradition became important in Bengal with Chaitanya and exists today in the Hare Krishna movement. While the Bhagavatas formulated the idea of God being born into the world during times of trouble, as expressed in the *Bhagavad Gita*, another Vaishnava sect, the Pancharatra, developed the idea that God (ie Vishnu) is manifested in a series of stages or emanations (*vyuhas*). The Pancharatra sect is mentioned in the *Mahabharata*, but comes to prominence in the 4th to 7th centuries CE with the production of a vast body of Tantric Vaishnava texts. These are concerned with ritual, mantras and temple worship. Some of these texts, notably the *Lakshmi Tantra*, are focused on Vishnu's consort Lakshmi as the power behind the universe. The Shri Vaishnava tradition which developed in South India is a fusion of the Bhagavata cult of Krishna, the Pancharatra tradition and the Tamil devotional or bhakti tradition of the Alvars. Vaishnavism has produced some notable theologians such as Ramanuja (11th–12th centuries), Madhva (13th century), Vallabha (1479–1531) and Nimbarka (12th century). Vaishnavas can often be distinguished by a v-shape painted on their foreheads. ▷ Alvar; avatara; Bhagavad Gita; Bhagavata Purana; bhakti; Chaitanya; Krishna; Lakshmi; Madhva; Mahabharata; moksha; Nimbarka; Radha; Rama; Ramanuja; Shaivism; Tamil Hinduism; Upanishads; Vallabha; Veda; Vishnu

Vaishyas (Vaiśyas) The lowest of the three Aryan or twice-born classes which came into Indian society. They were the 'mass of common people', the merchants and artisans, and were equated with the 'all gods', the corresponding mass of divine beings. In the *Rig Veda* (10.90: 11–12) the Vaishyas were said to emanate from the thighs of the primal being, *purusha*. ▷ purusha; varna

Valhalla In Norse mythology, a great hall built by Odin to house warriors who die bravely in battle. Every night they get drunk, and every day fight to the death and rise again. After this intensive training they will form an army to help the gods in the Last Battle. ▷ Germanic religion; Odin; Ragnarok

Valkyries In Norse and German mythology, the Maidens of Odin, who were also called Choosers of the Slain. They rode out with the Wild Hunt, or appeared as swans, in order to collect warriors killed in battle for Valhalla. ▷ Germanic religion; Odin; Valhalla

Vallabha (1479–1531) Hindu Vaishnava theologian, founder of the Shuddhadvaita ('Pure non-dualist') Vedanta school. A devotee of Krishna, he tried to combine devotion (bhakti) with non-dualism and wrote commentaries on the *Brahma Sutra* and the *Bhagavata Purana*, which he regarded as Krishna's final revelation or authority. Vallabha rejected Shankara's idea that the world is illusion (*maya*), believing instead that it is real and is identified with Brahman or Krishna: in other words, that God and the world are one. He advocates a path of personal devotion and surrender to the deity, the *pushtimarga* or 'way of nourishment', which culminates in great longing for Krishna, akin to the longing felt by the cowgirls (*gopis*). In this way the devotee, like the gopis, participates in Krishna's 'play' (*lila*). ▷ Bhagavata Purana; bhakti; Brahman; Krishna; lila; maya; Shankara

Valmiki (Vālmīki) The reputed author of the *Ramayana*. Legends say he was a vagabond discovered by the Rishi Narada, who encouraged him to study. He was visited at his hermitage at Chitrakuta on numerous occasions by Rama and Sita, and played host to Sita when she was banished by her suspicious husband. Inspired to poetry after seeing a heron grieving for her mate, which had been killed by a hunter, Valmiki, on the advice of Brahma mediated through Narada, wrote the adventures of Rama and Sita in metrical form. ▷ Brahma; Rama; Ramayana

Vanir ▷ Aesir and Vanir

varna (varṇa) (literally 'colour') A word which denotes the four divisions or classes of Hindu society. This hierarchical system of social ranking has been regarded as sacred in Hinduism. Mythologically the idea of varna is expressed in the 'Hymn to the Divine Person' (*Purusha Sukta*) in the *Rig Veda* (10.90) in which the primal man was sacrificed, from whose body arose the natural and social order. The priestly class (Brahmans) came from his mouth, the warrior class (*kshatriyas*) from his arms, the common people or merchants and artisans (*vaishyas*) from his thighs and the serfs (*shudras*) from his feet. The primal giant is thus a model of social ranking. The first three classes are called the twice-born (*dvija*) because all males undergo an initiation ceremony which enables them to participate in Vedic rites. This ceremony is theoretically undergone as a young adolescent, though is often performed at a young man's wedding. Beneath the four varnas, or as a subset of the fourth set are the untouchables, the 'fifth' class of 'outcastes' called *dalit* (the oppressed). Gandhi called them *harijans*, children of God. Article 17 of the Indian constitution of 1949 abolished untouchability and forbade its practice in any form. By law all now have an equal right to draw water from any well, to worship in any temple and to enter any profession. However, in real terms their status has not been substantially altered. Class (varna) and caste (*jati*) have become intermeshed in Hindu society. While castes remain distinct from each other, separated by powerful notions of purity and pollution, class members in contemporary Hindu communities do not always follow their traditionally designated roles. For example, Brahmans, traditionally priests, may own land, run businesses or work in the food industry (being ritually pure). Similarly Kshatriyas, traditionally associated with the army and government, are today found in most occupations. Vaishyas tend to remain merchants and artisans, while shudras retain their original place in serving the other three classes. ▷ Brahmans; caste; Gandhi, Mohandas Karamchand; Harijan; Kshatriyas; jati; Veda

vassa A Buddhist word meaning 'monsoon', used for the *vassa* festival that is held during the monsoon season that lasts from July to October. It is sometimes referred to as the Buddhist Lent. It appears to be the case that at the beginning of the Buddhist tradition, perhaps even during the lifetime of the Buddha himself, small groups of Buddhists would meet together communally in order to use the monsoon period to the best advantage, and this may have been the origin of the idea of a settled monastery. Vassa is now used by monks as a time of retreat when they stay in their own monastery to study and meditate and teach layfolk. Some Buddhists take ordination as monks during this period, although they are not monks for the rest of the year, and a monk's service is reckoned by the vassas, not the years, that he has spent in the *sangha*. Thus there are more people operating as monks during the vassa period, and there are more laymen attending monasteries in order to hear sermons and gain instruction from the monks. ▷ Buddha; Lent; sangha

Vasubandhu Traditionally Vasubandhu is said to have been born at what is now Peshawar in Gandhara at the end of the 4th century CE. He became a Sarvastivadin and wrote an influential work, the *abhidharma-kosa*, which remained the classical statement of *abhidharma* thought in North India. He was then, according to tradition, converted to the Mahayana position by his half-brother Asanga, and he helped Asanga to establish the *Yogacara* school of Mahayana Buddhism. He expanded his views in various treatises, including the *Vimsatika, Treatise in Twenty Stanzas on Consciousness Only*. His school argued that the mind is basically the only reality and that outward objects are projections of the mind. Like the consciousness of dream-objects, consciousness of external objects is vivid yet lacking in objective reality. In a number of ways Vasubandhu and his Yogacara companions bolstered their view of what would now be called subjective idealism against the 'materialism' of their day. Their school was later very important outside India, especially in Tibet. Scholarship has raised the question as to whether there were two Vasubandhus (a *Sarvastivadin* one and a *Yogacara* one) rather than one; the question is still not resolved. ▷ Asanga; Sarvastivada; Yogacara

Vatican Councils Two councils of the Roman Catholic Church. The First (1869–70) was called by Pope Pius IX to deal with doctrine, discipline and canon law, foreign missions, and the relationship between Church and State. It is best remembered for the decree on papal infallibility and the triumph of the Ultramontanists. The Second (1962–5) was called by Pope John XXIII, with the task of renewing religious life and bringing up to date the belief, structure, and discipline of the Church (aggiornamento). Its reforms in liturgy and its ecumenical tendencies have had far-reaching effects throughout the Christian world. ▷ aggiornamento; canon law; Council of the Church; ecumenism; John XXIII; liturgy; Pius IX; Roman Catholicism; Ultramontanism

Veda The 'sacred knowledge' of the Hindus, dating from c.1500BCE, contained in the four collections called the Vedas, the *Brahmanas* appended to them, and the Aranyakas and Upanishads which serve as an epilogue or conclusion. Originally the Veda consisted of the *Rig Veda* (sacred songs or hymns of praise), *Sama Veda* (melodies and chants used by priests during sacrifices), and *Yajur Veda* (sacrificial formulae); to which was later added the *Athara Veda* (spells, charms, and exorcistic chants). The Aranyakas and Upanishads deny that ritual sacrifice is the only means to liberation, and introduce monistic doctrine. They were eventually understood as the fulfilment of Vedic aspirations, and are called the Vedanta ('the end of the Veda'). ▷ Brahmanas and Aranyakas; Hinduism; monism; Upanishads; Vedanta

Vedanta (Vedānta) The most influential of the six orthodox (*astika*) schools of Hindu philosophy. The term means 'the end of the Veda' and at one level refers to the teachings of the last section of the Veda, the Upanishads, though it implies the 'essence of knowledge or wisdom' as well. The Vedanta is also called the Later (Uttara) Mimamsa as opposed to the Early (Purva) Mimamsa: the Vedanta emphasizing renunciation and the search for salvation or liberation (*moksha*), the Mimamsa emphasizing dharma, the performance of moral and ritual obligations in society. Apart from the Upanishads, the *Bhagavad Gita* is an influential text along with Badarayana's Brahma or *Vedanta Sutras*. Vedanta philosophers of different persuasions wrote commentaries on the Upanishads, the Gita and especially the Vedanta Sutras. Four statements found in the Upanishads are of particular importance in the Vedanta, namely: 'I am the Absolute' (*aham brahmasmi*); 'This self is the Absolute' (*ayam atma brahma*); 'All this is indeed the Absolute' (*sarvam khalu idam brahma*); and 'Thou art that' (*tat-tvam-asi*). These statements were interpreted by opposing schools of Vedanta. The Non-dual or Advaita Vedanta of Shankara (788–820) understood such statements in a monistic way: that there is only one reality with which the self is identical, all worldly distinctions being an illusion (*maya*). The 'qualified non-dualism' or Vishishtadvaita of Ramanuja (12th century) maintained that such statements implied the soul's being united with the Absolute, but not identical, whereas the Dualist or Dvaita Vedanta of Madhva (13th century) interpreted these statements to mean that the self is distinct from the absolute. Vedanta has strongly influenced contemporary Hinduism through the Hindu renaissance in the 19th century, especially the work of Vivekananda. ▷ Advaita Vedanta; Bhagavad Gita; dharma; Madhva; Mimamsa; moksha; Ramanuja; Shankara; Upanishads; Veda; Vedanta

veiling In Islam, the custom of covering the face practised by women. It is described by the term *hijab* in Arab countries, and by the term *purdah* in Indo-Persian lands. Quran 33.59 advised Muhammad's wives to go veiled, and Quran 24.31 advised the veiling of female adornments so that outsiders could not see them. However, the tradition of veiling the face did not become common before the time of the Abbasid caliphs (750–1258). The veil was not worn by girls, but was taken up at the time of transition to puberty. Muslim law schools do not prescribe the wearing of a veil, although they do prescribe the covering of the body to preserve modesty in public places. In practice, Muslim women who work outdoors or in rural communities in places such as South-East Asia and Bedouin lands have rarely used it, and wearing the veil has been a cultural as much as a purely religious tradition. While Islamic modernism has suggested that the veil is a symbol of the subjugation of women and should be removed, Islamic fundamentalism is exercising pressure upon Muslim women to introduce or reintroduce it. ▷ Abbasids; Islam, women in; Islamic law schools; Islamic modernism; Mara (Islamic); Quran

Venus Originally an obscure Italian deity of the vegetable garden, she was identified with Aphrodite, and, as a Roman goddess, took over the latter's mythology and attributes. ▷ Roman religion

Venus of Willendorf A famous female figurine, made of limestone, discovered at Willendorf near Wachau in Austria. She is the best known of a number of Venus figures that appeared during the later palaeolithic period. She has a large body and ample breasts which appear to signify pregnancy, but no arms or feet. She has no clear face, but does have stylized hair. It is clear that her body was carved to emphasize aspects of life associated with pregnancy, birth and nuture, and therefore it is reasonable to assume that she was connected in some way with fertility, for example as a fertility goddess. It is also possible that she was a protector of the dwellings where she was found. More speculative theories about the Venus figures include the notions that they were underworld deities, mothers of animals, hunt goddesses, and protectors of nature. ▷ goddess worship; palaeolithic religion

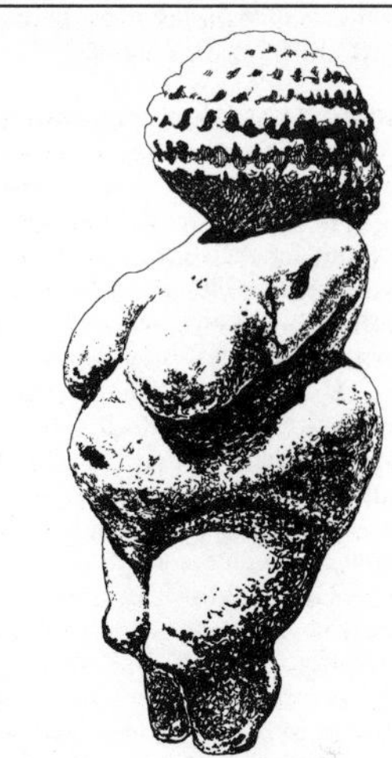

Venus of Willindorf

Vespers The evening hour of the divine office of the Western Church. In monastic, cathedral, and collegiate churches in the Roman Catholic Church it is sung daily between 3 and 6 pm. ▷ liturgy; Roman Catholicism

Vestal Virgins In ancient Rome, the aristocratic, virgin priestesses of Vesta, the goddess of the hearth. They tended the sacred flame which burned perpetually in the Temple of Vesta near the forum. ▷ Roman religion

vestments Special and distinctive garments worn by clergy in the worship and liturgy of the Christian Church. ▷ liturgy

vicar (Latin *vicarius*, 'substitute') Literally one who takes the place of another; for example, the pope is said to be the Vicar of Christ. In Anglican Churches, the term applies technically to the priest acting for the

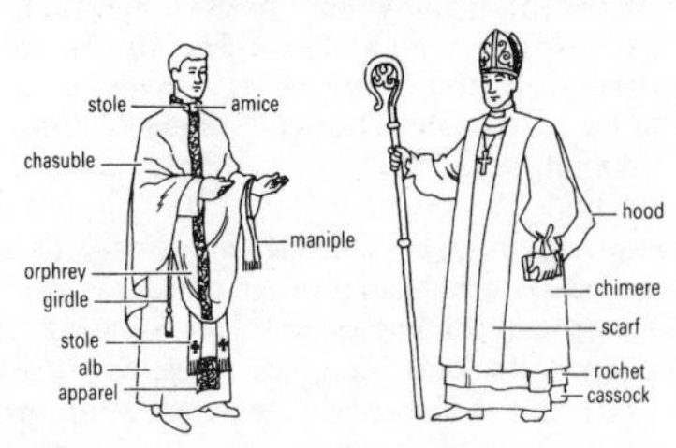

religious vestments

rector, but is widely used for any parish priest or minister. ▷ Church of England

vices, Sikh The Sikh tradition stresses five vices as being particularly harmful; lust, which is defined as undue sexual longing; wrath, or uncontrolled anger; greed—the pursuit of worldly goods for their own sake; attachment, which is defined as clinging to a person or a thing in such a way that one cannot become united with God; and egoism—reliance on self rather than having faith in God. These five vices lead to a lack of self-control and a flawed spirituality, whereas what is needed is the ability to live in the world where these five vices exist like a lotus in a muddy pool that flourishes untouched by its surroundings. Insofar as God is absolute reality and the creator of the world, it is he who gives the potentiality for goodness and for vice, both of which are present in human beings. The aim of life is to overcome vice and to know God. This involves leading a good life, but it means above all being united with God by reliance on his Grace. ▷ evil; grace

Vico, Giovanni Battista (Giambattista) (1668–1744) Italian philosopher and historian, born in Naples. He lived there for most of his life, apart from a period from 1686 to 1695 when he was tutor to the Rocca family at the castle of Vatolla, south of Salerno. He read prodigiously, if erratically, among classical and Renaissance writers and was appointed to the chair of rhetoric at the University of Naples in 1699, which was also the year of his marriage. The chair carried a poor stipend and as Vico subsequently had eight children he had to augment his income with commissions to compose ceremonial orations, official histories, biographies and the like. His own published work was extremely wide-ranging, extending into social and political theory, jurisprudence, philology, anthropology, history and rhetoric; but his major work is undoubtedly the *Scienza Nuova* (*The New Science*) which went through three major editions (1725, 1730 and 1744). He presents an original, and often strikingly modern, view of the methods and presuppositions of historical enquiry; he explains the fundamental distinctions between scientific and historical explanation, rejects the idea of a single, fixed, human nature invariant over time, and argues that the recurring cyclical developments of history can only be understood through a study of the changing expressions of human nature through language, myth and culture. His other works include the *Autobiography* (not published until 1818), *De nostri temporis studiorum ratione* (1709, 'On method in contemporary fields of study'), *De antiquissima Italorum sapientia* (1710, 'On the ancient wisdom of the Italians'), and two volumes jointly titled *On Universal Law* (1720–2).

vihara (vihāra) A Buddhist word meaning 'dwelling-place', which is the name used for a Buddhist monastery. At first the original Buddhists wandered around India, but from an early period they lived during the rainy season in small groups in settled communities, which evolved into permanent monasteries. The vihara eventually came to have a number of features, including a boundary wall, gardens, a stupa, a bodhi tree, dwelling-houses for the monks, and a worship-hall containing one or more Buddha images. The vihara is the communal focus for the monks and the local Buddhist community, both for general worship and for worship on special holy days. Sometimes, as for example in Thailand and Sri Lanka, the vihara is restricted in meaning to signify a large hall or sanctuary containing a Buddha image which lies within the wider complex of buildings. In the earlier history of the Buddhist tradition viharas became separate from cave monasteries (*guhas*) because they were free-standing buildings. Viharas in the general sense developed in different sizes, shapes and aesthetic styles, ranging from a tiny village building in Ceylon to a gigantic set of buildings at a place like Lhasa in Tibet, and to classical Zen monasteries in Japan. ▷ Buddha image; uposatha; Zen Buddhism

Vikings Raiders, traders, and settlers from Norway, Sweden, and Denmark, who between the late 8th century and the mid 11th century conquered and colonized large parts of Britain, Normandy, and Russia; attacked Spain, Morocco, and Italy; traded with Byzantium, Persia, and India; discovered and occupied Iceland and Greenland; and reached the coast of North America. As sea-borne raiders they gained a deserved reputation for brutality and destructiveness, but as merchants and settlers they played an influential and positive role in the development of medieval Europe. Their earliest overseas settlements were in the Orkney and Shetland Islands, which remained united to the Norwegian crown until 1472. ▷ Germanic religion

vinaya-pitaka (vinaya-piṭaka) The first section or basket (*pitaka*) of the Buddhist scriptures known as the *tipitaka* or Pali Canon. It deals with monastic discipline, and the other two sections focus on the discourses of the Buddha (*sutta-pitaka*), and the logical analysis of Buddhist doctrines (*abhidharma-pitaka*). The *vinaya-pitaka* deals with the early setting-up of the Buddhist community by the Buddha, and with the general rules that govern the life of the community and the particular code of conduct for individual monks and nuns. It focuses on three particular matters: rules for monks; rules for nuns; and special topics such as the ordination, holy days, dress, food, medicine, and living quarters of monks and nuns. Probably the original core of this section was the code of ethical precepts for monks known as the *Patimokkha*, which is still recited by local assemblies on two holy days every month. The centrality of monks, and to a lesser extent nuns, is a striking fact that contrasts Buddhism with other religious traditions. Nowhere else has a third portion of the scriptures been devoted to monks and nuns. Although there are other versions of the *vinaya-pitaka* in Sanskrit, Chinese and Tibetan, they do not differ greatly from that in the tipitaka, and all schools of Buddhism accept that monks are exemplary figures. ▷ Abhidharma; Patimokkha; sangha; sutta-pitaka; tipitaka

vipassana (vipassanā: Sanskrit: vipaśyanā) A form of Buddhist meditation known as 'insight meditation'. Vipassana is a direct awareness of reality, and it can arise spontaneously without the practice of meditation, but is more usually gained as a result of long concentration and meditational discipline. This is based upon the careful practice of mindfulness, especially mindfulness of each passing object. It is aimed at developing mindfulness of four things: the body as one sits or walks or performs bodily functions, feelings as they come and go, states of mind as they arise and fall, and the mental processes or dharmas. The ultimate goal and result of insight meditation is to see into the impermanence (*anicca*), unsatisfactory nature (*duhkha*), and lack of self or substance (*anatman*) in all things. It is often preceded by the practice of quietening the mind through 'calm meditation' (*samatha*), although Buddhist schools differ in their view of the relationship between these two forms of meditation. The counsel of a practitioner or master is usually considered necessary for fruitful vipassana, and different levels of insight can be obtained. Indeed, in Buddhaghosa's 'The Path of Purification' seven stages of purification are described, the last five of which refer to insight. At the highest levels, there is a break-through to a 'transcendent' level of insight, although even this is not yet equivalent to nirvana. ▷ anatman; bhavana; Buddhaghosa; dharma; duhkha; nirvana; samatha

Viracocha, or **Huirocochа** The supreme being in the state religion of the Inca empire. The meaning of the word, and even the language of origin, is unknown, and it may be a title rather than a name (even in modern times it can be used as an honorific address). The Inca, and no doubt other Andean peoples, recognized the creator deity under this name, which may have been used in the Tiahuanaco culture. Hatun Tupac Inca, 8th emperor, had a vision of Viracocha, took the name as his title and built temples to him at Cuzco and Cacha. The ninth emperor, Pachacuti, a great imperialist and religious reformer, established the worship of Viracocha as supreme being throughout the empire. Viracocha's statue, in human form, all gold, dominated the scene in the Temple of the Sun at Cuzco, the ideological centre of the empire. Divinities of conquered nations had to take a subordinate place, except for Pachacamac, whose prestige was too widespread, and who was declared to Viracocha under another name. In some Inca myths, Viracocha is seen setting up the sun and moon from Lake Titicaca, destroying the first disobedient world by a flood, and allotting the nations their respective locations, bases of livelihood and places of worship in the remade universe. Other stories suggest that Viracocha was a culture hero of the golden age and would one day return. Indeed, the Inca first took the Spaniards to be forces of the returning Viracocha, just as the Aztec saw them as those of Quetzalcoatl. The Spanish conquest, the collapse of the Inca empire and the years of disaster and depopulation seem to have broken Viracocha's dominance in the Andes. In years to come the Andean peoples combined the Christian God and local belief systems in various ways. ▷ Inca religion; Pachacamac; Pachacuti; Quetzalcoatl

Virgin Birth ▷ Immaculate Conception

Vishnu (Viṣṇu) A major Hindu deity, second in the triad (Trimurti) of gods manifesting the cosmic functions of the Supreme Being (the other two being Brahma and Shiva). The preserver of the universe and the embodiment of goodness and mercy, he is believed to have assumed visible form in nine descents (avataras): three in non-human form, one in hybrid form, and five in human form, of which his appearances as Rama and Krishna are the most important. Vaishnavites, his followers, consider him the ultimate God, and repeat his '1000 names' as an act of devotion.

Vishnu

He is generally depicted as either standing, holding weapons, or reclining on a serpent. He is usually dark-skinned, as his human incarnations have been. ▷ avatara; Brahma; Hinduism; Krishna; Shiva; Trimurti

vision quest A widespread Native American institution found, with variations, amongst Algonquin and other eastern peoples, and amongst people of the Plains and the Western Plateau. Typically, it was a young man's proving experience. He would prepare carefully by self-purification in the sweat lodge, by sacred smoking and intense prayer, by ordeal, including fasting and thirst, and by arduous seclusion in mountain or forest. In return he could receive a vision of his personal guardian spirit (often in animal form), learn of special powers now granted to him and the rules and tabus needed to keep them intact; and find the nature of his personal medicine bundle. Some by these means learned their vocation to be a medicine man or shaman; indeed, it has been debated whether the vision quest originated in a rite of passage at puberty or out of the shaman's call vision. Among Plains peoples, some adults sought and gained visions several times, as the story of Black Elk shows. Among West Coast peoples, the guardian spirit was inherited rather than separately identified. Vision quest declined with the passing of warrior culture and the breakdown of traditional life; peyote use has often become a functional substitute. ▷ Algonquin religion; Black Elk; calumet; medicine bundle; peyote; Sioux religion; sweat lodge

visions ▷ **dreams and visions**

Visser 'T Hooft, Willem Adolf (1900–85) Dutch ecumenist, born in Haarlem. He graduated in theology at Leiden and served young people's organizations until his appointment in 1938 as general secretary of what was to become the World Council of Churches, a post he held until retirement in 1966. In that role he proved himself the foremost ecumenical statesman of his generation. He insisted that the younger churches be regarded as equal partners in the common Christian task. A versatile scholar who spoke several languages fluently, he wrote many books, among which were *None Other Gods* (1937), *The Struggle of the Dutch Church* (1946), and his *Memoirs* (1973). ▷ ecumenism; World Council of Churches

Vivekananda (Vivekānanda), originally **Narendranath Datta** (1863–1902) Hindu thinker and reformer, born to a Bengali *kshatriya* family. He was educated at the Mission College in Calcutta, where he read European Philosophy with great success. His background was one of increasing Westernization and for a number of years he remained on the fringes of the Brahmo Samaj. Eventually, however, he was forced to leave as he could not accept the movement's opposition to the path of renunciation (*samnyasa*). In 1881 he met Ramakrishna, an uneducated devotee of the goddess Kali, whom Narendranath accepted as his guru. Ramakrishna led him to a personal experience of Kali and duly appointed him as his successor. In 1886 Ramakrishna died and Narendranath spent the next few years wandering the countryside. This time proved to be most productive for him as he slowly came to a position that combined the non-dualist ideas of Sankara with the devotional insight of Ramakrishna. In 1893 Narendranath obtained patronage from the Raja of Khatri to visit the World Parliament of Religion in Chicago. The Raja also suggested that he adopt the spiritual name of Vivekananda. During the Parliament, Vivekananda was a most popular speaker. Although there were other Hindus in attendance, he was the only one who gained recognition. He spoke powerfully on the subject of Hinduism as the universal truth, whilst at the same time stressing the need for tolerance. As a consequence of this success he embarked on an extensive lecture tour of the USA and Europe. In these lectures Vivekananda stressed self-reliance, arguing that people should look to themselves and not to external sources for their religious objectives. He attacked Christianity for its formality and lost spirituality. He believed that the spirituality of the East and the science and rationality of the West could come together, finding their ultimate meaning in the Vedanta. Thus he could be described as taking something of a 'Hindu inclusivist' view of religion. On returning to India he set up the Ramakrishna Mission. Although the Mission did not make the impact that Vivekananda might have hoped for, its importance should not be overlooked because of its pioneering stance on social issues. ▷ Advaita Vedanta; Brahmo Samaj; Kali; Ramakrishna Paramahasa; samnyasa; Shankara

vocation A calling to a particular way of life, service or profession. The original meaning of the term is religious. It refers to God's election of an individual to carry out his purposes. Examples of such religious vocations can be found in the calls of Samuel (I Samuel 3), Isaiah (Isaiah 6.18), Ezekiel (Ezekiel 2.1–3.11)), Paul (Acts 9; 13.2; Galatians 1.15) and Barnabas (Acts 13.2). On many occasions the call is not willingly accepted by the recipient. Thus Jeremiah resists his call on the grounds that he is 'only a youth' (Jeremiah 1.6), and Jonah 'rose to flee to Tarshish from the presence of the Lord' (Jonah 1.3). But vocation is not a phenomenon restricted exclusively to outstanding religious individuals. All human beings are called to God's service and there are a variety of ministries in which they can respond to this call. This universality of vocation was particularly stressed by Luther and Calvin, who emphasized the priesthood of all believers and applied the concept of vocation to secular occupations. Although it still retains its religious dimension, in current usage the term 'vocation' is applied to a series of professions such as medicine, teaching, engineering, law, etc, for which a higher degree of commitment is required than for non-vocational occupations. In this sense, 'vocation' is merely a synonym for 'profession'.

Voluspa (Voluspà) Literally meaning 'prophecy of the volva', this is the greatest of Norse poems. It is presented as an address, sometimes to a world audience of gods and humans, sometimes to Odin, by a prophetess who was present when the universe was formed and who foresees its end. It tells of the creation, of tragic conflicts and treachery, the death of Balder, the gods' revenge on Loki, and the day of Ragnarok when gods, monsters and universe are all destroyed and the world tree Yggdrasil splits apart. A fresh, renewed world is born in which Balder returns, reconciled with his unintentional killer, and a mighty ruler of all comes into his own. The extent of Christian influence in *Voluspa* is disputed; the poem probably comes from the period when Christianity was newly making its way in Iceland. Perhaps its author, himself of the old faith, has used some of the imagery of the new one. ▷ Balder; Loki; Odin; Ragnarok; volva; Yggdrasil

volva (vǫlva) A female seer or shaman in the old Norse religion who offered divination or fortune telling. The art was seen as belonging to the Vanir, for Freya is said to have taught it to the Aesir. The volva would sit on a high platform above her enquiring audience. A singer—on occasion, a whole choir—sang invocations of the spirits. The volva went into trance, heard spirit voices, and then announced future happenings. There is a vivid description in the saga of Erik the Red of a volva who appeared in Greenland during a famine. The story suggests that consultation of volvas continued, though with increasing rarity, in Christian times. ▷ Aesir and Vanir; divination; Freya; sagas; shamanism; Voluspa

voodoo The popular religion of Haiti, also found in the West Indies and parts of South America. The followers of this blending of Roman Catholicism with West African religion attend both the church and the voodoo temple, where a voodoo priest or priestess leads a ritual invoking of the spirits of the voodoo world through magical diagrams, songs, and prayer. The spirits possess the members in trance. ▷ magic; Roman Catholicism

vows and oaths A vow is a voluntary promise and personal commitment made to something held sacred, such as God, or to some other highest principle, such as the crown, the people, a saint, or even oneself. Vows are orientated towards the future. They commit the vow-taker to a course of action or mode of behaviour. Although they are self-imposed, vows are held to be binding and stigma is attached to any breach or failure to fulfil them. Vows can be made with regard to most human activities. The most common vows are associated with marriage or with the decision to enter a religious community, but vows can also be temporary in nature, as is the case, for example, with vows of fasting. All the major religions warn against excessive vow-taking and prescribe rules for their use. Like vows, oaths are voluntary, binding commitments. There are three main distinctions between vows and oaths. Firstly, the oath is not merely a personal act but involves the society of which the oath-taker is a member. Consequently, whereas only stigma is attached to the breaking of a vow, failure to fulfil an oath is a punishable offence. Secondly, in swearing an oath one commits one's life, honour, property or some other object of value as a pledge. These are forfeited in the event of a breach of the oath. Thirdly, an oath is a means of guaranteeing or confirming the truth of a statement, while at the same time binding the oath-taker to his statement. This accounts for the importance of the oath in legal proceedings. The Bible warns against using oaths too liberally and taking Yahweh's name in vain (cf Leviticus 19.12; Numbers 30.2; Deuteronomy 23.21; Matthew 5.34–7, 23.16–22; James 5.12).

Vratyas (Vrātyas) A sacred brotherhood in ancient India. The Vratyas were originally a military force who may have been among the first of the Aryans to enter India, thoug looked upon with disdain by Aryans wh came after. Non-Aryan ideas may have bee absorbed into orthodox brahmanical Hindu ism via the *Vratyas* and yogic techniques ecstasy, such as breath control, may hav originated with them. Some Vratyas practise celibacy and during midsummer rituals sexu intercourse was enacted between a 'prostitut (*pumshcali*) and a 'bard', a rite which may b a precursor of later Tantric rituals and th idea of the divine as possessing complemen tary male and female aspects. This rite wa known as the 'great vow' (*maha-vrata*). ▷ Aryans; Tantric Hinduism; yoga

Vulgate The Latin translation of the Chris tian Bible, originating with Jerome (c.405 who attempted to provide an authoritativ alternative to the confusing array of Old Lati versions in his day. From about the 7t century it emerged in Western Christianity a the favourite Latin version (*vulgate* meanin the 'common' edition), but was itself revise and corrupted through the centuries. In 154 the Council of Trent recognized it as th official Latin text of the Roman Catholi Church. ▷ Bible; Jerome, St; Roman Cath olicism; Trent, Council of

W

Wach, Joachim (1898–1955) German scholar of religion, born in Saxony. He was educated at Leipzig and taught there, but he left Germany during the Nazi era to teach at Brown University, Providence, Rhode Island, in the USA, and finally became Chairman of the history of religions programme at Chicago University, where he taught from 1945. His interests were wide and they centred upon the sociology of religion and comparative religion (*Sociology of Religion*, 1944, *The Comparative Study of Religions*, 1958), but he also wrote on religious experience and hermeneutics (*Types of Religious Experience—Christian and non-Christian*, 1951), *Understanding and Believing: Essays*, 1968), and in German on Mahayana Buddhism, particular themes in the study of religion, and general methodological problems. Although interested in theology, he differentiated it from the science of religion with its branches of phenomenology, history, psychology, and sociology of religion. In the latter field his wide-ranging analyses of different religious groups based on family, on religious institutions, on status, on relation to the state, and on charismatic authority, influenced later sociologists of religion. ▷ comparative religion; Eliade, Mircea; sociology of religion; study of religion; Religionswissenschaft

Wahhabis (Wahhābis) An Islamic movement which derives from Muhammad ibn Abd al-Wahhab, a religious reformer from Uyaina near Riyadh, and Muhammad ibn Saud, the ancestor of the present rulers of Saudi Arabia. The alliance was to lead to the unification in the 18th century of most of the peninsula under the Saudi banner. The modern reunification of the kingdom was carried out between 1902 and 1932 by King Abd al-Aziz, otherwise known as 'Ibn Saud'. Arabs call the followers of Abd al-Wahhab *muwahhidun* or 'unitarians' rather than Wahhabis, which is an anglicism. The movement maintains that legal decisions must be based exclusively on the Quran and the Sunnah. The original Wahhabis banned music, dancing, poetry, silk, gold, and jewellery, and in the 20th century, the *ikhwan* ('brotherhood') have attacked the telephone, radio, and television as innovations not sanctioned by God. ▷ Islam; Quran; sunnah

Waldenses, or **Waldensians** A small Christian community originating in a reform movement initiated by Peter Waldo in Lyon, France, in the 12th century. They rejected the authority of the pope, prayers for the dead, and veneration of the saints. Excommunicated and persecuted, they survived through the Middle Ages. After the Reformation, as Protestants, they continued mainly in northern Italy, with missions in South America. ▷ Protestantism; Reformation

wali (walī) The notion of a saint or holy man within the Muslim tradition, derived from the phrase *wali Allah*, 'friend of God', in Quran 10.63. Popular Islam recognizes different degrees of saintliness and different ranks of saints. At one level there is the person who is accounted to be pure; at another level there is the person who performs extraordinary acts and purveys charisma; at a higher level there is considered to be an unseen hierarchy of saints who have a cosmic significance. At the level of folk Islam, saints are very important as healing, helping and praying figures. Their tombs are often places of pilgrimage, with their distinctive domes which rest upon octagonal drums which in turn rest upon cubic structures, symbolizing the role of the saint as mediating between earth and heaven. The cult of saints has been especially important in India and North Africa. Furthermore, Sufi leaders have often been seen as saints and Sufi orders have formed around them, attracting devotion to their persons and pilgrimages to their tombs. However, some traditional Islamic groups such as the Wahhabis have questioned the cult of saints on the grounds that it is incompatible with the absolute oneness of God, *tawhid*. ▷ Allah; Folk Islam; Quran; saints in Islam; Sufism; tawhid; Wahhabis

Wali Allah, Shah (Walī Allāh, Shāh) (1703–62) Indian Muslim religious leader who lived mainly in Delhi. He grew up while the Islamic Mughal empire in India was declining, and his aim was to reform and revive Islam inwardly in India, and at the same time to defend Islam from potential attacks by non-Muslims. He did not completely reject medieval Islam like his contemporary reformer in Arabia, al-Wahhab (1703–87), but sought to synthesize Islamic law, mysticism and theology into a new integral vision that would refashion Indian Islam. He succeeded his father as local leader of the Naqshbandi Sufi order in 1719, and he attempted to purify Sufism and to join it to a purified traditional Islam (sunnah). He expounded his theories in writings such as *Hamat*, and the social and political implications of his work were developed by his son Abdul-l-Aziz (1746–1824) and his grandson Ismail (1781–1831). His dream of a revived Indo-Muslim power survived into the 20th century with consequences for Islam itself and for the states of India and Pakistan. ▷ Mughal Empire; Naqshbandiyyah; Sufism; sunnah; Wahhabis

Walker, Sir Alan Edgar (1911–) Australian Methodist clergyman and social activist, born in Sydney. He graduated there and in 1935 was ordained. His ministry in a coal-mining area of New South Wales first prompted his Christian social views, further developed while superintendent of the Waverley Methodist Mission (1944–54), and in the influential Sydney Central Methodist Mission (1958–78). He began a telephone counselling ministry that soon spread throughout the world, and after official retirement became the World Methodist Council's Director of Evangelism. His publications include *The Whole Gospel for the Whole World* (1957), *God the Disturber* (1973), *Standing up to Preach* (1983), and *Life in the Holy Spirit* (1986). ▷ evangelist; Methodism

Wang Yang-Ming (1472-1529) Chinese neo-Confucian philosopher, born in Yueh in the present Chekiang. His father was of noble birth, and he himself had a distinguished governmental career, which began in 1510 when he became a magistrate and included the suppression of a rebellion just before his death in 1529. He was the outstanding figure in the idealistic school of neo-Confucianism known as the school of Mind. Before his time Chu Hsi's school of Principle had been in the ascendant with its distinction between principle (*li*), which is unchanging and derives from the Supreme Ultimate, and substance (*chi*), which determines change. In his *Enquiry on the Great Learning*, Wang Yang Ming outlines his teaching: principle is identified with the mind; principle can be discovered by investigating the mind, through ethical reflection and meditation; the highest good is already innate in the mind; and by living out the innate knowledge of moral goodness already present in the mind the good life will certainly ensue. Wang Yang Ming's emphasis was monistic and moral whereas Chu Hsi's had been more intellectual and was influential in China and Japan. ▷ Chu Hsi; li; neo-Confucianism

waqf A Muslim term for the giving of property or money by pious endowment for charitable purposes. The gift could be used to maintain or build up an educational enterprise, a hospital, a mosque, or a Sufi establishment. It was normally donated permanently and could not be regained by the original donor. However, it became possible to set up a waqf for one's own family, whereby the right to manage the trust continued within the family. The custom has been very beneficial to Islamic enterprises, but in modern times has promoted two competing problems because of the extensive nature of waqf lands. On the one hand, Islamic governments have attempted to diminish the importance of family waqfs and to place them under greater government control; on the other hand, where waqf land administered by the state has become very extensive and has induced economic dilemmas, there have sometimes been attempts to divert it to more efficient and perhaps private ownership. ▷ mosque; Sufism

Way International A new religious movement within the Christian tradition. It was founded by an American evangelical Christian named Dr Victor Paul Wierwille, and it engages in teaching and research in connection with the Bible. However, it stresses the New Testament rather than the Old Testament, and it interprets the New Testament through Wierwille's eyes. It offers a course called *Power for Abundant Living*, which outlines Wierwille's interpretations and also instructs in speaking in tongues. It does not accept the Hebrew Old Testament as being authentic and it views Jesus as a perfect man but not as God, thereby becoming suspect in the eyes of Christian orthodoxy. It has, however, achieved some success because of the fervour and simplicity of its message. ▷ Jesus Christ; new religious movements in the West; New Testament; Old Testament

Weber, Max (1864–1920) German sociologist. Born in Erfurt, he was educated at the universities of Heidelberg, Berlin and Göttingen. He taught law at Berlin from 1892, political economy at Freiburg from 1894, and economics at Heidelberg from 1897. Not until the end of his life did he consider himself a sociologist. In 1897, following the death of his father, he suffered a serious nervous break down, and was given leave to recover. Until 1918, when he accepted a Chair of Sociology in Vienna, he lived largely as a private scholar. In 1919 he took over the Chair of Sociology at Munich. Weber is regarded as one of the founders of sociology. One of his main interests was his theory that religious and ethical concepts play a major role in shaping society. This he outlined in *Die protestantische Ethik und der Geist des Kapitalismus* (1904–5, trans as *The Protestant Ethic and the Spirit of Capitalism*, 1930). He later tried to determine what aspect of Western spiritual culture shaped the formation of capitalism, publishing his results in the three-volume *Gesammelte Aufsätze zur Religionssoziologie* (1920–1, trans as *The Religions of the East Series*, 1952–8). His work is extremely wide-ranging, with perhaps his greatest achievements being his comparative and historical studies of large-scale social institutions. He was also an advocate of the interpretive approach to social science.

Weil, Simone (1909–43) French philosopher and religious writer, born in Paris. She came from a Jewish intellectual family and had a brilliant academic career at school and university in Paris. Throughout her short life she combined the most sophisticated scholarly and philosophical interests with an extreme moral intensity and a dedicated identification with the interests of the oppressed and exploited. She taught philosophy in schools from 1931 to 1938, interspersing this with periods of hard manual labour on farms and at the Renault works in order to experience directly working-class life. Her political commitment was intensified in 1936 when she served in a non-military capacity with the Republican side in the Spanish Civil War. In 1941 she settled briefly in Marseille where, under the influence of the Dominican Father Perrin and Gustave Thibon, she developed a deep mystical feeling for the Catholic faith, yet a profound temperamental reluctance to join any organized religion or institutional framework. She left France in 1942, first for the USA, then Britain, where she worked for the French resistance in London. She finally starved herself to death, refusing to eat while the victims of World War II still suffered. Her posthumously-published writings are highly individual, often combining severe argumentation with impassioned spiritualism, and they have reached a large popular readership. They include: *La Pesanteur et la Grâce* (1947, trans as *Gravity and Grace*, 1952), *L'Enracinement* (1949, trans as *The Need for Roots*, 1952), *Attente de Dieu* (1950, trans as *Waiting for God*, 1951), *Oppression et Liberté* (1955, trans as *Oppression and Liberty*, 1958), and *Leçons de Philosophie* (1933–4, trans as *Lectures on Philosophy*, 1978). ▷ mysticism; Roman Catholicism

Wellhausen, Julius (1844–1918) German biblical scholar, born in Hameln. He was professor at Greifswald (1872), Halle (1882), Marburg (1885) and Göttingen (1892), and is best known for his investigations into Old Testament history and source criticism of the Pentateuch. He published several works, notably the *Prolegomena zur Geschichte Israels* (1883, trans as *History of Israel* 1885). ▷ Old Testament; Pentateuch

Wesley, Charles (1707–88) English hymn-writer and evangelist, brother of John Wesley, born in Epworth, Lincolnshire, son of the rector there. He studied at Christ Church College, Oxford, where he formed (1729) a small group of fellow students, nicknamed the 'Oxford Methodists', or the 'Holy Club', later joined by his brother. Ordained in 1735, he accompanied John to Georgia as secretary to Governor James Oglethorpe, returning to England in 1736. He was the indefatigable lieutenant of his more famous brother; after an evangelical conversion in 1738, he wrote over 5500 hymns, including such well-loved favourites as 'Jesu, Lover of my soul', 'Hark, the Herald Angels sing', and 'Love divine, all loves excelling'. ▷ evangelist; Wesley, John

Wesley, John (1703–91) English evangelist and founder of Methodism, brother of Charles Wesley, and son of the rector of Epworth, Lincolnshire. In 1720 he passed from the Charterhouse to Christ Church College, Oxford. He was ordained deacon in 1725, and in 1726 became a fellow of Lincoln and Greek lecturer. In 1727 he left Oxford to assist his father. In 1728 he was ordained a priest, and the following year returned to Oxford as a tutor. At this time he was much influenced by the spiritual writings of William Law. He became leader of a small dedicated group which had gathered round his brother Charles, nicknamed the 'Holy Club' or the 'Oxford Methodists', a name later adopted by John for the adherents of the great evangelical movement which was its outgrowth. The members of the club, who in 1730 were joined by James Hervey and George Whitefield, practised their religion with a then extraordinary degree of devotion, in strict accordance with the rubrics. On his father's death (1735), accompanied by Charles, he went as a missionary to Georgia, where his lack of experience led him to make many mistakes and aroused the hostility of the colonists. After an unfortunate love-affair he returned to England (1738). He had been influenced by Moravians on the voyage out, and now he met Peter Böhler, and attended society meetings. At one of these, held in Aldersgate Street, during the reading of Luther's preface to the epistle to the Romans, he experienced an assurance of salvation which convinced him that he must bring the same assurance to others. But his unwonted zeal alarmed and angered most of the parish clergy, who closed their pulpits against him; this intolerance, Whitefield's example, and the needs of the masses drove him into the open air at Bristol (1739). There he founded the first Methodist chapel. He preached in, and bought, the ruinous Foundry in Moorfields, London, Methodist anniversaries sometimes being reckoned from this event; the Foundry was for long the headquarters of Methodism in the capital. During his itinerary of half a century, 10000 to 30000 people would wait patiently for hours to hear him. He gave his strength to working-class neighbourhoods; hence the mass of his converts were colliers, miners, foundrymen, weavers, and day-labourers in towns. His life was frequently in danger, but he outlived all persecution, and the itineraries of his old age were triumphal processions from one end of the country to the other. During his unparalleled apostolate he travelled 250000 miles and preached 40000 sermons. Yet he managed to do a prodigious amount of literary work, and produced grammars, extracts from the classics, histories, abridged biographies, collections of psalms, hymns and tunes, his own sermons and journals, and founded the *Methodist Magazine* (1778). His works were so popular that he made £30000, which he distributed in charity during his life. He founded charitable institutions at Newcastle and London, and Kingswood School in Bristol. Wesley broke with the Moravians in 1745, and his acceptance of what was then known as an Arminian theology led to divergences with Whitefield in 1741, a separate organization of Calvinistic Methodists under the Countess of Huntingdon, and to an acute controversy (1769–78) with Augustus Toplady. Wesley was determined to remain loyal to the Church of England and urged his followers to do the same; but increasing pressures were brought to bear on him and in 1784 he himself ordained one of his assistants (Francis Asbury) for work in the USA (much to his brother's distress), a practice which he later extended. However, he always regarded Methodism as a movement within the Church and it remained so during his lifetime. In 1751 he married the widow Mary Vazeille, who deserted him in 1776. His journeys and spiritual odyssey were recorded in his *Journal* (1735–90). ▷ Asbury, Francis; evangelicalism; Jesuits; Law, William; Locke, John; Luther, Martin; Methodism; Moravian Brethren; Wesley, Charles; Whitefield, George

Western magical tradition With the triumph of Christianity in the West, older Western magical traditions either disappeared or merged inconspicuously into popular rural Christianity. There was, however, a revival of interest in a more sophisticated version of magic at the time of the Renaissance through the work of Pico della Mirandola (1463–94) and Marsilio Ficino (1433–99). They uncovered some of the hidden insights of Hermetism, the Kabbalah and neo-platonism and used this revised notion of magic for spiritual rather than merely functional ends. Although ritual techniques were used whereby one could atune oneself to the universe, the aim was not so much to change the world as to change oneself so that one became a more spiritual person and a better vessel for God's purposes. Important thinkers fed into this tradition, notably Paracelsus with his stress on healing and his mystical theosophy based on neo-platonism. The heyday of the scientific revolution in the 17th century brought a decline in interest in magic, but since the mid-19th century there has been a new concern for magic as part of the occult. The Hermetic Order of the Golden Dawn, founded in 188 by S Liddell MacGregor Mathers (1854–1918), was an important influence in the mini-revival of magic in the West, as was the work of A L Constant (1810–75) with Tarot Cards, and the more high-profile activities of individuals such as Aleister Crowley. The practice of magic continues in the West through the group of organizations spawned by the Golden Dawn Order, and in more informal ways. ▷ Crowley, (Edward) Aleister; Ficino, Marsilio; Hermetica, Hermetism; Kabbalah; neo-platonism; Paracelsus; Tarot

Westminster Confession of Faith The main Presbyterian Confession of Faith adopted by the Westminster Assembly, England, in 1643. It sets forth the main doctrines of the Christian faith from a Calvinistic perspective, and became the major confessional influence among Reformed Churches of the English-speaking world. ▷ confession 1; Calvinism; Reformed Churches

wheel of law, Buddhist (wheel of dharma) In his first sermon, the Buddha is said by Buddhists to have 'set in motion the wheel of the dharma'. After his enlightenment at Bodhgaya, he went on a journey that took him to the deer park at Sarnath just outside Banaras, and there he preached this famous sermon to five ascetics who had formerly been his companions when he himself had tried the way of asceticism. It marks the effective beginning of the Buddhist tradition. It was one of the four key events in the life of the Buddha, the others being his birth at Lumbini, his enlightenment at Bodhgaya, and his death at Kusinara. The teaching or dharma of the sermon, the wheel of which the Buddha set in motion at Sarnath, commended the middle way between the extremes of luxury and asceticsm, and emphasized the importance of the four noble truths that lay at the core of the message of the Buddha: all life is suffering; suffering results from craving; suffering can be ended by the elimination of craving; and this can happen in practice by following the eightfold path outlined by the Buddha. In early Buddhism the wheel became the symbol of the Buddha's teaching, and one of the key gestures made by the Buddha on Buddha images is to form a wheel with his hands to symbolize his teaching which, according to Buddhists, is superior to that of any earthly ruler. ▷ ariya sacca; Banaras; Bodhgaya; Buddha; Buddha image; dharma; eightfold path; Kusinara; Lumbini; Middle Way; mudras; Sarnath

wheel of life A Tibetan Buddhist symbol of the cosmos and the processes of karma and rebirth. The wheel of life is depicted as a large circle in the arms and jaws of Yama, the Lord of death. Within the circle are six, or sometimes five, realms (*gati-s*) in which beings can be reborn. These are (clockwise from the top) as follows: the heavenly realms of the gods (*deva-s*), experiencing bliss and pleasure; the realm of the jealous gods (*asuras*) who seek power and are constantly at war; the animal realm, characterized by dullness; the hell realm, where beings are tormented for their evil deeds; the realm of the hungry ghosts (*preta-s*) driven by insatiable thirst; and finally the human realm, characterized by birth, old age and death. Bodhisattvas are depicted teaching, out of compassion, in all these realms according to beings' levels of understanding. A being can be reborn anywhere in this wheel depending upon its karma. The outer circle of the wheel depicts in vivid images the 12 links of dependent origination (*pratityasamutpada*) which are the psychological processes of karma formation. At the hub of the wheel a cock, a snake and a pig chase each other, representing the root causes of human suffering: delusion or egotism, hate and greed. There is hope, however, and the white path of enlightenment leads out of hell. The wheel of life is a multi-levelled symbol used as a teaching device and understood in both psychological and cosmological terms. ▷ bodhisattva; dependent origination; karma; rebirth

White Eagle Lodge The centre of a new religious movement in Britain which makes available the teaching of an American Indian named White Eagle. His teachings are channelled through Grace Cooke and to this extent fit into the channelling model that is sometimes part of new age religion. White Eagle's teachings centre on the notion of communion with God by means of inner spirituality, and they include elements of astrology, ecology, healing, holism and rebirth. They advocate living in accord with the rhythms of nature and the rhythms of life, and are thus an attempt to adapt some of the strands of American Indian religion to a Western context. ▷ astrology; new age religion; new religious movements in the West; rebirth

Whitefield, George (1714–70) English evangelist, one of the founders of Methodism, born in the Bell Inn, Gloucester. At 18 he entered Pembroke College, Oxford, as a servitor. The Wesleys had already laid the foundations of Methodism at Oxford, and Whitefield became an enthusiastic evangelist. He took deacon's orders in 1736, and preached his first sermon in the Crypt Church, Gloucester. In 1738 he followed John Wesley to Georgia and was appointed minister at Savannah. He returned to England in 1739 to be admitted to priest's orders, and to collect funds for an orphanage. Religious interest was low, and Whitefield was actively opposed by his fellow churchmen, but when the parish pulpits were denied him he preached in the open air, the first time with great effect, on Kingswood Hill near Bristol. He quickly returned to Georgia and made extensive preaching tours. About 1741, differences on predestination led to his separation as a rigid Calvinist from John Wesley as an Arminian. His supporters now built him a chapel in Bristol and the Moorfields 'Tabernacle' in London. He reached immense audiences, but founded no distinct sect, and many of his adherents followed the Countess of Huntingdon in Wales and ultimately helped to form the Calvinistic Methodists. The Countess appointed him her chaplain, and built and endowed many chapels for him. He made seven evangelistic visits to America, and spent the rest of his life in preaching tours through England, Scotland (1741) and Wales. He compiled a hymn book in 1753. He set out for America for the last time in 1769, and died near Boston. ▷ Arminius, Jacobus; Calvinism; evangelist; Methodism; predestination; Wesley, Charles; Wesley, John

White Friars ▷ Carmelites

Whitehead, Alfred North (1861–1947) English mathematician and idealist philosopher, born in London. He was educated at Sherborne and Trinity College, Cambridge, where he was senior lecturer in mathematics until 1911. He became Professor of Applied Mathematics at Imperial College, London (1914–24), and of Philosophy at Harvard (1924–37). Extending the Booleian symbolic logic in a highly original *Treatise on Universal Algebra* (1898), he contributed a remarkable memoir to the Royal Society, 'Mathematical Concepts of the Material World' (1905). Profoundly influenced by Giuseppe Peano, he collaborated with his former pupil at Trinity, Bertrand Russell, in the *Principia Mathematica* (1910–13), the greatest single contribution to logic since Aristotle. In his Edinburgh Gifford Lectures, *Process and Reality* (1929), he attempted a metaphysics comprising psychological as well as physical experience, with events as the ultimate components of reality. Other more popular works include *Adventures of Ideas* (1933) and *Modes of Thought* (1938). He was awarded the first James Scott Prize (1922) of the Royal Society of Edinburgh. ▷ Aristotle; idealism; Russell, Bertrand Arthur William

White Lotus Society One of the most famous of a number of sects that have arisen in Chinese history, an earlier one being the Yellow Turbans who rebelled against the Han dynasty in 184CE. The White Lotus Society arose within Pure Land Buddhism during the southern Sung dynasty (1127–1279), but went in its own direction, developed its own rituals and temples, allowed its priests to marry, and included elements from Taoism and Chinese folk religion. In the early 14th century its more radical leaders borrowed features from the Manichaeans and Maitreya Buddhism, including the notion of a future saviour who would usher in a third stage of history when there would be a paradise on earth. It fomented a rebellion in 1351, and took part in the movement that overthrew the Mongol rulers of China in 1368. It later instigated the so-called White Lotus rebellion between 1796 and 1805. Although authentically religious societies such as the White Lotus tended to be drawn into anti-government activities because of their popular and radical character. ▷ folk religion; Maitreya; Manichaeism; Mongols; Pure Land Buddhism

Williams, Roger (c.1604–1683) English-born American clergyman, the founder of Rhode Island. Born in London, educated at the Charterhouse and Pembroke College, Cambridge, he took Anglican orders, became an extreme Puritan, and emigrated to New England in 1630. He refused to join the congregation at Boston because it would not make public repentance for having been in communion with the Church of England; he therefore went to Salem, but was soon in trouble for denying the right of magistrates to punish Sabbath-breaking. For his opposition to the New England theocracy he was driven from Salem, and took refuge in Plymouth. Two years later he returned to Salem, only to meet renewed persecution and banishment (1635). He escaped to the shores of Narragansett Bay on Rhode Island, where he purchased lands belonging to the Indians, founded the city of Providence (1636), and established a pure democracy. Having adopted the tenet of adult baptism, he established (1639) the first Baptist church in America. In 1643 and 1651 he went to England to procure a charter for his colony, and published a *Key into the Language of America* (1643), *The Bloudy Tenent of Persecution for Cause of Conscience* (1644), *The Bloudy Tenent yet more bloudy by Mr Cotton's Endeavour to wash it White in the Blood of the Lamb* (1652), and other works. He returned to Rhode Island in 1654, and was president of the colony till 1658. Renowned as an apostle of religious toleration, he refused to persecute the Quakers, but had a famous controversy with them—recorded in *George Fox digged out of his Burrowes* (1676). ▷ Anglican Communion; Fox, George; Puritanism; Friends, Society of

windigo The Ojibwa term for a monster known to Algonquin peoples. The windigo was originally a hunter who was led by hunger to eat human flesh. Now he lives in the forests and dangerous places, tracking and devouring unsuspecting humans. Anyone who eats human flesh (famine was a constant hazard for many Algonquin groups) will turn into a windigo. ▷ Algonquin religion

wine An alcoholic beverage made from fermented grape juice. In many cultures wine, due to its resemblance to blood, was offered as a sacrificial libation or as a gift to the gods or the ancestral dead. At the same time many religious traditions have prohibited excessive indulgence in wine and condemned drunkenness. ▷ Eucharist; food and drink

wine in Islam Strictly speaking alcohol, drugs, and all other intoxicants that affect consciousness, are forbidden in Islam. However, the situation is complicated by the fact that in Sufi (mystical) Islam wine is a symbol of divine knowledge, and a famous mystical 'wine ode' was written by Ibn al-Farid (1181–1235), a well-known Arab Sufi poet. In addition, the Quran states that in paradise there will be rivers of wine. Wine has been allowed in Islam for medicinal purposes, and in modern civil codes alcohol has been licensed for sale in some Islamic countries. However, whatever loopholes there may have been, the general Islamic practice is prohibition of alcohol, and this has been reinforced by the recent rise of Islamic fundamentalism. ▷ Paradise; Quran; Sufism

wisdom Practical knowledge gained through experience and observation of the universe and human nature. The basic principle of wisdom is to discover the laws underlying reality and thereby provide the human being with the ability to cope successfully with everyday life. Wisdom literature contains observations of the cosmos, studies of human and animal behaviour, discussions of the meaning of life, as well as practical advice and warnings concerning marriage, adultery, the dangers of alcohol, the folly of a loose tongue, etc. In many cultures wise sayings were collected and set down on paper. Thus wisdom literature can be found in ancient Egypt, Mesopotamia, Israel, Persia, and China. Examples of wisdom literature in the Bible and Apocrypha are Proverbs, Ecclesiastes, Job, Sirach, the Wisdom of Solomon, Tobit and IV Maccabees. The basic form of this literature is the proverb, but as wisdom literature developed greater use was made of lengthy discourses. Although wisdom was originally concerned with everyday, secular issues, it very rapidly became theologized. In learning about the workings of the universe and what is good for humankind, it was held that one was also discovering God's will for humankind. Living in harmony with the universe thus became synonymous with living in harmony with God's will. Wisdom also came to be seen as an attribute of God. There was also an increasing tendency to identify wisdom with revelation. A wise man thus became a person who ordered his life according to divine revelation. In Christianity a new development took place in Paul's contrast between earthly and divine wisdom. From the perspective of earthly wisdom, the cross of Christ is foolishness, but this earthly wisdom is itself made foolish by the cross (I Corinthians 1.18–22, 2.6–8). Elsewhere in the New Testament Christ himself is identified with wisdom (Luke 7.35; Luke 2.40, 52; 12.42, 11.31).

Wisdom, Book of ▷ Wisdom of Solomon

wisdom literature In the Hebrew Bible, a group of writings, usually including Proverbs, Ecclesiastes, the Song of Songs, and Job, although the influence of wisdom may also be found in other biblical stories (eg Esther) and in some of the Psalms. Amongst the Apocrypha, it also includes Ecclesiasticus and the Wisdom of Solomon. The literature is usually traced to a special class of sages in Israel who sought to draw lessons for life from general human experience rather than from revealed religious truths, although in fact their humanistic observations were often integrated with a belief in Yahweh and his law. ▷ Ecclesiastes/Ecclesiasticus/Job/Proverbs, Book of; Old Testament; Solomon; Wisdom of Solomon

wisdom literature, Ancient Egyptian Genre of instructive literature found in Egypt from the Old Kingdom (c.2686–2181BCE) onwards. The texts are normally presented as the address of a wise man to his son in the form of a collection of sayings or precepts. These contain pragmatic advice for correct behaviour and a life in accordance with Maat, the divine order. The genre is very similar to Israelite wisdom, and may have influenced it. Indeed one Egyptian text, *The Instruction of Amenemope*, bears so many similarities to part of the Book of Proverbs that there is probably a literary relationship between the two. ▷ literature, Ancient Egyptian; Maat; Proverbs, Book of

Wisdom of Jesus, the Son of Sirach ▷ Ecclesiasticus, Book of

Wisdom of Solomon, or **Book of Wisdom** A book of the Old Testament Apocrypha, or deuterocanonical work in the Catholic Bible, purportedly by Solomon, but usually attributed to an unknown Alexandrian Jew c.1st century BCE. Like other Jewish wisdom literature it praises the figure of Wisdom above ungodliness, but is a mixture of poetry and philosophical prose rather than short aphorisms. The follies of idolatry are emphasized, and reinforced by examples from Exodus of the contrasting fates of the faithful Israelites and idolatrous Egyptians. ▷ Apocrypha, Old Testament; Solomon

Wise Men ▷ Magi

Wishart, George (c.1513–1546) Scottish reformer and martyr, born in Angus; his eldest brother was a lawyer (king's advocate). In 1538 George was a schoolmaster at the grammar school in Montrose, where he incurred a charge of heresy for teaching the Greek New Testament. In 1539 he was in Bristol, and had to abjure heresy again. The next few years he spent on the Continent, and during this period translated the Swiss *Confession of Faith.* In 1543 he accompanied a commission sent to Scotland by Henry VIII to negotiate a marriage contract between his infant son, Prince Edward (the future Edward VI) and Mary, Queen of Scots; and he preached the Lutheran doctrine of justification by faith at Dundee and Montrose, in Ayrshire and East Lothian. At Cardinal David Beaton's insistence he was arrested in 1546, and burned at St Andrews on 1 March. John Knox was first inspired by Wishart. ▷ heresy; Knox, John

witchcraft A term that can be used in three different senses. In primal societies it is considered to be a psychic power usually held by women, and which is often (but not always) used in mysterious ways to harm people. In primal and especially African societies witchcraft is often used to explain mysterio calamity and death. The psychic power of witch is often unconscious in contrast to th of a sorcerer, which is more premeditated ar evil. In medieval Europe from the 14th ce tury onwards witchcraft was seen as a satan heretical religion involving a pact with t devil, and it was condemned by a papal bu of 1484. Accusations that witches engaged black masses, flew on broomsticks, had pe sonal devils as 'familiars' and so on sprea and by 1700 it is estimated that over 2000 people had been executed for witchcraft, ar outbreaks of witch-hunting, like that at Sale Massachusetts in 1692, became notorious. the modern West witchcraft in the form neo-paganism has emerged as a new religio movement. Influenced by the anthropologic theories of Margaret Murray (1863–1963) ar the work of Gerald Gardner (1884–1964) looks back to roots in pre-Christian paganis involving fertility rituals, nature religion, ar the worship of a Mother Goddess. Hundre of covens of neo-pagan witches are said practise semi-secretly in different parts of t Western world. ▷ neo-paganism; Satan

Alaskan puffin-beak rattle, used by witches to create storms

witchcraft and sorcery, African Followi E E Evans Pritchard in relation to the Zan people, it is common to distinguish witchcra (an innate power and desire to hurt othe without using instruments or 'medicine') fro sorcery (the use of means to bring harm others supernaturally). In principle, anyo may use sorcery (though there are specialis in it), whereas witches are physically so const tuted, often by heredity. Witchcraft, as th more insidious and unpredictable, is the mo dangerous threat to a community. Witchcra is typically believed to occur within a fami or among neighbours ie not among natur enemies but among those who ought to b friends. It threatens trust and harmony; su picion on a large scale suggests a society danger of disruption. Traditionally, witchcra accusations required legal process, and oft an ordeal by poison or other hazard. It wa the function of the 'witch doctor' to assist th detection of witch activity and the identif cation of culprits. Times of high stress som times produced witch-finding movemen aimed at smelling out concealed saboteurs the community. Colonial governments, anx ous to protect innocent victims, outlawed th ordeal and the witch-finding groups, and th independent African governments hav retained that legislation. But removing leg means of prosecuting witches did not remov fear of witch activity, and in some cas probably increased it. Part of the significan of the prophet-healing African Independent churches is their confrontation of witch beliefs. Not only do they offer hope of protection against witches, but also hope of cleansing for witches, since people confess to witchcraft and desire to be free of it. The procedures of the new religious movements suggest that in many cases what is identified as witchcraft can be interpreted as hatred and malice objectified. ▷ African Independent churches; Evans-Pritchard, Sir Edward Evan

Wittgenstein, Ludwig Josef Johann (1889–1951) Austrian-born British philosopher who became one of the most influential and charismatic figures in British philosophy this century. He was born in Vienna into a wealthy and cultivated family, the son of an industrialist. He was educated at home until the age of 14, then at an Austrian school for three years; he went on to study mechanical engineering at Berlin (1906–8) and at Manchester (1908–11), where he did research on aeronautics and designed a reaction jet propeller. He became seriously interested in mathematics, and then in the foundations of mathematics, and in 1911 abandoned his engineering research and moved to Cambridge to study mathematical logic under Bertrand Russell (1912–13). He studied with enormous intensity and Russell said admiringly that he 'soon knew all that I had to teach'.

Wittgenstein served in World War I in the Austrian army as an artillery officer and was taken prisoner on the Italian front in 1918. Throughout the war he had continued to work on problems in logic, carrying his notebooks round with him in his kitbag, and in the POW camp near Monte Cassino he completed his first work, the only one published in his lifetime, and sent it to Russell in England. It was eventually published in 1921 under the title *Logisch-philosophische Abhandlung* (and then in 1922, with a parallel German-English text and an introduction from Russell, as *Tractatus Logico-Philosophicus*). This was a novel, rather startling work, consisting of a series of numbered, aphoristic remarks centred on the nature and limits of language. Meaningful language, he conceived, must consist in propositions (or combinations of propositions) that are 'pictures' of the facts of which the world is composed. On this criterion we must discard as literally meaningless a lot of our conventional discourse, including judgements of value, and many of the claims of speculative philosophy. And since the limits of language are also the limits of thought, he reaches the rather portentous conclusion 'whereof one cannot speak, thereof one must be silent'.

This scheme for a logically foolproof language, a perfect instrument for meaningful assertion, seemed to represent a kind of terminus and Wittgenstein now turned away from philosophy to find another vocation. He gave away the money he had inherited and lived a simple ascetic life, working as an elementary schoolteacher in Austrian country districts (1920–6), a gardener's assistant in a monastery, and an amateur architect and builder commissioned by one of his sisters. In the late 1920s he was sought out by various philosophers who had found inspiration in the *Tractatus*, particularly Friedrich Schlick and the logical positivists of the Vienna Circle, and he revived his philosophical interests and returned to Cambridge in 1929, first as a research fellow of Trinity College and then as Professor of Philosophy (1939–47), interrupted only by a period of war service as a porter at Guy's Hospital, London, and a lab assistant at the Royal Victoria Infirmary in Newcastle. He became a naturalized British subject in 1938. At Cambridge his philosophy began to take a quite new direction; he attracted a group of devoted pupils and through his lectures and the circulation of his students' notes he came to exert a powerful influence on philosophy throughout the English-speaking world. The work of this second period of his philosophical career is best summarized in the posthumous *Philosophical Investigations* (1953), a discursive and often enigmatic work which rejects most of the assumptions and conclusions of the *Tractatus*. In the *Investigations* Wittgenstein no longer tries to reduce language to a perfect logical model, but rather points to the variety, open-endedness and subtlety of everyday language and explores the actual communicative and social functions of different modes of speech or 'language games'. Language is seen as a toolkit not a calculus. Philosophy then becomes a therapeutic technique of 'assembling reminders' of usage, which reveal the source of many philosophical paradoxes in the misunderstanding of ordinary language and the obsessive search for unity or simplicity where none exists. Instead of expecting each concept to have a single, defining essence we should rather look for a range of overlapping 'family resemblances'. Wittgenstein died of cancer in Cambridge, and there has been a continuous stream of posthumously edited publications from his prolific notebooks and manuscripts, including *Remarks on the Foundations of Mathematics* (1956), *The Blue and Brown Books* (1958), *Philosophische Bemer-*

kungen (1964) and *On Certainty* (1969). ▷ logical positivism; Russell, Bertrand Arthur William

wives of the Prophet Muhammad's first wife was a widow, Khadijah, whom he married in 595 when he was 25 and she was 40. Although she died in 619, three years before the crucial migration from Mecca to Medina, she had a great influence upon Muhammad, giving him vital encouragement in his sense of mission. She bore him four daughters, one of whom, Fatima, married Muhammad's cousin Ali and had a son, Husayn, who became revered among Shiite Muslims. After Khadijah died Muhammad married a number of other wives. Although Islam limited marriage to four wives at a time, Muhammad was able to marry more widely through special revelation. Most of his marriages were to widows or were contracted for political rather then personal reasons. One exception was Aishah (613–78), who was betrothed to Muhammad at the age of six, and to whom he was emotionally and spiritually close. Muhammad claimed that spiritual inspiration did not come to him in bed unless he was with Aishah. Another exception was Zaynab bint Sahsh. In all Muhammad married 11 times, and this was in line with prophetic precedents such as David, who also married a number of wives. ▷ Ali; David; Husayn; hegira; Khadijah; Mecca; Medina; Muhammad; Shiism

Wojtyla, Karol Jozef ▷ **John Paul II**

Wolsey, Thomas (c.1475–1530) English prelate and statesman, born in Ipswich, the son of a prosperous butcher and grazier. He studied at Magdalen College, Oxford, succeeding to a fellowship and obtaining a post as master in the seminary attached to the foundation. After 19 years at Oxford the living at Lymington in Somerset was bestowed on him, and influence brought him the post of secretary and domestic chaplain to the Archbishop of Canterbury. With the primate's death in 1502 Wolsey was endowed with the chaplaincy of Calais, where his ability brought him to the notice of Henry VII. Appointed a chaplain to the king (1507), he was careful to cultivate the favour of Bishop Fox, the Lord Privy Seal, and that of the treasurer of the royal household, Sir Thomas Lovel. Entrusted with the transaction of much of the sovereign's private business, the skill in negotiation he exhibited in his embassies to Scotland and the Low Countries brought him the lucrative deanery of Lincoln.

With the accession of Henry VIII, Wolsey strove to render himself indispensable. From almoner to royal councillor, from the registrarship of the Order of the Garter to a Windsor canonry, his progress to the deanery of York was steady and encouraging for a pluralist whose growing need for money was only matched by his increasing arrogance. In 1513 Wolsey accompanied the king to France; and with the English monarch ready to come to terms with Francis I, Wolsey's conduct of the negotiations brought him the bishopric of Lincoln, the archbishopric of York (1514), a cardinalate (1515), and the promise of Gallic support for further claims to preferment. In the same year, he was made Lord Chancellor and his very considerable estates were augmented by Henry's award of the administration of the see of Bath and Wells and the temporalities of the wealthy abbey of St Alban's. Wolsey even hazarded a breach of the Statute of Praemunire by accepting the appointment of papal legate from Leo X.

Deep in the king's confidence, the cardinal had attained a position more powerful than that enjoyed by any minister of the Crown since Thomas à Becket. As the controller of England's foreign policy he lent support to France and Germany alternately, entering into a secret alliance with the emperor Charles V against Francis I, always seeking to improve England's position. His aim in England was absolute monarchy with himself behind the throne. He established Cardinal's College (later Christ Church College) at Oxford and a grammar school at Ipswich. Wolsey's downfall originated in his prevarication and evasiveness over the question of Henry's divorce from Catherine of Aragon. This not only provoked the king's angry impatience but aroused the bitter enmity of the Anne Boleyn faction and of many other enemies, outraged by the cardinal's haughtiness, his parvenu display, and his punishing fiscal exactions. In effect, Wolsey's outmoded assertion of the ecclesiastical right to dominate secular policy had proved entirely unacceptable to the upstart but powerful aristocracy of the counting-house bred by the new spirit of mercantilism. Prosecuted under the Statute of Praemunire in 1529, the cardinal had to surrender the Great Seal and retire to Winchester. Impeachment by the House of Lords was followed by the forfeiture of all his property to the Crown. Arrested again on a charge of high treason, he died while journeying from his York diocese to London. ▷ Becket, St Thomas à

women in religion In many religious traditions women have been regarded as inferior and subordinate to men. Their role in such religions has been restricted to menial and secondary roles, and they have not for the most part been permitted to lead religious services. In religions where fertility is central, however, women have tended to play a more prominent role and have often been involved at the centre of divine worship. ▷ Christianity, women in; feminist theology; gender roles; harem; Islam, women in; Judaism, women in; menstruation

wondjina, or **wandjina** The name used by the Worora, Ngarinyin and other aboriginal peoples of the Kimberley area of Western Australia for ancestral beings of the Dreaming or altjiranga (the fundamental, creative, timeless epoch of the world). They created everything in the local environment, and continue to provide the rain that sustains life. They are represented in profusion in rock paintings in the area, usually shown head and shoulders, though occasionally full figure; their faces show eyes and nose, but no mouth; a form like a large halo appears behind the head. The figures occur singly or in groups, often accompanied by representations of animals, birds, plants, reptiles and heavenly bodies. Local people believe that the images were imprinted by the wondjina themselves, and that they still transmit their active presence. Other parts of Australia show different figures of the Dreaming. In Arnhem Land the rainbow serpent predominates, and certain human figures occur in the rock paintings of Eastern Australia. Central Australia seems to lack an equivalent; here local totemic ancestors are more important than such figures of the Dreaming. ▷ altjiranga; Australian Aboriginal religion

World Council of Churches An interdenominational Council of Churches, formed in Amsterdam in 1948. Originating in the ecumenical movement of the early 20th century, its main task is to seek the unity of the Church. It comprises most of the main-line Christian denominations with the exception of the Roman Catholic Church, with which, however, it keeps close contact. Its headquarters are in Geneva, and its ruling body, a representative Assembly, meets every six or seven years. ▷ Christianity; ecumenism

worship The acknowledgement, reverence and veneration of a God or gods. It can also be employed in a metaphorical sense to refer to something a person holds dear. Worship involves a diversity of activities such as praise, adoration, confession, thanksgiving, intercession, and petition. Most religions have developed ritual in order to structure and regulate worship. This ritual often involves re-enacting the core events of the particular religious tradition. ▷ rituals

Harimandir or Golden Temple, the holiest Sikh place of worship

worship, Christian To worship or serve God is to honour him (as the Anglo-Saxon *weorthscipe* implies) for what he is and for what he has done. Christian worship is a primary response of praise and thanksgiving for the revelation of God in creation, scripture, Christ and the Holy Spirit. The formulation and explanation of this revelation is secondary: Christ was worshipped as God decades before creeds and Councils attempted to understand how he could be both human and divine or one of the three Persons of the Trinity.

Christian worship, whether public and corporate or private and individual, typically includes elements of praise (in prayer or song), thanksgiving, confession of sin, and prayers for other people. In public worship the reading of the Bible is usually followed by a sermon (an important emphasis of Protestantism) or other commentary. There may also be a celebration of the Lord's Supper or Eucharist. Public worship is generally led by a priest, minister or other ordained or authorized person, although there is an increasing trend for participation by ordinary church members (commonly, if mistakenly, described as the 'laity') in parts of the service. The order of service (liturgy) and the prayers may be formal (following a traditional and widely accepted pattern, perhaps from a printed book such as the Church of England's *Book of Common Prayer* (1662) or *Alternative Service Book 1980*) or more informal and impromptu (as in charismatic or Pentecostal worship, although unwritten, if local traditions soon develop). Songs and music can also vary in style. As Christian worship may take place anywhere, its outward forms and the musical, artistic or architectural setting are felt important by some Christians and less so by others, such as members of the Society of Friends, who emphasize the inward and spiritual nature of worship. ▷ architecture, Christian; architecture, Christian; Council of the Church; Creeds, Christian; doctrine, Christian; Friends, Society of; Lord's Prayer; music, Christian; Orders, Holy; prayer, Christian

worship, Hindu Worship in Hinduism is practised in many forms. Ritual is essential in all Hindu worship, being seen as necessary to maintain and improve the position of the worshipper. Benefits range from alleviating disease to liberation (*moksha*) from rebirth (*samsara*). One of the central themes in Hindu worship is the maintenance of ritual purity, this being related to food and hygiene laws, and especially to the social hierarchy of the caste system. Also important is the notion of presenting offerings to deities in order to appease or petition them. There are a number of principal forms of practice within Hinduism which include festivals, sacrifice, meditation, renunciation, rituals, worship of deities and ancestor worship. These, of course, vary widely according to tradition, geography and chronology, the variations giving rise to innumerable rites and practices. ▷ domestic observances; jati; moksha; samnyasa; samsara; tapas

worship, Jewish The Hebrew word for worship is *avodah*, meaning 'service'. In Judaism, all religious activity constitutes such service of God, including study and obedience to the mitzvot. One element is worship proper, in which praise and petition are offered to God on behalf of the community and the individual. It may take place in both private and public spheres and, although spontaneous worship is by no means disallowed, set times and forms have developed. Private worship is centred in the home around the table, eg on Sabbaths and Passover. Public worship takes place in the synagogue and requires the presence of 10 men (or 10 men and women in Reform Judaism) to make up a *minyan* or quorum; this happens three times a day, with extra services on holy days. The liturgy focuses on two main rubrics: the Shema and the Tefillah. The former, consisting of Deuteronomy 6.4–6 and 11.13–21, and Numbers 15.37–41, is something like a creed and is recited morning and evening; its title comes from the first phrase, *shema yisrael* ('Hear O Israel'). The Tefillah ('Prayer') or Amidah ('standing') is recited three times a day in a standing position and consists of 19 benedictions/petitions, some of which are constant. Others are for use on weekdays and are replaced by different material on other occasions. On sabbaths and festivals changes and additions appropriate to the season and theme of the service are made. ▷ hagim; mitzvah; Shema; siddur; synagogue

Wulfila ▷ Ulfilas

Wycliffe, John (c.1329–1384) English religious reformer, born near Richmond in Yorkshire, probably of a family which held the manor of Wycliffe on Tees. He distinguished himself at Oxford, where he was a popular teacher. In 1360 he was Master of Balliol College, but resigned soon afterwards on taking the college living of Fillingham, which he exchanged in 1368 for Ludgershall, Buckinghamshire. He was possibly warden of Canterbury Hall for a time. He also held some office at court, where he was consulted by government and employed as a pamphleteer. In 1374 he became rector of Lutterworth, and the same year was sent (doubtless as a recognized opponent of papal intrusion) to Bruges to treat with ambassadors from the pope concerning ecclesiastical abuses. His strenuous activity gained him support among the nobles and the London citizenry. In 1376 he wrote *De Dominio Divino*, expounding the doctrine that all authority is founded in grace and that wicked rulers (whether secular or ecclesiastical) thereby forfeited their right to rule.

His maintenance of a right in the secular power to control the clergy was offensive to the bishops, who summoned him before the archbishop in St Paul's in 1377; but the council was broken up by an unseemly quarrel between the Bishop of London and Wycliffe's supporter, John of Gaunt (Duke of Lancaster). Pope Gregory XI now banned him, and addressed bulls to the king, bishops and University of Oxford, bidding them to imprison Wycliffe and make him answer before the archbishop and the pope. When at last proceedings were undertaken, at Lambeth in 1378, the prosecution had little effect upon Wycliffe's position. The whole fabric of the Church was now (1378) shaken by the Great Schism and the election of an antipope. Hitherto Wycliffe had attacked the manifest abuses in the Church, but now he began to strike at its constitution, and declared it would be better without pope or prelates. He denied the priestly power of absolution, and the whole system of enforced confession, of penances, and indulgence, and asserted the right of every man to examine the Bible for himself. Up to this time his works had been written in Latin; he now appealed to the people in their own language, and by issuing popular tracts became a leading English prose writer. He organized a body of itinerant preachers, his 'poor priests', who spread his doctrines widely through the country, and he began a translation of the Bible, of which as yet there was no complete English version. The work was completed rapidly, and widely circulated. He entered upon more dangerous ground when in 1380 he assailed the central dogma of transubstantiation. A convocation of doctors at Oxford condemned his theses; he appealed without success to the king. In 1382 Archbishop Courtenay convoked a council and condemned Wycliffite opinions. Wycliffe's followers were arrested, and all compelled to recant; but for some unknown reason he himself was not judged. He withdrew from Oxford to Lutterworth, where he continued his incessant literary activity.

His work in the next two years, uncompromising in tone, is astonishing in quantity, and is consistently powerful. The characteristic of his teaching was its insistence on inward religion in opposition to the formalism of the time; as a rule he attacked the established practices of the Church only so far as he thought they had degenerated into mere mechanical uses. The influence of his teaching was widespread in England, and, though persecution suppressed it, continued to be exerted up to the Reformation. His supporters came to be derisively known as 'Lollards' (from a Dutch word meaning 'mumblers'); Huss was avowedly his disciple; and there were Lollards or Wycliffites in Ayrshire down to the Reformation. Thirty years after Wycliffe's death, 45 articles extracted from his writings were condemned as heretical by the Council of Constance, which ordered his bones to be dug up and burned and cast into the Swift—a sentence executed in 1428. ▷ antipope; Council of the Church; Great Schism; Huss, John; Lollards; Reformation; transubstantiation

Wyszynski, Stefan (1901–81) Polish prelate and cardinal, born in Zuzela, near Warsaw. He was educated at Wloclawek seminary and Lublin Catholic University. He was professor at the Higher Seminary, Woclawek (1930–9), and founded the Catholic Workers University there (1935). During World War II he was associated with the resistance movement during the German occupation of Poland. In 1945 he became Rector of Wloclawek Higher Seminary, in 1946 Bishop of Lublin and in 1949 Archbishop of Warsaw and Gniezno and Primate of Poland. He was made a cardinal in 1952. In 1953, following his indictment of the communist campaign against the Church, he was suspended from his ecclesiastical functions and imprisoned. He was freed after the 'bloodless revolution' of 1956 and agreed to a reconciliation between Church and State under the 'liberalizing' Gomulka régime, but relations became increasingly strained, culminating in the acrimonious 1966 celebrations of 1000 years of Christianity in Poland. A further attempt at co-existence was made after widespread strikes in 1970, but uneasiness remained. ▷ Roman Catholicism

Xavier, St Francis ▷ Francis Xavier, St

Y

Yahweh, or **YHWH** The name of the God of Israel, perhaps deriving from Israel's experiences at Sinai, although also found in biblical stories of the patriarchs. The name is usually taken to mean 'he is/will be', 'he comes to be/creates', or 'he causes to fall'. The unvocalized YHWH (known as the Tetragrammaton) is considered by Jews too sacred to pronounce aloud, except by the high priest in the Holy of Holies on the Day of Atonement, and is usually replaced orally by Adonai ('Lord') when it is read from the Bible. Christians erroneously vocalized it as Jehovah. ▷ Bible; Elohim; God; Holy of Holies; Jehovah

Yamuna (Yāmuna) (c.916–1036) Tamil philosopher, poet and theologian who wrote in Sanskrit and is generally credited with the foundation of the Vaishnava school known as the *Shri Vaishnavas*. He was influenced by the *alvars*, this being particularly reflected in his devotional hymns to Vishnu and Shri (Lakshmi). His inclusion of Tamil devotional poetry with Sanskrit texts did much to widen the scope of Hindu literature generally. This combination resulted in the Shri Vaishnavas fusing both Brahmanic or Vedic and non-Brahmanic devotional ideas. It is generally believed that Yamuna's principal contribution to the Shri Vaishnava tradition was that, through his writings, he attracted Ramanuja as the sixth *acarya* of the school, and it was Ramanuja who gave the school much of its philosophical respectability. ▷ Alvar; bhakti; Lakshmi; Ramanuja; Shri Vaishanavas; Tamil Hinduism; Vishnu

yantra A form of mystical diagram used in Tantric Buddhism and Hinduism as a focus for meditation and worship. In contrast to mandalas, which also represent plans of the transcendent world in the form of circular diagrams, yantras often adopt symbols from the sexual realm to indicate the continuing dance and activity of creation. The most complex yantra in colour, design and imagery is known as the Shri Yantra, which is regarded as the most powerful of yantras. This is a complex design of nine intersecting triangles within a square surrounded by six concentric circles, with lotus petals on the outer circles. This diagram is a model of the Hindu cosmos with a point (*bindu*) at the centre representing the ineffable absolute from which all is manifested. The triangles show the interpenetration of Shiva and Shakti, the upward-pointing triangles representing Shiva, the male aspect of the cosmos, the downward-pointing triangles Shakti, the female force. The yantra is drawn on the ground, on cloth or on stone and is the object of worship (*puja*) and meditation (*dhyana*) as a deity (*devata*) in itself. The Tantric practice of visualization is sometimes used in regard to yantras whereby the adept draws on the energies and qualities of the visualized diagram by thinking him- or herself psychologically into the inner meaning of the yantra. ▷ dhyana; mandala; Tantric Buddhism; Tantric Hinduism

kali-yantra

yasna An Avestan word meaning 'act of worship'. This is the most important and central of all Zoroastrian rituals, and should ideally be performed every day. The rite can only take place in a consecrated place (*Dar-e Mehr*), and must be performed by priests who are in a state of ritual purity. Although the ceremony is now normally performed by two priests, older texts mention as many as eight celebrants, each with his own distinctive function. The initial part of the ceremony, the Paragna, consists of elaborate and ritualized preparations, such as the purification and consecration of the implements and substances to be used in the ceremony. This is followed by the yasna proper, which is introduced by the formal dedication of the rite to one or more divinities, and consists essentially of the ritual consumption of a special sort of bread (*darun*) with a little butter, and the juice of the haoma plant; offerings are also made to the fire and to water. These ritual acts are accompanied by a long liturgy, also called yasna, at the centre of which are Zoroaster's own *Gathas*, and which includes hymns of praise to the divinities Haoma and Sraosha. It is held to be significant that the seven elements of which Ahura Mazda's good creation consists (*Amesha Spentas*) are all symbolically present in the ritual. ▷ Ahura Mazda; Amesha Spentas; Avesta; haoma; Zoroastrianism

Yavneh ▷ Jabneh

yazata An Avestan term meaning 'one who receives worship'. In Zoroastrian sources the term yazata and its Middle Persian equivalent *yazad* can denote all divine beings who are worshipped in the ritual. The later Zoroastrian tradition prefers the word *fereshteh*, 'angel', for divine beings other than Ahura Mazda, presumably in order to avoid charges of polytheism by Muslims. In later Middle Persian and New Persian texts, the plural of the word, *yazdan*, could be used for God (ie Ahura Mazda), a development similar to that of Hebrew *Elohim*. ▷ Ahura Mazda; Avesta; Elohim; Zoroastrianism

Yggdrasil In Norse mythology, a giant ash, the World-Tree, which supports the sky, holds the different realms of gods and men in its branches, and has its roots in the underworld. ▷ Germanic religion; underworld

yin and **yang** Two basic contrary forces in ancient Chinese thought, elaborated in Han dynasty Confucianism. Yang is associated with male, heat, light, heaven, creation, dominance; yin with female, cold, dark, earth, sustenance, passivity. Yin and yang forces are alleged to exist in most things, and operate cyclically to produce change. ▷ Confucianism

yoga In Indian religious tradition, any of various physical and contemplative techniques designed to free the superior, conscious element in a person from involvement with the inferior material world. More narrowly, yoga is a school of Hindu philosophy which seeks to explain and justify the practices of yogin discipline. ▷ Bhakti Yoga; dhyana; Hinduism; Karma Yoga

Yogacara (Yogācāra) An important school of Mahayana Buddhist philosophy which contends that ultimately consciousness alone is real, whereas the objects of consciousness which seem to be real are not. It has similarities to some Western theories of subjective idealism, in that it opposes materialism and denies the independent existence of matter. It began as a school of thought in India in the 4th and 5th centuries CE due to the work of Asanga, Vasubandhu and their successors, and later became very important in Tibet. Underlying the work of the school was the presupposition that meditation was important as a way to develop the wisdom that would give true insight into the nature of reality. The *Yogacara* school had a deeper spiritual concern than its rival *Madhyamika* school, which was more interested in philosophical critiques. The Yogacarins gave systematic shape to a number of earlier Mahayana notions including the theory of the three bodies of the Buddha: his earthly body, his blissful body, and his cosmic body. They related this theory to the notion that there are three levels of truth: conventional truth, examined truth, and ultimate truth. They paved the way for two very different later developments. One, led by Dinnaga and Dharmkirti (7th century CE), took Indian Yogacara in a more logical direction; and the other, with its stress upon ritual, practice, mysticism and meditation, fed into the Tantric Buddhism which developed so successfully in Tibet. ▷ Asanga; bhavana; Madhyamika; Mahayana Buddhism; prajna; Tantric Buddhism; trikaya; Vasubandhu

Yoga Darshana (Yoga Darśana) From the root '*drs*', to see, and usually translated as 'viewpoint'. There have been six orthodox Hindu *darshanas*, or systems of philosophy, each playing a key role in the shaping of Hinduism. Traditionally, the founder of the Yoga Darshana was Patanjali, the reputed author of the *Yoga Sutra* (200BCE–500CE). The Samkhya, an abstract non-theistic description of the universe, dealing with the relationship between the soul and matter (*purusha* and *prakriti*) and the evolution of matter into multiplicity, provides the metaphysics of yoga. The Yoga Darshana defines the religious path engendered by this description. Some scholars highlight the tenuous nature of the link between the two schools since the Yoga Darshana, unlike the Samkhya, is provisionally theistic, but this difference can be conflated on a philosophical level. The word 'yoga' is cognate with both 'yoke' and 'union', implying that through discipline, a religious goal (*moksha*—which is sometimes defined as the union of the soul with God) can be achieved. Yogic discipline includes the practice of virtue, the control of the body and the senses through the exercise of breath control (*pranayama*), concentration, and withdrawal from the world, in order to precipitate a transformation of consciousness. God (*Ishvara*) is used as an object of meditation. The word yoga is also used in connection with other paths, not set out by Patanjali in the Yoga Sutra, such as Bhakti, Karma and Jnana Yoga, so its meaning has been expanded to embrace all religious paths to moksha. ▷ bhakti; dhyana; Ishvara; Karma Yoga; moksha; prakriti; purusha; yoga

Yohanan, or **Yochanan ben Zakkai** (1st century) Rabbi, about whom it is difficult to distinguish fact from legendary embellishment. According to rabbinic literature he escaped from Jerusalem, when it was besieged by the Romans prior to its destruction in 70CE, by being carried out in a coffin as though dead. Thereupon he received permission from the Roman general Vespasian, whom he correctly predicted would become the next emperor, to move to Yavneh (or Jamnia) near the Judaean coast accompanied by other colleagues. There he set up an academy, and this constituted the start of the reconstruction of Judaism after 70CE, with the Torah at its centre; the Temple and priesthood were still important theologically but their restoration was to be left to God. Geographically the focus of Judaism shifted from Jerusalem to Yavneh until a move to Galilee in the 2nd century. ▷ rabbi; Talmud; Temple, Jerusalem; Torah

Yom Kippur The Day of Atonement, a Jewish holy day (10 Tishri) coming at the end of ten days of penitence which begin on Rosh Hashanah. It is a day devoted to fasting, prayer and repentance for past sins. ▷ calendar, Jewish; fasts, Jewish

yoni ▷ **linga**

Young, Brigham (1801–77) American Mormon leader, born in Whitingham, Vermont. He was a carpenter, painter, and glazier in Mendon, New York. He first saw the 'Book of Mormon' in 1830, and in 1832, converted by a brother of Joseph Smith, was baptized and began to preach near Mendon. Next he went to Kirtland, Ohio, was made an elder, and preached in Canada (1832–3). In 1835 he was appointed to the Quorum of the Twelve Apostles of the Church and directed the Mormon settlement at Nauvoo, Illinois. In 1844 he succeeded Joseph Smith as president, and when the Mormons were driven from Nauvoo, he organized and led the trek to Utah in 1847. From 1839 to 1842 he visited England and made 2000 proselytes. In 1847 the great body of Mormons arrived at Utah, and founded Salt Lake City; and in 1850 President Fillmore appointed Brigham Young Governor of Utah Territory. The Mormon practice of polygamy occasioned growing concern, and in 1857 a new governor was sent with a force of US troops under Albert Sidney Johnston to suppress it; the appointment in 1869 of another 'Gentile' governor further reduced Young's authority. Practical and farseeing as an administrator, he encouraged agriculture and manufactures, made roads and bridges, and carried through a contract for 100 miles of the Union Pacific Railroad. He died leaving $2500000 to 17 wives and 56 children. ▷ Mormons; Smith, Joseph

Yuan Tan (Yüan Tan) The Chinese New Year Festival, which is the most important in the Chinese calandar, falling as it does on the first day of the first lunar month. A week beforehand the stove god, whose picture is present above the chimney in Chinese homes, goes off to report to the Jade Emperor (Yu-Huang) in heaven about the family's conduct during the past year. His picture is burnt to symbolize his departure, and often sweetmeats are thrown in the fire as well to make sure he gives a favourable report. Other gods are thanked and worshipped too, and on New Year's Eve the stove god returns to be welcomed back with firecrackers and to be placed again above the chimney. The books are balanced for New Year, and a three-day holiday festival is held, when the shops are closed and the streets are empty. Families come

Chinese gods of wealth, associated with the Chinese New Year

together; offerings are made to the ancestors, the household gods, and to earth and heaven; and a good time of feasting is had by all—although meat and fish are not eaten, and work is done about the house to prevent accidents. New Year cards are exchanged, and prayers wrapped in auspicious red paper are fixed to the doorposts. On the third day families visit each other with presents, food and cards, and children are given gifts of money enclosed in red paper. Shortly after the New Year festival candles, drink, food and incense are offered to the relevant gods to achieve protection from ghosts during the new year. ▷ ancestor reverence, Chinese; Chung Yuan; festivals, Chinese; Yu-Huang

yugas In Hindu cosmology the universe has no beginning and no ending, being instead a constant cycle of creation, maintenance and devolution. This cycle is variously depicted and different scriptural sources vary tremendously in the time-scales they posit. Generally, one day of Brahma embraces one of these cycles, and one night of Brahma indicates the period of hundreds of thousands of years in which the world is reduced to chaos, and in which souls do not transmigrate. Each day of Brahma, or *kalpa*, is broken down into four qualitatively different *yugas* or ages. These yugas are named after throws of the dice, the first and longest being the *kritayuga*, followed in diminishing length by the *tretayuga*, the *dvaparayuga*, and the present age, the *kaliyuga*. During each age there is a decline in the quality and length of life, and at the end of the kaliyuga comes the *pralaya*, or doomsday period, during which Brahma falls into a dreamless sleep and the three worlds are plunged into chaos. The kaliyuga is said to have begun at the end of the great war documented in the *Mahabharata*, which in itself has overwhelming apocalyptic themes. This age may last anything up to 432000 years, and after the ensuing aeon of chaos, Brahma will awake and the cycle will begin again. This description is only one permutation of the yuga theory; others are to be found in the *Puranas* and other Indian literature. The didactic purpose of such theories is to elucidate the impermanence of worldly things. ▷ Brahma; Mahabharata; pralaya; Purana; yugas

Yu-Huang (Yü-Huang) (Jade Emperor) The chief deity in Chinese popular religion. The notion of the rule of an emperor in the civil sphere was a cardinal element of Chinese life and thought, and this applied in the celestial realm too. The Jade Emperor emerged supreme in the Chinese popular pantheon of gods around the 10th century CE, and the cult and doctrine of the Jade Emperor arose during the heyday of the mighty Tang dynasty (618–906). In the Jade Emperor's court were various ranks of deities, and in 1017 a state cult was set up for the 'Great Heavenly Emperor, Majesty of Jade Purity'. His role was to superintend the divine pantheon and the investiture of rulers. Even so he was viewed as carrying out the orders of the Taoist Three Pure Ones, who were too remote for popular acclaim, whereas he was not. The Jade Emperor's festival takes place on the ninth day of the first lunar month, and he is portrayed as a dragon-robed emperor on a throne, served by his courtiers. A scripture devoted to him plays a role in Taoist ritual worship. ▷ Chinese pantheon; Chinese religion in Taiwan and Hong Kong (20th century); Chinese religion on the China mainland (20th century)

Z

Zacharias ▷ Zechariah, Book of

Zadokites Descendants of Zadok, a priest apparently of Aaronic lineage and of the family of Eleazar, who opposed the conspiracy of Abiathar against Solomon and was appointed high priest, serving in Solomon's temple. His family continued to hold this office until Jerusalem fell in 587BCE, and again later in the Second Temple period until the office became a political appointment of the occupying power under Antiochus IV (c.171BCE). The Qumran community continued to look for a renewal of the Zadokite priesthood, and described its own priestly members in these terms. Some derive 'Sadducees' from Zadokites. ▷ Aaron; Qumran, community of; Sadducees; Solomon; Teacher of Righteousness

Zaehner, Robert Charles (1913–74) English scholar of comparative religion, educated at Tonbridge School and Oxford and Cambridge universities. At the age of 20 he had a mystical experience of nature which gave him an interest in mysticism, and his conversion to Roman Catholicism in 1946 influenced his academic studies. Service in Teheran in World War II led him into important researches into Zoroastrianism, and he held the Spalding Chair of Eastern Religions and Ethics at Oxford from 1953 to 1974. His works, written in a fluent and accessible style, helped to popularize the study of religion at a time when it was developing in the Western world. His books on Zoroastrianism, Hinduism and (to some extent) mysticism, were intended to be objective studies of these traditions. In other works his Catholic convictions and theological interests were more obvious, and he operated as a fulfilment theologian who saw other religions as being fulfilled in Catholic Christianity. His comparison of religions centred upon India and Israel, and of different kinds of mysticism, was interesting for the significant differences he observed between religions, as well as their similarities. ▷ comparative religion; mysticism; theological attitudes

zakat (zakāt) The alms tax obligatory on all Muslims, and the third of the five 'pillars' of Islam. Traditionally, it consisted of a $2\frac{1}{2}$ per cent annual levy on income and capital. ▷ Islam

Zarathustra ▷ Zoroaster

zazen A Zen Buddhist practice made famous by the Soto Zen school, founded in Japan in 1227 by Dogen. It involves sitting upright, with legs crossed, in deep meditation. This includes regulation of the breathing, the correct posture of the body (usually in the lotus position), and deep concentration of the mind. By this method the mind is freed from all attachments and desires and one achieves satori, or enlightenment. The Rinzai school of Zen differed from the Soto school in its interpretation of zazen. According to Rinzai it was a channel for the systematic use of koans, paradoxical sayings and exercises aimed at jerking the mind out of its usual channels into sudden enlightenment. Dogen's Soto Zen school used koans less and stressed the importance of zazen as just sitting in quiet meditation which could in itself constitute enlightenment rather than being a means to enlightenment. As such it followed a system of meditation in five stages, moving from the 'seeming-self' up to an awareness of oneness with ultimate reality. ▷ Dogen; koans; Rinzai; satori; Soto

Zebulun, tribe of One of the 12 tribes of ancient Israel, purportedly descended from the sixth son of Jacob by Leah. Its territory was in North Israel, a fertile part of later 'Galilee' between the sea of Galilee and the Mediterranean coast, but buffered on each side by other tribes; to the south it was bounded by the tribes of Issachar and Manasseh. ▷ Israel, tribes of; Jacob; Old Testament

Zechariah, or Zacharias, Book of One of 12 so-called 'minor' prophetic writings of the Hebrew Bible/Old Testament, attributed to Zechariah, writing c.520–518BCE after returning to Jerusalem from exile. It presents visions of the building of Jerusalem's Temple and of a new messianic age. Chapters 9–14, however, are often considered the work of later hands (c.5th–3rd century BCE), when the Temple rebuilding was no longer in view and when increasing disillusionment gave rise to stronger hopes for the future vindication of

Israel. ▷ Haggai, Book of; messianism; Old Testament; Temple, Jerusalem

Zen Buddhism A meditation school of Buddhism introduced into Japan by monks returning from China in the 12th century. It originated in India, and spread to China, where it incorporated elements of Taoism. Zen stresses the personal experience of enlightenment based on a simple life lived close to nature, and upon methods of meditation which avoid complicated rituals and abstruse thought. In Japan there are two main Zen bodies: Rinzai, introduced by Eisai (1141–1214), and Soto, introduced by Dogen (1200–53). Rinzai seeks spontaneous enlightenment, while Soto teaches a form of meditation in which enlightenment is a more gradual process. ▷ Buddhism; Chan; meditation; Taoism

Zeno of Citium (334–262BCE) Greek philosopher, the founder of Stoicism. He was born in Citium, Cyprus, went to Athens as a young man and did the rounds of the various philosophy schools there. In about 300 he set up his own school in the *Stoa Poikile* (Painted Colonnade), which gave the Stoics their name, and had a formative role in the development of Stoicism as a distinctive and coherent philosophy. None of his many treatises survives, but his main contribution seems to have been in the area of ethics, which was in any case always central to the Stoic system. He supposedly committed suicide, after a long life. ▷ Stoicism

Zephaniah, Book of One of 12 so-called 'minor' prophetic writings of the Hebrew Bible/Old Testament, attributed to Zephaniah, son of Cushi and descendant of Hezekiah, active in Josiah's reign (7th century BCE), but unknown apart from this work. It strongly denounces influences from heathen cults on Jewish religion, presumably preparing for Josiah's reforms, and proclaims God's judgement on Israel's enemies, but consolation for the remnant in Jerusalem who loyally await the 'Day of the Lord'. The medieval Latin hymn, *Dies irae*, was inspired by Zephaniah's account of the coming day of wrath. ▷ Josiah; Old Testament; prophet

ziggurat A temple tower, in the shape of a mountain, found throughout ancient Sumeria and the adjacent region of Elam. It consisted of a high, pyramidal mound, constructed in stages and surmounted by a shrine. Access to the shrine was by a series of external stairways or ramps. Good examples come from Eridu,

ziggurat at Ur

Ur, Uruk, and Choga Zanbil near Susa. ▷ architecture, Sumerian and Assyrian

Zinzendorf, Nicolaus Ludwig, Graf von (1700–60) German religious leader, refounder of the Moravian Brethren, born in Dresden. He studied at Wittenburg, and held a government post at Dresden. He invited the persecuted Hussite refugees from Moravia to his Lusatin estates in Saxony, and there founded for them the colony of Herrnhut ('the Lord's keeping'). His zeal led to troubles with the government, and from 1736 to 1748 he was exiled. He visited England, and in 1741 went to America. During his exile from Saxony he was ordained at Tübingen, and became Bishop of the Moravian Brethren. He died at Herrnhut, having written over 100 books. His emphasis on feeling in religion influenced German theology. ▷ Hussites; Moravian Brethren

Zion, or **Sion** (Hebrew, probably 'fortress' or 'rock') Term used in the Old Testament and Jewish literature in various ways: for one of the hills in Jerusalem; for the mount on which the Temple was built; for the Temple itself; and symbolically for Jerusalem or even Israel as a whole. Today 'Mount Zion' usually denotes the south-west hill in Jerusalem just south of the city wall. ▷ Temple, Jerusalem; Zionism

Zionism The movement which sought to recover for the Jewish people their historic Palestinian homeland (the *eretz Yisrael*) after centuries of dispersion. The modern movement arose in the late 19th century with plans for the Jewish colonization of Palestine, and under Theodor Herzl also developed a political programme to obtain sovereign state rights over the territory. Gaining support after World War I, its objectives were supported by the British Balfour Declaration in 1917, as long as rights for non-Jews in Palestine were not impaired. After World War II the establishment of the Jewish state in 1948 received United Nations support. Zionism is still active as a movement encouraging diaspora Jews to immigrate to and take an interest in the Jewish state. ▷ Diaspora Judaism; eretz Yisrael; Herzl, Theodor; messianism; Zion

Zionist churches The usual designation for African Independent churches of the prophet-healing type in Southern Africa. Many include the word Zion in their title, the historical reason being an early association of one branch of the movement with the charismatic utopian Christian Catholic Apostolic Church founded in Zion City, Illinois, by J A Dowie (1847–1907). Nowadays 'Zion' is usually given a transcendent meaning, though sometimes attached to the church's sacred city or settlement. Among characteristics of Zionist churches that have been adduced are: baptism by immersion, healing through prayer, revelatory messages through prophecy and tongues, observance of the seventh day (rather than Sunday) as sacred, the admission of African traditional elements in worship, establishment of a holy city or camp, seasonal festivals, rejection of tobacco, alcohol and medicines (whether traditional or modern) and toleration of polygamy. Not all these features, however, are found in all Zionist churches, which vary in many respects. They are especially prominent in Zululand and Swaziland, and are the first point of contact with Christianity for large numbers of adherents of the traditional religions of Africa. ▷ African Independent churches; aladura

Zohar The main text of the Jewish Kabbalah. Discovered in Spain in the late 13th century, it was said to be the mystical teachings of Rabbi Simeon bar Yochai and his followers, who lived in Palestine in the 2nd/3rd century. There have always been doubts about its authenticity, but Kabbalistic tradition accepts it as genuine. ▷ Judaism; Kabbalah

Zoroaster, Grecized form of **Zarathustra** (c.1000BCE) Iranian religious leader and prophet, the founder or reformer of the ancient Parsee religion known as Zoroastrianism. The *Gathas* (the earliest portion of the *Avesta*, the sacred book of Zoroastrianism), which is written in older dialect, may represent his own words, and he is thought to have converted King Vîshtâspa, under whose protection he lived and preached. He believed that the world and history exhibit the struggle between Ahura Mazda and Angra Mainyu (the creator or good spirit, and the evil principle, the devil), in which finally evil will be banished and the good reign supreme. ▷ Ahura Mazda; Angra Mainyu

Zoroastrianism The religion which was founded by Zoroaster, or evolved from his teachings. Zoroaster was a highly trained priest, schooled in the religious tradition of his people. At one stage, the ancient (Indo-) Iranian religion prominently worshipped divinities who guarded and maintained 'Right Order' and stability in the universe and in society, such as Mithra, Lord of the Covenant or Contract. Probably during the period of their migrations southward from the Central Asian steppes, however, some of these tribes became ardent devotees of divinities whose qualities better reflected their own heroic and adventurous age, notably the war-like, amoral Indra. Zoroaster vehemently rejected the cult of such 'gods' (*daevas*), whom he regarded as wholly evil, and restricted worship to the moral *ahuras*, such as Ahura Mazda, Mithra, and the Amesha Spentas. Zoroastrianism understands the world as a theatre of war, limited in space and time, in which the powers of good and evil can fight to a conclusion. At the End of Time (*Frashokereti*), Angra Mainyu will be defeated, and the universe will be perfect, without even the latent threat of evil which existed during Ahura Mazda's original Creation (*Bundahishn*). All creatures and phenomena in the world, with the exception of humans, were created either by Ahura Mazda or by his evil opponent, and therefore cannot help being good or evil. The elements of the good Creation (such as fire, water, earth, useful plants, beneficent animals, and righteous people), are held to deserve reverence. Humans are the only creatures capable of moral choice, and each individual is required to make his or her choice in favour of Ahura Mazda, thus helping to bring about the ultimate defeat of Angra Mainyu. After death, the soul will be judged at the Chinvat Bridge, and sent to heaven or (temporarily) to hell or purgatory, depending on the balance between its good and wicked thoughts, words and deeds on earth.

Zoroastrianism first evolved in eastern Iran, becoming prominent in western parts of that country, it seems, with the rise to power of the Achaemenian dynasty (559–323BCE). Under the Achaemenians, it became the major religion of a great empire, developing in response to the demands made upon an Imperial faith, and also under the influence of such great cultures as that of Mesopotamia, to which the rise of Zurvanism may partly owe its origin. The victory of Alexander the

Great (known to the Zoroastrian tradition as 'the accursed') brought about the end of the Achaemenian era, and brought Iran into close contact with Hellenistic thought and culture. However, Zoroastrianism, with its deep roots in Iranian culture and its coherent teachings, appears to have been only superficially influenced by Hellenism. Later, the Sasanian dynasty (226–mid 7th century CE), which regarded itself as the defender of Zoroastrian orthodoxy, sought to remove all traces of Greek influence from the faith. When the Sasanians were defeated in their turn by the Muslim armies, Zoroastrianism gradually became a marginal religion in Iran. Its dwindling congregations could no longer support priestly scholarship for its own sake, and Zoroastrian learning naturally suffered. Faced with this threat, the priesthood wrote down as much as possible of its traditions in the 9th and 10th centuries. The 10th century saw the departure of a group of Zoroastrians from north-eastern Iran to India, where they became known as Parsis ('Persians'). Later, under British rule, the Parsis became a very prosperous community; they were in close contact with Western culture, and were forced to respond to its challenges. The Parsis helped and defended their Iranian co-religionists who suffered great hardships in the 19th century. Under the Pahlavi dynasty (1926–79) the social position of the Iranian Zoroastrians improved considerably. At present the numbers of the Parsi community are decreasing alarmingly, largely due to emigrations and mixed marriages, whereas those of the Iranian Zoroastrians are said to have increased spectacularly since the Islamic revolution. ▷ Ahura Mazda; ahuras; Amesha Spentas; Angra Mainyu; Bundahishn; Chinvat Bridge; daevas; fire; Frashokereti; heaven; hell; Indra; khvarenah; Mithra; Pahlavi; Parsi religious reforms; Zoroaster; Zoroastrianism; Zurvan

Zurvan God of Time, venerated by a branch of Zoroastrianism, probably from Achaemenian times (529–323BCE) until after the Islamic conquest of Iran in the mid 7th century CE. Non-Zurvanite Zoroastrians clearly objected strongly to the tenets of this sect, and anti-Zurvanite priests probably expunged most traces of it from the Pahlavi books. Most of our information about Zurvanite beliefs therefore derives from non-Zoroastrian (notably Armenian and Syriac) sources. These inform us that the Zurvanites believed that Zurvan, the God of Time, existed before all things. He longed to have a son, and offered sacrifice for a thousand years in order to see his wish fulfilled. In the course of that time, however, he had doubts as to the efficacy of his sacrifice. We are told that it was this doubt that led to the birth of the Evil Spirit, Angra Mainyu or Ahriman, whereas the sacrifice itself led to the birth of Ahura Mazda. Ahriman was born first, and as Zurvan had vowed to make his first-born king of the world, he unwillingly gave Ahriman authority over it for a long time (some sources mention a period of 9000 years). After that power will pass to Ahura Mazda. Both spirits then began to create their creations. The extant accounts seem to suggest that Zurvan then became a *deus otiosus*, a divinity who has set the world in motion but does not intervene in its affairs. There is evidence, however, to show that some Zurvanites did think of Zurvan as an active and powerful god. A belief in fate and astrology appears to have been a prominent element in Zurvanite thinking, which indicates that the religious ethos promoted by Zurvanism was very different to that of other forms of Zoroastrianism, which stress the individual's complete responsibility for his own actions. Such differences may account for the radical excision of all Zurvanite lore from the later Zoroastrian tradition. The cult of a god of Time may have had its origin in Western Iran, under Babylonian influence. ▷ Ahriman; Ahura Mazda; Angra Mainyu; Bundahishn; Pahlavi; Zoroastrianism

Zwemer, Samuel Marinus (1867–1952) American missionary to Islam, born in Vriesland, Michigan. Starting out initially (1890) under the auspices of the independent Arabian Mission which he had founded (with two colleagues), his work in Basrah, Bahrain and Muscat was adopted by the mission board of the (Dutch) Reformed Church in the USA in 1894. As a scholar, preacher and evangelist he worked tirelessly to spread Christianity in Islamic countries and to arouse interest in missions in the USA and Europe, writing numerous popular books and founding and editing *The Moslem World* (1911–). He was Professor of Christian Missions at Princeton (1929–37). His early missionary career is recalled in *The Golden Milestone* (1938). ▷ missions, Christian; Reformed Churches

Zwingli, Huldreich, Latin **Ulricus Zuinglius** (1484–1531) Swiss reformer, born in Wildhaus in St Gall. He studied at Bern, Vienna and Basel, and became priest at Glarus in 1506. Here he taught himself Greek, and twice went to war in Italy as field-chaplain with the Glarus mercenaries, taking part in the battles of Novara (1513) and Marignano (1515). Transferred in 1516 to Einsiedeln, whose Black Virgin was a great resort of pilgrims, he made no secret of his contempt for such superstition. In 1518 he was elected preacher at the Grossmünster in Zürich, and roused the council not to admit within the city gates Bernhardin Samson, a seller of indulgences. He preached the gospel boldly, and in 1521 succeeded in keeping Zürich from joining the other cantons in their alliance with France. The Bishop of Constance sent his vicar-general, who was quickly silenced in debate with Zwingli (1523), in presence of the council and six hundred; whereupon the city adopted the Reformed doctrines as set forth in Zwingli's 67 theses. A second disputation followed (1523), with the result that images and the mass were swept away. On Easter Sunday 1525 he dispensed the sacrament in both kinds; and the Reformation spread widely over Switzerland.

Zwingli first made public his views on the Lord's Supper in 1524. At Marburg in 1529 he conferred with other Protestant leaders, and there disagreed with Martin Luther over the Eucharist, a dispute which was destined to rend the Protestant Church. He rejected every form of local or corporeal presence, whether by transubstantiation or consubstantiation. Meantime the progress of the Reformation had aroused bitter hatred in the Forest Cantons. Five of them formed an alliance in 1528, to which the Archduke Ferdinand of Austria was admitted. Zürich declared war in 1529 on account of the burning alive of a Protestant pastor seized on neutral territory, but violence was averted for a time by the first treaty of Cappel (1529).

Then, in October 1531, the Forest Cantons made a sudden dash on Zürich with 8000 men, and were met at Cappel by 2000, including Zwingli. The men of Zürich made a desperate resistance, but were completely defeated, and Zwingli was among the dead. Zwingli preached substantially the Reformed doctrines as early as 1516, the year before the appearance of Luther's theses. Original sin he regarded as a moral disease rather than as punishable sin or guilt. He maintained the salvation of unbaptized infants, and he believed in the salvation of such virtuous heathens as Socrates, Plato, Pindar, Scipio and Seneca. On predestination he was as calvinistic as Calvin or Augustine. Less fiery and powerful than Luther, he was the most open-minded and liberal of the Reformers. Zwingli's *Opera* fill four folios (1545). The chief is the *Commentarius de vera et falsa religione* (1525); the rest are mainly occupied with the exposition of scripture and controversies on the Eucharist, and other subjects.

▷ Eucharist; Luther, Martin; Protestantism; Reformation

Appendices

Population Distribution of Major Beliefs

Figures have been compiled from the most accurate recent available information and are in most cases correct to the nearest 1%.
Where possible within Islam the relative proportion of Sunnis and Shiites is indicated.
No precise information was available for the following: Cyprus, Hong Kong, Lebanon, Micronesia, Mongolia.

Afro-Cuban syncretism

Cuba 2%

Animism

Cameroon 25%
Côte d'Ivoire 60%
Zimbabwe 40%

Bahaism

Bolivia 3%
French Guiana 1%
Kiribati 2%
Panama 1%
Papua New Guinea 1%
Tuvalu 1%
Virgin Islands (USA) 1%

Buddhism

Australia 1%
Bangladesh 1%
Bhutan 70%
Brunei 12%
Burma 89%
Cambodia 88%
China 6%
India 1%
Indonesia *unavailable*
Japan 38%
Korea, North 2%
Korea, South 18%
Laos 58%
Macau 45%
Malaysia 17%
Nepal 5%
Singapore 28%
Sri Lanka 69%
Taiwan 43%
Thailand 95%
Vietnam 55%

Chinese folk religion

China 20%
Laos 1%
Malaysia 12%
Taiwan 49%

Chondogyo

Korea, North 14%

Christianity

Protestantism (includes all non-Roman Catholic denominations)

Andorra 1%
Angola 21%
Antigua and Barbuda 86%
Aruba 9%
Australia 47%
Austria 8%
Bahamas 75%
Barbados 65%
Belize 31%
Benin 3%
Bermuda 73%
Botswana 41%
Brazil 6%
Bulgaria 27%
Burkina Faso 2%
Burundi 7%
Cameroon 18%
Canada 42%
Central African Republic 50%
Chad 12%
Chile 6%
Côte d'Ivoire 5%
Commonwealth of Independent States 35%
Congo 39%
Cuba 3%
Czechoslovakia 26%
Denmark 91%
Djibouti 2%
Dominica 16%
Ethiopia 53%
Faeroe Islands 94%
Finland 90%
France 4%
French Guiana 4%
French Polynesia 55%
Gabon 31%
German Democratic Republic (East Germany) 47%
Germany, Federal Republic of (West Germany) 42%
Ghana 44%
Greece 98%
Greenland 98%
Grenada 35%
Guam 17%
Guatemala c.25%
Guyana 31%
Haiti 16%
Honduras 10%
Hungary 24%
Iceland 97%
Indonesia 7%
Ireland 3%
Jamaica 56%
Kenya 47%
Kiribati 42%
Korea, South 41%
Laos 1%
Lesotho 49%
Liechtenstein 8%
Luxembourg 1%
Macau 1%
Madagascar 25%
Malawi 37%
Malta 1%
Martinique 12%
Mauritius 4%
Mexico 3%
Mozambique 8%
Namibia 62%
Netherlands Antilles 10%
Netherlands, The 27%
New Zealand 47%
Nigeria 37%
Norway 88%
Panama 5%
Papua New Guinea 64%
Paraguay 2%
Philippines 10%

Christianity

Protestantism (includes all non-Roman Catholic denominations) cont.

Portugal 1%
Puerto Rico 5%
Romania 80%
Rwanda 9%
Saint Kitts and Nevis 83%
Saint Lucia 11%
Saint Vincent and the Grenadines 77%
Seychelles 8%
Sierra Leone 6%
Solomon Islands 78%
South Africa 68%
Sudan, The 2%
Suriname 19%
Swaziland 66%
Sweden 90%
Switzerland 44%
Togo 7%
Tonga 73%
Trinidad and Tobago 28%
Tuvalu 98%
Uganda 29%
UK 74%
Uruguay 3%
USA 58%
Vanuatu 67%
Virgin Islands (USA) 64%
Western Samoa 72%
Yugoslavia 46%
Zaire 46%
Zambia 46%
Zimbabwe 33%

Roman Catholicism

Algeria 1%
Andorra 94%
Angola 69%
Antigua and Barbuda 10%
Argentina 93%
Aruba 89%
Australia 26%
Austria 84%
Bahamas 19%
Barbados 4%
Belgium 90%
Belize 62%
Benin 19%
Bermuda 14%
Bolivia 93%
Botswana 9%
Brazil 88%
Bulgaria 1%
Burkina Faso 10%
Burundi 78%
Cameroon 3 5%
Canada 47%
Cape Verde 98%
Central African Republic 33%
Chad 21%
Chile 81%
Côte d'Ivoire 15%
Colombia 95%
Commonwealth of Independent States 2%
Congo 54%
Costa Rica 89%
Cuba 40%
Czechoslovakia 66%
Denmark 1%
Djibouti 4%
Dominica 77%
Dominican Republic 92%
Ecuador 94%
El Salvador 93%
France 76%
French Guiana 87%
French Polynesia 39%
Gabon 65%
German Democratic Republic (East Germany) 7%
Germany, Federal Republic of (West Germany) 43%
Ghana 19%
Grenada 59%
Guadeloupe 91%
Guam 80%
Guatemala c.75%
Guyana 11%
Haiti 80%
Honduras 85%
Hungary 62%
Iceland 1%
Indonesia 3%
Ireland 93%
Italy 83%
Jamaica 5%
Kenya 26%
Kiribati 53%
Korea, South 3%
Laos 1%
Lesotho 44%
Liechtenstein 87%
Luxembourg 93%
Macau 7%
Madagascar 26%
Malawi 28%
Malta 97%
Martinique 88%
Mauritius 26%
Mexico 93%
Monaco 90%
Mozambique 31%
Namibia 20%
Netherlands Antilles 84%
Netherlands, The 36%
New Caledonia 63%
New Zealand 15%
Nicaragua 88%
Nigeria 12%
Panama 84%
Papua New Guinea 33%
Paraguay 96%
Peru 92%
Philippines 84%
Poland 95%
Portugal 95%
Puerto Rico 85%
Réunion 90%
Rwanda 65%
Saint Kitts and Nevis 7%
Saint Lucia 86%
Saint Vincent and the Grenadines 19%
San Marino 95%
São Tomé and Príncipe c.84%
Senegal 6%
Seychelles 91%
Sierra Leone 2%
Solomon Islands 19%
South Africa 10%
Spain 97%
Sudan, The 6%
Suriname 23%
Swaziland 11%
Sweden 2%
Switzerland 48%
Togo 22%
Tonga 16%
Trinidad and Tobago 32%
Uganda 50%
UK 13%
Uruguay 60%
USA 30%
Vanuatu 15%
Venezuela 92%
Vietnam 7%

Virgin Islands (USA) 34%
Western Samoa 22%
Yugoslavia 26%
Zaire 48%
Zambia 26%
Zimbabwe 12%

Unspecified

Albania 5%
Bahrain 7%
Brunei 9%
Burma 5%
Egypt c.10%
Equatorial Guinea 89%
Ethiopia 5%
Fiji 53%
Gambia, The 4%
Guinea 2%
Guinea-Bissau 5%
India 2%
Iran 1%
Iraq 4%
Israel 2%
Japan 4%
Jordan 5%
Korea, North 1%
Kuwait 8%
Liberia 68%
Malaysia 6%
Mali 1%
Mayotte 3%
Morocco 1%
Pakistan 2%
Qatar 6%
Saudi Arabia 1%
Singapore 19%
Sri Lanka 8%
Syria 9%
Taiwan 7%
Tanzania 34%
Thailand 1%
United Arab Emirates 4%

Druze

Israel 2%

Hinduism

Bangladesh 12%
Bhutan 25%
Burma 1%
Fiji 38%
Guyana 37%
India 83%
Indonesia 2%
Kuwait 2%
Malaysia 7%
Mauritius 53%
Nepal 90%
Oman 13%
Pakistan 2%
Qatar 1%
Seychelles 1%
Singapore 5%
South Africa 2%
Sri Lanka 16%
Suriname 27%
Trinidad and Tobago 24%
UK 1%

Islam

Afghanistan 99%
(Shiite 25%
Sunni 74%)
Albania 21%
Algeria 99% (Sunni)
Australia 1%
Austria 1%
Bahrain 85%
(Shiite 51%
Sunni 34%)
Bangladesh 87%
Belgium 1%
Benin 15%
Bhutan 5%
Brunei 67%
Bulgaria 8%
Burkina Faso 43%
Burma 4%
Burundi 1%
Cambodia 2%
Cameroon 22%
Central African Republic 3%
Chad 44%
China 2%
Côte d'Ivoire 20%
Commonwealth of Independent States 12%
Comoros 100% (Sunni)
Djibouti 94% (Sunni)
Egypt c.90% (Sunni)
Equatorial Guinea 1%
Ethiopia 31%
Fiji 8%
France 3%
French Guiana 1%
Gabon 1%
Gambia, The 95%
Germany, Federal Republic of (West Germany) 3%
Ghana 16%
Greece 2%
Guinea 85%
Guinea-Bissau 30%
Guyana 9%
India 11%
Indonesia 87%
Iran 99%
(Shiite 91%
Sunni 8%)
Iraq 96%
(Shiite 54%
Sunni 42%)
Israel 14%
Jordan 93% (Sunni)
Kenya 6%
Kuwait 90%
(Shiite 27%
Sunni 63%)
Laos 1%
Liberia 14%
Libya 97% (Sunni)
Madagascar 2%
Malawi 16%
Malaysia 53%
Maldives 100% (Sunni)
Mali 90%
Mauritania 99%
Mauritius 13%
Mayotte 97% (Sunni)
Morocco 99% (mostly Sunni)
Mozambique 13%
Nepal 3%
New Caledonia 4% (Sunni)
Niger 80% (Sunni)
Nigeria 45%
Oman 86%
Pakistan 97%
Panama 5%
Philippines 4%
Qatar 92% (mostly Sunni)
Réunion 1%
Romania 1%
Rwanda 9%
Saudi Arabia 99% (mostly Sunni)
Senegal 91% (Sunni)
Sierra Leone 39% (Sunni)
Singapore 16%
Somalia 100% (Sunni)
South Africa 1%
Sri Lanka 8%

Islam cont.

Sudan, The 73%
Suriname 20%
Syria 90% (mostly Sunni)
Taiwan 1%
Tanzania 33%
Thailand 4%
Togo 12%
Trinidad and Tobago 6%
Tunisia 99% (Sunni)
Turkey 99% (Sunni)
Uganda 7%
UK 1%
United Arab Emirates 95%
(Shiite 20%
Sunni 80%)
USA 2%
Vietnam 1%
Yemen, Republic of 100%
(Shiite 47%
Sunni 43%)
Yugoslavia 10%
Zaire 1%

Jainism

India 1%

Judaism

Canada 1%
Commonwealth of Independent States 1%
Hungary 1%
Israel 82%
UK 1%
Uruguay 2%
USA 3%

Non-religious belief

Albania 74%
Aruba 2%
Australia 13%
Austria 6%
Barbados 18%
Belgium 8%
Belize 1%
Bermuda 8%
Brazil 1%
Brunei 9%
Bulgaria 65%
Canada 7%
Chile 13%
China 71%
Commonwealth of Independent States 50%
Cuba 55%
Equatorial Guinea 6%
Finland 9%
France 3%
French Guiana 3%
French Polynesia 5%
Guyana 4%
Haiti 1%
Hungary 13%
Iceland 1%
Italy 16%
Jamaica 18%
Korea, North 68%
Korea, South 36%
Laos 5%
Mexico 3%
Netherlands Antilles 3%
Netherlands, The 33%
New Zealand 16%
Norway 3%
Portugal 4%
Romania 16%
San Marino 3%
Singapore 18%
Solomon Islands 3%
Spain 3%
Trinidad and Tobago 1%
UK 9%
Uruguay 35%
USA 7%
Vanuatu 1%
Virgin Islands (USA) 1%

Rastafarianism

Antigua and Barbuda 1%
Jamaica c. 5%

Shintoism

Japan 40%

Sikhism

Fiji 1%
India 2%

Spiritism

Brazil 4%
French Guiana 2%

Taoism

Singapore 13%

Traditional beliefs

Angola 10%
Benin 61%
Botswana 49%
Burkina Faso 45%
Burma 1%
Burundi 14%
Central African Republic 12%
Chad 23%
Congo 5%
Equatorial Guinea 5%
Ethiopia 11%
French Guiana 2%
Gabon 3%
Ghana 21%
Guinea 5%
Guinea-Bissau 65%
Kenya 19%
Korea, North 16%
Laos 34%
Lesotho 6%
Madagascar 47%
Malawi 19%
Mali 9%
Mozambique 48%
Niger 20%
Nigeria 6%
Papua New Guinea 3%
Rwanda 17%
Senegal 3%
Sierra Leone 52%
Sudan, The 17%
Swaziland 21%
Togo 59%
Vanuatu 8%
Zaire 3%
Zambia 27%

Major World Festivals

Bahaism

Martyrdom of the Bab	9 July
Anniversary of the birth of the Bab	20 October
Anniversary of the birth of Bahaullah	12 November
Nawruz (New Year's Day)	21 March
Ridvan (commemoration of the foundation of Bahaism and period of election of spiritual assemblies)	22 April–2 May
Anniversary of the Declaration of the Bab	23 May
Anniversary of the ascension of Bahaullah	29 May

Buddhism

Festivals do not hold great significance within Buddhism, and the observance of various days varies between country and tradition. The following are only some of the dates marked by Buddhists.

Parinirvana	15 February
Puja (Buddha's birthday)	8 April
Wesak/Vaisakha	16 May
Padmasanbhava Day	10 July
Dhamma Day/Asala	14 July
Kathina Day	October
Sangha Day	10 November
Bodhi Day	8 December

Chinese religion

	Chinese date
Chung Yuan	Shi Yue (9th day)
Yuan Tan	Er Yue (10th day)
Ch'ing Ming	San Yue (5th day)
Dragon Boat Festival	Liu Yue (5th day)

Chinese months	Gregorian equivalent
Yi Yue	January
Er Yue	February
San Yue	March
Shi Yue	April
Wu Yue	May
Liu Yue	June
Qi Yue	July
Ba Yue	August
Jiu Yue	September
Shi Yue	October
Shi Yi Yue	November
Shi Er Yue	December

Christianity

Solemnity of Mary, Mother of God	1 January
Epiphany	6 January
Christmas Day (Eastern Orthodox)	7 January
Baptism of Jesus	11 January
Conversion of Apostle Paul	25 January
Presentation of Jesus (Candlemas Day)	2 February
Ash Wednesday (First day of Lent)	between 4 February and 10 March
The Chair of Peter, Apostle	22 February
Easter Sunday	between 22 March and 25 April
Annunciation of the Virgin Mary	25 March
Ascension	between 30 April and 3 June
Whit Sunday	between 10 May and 13 June
Birth of John the Baptist	24 June
Transfiguration	6 August
Assumption of the Virgin Mary	15 August
Queenship of Mary	22 August
Birthday of the Virgin Mary	8 September
Exaltation of the Holy Cross	14 September
Guardian Angels	2 October
All Saints	1 November
All Souls	2 November
Dedication of the Lateran Basilica	9 November
Presentation of the Virgin Mary	21 November
Advent	end November/early December
Immaculate Conception	8 December
Christmas Day	25 December
Holy Innocents	28 December

Major World Festivals

Hinduism

	Hindu date*
Ramanavami (Birthday of Lord Rama)	Chaitra S 9
Rathayatra (Pilgrimage of the Chariot at Jagannath)	Asadha S 2
Jhulanayatra ('Swinging the Lord Krishna')	Sravana S 11–15
Rakshabandhana ('Tying on lucky threads')	Sravana S 15
Janamashtami (Birthday of Lord Krishna)	Bhadrapada K 8
Durga-puja (Homage to goddess Durga) (Bengal)	Asvina S 7–10
Navaratri (Festival of 'nine nights')	Asvina S 1–10
Lakshmi-puja (Homage to goddess Lakshmi)	Asvina S 15
Diwali, Dipavali ('string of lights')	Asvina K 15
Guru Nanak Jananti (Birthday of Guru Nanak)	Kartikka S 15
Sarasvati-puja (homage to goddess Sarasvati)	Magha K 5
Maha-sivaratri (Great Night of Lord Shiva)	Magha K 13
Holi (Festival of Fire)	Phalguna S 14
Dolayatra (Swing Festival) (Bengal)	Phalguna S 15

*S: Sukla, 'waxing fortnight'
K: Krishna, 'waning fortnight'

Hindu months*	Gregorian equivalent
Chaitra (29 or 30)	March–April
Vaisakha (29 or 30)	April–May
Jyaistha (29 or 30)	May–June
Asadha (29 or 30)	June–July
Dvitya Asadha (certain leap years)	
Sravana (29 or 30)	July–August
Dvitiya Sravana (certain leap years)	
Bhadrapada (29 or 30)	August–September
Asvina (29 or 30)	September–October
Kartikka (29 or 30)	October–November
Margasirsa (29 or 30)	November–December
Pausa (29 or 30)	December–January
Magha (29 or 30)	January–February
Phalguna (29 or 30)	February–March

*(Basis: Moon) Number in brackets: number of solar days in each month

Islam

	Islamic date
New Year's Day (starts on day which celebrates Muhammad's departure from Mecca to Medina in 622 CE)	1 Muharram
Birthday of Muhammad (celebrated throughout the month of Rabi I)	12 Rabi I
Laylat al-Miraj ('Night of Ascent' of Muhammad to heaven)	27 Rajab
Ramadan (a month of fasting during daylight hours)	Ramadan
Laylat al-Qadr ('Night of Power', celebrating the sending down of the Quran to Muhammad)	27 Ramadan
Id al-Fitr ('Feast of breaking the Fast', marking the end of Ramadan)	1 Shawwal
Annual pilgrimage ceremonies at and around Mecca; month during which the great pilgrimage (Hajj) should be made	8–13 Dhu 'I-Hijja
Id al-Adha (Feast of the Sacrifice)	10 Dhu 'I-Hijja

Islamic months	Gregorian equivalent
Muharram	September–October
Safar	October–November
Rabi	November–December
Rabi II	December–January
Jumada I	January–February
Jumada II	February–March
Rajab	March–April
Shaban	April–May
Ramadan	May–June
Shawwal	June–luly
Dhu 'I-Qada	July–August
Dhu 'I-Hijja	August–September

Jainism

	Jain date*
Paryushana Parva (period of contemplation and confession)	Sravan K 12
Mahavira Jayanti (birthday of Mahavira Jayanti)	Chaitra S 13

*S: Sukla, 'waxing fortnight'
K: Krishna, 'waning fortnight'

Jain months

Same as *Hindu months*

Japanese religion

Oshogatsu (New Year)	1–3 January
Ohinamatsuri (Dolls' or Girls' festival)	3 March
Tango no Sekku (Boys' Festival)	5 May
Hoshi matsuri/Tanabata (Star Festival)	7 July
Obon (Buddhist All Souls)	13–31 July

Judaism

	Jewish date
Rosh Hashana (New Year)	1–2 Tishri
Tzom Gedaliahu (Fast of Gedaliah)	3 Tishri
Yom Kippur (Day of Atonement)	10 Tishri
Sukkot (Feast of Tabernacles)	5–21 Tishri
Shemini Atzeret (8th Day of the Solemn Assembly)	22 Tishri
Simkhat Torah (Rejoicing of the Law)	23 Tishri
Hanukkah (Feast of Dedication)	25 Kislev–2–3 Tevet
Asara be-Tevet (Fast of 10th Tevet)	10 Tevet
Taanit Esther (Fast of Esther)	13 Adar
Purim (Feast of Lots)	14–15 Adar
Pesach (Passover)	15–22 Nisan
Israel Independence Day	5 Iyar
Shavout (Feast of Weeks)	6–7 Sivan
Shiva Asar be-Tammuz (Fast of 17th Tammuz)	17 Tammuz
Tisha be-Av (Fast of 9th Av)	9 Av

Jewish months	Gregorian equivalent
Tishri	September–October
Heshvan	October–November
Kislev	November–December
Tevet	December–January
Shevat	January–February
Adar	February–March
Nisan	March–April
Iyar	April–May
Sivan	May–June
Tammuz	June–July
Av	July–August
Elul	August–September

Rastafarianism

Birthday of Haile Selassie I	23 July
Ethiopian New Year's Day	11 September
Anniversary of the crowning of Haile Selassie I	2 November

Sikhism

	Sikh date*
Divali	Asvina K 15
Birthday of Guru Nanak	Kartikka S 15
Martyrdom of Guru Tegh Bahadur	Magha S 5
Birthday of Guru Gobind Singh	Pausa S 7
Baisakhi	Vaisakha K 15
Martyrdom of Guru Arjan Dev	Jyaistha S 4

*S: Sukla, 'waxing fortnight'
K: Krishna, 'waning fortnight'

Sikh months

Same as *Hindu months*

Zoroastrianism

Farvardigan	14–23 August
No Ruz	24 August
Khordad Sal	30 August
Jamshedi Noruz	21 March
Zartusht-No-Diso	31 May

Entries by Subject

African religion

African religions
ancestors, African
Dinka religion
divination, African
fetish
Modimo
Mulungu
Mwari
Nganga
Nuer religion
Nzambi
obi
Shilluk religion
witchcraft and sorcery, African

Ancient Egyptian religion

afterlife, Ancient Egyptian concept of
Akhenaton
Amun
Ancient Egyptian religion
animal cults
ankh
Anubis
Apis
art, Ancient Egyptian
Atenism
Atum
ennead
funerary practices, Ancient Egyptian
Hathor
Heliopolis theology
hieroglyphics
Horus
Imhotep
Isis
Ka
literature, Ancient Egyptian
Maat
magic, Ancient Egyptian
Memphite Theology
mummification
Nephthys
Nile
Nun
Osiris
pharaoh
primeval hill
Ptah
pyramid
Re
Reshef
scarab
Serapis
Seth
Shay
sphinx
temples, Ancient Egyptian
Thebes
Thoth
Tutankhamen
uraeus
wisdom literature

Ancient European religion

Aesir and Vanir
Altamira
Arthur
Balder
Cernunnos
Dagda, the
Druids
Edda
Fenrir
Freya
Frigg
frost giants
fylgja
Germanic religion
giants
head cult (Celtic)
Hel
Land of Youth
Loki
Lug
Mabinogion
matres, matrones
Merlin
Odin
Ragnarok
sagas
Samhain
ship burial
Slavic religion
Sturluson, Snorri
Sutton Hoo ship burial
Thor
Tuatha Dé Danann
Tyr, Tiwaz, Tu
Valhalla
Valkyries
Vikings
Voluspa
volva
Yggdrasil

Ancient Near Eastern religion

afterlife, Ancient Near Eastern concept of
Ahab
Akitu
Anat
Ancient Near Eastern religions
Aramaean religion
architecture, Sumerian and Assyrian
art, Assyrian
art, Babylonian
Asherah
Asshur
Assyria
Assyrian religion
Astarte
astrology, Ancient Near Eastern
Baal
Babylon
Babylonian religion
Canaan
Canaanite religion
cosmogony, Ancient Near Eastern
cosmology, Ancient Near Eastern
Dagan
divination, Ancient Near Eastern
El
Elam
Elamite religion
Enlil
evil, Ancient Near Eastern concept of
festivals, Ancient Near Eastern
Gilgamesh Epic
Hammurabi
Hittite religion
Hurrian religion

Bahaism

Buddhism

Chinese Buddhism

Chinese religion

Christianity

early religion

general subjects

Greek religion

Hinduism

Islam

Jainism

Japanese Buddhism

Japanese religion

Jewish Bible and Christian Old Testament

Naphtali, tribe of
Nathan
Nehemiah, Book of
Nimrod
Nineveh
Noah
Numbers, Book of
Obadiah, Book of
Old Testament
Ophir
penitential psalms
Pentateuch
Proverbs, Book of
Psalms, Book of
Rachel
Red Sea
Reuben, tribe of
Ruth, Book of
sacrifice, Ancient Israelite
Samson
Samuel
Samuel, Books of
Sarah, or Sarai
Saul
Septuagint
seraphim
Shechem
Shem
Sheol
Shiloh
Simeon, tribe of
Sinai, Mount
Sodom and Gomorrah
Solomon
Solomon, Psalms of
Song of Solomon
Song of the Three Young Men
Susanna, Story of
Ten Commandments
Ten Lost Tribes of Israel
testament literature
Tobit, Book of
wisdom literature
Wisdom of Solomon
Zadokites
Zebulun, tribe of
Zechariah, Book of
Zephaniah, Book of
Zion

Judaism

Aggadah
Akiva ben Joseph
Amidah
angels, Jewish
animal slaughter, Jewish
Annas
anti-Semitism
apocalypse
Apocrypha, Old Testament
Aqedah
art, Jewish
Ashkenazim
Baal Schem Tov
Babylonian Captivity
Baeck, Leo
Bahya ibn Paquda
Bar Kokhbah
Bar Mitzvah
Buber, Martin
calendar, Jewish
cantor
Conservative Judaism
conversion, Jewish
cosmogony, Jewish
covenant
Dead Sea Scrolls
Diaspora
Diaspora Judaism
Ebionites
Elohim
eretz Yisrael
Essenes
exile
exodus theme
fasts, Jewish
Gehenna
Gemara
Gentiles
Haggadah/Passover Haggadah
hagim
Halakhah
Halevi, Jehuda
Hanukkah
Hasidim
Hasidism
Hellenistic Judaism
Herzl, Theodor
Heschel, Abraham Joshua
high priest
Hillel I
Holocaust
Holy of Holies
humankind, Jewish view of
Israel, State of
Jabneh
Jehovah
Jericho
Jewish languages
Johanan ben Zakkai
Josephus, Flavius
Judah, kingdom of
Judaism
Judaism, women in
Judaism in Europe
Judaism in North America
Kabbalah
Kaddish
Kaplan, Mordecai Menahem
kashrut
kehillah
kiddushin
Kook, Abraham Isaac Hacohen
kosher
Liberal Judaism
Lilith
literature, Jewish
Luria, Isaac
Maccabees, Books of the
magen David
Maimonides
marrano
marriage/divorce, Jewish
Masoretes
Mendelssohn, Moses
menorah
menstruation, Jewish attitude towards
Merkavah Mysticism
Messiah
messianism
Methuselah
mezuzah
midrash
miqveh
Mishnah
mitzvah
Moabite Stone
Moses
music, Jewish
Nag Hammadi texts
Nahmanides
Nahman of Bratslav
Nazirites
Olam haBa
Old Testament
Orthodox Judaism
Passover
patriarch
Pharisees
Philo Judaeus
philosophy, Jewish

magic, astrology and the occult

Meso-American religion

Native American religion

new religious movements in primal societies

new religious movements in the West

Pacific religion

Roman religion

secular alternatives to religion

Sikhism

South American religion

study of religion

Tibetan religion

astrology, Tibetan
bardo
Bon, Bon po
Buston
chod
Dalai Lama
Gampopa
Gelugpa
Gesar
Jonangpa
Kadampa
Kagyupa
Kanjur
lama
Lamaism
lha and dre
Lhasa
Marpa
Milarepa
Naropa
Nyingmapa
Padmasambhava
Panchen Lama
Potala Palace
Red and Yellow Hats
Rime
Sakyapa
Shambala
Srongtsan Gampo
tanka
Tantra
Tibetan religion
Tilopa
Tsongkapa
tulku
Tun Huang
wheel of life

Zoroastrianism

Ahriman
Ahura Mazda
ahuras
Airyanam Vaejah
Amesha Spentas
Anahita
Angra Mainyu
Ateshgah
Avesta
Bundahishn
Chinvat Bridge
daevas
dakhma
Frashokereti
fravashi
Gahambars
haoma
Indo-Europeans
khvarenah
Magi
Mandaeans
Mani
Manichaeism
Minoan religion
Mithra
Mithraism
Mycenaean religion
naojote
Pahlavi
Parseeism
Parsi religious reforms
Saoshyant
shah
tripartite ideology
yasna
yazata
Zoroaster
Zoroastrianism
Zurvan